HANDBOOK OF
Reading Research

HANDBOOK OF
Reading Research

EDITOR

P. David Pearson

SECTION EDITORS

Rebecca Barr

Michael L. Kamil

Peter Mosenthal

Longman
New York & London

Handbook of Reading Research

Longman Inc., 1560 Broadway, New York, N.Y. 10036
Associated companies, branches, and representatives
throughout the world.

Developmental Editor: Lane Akers
Editorial and Design Supervisor: Russell Till
Interior Designer: Joan Matthews
Production Supervisor: Ferne Y. Kawahara
Composition: Kingsport
Printing and Binding: Vail Ballou

Library of Congress Cataloging in Publication Data

Main entry under title:

Handbook of reading research.

118520

Bibliography: p.
Includes index.
1. Reading—Addresses, essays, lectures.
2. Reading—Research—Methodology—Addresses, essays,
lectures. I. Pearson, P. David.
LB1050.H278   1984   428.4'072   83–26838
ISBN 0–582–28119–9

MANUFACTURED IN THE UNITED STATES OF AMERICA
9 8 7 6 5 4 3 2 1   92 91 90 89 88 87 86 85 84

Contents

PART ONE
Methodological Issues
Peter Mosenthal, Editor

Contributors

Richard L. Allington is chairman of the Department of Reading at the State University of New York at Albany. He received his Ph.D. in elementary and special education from Michigan State University. He has served as co-editor of *The Journal of Reading Behavior* and co-authored, with Michael Strange, the text *Learning through Reading* (Heath, 1980). His research interests are the study of reading and learning disabilities and classroom teaching processes.

Richard C. Anderson is director of the Center for the Study of Reading and a professor of psychology and education at the University of Illinois at Urbana–Champaign. He received his doctorate from Harvard University. Dr. Anderson is a past president of the American Educational Research Association. He has published extensively in the areas of instructional research and cognitive psychology.

Thomas H. Anderson is an associate professor of educational psychology and co-director of the Center for the Study of Reading at the University of Illinois at Urbana–Champaign. After completing doctoral work at the University of Illinois in the psychology of learning and instruction, he joined the faculty at Arkansas Polytechnic University and Indiana State University before returning to Illinois. His current research interests are text features that affect studying and computer-based instruction.

Bonnie B. Armbruster is a visiting assistant professor at the Center for the Study of Reading at the University of Illinois at Urbana–Champaign. She received her Ph.D. from the University of Illinois in educational psychology. Her research interests are content area reading/studying/writing and instructional development.

Steven R. Asher is professor of educational psychology and psychology at the University of Illinois at Urbana–Champaign. He also serves there as director of the Bureau of Educational Research. Dr. Asher received his Ph.D. in psychology from the University of Wisconsin. He has done research on interest effects on reading comprehension, children's referential communication skills, and children's peer relations and social competence. Dr. Asher is a Fellow of the American Psychological Association. He has served on the Editorial Board of *Child Development,* and he currently serves on the Editorial Boards of *Merrill-Palmer Quarterly* and the *Journal of Social and Personal Relationships.*

Linda Baker is an assistant professor of psychology at the University of Maryland Baltimore County. She received her Ph.D. in cognitive psychology from Rutgers University and spent two years at the Center for the Study of Reading as a visiting researcher. She is interested in the development and use of effective strategies for monitoring comprehension and in other metacognitive aspects of reading.

Rebecca Barr is a professor of education at National College of Education and a research associate at the University of Chicago. She received her Ph.D. in educational psychology from the University of Chicago. She then taught at the University of British Columbia before returning to the University of Chicago, where she was director of the Reading Clinic. Her current research centers on classroom instruction, and she is presently completing a four-year study on the organization of classroom instruction. Dr. Barr is the author (with R. Dreeben) of *How Schools Work* (Univ. of Chicago Press, 1983) and is currently working on a book (with M. Sadow) entitled *Reading Diagnosis for Teachers,* to be published in 1985 by Longman Inc.

James F. Baumann is an assistant professor of education at Purdue University, where he also serves as director of the Purdue Reading Clinic. He received his Ph.D. in curriculum and instruction from the University of Wisconsin—Madison. His current interests include the measurement of reading ability, especially in disabled readers, vocabulary development, and the application of teacher effectiveness research to comprehension instruction. He has had articles published in many reading education journals and is editor of *Reading Instruction and the Beginning Teacher: A Practical Guide* (Burgess, 1984).

David Bloome is an assistant professor of education at the University of Michigan. He received his Ph.D. in curriculum and instruction from Kent State University. His research interests are in the social and communicative dimensions of reading and reading instruction, the interrelationships between cognitive and social processes involved in literacy learning, literacy learning across home and school contexts, and the study of classroom processes.

Ann L. Brown is a professor of psychology and educational psychology at the University of Illinois at Urbana–Champaign. She received her Ph.D. in psychology from Bradford College of the University of London. Her current research interests are in the areas of Metacognition and reading and training comprehension. She is a frequent contributor to the professional literature.

Robert Calfee is an experimental cognitive psychologist. He earned his degrees at the University of California, Los Angeles, did postgraduate work at Stanford University, and spent five years in the Psychology Department at the University of Wisconsin. He returned to Stanford as associate professor in the

School of Education, and at present is professor of education and psychology. His interests have evolved over the past several years—beginning with research on prereading skills, methods for assessing reading, and instruction in reading. Dr. Calfee's current interests are the broader questions of how education influences human cognition and how an understanding of cognitive processes can be used to improve practice.

James W. Cunningham is associate professor of education at the University of North Carolina at Chapel Hill, where he teaches undergraduate and graduate courses in the teaching of reading and writing. He received his BA from the University of Virginia and his MA and Ph.D. degrees in reading education from the University of Georgia. He is co-author of three published textbooks and one in preparation. He is a member of the Editorial Advisory Board of the *National Reading Conference Yearbook* and *Reading Research Quarterly*. He has taught at the elementary and secondary levels in public schools of Tennessee, Georgia, and rural North Carolina.

Roger G. Eldridge is an assistant professor of education at East Carolina University. He received his Ph.D. from the University of Wisconsin. He is a former elementary teacher and reading specialist. At East Carolina, he teaches reading courses designed to train teachers in the use of remedial reading techniques. His research interests include the use of qualitative methods in reading research, the teaching of reading comprehension in schools and teacher training and practices in teaching reading. Dr. Eldridge is a consulting editor of the *Journal of Educational Research*. He has authored practitioner-based articles and book chapters on remedial techniques for classroom use.

Philip B. Gough is professor of psychology, professor of education, and co-director of the Center for Cognitive Science at the University of Texas at Austin. He received his Ph.D. from the University of Minnesota, and previously taught at Minnesota, Indiana, and U.C.L.A. His research interests include the reading process, reading acquisition, and reading disability.

Judith Green is associate professor of education in the Department of Policy and Leadership in the College of Education at the Ohio State University. Her research interests include explorations of teaching and learning as linguistic processes, ethnography of communication in educational situations, and effective instructional practices. Among her recent publications are *Ethnography and Language in Educational Settings* (with Cynthia Wallat, Ablex, 1981), Research on Teaching as a Linguistic Process: A State of the Art (in E. Gordon, ed., *Review of Research in Education*, 10, 1983), Exploring Classroom Discourse: Linguistic Perspective on Teaching-Learning Processes (*Educational Psychologist*, 18, 1983) and Ethnography and Reading: Issues, Approaches, Criteria and Findings (with D. Bloome, *Yearbook of the National Reading Conference*, 1983).

Larry F. Guthrie is a project director at Far West Laboratory for Educational Research and Development, San Francisco. He received his Ph.D. in educational psychology from the University of Illinois, where he spent three years at the

Center for the Study of Reading. His interests are in social and cultural issues in education, and his research has focused on children's language use in and out of school, instruction in bilingual education, and reading. He is currently conducting a series of policy case studies which examine opportunity structures for science learning in high school.

William S. Hall is professor of psychology at the University of Maryland. He was formerly a director of the center for the Study of Reading at the University of Illinois at Urbana-Champaign. Hall received his Ph.D. from the University of Chicago, in March of 1968. He has been an associate research psychologist at the Educational Testing Service, and a member of the faculty at Vassar, New York University, Princeton, and the Rockefeller University. At Rockefeller he also served as co-director of the Institute for Comparative Human Development.

James H. James is employed at Bell Laboratories, Holmdel, New Jersey, as a researcher in the area of speech perception. He received his Ph.D. in experimental psychology from Northern Illinois University, and thereafter was at Yale University as a NIMH postdoctoral fellow, where he did research on attention. His current research interests are in the areas of language acquisition and the attention process. Dr. James has authored many articles in the professional literature, and was a consultant to the National Institute of Education.

Dale D. Johnson is a professor of curriculum and instruction at the University of Wisconsin—Madison, where he also serves as a principal investigator in the Wisconsin Center for Education Research. His research interests include vocabulary and comprehension development and the assessment of word identification skills. Among his books are *Teaching Reading Vocabulary*, 2nd edition (Holt, Rinehart and Winston, 1984), *Teaching Children to Read*, 2nd edition (Addison-Wesley, 1980), and *The Ginn Word Book for Teachers* (Ginn and Company, 1983). He serves on the Board of Directors of the International Reading Association.

Peter H. Johnston is an assistant professor in the Reading Department at the State University of New York at Albany. His BSc, M.A., and teacher training were received in his native New Zealand, where he also taught elementary school. He received his Ph.D. in Educational Psychology from the University of Illinois at Urbana–Champaign working largely at the Center for the Study of Reading. He is responsible for teaching graduate classes in diagnosis, remediation, and prevention of reading difficulties, and in reading research methods. Recent work such as his monograph *A Cognitive Basis for the Assessment of Reading Comprehension* (1983) reflects his interest in assessment in reading and how it relates to instruction and research.

Michael L. Kamil is associate professor of education at the University of Illinois, Chicago. He received his Ph.D. in experimental psychology from the University of Wisconsin–Madison. His research interests are in the application of computer technology to instruction, theories in models of the reading process, and teacher decision-making behavior. He was recently awarded the

Milton D. Jacobson Readability Research Award for work on cloze techniques. He has been editor of the *National Reading Conference Yearbook* and has recently published the edited work (with L. Gentile and J. Blanchard) *Reading Research Revisited*.

George Klare is Distinguished Professor of Psychology at Ohio University, Athens, Ohio, where he has also served as chairman of the Psychology Department and dean of the College of Arts and Sciences. He received his Ph.D. from the University of Minnesota; before going to Ohio University, he was a staff psychologist at the Psychological Corporation, and a research associate at the University of Illinois at Urbana–Champaign. His research has been in the area of the measurement of readability. Professor Klare's publications include *Know Your Reader* (1954), *The Measurement of Readability* (1963), *Elementary Statistics: Data Analysis for the Behavioral Sciences* (1967), and *A Manual for Readable Writing* as well as numerous journal articles and book chapters. He was the 1981 recipient of the National Reading Conference Oscar Causey Award.

Jana M. Mason is an associate professor in the Department of Educational Psychology and a research professor at the Center for the Study of Reading at the University of Illinois at Urbana–Champaign. She received her Ph.D. from Stanford University, where her studies focused on the reading process, beginning reading, and educational practices in reading. Her publications include *Comprehension Instruction: Perspectives and Suggestions* and a forthcoming book on reading instruction.

Dominic W. Massaro has been professor of psychology at the University of California, Santa Cruz since 1980. After completing graduate school at the University of Massachusetts and a postdoctoral position at the University of California, San Diego, he joined the faculty at the University of Wisconsin. He taught at Wisconsin for ten years. He has received research fellowship awards from both the National Institutes of Mental Health and the Guggenheim Foundation. His research interests are human information processing, speech perception, and reading. Among his publications are *Experimental Psychology and Information Processing* (Rand McNally, 1975); *Understanding Language: An Information-Processing Analysis and Speech Perception, Reading, and Psycholinguistics* (Academic Press, 1975); and *Letter and Word Perception* (North Holland, 1980).

Bonnie J. F. Meyer is a professor in the Department of Educational Psychology at Arizona State University. She received her Ph.D. in Educational Psychology from Cornell University. Her research interests focus on discourse analysis, reading life-span differences in learning from text, and teaching readers and writers to use organization effectively in expository text. She was the recipient of the 1982 Arizona State University Faculty Research Award. For the past six years, she has been examining learning and memory from discourse by young, middle-aged, and old adults through support from the National Institute of Mental Health and the National Institute on Aging

Peter Mosenthal is an associate professor of reading and language arts at Syracuse University. He received his B.S. from the College of Wooster, Wooster, Ohio, and both his M.A. and Ph.D. from Ohio State University, Columbus. From 1977 to 1980 he was first associate director and then director of the Center for the Study of Reading at SUNY, Albany. Professor Mosenthal is the author, with L. Tamar and S. Walmsley, of *Research for Writing: Principles and Methods* (Longman, 1983). He has also written numerous journal articles and chapters in edited volumes. Professor Mosenthal began his career in education as an elementary school teacher in Ohio. He taught at SUNY, Geneseo, and SUNY, Albany, before assuming his current position at Syracuse University.

Ann Myers is a graduate student in educational psychology at the University of Illinois at Urbana–Champaign. She has also been an elementary school teacher and has supervised remedial reading programs.

Andrew Ortony is a professor of psychology and of educational psychology and a senior scientist in the Center for the Study of Reading at the University of Illinois at Urbana–Champaign. He is a cognitive scientist with a Bachelor's degree in philosophy and a Ph.D. in computer science from the University of London. His main research interests are in the comprehension of (especially figurative) language, and in the interactions between affect and cognition. His publications include *Metaphor and Thought* (1979) and (with Gerald L. Clore) *Affect and Cognition* (forthcoming).

Wayne Otto is professor and chair in the Department of Curriculum and Instruction, School of Education, University of Wisconsin—Madison. He received the Ph.D. from the University of Wisconsin–Madison in reading education and, prior to his present position, he was on the faculty of the University of Oregon and the University of Georgia. He was principal investigator of a project that developed *The Wisconsin Design for Reading Skill Development* at the Wisconsin Research and Development Center. His publications include *Corrective and Remedial Teaching*, 3rd ed. (with Smith, 1980), *The School Reading Program* (with Smith and Hanson, 1978), and *Reading Expository Text* (ed. with Sandra White, 1982).

P. David Pearson is a professor in the Department of Elementary and Early Childhood Education at the University of Illinois at Urbana–Champaign, where he also holds an appointment at the Center for the Study of Reading. He received his B.S. from the University of California, Berkeley, and his Ph.D. from the University of Minnesota at Minneapolis. His publications include two books, *Teaching Reading Comprehension* and *Teaching Reading Vocabulary*, with Dale D. Johnson of the University of Wisconsin, as well as numerous articles and monographs. With S. Jay Samuels of the University of Minnesota, he edits the *Reading Research Quarterly*. Professor Pearson taught elementary school in California before entering higher education; he taught for several years at the University of Minnesota, Minneapolis before going to the University of Illinois.

Dorothy Piontkowski is an associate professor of psychology at San Francisco State University. She received her Ph.D. in educational psychology from Stanford University. Her research interests include cognitive processes underlying reading acquisition and relations between learners' knowledge systems and classroom instruction. She is currently engaged in research of cognitive-process instruction aimed at improving college students' reasoning skills.

G. Elizabeth Rice is currently adjunct assistant professor in the departments of Educational Psychology and of Anthropology at Arizona State University. She received a Ph.D. in social sciences from the University of California, Irvine. Her current research interests in the field of prose comprehension center on cultural influences on the comprehension process. She has authored and co-authored several articles on prose comprehension.

Barak Rosenshine is a professor of educational psychology in the College of Education at the University of Illinois. He received his Ph.D. in Education at Stanford University. His interests include research on classroom instruction and instructional design.

S. Jay Samuels is professor of educational psychology and curriculum and instruction at the University of Minnesota. He is also a member of the Center for Research in Human Learning and was a member of research institutes on learning disabilities and educational handicaps at that institution. Professor Samuels is currently co-editor of *Reading Research Quarterly* and is a Fellow of the American Psychological Association. His research interests include characteristics of outstanding reading programs, text processing, and models of word recognition and reading.

Rand J. Spiro is a professor of educational psychology at the University of Illinois at Urbana–Champaign and a senior scientist at the Center for the Study of Reading. He received his Ph.D. in experimental psychology from the Pennsylvania State University. He has worked for the Artificial Intelligence Laboratory at Yale University, with appointments in computer science and psychology. His publications include *Schooling and the Acquisition of Knowledge* (with Anderson and Montague, 1977), *Theoretical Issues in Reading Comprehension* (with Bruce and Brewer, 1980), and various articles on the cognitive psychology of text processing.

Robert Stevens is a postdoctoral fellow at the Learning Research and Development Center, University of Pittsburgh. He received his Ph.D. in Educational Psychology at the University of Illinois. His interests are classroom instruction, cognitive task analysis, and instructional design.

Thomas G. Sticht is adjunct research professor of industrial psychology at the United States Naval Postgraduate School in Monterey, California; he is also president of Applied Behavioral and Cognitive Sciences, Incorporated, a nonprofit corporation which conducts research and development leading to improved methods of education and training undergraduate youth and adults. Previously, he was associate director of the National Institute of Education in the United States Department of Education, and he is a member of UNESCO's international literacy jury. He is senior author of a 1974 volume on listening and reading entitled *Auding and Reading: A Developmental Model*. He received his Ph.D. in experimental psychology from the University of Arizona in Tucson.

Robert J. Tierney is an associate professor at the Center for the Study of Reading at the University of Illinois, Urbana–Champaign. Over the past few years his major interests have focused upon instructional research issues and, most recently, the nature of composing. During 1981 and 1982, Dr. Tierney was a member of the faculty at Harvard University, where he taught courses dealing with reading comprehension and writing processes. From 1979 to 1983 he was a visitng research associate professor at the Center for the Study of Reading, where he was involved in a number of studies applying theoretical and research developments in reading comprehension to the classroom. From 1974 to 1978, he was a member of the Reading Department at the University of Arizona. Prior to that time, he completed studies at the University of Georgia and was a classroom teacher in Sydney, Australia, where he taught and studied for a number of years. He has been a major co-author of two basal reading programs published by Scott, Foresman, and he has authored and edited numerous articles and college textbooks.

Richard L. Venezky is the Unidel Professor of Educational Studies at the University of Delaware, with a joint appointment in Computer and Information Sciences. Prior to this, he was professor and chairman of Computer Sciences at the University of Wisconsin and a principal investigator at the Wisconsin Research and Development Center for Cognitive Learning. He holds a Bachelor of Electrical Engineering degree and a Master's degree in linguistics from Cornell University and a Ph.D. in linguistics from Stanford University. His research interests include alphabets and writing systems, reading instruction, the perception of printed words, and school factors that influence reading. Among his publications on reading are *The Structure of English Orthography* (Mouton, 1970), *Letter and Word Perception* (with D. Massaro et al, North-Holland, 1980, and *Orthography, Reading and Dyslexia* (edited with J. Cavanaugh, University Park Press, 1980). He is a consultant to the *Oxford English Dictionary Supplement* and to the *Dictionary of Old English*, and he serves on the editorial boards of several professional journals. Professor Venezky has also developed for national distribution instructional programs for teaching kindergarten children prereading skills, spelling, and elementary reading. He is currently working on a history of American reading instruction and on the formalization of instructional processes and instructional planning.

Allan Wigfield received his Ph.D. from the Human Development Program in the Department of Educational Psychology at the University of Illinois at Urbana–Champaign. He is currently a postdoctoral fellow in the Department of

Psychology at the University of Michigan and a faculty associate at the Institute for Social Research. His main research interest is achievement motivation, particularly how children's achievement motivation develops and the relationship among children's achievement motivation, achievement beliefs, and school performance. He is also interested in developing intervention programs to foster positive achievement motivation in the classroom. He has authored several articles for professional journals on the subject of achievement motivation.

Anne Wolf is currently a curriculum specialist with the Division of Curriculum and Instruction, New York City Board of Education. Dr. Wolf earned her doctoral degree at the University of Wisconsin—Madison and was assistant professor at the University of Wisconsin—Eau Claire when this chapter was written. Dr. Wolf's teaching interests center on reading in the content areas and the diagnosis and remediation of reading problems. Her research interests include the kinds and amounts of reading in content area classes and students' and teachers' attitudes toward reading.

Foreword

Approximately sixty years ago William S. Gray published the first summary of investigations related to reading. In that 1925 monograph Gray annotated and summarized 436 reports of reading research published in the United States and England prior to July, 1924. He suggested that the research summary should be useful to school officers and teachers in their efforts to reorganize courses of study in reading and to improve instructional techniques. He also emphasized the potential value of his summary in suggesting future directions for research and reading.

Gray's pioneer effort not only provided direction to curriculum builders, teachers, administrators, and researchers; it also established a mind-set that systematic collation and analysis of reading research was important. Subsequent to the publication of Gray's 1925 monograph he and a number of successors have produced to the present time annual summaries of reading research. From 1925 through the early 1960s between 75 and 150 published reports of research in reading were reviewed and summarized each year. By 1980 the number of published research reports approximated 1000 per year. The high degree of interest in the study of reading is further illustrated by the fact that in producing the most recent summaries more than 350 professional journals were monitored because of the likelihood of their including relevant research.

These annual summaries have certainly facilitated (if not made possible) our keeping abreast of current research in reading. Given the widespread interest in reading and the large number of studies published each year, it is difficult to imagine what our professional life would be like if Gray and his successors had not been so diligent and industrious. What has been lacking, however, is a comprehensive analysis and interpretation of this rich cumulative data base. The *Handbook of Reading Research* fills this void admirably. Contributors to the volume represent a variety of research interests in reading. Each, however, is well-matched with a particular aspect of research he or she has been asked to organize, summarize, and interpret. The qualifications of contributors are impressive. Indeed the authors constitute a veritable "Who's Who" in reading research. What is equally important, however, is that they have taken their task seriously. The reviews are comprehensive, authoritative, and effectively written.

The guiding hand of P. David Pearson in this impressive work is readily apparent. Pearson has the rare ability to work equally well in the laboratory and the classroom; to communicate effectively with both scientists and teachers; and to understand and appreciate the problems, frustrations, and needs of both groups. The wide scope of his interests in the complex field of reading research is reflected in the comprehensiveness of this volume. Chapters on "Beginning Reading Instruction" and "Managing Instruction" share equal billing with heady pieces on "Building and Testing Models of Reading Processes" and "A Schema-Theoretic View of Basic Processes in Reading Comprehension." The structure of text competes for the attention of the reader with oral reading and readability. Research on understanding figurative language is given similar consideration to that which speaks to the issue of teaching word identification skills to beginning readers. Classroom research and classroom instruction, moreover, both receive their fair share of attention. The *Handbook of Reading Research* has the breadth to appeal to a wide audience, yet the depth to speak authoritatively to various subgroups within that audience.

If William S. Gray were alive today he would most certainly applaud this long-awaited and long-overdue complement to his early efforts. Most assuredly, the *Handbook* will require frequent revising and updating. With approximately 1000 pieces of published reading research being added to the data each year, any state-of-the-art analysis will be outdated to some extent by the time it finds its way into print. The major task, however—that of pulling together 100 years of research—has now been accomplished. All of us, whether we are scientists, teacher educators, school administrators, graduate students, publishers of instructional materials, or most importantly, those who have not yet become literate, will be the benefactors of the persistence, dedication, and wisdom of those responsible for this scholarly work.

Robert Dykstra
University of Minnesota

Preface

If the gestation period of books, like those of animals, varies directly as a function of adult body weight, then the six-year pregnancy of this volume may be justified. It has been a labor of love, anger, frustration, awe, surprise, and serendipity. In short, it has progressed like any good marriage of authors, editors, and publishers.

Those of us who participated in the conception, labor, and birth hope that the offspring will prove, above all, to be useful to the reading research community— to those who will produce the next generation of reading research, to those who produced the previous generation of research, and to those who use reading research to guide their work in developing reading curricula, reading materials, and reading instruction.

We have chosen the term *Handbook* to serve as part of the title intentionally, for we hope that the book will be regarded as much a reference tool as it is a textbook. We have tried to provide, in a single volume, a characterization of both our current state of methodological prowess and our cumulative research-based knowledge. The chapters in Part One have been written in order to provide the reader with a perspective on important methodological issues and tensions in conducting reading research. Richard Venezky's opening salvo on the history of reading research, followed by Michael Kamil's spritely characterization of the reading research scene today, set the context for not only the rest of Part One, but really for the entire volume. The remaining four chapters in Part One are a mixture of "how to" advice and "you ought to be careful about X" admonitions that researchers need to consider as they plan and implement research endeavors. Part Two (basic process in reading) and Part Three (instructional practices in reading) contain reviews of research in important areas of reading. The authors of these chapters were asked to write reviews that were as "current and comprehensive" as possible, given the time constraints on moving from manuscript to bound books. These chapters, several of which have already become "classics" in their own right in pre-publication form, should provide convenient jumping-off points for scholars who wish to pursue research in particular areas. They should also serve as "landing areas" for these readers who simply want to know what the research has to say about a given topic.

We have tried to provide a number of features that we hope readers find helpful. While the subheadings in Parts Two and Three vary from chapter to chapter according to the taste and style of individual authors, there is a consistent structure across chapters. Each begins with a brief (this term, de facto, is defined as between 100 and 5000 words) history of the particular endeavor under study. Then comes what might be labeled a decompostion of the problem, a section in which the topic is broken down in order to study more specific lines of research in greater detail. Usually this is followed by a brief summary and "where do we go from here" reprise. This organization is intentionally violated in two particular chapters. Because of their widespread distribution as technical reports when they first appeared in about 1980, we have let the Baker and Brown chapter on metacognition in Part Two and the Tierney and Cunningham chapter on comprehension instruction in Part Three appear more or less as they first came out, with the addition of ending commentary about recent developments and new thoughts and perspectives. In these instances we took this stance more or less for archival purposes.

We have listed references at the end of each chapter in order to facilitate the kind of quick see–saw comparison of citations against references that many readers engage in. We provide a complete author index at the end of the volume; again we have tried to provide extra help to our readers by distinguishing between pages that contain citations (regular typeface) and those that contain references (italics). Our subject index is, we hope, equally helpful to our readers in its breadth and depth.

A BRIEF HISTORY OF THE ORIGINS OF THE VOLUME

Since my days as a graduate student at the University of Minnesota, I thought it odd that the field of reading research did not have a handbook comparable to what was available for field of teaching or child development. Granted, each year we had available to us the valuable summaries of research begun by William S. Gray and continued by Helen Robinson and, most recently, Sam Weintraub. But we did not have, in a single volume, current and comprehensive reviews of all the important issues in the field. Thus it was hard for us to see how our research efforts could become cumulative in the sense that we could continue our own work in a way that would add to what we already, as a field, knew. The danger, I thought (and still think), was that we would reinvent wheels, work at cross purposes with our heritage, or—worst of all—simply exhibit ignorance of that heritage. So, 10 years later, when I had the luxury of taking a leave from Minnesota to study and work for a year at the Center for the Study of Reading, I began by drafting a letter to 28 different scholars in the field, inviting them to become a part of this effort. Most accepted the invitation , some declined it, and a few did not respond.

Like many efforts of this sort, when so many are involved, manuscript completion deadlines were met by most, postponed by some, and ignored by a few. By the fall of 1980 the manuscript was 65% complete (40% of the chapters were 100% complete, 50% were 50% complete, and 10% were 0% complete). We hobbled along for the next two years, trying to reach closure. I engaged the able services of Peter Mosenthal as an additional reviewer so that someone besides myself would see the entire range of contributions. But we were reluctant to complete the final review and round of revisions until we had chapters from everyone (the obvious issue was potential overlap). This was a time of despair for all concerned. Some authors were angry at me; I was angry with other authors; the managing editor, Lane Akers, was upset with everyone!

Something had to be done! In the fall of 1982, Lane Akers and I decided that the only way we were ever going to accomplish the task was to secure the services of some additional developmental editors. We wanted people who would be knowledgeable about the field (so that they could accomplish the difficult task of giving authors direction about revisions) and who had reputations as fair but tough-minded scholars (so they could keep all the authors and the general editor on task and on time). We chose wisely. We asked Peter Mosenthal to serve as editor of Part One; Michael Kamil, Part Two; and Rebecca Barr, Part Three. We met at the National Reading Conference meeting in Clearwater in December of 1982. We took stock of our situation: what was complete, what was near completion, and what still needed to get started. We set up a new schedule for revisions and a new plan for communicating with our authors and among one another. We issued new invitations to some new authors to fill what we thought were holes in our overall scheme. And we did it! By August, 1983, we had a complete manuscript. All missing chapters had been written and revised, all previously completed chapters had been updated to accommodate research completed between 1980 and 1983, and what overlap we thought excessive had been eliminated.

The search for overlap proved both interesting and illuminating. We knew in advance that many authors would reference the same studies and, perhaps, even review the same bodies of research. As we undertook the process of comparing chapters for excessive overlap, we were struck by how differently different authors would treat and regard a study or set of studies. It was then we realized what we should have known all along: That the context within which some body of knowledge is viewed and regarded alters the interpretation and contribution of that knowledge. Consequently, we have let overlap stand intentionally so that readers may observe this phenomenon for themselves.

A word about the future prospects of this volume: In view of the fast pace of reading research, we think that this volume will experience a half-life of about three years. In other words, it will need update about twice every decade. This is both a curse and a blessing. The curse is that the book will be obsolete, save for archival interest, by 1990. The blessing, or course, is that the field will have progressed far enough to make it obsolete. I suppose this means that we should all hope—and do our best to ensure—that it does become obsolete!

One other note about future prospects: To the reader who notes some obvious omissions we can only say that we do too. Some of the omissions exist because certain topics have only very recently come to stand alone as extant lines of research: effective schools, change and the implementation of innovative reading programs, the application of semiotics or pragmatics to the study of reading, or vocabulary. In the present volume, these bodies of research are reviewed under other rubrics, if at all (e.g., vocabulary under reading comprehension instruction). There is one other notable omission in Part Three: There could have been a chapter dealing specifically with individual differences as they relate to schooling to parallel Spiro and Myers's chapter in Part Two. We chose instead to disperse that research across other topics such as word identification or comprehension instruction, prereading, beginning reading, and the like. In retrospect, it might have been advisable to put it all together in one place and simply to live with whatever overlap resulted.

I want to thank my colleagues who participated in the effort required to make this volume a reality. To the authors of the various chapters, I acknowledge both their gritty patience in sticking with an endeavor that moved so slowly and their intellectual prowess so evident in the pages that follow. To Lane Akers, the managing editor at Longman, I acknowledge his tireless support, his enduring belief in the project, and his muscle in bringing it into being. To the production editors, Joan Matthews and Russell Till, I acknowledge their painstaking work in getting things right. And to the section editors—Rebecca Barr, Michael Kamil, and Peter Mosenthal—I acknowledge the fact that without their good counsel, hard work, and careful monitoring of my editorial efforts this volume would never have been born.

I want to thank my family—Mary Alyce, Matthew, and Susan—for their patience with me and for the time I had to steal to complete the project.

It is our hope that those of you who read it will learn half as much as we who wrote it.

P. David Pearson
Urbana, Illinois

PART ONE

Methodological Issues

Peter Mosenthal, Editor

1 THE HISTORY OF READING RESEARCH

Richard L. Venezky

Like Joseph's coat, the history of reading research is a thing of many colors. It is not a single, continuous stream of human endeavor but at least four and perhaps as many as six independent threads, each with its own methods and each moving to the beat of a different drummer. Basic research on reading processes occupies the most visible and prestigious position among these strands, but it has influenced reading practice the least. Research on reading instruction, although lacking suitable methodologies and often done by careless researchers, has nevertheless had a larger impact on practice. The testing movement has also had a major impact on reading instruction, and its origins are found neither in the concern for human variability that prompted research on reading processes in the late 1800s nor in attempts to improve school practices that began in the mid-1800s with the efforts of Horace Mann and Henry Barnard and that formed the immediate antecedents of the scientific study of education. Instead, the testing movement began with the French Enlightenment of the early nineteenth century, in particular with the desire to provide humane treatment for the mentally retarded.

Finally, the study of literacy and the role it has played in society throughout history represent a fourth area of reading research and one that is again distinct from the first three. The interest this area holds for historians and sociologists has been represented most recently by the publication of Kenneth Lockridge's *Literacy in Colonial New England* (1974) and Jack Goody's *The Domestication of the Savage Mind* (1977), books that explore anew the extent and consequences of literacy and bring to attention methodological issues in ascertaining literacy levels of previous generations. This latter issue was raised in 1935 by Galbraith in a study of literacy among the medieval English kings, but it was not attended to seriously until fairly recently (Schofield, 1968).

These kinds of research on reading can be identified currently. But several topics that I include with instruction may be elevated to a status parallel with them: research on legibility, readability, and reading disabilities. Legibility stud-

Source: This chapter is based in part on an earlier article by the author on the history of research on the reading process. See Venezky (1977) in the References at the end of this chapter.

ies, which began at the end of the eighteenth century, are the most curious of this group in that they have been and remain totally atheoretical. No conceptual framework for vision or reading has been invoked for guiding legibility research; no serious legibility models have been proposed, and consequently no theories of legibility exist. Yet careful and highly useful studies have been done on the relative legibilities of almost every printing variable from type style to page layout.

This chapter traces the development of two research trends, reading processes and reading instruction, from their beginnings in the 1870s until roughly 1970. A third trend, testing, is treated briefly in the discussion of instructional research. Within each of these minihistories, an attempt is made to relate research interests and methods to the scientific and cultural environments within which each trend operated, both in terms of the influence that the wider field had on reading research and, where appropriate, the influence that reading research had on educational practice. This plan draws upon, but does not closely follow, approaches to the history of science organized by paradigms (e.g., Kuhn, 1970), research programs (e.g., Lakatos, 1970), and intellectual ideas (Newell, 1982). But it deviates noticeably from a recent suggestion by Button (1979) that a history of educational research should emphasize the effects of research results and the biographies of the researchers. Unlike medicine, chemistry, agriculture, or physics, educational practice is firmly entrenched in, and controlled by, the society it serves. Schools have fuzzy goals, thus making school effectiveness difficult to assess (Sieber, 1968); in addition, because of the number of variables that enter into classroom instruction, schooling practices are difficult to evaluate. The effectiveness of a new fertilizer or a new switching circuit can be assessed with whatever accuracy is desired; and their costs for production, distribution, and implementation can be accurately estimated. But a new teaching method or a new textbook cannot be evaluated with similar precision. Moreover, new ideas in education seem to enter the classroom more by cultural diffusion than by direct means (Clifford, 1973). For research on reading processes, direct effect on practice has never been a primary goal. Like all other basic psychological research, the objective of basic reading research has been to increase our knowledge about fundamental processes.

Some space in this chapter is devoted to biography, but mainly for embellishment and relief. This is not to say that reading researchers were, or are, a dull lot. Accounts of Cattell's initial presentation of himself to Wundt or Thorndike's peregrinations with his trained chickens could easily dispel that notion. But one can deduce little about the direction or procedures of reading research from the personalities involved.

Finally, history is, as Gay (1974) emphasizes, as much literature as science. The ability to tell a good story is what distinguishes a Tacitus or a Sarton from a pedantic annalist. Thus, no matter what else the present work does, it should not be judged successful unless it places in a readable and informative format the material it purports to record.

READING PROCESSES

The history of research on reading processes is for the most part the history of cognitive psychology, starting with Wilhelm Wundt's laboratory in Leipzig in the late 1870s and continuing to the present day. Whether we focus on James McKeen Cattell or Raymond Dodge, or on Rudolph Pintner or Edward L. Thorndike, or on the Project Literary staff, or on any of the present-day schema theorists, we find cognitive psychologists who examined traditional psychological problems, and who occasionally found reading processes to be a convenient vehicle for these interests. Their research goals usually did not begin with instructionally defined problems, nor were their results often carried to instructional conclusions. In general, the psychological issues that researchers pursued defined the extent of their interests in reading. When psychological interests changed, concern for reading usually changed also. In the review that follows, research on perceptual processes in reading is discussed first, followed by a shorter treatment of comprehension.

Perception of Print

Beginnings

The study of perceptual processes in reading began in Europe during a period of considerable turmoil and change. By the late 1870s when Wundt established his laboratory for experimental psychology in Leipzig, the effects of the industrial revolution were being felt throughout the Western world. An economic depression lingered on after the American stock market crash of 1873. The older liberalism was giving way to the new imperialism as new markets and new sources of raw materials were sought. The Ottoman Empire was breaking apart, England was gaining control of the Suez Canal and India, and Henry Morton Stanley (of Stanley and Livingstone fame) was conspiring with Leopold II of Belgium to open the interior of Africa to colonization. Against this background, Wundt accepted the chair of philosophy at Leipzig in 1875 and within four years had founded the world's first experimental psychology laboratory. According to Cattell (1888), foremost among the laboratory's interests were "(1) The Analysis and Measurement of Sensation; (2) The Duration of Mental Processes; (3) The Time-Sense; (4) Attention, Memory and The Association of Ideas." It was the second of these interests that led to a focus, however brief, on reading. Reaction-time experiments were part of psychometry, which had as its goal measuring the rapidity of mental events. Reaction times for responses to briefly exposed letters and words provided a means, through the subtractive procedures originated by the Dutch physiologist F. C. Donders (1818–1889), for determining the speeds of various mental events.[1]

The central figure in the reading studies at Leipzig was not Wundt but James McKeen Cattell, an American who was Wundt's first assistant and who spent three years in Leipzig, receiving his Ph.D. from there in 1886. Cattell's major concern was not reading per se, but individual differences; yet his work on letter and word recognition, legibility of letters and print types, and span of attention stimulated an interest in the experimental study of reading processes.[2]

Cattell's 1886 article "The Time It Takes to See and Name Objects" summarized in English two of the most important reading experiments to come out of Wundt's Laboratory.[3] In the first, Cattell mounted letters on a rotating drum so that they could be observed only while they were passing a narrow slit. When a single letter could be seen, the naming time was about one-half second. When the slit was widened so that the second letter came into view before the first disappeared, the naming time dropped to between one-third and one-fifth second; the time continued to decline as the slit was widened so that more letters came into view at once. Of the nine university teacher and student subjects, four read letters faster when five letters were in view at once, but were not helped by the sixth; three subjects were not helped by the fifth letter, and two were not helped by the fourth. This experiment on the "limits of consciousness" demonstrated not only that several processes could proceed in parallel but that the simple subtractive model for determining the speed of mental events was not always applicable. (The overlapping of seeing and naming that takes place in this study involves the eye-voice span, a phenomenon first reported for oral reading by Quantz, 1897, but not investigated extensively until Buswell, 1920.)

In the second experiment, Cattell measured the time required for reading aloud connected and unconnected words and letters. He found that subjects required twice as much time to read aloud unconnected words as connected ones (i.e., sentences) or unconnected letters as connected ones (i.e., words). This result was ignored until the 1950s when information theory applications prompted experiments based on reading and memorizing sentences that were controlled approximations to printed English.

In an earlier study, Cattell (1885) demonstrated that at a very brief exposure time, skilled readers could read three or four unconnected letters or two unconnected words. This result appeared to contrast with claims by Valentius (cited in Schmidt, 1917) that letters were perceived separately in word recognition, and it was often cited by reading "experts" as a justification for the whole-word approach to initial reading instruction.

Besides his work on basic reading processes, Cattell had a large indirect influence on reading through his work on mental tests and measurements. After leaving Leipzig, Cattell worked for a short time in Francis Galton's anthropometric laboratory in London where Galton was attempting to develop a standard series of measurements for such human traits as weight, height, and strength of pull. Cattell extended the idea of standard tests into the realm of mental processes after his return to the United States. In an 1890 study, Cattell introduced the term "mental tests" and proposed a series of ten tests for gathering normative data throughout the country. In the same study he suggested that through mental tests, "experimental psychology is likely to take a place in the educational plan of our schools and universities" (p. 380)—a remarkable understatement!

Cattell's legacy to reading research was not only his research but also his students, among whom were Edward L. Thorndike, Robert S. Woodworth, Walter F. Dearborn, and Arthur I. Gates. His concern for the science of psychology led him to consider many of the epistemological questions that experimental psychologists are still wrestling with today, particularly in reading research. A typical example is found in the introduction to "The Time It Takes to See and Name Objects," where he cited as one of the three major problems in experimentation (i.e., psychometry) what is now called the problem of ecological validity.

> The other difficulty lies in the fact the times measured are artificial, not corresponding to times taken up by mental processes in our ordinary life.

The conditions of the experiment place the subject in an abnormal condition, especially as to fatigue, attention, and practice (Cattell, 1886, p. 63).

Although Cattell was the most versatile and imaginative experimentalist during the earliest reading research, one other important experimentalist worked on reading during this period. Prior to Cattell's arrival at Wundt's laboratory, Emile Javal had undertaken a series of studies at the University of Paris on eye movements. The first report on these studies was published at about the same time that Wundt established his laboratory at Leipzig (Javal, 1879). Javal's observation that eye movements in reading occurred in jumps ("per saccades") contrasted sharply with the prevailing wisdom of the time.[4] Javal also studied the legibility of print. (His results in this latter area are discussed below under "Instruction.")

The Golden Years

Toward the end of the 1880s, reading processes moved to stage center in experimental psychology. In about twenty years most of the basic processing problems considered important today were examined, including cues for word recognition, the eye-voice span, the role of peripheral vision in reading, memory for connected text, and subvocalization.

These investigations, hardly thorough or reliable by modern standards and often based on the performance of a few subjects, nevertheless constitute the most creative analysis of reading processes ever undertaken. It is considerably more than curiosity that has led to the current interest in Huey's 1908 text *The Psychology and Pedagogy of Reading.* In the introduction to the 1968 reissue of this book, Kolers notes appropriately that "remarkably little empirical information has been added to what Huey knew, although some of the phenomena have now been measured more precisely" (p. xiv).[5]

Although the earliest studies were performed in Europe, principally at the University of Paris (Javal, Lamare), the University of Halle (Erdmann, Dodge), and the University of Leipzig (Cattell), the locus of experimentation had shifted by 1900 to American universities, in particular to Yale (Judd, McAllister, Steele), Brown (Delabarre), Columbia (Cattell), Wesleyan (Dodge), Clark (Huey), and Wisconsin (Quantz, Dearborn).

During this period three summaries of research on the psychology of reading were published: Quantz (1897), Dearborn (1906), and Huey (1908). Quantz's "Problems in the Psychology of Reading," which summarizes a series of studies done in Jastrow's laboratory at the University of Wisconsin, is the first systematic study of the reading process ever published and foreshadows much of today's work by positing a stage-by-stage reading model. These studies cover the eye-voice span, speed of reading, eye versus ear mindedness, lip movements during silent reading, and quickness of visual perception. Quantz was the first to publish on the eye-voice span, using as evidence data gathered from a single subject. In a brief summary of his 1897 publication, Quantz stated: "In reading aloud, furthermore, if it is to be intelligent and intelligible, words must be perceived some distance in advance of those which the voice is uttering. The rapid reader has the greatest interval between eye and voice" (Quantz, 1898, p. 436).

Of more importance for present-day work than specific results are Quantz's attempt to formulate stages for information processing during word recognition. Although his description lacks reference to iconic storage and short-term memory, analogues to these constructs are implicit in references elsewhere in his publication to "after-images" and "primary memory images."

Dearborn's (1906) study, undertaken for a dissertation at Columbia University under Cattell, is a thorough and important description of eye movements and the perceptual span during reading. (Besides Cattell, Dearborn acknowledged the assistance of Robert S. Woodworth, also on the Columbia faculty, Edward L. Thorndike, Teachers College, and Raymond Dodge, Wesleyan University.) Dearborn's work, which is discussed more fully later in this chapter, covered among other topics the number and duration of fixation pauses, refixations, perception during eye movements, span of attention, location of fixations, and eye fatigue in reading.

The most comprehensive treatment of reading by far during this period was Edmund Huey's (1908) text, which treated not only the experimental work on perception and rate of reading but also discussed at length the function of subvocal speech, the nature of meaning, the history of reading and reading methods, and reading instruction. Huey also attempted to relate research to pedagogy, especially in the visual domain: appropriate type sizes, lengths of printed lines, and so on. The book's major virtue, as summarized by a reviewer of the time, is no less important today: "Probably its most striking feature is the tempered, yet progressive mixture of science and practice" (Buchner, 1909, p. 149).[6]

The processing issues investigated during this period are discussed below under the general topics of eye movements, field of vision, perceptual span, and word recognition. These topics were pursued during an era in which big business came to dominate American life, when the telephone was becoming a commonplace fixture and the electric light bulb, the phonograph, and the internal combustion automobile were invented. When Cattell founded the *Psychological Review* in 1894, the population of the United States was less than 76 million; when Cattell was expelled from Columbia 23 years later because of (among other reasons) his pacifist views, the population had grown by almost 33 percent.

When Javal and Lamare first observed saccadic movements in reading, almost 20 percent of the population in America was illiterate. By the time Thorndike founded the *Journal of Educational Psychology* in 1911, illiteracy had been reduced by almost 50 percent. During this period the practice of reading underwent a number of changes that bore no relationship to the process research so enthusiastically pursued throughout college and university laboratories. The content of readers came to be dominated by "good literature," the whole-word method became the dominant approach to instruction, elocution was deemphasized, and reading disabilities were discovered. Nevertheless, process studies created an illusion of understanding that school psychologists used to promote particular methods of instruction.

Eye Movements[7]

The most controversial issue of the time concerned the nature of perception during reading, especially the question whether perception occurred while the eyes were moving. Cattell had suggested that it did, but experiments by Erdmann and Dodge (1898) and Dodge (1900, 1907) produced evidence to the contrary.[8] For those who held that visual perception did not occur during eye movements, a further controversy developed over the inhibitory mechanism. Dodge (1900) held that optical blurring was the cause, while Holt (1903) attributed it to a central inhibitory process. (Demonstrations of the correctness of Dodge's position were published by Volkmann, 1962, and Uttal and Smith, 1968.) Related to this issue was a conflict over the regularity of eye movements. Javal claimed that the eyes paused on every tenth letter in reading. Huey (1908), while not supporting the specific span of ten letters, nevertheless held that eye movements were rhythmic. Erdmann and Dodge (1898), on the other hand, stressed that irregularities in eye movements reflected individual differences in reading habits and differences in reading materials. In contrast to this view, Dearborn (1906) concluded that length of line, not sentence form or subject matter, conditioned the fixation pattern. He nevertheless found large individual differences in motor habits and noted especially the differences evidenced by the same subject in successive readings of the same passage.

Much less controversial were conclusions drawn about the nature of fixations during reading. Huey (1898) observed that fixations often involved small movements of the eye around a limited area. Both McAllister (1905) and Dearborn (1906) investigated this phenomenon, the latter finding that readjustments tended to occur primarily during the fixations at the beginning and end of a line.

Data were also accumulated on the number of fixations made on lines of different lengths, on the negative relationship between this variable and reading speed, and on the places within a line where the eyes are most likely to fixate. Investigation of this last variable is perhaps the most important contribution of Dearborn's (1906) dissertation. By comparing eye movements during successive rereadings of the same passages, Dearborn concluded that sequences of small function words required relatively more fixations than longer content words because they could not readily be fused into larger units: "Since they [prepositions, conjunctions, etc.] occur now with one word and now with another, they cannot without danger of error be fused into larger wholes, and, for that reason, they must, except where the content gives the connection, be separately perceived" (p. 85).

Dearborn (1906) was also the first to investigate the role of orthographic structure and pronounceability in reading. Using rows of unrelated nonsense words (five words per row) as stimuli, Dearborn obtained eye movement records from adult readers. From an analysis of these records and the structure of the nonsense words, he concluded the following:

> The length of the [fixation] pause is due in part to the sequence of letters. If that is the normal or more common sequence of words, such as "werq," "wopi," "gero," "apli," "enfa," the association process is less interfered with; such combinations as "ciuo," "weao," "dpin" disappoint the association expectancy and the time taken for perception is longer. A second and perhaps more important element is that of the ease of pronunciation . . . articulation or some form of motor expression is undoubtably one of the factors which determine the length of the fixation pauses in general (p. 65).

Although Dearborn's concept of common (i.e., English-like) letter sequences is slightly askew (the final *q* in "werq," for example, does not occur in English spelling), his suggestions about the role of orthographic structure and pronounce-ability were remarkable for his time. Not until the work of E. J. Gibson and her colleagues in the early 1960s (e.g., Gibson, Pick, Osser, and Hammond 1962) was this issue revived, and it remains unresolved today (cf. Kavanagh and Venezky 1980).

Field of Vision

The field of vision using letters as stimuli was studied continually throughout this period, but the most important contribution was that of Ruediger (1907). Using recognition of the letters *n* and *u*, Ruediger found that "the extent of the field varies with the size, legibility, and distance from the eye of the test units." By measuring the reading rates and number of fixations per line for his subjects, Ruediger also found that the size of the visual field did not relate to either reading speed or fixation pattern. He concluded that "reading rate is in the main determined centrally by the rapidity with which meaning is aroused after the words are seen."

Perceptual Span

Cattell's studies established that the field of distinct vision and the perceptual span were different entities, the latter depending upon the subject's ability to group stimuli into larger units. Erdmann and Dodge (1898) found similar results using isolated letters, words, and sentences. Quantz (1897) approached this problem by interrupting the reading stimulus during reading and counting the number of words that could be produced beyond this point. The resulting eye-voice span was found to vary not only by individual but also by place in the line where the interruption occurred. The span was longest at the beginning of the line and shortest at the end. Like Cattell (1886) and Erdmann and Dodge (1898), Hamilton (1907) used a tachistoscopic exposure of sentences but asked her subjects to report everything they could resolve of the stimulus, including image shape and first letters. She found that even when whole words were not resolved, various word features were nevertheless correctly retained.

More typical of work on span of attention during this period is a study by Griffing (1896) in which subjects from first grade through college attempted to identify briefly exposed capital letters. Each exposure contained six randomly drawn letters, which were arranged in two rows of three letters each. Exposure durations were one-tenth of a second and one second; each subject received ten trials at each exposure duration. Subjects showed continual improvement with increasing grade level, with the advantage of increased exposure time decreasing steadily over the same age span. Although Griffing's main concern was attention, he was not willing to attribute the entire experimental effect to this factor. He was clearly aware of immediate memory problems, mentioning the "ability to receive and retain a number of simultaneous retinal impressions."

Word Recognition

A major controversy centered on the cues for word perception. Erdmann and Dodge (1898) demonstrated that words could be read at a distance at which their constituent letters could not be identified. This result, which was later misinterpreted as support for a whole-word instructional strategy, was consistent with Cattell's earlier findings (1886) that the perceptual span for letters in meaningful words was considerably greater than the span for letters in random strings. Adding further support to the holistic explanation was a study reported by Pillsbury (1897) in which subjects were asked to identify words in which a letter was either omitted, blurred with an overtyped x, or replaced by another letter. These words were exposed for brief durations, and subjects were asked not only to identify each word but to comment on any letters that were not clearly seen. Subjects tended not to report the altered letters, and in some cases even insisted that a replaced letter was clearly seen. (Omissions were detected in 40 percent of the cases, replacements in 22 percent, and blurs in only 14 percent.)[9]

Opposed to the whole-word school were Goldscheider and Müller (1893), who found that misreadings of briefly exposed words were more frequent if "determining letters" were absent than if "indifferent letters" were missing. Also opposed were Messmer (1904) and Zeitler (1900), who derived a theory of "dominant letters" from studying which letters were reported most accurately in misreadings of tachistoscopically presented words.

In general, German psychologists supported the view that word recognition was mediated by letters and letter groups, while American psychologists argued for total form. An exception on this side of the Atlantic was Hamilton (1907), who seemed to support neither a pure word shape nor a dominant letter theory. Dearborn (1906) attempted to resolve this controversy through eye movement recordings, but he mistakenly assumed that changes in attention, as would occur during word perception mediated by letters, would necessarily be accompanied by fixation changes. Not finding any, he declared firmly for word shape. Huey (1908), while concluding that word form was the primary cue for recognition, hedged somewhat on the role that letters might play in this process. The general condition of word-perception theories in the early twentieth century was aptly described by Huey (1908), who wrote, perhaps for the entire century, "it is very difficult to draw final conclusions concerning visual perception in reading" (p. 102).

Other Issues

These were not the only topics investigated during this period. Subvocalization during reading was examined by, among others, Quantz (1897), Curtis (1899), and Secor (1900); word blindness was studied by Morgan (1896); and the integration of information across fixations was puzzled over by a number of investigators, including Dearborn (1906) and Dockeray (1910). But in general these were the main issues discussed, debated, and investigated empirically, and as a group they cover remarkably well the main processing issues under investigation today in reading.

Transition to Applied Research

Within a few years after the publication of Huey's book, the emphasis in reading research turned from basic perceptual processes to teaching and testing. These were, in Boring's terms, in the "spirit of the times." Individual differences and learning disabilities were incorporated into Dewey's progressive education, and from the interest in these came a need to measure progress objectively. By 1911 Binet's intelligence test had undergone two revisions, Volume 1 of the *Journal of Educational Psychology* had been issued, Thorndike's handwriting scale had been published, and the whole-word method of reading was in its ascendancy. From 1910 to 1920, a movement away from perceptual research occurred, with experimental psychologists shifting their interests to behaviorism and thereby abandoning research on basic reading processes to the educational psychologist.

For almost 40 years afterward, research on perceptual processes in reading received little emphasis. Some work of high quality did occur during the transition, including studies of reading speed (Pintner, 1913b; Mead, 1915; Oberholtzer, 1915), subvocalization (Pintner, 1913a), and eye movements, including the eye-voice span (C. T. Gray, 1917; Buswell, 1920; Judd & Buswell, 1922). But the intensity and excitement of the earlier period was lacking. Vernon lamented in 1931: "There had been little experimental work since the publication of Huey's *Psychology and Pedagogy of Reading* upon adult perception in reading, and the majority of the work upon children's perception in reading, though possibly of much pedagogical value, has been too disconnected and uncontrolled to provide results of much reliability or psychological interest" (Vernon, 1931, p. xiv). Competent studies of the eye-voice span (Tiffin, 1934; Fairbanks, 1937) and eye movements (Tinker, 1936, 1946; I. H. Anderson, 1937; Ballantine, 1951) continued to appear, but the major emphasis in reading research was on applied areas, particularly on diagnosis and assessment, as characterized by the studies of Arthur I. Gates and his colleagues (see pages 19–20).

Between about 1910 and the reentry of psychologists into reading research in the late 1950s, the total contribution to our understanding of perception in reading was small in comparison to the output up to 1910 and minuscule when considered relative to the number of psychological studies reported in each period.[10] Two major factors account for the lack of research on basic processes after 1910: (1) the domination of behaviorism in psychology and (2) the preoccupation with assessment within education. Another factor that may have been important but that is difficult to assess was funding. Educational research was never heavily funded prior to the passage of the Cooperative Research Act in 1954, and from the onset of the Great Depression until the late 1950s, research support was very difficult to obtain, especially for theoretical work. The Works Project Administration and several other agencies set up during the depression supported research at colleges and universities but tended to favor projects that employed large numbers of workers, such as normative studies of vocabulary or articulation ability. Communication of researchers across disciplines was also greatly reduced during this period, leading to a near stagnation of the field for at least 30 years.

Comprehension

Causes for Neglect

Romanes, a friend of Charles Darwin who extended the concept of evolution to the measurement of individual differences in animals and humans, reported the first study of reading comprehension in 1884. Adults read a ten-line paragraph during a fixed time period, after which they wrote down everything they could remember. Romanes found a 4–1 difference in reading rates among his subjects and observed that the more rapid readers recalled the most. He also noted that although recall was usually imperfect after the first reading, on a second reading many nonrecalled items were immediately recognized as familiar. This difference between recognition and recall he attributed to the "latency of ideas."

Occasional studies of comprehension followed over the next 75 years, but the investigation of cognition in reading comprehension up to the 1960s was never pursued as systematically as word recognition was. Part of the cause of this neglect was the dominating influence that Ebbinghaus had over the study of memory. The serial learning of nonsense syllables and lists of real words of various kinds was the central concern of verbal learning studies from the late 1800s until the revitalization of cognitive psychology after World War II. Memory for meaningful materials was studied throughout this period, as reviews by Whipple (1915) and Welborn and English (1937) demonstrate, but the critical mass of activity required to provide a fruitful contrast and testing of ideas was lacking.

It should also be noted that the present-day importance given to comprehension in reading research is a phenomenon of the last two or three decades. Through the first decade of this century, "reading" usually meant oral reading, wherein understanding was generally assumed when pronunciation was correct and natural. With the development of testing instruments and the shift in instructional emphasis to silent reading from 1915 to 1920, understanding gained in importance. Yet research on comprehension processes was so sparse up to the 1950s that even the phrase "reading comprehension" was seldom found. Woodworth (1938), for example, does not use the phrase at all in his chapter on reading, and devotes no space whatsoever to the topic. Anderson and Dearborn (1952), which claims to be "a text for professional courses on the psychology and teaching of reading," offers no general treatment of comprehension. The term appears here and there, but mostly in relation to methods of teaching reading or to testing. In contrast, both eye movements and word perception are afforded entire chapters. W. S. Gray (1938), in summarizing the contributions of the scientific movement in education to reading, stated just prior to the outbreak of World War II: "As to comprehension, the problems have proven even more challenging. The varied nature of comprehension has been emphasized by the wide variety of objective tests that have been used in measuring it; in fact, there is ample evidence now that the term is too loosely used" (p. 104).

Another factor that delayed the study of text comprehension was the emphasis on vocabulary that pervaded considerations of comprehension beginning before the middle of the nineteenth century. Ease or difficulty of understanding reading materials was attributed primarily to the difficulty of their vocabularies. According to W. S. Gray (1937), this belief is first evidenced in the McGuffey Readers, which were initially published between 1836 and 1844. By the early 1900s, vocabulary had become a major concern not only in reading but in intelligence testing as well. Chambers (1904), for example, gathered normative data on children's understanding of six vocabulary words (*monk, peasant, emperor, armor, nation, school*) through a survey carried out by almost 3000 teachers. The publication in 1921 of *The Teacher's Word Book* by Thorndike provided for both researchers and teachers a practical approach for manipulating vocabulary in reading (Klare, 1963; Clifford, 1978). Correlational studies by Hilliard (1926) and others also reinforced the primacy of vocabulary among those factors in comprehension that could be influenced by schooling.[11] (Correlational work was also pursued in more general studies of reading comprehension, as represented by Irion, 1925, and Dewey, 1935, which presented intercorrelations of scores on reading comprehension subtests, and by Davis, 1944, 1968, which used factor analytic techniques to isolate memory for word meanings and reasoning in reading as the two most important skills in reading comprehension. While interesting in themselves, these works failed either to fit into existing epistemological traditions or establish new ones. They remained, therefore, as singularities on a multicolored landscape of research trends.)

Even with these problems, research on comprehension processes prior to World War II made two notable contributions. The first, represented most prominently by the work of Henderson (1903) and Bartlett (1932), demonstrated the role of memory organization and prior experience in the recall of narrative and expository materials. The second, represented by Thorndike (1917a), established the view that reading comprehension was an active process, akin to problem solving.

Memory Organization

That the learning of new material is aided by knowledge already acquired has been common knowledge for at least 80 years. William James informed teachers of its validity in the 1890s (James, 1899/1958). Two years after Teddy Roosevelt became President, Laing (1903) presented the same notion in a manual for teachers of reading: "He [the child] interprets the new by means of the old concept" (p. 27). But Henderson (1903), in studying memory for connected discourse, seems to be the first to demonstrate this idea empirically.

Henderson, an educational psychologist, was interested in classroom learning, particularly in memory. "Any test of the result of school work," Henderson begins, "is at bottom a test of memory." Among the memory studies he describes, the most relevant for the present discussion involves successive recall of short (125 to 180 words) narrative and expository passages. Several hundred students, ranging from public school first-graders to Columbia University graduate students, were given passages to commit to memory. Three minutes were allowed for reading and rereading each passage, with stress on verbatim recall. At the end of the reading period the subjects were asked to write as much of the passage as they could. A second written reproduction was attempted two days later and a third four weeks later.

The scoring of responses was done in terms of the number of topics, subtopics, details, and words recalled. (This attempt to quantify the semantic content of reading materials was unusual for this period; it did not become a common research practice until almost 60 years later.) The most common changes found across successive reproductions were (1) regroupings, wherein related elements that appeared in different places in the original passage were brought together in recall; (2) simplification, generally through loss of detail; and (3) modification, "sometimes made in order to make the ideas consistent with the experience or preconceptions of the individual." Although Henderson's instructions to the subjects stressed verbatim recall, his results showed the dominance of conceptual organization in memory, with prior experience exerting an increasingly stronger role with each successive recall.

Bartlett (1932), who employed the same method of repeated reproduction in one study of remembering, arrived at similar conclusions. For stimulus materials, Bartlett employed eight different passages, but only one, adapted from a North American folk tale, was reported in detail. Twenty subjects, apparently all students at the University of Cambridge, were asked to read the passage twice to themselves. Fifteen minutes after completion of reading, each subject was asked to reproduce as much of the story as possible in writing. Successive reproductions were requested at varying intervals ranging from two weeks to ten years.

As with Henderson's responses, regroupings, simplifications, and modifications occurred, with the culturally different elements dropped or modified earliest. In summarizing his remembering studies, Bartlett concluded that the general "scheme or plan of a prose passage" tended to persist across all reproductions. In his theory of remembering, Bartlett reluctantly adopted Sir Henry Head's label "schema" to refer to "an active organization of past reactions, or of past experiences, which must always be supposed to be operating in any well-adapted organic response." Schemata are built from past experience, sometimes in a hierarchical fashion, with sensory "impulses" at the lowest level and common experiences (e.g., art, literature) at a higher level. Remembering is a constructive process, drawing on schemata that are often not closely connected.

This sketch does not do full justice to a work as innovative as Bartlett's *Remembering* was, but it does show the debt that present-day schema theory (and story grammars) owe to Bartlett.[12] Two further matters deserve brief mention here. First, Bartlett did not discuss Henderson's (1903) work. Both used the method of repeated reproduction, which according to Bartlett, originated with Philippe (1897). Second, the heavy influence of Ebbinghaus, dead for 24 years when *Remembering* was published, is exhibited continually through justifications for not employing nonsense syllables. For example, early in Chapter 1, Bartlett (1932) stated: "I have dealt at this length with the nonsense syllable experiments, partly because they are generally regarded as occupying a supremely important place in the development of exact method in psychology, and partly because the bulk of this book is concerned with problems of remembering studied throughout by methods which do not appear to approach those of the Ebbinghaus school in rigidity of control" (p. 6). Nonsense syllables may have provided an exact approach to the study of memory, but with far less substance than Bartlett attended to with his subjective procedures.

Reading as Thinking

Thorndike's contribution to the study of comprehension processes resulted from data gathered in field testing a reading comprehension test. The test consisted of paragraphs followed by open-ended questions. From a review of incorrect responses, Thorndike (1917a) concluded that incorrect responses resulted from three kinds of errors: (1) failure to identify the correct meaning of a word ("wrong connections with the words singly"), (2) assigning too little or too much importance to a word or idea ("over-potency or under-potency of elements"), or (3) failure to test seriously responses (or conclusions) drawn from reading ("failure to treat the ideas produced by the reading as provisional, and so to inspect and welcome or reject them as they appear").[13]

The first two categories were inferred from the frequent occurrence of particular words or phrases from the test paragraphs in incorrect responses. The third category was created to explain mostly nonsensical and illogical responses, such as "the day is age eleven" and "impassable roads are a kind of illness." Thorndike concluded that reading was not a passive, mechanical process but a highly active one involving "the same sort of organization and analytic action of ideas as occur in thinking of supposedly higher sorts." Moreover, errors in paragraph reading were attributed not to faulty organization or recall of material correctly interpreted but to a failure to comprehend the material during reading, a failure that the child seldom realizes. "Many of the children who made notable mistakes would probably have said that they understood the paragraph and, upon reading the questions on it, would have said that they understood them" (p. 331).

Since Thorndike's work, the analysis of reading errors has continued to be a fruitful approach to understanding reading behavior, yet few researchers have been able to probe as far beyond categorization as Thorndike did. Touton and Berry (1931), for example, classified 20,003 comprehension errors made by junior college entrants in such categories as "failure to grasp or retain ideas essential to the understanding of additional concepts" and "failure to see the setting or the context as a whole." Bennett (1942) classified 34,274 oral reading errors of middle-grade remedial readers according to stimulus-error overlap (e.g., same part of speech, real word versus nonsense word).[14] A more creative use of reading errors was demonstrated by Biemiller (1970), who used oral reading errors to infer reading strategies. Biemiller hypothesized three stages in first-grade reading: a context-dependent stage where substitution errors fit the context of the sentence but not usually the orthographic/phonological form of the target, a nonresponse stage where the reader generally gave no response to difficult words, and a flexibility stage wherein substitution errors on common words tended to be contextually driven and on difficult words were graphically driven.[15]

Thorndike's work on reading as thinking was reflected in the 1940s and 1950s in instructional studies of critical thinking and critical reading. His observations on children's abilities to recognize their mistakes, however, were not pursued empirically until recently, when metacognition studies became fashionable.

READING INSTRUCTION

The twelve labors of Hercules, from killing the Nemean Lion to bringing back Cerberus from Hades, approximate in difficulty the task of organizing the published research on reading instruction. This collection of over 15,000 books, pamphlets, articles, and occasional records of educational verbosity is an enduring testimony to the patience of the American printer and the vulnerability of American forests. From the insightful and innovative work of William S. Gray, Arthur I. Gates, and a couple of dozen others, to the most thoughtless correlation of ability A with ability B, this body of research incorporates every imaginable method and topic of investigation. To read, comprehend, and evaluate even 1 percent of it is a staggering and not entirely enjoyable task.

The central problem is not simply that the research is poorly executed; a bad study of an important issue can be more informative than an elegant study of a meaningless issue. Instead, the problem is discerning why a great majority of the studies were done at all, other than to satisfy some academic or professional requirement. A major portion of this literature can be classed as fishing expeditions, that is, as almost random searches for relationships, unanchored by any theoretical frameworks and often unbothered by the limitations of the methods employed. Rather than belabor these shortcomings, a brief sketch is presented here of the general trends in instructional research over the last 90 years, with emphasis on representative works. No attempt is made to cover completely the topics investigated or the methods employed. Some useful and important studies no doubt have been missed, but perhaps such shortcomings will encourage others to probe more deeply into these topics.

Scientific Education and Reading

The most important educational trend that affected reading instruction research was the scientific movement in education, which began in the late 1800s and accelerated rapidly after the turn of the century with the entry of efficiency studies and scientific management into business and industry (Callahan, 1962). At the turn of the century, school efficiency was a major issue. Money, space, and time were in short supply, particularly in the major cities where new immigrants and refugees from farmlands were flooding in. Thorndike, among others, held that with the help of science, schools could be run more efficiently, and educators, trained in scientific pedagogy, could gain control of education.

The School Survey

One direction that the scientific movement took was the school survey, which began with studies of teaching methods undertaken by Joseph Mayer Rice (1893). Although Rice concentrated on spelling and mathematics, his techniques were soon adapted for studying other curricular components, including reading.[16] By 1910 the school survey was the primary weapon used by school reformers to promote educational change (Tyack, 1974). A major study of the Cleveland, Ohio, school system, undertaken in 1915–1916 under the direction of Leonard P. Ayres, utilized reading tests for the first time on a large scale (Moley, 1923; Caswell, 1929).

The Cleveland survey, like many before and after it, focused on the complete educational system, from the superintendent to classroom materials and teaching methods. For reading, this meant analyses of the goals of reading instruction, the training of teachers, the methods and materials and time used, and the achievements of students in different components of reading. This in turn prompted studies of educational change, whereby the results of such surveys were converted to suggestions for organizational or instructional change and then the results of the changes were monitored. Maple (1917), for example, reported on the results in reading achievement that derived from changes in both school organization and instructional methods in the Vincennes, Indiana, schools.

Similarly, Neal and Foster (1926) described how, as a result of a survey, improvements were made in the teaching of comprehension in grades 4 and 5 of the San Antonio, Texas, schools. In this study, teachers were assisted in developing five new methods for teaching comprehension of reading materials. These methods centered on (1) finding answers to factual questions posed before reading; (2) finding answers to factual questions posed after reading; (3) finding answers that required organization of ideas from several sentences, paragraphs, or pages; (4) generating titles for paragraphs; and (5) outlining. According to Neal and Foster, the methods that the teachers developed for teaching each of these skills produced "marked" pupil progress.

The most thorough of these studies is that of W. S. Gray (1933), which reported on a multiyear reading improvement study in a small number of Chicago schools. With the results of intensive surveys of the five participating schools, including (besides organizational factors) assessment of the reading scores and reading habits of the pupils, conferences were held with the administrators of each school to assist them in analyzing their problems. The project staff then worked with the school staff to develop and implement improvement plans. Finally, reading achievement was reassessed one and two years after the changes. The importance of this particular study is not in its specific results but in the methodology employed, which borders on a *natural experiment* in the sense proposed by Bronfenbrenner (1976). Participant-observer techniques were employed, diaries were kept, and both subjective and quantitative data were reported. In addition, this study offers a model for planned instructional improvement and evaluation that seems as applicable to reading instruction today as it was 50 years ago.

Surveys of reading practices were not a major concern of reading research again until the late 1950s when the Carnegie Corporation sponsored a series of survey studies. Austin, Morrison, et al. (1961) was the first of these to be published, covering the preservice training of reading teachers. This was followed by Austin and Morrison (1963), which surveyed the inservice training of reading teachers. Barton and Wilder (1964) dealt with the communication of reading research into practice, but also analyzed the backgrounds and attitudes of the "reading experts." The last of these reports, Chall (1967), on the controversy over methods for teaching reading, was instrumental in focusing attention on phonics instruction.

In 1971 the publication of George Weber's survey of successful inner-urban schools initiated a new wave of school surveys based on a case-study methodology. Unlike the W. S. Gray (1933) study, more recent surveys have focused primarily on schools that succeed, in an attempt to isolate school-wide factors that account for unexpectedly high achievement. Although methodological rigor is often lacking in these studies, particularly in the procedures used for defining school success, they have had a positive impact on schooling practices.

A second direction the scientific movement took was in the development of objective measures for educational outcomes. Through the efforts of Cattell and Thorndike, a psychological basis for mental testing was established in this country early in the twentieth century. In 1910 Thorndike published his handwriting scale, and in 1914 his reading scales and tests. (Thorndike's 1917 papers on reading comprehension were based on the data obtained in field testing these instruments.) William S. Gray, a student of Thorndike, published the Gray Standardized Oral Reading Paragraphs in 1915 (Smith, 1965), and Courtis (1915) reported standard scores for measuring various components of reading.[17] Within a short time, reading achievement tests and then diagnostic tests became an indispensable component of the schooling ritual, a position they still hold today.

With the availability of standardized reading tests, instructional research shifted quickly to assessing teaching methods and identifying components of reading ability. Although much of this effort is flawed for one reason or another, the work of Arthur I. Gates and his colleagues remains a major contribution to an understanding of both reading assessment and reading instruction. Gates received his bachelor's and master's degrees from the University of California (Berkeley) and then went to Columbia for his Ph.D. in psychology under Cattell in 1917. He was immediately appointed to the faculty of Teachers College, where he remained until his retirement in 1956.

Gates (1921) explored the relationship between reading ability and intelligence in elementary school children through measures of oral and silent reading (including both reading speed and comprehension), vocabulary knowledge, and intelligence, and drew two important conclusions from the resulting correlation matrix. First, he found no evidence in the data to justify the notion of a general reading factor; instead, he found evidence for a number of moderately independent factors. Second, he found that the correlation of reading ability with intelligence increased from grade to grade, a result that he interpreted as evidence for at least two stages in reading: (1) a basic mechanics stage, which is not highly related to intelligence; and (2) a higher-level comprehension stage, which is.

> Since the inter-correlations among reading tests were as high in the lower grades as in the higher, the increasing correlation with mental age may be interpreted to mean that intelligence, as measured by Stanford-Binet, shows itself only when the mechanics of reading are fairly well mastered (Gates, 1921, pp. 458f).

In a later study Gates (1926) examined the relationship between reading ability and the perception of words, geometric forms, and digits. Although the perception of words correlated at a relatively high level with silent reading (even with IQ removed), the perception of geometric forms and digits did not. Moreover, the correlation of word perception with form or digit perception was low.

The implications of this study for prereading training are obvious, yet they are ignored in many reading readiness programs, which concentrate on identification and matching of geometric forms.

These correlational studies in the 1920s led in the 1930s to attempts by Gates and others to develop tests for predicting reading success. Wilson and Flemming (1938) and Gates, Bond, and Russell (1939) explored the predictive value of such abilities as oral vocabulary, intelligence, letter-name knowledge, and visual perception for end-of-first-grade reading success. In contrast to interpretations given years later by reading specialists, neither study found letter-name knowledge to be the best single predictor of later reading success. In comparing the results of these two studies, Gates, Bond, and Russell (1939) concluded: "The most useful reading readiness tests are tests of ability clearly involved in learning to read" (p. 29). Similar studies of predictive tests continued into the 1960s (Durrell, 1958; Weiner & Feldmann, 1963; deHirsch, Jansky & Langford, 1966), although the contribution of such studies either to classroom practice or to a basic understanding of reading is questionable, especially when factors that the schools have no control over are used for prediction.

Time Spent

With the focus on assessment of process and outcome that the scientific movement in education nurtured, a concern for time spent in schooling was a natural consequence. Rice (1893) was the first to investigate the relationship between instructional time and learner outcomes, finding that for spelling, time spent past a minimum amount did not lead to further achievement. The first study of time spent on reading was performed by Charles W. Eliot, president of Harvard University, who in the 1890s found through a simulation experiment that although the school curriculum guides specified that about 37 percent of the school day was to be devoted to reading and English language, the total time children spent in reading throughout the first six grades totaled only 46 hours (Eliot, 1898). Eliot, who founded the Harvard classics and promoted the college elective system, campaigned vigorously for the widespread introduction of "good literature" into the public schools. The extant school readers he called "ineffable trash."

Although Eliot advocated more school time for real literature, by the turn of the century educators like John Dewey were presenting schemes for shortening the number of years spent in elementary schooling. Before World War I, both the National Council of Education and the National Society for the Study of Education had appointed committees to study the time required for different curricular subjects, with the expressed aim of cutting one or more years from the elementary-secondary schedule (Holmes, 1915). The Simplified Spelling Board (1906) contributed its own form of irrationality to the time issue by declaring that the current "intricate and disordered spelling . . . wastes a large part of the time and effort given to the instruction of our children, keeping them, for example, from one to two years behind the school children of Germany . . ." (p. 7).

Although investigations of time actually spent in reading instruction were published periodically (e.g., *Fourteenth Yearbook of the NSSE*, 1915), and surveys of reading instruction included assessments of instructional time (e.g., W. S. Gray, 1933), few attempts were made prior to Harris and Serwer (1966) to relate instructional time directly to achievement. Thiesen (1921), summarizing several studies of questionable quality, reported that no significant relationship was found between the amount of time given to reading and phonics (grades 1, 3, 4, and 5) and reading ability. In these studies, however, *time* was not measured by observation, but by teacher report. The present focus in instructional studies on time on task (e.g., Stallings and Kaskowitz, 1974), although representing methodological refinement over the work done by Rice and the early-twentieth-century experimenters, has yet to progress beyond the general conclusions reached by Harris and Serwer (1966) that some instructional tasks are productive for learning and some are not. Thiesen (1921) concluded similarly, "it is entirely possible, e.g., that many children may gain more from ten minutes spent in independent silent reading than they would in a twenty-minute oral-reading recitation period of the conventional type" (p. 3).

From Oral to Silent Reading

The emphasis on meaning in reading instruction, which Horace Mann and other nineteenth-century educational reformers promoted, led by the end of the first decade in this century to a change in instructional emphasis from oral to silent reading. Where a popular manual for reading instruction declared before the turn of the century, "there can be no good reading without the ability to call words readily . . ." (Pollard, 1889), by the 1920s the prevailing wisdom had shifted. "The social needs of former days required the teaching of expressive oral reading . . . the social needs of the present require the teaching of effective rapid silent reading" (S. C. Parker, quoted in Wheat, 1923, p. 6). The change to silent reading resulted from general changes in American society. The change from a rural, cottage-industry society to an urban, mass-production society, which accelerated during this time, increased the need for literacy both in occupations and in everyday affairs. Advances during the 1870s and 1880s in the production of cheap paper and in high-volume printing techniques led to a significant increase in the production of inexpensive reading materials of all kinds. And the growing wealth of the country accelerated an emphasis on cultural activities, including the reading of all forms of literature.

These technical and social forces, coupled with the scientific movement in education that began with the school studies of Joseph Mayer Rice in the 1890s, led to analyses of silent reading abilities and, to a lesser degree, to the study of how vocabulary was acquired. Comparisons of reading rates for oral and silent reading were made by Huey (1908), who found that good readers could read one and a half to two times faster silently than orally. Pintner and Gilliland (1916), among others, compared comprehension abilities in oral and silent reading and found no significant differences in the number of ideas retained. Related studies by Mead (1915), C. T. Gray (1917), Judd (1918), and Judd and Buswell (1922) were used effectively, although not always objectively, by instructional reformers of that era, particularly at the University of Chicago (e.g., W. S. Gray, Judd, and Buswell) to promote an emphasis on silent reading in instruction.

The issues raised during this period on the differences between oral and silent reading continued to be investigated for another 30 years. While Judd and Buswell had emphasized the differences in oral and silent reading habits, particularly as revealed by eye movement studies, Anderson and Swanson (1937), Swanson (1937), and Fairbanks (1937) demonstrated a high similarity between the two kinds of reading. Anderson and Swanson (1937) showed that for college students, eye movements in oral and silent reading, as measured by pause duration, fixation frequency, and reading rate, were highly correlated. Swanson (1937) and Fairbanks (1937) both found high correlations between oral and silent reading errors (for college students). Anderson and Dearborn (1952), in an insightful review of the oral-silent reading issue, hypothesized that "oral and silent reading may be the overt and implicit expressions, respectively, of the same fundamental process."

This issue illustrates one of the difficulties in relating research to practice. W. S. Gray (1938), among other educators, attributes the change in instructional practice cited above to research results. An equally valid hypothesis is that by common sense and other subjective approaches, influential educators decided to encourage silent reading, and then through their own investigations and through selective interpretations of other works, marshaled support for their position. By modern standards, oral reading was overemphasized in the curriculum of the late nineteenth and early twentieth centuries. However, what should have constituted scientific proof of this hypothesis at that time (or even now) is difficult to assess. The issue, unfortunately, reduces to human motives; that is, were W. S. Gray, Judd, Buswell, and others motivated by an objective evaluation of empirical data, or were they driven by a need to justify their opinions? Perhaps the problem was simply that what had become obvious to objective observers—that schools needed to emphasize silent reading—was not provable empirically. One could invoke empirical data to justify certain aspects of silent reading instruction, but the need to teach silent reading depended on interpretations of unquantifiable social, cultural, and occupational factors.[18]

Legibility

Research on legibility represents the most ancient line of reading research, dating from at least the 1790s; yet it also represents one of the most curious to render into psychological terms because its goal is not an improved understanding of human behavior but the improved design of printed materials. For this reason, legibility studies have been derived from practical considerations of typographical variables (type face, type size, line length, etc.) rather than from hypotheses about visual or psychological processes. Consequently, these studies have not produced theories (interesting or otherwise) about either reading or the effects of typographical variation on psychological or physiological abilities. A secondary effect of this atheoretical stance has been the failure of legibility researchers to agree on appropriate dependent measures.

The earliest studies utilized distances at which print was still readable (Anisson, cited in Wiggins, 1967), visibility under dimmed lighting (Javal, 1879), speed of perception (Dockeray, 1910), and eye movements (Huey, 1908). Later research added visual fatigue (Carmichael & Dearborn, 1947), speed of reading (Paterson & Tinker, 1929), peripheral vision (Weiss, 1917), and a bevy of psychophysiological measures including blink rate, pupillary changes, heart rate, nervous muscular tension, and fatigue of the extrinsic eye muscles (Lukiesch & Moss, 1942).[19] Pyke (1926) decided on length of sentence that could be read during a limited tachisto-scopic exposure (3 seconds) as his measure of legibility, but Vernon (1931) sug-gested that the only valid measure for adults is fatigue. Whatever the merits of this issue, the main intention here is only to sketch the progression of legibility studies over the last 180 years or so and define the major results and lingering problems of this field. The most comprehensive review of this field from a typo-graphic viewpoint is Spencer (1968). Pyke (1926) gives a summary of research results from 1825 until 1925, while Tinker (1965) and Zachrisson (1965) summa-rize research techniques. Current research reports can be found in the journal *Visible Language* (before 1970 called the *Journal of Typographic Research*).

Anisson's study consisted of a comparison between a modern Roman face (Didot) and a Garamond style. Expert judges found that they could read the Garamond specimen at a greater distance than the Didot specimen. In the late 1820s, Charles H. Babbage (1791–1871), remembered best for his design for an analytical engine, also employed a majority vote in assessing the effects of different colors of paper on readability of print. But the first serious studies of legibility were performed by Emile Javal of the University of Paris, whose work on eye movements was described earlier in this chapter. Javal published extensively on legibility. In addition, he designed a type style he claimed gave maximal legibility to all letters, a claim that found limited support from his contempo-raries.[20] The maximal distance approach and visibility under reduced illumination were the primary methods used by Javal, although strong opinion was also utilized, particularly in defense of his alphabet.

With the primary role that reading played in the early history of experimen-tal psychology, a number of studies performed from an interest in mental pro-cesses also contributed to the growing concern with legibility. Among these were Huey (1898) on the distinctiveness of different parts of the word, Cattell (1885) on the distinctness of lowercase letters, Sanford (1888) on letter confusions, and Dockeray (1910) on the width of the field of distinct vision for letters of the alphabet. Dockeray's study employed a Dodge mirror tachistoscope and a Cattell fall chronoscope to control the exposure of letter pairs spaced at variable distances from a fixation point. From the 15,000 exposures given to three subjects, Dockeray concluded that "probably the fields of distinct vision overlap in successive fixa-tions."

Unlike basic process research, studies of legibility were unaffected either by the advent of behaviorism or educational psychology. Before 1920, legibility studies were being sponsored by printers and industries, one of the earliest being a study of indenting sponsored by the New York City Telephone Company to improve the legibility of their directories (Baird, 1917).[21] Engineering, printing, and school hygiene societies showed an interest in legibility as early as 1911 (Pyke, 1926).

By the early 1930s, when relatively large amounts of research on legibility were beginning, the major problems in methodology faced today were clearly defined. Pyke (1926) had already shown that no relationship existed between the relative legibility of type faces rendered by nonsense words and those ren-dered by meaningful materials. He found, moreover, that the type styles readers were most familiar with were the most legible to them and that relatively large changes in type size were necessary for producing measurable changes in reading habits. Both Pyke (1926) and Vernon (1931) argued for the use of natural reading situations for measuring legibility.

Through the 1930s and 1940s, reading speed became the most important measure of legibility, primarily through the work of Donald G. Paterson and Miles A. Tinker (e.g., Paterson & Tinker, 1929, 1938; Tinker, 1926, 1936). Their basic paradigm involved a 30-word sentence in which one word was incongruous. The subject's speed in locating and crossing out this word was measured. Although this technique was attacked for requiring too low a level of comprehension and for placing the rapid skimmer at a disadvantage, it nevertheless produced a large volume of data on different typographic variables. By the 1950s, the major variables of interest were still size of type, type face, leading and line length, papers and ink, and other format characteristics (indenting, margins, etc.).

Among the major post–World War II works on legibility is a text on research by Burt (1959); several major works by Tinker (1963, 1965), including his annotated bibliography of studies on legibility (Tinker, 1966); and Spencer's (1968) handsomely printed summary. (Spencer, 1968, presents a concise summary of the results of the last 180 years of legibility research.)

Readability

The desire to control the reading difficulty of instructional materials developed slowly through the first half of the nineteenth century, prompted primarily by the child-centered schooling philosophies of Pestolazzi (1746–1827) and Herbart (1776–1841). Prior to the McGuffey Readers, rare and obsolete vocabulary was as likely to occur in instructional materials as were common words. For example, in the 1813 edition of the *American Primer*, a popular alternative to the Webster Spellers for teaching reading and spelling to children, the list for teaching first-syllable accent for three-syllable words includes *abdicate, battledore, equipage, foppery, niggardly,* and *ominous,* among slightly less rarefied exemplars. With the McGuffey Readers, vocabulary became the dominant method for controlling reading difficulty. Not until the end of the nineteenth century were sentence length and sentence type investigated as indicators of style (Sherman, 1893; Gerwig, 1894). These were not, however, incorporated into evaluations of readability until almost 30 years later. Word length, measured by number of syllables, was suggested as a readability measure in the late 1920s (Bear, 1927, cited in Klare, 1963) and was incorporated into a readability formula within a few years (Johnson, 1930).

Interest in controlling vocabulary for foreign language materials began in the late nineteenth century. By 1910, vocabulary counts for Russian, German, and Latin had been made as a step toward standardizing reading materials for instruction in these languages. These lists, according to Clifford (1978), were probably instrumental in initiating Thorndike's interest in compiling a vocabulary list for English, an activity that he apparently began around 1911. The resulting product, published in 1921 as *The Teacher's Word Book,* quickly became the standard frequency list for English and in one form or another remained so until the computer-generated word counts of the 1960s and 1970s (e.g., Kučera & Francis, 1967; Carroll, Davies, & Richman, 1971).

In what Chall (1958) claims to be the first readability formula, an estimate of the vocabulary difficulty of a book was generated from a sample of 1000 words selected throughout the text (Lively & Pressey, 1923). The weighted median index number that this formula generated was based on the word frequencies given in Thorndike's *Word Book*. Washburne and Vogel (1926) tested the validity of the Lively-Pressey formula by correlating the formula-generated grade levels of selected books with those derived from the median grade-level reading abilities of children who had read and claimed to enjoy these books. (A correlation of .80 was found for the 700-book sample.)

Vogel and Washburne (1928) developed a new readability formula from a subset of the Washburne and Vogel (1926) reading sample, using four different weighted variables computed on a random sample of 1000 words. The formula was:

$$\text{Reading score} = 17.43 + .085w + .101p + .604x - .411s,$$

where w = number of different words in the 1000-word sample

p = number of prepositions in the 1000-word sample

x = number of words in the 1000-word sample not on the Thorndike (1921) list

s = number of simple sentence in a sample of 75 sentences drawn from the text.

By combining variables linearly, Vogel and Washburne (1928) established the prototype for almost every readability formula that followed. Klare (1963) lists 39 formulas published between 1928 and 1959, almost all of which derive a measure from some subset of scores based on word type, word frequency, syllables or letters per word, sentence length, sentence type, and part of speech. The most important alternative to this form of readability estimation is the cloze procedure (W. L. Taylor, 1953), which utilizes a paradigm that Ebbinghaus employed in the 1890s.

Since the 1920s, both reliability and validity of readability formulas have been worked over repeatedly, but little can be concluded definitively except that with whatever faults these formulas have, they have become permanent fixtures in the instructional landscape. No serious reading series is generated without guidance from them, and few major adoptions of reading materials are made without at least paying lip service to readability levels.

RETURN TO PROCESS RESEARCH

In the late 1950s, experimental psychologists, motivated by a renewed interest in cognitive processes and encouraged by federal funding for basic research related to the improvement of education, returned to the study of reading processes. Most notable of the studies done at the beginning of this revival were those produced by an interdisciplinary team at Cornell University, which later evolved into Project Literacy.[22] The first group of these studies (Levin et al., 1963) included work on letter recognition, letter-sound correspondences, children's abilities to segment words into separate sounds, and a variety of other topics related to perception and learning. Later studies added comprehension, oral reading errors, and the eye-voice span.

Other basic investigations were also carried out in the 1950s and 1960s. Gilbert (1959), for example, investigated the relationship between speed of word recognition and comprehension. Tulving and Gold (1963) and Morton (1964) examined the influence of sentence context on visual word recognition. From Shannon's (1948, 1951) work on information measures arose a number of studies on word-recognition mechanisms (e.g., Miller, Bruner, & Postman, 1954). Hardyck and Petrinovich (1969), using feedback techniques, explored subvocal speech and its relationship to reading speed. These are only a few of the numerous psychological studies that originated in the 1950s and 1960s, drawing on psychological traditions that varied from behaviorism through verbal learning and information processing.

One impetus for this renewed interest was the Cooperative Research Act of 1954, which authorized the commissioner of the U.S. Office of Education to enter into "contracts or jointly financed cooperative arrangements with universities and colleges and state educational agencies for the conduct of research, surveys, and demonstrations in the field of education" (U.S. Congress, 1954). The Office of Education, besides funding separate, field-initiated studies on reading, attempted both to coordinate research studies and to focus research on selected objectives. The former effort was represented by the Cooperative Research Program in Primary Reading Instruction, which attempted to compare outcomes from 13 independent instructional studies (Bond & Dykstra, 1967; Dykstra, 1968) and the latter by the Targeted Research and Development Program on Reading, which attempted to apply a convergence technique, borrowed from medical research, to the planning and management of reading research programs (Gephart, 1970). Results of the Primary Reading Project remain controversial; the Convergence Technique has, like the V-12 engine and the triplane, been quietly laid aside. The latter technique did, however, produce a major synthesis of the contemporary literature on reading research (Davis, 1971).

In 1972 the National Institute of Education was founded, with the goals (among others) of strengthening the scientific and technological foundations of education and building an effective educational research and development system. Since its creation, NIE has given a high priority to reading research; however, its commitment to ongoing curriculum development projects inherited from the Office of Education and the Office of Economic Opportunity and its failure to win substantial financial backing from the Congress in recent years have limited the funds available for basic studies.[23]

FROM THE PAST TO THE FUTURE

The last hundred years of reading studies have been rich in lessons for modern research. The work of Dodge (1906), Dearborn (1906), and Huey (1908), as a beginning, demonstrates how early in this century experimental psychologists confronted the most basic perceptual problems under investigation today, and how little conceptually has been gained since their time on these issues. Henderson (1903) and Bartlett (1932) deviated from the accepted scientific methods of their times, yet their insights into text processing are comparable to those gained from the most rigorously controlled experiments of today. For those interested in field methodologies in reading research, the school surveys (e.g., W. S. Gray, 1933) and the early case studies of individual learners (e.g., Monroe, 1932) are informative reading. But the study of reading instruction is still in search of an adequate methodology. Perhaps the suggestions of Piaget (1935/1970) for an *experimental pedagogy,* or the naturalistic methods currently in vogue, will move the investigation of reading instruction closer to the level of acceptability already attained by process research.

In reflecting on this history, it is difficult to ignore its fragmented, staccato nature. Reading research has not made a disciplined journey over the landscape of time. Instead, it has started and stopped, then gushed forth again for a few years here and there, sometimes in many places at once, but seldom with the continuity that accumulates strength and definition with the addition of each merging stream. Ideas were pursued vigorously and then abandoned, some to be rediscovered many years later and others to be ignored. No single cutting edge was ever definable; only a series of different foci that waxed and waned, often without sight of each other. Great men and women labored at the task, but their influence often derived more from their opinions about reading instruction than from the quality and results of their studies. And the component of research that found its way into practice could seldom be predicted from the validity and value of the research itself (cf. Singer, 1970).

The current revival of interest from experimental psychologists in basic reading research has led to interesting controversies, especially in perceptual processing and comprehension. Yet certain conditions under which the work is being done may limit its potential for improving reading instruction or even for gaining a clearer understanding of the reading process. Most present-day studies on reading processes are not motivated by an interest in reading per se. Much of the work on word recognition, for example, is aimed toward the construction of information processing models for vision, rather than toward reading models or even toward an understanding of how words are recognized in normal reading. Although the results of these endeavors may someday contribute to the improvement of literacy, the lack of attention to ecologically valid tasks reduces this possibility.

But even if the studies being done today were directed toward an improved understanding of reading, a chasm between research results and reading instruction would remain. First, adults and not children are the favored subjects for most of the studies now being reported on reading processes. What we are learning from these studies is therefore about the overpracticed abilities of accomplished readers and not, in general, about how these abilities are acquired.[24] We still do not know, for example, if the word-recognition processes of poor readers develop through stages that differ qualitatively from those experienced by good readers, or if only the rates at which these stages develop differ. Moreover, the few learning studies of reading processes reported tend to be based on short laboratory sessions (30 to 60 minutes per subject) rather than sustained learning in classroom settings.

Second, investigations on learning processes do not within themselves answer instructional questions. The what and how of instruction are functions of available resources, teacher competencies and attitudes, and entry-level abilities and interests of students as much as they are functions of processing strategies. An abiding appreciation of the complexities of curricular design and classroom practice are required for translating research results into improved instruction, yet, as is discussed below, few experimental psychologists who work on reading have involved themselves in these areas. Whether or not a true science of instruction is possible remains to be resolved. Perhaps William James (1901) was correct when he said, "You make a great, a very great mistake, if you think that psychology, being the science of mind's laws, is something from which you can deduce definite programmes and schemes and methods of instruction for immediate schoolroom use. Psychology is a science, and teaching is an art, and sciences never generate arts directly out of themselves" (pp. 7f).

In the communication of research results to other researchers and teaching specialists, conditions today appear to be much less favorable than those of 80 years ago. At the turn of the century, controversies over reading were a prominent part of the psychological literature. The journals were fewer in number: *Psychological Review* and *American Journal of Psychology* in the United States, *Mind* in England, and *Philosophische Studien* and one or two others in Germany and France. Experimenters in different laboratories were in frequent communication, and competition was at a professional level, much like that which has occurred in the present-day field of genetics (Watson, 1968). Today most reading research is fragmented and isolated, even though professional organizations have attempted to improve communication through special interest groups, and governmental funding agencies have attempted to bring researchers together to discuss their work or draft priority lists for research funding.

Finally, a concern must be expressed for the rationale that most funding agencies now give for support of basic reading research, that is, improving reading instruction. Although some knowledge about the reading process is needed for improving instruction, the claim that any basic research on reading can do this is bound to crack under even the most casual examination. Investigations of letter recognition, for example, are definitely part of basic reading research, and a thorough understanding of how letters are discriminated would provide a valuable insight into visual processing. But such information could do little to improve reading instruction because no major instructional problems are associated with letter discrimination. The issue is not the support of letter-discrimination studies, but the justification of such support under the guise of instructional improvement.

The other side of this issue is the diversion of instructional funds to research that has a low potential for improving the acquisition of literacy. Much remains to be learned about how reading ability is acquired and especially about how home and school factors influence this process, yet it is naive to assume that such knowledge will result from heavy funding of experimental psychologists who are not committed to practical applications in reading. If reading research is to influence instruction, then more experimental psychologists will have to be persuaded to interact professionally with teachers and curriculum developers, and to concern themselves with the practical side of reading. There is little chance that articles in professional publications will be sufficient to influence practice, or that practitioners will find the time and training to do good basic research. While it is reasonable to predict that a history such as this, written 25 years hence, will have a significantly augmented research literature to draw from, there is less chance that with the continuation of the current research procedures, significant advances in instruction will have resulted.

NOTES

1. Nevertheless, according to Woodworth (1944), Cattell's approach to reaction-time studies differed radically from Wundt's; in particular, Cattell rejected the partitioning of reaction time into time intervals for constituent processes (e.g., perception, choice, association). On Donders and the reaction experiment, see Boring (1950, pp. 174ff). Donder's original description of the subtractive method, published in 1868 under the title "Die schnelligkeit psychisher" (On the speed of mental process), has been translated by Koster (1969).

2. Many of Cattell's works have been reprinted in *James McKeen Cattell: Man of Science, 1860–1944*, 2 vols. (Lancaster, Pa.: Science Press, 1947). In addition, his work on reading is summarized by Dearborn (1914). Sokal (1971) contains Cattell's unpublished (and brief) autobiography. For perceptual studies on reading prior to Cattell's work, see Schmidt (1917).

3. These studies and others by Cattell were more fully described a year earlier in Wundt's new journal, *Philosophische Studien* (Cattell, 1885).

4. The discovery that eye movements in reading occurred in jumps was made jointly by Javal and Lamare, who was working under Javal (1878).

5. The original Huey text is referenced as Huey (1908). The reissue, with a foreword by John Carroll and an introduction by Paul Kolers, as Huey (1908/1968).

6. This quote is also given in John Carroll's Foreword to the 1968 reissue of Huey's text, which contains, in addition, a brief but highly informative biography of Huey.

7. Historical reviews of eye movements in reading are found in Crosland (1924), Woodworth (1938), and Anderson and Dearborn (1952). E. A. Taylor (1937) reviews the development of instrumentation for eye movement recording.

8. As Huey (1908) points out, Cattell later acknowledged the untenability of his position.

9. Walter Bowers Pillsbury was a student of Titchener at Cornell and was clearly in the Titchener camp on the role of introspection in psychological research. The work cited here was Pillsbury's dissertation study, done at Cornell over a three-year period, beginning in the fall of 1893. Five subjects in all were involved, of whom one was Titchener himself and one was Margaret Washburn, another member of the Cornell faculty. According to Pillsbury (1897), both Titchener and Washburn "knew the object of the experiments and had given advice in the preparation of the apparatus, material, etc." (p. 344). The data for these two subjects were markedly different from that of the other three subjects.

10. There does not exist a comprehensive bibliography on basic reading research. Gray (1925) provides a selective survey of work done up to July 1924, but the number of studies that Gray reports has become the basis for a modern-day cabalism that is both misleading and inaccurate. Duker and Nally (1956) and Mathews (1966) ignore Gray's ommission of the European works and present his figures as absolutes, without reservation, for all reading research. Smith (1965) qualifies one of these counts as being based on investigations in England and in the United States: "By 1910 only

34 studies had been reported altogether by investigators in England and the United States" (p. 154). Even if Gray's caveat had been noticed, his figures would still not accurately reflect the research done during this period because Gray was selective, not exhaustive, and he was primarily interested in pedagogical matters. Huey (1908), for example, cites dozens of works in English up to 1908 that Gray did not include. Perusal of the first 15 volumes of the *Psychological Review* (1895–1908) reveals further works on reading not counted by Gray. Finally, the emphasis on absolute numbers, especially with the modifier "only," gives a mistaken impression of paucity. Taken in perspective, a relatively large amount of material was published during this period.

11. Wiley (1928) was apparently the first to question the appropriateness of frequency-based lists for children. Wiley suggested that latency to respond to a word in a free-association task might be a better predictor of a person's knowledge of a word than its frequency of occurrence in print.

12. On schema theory in reading research, see R. C. Anderson (1977) and Spiro (1977).

13. Thorndike stretched these observations across three articles (1917a, 1917b, 1917c), occasionally using identical examples and arguments.

14. R. M. Weber (1968) reviews the major studies done on oral reading errors, starting in the 1940s. Interesting earlier studies that attended to the kinds of errors children made in reading include Bowden (1911) and Gates and Boeker (1923).

15. Barr (1974) shows that Biemiller's results may have been instructionally dependent.

16. No adequate biography of Joseph Mayer Rice has been published. The best available source of information on him is an unpublished dissertation (Nobel, 1970), which is based in part on the Rice papers in the Teachers College manuscript collection. Brief sketches of his life can be found in *Who's Who in America* (Chicago: Marquis, 1898–1932), the *Encyclopedia Judaica* (Jerusalem: Keter, 1971), and in a *New York Times* obituary (June 25, 1934, p. 15).

17. William Scott Gray (1885–1960) dominated the field of reading instruction for over 30 years. He graduated from Illinois State Normal University in 1910 and then, after teaching and further degree work, studied under Thorndike at Columbia University, where he began his interest in reading tests. After receiving his master's degree in 1914, Gray returned to a faculty position at the University of Chicago, where he received a Ph.D. in 1916. From 1917 to 1931 he served as dean of the college of education. Before retiring from the Chicago faculty in 1950, he had initiated the "Dick and Jane" reading series, helped establish the International Reading Association, and published on almost every applied area in reading.

18. The role of oral reading in school programs from 1880 to 1941 is discussed by Hyatt (1943).

19. Pyke (1926) summarizes 15 criteria used by 1925 in legibility studies.

20. Javal's major studies on reading are drawn together in his book *Physiologie de la lecture et de l'écriture* (Paris: Felix Alcan, 1905).

21. John Wallace Baird was a student of Titchener and a founder, with his Clark University colleagues G. Stanley Hall and L. R. Geissler, of the *Journal of Applied Psychology*. All three published in the first issue of the journal. Baird's contribution, which is cited here, resulted from consulting work he did for the Engineering Department of the New York City Telephone Company.

22. Project Literacy was organized at Cornell University on February 7, 1964, by a developmental projects award from the Cooperative Research Branch of the United States Office of Education. The Preface to the first *Report* stated: "The purpose of Project Literacy is to organize, in various universities, laboratories and state departments of education, research which is essential to understand the acquisition of reading skills. The major initial effort is to bring together researchers and educators from a variety

of disciplines to plan research which, when taken as a whole, will give us more substantial results than any single study can provide." Much of the work initiated by Project Literacy is discussed in Gibson and Levin (1975).

23. How priorities for research funding are set by agencies such as the Office of Education and the National Institute of Education merits more open discussion than is now found. This matter is unfortunately too complex to be treated here. Useful background materials on the plans and priorities of the National Institute of Education are found in *Building Capacity for Renewal and Reform* (1973), *NIE: Its History and Programs* (1974), and *Conference on Studies in Reading* (1975).

24. This issue was raised recently in a review of a text on schema theory and education. "Little of the research that is reported presents data that comes from classrooms. Most data were collected from the proverbial college sophomores and the results may or may not be applicable to elementary or secondary schools" (Kifer, 1979, p. 84).

REFERENCES

Anderson, I. H.   Studies in the eye movements of good and poor readers. *Psychological Monographs*, 1937, *43*, 1–35.

Anderson, I. H., & Dearborn, W. F.   *The psychology of teaching reading*. New York: Ronald Press, 1952.

Anderson, I. H., & Swanson, D. E.   Common factors in eye-movements in silent and oral reading. *Psychological Monographs*, 1937, *48* (3), 61–69.

Anderson, R. C.   The notion of schemata and the educational enterprise. In R. C. Anderson, J. R. Spiro, & W. E. Montague (Eds.), *Schooling and the acquisition of knowledge*. Hillsdale, N.J.: Erlbaum, 1977.

Austin, M. C., Morrison, C., et al.   *The torch lighters: Tomorrow's teachers of reading*. Cambridge, Mass.: Harvard Graduate School of Education, 1961.

Austin, M. C., & Morrison, C.   *The first R*. New York: Macmillan, 1963.

Baird, J. W.   The legibility of a telephone directory. *Journal of Applied Psychology*, 1917, *1*, 30–37.

Ballantine, F. A.   Age changes in measures of eye-movements in silent reading. In *Studies in the Psychology of Reading* (Monographs in Education, No. 4). Ann Arbor: University of Michigan Press, 1951.

Barr, R.   The effect of instruction on pupil reading strategies. *Reading Research Quarterly*, 1974, *10*, 555–582.

Bartlett, F. C.   *Remembering*. Cambridge, England: Cambridge University Press, 1932.

Barton, A. H., & Wilder, D. E.   Research and practice in the teaching of reading: Progress report. In M. B. Miles (Ed.), *Innovation in education*. New York: Teachers College, Columbia University, 1964.

Bennett, A.   An analysis of errors in word recognition made by retarded readers. *Journal of Educational Psychology*, 1942, *33*, 25–38.

Biemiller, A.   The development of the use of graphic and contextual information as children learn to read. *Reading Research Quarterly*, 1970, *6*, 75–96.

Bond, G. L., & Dykstra, R.   The Cooperative Research Program in first-grade reading instruction. *Reading Research Quarterly*, 1967, *2*, 5–141.

Boring, E. G.   *A history of experimental psychology* (2nd ed.). New York: Appleton-Century-Crofts, 1950.

Bowden, J. H.   Learning to read. *Elementary School Teacher*, 1911, *12*, 21–23.

Bronfenbrenner, U.   The experimental ecology of education. *Teachers College Record,* 1976, *78,* 157–204.

Buchner, E. F.   Review of E. B. Huey: The psychology and pedagogy of reading. *Psychology Bulletin,* 1909, *6,* 147–150.

Building capacity for renewal and reform.   Washington, D.C.: National Institute of Education, December 1973.

Burt, C.   *A psychological study of typography.* New York: Cambridge University Press, 1959.

Buswell, G. T.   *An experimental study of the eye-voice span in reading* (Supplementary Educational Monographs, No. 17). Chicago: University of Chicago Press, 1920.

Button, H. W.   Creating more useable pasts: History in the study of education. *Educational Researcher,* 1979, *8* (5), 3–9.

Callahan, R. E.   *Education and the cult of efficiency.* Chicago: University of Chicago Press, 1962.

Carmichael, L., & Dearborn, W. F.   *Reading and visual fatigue.* Boston: Houghton Mifflin, 1947.

Carroll, J. B., Davies, P., & Richman, B.   *American Heritage word frequency book.* Boston: Houghton Mifflin, 1971.

Caswell, H. L.   *City school surveys: An interpretation and appraisal.* New York: Teachers College, Columbia University, 1929.

Cattell, J. M.   Über die Zeit der Erkennung und Benennung von Schriftzeichen, Bildern and Farben. *Philosophische Studien,* 1885, *2,* 635–650.

Cattell, J. M.   The time it takes to see and name objects. *Mind,* 1886, *11,* 63–65.

Cattell, J. M.   The psychological laboratory at Leipsig. *Mind,* 1888, *13,* 37–51.

Cattell, J. M.   Mental tests and measurements. *Mind,* 1890, *15,* 373–380.

Chall, J. S.   *Readability: An appraisal of research and application.* Columbus: Bureau of Educational Research, Ohio State University, 1958.

Chall, J. S.   *Learning to read: The great debate.* New York: McGraw-Hill, 1967.

Chambers, W. G.   How words get meaning. *Pedagogical Seminary,* 1904, *11,* 30–50.

Clifford, G. J.   A history of the impact of research on teaching. In R. M. W. Travers (Ed.), *Second handbook of research on teaching.* Chicago: Rand McNally, 1973.

Clifford, G. J.   Words for schools: The applications in education of the vocabulary researches of Edward L. Thorndike. In P. Suppes (Ed.), *Impact of research on education: Some case studies.* Washington, D.C.: National Academy of Education, 1978.

Conference on studies in reading.   Washington, D.C.: National Institute of Education, 1975. (Issued in ten fascicles.)

Courtis, S. A.   Standards in rates of reading. In *Fourteenth Yearbook of the National Society for the Study of Education* (Part 1). Chicago: University of Chicago Press, 1915.

Crosland, H. R.   *An investigation of proofreaders' illusions* (University of Oregon Publication Series, Vol. 2, No. 6). Eugene, Ore.: University of Oregon Press, 1924.

Curtis, H. S.   Automatic movements of the larynx. *American Journal of Psychology,* 1899, *11,* 237–239.

Davis, F. B.   Fundamental factors of comprehension in reading. *Psychometrika,* 1944, *9,* 185–197.

Davis, F. B.   Research in comprehension in reading. *Reading Research Quarterly,* 1968, *3,* 499–545.

Davis, F. B.   *The literature on research in reading with emphasis on models* (Final Report, U.S. Office of Education Project No. 0–9030). New Brunswick, N.J.: Graduate School of Education, Rutgers—The State University, 1971.

Dearborn, W. F.   Professor Cattell's studies of perception and reading. *Archives of Psychology,* 1914, *4* (30), 34–45.

Dearborn, W. F.   The psychology of reading: An experimental study of the reading pulses and movements of the eye. *Archives of Philosophy, Psychology and Scientific Methods,* 1906, *4* (4).

deHirsch, K., Jansky, J. J., & Langford, W. S.   *Predicting reading failure.* New York: Harper & Row, 1966.

Dewey, J. C.   The acquisition of facts as a measure of reading comprehension. *Elementary School Journal,* 1935, *35,* 346–348.

Dockeray, F. C.   The span of vision in reading and the legibility of letters. *Journal of Educational Psychology,* 1910, *1,* 123–131.

Dodge, R.   Visual perception during eye movement. *Psychological Review,* 1900, *7,* 454–465.

Dodge, R.   Recent studies in the correlation of eye movement and visual perception. *Psychological Bulletin,* 1906, *3,* 85–92.

Dodge, R.   An experimental study of visual fixation. *Psychological Review Monograph Supplements,* 1907, *3* (4), 1–96.

Duker, S., & Nally, T. P.   *The truth about your child's reading.* New York: Crown, 1956.

Durrell, D. D.   First grade reading success study: A summary. *Journal of Education,* 1958, *140,* 2–6.

Dykstra, R.   Summary of the second-grade phase of the Cooperative Research Program in primary reading instruction. *Reading Research Quarterly,* 1968, *4,* 49–70.

Eliot, C. W.   *Educational reform.* New York: Century, 1898.

Erdmann, B., & Dodge, R.   *Psychologische Untersuchungen über das Lesen auf Experimenteller Grundlage.* Halle: Neimeyer, 1898.

Fairbanks, G.   The relation between eye-movements and voice in the oral reading of good and poor silent readers. *Psychological Monographs,* 1937, *48,* (3), 78–107.

Fourteenth Yearbook of the National Society for the Study of Education.   Chicago: University of Chicago Press, 1915.

Galbraith, V. H.   The literacy of medieval English kings. *Proceedings of the British Academy,* 1935, *21,* 201–238.

Gates, A. I.   An experimental and statistical study of reading and reading tests (in three parts). *Journal of Educational Psychology,* 1921, *12,* 303–314, 378–391, 445–465.

Gates, A. I., & Boeker, E.   A study of initial stages in reading by pre-school children. *Teacher College Record,* 1923, *24,* 469–488.

Gates, A. I.   A study of the role of visual perception, intelligence, and certain associative processes in reading and spelling. *Journal of Educational Psychology,* 1926, *17,* 433–445.

Gates, A. I., Bond, G. L., & Russell, D. H.   *Methods of determining reading readiness.* New York: Teachers College, Columbia University, 1939.

Gay, P.   *Style in history.* New York: McGraw-Hill, 1974.

Gephart, W. J.   *Application of the convergence technique to basic studies of the reading process.* Bloomington, Ind.: Phi Delta Kappa, 1970.

Gerwig, G. W.   On the decrease of prediction and of sentence weight in English prose. *University of Nebraska Studies,* 1894, *2,* 17–44.

Gibson, E. J., & Levin, H.   *The psychology of reading.* Cambridge, Mass.: MIT Press, 1975.

Gibson, E. J., Pick, A., Osser, H., & Hammond, M.   The role of grapheme-phoneme correspondence in the perception of words. *American Journal of Psychology,* 1962, *75,* 554–570.

Gilbert, L. C.   Functional motor efficiency of the eyes and its relation to reading. *Education,* 1953, *11,* 159–232.

Gilbert, L. C.   Speed of processing visual stimuli and its relation to reading. *Journal of Educational Psychology,* 1959, *55,* 8–14.

Goldscheider, A., & Müller, R. F.   Zur Physiologie und Pathologie des Lesens. *Zeitschrift für klinische Medicin*, 1893, *23*, 131–167.

Goody, J.   *The domestication of the savage mind.* Cambridge, England: Cambridge University Press, 1977.

Gray, C. T.   *Types of reading ability as exhibited through tests and laboratory experiments* (Supplementary Educational Monographs, No. 5). Chicago: University of Chicago Press, 1917.

Gray, W. S.   *Summary of investigations relating to reading* (Supplementary Educational Monographs, No. 28). Chicago: University of Chicago Press, 1925.

Gray, W. S.   *Improving instruction in reading* (Supplementary Educational Monographs, No. 40). Chicago: University of Chicago Press, 1933.

Gray, W. S.   The nature and types of reading. In *Thirty-sixth Yearbook of the National Society for the Study of Education* (Part 1). Bloomington, Ill.: Public School Publishing, 1937.

Gray, W. S.   Contribution of research to special methods: Reading. In *Thirty-seventh Yearbook of the National Society for the Study of Education* (Part 2). Bloomington, Ill.: Public School Publishing, 1938.

Griffing, H.   On the development of visual perception and attention. *American Journal of Psychology*, 1896, *7*, 227–236.

Hamilton, F. M.   The perceptual factors in reading. *Archives of Psychology*, 1907, *9*, 1–56.

Hardyck, D., & Petrinovich, L. F.   Treatment of subvocal speech during reading. *Journal of Reading*, 1969, *12*, 361–368, 419–422.

Harris, A. J., & Serwer, B. L.   The CRAFT project: Instructional time in reading research. *Reading Research Quarterly*, 1966, *2*, 27–56.

Henderson, E. N.   A study of memory for connected trains of thought. *Psychological Monographs*, 1903, *5* (6), 1–94.

Hilliard, G. H.   Probable types of difficulties underlying low scores in comprehension tests. In C. L. Robbins (Ed.), *University of Iowa Studies in Education* (Vol. 2). Iowa City: University of Iowa Press, 1926.

Holmes, H. W.   Time distribution by subjects and grades in representative cities, minimum essentials in elementary school subjects and standards and current practices. In *Fourteenth Yearbook of the National Society for the Study of Education* (Part 1). Chicago: University of Chicago Press, 1915.

Holt, E. B.   Eye-movement and central anaesthesia. *Harvard Psychological Studies* (Vol. 1) (issued as *Psychological Monographs*, Vol. 4), 1903, 3–48.

Huey, E. B.   Preliminary experiments in the physiology and psychology of reading. *American Journal of Psychology*, 1898, *9*, 575.

Huey, E. B.   *The psychology and pedagogy of reading.* New York: Macmillan, 1908. (Republished: Cambridge, Mass.: MIT Press, 1968.)

Hyatt, A. V.   *The place of oral reading in school program: Its history and development from 1880–1941.* New York: Teachers College, Columbia University, 1943.

Irion, T. W. H.   *Comprehension difficulties of ninth-grade students in the study of literature.* New York: Teachers College, Columbia University, 1925.

James McKeen Cattell: Man of Science, 1860–1944 (2 Vols.). Lancaster, Pa.: Science Press, 1947.

James, W.   *Talks to teachers on psychology.* New York: Holt, 1901.

Javal, E.   Essai sur la physiologie de la lecture. *Annales d'Oculistique*, 1879, *82*, 242–253.

Javal, E.   *Physiologie de la lecture et de l'écriture.* Paris: Felix Alcan, 1905.

Johnson, G. R.   An objective method of determining reading difficulty. *Journal of Educational Research*, 1930, *21*, 283–287.

Judd, C. H. *Reading: Its nature and development* (Supplementary Educational Monographs, No. 10). Chicago: University of Chicago Press, 1918.

Judd, C. H., & Buswell, G. T. *Silent reading: A study of the various types* (Supplementary Educational Monographs, No. 23). Chicago: University of Chicago Press, 1922.

Kavanagh, J. F., & Venezky, R. L. *Orthography, reading, and dyslexia.* Baltimore: University Park Press, 1980.

Kifer, E. Review of Anderson, R. C., Spiro, R. J. & Montague, W. E. (Eds.) *Schooling and the acquisition of knowledge.* Hillsdale, N.J.: Erlbaum, 1977. *American Educational Research Journal*, 1979, *16*, 83–85.

Klare, G. R. *The measurement of readability.* Ames, Iowa: Iowa State University Press, 1963.

Koster, W. G. (Ed.). *Attention and performance* (Vol 2). Amsterdam: North Holland, 1969. (Reprinted from *Acta Psychologica*, 1969, *30.*)

Kučera, H., & Francis, N. W. *Computational analysis of present-day American English.* Providence: Brown University Press, 1967.

Kuhn, T. S. *The structure of scientific revolutions* (2nd ed.). Chicago: University of Chicago Press, 1970.

Laing, M. E. *Reading: A manual for teachers.* Boston: Heath, 1903.

Lakatos, I. Falsification and the methodology of scientific programmes. In I. Lakatos and A. Musgrove (Eds.), *Criticism and the growth of knowledge.* London: Cambridge University Press, 1970.

Levin, H., Gibson, E. J., Baldwin, A. L., Gibson, J. J., Hockett, C. F., Ricciuti, H. N., & Suci, G. J. *A basic research program on reading.* Cornell University, Ithaca, N.Y., 1963. (Mimeograph.)

Lively, B. A., & Pressey, S. L. A method for measuring the 'vocabulary burden' of textbooks. *Educational Administration and Supervision*, 1923, *9*, 389–398.

Lockridge, K. A. *Literacy in colonial New England.* New York: Norton, 1974.

Luckiesh, M., & Moss, F. K. *Reading as a visual task.* New York: Van Nostrand, 1942.

McAllister, C. N. The fixation of points in the visual field. *Psychological Review Monograph Supplements*, 1905, *7* (1, Whole No. 29).

Maple, E. O. Teaching reading in Vincennes, Indiana. *Elementary School Journal*, 1917, *18*, 138–140.

Mathews, M. M. *Teaching to read, historically considered.* Chicago: University of Chicago Press, 1966.

Mead, C. D. Silent versus oral reading with one hundred sixth-grade children. *Journal of Educational Psychology*, 1915, *6*, 345–348.

Messmer, O. Zur Psychologie des Lesens bei Kindern und Erwachsenen. *Archiv für die gesamte Psychologie*, 1904, *2*, 190–298.

Miller, G. A., Bruner, J. S., & Postman, L. Familiarity of letter sequences and tachistoscopic identification. *Journal of General Psychology*, 1954, *50*, 129–139.

Moley, R. The Cleveland surveys—net. *The Survey*, 1923, *50*, 229–231.

Monroe, M. *Children who cannot read.* Chicago: University of Chicago Press, 1932.

Morgan, W. P. A case of congenital word-blindness. *British Medical Journal*, 1896, *2*, 1612–1614.

Morton, J. A. The effects of context on the visual duration threshold for words. *British Journal of Psychology*, 1964, *55*, 165–180.

NIE: Its history and programs. Washington, D.C.: National Institute of Education, 1974.

Neal, E. A., & Foster, I. A program of silent reading. *Elementary School Journal*, 1926, *27*, 275–280.

Newell, A. *Intellectual issues in the history of artificial intelligence* (Department of Computer Science Technical Report CMU-CS-82-142). Carnegie-Mellon University, 1982.

Noble, G. *Joseph Mayer Rice: Critic of the public schools and pioneer in modern educational measurements.* Doctoral dissertation, State University of New York at Buffalo, 1970). *Dissertation Abstracts International,* 1971, *31;* 4323A–4945A. (University Microfilms No. 71–6100.)

Oberholtzer, E. E. Testing the efficiency in reading in the grades. *Elementary School Journal,* 1915, *15,* 313–322.

Paterson, D. G., & Tinker, M. A. Studies of typographical factors influencing speed of reading: III. Length of line. *Journal of Applied Psychology,* 1929, *13,* 209–219.

Paterson, D. G., & Tinker, M. A. The part-whole proportion illusion in printing. *Journal of Applied Psychology,* 1938, *22,* 421–425.

Philippe, J. Sur les transformations de nos images mentales. *Révue Philosophie,* 1897, *43,* 481–493.

Piaget, J. [Science of education and the psychology of the child.] Translated by D. Coltman. New York: Orion Press, 1970. (Originally published 1935.)

Pillsbury, W. B. A study in apperception. *American Journal of Psychology,* 1897, *8,* 315–398.

Pintner, R. Inner speech during silent reading. *Psychology Review,* 1913, *20,* 129–53. (a)

Pintner, R. Oral and silent reading of fourth-grade pupils. *Journal of Educational Psychology,* 1913, *4,* 333–37. (b)

Pintner, R., & Gilliland, A. R. Oral and silent reading. *Journal of Educational Psychology,* 1916, *7,* 201–212.

Pollard, R. S. *A complete manual for Pollard's synthetic method of reading and spelling.* Chicago: Western Publishing, 1889.

Pyke, R. L. *Report on the legibility of print* (Medical Research Council Special Report Series, No. 110). London, England, 1926.

Quantz, J. O. Problems in the psychology of reading. *Psychological Monographs,* 1897, *2* (1, Whole No. 5). (Summary in *Psychological Review,* 1898, *5,* 434–436.)

Rice, J. M. *The public school system of the United States.* New York: Century, 1893.

Romanes, G. J. *Mental evolution in animals.* New York: Appleton, 1884.

Ruediger, W. C. The field of distinct vision: With reference to individual differences and their correlations. *Archives of Psychology,* 1907, *1* (5), 1–68.

Sanford, E. C. Personal equation. *American Journal of Psychology,* 1888, *2,* 5–38.

Schlesinger, I. M. *Sentence structure and the reading process.* The Hague: Mouton, 1968.

Schmidt, W. A. *An experimental study of the psychology of reading* (Supplementary Educational Monographs, No. 2). Chicago: University of Chicago Press, 1917.

Schofield, R. The measurement of literacy in preindustrial England. In J. Goody (Ed.), *Literacy in traditional societies.* Cambridge, England: University of Cambridge Press, 1968.

Secor, W. B. Visual reading: A study in mental imagery. *American Journal of Psychology,* 1900, *11,* 225–36.

Shannon, C. E. A mathematical theory of communication. *Bell System Technical Journal,* 1948, *27,* 379–423; 622–656.

Shannon, C. E. Prediction and entropy of printed English. *Bell System Technical Journal,* 1951, *30,* 50–64.

Sherman, L. A. *Analytics of literature.* Boston: Ginn, 1893.

Sieber, S. D. Organizational influences on innovative roles. In T. L. Eidell & J. M. Kitchel (Eds.), *Knowledge production and utilization in educational administration.* Eugene, Ore.: Center for Advanced Study of Educational Administration, University of Oregon, 1968.

Simplified Spelling Board. *Simplified Spelling* (1st ed.). Washington, D.C.: U.S. Government Printing Office, 1906.

Singer, H.   Research that should have made a difference. *Elementary English*, 1970, *47*, 27–34.

Smith, N. B.   *American reading instruction*. Newark, Del.: International Reading Association, 1965.

Sokal, M. M.   The unpublished autobiography of James McKeen Cattell. *American Psychologist*, 1971, *26*, 626–635.

Spencer, H.   *The visible word* (2nd ed.). New York: Hastings House, 1968.

Spiro, R.   Remembering information from text: The "state of schema" approach. In R. C. Anderson, R. Spiro, & W. Montague (Eds.), *Schooling and the acquisition of knowledge*. Hillsdale, N.J.: Erlbaum, 1977.

Stallings, J. A., & Kaskowitz, D.   *Follow-through classroom observation evaluation, 1972–73*. Menlo Park, Calif.: Stanford Research Institute, 1974.

Swanson, D. E.   Common elements in silent and oral reading. *Psychological Monographs*, 1937, *48*, 36–60.

Taylor, E. A.   *Controlled reading*. Chicago: University of Chicago Press, 1937.

Taylor, W. L.   Cloze procedure: A new tool for measuring readability. *Journalism Quarterly*, 1953, *30*, 415.

Thiesen, W. W.   *Factors affecting results in primary reading* (*Twentieth Yearbook of the National Society for the Study of Education*, Part 2). Bloomington, Ill.: Public School Publishing, 1921.

Thorndike, E. L.   The measurement of ability in reading. *Teachers College Record*, 1914, *15*, 207–227.

Thorndike, E. L.   Reading as reasoning: A study of mistakes in paragraph reading. *Journal of Educational Psychology*, 1917, *8*, 323–332. (a)

Thorndike, E. L.   The psychology of thinking in the case of reading. *Psychological Review*, 1917, *24*, 220–234. (b)

Thorndike, E. L.   The understanding of sentences: A study of errors in reading. *Elementary School Journal*, 1917, *18*, 98–114. (c)

Thorndike, E. L.   *The teacher's word book*. New York: Teachers College, Columbia University, 1921.

Tiffin, J.   Simultaneous records of eye-movements and the voice in oral reading. *Science*, 1934, *80*, 430–431.

Tinker, M. A.   Reading reactions for mathematical formulae. *Journal of Experimental Psychology*, 1926, *9*, 444–467.

Tinker, M. A.   Time taken by eye movements in reading. *Journal of Genetic Psychology*, 1936, *48*, 468–471.

Tinker, M. A.   The study of eye movements in reading. *Psychological Bulletin*, 1946, *43*, 93–120.

Tinker, M. A.   *Legibility of print*. Ames, Iowa: Iowa State University Press, 1963.

Tinker, M. A.   *Bases for effective reading*. Minneapolis: University of Minneapolis Press, 1965.

Tinker, M. A.   Experimental studies on the legibility of print: An annotated bibliography. *Reading Research Quarterly*, 1966, *1*, 67–118.

Touton, F. C., & Berry, B. T.   Reading comprehension at the junior college level. *California Quarterly of Secondary Education*, 1931, *6*, 245–251.

Tulving, E., & Gold, C.   Stimulus information and contextual information as determinants of tachistoscopic recognition of words. *Journal of Experimental Psychology*, 1963, *66*, 319–327.

Tyack, D. B.   *The one best system*. Cambridge, Mass.: Harvard University Press, 1974.

U.S. Congress.   *An Act to Authorize Cooperative Research in Education* (Public Law 531, Chapter 576, 83rd Congress). Washington, D.C.: U.S. Government Printing Office, 1954.

Uttal, W. R. & Smith, P.   Recognition of alphabetic characters during voluntary eye movement. *Perception & Psychophysics*, 1968, *3*, 257–264.

Venezky, R. L.   Research on reading processes: An historical perspective. *American Psychologist*, 1977, *32*, 339–345.

Vernon, M. D.   *The experimental study of reading*. Cambridge, England: University of Cambridge Press, 1931.

Vogel, M., & Washburne, C.   An objective method of determining grade placement of children's reading material. *Elementary School Journal*, 1928, *28*, 373–381.

Volkmann, F. C.   Vision during voluntary saccadic eye movements. *Journal of the Optical Society of America*, 1962, *52*, 571–578.

Washburne, C., & Vogel, M.   What books fit what children? *School and Society*, 1926, *23*, 22–24.

Watson, J. D.   *The double helix*. New York: Atheneum, 1968.

Weber, G.   *Inner-city children can be taught to read: Four successful schools* (Occasional Papers, No. 18). Washington, D.C.: Council for Basic Education, 1971.

Weber, R. M.   The study of oral reading errors: A survey of the literature. *Reading Research Quarterly*, 1968, *4*, 96–119.

Weiner, M., & Feldmann, S.   Validation studies of a reading prognosis test for children of lower and middle socio-economic status. *Educational and Psychological Measurement*, 1963, *23*, 807–814.

Weiss, A. P.   The focal variator. *Journal of Experimental Psychology*, 1917, *2*, 106.

Welborn, E. L., & English, H.   Logical learning and retention: A general review of experiments with meaningful verbal materials. *Psychological Bulletin*, 1937, *34*, 1–20.

Wheat, H. G.   *The teaching of reading*. New York: Ginn, 1923.

Whipple, G. M.   *Manual of mental and physical tests* (2nd ed.). Baltimore: Warwick & York, 1915.

Wiggins, R. H.   Effects of three typographical variables on speed of reading. *Journal of Typographic Research*, 1967, *1*, 5–18.

Wiley, W. E.   Difficult words and the beginner. *Journal of Educational Research*, 1928, *17*, 278–289.

Wilson, F. T., & Flemming, C. W.   Correlations of reading progress with other abilities and traits in grade 1. *Journal of Genetic Psychology*, 1938, *53*, 33–52.

Woodworth, R. S.   *Experimental psychology*. New York: Holt, 1938.

Woodworth, R. S.   James McKeen Cattell: 1860–1944. *Psychological Review*, 1944, *51*, 201–209.

Woodworth, R. S., & Schlosberg, H.   *Experimental psychology*. New York: Holt, 1954.

Zachrisson, B.   *Studies in the legibility of printed text*. Stockholm: Almquist & Wiksell, 1965.

Zeitler, J.   Tachistoskopische Untersuchungen über das Lesen. *Philosophische Studien*, 1900, *16*, 380–463.

Although Singer limits the hypotheses to reading comprehension, the scheme implicitly presumes some sort of taxonomy of instructional studies.

Duffy and Roehler (1982) have generated eight categories, divided into rhetorical (what and how to teach), global (textbook-bound or designed instruction) and pedagogical (organization of and interaction in classrooms) strategies. While all possibilities have not been realized in current instructional research studies, they have at least been mentioned on theoretical levels.

Pearson and Gallagher (in press) have identified four "traditions" of instructional research: existential descriptions (studies of what exists in educational settings), existential proofs (studies to determine whether certain variables work), pedagogical experiments (studies of intervention techniques) and program evaluations (studies of the institutionalization of variables). Examples of each of these types exist in the literature. Nevertheless, the limited number of categories (even when some are subdivided) obscures some important distinctions made, for example, in Duffy and Roehler's work.

For now, these taxonomies can be viewed as approximations. It is obvious, however, from these illustrations that there is no consolidated paradigm of instructional research. The possibility that there will never be such a paradigm is discussed in the next section.

Philosophical Underpinnings of Reading Research

It has often been assumed that social sciences are not different, in principle, from physical sciences. Nagel (1961) wrote: ". . . none of the methodological difficulties often alleged to confront the search for systematic explanation of social phenomena is unique to the social science or is inherently insuperable." This is not a universally held opinion. Mitroff and Mason (1981) suggest a variety of methodologies for science and a dialectical method for social science in particular. Foucault (1972) believes that the differences among sciences are the result of differences at a definitional level. He does not necessarily believe that these differences are absolute. Mosenthal (in press), however, suggests that there may indeed be no way to resolve the discrepancies inherent in different approaches to science.

Implicitly, all these positions equate educational research with research in the social sciences. One examination of the problems with translating philosophies of science to a variety of fields can be found in the exchange between Phillips (1983) and Eisner (1983).

The debate centers on the positivist notion that there is "Truth" that can be discovered by science versus the relativist position that scientific findings depend on many factors, such as the paradigm used or the culture within which the research was conducted. Kuhn (1962) has been interpreted as arguing for relativism as the general principle of science (Phillips, 1983). Jenkins (1979) has incorporated such a notion in a model of experiments on memory processes. The issues here can be stated rather simply: What is knowledge? What is meaning? How can we know when someone "knows" something? These are old epistemological questions; only the debaters are new. When and if these issues are resolved philosophically, reading research will benefit by being able to adopt one or more consistent paradigms. An alternative view of these issues can be found in Lakatos

---

2 CURRENT TRADITIONS OF READING RESEARCH

Michael L. Kamil

Contemporary reading research is a rich mixture of influences from cognitive and physiological psychology, linguistics, anthropology, computer sciences, social psychology, learning theory, and educational practice. The influences range from the most abstract, theoretical points of view to the most practical, applied situations. Current research in reading consequently has at least two clear, definable thrusts. First, research is aimed at understanding the basic nature of the reading process. Attempts to do this include the generation of models and theories of the reading process. Summaries of much of the earlier work in modeling and theory construction can be found in Singer and Ruddell (1970, 1976) and Davis (1971). The currency of this line of effort is evidenced by recent work by Carver (1977–1978), Gough (1972), Gough and Cosky (1975), Gough, Alford, Jr., and Holley-Wilcox (1979), Herndon (1978), Rumelhart (1977), Stanovich (1980), and others. LaBerge and Samuels (1983) continue extending and refining the modeling of the reading process. The second thrust is a renewed and increasingly intense search for better methods of teaching with the ultimate goal of improving education and reducing illiteracy.

This chapter is intended to be a nonexhaustive survey of the status of current reading research. Examples have been chosen to reflect developments appearing most recently in the literature; all possible examples cannot be listed. Historical examples are added where necessary to clarify the perspective. Reviews are cited when they treat specific areas more thoroughly.

CHANGES IN READING RESEARCH

Reading research is, and has been, undergoing changes that seem similar to what Kuhn (1962) has termed a paradigm shift. The pressures for the changes have been (1) an emphasis on the reader as an active information processor, (2) the development of comprehensive systems of discourse analysis that could be applied to reading (e.g., Fredericksen, 1975; Halliday & Hasan, 1976; Kintsch, 1974; Kintsch & van Dijk, 1978; Thorndyke, 1977), and (3) an increased interdisciplinary interest in precisely translating research into practice.

It is, however, too easy to overlook a large body of research that has not been the result of these changes. In short, what has looked like a shift has not consolidated, despite the use of seemingly appropriate jargon in much published reading research on traditional problems.

Publication of Reading Research

Significant changes in the outlets for publishing reading research have occurred. Most reading research is still reported in journals, but there seems to be a virtual explosion of theoretical and synthetic work reflected in book chapters as a basic unit of publication. The book chapter has become a new academic art form. This phenomenon is not limited to reading research; a similar trend can be seen, for example, in experimental psychology.

At the same time, in reading there are signs that research is less dependent on formal, highly explicit models (for such examples, see Massaro's chapter in this volume) than it was even a few years ago. The influence of schema theory has been largely responsible for a good portion of the change in "research style." (Much of this can be seen in the work of Anderson and his colleagues, e.g., Anderson, Spiro, & Montague, 1977.)

The most obvious symptoms of this change in research style is a greater reliance on prose rather than a set of diagrams and mathematical formulas to represent the models and relationships among component processes. The substantive change is that schema-theoretic models are at the same time more powerful and less constrained than their predecessors. They explain flexible behaviors in reading well. They also explain other behaviors, however, including logically inconsistent ones. (See the discussions by Thorndyke & Yekovich, 1979, and by Anderson and Pearson in this volume.) Together the book chapter phenomenon and the lack of formal models make an interesting contrast. The rules for data and evidence that must be observed for successful publication in a well-refereed journal are not so stringent when applied to book chapters. For book chapters, authors seem to be freer to make speculative conclusions and conjectures on much less substantial evidence, thus providing interesting and provocative notions to guide further research.

It is also true that many authors of book chapters produce work equal to that found in the highest-quality journals regardless of the evaluation criteria. In these cases, the general trend is clearly toward dealing with larger chunks of behavior in context. The larger units in reading have to do both with the scope of individual studies (e.g., moving from words and sentences to discourse and stories) and the nature of the interdisciplinary efforts (e.g., influences from computer science, cognitive psychology, and anthropology). All this seems to be a reaction against a more mechanistic view of reading research that prevailed only a few years ago. (Again, similar phenomena can be found in other fields, such as experimental psychology.)

A major drawback to the use of book chapters as units of publication is the delay involved in publication. Similar delays are, however, to be found in many major journals. One solution has been a dependence on technical reports and other informal publications primarily from research institutions (e.g., centers, laboratories, and institutes).

An even more prevalent form for presenting data continues to be the conference presentation. It offers a researcher the opportunity to present findings to a small group of interested colleagues much sooner than is possible with journal articles or book chapters. A major trend is to hold conferences on relatively narrow topics and to publish the proceedings. Examples can be seen in recent preconference institutes or workshops on field-based research and translating research into practice.

Mention also must be made of the pressures to "publish or perish." The end result of an overemphasis on numbers of publications is a glut of short-term studies that require little in the way of analysis. Young scholars and researchers are discouraged from performing the long-range studies that might be most important. In turn, they are encouraged to produce high volumes of work. In the absence of dependable funding for individuals, the trend is rarely reversed. The solution to this set of problems is obvious, but it is difficult to implement: The criteria for promotion and tenure need to be revamped. Until this is accomplished, programmatic research efforts will be restricted to institutions where funding is stable or to tenured individuals who are not subject to the publishing pressures.

Instructional and Classroom Research in Reading

A significant thrust of reading research is directed at identifying and improving educational practices in classrooms and other instructional settings. These efforts include observation of behaviors in natural instructional settings in an ethnographic framework as well as highly controlled manipulation of variables affecting reading instruction. Examples of these efforts can be found in the work of Durkin (1978–1979) and Calfee and Piontkowski (1981).

Researchers have mounted major efforts to accomplish the task of studying instruction in a systematic manner, for example, at the Institute for Research on Teaching at Michigan State University or the Center for the Study of Reading at University of Illinois at Urbana-Champaign.

The emphasis on paradigmatic instructional research has spawned attempts to create taxonomies for the expanding range of studies. Singer (1981) has enumerated a number of hypotheses in reading comprehension that are "in search of classroom validation." These hypotheses are grouped in three general categories. First, there are hypotheses about *input stimuli*: Materials should be modified to fit readers' abilities. Readers should then be brought to higher levels of ability on relevant variables. Some of the variables include conceptual level, syntactic level, and text organization.

The second set of hypotheses concern *mediational processes*: Instructional procedures should promote development of processes for the encoding, storage or retrieval of information. Variables involved in these hypotheses include questioning strategies, verbalization, concepts and schemata, and reasoning about print.

The final hypotheses are about *output products*: The type of measurement should correspond to the readers' purposes, processing, and demands of the materials. Examples of variables here include level of macro- and microstructure, hypothesis testing and print sampling, and coherence in teaching and test

and Musgrave (1970). They have collected a number of papers that examine the problems of Kuhn's notions of paradigmatic science, although they do not do a synthesis to arrive at an answer to the debate.

It can be argued that Kuhn's (1962) notions of paradigm can apply only to certain aspects of educational research. While the notion of paradigm seems adequate for some sciences, where it begins to break down is precisely where instructional research begins. Instructional research involves the empirical testing of epistemological considerations. Although other scientific fields may have disagreements about philosophical assumptions, educational research seems to make them the basic data of interest. Consequently, much educational research undertakes to verify or validate what amount to epistemological beliefs. For example, it is often the goal of instructional research to determine the most efficient methods for student learning. Underlying such research are epistemological assumptions about what knowledge is, how it is obtained, and how it is used.

A bothersome consequence of this problem is that as assumptions on a philosophical level differ, so too do the techniques involved in research differ. Empirical testing of assumptions is inappropriate; there are always alternative positions that will not be subject to verification by researchers of different beliefs.

The current debate in reading research over the locus of meaning (in the text versus in the head) is an example of conflict in assumptions rather than conflict of empirical data. An interesting perspective on this issue can be found in Olson's (1977) essay. He contends that written and oral language are radically different in their loci of meaning. Utterances require meaning "in the head"; written texts have meaning "in the text." Olson's position emphasizes differences between speaking/listening and reading/writing. In contrast, Sticht's chapter (this volume) deals with the listening-reading issue by emphasizing their similarities.

Another example of the philosophical problem is to be found by examining schema theory. Schema theory has, at base, some important philosophical assumptions that are often ignored. In general, schema theory is derivative from Platonic philosophy. Throughout the history of Western thought, this has been one of two dominant positions; Aristotelian philosophy was the other.

While schema theory is a powerful explanatory device, the basic questions of epistemology are still unanswered. ("Explanatory" is used here, and throughout this chapter, in contrast to "descriptive" or "predictive." That is, explanation entails establishing cause-effect relationships that can be absent in description or simple prediction.) It is still (after many years) not clear how one "gets" a schema if one does not have it in the first place. Moreover, the process of selecting a schema from all those available presents major logical difficulties. For example, if the schema is necessary to interpret the text, then it must be instantiated before it is needed. How is one to know what to instantiate prior to encountering the text? Or are all schemata always instantiated? If so, how is the choice made? A related discussion of similar issues, dealing with problems in psycholinguistics, can be found in Weimer's (1973) work.

Conducting beginning research with incomplete or inconsistent theoretical positions results in the fragmentation of research into isolated or only partially related studies. It is imperative that theories be explanatory, and, consequently, consistent. Without the guidance of such theories, research is far less effective, and the accumulation of knowledge is impeded. Perhaps what is needed is a philosophy of science that approximates what an educational researcher really does. This might be akin to Bronowski's (1977, pp. 83ff.) solution to the problems inherent in Popper's formulation of the falsification principle. Popper's position was that a scientist had to specify the conditions under which a statement could be falsified, as opposed to verified. Bronowski points out that a scientist's real goal is to find statements that are true, not those that are false. Educators, similarly, are interested in determining what works and why rather than what does not work.

An alternative to the use of theory is a reliance on descriptive data collection. In this approach, for educational research, the emphasis is on the description of educational practice, not validation. A goal might be to identify "successful" or "nonsuccessful" instructional components, methods, or environments. Subsequent efforts may or may not involve validation of the findings. These techniques may have real advantages over methods based in incomplete theory, given the arguments over assumptions. While descriptive techniques are not necessarily nontheoretical, they may approach that state (see Rosenshine and Stevens, this volume, for a review of much of this correlational work).

Basic versus Applied Research

Kerlinger (1977) has pointed out the paradox in talking about "applied" research. The present state of affairs in reading research reflects a similar confusion. It is rare that researchers from either end of the basic-applied continuum interact to generate mutually interesting research problems.

Reading practitioners have been impatient with a perceived lack of consensus among reading researchers, leading to a lack of consistency in recommendations for improving classroom practice. Researchers have similarly been loath to tackle the "messy" problems of reading instruction without knowing precisely the parameters of the reading and teaching processes in isolation. There is evidence in other fields that the returns from "basic" research may be greater than those from "applied" efforts (cf. Kerlinger, 1977). The hope for reading research would seem to lie in increased dialogue between researchers and practitioners. Such dialogue could focus research on "relevant" aspects of the reading process without giving in to the press for highly specific program-bound studies or evaluations.

The split between practitioners and theorists has produced a predictable difference in kinds of reading research efforts. On the practical side, there is a preponderance of "one-shot" studies or evaluations of individual programs, methods, or techniques. The question in each case is whether one program or method produces "better" learning than another. (This may seem an oversimplification, but it is not intended to be. Many of these studies are highly complex and well designed. It is not suggested that the methodology is simple. However, the generalizability of the results is limited. Such studies will not, typically, add much to the store of basic knowledge about the reading process.)

There is a tendency for theoreticians to generate programs of research in which the outcome of each study bears on the design of the next. As a rule, an organizing framework, point of view, or theory guides the selection of variables and methodologies. Often, but not always, the outcomes of studies are used as feedback to revise the framework or model governing the research program. Uncertainties about the reliability of collected data often make researchers feel more confident with logical than with empirical arguments.

It is, of course, impossible to state that *either* logic or data is a superior basis for argument. Nevertheless, primary reliance on logic in many cases has produced research endeavors that have as goals the validation of models rather than the explanation of the reading process. In turn, this has often led to some confusion about appropriate research methodologies. It may also be that ethnographic techniques are attempts to make data predominate in research efforts. (Discussions of ethnographic research techniques and findings are included in Green and Bloome's and Guthrie and Hall's chapters in this volume.)

GOALS OF READING RESEARCH

There would seem to be several distinctly indentifiable goals for current reading research.

1. *Research to generate a theory of reading.* This is a goal of many basic research studies. Attempts to explain the underlying processes in reading often fall in this category (e.g., Montare, Elmon, & Cohen, 1977; or Spilich, Vesonder, Chiesi, & Voss, 1979).
2. *Research to generate or validate a model of reading.* Many basic research studies stop short of having *explanation* as a goal. They are often directed at identification of components of the reading process and their relation to each other. The distinction is not clear-cut when trying to distinguish between the terms *theory* and *model.* While they have been used interchangeably by many, it has been argued that they should not be (see Kamil, 1978, or Pearson and Kamil, 1977–1978, for a discussion of this issue.)
3. *Research to collect data.* Many of these studies span the basic-applied distinction. Studies of this sort are designed to obtain such information as imagery or frequency values of words or characteristics of language and text (Coleman, 1970; Carver, 1975–1976; Rubin, 1978a; Sakiey, 1979). Often these studies are conducted to obtain data for use in future research studies. At other times, these studies are designed to collect data for use in making instructional decisions, such as how to sequence or construct materials (Canney & Schreiner, 1976–1977; Finn, 1977–1978).
4. *Research to make instructional decisions.* Most studies in this category fall on the "applied" end of research. Test construction procedures often belong in this category. Program evaluations, materials development, and classroom procedures are all included in this category (e.g., Kurth, 1978; Sheehan & Marcus, 1977; Tharp, 1982). What are important are the relative merits of alternatives rather than explanations, extensions, or validations of theories or models.

THE ROLE OF USERS IN SHAPING CURRENT RESEARCH

Three groups of reading professionals shape current trends in reading research. One group is the experimentalists. The focus for experimentalists tends to be examination of the "basic" processes without regard for the relevance or direct applicability of the findings to instructional situations. Thus, for example, it is difficult to assess the immediate and direct implications of studies that use reaction time as a variable and find significant differences on the order of milliseconds among treatment conditions, as in Steinheiser and Guthrie (1977) or Massaro, Venezky, and Taylor (1979).

This last statement is not meant to be an indictment of pure experimentalism. Good experimental research is directed at explanation. If the entire reading process were explainable, it would be highly likely that the implications for instruction of any given study would be obvious. Because we do not have sufficient knowledge of the entire process, it is not possible to explain fully the reading process with absolute precision. Thus, the instructional implications are distanced from the research conclusions. As knowledge of both basic processes and instructional processes accumulates, and as the two efforts converge, this task should become more manageable.

The second professional group that shapes reading research is the practitioners—the group that has direct contact with learners. In the vernacular, many members of this group need to know "what to do tomorrow morning." Because practitioners need or want guidance, they exert a strong force on the questions being asked by reading researchers and funding agencies. That is, they want evaluations of methods, validation of tests, and identification of crucial variables in instruction. The question practitioners ask is whether the research is relevant or, in other terms, ecologically valid (cf. Bronfenbrenner, 1976). That is, can the findings be translated directly into practice? Additional pressure for this kind of relevant research comes from funding, which often emphasizes products rather than basic data.

The final group exerting influence on reading research is the "translators." A relatively small, but growing, group, translators have some stake in both the experimentalist and the practitioner camps. Translators have two tasks. First, they speculate on the implications of experimental research and theory for instruction. Second, they point out the need for further research on instructional questions (Weaver & Shonkoff, 1978).

This third group has the job of synthesizing experimental results and generating new instructionally related research problems. It is composed of researchers who have interests in improving the teaching and learning of reading. Because of the complexity and esoteric nature of contemporary reading research, this group is becoming increasingly important in helping teachers understand new developments in research.

CHARACTERISTICS OF CURRENT READING RESEARCH

Experimental Designs in Current Reading Research

Not all reading research should or must be designed to yield explanatory information. Some effort certainly has to be expended in collecting descriptive data. Often, descriptive data are needed to identify or clarify problems in reading. For example, word lists or frequency counts are the results of descriptive research.

Until it is certain that there are measurable and stable differences in such variables, research manipulating those variables is futile.

Causal explanations are the seldom-attained goals of much reading research. Nevertheless, many correlation or factor analytic and multiple regression studies are found in reading research, even though no causal inferences can be drawn (e.g., Entin & Klare, 1978; Maxwell, 1978; O'Reilly & Streeter, 1977; Yap, 1979). Cause-and-effect relationships require experimental designs that allow the attribution of effects to (and only to) the manipulated variables. Correlational studies can be very useful when variables cannot be manipulated or for generating tentative hypotheses.

Reading research is also shaped by the environment in which it is conducted. The choices are often polarized as being either in the field or in the laboratory. It is more difficult, but not impossible, to conduct experimental research in the field. In fact, descriptive data are difficult, but not impossible, to collect in a laboratory, as Carnine and Carnine (1978) and Carver (1975–1976) have shown.

Similarly, experimental research is easiest to conduct in a laboratory. The control of extraneous variables may produce ideal experimental conditions at the expense of ecological validity. The use of randomized procedures, replications, and other techniques, however, can compensate for the lack of control in the field (see Carver, 1978, and Shaver & Norton, 1980, for specific methods). In addition, the use of complex designs can help. Some of these are discussed by Calfee and Piontkowski (this volume).

Prototypically, an experimenter manipulates variables and observes changes in performance. Many problems in reading research cannot (for many reasons, including ethical considerations) be studied this way. For example, one cannot induce reading disability to study the effectiveness of methods of remediation. The case-history method is often used to study these sorts of problems.

In a case-history study, an attempt is made to observe an individual for an extended period of time and to depend on other records (if necessary) for supporting or supplementary aid. The potential flaw in this design is that the history is not (or was not) under the control of the investigator. Full and complete records may not be available, and the necessary information may never have been recorded. The inference of causality in this design is, at best, risky for several reasons. First, the history for a particular individual may be unique. Generalizing to other members of the population may be inappropriate. Second, extraneous variables may have influenced the treatments. Thus, no unambiguous conclusion can be made with regard to the relationship between treatments and behavior. Third, all the relevant data may often not have been recorded. (A variant of this is that different techniques of data collection or recording may be used over the time span of the study. Here, too, conclusions cannot be unambiguous.) Finally, there can be bias in the data collection since the experimenter is often the only individual responsible for collection procedures. Despite these problems, case histories are useful when there *are* no other ways to perform an experiment (e.g., remedial techniques, like those in Moyer, 1979). Case histories can and should be thought of as important for initial (pilot studies or preliminary, suggestive studies) or final phases of a research program when one desires a complete validation of findings.

Another common method of doing research outside the laboratory is the correlational study. A correlational study is one in which the variables are not directly manipulated. Rather, the variables are measured, and a relationship is determined among them. (Discussions of research designs and kinds of variables can be found in Campbell & Stanley, 1963; Cook & Campbell, 1979; Popham, 1972; Resta & Baker, 1972; Sullivan, 1972.) This technique is common when the variables of interest are not directly manipulable. The use of good and poor readers as an independent variable produces many correlational studies. These studies are really correlational, even though they often use other statistical analyses, such as analyses of variance. That is, the observed differences in performance are correlated with, but not necessarily caused by, differences in reading ability. Examples of these kinds of studies include Allington (1978), Condon and Hoffman (1979), Marr (1979), and a host of others.

It is important to underscore the notion that correlational studies also do not strictly allow causal conclusions. Nevertheless, although correlation does not logically imply causation, high correlation values should *suggest* causal relationships. Such suggested relationships have to be verified by other experimental means. When regression analyses are used, precise prediction is possible, but causal explanation still does not result. The situation is similar when it comes to multiple correlation and regression. What changes is the number of variables that can be accounted for and the accuracy of prediction (see Coker & Lorentz, 1977; McCormick & Samuels, 1979; Park, 1978–1979; Zinck, 1978).

Factor analytic studies are yet another way of analyzing descriptive data. Factor analysis has enjoyed greater popularity than it does today (Davis, 1968). However, many problems can be studied in a preliminary fashion by using factor analysis. Attitudes are particularly amenable to study by this method (e.g., Duffy & Metheny, 1979). While factor analysis does not allow true causal inferences, the technique is valuable for preliminary work in "messy" problem areas. Taylor, Pearson, and Anderson (in press) have used factor analysis to identify key variables that they later used in a cleaner, less complicated data analysis.

The most common experimental design in reading research has been a simple two-group study. Cunningham (1977) and Haburton (1977) provide examples of studies using this design. One group is given a treatment; the other functions as a control group or receives a different treatment. Indications are that the most common experimental design is probably now some form of a factorial design (e.g., Froese & Kurishima, 1979; Mosenthal, 1978; Wood & Brown, 1979); that is, two or more independent variables are manipulated in the same study. All values of each variable are combined with all values of the other variables to produce treatment groups. This is, on one level, only a more complex form of the two-group design. However, the use of factorial designs allows the effects of several variables to be studied simultaneously. In addition, interactions among variables can be studied. The greater the number of variables manipulated in a given setting, the less artificial the situation will be. The desirability of this "ecological validity" has been argued carefully by Bronfenbrenner (1976).

Psychological researchers have for a long time recognized the difficulties inherent in using group data in analyses (see, e.g., Deese & Hulse, 1967). Some researchers in learning have consistently advocated studying single subjects across an extended range of time and/or behaviors. Noted among these in experimental psychology has been Skinner (1957). Staats and his colleagues have applied this methodology in reading (Staats, Staats, Schutz, & Wolf, 1962). The literature on exceptional children, particularly learning-disabled children, is replete with such designs.

Perhaps the most prevalent paradigm in reading research using the single/ small N methodology has been that of miscue analysis (e.g., Goodman, 1969). Most miscue studies utilize analysis of extensive data collected in individual sessions with, at most, a few readers. A primary argument for this methodology is that the relationships among responses are often as important as the content of them.

Because only a few subjects are involved, the collected data can be analyzed intensively. Much of miscue methodology is based on "error" analysis. (Goodman is unwilling to refer to these miscues as errors. They are, clearly, mismatches between text and oral reading.) There is also a similar growing emphasis in psychological research on analysis of errors (Pachella, 1974). Different approaches to errors and error analysis can be found in Nicholson (1978–1979) and Healy (1980). A recent review of oral reading error analysis can be found in Leu's (1982) review and in Allington's chapter (this volume).

Substantial risks are involved in doing research with single/small N samples. Foremost among them is the potential for studying nonrepresentative individuals. Conclusions based on a nonrepresentative sample are inappropriate for extended applications. The smaller the sample, the greater the risk of sampling error. This paradigm necessitates repeated measures, and both the benefits and disadvantages of repeated-measure designs are involved. Repeated measures allow each individual to serve as his or her own control, reducing the variance and increasing the precision of the statistical tests. When repeated measures are used, however, contrast effects may arise. That is, subjects may react differentially to the different treatments only because they realize the treatments are different. In addition, repeated measures are subject to practice and fatigue effects, further limiting their use.

A variant of single/small N designs is the time-series design. In this kind of study, measurements are made many times, before and after the administration of a treatment. Changes in performance can be observed over time as well as a function of the treatment. It is not necessary to have a small or single N to use a time-series design, but the extensive data collection makes it less practical for types of large samples (see Leslie & Osol, 1978, or Palincsar and Brown, in press, for examples of this design).

More sophisticated designs for experimental and quasi-experimental studies in reading are available (see the chapter by Calfee and Piontkowski in this volume.) Much of the impetus for using more complex designs has come from two sources. First, researchers have realized the inadequacies of some conventional methods of collecting data. Bronfenbrenner's notions of ecological validity necessitate collection of much more data than traditionally required. Second, there is a trend toward conducting experiments that require greater effort in data reduction than in the actual data analysis (Marshall & Glock, 1978–1979; Tierney, Bridge, & Cera, 1978–1979). The use of computers has made the analysis of large amounts of data in complex designs a routine matter. For example, a simple *t*-test should take no more than a few minutes to calculate, even by hand. The amount of time required to do a multifactor analysis of variance would clearly be prohibitive without computers. It is still relatively rare, however, to see complex designs like split plot and Latin Square in reading research. As more researchers study complex problems, even these rare, complex designs should become even more common. (There are examples of these complex designs in Gipe, 1978–1979; Perfetti & Goldman, 1976; and Richek, 1976–1977.)

A final class of designs for reading research is the ethnographic design, which is used when the researcher needs to, or wishes to, remain unobtrusive and nonreactive with the environment. Ethnographic studies have high ecological validity because there are no predetermined analytic schemes. Ethnographic studies have produced interesting and provocative results; they have uncovered new variables, relationships, and social dynamics that were masked by more manipulative designs. When decision rules and rules of evidence have been rigorously and consistently formulated and used, ethnography has proven to be a powerful addition to the reading research field. (A full treatment of ethnographic methodologies is given by Hall and Guthrie in this volume. Findings from ethnographic studies are discussed by Green and Bloome in this volume.)

Manipulation of Variables in Reading Research

Reading research often can be characterized by the number of factors manipulated. Much reading research has involved manipulating only a single variable. It is becoming increasingly common for researchers to use designs that manipulate several variables simultaneously. This reflects a realization that clusters of variables have to be studied to arrive at a thorough description or explanation of the reading process. (A *thorough* description is, by nature, ecologically valid, since it encompasses *all* possible variables.) The growing use of designs with a larger number of variables also reflects a growing sophistication among reading researchers. Greater reliance on computer-aided analysis will make the use of these designs more manageable and more likely to be used.

Other manipulations are systematic over a specified range of values. These manipulations usually (but not always) require more controlled conditions than other manipulations. In these studies an attempt is made to determine the effect on performance along a variable dimension. These manipulations are different from manipulations of a qualitative nature, even though the analysis is the same. The best examples of these sorts of studies are found in medical research, where, for example, a range of dosages of a drug might be administered under a variety of conditions. These designs are not commonly used in education.

Finally, there are evaluative manipulations in which a single value of a variable is used to determine whether there is some effect on behavior. Examples might be in test development or in testing a single teaching method or technique (Andrich & Godfrey, 1978–1979; Goldstein, 1976; Sheehan & Marcus, 1977; and Talmage & Walberg, 1978). These studies once dominated reading research, but seem to be less prevalent now than some years ago.

Reading Research Limits the Kinds of Variables

The nature of any phenomenon limits the variables researchers can study. In reading, three major classes of variables can be identified. The first is the class of instructional variables, including, among others, instructional format (Rusted & Coltheart, 1979; Samuels, 1970; Singer, Samuels, & Spiroff, 1974; Willows, 1978), time on task (Wyne & Stuck, 1979; Rosenshine & Stevens, this volume), and materials (Bradley & Ames, 1977; Peoples & Nelson, 1977). This class of variables is a mixture of the traditional (time on task, grouping, or instructional method) and the new (teacher beliefs) (Harste & Burke, 1977; Duffy & Metheny, 1979). New variables also include teacher decision-making processes and indirect measures of effectiveness (e.g., error rate or content covered). Teacher-student interactions variables are discussed in Mosenthal and Na (1980).

A second group of variables, reader/learner factors, can be divided into individual variables like language competence and language development (Byrne & Shea, 1979; Day & Day, 1979; Kleiman, 1975; Shankweiler, Liberman, Mark, Fowler, & Fischer, 1979; Tzeng, Hung, & Wong, 1977; Wisher, 1976), cognitive processes and cognitive development (Britton, Holdgredge, Curry, & Wesebrook, 1979; Marsh, Desberg, & Cooper, 1977; Moeser, 1978; Thorndyke, 1976; and Spiro's chapter in this volume), and more global variables like self-concept (Brady & Richards, 1979) and socioeconomic and cultural factors (Cunningham, 1976–1977; Greenwald & Dulin, 1979; Steffensen, Chitra, & Anderson, 1979).

A final group of variables might be classified as environmental. This group includes classroom design and organization (Cohen & Mosenthal, 1979; LaPorte & Nath, 1976; Rupley & McNamara, 1979), teacher-student interaction patterns (Au & Mason, 1981; Collins, 1983; McDermott & Aron, 1978), and a number of other socio-psycho-linguistic variables dealing with life in classrooms (see the chapter by Greene and Bloom in this volume).

Much of the work on text organization (Yekovich & Kulhavy, 1976) or adjunct aids (Mayer, 1979; Rickards, 1979; Rickards & Hatcher, 1977–1978) falls under the category of instructional format variables. It is a sufficiently large body of literature to deserve mention on its own. Other rapidly developing traditions include schema theory, background knowledge, and generative processing (Bower, Black, & Turner, 1979; Doctorow, Wittrock, & Marks, 1978; Pichert & Anderson, 1977; Reder, 1979), textual characteristics affecting reading (Britton, Meyer, Simpson, Holdredge, & Curry, 1979; Dooling & Christiaansen, 1977; Hayes-Roth & Thorndyke, 1979; Kieras, 1978; Lesgold, Roth, & Curtis, 1979; Rubin, 1978b), and story grammars (Baker, 1978; Black & Bower, 1979; Kintsch & Kozminsky, 1977; Mandler & Johnson, 1977; Rumelhart, 1978; Stein & Glenn, 1977; Stein & Nezworski, 1978; Thorndyke, 1977).

Metacognition has also assumed an important role in reading research. With roots in early work by Flavell, Paris, Brown, and others, the study of "knowing what one knows" about reading has grown into a mature field. The classic paper on metacognition in reading, with thorough updates, is included in the present work (see Baker and Brown in this volume).

An old and enduring line of research, the study of eye movements, has been revitalized. Recent findings from the study of eye movements have been used to model high-level cognitive processes (Ehrlich & Rayner, 1983; Just & Carpenter, 1980). Just and Carpenter have generated a model of the reading process. A thorough review of eye-movement research can be found in Rayner (1978).

Another major current trend is the focus of reading researchers on writing, either by itself or in conjunction with reading. Mosenthal (1982) has dealt with some of the issues in modeling the writing process.

Of central interest is the effect of teaching writing on reading, or vice versa. Extensive discussions of the issues involved can be found in Applebee (1977), Shanahan (1980) and Stotsky (1982). Shanahan (in press) has raised doubts about the transfer to reading of instruction in writing.

COSTS AND BENEFITS IN READING RESEARCH

Before looking ahead to future trends, a few observations about advantages and disadvantages of various research methods are in order. It is not possible to identify one research method or paradigm as the "best." Nevertheless, de Beaugrande (1981) has attempted to identify design criteria for models of reading that might bear on the issue of "best" in that context. (If it were possible, the method might be so general as to be only trivially "best.") Each technique of collecting or analyzing data involves some costs and some benefits. Mosenthal (in press) has approached this problem from a perspective of partial specification. That is, he suggests that there are too many variables involved in literacy events to allow research generalizations that can be used across contexts or linguistic communities. His solution is to limit the domain of the research effort *and* the conclusions one draws from research.

Perhaps the most obvious example can be seen in the dispute between the proponents of ethnographic/descriptive versus experimental methods. On one side is a method that is rich in the number of environmental variables that can be dealt with at one time. The other side is a method with precise controls over effects in the environment that can be attributed to a relatively small set of variables.

Data analysis procedures involve tradeoffs as well. A minimal effort may be required to collect correlational data. However, it is not possible to infer causation from those data. Parametric hypothesis testing may allow causal inference, but the cost will be extensive efforts in design and data collection.

It is important for researchers to be aware of the choices they have made and the consequences of those choices. Converging operations (Garner, Hake, & Erikson, 1956) are essential for reading researchers to take seriously in their research. Briefly, a converging operation is an attempt to verify a research finding by an alternate methodology, particularly one that is independent of the methodology used originally. (This is similar to the notion of triangulation in ethnographic work.) Converging operations attempt to eliminate possible confounding variables, experimenter effects, and the like. This is done by altering the experimental situations and "replicating" the study or experiment under the new conditions. Not only does this assure a higher degree of generalizability but it also narrows the range of possible cause-and-effect relationships.

FUTURE TRENDS IN READING RESEARCH

It will become increasingly difficult to defend reading research studies that do not have ecological validity. Educational researchers will be ever more concerned about instructional relevance in their studies of reading. Reading research will continue to evolve under pressure from several sources. There will be more institutional and less individual research as a result of funding patterns of Research and Development centers, laboratories, and institutes. Concerted, programmatic efforts will account for a larger portion of reading research. These trends can already be seen in the efforts, for example, of the Center for the Study of Reading and the Institute for Research on Teaching. Only in such concentrated research efforts can the long-term, consistent, and related studies needed to unravel the reading process be implemented. At the same time, the demand for relevance will increase where federal funding has influence. In spite of admonitions similar to Kerlinger's (1977) arguments, emphasis in reading research will be dominated by the demand for "product."

There will continue to be increasing inputs from other fields, notably computer science, linguistics, anthropology, cognitive psychology, and physiological psychology. These inputs will be both methodological and substantive. As a result, models and theories of the reading process will become more comprehensive, even though they may be less formal or testable. New methodologies will also be involved. Many more techniques from experimental psychology will be adopted. These will likely include physiological or sensory recording techniques (eye movements, neural recording, and the like). All this will have the effect of providing a set of converging operations on findings in reading research.

There will be additional important inputs from ethnographically oriented methodologists, which will guide future research in reading. In particular, complex clusters of important variables will be identified and related to practice in teaching reading.

Eventually there should be an interactive blending of methodologies. One possible outcome of such blending may be a "division of labor." Descriptive methods may be used to shape and define questions and variables. Experimental and quasi-experimental methods may be used to verify instructional efficacy.

There will be fewer *new* variables, although there may be new methods for deriving them. Some *old* variables will be dropped from the repertoire. For example, traditional measures of readability will probably be dropped in favor of expanded measures to include such considerations as concept load, text structure, and background knowledge. A new series of factor analytic or multiple regression studies will begin to isolate and identify clusters of important text, teaching, and individual variables. Much effort will be expended in refining text analysis procedures for describing discourse quantitatively. These efforts will also relate psychological and sociological processes to the analyses. Similarly, the details of certain schema processes will have to be clarified or dropped in favor of new explanations. (See Anderson and Pearson, this volume, for a related discussion.)

There will be increased reliance on technology for data collection. Microcomputers will play a major role. Far more data in experimental situations will be collected. Analyses will be complex, but additional reliance on computers will keep the tasks within manageable bounds. The dissemination of information will be faster as the use of computer technology becomes more widespread. Technology will also facilitate cooperative research efforts. There will also be profound effects on teaching and learning as a result of the use of technology, particularly microcomputers, but those effects are not clear-cut (Kamil, 1982).

To accommodate the new changes in theory and methodology, there will be improved training of graduate students in research techniques. This will sustain a decided trend from the recent past. As more interdisciplinary efforts are mounted, graduate training will be cross-fertilized further, and the ultimate result will be even greater increases in sophistication of reading research.

The development of meta-analysis (Glass, 1977) has spurred interest in quantifying reading research findings. While there are alternatives (Cooper, 1982; Ladas, 1980; Shapiro, 1982) and problems that may not have been overcome (Rosenthal, 1980), meta-analyses are becoming more common in reading research (e.g. Pflaum, Walberg, Karegianes, and Rasher, 1980). More emphasis will be placed on determining what research has really shown, either by meta-analyses, by synthesizing reviews, or by other means.

There will be more intensive efforts at translating research findings into instructional practice. A strong trend of interpreting research is already evident. Major works by Anderson et al. (1977), Gibson and Levin (1975), Guthrie (1981), Harste and Carey (1979), Johnson and Pearson (1978), Langer and Smith-Burke (1982), and Pearson and Johnson (1978) are but a small sample of the prevalence of translating endeavors. As reading research proceeds, translation into practice of course will be easier and more direct. As reading researchers become more adept at interpreting complex clusters of variables, the jump to practice will be much easier. Ultimately instructional practices will be substantially improved. It is not a goal that will be reached immediately. Meanwhile, striving for such a goal will yield large dividends.

REFERENCES

Allington, R. L.   Sensitivity to orthographic structures as a function of grade and reading ability. *Journal of Reading Behavior*, 1978, *10*, 437–439.

Anderson, R. C., Spiro, R. J., & Montague, W. E. (Eds.).   *Schooling and the acquisition of knowledge*. Hillsdale, N.J.: Erlbaum, 1977.

Andrich, D., & Godfrey, J. R.   Hierarchies in the skills of Davis' Reading Comprehension Test, Form D: An empirical investigation using a latent trait model. *Reading Research Quarterly*, 1978–1979, *14*, 182–200.

Applebee, A.   Writing and reading. *Journal of Reading*, 1977, *20*, 534–537.

Au, K. H., & Mason, J. M.   Social organizational factors in learning to read: The balance of rights hypothesis. *Reading Research Quarterly*, 1981, *17* (1), 115–152.

Baker, L.   Processing temporal relationships in simple stories: Effects of input sequences. *Journal of Verbal Learning and Verbal Behavior*, 1978, *17*, 559–572.

Black, J. B., & Bower, G. H.   Episodes as chunks in narrative memory. *Journal of Verbal Learning and Verbal Behavior*, 1979, *18*, 309–318.

Bower, G. H., Black, J. B., & Turner, T. J.   Scripts in memory for text. *Cognitive Psychology*, 1979, *11*, 177–220.

Bradley, J. M., & Ames, W. S.   Readability parameters of basal readers. *Journal of Reading Behavior*, 1977, *9*, 175–183.

Brady, P. J., & Rickards, J. P.   How personal evaluation affects the underlining and recall of prose material. *Journal of Reading Behavior*, 1979, *11*, 61–68.

Britton, B. K., Holdredge, T. S., Curry, C., & Westbrook, R. D.   Use of cognitive capacity in reading identical texts with different amounts of discourse level meaning. *Journal of Experimental Psychology: Human Learning and Memory*, 1979, *5*, 262–270.

Britton, B. K., Meyer, B. J. F., Simpson, R., Holdredge, T. S., & Curry, C.   Effects of the organization on text on memory: Test of two implications of a selective attention hypothesis. *Journal of Experimental Psychology: Human Learning and Memory*, 1979, *5*, 491–506.

Bronfenbrenner, U.   The experimental ecology of education. *Educational Researcher*, 1976, *5*, 5–15.

Bronowski, J.   *A sense of the future*. Cambridge, Mass.: MIT Press, 1977.

Byrne, B., & Shea, P.   Semantic and phonetic memory codes in beginning readers. *Memory and Cognition*, 1979, *7*, 333–338.

Calfee, R., & Piontkowski, D.   The reading diary: Acquisition of decoding. *Reading Research Quarterly*, 1981, *16*, 346–373.

Campbell, D. T., & Stanley, J. C.   *Experimental and quasi-experimental designs for research*. Chicago: Rand McNally, 1963.

Canney, G., & Schreiner, R.   A study of the effectiveness of elected syllabication rules and phonogram patterns for word attack. *Reading Research Quarterly*, 1976–1977, *12*, 100–124.

Carnine, L., & Carnine, D.   Determining the relative decoding difficulty of three types of simple regular words. *Journal of Reading Behavior*, 1978, *10*, 440–441.

Carver, R. P.   Measuring prose difficulty using the rauding scale. *Reading Research Quarterly*, 1975–1976, *11*, 660–685.

Carver, R. P.   Toward a theory of reading comprehension and rauding. *Reading Research Quarterly*, 1977–1978, *13*, 8–63.

Carver, R. P.   Sense and nonsense about generalizing to a language population. *Journal of Reading Behavior*, 1978, *10*, 25–33.

Cohen, M. W., & Mosenthal, P.   The relationship between teacher-student interaction and students' reading comprehension. In M. L. Kamil & A. J. Moe (Eds.), *Reading research: Studies and applications* (Twenty-eighth Yearbook of the National Reading Conference). Clemson, S.C.: National Reading Conference, 1979, 239–245.

Coker, H., & Lorentz, J. L.   Growth in reading as a correlate of pupil classroom behavior. In P. D. Pearson (Ed.), *Reading: Theory, research and practice* (Twenty-sixth Yearbook of the National Reading Conference). Clemson, S.C.: National Reading Conference, 1977, 118–125.

Coleman, E. B.   Collecting a data base for a reading technology. *Journal of Educational Psychology Monograph*, 1970, *61*, 1–23.

Collins, J.   *Linguistic perspectives on minority education* (Technical Report No. 2–75). Urbana-Champaign: University of Illinois, Center for the Study of Reading, 1983.

Condon, M. W. F., & Hoffman, J. V.   A comparison of context usage by good and poor readers in word boundary tasks. In M. L. Kamil & A. J. Moe (Eds.), *Reading research: Studies and applications* (Twenty-eighth Yearbook of the National Reading Conference). Clemson, S.C.: National Reading Conference, 1979, 39–44.

Cook, T., & Campbell, D.   *Quasi-experimentation*. Boston: Houghton Mifflin, 1979.

Cooper, H.   Scientific guidelines for conducting integrative reviews. *Review of Educational Research*, 1982, *52*, 291–302.

Cunningham, P. M.   Teacher's correction responses to black-dialect miscues which are non-meaning-changing. *Reading Research Quarterly*, 1976–1977, *12*, 635–653.

Cunningham, P. M.   Investigating the role of meaning in mediated word identification. In P. D. Pearson (Ed.), *Reading: Theory, research and practice* (Twenty-sixth Yearbook of the National Reading Conference). Clemson, S.C.: National Reading Conference, 1977, 118–125.

Davis, F. B.   Research in comprehension in reading. *Reading Research Quarterly*, 1968, *3*, 499–545.

Davis, F. B. (Ed.).   *The literature of research in reading with emphasis on models*. New Brunswick, N.J.: Graduate School of Education, Rutgers University, 1971.

Day, K. C., & Day, H. D.   Development of kindergarten children's understanding of concepts about print and oral language. In M. L. Kamil & A. J. Moe (Eds.), *Reading research: Studies and applications* (Twenty-eighth Yearbook of the National Reading Conference). Clemson, S.C.: National Reading Conference, 1979, 19–22.

de Beaugrande, R.   Design criteria for process models of reading. *Reading Research Quarterly*, 1981, *16*, 261–315.

Deese, J., & Hulse, S. H.   *The psychology of learning* (3rd ed.). New York: McGraw-Hill, 1967.

Doctorow, M., Wittrock, M. C., & Marks, C.   Generative processes in reading comprehension. *Journal of Educational Psychology*, 1978, *70*, 109–118.

Dooling, D. J., & Christiaansen, R. E.   Episodic and semantic aspects of memory for prose. *Journal of Experimental Psychology: Human Learning and Memory*, 1977, *3*, 428–436.

Duffy, G., & Metheny, W.   The development of an instrument to measure teacher beliefs about reading. In M. L. Kamil & A. J. Moe (Eds.), *Reading research: Studies and applications* (Twenty-eighth Yearbook of the National Reading Conference). Clemson, S.C.: National Reading Conference, 1979, 218–222.

Duffy, G., & Roehler, L.   An analysis of the instruction in reading instructional research. In J. Niles & L. Harris (Eds.), *New inquiries in reading research and instruction* (Thirty-first Yearbook of the National Reading Conference). Rochester, N.Y.: National Reading Conference, 1982.

Durkin, D.   What classroom observations reveal about reading comprehension instruction. *Reading Research Quarterly*, 1978–1979, *14*, 481–538.

Ehrlich, K., & Rayner, K.   Pronoun assignment and semantic integration during reading: Eye movements and immediacy of processing. *Journal of Verbal Learning and Verbal Behavior*, 1983, *22*, 75–87.

Eisner, E.   Anastasia might still be alive, but the monarchy is still dead. *Educational Researcher*, 1983, *12* (5), 13–14, 23–24.

Entin, E. B., & Klare, G. R.   Factor analyses of three correlation matrices of readability variables. *Journal of Reading Behavior*, 1978, *10*, 279–290.

Finn, P. J.   Word frequency, information theory, and cloze performance: A transfer feature theory of processing in reading. *Reading Research Quarterly*, 1977–1978, *13*, 508–537.

Foucault, M.   *The archaeology of knowledge.* London: Travistock, 1972.

Fredericksen, C.   Representing logical and semantic structure of knowledge acquired from discourse. *Cognitive Psychology*, 1975, *7*, 371–458.

Froese, V., & Kurishima, S.   The effects of sentence expansion practice on the reading comprehension and writing ability of third-graders. In M. L. Kamil & A. J. Moe (Eds.), *Reading research: Studies and applications* (Twenty-eighth Yearbook of the National Reading Conference). Clemson, S.C.: National Reading Conference, 1979, 95–99.

Garner, W., Hake, H., & Erikson, C.   Operationism and the concept of perception. *Psychological Review*, 1956, *63*, 149–159.

Gibson, E. J., & Levin, H.   *The psychology of reading.* Cambridge, Mass.: MIT Press, 1975.

Gipe, J.   Investigating techniques for teaching word meaning. *Reading Research Quarterly*, 1978–1979, *14*, 624–644.

Glass, G.   Integrating findings: The meta-analysis of research. *Review of research in education* (Vol. 5). Itasca, Ill.: Peacock, 1977.

Goldstein, D. M.   Cognitive-linguistic functioning and learning to read in preschoolers. *Journal of Educational Psychology*, 1976, *68*, 680–688.

Goodman, K. S.   Analysis of oral reading miscues: Applied psycholinguistics. *Reading Research Quarterly*, 1969, *1*, 9–30.

Gough, P. B.   One second of reading. In J. F. Kavanagh & I. G. Mattingly (Eds.), *Language by ear and by eye.* Cambridge, Mass.: MIT Press, 1972.

Gough, P. B., Alford, J. A., Jr., & Holley-Wilcox, P.   Words and contexts. In M. L. Kamil & A. J. Moe (Eds.), *Reading research: Studies and applications* (Twenty-eighth Yearbook of the National Reading Conference). Clemson, S.C.: National Reading Conference, 1979, 72–75.

Gough, P. B., & Cosky, M.   One second of reading again. In J. Castellan, D. Pisoni, & G. Potts (Eds.), *Cognitive theory* (Vol. II). Hillsdale, N.J.: Erlbaum, 1975.

Greenwald, M. J., & Dulin, K. L.   Male and female college-age readers' affective response to formal, colloquial, and substandard dialogue of male and female literacy characters. In M. L. Kamil & A. J. Moe (Eds.), *Reading research: Studies and applications* (Twenty-eighth Yearbook of the National Reading Conference). Clemson, S.C.: National Reading Conference, 1979, 246–248.

Guthrie, J. (Ed.).   *Comprehension and teaching: Research reviews.* Newark, Del.: International Reading Association, 1981.

Haburton, E.   Impact of an experimental reading-study skills course on high-risk student success in a community college. In P. D. Pearson (Ed.), *Reading: Theory, research and practice* (Twenty-sixth Yearbook of the National Reading Conference). Clemson, S.C.: National Reading Conference, 1977, 110–117.

Halliday, M., & Hasan, R.   *Cohesion in English.* London: Longman, 1976.

Harste, J. C., & Burke, C.   A new hypothesis for reading teacher research: Both the *teaching* and *learning* of reading are theoretically based. In P. D. Pearson (Ed.), *Reading: Theory, research and practice* (Twenty-sixth Yearbook of the National Reading Conference). Clemson, S.C.: National Reading Conference, 1977, 32–40.

Harste, J. C., & Carey, R. F. (Eds.).   *New perspectives on comprehension.* Bloomington, Ind.: Indiana University Press, 1979.

Hayes-Roth, B., & Thorndyke, P. W.   Integration of knowledge from text. *Journal of Verbal Learning and Verbal Behavior,* 1979, *18,* 91–108.

Healy, A. F.   Proofreading errors on the word the: New evidence on reading units. *Journal of Experimental Psychology: Human Perception and Performance,* 1980, *6,* 45–57.

Herndon, M. A.   An approach toward the development of a functional encoding model of short term memory during reading. *Journal of Reading Behaviors,* 1978, *10,* 141–148.

Jenkins, J. J.   Four points to remember: A tetrahedral model of memory experiments. In L. S. Cermak & F. I. M. Craik (Eds.), *Levels of processing in human memory.* Hillsdale, N.J.: Erlbaum, 1979.

Johnson, D. J., & Pearson, P. D.   *Teaching reading vocabulary.* New York: Holt, Rinehart & Winston, 1978.

Just, M., & Carpenter, P.   A theory of reading: From eye fixations to comprehension. *Psychological Review,* 1980, *87,* 329–354.

Kamil, M. L.   Models of reading: What are the implications for instruction in comprehension? In S. Pflaum-Connor (Ed.), *Aspects of reading education.* Berkeley, Calif.: McCutcheon, 1978, 63–88.

Kamil, M. L.   Technology and reading: A review of research and instruction. In J. Niles & L. Harris (Eds.), *New inquiries in reading research and instruction* (Thirty-first Yearbook of the National Reading Conference). Rochester, N.Y.: National Reading Conference, 1982, 251–260.

Kerlinger, F. N.   The influence of research on educational practice. *Educational Researcher,* 1977, *6,* 5–12.

Kieras, D. E.   Good and bad structure in simple paragraphs: Effects on apparent theme, reading time, and recall. *Journal of Verbal Learning and Verbal Behavior,* 1978, *17,* 13–28.

Kintsch, W.   *The representation of meaning in memory.* Hillsdale, N.J.: Erlbaum, 1974.

Kintsch, W., & Kozimsky, E.   Summarizing stories after reading and listening. *Journal of Educational Psychology,* 1977, *69,* 491–499.

Kintsch, W., & van Dijk, T.   Toward a model of text comprehension and production. *Psychological Review*, 1978, *85*, 363–394.

Kleiman, G. H.   Speech recording in reading. *Journal of Verbal Learning and Verbal Behavior*, 1975, *14*, 323–339.

Kuhn, T. S.   *The structure of scientific revolutions*. Chicago: University of Chicago Press, 1962.

Kurth, R. J.   Evaluations of an objective-based curriculum in word attack. *Journal of Reading Behavior*, 1978, *10*, 445–446.

LaBerge, D., & Samuels, S. J.   A critique of "Toward a theory of automatic information processing in reading." In L. Gentile, M. Kamil, & J. Blanchard (Eds.), *Reading research revisited*. Columbus, Ohio: Merrill, 1983.

Ladas, H.   Summarizing research: A case study. *Review of Educational Research*, 1980, *50*, 597–624.

Lakatos, I., & Musgrave, A. (Eds.).   *Criticism and the growth of knowledge*. London: Cambridge University Press, 1970.

Langer, J., & Smith-Burke, M. (Eds.).   *Reader meets author/Bridging the gap*. Newark, Del.: International Reading Association, 1982.

LaPorte, R. E., & Nath, E.   Role of performance goals in prose learning. *Journal of Educational Psychology*, 1976, *68*, 260–264.

Lesgold, A. M., Roth, S. F., & Curtis, M. E.   Foregrounding effects in discourse comprehension. *Journal of Verbal Learning and Verbal Behavior*, 1979, *18*, 291–308.

Leslie, L., & Osol, P.   Changes in oral reading strategies as a function of quantities of miscues. *Journal of Reading Behavior*, 1978, *10*, 442–445.

Leu, D. J., Jr.   Oral reading error analysis: A critical review of research and application. *Reading Research Quarterly*, 1982, *17*, 420–437.

McCormick, C., & Samuels, S. J.   Word recognition by second graders: The unit of perception and interrelationships among accuracy, latency and comprehension. *Journal of Reading Behavior*, 1979, *11*, 107–118.

McDermott, R. P., & Aron, J.   Pirandello in the classroom: On the possibility of equal educational opportunity in American culture. In M. C. Reynolds (Ed.), *Futures of exceptional students: Emerging structures*. Reston, Va.: Council for Exceptional Children, 1978.

Mandler, J. M., & Johnson, N. S.   Remembrance of things parsed: Story structure and recall. *Cognitive Psychology*, 1977, *9*, 111–151.

Marr, M. B.   Children's comprehension of pictorial and textual event sequences. In M. L. Kamil & A. J. Moe (Eds.), *Reading research: Studies and applications* (Twenty-eighth Yearbook of the National Reading Conference). Clemson, S.C.: National Reading Conference, 1979, 104–108.

Marsh, G., Desberg, P., & Cooper, J.   Developmental changes in reading strategies. *Journal of Reading Behavior*, 1977, *9*, 391–394.

Marshall, N., & Glock, M.   Comprehension of connected discourse: A study into the relationships between the structure of text and information recalled. *Reading Research Quarterly*, 1978–1979, *14*, 10–56.

Massaro, D. W., Venezky, R. L., & Taylor, G. A.   Orthographic regularity, positional frequency, and visual processing of letter strings. *Journal of Experimental Psychology: General*, 1979, *108*, 107–124.

Maxwell, M.   Learning style and other correlates of performance on a scanning experiment. *Journal of Reading Behavior*, 1978, *10*, 49–55.

Mayer, R. E.   Can advance organizers influence meaningful learning? *Review of Educational Research*, 1979, *49*, 371–383.

Mitroff, I., & Mason, R.   *Creating a dialectical social science*. Dordrecht, Holland: Reidel, 1981.

Moeser, S. D.   Effect of questions on prose utilization. *Journal of Experimental Psychology: Human Learning and Memory*, 1978, *4*, 290–303.

Montare, A., Elmon, E., & Cohen, J.   Words and pictures: A test of Samuels' findings. *Journal of Reading Behavior*, 1977, *9*, 269–285.

Mosenthal, P.   The new and given in children's comprehension of presuppositive negatives in two modes of processing. *Journal of Reading Behavior*, 1978, *10*, 267–278.

Mosenthal, P.   Toward a paradigm of children's classroom writing competence. In B. Hutson (Ed.), *Advances in reading/language research* (Vol. 1). Greenwich, Conn.: JAI Press, 1982.

Mosenthal, P.   The problem of partial specification in translating reading research into practice. *Elementary School Journal*, in press.

Mosenthal, P., & Na, T.   Quality of children's recall under two classroom testing tasks: Towards a socio-psycholinguistic model of reading comprehension. *Reading Research Quarterly*, 1980, *15*, 504–528.

Moyer, S.   Rehabilitation of alexia: A case study. *Cortex*, 1979, *15*, 139–144.

Nagel, E.   *The Structure of Science*. New York: Harcourt, 1961.

Nicholson, T.   The relative effects of different error types on children's understanding of connected discourse (abstracted). *Reading Research Quarterly*, 1978–1979, *14*, 259–264.

Olson, D.   From utterance to text: The bias of language in speech and writing. *Harvard Educational Review*, 1977, *47*, 157–181.

O'Reilly, R. P., & Streeter, R. E.   Report on the development and validation of a system for measuring literal comprehension in a multiple-choice close format. *Journal of Reading Behavior*, 1977, *9*, 45–69.

Pachella, R. G.   The interpretation of reaction time in information-processing research. In B. H. Kantowitz (Ed.), *Human information processing: Tutorial in performance and cognition*. Hillsdale, N.J.: Erlbaum, 1974.

Palincsar, A., & Brown, A.   *Reciprocal teaching of comprehension-monitoring activities*. Urbana-Champaign, Ill.: Center for the Study of Reading, in press.

Park, R.   Performance on geometric figure copying tests and predictors of types of errors in decoding. *Reading Research Quarterly*, 1978–1979, *14*, 100–118.

Pearson, P. D., & Gallagher, M.   The instruction of reading comprehension. *Contemporary Educational Psychology*, in press.

Pearson, P. D., & Johnson, D. J.   *Teaching reading comprehension*. New York: Holt, Rinehart & Winston, 1978.

Pearson, P. D., & Kamil, M. L.   What hath Carver raud? A reaction to Carver's "Toward a theory of reading comprehension and rauding." *Reading Research Quarterly*, 1977–1978, *13*, 92–115.

Peoples, A. C., & Nelson, R.   The differential effects of phonics versus sight-recognition methods of teaching reading on the eye movements of good and poor second-grade readers. *Journal of Reading Behavior*, 1977, *9*, 327–337.

Perfetti, C. A., & Goldman, S. R.   Discourse memory and reading comprehension skill. *Journal of Verbal Learning and Verbal Behavior*, 1976, *14*, 33–42.

Pflaum, S., Walberg, H., Karegianes, M., & Rasher, S.   Reading instruction: A quantitative analysis. *Educational Researcher*, 1980, *9*, 12–18.

Phillips, D.   After the wake: Postpositivistic educational thought. *Educational Researcher*, 1983, *12* (5), 4–12.

Pichert, J., & Anderson, R.   Taking different perspectives on a story. *Journal of Educational Psychology*, 1977, *69*, 309–315.

Popham, W. J.   *Simplified design for school research*. New York: American Book, 1972.

Rayner, K.   Eye movements in reading and information processing. *Psychological Bulletin*, 1978, *85*, 618–660.

Reder, L. M.   The role of elaborations in memory for prose. *Cognitive Psychology*, 1979, *11*, 221–234.

Resta, P. E., & Baker, R. L.   *Selecting variables for educational research*. New York: American Book, 1972.

Rickards, J. P.   Adjunct postquestions in text: A critical review of methods and processes. *Review of Educational Research*, 1979, *49*, 181–196.

Rickards, J. P., & Hatcher, C. W.   Interspersed meaningful learning questions as semantic cues for poor comprehenders. *Reading Research Quarterly*, 1977–1978, *13*, 538–553.

Richek, M. A.   Reading comprehension of anaphoric forms in varying linguistic context. *Reading Research Quarterly*, 1976–1977, *12*, 145–165.

Rosenthal, R.   Combining probabilities and the file drawer problem. *Evaluation in Education*, 1980, *4*, 18–21.

Rubin, D. C.   Word-initial and word-final NGRAM frequencies. *Journal of Reading Behavior*, 1978, *10*, 171–183. (a)

Rubin, D. C.   A unit of analysis of prose memory. *Journal of Verbal Learning and Verbal Behavior*, 1978, *17*, 599–620. (b)

Rumelhart, D. E.   Toward an interactive model of reading. In S. Dornic (Ed.), *Attention and performance* (Vol. 6). Hillsdale, N.J.: Erlbaum, 1977.

Rumelhart, D. E.   Understanding and summarizing brief stories. In D. Laberge & S. J. Samuels (Eds.), *Basic process in reading: Perception and comprehension*. Hillsdale, N.J.: Erlbaum, 1978.

Rupley, W. H., & McNamara, J. F.   Effects of instructional emphasis and pupil engaged time on reading achievement. In M. L. Kamil & A. J. Moe (Eds.), *Reading research: Studies and applications* (Twenty-eighth Yearbook of the National Reading Conference). Clemson, S.C.: National Reading Conference, 1979, 199–203.

Rusted, J., & Coltheart, M.   Facilitation of children's prose recall by the presence of pictures. *Memory and Cognition*, 1979, *7*, 354–359.

Sakiey, E.   The commonest syllables. In M. L. Kamil & A. J. Moe (Eds.), *Reading research: Studies and applications* (Twenty-eighth Yearbook of the National Reading Conference). Clemson, S.C.: National Reading Conference, 1979, 204–209.

Samuels, S. J.   Effects of pictures on learning to read, comprehension and attitudes. *Review of Educational Research*, 1970, *40*, 397–407.

Shanahan, T.   The impact of writing instruction on learning to read. *Reading World*, 1980, *19*, 357–368.

Shanahan, T.   The nature of the reading-writing relationship: A multivariate approach. *Journal of Educational Psychology*, in press.

Shankweiler, D., Liberman, I. Y., Mark, L. S., Fowler, C. A., & Fischer, F. W.   *Journal of Experimental Psychology: Human Learning and Memory*, 1979, *5*, 531–545.

Shapiro, J.   *On the use of bayesian statistics for the meta-analysis of research*. Paper presented to the joint meeting of the Philadelphia and New Jersey Educational Research Associations, Philadelphia, May 1982.

Shaver, J. P. & Norton, R. S.   Randomness and replication of ten years of the *American Educational Research Journal*. *Educational Researcher*, 1980, *9*, 9–16.

Sheehan, D. S., & Marcus, M.   Validating criterion referenced reading tests. *Journal of Reading Behavior*, 1977, *9*, 129–135.

Singer, H.   Hypotheses on reading comprehension in search of classroom validation. In M. Kamil (Ed.), *Directions in reading: Research and instruction* (Thirtieth Yearbook of the National Reading Conference). Washington, D.C.: National Reading Conference, 1981.

Singer, H., & Ruddell, R. B. (Eds.).   *Theoretical models and processes of reading*. Newark, Del.: International Reading Association, 1970.

Singer, H., & Ruddell, R. B. (Eds.).   *Theoretical models and processes of reading* (2nd ed.). Newark, Del.: International Reading Association, 1976.

Singer, H., Samuels, S. J., & Spiroff, J.   The effect of pictures and contextual conditions on learning responses to printed words. *Reading Research Quarterly,* 1974, *9,* 555–567.

Skinner, B. F.   The experimental analysis of behavior. *American Scientist,* 1957, *45,* 343–371.

Spilich, G. J., Vesonder, G. T., Chiesi, H. L., & Voss, J. F.   Text processing of domain-related information for individuals with high and low domain knowledge. *Journal of Verbal Learning and Verbal Behavior,* 1979, *18,* 275–290.

Staats, A., Staats, C., Schutz, R., & Wolf, M.   The conditioning of textual responses using "extrinsic" reinforcers. *Journal of Experimental Analysis of Behavior,* 1962, *5,* 33–40.

Stanovich, K.   Toward an interactive-compensatory model of individual differences in the development of reading fluency. *Reading Research Quarterly,* 1980, *16,* 37–71.

Steffensen, M. S., Chitra, J., & Anderson, R. C.   A cross-cultural perspective on reading comprehension. *Reading Research Quarterly,* 1979, *15,* 10–29.

Stein, N., & Glenn, C.   An analysis of story comprehension in elementary school children. In R. Freedle (Ed.), *Discourse production and comprehension* (Vol. 1). Norwood, N.J.: Ablex, 1977.

Stein, N. L., & Nezworkski, T.   The effects of organization and instructional set on story memory. *Discourse Processes,* 1978, *1,* 177–193.

Steinheiser, R., & Guthrie, J. T.   Perceptual and linguistic processing of letters and words by normal and disabled readers. *Journal of Reading Behavior,* 1977, *9,* 217–225.

Stotsky, S.   The role of writing in developmental reading. *Journal of Reading,* 1982, *24,* 330–339.

Sullivan, H. J.   *Classifying and interpreting educational research studies.* New York: American Book, 1972.

Talmage, H., & Walberg, H. J.   Naturalistic, decision-oriented evaluations of a district reading program. *Journal of Reading Behavior,* 1978, *10,* 185–195.

Taylor, M., Pearson, P. D., & Anderson, R.   *Reading comprehension and creativity in black language use: You stand to gain by playing the sounding game.* Urbana-Champaign, Ill.: Center for the Study of Reading, in press.

Tharp, R. G.   The effective instruction of comprehension: Results and description of the Kamehameha Early Education Program. *Reading Research Quarterly,* 1982, *17* (4), 503–527.

Thorndyke, P. W.   The role of inferences in discourse comprehension. *Journal of Verbal Learning and Verbal Behavior,* 1976, *15,* 437–446.

Thorndyke, P. W.   Cognitive structures in comprehension and memory for narrative discourse. *Cognitive Psychology,* 1977, *9,* 77–110.

Thorndyke, P. W., & Yekovich, F.   A critique of schemata as a theory of human story memory. *Poetics,* 1979, *2,* 113–126.

Tierney, R. J., Bridge, C. A., & Cera, M. J.   The discourse processing operations of children. *Reading Research Quarterly,* 1978–1979, *14,* 539–573.

Tzeng, O. J. L., Hung, D. L., & Wong, W. S-Y.   Speech recoding in reading Chinese characters. *Journal of Experimental Psychology: Human Learning and Memory,* 1977, *3,* 621–630.

Weaver, P., & Shonkoff, F.   *Research within reach.* St. Louis: CEMREL, 1978.

Weimer, W.   Psycholinguistics and Plato's paradoxes of the *Meno. American Psychologist,* 1973, *28,* 15–33.

Willows, D. M.   A picture is not always worth a thousand words: Pictures as distractors in reading. *Journal of Educational Psychology,* 1978, *70,* 255–262.

Wisher, R. A.   The effects of syntactic expectations during reading. *Journal of Educational Psychology,* 1976, *68,* 597–602.

Wood, M., & Brown, M.   Beginning readers' recognition of tough words in various contextual settings. In M. L. Kamil & A. J. Moe (Eds.), *Reading research: Studies and applications* (Twenty-eighth Yearbook of the National Reading Conference). Clemson, S.C.: National Reading Conference, 1979, 55–61.

Wyne, M. D., & Stuck, G. B.   Time-on-task and reading performance in underachieving children. *Journal of Reading Behavior*, 1979, *9*, 119–128.

Yap, K. O.   Vocabulary-building blocks of comprehension? *Journal of Reading Behavior*, 1979, *11*, 49–59.

Yekovich, F. R., & Kulhavy, R. W.   Structural and contextual effects in the organization of prose. *Journal of Educational Psychology*, 1976, *68*, 626–635.

Zinck, R. A.   The relation of comprehension to semantic and syntactic language cues utilized during oral and silent reading. In P. D. Pearson & J. Hansen (Eds.), *Reading: Disciplined inquiry in process and practice* (Twenty-seventh Yearbook of the National Reading Conference). Clemson, S.C.: National Reading Conference, 1978, 154–160.

3 DESIGN AND ANALYSIS OF EXPERIMENTS

Robert Calfee and Dorothy Piontkowski

The researcher's role in behavioral experimentation is an active one. The researcher arranges the conditions for observing behavior, imposes systematic changes on these conditions, and measures the effects of these changes on behavior. These activities contrast with the researcher's role when behavior is studied naturalistically, when observational or correlational approaches are used. Most research on how young children learn to read in school settings is of the latter sort. Researchers have relied mainly on observation of naturally occurring behavior and have employed correlational statistics to describe relations among variables. In this chapter we explore the techniques and the advantages and disadvantages from the systematic application of experimental design concepts and procedures to research on relations between reading instruction and acquisition.

The goal of behavioral experimentation is to obtain rational and trustworthy evidence about the phenomena of interest. The researcher designs each experiment so that it adds information to accumulated knowledge on the influential variables underlying human behavior. The experimenter begins with a rational analysis of the nature of the behavior to be investigated. At the same time the experimenter aims to link the analysis to a theoretical model of the underlying mental processes. The model guides decisions about the selection of variables and the amount and kind of information needed. Experiments often include many variables and are rich in information—to be sure, complicated studies are difficult to carry out and interpret. Simpler studies with less control and fewer variables are less demanding of time, energy, and resources, but they seldom provide the information needed to answer the research question. The researcher is always deciding how to make the most efficient use of resources in order to obtain clear answers to the experimental question.

In this chapter we discuss the design and analysis of experiments for research on reading. We begin with a general discussion of the methods and procedures for carrying out experiments, with special emphases on the additive model for data analysis and on design efficiency. We then illustrate the application of the experimental approach to two problems specific to reading: the development and evaluation of curriculum programs, and the design of an instrument for the assessment of reading comprehension.

RESEARCH METHODOLOGY

Experimental research begins with a question that is clearly stated, precise, and answerable. This question is the basis for planning the research design. The task of planning the design involves reflective and analytic thinking about the likely structure of the problem. The goal throughout experimental research is the achievement of control—the degree to which the investigation is planned, conducted, and analyzed so that the researcher arrives at a clear and precise answer to the experimental question. There are numerous pitfalls along the way, and experimental design techniques help the investigator avoid these traps.

Planning the Design

Experimental designs are comprised of three elements: factors, levels, and measures. A *factor* is a systematic variation incorporated in the design to determine the effect of that variation. Factors, also referred to as independent variables, include such dimensions as the instructional method (phonics versus whole word), the amount of practice (20 minutes versus 40 minutes a day), and the time of testing (morning versus evening).

We distinguish among three categories of factors: treatment factors; subject-classification factors; and control, or nuisance, factors. A treatment factor is directly controlled by the experimenter; an example of a treatment factor would be the method of reading instruction. A subject-classification factor is a characteristic of the subjects that cannot be readily modified by the experimenter but is controlled by the manner of selecting subjects; for example, both age and sex might be taken into account. Nuisance factors include variables that are not of particular interest to the experimenter but that must be built into the design in order to avoid problems of interpretation; for example, if subjects are tested repeatedly during an experiment, testing time would be included as a nuisance factor in order to take into account the possible influence of learning or boredom on performance.

A specific value of a factor is called a *level*. For some factors, the range of levels is small in number. For instance, male and female are the only levels for the factor of sex. Levels may be defined by the presence or absence of a treatment. Thus, a novel reading program may be contrasted with the absence of such a program, or reward (a nickel for each correctly pronounced word) may be contrasted with no reward. Many factors are quantitative in nature and hence have numerous levels. Age, amount of practice, and length of a reading passage are examples of such factors. Other factors have numerous levels because of their inherent complexity. For example, in the study of Planned Variation in Follow Through, a large number of reading programs constituted the levels of the treatment factor. Because instructional programs could vary in so many ways, the number of potential levels was very large.

The various indexes of the individual performance are referred to as *response measures* or dependent variables. These measures may be either quantitative or qualitative—number correct on a test, what is said or done, how long an action takes, how the person reports what he feels, and so on.

In planning the experiment, a researcher makes many decisions. Primary design decisions are the choice of factors to vary and to hold constant, the levels of each factor to include in the design, the manner of selecting subjects, and the planning of specific experimental procedures. During this decision making, three issues are of paramount importance: variability, confounding, and interaction.

Variability in this context refers to the fluctuations that commonly occur in human behavior. Some variations in performance reflect random, unpredictable changes; other variations reflect systematic and predictable change. In designing an experiment, the aim is to minimize random variability, to identify systematic changes, and thereby to converge on the true value of each measure.

Because we are usually interested in the average performance of the individual under some set of conditions, we can reduce the influence of random variability by increasing the number of observations. If we collect only one or two observations, these may differ substantially from the true value. With a larger number of observations, the average value tends toward accuracy; there is less chance that the mean will reflect a large margin of error. All other things being equal, in order to establish confidence in the accuracy of the estimate of performance, the experimenter should plan either to test each subject several times or to test a large number of subjects.

Random variability or error is also reduced by establishing control over the conditions of measurement. One method is to maintain a constant environment insofar as possible. A second method is to identify the nuisance factors that may produce variability and either maintain them at a constant level or include them in the experimental design so that their effects can be determined. For example, suppose an experimenter is evaluating the effects of a cross-age tutorial reading program on students' achievement scores and wants to establish control in the design over variability due to testing environments. The experimenter knows that under "normal conditions," the student will be tested under a variety of environments ranging from individual testing in a quiet room to group testing in a noisy classroom. One approach the experimenter can adopt is to insist that the evaluation provide for optimal individualized testing of each student. Control can also be attained by arranging for the achievement test to be administered in two ways. Half the students from each treatment group (tutorial program and nonprogram) are given the test individually by a trained tester, who makes sure each student understands the task and does his or her best. The rest of the students are tested by the regular teacher under normal conditions; the teacher reads the directions aloud to the entire class and monitors behavior in a general way.

Figure 3.1 illustrates how control over variability can determine the detectability of treatment effects. In both testing situations, students who receive tutorial assistance average ten points higher than students who do not. The amount of variability in the data, however, is influenced by the testing condition. Under group testing (Figure 3.1, upper panel), the results are unclear because variability within each group leads to considerable overlap in the performance of individuals in the two treatments. Under individual testing, the beneficial effect of the tutorial program is much more obvious (Figure 3.1, lower panel). The distributions of the two groups overlap only slightly; nearly all students in the tutored group scored above the highest-scoring students in the nontutored group.

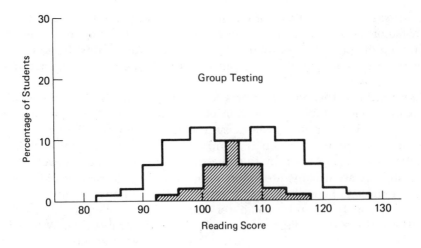

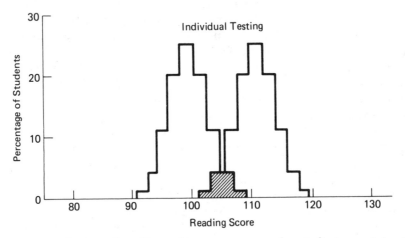

FIGURE 3.1 Distribution of reading achievement scores for students receiving tutoring and not receiving tutoring, when tested individually or in large groups.

A fundamental principle in statistics is that the effect of variation in a factor is measured relative to the amount of residual variability in the data. In our example, the greater within-group variability under group testing leads to uncertainty about whether to trust the difference in average performance between the two groups. The lesser variability with individual testing provides a clearer picture of the effects of the special program and allows for more direct and confident interpretation of the experimental results. To put it another way, we observe a higher degree of experimental control with individual testing than with group testing in this illustration.

A major source of uncontrolled variability in behavioral research comes from differences between individuals. When the researcher decides to assign different subjects to each condition, this decision also determines analytic procedures; treatment effects must be evaluated relative to variability between subjects in each group. This between-subject variability includes all differences the subjects bring to the experimental condition. A potent method for gaining control over between-subject variability is to test each subject under all conditions, rather than testing different subjects in each condition. The treatment effects can then be measured against random error within the same individual, rather than against the much larger random error that occurs between individuals. We return to this matter when we discuss within-subject designs.

Confounding occurs when conditions covary on factors other than those defined by the experimenter. In designing an experiment, the researcher assigns each experimental group to a different level of treatment factor. For comparisons among conditions to be interpretable, the treatment levels must differ only as defined by the experimenter. Otherwise a confounding exists, and the results of the experiment are inalterably ambiguous. There is no way to determine whether differences between groups result from the influence of the treatment factor or the confounded factor or both.

In our example on tutorial versus regular reading programs, for instance, several confoundings may have occurred. There may have been problems in how students were assigned to tutorial or nontutorial groups. If the more tractable students were paired with tutors, any changes in performance might reflect only this personality attribute. One way to avoid this confounding is to assign students to groups randomly. Another approach is to match pairs of students on tractability and assign members of each pair to each of the conditions.

Second, the teachers in the tutorial group may have received supplementary training or special status of some sort. If so, again these effects can account for at least part of any observed effects. The novelty of being part of an "experimental" condition can produce effects on behavior in and of itself. The Hawthorne effect, as it is sometimes called (Homans, 1941), may result partly from increased motivation and the subject's feeling that he should try harder, and partly from changes in the way the task is approached, in the learning strategies, and in attentional processes.

Another source of confounding is the link between test instruments and treatments. Not too surprisingly, students perform better on tests that directly measure what they are taught (Walker & Schaffarzick, 1974). It is usually advisable to measure performance in several ways, which tap overall performance as well as the special features of each treatment condition.

Finally, it is possible that the testers were aware of the students' treatment conditions before they administered the tests. If so, they may alter the testing procedures in subtle ways that modify students' performances in expected directions. To rule out such experimenter-produced bias, a "blind" procedure should be used in which the tester is kept unaware of whether the student is enrolled in the tutorial or nontutorial program.

It is virtually impossible to eliminate all sources of confounding in a study. The important point here is that the researcher should be alert to potential sources of confounding and should weigh the likely influence of each confounded variable against the cost of gaining increased control. The decision to be watchful but to tolerate a confounding is far better than to discover its existence after the data are in.

Interactions occur when the effects of a factor vary from one level to the next of a second factor. Interactions are not inherently wrong. Indeed, many research questions are designed to investigate the character of specific interactions (Cronbach & Snow, 1977). An experimenter who suspects that two factors interact, however, must use special care in the design, analysis, and interpretation of the study. An adequate account requires consideration of both the joint effects and the separate effects of the factors. The exact nature of the interaction needs description, and the interpretation must include consideration of the interaction.

To determine if an interaction exists, the investigator must plan a *factorial design,* which includes all combinations of two or more factors. Suppose in the example of the tutorial reading program that the researcher includes students in two grades, first and third. Grade and treatment program constitute two factors with two levels in each, making a total of four possible combinations. The hypothetical results, plotted in Figure 3.2, illustrate the concept of interaction. The effects of tutoring on test performance differ at the two grade levels: first-graders benefit far more from tutoring than do third-graders.

The results of any single experiment are of interest only insofar as they generalize to a larger set of situations. If interactions go undetected, the results can lead to false generalizations. For instance, if only first-grade students had been included in the design, the effects of tutoring would have been overestimated; if only third-grade students had been included, the results would have been underestimated. Interactions are most often undetected because of inadequate designs. The experimenter must make thoughtful decisions about the conditions and kinds of people to which he wishes to extend the results. To be sure, it is impossible to include all potentially relevant factors of a research problem in a single study. The aim during planning must be to consider the existence of interactions and build into the design those factors that are representative of the situations of interest.

Within- and between-subject designs   A major decision in experimental design is the choice of the unit for variation of each factor. This decision is often thought of as the contrast of between-subject and within-subject designs. The decision is actually not this simple, but because it is the most familiar situation, let us begin with it.

Often each subject is assigned to a single treatment condition. Such designs,

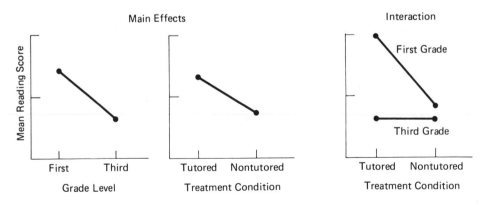

FIGURE 3.2 Hypothetical mean reading scores examined for main effects (grade level, treatment condition), and for grade level × treatment interaction.

called *between-subject designs,* avoid contamination of one condition by another. Further, the researcher does not need to worry about practice or fatigue effects, or about other temporal changes that might occur with repeated testing. Finally, some experimental problems restrict the investigator to a single observation per subject. For instance, not only do people learn, they learn how to learn. Learning studies therefore are typically limited to between-subject designs. Once a student has learned to read under one approach, that is necessarily the end of the study for that student.

The major advantages of a *within-subject design* are improved control and reduced random variability. Repeated observations on a single subject produce less variable data than do observations collected from different subjects. This means that to establish the importance of a treatment effect of a given size, fewer observations are required using a within-subject design than a between-subject design.

Often it is more convenient to collect a large number of observations using a within-subject design. If substantial time is required for instructions and preliminary training on a task, it seems sensible to obtain as much information as possible before releasing a subject from the experiment. When it takes only a moment or so to collect an observation, as in a short-term memory test, then it is reasonable to collect several observations on each subject.

A within-subject design may be required by the nature of the experimental problem. Certain factors affect performance only when a subject is exposed to different levels of the factor. A good illustration is the phenomenon known as reward contrast. A between-subject design is planned to measure the effects of differential payoff on subjects' ability to read as many words as possible in 30 seconds. One group receives the basic instructions. Two other groups are given similar instructions, but subjects in the second group are told they will receive a nickel and subjects in the third group a dime for each word read within the time limit.

Available research (Grice, 1966) suggests that the performance of the three groups will differ only slightly, if at all. The results seem surprising, given the importance of money in our society. Of course, the actual amounts of payoff are relatively small in this study. Experimenters are unfortunately not in a position to up the ante to a significant level.

If each subject is tested at all three reward levels, however, the amount of payoff will have a substantial influence on behavior. The effect depends on how payoff conditions are ordered. If the subject receives a large payoff following a small payoff, performance will improve markedly (this is referred to as "positive contrast"). If the sequence is reversed (small payoff following large), then performance will decline ("negative contrast").

A nickel may not seem like much in the abstract. But if you have been getting a dime, it seems even smaller, and if you have been working for nothing, then it seems like quite a lot. Subjects can make such comparisons only in a within-subject design.

It is sometimes essential to test a subject under several conditions in order to provide an adequate experimental test of a theory. For instance, suppose that a particular theoretical model predicts that when a person is trying to remember some facts, the amount remembered varies in direct proportion with the amount of time spent in study. According to this model, recall should increase in a straight-line fashion with study duration, as is shown in Figure 3.3 for four subjects. Some subjects acquire information at a faster rate than others, but for all subjects in this example, the relation between recall and study time is a straight line. If each subject were tested at all four levels of the study-time factor, the data would confirm the theoretical hypothesis.

The evidence might be less convincing if a between-subject design was used in this situation. The problem is that although the basic relation is a straight line for all subjects, the slope of the line varies considerably from subject to subject. If subjects were assigned to levels of the treatment factor, as indicated by the X set, the data suggest that the theoretical model is correct (see Figure 3.4). However, if the Y selection was chosen at random, the experimenter might be led to reject the theoretical model.

Whenever a subject's performance in one or more treatment conditions is to be compared to a baseline condition for that subject, then a within-subject design is essential. The most frequent application of this principle is the pre-post design. Here a subject's pretest performance is established under neutral conditions prior to some experimental manipulation. Next a treatment is administered and then a posttest is given. The size of the difference between pre- and posttest measures reflects the magnitude of the treatment effect.

Finally, we should emphasize that the choice of within- or between-subject design is not an all-or-none decision. In a factorial design, the decision whether subjects should receive one level or all levels must be made for each component factor. If some factors in a design are varied within subjects and others are varied

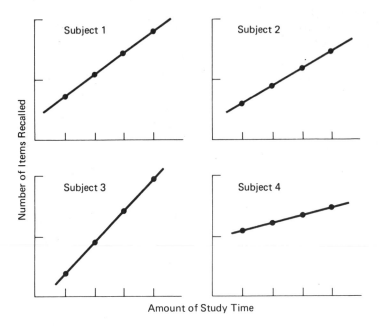

FIGURE 3.3 Hypothetical data from four subjects in an experiment on relation of study time to amount recalled. Some subjects learn at a faster rate than others, but the relationship is a straight line for every subject. (*After Calfee, 1975.*)

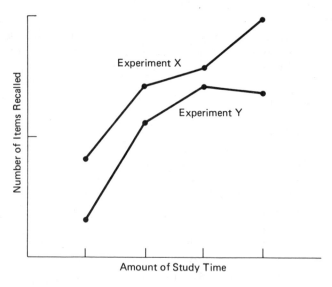

FIGURE 3.4   Illustration of how a between-subject design may or may not reveal the character of an individual subject's performance. Data are from Figure 3.3. In Experiment X the relationship between study time and performance is a straight line. Experiment Y suggests that there is an upper limit on performance.

between subjects, the result is called a mixed design. Thorough analysis of a problem generally yields this kind of design.

   Quasi-experimental designs   Some situations require that the researcher deal with previously existing groups of conditions and subjects. When the assignment of subjects to conditions is not random, and when the treatment is only partly under the researcher's control, the investigation is often referred to as a quasi experiment (Cook & Campbell, 1979).

   Both true experiments and quasi experiments aim to assess the effect of particular treatments on behavior. In both cases, the researcher poses the primary experimental question and then identifies other relevant factors in the design. The main difference between the two experiments is that control over conditions and subject arrangements is compromised in a quasi-experimental design. As a result, there is a greater chance that factors will be confounded, and the results of the study will therefore be ambiguous and difficult to interpret.

   In quasi-experimental research, the effect of the treatment is typically measured against a control condition that serves as a comparison baseline. This single control condition is frequently defined only by the absence of the experimental treatment. Definition by exclusion scarcely tells us what actually happened in the control situation, nor does it reveal the ways in which the experimental and control groups actually differ. If the treatment appears effective, these other sources of variation may in fact be responsible for the effect. A more analytic approach is to include as many control groups as there are differentiating facets in the experimental treatment (Campbell, 1957; Campbell & Stanley, 1963).

   Design efficiency   Factorial designs are frequently conceived as between-subject arrangements of all the combinations of two or three factors, with ten or more subjects assigned to each combination. The high cost of factorial designs might appear to severely restrict the experimenter's ability to investigate complex problems. With three two-level factors, there are $2 \times 2 \times 2$ or eight combinations, which with ten subjects per combination amounts to 80 subjects. There is a geometric increase with additional factors and levels per factor. Designs with more than five factors are impractical because of the cost, even if the subjects are students. If they are teachers or programs, the constraints are even tighter; designs with one or two factors may be the upper limit.

"As everyone knows," sample size must be large in each factorial combination, or the statistical test of the treatment effect lacks power. In fact, this "large-sample-size-per-cell" requirement is based on a common misunderstanding about the character of factorial designs, and the nature of statistical tests based on such designs. In general, it is not the number of observations per combination that matter but the number of observations that enter into each *comparison*. For instance, a $2 \times 2 \times 2$ design with five subjects per cell provides 40 subjects for each of the main treatment levels, certainly an adequate sample size. For the two-way interactions, there are 20 subjects in each combination, but the statistical test is still based on a comparison between two groups of 40 subjects.

One way to achieve greater efficiency is to adopt a within-subject design. When each subject is tested under several factorial combinations, the statistical tests are sensitive because treatment effects are measured against variation within the individual. Usually the subject is tested only once under each combination, and the within-combination sample-size requirement is conveniently overlooked in these designs. Control for order and material variables is usually achieved with a Latin square or Greco-Latin square design. The analysis of correlated data from such designs raises some problems, but techniques for handling these difficulties have reached a high level of refinement. When appropriate, within-unit designs constitute a powerful experimental methodology.

Even here, there are practical limits to the number of factors that can be examined as long as *full* factorial designs are employed. A design with six two-level factors has 64 combinations. This number of combinations can be unmanageable, even given a within-subject design and one observation per cell. If each treatment combination takes a minute or more, the "50-minute hour" that is the typical limit of much psychological research is violated. In educational research, we may be talking about treatment combinations that require days, weeks, or months to administer. If this problem calls for a between-subject design, then each additional factor doubles or triples the number of subjects required for a study. Given the cost implications of the situation, it is not surprising that most researchers have been conservative when deciding on the number of factors to include in a design.

Fractional designs provide an efficient alternative to full factorial design. These designs are not new; the basic procedures have been available for at least 40 years and are described in a number of standard texts (Kirk, 1968; Winer, 1971). For some reason, they have seen little use in the behavioral sciences, except for the special case of Latin and hyper-Latin squares.

Two related design procedures constitute what are referred to as fractional designs: fractional-factorial and confounded-blocks designs. In a *fractional-facto-*

rial design the experimenter selects a balanced subset or fraction of cells from the full design. In a *confounded-blocks design* the full design is divided into orthogonal blocks, each of which is assigned to a different experimental unit. Many applications involve both techniques; a fraction of the full design is selected and then broken into blocks, each of which is assigned to a different unit (U.S. Department of Commerce, 1962).

The basic concepts of fractional-factorial and confounded-blocks designs with two-level factors are illustrated by an example with three two-level factors, shown in Figure 3.5. In a 2^3 design, eight degrees of freedom are available for estimating the grand mean, main effects, and interactions, each with one degree of freedom. This is the most compact design that permits illustration of the concepts. The situation is far too simple for practical application, but the simplicity should make the ideas clear.

The complete design shown in Figure 3.5 has been divided into two subsets (X_+ and X_-), each subset comprising one-half the full design. A design can be fractionalized into balanced, orthogonal chunks in this way by using a high-order interaction as the defining contrast. Figure 3.6 illustrates the procedure. Suppose we conduct an experiment using only X_+ cells in the design. Notice that all the main effects are perfectly counterbalanced. For instance, B_0 and B_1 are both combined with A_0 condition, as are both C_0 and C_1. The fractional design provides one degree of freedom for estimating the grand mean, and three degrees of freedom for estimating treatment effects. The *ABC* effect in this fractional design

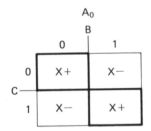

FIGURE 3.5   A full 2^3 design, with three treatment factors, *A*, *B*, and *C*, each at two levels, 0 and 1. Cells containing pluses and minuses represent the two levels of the *ABC* interaction.

FIGURE 3.6   The procedural layout for fractionalizing a 2^3 design into two subsets of orthogonal blocks using the *ABC* interaction as the defining contrast.

Factor								
A	0				1			
B	0		1		0		1	
C	0	1	0	1	0	1	0	1
Contrasts								
A	+	+	+	+	−	−	−	−
B	+	+	−	−	+	+	−	−
C	+	−	+	−	+	−	+	−
A*B*C	+	−	−	+	−	+	+	−

Source	DF	Alias
Mean	1	ABC
A	1	BC
B	1	AC
C	1	AB

FIGURE 3.7 ANOVA table for a half replicate of a 2^3 design with *ABC* as the defining contrast.

is the same as the grand mean; hence, there is no independent information about *ABC*. Furthermore, the estimates for the pairs of main effects and two-way interaction effects are also confounded. A pair of confounded effects like *A* and *BC* are referred to as aliases—as shown in the ANOVA source table for the fractional-factorial design (Figure 3.7). Only one of the entries in each pair of aliases can be independently estimated. The cost of slicing the full design in half is that information about interactions is lost. As a consequence, the experimenter who plans a fractional design must think seriously about which hypotheses are really worthy of investigation. This seems to us a highly desirable consequence.

Next, let us look briefly at the confounded-blocks design based on a 2^3 design. In this case we again use the *ABC* interaction to divide the full design into two equally balanced fractions or orthogonal blocks (the pluses and minuses in the figure). Each block is assigned to a different experimental unit or subject. This plan yields one degree of freedom for the grand mean, and seven degrees of freedom for estimating treatment effects. We introduce a "dummy" variable for blocks, designated by $X+$ or $X-$, so that each level is associated with one level of the *ABC* interaction. Since each level of this variable is assigned to a different experimental unit, it constitutes a between-unit effect. The aliasing patterns for the remaining factors, all of which are within-unit effects, are shown in Figure 3.8. The design allows for a test of all the main effects, including the block factor, as well as selected two-way interactions.

This brief account is intended only to sketch the concepts of design efficiency. The techniques are relatively simple in practice, though most discussions

Source	DF	Alias
Mean	1	
A	1	BCX
B	1	ACX
C	1	ABX
AB	1	CX
AC	1	BX
BC	1	AX
ABC	1	X

FIGURE 3.8 ANOVA table for the analysis of a 2^3 design run in two blocks. Each level of the blocks factor, *X*, was assigned to a different experimental unit and is therefore a between-unit factor.

of the methods are unfortunately complex. We present a more realistic illustration of the methods later in the chapter.

Experimental Procedures

Once the design has been formulated, there are several "nondesign" details, generally referred to as experimental procedures, that must be arranged. Whereas design decisions involve the selection of factors and levels of factors that are to be systematically varied, procedural decisions entail the specification of conditions that are to remain constant throughout the experiment. For example, materials and techniques must be selected or developed; the experimental task and testing arrangements must be specified; the time and place of the study must be chosen. As with design decisions, procedural decisions must be based upon the research question and nature of the population to which the results are to be generalized.

The flaws in many experiments apparently have their roots in the planning of procedures. These are often the last details to be worked out, and they often evolve in haste, depending on convenience and necessity for their resolution. The overriding consideration is that, since the investigator has already "used up" all the degrees of freedom available for systematic variation, he must now settle on fixed ways of doing everything else or simply ignore the problem and hope the "randomness" will override any substantial bias or confounding.

We do not try in this brief space to explore all the pitfalls along this particular path, but a few words of advice can be given. First, the context in which an experiment is conducted, while it may not be of central interest to the experimenter, is likely to be associated with substantial variance in performance. At worst, uncontrolled variations in context factors may turn out to be confounded with variables of focal importance, in which case the interpretation of the results may be substantially compromised. Even though confounding may be avoided, it is nonetheless true that uncontrolled variance does not disappear because the experimenter chooses to ignore it. Instead, it becomes part of the "random error variance" against which systematic treatment effects are evaluated.

Second, a thorough analysis of virtually any research question in the behavioral and social sciences will turn up a multitude of factors with substantive bearing on the question. Even if only a few factors have impact through main effects, several other factors usually have the potential for secondary influence through interaction with the primary factors. We are not in agreement with Cronbach (1975) that the number of such influences is enormous, a virtual hall of mirrors. Nevertheless, in the absence of clarifying theories, it is hard to rule out a large number of candidate factors for almost any research question. As long as we are stumbling around in the empirical darkness, the world will seem fairly complicated.

Given the preceding comments, it seems to us that the best advice in arranging the procedures for an experiment is to treat the procedures as part of the design process. That is, rather than select the materials, instruction, environment, and other procedural variables at the last moment by a "cut and paste" approach, the experimenter should pin down the significant dimensions on which the procedural facets of the study can vary. This analysis should be carried out at the same time as the examination of the primary factors. The experimenter can then decide on the plan of the study from a broader vantage point—choosing which factors to vary and which to keep constant. If our experience is any guide, "throwaway factors" will assume a substantially greater role in experimental designs.

Selection of Subjects

The results of an experiment are of interest only to the extent that they can be generalized to some larger collection of entities beyond those included in the study. Ideally, the researcher selects a random sample of subjects from the population to which he intends to generalize the results and then randomly assigns the sample of subjects to treatment conditions. Random sampling yields a subset of individuals who are representative of some larger population and are not biased toward any subgroups in the population. This ideal is often compromised in ways that seriously curtail accurate generalizations.

For example, most reading research has the implicit goal of discovering general principles that apply to "normal" reading by "typical" students. In fact, a truly random sample of all readers in all American schools is virtually impossible to obtain. As a practical approach, the researcher selects a "handy random sample" of subjects from local schools and then generalizes with less confidence to students who differ in definable ways from the original population. The trustworthiness of any generalizations depends altogether on the match to the subpopulation "available" to the experimenter (e.g., the population that suits resources and level of convenience). College students provide an easily accessible pool of subjects for many researchers, and for this reason a great deal of research on reading is carried out on this population. It may be safe to generalize experimental results from a sample of college students to the adult population of high school graduates. It is less safe to generalize the results of these studies to illiterate first-graders.

The experimenter can achieve control over extraneous variability due to random sampling by including subject-classification factors in the research design. These include such variables as age, sex, ability, socioeconomic status, and stylistic preferences. In choosing subject factors, the purpose of the experiment and the ease with which a subject factor can be incorporated in the design are important considerations. Interactions between treatment factors and subject variables are not uncommon; the researcher must decide whether subject factors are critical for measuring interactions in the study. Control over subject variables can forestall confounding with treatment conditions or confounding among subject factors. Suppose, for example, that the primary goal of a study is to isolate the effects of sex, age, ability, or other subject factors. These factors are often correlated with one another in the "real world." Young boys generally score lower on verbal intelligence than girls do, so verbal ability and sex are ordinarily confounded. Assignment to conditions on the basis of intelligence means assignment partly on the basis of sex. Contrariwise, assignment by sex means a difference in intelligence scores between the groups. For another instance, a child's score on a reading readiness test frequently determines the books and methods used in teaching him or her to read. Hence, ability is easily confounded with the method of reading instruction.

Subject-selection procedures also help avoid biased selection by controlling the distribution of individual-difference factors over treatment conditions. In essence, these procedures are equivalent to incorporating these factors in the design of the experiment. If kindergartners are to participate in an experiment on short-term memory, it would be quite easy to include sex as a factor in the design. If information on verbal fluency is available, this factor might also be incorporated as a subject variable, especially if the study has to do with short-term memory for words. Ideally, each treatment condition in the experiment would be assigned the same number of children above and below the average intelligence level of the class, as well as the same proportion of boys and girls. To ensure proportionate samples in all cells of the design, the investigator might wish to classify students as high and low verbal ability within each level of the sex factor—each boy would be rated against the mean for boys, and each girl rated against the mean for girls. This procedure ensures a balanced sample of students in each condition and provides an opportunity to investigate potential interactions between subject and treatment factors. As always, the gain from improved experimental control and additional information must be weighed against the cost of a more complex design. Moreover, the meaning of high and low ability must be considered in the light of the method used to define the levels of the factor.

In discussing subject-selection factors, we alluded to a difference between *fixed factors* and *random factors.* This distinction holds for all kinds of factors, but is especially important when considering people and material.

Fixed factors include within the research design *all* the levels to which the researcher intends to generalize. Thus, if the experimenter studies second- and fifth-grade students, and intends to apply the results to those grade levels only, then grade level is functioning as a fixed factor. *Random factors* are those for which there exists a population of levels, and only a sample of these levels is included in the design. Thus, if the experimenter includes "school" as a factor in the design, and selects 20 sample schools from a population of 500 available schools, then "school" is functioning as a random factor.

A fixed factor usually calls for evaluation by the conventional "test of statistical significance." Are the observed effects of the factor large enough, compared with the random variability in the study, to justify rejection of the hypothesis that the real effect is zero? The emphasis here is on *observed effects* because a replication of the experiment entails the same levels of the factor.

A random factor calls for an evaluation of the reliability or generalizability of the factor. For instance, given the variability among the schools in a random sample, are the differences large enough to believe that in another random sample (or in the population at large) the projected differences would again be large enough to take seriously? The levels of a random factor have no intrinsic meaning—a positive answer to the preceding question simply means that something is happening. The emphasis here is on *population effects*, which are over and above those actually observed in a particular sample.

Finally, we should note that many factors are neither fixed nor random. The experimenter chooses levels of a factor that are close to the levels of interest for generalization—the match between what is observed and what is of interest is almost, but not quite, exact. The investigator wants to generalize to the difference between primary and upper elementary grades, and so he studies second and fifth grades. The factor is almost fixed, but some degree of uncertainty remains. As is true of most problems in the arts and sciences, the interpretation is partly art and partly science.

THE APPLICATION OF DESIGN PRINCIPLES

In the next two sections we illustrate the application of ideas we have sketched above. Because the "real world" is complicated by multiple variables, the experimental designs we present are complex. These examples reflect the level of analysis that we think is reasonable for well-controlled experiments. First, we lay out plans for a fractional-factorial experiment on a reading curriculum. Then we follow this with ideas for the development of a multidimensional assessment system to test reading skills.

An Experiment on Beginning Reading Curricula

A reading curriculum is an organized structure for carrying out instruction. The structure encompasses content (what is taught) and sequence (the order in which things are taught). Both content and sequence require that the curriculum developer make a large number of decisions. How can we gather evidence during the planning and development of a curriculum about the conditions under which it does the job intended? How can we identify the conditions under which a curriculum can be effectively "installed" in a classroom to best meet the needs of the teacher and students?

It seems to us that progress in solving these problems requires that experimental control be established over the major decision factors in the curriculum plan, and over subsidiary factors (e.g., installation techniques) where feasible. Too often a new curriculum represents a single set of decisions about content, sequence, method of delivery, and context. Under these conditions, there is no way to obtain evidence about possible outcomes under alternative decisions. A comparison of two curricula in which choices are varied in an unsystematic manner is also uninformative, because of uncontrolled confoundings. The recent history of curriculum research and development is rather unencouraging, to say the least. Virtually every new curriculum program seems to get into the air on its maiden voyage, but all come crashing to earth thereafter. At least in the area of reading, we know of no "approach" with guaranteed and substantial effectiveness compared with other approaches.

Experimental curriculum research requires identification of the important factors both in the curriculum and in classroom conditions. One procedure for undertaking this analysis entails a structural description of the existing curriculum in order to highlight the decisions actually embodied in the course of study—decisions about learning goals, organization of content, instructional sequence, and requisite entry behaviors (Figure 3.9). The designer should explore the assumptions behind the teaching methods, content, and materials, and should examine the priorities assigned to various learning goals.

An important consideration—and one that is usually overlooked—in the evaluation of a curriculum is the degree to which the curriculum is effective

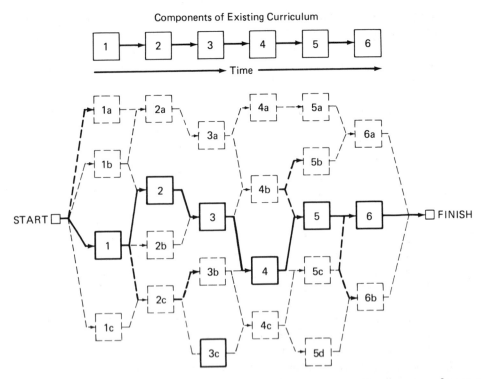

FIGURE 3.9   Structural analysis. At the top are blocks representing the sequence of components (or lessons) of the existing curriculum. One block might represent a module in which
the child is taught a set of "sight" words, or is taught the principle of adding two-digit
numbers with a carry. Below, these components are placed in a decision network illustrating a hypothetical set of choices made by the curriculum planner. Thus, 1a, 1b, and 1c,
along with 1, were all candidates for the first component. In choosing 1, the planner made
a decision that limited the available components for the next stage to 2, 2b, and 2c.
The most significant decisions, as identified by the designer and other experts, are indicated
by dotted lines. These serve as the basis for constructing alternative curriculum strands
for experimental evaluation. (*After Calfee, 1974.*)

under the varied contexts of real classrooms. The evaluator may try out the
program in a handy random sample or may actually seek out a set of teachers
committed to the success of the program in order to test the approach under
"hothouse" conditions. In neither instance are the results trustworthy for generalization to the larger population of classes, schools, and teachers.

Control over external variation requires the researcher to identify potentially relevant factors and select a sample of schools, teachers, and students in
such a fashion as to isolate main effects and interactions associated with those
factors. It is especially important to measure interactions between curriculum
factors and contextual factors. If these interactions are substantial, then the researcher must be careful to specify the contextual conditions under which one
or another version of the curriculum is most effective.

Let us turn to the planning of an evaluative experiment for a beginning
reading curriculum. The purpose of the experiment is to obtain information
about the relative merits of different elements in the "experimental" program.

The developer thinks it feasible to create as many as 16 variations on the basic curriculum program, each to be implemented within at least two first-grade classrooms. We focus on three design elements: content, materials and format, and management system. Let us assume that preliminary discussions have directed attention on the following questions:

A. Content: basic reading instruction
1. What is the value of a relatively strong emphasis on phonics/decoding skills versus a relatively strong emphasis on comprehension/"reading for meaning"? The planner hopes to incorporate both components in the curriculum but would like information about the effectiveness of allocating more or less time on each topic. The question leads to the "fuzzy" specification of two levels of this factor—relatively more time expended on phonics versus relatively more time given to vocabulary and comprehension.
2. Within the phonics and meaning programs, two subquestions are posed:
   a. Is phonics most effectively presented by a rule orientation (learning letter-sound associations and blending) or by a word-based orientation (e.g., following Bloomfield and Barnhart, 1961)?
   b. How important is vocabulary control in a "reading for meaning" program? Is a comprehension-based program best taught with high-frequency words that are likely to be irregularly spelled, or can the program be based on somewhat less frequent words that are regularly spelled and might have greater transfer to decoding skills?
B. Content: skill development
1. Does it matter whether visual-skill worksheets are included in a module?
2. Ditto for auditory-skill materials?
C. Content: literature
1. Does it matter whether or not materials for storytelling and poetry are included in a module?
D. Materials
1. Should student workbooks be included along with the basic textbook materials?
E. Management
1. Does it matter whether a module is constructed around a learning-to-mastery emphasis, as opposed to a minimal-competence or remedial model?
2. Should an assessment and recordkeeping system be provided?

Question A is of fundamental importance to the evaluation and refinement of curricular content in the final version of the program. Questions B through E are mostly yes-no questions. Answers to these might deter the tendency to throw everything including the kitchen sink into the curricula. This smorgasbord approach costs money, makes it more difficult for a teacher to pick out the vital components, and is of uncertain benefit.

The questions above constitute a set of eight two-level factors. To create a particular instructional module, we respond to each of eight design questions where there are two possible answers to each question. For instance, one module might have (A.1) a strong *phonics* emphasis; (A.2.a) a *rule orientation;* (B.1) *no visual-skill* materials; but (B.2) *auditory* materials; (C.1) *storytelling* materials;

and (D.1) *no workbooks;* but (E.1) a *learning-to-mastery* emphasis with (E.2) an *assessment and recordkeeping system.*

If all combinations of these factorial variations were to be investigated, the complete design would include 2^8, or 256, cells. This is clearly too large a set of curricular variations for practical implementation as a research and development study—we have already noted that the resources available for this illustrative study permit only 16 alternate programs. Moreover, most of the information gained from the complete design is of questionable value; interactions involving four or more factors are unlikely to be either practically or statistically significant, nor are such complex patterns likely to be interpretable.

The procedures for constructing a balanced fractional design for this problem operate as follows:

Step 1. Plan the complete factorial design, listing all potentially relevant factors in an organized fashion, deciding the relative importance of each factor, and identifying any interactions of particular importance. This step was described at the beginning of this section. The primary interest is in the main effects of each factor. A small number of two-way interactions might be worth exploring, but we will ignore the matter for now.

Step 2. Decide how many and what kinds of observations can be obtained with the resources available to you. This issue was also discussed above for the present example. A more intensive examination of the problem might turn up alternatives to what is being proposed. For example, we are assuming that the treatment factors remain constant for the duration of the program. In fact, some of the factors might be varied within classrooms (e.g., a class might use workbooks for the first half of the school year and not for the second, or vice versa).

Step 3. Decide on a fractional subset of the full design, and select the cell combinations for the fraction. The present study calls for 2^4, or 16, cells to be selected out of the total of 2^8, or 256, cells in the complete design. Conceptually, we need to divide the full design into 16 balanced fractions with 16 cells each and then pick one of the fractions at random for the investigation. This task would pose a challenge if we had to do it from scratch. Fortunately, a set of tables of fractional designs has been prepared for the purpose (U.S. Department of Commerce, 1962).

The 16 curriculum programs in Figure 3.10 are perfectly balanced. For each of the eight factors, two levels each occur the same number of times. Each factor level occurs equally often with every other factor level. There is no confounding of any of the main effects, and several of the two-way interactions are also testable. The plan contains 16 cells, and so there are 15 degrees of freedom for testing specific hypotheses. Eight degrees of freedom are used for evaluation of main effects. One could test up to seven two-way interactions with this design (e.g., the two instructional factors). The degrees of freedom for error are available because each curriculum is installed in at least two classrooms.

It should be clear that the experimenter pays a cost for the efficiency gained by fractionalization; not all interactions can be tested, and the investigator has to plan the design with care and ensure that the design is implemented exactly as planned. Nevertheless, the gain in control over main effects is considerable.

Fractional designs can be used as building blocks. For instance, in selecting the 32 teachers and classrooms, the experimenter would be well advised to plan

Curriculum Number	Instruction: Phonics by Generalization (PG) or Example (PE), or Meaning by Familiar (MF) or Regular Words (MR)		Skills: Visual Skills, Yes (Y) or No (N); Auditory Skills, Yes (Y) or No (N)		Literature: Story-telling, etc., Yes (Y) or No (N)	Workbooks: Yes (Y) or No (N)	Management: Mastery (M) or Remedial (R); Assessment/Record-keeping, Yes (Y) or No (N)	
1	P	G	Y	N	Y	Y	M	Y
2	P	G	N	N	N	N	N	Y
3	M	R	N	N	Y	Y	M	Y
4	M	R	Y	Y	N	N	M	Y
5	M	R	N	N	N	N	R	N
6	M	R	Y	Y	Y	Y	R	N
7	P	G	Y	Y	N	N	R	N
8	P	G	N	N	Y	Y	R	N
9	M	F	Y	Y	Y	N	R	Y
10	M	F	Y	N	Y	N	R	Y
11	P	E	Y	N	N	Y	M	N
12	P	E	N	Y	N	Y	R	Y
13	P	E	Y	N	N	Y	M	N
14	P	E	N	Y	Y	N	M	N
15	M	F	N	Y	N	Y	M	N
16	M	F	Y	N	Y	N	M	N

FIGURE 3.10   Fractional design for evaluation of reading components; $\frac{1}{16}$ fraction of 2^8 design.

the sample selection in a systematic fashion. For example, the following school and teacher factors would be reasonable candidates in the illustrative study:

A. School characteristics
   1. Urban/suburban
   2. High/low socioeconomic neighborhood
B. Teacher characteristics
   1. Experienced/beginning

2. Prefers to follow curriculum and teacher manual closely/prefers to adapt curriculum to own program
3. Prefers large-group instruction/small-group, independent work.

These five two-level factors, together with the four factors needed to describe the 16 curriculum variations, constitute a 2^9 design. By selecting a 2^4 fraction of the full design, one cell is provided for each of the 32 teachers in the sample (cf. Calfee, 1974, for an example of this approach). Control is maintained over school and teacher factors, and over the assignment of curriculum factors to classes. The main effects of school and teacher factors are all testable. Equally important, it is possible to test hypotheses about interactions between school/teacher factors and curriculum factors. For instance, the researcher might want to arrange the design to measure the effect of a learning-to-mastery component for teachers who prefer large-group instruction compared with those who adopt a more individualistic approach.

Our main point in this discussion should now be clear. *It is feasible to plan designs that handle the complexities that arise in curriculum evaluation and development and that achieve the rigor of control deemed necessary in behavioral experiments without increasing the observations over the number required for a much simpler design with less adequate control.*

Systematic Designs for the Assessment of Reading Skills

Research on reading generally requires the development of an "instrument package" for measurement. We concentrate in this section on the assessment of students' reading skills, but our comments apply more generally to the measurement of teacher knowledge, to observation of classroom activities, and to diagnosis of learning difficulties (Calfee & Shefelbine, 1981).

Current practices in the development of reading tests are atheoretical and rely on the simplest of design concepts. Most often, a set of topics or objectives is designated as the basis for writing items. For instance, standardized tests of reading often combine three or four topical areas (e.g., vocabulary, comprehension, and study skills) with a dimension of graduated difficulty (the levels of the test and item difficulty within each level). Criterion-referenced tests begin with a specification of dozens or hundreds of objectives, each of which serves as a basis for writing one or more items.

The unidimensionality of present-day test designs means that many of the factors that affect reading achievement are uncontrolled. For instance, how is the test writer to prepare items to assess "the student's knowledge of short vowel correspondences"? The content to be included under this heading is relatively easy to settle on. But what about the other decisions that must be made in order to write an item? What tasks should be employed for the assessment? What kinds of words should be used? What should the instructions be? Questions of this sort generally remain unanswered, and so it is up to the test writer to decide on these matters. The result is that the test items measure the student's knowledge of short vowel correspondences plus the student's ability to handle the tasks, the words, and the instructions that form the context for assessment.

We think that the construction of a measurement system should rest on an analysis of the underlying cognitive processes. Current research on information processing provides relevant theoretical guidance here (Sternberg, 1969; Kavanaugh & Mattingly, 1972; Haber & Hershenson, 1973). Information-processing models take the form of sequentially or hierarchically organized structures of cognitive processes. In postulating a structural model for a given task, the psychologist identifies the specific processes and factors affecting each process and then turns to experimental designs to obtain evidence about the operation of these processes.

One theoretical basis for designing reading assessment systems is the independent-process approach. As we have applied this concept to reading, the set of independent processes is derived from a curriculum-based analysis of the component skills that make up reading—decoding, vocabulary, and so on. The original conception of independent processes was by Sternberg (1969), who pointed out that once the theorist has postulated that a cognitive task proceeds through a series of stages, he should be prepared to list one or more factors that have a major impact on the operation of each stage. Each factor set should influence performance measures associated with that stage and that stage only.

The approach was extended by Calfee (1976), who proposed a more general technique for showing how each component process could be linked to a unique set of factors and a well-defined set of measures (Figure 3.11). To establish the independence of the processes in a model, a set of factors is defined for each process along with a set of complementary measures. The factor-measure combinations take practical shape as a collection of highly structured subtests. The model predicts that variation in factors associated with a given process will affect only the measure(s) for that process. Notice that we are *not* assuming that the various processes are totally unrelated. It is clear that for a word to be understood,

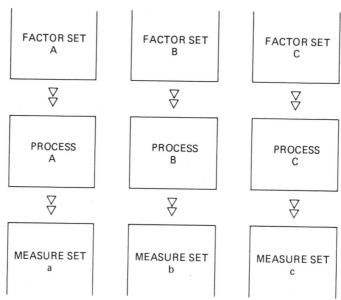

FIGURE 3.11   The generalization of the independent process model. Associated with each component process is a set of factors and a set of measures, each assumed to be uniquely linked to the process. (*After Calfee, 1976.*)

the student must decode it; for a paragraph to be comprehended, decoding, vocabulary, and syntax must all function properly. When we speak of processes as independent, we mean that each step of the operation is affected by a unique set of factors and can be measured in a distinctive manner. Moreover, as long as a given process provides the appropriate information to the next process down the line, it does not matter how that information is generated.

Let us turn to a concrete example of this approach. Assume that the skilled reader proceeds in the analytic fashion shown by the independent-process model in Figure 3.12. Notice that the independent processes in the diagram are closely linked to what is taught. The model is tested by varying factors for each process and measuring responses to each such variation. Practically speaking, the approach is to measure what has been taught, with systematic variations in the conditions of assessment. The figure gives examples of the kinds of factors and measures that might be included in a factorial assessment system on reading. Each individual student is tested under various combinations of the factors, with performance being measured for each of the processes in the figure.

Figure 3.13 illustrates the approach with a couple of combinations. Each combination is the equivalent of a set of test items and provides measures of student performance in several skill areas. However, the measures are controlled and coordinated by the fact that they fit into an overall design. Rather than measure each skill in total isolation, the tester proceeds in sequence through the theoretically separable components that go together to make up the totality that we refer to as reading. The data provide a basis for evaluating relative strengths and weaknesses as each factor is varied. Moreover, as problems are identified during the testing of a given combination, the tester can provide immediate remediation before proceeding further. For instance, if the student mispronounces a word, it makes little sense to ask the student what the word means until the pronunciation is corrected. Likewise, asking the child to comprehend the passage without first determining the status of the contributing processes—the state of the child's abilities on the particular conditions underlying the passage—is to obtain an uninterpretable measure of comprehension. Perhaps decoding is at fault, perhaps vocabulary is inadequate, perhaps syntax is a problem, perhaps comprehension itself is incomplete—when any and all of these are possibilities, the validity of the test results seems thoroughly compromised.

The independent-process approach, by constructing a multidimensional experimental design, provides a systematic examination of the student's relative strengths and weaknesses. We can envision each student's performance in the multidimensional space represented by the factorial combinations from the design in Figure 3.12. The task of the tester is to create the student's profile in this space, in the sense that the tester can portray how accurately and quickly the student performs in each combination. One can conceive of a "trace" through the testing space of the boundary between success and failure for the student. The most efficient test would focus on exploration of this boundary. In experimental design, this task calls for the technique known as response-surface methodology (Box, Hunter, & Hunter, 1978). In testing, Lord (1974) discusses this approach for the unidimensional situation under the label "tailored testing"; the multidimensional case for testing remains to be developed, to the best of our knowledge.

Complementing the factorial approach to test design is the idea of "clean"

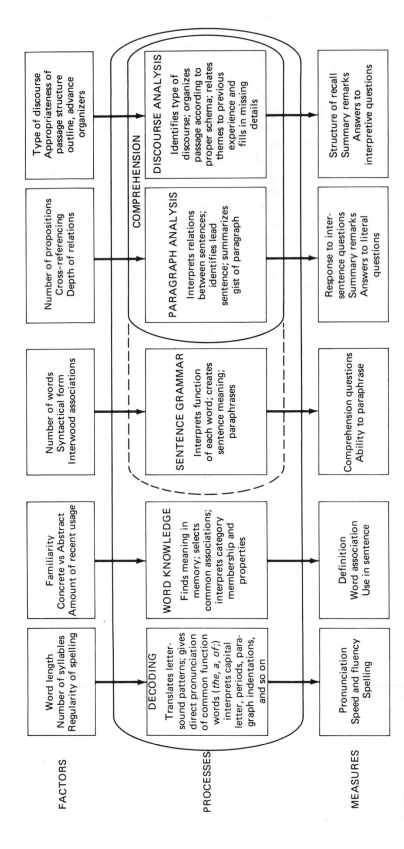

FIGURE 3.12 Examples of factors and measures that might be included in a factorial assessment system on reading.

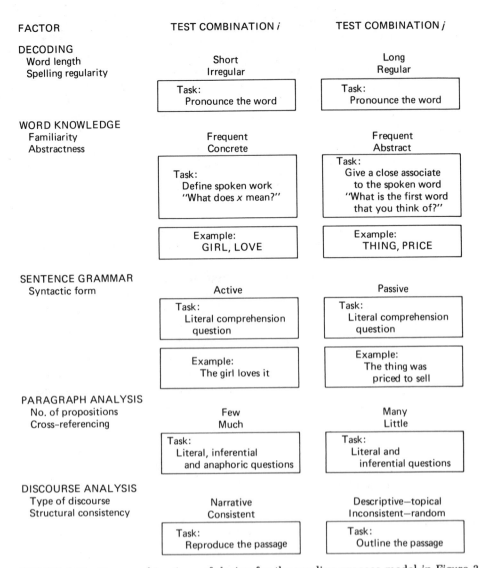

FIGURE 3.13   Two combinations of design for the reading process model in Figure 3.12.

tests. Clean tests place minimal demands on the student, other than the skill under examination, in order that a single, well-defined component can be examined (Calfee, Chapman, & Venezky, 1972). Developing a clean test requires working backward, asking the question, "What must the student know to be able to succeed in this task?" By pursuing this question, the test designer searches for simpler and more direct testing formats. Testing begins with a set of tasks and materials so simple and direct that no student should make an error. The tester is then assured that the student understands the nature of the test and can handle general test-taking requirements. After a successful performance on that combination, the difficulty of the test can be increased systematically. As errors occur, they reveal conditions under which the student experiences difficulty.

An experimentally designed assessment system such as we propose is comprehensive as well as precise. Cronbach (1970) refers to these measurement attributes as "band-width" and "fidelity." From the perspective of the cognitive psychologist, what we have described are within-subject factorial experiments. From the perspective of the educational psychologist or curriculum evaluator, these systems can be viewed as tests or assessment instruments. The data can be analyzed in a straightforward way to answer questions about the relative importance of each factor, and about sources of substantial individual differences (cf. linear contrast analysis, Dayton, 1970). There is no need to resort to factor analysis or attempt to construct "factor-pure" tests. The experimental design is self-confirming and self-correcting as to the validity of the underlying process model.

PROS AND CONS OF FISHERIAN
EXPERIMENTAL DESIGNS

We have emphasized the establishment of adequate control by the application of experimental design procedures. Factorial designs provide a particularly powerful approach to untangling complex variables in psychological and educational research. Over the past three decades, hierarchical designs have become commonplace, and Latin and Greco-Latin squares are often used for the control of nuisance factors. The methodology is scarcely novel; most of the techniques derive from the work of R. A. Fisher (1935). To be sure, recent years have seen further sophistication in the statistical and interpretive analysis of test designs, especially with regard to questions on generalization to various populations (Cronbach, Gleser, Nanda, & Rajaratnam, 1972).

The experimental design approach does have its detractors, who argue that tight control over school-related field-based research is impractical or unnecessary (cf. Stufflebeam, 1970). Other critiques, focusing on analysis rather than design, promote multiple regression as more appropriate than analysis-of-variance techniques. In fact, one procedure is sometimes more suitable than the other; both are based on the same underlying model, and they generally give similar if not identical results. There does tend to be a link between methods of design and analysis—multiple regression tends to be applied to naturalistic "designs" with little effort at control, while analysis of variance is used with experimental designs.

Compared with naturalistic samples, the Fisherian design requirements of *a priori* arrangement of factors into orthogonal structures substantially increase the sensitivity of an investigation. These requirements include the selection of experimental units and the balanced assignment of treatments to these units. It is, of course, easier to locate a convenient school that will let you carry out research than to try to gain entry to a school with the characteristics called for by the design. It is also easier if a teacher volunteers for a treatment than to persuade a teacher to follow a treatment according to a design. To be sure, it sometimes makes sense for the investigator to cast around for preexisting treatment-unit combinations and see what sort of design he winds up with. At other times, a naturalistic design can be "helped along" so that a degree of orthogonal control is achieved (e.g., Cohen, 1970). This technique can be combined with more direct experimental control to good advantage. However, none of these approaches the power of an orthogonal plan based on random assignment.

Experimental design is only one component in the planning of a research study. Careful description, as represented by ethnographic methods, for example, is an essential element (and the "principles" of good design may be essential to a competent enthnographic study; cf. Basso, 1979). Correlational and factor analytic techniques are important tools in searching for structure in data. It is difficult for us to imagine a well-planned investigation that does not bring into play all these methods, and others.

The significance of experimental design is that it leads to a deeper level of analysis and a more trustworthy degree of control than other methods. The field of reading research has reached the point where the experimental paradigm can be applied to good advantage, both for support of theory development and for practical matters such as curriculum evaluation. We think that the complexity of reading and reading instruction, while by no means overwhelming, does call for a relatively high level of sophistication in design. Techniques of considerable power and efficiency are available. We trust that our examples point the way to what is possible, and to what can be achieved.

REFERENCES

Basso, K. H.   Children and ethnographers. *Science,* 1979, *206,* 823–824.

Bloomfield, L., & Barnhart, C. L.   *Let's read: A linguistic approach.* Detroit, Mich.: Wayne State University Press, 1961.

Box, G. E. P., Hunter, W. G., & Hunter, J. S.   *Statistics for experimenters.* New York: Wiley, 1978.

Calfee, R. C.   *The design of experiments and the design of curriculum.* Paper presented at Stanford Evaluation Consortium, Stanford University, Stanford, Calif., 1974.

Calfee, R. C.   *Human experimental psychology.* New York: Holt, Rinehart & Winston, 1975.

Calfee, R. C.   Sources of dependency in cognitive processes. In D. Klahr (Ed.), *Cognition and instruction.* Hillsdale, N.J.: Erlbaum, 1976.

Calfee, R. C., Chapman, R., & Venezky, R. L.   How a child needs to think to learn to read. In L. W. Gregg (Ed.), *Cognition in learning and memory.* New York: Wiley, 1972.

Calfee, R. C., & Shefelbine, J. L.   A structural model of teaching. In A. Levy & D. Nevo (Eds.), *Evaluation roles in education.* New York: Gordon and Breach, 1981.

Campbell, D.   Factors relevant to the validity of experiments in social settings. *Psychological Bulletin,* 1957, *54,* 297–312.

Campbell, D. T., & Stanley, J. C.   *Experimental and quasi-experimental designs for research.* Chicago: Rand McNally, 1963.

Cohen, E. G.   *A new approach to applied research: Race and education.* Columbus, Ohio; Merrill, 1970.

Cook, T. D., & Campbell, D. T.   *Quasi-experimentation: Design and analysis for field settings.* Chicago: Rand McNally, 1979.

Cronbach, L. J.   *Essentials of psychological testing* (3rd ed.). New York: Harper & Row, 1970.

Cronbach, L. J.   Beyond the two disciplines of scientific psychology. *American Psychologist,* 1975, *30,* 116–127.

Cronbach, L. J., Gleser, G. C., Nanda, H., & Rajaratnam, J.   *The dependability of behavioral measurements: Theory of generalizability for scores and profiles.* New York: Wiley, 1972.

Cronbach, L. J., & Snow, R. E. *Aptitudes and instructional methods.* New York: Irvington, 1977.

Dayton, C. M. *The design of educational experiments.* New York: McGraw-Hill, 1970.

Fisher, R. A. *The design of experiments.* Edinburgh, Scotland: Oliver & Boyd, 1935.

Grice, G. R. Dependence of empirical laws upon the source of experimental variation. *Psychological Bulletin,* 1966, *66,* 488–498.

Haber, R. N., & Hershenson, M. *The psychology of visual perception.* New York: Holt, Rinehart, & Winston, 1973.

Homans, G. H. Group factors in worker productivity. In *Fatigue of workers: Its relation to industrial production.* New York: Reinhold, 1941. (Reprinted in E. Maccoby, R. Newcomb, & E. Hartley (Eds.), *Readings in social psychology* (3rd ed.). New York: Holt, Rinehart, & Winston, 1958, 583–595.)

Kavanagh, J. F., & Mattingly, I. G. *Language by ear and by eye.* Cambridge, Mass.: MIT Press, 1972.

Kirk, R. E. *Experimental design: Procedures for the behavioral sciences.* Belmont, Calif.: Brooks/Cole, 1968.

Lord, F. M. Individualized testing and item characteristic curve theory. In D. H. Krantz, R. C. Atkinson, R. D. Luce, & P. Suppes (Eds.), *Contemporary developments in mathematical psychology* (Vol. 2): *Measurement, psychophysics and neural information processing.* San Francisco: Freeman, 1974.

Sternberg, S. The discovery of processing stages: Extensions of Donder's method. In W. G. Koster (Ed.), *Attention and performance* (Vol. 2). Amsterdam: North-Holland, 1969.

Stufflebeam, D. L. *The use of experimental design in educational evaluation.* Paper presented at the annual meeting of the American Educational Research Association, Minneapolis, Minn., April 1970.

U.S. Department of Commerce. National Bureau of Standards. *Fractional factorial experimental design at two levels* (Doc. C.13.32.48). Washington, D.C.: U.S. Department of Commerce, Applied Math Series, 1962.

Walker, D. F., & Schaffarzick, J. Comparing curricula. *Review of Educational Research,* 1974, *74,* 83–111.

Winer, B. J. *Statistical principles in experimental design* (2nd ed.). New York: McGraw-Hill, 1971.

4 ETHNOGRAPHIC APPROACHES TO READING RESEARCH

Larry F. Guthrie and William S. Hall

Within the educational research community, ethnography and ethnographic methods have been gaining in prominence as a means of studying schools and educational processes. The situation is no different in reading research. "Ethnography" is approaching the status of a catchword. All manner of reading researchers toss around the terms *ethnographic research, qualitative methods,* and *observational studies* with abandon. References to an *ethnographic approach* or *ethnographic component* have become essential parts of funding agencies' requests for proposals, and studies claiming to employ ethnographic methods have crept into professional reading research journals. There have been calls for a more qualitative approach and a less narrow perspective on the process of reading and the acquisition of reading skills. In other words, ethnography is achieving credibility.

An unfortunate aspect of this phenomenon is that many of those who talk about ethnographic research—and even those who claim to do it—do not have a firm grasp on what "ethnographic," "qualitative," and "observational" mean and how they should be distinguished. All too often, they are used interchangeably. In addition, while most reading researchers may talk about ethnographic approaches, they really take a somewhat dim view of such "soft" research. Because educational anthropologists conduct research and present findings in ways different from those employed in the standard experimental approach, their methods are to a large degree suspect. Ethnographic studies are interesting, but questionable. They are considered to be little more than curiosities because of perceived problems in reliability and generalizability. From the perspective of mainstream educational research, ethnography is basically a method that relies on a small sample, observations, note taking, and a lot of intuition. Because ethnographers generally do not employ statistical procedures, their research is regarded as more anecdotal than scientific, and as lacking in rigor.

To complicate matters, another group of researchers, those coming out of a more ethnographic tradition, have become critical of some of the work done recently under the guise of ethnography. Rist (1980), for example, has taken offense at what he calls "blitzkrieg ethnography." His point is that much of the current "ethnographic" work is not ethnography at all. It may only have some of the trappings of ethnography. Lutz (1981) makes a similar point, distinguishing between "ethnography" and "ethnographic." Certain criteria determine what ethnography is; the isolated use of observations, fieldnotes, videotape, or interviews does not in itself constitute ethnography.

One purpose of this chapter is, then, to attempt to clarify exactly what is and is not ethnography. Our theoretical perspective is that of anthropology. While we recognize that qualitative research, and ethnography, is part of other disciplines as well (e.g., sociology), it is with anthropology that the method is most often associated. We present a general description of the ethnographic process and outline a series of standard ethnographic data-collection procedures. Part of this discussion focuses on the distinction between microethnography and macroethnography. Next, we explain why an ethnographic approach is both appropriate and necessary for research on reading. We attempt to show what evidence these techniques can provide that other methods cannot. We feel that it is essential that those engaged in reading research and interested in qualitative or ethnographic approaches at least have a clear idea of the standard ethnographic methodology. We realize that we cannot, in this brief overview, present a thorough account of how to conduct ethnographic research. What we can hope to do is at least introduce a different methodology to the reading research community and clear up some of the misconceptions surrounding that approach. More thorough accounts of how to conduct ethnographic and qualitative research are available—for example, Agar (1980), Pelto and Pelto (1973), Schatzman and Strauss (1974), and Spindler (1982).

A second purpose of this chapter is to present examples of research on reading done within the ethnographic paradigm. This work, though somewhat scarce, is opening up new areas for investigation and paving the way toward a fruitful line of research.

Third, and finally, we discuss in some detail some future directions for ethnographic research on reading and how it might proceed. We attempt to cover some representative areas of reading research that would be appropriate for ethnographic investigation.

ETHNOGRAPHIC RESEARCH

Ethnography has traditionally been the study of other cultures. It is based on the belief that each culture has its unique world-view and ways of assigning meaning to human behavior. Members of a culture possess their particular sociocultural knowledge about, for example, how to interact with different people and in different situations. Much of it, however, is at a subconscious level. The task of the researcher, then, is to capture as clearly as possible a picture of that world-view and sociocultural knowledge. To do so, the researcher tries to experience the world as members of the culture in question do. The ethnographer's goal is to understand the social and cognitive world they occupy and to learn what one needs to know in order to be a competent member of that society. As Bauman (1972, p. 157) put it, ethnography is "the process of construction through direct personal observation of social behavior, a theory of the working of a particular culture in terms as close as possible to the way members of that culture view the universe and organize their behavior within it."

Such insights into another culture's perspectives do not come easily—or overnight. To arrive at them requires the use of a set of specialized techniques over an extended period of time. Notions of how other people construct their world normally emerge only after many months (or years) in the field.

Ethnographic studies, of course, need not be restricted to other continents or societies. As Spindler put it:

> The ethnographic world view assumes that any classroom, any school, any group or community is a variant adaptation within a regional, national, and world-wide variation in culture and social organization (1982, p. 491).

Several ethnographic studies in education, particularly in reading, have been conducted in ways similar to those employed in these forays into other people's worlds. The basic tenets and methods for research still hold, and while the subject of study may not be in some exotic clime, the underlying goals are the same: to "grasp the native's point of view, his relation to life, to realize *his* version of *his* world" (Malinowski, 1935, p. 25).

An essential part of ethnographic research is that ethnographers enter the field with an open mind. They try to be as free from preconceived notions as possible. And while ethnographers may at times narrow the subject of their studies somewhat in advance, they strive throughout to remain open and not impose their own cultural categories (G. Guthrie & Hall, 1981).

A second basic tenet is that the research methodology is in a sense open-ended. This aspect of ethnographic research is perhaps the most difficult for researchers accustomed to the experimental paradigm to comprehend. It is a misconception, however, to think of ethnographic research as unstructured and without reason. While the exact direction the research takes is unspecified, it is not a random operation. As Malinowski put it, the ethnographer does not merely "spread his nets in the right place and wait for what will fall into them" (1935, p. 7). He must actively pursue information that will contribute to his picture of the community under study. The search is for the "native's" perspective, and whatever means the researcher must employ to get at that perspective, he will. The precise ethnographic methods to be utilized, then, will differ from one study to another, and from one ethnographer to another. Despite popular belief, ethnographers do not rely solely on participant observation to collect their data. Most will, in fact, employ a variety of techniques, of which participant observation is usually an essential component.

For these reasons, ethnography is perhaps best seen as a process rather than a set of methods or techniques. As the research progresses, the ethnographer alternately develops hypotheses and tests them, and, depending upon the question being asked, employs the method(s) that seem most appropriate. The ethnographic process has been described both as cyclical (G. Guthrie, 1982; Spradley, 1980) and as composed of stages (Gearing & Epstein, 1982; Spindler, 1982). In either case, the procedures are basically the same.

In terms of stages, three have been identified. The ethnographer first orients himself to the setting (e.g., the community and school). This Spindler (1982) calls the *reconnaissance* phase. Data sources may include census data, newspaper and journal articles, and other published documents—anything that may provide some preliminary information about the site. It is at this stage, too, that the ethnographer begins to negotiate entry into the site. In the second stage, called *reconnoiter* by Spindler, the ethnographer makes initial observations of the site, first engaging people in casual conversations and then conducting more structured observation and interviewing. During this stage, various relationships between people and events are sorted out. Gearing and Epstein (1982) refer to this as the *event structure* phase, where one seeks to pick out what is important in the interaction of activities and persons. As the research progresses, and the ethnographer learns more about the culture, he (or she) is able to narrow the focus of the investigation. He develops hypotheses about what is important to the subjects of the study and then goes about the task of testing them. While not explicitly labeled by Spindler, we can call this the hypothesis-testing phase. To test hypotheses, the ethnographer may employ any number of different methods, or combinations of methods. He or she may conduct additional (more focused) interviews, develop and distribute questionnaires, use observational schedules, or make audio or videotapes. In the next section, these various methods are briefly described.

The cyclical nature of the method may appear at any point throughout the ethnographic enterprise. Because the direction of the research is not made explicit in advance, the ethnographer may, upon analyzing data from one phase of the study, return to collect additional data or data of another type. In the analysis of ethnographic interviews, for example, the researcher may encounter information from one informant that causes him (or her) to seek confirmation from others. He then reenters the field, checking out the information. In this way, the ethnographer may move again and again in a cyclical fashion until finally satisfied that the picture is accurate and complete (G. Guthrie, 1982; Spradley, 1979, 1980).

The end product of this endeavor is then a "thick description" (Geertz, 1963) of the other culture and its world-view. The ethnographer produces an account of the people's beliefs and customs, the important events and systems that structure their lives. The ethnographer tries to show, once again, what one needs to know to be a member of that culture. As Lutz put it:

> Ethnography is a holistic, thick description of the interactive process involving the discovery of important and recurring variables in the society as they relate to one another, under specified conditions, and as they affect or produces certain results and outcomes in a society (1981, p. 52).

This brings us to the issue raised recently by Rist (1980), Lutz (1981), and others regarding the use and misuse of ethnography. Their argument is that an essential part of ethnography is the contextualization of information and multiple perspectives on a subject. Through the use of a variety of data-collection strategies, the validity of the research is increased (Wilcox, 1982); when techniques of ethnography are taken and used in isolation, the research is no longer ethnography. It is here that Lutz draws the distinction between ethnography and ethnographic.

MICROETHNOGRAPHY

Microethnographic studies are characterized primarily by the fact that they employ ethnographic and sociolinguistic techniques to examine in detail small pieces of human behavior. In contrast to such studies, more traditional ethnographies have been labeled macroethnographies. A certain amount of controversy concerning micro- and macroethnography has arisen in the last few years (for a discussion, see Ogbu, 1981). Within the framework presented here, however, the dichotomy is a false one; from this perspective, microethnography is the portion of the holistic ethnography that may constitute the third stage of investigation.

The basic rationale for microethnographic approaches is that in the interactional give-and-take of everyday conversation, people negotiate their understanding of one other and the world. Unless educational research can get at how these interactions are conducted, it is argued, important features of the processes of teaching and learning will be overlooked. (More of the arguments behind this approach are presented in the following section.)

Microethnographies, like any research method, take a number of forms and labels. What Erickson and Schultz (1981) call "microethnography," Mehan (1979) calls "constituitive ethnography," Hymes (1981) calls "ethnographic monitoring," and others call "selective ethnography." They are all basically the same thing: the study of how people structure their interactional accomplishments. Employing audio or audiovisual equipment, the researcher is able to examine the behaviors thoroughly and repeatedly. Social interaction is so complex that any on-the-spot recording of behavior is suspect. When one looks at the same piece of interaction over and over, a more complete and accurate description of that event will emerge. Another feature of this approach implicit in the terms "selective ethnography" and "ethnographic monitoring" is that representative aspects of the totality of behavior are selected for analysis. Without the first and second stages of analysis, through which the event structure of the culture is determined, the selection of events for further study is arbitrary. Those engaged in microethnography, on the other hand, are concerned that traditional ethnographers may stop at the second stage, a point made by Spindler (1982). According to Mehan (1979), traditional ethnographic approaches in classroom research (e.g., Smith & Geoffrey, 1968) produce in-depth, often revealing accounts of everyday life in a classroom. Without the close examination possible through a microethnographic approach, they tend to be anecdotal and fail to specify how the decision to include or exclude information is made, and which behaviors are typical or atypical.

ETHNOGRAPHIC METHODS

In this section, we briefly describe some standard tools of the trade of ethnographers. These methods, used in combination, are what the ethnographer does. In a later section, we point out examples from reading research that have utilized each method. Participant observation is described first because it is the basic ethnographic approach. Next come interviews and quantification schemes. Finally, there is a brief discussion of the use of technology, audio- and videotapes.

Participant Observation

In participant observation, the investigator attempts to immerse himself (or herself) in the daily lives and activities of the people being studied (cf. Spradley, 1980). Whether they are a village of Pacific Islanders or a classroom of American schoolchildren, the researcher spends as much time as possible with them, trying to learn their ways of behaving and organizing their world. This process usually takes several months, during which the researcher ideally becomes like a fixture in the community. Because people get used to having the researcher around, they tend to become less self-conscious and more natural.

To be effective, the participant observer must be more than just a casual onlooker. He must know what to look for, what to observe, and must try to remain objective. Although the method is in a sense unsystematic, in that is not preplanned, it is by no means haphazard. From the beginning, the researcher records everything that might be of importance and does not rely on memory. As much or more time may be spent in daily note taking as in observation. To a large extent, the effectiveness of this endeavor depends on the individual researcher's sensitivity and skills as an observer.

Naturally, educational ethnographies all involve school and classroom observation to some extent. This may range from what Smith (Smith & Geoffrey, 1968) called nonparticipant observation, in which the researcher merely observes, to real participant observation, in which the researcher assumes the role of teacher's aide or helper (Cook-Gumperz, Gumperz, & Simons, 1981; G. Guthrie, 1982; Hart, 1982). The amount of time in the school varies as well. In McDermott's (1976) microethnographic study of reading groups, he spent an entire year as a participant observer in the class; others have restricted their observations to several visits.

Interviews

The ethnographer employs a variety of interviewing techniques. A brief overview of three basic techniques is provided here: ethnographic interviews, structured interviews, and semistructured interviews. For a more detailed presentation of techniques of ethnographic interviewing, see Agar (1980) and Spradley (1979). Since interviewing is such an integral part of the ethnographic process, virtually all educational ethnographies utilize some form of interview.

Key informant   A common approach among anthropologists today is to enlist what is known as a key informant. The key informant becomes an essential part of the research in that the ethnographer not only interviews the person but discusses the research and checks out hypotheses and hunches with him or her. This person should be someone with knowledge of the culture, and with sensitivity. The key informant should also be someone who is articulate and can report on his or her own behavior. In working with the researcher, the good key informant comes to learn what sorts of things the researcher is interested in and begins to see the culture more from a social scientist's perspective.

What the interviewer learns from this informant is only one person's opinion, of course, and an untrained one at that. Nevertheless, it may enable the researcher to acquire information that might otherwise not be available. From the key informant, for instance, a perspective of the culture is always available. The observer who sees something interesting or peculiar can immediately question the informant about it, getting a native's point of view.

In the study of schools and schooling, the most obvious point at which a key informant might be useful is at the community level, given the more formal structure of schools and classrooms. A particular teacher might also become a key informant, and become engaged in prolonged interviewing. In the course of the study, as the researcher notices differences in reading practices, for example, the teacher could be consulted for a native's interpretation.

A variation on this procedure might be to utilize a process of "indefinite triangulation" (Cicourel, 1974), in which subjects are asked to interpret their own data, such as audio- or videotapes (e.g., Cicourel, Jennings, Jennings, Leiter, MacKay, Mehan, & Roth, 1974; Mehan, 1979; Mehan, Hertweck, Combs, & Flynn, 1982).

Structured interviews   Once particular hypotheses or research questions have been formulated, the ethnographer may choose to employ structured interviews. These make data quantifiable and comparable, and can be administered to exact procedures. In addition, by sampling a larger number of subjects, it can be argued that these interviews are representative of the population as a whole.

At the orienting stage, structured interviews might be used to elicit demographic data (name, ages, clan and ethnic affiliation, birth date and place, etc.), as well as facts about socioeconomic status, living conditions, educational level, and educational goals. The information can of course then be checked through other techniques. An essential point in the development of an interview schedule is that the researcher must somehow know what to ask, even at the beginning of a study. A conscientious researcher therefore spends time observing first, getting a notion about what kinds of questions will be significant and what kind superfluous.

Information relevant to reading research that might be explored through this procedure include teacher's age, educational background, inservice training, and curriculum materials.

Semistructured interviews   Semistructured interviews follow an open-ended format. The researcher approaches the interview with a set of questions or topics that he wishes to explore, but does not follow a rigid pattern of questioning. The researcher covers all the areas of interest, but is open to explore other areas as well. This format allows the interviewer to investigate topics that may not have been considered ahead of time. The less-structured format also tends to put the subject at ease, thus helping to elicit information that otherwise might not have been available.

In reading research, it may be important to inquire about the teacher's curriculum, how she organizes her class, how she grades, and so on. Through a semistructured interview, this information is readily obtained.

Quantification Schemes

Checklists and rating scales are two methods researchers have devised in an attempt to quantify the analysis of behavior. In using prepared checklists, the researcher (or team of researchers) tabulates the occurrence of particular behaviors of interest. In regard to social interaction, perhaps the best-known checklist approach is that developed by Bales (1950), Interaction Process Analysis. Similar checklist approaches have been employed in the study of classroom interaction (e.g., Amidon and Flanders, 1963; Fisher, Berliner, Filby, Marliave, Cahen, & Dishaw, 1980; Flanders, 1970; Stallings, 1975). Using basically the same method, but a different checklist of course, coders categorize the behaviors of teachers and students. Quantification schemes can be used to answer any number of questions about the interaction of participants in an event. In a reading group, for instance, a schedule might be developed to count students' turns at reading, correct answers, reading miscues, or any number of behaviors considered worthy of investigation.

While this approach gives a general picture of classroom interaction and organization, in isolation, it does have important weaknesses (cf. Mehan, 1979). Many behaviors (e.g., students') in a group as large as a class may be missed altogether, behaviors that participants may not miss. Nonverbal behavior is also often ignored. Additionally, by coding language on the spot, the multiple functions of language are missed. Finally, there is no depiction of the context or the flow of interaction using a checklist approach, a critical point, especially if educational research done using checklists relies exclusively on those data. Once again, an essential criterion of an ethnography is that it employs a range of data-collection methods, of which checklists are only a part.

Diary Studies

This method is closely related to the case-study approach, for it is an in-depth account of one person's life. In fact, it is often treated as a variation of the case-study method. In the literature, two kinds of diary studies can be found: those involving the investigator's diary, and those involving a subject's diary.

Investigator's diary   Some researchers find it useful to keep a diary. One advantage to this is that it may reveal the investigator's own thoughts and feelings, expressions of self that normally might not become public. If the researcher keeps a diary during a field experience, then it will additionally provide a check on other data. The circumstances under which the data were collected, as well as the investigator's own emotional state, will be revealed. A further advantage to the diary is that it is relatively free from the reconstructions of memory, having been written close to the experience.

Subject's diary   A researcher may also want to draw information from a diary kept by one or more subjects. How they react to critical events and interpret those events can be of great interest. The researcher may then gain insights into the subjects and the larger culture of which they are a part. The intimacy of such a journal, and the fact that it may be less distorted by the researcher's presence or questions, or by the subject's self-consciousness, can make it very valuable.

In his study of education in a rural American community, Peshkin (1978) asked students to keep diaries of their experiences in and out of school. An application of this procedure to reading research might be to have students keep a record of everything they read throughout the day.

Case Studies

Case studies can focus on individuals, groups, or organizations. They are attempts to depict as accurately and reliably as possible the subject's life experiences and interpretations of those life experiences. In case studies of individuals, the standard method is the prolonged interview, in which the investigator and the subject interact and establish a rapport over time. It is of little consequence that this person will often be exceptional rather than typical. Nor is truth necessarily of the greatest concern. What is important is that beliefs, conceptions, and life experiences are captured. They reveal how the subject sees the world.

Case studies can also be conducted on groups of people, such as schools or classrooms; the chief difference from ethnography being one of scope. Hart (1982) conducted what might be considered a case study of reading in an elementary school. Working as a helper, tutor, and observer, she was able to document the ways in which social organization of reading is established.

The Use of Technology

Microethnographers have, in the past several years, developed some ingenious ways of analyzing behavior through the use of modern technology, namely audio and audiovisual equipment. Because such procedures provide a permanent record of selected events, they can be viewed and analyzed repeatedly, and are available for analysis by others. For comprehensive descriptions of some of the procedures employed, see Erickson and Schultz (1981) and Erickson and Wilson (1982).

Not only anthropologists but sociolinguists, psychologists, and sociologists have employed audio and videotape equipment in the analysis of student interaction. The standard procedure is that a taped record made of selected episodes is analyzed according to some coding system, either developed for that study or borrowed from a previous one. Coding may focus on verbal behavior, nonverbal behavior, or a combination (e.g., see papers in Ervin-Tripp & Mitchell-Kernan, 1977; Freedle, 1977; Green & Wallat, 1981; Trueba, G. Guthrie, & Au, 1981; Wilkinson, 1982).

WHY AN ETHNOGRAPHIC APPROACH TO READING RESEARCH?

Now consider some of the arguments for the use of ethnography in the conduct of reading research. To date, most of the studies in this area have focused on minority populations and the difficulties they have in learning to read (cf. for example, Cook-Gumperz et al., 1981; McDermott, 1976; Piestrup, 1973; Rist, 1973).

One of the reasons the experimental and correlational research on reading for minority children is so equivocal and not very informative is that it, in effect, is a measurement of the wrong thing. It tells us where children stand in relation to others, but it says nothing about how they got there. In this section we discuss a growing disenchantment with traditional approaches to the study of problems facing minority education. A common thread running through this research is the belief that only by looking at the interactional process of education, only by looking at what is really happening between teacher and students when children learn, or are taught, will we really gain any significant insight into the problems facing poor readers.

This line of research asks some basic questions about the nature of reading. For children, reading—and reading instruction in particular—is more than a solitary, cognitive process. For them, reading is something one does in groups, led by a teacher. It is a social, interactional activity. As Cazden (1979) points out, learning to read is deeply embedded in the interaction that takes place between teachers and peers in reading group. How the teacher organizes that reading group, how she or he assigns turns, gives praise, asks questions, and so on, can have a profound effect on whether a child learns to read. Similarly, how children conduct themselves in the group in bidding for turns, reading aloud, answering questions, and responding to other students can in a very real sense determine whether they learn to read.

This notion is commensurate with work on classroom interaction, the ethnography of communication (Hymes, 1974), and the functions of language in the classroom (Cazden, John, & Hymes, 1972; Trueba et al., 1981). While not dealing with reading in particular, this research is directly related to the study of reading as a social activity. It has been shown, among other things, that different groups of people use language in different ways, ways that can be of critical importance to them on social and educational levels. As McDermott (1977) says, "in any given community, different people appear to know different things about how to get along linguistically, and they use these differences to negotiate statuses and roles" (pp. 154–155). When members of these groups come in contact, miscommunication can result, not just on the basis of linguistic interference, but because of mismatches between language function and use. Further, if these breakdowns are not repaired, or are not even recognized, they can have a negative effect on how people relate to one another, and in turn, on children's performance.

This argument is sometimes expressed as a variant of the home-school mismatch hypothesis, which suggests that minority children's ways of speaking and acting, while not inferior or deficient, happen not to coincide with those particular behaviors that form the basis for school success. The rules that regulate classroom interactions are essentially middle-class rules, and children from nonmainstream backgrounds have to learn them if they are to navigate the school environment successfully (L. Guthrie & Hall, 1983; Hall & L. Guthrie, 1981a, 1981b). For example, children must learn the structures of daily activities, how transitions are signaled, and how to get the teacher's or other students' attention. It is perhaps here that their initial difficulties lie: not in the rules listed on the classroom wall, but in the implicit, out-of-awareness rules for social interaction and classroom organization.

For children learning to read, the relational structure of the reading group can be crucial to success. People in interaction negotiate with each other; it is a mutually constructed phenomenon. If because of different ways of speaking or viewing the world, teachers and students define the situation of learning to read differently, then their chances for success in that endeavor are limited. The teacher may develop a negative attitude or low expectations toward the child; she or he may select a method of instruction that is incompatible with the child's experiences and ways of behavior; the child may simply turn off.

The rationale behind this research is that if we can uncover the dynamics of the interactions between teachers and students and locate those points of misunderstanding, then we might be able to find more successful ways to bring all children to read. We want to discover what it is "about how teachers and children hold each other accountable that has them either making sense of each other or at each other's throats. . . . A good ethnography of classrooms should answer this question" (McDermott, 1977, p. 164).

Children also have their own view of reality. In a series of interviews with young children who had taken the California reading tests (Cicourel et al., 1974; Mehan & Wood, 1975), Mehan uncovered some startling discrepancies between the adult and child views of the examination. A child who matched the word "fly" with an elephant because it looked like Dumbo, the flying elephant, was of course marked down. Similar discrepancies must exist between the child and adult views of particular reading passages, as well as the process of reading. How children conceive of reading and what they understand it and its purposes to be can also have a very real effect on their learning. By taking the anthropologist's view and treating the "native" or "subject" as an expert on his culture (Spindler, 1982), reading research can learn a lot about children's reading and reading problems.

The argument for studying the process of teaching and learning as *interaction* is made effectively by both Mehan (1979) and McDermott (1977); critical of the traditional methods of educational psychology, they call for more ethnographic approaches. Mehan notes that the predominant and most pervasive kind of educational research is correlational. Input factors are compared with output factors, and decisions are made on the basis of their degree of correlation. Whether on the level of schools or programs, classrooms or groups of individuals, the procedure is essentially the same. Factors such as social class, age, sex, teacher attitudes, and classroom size, as well as variations in reading text, orthography, or syntax, are correlated with student achievement. What is left out of most research is an image of the actual process of reading. What really happens in the relations of the thousands of students and their teachers that reports discuss is seldom touched on.

McDermott (1977) is critical of research that treats teaching as a bag of tricks out of which teachers, supervisors, and principals pick solutions. If one thing does not work, try another. It is not fair, McDermott claims, to assume that poor readers, for example, are missing some cognitive skill purely on the basis of experimental research. He insists, rather, that it is the relational fabric of the classroom that decides, or lets children decide, whether learning takes place. Given this, and faced with the reality of a high rate of functional illiteracy among inner-city black children, he sees two possible explanations: (1) There is something lacking in their culture; (2) there is something inadequate about the situations in which they are asked to learn how to read. Evidence from anthropology shows that virtually no culture socializes children so that they cannot learn how to read; McDermott therefore rejects the first explanation. He concludes that it is in terms of interactional conflicts that we should search for possible causes. Mehan (1979) takes a similar position: "In order to understand the influence of schooling, we need research strategies that examine the living processes of education that occur within classrooms, on playgrounds, at home, and on the streets" (p. 10). He calls for going into the classrooms and observing directly what is going on, what teaching and learning really are.

Mehan and McDermott are not the first to have made these arguments. Similar calls for observational studies of classroom interaction have resulted in another widely used strategy, which Mehan also criticizes: quantification schemes. When not thoroughly grounded in an ethnographic research effort, the implementation of quantification schemes may, as mentioned, be problematic. Prearranged categories may be applied arbitrarily; teacher behavior may be studied in isolation from the contribution of students; critical verbal and nonverbal information, as well as the sequential flow of events, may be obscured; and the multiple functions of language may be lost.

In order to see how ethnographic methods have been implemented in reading research, we present in the next section three representative examples.

STUDIES OF READING AS A SOCIAL ACTIVITY

Ethnographic studies of reading, compared to more experimental approaches, are rare. As the dissatisfaction with standard methodologies becomes more widespread, however, their numbers are increasing. In this section we review four such studies, focusing primarily on the methods the researchers employed. As will become evident, in each of the examples provided the researchers followed a reasoned procedure similar to that outlined above.

McDermott: "Kids Make Sense"

McDermott (1976, 1977) conducted a microethnography of two 30-minute reading groups, one high, one low. Using videotape data, he analyzed the speech and nonverbal behaviors of the teacher and students frame by frame. McDermott's analysis was not based solely on one hour of videotape, however. During the course of his research, he spent an entire school year visiting the classroom under study several times a week. McDermott's basic microethnographic technique of analyzing minute nonverbal behaviors was supplemented by a more macrolevel approach, and the categories and interpretations he made were possible only after an extended period of participant observation. Any conclusions he made were drawn not just from a small sample of isolated behavior but from his own insights into the structure of the class—the result of hundreds of hours of observation. His interpretations of the taped behaviors were thus more nearly like those of a participant in the culture of the classroom than an interested but casual observer. McDermott's observational field notes provided him with the supporting data and the context on which to base his conclusions.

From this combination of sources, he was able to determine significant differences in the environment of each group. In regard to time, children in the high group were found to spend three times as much time on task as those in the low group. Further, in the high group, turns to read were allocated in order, a fixed number of pages per child; in the low, turns were bid for and negotiated in no fixed order. Thus, more time was taken in the low group just deciding who should read next. Interruptions, many initiated by advanced-group students and some teacher-initiated, were 20 times more frequent in the low group.

McDermott concluded that these groups constituted an instance when the social organization and the relational fabric of the class make it difficult for certain children to learn to read, having been offered different environments for learning. The circumstances under which the low group had to get organized and on task were not the same as for the high group and, more important, probably were inappropriate for them in the long run.

The differential treatment in the reading groups did not appear to have been consciously imposed by the teacher. The different turn-taking mechanisms, for example, came about because certain children in the low group were simply unable to read when given a turn. The constant renegotiation of turns was a way of avoiding embarrassment, both of the students and the teacher. Thus their behavior, under the circumstances, was understandable; as McDermott (1976) put it, "kids make sense."

The School Home Ethnography Project

Cook-Gumperz et al. (1981) recently completed a major study of language use at home and school, the School Home Ethnography Project (SHEP). Their focus was the acquisition of literacy in urban communities, and they approached the problem from a theoretical perspective similar to that of Mehan, McDermott, and others. In other words, they saw the problem as a function of social processes: what is important is what is communicated in school. While they began with a notion of what to focus on, they did not attempt to predict in advance what was important.

They utilized what they call the "typical case" method, similar to a "constitutive" or "selective" ethnography, and proceeded in the following way: First, ethnographic information on classroom interaction and students' cultural background and peer networks was gathered. This was accomplished through participant observation, selective audio- and videotaping, and interviews and questionnaires. Both the home and the school were investigated. In the course of this initial stage of investigation, particular attention was paid to instances of apparent miscommunication. In addition, an attempt was made to formulate notions of a typical school day, participant structures, the social network of the family, and the particular discourse styles of children and adults. Mothers were enlisted to help in the taping and by keeping diaries.

On the basis of these data, *key situations* were identified. These were situations in which access to educational or occupational opportunities appeared to be controlled. In key situations, one's interactional strategies can be important in determining how one emerges from the situation. In the School Home Ethnography Project, several issues that would help identify these situations were explored. Among these were (1) differential treatment of children, (2) teacher expectations, (3) children's attention-getting strategies, and (4) peer-group networks.

Once key situations were identified, they were subjected to a conversational analysis. This analysis was based on Gumperz's notion of conversational inference, the "situated process by which participants in a conversation assess other participants' intentions and on which they base their responses" (Gumperz, 1981, p. 12). The assumption is that people rely on their own sociocultural knowledge of linguistic and interactional rules and conventions in order to participate in an activity. The goal of the analysis is to identify particular cues by which people establish and maintain their involvement.

One of the key situations that the SHEP research team identified was "sharing time," or "show and tell" as it is sometimes called (Michaels & Cook-Gumperz, 1979). These daily episodes became settings for "oral preparation for literacy." As the teacher guides children through their discourse presentations through questions and instructions, he or she reveals personal notions of what narrative discourse should be. Based on the recorded data from over 50 sharing sessions, Michaels identified ways in which the home-based narrative styles of children afforded them differential treatment. Children's styles were found to be one of two basic types: topic-centered and topic-chaining. Topic-centered narratives seemed to fit the teacher's scheme of a narrative, while narratives that employed topic-chaining did not. This was evident not only in the teacher's instructions ("tell about one thing") but in understanding and handling the discourse. With the white children in the class, there was a match between their discourse styles and that of the teacher. In effect, they and the teacher produced the oral narratives collaboratively. In the case of black children, who employed topic-chaining techniques, the teacher was often unable to follow the topic; teacher comments and questions were ill-tuned, and so they interrupted and confused the child. Michaels is careful to point out that the examples she discusses were not isolated but were instances of a consistently recurring phenomenon.

The implications for these findings are that those children who use the topic-centered style will become more proficient at structuring oral (and written) narratives in the way required by the teacher and literacy convention. They will also develop a different sense of narrative structure and how to interpret it. As a result, they will be placed in higher reading groups. The topic-chaining children presumably will not.

A comparison was also made between high- and low-ability groups (Collins, 1981). It was found in this fine-grained analysis that in the low group, the teacher encouraged word-by-word reading and provided primarily decoding cues; in the high group, comprehension-based reading was developed. These findings complement those of McDermott (1976).

The Kamehameha Early Education Program

The Kamehameha Early Education Program (KEEP) in Hawaii provides an example of how traditional ethnographic research can contribute directly to the development of a successful reading program. As documented in a number of sources (Au, 1980; Au & Jordan, 1981; Calfee, Cazden, Duran, Griffin, Martus, & Willis, 1981; Tharp, 1982), KEEP has used features of Hawaiian culture derived from ethnographic study to dramatically raise the reading scores of Hawaiian children when apparently all other approaches had failed.

Hawaiian children have traditionally scored very low on standardized tests of reading; in fact, Calfee et al. report on recent statewide testing that showed average fourth-grade scores in the tenth percentile. However, efforts at the KEEP school have shown that with the proper approach, an approach that is culturally compatible, these children do learn to read. Hawaiian children who have been taught with the KEEP curriculum now score at grade level or above.

In the course of a multiyear project, researchers collected a variety of traditional ethnographic data on the Hawaiian community in the form of observational field notes, interviews, and demographic information. They were able to identify, among other things, "talk-story," an important speech event in Hawaiian culture that could be applied to the classroom. Talk-story is a way of mutual storytelling in which participants narrate the story together.

Although young Hawaiian children do not normally participate in talk-story, they are of course familiar with it and will co-narrate stories under the right circumstances (Watson-Gegeo & Boggs, 1977). When features of the talk-story process were incorporated into the KEEP reading curriculum, the reading scores of the native Hawaiian children went up.

The researchers at KEEP (e.g., Au, 1980) are careful to point out that their lessons are not replicas of community speech events. They do not re-create exactly the informal learning styles of the community into the classroom. What they have done is isolate certain aspects of talk-story, such as co-narration, and an interested nonthreatening adult into the curriculum. Prior to that, a number of standard curricula were tried, and despite the fact that on-task behavior was achieved, the reading scores remained low (Tharp, 1977, 1982). What seems to have made a difference in this case is that the activity of reading was made culturally relevant.

Au (1980; Au & Jordan, 1981), using the microethnographic method perfected by Erickson (Erickson et al., 1981), has sought to document the critical interactional differences present in the KEEP reading program. To the casual observer, it seems, the KEEP lessons look much like other school lessons, but by focusing on subtle differences in the participant structures, Au was able to specify ways in which the lessons reflected Hawaiian culture.

DIRECTIONS FOR FURTHER RESEARCH

One thing that should be obvious from the above review and discussion is that macroethnographic and microethnographic approaches should go hand in hand and be used to complement each other. As Ogbu (1981) suggests, the distinction between the two may be a false one.

As the studies reviewed here show, it is often in the communicative exchanges in the classroom that the causes of reading failure originate. Without some knowledge of the child's world outside the class, however, without data on home and community interactional patterns, the usefulness of these data is limited. In the Hawaiian case, it was only because of a knowledge of the talk-story speech event that the KEEP personnel were able to develop a successful curriculum. Despite the unquestioned value of his extended exposure to classroom activities, McDermott's data was not community based, and thus sources of the differential treatment he identified are available only at the level of speculation. Research on classroom interaction does not end with the identification of communicative conflict; that is where it begins.

More research is needed on the key situations of the classroom: reading groups, sharing time, and others. In regard to minority-culture children and their classroom experiences, research should continue to delineate the interactional components of situations that may result in differential treatment of limited access to opportunity. These situations may be site specific, culture specific, or both, and only through a careful charting of the children's school experiences will we begin to be able to single them out. In short, we need to know more precisely how minority cultural norms of interaction interface with those operative in the classroom, and how both fit in with the reading curriculum.

As should be clear from the above reviews, what is compatible with one cultural group may not be with another. One finding of McDermott's study was that the turn-taking strategy the teacher employed in the low group resulted in less actual reading time. But more efficient strategies are not always more effective, as the Hawaiian experience so clearly shows.

Ethnographic methodologies need also to be applied to populations of majority-culture children. The critical factor for the children in McDermott's study was not that they were black or lower class but that they had been placed in the low reading group. Does membership in a low reading group really ensure failure, as McDermott (1976, 1977) and Rist (1973) have suggested? McDermott's focus was on nonverbal behavior and organization (e.g., turn taking). How teachers and students organize discourse in reading groups is a ripe area for examination. Collins's (1981) study of differences in instructional strategies actually only scratched the surface.

Once differences in communicative and/or teaching strategies have been identified—whether cultural or not—an effort should be made to apply that knowledge to the classroom. As at KEEP, researchers should work closely with practitioners searching for ways in which to adapt the results of research to the classroom. Where these findings have a positive affect on learning, they can be incorporated into the curriculum.

A final word to more quantitatively oriented reading researchers. Some of the ethnographic techniques described in this chapter could prove very useful in their research, particularly in the identification of areas for experimentation. Unfortunately, much of the experimental research done today in the area of reading has little or no relationship to reality. All too often, an aspect of text is manipulated for little reason other than the sake of manipulation. In training studies, children are often taught to perform complicated operations on narrative text under the guise of improving their reading skills, with no regard for whether those operations are necessary or even useful. At a conference recently, a colleague summarized a research plan in which he intended to train children to organize passages into "information units." It looked very much like outlining. When asked about the usefulness of such an endeavor, whether students really needed to outline passages, the colleague seemed confused. He seemed unable to consider the basic question whether what he intended to train children to do was something a proficient reader actually does or needs to do.

What we are calling for here is the grounding of reading research in an ethnographic base. Before coming up with his outlining project, our colleague might have spent some time in classrooms watching what good and poor readers do when they read. He might have asked some students (or adults) whether outlining was something they might find useful and practical. He might have tape-recorded lessons and tried to identify other weaknesses in the reading strategies of some children. Whichever of these things he did, or others, he would very likely have gained some insight into what reading is for children and what type of training might really contribute to an improvement in their reading skills. In Lutz's (1981) terminology, his research would not have been an ethnography, but it would have been ethnographic.

We might suggest that our colleague first conduct a thorough ethnography of the classroom and community in question; then, on the basis of evidence derived from this study, he could test out his ethnographic findings experimentally. For most researchers, however, this approach is neither practical nor feasible. Ethnography is time-consuming and requires training and practice. Most reading researchers are not trained as ethnographers; their area of expertise lies in the experimental approach. For them, two possibilities remain open. First, they can develop research topics out of the classroom ethnographies of others. For example, the identification of differential turn-taking mechanisms as a factor that might contribute to student success (McDermott, 1976) has prompted considerable sociolinguistic research (e.g., articles in Wilkinson, 1982). A second approach would be to follow the procedure suggested above and employ some ethnographic techniques on their own. This would, of course, not be an ethnography; but it would at least help to ensure a degree of ecological validity in the study.

REFERENCES

Agar, M. *The professional stranger: An informal introduction to ethnography.* New York: Academic Press, 1980.

Amidon, E., & Flanders, N. *The role of the teacher in the classroom.* Minneapolis: Amidon, 1963.

Au, K. H. On participation structures in reading lessons. *Anthropology and Education Quarterly,* 1980, *11,* 91–115.

Au, K. H., & Jordan, C. Teaching reading to Hawaiian children: Finding a culturally appropriate solution. In H. Trueba, G. P. Guthrie, & K. H. Au (Eds.), *Culture and the bilingual classroom: Studies in classroom ethnography.* Rowley, Mass.: Newbury House, 1981.

Bales, R. F. *Interaction process analysis.* Cambridge, Mass.: Addison-Wesley, 1950.

Bauman, R. An ethnographic framework for the investigation of communicative behavior. In R. Abrahams & R. Troike (Eds.), *Language and cultural diversity in American education.* Englewood Cliffs, N.J.: Prentice-Hall, 1972.

Calfee, R., Cazden, C., Duran, R., Griffin, M., Martus, M., & Willis, H. D. *Designing reading instruction for cultural minorities: The case of the Kamehameha Early Education Program.* Honolulu: Kamehameha Early Education Program, 1981.

Cazden, C. B., John, V. P., & Hymes, D. (Eds.). *Functions of language in the classroom.* New York: Teachers College Press, 1972.

Cazden, C. B. Learning to read in classroom interaction. In L. B. Resnick & P. A. Weaver (Eds.), *Theory and practice in early reading* (Vol. 3). Hillsdale, N.J.: Erlbaum, 1979.

Cicourel, A. V. *Cognitive sociology.* New York: Free Press, 1974.

Cicourel, A. V., Jennings, S. H. M., Jennings, K. H., Leiter, K. C. W., MacKay, R., Mehan, H., & Roth, D. R. *Language use and school performance.* New York: Academic Press, 1974.

Collins, J. Differential treatment in reading instruction. In J. Cook-Gumperz, J. Gumperz, & H. Simons, *School home ethnography project* (Final Report). Washington, D.C.: National Institute of Education, 1981.

Cook-Gumperz, J., Gumperz, J. T., & Simons, H. *School Home Ethnography Project* (Final Report). Washington, D.C.: National Institute of Education, 1981.

Erickson, F., & Schultz, J. When is a context? In J. Green & Wallat (Eds.), *Ethnography and language in educational settings.* Norwood, N.J.: Ablex, 1981.

Erickson, F., & Wilson, J. *Sights and sounds of life in schools: A resource guide to film and videotape research and education* (Research Series No. 125). East Lansing: Michigan State University, Institute for Research on Teaching, 1982.

Ervin-Tripp, S., & Mitchell-Kernan, C. (Eds.). *Child discourse.* New York: Academic Press, 1977.

Fisher, C., Berliner, D., Filby, N., Marliave, R., Cahen, L., & Dishaw, M. Teaching behaviors, academic learning time, and student achievement: An overview. In C. Denham & A. Lieberman (Eds.), *Time to learn.* Washington, D.C.: National Institute of Education, 1980.

Flanders, N. *Analyzing teaching behavior.* Reading, Mass.: Addison-Wesley, 1970.

Freedle, R. O. (Ed.). *Discourse production and comprehension* (Vol. 1). Norwood, N.J.: Ablex, 1977.

Geertz, C. *The interpretation of cultures.* New York: Basic Books, 1973.

Green, J., & Wallat, C. (Eds.). *Ethnography and language in educational settings.* Norwood, N.J.: Ablex, 1981.

Gumperz, J. J. Conversational inference and classroom learning. In J. L. Green & C. Wallat (Eds.), *Ethnography and language in educational settings.* Norwood, N.J.: Ablex, 1981.

Guthrie, G. P. *An ethnography of bilingual education in a Chinese community.* Doctoral dissertation, University of Illinois at Urbana-Champaign, 1982.

Guthrie, G. P., & Hall, W. S. Introduction. In H. Trueba, G. P. Guthrie, & K. Au (Eds.), *Culture and the bilingual classroom: Studies in classroom ethnography.* Rowley, Mass.: Newbury House, 1981.

Guthrie, L. F. *The task variable in children's language use: Cultural and situational differences.* Doctoral dissertation, University of Illinois at Urbana-Champaign, 1981.

Guthrie, L. F., & Hall, W. S. Continuity/discontinuity in the function and use of language. In E. Gordon (Ed.), *Review of research in education* (Vol. 10). Itasca, Ill.: Peacock, 1983.

Hall, W. S., & Guthrie, L. F. Cultural and situational variation in language function and use: Methods and procedures for research. In J. Green & C. Wallat (Eds.), *Ethnography and language in educational settings.* Norwood, N.J.: Ablex, 1981. (a)

Hall, W. S., & Guthrie, L. F. The dialect question and reading. In R. J. Spiro, B. C. Bruce, & W. F. Brewer (Eds.), *Theoretical issues in reading comprehension.* Hillsdale, N.J.: Erlbaum, 1981. (b)

Hart, S. Analyzing the social organization of reading in one elementary school. In G. Spindler (Ed.), *Doing the ethnography of schooling.* New York: Holt, Rinehart & Winston, 1982.

Hymes, D. *Foundations in sociolinguistics.* Philadelphia, Pa.: University of Pennsylvania Press, 1974.

Hymes, D. Ethnographic monitoring. In H. Trueba, G. P. Guthrie, & K. H. Au (Eds.), *Culture and the bilingual classroom: Studies in classroom ethnography.* Rowley, Mass.: Newbury House, 1981.

Jackson, P. *Life in classrooms.* New York: Holt, Rinehart, & Winston, 1968.

Jordan, C., Weisner, T. Tharp, R. G., & Au, K. *A multidisciplinary approach to research in education: The Kamehameha Early Education Program* (Technical Report No. 81). Honolulu: Kamehameha Early Education Program, 1979.

Lutz, F. W. Ethnography—The holistic approach to understanding schooling. In J. Green & C. Wallat (Eds.), *Ethnography and language in educational settings.* Norwood, N.J.: Ablex, 1981.

McDermott, R. P. *Kids make sense: An ethnographic account of the interactional management of success and failure in one first grade classroom.* Doctoral dissertation, Stanford University, Stanford, Calif., 1976.

McDermott, R. P. The ethnography of speaking and reading. In R. Shuy (Ed.), *Linguistic theory: What can it say about reading?* Newark, Del.: International Reading Association, 1977.

Malinowski, B. *Argonauts of the Western Pacific.* New York: Dutton, 1932.

Mehan, H. *Learning lessons.* Cambridge, Mass.: Harvard University Press, 1979.

Mehan, H., & Wood, H. *The reality of ethnomethodology.* New York: Wiley, 1975.

Mehan, H., Hertweck, A., Combs, S. E., & Flynn, P. J. Teachers' interpretations of students' behaviors. In L. C. Wilkinson (Ed.), *Communicating in the classroom.* New York: Academic Press, 1982.

Michaels, S., & Cook-Gumperz, J. A study of sharing time with first grade students: Discourse narratives in the classroom. In *Proceedings of the Berkeley Linguistic Society,* 1979, *5,* 87–103.

Ogbu, J. School ethnography: A multilevel approach. *Anthropology and Educational Quarterly,* 1981, *12,* 3–29.

Pelto, P. J., & Pelto, G. H. Ethnography: The fieldwork enterprise. In J. J. Honighann (Ed.), *Handbook of social and cultural anthropology.* Chicago: Rand McNally, 1973.

Peshkin, A. *Growing up American: Schooling and the survival of a community.* Chicago: University of Chicago Press, 1978.

Piestrup, A. *Black dialect interference and accomodation of reading instruction in first grade.* Berkeley, Calif.: Monographs of the Language Behavior Research Laboratory, 1973.

Rist, R. *The urban school: A factory for failure.* Cambridge, Mass.: MIT Press, 1973.

Rist, R. Blitzkrieg ethnography: On the transformation of a method into a movement. *Educational Researcher,* 1980, *9,* 8–10.

Schatzman, L., & Strauss, A. *Field research strategies for a natural sociology.* Englewood Cliffs, N.J.: Prentice-Hall, 1974.

Smith, L. M., & Geoffrey, W. *The complexities of an urban classroom: An analysis toward a general theory of teaching.* New York: Holt, Rinehart, & Winston, 1968.

Spindler, G. (Ed.). *Doing the ethnography of schooling: Educational anthropology in action.* New York: Holt, Rinehart & Winston, 1982.

Spradley, J. P. *The ethnographic interview.* New York: Holt, Rinehart & Winston, 1979.

Spradley, J. P. *Participant observation.* New York: Holt, Rinehart & Winston, 1980.

Stallings, J. Implementations and child effects of teaching practices in Follow Through classrooms. *Monographs of the Society for Research in Child Development,* 1975, *40,* 50–93.

Tharp, R. G. The effectiveness of comprehension: Results and description of the Kamehameha Early Education Program. *Reading Research Quarterly, 18,* 1982, 503–527.

Trueba, H., Guthrie, G. P., & Au, K. (Eds.). *Culture and the bilingual classroom: Studies in classroom ethnography.* Rowley, Mass.: Newbury House, 1981.

Watson-Gegeo, K., & Boggs, S. T. From verbal play to talk story: The role of routines in speech events among Hawaiian children. In S. Ervin-Tripp & C. Mitchell-Kerman (Eds.), *Child discourse.* New York: Academic Press, 1977.

Wilcox, K.   Ethnography as a methodology and its applications to the study of schooling: A review. In G. Spindler (Ed.), *Doing the ethnography of schooling: Educational anthropology in action.* New York: Holt, Rinehart & Winston, 1982.

Wilkinson, L. C. (Ed.).   *Communicating in the classroom.* New York: Academic Press, 1982.

5 BUILDING AND TESTING MODELS OF READING PROCESSES
EXAMPLES FROM WORD RECOGNITION

Dominic W. Massaro

Theories are nets cast to catch what we call "the world": to rationalize, to explain, and to master it. We endeavor to make the mesh ever finer and finer.

Karl R. Popper, 1959, p. 59

The measure of success in moving toward scientific explanation is the degree to which a theory brings out relationships between otherwise distinct and independent clusters of phenomena.

William K. Estes, 1979, p. 47

In the field of empirical sciences, . . . [the scientist] constructs hypotheses, or systems of theories, and tests them against experience by observation and experiment.

Karl R. Popper, 1959, p. 27

A theory is only overthrown by a better theory, never merely by contradictory facts.

J. B. Conant, 1947, p. 36

. . . To completely analyze what we do when we read would almost be the acme of a psychologist's achievements. . . .

E. B. Huey, 1908, p. 6

Building and testing models of reading processes advance our understanding of what the reader does while reading. We seek to know not only the nature of reading behavior but, more importantly, the internal mental machinery guiding the observable behavior. In this chapter, I discuss the logic of scientific endeavor in reading-related research. In addition, I present specific instances to

Source: The writing of this paper was supported, in part, by funds from the National Institute of Education and the National Institute of Mental Health. I appreciate the comments of Lola L. Lopes and Peter Mosenthal on an earlier version of this chapter.

illustrate some of the methods and techniques involved in the art of model building and testing. Consonant with my research interests and experience, the focus of specific models discussed here is word recognition in reading. The discussion is illustrative of model building and testing in general, however, and ought to apply to other aspects of reading conduct.

Although students of reading are fundamentally concerned with actual reading, seldom is an empirical or theoretical study directly concerned with normal reading. As is common in most areas of scientific endeavor, investigators feel it necessary to abstract for study only one or two components from the phenomenon of interest. The phenomenon of reading is complex in its entirety, and usually little knowledge is gained without some simplification and control in its investigation. Although some influential researchers (e.g., Neisser, 1976) are unhappy with the analysis of specific experimental situations, the most advanced state of the art in reading rests on exactly this kind of analysis (Baron, 1978; Estes, 1978; Gibson & Levin, 1975; LaBerge & Samuels, 1977; Massaro, 1975a, 1978, 1979b).

Given this state of affairs, we are concerned here with models of specific processes that occur in reading, rather than with general viewpoints of normal reading. These models of reading processes are usually developed and tested within the framework of laboratory experiments, and their exact relationship to normal reading is necessarily indirect. I do not mean to free the scientist from justifying a relationship between the simpler laboratory situation and the more complex act of normal reading. External validity, or the generalization from experiment to application, must be of constant concern. As an example, tachistoscopic studies reveal that visual perception during a given eye fixation is limited to a small area around the fixation point (Woodworth, 1938). That this limitation also exists in normal reading has been verified by manipulating the amount of text in view during any fixation in reading continuous text (McConkie & Rayner, 1975). Past experience in both the physical and psychological sciences supports the laboratory approach, although indirect, as the best choice for the researcher and theorist seeking an understanding of what we do when we read.

PSYCHOLOGICAL VERSUS PHYSIOLOGICAL MODELS

We are concerned with model building and testing in the study of psychological processes fundamental to reading. Models in this domain aim at a psychological rather than physiological level of description. Although a psychological model may one day be reduced to a physiological level of description, the psychological level will probably continue to be valuable. A good model enhances our understanding and leads to productive advances in research and practice. A psychological model may be easier to apply to the study of reading because its level of description may be more appropriate for assessment, intervention, and control.

The student may question whether the scientist can achieve a model of psychological processes that is independent of an understanding of the underlying physiological hardware. Consider the arrival on our planet of intelligent machines from outer space, intrigued by these general-purpose computing devices called people. The machines have no knowledge of, or experience with, living organisms.

Our visitors could learn a great deal about how we function without addressing the unique properties of living matter. Their models of our behavior would resemble psychological models. The basic components of the models would involve hypothetical structures and processes that would relate certain observable behaviors to certain environmental situations. We do not doubt that these intelligent machines could develop something of truth in their psychological models. People are relatively good at understanding other people, even without great insights into underlying physiological mechanisms.

A psychological model is analogous to a model of a computer's software programs rather than its physical hardware. A computer can be built with vacuum tubes, magnetic chips, or large-scale integrated circuits. The underlying physical components are largely irrelevant to what programs can or cannot be run on the machine. Therefore, the potential user of the machine benefits more from learning about the machine's programs and how they are implemented than from studying its physical hardware. In some instances the machine's hardware constrains certain programming operations. This is analogous to the limitations in our visual acuity in reading, given the physiological makeup of the visual system. On the other hand, it is not apparent how any knowledge of underlying physiology can address the precise role of speech recoding in reading. Given the current state of the art, psychological models can provide the most valuable insights into reading processes.

SCIENTIFIC FRAMEWORKS

Models are usually developed and tested within general scientific frameworks, whether these frameworks are explicitly defined or only implicitly assumed. One framework for scientific endeavor has been expressed most succinctly by Popper (1959). The central assumption is that model building and testing must follow deductive rather than inductive methods. Following Hume, Popper claims that we are not justified in inferring universal statements from singular ones. Any conclusion drawn inductively may turn out to be false. Although we may have many instances of bright graduate students, this does not justify the conclusion that all graduate students are bright. Therefore the scientist should not try to verify a theory by demonstrating that it works in specific instances. Since new instances can always lead to the rejection of the theory, no experimental observation can verify a theory.

Popper proposes that theories,[1] once constructed, must be subjected to the following analyses: The investigator begins by comparing the conclusions derived from the theory in order to determine whether they are internally consistent. An analysis of the conclusions also indicates whether the theory is testable. By contrasting this theory with other theories, the investigator then determines whether the theory is unique and whether it would constitute a scientific advance if it survived experimental tests. Finally, if the conclusions drawn from the theory meet these requirements, then it is worthwhile to test the theory by subjecting its conclusions to experimental tests.

Experimental tests decide how well the theory survives. If it survives the experimental tests, we should not discard the theory. If experimental tests falsify conclusions drawn from the theory, then the theory should be rejected or modified accordingly. Surviving a particular experimental test only temporarily supports the theory because another investigator may provide a test that overthrows it. A critical feature of Popper's metatheoretical framework for building models is that verifiability and falsifiability of models do not have a symmetrical relationship. Although models can be falsified, they cannot be truly verified. Popper proposes that it is best to conclude that positive results only corroborate a particular theory; they do not verify it.

In a slightly different approach to scientific endeavor, Platt (1964) encourages scientists to employ a strong inference strategy of testing hypotheses. In contrast to generating a particular model, Platt would have the scientist generate multiple hypotheses relevant to a phenomenon of interest. The experimental test would be designed to eliminate (or in Popper's words, falsify) as many hypotheses as possible. The results of the experimentation would allow the generation of new hypotheses, which could be subjected to further tests. Both Platt and Popper adhere to David Hume's axiom prohibiting inductive arguments. The message is that the scientist should not attempt to confirm a single pet hypothesis. Platt's solution seems more productive, however, in that at least one of the multiple hypotheses under test should fail, and therefore the corresponding model can be rejected.

Given some ideal of model building and testing in empirical science, it becomes important to determine our natural disposition in formulating and testing hypotheses. An ingenious experiment carried out by Mynatt, Doherty, and Tweney (1977) was aimed at exactly this question. These researchers created an artificial research environment and allowed college subjects to make preliminary alterations in the environment. After observing the environment, the participants were instructed to formulate a hypothesis to account for the behavior of objects in the environment. The subjects were then given the opportunity to test their hypotheses. One group of subjects was instructed that the job of the scientist was to confirm hypotheses. Another group was told that the job was to disconfirm hypotheses. A third group was given neutral instructions in terms of simply testing hypotheses. Subjects were shown hypothetical environments that would allow tests of their hypotheses. Given a pair of environments, a subject was asked to choose one member of the pair to test the hypothesis. By evaluating these choices against the subject's original hypothesis, the authors determined whether the subjects chose situations to confirm or disconfirm their hypotheses.

Subjects chose a situation to confirm their hypothesis about seven times out of ten, regardless of how they were instructed. These results and other evidence adduced by the authors revealed a strong confirmation bias in this simulated research inquiry. People chose hypothetical situations to confirm their hypothesis and avoided consideration and testing of alternative hypotheses. A second result revealed that subjects faced with disconfirming evidence changed to a new hypothesis. Negative results were usually effective in changing the participant's opinion of the truth of the hypothesis. Although subjects may not seek disconfirmatory evidence, they use it correctly when it is available.

In a second study by the same authors (Mynatt, Doherty, & Tweney, 1978), subjects were faced with a much more complex research environment. Subjects attempted to determine how 27 fixed objects influenced the direction of a moving particle in a two-dimensional display. The objects differed in size, shape, and brightness, and their influence on the particle varied as a function of these dimensions. A confirmation bias was again observed and could not be modified with highly explicit training in strong inference. In contrast to the previous study, subjects often kept or returned to their disconfirmed hypotheses. The more complex environment seemed to limit the generation of new hypotheses, and subjects therefore kept alive the few ideas they had. This is reminiscent of the compulsive gambler's dilemma: "I know the game is crooked, but it's the only game in town." A final result indicated that complete abandonment of a disconfirmed hypothesis also proved unproductive. For example, a general hypothesis of how objects influence particle direction was abandoned when it failed experimental tests. Nevertheless, the principle itself was correct, but only for some of the objects. Accordingly, it can be worthwhile to modify disconfirmed hypotheses based on previous results rather than reject all aspects of the disconfirmed hypothesis.

Continuing their research, Doherty, Mynatt, Tweney, and Schiano (1979) had subjects decide from which of two islands an archeological find had come. Subjects usually asked for information relevant only to their preferred island, not for information relevant to both islands. The requested information was useless because knowing that a characteristic of the found object is representative of one island does not provide information about whether the characteristic is also representative of the other island. This confirmation bias led to an inappropriate confidence in the subject's hypothesis. For example, if the subject believes that the pot with a curved handle comes from one island and then finds out that 80 percent of the pots from that island have curved handles, he or she becomes even more convinced that the pot is from that island. What the subject fails to realize is that pots from the other island may be even more likely to have curved handles.

Although the behavior of subjects who are not scientists in a simulated research environment cannot be generalized to empirical science, the results are illuminating and thought provoking. Interviews with NASA scientists, in fact, reveal a strong confirmation bias (Mitroff, 1974). A scientist tends to view the world in terms of a personal theory; he or she may be the least-equipped person to invent a critical test of the theory. Empirical tests usually turn out to provide results consistent with the theory without really providing a critical test of the theory. Given the conditional statement "If p, then q," where p is a statement concerning one side of a card and q a statement concerning the other side, and the alternatives are p, q, not-p, and not-q, what cards would you turn over to test the hypothesis? Most people choose only "p" or "p and q," when in fact "p and not-q" are the only critical tests of the hypothesis.

Most of the theoretically driven research in reading aims at supporting, not falsifying, theories. Given a natural predisposition for the scientist to verify rather than falsify a pet theory, it is important that the scientific endeavor remain competitive. The competitive dimension is probably as fundamental to the game of scientific endeavor as it is in most games (McCain & Segal, 1973). Scientists are much more willing to falsify other theories while seeking support for their own. If one accepts the ideal of falsifying models, the scientists are usually making most progress when they test someone else's theory, not their own. A model is a good model to the extent that its conclusions are easily tested by other scientists. Experimental tests should not only allow falsification of the model but also should provide clues to building new models if falsification occurs. Of course, these new models must also be easily testable.

Popper's and Platt's framework may be most appropriate for a relatively mature scientific discipline. In an early stage of model development, an empirical scientist may have to be content with a relatively facile acceptance of models or systems from other domains. As an example, Descartes used the machine as an analogue of overt behavior of people; the behavior of a person was viewed as following the same principles as those for machines. Models derived from analogues can be tested to some extent in that conclusions drawn from the analogue can be tested in the system of interest. Using the pump as an analogue for a model of the circulatory system, it is possible to derive certain relationships between pressure and output flow in pumps and test whether this relationship holds in the circulatory system.

Roediger (1980) discusses analogies used for models of memory. As examples, a house, purse, leaky bucket, dictionary, and garbage can serve as analogues of memory processes. A familiar example in cognitive psychology is that of the computing device as a model for some human mental functioning. The computing device can be described in terms of a number of stages beginning with input to the computer, operations on this input with respect to information stored in the memory of the computer, and output of the outcomes of the operations. In order to test whether the computer provides a good analogue to mental functioning, a more specific analogue is necessary to generate testable hypotheses. As an example, one could develop computer programs that carry out specific kinds of memory search and test if any of them describe how humans carry out memory search.

In some situations, an analogue can be shown to produce the same outcome as a human, but with an entirely different set of processes. If this is the case, the analogue is a poor model, even though it makes correct predictions. Work in artificial intelligence has encouraged psychologists to adopt working systems in this area as models of psychological processing. For example, speech-understanding systems have been used to guide the development of a model of reading (Allport, 1977; Rumelhart, 1977). One problem with this artificial system as a model for psychological functioning is that its computing capacity and speed can compensate for the deficiency of certain intelligent processes by sheer processing energy and time. Although an artificial system may be shown to perform some task, such as reading, the critical question is whether the artificial system performs the task in the same way as humans do. This requires the investigator to compare the nature and time course of the internal processes in humans to those of the artificial system. Only if the internal processes are similar can we say that the artificial system is a good model of the human system.

As students of reading processes, we are interested in whether a model holds up to its experimental tests and whether practical applications can be derived from the model. Although the model helps us understand the behavior, we also want it to help us modify it. An obvious example is whether a model proves useful in an assessment of reading skills and the development of reading instruction. A model's adequacy in providing assessment and guiding instruction provides additional tests of the model. If a model assumes that a reader must have some knowledge of spelling constraints (orthographic structure) in order to recognize words for rapid reading, then readers without this knowledge should reveal reading problems. Acquiring this knowledge should lead to rapid reading if no other deficits exist.

The student of reading may not readily discover any consistent approaches to building and testing models in research on reading. The prescriptions of a theory of model building and testing are not always apparent in actual practice. Each substantive area of investigation has a unique history and state of the art; the scientist cannot easily avoid these influences. In this chapter, I discuss model building and testing in four or five substantive areas of reading research. Given the relatively advanced state of the art in letter and word recognition, this domain offers an ideal research environment for the discussion of model building and testing in reading research. My goal is to present to the student some tools for building and testing models in the context of actual investigation. The present framework for research is highly biased, as any informative and internally consistent framework must be. For alternative approaches to the study of reading, the student is referred to Guthrie and Hall and to Kamil in this volume.

Before initiating our discussion of specific models, it is necessary to mention the restricted domain of the models we will discuss. I am using the term *psychological model* to signify a formal description of some psychological phenomenon. In addition, the models to be discussed are concerned with information-processing characteristics of reading: how the reader travels from one state of knowledge to another by way of the printed medium. Unfortunately, there has been very little development of formal models of personality, social, cultural, and affective contributions to reading. Models within the genre of information processing may have *nothing* to say about what or why people read. Motivation, goals, and interests are critical to a complete understanding of reading, as they are in all other aspects of psychological functioning. Our modest, although not easily achieved, goal is to understand perceptual and cognitive functioning unique to reading. After some mastery of this domain, it will be necessary to extend the analysis to include the affective dimensions, accounting for why or what we read.

LETTER RECOGNITION

The role of model building in reading can be illuminated in the substantive area of letter recognition. How does a reader recognize some squiggles on the page as a familiar letter? There have been two basic approaches in building models of letter recognition: templates and features. Palmer (1978) provides an informative analysis of the properties of template and feature theories. He points out that the two theories are not easily distinguished. I believe the important difference between the two theories is their differences in explanatory power. In the template model, the implicit assumption is that letters are essentially Gestalt units that cannot be further analyzed or reduced in terms of other characteristics. Therefore, a sequence of letters in a text would consist of a sequence of indivisible patterns. Visual analysis of these patterns would be limited to some kind of scheme in which the reader would match a series of templates stored in memory with the visual pattern of each letter. A unique template is needed for every unique visual pattern. When a match is found, recognition occurs.

The central criticism of the template matching scheme is that it is very inflexible (Neisser, 1967). Size or orientation differences between the template and the visual pattern will baffle a direct matching between memory templates and visual information. It is possible to develop normalization routines, however, that allow modification of the visual pattern to put it into a format that corresponds more closely to the templates in memory. Given a set of normalization routines, variations in size and orientation are not necessarily an insurmountable obstruction for successful template matching.

A more critical problem with the template matching scheme is a metatheoretical[2] one. The template matching scheme provides little analysis or understanding of the phenomenon of interest. The template matching scheme may be interpreted as nothing more than a restatement of the problem. Although it postulates little theoretical machinery, the template matching scheme has no predictive power; for every item to be recognized, a template must be stored in memory. In order to predict the recognition of 26 letters, a template matching model must assume 26 templates. A good model must predict more than it assumes.

Each template must be considered a free parameter since the template matching model does not predict the nature of the templates. Although the concept of a free parameter is not easily articulated, an example of its use usually provides a sufficient explanation. Every quantitative description of some state of affairs has a set of parameters. As an example, Fechner's (1860/1966) psychophysical law was formulated and expressed as

$$S = K \log_{10} I,$$

where S measures the magnitude of the sensation, I the intensity of the stimulus, and K is a constant of proportionality. In this model, K and I serve as parameters. The stimulus intensity I is directly measurable in that Fechner specified exactly how it should be measured. The value of K cannot be measured directly and therefore is a free parameter. In other words, Fechner's law cannot predict the magnitude of sensation, given the stimulus intensity, until some K value is assumed. In testing the law, the obvious question is what K value should be assumed. The answer is, the K value that optimizes the predictions of the law. Any other value would produce an unfair test of the law because it would always be possible to find a K value that would violate the predicted relationship. More specifically, we want to find the K value that minimizes the differences between the observed and predicted values. For Fechner's law, a simple mathematical solution is possible; for more complicated models, iterative computer routines (e.g., Chandler, 1969) are available.

The predictive power of a model is determined by evaluating how much can be predicted relative to how much has to be assumed. To return to Fechner's law, it cannot be disproven if it is tested at only one stimulus intensity. Regardless of the sensation S, some value of K exists to predict it exactly. This would not be the case with two or more levels of stimulus intensity. To the extent that a single free parameter K can predict the sensation at a large number of stimulus intensities, we gain confidence in the model. If Fechner's law holds for three or four intensity levels, we are somewhat impressed; if it holds across the complete range of audible intensities, we are very impressed. The student should be warned that there is no convenient measure of how well a model describes some set of outcomes relative to the number of free parameters needed to predict those outcomes. It is difficult to choose between two models when the model with the more accurate description also requires more free parameters.

For each unique letter to be recognized in the template matching model, a unique template is assumed, which requires another free parameter. Given this situation, the model has very little predictive value for the phenomenon of interest. One goal of a theory of letter recognition would be to devise a scheme for letter recognition that would allow the recognition of more letters than there are templates. In order to accomplish this, some theoretical process must be formalized to allow letter recognition on the basis of a relatively small amount of memory storage.

One scheme that accomplishes efficient recognition is called feature analysis and was primarily inspired by work in linguistics and artificial intelligence (Jakobson, Fant, & Halle, 1961; Selfridge, 1959). In linguistics Trubetzkoy and his colleagues of the Prague school questioned the idea that spoken language consists of minimal units called phonemes. Phoneme units could not be further divided, and therefore some kind of template matching scheme would be required for their recognition. Trubetzkoy and his colleagues, however, assumed that the phoneme units could be further analyzed in terms of distinctive features that represent similarities and differences with respect to other phonemes. The goal of this theoretical perspective was to analyze all the phonemes of a given language in terms of a small set of distinctive features. To the extent that the number of distinctive features was significantly less than the number of phonemes, the theory would have strong predictive value.

There are two important dimensions of a model of feature analysis of letter recognition. These are the structural aspects and process aspects of the model. Miller and Johnson-Laird (1976) propose that an important psychological problem is to characterize the *contents* of the perceptual world to account for other psychological phenomena. This problem would be addressed by the structural dimension of a model. Essentially, the world of experience is characterized in terms of variations in the stimulus world. In terms of a model of letter recognition, the goal would be to determine which characteristics of written letters are important in their recognition. The process component of a model is an attempt to account for the *generation* of the perceptual world, rather than the specific contents of the perceptual world. In this case, the emphasis would be, not on the characteristics of the letters that are critical for letter recognition, but on how the perceived characteristics are evaluated and integrated together in order to arrive at letter recognition. The goal would be to articulate rules for combining the perceived characteristics to produce the desired psychological outcome. Both the contents and the generation of the perceptual experience are important issues for a theory of letter recognition. A review of the visual features used in letter recognition and the processes involved is given by Massaro and Schmuller (1975). More recent work in this area can be found in Oden (1979), Naus and Shillman (1976), and Massaro (1979b).

WORD RECOGNITION

Disagreements in scientific endeavor prove productive if the researchers follow Platt's advice and test between opposing views. One question debated since the inception of reading-related research (Cattell, 1886; Gibson & Levin, 1975; Huey, 1908/1968; Massaro, 1975b) is to what extent word perception[3] is mediated by letter perception. According to one view, word perception follows naturally from perception of the letters in the word and the appropriate knowledge in the mind of the reader. The opposing view claims that a word is perceived as a unique configuration. These two theories have at various times served as the basis for the phonics and sight-word methods of reading instruction (Chall, 1967; Smith, 1971).

How does the scientist proceed to test between these views? First, each view must be explicitly developed in the form of a specific model. It is not possible to test between the two general statements given in the preceding paragraph, and therefore these statements must be transformed into specific models. Given a specific model, conclusions can be derived and can be checked for internal consistency and the possibility of being tested. The models derived from the different views should be contrasted to see if the conclusions are significantly different from one another. In many cases, two apparently discrepant views are transformed into very similar models when they are precisely formulated. If the two models make opposing conclusions, the scientist should still evaluate whether the conclusions are worth testing in terms of what knowledge would be gained. If the answer is positive, the researcher faces the challenge of mapping these conclusions into an experimental test.

I followed the above procedure in testing between the two theories of word perception (Massaro, 1979a). The theories were explicitly developed in a generally accepted view of word perception in reading. In this view, a printed pattern is first transduced by the visual receptor system, and featural analysis makes available a set of visual features. The word-perception process combines this visual information with other nonvisual knowledge and arrives at a perceptual experience of the printed pattern. The two theories seemed to differ in terms of whether or not the feature analysis of each letter is independent of the orthographic context imposed by the surrounding letters. If letters mediate word perception, feature analysis of the letters should not be modified by orthographic context. If a word is a unique configuration, feature analysis should be modified by orthographic context. A critical test between the two classes of models, therefore, could ask whether orthographic context influences feature analysis. The first theory says that orthographic context and featural analysis are independent; the second theory says that they are not. These will be referred to as independence and nonindependence theories.

Current models of word recognition were classified in terms of whether featural analysis and orthographic structure make independent contributions to letter perception. Consistent with the advice of Broadbent (1973), the goal of the experiment was to obtain results that would be probable under one class of models and improbable under the other class of models. The contrasting theories can be clarified by an analysis of recent formulations of specific models. Nonindependence views have taken the form of feature-analysis differences, higher-order units, and hypothesis-testing mechanisms.

A letter in a word is recognized more often than a letter presented alone or presented in a nonword under the same conditions (Johnston & McClelland, 1973; Reicher, 1969; Thompson & Massaro, 1973). This result obtains even when a simple guessing advantage for words is precluded by constraining the response alternatives. One of the primary interpretations of these findings is that the word context enhances the visual feature analysis of the component letters. If feature analysis were a limited-capacity process and subject to attentional control, then it might be expected that the familiarity of a word pattern would produce better feature analyses of the component letters. After an exhaustive and careful review of the literature, Krueger allows the possibility that the familiarity of orthographic context might influence the feature-analysis stage (Krueger, 1975, Table 1). According to this interpretation, readers would have a greater number of features and/or a better resolution of the features in a word than in a nonword context. This would mean that readers should be able to report more accurate detail about the visual characteristics of the letters in a word than in a nonword context.

In the second kind of nonindependence models, higher-order units intervene in the processing sequence and change the features and/or featural analyses employed. As an example, some models assume specific memory codes for spelling-pattern units, and some visual features are defined in terms of these higher-order units (Juola, Leavitt, & Choe, 1974; LaBerge & Samuels, 1974; Neisser, 1967; Smith & Haviland, 1972; Taylor, Miller, & Juola, 1977; Wheeler, 1970). As an example, the frequent spelling pattern *st* could function as a perceptual unit, and the top extent of the *s* and the horizontal cross of the *t* might function as a single supraletter feature. In this case, perception of the spelling pattern *st* might be easier than perception of either letter presented alone, since the presence of supraletter features gives the reader additional visual information (Wheeler, 1970).

In contrast to assuming a facilitative effect of higher-order units, other models in this set assume that word context can override the perception of the letters that make it up. In Johnson's (1975) model, for example, the feature set assigned to a letter sequence is determined by the entire sequence and higher-order memorial feature sets. In this case, a letter is assigned different features in different orthographic contexts. Johnson's model makes the prediction that the higher-order memorial feature sets camouflage the component letters and that therefore readers may know less about the visual characteristics of a particular letter in a word than that same letter presented alone or in a nonword string.

A final class of nonindependence models assumes that expectancy and hypothesis testing play an important role in the initial stage of visual analyses. In hypothesis-testing models, the current hypothesis directs feature analysis (Goodman, 1976a, 1976b; Wheeler, 1970). In the hierarchical feature-testing model of Wheeler (1970), for example, the detection of some features guides the detection of other features. Osgood and Hoosain (1974) have also made this kind of nonindependence assumption in their view of word perception. Their specific idea of nonindependence involves the derivation of the meaning of the word to feed back and influence the information passed on by peripheral sensory processes (feature detection in the present framework). This assumption is similar to an observing response model (Broadbent, 1967) in which the feature detection is biased by context and the solution given by Erdelyi (1974) for findings in the perceptual defense literature. The distinguishing attribute of this class of models is that feature processing is directly dependent on the guiding hypothesis; for example, a hypothesis that the word is *Philadelphia* might guide the feature analysis to test for an initial capital letter and a relatively long word. Accordingly, the visual features passed on by feature analysis vary as a function of the guiding hypothesis. The reader should know more about the visual characteristics of the segment of word that are relevant to the current hypothesis and less about the visual characteristics that are not relevant.

The current analysis makes transparent that nonindependence views of reading do not make the same predictions about how visual feature analysis is modified by orthographic context. However, in contrast to independence models, all nonindependence models assume that orthographic context changes the visual information passed on by feature analysis to the next stage of word recognition process.

Independence models follow in the tradition of Morton's (1969) logogen model in which higher-order context and visual information provide independent contributions to word recognition. Broadbent's (1971) model of the biasing effects of context and probability also qualifies as an independence model, since changes in these variables do not modify the intake of visual information. Although the issue of orthographic context was not addressed in these models, another independence model has been articulated in terms of word recognition as a direct consequence of featural information and orthographic context (Massaro, 1973, 1975a; Thompson & Massaro, 1973). The model was developed on the basis of experiments carried out using variants of the Reicher paradigm (Reicher, 1969; Wheeler, 1970). Subjects were presented with either a word or a single letter for a short duration, followed immediately by a masking stimulus and two response alternatives. The response alternatives would both spell words in the word condition; for example, given the test word *WORD*, the response alternatives -*D* and -*K* would be presented. The corresponding letter condition would be the test letter *D* followed by the response alternatives *D* and *K*. Performance was about 10 percent better in the word than in the single-letter condition.

Given the two-alternative forced-choice control, it was argued that the reader was able to utilize orthographic context to eliminate possible alternatives during the perception of the test display before the onset of the masking stimulus (Thompson & Massaro, 1973). As an example, given recognition of the context *WOR* and a curvilinear segment of the final letter, the reader could narrow down the alternatives for the final letter to *D*, *O*, and *Q*. Given that *O* and *Q* are orthographically illegal in the context *WOR-*, the letter *D* represents an unambiguous choice. The reader will therefore perceive the word *WORD* given just partial information about the final letter. If the reader has recognized the same curvilinear segment in the corresponding letter condition, however, any of the three letters (*D, O,* and *Q*) are still possible, and the perceptual synthesis will result in *D* only one out of three times. What is critical in this analysis is that a word advantage is obtained even though the visual information available to the perceptual process is equivalent in the word and letter conditions. The orthographic context of the word simply provides an additional but independent source of information. The featural information available to the recognition process does not change with changes in orthographic context. In this view, although orthographic context facilitates word perception, it does not modify the feature analysis of the printed pattern.

An experiment was carried out to test between the two general classes of nonindependence and independence models. The logic of the experiment to test between these two theories centered on the question whether context and featural processing make independent contributions to letter perception. The experiment involved the independent variation of the visual information about a letter and its orthographic context in a letter perception task. Consider the lowercase letters *c* and *e*. It is possible to gradually transform the *c* into an *e* by extending the horizontal bar. To the extent the bar is long, the letter resembles *e* and not *c*. If the letter is now presented as the first letter in the context *-oin*, the context would support *c* but not *e*. Only *c* is orthographically legal in this context because three consecutive vowels would violate English orthography. This condition is defined as *e* illegal and *c* legal ($\bar{e} \wedge c$). Only *e* is valid in the context *-dit* since the cluster *cd* is an invalid initial pattern in English. In this case, the context *-dit* favors *e* ($e \wedge \bar{c}$). The contexts *-tso* and *-ast* can be considered to favor neither *e* nor *c*. The first remains an illegal context whether *e* or *c* is present ($\bar{e} \wedge \bar{c}$), and the second is orthographically legal for both *e* and *c* ($e \wedge c$).

The experiment factorially combined six levels of visual information with these four levels of orthographic context, giving a total of 24 experimental conditions. The bar length of the letter took on six values going from a prototypical *c* to a prototypical *e*, as shown in Figure 5.1. In addition, the figure shows that the test letter was also presented at each of the four letter positions in each of the four contexts. A single test string was presented for a short duration, followed after some short interval by a masking stimulus composed of random letter features. In all cases, the subject indicated whether an *e* or *c* was presented in the test string.

Nonindependence theory assumes that featural processing is dependent on context. One direct measure of featural processing in the present experiment is the degree to which the reader can discriminate the bar length of the test letter. This discrimination can be indexed in the present experiment by the degree of differential responding to the successive levels of the bar length of the test letter. Better featural processing of the test letter is assumed to occur to the extent the subject responds *e* to one length and *c* to another. In the ($e \wedge c$) context, both letters spell words, whereas neither letter spells a word in the ($\bar{e} \wedge \bar{c}$) context. If the word context influences featural processing, as assumed by nonindependence theory, then the discrimination of bar length should differ in word and nonword contexts. If it does not, this would provide

```
cdit scll slcd panc          cast scar duct talc
cdit scll slcd panc          cast scar duct talc
cdit scll slcd panc          cast scar duct talc
edit scll slcd panc          cast scar duct talc
edit sell sled pane          east sear duet tale
edit sell sled pane          east sear duet tale
```

```
coin scum pack zinc          ctsa acsr dtcu tlac
coin scum pack zinc          ctsa acsr dtcu tlac
coin scum pack zinc          ctsa acsr dtcu tlac
eoin scum pack zinc          ctsa acsr dtcu tlac
eoin scum paek zine          etsa aesr dteu tlae
eoin scum paek zine          etsa aesr dteu tlae
```

FIGURE 5.1 The 96 test items generated by the factorial combination of six bar lengths of the test letter, four serial positions of the test letter, and four orthographic contexts. (*After Massaro, 1979a.*)

a critical failure of nonindependence theory. The results indicated that context did not influence the discrimination of bar length, a critical failure of the nonindependence theory (Massaro, 1979a).

A qualitative test of the independence model was not available, and it was necessary to develop the model quantitatively. I now describe the quantitative model and how it was tested. In the experimental task, two independent sources of information are available: the visual information from the critical letter and the orthographic context. The first source of information can be represented by V_i where the subscript i indicates that V_i changes only with bar length. For the *e-c* identification, V_i specifies how much *e*-ness is given by the critical letter. This value lies between zero and one and is expected to increase as the length of the bar is increased. With these two letter alternatives it is reasonable to assume the visual information supporting *c* is simply one minus the amount of *e*-ness given by that same source. Therefore, if V_i specifies the amount of *e*-ness given by the test letter, then $(1 - V_i)$ specifies the amount of *c*-ness given by that same test letter.

The orthographic context provides independent evidence for *e* and *c*. The value C_j represents how much the context supports the letter *e*. The subscript *j* indicates that C_j changes only with changes in orthographic context. The value of C_j lies between zero and one and should be large when e is legal and small when e is illegal. The degree to which the orthographic context supports the letter c is indexed by D_j and is independent of the value of C_j. The value of D_j also lies between zero and one and should be large when c is legal and small when c is illegal.

Faced with two independent sources of information, the reader evaluates the amount of e-ness and c-ness from these two sources. The amount of e-ness and c-ness for a given test display can therefore be represented by the conjunction of the two independent sources of information:

$$e\text{-ness} = (V_1 \wedge C_j) \tag{1}$$

$$c\text{-ness} = ((1 - V_i) \wedge (D_j)). \tag{2}$$

The e-ness and c-ness values given by both sources can be determined once conjunction is defined. Research in other domains has shown that a multiplicative combination provides a much better description than an additive combination (Massaro & Cohen, 1976; Oden, 1979; Oden & Massaro, 1978). Applying the multiplicative combination, Equations (1) and (2) are represented as:

$$e\text{-ness} = V_i \times C_j \tag{3}$$

$$c\text{-ness} = (1 - V_i) \times (D_j). \tag{4}$$

A response is based on the e-ness and c-ness values: a choice of e is assumed to be made by evaluating the degree of e-ness relative to the sum of e-ness and c-ness values. This choice rule is a direct application of Luce's (1959) choice axiom. The probability of an e response, $P(e)$, is expressed as

$$P(e) = \frac{V_i C_j}{V_i C_j + (1 - V_i)(D_j)}. \tag{5}$$

To derive $P(e)$ for the four orthographic contexts, the central assumption about context is that a given alternative is supported to the degree x by a legal context and to the degree y by a illegal context, where $1 \geq x \geq y \geq 0$. The values x and y do not have subscripts since they depend only on the legality of the context. Therefore, C_j is equal to x when e is legal in a particular context and equal to y when e is illegal. Analogously, D_j is equal to x when c is legal in a particular context and equal to y when c is illegal.

Given the context with e legal and c illegal,

$$(e \wedge \bar{c}): P(e) = \frac{V_i x}{V_i x + (1 - V_i) y} \tag{6}$$

since the e-ness is given by $V_i x$ and the c-ness by $(1 - V_i)y$. Analogous expressions for the other three contexts are

$$(e \wedge c): P(e) = \frac{V_i x}{V_i x + (1 - V_i) x} = V_i \tag{7}$$

$$(e \wedge \bar{c}): P(e) = \frac{V_i x}{V_i x + (1 - V_i)y} \tag{8}$$

$$(\bar{e} \wedge c): P(e) = \frac{V_i y}{V_i y + (1 - V_i)x} . \tag{9}$$

Equations (6) and (9) predict an effect of context to the extent a legal context gives more evidence for a particular test letter than does an illegal context (i.e., to the extent $x > y$). A second feature of this model is that $P(e)$ is entirely determined by the visual information when the context supports both or neither of the test alternatives; Equations (7) and (8) both predict $P(e) = V_i$.

This form of the independence model was tested against the observed results. Figure 5.2 gives the observed and predicted values. The results showed large effects of bar length and orthographic context on the identification of the

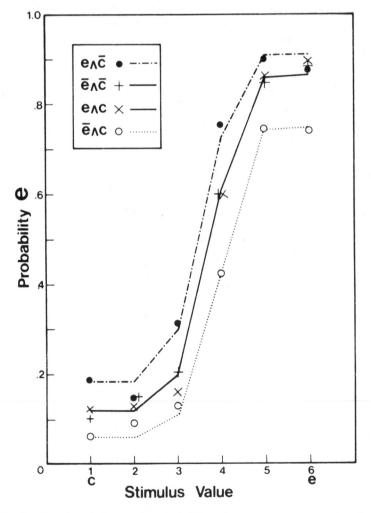

FIGURE 5.2   Predicted and observed probabilities of an e response as a function of orthographic context and stimulus value.

test letter. In order to fit the model to the data, it was necessary to estimate six values of V_i for each level of bar length of the critical letter and an x value for a legal context and a y value for an illegal context. The parameter values were estimated using the iterative routine STEPIT by minimizing the deviations between predicted and observed values (Chandler, 1969).

The model provided a good description of the results, considering that 24 independent observations are predicted with eight free parameters. In addition, the parameter estimates are psychologically meaningful. The value of V_i increased with increases in the length of the bar of the critical letter. The values were .11, .11, .19, .60, .85, and .86 for the six levels. The value of x was .76 for legal context, and the value of y was .40 for the illegal context.

Following the caveat of Hume, Popper, and Platt, the results do not verify the independence model; they simply corroborate it. Nevertheless, these results were sufficient to falsify the predictions of nonindependence theories. The proper conclusion is that there is no evidence to reject the idea of the independence of visual information and orthographic context in word perception in reading. Some theorists may not want to abandon the nonindependence view because of this single failure to find a difference where one should have occurred. The theorist may want to interpret the negative result as a sampling error; the null result could have been due to sampling variability overwhelming the underlying difference between the experimental conditions. This view is difficult to defend because there were large and systematic effects of the independent variables in the experiment. In addition, identical results were obtained with another stimulus set of items. The nonindependence theorist may also argue that the experimental test is irrelevant since its method and procedure placed it outside the domain of the theory. Some justification for this interpretation would be necessary if it is to be taken seriously. As with most experiments, however, certain deficiencies may be discovered and additional research will be necessary to resolve the issue. The ideal of a critical experiment may not be obtainable, and we may have to be content with the gradual accumulation of knowledge in scientific endeavors. Hence the need for highly energetic and persevering researchers.

TEMPORAL COURSE OF READING

A concept central to models of reading processes is time. Reading is an event over time, and any model of reading processes must include time as a dimension of empirical and theoretical analysis. It follows that the time taken by certain reading tasks becomes a crucial dependent measure for students of reading. In addition, it was discovered that the early stages of visual information processing in reading could be terminated at various times after their initiation. In this situation, performance accuracy could be used to index the processing activity up to its termination. The first paradigm is called a reaction-time task and the second is called backward recognition masking.

Reaction Time

The goal is to build models of performance in these tasks while making the critical assumption of a correspondence between some processes in the task and processes occurring in natural reading. Reaction-time research is carried out in a relatively intuitive theoretical framework. The framework was first articulated over a hundred years ago by Donders, a Dutch scientist best known for his work in ophthalmology. Donders (1868–1869/1969) assumed that a simple performance task involved a strict sequence of processes between the presentation of some stimulus event and the initiation of some response on the part of the observer. Donders developed a theoretical and methodological paradigm in order to measure the time of these intervening processes. Donders took issue with the then commonly accepted notion that responses to stimuli were infinitely short. He cited Helmholtz's work, which allowed the measurement of the time between the presentation of some stimulus on the skin and an involuntary reflex to that stimulus. Donders reasoned that it would be possible to devise two experimental situations in which the processing required would be very similar, except that one additional process would be required in one experimental situation relative to the other. The additional time required by the task with the additional process would be the time taken by the additional process. This was called the subtractive method.

One of the first questions to be addressed was the time taken to recognize a stimulus. Donders developed two tasks to study the time for recognition. In the first task, the subject was required to make a predetermined response whenever any visual stimulus was presented. The second task required the subject to make the same predetermined response only when a *particular* visual stimulus was presented. Donders reasoned that the subject would simply have to detect the presence of a visual stimulus before initiation of the response in the first task, whereas the stimulus would also have to be recognized as the appropriate alternative before initiation of the response in the second task. Since Donders believed that if all other aspects of the task were held constant, such as the response required, then the difference in reaction times between the two tasks should be a pure measure of the recognition time of the stimulus as the appropriate alternative. Donders's results were very promising in that he observed that recognition time was on the order of one-twentieth of a second. Therefore, the results of the experiment tended to support both the general framework of the subtractive method for measuring the time for mental events and provided specific information about the time taken for recognition.

Donders and others extended this subtractive method to a variety of experimental conditions and provided quantitative measures of such mental processes as recognition, discrimination, and response selection.

Donders's tasks did not go unchallenged. A number of investigators at the turn of the century criticized the central assumption made in the subtractive method. They argued that the assumption that one mental process can be added to a task without affecting the time to complete other mental processes was not valid. Changing the task to add a single stage probably affected the time it took for other stages. These critics did not provide any evidence supporting this criticism but simply relied on the introspective reports of their observers. Although the criticism was without empirical foundation, investigators lost interest in Donders's subtractive method as a tool for studying mental processes.

Other research could have also contributed to the downfall of the subtractive method. A century ago, James McKeen Cattell reported a series of experiments that created difficulty for the idea of completely successive mental processes.

Of particular interest to us are Cattell's studies of the processing stages in reading. The subjects in Cattell's (1886, 1888/1947) experiment included Cattell himself, George Stanley Hall, John Dewey, and Joseph Jastrow—a pretty impressive bunch of readers. Cattell modified Donders's recognition task to make it continuous. Letters were printed on a rotating cylinder that could be viewed through a slit. The size of the slit and the speed of rotation of the cylinder could be varied. The task of the subject was to name the letters, one by one, as they were exposed in the slit. The main independent variable was the size of the slit. The dependent variable was the rotation speed of the cylinder required by the subject to manage the task without error. If the window allowed only one letter at a time to be exposed, subjects required 360 milliseconds (msec) per letter in order to perform the naming task. On the other hand, by increasing the size of the window to expose more than one letter, the time needed per letter decreased from 360 to 225 msec with increases between one and four letters. Further increases beyond four letters did not speed up the task.

Cattell used these results to argue against the strict sequence of intervening processes assumed by Donders. If processing was purely sequential in that the naming of the second letter could not begin until the naming of the preceding letter was completed, then increasing the size of the window to expose more letters should have made no difference. The fact that increasing the size of the window did facilitate performance provides evidence for overlapping psychological processes. The processing of a second letter can begin while the first is still being processed.

Although Cattell did not analyze his result in the framework of a formal model, three interpretations can be formalized. First, Donders's sequential model may still be correct in terms of the processing of any single letter, but the processing of the second letter can begin before the processing of the preceding letter can be completed. That is, it could be the case that the subject, having recognized the first letter, and beginning to select the response to the first letter, can proceed to recognize the second letter, even though the response selection stage is not completed. Therefore, with respect to any given letter, Donders's sequential stage is valid but there is an overlapping of processes for the different letters.

A second explanation of Cattell's results is that the subject did not process the letters in a completely serial manner. Two or more letters could be recognized in parallel or simultaneously. Similarly, the response selection could occur in parallel for two or more letters. Both explanations do not necessarily invalidate Donders's sequential model but simply show that the unit of analysis at each stage is not necessarily the single letter. Although subjects can process two or more letters simultaneously, it does not invalidate Donders's assumption that response selection cannot begin until recognition is completed.

A third example rejects the notion that response selection does not begin until recognition is complete. Partial recognition of the first letter could allow some response selection to take place. As an example, subjects may recognize the first letter as one of five alternatives and pass this information on to the response selection stage. The response selection stage could then proceed to make these five letters available, waiting for additional information from the recognition stage.

Donders's subtractive method was revived a century later by Sternberg's modification and formal development of the additive-factor method (Sternberg,

1969a, 1969b). The additive-factor method is a powerful tool for studying models of reading processes. Other developments (e.g., McClelland, 1979) even permit a formal analysis of the reaction-time results when the intervening processes are not perfectly sequential but overlap in time. Research and model testing using the additive-factor method can be found in Massaro (1975a), Meyer, Schvaneveldt, and Ruddy (1975), and Theios (1975). The value of breaking down reaction times into times for separate psychological processes is illustrated in the discussion of building and testing models of phonological mediation in reading.

Backward Recognition Masking

Work in backward recognition masking began about the same time as Donders's work using the reaction-time paradigm. Baxt, in 1871, was interested in the time required to recognize letters. Baxt (cited in Sperling, 1963) did not have the distinguished subjects available to Cattell, so he used himself. He presented himself with a display containing a number of letters for a very short duration of about five msec. The display of letters was followed by a bright light flash. Baxt assumed that the bright light flash would terminate any further processing of the letters. The dependent measure in the task was the number of letters that could be seen as a function of the time between the presentation of the display and the presentation of the bright light. Baxt apparently could see one additional letter for every additional ten msec of time between the display and the bright flash. Therefore, he estimated recognition time for each letter as ten msec.

Sperling (1963) set out to replicate these results. Rather than use a bright light as a means of terminating processing of the letters, Sperling used a noise field, which was a series of random bits of letters. However, instead of presenting the display for a fixed duration and varying the blank interval between the display and the noise mask, the display remained on during the interval before the onset of the noise mask. Sperling replicated Baxt's results exactly. For every increase in presentation time of ten msec, Sperling's subjects were able to read out an additional letter. Maximum performance, of course, was only about four or five letters because of what would be expected from a short-term memory limitation. Sperling's results rest on the assumption that the noise mask terminated further processing of the test display. Given the short interval between the test display and the noise mask, however, it is possible that the two stimuli were visually integrated, and the subject was actually perceiving the letters after the noise mask was presented. More recent experiments have shown that this is probably the case (Eriksen & Eriksen, 1971). Therefore, Baxt's experiment and Sperling's experiment do not necessarily provide information about the time it takes to recognize letters.

Although these experiments are problematic, experimental situations can be designed so that backward masking can provide information about the temporal course of letter and word recognition. The paradigm also allows a more direct assessment of the dynamic utilization of orthographic context by the reader. A couple of studies have looked at the perceptual advantage of words over single letters in the Reicher (1969) task. On each trial, either a single letter or a complete word is presented. On both kinds of trials, a pair of one-letter alternatives is presented, one of which had appeared in the original stimulus. The subject's task is to state which of the two letters had appeared. For example, on word trials the subject might be presented with the word *WORD* for a very brief time. When the task was to name the fourth letter of the word, the alternatives *D* and *K* would be presented above the former location of the fourth letter. The subject would have to choose from one of these two alternatives. On single-letter trials, the letter *D* might be presented, and the subject would have to choose between the alternatives *D* and *K*. Reicher (1969) and Wheeler (1970) found that performance was about 10 percent more accurate for words than for single letters.

Johnston and McClelland (1973) discovered that the word-letter difference was a function of the masking condition and, therefore, the processing time available. Three kinds of visual displays were tested: word, single letter, and a single letter embedded in a nonalphabetic symbol, #. In one experiment the test stimulus was followed immediately by a pattern mask. The test stimulus was presented at a high figure-ground contrast so that a relatively clear image was seen for a short period. As discussed earlier and in Massaro (1975b), the pattern mask interferes with any further processing of the test stimulus. Words were recognized 14 percent better than single letters and single letters embedded in # symbols. Performance did not differ for the two kinds of single-letter trials. In a second experiment the test stimulus was presented at a lower luminance and was followed by a plain white field of the same luminance as the test field. In this case, the white field would not interfere with the image of the test stimulus, and the subject would see a fuzzy image for a relatively long period. Single letters were now recognized as well as words, and these displays were recognized 8 percent better than the letters embedded in # symbols.

Johnston and McClelland (1973) proposed three alternative interpretations for the results. First, different systems could be responsible for processing letters and words. More specifically, it could be the case that letters in a word are protected from the detrimental effects of the pattern mask. With reference to our previous discussion of the use of analogy in model building, an analogue for this explanation came from the literature attempting to show that speech is not processed by the same mechanisms used to process nonspeech sounds (Liberman, Cooper, Shankweiler, & Studdert-Kennedy, 1967). A second interpretation of the results is based on the process of lateral masking, which is a degradation of perception of a letter caused by the adjacent contours of surrounding letters. If the same neural mechanism were responsible for backward masking and lateral masking, then the interference might follow a law of diminishing returns. This means that less lateral masking would be observed in the pattern-mask condition than in the white-field condition. Lateral masking would be responsible for the elimination of the word advantage in the white-field condition. This explanation accounts only for the differences in the word advantage between the two masking conditions; it does not account for the word advantage itself. The third explanation is that letters in words are processed faster than letters presented alone or in # symbols. The word advantage occurs when processing time is limited with the pattern mask, but not when there is no limit on processing time in the white-field masking condition.

Johnston and McClelland (1973) evaluated the differences between a pattern mask and essentially a no-mask condition. The white field following the display does not mask or terminate perceptual processing. To evaluate the effect of pattern masking on the word advantage, it is important to assess performance continuously during the temporal course of letter recognition. Therefore it is necessary to vary systematically the interval between the test and masking stimuli in the recognition task. Following this logic, Massaro and Klitzke (1979) replicated and extended Johnston and McClelland's (1973) study in order to assess how the contribution of orthographic context varies with the pattern masking interval. Letter, letter embedded in $'s, word, and nonword test displays were presented in Reicher-Wheeler task in a backward recognition masking experiment. The masking stimulus followed the test display after a variable silent interval, and on some trials no mask was presented.

The results revealed highly systematic effects of the test displays and the masking interval. For all test conditions, performance improved systematically with increases in the interval between the test and mask displays. What is of interest is the rate of improvement with increases in masking interval for each of the test displays. There was no difference between the nonwords and the letters embedded in $'s, and these will be referred to simply as nonword displays. However, rate of improvement is a theoretical construct and must be defined explicitly with a particular model of performance. For their model, Massaro and Klitzke used a model that had proved successful in a variety of other domains (Massaro, 1970, 1975a).

In this model, the quantitative formulation of the time course of recognition describes the temporal course of letter perception by the simple equation

$$d' = \alpha(1 - e^{-\theta t}), \tag{10}$$

where d' represents the perceptibility of the letter in z units, α represents maximal perceptibility with unlimited processing time, t is the processing time measured from the onset of the test stimulus to the onset of a masking stimulus, θ is the rate of processing, and e is the natural logarithm. Perceptibility is assumed to be a negatively accelerating growth function of the processing time available. The value α is dependent on the properties of the visual display and the acuity of the visual system. If the perceptibility of a letter is lowered by the lateral masking of a neighboring letter, this should result in a lower value of α. The value of θ reflects the rate of perceptual processing—how quickly primary recognition occurs. The value of θ can be expected to be dependent upon process variables such as selective attention to a particular letter (Lupker & Massaro, 1979) and the degree to which the reader utilizes orthographic context to recognize a test letter.

The primary support for this description of the temporal course of letter recognition comes from backward recognition masking experiments. In this task, a target stimulus is presented for a short duration and is followed after some blank interval by a masking stimulus superimposed at the same location as the target. The basic finding is that recognition of the target improves with increases in the blank interval before the onset of the mask. Before applying the model to the issue of letter and word recognition, some clarification of backward masking is necessary. There seems to be a general misunderstanding of what backward masking does and how it is interpreted in serial-stage models of information processing. One common misinterpretation is that a backward mask somehow works retroactively; it eliminates all perceptual information about the visual display. Thus, unless subjects manage to encode the display into abstract representation, they will not be able to report anything about what was presented. In the present view of backward masking, however, the mask simply terminates any further perceptual resolution; the resolution that occurs before the mask is presented is continuously passed on to the next stage. This information is not eliminated by the mask, although the mask may also function to interfere with the information at this level (Kallman & Massaro, 1979; Massaro, 1975a, Chapter 24). The gradual improvement in performance with increases in the masking interval reflects the continuous perceptual resolution before the mask is presented.

Massaro and Klitzke (1979) used the model of processing described by Equation (10) to predict systematic changes in the contribution of orthographic context with processing time in the backward recognition masking task. Two relevant factors in single-letter and nonword perception are assumed to operate identically in word perception. They are (1) the processing time available between the onset of a test letter and the onset of a masking stimulus and (2) the lateral masking of the perceptibility of a letter by its neighboring letters. In the model, lateral masking and orthographic context are identified with different parameters in Equation (10), describing performance as a function of processing time t. Adjacent letters that degrade the perceptibility of a neighboring letter should influence the α value for that letter. Adjacent letters that reduce the uncertainty of a given letter should increase θ, the rate of processing the information in that letter.

It is important to consider how orthographic context functions to reduce the uncertainty of a given letter and modify the rate of processing of that letter. Consider the case in which the single letter c is presented. Perceptual resolution of the letter is assumed to be a temporally extended and continuous process. As an example, when $t = 100$ msec, the letter may be resolved sufficiently to reduce the alternatives to c, e, and o; 200 msec might be needed to completely resolve the letter c. In the word test condition, the letter c may be presented in the context *coin*. In this case, because of lateral masking, c may not be resolved completely but may be seen at only 90 percent clarity even with unlimited processing time. Hence the α value for c would be lower in the word than in the single-letter condition. But the word context should also enhance the rate of processing the information in the letter c. If the context *-oin* is resolved completely and the alternatives for the first letter are limited to c, e, and o, no further visual processing is necessary given this visual information and the orthographic regularity of the written language. The strings *eoin* and *ooin* are illegal in the context *-oin*. Therefore, c is the only valid alternative for the first letter. Given limited visual information, c can be recognized exactly in the word context. When c is presented as a single letter, complete visual information is necessary for correct recognition.

The operation of lateral masking and the utilization of orthographic context leads to an expected interaction between the letter and word conditions and the processing time available. When processing time is maximal, rate of processing is unimportant, and the letter condition should show an advantage because the perceptibility of a letter in a word is reduced by lateral masking. With intermediate processing times, the advantage of orthographic context in the word condition should enhance the rate of processing of the test letter and therefore offset the deficit of lateral masking.

This model makes certain predictions for the Massaro and Klitzke experiment. First, performance on nonwords should be equivalent to that on letters in dollar signs at all masking intervals. Both have the disadvantage of lateral masking, and both possess no orthographic context. Second, letters in words should be recognized at a faster rate than letters in nonwords. Third, with very long processing times, single letters should be better recognized than letters in words because of the lateral masking in word strings. Fourth, and most important, the model also predicts that the disadvantage of lateral masking in words relative to single letters (different α's) can be overridden at the shorter masking intervals by the faster rate of processing letters in words (different θ's) because of the utilization of orthographic context.

The results of critical interest are the masking functions for each of the test strings. Since the model predicts d' values, it was necessary to compute observed d' values for the letter, word, and nonword conditions as a function of stimulus onset asynchrony, the time between the onset of the test display and the onset of the masking stimulus. The nonword and the letter-in-$ conditions were also averaged before the d' values were computed, since there was no significant difference between these conditions. The d' values were computed from the average percentage correct values. In this analysis, the hit rates correspond to the percentage correct values and one minus these values are the false alarm rates.

Figure 5.3 plots the observed d' values as a function of orthographic context and the stimulus onset asynchrony. A monotonic masking function was observed for each context condition, and the functions seem to rise at different rates and to different asymptotes in the different conditions. Although the perceptibility of a letter in a word is greater than a letter presented alone at short processing times, the opposite is the case for long processing times. This interaction is exactly what is predicted by the present formulation. In terms of the model, α should be larger for single letters than for words or nonwords because of the reduced signal-to-noise ratio due to the lateral masking of adjacent letters in the word and nonword conditions. The rate parameter θ, however, should be larger for words than for single letters or nonwords because orthographic constraints allow the reader to arrive at a decision about which letters are present at a faster rate in the word condition than in the single-letter condition. The clarity of the features for a letter in a word is less for a letter presented alone, but fewer of these features are necessary to arrive at a decision in the word condition than in the single-letter condition.

In fitting the model to the results, one α was estimated for the single-letter condition and another for the word and nonword conditions. The word and nonwords should have the same value of α since lateral masking should be equivalent in these two cases. With respect to the rate of processing, θ, letters in words should be processed at a faster rate than letters in nonwords or a letter presented

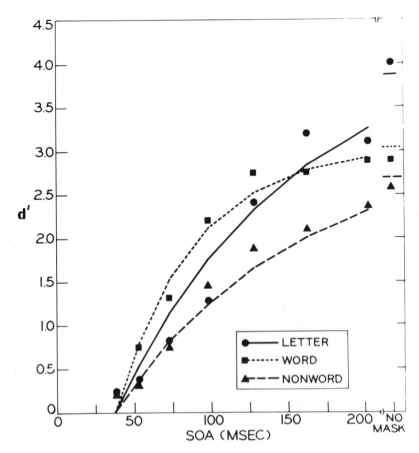

FIGURE 5.3 Predicted and observed d' values for the word, nonword, and single-letter conditions as a function of SOA.

alone. It follows that one value of θ should be estimated for words and another for letters and nonwords. Since the masking stimulus was more intense than the test stimulus, the mask would have a faster arrival time at the visual processing area than would the test stimulus. Therefore, it was also necessary to estimate a dead time, since the masking interval probably overestimated the true processing interval. Finally, it was necessary to estimate the duration that the display information was maintained in the visual processing center. This duration, t_D, gives the maximum processing time for very long masking intervals and the no-mask condition. If the masking interval exceeded t_D, then t_D was inserted in the equation.

The observed d' values were fit with the predictions of the model by estimating the six parameter values using the minimization subroutine STEPIT (Chandler, 1969). The α value for the letter alone condition was 4.32—significantly larger than the α value of 3.06 for words and nonwords. The θ value for words was 18.95—significantly larger than the θ value of 8.45 for letters and nonwords. The dead time was estimated to be 37 msec, and 266 msec was the estimated duration of preperceptual visual storage. The model provided a reasonably good description of the results, considering that 24 independent data points were described with just six parameter values. One test of the adequacy of the model is to see if the description would be improved when the constraints on α and θ were removed and two additional parameters are estimated. Therefore, if the α value for words differs from the α value for nonwords, and the θ value for letters differs from the θ value for nonwords, the description of the new model should be greatly improved. It was not, providing additional support for the original model.

The good description of the results by the model allows an assessment of the three interpretations offered by Johnston and McClelland (1973). First, it is not necessary to assume that letters and words were processed by qualitatively different mechanisms. The only difference for words is that readers have the added benefit of utilizing orthographic context. Second, it was not necessary to assume a tradeoff between backward masking and lateral masking mechanisms; the observed tradeoff is simply a natural outcome of the temporal course of processing. Third, words are processed faster than nonwords or letters alone due to the utilization of orthographic context. By providing results consistent with the third explanation, the experiment reveals that the first two interpretations are not necessary to explain the results of either the Johnston and McClelland (1973) or the Massaro and Klitzke (1979) experiments.

PHONOLOGICAL MEDIATION[4]

A very old question in reading-related research, one that is probably as old as reading itself, is whether the reader must translate print into some form of speech before meaning is accessed. This question can be formalized in terms of models in which speech mediation either does or does not occur in a derivation of meaning. Figure 5.4 presents a schematic diagram of both models. The top model assumes that phonological mediation must occur in order for the meaning of a message to be determined. In this model a letter string is presented, and the letters are identified by evaluating the visual information against feature lists of letters in long-term memory. The letters then are translated into sound or a soundlike medium by the spelling-to-sound correspondences of the language. One example of a spelling-to-sound rule would be that a medial vowel is usually pronounced as short unless it precedes a consonant followed by a final *e*. Thus, we have *fin* and *fine* or *fat* and *fate*. The speech code derived from spelling-to-sound rules is then used to access the lexicon in order to recognize the meaning of the word. The critical assumption of this model is that lexical access is achieved only by way of a speech code.

The bottom model in Figure 5.4 assumes that a speech code becomes available only after lexical access is achieved. The letters are identified in the same way as in the speech mediation model. However, the meaning of the letter string is determined by utilizing a visual code to achieve lexical access. The important assumption in this model is that the reader has information about what letter sequences represent what words. In this model the speech code becomes available only after lexical access is achieved. Given these two formal models, one would expect that it would be relatively easy to distinguish between

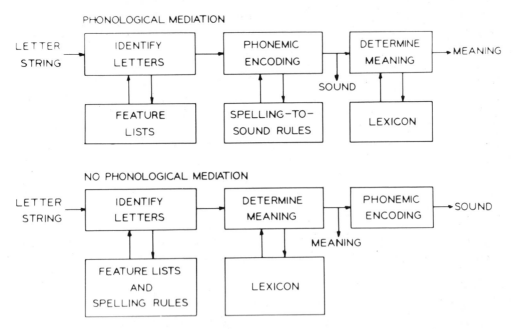

FIGURE 5.4   Two-stage models of the role of phonological mediation in reading.

them. Yet there is no consensus on which of these models is more likely to be correct.

Experiments have been done utilizing the time needed for lexical access in order to test between the models. Consider an experiment carried out by Gough and Cosky (1976). Subjects were asked to read aloud words that either obeyed or violated spelling-to-sound rules. One example of a word that violates a spelling-to-sound rule would be the word *give;* the vowel is not pronounced as long as it should be, as, for example, in the word *hive.* If subjects recognize words via speech mediation and utilize spelling-to-sound rules to achieve the speech code, then recognition of the word *give* should take longer than recognition of the word *hive.* Utilizing spelling-to-sound rules the reader would first interpret the letters *give* as [giyv] (rhymes with *hive*). Failing to achieve lexical access, a backup strategy would be initiated, and the short form of the vowel would be inserted giving the pronunciation [gIv]. In this case, lexical access would be achieved on the second try. Given the word *hive,* recognition would occur directly from the speech code [hiyv] produced by spelling-to-sound rules. The obvious hypothesis is that the pronunciation time for exception words, such as *give,* should be longer than the pronunciation times for regular words, such as *hive.* Gough and Cosky found that the pronunciation times for the exception words were in fact 27 msec longer than the pronunciation times for regular words. This result would seem to provide evidence for the speech mediation model.

Before these results can be interpreted as supporting the speech mediation model, however, it is necessary for the investigator to locate the differences in reaction time at the word-recognition stage of processing. The naming task requires a number of processing stages, and it is necessary to perform a stage analysis of the naming task. Naming a written pattern includes word-recognition and naming response operations. In terms of this analysis, reaction time between the onset of the written pattern and the onset of the spoken response is a composite of these two component times plus the times for other processes.

It is necessary to ask whether the reaction-time differences observed by Gough and Cosky are due to word recognition (lexical access), as they assume, or are due to naming response operations. It could be that lexical access time did not differ for exception and regular words but that the time for the subjects to program the naming response on achieving lexical access differed for exception and regular words. It could be that exception words are more difficult to pronounce once they are recognized and therefore require more time in the pronunciation task. Until the stage of processing is localized, these results cannot be taken as evidence for the speech mediation model. One possible control would have been to present the words auditorily and see if naming times differ in this situation. If they did not, this would provide some evidence that the differences in naming time were due to differences in time to achieve lexical access in the visual presentation condition.

Another way to test the differences between the exception and regular words, without confounding response selection and programming, would be to require a category judgment task. Here subjects could be asked to categorize the words, such as being nouns or verbs. The differences in the times to complete the categorization task would not be confounded with response processes because the response of categorization is identical for the exception and regular words. Following this logic, Bias (cited by McCusker, Hillinger, and Bias, 1981) found differences between exception and regular words using animal/nonanimal judgments. Further evidence against a response account of spelling-to-sound influences comes from a study in which both pronunciation and lexical decision[5] times were shorter for regular than for exception words.

Even if lexical access is slower for exception than for regular words, speech mediation may not be responsible. Differences between exception and regular words could be the result of differences in the times to process the letters of the words. There is good evidence that readers utilize orthographic structure to facilitate letter processing in word strings (Krueger & Shapiro, 1979; Massaro, 1979a). It could be that exception words have less orthographic structure than regular words, and letter recognition is therefore faster for regular than for exception words. Controlling for orthographic structure differences is difficult because an exact description of structure has not been validated. It is necessary to test for differences between these two classes of words in tasks that do not involve lexical access. As an example, a control experiment could have subjects search for a given target letter in regular and exception words. If the letter strings did not differ with respect to orthographic structure, then the time to search for a target letter in the strings would not differ for exception and regular words.[6]

SENTENTIAL CONTEXT

One of the oldest questions in reading-related research is the extent to which syntactic-semantic context influences word recognition. Many experiments have been carried out to demonstrate that sentential context influences word recognition. In contrast to the plethora of experimental work, there have been few models of how context works in word recognition. Gough, Alford, and Holley-Wilcox (1978) discuss a model that assumes the contribution of context is independent of the extraction of visual information from the word. This assumption is similar to the assumption of the independence of featural analysis and orthographic context in the independence model given in the section on word recognition. The Gough et al. model was formulated by Tulving, Mandler, and Baumal (1964). These authors proposed that the independence assumption made the following prediction: Assume that f is the probability of recognition of a word presented without any context, and c is the probability of recognizing the same word given only the context. If the visual information and context are processed independently, then p, the probability of recognizing the word, given both the stimulus presentation and context, should be

$$p = f + c - fc, \tag{11}$$

which is the equation given by probability theory for describing the summation of two independent probability events.

Some of the original studies of the combination of sentential context and stimulus information in word recognition were performed by Tulving and his colleagues (Tulving & Gold, 1963; Tulving et al., 1964). Tulving et al. (1964) combined eight exposure durations with four context lengths in a word-recognition task in which a tachistoscopic presentation of a word followed the reading of the context. Subjects read either the last zero, two, four, or eight words of the context part of the sentence, and the test word was presented at either 20, 40, 60, 80, 100, 120, or 140 msec. This gives a total of 32 experimental conditions. Subjects were instructed to write down the test word and guess if they were not sure of their answer. They were told that the context words might be helpful in recognition of the test word.

Figure 5.5 presents the percentage of correct responses as a function of the duration of the test word; context length is the curve parameter. The context with two words is not presented because it produced results roughly identical to the context with four words. As expected, performance improved with increases in word duration. Performance also improved with increases in sentential context. The results show a larger contribution of sentential context when the exposure duration is intermediate and performance is neither very poor nor very good. This result indicates that context is most effective when subjects have some, but not relatively complete, featural information about the test word.

Tulving et al. (1964) tested the independence idea given by Equation (11) against the results of their experiment. A straightforward interpretation of Equation (11) would assume that the duration of the stimulus can influence f and that the number of context words can influence c. Therefore, eight parameter values of f and four parameter values of c must be estimated before the model can be evaluated. The estimates of f were assumed to be the probabilities of a correct response at the zero context condition. Similarly, the estimates of c were obtained from the response probabilities at the zero exposure duration. To test the model, the authors compared the observed probabilities under the 21 other experimental conditions to those predicted by Equation (11), given the appropriate estimates of f and c. The observed recognition probabilities were in every

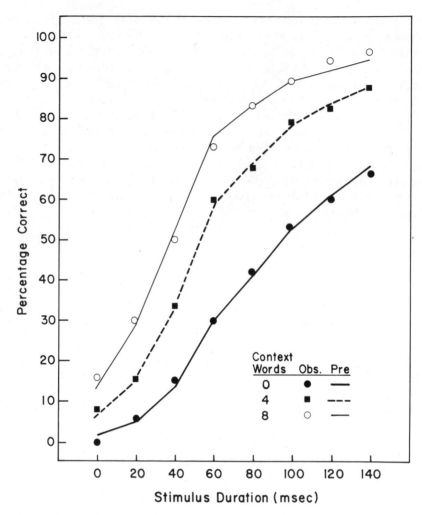

FIGURE 5.5 Observed (points) and predicted (lines) percentage correct identifications as a function of stimulus duration and the number of context words.

case larger than that predicted by the independence equation (11). Therefore, the idea of independence of stimulus information and context was rejected.

The rejection of independence may have been premature. As Gough et al. (1978) pointed out, the response probabilities at the zero context or zero duration conditions may not be valid estimates of c and f. All the observed data should be used to make the parameter estimates. Tulving et al. did not have a computer to estimate the parameters by minimizing the deviations between the predicted and observed recognition probabilities. A more critical problem in the application of the model is the implicit assumption that c is zero when no context is presented. It is possible that the experience of the readers in the experiment allowed them to utilize some knowledge about the set of target words even in the zero context condition. If this was the case, the model may also have failed for this reason.

It should also be stressed that the formulation of Tulving et al. is only one instance of an independence model. A critical although implicit component of their formulation is that recognition via context and stimulus is all or none. Context either allows recognition of a word or it does not; it does not allow the contribution of partial information about the word. This is also true for stimulus information. This stands in sharp contrast to the idea of continuous information discussed in previous sections of this chapter. Moreover, the Tulving et al. formulation makes the implicit assumption that false information is not possible because there is no rule to apply if stimulus information triggers one alternative and context information another. In the fuzzy-logical model of Massaro (1979a), however, the reader has partial information from both context and stimulus presentation. The integration of these sources of partial information is analogous to the integration of letter information and orthographic context, discussed in the section on word recognition.

In the framework of the fuzzy-logical model, the reader has two sources of information about the test word; the visual information is indexed by V_i and the context by C_j. The reader evaluates both sources of information to arrive at the amount of support for a particular word alternative. The overall degree of support for the correct word can be indexed by g(correct word, S_{ij}), where S_{ij} is the stimulus condition corresponding to the ith level of visual information and the jth level of context. Combining the two sources of information would give

$$g(\text{correct word}, S_{ij}) = V_i \times C_j. \tag{12}$$

In Equation (12), V_i is the visual information, and C_j is the sentential context information. Before the overall degree of support for the correct alternative can be used to indicate the likelihood of a correct response, the support for all other alternatives must be taken into account. For simplicity, it seems reasonable to assume that there is a relative tradeoff between the correct and incorrect alternatives for each source of information. In this case, if V_i represents the degree of visual support for the correct alternative, $(1 - V_i)$ would represent the degree of support for all incorrect alternatives. Similarly, $(1 - C_j)$ would represent the degree of support for all incorrect alternatives given by sentential context. Therefore, the likelihood of a correct response should be equal to the support for the correct word relative to the total support for all alternatives:

$$P(\text{correct}) = \frac{V_i C_j}{V_i C_i + (1 - V_i)(1 - C_i)}. \tag{13}$$

In order to fit the model to the observed results, eight values of V_i and four values of C_j must be estimated as parameters in Equation (12). Figure 5.5 also presents the predictions of the fuzzy-logical model. The model provides a reasonably good description of the results, with a root mean square deviation of 2.1 percent.

We began with some general considerations in building and testing psychological models. These general considerations were an important aspect of the discussion of six or seven research problems within the domain of letter and word recognition in reading. Overall, the approaches seem to comply with the established frameworks for scientific endeavor. Scientists value theories that are parsimonious, that are capable of being falsified, and that make unique predictions in the domain of interest. We guard against confirmation biases by primarily having a highly interactive and competitive research area. No claims go unchallenged, and the theoretician is vulnerable to disconfirmation from other members in the field. Although one might believe that a good theory is one that is easily disproven, it is important to remember that rejection of a theory requires a viable alternative for significant progress in the field.

Our venture into model building and testing in reading research has revealed a parallel between reading and scientific endeavor. Both rely on basic perceptual, cognitive, and emotional processes of the individual. Reading, like scientific endeavor, begins with a large and unwieldy data base or knowledge structure. New information is processed and assimilated into the structure. Curiosities are developed, and hypotheses are generated, formulated, and tested against available data. Novel situations are explored and created in a continuous search for resolution and hope of completeness. To paraphrase Huey (1908/1968), to understand what we do in the scientific process would not only illuminate the process itself but might provide a fundamental understanding of those processes so characteristic of the only known species of readers.

NOTES

1. For our purposes, the terms *models* and *theories* can be used interchangeably, although models may be considered to be less general and more formal (precise) than theories.
2. The term *metatheory* is used to signify a philosophical framework that cannot be empirically tested. A metatheoretical issue is a point of logical debate; empirical evidence may come into play by evaluating the success of specific models derived within certain metatheories.
3. The terms *perception, recognition,* and *identification* are usually used interchangeably in reading research.
4. The terms *phonological* and *phonemic* are used to mean a speechlike code of a visible letter string.
5. A lexical decision involves classifying a letter string as a word or nonword without any overt pronunciation of the string.
6. One limitation with this control study is that lexical status also facilitates target search (Krueger, 1975; Massaro, Taylor, Venezky, Jastrzembski, & Lucas, 1980). If lexical access is achieved faster for regular than for exception words, we would expect faster target search for the regular than for the exception words. An advantage of regular words in the target-search task would not be informative. Only if performance is equivalent in the target-search task for regular and exception words do we have evidence that these strings are roughly equivalent in orthographic structure. In addition, these results would indicate that lexical access was not achieved faster for the regular than for the exception words. It would follow that the differences between these two classes of words in the naming experiment were probably due to differences in a response rather than a recognition operation.

REFERENCES

Allport, D. H.   On knowing the meaning of words we are unable to report: The effects of visual masking. In S. Dornic (Ed.), *Attention and performance VI.* Hillsdale, N.J.: Erlbaum, 1977.

Baron, J.   The word-superiority effect: Perceptual learning from reading. In W. K. Estes (Ed.), *Handbook of learning and cognitive processes*. Hillsdale, N.J.: Erlbaum, 1978.

Broadbent, D. E.   Word-frequency effect and response bias. *Psychological Review*, 1967, *74*, 1–15.

Broadbent, D. E.   *Decision and stress*. New York: Academic Press, 1971.

Broadbent, D. E.   *In defense of empirical psychology*. London: Methuen, 1973.

Cattell, J. M.   The time it takes to see and name objects. *Mind*, 1886, *11*, 63–65.

Cattell, J. M.   The time it takes to think. *Popular Science Monthly*, 1888, *32*, 488–491. (Reprinted in *James McKeen Cattell: Man of Science* (Vol. 2): *Addresses and formal papers*. Lancaster, Pa.: Science Press, 1947.)

Chall, J.   *Learning to read: The great debate*. New York: McGraw-Hill, 1967.

Chandler, J. P.   Subroutine STEPIT—Finds local minima of a smooth function of several parameters. *Behavioral Science*, 1969, *14*, 81–82.

Conant, J. B.   *On understanding science*. New Haven: Yale University Press, 1947.

Doherty, M. E., Mynatt, C. R., Tweney, R. D., & Schiano, M. D.   *Pseudodiagnosticity (Acta Psychologica)*, 1979, *43*, 111–121.

Donders, F. C.   *On the speed of mental processes, 1868–1869*. Translated by W. G. Koster. In W. G. Koster (Ed.), *Attention and performance II (Acta Psychologica)*, 1969, *30*, 412–431.

Erdelyi, M. H.   A new look at the new look: Perceptual defense and vigilance. *Psychological Review*, 1974, *81*, 1–25.

Eriksen, C. W., & Eriksen, B. A.   Visual perceptual processing rates and backward and forward masking. *Journal of Experimental Psychology*, 1971, *89*, 306–313.

Estes, W. K.   Perceptual processing in letter recognition and reading. In E. C. Carterette & M. P. Friedman (Eds.), *Handbook of perception* (Vol. 9). New York: Academic Press, 1978.

Estes, W. K.   On the descriptive and explanatory functions of theories of memory. In L. Nilsson (Ed.), *Perspectives on memory research*. Hillsdale, N.J.: Erlbaum, 1979.

Fechner, G. T.   *Elements of psychophysics* (Vol. 1), 1860. Translated and edited by H. E. Adler, D. H. Howes, & E. G. Boring. New York: Holt, Rinehart, & Winston, 1966.

Gibson, E. J., & Levin, H.   *The psychology of reading*. Cambridge, Mass.: MIT Press, 1975.

Goodman, K. S.   Behind the eye: What happens in reading. In H. Singer & R. B. Ruddell (Eds.), *Theoretical models and processes of reading*. Newark, Del.: International Reading Association, 1976. (a)

Goodman, K. S.   Reading: A psycholinguistic guessing game. In H. Singer & R. B. Ruddell (Eds.), *Theoretical models and processes of reading*. Newark, Del.: International Reading Association, 1976. (b)

Gough, P. B., Alford, J. A., Jr., & Holley-Wilcox, P.   *Words and contexts*. Paper presented at the annual meeting of the National Reading Conference, St. Petersburg Beach, Fla., December, 1978.

Gough, P. B., & Cosky, M. J.   One second of reading again. In N. J. Castellan, Jr., D. B. Pisoni, & G. R. Potts (Eds.), *Cognitive Theory* (Vol. 2). Hillsdale, N.J.: Erlbaum, 1976.

Huey, E. B.   *The psychology and pedagogy of reading*. New York: Macmillan, 1908. (Republished by MIT Press, 1968.)

Jakobson, R., Fant, C. G. M., & Halle, M.   *Preliminaries to speech analysis: The distinctive features and their correlates*. Cambridge, Mass.: MIT Press, 1961.

Johnson, N. F.   On the function of letters in word identification: Some data and a preliminary model. *Journal of Verbal Learning and Verbal Behavior*, 1975, *14*, 17–29.

Johnston, J. C., & McClelland, J. P.   Visual factors in word perception. *Perception and Psychophysics*, 1973, *14*, 365–370.

Juola, J. F., Leavitt, D. D., & Choe, C. S.   Letter identification in word, nonword, and single letter displays. *Bulletin of the Psychonomic Society,* 1974, *4,* 278–280.

Kallman, H. S., & Massaro, D. W.   Similarity effects in backword recognition masking. *Journal of Experimental Psychology: Human Perception and Performance,* 1979, *5,* 110–128.

Krueger, L. E.   Familiarity effects in visual information processing. *Psychological Bulletin,* 1975, *82,* 949–974.

Krueger, L. E., & Shapiro, R. G.   Visual search for intact and mutilated letters through rapid sequences of words and nonwords. *Journal of Experimental Psychology: Human Perception and Performance,* 1979, *5,* 657–673.

LaBerge, D., & Samuels, S. J.   Toward a theory of automatic information processing in reading. *Cognitive Psychology,* 1974, *6,* 293–323.

LaBerge, D., & Samuels, S. J. (Eds.).   *Basic processes in reading: Perception and comprehension.* Hillsdale, N.J.: Erlbaum, 1977.

Liberman, A. M., Cooper, F. S., Shankweiler, D. P., & Studdert-Kennedy, M.   Perception of the speech code. *Psychological Review,* 1967, *74,* 431–461.

Luce, R. D.   *Individual choice behavior.* New York: Wiley, 1959.

Lupker, S. J., & Massaro, D. W.   Selective perception without confounding contributions of decision and memory. *Perception and Psychophysics,* 1979, *25,* 60–69.

McCain, G., & Segal, E. M.   *The game of science.* Monterey, Calif.: Brooks/Cole, 1973.

McClelland, J. L.   On the time relations of mental processes: An examination of systems of processes in cascade. *Psychological Review,* 1979, *86,* 287–330.

McConkie, G. W., & Rayner, K.   The span of the effective stimulus during a fixation in reading. *Perception and Psychophysics,* 1975, *17,* 578–586.

McCusker, L. X., Hillinger, M. L., & Bias, R. G.   Phonological recoding and reading. *Psychological Bulletin,* 1981, *89,* 217–245.

Massaro, D. W.   Perceptual processing and forgetting in memory tasks. *Psychological Review,* 1970, *77,* 557–567.

Massaro, D. W.   Perception of letters, words, and nonwords. *Journal of Experimental Psychology,* 1973, *100,* 349–353.

Massaro, D. W.   *Experimental psychology and information processing.* Chicago: Rand McNally, 1975. (a)

Massaro, D. W. (Ed.).   *Understanding language: An information processing analysis of speech perception, reading, and psycholinguistics.* New York: Academic Press, 1975. (b)

Massaro, D. W.   A stage model of reading and listening. *Visible Language,* 1978, *12,* 3–26.

Massaro, D. W.   Letter information and orthographic context in word perception. *Journal of Experimental Psychology: Human Perception and Performance,* 1979, *5,* 595–609. (a)

Massaro, D. W.   Reading and listening. In P. A. Kolers, M. Wrolstad, & H. Bouma (Eds.), *Processing of Visible Language* (Vol. 1). New York: Plenum, 1979, 331–354. (b)

Massaro, D. W., & Cohen, M. M.   The contribution of fundamental frequency and voice onset time to the /zi/-/si/ distinction. *Journal of the Acoustical Society of America,* 1976, *60,* 704–717.

Massaro, D. W., & Klitzke, D.   The role of lateral masking and orthographic structure in letter and word perception. *Acta Psychologica,* 1979, *43,* 413–426.

Massaro, D. W., & Schmuller, J.   Visual features, preperceptual storage, and processing time in reading. In D. W. Massaro (Ed.), *Understanding language: An information processing analysis of speech perception, reading, and psycholinguistics.* New York: Academic Press, 1975.

Massaro, D. W., Taylor, G. A., Venezky, R. L., Jastrzembski, J. E., & Lucas, P. A.   *Letter and word perception: Orthographic structure and visual processing in reading.* Amsterdam: North Holland, 1980.

Meyer, D. E., Schvaneveldt, R. W., & Ruddy, M. G.   Loci of contextual effects on visual word-recognition. In P. M. A. Rabbitt & S. Dornic (Eds.), *Attention and Performance V.* New York: Academic Press, 1975.

Miller, G. A., & Johnson-Laird, P. N.   *Language and Perception.* Cambridge, Mass.: Belknap, 1976.

Mitroff, I. I.   *The subjective side of science.* Amsterdam: Elsevier, 1974.

Morton, J.   Interaction of information in word recognition. *Psychological Review,* 1969, *76,* 165–178.

Mynatt, C. R., Doherty, M. E., & Tweney, R. D.   Confirmation bias in a simulated research environment: An experimental study of scientific inference. *Quarterly Journal of Experimental Psychology,* 1977, *29,* 85–95.

Mynatt, C. R., Doherty, M. E., & Tweney, R. D.   Consequences of confirmation and disconfirmation in a simulated research environment. *Quarterly Journal of Experimental Psychology,* 1978, *30,* 395–406.

Naus, M. J., & Shillman, R. J.   Why a Y is not a V: A new look at the distinctive features of letters. *Journal of Experimental Psychology: Human Perception and Performance,* 1976, *2,* 394–400.

Neisser, U.   *Cognitive psychology.* New York: Appleton-Century-Crofts, 1967.

Neisser, U.   *Cognition and reality.* San Francisco: Freeman, 1976.

Oden, G. C.   A fuzzy logical model of letter identification. *Journal of Experimental Psychology: Human Perception and Performance,* 1979, *6,* 336–352.

Oden, G. C., & Massaro, D. W.   Integration of featural information in speech perception. *Psychological Review,* 1978, *85,* 172–191.

Osgood, C. E., & Hoosain, R.   Salience of the word as a unit in the perception of language. *Perception and Psychophysics,* 1974, *15,* 168–192.

Platt, J. R.   Strong inference. *Science,* 1964, *146,* 347–353.

Popper, K.   *The logic of scientific discovery.* New York: Basic Books, 1959.

Reicher, G. M.   Perceptual recognition as a function of meaningfulness of stimulus material. *Journal of Experimental Psychology,* 1969, *81,* 275–280.

Roediger, H. L., III.   Memory metaphors in cognitive psychology. *Memory and Cognition,* 1980, *8,* 231–246.

Rumelhart, D. E.   Toward an interactive model of reading. In S. Dornic (Ed.), *Attention and performance VI.* Hillsdale, N.J.: Erlbaum, 1977.

Selfridge, O. G.   Pandemonium: A paradigm for learning. In *Symposium on the mechanization of thought processes.* London: Her Majesty's Stationery Office, 1959.

Smith, E. E., & Haviland, S. E.   Why words are perceived more accurately than nonwords: Inference versus unitization. *Journal of Experimental Psychology,* 1972, *92,* 59–64.

Smith, F.   *Understanding reading.* New York: Holt, Rinehart, & Winston, 1971.

Sperling, G.   A model for visual memory tasks. *Human Factors,* 1963, *5,* 19–31.

Sternberg, S.   Memory scanning: Mental processes revealed by reaction-time experiments. *American Scientist,* 1969, *57,* 421–457. (a)

Sternberg, S.   The discovery of processing stages: Extensions of Donders' method. *Acta Psychologica,* 1969, *30,* 276–315. (b)

Taylor, G. A., Miller, T. J., & Juola, J. F.   Isolating visual units in the perception of words and nonwords. *Perception and Psychophysics,* 1977, *21,* 377–386.

Theios, J.   The components of response latency in human information processing. In S. Dornic & P. M. A. Rabbitt (Eds.), *Attention and Performance V.* New York: Academic Press, 1975.

Thompson, M. C., & Massaro, D. W.   The role of visual information and redundancy in reading. *Journal of Experimental Psychology,* 1973, *98,* 49–54.

Tulving, E., & Gold, C.   Stimulus information and contextual information as determinants of tachistoscopic recognition of words. *Journal of Experimental Psychology,* 1963, *66,* 319–327.

Tulving, E., Mandler, G., & Baumal, R.   Interactions of two sources of information in tachistoscopic word recognition. *Canadian Journal of Psychology,* 1964, *18,* 62–71.

Wheeler, D. D.   Processes in word recognition. *Cognitive Psychology,* 1970, *1,* 59–85.

Woodworth, R. S.   *Experimental psychology.* New York: Holt, Rinehart & Winston, 1938.

6 ASSESSMENT IN READING

Peter H. Johnston

This chapter examines the development and current status of the assessment of reading. While reading assessment is "as old as the first mother or teacher who questioned and observed a child reading" (Farr & Tone, in press), its documented development goes back only a short distance into the last century. The issues involved in the assessment of reading include (at least) the diverse areas of sociology, education, politics, philosophy, and all branches of psychology. The organization of such a chapter cannot be discrete, thus certain issues recur in different contexts in the various sections. The organization was selected on the basis of personal bias.

The chapter begins with a brief historical overview in which it is claimed that certain early developments set up a paradigm that all but determined our current assessment practices. As Haney (1981) comments, ". . . standardized tests appear to be social artifacts as much as scientific instruments" (p. 1030). The second section briefly addresses some often overlooked aspects of the construction and use of questions in assessment instruments. The third section describes some issues involved in the conflict between two opposing models of testing, and the fourth section discusses some issues involved in the concept of validity. The fifth section comments on trends in the deployment of assessment efforts.

Inertia and the various factors noted by Kuhn (1962) tend to allow us to maintain our basic paradigm without seriously evaluating it with a view to radical renewal. One constructive way for us to examine our current status is to challenge the assumptions of the existing paradigm, thus forcing a complete justification by those supporting the status quo. Consequently, the sixth section, in order to uncover some of the weaknesses in the state of the art, investigates where we might be now had we not pursued the current assessment approach. Finally, a brief summary is presented.

I am indebted to my colleagues Dick Allington, Peter Mosenthal, Fred Ohnmacht, David Pearson, and Jaap Tuinman for helpful comments on an earlier version of this paper, and particularly to David Pearson for getting me involved in it in the first place.

SOME HISTORY

The Beginnings of Reading Assessment

The formal assessment of reading as a cognitive activity probably originated in the Leipzig psychological laboratory of Wilhelm Wundt around 1880 (see Venezky's chapter in this volume). James McKeen Cattell was Wundt's research assistant in his attempts to measure the speed and nature of mental events. While reading per se was not the focus of this work, Cattell was concerned with word and letter perception and the standardization of tasks with which to measure this perception (Cattell, 1886). Around the same time, Javal (1879, cited in Anderson & Dearborn, 1952) was relating eye movements to the reading process. Javal simply watched readers' eyes and described how the eyes moved "par saccades." By making a small hole in the middle of a page, Miles and Segal (1929) observed eye movements as a clinical assessment method. This technique was later developed as an assessment device called the Ophthalm-O-Graph (American Optical Company, 1936). The corneal reflection method, first used by Dodge and Cline (1901), is still in use in the investigation of dyslexia (Pavlidis, 1981). In 1897, Quantz began the systematic study of eye-voice span, which was later used as a form of assessment of reading ability in experimental work (e.g., Buswell, 1920).

Before the turn of the century, Binet (1895, cited in Freeman, 1926) had also made some initial progress in developing reading comprehension tests, though his motivation was to use these comprehension tests as an element in his attempts to assess intelligence. This relationship between reading and intelligence was echoed by Edward Thorndike (1917), who, in trying to measure reading, concluded that "reading is reasoning." Indeed, for a considerable period of time, it was difficult to tell apart intelligence tests and reading tests. For example, the following item is drawn from an early intelligence test (L. L. Thurstone, n.d.).

> "Every one of us, whatever our speculative opinions, knows better than he practices, and recognizes a better law than he obeys" (Froude.) Check two of the following statements with the same meaning as the quotation above:
> —— To know right is to do the right.
> —— Our speculative opinions determine our actions.
> —— Our deeds fall short of the actions we approve.
> —— Our ideas are in advance of our every day behavior.

The item could easily have come from a reading test. Interestingly, a good proportion of the people developing reading tests were also producing intelligence tests. The difficulties of this (reading-reasoning) relationship have persisted to the present time (cf. Johnston, 1983; Tuinman, 1979).

The measurement of reading as an educational achievement (as opposed to a psychological process) was brought to America by Rice, who had also studied at Leipzig. He developed the notion of assessing instructional effectiveness with specific tests. He began in 1894 with a comparative assessment of spelling performance that, along with his other suggestions, was received with derision at the 1897 meeting of the Department of Superintendence of the National Education

Association. By 1914, however, Rice's ideas had gained general acceptance, and large-scale surveys of educational progress were well under way (Ayers, 1918), developing full momentum in the 1920s and never really looking back.

Two driving forces were behind the testing movement. One of these was the intention to make psychology worthy of the term *science,* and this seemed entirely dependent on quantification and "objectivity." The second motivating factor was the rapidly increasing number of children enrolled in education programs and the press for educational accountability. Immigration and population growth in the two decades on either side of the turn of the century caused part of the increase. But the problems were exacerbated by the growth of compulsory schooling and child labor laws (Landes & Solomon, 1972; Resnick, 1982), and by increased societal expectations for literacy. The high failure rate in schools meant that one in six were retained in first grade; by eighth grade, one in two were behind their age peers (Ayers, 1909, 1918). To monitor this problem, school surveys were instituted. This group testing movement, already institutionalized, had its future ensured in 1935 when the IBM 805 was introduced to score tests, the effect being to reduce the cost of testing by about a factor of ten (Downey, 1965; Resnick, 1982).

Educational testing initially served a gatekeeping function between school grades (a function to which it has recently returned). Although it pointed to some difficulties with curriculum and instruction, the major function of educational testing did not turn out to be assisting teachers in their instructional planning. Indeed, there was considerable opposition from teachers to the testing. Support for comparative testing initially came from school administrators, who were particularly pleased about the accountability function of the tests (Resnick, 1982).

This group focus, along with the silent reading emphasis, which had also reached a peak (see Allington's chapter in this volume), produced a climate in which a certain kind of test would survive. Thus, while diverse approaches were developed initially, the fittest in terms of efficiency soon surfaced. Reading tests came to consist of the silent reading of a passage, followed by the solving of brief, generally text-related, problems; usually questions. Thorndike, in developing his 1917 prototypical test, might be considered the father of modern group tests of reading. Parenthetically, Thorndike's influence did not stop with the form of the test. He was also the father of modern reliability theory, which forms the basis of test evaluation. In his 1904 text, he comments that "we measure the unreliability of any obtained measure by its probable divergence from the true measure" (p. 136). While this theory has formed the basis of psychometrics for three-quarters of a century, it is fundamentally flawed in several ways (Lumsden, 1976). Nonetheless, it pervades all reading tests that report statistical data.

By the time Gertrude Hildreth published her *Bibliography of Mental Tests and Rating Scales* (1933), most of the tests available were of silent reading. The proliferation of silent reading group tests is also attested to by Gray (1938), who commented: "During 1914–1915 two thirds of the (reading) studies reported dealt with the organization, standardization, and application of silent reading tests" (p. 102). Clearly, mainstream reading measurement has been heavily oriented toward the group assessment of silent reading. Consequently, the theory surrounding the group silent reading test has developed to a highly sophisticated level. Few question the scientific nature of psychometrics; this was, after all, one of the major reasons for its existence.

Methodology

With the increased interest in reading and its assessment, the first two decades of this century saw considerable diversity in approaches to the problem of measuring reading performance systematically. The most labor-intensive approach was probably that of scoring verbatim free recalls. Several methods of accomplishing this were proposed. Courtis (1914) advocated counting the number of idea units reproduced and interpreting it in terms of the number of units possible. This method was also supported by Brown (1914), and it is a primitive version of current propositional-analysis techniques (e.g., Kintsch & van Dijk, 1978; Turner & Greene, 1977).

Starch (1915) used a timed reading with free recall. Thirty seconds' reading time was allowed, and unlimited recall time. He suggested using the ratio of "relevant words" to the total number of words. This simpler measure was calculated by deleting "wrong" and "irrelevant" words and repetitions to leave the relevant words, a procedure not unlike that currently used in experimental studies of children's summarizing strategies (Winograd, 1982). Gray (1917) supplemented this scoring procedure with ten questions for each passage to provide greater validity. These scores were averaged to increase the reliability. The use of oral recalls represented an improvement in terms of the validity of the test for less able writers. The use of multiple indicators was also prominent in the *Dearborn-Westbrook Reading Examination* (Dearborn & Westbrook, 1920). That test used five different measures to determine the extent to which the reader had comprehended a story. Multiple measures are still advocated as an effective assessment strategy (Johnston, 1983).

The "reproduction" approach began to fall into disrepute early because, as Kelly (1916) pointed out:

> It is generally agreed, I think, that the ability to reproduce is quite a separate ability from the ability to get meaning, and, therefore, the ability to get meaning which involves a minimum of reproduction (p. 64).

While the approach survived in the Silent Reading subtest of the *Durrell Analysis of Reading Difficulty* (Durrell, 1937, 1955), it was generally dropped until Goodman and Burke (1970) revived it in a slightly different form called the "retelling." Retellings were not to be verbatim, were prompted, and were scored according to a "story grammar" model (e.g., Mandler & Johnson, 1977; Stein & Trabasso, 1982) adapted by awarding points for character analysis, theme, plot, events, and additional information. The procedure is very time-consuming and is not commonly used.

Kelly (1916) proceeded to develop the Kansas Silent Reading Test in which students were allowed five minutes to complete as many as possible of 16 exercises. Each exercise consisted of a brief paragraph forming a very simple task such as modified cloze, verbal logic problems, or convoluted instructions to follow. A similar technique of brief paragraphs each followed by single responses was used by Monroe (1918), although the requisite response was the underlining of a word that answered a question. Haggerty (1919) used sentence and paragraph comprehension with yes-no questions to assess reading ability. The format was not unlike that still found in the Stanford (Karlsen, Madden, & Gardner, 1976), though the response requires the selection of one of four words to complete a sentence. Courtis (1917) also developed a unique test in which the reader had three minutes to read as much as possible of a two-page story, followed by five minutes with the same passage broken into paragraphs each with five yes-no questions. As an assessment technique, this seems to have been a terminal evolutionary line.

Chapman's (1924) task of detecting erroneous words in the second half of paragraphs fell into disuse until recently. A modified form using irrelevant clauses was developed for use with college students (Eurich, 1936). Both were criticized (e.g., Anderson & Dearborn, 1952) and cast aside. Nevertheless, interest has recently been renewed in the technique in a research context (Markman, 1977; Winograd & Johnston, 1982) and in an early reading context (Clay, 1979). Clay uses the approach to test children's knowledge of letter order and line order.

In describing "devices for guiding and measuring comprehension," Gates (1937) describes a number of alternative devices for the assessment of reading. He lists:

1. the selection of the best illustration to describe a paragraph.
2. pupil illustrating the paragraph.
3. marking parts of a picture either with an X or so as to complete it to represent the paragraph.
4. making titles for an illustration with respect to the paragraph.
5. executing directions given in the text.
6. questions—multiple choice—true/false statements—true and nonsense statements—completion.

The completion task that Gates suggests is the cloze task. Currently a common assessment technique, this was popularized by Taylor (1953), but its roots go back to the completion tasks used by Ebbinghaus in 1897 in his efforts to find a measure of mental fatigue. Though Ebbinghaus found it unsatisfactory for this purpose, he noted its excellence as a measure of intellectual ability (Freeman, 1926; Webb & Shotwell, 1932). Gates's "execution task" was often a picture accompanied by a paragraph describing what marks to draw on it. For example, the May Ayres Burgess Scale for Measuring Ability in Silent Reading (Burgess, 1921) required such performances as putting a woman's shoe on by blackening her foot in the picture, or drawing smoke coming from a man's pipe and billowing in a particular direction.

The number and length (roughly inversely related) of texts used in tests over the years has varied considerably. Gray (1917) used three relatively long texts, each child reading but one. Starch (1915) had each child read two lengthy texts. One, on the reader's grade placement, was read on the first day, and on the second day an easier one was read. Kelly (1916) used 16 very brief paragraphs, and some of those used by Thorndike (1917) were only a sentence long. Currently, while there is some variability in this, the texts used in reading comprehension tests tend to be many and brief.

Further early developments in the field of reading assessment were noted by Gates (1937), who stated:

A survey of published standardized tests for grades IV to VIII shows a large number and great variety. Among the tests located, twenty-seven measure *speed* of reading materials of uniform difficulty and five of these measure both *speed* and *accuracy,* and twenty-three measure *level* or *power* of comprehension. Fourteen tests of vocabulary or word knowledge were found. It is apparent, moreover, that there is an increased tendency to produce series, or batteries, of tests which include measures of several phases or types of reading . . . (pp. 382–383).

The increase in the number of available batteries was driven by the dual emphases on diagnosis and standardized development.

Oral reading errors were also used in assessment, but they drew little comment in the literature of the first two decades of the century (see Allington's chapter in this volume). Oral reading had fallen into disrepute by the end of the first decade of this century. Complaints generally revolved around oral reading not dealing with understanding and not being the most important kind of reading. Nonetheless, such tests continued to be developed, if slowly.

Gray's (1915) Standardized Oral Reading Paragraphs consisted of a graded series of paragraphs to be read aloud for the examiner to code errors and reading time. Norms for reading time were provided, and error types included omissions or additions (of sounds or words), substitutions, mispronunciations, repetitions, self-corrections, words given assistance on, and the ignoring of punctuation. The recording procedures became more refined with Gates (1937) adding the error of hesitation and not coding self-corrections as errors. The latter advance was ignored until 1970 when Goodman and Burke produced their Reading Miscue Inventory. This fact is indicative of the manner in which reading errors were interpreted. They were basically considered faults to be corrected. While descriptive and comparative studies of errors increased in frequency (e.g., Daw, 1938; Duffy & Durrell, 1935; Madden & Pratt, 1941), there were few attempts to use errors to model the processes, knowledge, and misunderstandings that produced them. Goodman and Burke's scoring method developed this element in the assessment literature. Their scoring system was comprehensive and systematic, and their analysis of error patterns ("miscues") was directed toward discovering the nature and balance of strategies used by the reader. This approach was suggested much earlier, for example by Gates (1937). However, it does not seem to have held great appeal at the outset.

A conceptual shift occurred with Durrell's (1937) use of error rates to describe task difficulty rather than reader ability. He stated: ". . . we assume that one error in twenty running words is the maximal difficulty of material for this grade . . ." (p. 335). Betts (1946) developed this concept further. If the error rate was 1 percent, the material was at the reader's independent level. Material read with a 2 to 5 percent error rate was at the reader's instructional level, and material with a greater than 5 percent error rate was "frustration" level. Corresponding levels of accuracy at answering questions were suggested as 90, 75, and 50 percent. Unfortunately, these scoring criteria were developed using only fourth-graders who preread the text. Arguments over the adequacy of these criteria adorn the literature without resolution (Fuchs, Fuchs, & Deno, 1982; Powell, 1970; Weber, 1968).

These arguments notwithstanding, the development of oral reading assessment has been painfully slow. Even the problems involved in one-to-one oral reading have been slow to surface. For example, the fact that an oral reading diagnosis is in a sense "negotiated" by the examiner and examinee via their verbal and nonverbal interaction has been a recent realization (McGill-Franzen & McDermott, 1978; Mehan, 1978). Note, too, that statistical evaluation procedures have not generally been applied to oral reading techniques. For example, while considerable statistical effort has been devoted to examinations of the multi-dimensionality of group tests (e.g., Davis, 1944, 1972; Drahozal & Hanna, 1978; Spearitt, 1972), similar statistical effort has been applied to oral reading errors only recently (e.g., Haupt & Goldsmith, 1982). This slow development is unusual considering the early start that the field had on other disciplines. Only recently has mathematics been highly involved in the analysis of arithmetic error patterns as indicators of underlying misconceptions or information deficits (e.g., Brown & Burton, 1978). The reason informal oral reading tests were downplayed was probably partly because of their lack of "objectivity." "Subjectivity" is generally frowned upon.

The major approach to the assessment of reading that is currently in use (largely group silent reading tests) seems to have been the result of an ideological thrust that favored ease of use over all else. The reasoning is probably best captured by Anderson and Dearborn (1952):

> If the reader will now ask himself this double-headed question as to (1) just how he is going to find out how much and how well the individual pupils in a class understand or comprehend what they have read silently, and (2) just how he is going to make it easy for the teacher or tester to score the findings in terms of age and grade norms, he will come to understand why the tests of silent reading are as and what they are, and why they have so many shortcomings or limitations (p. 301).

From the brief historical account presented here, it can be seen that the current situation exists largely through accident rather than design and that it has been maintained more through societal press than scientific process. As Anderson and Dearborn note, the approach has a number of substantial flaws, some of which are explored in the remainder of this paper. Because questioning has been intrinsic to most forms of reading assessment, this aspect is addressed first.

SOME QUESTIONS ABOUT QUESTIONS

Historically, and currently, most of our attempts to assess reading performance involve the use of questions. Thus, the present section addresses some unresolved and unrecognized issues associated with this mode of information gathering. Since we cannot see comprehension, the pupil must

> . . . do something else to indicate how much and how well he has understood, and that something may make the test . . . just so much less a simon-

pure test of reading and thus in part a test of something else beside reading
. . . (Anderson & Dearborn, 1952, p. 302).

The Nature of Questions

The "something else" that the pupil must do depends somewhat on the nature
of the question and its relationship to the text. Attempts to systematize the production of comprehension questions have met with limited success (Anderson,
1972; Bormuth, 1970). Attempts at post hoc classification have met with more
success. However, research does present an increasingly coherent picture of what
comprehending from text involves, and this has considerable importance for
our understanding of the important aspects of questions. Comprehending involves
building in one's head a model of the presumed intended meaning of a text. It
is accomplished by constructing a central causal chain and organizing information
from the text and from one's prior knowledge with respect to that chain (Johnston,
1983; Omanson, 1982; Schank, 1975). This process requires considerable use of
prior knowledge in order to tie together and assign degrees of relevance or
importance to the text information. From this description of reading, two potentially important dimensions of test questions arise: prior knowledge and centrality.
Since the construction of a central causal chain is of the essence in comprehension,
it is more important that the reader has a grasp of the "central" elements of
the text than of the peripheral elements. Centrality has not generally been considered to be an element in question classification or selection. Evidence suggests
that it should be (Johnston, in press, a). Related to this, when the text is available
to readers for referral while answering the questions, they do not have to construct
such a central chain. Rusch and Stoddard (1927) noted the problem over half a
century ago:

> Reading a paragraph, then finding the right answer to questions based on
> the reading (the paragraph remaining in view), is to some extent a matching
> exercise . . . it disregards the mechanics of the process . . . (p. 117).

In group-administered tests the passage is usually available. In individual tests
the text is usually not available for referral when the reader responds to questions.
It has been demonstrated (Johnston, in press, a) that this issue of availability
changes the nature of the question-answering task markedly. Text availability
is particularly a problem because the effects are different for different kinds of
questions. This casts doubt on the comparability of questions defined similarly
in group and individual tests. It also casts doubt on our use of the term *comprehension* as if it were the same under conditions of availability versus memory.

Questions and Prior Knowledge

The second dimension of questions raised by the description of reading is that
of prior knowledge. Pearson and Johnson (1978) have included this element in
their classification of questions. Questions whose answers rely partly on relevant
scriptal knowledge are called scriptally implicit. This distinction between script-
based (scriptally implicit) and text-based (textually implicit) questions is one way
to divide the classic "inference" question. Without knowing what the reader

knew before starting to read, however, one has no way of classifying with any certainty the source of the information (text or prior knowledge) unless the information could not have been gained from the text alone. Furthermore, making text-based inferences seems also to depend on some aspect of prior knowledge. Perhaps text-based inferences depend more on procedural knowledge of pragmatic language constraints, such as knowing that statements of effects often follow statements of causes.

For some time it has been felt that on standardized reading comprehension tests there are questions that children can answer without reading the text (e.g., Anderson & Dearborn, 1952). Research has supported this notion (Allington, Chodos, Domaracki, & Truex, 1977; Marr & Lyons, 1980; Tuinman, 1974; Weaver, Bickley, & Ford, 1969). The solution to the problem has been to administer test questions, without the texts, to many children and to see on which questions children, on average, perform better than chance. These items are then discarded. This does not solve the problem, though it may ameliorate it somewhat. At the population level, the effect is reduced, but for individuals, some items are still to some extent passage independent.

What causes a question to be passage independent? It is generally caused by the text being redundant with the reader's prior knowledge (cf. Hanna & Oaster, 1978). How can we completely prevent this? One way is to ask questions about unpredictable details that are peculiar to that passage alone. But this tends to increase the probability of selecting trivial rather than central items. A second method is to provide highly unfamiliar texts in order to prevent readers from using their prior knowledge. Unfortunately, these methods would tend to produce a testing instrument with very limited validity since by our earlier definition of reading comprehension, if readers do not or cannot use their prior knowledge, they will generally fail to comprehend the text.

Sternberg (1981) claims that the diagnostic goal of cognitive assessment is to find out whether various processing components are unavailable, inaccessible, or inefficiently executed; whether components are combined into suboptimal strategies; and whether the components and strategies operate on a suboptimal mental representation. Perhaps, he suggests, we need "cognitive contents" tests as well as "cognitive components" tests in order to assess both knowledge and processing deficiencies. Johnston (in press, a) has suggested and demonstrated the value of something along these lines in his proposal of a specific vocabulary test as a measure of prior knowledge. If one could know the extent and nature of relevant knowledge held by readers prior to their reading a passage, one would know much more about the nature of the task posed by questions following the text and the nature of the strategies that could be employed.

This approach might resolve the current ambivalence over the place of vocabulary questions in the scheme of things. The first vocabulary test associated with a reading test was developed by Haggerty (1919). It was used as a context within which to interpret the reading performance. In present tests of reading, vocabulary items are sometimes included as comprehension questions, sometimes placed in a separate test, and sometimes found in both places. If vocabulary questions were designed with a specific diagnostic objective—to assess text-relevant background knowledge—we might better realize what use to make of the information they provide.

While prior knowledge assessment may solve some problems, the approach will not solve the fundamental problem raised by Rosenblatt (1978): that we cannot assess readers' "aesthetic" responses to text. These responses are personal, and indeed any attempts to assess them would probably result in the readers' adopting an "efferent" mode of reading in order to answer the questions expected to follow the text. Rosenblatt's notion that the author's intended meaning is fundamentally unknowable also poses some awkward issues for test-item constructors. To satisfy yourself that these are problems, try to construct central questions about quality poetry including multiple-choice alternatives that are clearly right and clearly wrong regardless of your perspective, without "giving the show away."

Questions and Indexes of Processing

The major problem with questions is that they do not allow us to assess the *process* of reading comprehension. It may be possible to develop tests so that they provide information as to the processes, hypotheses, and misconceptions underlying the test performance. Our technical skill must progress considerably, however, before this is possible. First, we need some theory-driven method of question generation or classification so that we know what a response means. We need to be able to describe the task. Second, and most important, we need a theory-driven method for developing distractors or analyzing responses so that we understand the deep structure of error patterns. Until the nature of the error can be specified, only limited progress can be made.

If we could solve these two problems, there would be enough information with which to begin tailored diagnostic testing programs. Tailored testing involves the use of the computer to reduce some of the problems of group testing (e.g., Urry, 1977). There is normally considerable waste of time and effort in standardized group tests because able children spend most time on items that are too easy, and less able readers spend most time on items that are too difficult. A computer, armed with a large bank of validated items, would permit one to identify and adjust items to an optimal difficulty level for any given student, thus gathering maximal information in minimal time. So far, this can be done only to make rapid, refined estimates of general ability. With theory-derived questions and alternatives, however, we might have the computer select items and alternatives to test hypotheses about specific processing strategies. Another aspect of processing that might be examined via computer is sensitivity to various text cues. A computer would permit the manipulation of various cues and measurement of subject-controlled exposure times. Lookbacks and search strategies might also be examined. If a student got all easy and no hard items correct, this would imply a different strategy from that used by a student who got some of each correct. This development would take a very concerted interdisciplinary effort, though the benefits could be great. Microcomputers already are capable of handling such programs and are available in schools in increasing numbers.

Questions and Measurement Techniques

There remain some rather unyielding problems with our current statistical measurement techniques. Both test-retest and parallel-form methods of assessing reliability rely on the assumption that the questions represent equal interval scales so that practice and other influences will produce equivalent effects on the measures. Such an assumption is made also by the one-parameter item-response (Rasch) model of measurement. This assumption is very difficult to meet. One would need a set of questions that presented an even gradient of difficulty. There seem to be several ways to go about adjusting the difficulty of test items for this purpose, half of which involve manipulations of the text and the other half manipulations of the questions. One could increase the complexity of the sentence structures, the familiarity of the text, or the concept load of the text. A second method would be to increase the complexity of the question. A third method would be to increase the complexity or the distractive power of the alternatives in multiple-choice items.

Does it matter whether we adjust the difficulty one way or another? It probably does. If the difficulty is increased by manipulating one of these variables, then the increase is presumably related entirely to that variable. If we consistently use one method over another, our final score is more determined by that variable than by others. Because each method of manipulation seems to pose a different task for the learner, the validity of the test is threatened. Note also the problems this dilemma poses for the assumption in both classical reliability theory and item-response theory (IRT), that is, that ability is unidimensional. As far back as 1916, Thorndike (1916) noted that the "series of facts used as a scale must be varying amounts of the same sort of thing or quality" (p. 13). Similar problems relating to item development are yet to be solved. If we are to use sophisticated statistical models of assessment, we should feed them on data of suitable quality.

> If the model requires a unidimensional test, then a unidimensional test or near facsimile of one should be found or constructed. It is useless to run a Cadillac scaling method on paraffin item sets (Lumsden, 1976, p. 272).

MODELS OF FAILURE AND TEST REFERENCING

Two fundamentally opposing models of reading difficulty pervade our current approaches to assessment. They are distinguished by their underlying assumptions. The first might be termed an *ability* model and hypothesizes the presence or absence of underlying constitutionally fixed traits, such as "perceptual deficits." The model is exactly analogous to the common "Darwinian" conception of intelligence from which it derives. The second model might be termed a *learning* model; it hypothesizes the causes of failure to lie more in the instructional environment and makes failure external rather than internal to the learner.

The model from which stem our current assessments relating to reading failure is still based on the assumption of general neurological abilities—the diagnosis of deficits—rather than on the specific knowledge required for the reading task. While Gerald Coles (1978) in his classic paper on tests for learning disabilities left little of a positive nature to be said for such tests and the model supporting them, they are still well regarded in the field (Allington, 1982; Kavale, 1981). The following quotations from test manuals illustrate this fact.

> The Stanford-Binet Scale with its verbal and non-verbal tests or the Lorge-Thorndike Intelligence tests with their verbal and non-verbal scores will

help identify those who will profit most from reading instruction (Nelson & Denny, 1960, p. 23).

When a student with strong reading disabilities reaches an independent level higher than his or her instructional level, it is very probable that the student will respond to remedial help (Spache, 1981, p. 45).

It may take considerable time to remove a model that possesses such historical acceptance, such a clear relationship to the "medical model" (and support from that quarter), and such convenience as a defense for educators. The problem, of course, lies in the fact that diagnosis from such a perspective is, in a sense, terminal. Once a "learning disabled" classification has been reached, there is little that can be done for the child; the problem is considered neurological. Classification rather than remediation seems to be the dominant goal. Indeed, research suggests that once an initial classification has been made, less able readers become placed in instructional environments that will ensure their continued failure and apparent neurological weakness (e.g., Allington, in press; Gambrell, Wilson, & Gantt, 1981; McDermott, 1976).

The more recent "learning" model is most closely associated with Bloom (1976), who takes a fairly extreme "environmentalist" stand. His mastery-learning model places the burden of performance squarely on the instructional environment. This model, although threatening for educators because it does not leave an "out" for failure, provides a much more optimistic educational perspective. A considerable amount of classroom research also supports such a model (e.g., Bloom, 1976; also see Rosenshine's chapter in this volume).

The issue of the appropriateness of one or another model to reading is confounded by confusion over the nature of the task of learning to read. If reading is thought to be basically a decoding process, then "perceptual factors" such as visual and auditory discrimination assume central importance. If reading is regarded as a meaning-getting activity, however, perceptual issues assume less importance. Knowledge of "book language"; general experiential background; and knowledge of the functions of books, reading, and writing become more central issues. The two causal models are represented by two different approaches to test development. Abilities are tested with norm-referenced tests, whereas learning is tested with criterion-referenced tests. When the testing movement got under way in the early 1920s, assessment was almost entirely norm-referenced. Assessment in reading generally continued to be so until a change began in the mid-1960s. In the late 1950s, educators began to be concerned about describing behavioral outcomes, thus developing an aspect of criterion-referenced measurement (CRM), but by the late 1960s, CRM was well under way and at the same time the subject of much debate. At the present time most publishers of reading tests publish both criterion- and norm-referenced tests, and basal reader programs virtually all have some sort of objectives-based testing system.

Norm- versus Criterion-Referenced Measurement

Norm-referenced and criterion-referenced measurements differ in that the former uses the performance of an individual's peer group as the reference point against which an individual's score is to be evaluated, whereas the latter uses some absolute level (percent correct) of performance on a specific task as its reference point for judging the quality of learning. Neither concept is new. Thorndike in 1913 made the following observation:

> The marks given by any one teacher, though standing for some obscure standards of absolute achievement . . . in the teacher's mind, could stand, in the mind of anyone unacquainted with these meanings, only for degrees of relative achievement—for being at the top or at the bottom, for being above or below something. . . .
>
> Suppose, for example, that instead of the traditional 89s or "goods," a pupil had records of just how many ten-digit additions he could compute correctly in five minutes, of just how difficult a passage he could translate correctly at sight, and of how long it required, and the like. He could, of course, still compare himself with others, but he would not be compelled to do so (pp. 113–114).

Glaser (1963) contributed to the development of the notion by clearly distinguishing between the two testing criteria (norm group and absolute performance) and noting that the two approaches to assessment require different test-development techniques, particularly in terms of test-item selection. Later, Carver (1974) made the same distinction but on the basis of test function, using the terms "psychometric" (norm-referenced) and "edumetric" (criterion-referenced). Carver gave guidelines for evaluating the two test dimensions. The psychometric dimension requires item difficulties of about $p = .50$ so as to maximize variance and hence the reliability of the test. However, a good test item in edumetric terms would be one that no student got right before instruction and that all students got right after instruction. Such a test would show no variance on each administration, item p values being $p = 0$ on the pretest and $p = 1.0$ on the posttest. Coupled with the entirely different item-sampling needs—broad for psychometric and narrow for edumetric—the demands of the two test traditions are incompatible. Thus, certain reading tests, such as the Woodcock Reading Mastery test (Woodcock, 1973) or the Stanford Diagnostic Reading Test (Karlsen et al., 1976), which claim to be both norm- and criterion-referenced (i.e., serve both psychometric and edumetric functions), should be looked upon with considerable suspicion. In their attempts to serve two masters, they may serve neither adequately.

There are two general approaches to constructing CRTs. One is to write a sequence of enabling objectives and accompanying test items in order to test a child's attainment of the objectives at intervals (objectives-based assessment). A second approach (domain-referenced assessment) is to carefully define a domain of performance and then devise items that test the domain (Popham, 1978). In either case, one must first define the nature of the behavior considered to be appropriate evidence of success, and the notion of success is supposedly independent of the performance of one's peers (Walmsley, 1977). The model is appealing but has some flaws in its present form. Walmsley (1978–1979) has used this approach to successfully assess children's pronunciation of CVC clusters, but as he points out, the domain was chosen specifically for its highly restricted nature.

While Anderson, Wardrop, Hively, Muller, Anderson, Hastings, and Frederickson (1978) have applied the domain definition model to more complex aspects of comprehension, the resultant test is by their own admission somewhat unwieldy. Furthermore, the definition of the domain is dependent on one's theoretical perspective toward reading (Walmsley, 1981).

Currently, the CRM model is generally applied via the objectives-based approach, along with the concept of "mastery"; that is, there is built into the objective a criterion (e.g., eight of ten), the attainment of which signifies mastery. The outcome of this has been a belief that any test that has a criterion is a criterion-referenced test. This is not the case (Popham, 1978). Moreover, the actual setting of a criterion is a nontrivial and very subjective activity (Haney & Madaus, 1978; Rowley, 1982). Consequently, in practice, the distinction between criterion- and norm-referenced tests has become blurred. As Tuinman (1978) points out:

> In fact, what is happening is a process of delayed norm-referencing. In brief, this is the sequence of events: An objective is selected. Items are written. A level of performance mastery (80 percent, 90 percent) is specified. Then the test is used. . . . If, however, it turns out that too many students do not reach mastery, items are revised until the test is easy enough. To "pass" the test from here on out is a norm-referenced achievement (p. 171).

However, according to Popham (1978), one need not even have a criterion. That is, while variability is, in a sense, irrelevant to CRM (since one reaches a criterion or one does not), one need not ignore such variability as occurs. Nonetheless, considerable research effort is being invested in attempts to derive statistically defensible cutoff values (e.g., Huynh, 1976; Meskauskas, 1976).

A second problem also results from the fact that the CRM model is generally interpreted in the context of a "mastery learning" approach to instruction. Such an approach requires a sequential set of enabling objectives. Hierarchical models of reading have found little support in the literature, however, which tends to give more support to interactive models. Reading does not consist of a set of discrete subskills (but see Carnine & Silbert, 1979, for an opposing view), but involves the integration of a variety of declarative, procedural, and strategic knowledge in different ways, depending on the state of the comprehending system and the information available to it from various sources.

The dynamic interactive nature of the reading process does not lend itself well to specification in terms of discrete objectives with simple criteria. Such specification has tended to decontextualize and trivialize the process. When advantages are being touted, the examples given are always of discrete skills such as "identifying 80% of a list of 100 one-syllable words may be a criterion set for a student" (Ysseldyke & Marston, 1982). This problem has previously been alluded to by Kingston (1970):

> Measurement is dependent, in part, upon the careful delineation of the behavior to be measured . . . [however]. . . . We describe it as a complex rather than a simple skill, but then simply list the component parts. We ignore the process of integration . . . (p. 232).

CRM tends to result in a view of reading as separate subskills that must be assessed independently. The information provided by such assessment will ensure that teaching will follow the same model. The major problem is with the less able readers. These children are demonstrably less able to generalize and integrate, yet CRM indirectly results in leaving these tasks up to them.

Pearson and Johnson (1978) have pointed out a further reason why it may be unwise to apply a mastery-learning model to reading. They reject the notion of mastery as it applies to comprehension, seeing no reason to cease instruction on cause-effect relations simply because a student has answered eight of ten items correctly. The problem is, of course, that reading requires integrated performance from the start, on increasingly difficult text. If a mastery model is to be applied at all, it is to the integrated performance of reading on text of a given difficulty before proceeding to the next difficulty level. To operationalize such a model we need a method of ordering the difficulty of text: no mean task when the difficulty of text will vary from reader to reader because of the difference in the readers' relevant prior knowledge (Steffenson, Anderson, & Joag-Dev, 1979), interest (Anderson, Mason, & Shirey, 1983), and perspective (Anderson & Pichert, 1977; Bower, 1978). Clearly, readability formulas will not be adequate to perform this task (Bruce, Rubin, & Starr, 1981; Davison & Kantor, 1982; Davison, Lutz, & Roalef, 1981). We need to develop these notions substantially before further progress can be made.

VALIDITY

From books on measurement, one can generally derive the most important measurement commandment of all: "There are three great test virtues, reliability, usability, and validity, but the greatest of these is validity." Nevertheless, in reading test development we have tended to sacrifice the less easily quantifiable criterion of validity for increases in the more easily measured criterion of reliability and the more marketable criterion of usability. Current validity statements in reading assessment frequently emphasize content validity. The content consideration most important in reading test construction, however, is not the task content but the response processes employed in task performance (Lennon, 1956). This is more in the domain of construct validity. Indeed, Messick (1981) suggests that all measurement should be construct referenced, and that construct validity is by far the most important concern in assessment. Meaningful test interpretation is extremely difficult in the face of looseness in construct validity, which results in the subversion of responsible test use.

According to Gronlund (1976), evidence for this aspect of validity can be gathered from four different sources:

1. analyzing the mental processes required by test items,
2. comparison of scores of known groups (e.g., good/poor reader studies),
3. pre-test/post-test treatment studies, and
4. correlations with other tests.

The first three are rarely used by publishers in defense of their instruments. The predominant approach to construct validity in standardized reading tests seems to be the last of these sources: correlations with other tests. This is called "criterion-related" validity if the delay between testing is small, or "predictive" validity if the time delay is large. Unfortunately, it is the weakest of the four sources of evidence. This approach can naturally result in a rather circular argument, since two tests can intend to measure the same trait, be highly correlated, and still fail to measure what they were intended to measure. Indeed, to reverse the argument, tests of reading comprehension tend to be correlated well with tests of intelligence. Does this then make the intelligence test a valid test of reading comprehension (or vice versa), or does the finding make the reading comprehension test an invalid indicator of reading comprehension? Without a very strong conceptual argument, the empirical argument is futile.

It is important that test publishers develop alternative approaches to validity; in particular, it would be helpful to see some convincing training studies done. This becomes more imperative when one considers the changes that have occurred in the nature of the concept of validity over recent years. These changes are fundamental and may best be illustrated through issues relating to test bias. Test bias is commonly considered to be a measurement error that is nonrandom and thus systematically influences measurements of performance. Hunter and Schmidt (1976) provide an excellent discussion of five different statistical definitions of bias and three related ethical positions.

Bias   Judgments based on scores containing bias may be considered discriminatory. Consequently, the validity of reading tests can in many respects come to be a sociopolitical issue. In a 1969 case, *Hobson* v. *Hansen,* minorities questioned the constitutionality of the use of group tests of ability to determine group placement. The establishment, and group assessment devices, came off second best. More recent court cases (e.g., *Larry P.* v. *Riles,* 1980; *PASE* v. *Hannon,* 1980) have focused more on tests of intelligence (Drowatzky, 1981), though their impact may well be felt in the assessment of reading. In ruling against the California State Department of Education in the *Larry P.* case, the court mandated that the state meet certain standards before it could use intelligence tests. These standards were developed to deal with the issue of test bias and hence could readily be imposed on reading tests, for they too are used for within- and between-class placement. The tests were required to do the following:

1. Yield the same pattern of scores when administered to different groups of students.
2. Exhibit roughly equal means for all subgroups included in the standardization sample.
3. Correlate well with relevant criterion measures.

Which current reading tests could meet these criteria? Would we want them to? The implications of these constraints for tests of reading may well force the construction of tests that are invalid for other reasons. The problem to be dealt with is, What constitutes bias, and how can we best go about eliminating it? Consider what reading involves. It involves the active use of the individual's relevant prior knowledge to help predict, verify, self-correct, make inferences, and store information. Such demands as those imposed by the court would mean that test makers would have to face the task of constructing texts that were uninfluenced by differences in relevant prior knowledge. For example, it would be necessary to find domains of knowledge that exhibited no interracial differences and construct related texts whose structure was simultaneously similar to each of the various racial speech patterns (apart from numerous other considerations).

One proposed solution to the bias problem has been the use of population-specific tests, but these are not considered to be viable alternatives to standardized tests (Barnes, 1972). The only other sure way to create unbiased tests is to use texts based on information about which no group could have any knowledge. The problem then would be that the test would have relatively little to do with the normal demands of reading tasks. Thus, although the bias would be gone, the test would be invalid for an even more fundamental reason. Moreover, it is unlikely that such equating would produce an outcome that met the court guidelines. Minority groups tend to be disadvantaged economically and are less likely to secure exposure to a literate environment. Hence, diagnostically important differences in performance are likely to persist. Even if these differences relate to minority status, they should not be intentionally masked because they may provide the information essential to educators for planning more appropriate educational programs.

Almost as controversial as the sociopolitical dimension of reading test bias (validity) is the instructional dimension. The fact that minorities are overrepresented in Title I programs (Reschly, 1981) remains a social problem only if the assessment does not result in improved instruction for the individuals involved. Simply to decide that the test is biased because two different groups perform differently on it is unwise; there may well be a real difference in their skill development. The best thing to do, then, is to adapt instruction for different groups so that it is optimal for each. If decisions based on test scores result in more effective educational programs for all, the student group composition is irrelevant to bias or discrimination (Reschly, 1981).

If, however, the classification results in differential treatment that does not benefit students, then the test is exceedingly unfair. Unfortunately, the differential assignment of students to ability groups in reading seems unfair. The differences in the instruction accorded more and less able readers have received considerable attention recently (Alexander & McDill, 1976; Allington, in press; Hiebert, 1983; Rosenbaum, 1980). Such test outcomes (decisions) thus become unfair (invalid) not because of a flaw in the instrument, or even in the interpretation, but because of the instructional result of the decision. Note that this brings us back to the notion of training studies to provide important test validation information.

Thus there has been considerable change in the concept of validity over the years. An early, though still not uncommon, definition of validity relates to the "adequacy with which a test measures the qualities, abilities, skills, and informations it is designed and supposed to measure" (Greene & Jorgeson, 1935, p. 10). A more recent definition shifts the locus of validity from the test level to the interpretation level.

> We sometimes speak of the validity of a test for the sake of convenience but it is more appropriate to speak . . . of the validity of the interpretation to be made from the results (Gronlund, 1976, p. 81).

In this more recent definition it is the outcome of the decision that is to be judged valid or invalid, not simply the test or the score. This approach has been developed in mastery-testing models as "decision validity" or "discriminant validity" (Hambleton, 1980).

The previous discussion of bias suggests that the issue of validity can be shifted one step further, however, to the level of instruction, thus reuniting the teaching-testing functions. Cronbach and Gleser (1959) addressed this problem in relation to personnel decisions and suggested that a suitable way to approach such decision-making validity is by specifying for each score the exact benefit or loss from each possible decision, and they provided a logic for doing so. This "proof of the pudding" approach at least focuses the evaluation of construct validity on training studies (the third of Gronlund's methods noted above). Messick (1981) describes a "useful view of test validity" that is relevant for those of us interested in the measurement of reading performance. He describes a set of four questions that we might use to evaluate the validity of an assessment. These powerful questions are presented in tabular form in Table 6.1. They provide cause for serious self-examination and probably a collective red face in the field of reading. Current approaches to assessment in reading have not dealt with the fact that constructs such as competence, mastery, ability, and readiness are value laden and carry considerable ideological baggage. Where would we find evidence to suggest that current uses of assessment in reading are effective and not socially damaging? In fact, the evidence on differential treatment of students classified (on the basis of test scores) as more and less able suggests that the social and educational consequences may be damaging (e.g., Allington, in press; Hiebert, 1983; McDermott, 1976).

In summary, then, the issue of validity is considerably broader, more complex, and more important than the conventional wisdom suggests. We need to ask whether teachers and administrators who make decisions about tests, or about instruction or placement on the basis of students' test scores, have the expertise to do so or the knowledge of validity issues necessary to temper judgments. Even if they do, we have to admit that much of the information required for such decisions has not been produced by researchers or publishers. This problem

TABLE 6.1   FOUR QUESTIONS ON WHICH TO BASE THE ANALYSIS OF VALIDITY

	Interpretation	Use
Evidential	Which evidence supports the chosen test interpretation, and how does it weigh against counterevidence and data justifying rival hypotheses?	Which evidence supports the chosen test use in comparison with data supporting other possibilities based on alternative approaches including nontesting methods?
Consequential	The chosen test interpretation has value implications. What are they, and to what extent are the theoretical and value implications in harmony?	Consider the potential social consequences of the selected test use. To what extent do they help or hinder the intended purpose?

Source: Adapted from Messick, 1981.

of user expertise raises thorny issues relating to teacher and administrator training, a topic raised again in the last section of this chapter. Moreover, the current
emphasis on objectives-based content validity in reading tests is misplaced and
may be misleading. The content we ought to be concerned about—the content
we do not have in our current tests—relates to the processes employed in the
performance of the reading test. These are clearly the domain of construct
validity.

THE FOCUS OF ASSESSMENT

There are two current foci of testing effort in reading. One is on the less able,
remedial student. The second is at the tail end of schooling, represented by
the minimal competency testing (MCT) movement.

The first assumption that needs to be questioned is the belief commonly
held among the reading community that ". . . the poorer students, as defined
relative to a given instructional program, should receive more extensive assessment than the better students" (Venezky, 1974, p. 13). This belief misses an
important aspect of learning. The canon should instead be generalized to read
"the extent of assessment should be inversely related to the state of development
of the learner." The revised canon reduces the normative focus and allows for
more frequent and intensive assessment among less able readers, but it also
focuses more attention on the early stages of reading development.

The importance of this shift in focus can be understood by thinking of the
process in the following way: In the early stages of learning a skill, it is crucial
that the learner develop the appropriate hypotheses and "sets" because all future
hypotheses are based on the model of the task developed at the outset. If the
initial hypotheses are incorrect and if they persist, then the learner will become
ensnared in a web of confusion that will generate more incorrect hypotheses
and strategies. This danger is greatest at the beginning stages of development
because the data base from which the learner can build a model is so restricted.
By contrast, at later stages there are enough elements in the learner's model
of the task to generate more accurate hypotheses and strategies and to detect
flawed hypotheses. In early stages, inappropriate hypotheses can resist change
because of their occasional apparent correctness (variable ratio reinforcement
schedule). They also incline the learner to generate new inappropriate hypotheses
when he or she tries to accommodate existing hypotheses in order to make sense
out of reading. The learner ignores task features that should be most salient,
and a history of failure accumulates.

The suggested approach, then, is more preventive than patch-up. The main
assessment focus might thus be in the first three years of school. Until recently,
this model would have been difficult to apply because of the unreliability of
early reading tests. The area of "reading readiness" or "prereading" was relatively
late in developing. Whipple (1925) noted that standardized reading tests did
not at that time reach down into the prereading stage. Hildreth's (1933) *Bibliography of Mental Tests and Rating Scales* cited only three such tests. Reflecting
the "look-say" instruction of the day rather than a problem-solving approach
to reading, Gates (1937) pointed out,

unfortunately, it is particularly difficult to develop standardized tests suitable to all pupils during the first three quarters of a typical first year's progress. This is due primarily to the fact that, since children's reading is limited largely to the specific words they have learned, their showing depends greatly on the number of such words included in the test (p. 378).

Further, with the emphasis on remediation rather than prevention, and the disability criterion of performance one (or two) years below grade level, the only purpose for early assessment could be for grouping.

An additional problem has been that readiness test validity was, until recently, almost entirely predictive. It was based on the notion of neurological "readiness" ("ripeness"), a hangover from the work of Gesell (1928) and other medical people in child development in the 1920s (cf. Durkin, 1976). Following Morphett and Washburne (1931) and Washburne (1936), it was believed until relatively recently that a mental age of 6.5 years was necessary for a child to learn to read. While there were some extreme swings against this neurological maturation notion (e.g., Doman, Stevens, & Orem, 1963), the general feeling persisted (e.g., Heffernan, 1960). This persistence endured in spite of clear evidence presented by Gates (1937) that the notion was untenable. The neurological model still forms the basis of tests such as the Metropolitan Readiness Test (MRT) (Nurss & McGauvrin, 1976).

It was not until Clay (1972) developed her Concepts about Print Test (CAP), based on a careful analysis of the task of beginning reading, that early reading tests became construct referenced. The CAP is composed of clearly defined early reading tasks that are directly interpretable in terms of instruction. The test also represents a shift from an attempt to assess relatively fixed "abilities" or "traits" (psychometric approach) to an attempt to assess the state of knowledge (edumetric approach), particularly as reflected by the specificity of the domain of items.

In the early stages it is possible to directly assess the conceptual knowledge needed as a child learns to read: for example, knowledge of print conventions such as (in English orthography) left to right through the book, across the page, within the word, and even at the letter level. It will also be necessary at some point that the child distinguish letters from one another. The letter-recognition issue is an interesting one because it demonstrates clearly the psychometric and edumetric dimensions of current tests. Compare the MRT with the CAP. The MRT (a psychometric test) tests visual discrimination using a sample of letters and a mixture of symbols. The CAP (an edumetric test) tests this aspect using the whole domain of letters (54: upper and lower case, plus the alternate forms of *a* and *g*) and nothing outside that domain. The number of elements is not large enough to require sampling, and the knowledge of each letter is too important unless one is using the test to predict rather than make instructional decisions. Since it takes only about five minutes to test the whole domain, the increased time requirement of the individual test seems a small price to pay for such necessary information. In analyzing the task in the CAP, it is also clear that identification does not necessarily mean that children must name the letters, but merely that they provide evidence that they can distinguish letters one from another. A child may respond to a letter with a letter name, sound, or a word that starts with it (Clay, 1979).

Substantial progress has been made as a result of this careful task-analysis approach. Validity has been established more through the outcomes of subsequent training than through correlational means. However, in the United States the use of the CAP test and associated prevention model is minimal. The emphasis has come to be on the detection of failure (or a lack of match between actual and expected outcomes) at the end of schooling: minimum competency rather than prevention. In competency testing it only matters that students pass or fail; the cause of failure is unimportant.

Minimum competency testing thus represents an unusual function of assessment in reading instruction. It is not to be used to make informed instructional decisions but as a punishment for failure. It does seem a little late to decide at the end of high school whether academic performance (for whatever reason, from inappropriate instruction to personal problems to inattention) is adequate. On the other hand, the more reasonable prevention model represents a more challenging problem because individual achievement differences are smaller. It is not difficult to detect the very large differences in performance that develop by the end of high school.

Nonetheless, we are entering an age in which the focus is on minimum competency testing. In 1976, only eight states had legally imposed some form of competency assessment. By 1980, 38 states had such laws (Lerner, 1981). This intensive drive for mandating competence is driven by noneducators (Pipho, 1978) with lots of concern but little knowledge of the issues involved. Nevertheless, there is a common insistence on the importance of the basics and objective evidence of success or failure (Lerner, 1981). That this testing represents a gate-keeping function is illustrated by the fact that for about a third of the states using MCT, the main purpose is to certify the high school diploma (Resnick, 1982).

There are two problems involved in the use of MCT in reading. First, there is the problem of defining the domain. What is reading or literacy? The difficulty is that the answer is rather dependent on whom you ask, in terms of both the cognitive processes involved and the social demands. Graham (1981) defines it as "the ability to read, communicate, compute, make judgements, and take actions resulting from them" (p. 128). Resnick and Resnick (1977) have documented historical shifts in the nature of literacy. They note that the term "functional literacy" has come to refer to the ability to read newspapers, manuals, and other common texts, and to use the information gained usually to secure employment (see also Kirsch & Guthrie, 1977–1978). Unless we define minimal competency more adequately, testing it will be distinctly awkward.

Even if we are able to define the domain, there remains the second, and more difficult, problem of setting a criterion of competence. This latter problem is complex and is fundamentally an issue of human judgment. There will be a full range of performance on any test; the division of gray into black and white is arbitrary. One cannot defend such judgments on the basis of mathematical reasoning, only logical, social, or political reasoning, focusing particularly on the consequences of decisions based on the criterion (Haney & Madaus, 1978).

CHALLENGING THE ASSUMPTIONS: WHAT IF . . . ?

Underlying our current approaches to assessment, there are several assumptions that have gone unchallenged over the years. In this section some of these assumptions are challenged, particularly by creating a *what if* scenario. Rather than weigh the outcomes of our current approach to assessment against the consequences of no assessment, as suggested by Ebel (1964), the section speculates on the question of what might have happened had we not originally decided to invest so heavily in the group silent reading, product-oriented model of assessment. This section should be thought of as a gauntlet thrown at the feet of the supporters of the current model of assessment. At the same time, if the challenge cannot be answered, it might also be thought of as a *Where to now?* statement.

Suppose, for the sake of argument, that history had predisposed us toward an individualized, descriptive, process-oriented assessment model instead of the standardized group silent reading model. For example, suppose oral reading had not fallen into disrepute, and we had opted for the more direct descriptive observation of oral reading errors. Some fundamental differences between group and individual approaches to assessment allow for interesting contrasts, with similarly interesting consequences. It seems likely that had we originally adopted the alternative model, there would be some substantial differences not only in our techniques of assessment but in our instruction, and possibly in our social attitudes toward literacy. To begin then, let us challenge the fundamental premise that underlies group assessment, the belief that it is more efficient.

Efficiency

When educators set out to find a test, they are concerned about reality constraints that often come down to time and money, with classroom time having the highest priority. Thus we have the group test, which has been the source of a number of tradeoffs between time, reliability, and validity. The feeling is that if one had to test each child in one's class individually, the time devoted to testing would either detract from the instructional time or require additional personnel (increasing the financial burden). The underlying assumption is that the smaller investment of time and money in group tests compensates for the lower quality of information they give us. Perhaps the assumption is unwarranted. This premise has been questioned before without discernible effect on mainstream educational assessment. For example, Whipple (1925) comments:

> Periodic informal tests need not increase the burden of instruction. On the contrary, experiment shows that they actually simplify the teacher's problem and increase the effectiveness of instruction in a way which saves time (p. 263).

Some recent evidence also might cause the assumption to be challenged. Clay (1979) has shown that individual assessment of students after one year in school can detect incipient reading failure, which, if dealt with instructionally, can prevent the actual failure from developing.

Objectivity-Subjectivity

A second assumption that should be challenged relates to the notion of "subjectivity." The reason informal individual reading tests were downplayed was partly because of their lack of "objectivity." A test that is "subjective" is not looked upon well (e.g., Reschly, 1981). But what does it mean for a test to be objective? Thorndike (1916) held that ". . . a perfectly objective scale is a scale in respect to whose meaning all competent thinkers agree" (p. 11). However, we must be careful about our use of "subjective." Scriven (1972) distinguishes between subjective in the qualitative sense and in the quantitative sense. Quantitatively, subjective refers to the data being based on the judgment of one individual. Subjective in the qualitative sense means a matter of opinion, unreliable, and probably biased. Subjectivity in the former sense should not be scorned.

Usefulness

A third questionable assumption is the belief that group standardized tests give us instructionally useful information. To challenge this, we could simply take the test publishers' own advice more seriously. They have extreme reservations about their tests. Consider the following excerpt from the manual of a popular test:

> . . . test results . . . should be viewed as tentative until substantiated by additional information. . . . Accept the test results as a challenge to your ingenuity in finding out why the class or individual pupils obtained certain scores . . . (Nurss & McGauvrin, 1976, p. 16).

Reason enough, perhaps, to pursue the individual descriptive assessment in the first place, thus avoiding time wasted on the group test.

Internal-External Validity Tradeoff

The focus in the group assessment model has been on internal validity, that is, on the "tightness" of the design of the test materials. This concern has been evident regardless of the effects it might have on the test's external or ecological validity, the degree to which the task is representative of real reading tasks and situations. Thus, a fourth questionable assumption of the group assessment approach is that the tradeoffs between internal and external validity are acceptable. This assumption is held in spite of Cattell's (1886) warning that "the conditions of the experiment (test) place the subject in an abnormal condition, especially as to fatigue, attention and practice" (p. 63). The failure to heed Cattell's warning has allowed us to fall into an unfortunate situation. Currently, "reading assessment" can be substituted for "developmental psychology" in the following statement by Bronfenbrenner (1976):

> . . . much of developmental psychology is the science of the strange behavior of children in strange situations with strange adults for the briefest possible periods of time.

We have developed a sort of "Blitzkreig assessment," one that is devoid of context. Had we taken the path of individualized assessment, this focus would certainly have shifted toward an emphasis on the context and the external validity of tests.

Test Items and Analysis

Currently, we take for granted the notion of a test "item." Depending on the manner in which one measures reading, however, items can have a number of forms: a question, a cloze blank, a word to be identified, an error to be detected, and so on. Current item-response theory (IRT) identifies the item, independent of its context, and attributes to it specific characteristics. But the assumption that an item is independent of its context is not reasonable. The order in which questions or problems are presented tends to influence the manner in which individuals respond to them, by inducing cognitive response sets. The effect of context is very strong in cloze tasks in which the item (blank) cannot be removed from the specific context without changing most of its characteristics. This effect is reduced by having single isolated cloze sentences in some standardized reading tests. Indeed, an attempt is made in group tests (unlike individual oral tests) to make everything discrete.

On the other hand, consider the concept "item" in terms of an individual oral reading test. Since an item can be anything that has a success-failure outcome, one way to approach this issue would be to define each word as an item on which the child could succeed or fail. First, item selection on the basis of discriminating power would be foolish. Also, the same word (item) could elicit a different response on different occasions, especially if the context differed or if the immediately preceding error rate was higher on one occasion than on another. In this instance, the IRT assumption of independence of context is blatantly absurd. The IRT model may not have been developed. Indeed, the whole notion that an assessment model requires discrete success-failure instances may be unfortunate. The important aspect of oral reading analysis is the nature of the strategies used in attempting the word in a given context, regardless of the success or failure of the attempt.

Had we decided to invest in the individual recording of oral reading errors, we may have developed increased awareness of the importance of the patterns of errors (and other behaviors) that occur under different circumstances and may have searched for the underlying hypotheses and misconceptions that produced them. This aspect of descriptive assessment has been slow to develop and is still not well understood in the field. For example, Ysseldyke & Marston (1982) note:

> There are also problems with error analysis. Spache (1976) reported that student error patterns vary with passage difficulty; thus, finding the most valid error profile is problematic (p. 261).

The field of reading potentially had a large head start over other fields in this matter. In composition, only recently have error patterns come under this type of analysis (e.g., Bartholomae, 1980). Similarly, the concept of procedural networks in mathematics (Brown & Burton, 1978) uses the same notions but has become quite refined in a very short period of time.

This individual approach to assessment depends upon a framework for constructing diagnostic models that are capable of detecting students' misconceptions or inappropriate behaviors. The individual approach assumes that students behave in a rational, intelligent manner; therefore, ". . . in most cases, the students' behavior is not random or careless, but is driven by some underlying misconceptions or by incomplete knowledge" (Glaser, 1981, p. 926). The danger, of course, is that ideological differences between interpreters of test performance can cause them to infer different causal misconceptions and strategies (e.g., Weinshank, 1982). With adequate and continuing samples of behavior, however, the necessary inferences are not large, and can be tested with a variety of specific tasks.

Note that this approach represents a search for strengths more than weaknesses or deficits. Students' performances are evaluated, not on the basis of numbers of errors, but on the underlying misconceptions likely to have caused the patterns of errors. Indeed, sheer number of errors is more a function of the assessor's text selection than the child's reading strategies. Attempts to infer children's *learning strategies* rather than their *abilities* calls into question another assumption of current group tests of reading. Group diagnostic tests of reading are based on the assumption that difficulties are caused by reading-specific problems. Yet many of the reading problems that turn up in clinics are learning problems rather than problems specific to reading (Johnston, in press, b). They are caused by passive or inappropriate learning strategies, lack of awareness of the task demands, or lack of learning strategies. For example, Gates (1937) described some of these as:

> . . . whether the pupil uses quick and superficial or slow and laborious procedures. Tries persistently or gives up quickly. . . . Easily satisfied with any result or critical of results and willing to try again (p. 363).

Should we then be testing for such problems in diagnostic assessments, or should we simply worry about the reading problems as if their cause is always reading related? Even if we remediate a "deficient subskill," if we still have a "teacher watcher" (Holt, 1964), we have gained little.

Just Suppose . . .

How might the early adoption of the individual, process-oriented model have affected research? It may have turned our attention toward some aspects of the reading process and away from others. For example, our realization of the importance of prediction may have prevented a number of blind alleys from consuming large amounts of research effort. In other words, the kinds of research questions that seemed worth investigating may well have been radically different. Similarly, the manner in which we approached data collection may also have tended to emphasize external validity rather than internal validity; and what we would accept as evidence of change would probably have differed substantially. Fewer studies would probably have been done because one-to-one assessment requires a greater time investment than does group assessment.

Our instructional procedures may well have been altered too. For example, we may have tended toward individualized instruction rather than group instruction. At least grouping decisions would be different. We might group by strategy use rather than reading level. Indeed, we might not group at all. Consider also the division between comprehension and decoding, which is all too evident in group tests. In individual oral reading tests, these two aspects are completely intertwined. Decoding is dependent on comprehension, and vice versa. Self-corrections can be directed by comprehension or by graphophonic cues. Errors can be comprehension-based substitutions or based on partial graphophonic information, and can be corrected or not depending upon whether they affect the meaning of the text. Instruction may have also tended toward a more integrated approach, perhaps the "shared book experience" type of instruction (Holdaway, 1979).

Our approach to testing—and teaching—comprehension would probably be quite different. Currently, individual reading tests still generally use questions to address "pure comprehension," just as do group tests—although, as noted, the text is usually unavailable for review. While this format requires the reader to construct a model of the meaning of the text, it still does not get at the *process* of comprehending. If our investment had earlier been in these one-to-one measures, perhaps we would have developed a different approach to the problem. A recent paper by Nicholson (in press) provides rich data on children's content-area reading difficulties. The study involved the researchers interviewing students while they were engaged in content-area reading activities. The interview techniques suggested by Nicholson are reminiscent of Rogerian psychology (Rogers, 1942) or "mmhmm" therapy as it has been often dubbed. This reflective questioning may have been "discovered" by the reading assessment community much earlier than this had we taken the individual assessment path rather than the group one.

In line with this approach, a natural extension of the oral reading test might be the "think-aloud" approach (Kavale & Schriener, 1981; Olshavsky, 1977). This requires the student to verbalize his or her thought processes while reading. The technique is much used in the analysis of problem-solving strategies (Ericsson & Simon, 1980), and reading does involve considerable problem solving in all aspects. We would possibly have had to train students to do this properly and have had them practice to the point that the vocalization interfered little with normal processing, but such an approach would have changed radically our model of reading to be more in line with the currently emerging model of comprehension and comprehension failure (e.g., Collins & Smith, 1981). On the other hand, children may not require as much training in this as we think. In early stages of development they naturally think out loud, and in early shared-book-experience reading, it is hard to stop them from predicting and hypothesis testing out loud.

The zone of proximal development is a related idea that might have caught on earlier (Johnston, 1981). This has been a prominent concept in Soviet cognitive psychology (Brown & French, 1979; Vygotsky, 1978). A similar concept has been developed by Feuerstein (1979) in his "dynamic assessment" approach. The idea is that there is not only a point in a test at which the learner will fail but there is an area beyond that in which the learner will profit from instruction. Work from this perspective has shown, for example, that learning-disabled children tend to have a wider zone than do retarded children (e.g., Hall & Day, 1982). Flavell has spoken of this zone as an area of "production deficiency" in which the student has the relevant skills available, but does not have control of them and is unable to use them independently. Thus the focus would be directly on the interface of assessment and instruction, the two becoming part of the one dynamic process.

An example of this dynamic assessment in reading can be seen in Clay's "running records" when the teacher, observing a child to have read himself into a corner with consecutive errors, says "try that again" and records the responses *and* the prompt. Because the teacher-student interaction is recorded, the approach also represents a beginning in terms of assessing the environment that supports the child's behaviors. Such an assessment technique is most effective when used by the classroom teacher. Teachers can make regular records of children's reading, and the children are in a less threatening situation; it is not a "test." Moreover, since the teacher records his or her own behaviors at the same time, the approach has a teacher self-monitoring element as well. When teachers do this assessment themselves, they also get to "own" the information. It is more meaningful and important to them. On top of that, the cost is virtually zero, and there is no time required outside of the regular instructional time.

Had we developed such an individual assessment model, perhaps we would have considered a different approach to reliability, by expanding on the notion of stability over time. This notion is related to the state-trait issue in the psychology of personality, and to the tension between nomothetic science and ideographic assessment (e.g., Allport, 1966; Bem & Allen, 1974; Mischell, 1968). While it may be true that for some individuals their patterns of behavior are consistent in all contexts (the nomothetic-trait model), more often their patterns of behavior are consistent within context over time but not across contexts (the ideographic-state model).

Suppose one were to examine readers' behaviors in relation to one another over time, a model represented by the multiple-baseline single-subject design in behavioral research (Kratochwill, 1978). To begin with, one would be relieved of many of the problems of trying to construct parallel forms of a test. Clay's (1979) running records represent an approach not unlike this; it uses no specially designed texts, just whatever texts are part of the classroom instructional program. If one were interested in, for example, self-corrections, one would be interested in them in the context of the error rate, which indicates the difficulty of the task. We should not be surprised at low self-correction rates in the context of high error rates. Error rate has been used as a primary indicator of task difficulty for many years. However, there are still some researchers who feel that the group-based readability formulas are more accurate than the more direct individual error rate (e.g., Fuchs, Fuchs, & Deno, 1982).

This notion of the importance of error rate as a direct measure of difficulty is crucial. In constructing parallel forms, we are really concerned about comparability of tasks, and if the error rate is comparable, we have some reasonable assurance that the "forms" (or contexts) are equivalent. Perhaps there are other indicators that we should examine as further evidence of the equivalence of situations. Even if a chosen text turns out not to be equivalent, however, it can still yield useful information. The extent to which, and manner in which, self-correction and other strategies break down under increased task difficulty is of considerable interest to the diagnostician. In fact, such variability in context can occur within a given text. An important benefit of these individual running records is that one can maintain a record of change over time which is (1) unconfounded by practice effects, (2) ecologically (externally) valid, (3) more information laden, and (4) more instructionally relevant than conventional approaches to assessment.

The one-to-one descriptive process model may thus have altered the concept of reliability and its relationship to validity. Perhaps, contrary to current psychometric theory, a child's oral reading on a text can be valid but unreliable. The same item (particularly a word) may be approached using different strategies on different occasions, particularly if the item appears in different contexts. Some strategies may be successful and others unsuccessful, thus making the test unreliable. Such outcomes do not affect the validity of the test, however, since it represents an externally valid task. The *test* is valid; the *response* is unstable or unreliable. Indeed, the instability of the response generally tells us something about the learner. It may be that we need to look more into the context of the successes and failures across time. Or, alternatively, it may be that the response lies in the learner's zone of proximal development, in which he or she has the knowledge or strategies available but does not yet have control of them.

Under this model, if the child responds differently to the same item on different occasions in an individual test, we interpret that as telling us something about the *child*. The same outcome on a group test, we think, has *told* us something about the test. That is, our assumptions are different in the two situations. This distinction is not new either. For example, Freeman in 1926 made the following comment:

> It had been common to designate the differences among the individuals of a group of observers by the term *probable error*. . . . It became evident, in the course of experimentation, that these divergencies of individuals from the other individuals of the group are not due mainly to error, but constitute real differences in their . . . modes of behavior (pp. 33–34).

Had this approach been applied to reading, reliability theory would have been considered less tenable, and the 50 years of effort developing it may have been spent more profitably. Moreover, the focus would have had to shift toward individual "modes of behavior."

The real reliability concern in individual oral reading tests is between- and within-observer reliability, which is not so much a function of the test as of the user. The issues involved become quite different. For example, those discussed by Clay (1979) relate to the influences of the extent of observer training, error rate, and reader ability (because less able readers produce more complex patterns). A knowledge of factors beyond the data gathered in a test session is helpful because it gives a context within which to interpret the test performance (Harris & Sipay, 1975). At the same time, there are some problems caused by possession of such knowledge. Ysseldyke and Algozzine (1982) have demonstrated that even given perfectly normal test-score data, over half their sample of school professionals based a disabilities classification on referral data, including sex, looks (from a photograph), and SES (father's occupation). Thus it seems that invalidity in interpretation can occur even with ample "hard" data. Those administering the tests (or receiving test data) need to be wary of this. Such knowledge of context also can influence the scoring procedure in individual reading tests. Many gray areas occur in this scoring, such as decisions on dialect versus error or accuracy of answers to comprehension questions. McGill-Franzen and McDermott (1978) have described the reading diagnosis as "negotiated" in that the parameters of the testing interaction are tacitly debated and mutually agreed upon over the course of the assessment session. Again, teacher education on assessment is probably the best way to deal with these problems.

This shift of focus from the test to the user-teacher is important. The burden of decision quality (reliability and validity) is on the teachers rather than the tests, just as it is in clinical and counseling psychology. This may become a particular problem in view of the declining SAT scores of prospective education majors (Weaver, 1981) and the rather negative estimates of the quality of instruction they receive (Atkin, 1981). If we had originally selected the individual, process-oriented testing model, we would probably have been more concerned about the quality of teachers and teacher-training programs than about the quality of the testing instruments they used, since teachers would have had to become sensitive observers of students' reading behaviors.

CONCLUDING COMMENT

Since we have gone as far as we have down the current assessment path, it has become difficult for us to challenge the fundamental assumptions of our position. We have developed an awesome structure through three-quarters of a century of research and social and financial commitment. I hope that this chapter has made it clear that the model is based on tenuous assumptions. It is time for a thorough stock-taking of our approach to assessment in reading and the tradeoffs that we have been making. Too many assumptions have remained untested for too long.

There is a great need for researchers to reflect upon, and communicate the importance of their findings for assessment practice in applied settings. Research findings of late have tended to emphasize the importance of process over product, yet educators and researchers persist in depending on the more conveniently obtained product data. Metacognition has also recently been stressed in instructional research, yet many researchers continue to ignore the metacognitive components of reading in their assessment and the importance of metacognitive aspects of assessment for instruction. Both educators and researchers must bear in mind that children are rational beings who behave as such to the extent of their available knowledge. Instead of a concern over response outcomes, right or wrong, there needs to be greater concern over the reasons behind the responses. The bottom line is that we need to worry more about the assessment of process in the individual, and about the process of assessment in context.

In many ways the onus is on researchers to test assumptions and examine alternatives models. Researchers generally have fewer societal constraints to contend with than do other segments of the community involved with the assessment of reading. Since most research in reading involves some measurement (e.g., pretest-posttest), it is not only the measurement research community that needs to face the problem but virtually all those involved in reading research. Failure to challenge the status quo may be the worst form of intellectual complacency.

REFERENCES

Alexander, K. L., & McDill, E. L.   Selection and allocation within schools: Some cases and consequences of curriculum placement. *American Sociological Review,* 1976, *41,* 963–980.

Allington, R. L.   The persistence of teacher beliefs in facets of the visual perceptual deficit hypothesis. *Elementary School Journal,* 1982, *82,* 351–359.

Allington, R. L.   The reading instruction provided readers of differing reading abilities. *Elementary School Journal,* in press.

Allington, R. L., Chodos, L., Domaracki, J., & Truex, S.   Passage dependency: Four diagnostic oral reading tests. *Reading Teacher,* 1977, *30,* 369–375.

Allport, G. W.   Traits revisited. *American Psychologist,* 1966, *21,* 1–10.

American Optical Company, Southbridge, Mass.   Manufacturer of the Ophthalm-O-Graph, 1936.

Anderson, I. H., & Dearborn, W. F.   *The psychology of teaching reading.* New York: Ronald Press, 1952.

Anderson, R. C.   How to construct achievement tests to assess comprehension. *Review of Educational Research,* 1972, *42,* 145–170.

Anderson, R. C., Mason, J., & Shirey, L.   *The reading group: An experimental investigation of a labyrinth* (Technical Report No. 271). Urbana-Champaign, Ill.: University of Illinois, Center for the Study of Reading, February 1983.

Anderson, R. C., & Pichert, J. W.   *Recall of previously unrecallable information following a shift in perspective* (Technical Report No. 41). Urbana-Champaign, Ill.: University of Illinois, Center for the Study of Reading, July 1977.

Anderson, T. H., Wardrop, J. L., Hively, W., Muller, K. E., Anderson, R. I., Hastings, N. C., & Frederickson, J.   *Development and trial of a model for developing domain referenced tests of reading comprehension* (Technical Report No. 86). Urbana-Champaign, Ill.: University of Illinois, Center for the Study of Reading, May 1978.

Atkin, J. M.   Who will teach summer school? *Daedalus,* 1981, *110,* 91–103.

Ayers, L. P.   *Laggards in our schools: A study of retardation and elimination in city school systems.* New York: Russell Sage Foundation, 1909.

Ayers, L. P.   History and present status of educational measurements. In *Seventeenth Yearbook of the National Society for the Study of Education.* Bloomington, Ill.: Public School Publishing, 1918.

Barnes, E. T.   Cultural retardation or shortcomings of assessment techniques? In R. L. Lones (Ed.), *Black psychology.* New York: Harper & Row, 1972.

Bartholomae, D.   The study of error. *College Composition and Communication,* 1980, *31,* 253–269.

Bem, D. J., & Allen, A.   On predicting some of the people some of the time: The search for cross-situational consistencies in behavior. *Psychological Review,* 1974, *81,* 506–520.

Betts, E.   *Foundations of reading instruction.* New York: American Book, 1946.

Bloom, B. S.   *Human characteristics and school learning.* New York: McGraw-Hill, 1976.

Bormuth, J.   *On the theory of achievement test items.* Chicago: University of Chicago Press, 1970.

Bower, G. H.   Experiments on story comprehension and recall. *Discourse Processes,* 1978, *1,* 211–231.

Bronfenbrenner, U.   The experimental ecology of education. *Teachers College Record,* 1976, *78,* 157–205.

Brown, A. L., & French, L. A.   *The zone of potential development: Implications for intelligence testing in the year 2000* (Technical Report No. 128). Urbana-Champaign, Ill.: University of Illinois, Center for the Study of Reading, May 1979.

Brown, H. A.   The measurement of efficiency in instruction in reading. *Elementary School Teacher*, 1914, *14*, 477–490.

Brown, J. S., & Burton, R. R.   Diagnostic models for procedural bugs in basic mathematical skills. *Cognitive Science*, 1978, *2*, 155–192.

Bruce, B., Rubin, A., & Starr, K.   *Why readability formulas fail* (ERIC Document Reproduction Service No. ED 205 915). August 1981.

Burgess, M. A.   *A scale for measuring ability in silent reading.* New York: Russell Sage Foundation, 1921.

Buswell, G. T.   *An experimental study of the eye-voice span in reading* (Supplementary Educational Monographs, No. 17). Chicago: Department of Education, University of Chicago, 1920.

Carnine, D., & Silbert, J.   *Direct instruction reading.* Columbus, Ohio: Merrill, 1979.

Carver, R. P.   Two dimensions of tests: Psychometric and edumetric. *American Psychologist*, 1974, *29*, 512–518.

Cattell, J. M.   The time it takes to see and name objects. *Mind*, 1886, *11*, 63–65.

Chapman, J. C.   *Chapman unspeeded reading-comprehension test.* Minneapolis: Educational Test Bureau, 1924.

Clay, M. M.   *Reading: The patterning of complex behaviour.* Auckland, New Zealand: Heinemann, 1972.

Clay, M. M.   *The early detection of reading difficulties: A diagnostic survey with recovery procedures* (2nd ed.). Auckland, New Zealand: Heinemann, 1979.

Coles, G. S.   The learning disabilities test battery: Empirical and social issues. *Harvard Educational Review*, 1978, *48*, 313–340.

Collins, A., & Smith, E.   Teaching the process of reading comprehension In D. K. Detterman & R. J. Sternberg (Eds.), *How and how much can intelligence be increased?* Norwood, N. J.: Ablex, 1982.

Courtis, S. A.   Standard tests in English. *Elementary School Teacher.* 1914, *14*, 374–392.

Courtis, S. A.   *Courtis standard research tests in silent reading* (No. 2). Detroit: Courtis, 1917.

Cronbach, L. J., & Gleser, G. C.   Interpretation of reliability and validity coefficients: Remarks on a paper by Lord. *Journal of Educational Psychology*, 1959, *50*, 230–237.

Dana, R. H., & Leech, S.   Existential assessment. *Journal of Personality Assessment*, 1976, *38*, 428–435.

Davis, F. B.   Fundamental factors of comprehension in reading. *Psychometrika*, 1944, *9*, 185–197.

Davis, F. B.   Research in comprehension in reading. *Reading Research Quarterly*, 1972, *7*, 628–678.

Davison, A., & Kantor, R. N.   On the failure of readability formulas to define readable texts: A case study from adaptations. *Reading Research Quarterly*, 1982, *17*, 187–209.

Davison, A., Lutz, R., & Roalef, A.   Text readability. *Proceedings of the March, 1980, Conference Center for the Study of Reading.* Urbana, Ill., 1981.

Daw, S. E.   The persistence of errors in oral reading in grades four and five. *Journal of Educational Research*, 1938, *32*, 81–90.

Dearborn, W. F., & Westbrook, C. H.   *Dearborn and Westbrook reading examination.* Boston: Dearborn, Harvard University Graduate School of Education, 1920.

Dodge, R., & Cline, T. S.   The angle velocity of eye-movements. *Psychological Review*, 1901, *8*, 145–157.

Doman, G., Stevens, G. L., & Orem, R. C.   You can teach your baby to read. *Ladies Home Journal*, 1963, *80*, 62.

Downey, M. T.   *Ben D. Wood, educational reformer.* Princeton, N.J.: Educational Testing Service, 1965.

Drahozal, E. D., & Hanna, G. S.   Reading comprehension subscores: Pretty bottles for ordinary wine. *Journal of Reading*, 1978, *21*, 416–420.

Drowatzky, J. N.   Tracking and ability grouping in education. *Journal of Law and Education*, 1981, *10*, 43–59.

Duffy, G. B., & Durrell, D. D.   Third grade difficulties in oral reading. *Education*, 1935, *56*, 37–40.

Durkin, D.   *Teaching young children to read* (2nd ed.). Boston: Allyn & Bacon, 1976.

Durrell, D. D.   Individual differences and their implications with respect to instruction in reading. In *The teaching of reading: A second report* (Thirty-sixth Yearbook of the National Society for Studies in Education, Part 1). Bloomington, Ill.: Public School Publishing, 1937.

Durrell, D. D.   *Durrell analysis of reading difficulty*. New York: Harcourt, Brace & World, 1937, 1955.

Ebel, R. L.   *The social consequences of educational testing* (Proceedings of the 1963 Invitational Conference on Testing Problems). Princeton, N.J.: Educational Testing Service, 1964.

Ericsson, K. A., & Simon, H. A.   Verbal reports as data. *Psychological Review*, 1980, *87*, 215–251.

Eurich, A. C.   *Minnesota speed of reading test for college students*. Minneapolis: University of Minnesota Press, 1936.

Farr, R., & Tone, B.   Text analysis and validated modeling of the reading process (1973–1981): Implications for reading assessment. In *Reading comprehension from research to practice*. Hillsdale, N.J.: Erlbaum, in press.

Feuerstein, R.   *The dynamic assessment of retarded performers: The learning potential assessment device, theory, instrument and techniques*. Baltimore: University Park Press, 1979.

Freeman, F. N.   *Mental tests: Their history, principles and applications*. Chicago: Houghton Mifflin, 1926.

Fuchs, L. S., Fuchs, D., & Deno, S.   Reliability and validity of curriculum-based informal reading inventories. *Reading Research Quarterly*, 1982, *18*, 6–25.

Gambrell, L. B., Wilson, R. M., & Gantt, W. N.   Classroom observations of task attending behaviors of good and poor readers. *Journal of Educational Research*, 1981, *74*, 400–404.

Gates, A. I.   *The improvement of reading: A program of diagnostic and remedial methods*. New York: Macmillan, 1928.

Gates, A. I.   The measurement and evaluation of achievement in reading. In *The teaching of reading: A second report* (Thirty-sixth Yearbook of the National Society for Studies in Education, Part 1). Bloomington, Ill.: Public School Publishing, 1937.

Gesell, A. L.   *Infancy and human growth*. New York: Macmillan, 1928.

Glaser, R.   Instructional technology and the measurement of learning outcomes: Some questions. *American Psychologist*, 1963, *18*, 519–521.

Glaser, R.   The future of testing: A research agenda for cognitive psychology and psychometrics. *American Psychologist*, 1981, *36*, 923–936.

Goodman, Y. M., & Burke, C. L.   *Reading miscue inventory manual procedure for diagnosis and evaluation*. New York: Macmillan, 1970.

Graham, P.   Literacy: A goal for secondary school. *Daedalus*, 1981, *110*, 119–134.

Gray, W. S.   *Studies of elementary school reading through standardized tests* (Supplemental Educational Monographs No. 1). Chicago: University of Chicago Press, 1917.

Gray, W. S.   Contributions of research to special methods. In G. M. Whipple, (Ed.), *The scientific movement in education* (Thirty-seventh Yearbook of the National Society for the Study of Education). Bloomington, Ill.: Public School Publishing, 1938.

Greene, H. A., & Jorgenson, A. N.   *The use and interpretation of elementary school tests*. New York: Longman, 1935.

Gronlund, N. E.   *Measurement and evaluation in teaching* (3rd ed.). New York: Macmillan, 1976.

Haggerty, M. E.   *Haggerty reading examination*. Yonkers, N. Y.: World Book, 1919.

Hall, L. K., & Day, J. D.   *A comparison of the zone of proximal development in learning disabled, mentally retarded and normal children*. Paper presented at the annual meeting of the American Educational Research Association, New York, March 1982.

Hambleton, R. K.   Test score validity and standard-setting methods. In R. A. Berk (Ed.),

Criterion-referenced measurement: The state of the art. Baltimore: Johns Hopkins University Press, 1980.

Haney, W.   Validity, vaudeville, and values: A short history of social concerns over standardized testing. *American Psychologist,* 1981, *36,* 1021–1034.

Haney, W., & Madaus, G. F.   Making sense of the competency testing movement. *Harvard Educational Review,* 1978, *48,* 462–484.

Hanna, C. S., & Oaster, T. R.   Toward a unified theory of context dependence. *Reading Research Quarterly,* 1978, *14,* 226–243.

Harris, A. J., & Sipay, E. R.   *How to increase reading ability* (6th ed.). New York: Longman, 1975.

Haupt, E. J., & Goldsmith, J. S.   *Expanding the factorial structure of reading errors: Frequency, severity, and higher order components in reading errors.* Paper presented at the annual meeting of the American Educational Research Association, New York, March 1982.

Heffernan, H.   Significance of kindergarten education. *Childhood Education,* 1960, *36,* 313–319.

Hiebert, E. H.   An examination of ability grouping for reading instruction. *Reading Research Quarterly,* 1983, *18,* 231–255.

Hildreth, G. H.   *A bibliography of mental tests and rating scales.* New York: Psychological Corporation, 1933.

Hobson v. *Hansen.* 269 F.Supp. 401 (D. D.C. 1967), Aff'd sub. nom. *Smuck* v. *Hobson,* 408 F.2d 175 (D.C. Cir. 1969).

Holdaway, D.   *The foundations of literacy.* Sydney, Australia: Ashton Scholastic, 1979.

Holt, J.   *How children fail.* New York: Pitman, 1964.

Hunter, J. E., & Schmidt, F. L.   Critical analysis of the statistical and ethical implications of various definitions of test bias. *Psychological Bulletin,* 1976, *83,* 1053–1071.

Huynh, H.   Statistical consideration of mastery scores. *Psychometrica,* 1976, *41,* 65–78.

Johnston, P.   *A cognitive basis for the assessment of reading comprehension.* Newark, Del.: International Reading Association, 1983.

Johnston, P.   *Implications of basic research for the assessment of reading comprehension* (Technical Report No. 206). Urbana-Champaign, Ill.: University of Illinois, Center for the Study of Reading, May 1981.

Johnston, P.   Prior knowledge and reading comprehension test bias. *Reading Research Quarterly,* in press. (a)

Johnston, P.   Instruction and student independence. *Elementary School Journal,* in press. (b)

Karlsen, B., Madden, R., & Gardner, E. F.   *Stanford diagnostic reading test* New York: Harcourt Brace Jovanovich, 1976.

Kavale, K.   Functions of the Illinois Test of Psycholinguistic Abilities (ITPA): Are they trainable? *Exceptional Children,* 1981, *47,* 496–513.

Kavale, K., & Schreiner, R.   The reading processes of above average and average readers: A comparison of the use of reasoning strategies in responding to standardized comprehension measures. *Reading Research Quarterly,* 1979, *15,* 102–128.

Kelly, E. J.   The Kansas silent reading tests. *Journal of Educational Psychology,* 1916, *7,* 63–80.

Kingston, A. J., Jr.   The measurement of reading comprehension. In R. Farr (Ed.), *Measurement and evaluation of reading.* Chicago: Harcourt, Brace & World, 1970.

Kintsch, W., & van Dijk, T. A.   Toward a model of text comprehension and production. *Psychological Review,* 1978, *85,* 363–394.

Kirsch, I., & Guthrie, J.   The concept and measurement of functional literacy. *Reading Research Quarterly,* 1977–1978, *13,* 485–507.

Kratochwill, T. R. (Ed.).   *Single subject research strategies for evaluating change.* New York: Academic Press, 1978.

Kuhn, T. S.   *The structure of scientific revolutions.* Chicago: University of Chicago Press, 1962.

Landes, W., & Solomon, L.   Compulsory schooling legislation: An economic analysis of law and social changes in the nineteenth century. *Journal of Economic History*, 1972, *32*, 54–91.

Larry P. v. *Riles*. 495 F.Supp. 926 (N.D. Cal. 1979) appeal docketed, No. 80–4027 (9th Circ., Jan. 17, 1980).

Lennon, R. T.   Assumptions underlying the use of content validity. *Educational and Psychological Measurement*, 1956, *16*, 294–304.

Lerner, B.   The minimum competence testing movement: Social, scientific, and legal implications. *American Psychologist*, 1981, *36*, 1057–1066.

Lumsden, J.   Test theory. *Annual Review of Psychology*, 1976, 223–258.

McDermott, R. P.   Achieving school failure: An anthropological approach to illiteracy and social stratification. In H. Singer, & R. B. Ruddell (Eds.), *Theoretical models and processes of reading*. Newark, Del.: International Reading Association, 1976.

McGill-Franzen, A., & McDermott, P.   *Negotiating a reading diagnosis*. Paper presented at the National Reading Conference, St. Petersburg, Fla., December 1978.

Madden, M., & Pratt, M.   An oral reading survey as a teaching aid. *Elementary English Review*, 1941, *18*, 122–126.

Mandler, J. M., & Johnson, N. S.   Remembrance of things parsed: Story structure and recall. *Cognitive Psychology*, 1977, *9*, 111–151.

Markman, E. M.   Realizing that you don't understand: A preliminary investigation. *Child Development*, 1977, *48*, 986–992.

Marr, M. B., & Lyons, K.   Passage independence: An examination of three informal reading inventories. In M. L. Kamil & A. J. Moe (Eds.), *Perspectives in Reading Research and Instruction*. Clemson, S.C.: National Reading Conference, 1980.

Mehan, H.   Structuring school structure. *Harvard Educational Review*, 1978, *48*, 32–64.

Meichenbaum, D.   *Cognitive behavior modification: An integrative approach*. New York: Plenum, 1977.

Meskauskas, J. A.   Evaluation models for criterion-referenced testing: Views regarding mastery and standard-setting. *Review of Educational Research*, 1976, *46*, 133–158.

Messick, S.   Evidence and ethics in the evaluation of tests. *Educational Researcher*, 1981, *10*, 9–20.

Miles, W. R., & Segal, D.   Clinical observation of eye-movements in the rating of reading ability. *Journal of Educational Psychology*, 1929, *20*, 520–529.

Mischel, W.   *Personality and assessment*. New York: Wiley, 1968.

Monroe, W. S.   Monroe's standardized silent reading tests. Bloomington, Ill.: Public School Publishing, 1918.

Morphett, M. V., & Washburne, C.   When should children begin to read? *Elementary School Journal*, 1931, *31*, 496–503.

Nelson, M. J., & Denny, E. C.   *The Nelson-Denny Reading Test*. Revised by J. I. Brown. Boston: Houghton Mifflin, 1960.

Nicholson, T.   Is it "pecking" as in chicken or as in China? *Topics in Learning and Learning Disabilities*, in press.

Nurss, J. R., & McGauvrin, M. E.   *Teacher's manual (Part 2): Interpretation and use of test results*. New York: Harcourt, Brace, 1976.

Olshavsky, J. E.   Reading as problem solving: An investigation of strategies. *Reading Research Quarterly*, 1977, *12*, 654–674.

Omanson, R.   The relation between centrality and story category variation. *Journal of Verbal Learning and Verbal Behavior*, 1982, *21*, 326–337.

PASE v. *Hannon*. 506 F.Supp. 831 (N.D. Ill. 1980).

Pavlidis, G. Th.   Sequencing, eye movements and the early objective diagnosis of dyslexia. In G. Th. Pavlidis & T. R. Miles (Eds.), *Dyslexia research and its applications to education*. New York: Wiley, 1981.

Pearson, P. D., & Johnson, D. D.   *Teaching reading comprehension*. New York: Holt, Rinehart & Winston, 1978.

Pflaum, S. W., & Pascarella, E. T.   Interactive effects of prior reading achievement and training in context on the reading of learning disabled children. *Reading Research*

Quarterly, 1980, *16,* 138–158.

Pipho, C. Minimum competency testing in 1978: A look at state standards. *Phi Delta Kappan,* 1978, *59,* 585–588.

Popham, W. J. *Criterion referenced measurement.* Englewood Cliffs, N.J.: Prentice-Hall, 1978.

Powell, W. R. Reappraising the criteria for interpreting informal reading inventories. In E. L. DeBoer (Ed.), *Reading diagnosis and evaluation.* Newark, Del.: International Reading Association, 1970.

Quantz, J. O. Problems in the psychology of reading. *Psychological Review Monograph Supplements,* 1897 (Whole No. 1).

Reschly, D. J. Psychological testing in educational classification and placement. *American Psychologist,* 1981, *36,* 1094–1102.

Resnick, D. P. History of educational testing. In A. K. Wigdor & W. R. Garner (Eds.), *Ability testing: Uses, consequences, and controversies* (Part 2). Washington, D.C.: National Academy Press, 1982.

Resnick, D. P., & Resnick, L. The nature of literacy: An historical exploration. *Harvard Educational Review,* 1977, *47,* 370–385.

Rogers, C. R. *Counseling and psychotherapy.* Boston: Houghton Mifflin, 1942.

Rosenbaum, J. E. Social implications of educational grouping. In D.C. Berliner (Ed.), *Review of educational research* (Vol. 8). Washington, D.C.: American Educational Research Association, 1980.

Rosenblatt, L. M. *The reader, the text, the poem: The transactional theory of the literary work.* Carbondale, Ill.: Southern Illinois University Press, 1978.

Rowley, G. Historical antecedents of the standard-setting debate: An inside account of the minimal-beardedness controversy. *Journal of Educational Measurement,* 1982, *19,* 87–95.

Rusch, G. M., & Stoddard, G. D. *Tests and measurements in high school instruction.* Yonkers, N.Y.: World Book, 1927.

Schank, R. C. The structure of episodes in memory. In D. G. Bobrow and A. Collins (Eds.), *Representation and understanding: Studies in cognitive science.* New York: Academic Press, 1975.

Scriven, M. Objectivity and subjectivity in educational research. In L. G. Thomas (Ed.), *Philosophical redirection of educational research* (Seventy-first Yearbook of the National Society for the Study of Education, Part 1). Chicago: University of Chicago Press, 1972.

Spache, G. *Diagnosing and correcting reading disabilities.* Boston: Allyn & Bacon, 1976.

Spache, G. *Diagnostic reading scales.* Monterey, Calif.: McGraw-Hill, 1981.

Spearitt, D. Identification of subskills of reading comprehension by maximum likelihood factor analysis. *Reading Research Quarterly,* 1972, *8,* 92–111.

Starch, D. The measurement of efficiency in reading. *Journal of Educational Psychology,* 1915, *6,* 1–24.

Steffensen, M. S., Joag-Dev, C., & Anderson, R. C. A cross-cultural perspective on reading comprehension. *Reading Research Quarterly,* 1979, *15,* 10–29.

Stein, N. L., & Trabasso, T. What's in a story: An approach to comprehension and instruction. In R. Glaser (Ed.), *Advances in the psychology of instruction* (Vol. 2). Hillsdale, N.J.: Erlbaum, 1982.

Sternberg, R. J. Testing and cognitive psychology. *American Psychologist,* 1981, *36,* 1181–1189.

Taylor, W. Cloze procedure: A new tool for measuring readability. *Journalism Quarterly,* 1953, *9,* 206–223.

Thorndike, E. L. *An introduction to the theory of mental and social measurements.* New York: Science Press, 1904.

Thorndike, E. L. *Educational psychology* (Vol. 1). New York: Teachers College, Columbia University, 1913.

Thorndike, E. L. *An introduction to the theory of mental and social measurements* (2nd ed.). New York: Teachers' College, Columbia University, 1916.

Thorndike, E. L.   Reading as reasoning: A study of mistakes in paragraph reading. *Journal of Educational Psychology*, 1917, *8*, 323–332.

Thurstone, L. L.   *Psychological examination* (Test 4). Stoelting, n.d.

Tuinman, J. J.   Determining the passage-dependency of comprehension questions in five major tests. *Reading Research Quarterly*, 1974, *9*, 207–223.

Tuinman, J. J.   Criterion referenced measurement in a norm referenced context. In J. Samuels (Ed.), *What research has to say about reading instruction*. Newark, Del.: International Reading Association, 1978, 165–173.

Tuinman, J. J.   Reading is recognition—When reading is not reasoning. In J. C. Harste & R. R. Carey (Eds.), *New perspectives on comprehension* (Monograph in Language and Reading Studies, No. 3). Bloomington Ind.: Indiana University Press, 1979.

Turner, A., & Greene, E.   *The construction of a propositional text base* (Technical Report No. 63). Boulder: University of Colorado Press, April 1977.

Urry, V. W.   Tailored testing: A successful application of latent trait theory. *Journal of Educational Measurement*, 1977, *14*, 181–196.

Venezky, R. L.   *Testing in reading: Assessment and instructional decision making*. Urbana, Ill.: National Council of Teachers of English, 1974.

Vygotsky, L.   *Mind in society*. Cambridge, Mass.: Harvard University Press, 1978.

Walmsley, S. A.   Some persistent problems with objectives and objective-item congruence in criterion-referenced tests. *Improving Human Performance Quarterly*, 1977, *6*, 157–164.

Walmsley, S. A.   The criterion referenced measurement of an early reading behavior. *Reading Research Quarterly*, 1978–1979, *14*, 574–604.

Walmsley, S. A.   On the purpose and content of secondary reading programs: An educational ideological perspective. *Curriculum Inquiry*, 1981, *11*, 73–93.

Washburne, C.   Ripeness. *Progressive Education*, 1936, *13*, 125–130.

Weaver, W. T.   The talent pool in teacher education. *Journal of Teacher Education*, 1981, *32*, 32–36.

Weaver, W. T., Bickley, A. C., & Ford, F.   A cross-validation study of the relationship of reading test items to their relevant paragraphs. *Perceptual and Motor Skills*, 1969, *29*, 11–14.

Webb, L. W., & Shotwell, A. M.   *Standard tests in the elementary school*. New York: Farrar & Rinehart, 1932.

Weber, R. M.   The study of oral reading errors: A review of the literature. *Reading Research Quarterly*, 1968, *4*, 96–119.

Weinshank, A. B.   The reliability of diagnostic and remedial decisions of reading specialists. *Journal of Reading Behavior*, 1982, *14*, 33–50.

Whipple, G. M.   Reading tests—Standardized and informal. In G. M. Whipple (Ed.), *Report of the National Committee on Reading* (Twenty-fourth Yearbook of the National Society for the Study of Education, Part 1). Bloomington, Ill.: Public School Publishing, 1925.

Winograd, P.   *An examination of strategic difficulties in summarizing texts*. Doctoral dissertation, University of Illinois, Urbana-Champaign, January 1982.

Winograd, P., & Johnston, P.   Comprehension and the error detection paradigm. *Journal of Reading Behavior*, 1982, *14*, 61–76.

Woodcock, R. W.   *Woodcock reading mastery tests*. Circle Pines, Minn.: American Guidance Service, 1973.

Ysseldyke, J. E., & Algozzine, B.   Bias among professionals who erroneously declare students eligible for special services. *Journal of Experimental Education*, 1982, *50*, 223–228.

Ysseldyke, J. E., & Marston, D.   A critical analysis of standardized reading tests. *School Psychology Review*, 1982, *11*, 259–266.

PART TWO

Basic Processes:
The State of the Art

Michael Kamil, Editor

7 MODELS OF THE READING PROCESS

S. Jay Samuels and Michael L. Kamil

SOME CONTEXT

A Brief History of Models

Reading research is just a little more than 100 years old. In fact, it was the year 1879 when Emile Javal published his first paper on eye movements; James McKeen Cattell's still-cited paper on seeing and naming letters versus words (see Gough, this volume) was published in 1886. Surprisingly, serious attempts at building explicit models of the reading process—models that describe the entire process from the time the eye meets the page until the reader experiences the "click of comprehension"—have a history of a little more than 30 years, probably best marked by the publication in 1953 of Jack Holmes's famous and controversial substrata-factor theory of reading. A comparable, but earlier, emphasis on building models in the psychology of learning can be seen in the work of Hull (1943) and Tolman (1932).

This is not to say that early reading researchers were not concerned about all aspects of the reading process or that there were no scholarly pieces from which a model could be deduced fairly easily. One has but to read Huey (1908/1968), Woodworth (1938), or Anderson and Dearborn (1952) to refute such a claim. It is perhaps more accurate to speculate that until the mid-1950s and the 1960s, there simply was not a strong tradition of attempting to conceptualize knowledge and theory about the reading process in the form of explicit reading models.

There are a variety of factors that account for the observed burst in model-building activity from 1965, say, to the present. Surely the changes that occurred in language research and the psychological study of mental processes (see Kamil, this volume) played a major role by elevating reading research to a more respectable stature. Just as surely, the advent of what has come to be known as the psycholinguistic perspective (Goodman, 1967/1976, 1970; Smith, 1971) pushed the field to consider underlying assumptions about basic processes in reading, as did a geometrically accelerating body of empirical evidence about basic processes (see Venezky, this volume).

Holmes's attempts to build a reading model along with those of his colleague and successor to the efforts, H. Singer, are exemplary not only for the specific content or components of the model, but also for the approach they used to model building and model evaluation. Although Singer and Ruddell (1976) classify Holmes's model as a developmental model (indeed, it does try to account for changes in reading performance across ages), it is probably more accurate to call it a psychometric model. This classification seems justified because of the methodology used to evaluate the model—administer a large battery of component-skill subtests to readers of different developmental levels and then try to determine which component processes (or combinations of component processes) explain the greatest proportion of variance in a criterion variable, like comprehension or "reading power." What is exemplary about their efforts, expecially for an early model, is the emphasis on using empirically gathered evidence to evaluate the model. In fact, it is fair to conclude that Holmes and Singer used available data to derive the construction of their model. This approach is to be distinguished from that used by other model builders whose style is to build a logically consistent model and then devise experiments to evaluate the efficacy of its components.

During the 1960s and early 1970s, a number of scholars developed more-or-less formal models of the reading process. Hockberg (1970), Mackworth (1972), and Levin and Kaplan (1970) all speculated about what a model describing the processes of skilled reading must account for; however it is probably not fair to classify their attempts as model-building efforts because each discussed these issues within the context of another purpose. Carroll (1964) provided a definition of reading along with a simple one-way flow diagram from visual stimulus to an oral language recoding to meaning responses. Carroll's purpose was to be illustrative not definitive; consequently, his model leaves many stages imprecisely specified.

Ruddell (1969) developed a system of communication model of reading that differed categorically from its predecessors in its excruciating detail of component processes and stages. Ruddell's model incorporated components consistent with emerging concepts from the rapidly expanding body of research on language development and language competence. Ruddell offered no line of empirical work to evaluate the model; instead, he chose to cite existing research that supported the inclusion of severai of the components in the model (e.g., boxes for evaluating systactic and semantic input or transformational rewrite rules).

Goodman also worked out a model of reading over several years (1965, 1966, 1967/1976) that culminated in a relatively formal statement of the model's components and stages (1970), complete with a flow diagram. During that period and in the subsequent years, Goodman and his colleagues have amassed an extensive array of oral reading data to evaluate and support the model or at least the key features of the model. Often dubbed "reading as a psycholinguistic guessing game," its most distinctive characteristic is its procedural preference for allowing the reader to rely on existing syntactic and semantic knowledge structures, so that reliance on the graphic display and existing knowledge about the sounds associated with graphemes (graphophonemic knowledge) can be minimized. This is not to say that his model does not allow for a reader to go from symbol to sound to meaning—such mediation will not occur in predictable situations (as a function of familiarity and, perhaps, instructional history). It is more accurate to assert that his model always prefers the cognitive economy of reliance on well-developed linguistic (syntactic and semantic) rather than graphic information.

Another interesting distinction between Goodman's model and other models centers on his use of the term *decoding*. Whereas others typically reserve this term to describe what happens when a reader translates a graphemic input into a phonemic input, Goodman uses it to describe how either a graphemic input or a phonemic input gets translated into a meaning code. Goodman uses the term *recoding* to describe the process of translating graphemes into phonemes. Thus, *decoding* can be either direct (graphemes to meaning) or mediated (graphemes to phonemes to meaning). Most of the extensive research efforts of Goodman and his colleagues have been directed toward demonstrating the strong procedural preference readers of all ages have for relying upon the meaning (as opposed to the graphic and graphophonemic) cues available in the printed message. A final unique aspect of Goodman's model is that it, among all earlier and later models, has had the greatest impact on conceptions about reading instruction, particularly early instruction. So strong has been this impact that it is not uncommon to hear or read about *THE* psycholinguistic approach to reading or *THE* whole language approach to reading.

It is difficult to know what to say about Frank Smith's (1971) seminal work describing reading as a psycholinguistic process. It is not so much a model of reading as it is a description of the linguistic and cognitive processes that any decent model of reading will need to take into account. Like Goodman, he is careful to distinguish between mediated (through recoding to sound) and immediate meaning identification (print to meaning). Also, like Goodman, his account of reading exhibits a procedural preference for reliance on language factors instead of graphic information. But to call it a model of reading would misrepresent Smith's aim. Perhaps the greatest contribution of Smith's work is to explain how the redundancy inherent at all levels of language (letter features, within letters, within words, within sentences, within discourses) provide the reader with enormous flexibility in marshaling resources to create a meaning for the text at hand.

With the publication of Gough's (1972) model of reading, the impact of the information processing approach to studying mental processes is seen within the reading field. Controversial because of Gough's assumption that all letters in the visual field must be accounted for individually by the reader prior to the assignment of meaning to any string of letters, Gough's model has probably generated as much controversy about basic processes as Goodman's has about instructional practice. The appearance of LaBerge and Samuels's (1974) model emphasizing automaticity of component processes and Rumelhart's interactive model (1977) emphasizing flexible processing and multiple information sources, depending upon contextual circumstances, provided convincing evidence that the information processing perspective was here to stay within the reading field.

Since the publication of Rumelhart's model, there have been other notable efforts deserving mention. Carver (1977–1978) has provided us with a model that hearkens back to that of Gough (because of its unidirectional emphasis from letters to sounds to meaning) and to Holmes and Singer (because Carver, more than any other recent model builder, has emphasized the empirical evaluation of *all* aspects of his model). Stanovich (1980) has developed an interesting twist to the Rumelhart model. Kintsch and van Dijk (1978) have built a model emphasizing comprehension to the exclusion of word identification (most other models, including Rumelhart's, seem to have a bias for explaining word identification). Most recently, Just and Carpenter (1980) have built a model to account for comprehension processes based upon studies of eye movements.

With this brief history, we now turn to describing and explaining some of the models we have mentioned. Here, our own scholarly biases emerge. We have chosen to describe the Gough, LaBerge and Samuels, and Rumelhart models in some detail; following this, we will try to capsulize the advances made by Stanovich, Kintsch and van Dijk, and Carpenter and Just. Finally, we will offer some comparative comments about the models we have described. We have chosen to emphasize these three because they are the most formal of the extant models; thus, they provide a fair amount of detail about certain aspects of the reading process. But first, a few words about some thorny problems all models must address and about the nature of information processing models.

Some Problems in Model Evaluation

When researchers attempt to describe the reading process, we must be aware of two major problems that lead to misunderstandings among model builders. The first of these problems is that the developer of a model of reading has only a limited knowledge base to draw upon, and this knowledge base is influenced by the scientific philosophies and studies dominant within the historical context in which the model was developed. Thus, if one contrasts the models that were developed during the pre-1960 period of behaviorism with those developed during the post-1965 period of cognitive psychology, one can find conceptualizations and components in the newer models not found in earlier ones. Before the mid-1960s, because of the emphasis on behaviorism, the models attempted to describe how stimuli, such as printed words and word-recognition responses, became associated. During this period, because the emphasis was on directly observable events external to the individual, little attempt was made to explain what went on within the recesses of the mind that allowed the human to make sense of the printed page. After the mid-1960s, with the emergence of cognitive psychology as a major force, the models began to show how processes, such as memory and attention, which went on within the recesses of the human mind, played a role in reading. As more became known about comprehension, an attempt was made to model this process through conceptual networks.

Even during this current period, in which cognitive psychology dominates so much thinking about reading, one can observe how changes in thinking have influenced the models of human information processing. For example, the models of the 1970s tended to be linear information processing models, whereas the later models tended to be interactive with opportunities for feedback loops from components in the later stages to influence components in the earlier stages. Thus, as we attempt to evaluate the models of reading of the last three decades, we must do so in terms of the information available and the conceptualizations current during the period in which they were developed.

The second major problem which we must keep in mind as we study and evaluate these different reading models is that each scholar who describes the process is influenced by information gathered during experiments. Unfortunately, researchers have tended to ignore the fact that information gathered during an experiment is influenced by four interacting factors. These are the age and skill of the experimental subjects, the tasks which the subjects are asked to perform, the materials which are used, and the context (e.g., classroom, laboratory, type of school, etc.) which surrounds the study. A change in any of these variables can alter the results of a study and the researcher's view of the process. These four interactive variables can be seen in Figure 7.1 (adapted from Jenkins, 1979).

If, for example, a researcher does a series of studies using children but not adults, a view of the reading process would emerge which would be different from the view which would emerge had skilled adult readers been used. Similarly, the type of task used in an experiment has an important influence on the outcome

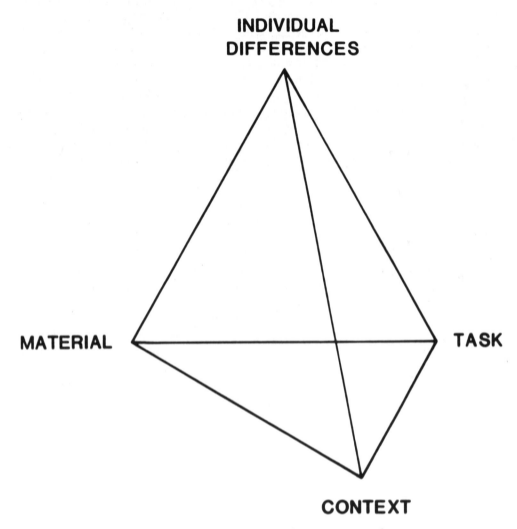

FIGURE 7.1   Four interacting factors which can alter experimental outcomes.

and conclusions of a study. For example, in a study of word recognition, one can use an oral response, semantic categorization, lexical decision, or a matching task. Each of these tasks can possibly lead to different results.

Still, other changes in addition to task and individual difference factors can alter the results of a study. The researcher may use high- or low-frequency words or the words may be presented in context or in isolation. Situational context can alter performance too. A student who knows she is in an experiment as a requirement to complete a college psychology course may not react to the task in the same way as a businessman reading the morning paper on a commuter train. Each of the variables in an investigation of word-recognition process—the skill of the experimental subjects, the nature of the experimental task, the difficulty of the words used, and contextual factors—will influence the experimental findings.

Because of the interactive nature of the variables in a study, we must attempt to evaluate the different reading models in terms of their generalizability. Each of the models presented in this article is an adequate description of the reading process for a particular set of conditions *but not for all conditions*. As we investigate and study the models, we ought to be asking questions, such as Does this model adequately describe both fluent and beginning reading? Does this model describe reading across a variety of tasks and purposes? Does the model describe the word recognition process as well as the comprehension process? Does the model describe the reading process for different materials as well as different contexts? At the present time, none of the models can do all of the above. Hence, our need to study the models carefully to know what they can and cannot do.

INFORMATION PROCESSING MODELS

Building Information Processing Models

To the information processing theorist, the human being is viewed as a communication channel with a capacity for taking in information from sensory organs, such as eyes and ears, and then transforming, storing, retrieving, and finally using this information when it is needed. In order to describe how this complex sequence of steps occurs, information processing theorists often create an analogy between what goes on in the human head and what happens in a manufacturing process.

In a manufacturing process, raw materials are taken in and by a series of stages machines transform the raw materials until a finished product emerges. Since, as often happens, some stages in the manufacturing process take less time than others, provision must be made to store the unfinished product until it can be taken up once again and moved along to its final completed form. Consequently, a schematic drawing of the manufacturing process should show an input stage for the raw materials, the machines which transform the raw material, and storage points where the unfinished product must rest for a period of time until it can be taken up again.

To continue the analogy between the manufacturing process—with its raw materials, machines, and storage facilities—and human information processing, we can say that the raw materials of reading consist of stimuli from the words in print. The principal structures (or machines) in the human head used to convert the raw material of reading into a more usable form include the eyes and the brain, while the storage facilities necessary in manufacturing are represented in human information processing by memory systems, such as visual information store, short-term and long-term memory.

While the eyes and the brain are important structures for converting the raw material of reading to another form, a case can be made to include the ears as well since they are also involved but in an indirect way. Our ability to hear is an important element in language acquisition, and language is obviously a critical element in reading. It is well known, for example, that those who have been deaf since birth have an extraordinarily difficult time learning to read.

So far, in schematic model building, we have mentioned the raw material of reading, the structures used to transform the raw materials, and the memory storage systems. In order to complete the picture, we need to describe the movement of materials through the system. To accomplish this, information processing theorists usually use flow diagrams to trace the path that the data take as they are moved along step by step and are finally processed into meaning. Thus, one may characterize an information processing model of reading as an attempt to explain by analogy how information from print is taken in and transformed into meaning. This goal is achieved by describing the machinery, the transformations, and the memory storage facilities which the information passes through on its journey from the printed words on a page to meaning within the human head.

Characteristics of Models

As we shall see, model building is a game which any number can play, but a good model has certain important characteristics. The three characteristics of a good model are: (a) it can summarize the past, (b) it can help us to understand the present, and (c) it can predict the future. Some models are developed only after a considerable amount of research has been done and data collected on a topic. When the model is developed, it can synthesize much of the information which was gathered in the past. Although Boyle's law is not a model, it can illustrate this point. This law shows the relationship between the volume of a gas and its temperature: gases which are heated increase in volume and gases which are cooled decrease in volume. This law was derived only after numerous separate experiments were done. However, once the law was developed, it helped to summarize those studies and findings which had been done previously. With the aid of a law, there is no need to memorize the data from separate experiments since one can recreate the data from the law.

The second function of models is that they help us to understand the present. It is unfortunate, but almost everything we are interested in turns out to be complex. Even so-called simple things, upon proper investigation, turn out to be extraordinarily complex. At one time, for example, psychologists thought the stimulus-response bond would turn out to be a simple, basic element in learning;

but the more they studied it, the more they found out that it too was complex, involving both stimulus learning and response learning as well as the problems of associating the two. Thus, the development of a model which can help us to understand a complex phenomenon can serve as a most important scientific and social function. It helps us to understand by eliminating the nonessential aspects of the phenomenon, by focusing our attention on the essential, and by showing how these essential parts interrelate and function.

The third characteristic of a good model is that it enables us to formulate hypotheses which are testable, that is, it helps us predict the future. As mentioned previously, model building is a game in which almost anyone can engage. We are all familiar with models which were developed in the past which, on the surface, helped us to understand complex phenomena but, in the face of testing, could not stand up to the facts. For example, at one time the Earth was thought to be flat. Models of the solar system showed the planet Earth as its center. However, Copernicus and, a century later, Galileo were able to destroy the old model that showed the centrality of the Earth in the solar system. Consequently, it is important that we test our models in order to eliminate the invalid ones and to retain the ones which deserve to be saved but may be in need of fine tuning. Thus, an absolutely critical characteristic of a good model is that it be precise enough to lead to testable hypotheses. It is only through the process of testing a model that we are able to determine its validity.

THREE CURRENT MODELS

The Gough Model

The first of the three models to be described is Gough's (1972) model of the reading process. It is a carefully worked out description of how text is processed from the time the eye first looks upon the printed words to the time that meaning is derived from the visual input. His model is shown in modified form in Figure 7.2.

Iconic Representation

As seen in Figure 7.2, the reading process begins when the eye fixates upon the words printed on the page. This eye fixation lasts for some 250 msec (Tinker, 1958) and takes in approximately 15 to 20 letters and spaces from the printed line of text. The movements of the eye, called saccadic movements, consist of fixations, regressions, as well as forward and backward sweeps of the eye. Each forward eye fixation will move some 10 to 12 letter spaces to the right and results in the formation of an iconic image from a portion of the page upon which the eye focuses.

The iconic image from the visual input persists for a brief period of time on the retina, usually for a fraction of a second, after the external stimulus from the page vanishes. Sperling (1963) has demonstrated that this iconic image, held in what may be called a visual information store or buffer, has reasonably large

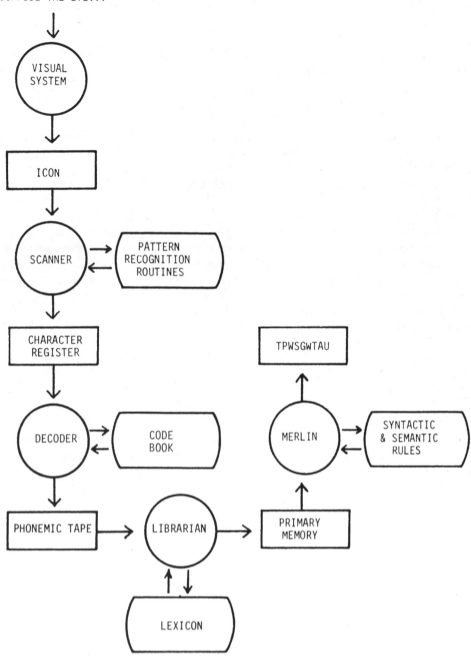

FIGURE 7.2

capacity. It can hold as many as 18 letters in an oval roughly 2-in. wide and 1-in. high.[1] The iconic image is thought to be in an "unidentified" or "precategorical" form, probably consisting of bars, slits, edges, curves, angles, and breaks and probably corresponding to the output feature detectors described by Hubel and Wiesel (1962).

Letter Identification

The identification of letters by fluent readers occurs rapidly. Even unrelated letters may be recovered from the iconic image at the rate of 10 to 20 msec per letter.

In a study by Stewart, James, and Gough (1969), words were presented that varied in length from three to ten letters. The visual recognition latency—the time between word presentation and onset of the pronunciation—varied from 615 msec for the three-letter words to 693 msec for the ten-letter words. In another study of how long it takes a person to decide if a string of letters is a word, Gough and Stewart (1970) found that four-letter words were processed 35 msec faster than six-letter words. Still another procedure was used by Samuels, LaBerge, and Brewer (1978) in which subjects were required to push a button if the word was a member of an animal category. Averaging across all age categories, the recognition latency ranged from 685 msec for three-letter words to 758 msec for six-letter words. These studies lead one to conclude that, under certain conditions, the addition of a letter to a word adds some 10 to 20 msec for readout from the icon.

In fact, Gough (1972, p. 353) states, "I see no reason, then, to reject the assumption that we do not read letter by letter . . . the weight of the evidence persuades me that we do so serially, from left to right (cf. White, 1969) . . . the letters in the icon emerge serially, one every 10 or 20 msec into some form of character register."

The Mapping Problem

This is the problem of explaining how one goes from the context of the character register to the lexicon (the mental dictionary of words and their meanings contained in the human head).

One possibility is that there is a direct association between the readout of the character register and meaning in the mental lexicon. The difficulty with this position is that this imposes a severe memory burden because thousands of associations between the printed words and their meanings would have to be learned.

A second possibility is that each printed word would be recoded into phonological form. Since the reader has a lexicon which is accessible through spoken words, all that one must do is go from print to speech and then on to lexical meaning. This possibility is rejected by Gough because the process from print to speech to meaning does not work fast enough to account for high-speed word recognition. Skilled readers can recognize a word faster than they can pronounce a word.

There is a third possibility, one which Gough suggests as a possibility, namely,

that the reader maps print not onto speech, but onto a string of systematic phonemes (Chomsky & Halle, 1968). These systematic phonemes are abstract representations of speech that are related to sounds but not the sounds themselves.
Thus, the contents of the character register are transposed into systematic phonemes.

Lexical Search

Having suggested a means whereby the output of the character register is mapped
onto a lexical entry, the next problem encountered is that of explaining how
strings of words in sentences are processed. According to Gough, words in a
sentence are understood serially from left to right.

An objection to this explanation hinges on what readers do when they encounter ambiguous words. If words are understood one at a time, there will be
frequent occurrences when a wrong meaning will be assigned. Gough cites experimental evidence suggesting that this is what happens when reading. Gough states
(1972, p. 339), "Thus, lexical search would appear to be a parallel process, with
the race going to the swift. When the first entry is located, its contents are
accepted as the reading of the word until it proves incompatible with subsequent
data."

The lexical entries from the individual words in a sentence must be stored
until they can be organized into a larger unit. The storage of the individual
words takes place in primary memory.

Primary Memory

The short-term memory system has a number of important characteristics. It is
capable of both rapid input and output of information, but the amount of time
in which it can store information without active rehearsal is severely limited.
Without active rehearsal, half the input can be lost within 5 sec (Peterson &
Peterson, 1959). While its capacity is rather small, in the neighborhood of six
to seven items, what constitutes an item can vary from a single letter to a multisyllabic word.

According to Gough, primary memory builds lexical items along with its
phonological syntactic and semantic information until the string of lexical items
can be comprehended. Once the contents of primary memory are understood,
its contents are cleared, and the sentence is deposited in the "Place Where
Sentences Go When They Are Understood" (PWSGWTAU). As soon as the contents of primary memory are cleared, then new items can be entered.

Primary memory serves as a brief storage system for the comprehension
device. Precisely how the comprehension device works is under investigation,
but it is assumed that this wondrous device, called Merlin, discovers the deep
structure of the word string held in primary memory. Once Merlin succeeds
in extracting the deep structure of the word string, the semantic content is
moved to the ultimate register—the PWSGWTAU.

This brief description of the Gough model will suffice for now. We will
examine it again briefly when we look for similarities and differences among
the various models of reading.

The LaBerge and Samuels Model

The LaBerge and Samuels model of human information processing has several functions. First, it attempts to show how attentional resources are displayed by beginning and skilled readers. Second, it describes a variety of routes which information may take as it flows through the processing system. Third, it attempts to describe how information is processed within each of the components in the system.

Since its first publication, this model has undergone several developments. First, a series of studies have been completed which test the visual-memory component of the model. This visual-memory component indicates that the size of the visual unit used in word recognition may vary from units as small as distinctive features and letters to units as large as the entire word. Second, feedback loops have been added in order to interconnect the components (Samuels, 1977), thus permitting the end products of comprehension to influence what occurs earlier in the processing sequence.[2] Third, since the model was first developed there has been an explosion of information on the comprehension process, and this has been incorporated into the model in order to help us better understand what happens in semantic memory.

As seen in Figure 7.3, there are five main components in the model labeled

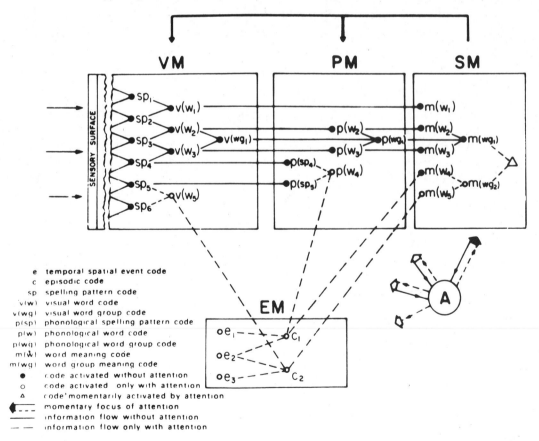

FIGURE 7.3

VM, PM, SM, EM, and A. These symbols stand for visual memory, phonological memory, semantic memory, episodic memory, and attention.

Attention

Since attention lies at the heart of the model, this component will be described first. The model assumes that attention is required in order to derive meaning from text and that the amount of attentional resource which any individual possesses is limited. This does not mean that the amount of attention one has is limited to some finite amount and that once it is used up, it is gone forever, but rather that for any given interval of time, there seems to be a limit to the amount available. In other words, attention is a renewable resource for text processing.

Since there is a limit to the amount of attention which is available over any unit of time, then attention, like any other scarce resource, must be allocated with care. How attention is allocated during reading is important if we are to understand an important aspect of the reading process.

In order to understand how attention is used we must consider two tasks we perform when we read. These two component tasks are decoding and comprehension. By decoding we mean going from the printed word to some articulatory or phonological representation of the printed stimulus. By comprehension we mean deriving meaning from the material we have decoded.

Both tasks, decoding and comprehension, require attention. In fact, we can assert that comprehension, under virtually all situations, requires attention, whereas decoding may require more or less attention, depending on the skill of the reader. How much attention is required by decoding and comprehension depends upon a number of factors. For example, the amount of attention required for decoding depends upon the reader's skill as well as the reader's familiarity with the words in the text. The amount of attention required for comprehension depends upon such factors as the number of propositions or ideas contained in a sentence as well as the degree to which the ideas presented by a writer are matched by the knowledge contained in the reader's head. Thus, we see that both decoding and comprehension require attention and the amount of attention required varies with decoding skill, familiarity with the words in the text, as well as the topic and density of idea units found in the text.

For the beginning reader, decoding the text is a difficult task. Consequently, the combined demands of decoding and comprehension may exceed the limited attention capacity of the student. When combined demands from these two essential tasks exceed the student's attentional capacity, the tasks cannot be performed simultaneously. In order to overcome this apparent impasse, the beginning reader uses a simple strategy, namely, that of attention switching. First, attention is used for decoding. After decoding is done, attention is switched to the comprehension task. This alternative switching of attention from decoding to comprehension is similar to the strategy used by beginning students of a foreign language who first work their way through a novel written in a foreign language by translating all the difficult words and then rereading the text again in order to understand it. In beginning reading, the strategy of attention switching allows the student to comprehend, but it comes at a cost. Attention switching is time consuming, puts a heavy demand on short-term memory, and tends to interfere with recall.

With time and practice, there is a transition from the attention switching characteristic of the beginning stage of reading to the skilled stage where attention switching is not required. The skilled stage occurs when the decoding task can be performed with little or almost no attention. When almost no attention is required, we can think of the student as being automatic at the decoding aspect of reading. Now, the skilled reader, who is automatic at decoding, can do two things simultaneously—decode and comprehend—whereas the beginning reader who is nonautomatic can do only one thing at a time, either decode or comprehend. The reason the skilled reader can decode and comprehend at the same time is that the decoding task requires so little attention that nearly all of the available attention can be allocated to the task of comprehension. Consequently, attention switching is only occasionally necessary in fluent reading.

It would be wrong to think that once the skilled reading stage was reached that all decoding would be automatic. There are several special circumstances which require additional amounts of attention, even for the skilled reader. For example, when words are encountered which are rare or unfamiliar or when words are printed in an unfamiliar type face, additional amounts of attention are required.

Having explained the differences between how attention is allocated by beginning and skilled readers, one additional but highly important point needs to be made—attention can be allocated in a variety of ways. If, for example, a skilled reader is proofreading a letter, then she may direct her attention to spelling patterns while ignoring meaning. A person looking at a handwritten manuscript to see if it is legible, may direct attention at the distinctive features of each letter. If, on the other hand, a person is reading a text to get a fast general overview, then she would direct attention at meaning and may fail to notice spelling errors. Depending upon the skill of the reader and the kind of task undertaken, attention can be directed at distinctive features embodied within letters, at each letter as a unit, at the spelling patterns within words, or at the entire word itself. This freedom to allocate attention to visual units, which vary in size from individual letters to the whole word, or to put a major portion of attention on meaning rather than decoding suggests that for the skilled reader, at least, there is no fixed pathway which must be followed in order to process a text.

Visual Memory

As seen in Figure 7.4, it is at the visual-memory component that the visual stimuli from the printed page are processed. Exactly what size visual unit is selected for processing (i.e., whether it is a distinctive feature, letter, spelling pattern, or word) depends upon several factors, such as the reader's skill, familiarity with the word, and purpose for reading.

As Figure 7.4 shows, stimuli from the sensory surface of the eye can be represented at any one of several levels. Thus, stimuli from letters could be analyzed into distinctive features, represented by $f3$ through $f8$. For example,

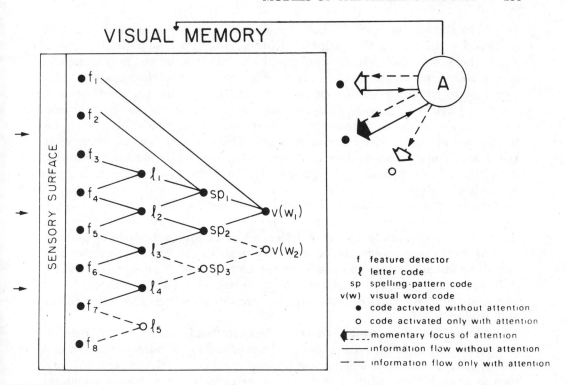

FIGURE 7.4

letters *b, d, p,* and *q* could be analyzed into verticals, circles, and a relational dimension, such as up-down and left-right. Letter *b* would be represented as a vertical element with a circle on the lower right, whereas letter *d* would be represented as a vertical with a circle on the lower left. It is highly probable that noting the distinctive features of letters is an early stage in letter recognition.

With practice, the distinctive features would be unitized into a letter code, represented by *l* in the Figure 7.4. Thus, the student who is able to recognize letters with speed and accuracy sees the letter as a single unit and not as a set of distinctive features. In fact, as skilled readers, it is hard to imagine any letter of the alphabet as a separate component since, with practice, the separate components are unitized or welded together. Of course, for purposes of analysis, we can separate out the components, but that is not how we tend to see them.

Again, with sufficient practice and exposure to certain recurrent letter combinations, we begin to see them as spelling patterns. These spelling patterns are represented by *sp* in Figure 7.4. The recurrent patterns of letters would not be processed by experienced readers as separate letters but as a single visual unit. For example, recurrent spelling patterns, such as *sch* in school, *gh* in ghost, *anti* in antiestablishment, or the *ed* or *ing* in jumped and jumping would be processed as a single visual unit.

At still a higher level of organization, as seen in Figure 7.4, spelling patterns are combined, so that the word itself is processed as a single visual word unit. This is represented by *v(w)* in the model of visual memory.

Thus far, we have shown how visual stimuli from printed words can be processed at the level of the distinctive feature, letter, spelling pattern, or whole word. There are still two other routes to the word. As indicated by $f1$, features such as word length, word contour, and the internal visual patterns (of one letter seen next to another one) may be used in word recognition. In words, such as *fat* and *friend* or *pay* and *penny*, we see how word length and contour may possibly serve as cues for recognition. There may be a combination of letter cues as well as word length and contour cues which are used in word recognition, as in *f* or *p*. These cues would be most useful when there is some context available as in "Because of overeating he became *f⎍*" or "He was broke and down to his last *p⎍*."

Code $f2$ indicates that certain highly common spelling patterns, such as prefixes, suffixes, and diagraphs, may be recognized as holistic units rather than through a blending of the individual letters which comprise the spelling pattern.

As mentioned previously, several empirical studies have been conducted to test the visual-memory component of the LaBerge and Samuels model. These studies provide information on the size of the visual unit used in word recognition. The units used in word recognition may vary in size from the letter to the entire word.

The methodology which is used in these studies is rather simple. Subjects are shown words which vary in length from three to six letters. The subjects are told that if the word which is shown is a member of a designated category, such as animal, they should press a button as quickly as possible. A computer measures the latency between presentation of the word and the button push. The reasoning underlying this procedure is that if the words are recognized by going through a letter-by-letter process, then the latency of response between word presentation and the button press should vary directly as a function of word length. On the other hand, if words are recognized as holistic units, then response latency should be insensitive to word length, up to some limit.

In one of our first studies, college students were shown common animal words in either regular or transformed (i.e., mirror-image) text. We found that common words in regular print were processed as holistic units, whereas the same words transformed were processed letter-by-letter (Terry, Samuels, La-Berge, 1976). This can be seen in Figure 7.5. For the words presented in normal print, there is no increase in latency as the words get longer, indicating holistic processing. For words printed in transformed (mirror image), there is an increase in latency as the words get longer, indicating component letter processing. The contribution of this study to our understanding of the reading process is that it demonstrates that with skilled readers, the size of the visual unit used in recognition may vary, depending upon task demands.

In another study, subjects from Grades 2, 4, 6, and college were shown common words in regular print. They found a developmental trend (see Figure 7.6) in the size of the perceptual unit used for word recognition (Samuels et al., 1978). For younger students (Grades 2 and 4), there is an increase in response latency as a function of word length. However, for sixth-grade students and for college students, there is no increase in latency for longer words. These results suggest that: (1) the students in Grade 2, with the least reading skill, were using component letter-by-letter processing; (2) with increasing skill, however, the size of the unit increased, so that by sixth grade, the unit of recognition was the entire word; (3) both sixth-grade and college students processed words as a single unit; (4) the only difference between college students and sixth graders was that the college students were faster overall at processing the words.

In another study on the unit of word recognition, McCormick and Samuels (1981) varied the basic procedure somewhat. They presented words found in first- and second-grade basal readers and required the second-grade students to say the words as quickly as possible into a voice-activated relay while a computer recorded the latency between word presentation and voice onset. As usual, the words varied in length. They found that the less-able students were processing letter by letter. In fact, on the second-grade words, each additional letter in-

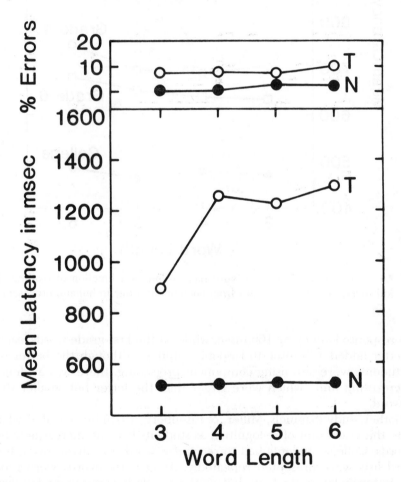

FIGURE 7.5   Speed and accuracy of response for normal (N) and transformed (T) text. Adults were responding to normal words as holistic units but using component letters for transformed text.

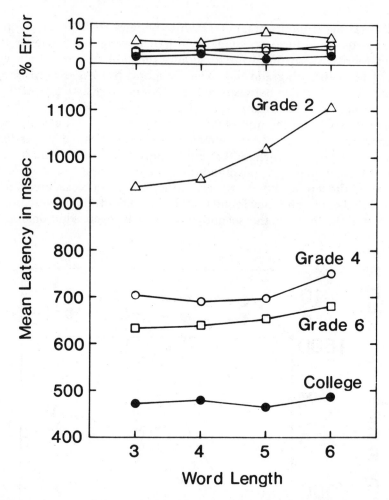

FIGURE 7.6   The size of the unit of word recognition as a function of reading skill. As reading skill increases there is a shift from component letter to holistic processing.

creased response latency by 160 msec, while on the first-grade words, each additional letter added 130 msec to response latency. Although the better second-grade students were also using component processing, there was evidence that they were using units which were larger than the letter but smaller than the entire word.

Another study (Samuels, Miller, & Eisenberg, 1979) investigated what happened to the visual unit of recognition as students became increasingly familiar with words. College students had to recognize words in mirror-image text, but the word lists were presented repeatedly. At first, the words were processed using a letter-by-letter strategy, but as the words became more familiar with each repetition, the size of the perceptual unit increased. However, throughout the experiment other common mirror-image words were presented only once.

These nonrepeated words contained many of the same letters as contained in the repeated words, yet there was no evidence that there was any increase in the size of the unit for the nonrepeated words. This suggests that there was virtually no transfer to new words, despite the overlap of letters between the repeats and the no-repeats. Thus, the practice effects seem to be specific to the practiced words. Whether or not transfer could occur to unpracticed words is still open to question since the training given in this study did not extend over days, weeks, and months, as occurs in the classroom.

The previous studies which have been described were done with words in isolation. However, since reading is usually done with words in context, we (Patberg, Dewitz, & Samuels, 1981) have also studied the size of the perceptual unit of recognition for words in context. Good and poor second- and fourth-grade students were asked to recognize words presented in context (cold snow) or in isolation (xxxx snow). Our results indicated that second-grade poor readers did letter-by-letter processing, regardless of whether words were presented in context or in isolation. The good second- and fourth-grade students did holistic processing for both the no-context and context conditions. The most interesting results were with our fourth-grade poor readers. They did letter-by-letter processing for words in isolation but holistic processing for words in context. We, therefore, find an important interaction between an inside-the-head factor, that is, reader skill, and an outside-the-head factor, that is, context. Thus, an inside-the-head factor and an outside-the-head factor can interact to increase the size of the perceptual unit used in word recognition.

The finding from the fourth-grade poor readers that indicates they use component-letter processing for words in isolation but holistic processing for words in context is interesting from the point of view that we have to provide mechanisms which will account for this difference in cognitive processing. These mechanisms must explain how the kind of processing taking place in the human mind is influenced by the context on the page. The first mechanism we must provide is one which is a memory store for the knowledge we have of the rules of grammar, word associations, rules of spelling, as well as the general knowledge we have of the world. This memory store is found in the semantic-memory component of the model (see Figure 7.3) and is capable of using the information provided in a text as it moves through the various buffers in our model. The second mechanism we must provide is one which can bring the knowledge contained in semantic memory to bear upon the kind of processing done in visual memory. This mechanism is provided by the feedback loop from semantic memory. Thus, the knowledge that we have allows us to take advantage of the context on the page which, in turn, will influence the size of the visual unit used in word recognition.

In summary, the experimental studies indicate that the size of the unit one uses in word recognition depends upon one's reading skill, familiarity with the word, and context. The LaBerge and Samuels model does not postulate a strict letter-by-letter sequence en route to word recognition. While the experimental evidence suggests that poor readers may have to go through an obligatory letter-by-letter sequence, regardless of the context in which the words are presented, the evidence also shows that skilled readers have optional sequences which they may pursue because attention can be allocated in a variety of ways, depending upon task demands. For example, with unfamiliar words, they may do component-letter processing, but with familiar words, they do holistic processing. For those who have assumed that the LaBerge and Samuels model presents an obligatory bottom-up sequence, the experimental evidence on the unit of recognition combined with the feedback loops among the components should show that this is not the case.

Phonological Memory

As seen in Figure 7.3, all the other components in the system feed information into phonological memory. It is assumed that phonological memory contains units that are related to acoustic and articulatory inputs. Although acoustic codes in a phonological system seems logical, one wonders why there would be articulatory codes. The reason is that in recent years, evidence has been gathered to the effect that certain kinds of articulatory-motor responses made in programming a speech sound may also be involved in perceiving that sound.

The organization of codes in phonological memory is somewhat similar to the organization of codes in visual memory. The units in visual memory increase in size from the distinctive features up to the word level. Similarly, the size of the units represented in phonological memory increase in size. The units in phonological memory include distinctive features, phonemes, syllables, and morphemes.

Phonological memory serves an important function in any system which attempts to explain how meaning is derived while reading. Its importance is underscored when one considers that phonological memory provides a mediating link between visual and semantic memory. In other words, whatever size unit is selected from visual memory for processing, it must be recoded and a counterpart found in phonological memory. For instance, the units in visual memory may be letters, spelling patterns, or words that would be recoded in phonological memory into letter sounds, syllables, or morphemes. For example, when a beginning reader encounters a new word, it may be broken down into parts and each part sounded out prior to the word's recognition. Once the visual unit is recoded into a phonological unit, the phonological information is passed on to semantic memory, where it is processed into meaning. Despite claims that skilled readers may be able to go directly from print to meaning without the need for a phonological recoding stage, there seems to be common agreement that beginning readers as well as skilled readers who are reading difficult text engage in phonological recoding.

Episodic Memory

Episodic memory is involved in the recall of specific events related to people, objects, location, and time. Information in episodic memory might well be organized around *wh* words, such as when (time), where (location), who (people), and what (objects). When we attempt to answer questions, such as "Who was my first-grade reading teacher?" or "What reading series did I use in first grade?" we are using episodic memory. There are special conditions under which episodic memory can be used in the reading process, for example, when a student uses a mnemonic, such as the long word is hippopotamus or the word with the tail on the end is monkey. Obviously, this type of recognition strategy and the use of episodic memory, in general, is not a major factor in fluent reading.

Semantic Memory

This will be the last component of the LaBerge and Samuels model which we will discuss. Semantic memory is involved in the recall of general knowledge, such as how to drive cars, act in restaurants, and behave in school. In a reading situation, semantic memory is used when we apply our knowledge of letter-sound correspondences and sound blending to decode unusual words or when we read and understand what we have read. It is in semantic memory that we store our general information about the world.

One way to represent the knowledge stored inside the head is through semantic-memory networks (e.g., Collins & Loftus, 1975; Lindsay & Norman, 1977). The semantic network is itself a model of how human knowledge can be represented. This representation resembles an intricate spiderweb. Each node in the web represents a concept, and the strands in the web link up each concept with all the other concepts in semantic memory.

Each concept in the semantic network is defined by other concepts. There are three parts to the definition of a concept: a higher-order class (a category to which the concept belongs), a listing of attributes or characteristics, and examples. For instance, the concept dog may be defined as an animal, it barks, has four legs, nurses its young, has nonretractable claws, and that poodles and collies are examples. We should notice, however, that each of the concepts used to define dog is itself subject to a three-part definition. For example, the definition of dog includes the concept animal. To understand this concept, we must know that animal is a living thing, it ingests and egests nutrients, reproduces and dies, and that dogs, cats, and birds are examples of animals. It is this proliferation of interrelated concepts which becomes the building blocks of this intricate web we call the semantic network. Thus, the semantic network becomes the store-house for the knowledge we possess.

Having explained how knowledge is represented in semantic memory, it is important to describe the comprehension process. At the risk of oversimplification, the process seems to work in the following manner. In order to make sense of what we are experiencing—or reading—we attempt to match the information coming in from outside the head with the knowledge stored in the semantic memory network. To the extent that there is a good match between the information coming in from the outside and the knowledge stored in memory, we are able to comprehend and make sense of the world. When there is a poor match between incoming information and stored knowledge, the incoming information seems to be incomprehensible.

As previously mentioned, we experience the click of comprehension when there is a match between textual information coming in from outside the head with the concepts stored inside the head. If this is true, then it is likely that our ability to understand the ideas in a text as well as our attitudes about this information is limited and colored to a large degree by the concepts already stored in memory. Thus, contrary to conventional wisdom, which states that comprehension is the process of getting meaning from a page, comprehension is viewed here as the process of bringing meaning to a text. It is this process of bringing meaning to a text which accounts for the fact that the same text can be interpreted so differently by so many people.

Since comprehension entails a linkup between incoming information and knowledge stored in memory, one might inquire as to the mechanism which guides this process. What we are trying to explain is the process which allows us to search through our memory network of concepts for the appropriate knowledge which will account for and make comprehensible the information coming in from the outside. To a considerable extent, it is the context and the environment which surrounds the object, text, or event we are trying to understand which guides us in the search for concepts which will give meaning to our experience. For example, a textbook provides a variety of cues which facilitate this search through memory for appropriate concepts. On a desk is a book with the title, *Educational Psychology*. Inside the cover is a table of contents listing topics, which include Basic Processes in Infancy, Curiosity and Exploratory Behavior, Transfer, Memory, and Forgetting. Each of the chapters contains side headings in bold type which indicate the major topics to be covered in that subsection and many of the paragraphs in the book contain topic sentences which signal what kind of information will be presented.

Each of the contextual cues found in a textbook, ranging from titles to side headings, guide the reader in the selection of concepts which can be used to interpret what is being read. To illustrate this process with a simple case, the ambiguous sentence, "The shooting of the hunters was terrible" becomes clear as soon as we add contextual cues, such as "marksmanship" or "murder." Still another example is the ambiguous sentence; "Reading teachers are novel lovers." The critical word here is novel, and the meaning is changed, depending on whether we add a cue indicating that it is used as an adjective or a noun. These examples illustrate that decontextualized sentences often appear to be ambiguous and it is the addition of contextual cues which allow us to remove the uncertainty and interpret the sentence in a particular way. Similarly, it is through the addition of contextual cues found in a textbook or in the reading environment that we are aided in the activation of those concepts and schemata which facilitate text comprehension.

The difference between literal and inferential comprehension is that with the former, all the information which is requested is contained in the text, while in the latter the information requested goes beyond the information contained in the text. For example, when given a sentence, such as "John kicked Mary," one can ask "Who kicked Mary?" or "Why did John kick Mary?" The answer to the first question involves literal comprehension, while the answer to the second question involves inferential comprehension.

In this section, two points need to be made: the first is that teachers are in error when they think that they can get an adequate measure of a student's comprehension when only literal questions are asked; the second point is that even literal comprehension requires some degree of inference in order to understand the text.

Let us begin with the first point, which states that literal comprehension questions are not an adequate test of comprehension. Assume that a text states, "*X* pligumed *Y* for *Z*." We can ask questions, such as "What did *X* pligum?" (the answer is *Y*) or "For whom was *Y* pligumed?" (the answer is *Z*) or "When did this action take place?" (the answer is in the past). All of these literal comprehension questions can be answered without a shred of real understanding of what is involved here.

It is not until we ask some inferential questions that we realize that no real understanding of the nonsense sentence occurred. For example, when we ask questions, such as "Where did the action probably take place?" or "What tools or utensils were used?" or "How did *Y* feel?", we discover that it is virtually impossible to answer these inferential questions with any degree of certainty about the truth value. Thus, the ability to answer literal questions does not necessarily mean that the student understood the text and that the ability to answer inferential questions may indicate if, indeed, there was any real comprehension.

The nonsense sentence, "*X* pligumed *Y* for *Z*," can be changed to a meaningful sentence of the same syntactic form by stating, "Mother cooked breakfast for Bill." Now we can ask inferential questions:

QUESTION: Where was breakfast cooked?

ANSWER: Probably in the kitchen, but it could have been at a campfire if they were on a camping trip.

QUESTION: What utensils were used?

ANSWER: Probably a stove, pots, and pans.

QUESTION: How did Bill feel?

ANSWER: He was probably hungry and, after eating, he was not hungry.

It is the ability to make reasonable inferences which go beyond the actual information contained in the sentence which indicates that the student comprehended the text.

Our second point is that even the simplest type of literal comprehension requires that we engage in inferencing. The reason for this is that there is an unwritten contract between a writer and a reader—or for that matter a speaker and a listener. This contract specifies that as a writer, we should provide no more information than the reader needs in order to make sense of what we are expressing. Thus, the writer must assess the potential audience and provide no more information than is needed. To violate this contract leads to some problems. If we provide too much detail, the reader may become bored, the text seem redundant, and the author appear to be condescending. On the other hand, if we provide less detail than the reader needs, the text appears to be incomprehensible. Thus, the writer provides only as much detail as the reader needs, and the writer relies on the stored knowledge of the reader in order to fill in the gaps left vacant in the text.

Let us look at two examples of inferencing which we must engage in to fill the information gaps in the text. Although the sentence, "The hiker's carelessly dropped cigarette led to one of the worst fires in the state's history" is easily understood, it requires considerable inferencing in order to understand it. This inferencing is made possible because of the rich network of association which we have about key words, such as hiker and cigarettes. For example, in order to comprehend this sentence, we have to make two assumptions, first, that the hiker was probably in a wooded area and that we are describing a forest fire; second, that the cigarette was lit. Both of these assumptions enable us to make sense of the sentence, although neither fact is expressly stated.

The second example of how inferencing is required in literal comprehension may be illustrated with a sentence, such as "Mr. Smith drank a quart of vodka in less than an hour." Although the sentence does not specifically state how this was done, we can make some highly probable guesses. Mr. Smith is a human being. Consequently, he probably used his arm, hands, and fingers to grasp the bottle (or the contents of the bottle), in order to bring the liquid to his mouth to ingest it. We also know the probable condition of Mr. Smith after drinking the vodka. Again, we must use our knowledge of what kind of liquid vodka is as well as our knowledge of the physical capacity of human beings to ingest alcoholic beverages to judge the probable condition of Mr. Smith. If we apply this knowledge, we assume that Mr. Smith is currently in poor health and may well be at death's door.

While this discussion of semantic memory has emphasized its role in comprehension, one brief comment is in order regarding its function in facilitating word recognition. The assignment for processing the letter strings on the page into words is given to the visual-memory component. However, the memory store for the schema knowledge relevant to the topic that one is reading about is assigned to semantic memory. Furthermore, as one reads, the contextual information that one picks up from the text one is reading is also located in semantic memory. This combination of information from schema knowledge, with its rich network of verbal concepts relevant to the text being read, and the specific context picked up while reading is potentially available for facilitating the word-recognition process.

To illustrate how the knowledge sources from semantic memory might influence the processing of a word in visual memory, imagine the following: a student is reading an article about precious jewels (schema activation), and encounters the sentence, "The jeweler handed me two beautiful rings, one with a green emerald and the other with a red r_____." Both sources of information from schema activation and prior context may combine to facilitate the recognition of the word ruby. In other words, less visual information may be required for the recognition of the target word when other sources of information are available from semantic memory.

The mechanism which permits the later processing stage to influence the processing of an earlier stage is made possible by the feedback loops from semantic to visual memory. The study (described earlier) on the unit of visual processing which found that the unit of processing was influenced by context and by the reader's skill (Patberg et al., 1981) illustrates how semantic memory may influence a process in visual memory. On the other side of the coin, however, Gough (1972) has presented evidence indicating that context effects can be minimal.

The description of what happens in semantic memory completes the discussion of this model. Our discussion has indicated that the model has undergone modification and continued research has been done since it was first published in 1974.

The Rumelhart Model

Information processing models tend to be linear and to have a series of noninteractive processing stages. Each stage in a noninteractive model does its work independently and passes its production to the next higher stage. According to Rumelhart (1977), linear models which pass information along in one direction only and which do not permit the information contained in a higher stage to influence the processing of a lower stage contain a serious deficiency.

Deficiencies in Linear Models

The deficiencies in linear models of reading are such that they have difficulty accounting for a number of occurrences known to take place while reading. However, an interactive model, which permits the information contained in higher stages of processing to influence the analysis which occurs at lower stages of processing can account for these well-known occurrences in reading.

What each of the well-known occurrences and observations share in common is that they can be explained with a model which permits the information found in a higher processing stage to influence the analysis of a lower stage. The first of these observations is that more letters can be apprehended in a given unit of time if they spell a word than if the same letters are used in a nonword (Huey, 1908/1968). For example, more letters are apprehended in a word like alligator than in a letter string like rllaagtio.

Similarly, more letters can be apprehended in a nonsense letter string which conforms to rules of English spelling than in a nonsense letter string which does not conform to English spelling rules (Miller, Bruner, & Postman, 1954), for example, vernalit as opposed to nrveiatl. To account for the fact that apprehension of letters is superior in real words and in nonsense strings which conform to English orthographic rules, one must posit a mechanism whereby the knowledge of lexical items and orthography contained in higher-order stages can influence the perception of letters which occurs earlier at lower stages in the information processing system.

The second category of observations pertinent to reading relates to syntactic effects on word perception. It is commonly observed that when an error in word recognition is made, there is a strong tendency for the word substitution to maintain the same part of speech as the word for which it was substituted (Kolers, 1970; Weber, 1970). In a now classic study, Miller and Isard (1963) found that auditory perception of words in a noisy environment was superior when normal syntax was used than when there was a violation of normal syntax.

The third type of observation about reading relates to the fact that semantic knowledge influences word perception. For example, using an experimental procedure in which the subject must decide as quickly as possible if a letter string spells a word, it was found that the decision can be made faster when a pair of words are semantically related, as in bread-butter or doctor-nurse than if they are semantically unrelated, as in bread and doctor or nurse and butter (Meyer & Schvaneveldt, 1971; Meyer, Schvaneveldt, & Ruddy, 1975). Using a different procedure, Tulving and Gold (1963) were able to demonstrate that speed of word recognition was progressively faster as increased amounts of a sentence were exposed prior to presenting the target word than if the target word was presented by itself.

The fourth observation is that perception of syntax for a given word depends upon the context in which the word is embedded. For example, if we compare the italicized words in "They are *eating apples,*" it is not clear whether the sentence is describing the act of consuming apples or if it is describing a type of apple, that is, eating apples as opposed to cooking apples. We can disambiguate the sentence if we precede the sentence in the following manner: "What are the children eating? They are eating apples." Or we can ask: "What kind of apples are these? They are eating apples." It is clear now that the first context leads to a decision indicating that we are describing the act of children consuming a fruit, while the second context is describing a type of apple.

The final observation offered by Rumelhart relates to the fact that our interpretation of what we read depends upon the context in which a text segment is embedded. For example, in the sentence, "The statistician was certain the difference was significant since all the figures on the right-hand side of the table were larger than any of those on the left," our interpretation of the word "figures" is that of numerals, whereas in the sentence, "The craftsman charged more for the carvings on the right since all the figures on the right-hand side of the table were larger than any of those on the left," the term relates to a wood or ceramic figure. Similarly, our interpretation of the ambiguous statement, "The shooting of the hunters was terrible" can be altered by prior context. For example, contrast the statement, "Their marksmanship was awful. In fact, the shooting of the hunters was terrible" with the statement, "Their cruelty was awful. In fact, the shooting of the hunters was terrible." We can observe in these examples that meaning is not constructed just from the particular text segment we are processing but from its surrounding environment.

Components of Rumelhart's Model

The examples which have been presented in the previous paragraphs have illustrated how syntactic, semantic, lexical, and orthographic information can influence our perceptions. In each of the illustrations, our higher-order knowledge influenced the processing at a lower stage of analysis. Consequently, Rumelhart's model of reading, as seen in Figure 7.7, has each of these knowledge sources exerting influence upon the text processing and our ultimate interpretation of the text.

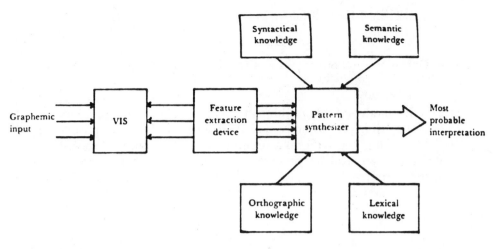

FIGURE 7.7

As seen in Rumelhart's model, information from syntactic, semantic, lexical, and orthographic sources converge upon the pattern synthesizer. These knowledge sources are providing input simultaneously and a mechanism must be provided which can accept these sources of information, hold the information, and redirect the information as needed. The mechanism which can accomplish these tasks is the message center.

The message center has several functions. As each of the knowledge sources feeds in information about the text being processed, the center holds this information in a temporary store. Each of the knowledge sources may use the information provided by one or more of the other sources. For example, lexical knowledge may search for information about spelling patterns or there may be a check for information about syntax. Rumelhart states:

> The message center keeps a running list of hypotheses about the nature of the input string. Each knowledge source constantly scans the message center for the appearance of hypotheses relevant to its own sphere of knowledge. Whenever such a hypotheses enters the message center, the knowledge source in question evaluates the hypothesis in light of its own specialized knowledge. As a result of its analysis, the hypotheses may be confirmed, disconfirmed and removed from the message center, or a new hypothesis can be added to the message center. This procedure continues until some decision can be reached. At that point the most probable hypothesis is determined to be the right one. (1977, pp. 589–590)

By means of separate knowledge sources and a message center which permits these sources to communicate and interact with others, the higher-order stages are able to influence the processing of lower-order stages. Thus, Rumelhart's model is able to accommodate the occurrences known to take place while reading which the linear models have difficulty accommodating.

RECENT DEVELOPMENTS IN MODEL BUILDING

Stanovich

The Stanovich model (1980) integrates concepts from a variety of sources. He states (p. 32):

> Interactive models of reading appear to provide a more accurate conceptualization of reading performance than do strictly top-down or bottom-up models. When combined with an assumption of compensatory processing (that a deficit in any particular process will result in a greater reliance on other knowledge sources, regardless of their level in the processing hierarchy), interactive models provide a better account of the existing data on the use of orthographic structure and sentence context by good and poor readers.

According to Stanovich, the earlier bottom-up reading models had a tendency to depict the information flow in a series of discrete stages, with each stage transforming the input and then passing the recoded information on to the next higher stage for additional transformation and recoding. Because the sequence of processing proceeds from the incoming data to higher-level encodings, these descriptions of the reading process are called bottom-up models. As I have already suggested, an important shortcoming of these models is lack of feedback, in that no mechanism is provided to allow for processing stages which occur later in the system to influence processing which occurs earlier in the system. Because of the lack of feedback loops in the early bottom-up models, it was difficult to account for sentence-context effects and the role of prior knowledge of text topic as facilitating variables in word recognition and comprehension. Stanovich states that because of this problem, "Samuels (1977) revised the LaBerge and Samuels (1974) model just for this reason," (p. 34).

Top-down models, on the other hand, conceptualize the reading process as one in which stages which are higher up and at the end of the information processing sequence interact with stages which occur earlier in the sequence. More important, the higher-order stages seem to be driving and directing the process and are doing the lion's share of the work. In top-down processing, since the reader is only sampling text information in order to verify hypotheses and predictions, reading is viewed as being conceptually driven by the higher-order stages rather than by low-level stimulus analysis. One way to look at the difference between top-down and bottom-up models is that the bottom-up models start with the printed stimuli and work their way up to the higher-level stages, whereas the top-down models start with hypotheses and predictions and attempt to verify them by working down to the printed stimuli.

Just as the bottom-up models have problems, so, too, do the top-down models. One of the problems for the top-down model is that for many texts, the reader has little knowledge of the topic and cannot generate predictions. A more serious problem is that even if a skilled reader can generate predictions, the amount of time necessary to generate a prediction may be greater than the amount of time the skilled reader needs simply to recognize the words. In other words, for the sake of efficiency, it is easier for a skilled reader to simply recognize words in a text than to try to generate predictions. Thus, while the top-down models may be able to explain beginning reading, with slow rates of word recognition, they do not accurately describe skilled reading behavior.

Stanovich has attempted to incorporate what is known about skilled and unskilled reading into the interactive-compensatory model. A key concept is that "a process at any level can compensate for deficiencies at any other level" (p. 36). Thus, if there is a deficiency at an early print-analysis stage, higher-order knowledge structures will attempt to compensate. For the poor reader, who may be both inaccurate and slow at word recognition but who has knowledge of the text topic, top-down processing may allow for this compensation. For example, if a beginning reader who is weak at decoding comes upon a word he does not know, such as emerald, in the sentence "The jeweler put the green emerald in the ring," he may use sentence context and knowledge of gems to decide what the word is.

On the other hand, if the reader is skilled at word recognition but does not know much about the text topic, it may be easier to simply recognize the words on the page and rely on bottom-up processes. In essence, Stanovich states, "Interactive models, . . . assume that a pattern is synthesized based on information provided simultaneously from several knowledge sources. The compensatory assumption states that a deficit in any knowledge source results in a heavier reliance on other knowledge sources, regardless of their level in the processing hierarchy" (p. 63). The Stanovich model, then, is interactive in the sense that any stage, regardless of its position in the system, may communicate with any other stage, and it is compensatory in the sense that any reader may rely on better developed knowledge sources when particular, and usually more commonly used, knowledge sources are temporarily weak.

Stanovich has made a unique contribution to reading models, because he has allowed us to explain, from a theoretical viewpoint, the apparent anomaly in many particular research studies; that is, under certain conditions poor readers exhibit greater sensitivity to contextual constraints than do good readers. They do so in those circumstances where featural, orthographic, and/or lexical knowledge (from Rumelhart's model as depicted in Figure 7.5) sources are weak in comparison to syntactic and semantic knowledge. The reason good readers are sometimes less sensitive to contextual effects is that their knowledge sources for these lower-level processes are seldom weak.

Just and Carpenter

Marcel Just and Patricia Carpenter and their students have developed a model of reading comprehension based on an extended series of studies (Carpenter & Daneman, 1981; Carpenter & Just, 1977; Just & Carpenter, 1976; 1978; 1980; Just, Carpenter, & Woolley, 1982). These studies have been based on eye-movement research with college-age readers.

Assumptions

Perhaps the most important fact to come from recent eye-movement studies is that readers average 1.2 words per fixation when the test is appropriate for their reading levels. The words that are most often skipped are high-frequency

function words, like *a, the, of,* and so on. In addition, there is a wide variability
in length of fixations. Fixations on function words are quite short; those on infrequent words or at ends of sentences are longer.

There are two basic assumptions that underly this model. The first assumption is that the reader attempts to interpret each content word, as it is encountered, even if guesses are made that later prove wrong. Interpretation for Just
and Carpenter (1980) means processing at several levels: encoding the word,
choosing a single meaning, assigning it to its referent, and determining its role
in both local and global context. This assumption means that interpretations
are not deferred; they occur immediately. The second assumption is that each
eye fixation lasts as long as the word is being processed. Thus, fixation time is a
direct index of processing time. While there is some debate over this position,
it is supported by eye-movement research in naturalistic situations (Carpenter
& Daneman, 1981; Carpenter & Just, 1977).

A schematic of the Just and Carpenter model is given in Figure 7.8. The
left-hand column shows the processing stages in their normal order of execution.
Knowledge is stored in long-term memory as well as the procedural information
needed to execute the processing. Working memory mediates the processes and
long-term memory.

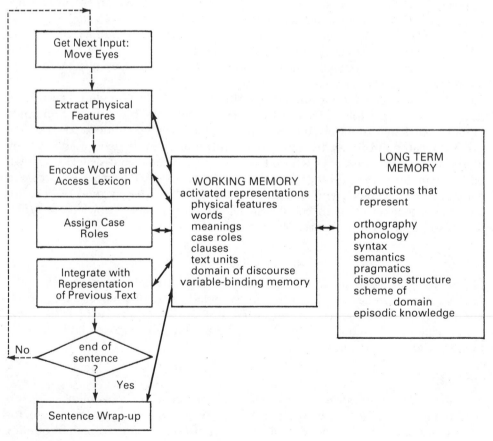

FIGURE 7.8

Processes

Get next input.   Get next input is a quite short stage in which a decision is made to move the eyes to a new fixation *if* all the necessary processing is completed. Just and Carpenter believe that this decision is made when a list of conditions is fulfilled. These conditions include general and specific reading goals. A general condition is that a meaning for a word must be accessed. A more specific condition might be that the word be transferred to memory.

When the conditions are filled, the get next input moves the fixation forward one or two words, unless the fixation is already at the end of a line. When the right margin is in the periphery of the fovea, the sweep returns to just short of the left margin, followed by a short correction. This get-next-input stage accounts for 5 to 10% of total reading time.

Word encoding and lexical access.   In the word-encoding and lexical-access stage, the word is perceptually encoded and the underlying concept is activated. The concept serves as a pointer to locate a more precise meaning representation. Carpenter and Just conceive of this as a narrow semantic network. Factors, like frequency and repetition, influence fixation durations.

Assigning case roles.   Assigning case roles is the first of the processes that determine relationships among words. Just and Carpenter assume that these can be approximated by case relationships (cf. Fillmore, 1968). This stage of processing includes a clausal segmentation procedure since case assignments are made within clauses. In this version of the model, there is no direct or differential mapping of particular cases and duration of processing.

Interclause integration.   Carpenter and Just (1977, p. 343) believe that "clauses and sentences must be related to each other by the reader to capture the coherence in the text." There are two major places where integration can occur. First, when each word is encountered, an attempt is made to relate it to previous information. The second is a running clause interpretation, updated as each word of the clause is read. Readers use two basic strategies to integrate old information with new. First, readers can check to see whether new information is related to the information already in working memory. This might entail trying to relate new information to a topic already active in working memory. A second strategy is to search for explicitly marked old information (as in a relative clause). It takes longer to use the second strategy than the first. It is during this stage that errors are encountered and corrections attempted. Readers do not, however, usually go to the beginning of the sentence to reinterpret. Rather, they use heuristics that allow them to detect the error more efficiently (Carpenter & Daneman, 1981).

Sentence wrap-up.   In the sentence wrap-up stage, the reader attempts to resolve any inconsistencies within the sentence and to search for referents that have not been assigned. The ends of sentences indicate that one thought has ended and another is to begin. Thus, the reader knows this is an appropriate place to attempt integration. Readers may also do some wrap-up at ends of clauses or at the end of units longer than a sentence.

Other Features of the Model

This is a flexible model, in that it can account for a large number of different types of reading behavior. It attempts to describe mechanisms for all stages of reading. The model is best described as somewhere between the extremes of top-down and bottom-up models. The top-down processes can influence the bottom-up ones. This model allows for any stage to be influenced by any stage executed earlier or simultaneously. Finally, the emphasis on production makes the model attractive to match human behavior.

The Kintsch Model

Kintsch and his colleagues and students have developed a reading model that focuses strictly on comprehension processes. The most complete version of the model is given by Kintsch and van Dijk (1978). Improvements, additions, revisions, and tests of the original model can be found in Kintsch and Vipond (1979), Miller and Kintsch (1980), Bates, Kintsch, Fletcher, and Giuliani (1980), and Kozminsky, Kintsch, and Bourne (1981).

Assumptions

The model assumes that comprehension is composed of several complex processes that can operate either in serial or parallel. A processing-capacity limitation is assumed. That is, all processing takes some capacity, and humans have a fixed capacity that can be devoted to tasks. For many of the operations, the demands on capacity are minimal. Memory storage and response production, however, are assumed to require a great deal of capacity. Finally, the meaning of the text can be expressed as a set of propositions. These follow the form described by Kintsch (1974) or Turner and Greene (1979). The propositional analysis is also discussed by Meyer, this volume.

Components of the Model

The Kintsch model is a processing model that specifies three types of operations. First, the meaning elements of a text are organized into a coherent whole. During this stage of processing, some elements are subjected to multiple processing which, in turn, leads to better differential retention among the text elements. Second, another set of operations compresses the full meaning of the text into its gist. The third component generates new texts from the memorial consequences of the comprehension processes. The ultimate goal of this model is to be able to specify how a text is processed sentence by sentence and to specify the outputs of the various stages of comprehension.

Additional Concepts in the Model

Input to the model, as described by Kintsch and van Dijk (1978), is a set of propositions representing the semantic surface structure of the text. The set is ordered by the semantic relations among the propositions. The semantic structure is characterized at two different levels by the microstructure and the macrostructure. Microstructure refers to the local level of the discourse, the structure of the individual propositions and their relations. Macrostructure is more global, characterizing the discourse as a whole. These two levels are related by a set of specific semantic mapping rules called macrorules.

Processing the Text

A discourse is coherent only if its respective sentences and propositions are connected and if they are also organized at the macrostructure level. The reader checks the text base (the set of propositions for input) for coherence. This checking is primarily for referential coherence. The reader must add appropriate inferences, but, because of memory limitations, this cannot be performed on the entire text base. To overcome memory limitations, the text is processed in cycles. Each chunk must be connected to those already processed.

Propositions are retained in a short-term memory. If connections are found between the new propositions and those in the buffer, the input is accepted as coherent. Otherwise, the reader searches through all the text propositions in long-term memory. If this isn't successful, an inference process is initiated that adds one or more appropriate propositions to the text to make it coherent.

The cyclical process is assumed to be automatic—making few demands on capacity. When no connections are found, the search of long-term memory is initiated. This search requires allocation of resources (capacity). An example of a text is given in Table 7.1. The text base is given in Table 7.2. Figure 7.2 shows the resultant cyclical processing.

Macrostructures are hierarchical, hence, they are applied in multiple cycles. More stringent criteria for relevance are applied at each succeeding cycle. At the lowest level of macrostructure, many propositions are selected as relevant. At the highest level, only one macroproposition is retained. This might, for example, be a title for the text unit.

Role of Schemata

The reader's goals control the application of the macro-operators, which transform the text base into macropropositions representing the gist of the text. The formal representation of these goals is the reader's schema. A specific schema always controls text comprehension since the schema dictates which micropropositions are relevant to the gist of the text.

If a reader has an appropriate goal, comprehension should be good. If a reader's goals are vague and the text structure is unconventional, the reader may set up different schemata from normal. Thus, the macro-operations would be unpredictable and comprehension would be poor.

TABLE 7.1   SAMPLE TEXT USED BY KINTSCH AND VAN DIJK (1978)

A series of violent, bloody encounters between police and Black Panther Party members punctuated the early summer days of 1969. Soon after, a group of Black students I teach at California State College, Los Angeles, who were members of the Panther Party, began to complain of continuous harassment by law enforcement officers. Among their many grievances, they complained about receiving so many traffic citations that some were in danger of losing their driving privileges. During one lengthy discussion, we realized that all of them drove automobiles with Panther Party signs glued to their bumpers. This is a report of a study that I undertook to assess the seriousness of their charges and to determine whether we were hearing the voice of paranoia or reality.

SOURCE: F. K. Heussenstam, Bumperstickers and cops, *Transaction*, 1971, *8*, 32.

TABLE 7.2 PROPOSITION LIST FOR THE BUMPERSTICKERS PARAGRAPH

PROPOSITION NUMBER	PROPOSITION
1	(SERIES, ENCOUNTER)
2	(VIOLENT, ENCOUNTER)
3	(BLOODY, ENCOUNTER)
4	(BETWEEN, ENCOUNTER, POLICE, BLACK PANTHER)
5	(TIME: IN, ENCOUNTER, SUMMER)
6	(EARLY, SUMMER)
7	(TIME: IN, SUMMER, 1969)
8	(SOON, 9)
9	(AFTER, 4, 16)
10	(GROUP, STUDENT)
11	(BLACK, STUDENT)
12	(TEACH, SPEAKER, STUDENT)
13	(LOCATION: AT, 12, CAL STATE COLLEGE)
14	(LOCATION: AT, CAL STATE COLLEGE, LOS ANGELES)
15	(IS A, STUDENT, BLACK PANTHER)
16	(BEGIN, 17)
17	(COMPLAIN, STUDENT, 19)
18	(CONTINUOUS, 19)
19	(HARASS, POLICE, STUDENT)
20	(AMONG, COMPLAINT)
21	(MANY, COMPLAINT)
22	(COMPLAIN, STUDENT, 23)
23	(RECEIVE, STUDENT, TICKET)
24	(MANY, TICKET)
25	(CAUSE, 23, 27)
26	(SOME, STUDENT)
27	(IN DANGER OF, 26, 28)
28	(LOSE, 26, LICENSE)
29	(DURING, DISCUSSION, 32)
30	(LENGTHY, DISCUSSION)
31	(AND, STUDENT, SPEAKER)
32	(REALIZE, 31, 34)
33	(ALL, STUDENT)
34	(DRIVE, 33, AUTO)
35	(HAVE, AUTO, SIGN)
36	(BLACK PANTHER, SIGN)
37	(GLUED, SIGN, BUMPER)
38	(REPORT, SPEAKER, STUDY)
39	(DO, SPEAKER, STUDY)
40	(PURPOSE, STUDY, 41)
41	(ASSESS, STUDY, 42, 43)
42	(TRUE, 17)
43	(HEAR, 31, 44)
44	(OR, 45, 46)
45	(OF REALITY, VOICE)
46	(OF PARANOIA, VOICE)

Note. Lines indicate sentence boundaries. Propositions are numbered for ease of reference. Numbers as propositional arguments refer to the proposition with that number.

SOURCE: W. Kintsch and T. van Dijk, Toward a model of text comprehension and production. *Psychological Review*, 1978. *85*, 377.

Production

The model accounts for outputs by using probability estimates for selecting propositions, retaining them in memory, and so on. A simulated recall protocol is given in Table 7.3. The model contains rules for applying transformations to the text base as well as reproduction, reconstruction, and production planning. There are also provisions for inclusion of metastatements in the protocols. Different sets of rules apply for other tasks related to comprehension, for example, producing summaries.

Comments on the Model

This is perhaps the only model which focuses exclusively on comprehension. In fact, the model requires (Kintsch & van Dijk, 1978) a proposition list (as in Table 7.2) as input. Later versions (e.g., Miller & Kintsch, 1980) discuss ways of going from text to propositions however. Nonetheless, word identification is not even discussed other than to acknowledge that it has to exist.

The other major feature of the model is its ability to simulate comprehension. This simulation can be based on parameter estimates of human performance and capacity. Thus, the model can be closely compared with performance on a wide variety of texts under a range of conditions. Future developments will likely make this model even more promising than it already is.

COMPARISON OF THE MODELS

Each of the models described has a specific focus, usually different from other models. Gough, LaBerge and Samuels, Stanovich, and Rumelhart all concentrate most of the power of their models on word-recognition processes. Within this group, the emphasis is either on strict linear processing (Gough or the early LaBerge and Samuels) or on interactive processing (Rumelhart, Stanovich, or the revised version of LaBerge and Samuels). The model of Just and Carpenter

TABLE 7.3 A SIMULATED RECALL PROTOCOL

REPRODUCED TEXT BASE
P1, P4, M7, P9, P13, P17, MP19, MP35, MP36, M37, MP39, MP40, MP42

Text base converted to English, with reconstructions italicized

In the sixties (M7) there was a series (P1) of riots between the police and the Black Panthers (P4). *The police did not like the Black Panthers* (normal consequence of 4). After that (P9), students *who were enrolled* (normal component of 13) at the California State College (P13) complained (P17) that the police were harassing them (P19). *They were stopped and had to show their driver's license* (normal component of 23). The police gave them trouble (P19) because (MP42) they had (MP35) Black Panther (MP36) signs on their bumpers (M37). *The police discriminated against these students and violated their civil rights* (particularization of 42). They did an experiment (MP39) for this purpose (MP40).

Note. The parameter values used were $p = .10$, $g = .20$, and $m = .40$. P, M, and MP identify propositions from Table 2.
SOURCE: W. Kintsch and T. van Dijk, Toward a model of text comprehension and production. *Psychological Review*, 1978, *85*, 384.

and that of Kintsch and van Dijk concentrate on comprehension, almost to the exclusion of letter-level processes. This lack of a common focus is the largest impediment to making comparisons among the models.

Model evolution over time also makes comparison difficult. For example, additional studies since the LaBerge and Samuels model was first introduced have extablished the text conditions and the developmental levels of reading skill under which component and holistic processing of words operate. Both the Gough and the LaBerge and Samuels models were originally formulated as serial, linear models, with the higher-order stages unable to influence lower-order stages, which must do their work earlier in the processing sequence. However, the revisions outlined in this chapter clearly indicate that the LaBerge and Samuels model now allows interaction between stages in the model.

Despite these difficulties, there have been attempts to compare models along sets of common dimensions. For example, deBeaugrande (1981) has generated a set of 16 categories for describing models of reading. Some of these categories include: the contribution of the processor (Is it top-down or bottom-up?), memory storage (abstractive, constructive, or reconstructive), automatization (whether some processes require little or no attention), processing depth (how much processing is required as a function of the task), and serial versus parallel processing (whether only one task or several can be performed concurrently).

Mosenthal (in press) has argued, however, that the comparison of models needs to include social and political criteria as well as statistical and logical criteria. His argument is that the scope of models should be limited by their "partial specifications." A partially specified model consists of *samples* of the features, procedures, and criteria that *approximate* a fully specified model's features, and so on. This means that since models are less than complete, the implications should also be viewed as incomplete. Certainly, model builders have been less than likely to assume that their models can account for *all* reading phenomena.

Each of the builders of reading models is describing the process from a somewhat different perspective, with a different focus. If there are discrepancies among the empirical studies reported in support of a particular model, it is probably the result of differences in materials used in the studies, the task subjects had to perform, the skill level of the experimental subjects, and the context of the studies.

While each model tends to draw upon conceptualizations of the reading process which have preceded it, it does not follow that the earlier models are no longer useful because each model describes a somewhat different aspect of reading. Thus, each model provides unique information about the reading process not found in the other models. In order to gain a more comprehensive view of reading, one should study each of the models. In fact, as one studies each of the models, one becomes impressed with how much experimental knowledge has been compressed with these few models.

Finally, we should recognize that our models have gaping holes in them. As we have developed some sophisticated ideas about how comprehension takes place and how metacognitive strategies are used to facilitate reading, the models have been slow to incorporate this information. It is as though there are separate knowledge entities in need of a cohesive force to integrate the disparate pieces of information into a unified model. However, before we attempt to build comprehensive models, it is important that we first establish partial models, such as the ones described in this article, that can be tested and modified as the need arises. At our present stage of development, we need partial models which can be tested more than we need comprehensive models which are more difficult to test. It should be most fascinating in the years to come to see what changes will occur in our models of reading as new knowledge accumulates about this process.

NOTES

1. What is fascinating to consider about the iconic image is that, despite the fact that the image is in the shape of an oval and contains information from four to five lines of print, when reading for meaning we seem to be oblivious or blind to the text above and below the line we are processing for meaning. On the other hand, when we merely look at a word on a page without trying to read it, we are then aware of the printed words above and below the word upon which we are focusing.
2. The addition of such a feedback loop makes it very much like some of the interactive models, such as the Rumelhart model and the Stanovich model examined later in this chapter.

REFERENCES

Anderson, I. H., & Dearborn, W. F. *The psychology of teaching reading.* New York: Ronald Press, 1952.

Bates, E., Kintsch, W., Fletcher, C., & Giuliani, V.   The role of pronominalization and ellipsis in texts: Some memory experiments. *Journal of Experimental Psychology: Human Learning and Memory,* 1980, *6,* 676–691.

Carpenter, P. A., & Daneman, M.   Lexical retrieval and error recovery in reading: A model based on eye fixations. *Journal of Verbal Learning and Verbal Behavior,* 1981, *20,* 137–160.

Carpenter, P. A., & Just, M. A.   Reading comprehension as eyes see it. In M. A. Just & P. A. Carpenter (Eds.), *Cognitive processes in comprehension.* Hillsdale, N.J.: Erlbaum, 1977.

Carroll, J. B. *Language and thought.* Englewood Cliffs, N.J.: Prentice-Hall, 1964.

Carver, R. P.   Toward a theory of reading comprehension and reading. *Reading Research Quarterly,* 1977–1978, *13,* 8–64.

Cattell, J. M.   The time it takes to see and name objects. *Mind,* 1886, *11,* 63–65.

Chomsky, N., & Halle, M. *The sound pattern of English.* New York: Harper & Row, 1968.

Collins, A. M., & Loftus, E. F.   A spreading-activation theory of semantic processing. *Psychological Review,* 1975, *82,* 407–428.

Cosky, M. J.   The role of letter recognition in word recognition. *Memory and Cognition,* 1976, *4,* 207–214.

deBeaugrande, R.   Design criteria for process models of reading. *Reading Research Quarterly,* 1981, *16,* 261–315.

Fillmore, C. J.   The case for case. In E. Back & R. T. Harms (Eds.), *Universals in linguistic theory.* New York: Holt, 1968.

Goodman, K. S.   A linguistic study of cues and miscues in reading. *Elementary English,* 1965, *42,* 639–643.

Goodman, K. S.   A psycholinguistic view of reading comprehension. In G. B. Schick &

M. M. May (Eds.), *New frontiers in college-adult reading* (15th Yearbook of the National Reading Conference). Milwaukee, Wisc.: National Reading Conference, 1966.

Goodman, K. S.   Behind the eye: What happens in reading. In K. S. Goodman & O. S. Niles (Eds.), *Reading: Process and program.* Urbana, Ill.: National Council of Teachers of English, 1970.

Goodman, K. S.   Reading: A psycholinguistic guessing game. In H. Singer & R. Ruddell (Eds.), *Theoretical models and processes of reading* (2nd ed.). Newark, Del.: International Reading Association, 1976. (Originally published, 1967.)

Gough, P. B.   One second of reading. In J. F. Kavanagh & I. G. Mattingly (Eds.), *Language by ear and eye.* Cambridge: MIT Press, 1972.

Gough, P. B., & Stewart, W. C.   *Word vs. non-word discrimination latency.* Paper presented at the Midwestern Psychological Association, 1970.

Gough, P. C., & Cosky, M. J.   One second of reading again. In J. Castellan & G. Pisoni, (Eds.), *Cognitive theory* (Vol. 2). Hillsdale, N.J.: Erlbaum, 1975.

Hockberg, J.   Components of literacy: Speculations and exploratory research. In H. Levin & J. P. Williams (Eds.), *Basic studies on reading.* New York: Basic Books, 1970.

Holmes, J. A.   *The substrata-factor theory of reading.* Berkeley: California Book, 1953.

Hubel, D. H., & Wiesel, T. N.   Receptive fields, binocular interaction and functional architecture in the cat's visual cortex. *Journal of Physiology,* 1962, *160,* 106–154.

Huey, E. B.   *The psychology and pedagogy of reading.* Cambridge: MIT Press, 1968. (Originally published, 1908.)

Hull, C. L.   *Principles of behavior.* New York: Appleton-Century-Crofts, 1943.

Javal, E.   Essai sur la physiologie de la lecture. *Annales d'oculistique,* 1879, *82,* 242–253.

Jenkins, J. J.   Four parts to remember: A tetrahedral model of memory experiments. In L. S. Cermak & F. I. M. Craik (Eds.), *Levels of processing in human memory.* Hillsdale, N.J.: Erlbaum, 1979.

Just, M. A., & Carpenter, P. A.   Eye fixations and cognitive processes. *Cognitive Psychology,* 1976, *8,* 441–480.

Just, M. A., & Carpenter, P. A.   Inference processes during reading: Reflections from eye fixations. In J. W. Senders, D. F. Fisher, & R. A. Monty (Eds.), *Eye movements and the higher psychological functions.* Hillsdale, N.J.: Earlbaum, 1978.

Just, M. A., & Carpenter, P. A.   A theory of reading: From eye fixations to comprehension. *Psychological Review,* 1980, *87,* 329–354.

Just, M. A., Carpenter, P. A., & Woolley, J. D.   Paradigms and processes in reading comprehension. *Journal of Experimental Psychology: General,* 1982, *111,* 228–238.

Kintsch, W.   *The representation of meaning in memory.* Hillsdale, N.J.: Erlbaum, 1974.

Kintsch, W., & van Dijk, T.   Toward a model of text comprehension and production. *Psychological Review,* 1978, *85,* 363–394.

Kintsch, W., & Vipond, D.   Reading comprehension and readability in educational practice and psychological theory. In L. Nilsson (Ed.), *Perspectives in memory research.* Hillsdale, N.J.: Erlbaum, 1979.

Kolers, P. A.   Three stages of reading. In H. Levin & J. P. Williams (Eds.), *Basic studies on reading.* New York: Basic Books, 1970.

Kozminsky, E., Kintsch, W., & Bourne, L., Jr.   Decision making with texts: Information analysis and schema acquisition. *Journal of Experimental Psychology: General,* 1981, *110,* 363–380.

LaBerge, D., & Samuels, S. J.   Toward a theory of automatic information processing in reading. *Cognitive Psychology,* 1974, *6,* 293–323.

Levin, H., & Kaplan, E. L.   Grammatical structure and reading. In H. Levin & J. P. Williams (Eds.), *Basic studies on reading.* New York: Basic Books, 1970.

Lindsay, P., & Norman, D.   *Human information processing* (2nd ed.). New York: Academic Press, 1977.

Mackworth, J. F.   Some models of the reading process: Learners and skill readers. *Reading Research Quarterly*, 1972, *7*, 701–733.

McCormick, C., & Samuels, S. J.   Word recognition by second graders: The unit of perception and interrelationships among accuracy, latency, and comprehension. *Journal of Reading Behavior*, 1981, *13*, 33–48.

Meyer, D. E., & Schvaneveldt, R. W.   Facilitation in recognizing pairs of words: Evidence of a dependence between retrieval operations. *Journal of Experimental Psychology*, 1971, *90*, 27–234.

Meyer, D. E., Schvaneveldt, R. W., & Ruddy, M. G.   Loci of contextual effects on word recognition. In P. M. A. Rabbitt & S. Dornic (Eds.), *Attention and performance V.* New York: Academic Press, 1975.

Miller, G. A., Bruner, J. S., & Postman, L.   Familiarity of letter sequences and tachistoscopic identification. *Journal of General Psychology*, 1954, *50*, 129–139.

Miller, G. A., & Isard, S.   Some perceptual consequences of linguistic rules. *Journal of Verbal Learning and Verbal Behavior*, 1963, *2*, 217–228.

Miller, J., & Kintsch, W.   Readability and recall of short prose passages: A theoretical analysis. *Journal of Experimental Psychology: Human Learning and Memory*, 1980, *6*, 335–354.

Mosenthal, P.   Problems of partial specification in translating reading research into practice. *Elementary School Journal*, in press.

Patberg, J., Dewitz, P., & Samuels, S. J.   The effect of context on the size of the perceptual unit used in word recognition. *Journal of Reading Behavior*, 1981, *13*, 33–48.

Peterson, L. R., & Peterson, J. M.   Short-term retention of individual verbal items. *Journal of Experimental Psychology*, 1959, *58*, 193–198.

Ruddell, R. B.   Psycholinguistic implications for a system of communication model. In K. Goodman & J. Fleming (Eds.), *Psycholinguistics and the teaching of reading.* Newark, Del.: International Reading Association, 1969.

Rumelhart, D.   Toward an interactive model of reading. In S. Dornic (Ed.), *Attention and performance VI.* Hillsdale, N.J.: Erlbaum, 1977.

Samuels, S. J.   Introduction to theoretical models of reading. In W. Otto (Ed.), *Reading problems.* Boston: Addison-Wesley, 1977.

Samuels, S. J., LaBerge, D., & Bremer, D.   Units of word recognition: Evidence for developmental changes. *Journal of Verbal Learning and Verbal Behavior*, 1978, *17*, 715–720.

Samuels, S. J., Miller, N., & Eisenberg, P.   Practice effects on the unit of word recognition. *Journal of Educational Psychology*, 1979, *71*, 514–520.

Singer, H.   The substrata-factor theory of reading and its history and conceptual relationship to interaction theory. In L. Gentiel, M. Kamil, & J. Blanchard (Eds.), *Reading research revisited.* Columbus, Ohio: Charles B. Merrill, 1983.

Singer, H., & Ruddell, R. (Eds.),   *Theoretical models and processes of reading* (2nd ed.). Newark, Del.: International Reading Association, 1976.

Smith, F.   *Understanding reading.* New York: Holt, Rinehart & Winston, 1971.

Sperling, G.   A model for visual memory tasks. *Human Factors*, 1963, *5*, 19–31.

Stanovich, K. E.   Toward an interactive-compensatory model of individual differences in the development of reading fluency. *Reading Research Quarterly*, 1980, *16*, 32–71.

Stewart, M. L., James, C. T., & Gough, P. B.   *Word recognition latency as a function of word length.* Paper presented at the Midwestern Psychological Association, 1969.

Terry, P., Samuels, S. J., & LaBerge, D.   The effects of letter degradation and letter spacing on word recognition. *Journal of Verbal Learning and Verbal Behavior,* 1976, *15,* 577–585.

Tinker, M. A.   Recent studies of eye movements in reading. *Psychological Bulletin,* 1958, *55,* 215–231.

Tolman, E. C.   *Purposive behavior in animals and men.* New York: Appleton-Century-Crofts, 1932.

Tulving, E., & Gold, C.   Stimulus information and contextual information as determinants of tachistoscopic recognition of words. *Journal of Experimental Psychology,* 1963, *66,* 319–327.

Turner, A., & Greene, E.   Construction and use of a propositional text base. *JSAS Catalog of Selected Documents in Psychology,* 1979, *8,* 58.

Weber, R. M.   First graders' use of grammatical context in reading. In H. Levin & J. P. Williams (Eds.), *Basic studies on reading.* New York: Basic Books, 1970.

White, M. J.   Laterality differences in perception: A review. *Psychological Bulletin,* 1969, *72,* 387–105.

Woodworth, R. S.   *Experimental psychology.* New York: Holt, 1938.

8 WORD RECOGNITION

Philip B. Gough

Word recognition is the foundation of the reading process.

To be sure, there is much more to reading than word recognition. The reader who would understand an aphorism, such as the following, must do much more than recognize 11 words.

A woman needs a man like a fish needs a bicycle.

He must, among other things, discern that MAN is a noun, not a verb, and that it is the object of the verb NEEDS, not the subject of that verb; he must, in short, discover the grammatical relations among the words in order to arrive at the meaning of the sentence. If he is to appreciate that meaning, he must draw upon his knowledge of men and women, fishes and bicycles. And if he is to understand its significance, he must integrate it into the discourse of which it is a part.

But before any of this can be done, those 11 words must be recognized. The reader must see that the sentence contains MAN, not FAN or MAT, and NEEDS, not FEEDS or NEARS, or the sentence will be misunderstood.

It behooves the student of reading, then, to understand something of word recognition.

Routine as it may seem, each instance of word recognition is an amazing feat. It begins with a pattern of light and dark cast onto the retina by reflection from the printed page; for the skilled reader, it ends less than a quarter of a second later and almost always with the correct word. In this time, the reader must find the word's meaning in memory, for only there is word form associated with meaning; he must locate a single item in a mental lexicon containing tens of thousands of entries (cf. Gough, 1975).

How this lexical search is accomplished remains essentially a mystery after nearly a century of research.

The first studies of word recognition were published by James McKeen Cattell (Cattell 1885, 1886/1947); these experiments were among the first to be conducted in the very first psychological laboratory, established in Leipzig in 1879 by Wilhelm Wundt. Cattell's attention soon turned to other matters, but his success in applying the new experimental methods to word recognition undoubtedly inspired its first body of research, engagingly reviewed by Huey (1908/1968). But for some reason (perhaps the rise of behaviorism), word recognition research then virtually ceased, resuming roughly 60 years later and increasing steadily over the past 15 years.

The volume of this research has grown well beyond the limits of a single chapter; a recent (and excellent) book surveying this literature (Henderson, 1982) contains 27 pages of references. The present chapter, then, cannot pretend to be comprehensive. Instead, we present what we take to be the major theoretical and empirical issues in word recognition and our current understanding of them.

We first state our methodological premises.

METHODOLOGY

The student of word recognition must begin by acknowledging that it cannot be studied directly. Word recognition is a central, presumably neural, event taking place in the eyes, optic nerves, and brain. We do not know what form it takes there, so we cannot observe or directly measure its occurrence. (Perhaps the closest we have come is through the measurement of evoked potentials accompanying the detection of semantic incongruities (Kutas & Hilliard, 1980). But even this is really indirect.)

What we can (and do) do is to ask a reader to perform some task which results in an overt response and then measure that response. Thus, we can ask a subject to read a word aloud (to name it), or to decide whether it is a word (as opposed to a string of letters), or whether it contains a given letter, or whether the object it names is bigger than a breadbox, and then measure his performance in this task. In fact, the number of such tasks is unlimited, so that there is potentially infinite variety in our methodology. But whatever task we choose, we face this fact: even the simplest task involves more than word recognition. Naming, for example, involves programming and executing a complex sequence of motor activities which are entirely subsequent to word recognition.

What this means is that we must make assumptions about how word recognition is manifested in the experimental task, about how word recognition is linked to the response we measure. Thus, the study of word recognition necessarily involves theoretical assumptions, and the methodology of word recognition inherently involves building a theoretical model. It is important, then, to consider the requirements for such a model.

At bottom, there is just one. To have explanatory power, a theoretical model must be falsifiable (cf. Platt, 1964; Popper, 1959).

The reason is this. A model, a theory, consists of a set of propositions, M ($=p_1 + p_2 + \cdots + p_n$). An empirical observation (a fact, datum, or bit of evidence) is another proposition, p_j. The model explains the observation if, assuming the model (i.e., $p_1 + p_2 + \cdots + p_n$) to be true, we can derive p_j, using strictly logical rules of inference (and their mathematical extensions). But the explanation rests squarely on the assumption that the model is correct, the theory true. And the paradox is that we can never prove that it is, for we can only disprove a theory.

The problem arises from the nature of logical inference. If p implies q and q is false, then p must be false, and we use this form of argument every time we attempt to refute a theory. That is, we use a theory to derive some prediction. We observe that the prediction is false, and we conclude that the theory is incorrect; at least one of the theory's propositions must be false.

But if p implies q and q is true, it does *not* follow that p is true; to conclude that it is would be to commit what logicians call the fallacy of affirming the consequent. If a model yields a prediction which is correct, we can only conclude that we have not yet disconfirmed that model; we may continue to assume that it is true and seek another way of falsifying it.

The result is, then, that the only way we make progress is by a kind of successive approximation. We try to formulate a model which not only explains the known facts, but also yields new and falsifiable predictions; when our model is falsified by some fact, then we seek a new one which explains that fact as well as the others. Then we try to falsify it, and so forth, *ad veritatem*.

It follows, then, that the first question we should ask about any proposed model, any theory, is this: What would prove it false? For the real danger in theorizing is not falsehood, but vacuity: to be compatible with known data by virtue of being compatible with *any* set of data. Such theories can have no explanatory value whatsoever. So, we ought never to be satisfied with theories which sound vaguely correct; rather, we should insist that they yield clear and falsifiable predictions.

We turn, then, to the methods by which models of word recognition can be disconfirmed.

Broadly speaking, there are two indexes of word recognition, accuracy and speed (or its reciprocal, latency). Each has advantages and disadvantages; we consider them in turn.

Accuracy

Under ordinary circumstances, accuracy is of little use with skilled readers, for they are seldom inaccurate. We do not know the incidence of errors in silent reading. But in oral reading of text displayed on a CRT, college students average less than one error in 50 words (Alford, 1980; Stevens & Rumelhart, 1975), and any video display is inferior to the average text in adequate light. So, one who wishes to study word recognition via accuracy must degrade the printed word in some way.

In principle, any way might do, and several have been employed. Thus, the word might be displayed at a distance too great (or, equivalently, in type too small) for recognition (e.g., see Erdmann & Dodge, 1898). Or the word might be projected too dimly (i.e., with too little contrast) to be read accurately (e.g., see Smith, 1969). But the oldest and by far the most popular manipulation is to reduce the duration of exposure of the word (Cattell, 1886/1947). Traditionally, this was done by means of a tachistoscope or tachistoscopic shutter; today, it is usually accomplished using a computer-controlled video display.

Whatever the means of reducing accuracy, the typical investigator uses a measure derived from accuracy, rather than accuracy itself, as a dependent variable. For example, duration of exposure is often reduced to the point of chance accuracy, then gradually increased until the target word is recognized; the duration at which this occurs is termed the *duration threshold*. The same can be done with any other form of word degradation, *mutatis mutandis;* for details, consult any textbook of psychophysics. But it is still, at bottom, accuracy—that is, probability of correct word recognition—which is being measured.

Until the 1970s, measures based on accuracy (using exposure duration in particular) were predominant in word recognition research, and they continue to be used for the study of certain questions. But in recent years, certain problems with these methods have become apparent. They are clearly associated with the duration threshold.

Consider, for example, Cattell's classic works. One of them is entitled, "The time taken up by cerebral operations" (Cattell, 1886/1947), and one of the cerebral operations which concerned him was, of course, word recognition. It might seem that one could directly measure "the time taken up by word recognition" by ascertaining how long a word must be exposed to a reader in order for it to be recognized (i.e., by measuring its duration threshold). But we now know that this duration is profoundly influenced by the nature of the prestimulus and poststimulus fields (i.e., what precedes and follows the word). For example, if the prestimulus and poststimulus fields are both dark (and the target word is black on white), it is next to impossible—given current instruments—to expose a word too briefly to be seen; an exposure of 1 msec will often suffice. The problem is that while we are controlling the exposure duration of the printed word itself, the *effective* stimulus (the firing of the retinal units initiated by the light reflected from that word) will continue for several hundred msec unless altered by some following stimulus (e.g., see Sperling, 1960). The obvious gambit is, then, to present another stimulus either before (a *forward mask*) or after (a *backward mask*) the target word, or both. But we have learned that the duration threshold depends crucially on the nature of those masks (e.g., Johnston & McClelland, 1980); there simply is no single duration threshold.

The problem is (as would be apparent to anyone who looked inside a tachistoscope) that brief exposures give partial information (always at least a rough idea of length, often general configuration, sometimes a letter here and there) so that the inference and the outright guess inevitably come into play.

But perhaps even more important than the inferential problem (which can be reduced by sophisticated design) is the pragmatic one. In order to use accuracy as a measure, you must have *in*accuracy. Therefore, a study of word recognition based on accuracy must include trials whose sole purpose is to produce error.

The alternative is to use speed or (equivalently) latency.

Speed

Speed (how quickly one does something) is simply the reciprocal of latency (how long it takes to do it) and vice versa. Investigators of word recognition almost universally measure and report latency, undoubtedly because it relates most directly tothe stage models and questions of serial and parallel processing (see chapter by Massaro, this volume) which they are testing. That is, many current models of word recognition posit that words are recognized through a sequence of operations, perhaps in series, perhaps in parallel, perhaps in cascade (McClelland, 1979). Whatever the case, the process of word recognition is conceived as extended in time, and the prediction of the time it takes to recognize a particular word (or class of words) is the explanatory target of such models. So, attempts to test these models inevitably involve measurement of response duration in some task involving word recognition.

As noted above, there is no limit, in principle, to the number of such tasks. But, in practice, only a few have been used, two predominantly. These two (as well as the other latency tasks) would share the advantage (over tasks manipulating accuracy) that all responses contribute directly to measurement; for that reason, such tasks are intended to minimize errors. Their advantages are much the same; their drawbacks differ.

Perhaps the simplest and most straightforward task is naming, where the subject must simply name each word as it appears; the onset of his or her response is detected by a voice-operated relay, and the interval between stimulus presentation and response initiation is measured as *naming latency*. The particular advantage of this task is that little beyond word recognition—only articulation—would seem to be required; its critics argue, however, that it may not really require word recognition (i.e., lexical access) at all, in that a word might be pronounced aloud using letter-sound correspondence rules without even contacting the internal lexicon. (Whether a word *is* named this way is clearly subject to empirical investigation; sadly—from a methodological standpoint—the evidence, as we shall see below, is mixed.)

The latter problem is avoided in another simple and popular task, the *lexical decision task* (LDT). Here, the subject is presented with a string of letters and must decide whether that string constitutes a word or not, usually indicating his or her response by pressing a button. The interval between word presentation and the subject's response is measured as the *lexical decision latency* for that word. At least if the foils (the nonword strings) are pseudowords (i.e., pronounceable and "wordy," like, say, PRASK or FLITCH), correct responses in excess of chance must depend upon true word recognition (i.e., contacting the corresponding item in the internal lexicon), and only that. But this statement acknowledges two disadvantages of the LDT. First, lexical decision latency for a given word depends not only on that word, but also on the character of the foils employed; the less "wordy" the foils, the shorter the latency for words. Second, a correct response does not guarantee word recognition. (In naming, the probability of a correct response by chance is virtually nil; here it is .50.)

Each of the common tasks, whether using accuracy or latency, has merits and demerits. The same could undoubtedly be said of any other task which has been, or might be, used to measure word recognition. For example, in one study (Terry, Samuels, & LaBerge, 1976), subjects were asked to decide whether each word (in a succession of words) named an animal. The advantage of such a task is clearly that true word recognition, involving access to the internal lexicon, is necessarily involved. But the disadvantages may be less obvious. First, response latency must depend crucially on the nature of the foils. Second, it must depend on semantic factors well beyond lexical access (e.g., the more "animal" the concept, the faster the response). Third, the task itself almost certainly must "prime" words in the animal category (as we shall see in our discussion of the effects of context on word recognition) and, so, override, or conceal, the effects of other variables.

We hope that this brief discussion of methodology in word recognition will make clear that there is no easy way—no way free of interpretive problems— to study word recognition. Each of our means of measurement, from tachisto-scopic duration threshold to semantic decision latency, is fraught with interpretive perils. But the astute reader will have noted that, in each case, the difficulties arise as objections to making direct translations from experimental observations to conclusions about the nature of word recognition. We have noted nothing which would stand in the way of an adequate theory, a model which would not only posit how words are recognized, but also how that process is incorporated in whatever experimental tasks an investigator might devise.

We end this brief discussion of methodology where we began, by offering this as the first and last methodological principle in word recognition: falsifiable theory is both the end and the means.

We turn now to matters of substance in word recognition. As noted above, our discussion is organized around four issues which we judge to be central. These are the question of the perceptual unit, the question of phonological media-tion, the question of word frequency, and the question of context.

THE PERCEPTUAL UNIT

The nature of the unit of word recognition has been the primary issue in word recognition since it was first broached by Cattell (1885, 1886/1947).

Common sense dictates the letter. Words are obviously composed of letters, and the fact that readers can spell (the reading and spelling subtests of the Wide Range Achievement Test correlate .86 for adults [Jastak & Jastak, 1978]) indicates that they are aware of those letters. Thousands of words differ from others only by a single letter, and it seems natural to assume that we distinguish them by distinguishing those letters. And since there is no way to anticipate where the distinguishing letter might fall (compare BOOK and LOOK, GOLDMAN and GOODMAN, SMITH and SMITE), it seems equally natural to assume that we simply register each of them and, so, recognize the word.

But at least since Cattell (if not before—cf. Balmuth, 1982, Chapters 24, 25), the role of the letter as the perceptual unit in word recognition has been challenged.

What Cattell found was that words could be read as rapidly as single letters in two senses. First, the exposure duration necessary for recognition of a word was slightly less than that for a letter. Second, a word's naming latency was also less than a letter's.

Cattell himself drew from these results the conclusion that "we do not therefore perceive separately the letters of which a word is composed, but [rather we perceive] the word as a whole" (Cattell, 1886/1947, p. 74). Henderson (1980) has pointed out that the meaning of Cattell's statement depends squarely on whether *perceive* is taken to denote the process of recognition or its result. But whatever Cattell's intent, many subsequent writers (e.g., Huey, 1908/1968) have taken the import of his work to be that word recognition cannot be mediated by letter recognition. More important, a considerable body of argument and research has been generated in the service of supporting, or refuting, this conclusion. This work is conveniently divided into two lines traceable to each of Cattell's seminal findings, one dealing with the accuracy of word and letter recognition, the other with their latencies.

Word- versus Letter-Recognition Accuracy

Cattell's initial observation that words could be recognized at an exposure duration too brief for single letter recognition was quickly reinforced by several related findings. Cattell himself further observed that an exposure duration which permitted 3 to 4 unrelated letters to be identified sufficed for two whole words—even four if they formed a sentence—to be grasped. In a similar vein, Erdmann and Dodge (1898) found that words could be read at a distance at which their letters, when presented singly, were unrecognizable. They also showed that with an exposure duration at which 4 to 5 unrelated letters could be read, their subjects could read single words containing as many as 22 letters.

The findings that more letters can be recognized if they are organized into words (and still more if into a sentence)—what Neisser (1967) called the *word apprehension effect*—have seldom, if ever, been taken as a serious threat to the idea that word recognition is mediated by letter recognition, for this effect can readily be ascribed to some factor (like greater memory loss for the unrelated letters) extraneous to those processes. But the repeated observation that words could be recognized under conditions where their letters could not be recognized seriously challenged the letter as the perceptual unit of the word.

If word recognition is mediated by letter recognition, then it would seem to follow that preventing letter recognition should prevent word recognition. Yet, the results consistently showed otherwise.

In the face of this fact, the letter's advocate had to argue that the chain of inference was flawed. In particular, he or she could challenge the argument that complete identification of each letter is a necessary condition for word recognition. In fact, we know that is not the case, for we know that there is often redundancy in words, and we can often readily identify words with missing letters or even with letters replaced by others (i.e., misspelled words). Given this, the defender of the letter could simply argue that word recognition in the apparent absence of letter recognition was really word recognition based on partial letter information and inference (cf. Goldscheider & Muller, 1893; Zeitler, 1900).

So, the matter rested until 1969, when Reicher published an amazing result. Using a tachistoscope, Reicher flashed a target letter, followed by a mask, and then asked his subjects to decide which of two letters had been presented. He noted that by varying the exposure duration of the target, he could produce variation in the probability of a correct response by his subject, ranging smoothly from chance (.5) at the shortest durations to perfect accuracy (1.0) at the longest, and he determined, for each subject, that duration which led to accuracy midway between these extremes (i.e., .75). Then, he presented, at exactly this duration, a four-letter word, followed by a mask, and asked his subject to decide which of two letters had been presented in the word.

The target letter contained in the word was identical to that previously presented in isolation, and the two alternatives presented after the word were the same as those presented after the single letter. Yet, when the word was presented at precisely the same duration which yielded a correct response probability of .75 with the single letter, it led to a response of probability .85.

Evidently, a letter embedded in a word can be recognized better than a letter in isolation. Or, in other words, a letter can be recognized when it is in a word where it cannot be recognized in isolation. And this effect *cannot* be attributed to partial letter recognition and inference, for each of the two alternatives provided to Reicher's subjects would form a word with the other letters. (For example, if the target letter *R* was presented in isolation and in the word RIPE, the foil in both conditions would be *W.*) Thus, Reicher evidently swept away the last defense of the letter as the unit of word recognition.

Subsequent studies by Wheeler (1970) and others (Johnston & McClelland, 1973; Juola, Leavitt, & Choe, 1974; Thompson & Massaro, 1973) amply confirmed Reicher's finding. But they also brought to light two additional facts of great importance to the interpretation of the word-superiority effect.

First, it was soon discovered that masking plays a significant role in this effect. Johnston and McClelland (1973) and Juola et al. (1974) found that the word-superiority effect disappeared when no mask followed the target, clearly indicating that the mask is, in some way, responsible for the effect. Moreover, the mask does it, as Bjork and Estes (1973) and Massaro and Klitzke (1979) showed, by producing greater interference with the single letter than with the word.

What these results indicated was that the mask did not simply interrupt and terminate the processing of the preceding item (i.e., the letter or word). But notice that this is just what was assumed in concluding that the word was processed in less time than one of its letters could have been. So, we cannot conclude from these results that a word is processed faster than its letters. Instead, we must believe that the processing of the word or letter continues after the arrival of the mask and that the processing of the mask commingles with the processing of the target to produce the effect.

What several writers (Johnston, 1981; McClelland & Rumelhart, 1981; Paap, Newsome, McDonald, & Schvaneveldt, 1982) have assumed to happen is this. When a word or letter is presented, it begins to activate letter detectors. As the letter detectors are activated, they begin to activate word detectors; the word detector, in turn, sends back activation to the letter detectors linked to it. When a mask arrives, composed (as it usually is) of letter fragments, it begins to activate other letter detectors than the target; these then compete with the target letter to reduce the subject's accuracy. But when the target letter had been presented in a word, it will receive feedback from word detectors linked to that letter and so performance will be improved in this condition.

It remains to be seen how this idea will survive further testing. But it is surely significant, if not ironic, that the best accounts currently available of the word-superiority effect, an effect thought to show that word recognition could not be mediated by letter recognition, assume that it is.

The second important development concerning the Reicher effect is that superiority over single letters is not limited to words. Several studies (Carr, Davidson, & Hawkins, 1978; Massaro & Klitzke, 1979; McClelland & Johnston, 1977) have shown that letters are recognized more accurately in *pseudowords* (i.e., pronounceable nonwords, like MAVE or GLAM) than in isolation. While words have a clear advantage over pseudowords (Adams, 1979; Juola et al., 1974; Manelis, 1974; McClelland, 1976; McClelland & Johnston, 1977), the advantage of pseudowords over single letters hints that at least some of the word-superiority effect must be due to some property of words other than their lexicality.

A variety of properties have been proposed, including letter-position redundancy, sequential redundancy, and pronounceability (see Massaro, Taylor, Venezky, Jastrzembski, and Lucas, 1980, for a careful review). But, again, the most successful attempts to explain the effects of orthographic structure on word recognition hold that they are mediated by its influences on constituent letter recognition.

Thus, the current state of our understanding of word-recognition accuracy is that word recognition *is* mediated by letter recognition.

Latency

We return to Cattell's second seminal finding, that words (at least short, familiar words) could be named as fast as single letters.

This result has also been used to challenge the letter-unit hypothesis, and understandably so. If word recognition is mediated by letter recognition, then word recognition must take longer than letter recognition, for whether they are performed in series or in parallel, the completion of a number of processes must take longer than the completion of any one of them. If naming could be equated with recognition, then Cattell's result would constitute incontrovertible evidence that word recognition cannot involve prior letter recognition.

But the catch is that letter naming cannot be equated with letter recognition. Letter naming obviously *includes* letter recognition, but it also involves, at the very least, formulating and initiating articulation of the letter's name. Similarly, even if word recognition is equated to the recognition of its letters, word naming necessarily involves additional processes. If we knew that the extraneous factors were the same in the two cases, then Cattell's result would prove that word recognition is faster than letter recognition and so refute the proposition that letter recognition precedes word recognition. But we have no reason to believe that the extraneous factors are the same in naming letters and words.

Exactly the same problem arises in every other attempt to evaluate the letter-unit hypothesis by comparing performance on words and single letters. For example, Johnson (1975, 1981) has found that it takes longer to match a letter with a word than to match two words, and he uses this to argue against the letter as the perceptual unit. But the matching task must involve more than recognition of the two stimuli (it requires their comparison, if nothing else), and we simply cannot rule out the possibility that the observed differences in latency should be ascribed to processes other than recognition.

The letter-unit hypothesis clearly entails that a letter must be recognized faster than a word containing that letter, but until we find a way of measuring recognition more directly, any attempt to evaluate the hypothesis by comparing word and letter recognition must be flawed. But the word-letter prediction is (only) a special case of a much broader one: the recognition of a set of letters must take longer than the recognition of any proper subset of those letters. It follows, therefore, that if word recognition is mediated by letter recognition, word-recognition latency must increase with word length in letters.

Whether it does is not yet settled.

There can be no doubt that word-naming latency increases with word length (Cosky, 1976; Forster & Chambers, 1973; Frederiksen & Kroll, 1976; Glushko, 1979; Mason, 1978; Seymour & Porpodas, 1980). But it has been argued (cf. Frederiksen & Kroll, 1976) that word naming can be accomplished by means other than word recognition; subjects who read PINT to rhyme with LINT provide proof of the point.

Clearer evidence ought to be obtained by using a task which does not require pronunciation, and the LDT has recommended itself to several investigators. Forster and Chambers (1973) found that lexical decision latency was greater for six- than four-letter words, but Frederiksen and Kroll (1976) found no such effect. Then Whaley (1978) measured the lexical decision latency for a large sample of words varying naturally on a variety of dimensions; multiple regression showed word length to be one of the two best predictors (the other was frequency).

The weight of the evidence, then, suggests that word-recognition latency increases with word length. More decisive research may show otherwise, but we conclude that the current evidence on word-recognition latency, like that on accuracy, is still consistent with the proposition that the letter is the perceptual unit of word recognition.

Summary

As we see it, the letter is still the best candidate as the perceptual unit of word recognition, if only because no other serious candidate has yet been put forward.

Few others have even been suggested. Eleanor Gibson (Gibson, 1965; Gibson & Levin, 1975; Gibson, Pick, Osser, & Hammond, 1962; Gibson, Shurcliff, & Jonas, 1970) proposed the *spelling pattern*, "a cluster of graphemes in a given environment which has an invariant pronunciation according to the rules of English." But this proposal was used only to explain why exchanging the consonant clusters in a pseudoword like SLAND (to yield NDALS) greatly reduced perceptibility (and interpretations of this fact involving the letter are easily found). Similarly, Smith (Smith & Haviland, 1972; Smith & Spoehr, 1974; Spoehr & Smith, 1973) proposed the vocalic center group (Hansen & Rogers, 1973), which roughly amounts to the syllable. But it served only to explain effects of syllabic length on recognition (and any which cannot be ascribed to letter length are very elusive; e.g., see Henderson, Coltheart, & Woodhouse, 1973).

The most common alternative offered by those who would reject the letter is the word itself. But this is not really an alternative; it is only the assertion of the negation of the letter hypothesis. Advocates of "holistic processing" (e.g., Terry et al., 1976) really proceed by deriving a prediction from the letter-unit hypothesis, and then state that their holistic model predicts the opposite. But in such cases, the letter-unit hypothesis does the work. This is not to deny that word recognition may ultimately prove holistic (i.e., unmediated by smaller units). But until a holistic model can be developed to yield falsifiable predictions of its own, we must consider it vacuous.

In the end, it is difficult to see how the letter can be avoided, if only because of what might be called the ransom note phenomenon. The ransom note (at least in fiction) is composed by clipping letters—varying conspicuously in case, font, and size (to say nothing of color)—and arranging them intowords. It seems incontrovertible that the only thing the resulting word tokens share with others of the same type is the identity of their letters. So, the words of a ransom note could *only* be identified by identifying their letters.

We know that such words are identified less readily than words in regular and ordinary fonts (Adams, 1979; McClelland, 1976). But it takes careful measurement to reveal these differences, for ransom note words are easily (i.e., quickly and accurately) read. They must be read by recognizing their letters, so, it seems to us incontrovertible that letter recognition is involved in word recognition.

It certainly does not follow that other cues might not contribute to word recognition. But none has yet been identified (influences of font distortion and word shape can easily be understood as influences on letter recognition itself), and we have good reason to look further. We would conclude that the letter *is* the perceptual unit of word recognition; the problem is to discover exactly how *the letter* is recognized and exactly how it leads to word recognition.

PHONOLOGICAL MEDIATION

The second major issue in word recognition is whether recognition of the printed word is mediated by some version of its spoken equivalent.

In broad form, this question is also a venerable one. Even before Cattell's pioneering studies, Egger (1881, p. 1) wrote, "Lire, en effet, c'est traduire l'écriture en parole" ['To read, in effect, is to translate writing into speech']. (Indeed, Henderson, 1982, p. 86, suggests that Aristotle held a similar view.) Ideas like this inspired a number of early investigations of "inner speech" and its role in reading, and Huey's (1908/1968) classic volume devotes two chapters to the matter.

To the modern reader, the early studies seem flawed by two confusions: they failed to distinguish speech (i.e., articulation) from language, and they failed to distinguish between "inner speech" which might occur before and after word recognition.

In the early 1970s, the issue was sharpened by a clear and strong theoretical proposition, the *phonological recoding hypothesis*, first offered by Rubenstein, Lewis, and Rubenstein (1971a).

The phonological recoding hypothesis holds that the recognition of a printed word is mediated by its phonological form. Starting from the premise that the mental lexicon is phonologically organized (see Gough, 1975), the phonological recoding hypothesis holds that word recognition is accomplished in two stages. First, the letter string is converted into a string of phonemes by means of grapheme-phoneme correspondence rules. (Thus, a string of letters, like THICK, would be converted into a string of phonemes, like /θɪk/.) Second, the mental lexicon is searched for an entry which matches this form; when it is found, the word is recognized. (Given /θɪk/, the reader arrives at its meaning.)

The phonological recoding hypothesis cleared both ambiguities from the inner speech issue. Obviously, it holds that "inner speech" plays a crucial role in the very recognition of a word, thus, it focuses the issue *pre*lexically. (It should be clear that this does not preclude the question of a postlexical role; this simply becomes a separate issue.)

But even more important, it exactly specifies the nature of the "inner speech" as a string of phonemes. In so doing, it denies that word recognition is mediated by any form of speech or subvocalization, for phonemes are abstract, hypothetical entities (see Chomsky & Halle, 1968; Gough, 1972). Hence, two traditional approaches are closed to us. We cannot employ direct measurements, for the phonemes are presumed to be central events; we assume they are neural, but we do not know where they might be or what form they might take wherever they are. Moreover, we cannot make use of interference, for we cannot assume with any confidence that some supposedly interfering task might engage the phonological recoding mechanisms (though some have tried, with mixed results: see Kleiman, 1975; Levy, 1975; Martin, 1978). We must, instead, seek to evaluate the claim indirectly by trying to falsify the model in which it is embedded, that is to say, the phonological recoding hypothesis.

The phonological recoding hypothesis yields three crucial sets of predictions concerning homophony, regularity, and ambiguity.

Homophony

The phonological recoding hypothesis yields several clear predictions concerning the effect of homophony. As Rubenstein et al. (1971a) pointed out, if the phonological recoding hypothesis is true, then a *pseudohomophone* (a nonword whose pronunciation corresponds to that of a real word, like BRANE, or LEEPH, or HOAM) should lead to the lexical entry for that word. If a subject were asked to decide whether letter strings were words or not, then pseudohomophones would be harder to reject than equally pronounceable and otherwise similar nonwords (like BRONE, or LOOPH, or GOAM). Using the LDT, Rubenstein et al. (1971a) found that both errors and latencies were greater for pseudohomophones than for appropriate controls (see also Coltheart, Davelaar, Jonassen, & Besner, 1977). Similar effects using other tasks are easily demonstrated; one of practical consequence is that spelling or typing errors which preserve a word's pronunciation, like WERK for WORK, are far harder to detect in proofreading than those, like WARK, which do not (Gough & Cosky, 1977; MacKay, 1968).

On first examination, then, the phonological recoding hypothesis seems promising: it yielded a clear and falsifiable prediction, and that prediction has been borne out. But, at the same time, we must recognize a certain conceptual difficulty with the hypothesis: given that BRANE will lead to the lexical entry for /breyn/, how then do we distinguish it from BRAIN? We may confuse the two in haste (as in the LDT), but under most circumstances, we certainly recognize that BRANE is, at best, a misspelling of the familiar word. So, if we are to maintain the phonological recoding hypothesis, we must suppose that the lexical entry for /breyn/ contains the spelling B-R-A-I-N (indeed, we must suppose this anyway if we are to account for the fact that the skilled reader can spell the word) and that after the lexical entry is accessed (whether from BRAIN, or BRANE, or BRAYN), the spelling is checked.

This problem was recognized by Rubenstein et al. (1971a), and their initial model contained a spelling check subsequent to lexical access. So, their model does "handle" the difficulty; the phonological recoding hypothesis is not invalidated—disconfirmed—by the fact that readers can distinguish pseudohomophones from their real counterparts. But the necessity of postulating a spelling check begins to undermine the appeal of the phonological recoding hypothesis.

The appeal of this hypothesis to many (cf. Gough, 1972; Gough & Cosky, 1977) is its apparent "cognitive economy." Our brains must contain the mechanisms for lexical search, given phonological form; we can, after all, recognize the spoken word. Add to this only some way of translating printed shapes into these forms and we have a mechanism for finding meaning from print; we have a reading machine. The parsimony of this simple additive formula is intrinsically appealing. But the necessity of including the spelling check in the phonological recoding hypothesis shows that at least the simplest version of the formula is inadequate.

Nevertheless, the phonological recoding hypothesis, augmented with the spelling check, yielded the prediction of the pseudohomophone effects; what was a falsifiable prediction was confirmed. The phonological recoding hypothesis thus survived its first test (and, at the same time, led to the discovery of several new phenomena).

But the skeptic—the critic of the phonological recoding hypothesis—could point out that each of these pseudohomophone effects was (by definition) obtained with nonwords. It is not hard to accept the idea that the skilled reader, confronted with an unfamiliar letter string, might convert it into phonological form; there is not much else that could be done with it. But it does not follow that the same thing must happen with familiar words. That is, the existence of pseudohomophone effects is hardly persuasive evidence that real words must be phonologically recoded before they can be recognized.

This is a cogent argument. After all, we knew, long before any experiments were conducted, that skilled readers *can* convert pseudowords into phonological form, for they can pronounce them. (Indeed, the pseudohomophone experiments could not even be conducted unless we knew which letter strings were homophonic with real words.) The pseudohomophone results are still revealing: they show that subjects *do* phonologically recode such strings, even when reading silently and even when it is to their disadvantage to do so. But the fact is that these results are all obtained with nonwords, and these nonword results do not show that skilled readers dothe same thing with real words. For this, we need evidence involving real words.

We need not look far. With the first explicit formulation of the phonological recoding hypothesis, Rubenstein et al. (1971a) recognized that it applied to real homophones exactly as it applied to pseudohomophones: if BRANE leads to /breyn/, which leads to the lexical entry for BRAIN, then SALE must lead to the lexical entry for /seyl/, which must (at least sometimes) lead to the lexical entry for SAIL. Thus, virtually the same derivation which leads to the prediction of the pseudohomophone effects leads to the parallel prediction of *homophone* effects.

Here the evidence is far less consistent. Using the LDT, Rubenstein et al.(1971a) reported that words with homophones, like SAIL (SALE) or FARE (FAIR), led to longer decision latencies than control words without homophones, like JAIL (*JALE) or CARE (*CAIR). But a reanalysis of their data by Clark (1973) cast doubt on the validity of their conclusion, and two subsequent studies by Coltheart leave the matter unsettled, for one (Davelaar, Coltheart, Besner, & Jonassen, 1978) found the effect, the other (Coltheart, Besner, Jonassen, & Davelaar, 1979) did not. The evidence for the predicted homophone effect in lexical decision is simply not conclusive.

Evidence for (or against) the homophone effect in other tasks is nonexistent. For example, while we know that misspellings are often "phonetic" (Sears, 1969), we have no idea whether misspellings which result in words, like THERE for THEIR, or TOO for TO, are harder to detect in proofreading than misspellings which do not, like PRIAR for PRIOR, DOO for DO.

The homophony results, then, do not provide strong support for the phonological recoding hypothesis. It correctly predicts pseudohomophone effects, but the corresponding predictions of homophone effects have not been confirmed. And to account for the skilled reader's ability to distinguish among homophones, it was necessary to augment the phonological recoding hypothesis with a spelling check which considerably reduces its parsimony.

Regularity

The second prediction engendered by the phonological recoding hypothesis concerns the effect of spelling-sound regularity.

According to the phonological recoding hypothesis, the first step in recognizing a word is to translate it into phonemes by means of spelling-sound correspondence rules. But then it must follow that irregular words, like PINT and CASTE (words which are exceptions to the rules), must cause difficulties: either they must be recoded wrongly, or some additional mechanism must be added to "correct" their mispronunciation. The phonological recoding hypothesis predicts, then, that the recognition of irregular words must be retarded relative to the recognition of regular words.

Several studies have tested this prediction, with mixed results. Evidently, irregularity does have the predicted result on naming latency. Baron and Strawson (1976), Gough and Cosky (1977), Stanovich and Bauer (1978), and Coltheart et al. (1979) all report longer naming latencies for exception words than for controls (though Seidenberg, Waters, Barnes, & Tanenhaus, in press, report that the effect holds only for low-frequency words). But with lexical decision, no such consistent finding is obtained: Stanovich and Bauer (1978) and Barron (1979) found the predicted effect, but neither Coltheart et al. (1979) nor Seidenberg et al. (in press) obtained this result.

These inconsistencies are in need of resolution; some of the differences are almost certainly due to differences in the criteria employed by different investigators to select exception words. But it seems most unlikely that the resolution will reveal the simple effect of irregularity predicted by the phonological recoding hypothesis.

Ambiguity

The third prediction entailed by the phonological recoding hypothesis involves ambiguity. The orthography of English is alphabetic; the spellings of English words correspond, in a systematic way, to the phonemes of their spoken forms. But few of these correspondences are one to one: most phonemes can be spelled in more than one way, and many spelling patterns correspond to more than one phoneme. For example, EA corresponds to one thing in LEAK, another in HEAD, and still another in STEAK (to say nothing of AREA). The spelling-sound correspondence rules assumed by the phonological recoding hypothesis must, therefore, include (at least) three different rules which must be applied to words (or nonwords) containing EA. So, the recoding of such phonologically ambiguous strings must be complicated relative to that of unambiguous strings (like MESH, or CLIFF, or DUCK). Thus, the phonological recoding hypothesis entails the prediction that phonologically ambiguous words must be more difficult to recognize than unambiguous ones.

This prediction appears to be false. Seidenberg et al. (in press) found no difference in either naming latency or lexical decision latency between words with ambiguous spelling patterns (e.g., DEAD, GOWN) and unambiguous controls (e.g., NOTE, BOIL).

Summary

In summary, the phonological recoding hypothesis is clearly insufficient, if not simply wrong. It correctly predicted the effect of homophony on pseudowords, but the parallel prediction with words has not been supported. Its prediction of an irregularity effect has been confirmed with naming, but not with lexical decision. Finally, its prediction of an ambiguity effect has found no support.

The experimental evidence, then, fails to support the phonological recoding hypothesis. There is also clinical evidence which casts doubt on it. Several investigators (e.g., Marshall & Newcombe, 1973; Patterson & Marcel, 1977; Saffran & Marin, 1977) have observed brain-damaged patients who have lost (if they ever had them) the spelling-sound correspondence rules presumed by the phonological recoding hypothesis. They cannot decode (i.e., name) pseudowords, but they can still correctly identify many (in at least one case thousands) of words. These cases clearly point to the existence of a route to the internal lexicon other than phonological recoding.

It is hard to escape the conclusion that the strong form of the phonological recoding hypothesis—that the skilled reader inevitably goes through phonological form en route to the lexicon—is simply wrong. But it is equally hard to conclude the opposite—that lexical access is simply direct and visual. For one thing, the hypothesis of "direct visual access" is not really an alternative; it is simply the negation of the phonological recoding hypothesis. As such, it offers no predictions, no falsifiable consequences, whatsoever. The phonological recoding hypothesis did the heuristic work; it predicted several new phenomena, and the "direct access hypothesis" simply stood around and collected the leavings.

But more important than this methodological point, some of the predictions of the phonological recoding hypothesis were correct. In particular, its prediction of pseudohomophone effects has been strongly supported. What these suggest is that skilled readers invariably do phonologically recode unfamiliar letter strings, even when it is to their disadvantage to do so. This has lead several investigators to propose *dual access* models in which the skilled reader is supposed to have two means of access to his or her lexicon, one direct, the other involving phonological recoding (see Coltheart et al., 1979; McCusker, Hillinger, & Bias, 1981; Meyer, Schvaneveldt, & Ruddy, 1974). The two mechanisms are thought to function in parallel, with the race going to the swift; word frequency is then supposed to influence the speed of the direct channel, but not phonological recoding, thereby accounting for the latter's effect on unfamiliar strings and the lack of its effects on familiar words.

It remains to be seen whether a dual access model which is compatible with all the data can be worked out. If it can, then the phonological recoding hypothesis has done its work: it generated falsifiable predictions, and they, in turn, generated a new and better model. The task, then, will be to disprove the new model.

FREQUENCY

Word frequency has earned a reputation as the single most important variable in word recognition. As measured by word counts like those of Thorndike and Lorge (1944), Kučera and Francis (1967), and Carroll, Davies, and Richman (1971), its effects have been found in virtually every task used to measure word recognition, from tachistoscopic recognition to semantic judgment. These effects are robust enough to be used routinely as laboratory demonstrations in experimental psychology, and every investigator must be aware of the need to control for word frequency in any experiment involving words.

The effects of frequency are consistent. With respect to accuracy, frequency has long been known to correlate with both visual duration threshold (Howes & Solomon, 1951; Postman & Adis-Castro, 1957) and luminance threshold (Baker & Feldman, 1956). More recently, it has been shown to correlate with latency in a variety of tasks ranging from matching or naming to syntactic and semantic decisions (e.g., see Chambers & Forster, 1975; Forster & Chambers, 1973; Frederiksen & Kroll, 1976; Whaley, 1978).

In each of these cases, the effect appears to be linear on the logarithm of word frequency. That is, the function relating the measure of word recognition to word frequency can be expressed as a linear equation

$$r = a(\log f) + b$$

where r is the dependent variable (e.g., duration threshold or lexical decision latency), f is word frequency (e.g., in the Kučera & Francis count), and a and b are constants. The import of this generalization (which might be called the Frequency Law of word recognition) is that comparable effects are produced by multiplicative, not additive, changes in word frequency. The difference in (say) lexical decision latency between words of frequency 5 and words of frequency 10 equals, not that between words of frequencies 50 and 55, but rather that between words of 50 and 100. (An important methodological consequence of this is that frequency must be controlled much more tightly with low-frequency words than with high-frequency words.)

Moreover, another generalization seems warranted by the data: the magnitude of the effect of frequency appears to depend directly on the difficulty of the task (in terms of the Frequency Law, a varies with b). For example, in the LDT, where typical latencies for college students range 700 to 1000 msec, latency evidently decreases 60 to 100 msec per log unit of frequency (e.g., see Rubenstein, Garfield, & Millikan, 1970). But in the naming task, where latencies can be as brief as 500 msec or less, the effect of frequency is less than half as great, averaging 15 to 35 msec per log unit of frequency for four- and five-letter words (Forster & Chambers, 1973; Frederiksen & Kroll, 1976).

The facts, then, seem clear, but their explanation is not. It may seem, at first glance, as if no explanation is needed: that familiar stimuli are easier to recognize than unfamiliar is something we knew all along, and the word-frequency effect is just another instance of this obvious principle. But the fact that these results seem obvious does not diminish their need of explanation; if we are truly to understand them, we must seek the mechanisms which underlie them.

The first demonstrations of the word-frequency effect involved tachistoscopic presentation: the word was presented too briefly or too dimly to be seen, then the duration or luminance was increased until the word was correctly reported. To someone who has never peered into a tachistoscope, it might seem that the duration or luminance threshold marks a clear boundary between those durations (or luminances) at which the word cannot be recognized, and those at which it can. But anyone who has looked into one knows that on subthreshold trials, some things are recognized: one usually can detect the word's length, often its general configuration, sometimes a letter here or there. Given such information, all but the most cautious subjects will quite reasonably try to infer (to guess) the identity of the word, and most will guess common words before rare. Given this, a common target must be arrived at before a rare target simply because it will be offered earlier as a guess—a point demonstrated in a methodological tour de force by Goldiamond and Hawkins (1958) who showed that the word-frequency effect was obtained when only blanks were exhibited in the tachistoscope and an arbitrary word was designated as target on each trial.

This explanation of the word-frequency effect in tachistoscopic recognition was formalized by Broadbent (1967) as the sophisticated guessing theory (sophisticated because the guesses are supposed to take advantage of whatever visual information is available). Broadbent rejected it in favor of what he called a criterion bias theory. The idea is drawn from signal detection theory, where the recognition of a stimulus is treated as a kind of statistical decision; the subject is supposed to adopt a lower decision criterion for common words than for rare words.

Whether there is any real difference between these two theories is questionable; if there is, it is subtle enough to have provoked a prolonged debate over its existence (Catlin, 1969, 1971; Nakatani, 1970, 1973; Treisman, 1971). But while sophisticated guessing theory seems like a natural account of the word-frequency effect in tachistoscopic recognition, it seems awkward when applied to speed tasks. Perhaps, for this reason, some version of the criterion bias idea is usually now invoked to explain the effects of word frequency on response latency in word-recognition tasks.

The most widely cited of these is the *logogen* model offered by Morton (1969, 1970, 1979). Morton coined the felicitous term logogen to label a hypothetical unit in the mental lexicon; the model assumes that there is a logogen corresponding to each of the words in our vocabularies. The function of the logogen is to integrate information from sources pertinent to the recognition of a word; in particular, it is intended to combine visual information with contextual. Whenever information arrives, whether from prior context or the printed word, the logogen is activated; when this activation reaches a certain threshold, the logogen fires and the word is recognized. To explain the word-frequency effect, Morton simply assumes that this threshold varies inversely with word frequency.

It should be clear, at least by the methodological standards proposed at the beginning of this chapter, that this is not an adequate explanation of the word-frequency effect. It really says only that high-frequency words are recognized faster than low-frequency words because the recognition thresholds of the high-frequency words are reached faster than those of the low-frequency words, and this comes close to saying that high-frequency words are recognized faster because high-frequency words are recognized faster. (While it does deny that sensory information is accumulated any faster for high-frequency words than for rare-frequency words, the substance of this claim is not clear.)

Evidently, what we lack is an account of the word-frequency effect which explains it, not as a consequence of a change in some parameter, but rather as one which shows how the process of word recognition might be altered by familiarity, how some cognitive operation might require fewer steps (or even be omitted) with increasing familiarity, or how the process might even undergo qualitative change. (An example is that offered by models assuming phonological recoding for low-frequency words, but not for high-frequency words.) It seems clear, then, that an adequate account of the word-frequency effect can only be provided by the development of a fuller model of word recognition than we now have.

At the same time, the nature of the word-frequency effect must constrain this development. There remain some significant empirical questions regarding the effect, all connected with the difficulty of measuring the word-frequency variable.

The first question is whether any variable except word frequency really influences word recognition. At least since Zipf (1935), students of word recognition have been aware that word frequency is correlated with many other word properties, including length, irregularity, bigram frequency, degree of ambiguity (i.e., number of meanings), and concreteness. Each of these variables has been thought to influence word recognition and each has been thought to interact with word frequency. Thus, for example, it seems apparent that both word length and regularity influence recognition less with high-frequency words than with low-frequency words.

To study such interactions, it is necessary to manipulate frequency and the potentially interacting variable orthogonally. In order to do this, investigators of the word-frequency effect routinely employ published word counts to define word frequency operationally. But no one supposes that frequency so defined is really the relevant variable (the frequency with which a word appears in the

New York Times can hardly have an effect on one who does not read it); rather it is tacitly assumed that these counts simply provide good estimates of the frequency with which experimental subjects have encountered those words in their own reading, that is, of word familiarity. At the upper end of the frequency distribution, this is certainly reasonable; words like THE and OF and IS are common in any and every sort of reading matter. But at the other end, this is certainly not so; the most casual skimming of the low-frequency words in (say) Kučera and Francis (1967) will show that they differ drastically in familiarity. The frequency counts thus exemplify a well-known statistical principle: The stability of an estimate of a probability will decrease with that probability.

It follows, then, that investigators must be careful in dealing with low-frequency words: that such words are equated in a word count does not ensure that they are equated in familiarity. A failure to observe this precaution appears to account for at least three apparently puzzling interactions of frequency with other variables (Gernsbacher, in press). One such is that between word and bigram frequency, where it was consistently found that bigram frequency had no significant effect on high-frequency words, but where conflicting results with low-frequency words had been reported by a number of investigators (Biederman, 1966; Broadbent & Gregory, 1968; McClelland & Johnston, 1977; Rice & Robinson, 1975; Rumelhart & Siple, 1974). Gernsbacher was able to show that each of the obtained results was attributable to familiarity and, thus, that there is no evidence in these effects that bigram frequency plays any role in word recognition. Similarly, she found that differential familiarity among low-frequency words could account for interactions which have been reported between frequency and concreteness (James 1975; Paivio & O'Neill, 1970; Richards, 1976; Rubenstein et al., 1970; Winnick & Kressel, 1965) and between frequency and degree of ambiguity or number of meanings (Forster & Bednall, 1976; Jastrzembski, 1981; Jastrzembski & Stanners, 1975; Rubenstein et al., 1970; Rubenstein, Lewis, & Rubenstein, 1971b).

It remains an intriguing possibility that, save for length and regularity, frequency is the only variable which influences word recognition. But the same time, it may be that it is not really frequency which counts.

As we have noted, frequency is correlated with many other variables. But there is one from which it is nearly inseparable, namely *recency*. By the very nature of things, frequent words tend to have been seen recently, rare words not so recently. Until a short time ago, recency has been a confounding variable in every study of the word-frequency effect.

To assess directly the effects of these two variables, it would be necessary to vary them independently. It is not easy to see how to manipulate recency while holding frequency constant. But it is easy to do the opposite (i.e., to hold recency constant while manipulating frequency): one simply shows words to the reader twice. The first time, frequency and recency are confounded, but on the second trial, all the words are of equal recency, so, only frequency remains. Several studies (Dixon & Rothkopf, 1979; Scarborough, Cortese, & Scarborough, 1977; Theios & Muise, 1976) have recently shown that repetition considerably reduces the frequency effect on word-recognition latency; Richards and Platnick (1974) report that it virtually eliminates frequency's effect on the visual duration threshold.

What is suggested by these results is that the word-frequency effect, rather than reflecting a permanent, structural modification of the reader's perceptual system, may instead reflect only the current state, the present arrangement, of that system. How this might change our model of word recognition remains to be seen.

CONTEXT

We finally take up the question of the role of context in word recognition. This question looms large in theoretical discussions of reading. As Rumelhart (1977) has noted, models of reading can be partitioned into three classes: the *bottom-up*, the *top-down*, and the *interactive*. Bottom-up models are those which (like Gough, 1972, or LaBerge & Samuels, 1974) view reading as beginning with the printed page, proceeding linearly from the visual data to meaning by a series of processing stages. Top-down models, in contrast, are those which (like Goodman, 1967, or Smith, 1971) see reading as beginning with the reader's generation of expectancies, hypotheses, or predictions about the printed word and the subsequent testing of these hypotheses against the visual data. Interactive models (e.g., Rumelhart, 1977) strive to synthesize these extremes by viewing reading as the subtle interplay of the conceptual and visual processes.

No theory of reading can deny the importance of context in *reading;* as Gough, Alford, and Holley-Wilcox (1981) point out, it is context which determines the referent of pronouns and other deictic terms; selects the form class of uninflected terms, like WALK and SNEEZE; and chooses the reading of homographs, like CHEST and TANK. But bottom-up models, in contrast to top-down and interactive models, hold that context has its effects *after* word recognition has taken place. Thus, any evidence of an effect of context on word recognition itself is an argument against bottom-up models.

On the face of it, context clearly does affect word recognition. Tulving and Gold (1963) showed that the presence of an appropriate sentential context in the preexposure field of a tachistoscope can substantially lower the recognition threshold of a target word, while an inappropriate context can raise it a like amount (see also Morton, 1964). But the relevance of these results to ordinary reading can easily be challenged (cf. Massaro, 1975; Meyer, Schvaneveldt, & Ruddy, 1975). In these studies, subjects had ample time to peruse the context and combine the product with information gathered in previous exposures to guess the target, a situation far different from that in ordinary reading, where the prior context is available only milliseconds before a target word. Such sophisticated guessing (to borrow the term from an analogous treatment of the word-frequency effect) would be perfectly compatible with the view that, under normal circumstances, reading is bottom-up.

But the bottom-up view was further discomfited by the observation that context can also influence word-recognition latency. Meyer et al. (1975) demonstrated that the lexical decision latency for a target like NURSE was significantly reduced by the prior occurrence of a related word like DOCTOR. The relevance of this *semantic priming* to ordinary reading may be challenged because associated words rarely occur together in print (cf. Forster, 1979; Gough et al., 1981), but Schuberth and Eimas (1977) then showed that lexical decision was facilitated by a congruous sentential context (compared to a context of random digit names), while an incongruous context had the opposite effect. Moreover, West and Stanovich (1978), in the first of a systematic series of studies (see Stanovich and West, 1983, for an overview), found that an appropriate sentential context facilitated even naming latency, perhaps the most "peripheral" (certainly the fastest) of word-recognition indexes. Interestingly, though, they did not find the inhibition effect of inappropriate context obtained by the previous investigators.

To account for these discrepant results (i.e., contextual facilitation and inhibition in some studies, only facilitation in others), Stanovich and West (1981, 1983) have adopted an idea (first proposed by Posner and Snyder, 1975, and further developed by Neely, 1976, 1977) that there are *two* contextual effects on word recognition. One is, like sophisticated guessing, based on slowly forming, perhaps conscious, expectancies; this results in contextual facilitation, but at the cost of contextual inhibition when those expectancies go wrong (cf. Gough et al., 1981). On the other hand, there is an automatic, fast, "cost-free" spreading activation mechanism which results in contextual facilitation without inhibition.

This analysis is consistent with much of the available data concerning the effect of sentential context on word recognition. And the notion of an automatic, fast, inhibitionless spreading activation mechanism is certainly incompatible with a bottom-up notion of reading: it clearly points to an interactive, if not top-down, word-recognition process.

But there are two problems in accepting this as the final answer to the question of the influence of context on word recognition.

The first is empirical. There is no doubt that prior research has conclusively demonstrated contextual facilitation of word recognition. But that effect is far from constant. For one thing, it varies considerably with stimulus quality: the more degraded the stimulus, the greater the effect of context (hence, the clearer the stimulus, the less the effect; see Stanovich and West, 1983, for a review). For another, the effect of context diminishes with reading ability. Context consistently shows larger effects with younger and poorer readers than with older and better ones (Stanovich, 1980). To account for these results, Stanovich (1980) has proposed an *interactive-compensatory model* of reading, the essence of which is that the reader uses context to compensate for difficulties in word recognition, whether caused by stimulus degradation or deficient ability.

It seems, then, that while the effects of context can be dramatic, those effects are diminished with the skilled reader reading clear text. It is even possible that they are normally absent, for the contexts studied to date are hardly representative. In every single study, the targets have been nouns, in sentence final position, and highly predictable. This "sample" of words is simply not representative of the average word, in that (1) nouns constitute only a fraction of content words, which together account for no more than half of the words in running text; (2) the average sentence (at least in the newspaper, see Kučera and Francis, 1967) is over 20 words in length, making words in the final position a distinct minority; and (3) the average predictability of content words in running text is only about .10 (Gough, 1983). It remains an open (and important) question whether the average context has any effect at all on the average word read by the skilled reader in good light. It is at least conceivable that skilled reading is, most of the time, bottom-up.

The second problem is conceptual. The phrase spreading activation, reminiscent as it may be of neurophysiological processes, really seems to have little content. It is hard to see how it differs from spreading facilitation. But if it does not, then its use as an explanation of contextual facilitation is simply circular, thus totally empty.

That context *can* and sometimes does influence word recognition cannot be denied, but whether it ordinarily does so remains to be seen. Whatever effects it may have are still in need of explanation.

PROSPECTUS

As the preceding discussions must show, there is much to be learned about word recognition. An optimist, noting the current level of activity in the area, might predict that new insights are just around the corner (and that this review will shortly be outdated). But there is also a pessimistic view, which holds that we are learning more and more about less and less.

It cannot be denied that some promising lines of investigation have recently been opened (or revived). One is the study of word recognition in contrasting orthographies (see Kavanagh & Venezky, 1980); of two worthy of note, one is Chinese, which is nonalphabetic (see Tzeng and Hung, 1980, for a recent review) and the other is Serbo-Croatian, which can be written in either of two alphabets (Roman and Cyrillic) with intriguing complications (see Lukatela and Turvey, 1980). Another is the use of eye-movement recording to study word recognition in situ (Rayner, 1983); in particular, the technique of changing the visual stimulus contingent upon eye movement seems ripe for exploitation.

But the pessimist will argue that what we most need is not more data, but rather better theory. Current models of word recognition are all of a piece. They assume that word recognition begins with the extraction of visual information from the printed word by feature detectors; the feature detectors activated by the word then activate letter detectors (sometimes called *codes* or *nodes*) which, in turn, activate word detectors. By carefully adjusting their parameters, it is possible to account for an impressive array of data (see McClelland & Rumelhart, 1981, and Rumelhart & McClelland, 1982, for an outstanding example).

Yet, in absolute terms, the variance these models try to account for is surprisingly limited. Take the longest, the most irregular, the rarest word in a reader's vocabulary, and that word will still be recognized in less than a second. (Indeed, take a random-letter string—at least one within the limits of short-term memory— and it will be recognized nearly as quickly.) But really to slow down word recognition, all we need do is obscure its letters.

It seems clear that to solve the problem of word recognition, we must solve the problem of letter recognition; we must develop a model of how we can recognize the underlying unity in the infinite variety of forms a letter can take (see Hofstadter, 1982a, 1982b, for a stimulating discussion of the problem).

The fundamental shortcoming of current models is that they do not really face up to this problem. In these models, one must look closely to find any mention of visual form, of line or slope, angle or curvature, concavity or connectedness; such matters are treated only in the customary preamble concerning feature extraction. And the notion of feature extraction itself, far from being an answer to the question of how form is processed, is instead a kind of explanatory nostrum which has never been shown to work; feature detectors which we know how to construct cannot be combined in any known way to yield letter detectors, while we have no idea how to build those which could. Thus, it might be said that our models begin where they should end (that is, they focus on processing which occurs after the registration of visual form) because they end where they should begin (they provide no account of how that is accomplished).

We conclude, then, that to solve the problem of word recognition we must solve the problem of pattern recognition. But to do that will be to solve the deepest problem in perception.

REFERENCES

Adams, M. J.   Models of word recognition. *Cognitive Psychology*, 1979, *11*, 133–176.

Alford, J. A.   *Lexical and contextual effects on reading time.* Unpublished doctoral dissertation, University of Texas at Austin, 1980.

Baker, K. E., & Feldman, H.   Threshold-luminance for recognition in relation to frequency of prior exposure. *American Journal of Experimental Psychology*, 1956, *69*, 278–280.

Balmuth, M.   *The roots of phonics.* New York: McGraw-Hill, 1982.

Baron, J., & Strawson, C.   Use of orthographic and word-specific knowledge in reading words aloud. *Journal of Experimental Psychology: Human Perception and Performance*, 1976, *2*, 386–393.

Barron, R. W.   Reading skill and phonological coding in lexical access. In M. M. Gruneberg, R. N. Sykes, & P. E. Morris (Eds.), *Practical aspects of memory.* New York and London: Academic Press, 1979.

Biederman, G. B.   The recognition of tachistoscopically presented five-letter words as a function of diagram frequency. *Journal of Verbal Behavior and Verbal Learning*, 1966, *5*, 208–209.

Bjork, E. L., & Estes, W. K.   Letter identification in relation to linguistic context and masking conditions. *Memory and Cognition*, 1973, *1*, 217–223.

Broadbent, D. E.   Word frequency effect and response bias. *Psychological Review*, 1967, *74*, 1–15.

Broadbent, D. W., & Gregory, M.   Visual perception of words differing in letter diagram frequency. *Journal of Verbal Behavior and Verbal Learning*, 1968, *7*, 569–571.

Carr, T. H., Davidson, B. J., & Hawkins, H. L.   Perceptual flexibility in word recognition: Strategies affect orthographic computation but not lexical access. *Journal of Experimental Psychology: Human Perception and Performance*, 1978, *4*, 674–690.

Carroll, J. B., Davies, P., & Richman, B.   *The American Heritage Word Frequency Book.* New York: Houghton Mifflin, 1971.

Catlin, J.   On the word-frequency effect. *Psychological Review*, 1969, *79*, 504–506.

Catlin, J.   In defense of sophisticated guessing theory. *Psychological Review*, 1971, *80*, 412.

Cattell, J. M.   The inertia of the eye and brain. *Brain*, 1885, *8*, 295–312.

Cattell, J. M.   The time taken up by cerebral operations. In A. T. Poffenberger (Ed.), *James McKeen Cattell.* New York: Basic Books, 1947. (Originally published, 1886.)

Chambers, S. M., & Forster, K. I.   Evidence for lexical access in a simultaneous matching task. *Memory and Cognition*, 1975, *3*, 549–559.

Chomsky, N., & Halle, M.   *The sound pattern of English.* New York: Harper & Row, 1968.

Clark, H. H.   The language-as-fixed-effect fallacy: A critique of language statistics in psychological research. *Journal of Verbal Learning and Verbal Behavior*, 1973, *12*, 335–359.

Coltheart, M.   Critical notice of E. J. Gibson and H. Levin, "The Psychology of Reading." *Quarterly Journal of Experimental Psychology*, 1977, *29*, 157–167.

Coltheart, M.   Lexical access in simple reading tasks. In G. Underwood (Ed.), *Strategies of information processing.* London and New York: Academic Press, 1978.

Coltheart, M., Besner, D., Jonassen, J. T., & Davelaar, E.   Phonological encoding in the lexical decision task. *Quarterly Journal of Experimental Psychology*, 1979, *31*, 489–507.

Coltheart, M., Davelaar, E., Jonassen, J. T., & Besner, D.   Access to the internal lexicon. In S. Dornic (Ed.), *Attention and performance VI.* Hillsdale, N.J.: Erlbaum, 1977.

Cosky, M. J.   The role of letter recognition in word recognition. *Memory and Cognition*, 1976, *4*, 207–214.

Davelaar, E., Coltheart, M., Besner, D., & Jonassen, J. T.   Phonological recoding hypothesis and lexical access. *Memory and Cognition*, 1978, *6*, 391–402.

Dixon, P., & Rothkopf, E. Z.   Word repetition, lexical access, and the process of searching words and sentences. *Journal of Verbal Learning and Verbal Behavior*, 1979, *18*, 629–644.

Egger, V.   *La parole intérieur.* Paris: Librairie Germer Baillière et Cie, 1881.

Erdmann, B., & Dodge, R.   *Psychologische Untersuchungen uber das lesen.* Halle: Niemeyer, 1898.

Forster, K. I.   Levels of processing and the structure of the language processor. In W. E. Cooper & E. Walker (Eds.), *Sentence processing: Psycholinguistic studies presented to Merrill Garrett.* Hillsdale, N.J.: Erlbaum, 1979.

Forster, K. I., & Bednall, E. S.   Terminating and exhaustive search in lexical access. *Memory and Cognition*, 1976, *4*, 53–61.

Forster, K. I., & Chambers, S. M.   Lexical access and naming time. *Journal of Verbal Learning and Verbal Behavior*, 1973, *12*, 627–635.

Frederiksen, J. R., & Kroll J. F.   Spelling and sound: Approaches to the internal lexicon. *Journal of Experimental Psychology: Human Perception and Performance*, 1976, *2*, 361–379.

Gernsbacher, M. A.   Resolving twenty years of inconsistent interactions between lexical familiarity and orthography, concreteness, and polysemy. *Journal of Experimental Psychology: General*, in press.

Gibson, E. J.   Learning to read. *Science*, 1965, *148*, 1066–1072.

Gibson, E. J., & Levin, H.   *The psychology of reading.* Cambridge: MIT Press, 1975.

Gibson, E. J., Pick, A. D., Osser, H., & Hammond, M.   The role of grapheme-phoneme correspondence in the perception of words. *American Journal of Psychology*, 1962, *75*, 554–570.

Gibson, E. J., Shurcliff, A., & Jonas, A.   Utilization of spelling patterns by deaf and hearing subjects. In H. Levin & J. P. Williams (Eds.), *Basic studies on reading.* New York: Basic Books, 1970.

Glushko, R. J.   The organization and activation of orthographic knowledge in reading aloud. *Journal of Experimental Psychology: Human Perception and Performance*, 1979, *5*, 674–691.

Goldiamond, I., & Hawkins, W. F.   Vexierversuch: The log relationship between word frequency and recognition obtained in the absence of stimulus words. *Journal of Experimental Psychology*, 1958, *56*, 457–463.

Goldscheider, A., & Muller, R. F.   Zur Physiologie und Pathologie des lesens. *Zeitschrift fur Klinische Medizin*, 1893, *33*, 131.

Goodman, K. S.   Reading: A psycholinguistic guessing game. *Journal of the Reading Specialist*, 1967, *6*, 126–135.

Gough, P. B.   One second of reading. In J. F. Kavanagh & I. G. Mattingly (Eds.), *Language by ear and by eye*. Cambridge: MIT Press, 1972.

Gough, P. B.   The structure of the language. In D. D. Duane & M. B. Rawson (Eds.), *Reading, perception, and language*. Baltimore: York Press, 1975.

Gough, P. B.   Context, form, and interaction. In K. Rayner (Ed.), *Eye movements in reading: Perceptual and language processes*. New York: Academic Press, 1983.

Gough, P. B., Alford, J. A., Jr., & Holley-Wilcox, P.   Words and contexts. In O. J. L. Tzeng & H. Singer (Eds.), *Perception of print: Reading research in experimental psychology*. Hillsdale, N.J.: Erlbaum, 1981.

Gough, P. B., & Cosky, M. J.   One second of reading again. In N. J. Castellan, D. B. Pisoni, & G. R. Potts (Eds.), *Cognitive theory* (Vol. 2). Hillsdale, N.J.: Erlbaum, 1977.

Hansen, D., & Rogers, T. S.   An exploration of psycholinguistic units in initial reading. In K. S. Goodman (Ed.), *The psycholinguistic nature of the reading process*. Detroit: Wayne State University Press, 1973.

Henderson, L.   Wholistic models of feature analysis in word recognition: A critical examination. In P. A. Kolers, H. Bouma, & M. Wrolstad (Eds.), *Processing of visible language* (Vol. 2). New York: Plenum, 1980.

Henderson, L.   *Orthography and word recognition in reading*. London and New York: Academic Press, 1982.

Henderson, L., Coltheart, M., & Woodhouse, D.   Failure to find a syllabic effect in number-naming. *Memory and Cognition*, 1973, *1*, 304–306.

Hofstadter, D. R.   Meta-font, metamathematics, and metaphysics: Comments on Donald Knuth's "The concept of a meta-font." *Visible Language*, 1982, *16*, 309–338. (a)

Hofstadter, D. R.   Metamagical themas: Variations on a theme as the essence of imagination. *Scientific American*, 1982, *247*, 20–28. (b)

Howes, D. H., & Solomon, R. L.   Visual duration threshold as a function of word-probability. *Journal of Experimental Psychology*, 1951, *41*, 401–410.

Huey, E. B.   *The psychology and pedagogy of reading*. Cambridge: MIT Press, 1968. (Originally published, 1908.)

James, C. T.   The role of semantic information in lexical decisions. *Journal of Experimental Psychology: Human Perception and Performance*, 1975, *1*, 130–136.

Jastak, J. F., & Jastak, S.   *The Wide Range Achievement Test Manual of Instructions*. Wilmington, Del.: Jastak Associates, 1978.

Jastrzembski, J.   Multiple meanings, number of related meanings, frequency of occurrence, and the lexicon. *Cognitive Psychology*, 1981, *13*, 278–305.

Jastrzembski, J., & Stanners, R.   Multiple word meanings and lexical search speed. *Journal of Verbal Learning and Verbal Behavior*, 1975, *14*, 534–537.

Johnson, N. F.   On the function of letters in word identification: Some data and a preliminary model. *Journal of Verbal Learning and Verbal Behavior*, 1975, *14*, 17–29.

Johnson, N. F.   Integration processes in word recognition. In O. J. L. Tzeng & H. Singer (Eds.), *Perception of print: Reading research in experimental psychology*. Hillsdale, N.J.: Erlbaum, 1981.

Johnston, J. C.   Understanding word perception: Clues from studying the word-superiority effect. In O. J. L. Tzeng & H. Singer (Eds.), *Perception of print: Reading research in experimental psychology*. Hillsdale, N.J.: Erlbaum, 1981.

Johnston, J. C., & McClelland, J. L.   Visual factors in word perception. *Perception and Psychophysics*, 1973, *14*, 365–370.

Johnston, J. C., & McClelland, J. L.   Experimental tests of a hierarchical model of word identification. *Journal of Verbal Learning and Verbal Behavior*, 1980, *19*, 503–524.

Juola, J. F., Leavitt, D. D., & Choe, C. S.   Letter identification in word, nonword and single-letter displays. *Bulletin of the Psychonomic Society*, 1974, *4*, 278–280.

Kavanagh, J. F., & Venezky, R. L. (Eds.)   *Orthography, reading, and dyslexia*. Baltimore: University Park Press, 1980.

Kleiman, G. M.   Speech recoding in reading. *Journal of Verbal Learning and Verbal Behavior*, 1975, *14*, 323–339.

Kučera, H., & Francis, W. N.   *Computational analysis of present-day American English*. Providence, R.I.: Brown University Press, 1967.

Kutas, M., & Hilliard, S. A.   Reading senseless sentences: Brain potentials reflect semantic incongruity. *Science*, 1980, *207*, 203–205.

LaBerge, D., & Samuels, J.   Toward a theory of automatic information processing in reading. *Cognitive Psychology*, 1974, *6*, 293–323.

Levy, B. A.   Vocalization and suppression effects in sentence memory. *Journal of Verbal Learning and Verbal Behavior*, 1975, *14*, 304–316.

Lukatela, G., & Turvey, M. T.   Some experiments on the Roman and Cyrillic alphabets of Serbo-Croatian. In J. F. Kavanagh & R. L. Venezky (Eds.), *Orthography, reading and dyslexia*. Baltimore: University Park Press, 1980.

MacKay, D. G.   Phonetic factors in the perception and recall of spelling errors. *Neuropsychologia*, 1968, *6*, 321–325.

Manelis, L.   The effect of meaningfulness in tachistoscopic word perception. *Perception and Psychophysics*, 1974, *16*, 599–614.

Marshall, J. C., & Newcombe, F.   Patterns of paralexia: A psycholinguistic approach. *Journal of Psycholinguistic Research*, 1973, *2*, 175–199.

Martin, M.   Speech recoding in silent reading. *Memory and Cognition*, 1978, *6*, 108–114.

Mason, M.   From print to sound in mature readers as a function of reader ability and two forms of orthographic regularity. *Memory and Cognition*, 1978, *6*, 568–581.

Massaro, D. W.   Primary and secondary recognition in reading. In D. W. Massaro (Ed.), *Understanding language*. New York: Academic Press, 1975.

Massaro, D. W., & Klitzke, D.   The role of lateral masking and orthographic structure in letter and word recognition. *Acta Psychologica*, 1979, *43*, 413–426.

Massaro, D. W., Taylor, G. A., Venezky, R. L., Jastrzembski, J. E., & Lucas, P. A.   *Letter and word perception*. Amsterdam: North-Holland Publishing Co., 1980.

McClelland, J. L.   Preliminary letter identification in the perception of words and nonwords. *Journal of Experimental Psychology: Human Perception and Performance*, 1976, *2*, 80–91.

McClelland, J. L.   On the time relations of mental processes: An examination of systems of processes in cascade. *Psychological Review*, 1979, *86*, 287–300.

McClelland, J. L., & Johnston, J. C.   The role of familiar units in perception of words and nonwords. *Perception and Psychophysics*, 1977, *22*, 249–261.

McClelland, J. L., & Rumelhart, D. E.   An interactive activation model of context effects in letter perception: Part 1. An account of basic findings. *Psychological Review*, 1981, *88*, 375–407.

McCusker, L. X., Hillinger, M. L., & Bias, R. G.   Phonological recoding and reading. *Psychological Bulletin*, 1981, *89*, 217–245.

Meyer, D. E., Schvaneveldt, R. W., & Ruddy, M. G.   Functions of graphemic and phonemic codes in visual word recognition. *Memory and Cognition*, 1974, *2*, 309–321.

Meyer, D. E., Schvaneveldt, R. W., & Ruddy, M. G.   Loci of contextual effects on word recognition. In P. M. A. Rabbitt & S. Dornic (Eds), *Attention and performance V.* New York: Academic Press, 1975.

Morton, J.   The effects of context upon speed of reading, eye movements, and the eye-voice span. *Journal of Experimental Psychology,* 1964, *16,* 340–355.

Morton, J.   The interaction of information in word recognition. *Psychological Review,* 1969, *79,* 165–178.

Morton, J.   A functional model for memory. In D. A. Norman (Ed.), *Models of human memory.* New York and London: Academic Press, 1970.

Morton, J.   Word recognition. In J. Morton & J. C. Marshall (Eds.), *Psycholinguistics* (Vol. 2). Cambridge: MIT Press, 1979.

Nakatani, L. H.   Comments on Broadbent's response bias model for stimulus recognition. *Psychological Review,* 1970, *77,* 574–576.

Nakatani, L. H.   On the evaluation of models for the word frequency effect. *Psychological Review,* 1973, *80,* 195–202.

Neely, J. H.   Semantic priming and retrieval from lexical memory: Evidence for facilitatory and inhibitory processes. *Memory and Cognition,* 1976, *4,* 648–654.

Neely, J. H.   Semantic priming and retrieval from lexical memory: Roles of inhibitionless spreading activation and limited-capacity attention. *Journal of Experimental Psychology: General,* 1977, *106,* 226–254.

Neisser, U.   *Cognitive psychology.* New York: Appleton-Century-Crofts, 1967.

Paap, K. R., Newsome, S. L., McDonald, J. E., & Schvaneveldt, R. W.   An activation-verification model for letter and word recognition: The word-superiority effect. *Psychological Review,* 1982, *89,* 573–594.

Paivio, A., & O'Neill, B. J.   Visual recognition thresholds and dimensions of word meaning. *Perception and Psychophysics,* 1970, *8,* 273–275.

Patterson, K. E., & Marcel, A. J.   Aphasia, dyslexia and the phonological coding of written words. *Quarterly Journal of Experimental Psychology,* 1977, *29,* 307–318.

Platt, J. R.   Strong inference. *Science,* 1964, *146,* 347–353.

Popper, K.   *The logic of scientific discovery.* New York: Basic Books, 1959.

Posner, M. I., & Snyder, C. R. R.   Attention and cognitive control. In R. Solso (Ed.), *Information processing and cognition: The Loyola Symposium.* Hillsdale, N.J.: Erlbaum, 1975.

Postman, L., & Adis-Castro, G.   Psychophysical methods in the study of word recognition. *Science,* 1957, *125,* 193–194.

Rayner, K.   *Eye movements in reading: Perceptual and language processes.* New York: Academic Press, 1983.

Reicher, G. M.   Perceptual recognition as a function of the meaningfulness of stimulus material. *Journal of Experimental Psychology,* 1969, *81,* 275–280.

Rice, G. A., & Robinson, D. O.   The role of bigram frequency in perception of words and nonwords. *Memory and Cognition,* 1975, *3,* 513–518.

Richards, L. G.   Concreteness as a variable in word recognition. *American Journal of Psychology,* 1976, *89,* 707–718.

Richards, L. G., & Platnick, D. M.   On the influence of pretraining on recognition thresholds for English words. *American Journal of Psychology,* 1974, *87,* 79–592.

Rubenstein, H., Garfield, L., & Millikan, J.   Homographic entries in the internal lexicon. *Journal of Verbal Learning and Verbal Behavior,* 1970, *9,* 487–494.

Rubenstein, H., Lewis, S. S., & Rubenstein, M. A.   Evidence for phonemic recoding in visual word recognition. *Journal of Verbal Learning and Verbal Behavior,* 1971, *10,* 645–657. (a)

Rubenstein, H., Lewis, S. S., & Rubenstein, M. A.   Homographic entries in the internal lexicon: Effects of systematicity and relative frequency of meanings. *Journal of Verbal Learning and Verbal Behavior,* 1971, *10,* 57–62. (b)

Rumelhart, D. E.   Toward an interactive model of reading. In S. Dornic (Ed.), *Attention and performance VI.* Hillsdale, N.J.: Erlbaum, 1977.

Rumelhart, D. E., & McClelland, J. L.   An interactive activation model of context effects in letter perception: Part 1. An account of basic findings. *Psychological Review*, 1981, *88*, 375–407.

Rumelhart, D. E., & Siple, P.   The process of recognizing tachistoscopically presented words. *Psychological Review*, 1974, *81*, 99–118.

Saffran, E. M., & Marin, O. S. M.   Reading without phonology: Evidence from aphasia. *Quarterly Journal of Experimental Psychology*, 1977, *29*, 515–525.

Scarborough, D. L., Cortese, C., & Scarborough, H. S.   Frequency and repetition effects in lexical memory. *Journal of Experimental Psychology: Human Perception and Performance*, 1977, *3*, 1–17.

Schuberth, R. E., & Eimas, P. D.   Effects of context on the classification of words and nonwords. *Journal of Experimental Psychology: Human Perception and Performance*, 1977, *3*, 27–36.

Sears, D. A.   Engineers spell acoustically. *College Composition and Communication*, 1969, *20*, 349–351.

Seidenberg, M. S., Waters, G. S., Barnes, M. A., & Tanenhaus, M. K.   When does irregular spelling or pronunciation influence word recognition? *Journal of Verbal Learning and Verbal Behavior*, in press.

Seymour, P. H. K., & Porpodas, C. D.   Lexical and non-lexical processing of spelling in developmental dyslexia. In U. Frith (Ed.), *Cognitive processes in spelling.* New York: Academic Press, 1980.

Smith, E. E., & Haviland, S. E.   Why words are perceived more accurately than nonwords: Inference vs. unitization. *Journal of Experimental Psychology*, 1972, *92*, 59–64.

Smith, E. E., & Spoehr, K. T.   The perception of printed English: A theoretical perspective. In B. H. Kantowitz (Ed.), *Human information processing: Tutorials in performance and cognition.* Hillsdale, N.J.: Erlbaum, 1974.

Smith, F.   Familiarity of configuration vs. discriminability of features in the visual identification of words. *Psychonomic Science*, 1969, *14*, 261, 263.

Smith, F.   *Understanding reading.* New York: Holt, Rinehart & Winston, 1971.

Spoehr, K. T., & Smith, E. E.   The role of syllables in perceptual processing. *Cognitive Psychology*, 1973, *5*, 71–89.

Stanovich, K. E.   Toward an interactive-compensatory model of individual differences in the development of reading fluency. *Reading Research Quarterly*, 1980, *16*, 32–71.

Stanovich, K. E., & Bauer, D. W.   Experiments on the spelling-to-sound regularity effect in word recognition. *Memory and Cognition*, 1978, *6*, 410–415.

Stanovich, K. E., & West, R. F.   The generalizability of context effects on word recognition: A reconsideration of the roles of parafoveal priming and sentence context. *Memory and Cognition*, 1983, *11*, 49–58. (a)

Stanovich, K. E., & West, R. F.   On priming by a sentence context. *Journal of Experimental Psychology*, 1983, *112*, 1–36. (b)

Stanovich, K. E., West, R. F., & Feeman, D. J.   A longitudinal study of sentence context effects in second-grade children: Tests of an interactive-compensatory model. *Journal of Experimental Child Psychology*, 1981, *32*, 185–199.

Stevens, A. L., & Rumelhart, D. E.   Errors in reading: analysis using an augmented transition network model of grammar. In D. A. Norman & D. E. Rumelhart (Eds.), *Explorations in cognition.* San Francisco: W. H. Freeman, 1975.

Terry, P., Samuels, S. J., & LaBerge, D.   The effects of letter degradation and letter spacing on word recognition. *Journal of Verbal Learning and Verbal Behavior*, 1976, *15*, 577–585.

Theios, J., & Muise, J. G.   The word identification process in reading. In N. J. Castellan and D. Pisoni (Eds.), *Cognitive theory* (Vol. 2). Hillsdale, N.J.: Erlbaum, 1976.

Thompson, M. C., & Massaro, D. W.   The role of visual information and redundancy in reading. *Journal of Experimental Psychology*, 1973, *98*, 49–54.

Thorndike, E. L., & Lorge, I.   *The teacher's word book of 30,000 words.* New York: Columbia University Press, 1944.

Treisman, A. M.   On the word frequency effect: Comments on the papers by J. Catlin and L. H. Nakatani. *Psychological Review*, 1971, *78*, 420–425.

Tulving, E., & Gold, C.   Stimulus information and contextual information as determinants of tachistoscopic recognition of words. *Journal of Experimental Psychology*, 1963, *66*, 319–327.

Tzeng, O., & Hung, D.   Reading in a nonalphabetic writing system: Some experimental studies. In J. F. Kavanagh & R. L. Venezky (Eds.), *Orthography, reading, and dyslexia.* Baltimore: University Park Press, 1980.

West, R. F., & Stanovich, K. E.   Automatic contextual facilitation in readers of three ages. *Child Development*, 1978, *49*, 717–727.

Whaley, C. P.   Word-nonword classification time. *Journal of Verbal Learning and Verbal Behavior*, 1978, *17*, 143–154.

Wheeler, D. D.   Processes in word recognition. *Cognitive Psychology*, 1970, *1*, 59–85.

Winnick, W. A., & Kressel, K.   Tachistoscopic recognition thresholds, paired-associate learning, and immediate recall as a function of abstractness-concreteness and word frequency. *Journal of Experimental Psychology*, 1965, *70*, 163–168.

Woodworth, R. S.   *Experimental psychology.* New York: Holt, Rinehart & Winston, 1938.

Zeitler, J.   Tachistoscopic Untersuchungen über das lesen. *Philosophische Studien*, 1900, *16*, 380–463.

Zipf, G. K.   *The psychobiology of language.* Boston: Houghton Mifflin, 1935.

9

A SCHEMA-THEORETIC VIEW OF BASIC PROCESSES IN READING COMPREHENSION

Richard C. Anderson
and P. David Pearson

. . . to completely analyze what we do when we read would almost be the
acme of a psychologist's dream for it would be to describe very many of the
most intricate workings of the human mind, as well as to unravel the tangled
story of the most remarkable specific performance that civilization has learned
in all its history.

(Huey, 1908/1968, p. 8)

Huey's eloquent statement about the goals of the psychology of reading is
as relevant today as it was when he wrote it in 1908. The quotation usually
precedes an apology for how little we have learned in the past 75 years. We
wish to break with that tradition and use Huey's statement to introduce an essay
in which we will try to demonstrate that while we have not fully achieved Huey's
goal, we have made substantial progress.

Our task is to characterize basic processes of reading comprehension. We
will not present a model of the entire reading process, beginning with the focusing
of the eye on the printed page and ending with the encoding of information
into long-term semantic memory or its subsequent retrieval for purposes of demonstrating comprehension to someone in the outer world. Instead, we will focus
on one aspect of comprehension of particular importance to reading comprehension: the issue of how the reader's *schemata*, or knowledge already stored in
memory, function in the process of interpreting new information and allowing
it to enter and become a part of the knowledge store. Whether we are aware
of it or not, it is this interaction of new information with old knowledge that
we mean when we use the term comprehension. To say that one has comprehended a text is to say that she has found a mental "home" for the information
in the text, or else that she has modified an existing mental home in order to
accommodate that new information. It is precisely this interaction between old
and new information that we address in this chapter.

Our plan for the chapter is straightforward. First, we will trace the historical antecedents of schema theory. Then we will outline the basic elements of the theory and point out problems with current realizations of the theory and possible solutions. Next, we will consider the interplay between the abstracted knowledge embodied in schemata and memory for particular examples. Then we will decompose the comprehension process in order to examine components of encoding (attention, instantiation, and inference) and retrieval (retrieval plans, editing and summarizing, and reconstructive processes). Finally, we will evaluate the contributions of schema theory to our understanding of the comprehension process and speculate about the directions future research should take.

HISTORY OF THE NOTION OF A SCHEMA

While Sir Frederic Bartlett (1932) is usually acknowledged as the first psychologist to use the term schema in the sense that it is used today, historical precedence must surely be given to the Gestalt psychologists. The starting point for Gestalt psychology was a paper by Max Wertheimer in 1912 reporting research in which Wolfgang Kohler and Kurt Koffka served as assistants. These three became the principal figures in the Gestalt movement.

The term Gestalt literally means shape or form. Gestalt psychology emphasized holistic properties. It was the study of mental organization. The Gestalt movement was a reaction against the Zeitgeist at the turn of the century, which held that perception, thought, and emotion could be resolved into elemental sensations. According to Wilhelm Wundt, the dominant figure in psychology during that period, the business of psychology "was (1) the *analysis* of conscious processes into *elements,* (2) the determination of the manner of *connection* of these elements, and (3) the determination of their laws of connection" (cited in Boring, 1950, p. 333). The popular metaphor was that psychology was "mental chemistry."

The insight of the Gestalt psychologists was that the properties of a whole experience cannot be inferred from its parts. Carrying the mental chemistry metaphor a step further, they liked to point out that the molecules of chemical compounds have emergent properties that cannot be predicted in a simple fashion from the properties of the constituent elements (cf. Kohler, 1947, p. 115).

The basic principle of Gestalt psychology, called the Law of Pragnanz, is that mental organization will always be as good as prevailing conditions allow (cf. Koffka, 1935, p. 110). In this definition, "good" embraces such properties as simplicity, regularity, and symmetry. The theory stresses that mental organization is "dynamic," which means that the tendency toward coherent organization is a spontaneous process that can happen without an external goad.

Gestalt ideas were applied especially to visual perception. A notable example, which had a considerable influence on subsequent thinking, was Wulf's (1922/ 1938) research on memory for geometric designs. Subjects were asked to make drawings that reproduced the designs shortly after exposure, after 24 hours, and after a week. As the interval lengthened, Wulf observed characteristic changes in the reproductions that he termed "leveling" and "sharpening." Leveling means smoothing an irregularity. Sharpening means emphasizing or exaggerating a salient feature. The overall effect generally was to "normalize" reproductions. Wulf (1922/1938, p. 140) illustrated the process with the design shown in Figure 9.1.

FIGURE 9.1   (*From Wulf, 1922/1938, p. 140.*)

Four subjects spoke of this as a "bridge," while another called it an "arch." In their reproductions of this figure, these subjects all lengthened the "supports." Wulf (1922/1938, p. 141) explained his results in these terms:

> In addition to, or even instead of, purely visual data there were also general types or schemata in terms of which the subject constructed his responses. . . . The schema itself becomes with time ever more dominant; visual imagery of the original disappears, . . . details contained in the original are forgotten and incorrectly reproduced, yet even the last reproduction will usually show a steady progress towards representation of the type or schema originally conceived.

According to Bartlett in his classic book *Remembering* (1932, p. 201) the term "schema" refers to "an active organization of past reactions, or past experience." The term active was intended to emphasize what he saw as the constructive character of remembering, which he contrasted with a passive retrieval of "fixed and lifeless" memories. "The first notion to get rid of," Bartlett wrote (1932, p. 204), "is that memory is primarily or literally reduplicative, or reproductive. . . . It is with remembering as it is with the stroke in a skilled game [of tennis or cricket]. . . . Every time we make it, it has its own characteristics."

Though he used phrases such as "mental set," "active organization," and "general impression" a great deal, Bartlett was never very clear about what he meant by them, other than to indicate a top-down influence:

> an individual does not ordinarily take . . . a situation detail by detail and meticulously build up the whole. In all ordinary instances he has an overmastering tendency simply to get a general impression of the whole; and, on the basis of this, he constructs the probable detail. Very little of his construction is literally observed. . . . But it is the sort of construction which serves to justify his general impression. (1932, p. 206)

Bartlett was vague about just how schemata work. For example, he said several times that a central idea in his theory was "turning around on one's schemata." He apparently meant deducing the way the past must have been from one's current schema. But he never explicated the idea. Indeed, he admitted, "I wish I knew exactly how it was done" (1932, p. 206).

Bartlett's ideas resembled those of Gestalt psychology, and he even described research of his own on memory for pictorial material that was similar to Wulf's. Nevertheless, there is no indication that he was directly influenced by the Gestalt tradition. The only Gestalt psychologist that Bartlett cited was Kohler, and he in just a passing note that "recent general psychological theories are still in a fluid state" (1932, p. 186). At least one of the major Gestalt psychologists was aware of Bartlett's work. In *Principles of Gestalt Psychology,* Koffka (1935, p. 519) complained that he found Bartlett difficult to understand but acknowledged that there was "a great affinity between Bartlett's theory of memory and our own."

With respect to empirical research, Bartlett is best remembered for his study of the recall of the North American Indian folktale, *The War of the Ghosts.* He reported that, especially after a long interval, subjects' reproductions became simplified and stereotyped. Details that "fit in with a subject's preformed interests and tendencies" (1932, p. 93) were recalled. Other details were either omitted or "rationalized by linking them together and so rendering them apparently coherent, or linking given detail with detail not actually present . . ." (p. 94). As time passed, elaborations, importations, and inventions appeared in subjects' reproductions with increasing frequency. Usually these intrusions could be seen as contributing to the subject's rationalization of the text.

We turn now to a major figure in the recent history of education and psychology, David P. Ausubel. He has had a direct influence on the thinking of the current generation of educational research workers, including the present authors. His thinking, in turn, bears resemblances to that of Bartlett, the Gestalt psychologists and, perhaps even more, to nineteenth-century figures, such as Herbart, as Barnes and Clawson (1975) have pointed out. However, Ausubel himself has emphatically denied such intellectual debts (1978). It seems only fair to conclude that he reinvented the ideas associated with his name and gave them a distinctive flourish.

According to Ausubel (Ausubel, 1963; Ausubel & Robinson, 1969), in meaningful learning, already-known general ideas "subsume" or "anchor" the new particular propositions found in texts. This happens only when the existing ideas are stable, clear, discriminable from other ideas, and directly relevant to the to-be-understood propositions. The reader has to be aware of which aspects of his knowledge are relevant. Sometimes this will be obvious. Sometimes the text will be explicit. When neither of these conditions holds or the reader's grasp of the required knowledge is shaky, an "advance organizer" may be prescribed. An advance organizer is a statement written in abstract, inclusive terms deliberately introduced before a text and intended to provide a conceptual bridge between what the reader already knows and the propositions in the text that it is hoped he will understand and learn.

Ausubel has not called his theory a schema theory, but it clearly is. Ausubel's own research and the research of those inspired by him has dealt mainly with advance organizers, which have proved to have facilitative effects (Luiten, Ames, & Ackerson, 1980; Mayer, 1979).

Among educators, something like schema theory has driven conceptions about reading. Take, for instance, Huey's (1908/1968) conclusion about whether we read letter by letter or in larger chunks:

So it is clear that the larger the amount read during a reading pause, the more inevitably must the reading be by suggestion and inference from clews of whatsoever kind, internal or external. In reading, the deficient picture is filled in, retouched, by the mind, and the page is thus made to present the familiar appearance of completeness in its details which we suppose to exist in the actual page. (p. 68)

Implicit, if not explicit, in the philosophy of Francis Parker when he ran the laboratory school at the University of Chicago at the turn of the last century was the importance of building knowledge structures through experience as a prerequisite to reading (see Mathews, 1966). Ernest Horn (1937), famous for his work in spelling, recognized the active contribution of the reader: "[The author] does not really convey ideas to the reader; he merely stimulates him to construct them out of his own experience. If the concept is . . . new to the reader, its construction more nearly approaches problem solving than simple association" (Horn, 1937, p. 154). And, of course, William S. Gray recognized, both in his professional writing (1948) and in his suggestions for teachers in basal reader manuals, the necessity of engaging children's prior knowledge before reading.

But the full development of schema theory as a model for representing how knowledge is stored in human memory had to await the revolution in our conception of how humans process information spurred by the thinking of computer scientists doing simulations of human cognition (e.g., Minsky, 1975; Winograd, 1975). Hence, it was in the late 1970s that ambitious statements of schema theories began to emerge (Rumelhart, 1980; Schank & Abelson, 1977) and to be applied to entities like stories (e.g., Mandler & Johnson, 1977; Rumelhart, 1975; Stein & Glenn, 1979) and processes like reading (see Adams & Collins, 1979; R. C. Anderson, 1977, 1978). Concurrently, schema-theoretic notions became the driving force behind empirical investigations of basic processes in reading. Much of this research is described later in this chapter. First, however, we attempt to elucidate schema theory as a model of human knowledge.

SOME ELEMENTS OF SCHEMA THEORY

A schema is an abstract knowledge structure. A schema is abstract in the sense that it summarizes what is known about a variety of cases that differ in many particulars. An important theoretical puzzle is to determine just how much and what sort of knowledge is abstracted and how much remains tied to knowledge of specific instances. A schema is structured in the sense that it represents the relationships among its component parts. The theoretical issue is to specify the set of relationships needed for a general analysis of knowledge. The overriding challenge for the theorist is to specify the form and substance of schemata and the processes by which the knowledge embodied in schemata is used.

We will hang our discussion of these issues on a concrete case, the SHIP CHRISTENING schema. A possible representation of this schema is diagrammed in Figure 9.2. If for the sake of the argument, one takes this as a serious attempt to represent the average person's knowledge of ship christening, what does it say and what follows from it?

Figure 9.2 says that the typical person's knowledge of ship christening can

FIGURE 9.2

be analyzed into six parts: that it is done to bless a ship, that it normally takes place in a dry dock, and so on. In the jargon of schema theory, these parts are called "nodes," "variables," or "slots." When the schema gets activated and is used to interpret some event, the slots are "instantiated" with particular information.

There are constraints on the information with which a slot can be instantiated. Presumably, for instance, the ⟨celebrity⟩ slot could be instantiated with a congressman, the husband or wife of a governor, the secretary of defense, or the Prince of Wales, but not a garbage collector or barmaid.

Suppose you read in the newspaper that,

> Queen Elizabeth participated in a long-delayed ceremony in Clyde-bank, Scotland, yesterday. While there is still bitterness here following the protracted strike, on this occasion a crowd of shipyard workers numbering in the hundreds joined dignitaries in cheering as the HMS *Pinafore* slipped into the water.

It is the generally good fit of most of this information with the SHIP CHRISTENING schema that provides the confidence that ⟨part of the⟩ message has been comprehended. In particular, Queen Elizabeth fits the ⟨celebrity⟩ slot, the fact that Clydebank is a well-known shipbuilding port and that shipyard workers are involved is consistent with the ⟨dry dock⟩ slot, the HMS *Pinafore* is obviously a ship and the information that it "slipped into the water" is consistent with the ⟨just before launching⟩ slot. Therefore, the ceremony mentioned is probably a ship christening. No mention is made of a bottle of champagne being broken on the ship's bow, but this "default" inference is easily made.

The foregoing informal treatment of the process of schema "activation" can be made more precise. Assume that words mentioning any component of a schema have a certain probability of bringing to mind the schema as a whole. Assume also that, once the schema is activated, there is a certain probability of being reminded of each of the other parts. It is not necessary to assume that the likelihood that a part will remind a person of the whole schema is the same as the likelihood that the schema will remind the person of that part. It seems likely, for example, that a person's SHIP CHRISTENING schema is more likely to activate the component concept of a celebrity than the mention of a celebrity is to activate the schema. The reason is that ⟨celebrity⟩ is a component of many schemata and SHIP CHRISTENING is not very prominent among them; therefore, the probability that words about a celebrity will activate SHIP CHRISTEN-ING is low.

Some components of a schema are particularly salient; that is to say, words mentioning the component have a high probability of bringing to mind the schema and only that schema and, therefore, these words have great diagnostic value for the reader. One would suppose, for example, that words to the effect that a bottle was broken on the bow of a ship would be extremely likely to remind a person of ship christening.

A final assumption in this simple model of schema activation is that, when two or more components of a schema are mentioned, the aggregate probability of the whole schema being activated is a function of the sum of the probabilities that the individual components will activate the schema.

Ross and Bower (1981) worked out a formal, mathematical version of the schema-activation theory that has just been outlined and subjected it to experimental test. In one of their experiments, subjects studied 80 sets of four words, each related to a more or less obvious schema. For instance, one set was "driver," "trap," "rough," and "handicap," which relate to a GOLF schema. Another set was "princess," "mouth," "hold," and "dial," which relate to a TELEPHONE schema. After studying the word sets, subjects attempted to recall the words, given one or two words from each set as a cue. The schema model gave a good account of the recall patterns observed in this and two other experiments. In fact, it did better than a model based on S-R learning theory and traditional associationism.

To get a feeling for how a model of schema activation of this type might work with text, consider the following two sentences:

Princess Anne broke the bottle on the ship.

The waitress broke the bottle on the ship.

In the first case, the ⟨celebrity⟩ slot as well as the ⟨ship⟩ and ⟨bottle-breaking⟩ slots are matched and a ship christening interpretation is invited. If there is any hiatus over the end of the first sentence, it can be treated as elliptical for "broke the bottle on the bow of the ship." For most people, the second sentence does not suggest a ship christening but instead, perhaps, a scene in the ship's dining room. This intuition is consistent with the schema-activation model because a waitress will not fit in the ⟨celebrity⟩ slot and thus there is less evidence for a ship christening interpretation.

The simple model we are considering is likely to fail with the following sentence, though:

> During the ceremony on the ship, Prince Charles took a swig from the bottle of champagne.

Here many slots in the schema are matched and the model cannot resist predicting activation of the SHIP CHRISTENING schema. How could the model be made smarter so that, like a person, it would not come to this conclusion?

First, consider a nonsolution. As a general rule people are unlikely to include in their schemata knowledge of the form, "in a ship christening the ceremony does *not* take place on board the ship" and "the celebrity does *not* drink from the bottle of champagne." The problem is that there are infinitely many things that are not true of any given type of event. Thus, it seems reasonable to suppose that what is *not* true of a type of event is "directly stored" only in special circumstances. For instance, one might store that a warbler does not have a thick beak if this is the critical feature that distinguishes it from the otherwise very similar song sparrow.

In general, though, determining what is *not* true requires an inference from what is true or is believed to be true. In the case of the Prince Charles sentence, the inference chain might look like the following:

1. A ship christening takes place on a platform on the dock next to the bow of the ship (from stored knowledge).
2. The celebrity playing the key role in the ceremony stands on this platform (from stored knowledge).
3. If Prince Charles were the celebrity taking the principal part in a ship christening ceremony, then he would have been standing on this platform (inference).
4. A platform on the dock next to the bow of a ship is not on the ship (inference).
5. During the ceremony, Prince Charles was on the ship (given in to-be-interpreted sentence).
6. During the ceremony, Prince Charles was not on a platform used for ship christening (inference).
7. The ceremony in which Prince Charles was participating was not a ship christening (inference).

Converging evidence that the sentence is not about a ship christening might come from analysis of the fact that Prince Charles took a swig of the champagne. In this case, the reader might make a lack-of-knowledge inference (Collins, 1978), which would work something like the following:

1. I (the reader) do not have stored the information that the celebrity takes a swig from the bottle of champagne during a ship christening (computation based on stored knowledge).
2. I have many facts stored about ship christenings that are at the same level of detail as the information that the celebrity takes a swig from the bottle (computation based on stored knowledge).
3. If the celebrity's taking a drink from the bottle were a part of a ship christening, I would probably know that fact (inference).
4. A ceremony during which the celebrity takes a drink from a bottle of champagne is probably not a ship christening (inference).

5. Prince Charles took a swig from a bottle of champagne (from the to-be-interpreted sentence).
6. The ceremony in which Prince Charles is participating is probably not a ship christening (inference).

Plainly, the representation of the SHIP CHRISTENING schema diagramed in Figure 9.2 is not adequate to support the chains of inference required to deal with the Prince Charles sentence. One problem is that some pieces of knowledge, such as that the christening takes place on a platform under the bow of the ship, are missing. But this is the least of the problems with the representation.

The fundamental problem with the representation is that it does not make explicit the temporal, causal, spatial, part-whole, and member-set relations among the components of a ship christening. For instance, the representation does not include the information that it is the celebrity who breaks the bottle on the bow of the ship and that the reason for the breaking of the bottle is to bless the ship. Figure 9.3 shows some of the relationships among these components. Such relational knowledge is necessary for inferencing and, as we have just seen, inferencing can be necessary to get the right schema activated.

Because the representation of the SHIP CHRISTENING schema portrayed in Figure 9.2 is impoverished, the relationships among the parts and between the parts and the whole are arbitrary and unmotivated. It can be predicted with some confidence on the basis of accumulated experimental evidence that a person who possessed the knowledge, and only the knowledge, represented in Figure 9.2 would not only have trouble making perspicuous inferences, but also (a) would have trouble learning similarly arbitrary additional facts about ship christening, (b) would be vulnerable to confusions when attempting to recall and use facts about ship christening, and (c) would be relatively slow to retrieve even well-known facts. Each of the preceding problems would grow more severe as the number of arbitrarily related facts that were known increased.

Every schema theorist has emphasized the nonarbitrary nature of knowledge. Notably, John Bransford (e.g., 1983) has stressed that "seeing the significance" of the parts in terms of the whole is the sine qua non of a schema-theoretic view of comprehension. In one of a number of experiments that Bransford and his colleagues have done which provide evidence for this claim, Stein and Brans-

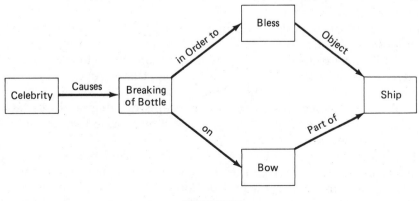

FIGURE 9.3

ford (1979) found that subjects were slightly worse at recalling core sentences, such as,

The fat man read the sign.

when the sentences were arbitrarily elaborated, as in,

The fat man read the sign that was 2-feet high.

In contrast, recall of the core sentences improved substantially when the core sentences were "precisely elaborated," as in,

The fat man read the sign warning of the thin ice.

A precise elaboration clarified the significance of the concepts in the core sentence and indicated how the concepts fit together.

Smith, Adams, and Schorr (1978; see also Clifton & Slowiaczek, 1981, and Reder & Anderson, 1980) have presented some strong evidence showing the benefits of integrating otherwise arbitrary information under the aegis of a schema. Subjects learnedpairs of apparently unrelated propositions attributed to a member of some profession. For instance,

The banker broke the bottle.

The banker did not delay the trip.

Then, a third proposition was learned that either allowed the subject to integrate the three sentences in terms of a common schema or which was unintegratable with the other two sentences, as is illustrated below:

The banker was chosen to christen the ship.

The banker was asked to address the crowd.

Subjects required fewer study opportunities to learn the third sentence when it was readily integratable than when it was unintegratable. Most interesting was the fact that after all of the sentences had been learned to a high criterion of mastery, it took subjects longer to verify that sentences from the unintegratable sets were ones they had seen.

The explanation for this subtle finding is that, in an unintegrated set, all of the propositions fan out from a single common node representing, for instance, "the banker." This means that each new proposition added to the set increases the burden of memory search and verification and, therefore, causes an increase in memory search time called the "fanning effect" (J. R. Anderson, 1976). In contrast, the interconnections among the concepts in integrated sets facilitate retrieval and verification; thus, adding a proposition to an integrated set causes little or no increase in search time.

Most discussions of schema theory have emphasized the use of schemata to assimilate information. Here, instead, we will deal with how a schema may be modified to accommodate new information. Obviously, a person may modify a schema by being told new information. For instance, a person might add to his or her SHIP CHRISTENING schema upon being informed that the platform on which the ceremony takes place is typically draped with bunting displaying the national colors.

Presumably, a logical person will check to make sure new information is consistent with the information already stored and, if it is not, will either reject the new information or modify the old. Presumably, a careful person will evaluate whether the source of new information is creditable or the evidence is persuasive before changing a schema. Lipson (1983) has evidence that suggests that even young readers will reject text information if it is inconsistent with an already possessed interpretation that they believe to be correct.

A primary source of data for schema change and development is experience with particular cases. In a process that is still not well-understood, even though thinkers have wrestled with how it happens since the time of the ancient Greeks, people make inductive generalizations based on perceptible or functional features or patterns of particular cases. Traditional psychological theories envisioned a slow, grinding process of generalization, so slow and uncertain that the wonder was that anyone acquired the knowledge of a five-year-old. Current theories envision powerful inferential heuristics and generalization from a few cases or even a single case. Now the wonder is how people avoid filling their heads with all sorts of inaccurate and farfetched beliefs. How, for instance, is the nonexpert in ship christening, upon reading the newspaper describing the putative christening of the HMS *Pinafore*, to be restrained from inferring that the purpose of a ship christening is to celebrate the end of a labor dispute?

We turn now to the question of the relationship between the knowledge embodied in schemata and the knowledge of particular scenes, happenings, or messages. An attractive theory is that a schema includes just the propositions that are true of every member of a class. For instance, a BIRD schema may be supposed to include the information that birds lay eggs, have feathers, have wings, and fly, that the wings enable flying, and so on.

Collins and Quillian (1969) proposed the interesting additional assumption that, for reasons of "cognitive economy," propositions about the general case are not included in the representation for particular cases. So, the representation for a robin is supposed to include propositions about distinctive features of robins: that they have red breasts, but not that they fly or lay eggs. These facts can be deduced from the fact that a robin is a bird and that a robin has any property ascribed to all birds. Similarly, the bird representation does not directly include the information that birds breathe since birds are animals and breathing is a property of all animals.

Collins and Quillian theorized that knowledge is organized in semantic networks that permit graphical representations of the type illustrated in Figure 9.4. Notice that there is an increasingly long path in the network from the canary node to the information (or predicate) in each of the following sentences:

Canaries are yellow.

Canaries lay eggs.

Canaries can breathe.

It is a straightforward prediction that the greater the distance in the network that must be traversed to find the stored information, the longer it will take to

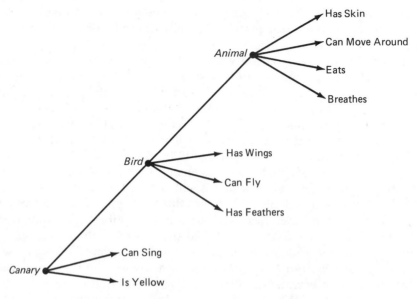

FIGURE 9.4   (*From Collins & Quillian, 1969, p. 241.*)

verify the proposition. This prediction has been confirmed many times in many laboratories.

The appeal of the cognitive-economy hypothesis is that, while long-term human memory capacity is no doubt very large, it is not infinite. People could save a lot of memory space if they stored information at the most inclusive possible levels in their knowledge representations. Furthermore, most people have probably never seen a canary lay an egg or a giant condor fly, so there is little reason to suppose that this information would be directly stored in their canary or condor representations.

But what about the information that a robin can fly? Surely the typical person has seen countless flying robins. It would be an odd theory of human information processing that could explain why this fact was not stored directly in a person's robin representation. To do so would require postulating a mental librarian who, when the senses return information about flying robins, steadfastly files it on a higher shelf.

Current theories of concepts posit that the information represented in specific concepts, such as robin, overlaps with the information in general concepts, such as bird (Smith & Medin, 1981). In fact, robin is a "good" example of a bird since the overlap is large, while penguin is a "poor" example because the overlap is small.

What is the best way in a theory of knowledge representations to cope with exceptional cases? In the first place, people probably place an implicit hedge on all the facts they think they know, of the form, "This proposition is true in only normal states of the world." At the very least, such a hedge helps fend off philosophers who ask questions like, "If a dog *is* a four-legged animal, what is a creature that has three legs but is otherwise a dog?"

The real theoretical problem, however, is not with abnormal cases such as dogs with three legs and hens that do not lay eggs, but with more mundane exceptions: most birds fly, however some, such as penguins, do not; canaries are often domesticated, however many more are wild; cups tend to be used to hold liquids, but they can be used to hold solids.

The classical issue in concept analysis was to specify the features that were individually necessary and jointly sufficient before a thing could rightly be called an instance of a concept. For example, following Katz (1972), some of the necessary features of bachelor are said to be ⟨male⟩, ⟨adult⟩, ⟨human⟩, and ⟨unmarried⟩. If a feature is *necessary*, then *all* instances of the concept display that feature. However, a feature that all instances possess may not be a necessary one. It may be safe to assume that every bachelor has a nose, but ⟨having a nose⟩ is not a necessary feature. If an unmarried, adult, human male without a nose did turn up, no one would be reluctant to call him a bachelor. In contrast, calling a married man a bachelor would be regarded as a non sequitur (or a joke or a metaphor). Thus, ⟨having a nose⟩ is a characteristic feature, while ⟨unmarried⟩ is a necessary feature, even though, by hypothesis, every bachelor displays both features.

The very idea that concepts or schemata (there is no principled distinction between the two) have necessary features has come under lethal attack in recent years. Wittgenstein (1953) noticed that it can be difficult, if not impossible, to specify the necessary features of most ordinary concepts. His famous analysis of games suggested that there are no features common to all games and that the relationship among games is most aptly characterized as one of "family resemblance." Putnam (1975; see also, Kripke, 1972) has shown that features of ordinary concepts that at first glance might seem to be necessary are really only characteristic. For instance, ⟨precious⟩ cannot be a necessary feature of gold because gold would no longer be precious if large quantities of it were discovered somewhere.

If there are few ordinary concepts with clearly necessary features and, indeed, not many with characteristic features true of all cases, the basis for positing that knowledge consists of abstract summaries of particular cases begins to erode. And this leads one to consider granting a greater role to memories for particular cases. It could be that much that passes for general knowledge is actually derived as needed by retrieving specific cases and making calculations based on what is known about them.

Let's do a thought experiment. What kind of nests do birds build? Try to pause before reading on and notice how your mind works as you answer this question.

Probably you answered the question by thinking of particular types of birds and then trying to remember occasions when you saw the nests of these birds, either in nature or in books. Probably, you began your search with a familiar, typical bird, such as a robin. If you know quite a bit about birds, your search probably turned up diverse kinds of nests, such as those of ducks, Baltimore orioles, barn swallows, and bald eagles.

Your intuitions were no doubt consistent with the hypothesized process of searching memories of specific cases. Experimental evidence, which does not rely on intuition, is also consistent with the hypothesized process. Walker (1975) asked subjects to accept or reject as quickly as possible propositions about a wide variety of things with quantifiable dimensions, such as the following:

A large dog could weigh 12 pounds.

Subjects quickly rejected this proposition and also quickly rejected sentences that ascribed an extremely heavy weight, such as 400 pounds, to a large dog. Furthermore, subjects quickly accepted statements ascribing a weight rated as typical of a large dog, such as 100 pounds. However, subjects were slow to accept or reject weights rated at the boundaries of a large dog, say 40 to 60 pounds.

It is very difficult to accommodate Walker's findings to a theory that says that people have directly stored as part of their general concept of a large dog that large dogs weigh from, say, 51 to 140 pounds. Such a theory would have to predict that people would be equally fast at accepting any weight between 51 and 140 pounds and equally fast at rejecting any weight outside this range. Moreover, the theory that people directly store as part of their knowledge of a class of objects generalizations about the range on each dimension along which the objects can be classified is highly implausible. Objects vary in innumerable dimensions. If a person has stored the range of weights of large dogs, why not the widths of their ears and the lengths of their tails? The more plausible and parsimonious theory, then, is that people make use of knowledge of specific cases in calculations such as the foregoing.

It is well established that words can have different meanings in different contexts, even when the words are being used in the same sense (Anderson, Pichert, Goetz, Schallert, Stevens, & Trollip, 1976; Anderson & Shiffrin, 1980). This fact poses a grave problem for any theory along the lines that the meaning of a compound is the product of the general meanings of the constituent words. This conventional theory does work in some cases. For instance, it seems to work in the case of the compound, *red dress*. The dress can be construed as having a typical shade of red.

Now consider the following compounds, however: *red strawberry, red barn, red sunset,* and *red hair*. The red visualized is different in each of these cases, as Halff, Ortony, and Anderson (1976) have demonstrated empirically. To explain this effect, we propose that specific memories of, for instance, red hair are retrieved and the range of hues calculated. We further suggest that the hue of the compound is predicted on the basis of the generic concept of red and the generic concept of the object only when the person has not experienced this combination before or when an indeterminate range of hues is possible.

Stating the foregoing theory in general form, word meanings are context sensitive because people treat words and phrases as instructions to locate specific examples in memory. The sense and reference of the terms are then refined on the basis of these examples. When specific examples representing the intersection of the sets of examples signified by the terms cannot be located, then the default inference of a typical meaning is made, based on the general schemata that the terms represent.

How are the phrases, "a particular case" and "a specific example," to be interpreted? A robin is a specific example of a bird, but notice that ROBIN is itself an abstracted and generic schema. Still more specific is the-robin-I-saw-nesting-in-the-hawthorne-tree-outside-my-front-door-this-morning.   Following Smith and Medin (1981), we assume that people have knowledge represented at various levels of specificity. Nothing about our thinking requires people always to get back to memories of cases experienced at particular moments in time and space.

In summary, the three main points of this section were that an adequate account of the structure of schemata will include information about the relationships among components, that a complete theory of schema activation will include a major role for inference, and that, during language comprehension, people probably rely on knowledge of particular cases as well as abstract and general schemata.

SCHEMATA AND INFERENCE

One of the key processes in a schema-theoretic account of cognitive processing is inferencing. In choosing to highlight inferences in a special section, we run the risk of suggesting that inferencing occupies some special stage in the comprehension process. We assert no such claim; in fact, we will demonstrate that inferences can occur either at the time of initial encoding of text information into memory *or* at the time that information is retrieved from memory. The reason for devoting a special section to inferences is to acknowledge their centrality to the overall process of comprehension. At least four kinds of inference can be identified in reading comprehension.

Inferences may be involved in the process of *deciding what schema among many should be called into play* in order to comprehend a text. It is rarely the case when reading that one is told directly what schema to use. Subtle cues are usually picked up from the text that allow schema selection. For example, to read a lead sentence from a newspaper article indicating that Princess Anne took part in a ceremony involving a new ship may provide sufficient evidence to allow a reader to infer that a SHIP CHRISTENING schema should be invoked.

Inference is also involved in the process of *instantiating slots* within a selected schema. A reader typically makes inferences when deciding that a particular character or item mentioned in a story is intended to fill a particular slot. Consider the earlier example about Queen Elizabeth in Clydebank. There was nothing explicitly stated in the text to tell the reader that Queen Elizabeth should fill the ⟨celebrity⟩ slot. The reader who decides she should fill that slot has made the inference that she, among all the characters and items in the text, is the most likely candidate to fill that slot. Furthermore a reader may fill a particular slot in a schema by *assigning default values* in the absence of any specifically substantiating information in the text. Again, using the SHIP CHRISTENING example, deciding that a bottle of champagne was used is an example of such a default inference. It should be stressed that filling slots by default is not a rare event. Rather, it is a routine aspect of the ongoing process of comprehension. Writers rely on the fact that there is a considerable amount of knowledge that they share with their audience. When it can be assumed that their audience will be able to infer accurately what shared knowledge has been omitted, writers will usually omit it (Clark & Haviland, 1977; Grice, 1975). It is this process of filling slots by default that most people think of when they are told that an inference has been made.

There is a fourth kind of inference involved in comprehension: it involves *drawing a conclusion based upon lack of knowledge.* It has the logic, "If X were true, I would know it were true. Since I do not know X to be true, it is probably false." Recall the earlier example in which this sort of inference was involved in deciding that since Prince Charles took a swig of champagne from the bottle, he must not be participating in a ship christening.

One paradigm of studies designed to investigate schema-selection inferences involves presenting students with an ambiguous text, written to permit two or more interpretations, and later asking them to recall it. Then on the basis of theme-revealing intrusions into subjects' recall protocols, one can infer the schema that a given reader selected to provide the best account of the data in the text.

The paradigm is illustrated in a study by Anderson, Reynolds, Schallert, and Goetz (1977), who presented college students with two texts. One text permitted the interpretation of a prisoner planning his escape from a cell or that of a wrestler trying to get out of his opponent's hold. The second permitted the interpretation of four people getting together to play cards or that of a quartet about to begin their weekly music practice. Physical education majors and music majors tended to select the specialized schema (wrestling or quartet) for only that passage consistent with their experience, selecting the more common schema (prison or cards) for the other passage. The study suggests these conclusions: (a) schema selection is often based upon inference, (b) the schema one selects influences the amount and nature of recall, and (c) once a schema has been selected, even by inference, it will drive other inferences, particularly slot-filling inferences (see section on Schemata and Remembering).

Evidence for the second kind of inference, using a schema already selected to guide the instantiation of slots within the schema, comes from a slightly different research paradigm. Subjects are given a passage written in language so general and vague that it is difficult to remember by itself, such as this one (used by Dooling & Lachman, 1971, and Bransford & Johnson, 1972):

The procedure is actually quite simple. First, you arrange the items into different groups. Of course one pile may be sufficient depending on how much there is to do. If you have to go somewhere else due to lack of facilities that is the next step; otherwise, you are pretty well set. It is important not to overdo things. That is, it is better to do too few things at once than too many. In the short run this may not seem important but complications can easily arise. A mistake can be expensive as well. At first, the whole procedure will seem complicated. Soon, however, it will become just another facet of life. It is difficult to foresee any end to the necessity for this task in the immediate future, but then, one never can tell. After the procedure is completed one arranges the materials into different groups again. Then they can be put into their appropriate places. Eventually they will be used once more and the whole cycle will then have to be repeated. However, that is part of life.

Some subjects are given the title, "Washing Clothes," before they read the passage, some after, others not at all. Passage recall is enhanced only for the condition in which subjects are given the title before reading. Without a title, which allows subjects to invoke a schema, a reader cannot decide what to do with the information in the text. Once a reader is able to activate the WASH-ING CLOTHES schema, however, even the vague terms in the text can be matched with the appropriate slots (e.g., "somewhere else" = laundromat). Hence, memory for the text is improved. Variations on this paradigm have used disambiguating pictures (Bransford & Johnson, 1972) or names of historical characters (Dooling & Lachman, 1971). The broader point to be made is that even normal texts, with no intentional ambiguity, are rarely completely clear about what text items ought to instantiate which slots within the schema that has been selected; usually, the reader herself has to decide, for example, which character is the heroine or why someone performed a particular act.

The third type of inference—using a selected schema to fill important slots by assigning a default value—is, as we have said, the normal sense of what we mean when we say someone has drawn an inference. And it is this type of inference that has been studied most often, particularly developmentally. The developmental research is ambivalent concerning precisely what accounts for the observed growth across age in the sheer number of inferences readers are able to draw. The work of Paris and his colleagues (e.g. Paris & Lindauer, 1976; Paris & Upton, 1976) suggests that younger children are simply not predisposed to draw inferences spontaneously. They found that five-year-olds were less able to infer the implied instrument in sentences like, "The man dug a hole," than were eight-year-olds. However, when the five-year-olds were told to act out the action in the sentence as they heard it, they were just as able as the eight-year-olds to infer the instrument in response to a later probe.

An alternative, although not mutually exclusive, argument is that age-related growth in inference ability is really a difference in the growth of knowledge available for drawing inferences. Omanson, Warren, and Trabasso (1978) concluded that it was available prior knowledge, not differences in memory capacity or control mechanisms, that accounted for differences in the quantity of inferences drawn by eight- versus five-year-olds. Pearson, Hansen, and Gordon (1979) found that differences in prior knowledge of the topic accounted for large differences in children's ability to answer inferential questions, but only for very modest differences in literal questions. Nicholson and Imlach (1981) have reported even more convincing evidence for the influence of knowledge on slot-filling inferences. They found that when children were given texts about familiar topics that they often resorted to prior knowledge to answer inference questions, even when the text provided explicit information that could have been used.

Regarding the fourth type of inference, the lack-of-knowledge inference, only anecdotal case study data are currently available to evaluate the role and frequency of this sort of inference. However, Collins (1978) does provide numerous examples of questions that it would appear that readers could answer only by invoking lack-of-knowledge inferences. One point about them: they seem to be made primarily at the point of retrieval or when an interrogator (teacher or experimenter) imposes a task upon the reader demanding such reasoning. Unlike default inferences, for example, they may not be made routinely during the ongoing comprehension process.

Two important questions about inferences that any good theory of comprehension will have to deal with are: (1) Which inferences, among the indefinitely large number that could be made, will a reader make during comprehension? and (2) When do readers make inferences, at the time of initial encoding of information into memory or at the time of retrieval?

Regarding the first question, the best evidence comes from a study by Goetz (1979). Goetz created alternative texts in which a target piece of information was either essential or unessential to understanding a story, and was either explicitly stated in the text or only implied by the information in the text. He then measured the probability that the target information would be recognized (Experiment 1) or recalled (Experiment 2) as a function of explicitness and importance. He found that importance was a good predictor of both the probability that the implied information would be recognized and the probability that it would be recalled. Interestingly, however, when the target information was stated explicitly, importance predicted recall but not recognition. Goetz's findings are significant because they provide insight into constraints on an otherwise unwieldy process. Without some criterion for deciding which inferences are to be made, there is no principled way for a theory to explain how the inference mechanism is stopped from churning out countless elaborations of the text.

The issue of when inferences are made, during encoding or retrieval, has a checkered experimental history. The usual paradigm for determining the locus of inferences is to give subjects a passage to read and to later test their recognition latency for information that was directly stated in the text in comparison to that which was only implied. Equivalent recognition latencies imply that the inferences must have been made during encoding; longer latencies for inferences imply that they must have been computed at the point of retrieval.

Kintsch (1974) reported three studies in which he found shorter times for explicitly stated information only when the recognition test was given immediately; with delays of either 20 minutes or 48 hours, there were no differences in the recognition latencies for explicit and implicit information. Singer, on the other hand, has consistently found shorter latencies for explicit information (Singer, 1979a, 1979b). However, in a more recent experiment, Singer (1980) found that importance, as indexed by how crucial the inference was to maintaining the coherence of the text, is a moderating factor. Necessary inferences were recognized as rapidly as explicit information. Both of these types were recognized about 245 milliseconds more rapidly than plausible but unnecessary inferences.

In summary, it is somewhat ironic that in order to fulfill the basic goal of creating a model of the meaning of a text that accounts for all the explicit information or as much of it as is possible, interpretations must be made that often go well beyond the text itself. Current evidence suggests that inferences important for a coherent understanding of the text will be made at the time the text is read. Other inferences will be drawn only when circumstances demand.

SCHEMATA AND THE ALLOCATION OF ATTENTION

Perhaps the most pervasive and consistent finding of research on discourse is that important text elements are more likely to be learned and remembered than less important elements. One attractive theory to explain this fact is that readers selectively attend to important elements. The following is a simple version of this theory:

1. The schema to which the text is being assimilated, already-processed text information, and an analysis of task demands provide a gauge for judging the importance of upcoming text elements.
2. As it is encountered, each text element is processed to some minimum level and then graded for importance.
3. Extra attention is devoted to elements that surpass a criterion of importance.
4. Because of the extra attention they receive, important text elements are learned better; because they are learned better, these text elements are also remembered better.

Recently there have been several attempts to test a selective-attention model, such as the foregoing, by directly measuring indicators of amount of attention. It should be emphasized that attention is a hypothetical construct that may be imperfectly reflected in any operational measure (see Kahneman, 1973). One index that has commonsense appeal, as well as a substantial history of use in experimental research, is the amount of time a subject takes to complete a task or a segment of a task. Other measures that have been argued to reflect aspects of attention include eye fixations, pupil dilation, brain waves, and latency of response to a secondary-task probe.

We will begin the review of empirical studies with ones that gave readers a task that almost certainly influenced the aspects of the text to which they paid attention. Rothkopf and Billington (1979) completed three experiments in which high school students memorized simple learning objectives before studying a 1481 word passage on oceanography. Readers got either five or ten objectives, all stated in specific terms and relevant to a single, readily identifiable sentence in the passage. For instance, one of the learning objectives was: What is the name of the scale used by oceanographers when recording the color of water? The test sentence that satisfied the objective was: Oceanographers record the color of the ocean by comparison with a series of bottles of colored water known as the Forel scale. The data confirmed that students who read with objectives in mind spent more time on sentences relevant to these objectives and less time on ones not relevant to the objectives than did students who read without objectives. In the third experiment, patterns of eye movements were found to be consistent with the reading-time results. In each study, subjects learned and remembered substantially more information relevant to assigned objectives. These experiments produced exactly the results that would be expected on the basis of the selective-attention hypothesis.

Questions inserted in a text have been hypothesized to cause readers to pay more attention to information of the type that the questions are about. Reynolds, Standiford, and Anderson (1979) investigated this hypothesis in an experiment in which college undergraduates were periodically questioned while they read a 48-page marine biology text. The questions were of a clear and distinctive type. For instance, one group of readers received questions every four pages that could always be answered with a proper name. Other groups were asked questions that could always be answered with a technical term or a number. Time to read the text was recorded for every four-line segment. The main result of the experiment was that readers who answered questions spent more time on the segments of the text that contained information from the category needed to answer the questions. Performance on a later test showed that questioned groups learned and remembered more question-relevant information than the nonquestioned groups. The results were entirely consistent with a simple selective attention theory.

Several studies by Britton and his associates (cf. Britton, Piha, Davis, & Wehausen, 1978) have used the length of time before a secondary task is performed as a measure of the amount of attention being devoted to reading. Subjects were told that comprehending the text was their primary task. They were also given the "secondary task" of depressing a key whenever an auditory signal, or probe, was sounded. The idea behind this procedure is that, when the mind is occupied with the primary task, there will be a slight delay in responding to the secondary task. To explain this more fully, there is an upper limit to the amount of attention, or "cognitive capacity," that people can devote to a task. Ordinarily, there is plenty of spare capacity when doing mental work such as reading. However, if a reader were to put substantial extra effort into a text element, this would place peak load demands on the cognitive system. Then there would be little capacity left over to process the probe and respond to it. Hence, the reaction to the probe would be delayed until capacity had been freed.

Britton, Piha, Davis, and Wehausen (1978) and Reynolds and Anderson (1982) have employed the secondary-task procedure to investigate whether periodic questions cause readers to allocate attention selectively. In the latter study, college students again read the 48-page marine biology text. They were asked either a proper-name question or a technical-term question every four pages. During each four-line text segment, the reader heard either zero, one, or two probes presented through earphones, at which points he or she was to push a key as quickly as possible. The results showed that readers took longer to respond to the probe when studying a segment that contained question-relevant information than when studying one that did not. Reading times were also longer on segments containing question-relevant information. Thus, using two different measures, this study supported the selective-attention interpretation of the effects of questions.

The selective-attention hypothesis provides a parsimonious and convincing interpretation of the effects of equipping readers with instructional objectives or occasionally asking them questions. It is much more problematical, though, that the reader's schema acts primarily as a device for allocating attention. To assimilate the following vignette, it may be supposed that most readers would employ a WHO DONE IT schema.

> Detective Lieutenant Bill Roberts bent over the corpse. It was apparent the victim had been stabbed. Roberts searched the room looking for evidence. There, near the foot of the bed, partly covered by a newspaper, he discovered the butcher knife.

The question is whether extra cognitive capacity will be devoted to processing the important information expressed by "the butcher knife." The selective attention hypothesis says yes. An alternative explanation is that the WHO DONE IT schema furnishes the "ideational scaffolding" (Ausubel, 1963; Anderson, Spiro, & Anderson, 1978) for the information in the text. Presumably the (murder weapon) occupies an important niche, or slot, in this structure. Furthermore, the second sentence of the text constrains the murder weapon to a sharp instrument. Thus, there is a slot established in the schema for which a knife is a leading candidate by the time the phrase, "the butcher knife," is encountered. As a consequence, according to the ideational-scaffolding hypothesis, the information about the knife will be readily assimilated and there is no reason why it ought to require, or will receive, extra attention.

Another alternative to the selective attention model outlined at the beginning of this section has been formulated by Kintsch and van Dijk (1978). They theorized that important propositions are maintained in working memory throughout more processing "cycles" than less important ones. This is a kind of selective-attention theory since Kintsch and van Dijk believe that important propositions are more memorable because of the greater amount of processing they receive. However, the extra attention is not given when the proposition is encoded but rather is said to come later when subsidiary propositions are being processed.

Still another alternative hypothesis, as will be explained at length in the next section, is that the greater likelihood of recall of important text elements may be attributable to a memory process rather than a learning process. This hypothesis, the ideational-scaffolding hypothesis, and the Kintsch and van Dijk multiple-cycles hypothesis are all rivals to the simple selective-attention hypothesis. Thus, the outcome of research on attention involving variations in schemata or text organization is not a foregone conclusion; and the results will be of genuine interest.

Goetz, Schallert, Reynolds, and Radin (1983) examined the effects of the reader's perspective on the allocation of attention. Policemen, people in training to be real estate agents, and college students were instructed to take the perspective of a burglar, a person interested in buying a home, or no particular perspective while reading a story ostensibly about what two boys did at one boy's home while playing hooky from school. The research confirmed previous research that has established that the reader's perspective strongly influences which information will be recalled from this story (Anderson & Pichert, 1978; Grabe, 1979; Pichert & Anderson, 1977). Persons playing the role of a burglar are more likely to recall, for instance, that money is kept in a desk drawer, whereas those imagining themselves to be home buyers more often reproduce, for example, the information that the place had spacious grounds. The new finding obtained by Goetz and his colleagues is that subjects spent more time reading sentences that contained information important in the light of the schema activated by perspective instructions. They also spent somewhat more time on sentences important in the light of their background. For instance, the policemen took longer to read sentences containing information important to burglars than the other subjects. Reynolds (1981) and R. C. Anderson (1982) have summarized research consistent with these findings.

Cirilo and Foss (1980) have reported two experiments in which time to read sentences was assessed when the sentences were of high importance in one story and low importance in another. The sentence, He could no longer talk at all, was highly important in a story in which it described the effect of a witch's curse on a wise king. The same sentence was of low importance in a story in which it described the momentary reaction of a simple soldier upon hearing that he would receive a large reward for finding a precious ring. In two experiments Cirilo and Foss found that readers spent more time on a sentence when it played an important role in a story.

Britton, Meyer, Simpson, Holdredge, and Curry (1979) have recently reported another test of the selective-attention hypothesis. The materials included two expository texts involving the energy crisis. In one, according to Meyer's (1975) analysis, a paragraph on the breeder reactor was high in the content structure; the passage said the fast breeder reactor is the solution to energy problems. In the context of the other passage, the paragraph was low in the content structure; the breeder reactor is only one of five possible solutions to the energy crisis. Subjects recalled more information from the critical paragraph when it was of high importance. However, they took the same amount of time to read the critical paragraph and the same amount of time to react to a secondary-task probe regardless of the paragraph's importance. Hence, the selective-attention hypothesis was not confirmed. Britton and his collaborators theorized that the superior recall of the critical paragraph when it was of higher importance was due to a memory process.

We don't know how to reconcile the conflicting results obtained by Cirilo and Foss (1980) and in our own research, on the one hand, and Britton et al. (1979), on the other. There were several differences in materials and procedures. Most notably, there were different definitions of what makes a text element "important." It is apparent that one ought to be cautious in assuming that every operation that can be said to make a segment of text salient, interesting, or important will affect processing in the same manner (see R. C. Anderson, 1982). An important task facing the field of reading research is a further explication of the notion of "importance."

Improvements in the simple, first-order theory of selective attention will be required before the theory can cope with the demands of texts of any complexity. For instance, readers often will be unable to gauge the importance of elements when first encountered. Indeed, in some literary forms, such as short stories and the detective novels, innocuous happenings frequently turn out to be significant at some later point.

What "fix-up strategy" (Alessi, Anderson, & Goetz, 1979) could readers use for dealing with text information whose significance was not initially appreciated? If the information were available in memory, perhaps in fragmentary and unassimilated form, it could simply be retrieved and processed further at the point at which its importance was discovered. If the information were not in memory, the reader could look back and reread the relevant section of the text. Efficient use of "look backs" (Alessi et al., 1979) would require the person to know where in the text the information could be found. Rothkopf (1971) has discovered that readers incidentally acquire a surprising amount of information about the geography of a text. Though they had not been forewarned that they would be asked where information was located, after reading a 3000-word passage people were able to report the page on which information appeared, and even the location within the page with much better than chance accuracy.

A fundamental question is why an extra allocation of cognitive capacity ought to be facilitative. Some would simply take it as axiomatic that attention is the precursor to learning, and let the argument rest there (cf. Schneider & Shiffrin, 1977; Shiffrin & Schneider, 1977). Our view is that ultimately this is not a satisfying level of explanation. A complete theory will require an analysis of what readers are doing with the cognitive capacity they invest. They could be rehearsing selected segments of the text in the traditional sense of implicitly repeating the segments to themselves, as actors learning their lines do. Rehearsal appears to be the operation that Rothkopf and Billington (1979) had in mind as the explanation for the effects of learning objectives. Another view is that readers pay extra attention to certain text segments in order to process them at a semantically deeper level. A problem with the depth-of-processing notion is that a semantic level of representation is required before a reader could have a basis for determining that a segment was important enough to deserve more attention. At this point the reader might engage in still "deeper" processing, but no one has been able to say exactly what that could mean, as critics of the idea have noted (Baddeley, 1978; Nelson, 1977). In any event, Craik and his associates, who introduced the phrase "depth of processing" (Craik & Lockhart, 1972), have abandoned the concept. He and his colleagues now speak in terms of the "elaboration" of to-be-learned material (Craik & Tulving, 1975) and the "distinctiveness" of the encoded representation (Jacoby, Craik, & Begg, 1979).

Our conjecture is that extra attention is invested in important propositions in a text in order to connect these propositions with the overall representation that is being constructed. So, if a person pretending to be a burglar reads that coins are kept in a desk drawer, the connection is made that the coins are potential loot and what a burglar is interested in is loot. Drawing such connecting inferences requires cognitive capacity. The fact that they are drawn is the reason, or part of the reason, for the superior recall of important text elements.

When a person is *studying* a text—that is, reading with the deliberate intention of learning ideas and information—some form of the selective-attention hypothesis would appear to give a highly plausible account of aspects of the reader's processing activities (see T. H. Anderson, 1979). However, as a characterization of the activity of a person who is *simply reading*, the hypothesis has much less *a priori* appeal. We would not be surprised to find no evidence of differential allocation of capacity on the part of an individual engrossed with the sports page or curled up with a novel. Such learning of information as takes place under these conditions is the incidental by-product of comprehension. The demand characteristics of laboratory experiments on discourse processes put subjects more in the mode of studying than simply reading. Direct, systematic study of what is happening when people are simply reading will not be easy since procedures for the real-time measurement of attention are especially intrusive.

A complete theory of the allocation of attention during reading will have to take account of all major demands on cognitive capacity. Included is the capacity needed to analyze words and access their meanings, to parse sentences into constituents, and to construct propositions. Many aspects of reading may be automatic, at least in the skilled reader, and, hence, require very little cognitive capacity (LaBerge & Samuels, 1974; Posner, 1978). Nevertheless, as a general rule, it is probably a safe bet that every level of linguistic analysis requires some attention. Even highly overlearned, largely habitual operations must be monitored because of occasional breakdowns.

Graesser, Hoffman, and Clark (1980) and Just and Carpenter (1980) have demonstrated that a range of language-processing operations do require cognitive capacity. In the former study, reading times were collected for 275 sentences in 12 passages. The sentences were analyzed in terms of three variables believed to relate to the text macrostructure—that is, the interrelationships among sentences and the organization of the passage as a whole. There were also three variables related to the microstructure, or linguistic units within sentences. Reading time was strongly influenced by macrostructure variables, especially whether the sentence was from a story or expository text, but also by the familiarity of the topic (see Steffensen, Joag-dev, & Anderson, 1979), and by the amount of new information in the sentence. The microstructure variables had smaller but still significant effects on overall reading time. When subjects were split into groups of fast and slow readers, there was no difference between groups on macrostructure components, but a substantial difference with respect to microstructure variables. The cost in time to process an additional word or proposition or to cope with unpredictable syntax was much greater for slow than fast readers. Graesser and colleagues went on to show that readers instructed to prepare for an essay, in contrast to a multiple-choice, examination devoted increasing amounts of time to difficult macrostructure components of the texts, whereas time to process microstructure components did not vary. This is a reasonable result since an essay exam requires an organized understanding of a text. Multiple-choice questions can be answered from a piecemeal representation.

In summary, despite some inconsistent findings and several unanswered questions, based on the evidence available at this time, the selective attention hypothesis looks promising.

SCHEMATA AND REMEMBERING

Thus far, we have dealt with processes supported by the person's schema when a message is being comprehended and aspects of its content learned. In this section we turn to the influence of schemata on processes that may be at work later when the information and ideas in the message are being remembered and used.

Much research that is ostensibly about remembering is really about comprehension and learning. In such research, the operational measure is recall, which seems to implicate memory, but in fact the measure is collected in order to make inferences about earlier processes that are not directly observable. Such research rests on the assumption that what gets stored is the major determiner of what can be remembered. Notice, however, that if learning entirely determines remembering, then remembering is an uninteresting, derivative process. Loosely speaking, any factor that affects performance on a recall test can be said to affect remembering. In a serious discussion, though, a result should not be attributed to remembering unless there is an effect above and beyond that which can be explained in terms of learning.

Pichert and Anderson (1977) obtained evidence which suggested that a person's schema has an effect on memory in addition to an effect on learning. Subjects read the passage already described about what two boys did at one boy's home while skipping school, or they read a passage about two gulls frolicking over a remote island. Readers' schemata were manipulated by assigning different perspectives. For the boys-playing-hooky-from-school passage, one-third of the subjects were instructed to read the story from the perspective of a potential home buyer, one-third were to read it from the perspective of a burglar, and one-third (a control group) were given no special perspective. For the gulls-frolicking-over-an-island story, one-third of the subjects were told to take the perspective of an eccentric florist who desired a remote place to raise exotic flowers, one-third were to read the story from the perspective of a shipwrecked person eager to stay alive and get home, and one-third were controls.

The passages were written so as to contain information of contrasting importance to the perspectives. For instance, the passage ostensibly about two boys playing hooky from school contained the information that the house had a leaky roof, which would be important to a real estate prospect but not a burglar, and the information that the family had a large color TV set, where the reverse would be true.

Subjects were asked to recall the passage shortly after reading and a week later. Table 9.1 summarizes the results. As can be seen, the importance of the information to the assigned perspective had a powerful influence on learning and also a positive, though small, influence on memory after one week. The index of memory was the proportion of information recalled, given that the same information had also been recalled on the first test shortly after reading a week earlier. This index is logically independent of level of recall on the first test. If the first test is regarded as representing level of learning, then the experiment provides evidence that a person's schema has separate effects on learning and memory.

This interpretation is open to challenge, however. It could be argued that the schema operative when a person is reading has an influence on learning that is not manifested in an immediate opportunity to recall. Text elements that are important in the light of the reader's schema might be overlearned because they receive more processing or deeper processing. As a result, these elements may have enough strength to appear at both immediate and delayed recall. On the other hand, a larger proportion of the less well-learned, unimpor-

TABLE 9.1 MEAN PROPORTION
RECALLED AS A FUNCTION OF IDEA
UNIT IMPORTANCE

	IDEA UNIT IMPORTANCE[a]		
	HIGH	MEDIUM	LOW
Learning[b]	.48	.36	.25
Memory[c]	.68	.65	.53

SOURCE: Pichert and Anderson, 1977, p. 311.
[a] Coded according to the perspective operative while the passage was read.
[b] Proprotion of idea units recalled on immediate test.
[c] Proportion of idea units recalled on delayed test given recall on immediate test.

tant elements may be above a recall threshold when the first test is given but below the threshold a week later.

Anderson and Pichert (1978) attempted to design a test of the effects of schemata on memory that would be free from possible latent effects of level of learning. Subjects read the boys-playing-hooky-from-school passage from one of the two perspectives, recalled the passage for a first time, changed perspectives—from home buyer to burglar or vice versa—and then recalled the passage for a second time. The data showed that people recalled additional, previously unrecalled information following the shift in perspective. There was a significant increase in recall of information important to the new perspective but unimportant to the one operative when the passage was read. It is impossible to explain this result in terms of a learning process since the switch of perspectives occurred after the material had been read and recalled once. The phenomenon must be attributed to a remembering process.

The finding that a change of perspective leads to an increment in recall of information important to the new perspective as well as a decrement in recall of information unimportant to the new perspective has been replicated a number of times under several variations of design and procedure. For example, Anderson, Pichert, and Shirey (1983) asked high school students to read a passage and recall it just once, either from the perspective operative during reading or a different perspective assigned prior to recall. Table 9.2 contains the results. As can be seen, there were independent effects of the reading perspective and the recall perspective on recall. The data plainly show that the schemata brought into place by perspective instructions affect both learning and remembering.

In a second experiment, Anderson et al. (1983) found that a new perspective had lost most of its power to reinstate previously unrecalled text information after an interval of a week. Similarly, Fass and Schumacher (1981) reported a diminished perspective shift effect after an interval of 24 hours. On the other hand, Flammer and Tauber (1982), in a study involving German-speaking Swiss university students, found only slightly reduced recall of information important in the light of the new perspective when the perspective was introduced 20 minutes after reading. Evidently unassimilated bits and pieces of information in the recesses of the mind will be irretrievably lost unless a complementary schema is introduced within a fairly short period after reading.

Exactly how does a person's schema influence remembering? In previous papers (e.g., R. C. Anderson, 1978), we have outlined three possible answers to this question, which we labeled the retrieval-plan hypothesis, the output-editing hypothesis, and the reconstruction hypothesis.

TABLE 9.2   MEAN PROPORTIONS OF TEXT ELEMENTS RECALLED

IMPORTANCE TO RECALL PERSPECTIVE	IMPORTANCE TO READING PERSPECTIVE	
	LOW	HIGH
High	.41	.51
Low	.32	.43

SOURCE: Anderson, Pichert, and Shirley, 1983.

According to the retrieval-plan hypothesis, the schema provides the framework for a "top-down" (Bobrow & Norman, 1975) search of memory. The idea is that search proceeds from the general concepts incorporated in the schema to the particular information related to these concepts that was learned while the passage was being read. According to the theory, a top-down, schema-guided search provides access to information important in the light of the schema, but it cannot turn up information unrelated to the schema.

The retrieval-plan hypothesis can be illustrated with reference to the burglar perspective on the hooky passage. Most peoples' BURGLARY schema will include the general concepts of entering the premises to be robbed, trying to avoid detection, finding objects that qualify as loot—namely, valuable objects that are easily moved and readily fenced—and making a clean getaway. The statement in the passage that the side door to the house is kept unlocked is likely to be made accessible when the general need of burglars to enter the premises is considered. The statement that tall trees hid the house from the road is a candidate for reinstatement by the AVOIDING DETECTION subschema. Similarly, various objects mentioned in the story, such as the color TV set and money in the desk in the den, are likely to occur to the rememberer when he thinks about loot. The general point is that, by reviewing his knowledge of what is true of most burglaries, the rememberer is reminded of the burglar-relevant information in the passage. Though the processes of remembering are not necessarily deliberate or conscious, a useful way to think about the retrieval-plan hypothesis is that the schema provides the rememberer with an outline of the questions he ought to ask himself.

A second possible hypothesis to explain effects on remembering is that the schema provides the basis and the motivation for output editing. By "output editing" we mean selection/rejection of information to report when recalling a passage. The hypothesis says that the criteria for this decision favor the currently operative schema. If a piece of information is relevant to his schema, a person might be willing to report it even though he is uncertain of his recollection. On the other hand, the person might impose high standards of certainty for evaluating information not relevant to his schema. The pattern of results that involves increased recall of important information and decreased recall of unimportant information could be explained in terms of perspective-induced shifts in standards for output editing.

A third hypothesis is that the rememberer's schema facilitates reconstruction. According to this hypothesis, the person generates inferences about what must have been in the passage based on his schema and aspects of the passage that can be recalled. For instance, a person attempting to recall the hooky passage from the perspective of a burglar will surely recall that the narrative involved an affluent, middle-class family. Knowing the lifestyle and spending habits of persons in this social stratum and the concern of a burglar with valuable, portable, fencible items, it may occur to the rememberer that the passage mentioned one or another small appliance, such as a food processer, color TV, camera, chain saw, sewing machine, or stereo. As a matter of fact, among these items only a color TV is mentioned. However, a person's degree of conviction that he "read" about a particular appliance may relate not only to whether the item was actually there, but also to such factors as the likelihood that a family of this type would have such an appliance and whether that appliance is typically part of a burglar's loot. Thus, a person might be fairly certain that he read about a stereo, even though none was mentioned. As Spiro (1977) has noted, a similar process could produce instances of correct recall. Suppose a person did not actually remember the information about the color TV set. He might infer its existence anyway and become convinced that he read about it because of the high likelihood of a color TV set in well-to-do-households. In this fashion, an inventive person with a slack criterion for output editing may be able to "remember" additional information from a text as well as produce fabrications (cf. Gauld & Stephenson, 1967).

Next, we will consider the evidence that bears on the mechanisms by which a schema affects remembering. The simplest and least interesting explanation is provided by the output-editing hypothesis. Indeed, one may wonder whether a change in criterion ought to be called a memory process.

Several studies have examined the output-editing hypothesis. Surber (1977) varied the incentive for recall. He reasoned that if the increment in recall observed among people who shift to a new perspective were due to the adoption of a lax criterion, then the increment would disappear under conditions of high incentive because then, presumably, everybody would apply a lax criterion. The results showed a difference in recall in favor of people who shifted perspective, regardless of whether a $.25 bonus was paid for each new idea.

Anderson and Pichert (1978) used a direct approach to see whether output editing was a creditable hypothesis. They interviewed subjects who had recalled a passage for the second time after changing perspectives. Of 12 subjects, 9 insisted that each time they recalled the passage they wrote down everything they could remember whether important or unimportant. In the words of one of them, "I tried to write down everything even if it seemed stupid, you know. I generally wrote what I could remember."

Two unpublished experiments by Anderson, Shirey, and Pichert have assessed the output-editing hypothesis using recognition memory. For one experiment, alternate versions of the boys-playing-hooky passage were written that contained different but comparable information of roughly equal attractiveness to burglars or to real estate prospects. For instance, a piece of information relevant to home buyers was a damaged ceiling due to a leaky roof. The comparable information in the other version was a crack in a wall due to a settling foundation. In this experiment, half the subjects read one of the versions of the passage, half read the other, and later everyone took a test based on information from both versions. The test required subjects to evaluate whether or not each of a series of sentences expressed a proposition that they had read. According to the output-editing hypothesis, people will apply a lenient criterion for evaluating items expressing information relevant to their perspective. As a consequence, they will tend to accept perspective-relevant items they have not actually seen. In the case being used for illustration, a person given the home buyer perspective would be expected to accept both the item about the settling foundation and the one about the leaky roof. This did not happen. Indeed, neither reading perspective nor recall perspective had any discernible effect on recognition memory in two large experiments using somewhat different materials and procedures.

Presumably, people can and do evaluate what they are saying according to criteria of relevance and veracity, and, presumably, these criteria change according to circumstances. Nonetheless, based on the accumulated evidence, it seems safe to conclude that output editing is not responsible for the changes in recall of passages that have been observed when people shift perspectives, at least under the conditions that have prevailed in the experiments reviewed in this chapter.

The retrieval-plan hypothesis is able to explain why perspective instructions have consistent effects on recall but no apparent effects on recognition. A recognition test item minimizes the need for retrieving information from memory since the information is provided in the item itself. The essence of the retrieval-plan hypothesis is that the schema is a structure that provides *access* to information in memory. Since access is not a problem on recognition items, the retrieval-plan hypothesis predicts no effect. Access is a critical process in free recall, so large effects are predicted there. Intermediate effects would be expected on a cued recall test that provided some guidance but did not eliminate the need for retrieval.

Anderson and Pichert (1978) obtained interview protocols that supported the notion of using a schema as the basis for a retrieval plan. The interviewer probed to determine why subjects thought they had come up with new information the second time they recalled a passage. Of the 16 subjects, 7 expressly stated that considering categories of information which were significant in the light of the perspective caused them to recall additional items of information from these categories. For instance, one subject who shifted from the home buyer to the burglar perspective said:

> I just thought of myself as a burglar walking through the house. So I had a different point of view, a different objective point of view for different details, you know. I noticed the door was open, and where would I go here, go there, take this, take that, what rooms would I go to and what rooms wouldn't I go to. Like, you know, who cares about the outside and stuff? You can't steal a wall or nothing. . . . I remembered [the color TV] in the second one, but not in the first one. I was thinking about things to steal, things you could take and steal. In the den was the money. China, jewelry, other stuff in other places. [Q: Why do you think you remembered the color TV the second time and not the first time?] Because I was thinking of things to steal, I guess.

In addition, 6 other subjects, who were less explicit about recall strategies, said that the new perspective "jogged" their memories or that, when given the new perspective, additional information "popped" into their heads. Hence, in all, 13 of 16 subjects made statements consistent with the retrieval-plan hypothesis.

A subtle prediction that can be made based on the retrieval-plan hypothesis is that rememberers ought to recall information in conceptually related clusters. The hypothesis asserts that memory search is organized in terms of the general categories that comprise the schema. So, for instance, a person pretending to be a home buyer might be expected to recall, one after another, several defects of the house that were discussed at locations scattered across the passage. We have failed to find much clustering in informal analyses of attempts to recall the hooky passage. One reason for this may be that the assigned perspective is not the only schema subjects are using to organize recall. Two other schemata that come into play involve the spatial organization of the house and the temporal organization of the plot, such as it is, involving the two boys. These supplementary schemata may tend to minimize clustering in terms of burglar or home buyers concerns.

Grabe (1979) has also investigated the role of schemata in recall organization. He used the boys-playing-hooky-passage and a passage about a nursery school which was recalled from the perspective of either a toy manufacturer or a child psychologist. Clustering was significantly greater among subjects assigned perspectives than among no-perspective control subjects, largely because of the strong results obtained with the nursery school material. In Grabe's (1979) study, the perspective was assigned before the passage was read, so, it can be assumed that it provided the framework for learning as well as remembering. A worthwhile project would be to see if recall organization changes when the perspective shifts after reading.

In summary, the retrieval-plan hypothesis gives a good account of several different kinds of data. It remains a plausible candidate to explain some of the effects of schemata on remembering.

There is a substantial research literature bearing on the inferential-reconstruction hypothesis. We will consider here only studies that provide a clear basis for distinguishing between memory effects and effects attributable to the representation built up when a message was initially interpreted. A memory effect must be involved when a person acquires a certain perspective *after* reading a message, as was the case in the research of Spiro (1977, 1980) and Snyder and Uranowitz (1978).

In the latter study, people read a case history of a woman named Betty K. Later some subjects were informed that Betty K. was living a lesbian lifestyle, while others were told she was a heterosexual. Although subjects were told that they were being tested for accuracy of memory for factual information in the case history, answers to a multiple-choice test indicated selective remembering of information that supported their current interpretation of Betty K's sexuality and also distortion of information that contradicted their current view. For example, subjects who were informed that Betty K. was a lesbian said she never went out with boys during high school, whereas some subjects given the information that she was a heterosexual said she had a steady boyfriend. The correct answer was that she occasionally dated boys.

Loftus and her colleagues have done some especially provocative research on reconstructive memory (cf. Loftus, 1979). In one study (Loftus & Palmer, 1974), people saw a film of an automobile accident and then answered questions about what they had seen. The question, "About how fast were the cars going when they smashed into each other?" elicited a higher estimate of speed than questions that used verbs such as *bumped* or *hit* in place of *smashed*. On a test administered one week later, those subjects who had heard the verb *smashed* were more likely to answer "yes" to the question, "Did you see any broken glass?" even though broken glass was not present in the film. This experiment (and many others using similar procedures) shows that related information is usually assimilated into a single schema, with the frequent result that people are unable to distinguish between information with a direct basis in experience and that which was not actually experienced but which is consistent with the schema.

Several studies show that the longer the interval between reading and recall, the larger the effects of the reader's schema. A remembering process is implicated, therefore, rather than a learning process because the effects of a learning process would be strongest immediately following a passage and would diminish thereafter. The schema manifests itself as an increase with time in the frequency of schema-consistent distortions in free recall (Bartlett, 1932) or in susceptibility to schema-consistent foils in recognition (Sulin & Dooling, 1974). This phenomenon is nicely illustrated in a study by Read and Rossen (1981). They asked people who were either strongly for or strongly against nuclear power to read a text about a fire at a nuclear power plant. The data revealed very little effect on a multiple-choice test given immediately after the story. However, when the test was given one or two weeks later, there was a substantial degree of acceptance of belief-consistent distortions of the original information. Subjects who were personally opposed to nuclear power correctly rejected spurious, pronuclear statements; however, they tended to accept incorrect antinuclear statements. Subjects who favored nuclear power produced the opposite pattern of results.

There have been studies that have failed to support a reconstructive view of memory (Brigham & Cook, 1969). In general, these studies have used arbitrary, disconnected material, have involved reading this material in an unnatural manner, or have given the test immediately after the material was exposed. Conversely, when people read lifelike prose in a normal manner so that their knowledge and belief about the world is actually engaged, and when the test is delayed for more than a few moments, typically the results strongly support the reconstructive hypothesis (Read & Rossen, 1981; Sheppard, 1981; Spiro, 1977).

In summary, available data support the ideas that the reader's schema is a structure that facilitates planful retrieval of text information from memory and permits reconstruction of elements that were not learned or have been forgotten.

FUTURE DIRECTIONS FOR RESEARCH
IN COMPREHENSION

In our judgment, Huey would have been delighted with the progress that reading research has made in unraveling "the tangled story of the most remarkable specific performance that civilization has learned in all its history" (1908/1968, p. 8). It is true, of course, that there are gaps in understanding and alternative explanations of phenomena for which the available evidence provides no resolution. Thus, there is still much work to be done in order to build THE definitive model of basic processes in reading comprehension.

We close by discussing some of the implications that basic research in comprehension holds for educational research and practice (see also the thoughtful review of research on comprehension instruction by Tierney and Cunningham, this volume). These ideas are offered in the spirit of conjecture, as hypotheses in need of elaboration and explication, and in need of testing in the laboratory and in the classroom.

First, poor readers are likely to have gaps in knowledge. Since what a person already knows is a principal determiner of what she can comprehend, the less she knows the less she can comprehend.

Second, poor readers are likely to have an impoverished understanding of the relationships among the facts they do know about a topic. Arbitrary information is a source of confusion, slow learning, slow processing, and unsatisfactory reasoning.

Third, poor readers are unlikely to make the inferences required to weave the information given in a text into a coherent overall representation. Poor readers do not seem consistently to appreciate that—using the analogy of Wilson and Anderson (in press)—comprehending a story or text is like completing a jigsaw puzzle: all of the information must be used, the information must fit into place without forcing, all of the important slots must contain information, and the completed interpretation must make sense. Forming a coherent representation requires drawing precise, integrating inferences, and drawing such inferences is not something poor readers do routinely and spontaneously (see Bransford, Stein, Nye, Franks, Auble, Merynski, & Perfetto, 1982, and the companion articles).

If the foregoing problems have been accurately identified and they are the central ones, then plausible solutions naturally suggest themselves: becoming a good reader demands a curriculum rich with concepts from the everyday world and learned fields of study. Becoming a good reader requires books that explain how and why things function as they do. Becoming a good reader depends upon teachers who insist that students think about the interconnections among ideas as they read.

We hope that these conjectures provide impetus for instructional researchers to conduct the kind of painstaking classroom and materials research necessary to build and validate better programs of comprehension instruction and for educators to begin to develop and evaluate instructional programs that will lead to the literate citizenry our future will demand.

REFERENCES

Adams, M. J., & Collins, A. M.   A schema-theoretic view of reading. In R. O. Freedle (Ed.), *Discourse processing: Multidisciplinary perspectives.* Norwood, N.J.: Ablex, 1979.

Alessi, S. M., Anderson, T. H., & Goetz, E. T.   An investigation of lookbacks during studying. *Discourse Processes,* 1979, *7,* 197–212.

Anderson, J. R.   *Language, memory and thought.* Hillsdale, N.J.: Erlbaum, 1976.

Anderson, R. C.   The notion of schemata and the educational enterprise. In R. C. Anderson, R. J. Spiro, & W. E. Montague (Eds.), *Schooling and the acquisition of knowledge.* Hillsdale, N.J.: Erlbaum, 1977.

Anderson, R. C.   Schema-directed processes in language comprehension. In A. Lesgold, J. Pelligreno, S. Fokkema, & R. Glaser (Eds.), *Cognitive psychology and instruction.* New York: Plenum, 1978.

Anderson, R. C.   Allocation of attention during reading. In A. Flammer & W. Kintsch (Eds.), *Discourse processing.* Amsterdam: North-Holland Publishing Co., 1982.

Anderson, R. C., & Pichert, J. W.   Recall of previously unrecallable information following a shift in perspective. *Journal of Verbal Learning and Verbal Behavior,* 1978, *17,* 1–12.

Anderson, R. C., Pichert, J. W., Goetz, E. T., Schallert, D. L., Stevens, K. V., & Trollip, S. R.   Instantiation of general terms. *Journal of Verbal Learning and Verbal Behavior*, 1976, *15*, 667–679.

Anderson, R. C., Pichert, J. W., & Shirey, L. L.   Effects of the reader's schema at different points in time. *Journal of Educational Psychology*, 1983, *75*, 271–279.

Anderson, R. C., Reynolds, R. E., Schallert, D. L., & Goetz, E. T.   Frameworks for comprehending discourse. *American Educational Research Journal*, 1977, *14*, 367–382.

Anderson, R. C., & Shiffrin, Z.   The meaning of words in context. In R. J. Spiro, B. C. Bruce, & W. F. Brewer (Eds.), *Theoretical issues in reading comprehension*. Hillsdale, N.J.: Erlbaum, 1980.

Anderson, R. C., Spiro, R., & Anderson, M. C.   Schemata as scaffolding for the representation of information in connected discourse. *American Educational Research Journal*, 1978, *15*, 433–440.

Anderson, T. H.   Study skills and learning strategies. In H. F. O'Neil, Jr., & C. D. Spielberger (Eds.), *Cognitive and affective learning strategies*. New York: Academic Press, 1979.

Ausubel, D. P.   *The psychology of meaningful verbal learning*. New York: Grune & Stratton, 1963.

Ausubel, D. P.   In defense of advance organizers: A reply to the critics. *Review of Educational Research*, 1978, *48*, 251–258.

Ausubel, D. P., & Robinson, F. G.   *School learning*. New York: Holt, Rinehart & Winston, 1969.

Baddeley, A. D.   The trouble with levels: A reexamination of Craik and Lockhart's framework for memory research. *Psychological Review*, 1978, *85*, 139–152.

Barnes, B. R., & Clawson, E. U.   Do advance organizers facilitate learning? Recommendations for further research based on an analysis of 32 studies. *Review of Educational Research*, 1975, *45*, 637–659.

Bartlett, F. C.   *Remembering*. Cambridge: Cambridge University Press, 1932.

Bobrow, D. G., & Norman, D. A.   Some principles of memory schemata. In D. G. Bobrow & A. M. Collins (Eds.), *Representation and understanding: Studies in cognitive science*. New York: Academic Press, 1975.

Boring, E. G.   *A history of experimental psychology*. New York: Appleton-Century-Crofts, 1950.

Bransford, J.   Schema activation—schema acquisition. In R. C. Anderson, J. Osborn, & R. C. Tierney (Eds.), *Learning to read in American schools*. Hillsdale, N.J.: Erlbaum, 1983.

Bransford, J. D., & Johnson, M. K.   Contextual prerequisites for understanding. Some investigations of comprehension and recall. *Journal of Verbal Learning and Verbal Behavior*, 1972, *11*, 717–726.

Bransford, J. D., Stein, B. S., Nye, N. J., Franks, J. F., Auble, P. M., Merynski, K. J., & Perfetto, G. A.   Differences in approaches to learning: An overview. *Journal of Experimental Psychology: General*, 1982, *3*, 390–398.

Brigham, J. C., & Cook, S. W.   The influence of attitude on the recall of controversial material: A failure to confirm. *Journal of Experimental Social Psychology*, 1969, *5*, 240–243.

Britton, B., Meyer, B., Simpson, R., Holdredge, T., & Curry, C.   Effects of the organization of text on memory: Tests of two implications of a selective attention hypothesis. *Journal of Experimental Psychology: Human Learning and Memory*, 1979, *5*, 496–506.

Britton, B. K., Piha, A., Davis, J., & Wehausen, E.   Reading and cognitive capacity usage: Adjunct question effects. *Memory and Cognition*, 1978, *6*, 266–273.

Cirilo, R. K., & Foss, D. J.   Text structure and reading time for sentences. *Journal of Verbal Learning and Verbal Behavior*, 1980, *19*, 96–109.

Clark, H. H., & Haviland, S. E.   Comprehension and the given-new concept. In R. O. Freedle (Ed.), *Discourse production and comprehension*. Norwood, N.J.: Ablex, 1977.

Clifton, C., Jr., & Slowiaczek, M. L.   Integrating new information with old knowledge. *Memory and Cognition*, 1981, *9*, 142–148.

Collins, A.   Fragments of a theory of human plausible reasoning. In D. L. Waltz (Ed.), *Theoretical issues in natural language processing-2*. Urbana-Champaign: University of Illinois, 1978.

Collins, A. M., & Quillian, M. R.   Retrieval time from semantic memory. *Journal of Verbal Learning and Verbal Behavior*, 1969, *8*, 240–247.

Craik, F. I. M., & Lockhart, R. S.   Levels of processing: A framework for memory research. *Journal of Verbal Learning and Verbal Behavior*, 1972, *11*, 671–684.

Craik, F. I. M., & Tulving, E.   Depth of processing and the retention of words in episodic memory. *Journal of Experimental Psychology: General*, 1975, *104*, 268–294.

Dooling, D. J., & Lachman, R.   Effects of comprehension on retention of prose. *Journal of Experimental Psychology*, 1971, *88*, 216–222.

Fass, W., & Schumacker, G. M.   Schema theory and prose retention: Boundary conditions for encoding and retrieval effects. *Discourse Processes*, 1981, *4*, 17–26.

Flammer, A., & Tauber, M.   Changing the reader's perspective. In A. Flammer & W. Kintsch (Eds.), *Discourse processing*. Amsterdam: North-Holland Publishing Co., 1982.

Gauld, A., & Stephenson, G. M.   Some experiments relating to Bartlett's theory of remembering. *British Journal of Psychology*, 1967, *58*, 39–49.

Goetz, E. T.   Inferring from text: Some factors influencing which inferences will be made. *Discourse Processes*, 1979, *2*, 179–195.

Goetz, E. T., Schallert, D. L., Reynolds, R. E., & Radin, D. I.   Reading in perspective: What real cops and pretend burglars look for in a story. *Journal of Educational Psychology*, 1983, *75*, 500–510.

Grabe, M. D.   Reader imposed structure and prose retention. *Contemporary Educational Psychology*, 1979, *4*, 162–171.

Graesser, A. C., Hoffman, N. L., & Clark, L. F.   Structural components of reading time. *Journal of Verbal Learning and Verbal Behavior*, 1980, *19*, 135–151.

Gray, W. S.   *On their own in reading*. Glenview, Ill.: Scott, Foresman, 1948.

Grice, H. P.   Logic and conversation. In P. Cole & J. L. Morgan (Eds.), *Syntax and semantics*, Vol. 3, *Speech acts*. New York: Seminar Press, 1975.

Halff, H. M., Ortony, A., & Anderson, R. C.   A context-sensitive representation of word meaning. *Memory and Cognition*, 1976, *4*, 378–383.

Horn, E.   *Methods of instruction in the social studies*. New York: Scribner's, 1937.

Huey, E. B.   *The psychology and pedagogy of reading*. Cambridge: MIT Press, 1968. (Originally published, Macmillan 1908.)

Jacoby, L. L., Craik, F. I. M., & Begg, I.   Effects of elaboration of processing as encoding and retrieval: Trace distinctiveness and recovery of initial context. *Journal of Verbal Learning and Verbal Behavior*, 1979, *18*, 585–600.

Just, M. A., & Carpenter, P. A.   A theory of reading: From eye fixations to comprehension. *Psychological Review*, 1980, *87*, 329–354.

Kahneman, D.   *Attention and effort*. Englewood Cliffs, N.J.: Prentice-Hall, 1973.

Katz, J. J.   *Semantic theory*. New York: Harper & Row, 1972.

Kintsch, W.   *The representation of meaning in memory*. Hillsdale, N.J.: Erlbaum, 1974.

Kintsch, W., & van Dijk, T. A.   Toward a model of text comprehension and production. *Psychological Review*, 1978, *85*, 363–394.

Koffka, K.   *Principles of Gestalt Psychology*. New York: Harcourt, Brace, 1935.

Kohler, W.   *Gestalt Psychology*, New York: Liveright, 1947.

Kripke, S.   Naming and necessity. In D. Davidson & G. Harman (Eds.), *Semantics of natural languages*. Dordrecht, The Netherlands: Reidel, 1972.

LaBerge, D., & Samuels, S. J.   Toward a theory of automatic information processing in reading. *Cognitive Psychology*, 1974, *6*, 293–323.

Lipson, M. Y.   The influence of religious affiliation on children's memory for text information. *Reading Research Quarterly*, 1983, *18*, 448–457.

Loftus, E. F.   The malleability of human memory. *American Scientist*, 1979, *67*, 312–320.

Loftus, E. F., & Palmer, J. C.   Reconstruction of automobile destruction: An example of the interaction between language and memory. *Journal of Verbal Learning and Verbal Behavior*, 1974, *13*, 585–589.

Luiten, J., Ames, W. S., & Ackerson, G.   A meta-analysis of the effects of advance organizers on learning and retention. *American Educational Research Journal*, 1980, *17*, 211–218.

Mandler, J. M., & Johnson, N. S.   Remembrance of things parsed: Story structure and recall. *Cognitive Psychology*, 1977, *9*, 111–151.

Mathews, M.   *Teaching to read: Historically considered.* Chicago: University of Chicago Press, 1966.

Mayer, R. E.   Can advance organizers influence meaningful learning? *Review of Educational Research*, 1979, *49*, 371–383.

Meyer, B. J. F.   *The organization of prose and its effects on memory.* Amsterdam: North-Holland Publishing Co., 1975.

Minsky, M.   A framework for representing knowledge. In P. Evinston (Ed.), *The psychology of computer vision.* New York: Winston, 1975.

Nelson, T. O.   Repetition and depth of processing. *Journal of Verbal Learning and Verbal Behavior*, 1977, *16*, 151–171.

Nicholson, T., & Imlach, R.   Where do their answers come from? A study of the inferences which children make when answering questions about narrative stories. *Journal of Reading Behavior*, 1981, *13*, 111–129.

Omanson, R. C., Warren, W. H., & Trabasso, T.   Goals, themes, inferences and memory: A developmental study. *Discourse Processing*, 1978, *1*, 337–354.

Paris, S. C., & Lindauer, B. K.   The role of inference in children's comprehension and memory. *Cognitive Psychology*, 1976, *8*, 217–227.

Paris, S. C., & Upton, L. R.   Children's memory for inferential relationships in prose. *Child Development*, 1976, *47*, 660–668.

Pearson, P. D., Hansen, J., & Gordon, C.   The effect of background knowledge on young children's comprehension of explicit and implicit information. *Journal of Reading Behavior*, 1979, *11*, 201–209.

Pichert, J. W., & Anderson, R. C.   Taking different perspectives on a story. *Journal of Educational Psychology*, 1977, *69*, 309–315.

Posner, M. I.   *Chronometric explorations of mind: The third Paul M. Fitts lectures.* Hillsdale, N.J.: Erlbaum, 1978.

Putnam, H.   The meaning of "meaning." In H. Putnam (Ed.), *Mind, language and reality.* Cambridge: Cambridge University Press, 1975.

Read, S. J., & Rossen, M. B.   *Rewriting history: The biasing effects of beliefs on memory.* Manuscript submitted for publication, 1981.

Reder, L. M., & Anderson, J. R.   A partial resolution of the paradox of interference: The role of integrating knowledge. *Cognitive Psychology*, 1980, *12*, 447–472.

Reynolds, R. E.   *Cognitive demands of reading.* Paper presented at the annual meeting of the American Educational Research Association, Los Angeles, April 1981.

Reynolds, R. E., & Anderson, R. C.   Influence of questions on the allocation of attention during reading. *Journal of Educational Psychology*, 1982, *74*, 623–632.

Reynolds, R. E., Standiford, S. N., & Anderson, R. C.   Distribution of reading time when questions are asked about a restricted category of text information. *Journal of Educational Psychology*, 1979, *71*, 183–190.

Ross, B. H., & Bower, G. H.   Comparisons of models of associative recall. *Memory and Cognition*, 1981, *9*, 1–16.

Rothkopf, E. Z.   Incidental memory for location of information in text. *Journal of Verbal Learning and Verbal Behavior*, 1971, *10*, 608–613.

Rothkopf, E. Z., & Billington, M. J.   Goal guided learning from text: Inferring a descriptive processing model from inspection times and eye movements. *Journal of Educational Psychology*, 1979, *71*, 310–327.

Rumelhart, D. E.   Notes on a schema for stories. In D. G. Bobrow & A. M. Collins (Eds.), *Representation and understanding: Studies in cognitive science*. New York: Academic Press, 1975.

Rumelhart, D. E.   Schemata: The building blocks of cognition. In R. J. Spiro, B. C. Bruce, & W. F. Brewer (Eds.), *Theoretical issues in reading comprehension*. Hillsdale, N.J.: Erlbaum, 1980.

Schank, R. C., & Abelson, R.   *Plans, scripts, goals and understanding*. Hillsdale, N.J.: Erlbaum, 1977.

Schneider, W., & Shiffrin, R. M.   Controlled and automatic human information processing: I. Detection, search and attention. *Psychological Review*, 1977, *84*, 1–66.

Sheppard, B. H.   *Opinions and remembering revisited: The case of the disappearing phenomena*. Manuscript submitted for publication, 1981.

Shiffrin, R. M., & Schneider, W.   Controlled and automatic human information processing: II. Perceptual learning automatic attending, and a general theory. *Psychological Review*, 1977, *84*, 127–190.

Singer, M.   Processes of inference in sentence encoding. *Memory and Cognition*, 1979, *7*, 192–200. (a)

Singer, M.   The temporal locus of inference in the comprehension of brief passages: Recognizing and verifying implications about instruments. *Perceptual and Motor Skills*, 1979, *49*, 539–550. (b)

Singer, M.   The role of case-filling inferences in the coherence of brief passages. *Discourse Processes*, 1980, *3*, 185–201.

Smith, E. E., Adams, N., & Schorr, D.   Fact retrieval and the paradox of interference. *Cognitive Psychology*, 1978, *10*, 438–474.

Smith, E. E., & Medin, D. C.   *Categories and concepts*. Cambridge: Harvard University Press, 1981.

Spiro, R. J.   Inferential reconstruction in memory for connected discourse. In R. C. Anderson, R. J. Spiro, & W. E. Montague (Eds.), *Schooling and the acquisition of knowledge*. Hillsdale, N.J.: Erlbaum, 1977.

Spiro, R. J.   Constructive processes in prose recall. In R. J. Spiro, B. C. Bruce, & W. F. Brewer (Eds.), *Theoretical issues in reading comprehension*. Hillsdale, N.J.: Erlbaum, 1980.

Snyder, M., & Uranowitz, S. W.   Reconstructing the past: Some cognitive consequences of person perception. *Journal of Personality and Social Psychology*, 1978, *36*, 941–950.

Steffensen, M. S., Joag-dev, C., & Anderson, R. C.   A cross-cultural perspective on reading comprehension. *Reading Research Quarterly*, 1979, *15*, 10–29.

Stein, B. S., & Bransford, J. D.   Constraints on effective elaboration: Effects of precision and subject generation. *Journal of Verbal Learning and Verbal Behavior*, 1979, *18*, 769–777.

Stein, N., & Glenn, C. G.   An analysis of story comprehension in elementary school children. In R. Freedle (Ed.), *New directions in discourse processing*. Norwood, N.J.: Ablex, 1979.

Sulin, R. A., & Dooling, D. J.   Intrusion of a thematic idea in retention of prose. *Journal of Experimental Psychology*, 1974, *103*, 255–262.

Surber, J. R. *The role of output editing in the recall of brief narrative.* Unpublished doctoral dissertation, University of Illinois at Urbana-Champaign, 1977.

Walker, J. H.   Real-world variability, reasonableness judgments, and memory representations for concepts. *Journal of Verbal Learning and Verbal Behavior,* 1975, *14,* 241–252.

Wertheimer, M.   Experimentalle Studien über das Seheu von Bewegung. *Zls. f. Psych,* 61, 1912, 161–265.

Wilson, P. & Anderson, R. C.   What they don't know will hurt them: The role of prior knowledge in comprehension. In J. Orsanu (Ed.), *Reading Comprehension: From research to practice.* Hillsdale, N.J.: Erlbaum, in press.

Winograd, T.   Frame representations and the declarative-procedural controversy. In D. G. Bobrow & A. M. Collins (Eds.), *Representation and understanding: Studies in cognitive science.* New York: Academic Press, 1975.

Wittgenstein, L.   *Philosophical investigations.* New York: Macmillan, 1953.

Wulf, F.   [Uber die Veränderung von Vorstellungen (Gedächtnis und Gestalt).] In W. D. Ellis (trans. and condensed), *A source book of Gestalt psychology.* London: Routledge & Kegan Paul, 1938.

10 LISTENING AND READING

Thomas G. Sticht and James H. James

D. P. Brown, a blind educator, completed his doctoral dissertation 30 years ago at Stanford University. In it, he analyzed relationships among oral and written language skills (Brown, 1954). He argued that listening to and comprehending spoken language is different from listening to nonlanguage sounds, which is something the prelanguage infant can do. He argued that, just as reading is not called looking, though it certainly involves looking while processing language symbols, listening while processing language signals should not be called merely listening. Listening, so he argued, is a parallel term to looking, and it causes confusion to have the term also serve as the oral language counterpart to reading. So, he coined the term auding to refer to the process of listening to language and processing it for comprehension.

In this chapter, we will use the term auding as defined by Brown; the term oracy (Wilkinson, 1971) to refer to the oral language skills of auding and speaking; and the term literacy to refer to the processes of reading and writing. Our goal for the chapter is to understand better the relationships among oracy and literacy skills, with a special concern for examining the various lines of evidence regarding the transfer of skills and knowledge used in comprehending oral language (auding) to the comprehension of written language (reading).

Practical Concerns

Understanding the nature of auding and reading and the relationships among these information processing skills has important implications for educational policy and practice. Regarding educational policy, it is notable that the federal government spends millions of dollars each year on preschool intervention programs that aim, in large part, to develop children's oral language (verbal IQ) skills, with the expectation that this development will subsequently facilitate, through some process of transfer, the acquisition of higher levels of reading ability (Ziegler & Valentine, 1979).

The importance of understanding relationships among auding and reading for educational practice is underscored by the fact that the teaching of reading through either code, meaning, or psycholinguistic approaches shares with federal intervention programs the assumption that oral language skills are fundamental to learning to read. For instance, Chall (1967), speaking from the code emphasis perspective, states, "Once the pupil has learned to recognize in print the words he knows (because they are part of his speaking and listening vocabulary), any additional work on decoding is a sheer waste of time" (p. 307).

Smith (1971), speaking from the meaning emphasis point of view, acknowledges "the fact that almost all children have acquired a good deal of verbal fluency before they face the task of learning to read" and that this provides "a basis of language that is obviously relevant to the process of learning to read— the written language is basically the same language as that of speech, even if it has special lexical, syntactic, and communicational aspects" (p. 45).

Addressing the relationships among oral and written languages from the psycholinguistic perspective, Goodman and Goodman (1979) state, "Written language development draws on competence in oral language, since both written and oral language share underlying structures and since, for most learners, oral language competence reaches a high level earlier. As children become literate, the two systems become interactive, and children use each to support the other when they need to" (p. 150).

ORACY TO LITERACY TRANSFER CONCEPTS

As indicated by the foregoing quotations, advocates of the code, meaning, and psycholinguistic approaches to reading all share three premises regarding relationships among oral and written languages: (1) oral language skills develop to a fairly high level prior to the development of written language, (2) oral and written languages share essentially the same lexicon (vocabulary) and syntax (grammar), and (3) beginning readers draw upon their knowledge of oral language in learning to read.

Setting aside, for the moment, the discussion of just how these three perspectives differ with regard to the precise procedures involved in drawing upon oral language knowledge in learning to read, we can identify three concepts implied by the three premises shared by these three theoretical perspectives. One is the concept of *reading potential*, which is the inference from the three premises that, if in learning to read, the person first learns to comprehend the written version of the earlier acquired oral vocabulary and syntax, then the person's oral language comprehension level establishes a goal or potential for what can be comprehended through reading, at least until the latter develops to the point where, as with oral language, new terms and syntactical constructions can be learned from print.

The second and third basic concepts are really corollaries to the concept of reading potential. The first of these is the concept of *transfer* from oral to written-language skills. This is the basis for the preschool intervention programs— that improvements in oral language will transfer to improvements in reading, that is, will raise the reading potential. The second corollary is the notion, alluded to in Chall's (1967, p. 307) quote above, that in learning to read, people *close the gap* between auding and reading skills, that is, they become capable of recognizing in printed form words and syntactic constructions they could previously recognize only in spoken form.

The remainder of this chapter reviews research literature dealing with the concepts of reading potential, transfer from oral to written language, and closing the gap between auding and reading. Major questions include: Are these concepts sound? Does the evidence support their veracity? What are the major educational implications of these concepts?

The Reading Potential Concept

The reading potential concept states that, in the typical case, people first develop vocabulary and comprehension skills by means of the oral language skills of auding and speaking. Then, when they begin to learn to read, they learn to comprehend by reading what they previously could comprehend only by auding. Stated otherwise, in the typical case of the person who is learning to read, he or she will begin training with a relatively large capability of comprehending the spoken language. In learning to read, then, one of the person's major tasks is to learn to comprehend the printed form of language with the same accuracy and efficiency as he or she comprehends the spoken form of language.

Because people typically learn to comprehend language by auding before they can comprehend it by reading, it is possible to consider that, in learning to read, they close the gap between the auding skill and the reading skill, both of which permit them to comprehend linguistic message displays. This process is illustrated in Figure 10.1, where it is seen that, at the beginning of schooling,

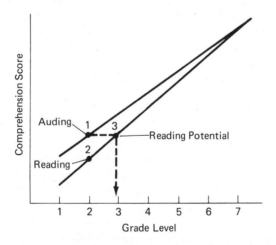

FIGURE 10.1   Schemata showing relationships among auding and reading comprehension scores as a function of school grade level. (Within the figure, 1 indicates the normative auding score for the second grade, called auding at the second-grade level; 2 shows the normative reading score for the second grade, called reading at the second-grade level; 3 shows conversion of the normative auding score to a reading potential score by drawing a horizontal from 1 to intersect with the reading curve and then dropping a perpendicular line to the abscissa. The example shows a reading potential score of third grade. Thus, the case illustrated shows a person auding and reading at the second-grade level, with a reading potential score at the third grade-level.)

pupils can comprehend language better by auding than by reading. As they progress through the school grades, they acquire more and more skill in reading and eventually close the gap between auding and reading skills.

We shall return to Figure 10.1 in discussing the concepts of oracy to literacy transfer and the closing of the gap between auding and reading. For the time being, however, we will focus on the concept of reading potential, according to which the pupil's capabilities in auding are considered to establish a potential for reading. In Figure 10.1, the auding curve represents, at each grade, the level to which reading would rise if, by some magical process, the pupil could be instantly taught reading decoding skills. Thus, if a pupil was unskilled in auding, his or her reading potential would be low, limited by poorly developed oral language skills. On the other hand, pupils highly skilled in auding would have the potential to become highly skilled in reading. In short, a positive correlation should exist between preschool or early-school oral language skills and subsequent achievement in reading.

Research demonstrating the above relationship has been obtained in a longitudinal study by Loban (1964). He presents data on reading achievement in Grades 4, 5, 6, 7, and 8 for children who were evaluated in kindergarten for oral language competency by means of a vocabulary test administered orally and teachers' ratings on (a) amount of language; (b) quality of vocabulary; (c) skill in communication; (d) organization, purpose, and control of language; (e) wealth of ideas; and (f) quality of listening. Nationally normed standardized reading achievement tests were used to assess reading.

Figure 10.2 presents data from Loban's (1964) research. High-language-ability students were those who scored two standard deviations above the mean of the oral language ratings obtained in kindergarten; low-language-ability students scored two standard deviations below the mean. The data clearly point to a strong relationship between oral language ability in kindergarten and subsequent reading ability, at least for extreme groups.

While Loban nowhere presented correlation coefficients for oral language and reading achievement for the total sample of students studied, he does present scatter diagrams for Grades 4, 6, and 8 respectively. From these diagrams, we have computed contingency coefficients: +.36, +.49, and +.52 for Grades 4, 6, and 8 respectively. Thus, for the total group as well as the extreme groups of Figure 10.2, there is a positive relationship between oral language and reading. Furthermore, the relationship grows with increases in grade level, which is consistent with the expectation that auding and reading-test performance will be more highly correlated *after* some skill in learning to read has developed. This may occur because much of the variability in reading-test performance found among children—all of whom are still in the process of initially acquiring reading skill—could reflect differences in the mastery of decoding skill rather than differences in the comprehension of language.

Additional data from a group of studies reporting correlations between auding and reading-test performance are presented in Figure 10.3. This figure is identical to that reported by Sticht, Beck, Hauke, Kleiman, and James (1974), with the exception that two correlations reported by Smiley, Oakley, Worthen, Campione, and Brown (1977) have been averaged and plotted at the seventh-grade level in the figure. The figure summarizes results from some three dozen

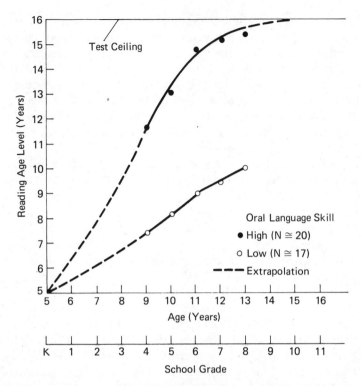

FIGURE 10.2 Relationship between chronological-age/school-grade level and median reading ability for students rated high or low in oral language skills in kindergarten. (Constructed by Sticht, Beck, Hauke, Kleiman, & James, 1974, from data presented in Loban, 1964, Table 16, p. 117.)

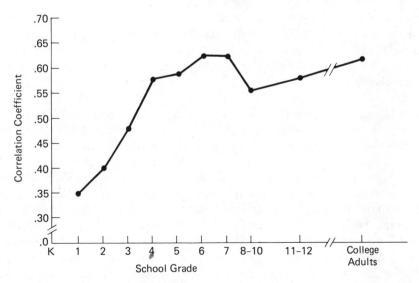

FIGURE 10.3 Correlation between auding- and reading-test performance for various studies, as a function of school-grade level.

studies distributed over the grade levels indicated. The orderly pattern seen in Figure 10.3 results despite a wide variety of auding and reading tests used in the various studies, suggesting that the pattern is quite generalizable, with the correlations increasing from +.35 in the first grade to around +.60 in the fourth grade and remaining fairly constant at that value beyond the fourth grade. These data should be contrasted with those of Hammill and McNutt (1980), who averaged over 297 correlation coefficients for auding and reading without regard to grade level, a practice that obscures the developmental characteristics implied by the reading-potential concept.

Both Loban's (1964) data and the data summarized in Figure 10.3 are consistent with the position that, in general, auding ability is indicative of potential for reading. Perhaps the limits of this relationship are indicated by comparing the rate of achievement in reading of the congenitally deaf to that of typical hearing children. In this case, the deaf have *no* auding ability. Data by Furth (reported by Gibson & Levin, 1975, p. 501) indicate that deaf students seem to reach a plateau at fourth-grade reading skill, even though they may stay in school until they are 19 or 20 years old. This contrasts with the typical high school graduate of 18 years who reads, by definition, at the twelfth-grade level.

The data for the deaf, like those of Loban (1964) and Figure 10.3, strongly support the concept of auding skill as an indicator of reading potential. However, the data for the deaf, which show that some deaf people *do* learn to read, also indicate that oral language is not *necessary* for the acquisition of at least a modicum of skill in reading. This is important, given the large amount of research effort expended in attempts to support or refute the hypothesis that, in reading, printed language *must* be recoded to spoken language (Levy, 1978, reviews much of this literature). Although not a necessity, for achieving lower levels of reading skill, apparently it helps in achieving higher-skill levels in reading if the person has the *option* of drawing upon oral language skills, as indicated by the higher achievement levels of hearing over deaf children. Though the exact advantages of having the option of recoding print to speech are not entirely understood, Kleiman (1975) suggests that recoding print to speech is especially helpful as a method of overcoming the limits of working memory, so that new information, such as introduced by relative pronouns, can be related efficiently to old information.

Auding rate and reading rate.   According to the reading potential concept, in learning to read, the person learns to turn the written representation of language into the same internal vocabulary and syntax as is used for speech, and the latter is then used to construct meaning or thoughts. In this way of thinking, then, the rate at which one can ultimately read will be limited by: (1) the rate at which internal language representations are formed and (2) the rate at which thinking can occur. Since these processes are supposed to be the same for auding and reading, both auding and reading have comparable upper limits in rate, though differences in external displays may actually limit the rate at which auditory information can be picked up in comparison to the rate of visual information pickup. For instance, speakers usually present speech at rates of around 100 to 150 words per minute, rates which do not appear to be due to how quickly internal language can be formed but seem to reflect the difficulty of forming thoughts at a fast rate (Lenneberg, 1967, p. 90). Such rates of speech obviously dictate how quickly the listener can aud.

Carver (1973a, 1973b) and Sticht et al. (1974) review extensive research, using time-compressed speech to accelerate spoken-word rates to as fast as 500 wpm with little signal distortion. Using this approach, it has been found that both auding and reading comprehension rates for college-level readers are *optimal* at around 300 wpm.

Fullmer (1980) indicates that *maximal* rates of reading, defined as the rate at which comprehension is no better than chance, may be somewhere in the neighborhood of 700 or so wpm, while auding may fail to produce comprehension above chance level at some 500 or so wpm. While these findings may reflect differences in the methods for controlling rate of presentation of information for auding and reading, it may also be indicative of separate language-processing mechanisms for auding and reading. It may also indicate that auding and reading utilize the same internal mechanism but that the auding display does not reach the limits of this mechanism in either ordinary speech or in time-compressed speech, where it may lose intelligibility due to signal distortion produced by the compression process. If the latter is the case, we might expect to find that, in the early stages of learning to read, auding is more efficient than reading. With extensive practice in reading, however, we might expect to find reading more efficient than auding. That is indeed what the review of literature summarized in Figure 10.4 (p. 305) reveals for a large part of the adult population.

Though the data on optimal and maximal auding and reading rates support the hypothesis that both reading and auding use the same, or similar, internal-language process (as suggested by the reading-potential concept), it does not rule out the possibility that it is the rate of thinking that limits information processing by eye and by ear, not the rate of some internal-language process (see Sticht et al., 1974, pp. 92–107, and Carver, 1981, for further analyses of these problems).

Whether it is thinking or internal languaging that is operating to set potential levels for reading rate, the fact that auding is acquired earlier than reading permits the use of auding rate as an indicator of potential reading rate, in the same manner that auding comprehension is an indicator of potential-reading comprehension, as suggested by the research of Loban (1964) and that summarized in Figure 10.3. This concept is discussed further later. For applications of the reading potential concept to the assessment of auding and reading skills, see Sticht and Beck (1976) and Carroll (1977).

The Auding to Reading Transfer Concept

If reading builds upon a foundation of the person's earlier acquired oral language competence, as suggested in the code, meaning, and psycholinguistic approaches to reading, then it follows that raising the oral language base should elevate reading ability. This is the basis for preschool language and experiential enrichment programs.

In this section, we will consider six lines of research that explore the auding to reading transfer concept: (1) research using the simultaneous auding and reading of messages which involves the transformation of auding and reading inputs into some comparable internal form for the making of same-different judgments;

(2) research involving the auding of messages and the subsequent reading of the same messages, with interest in whether or not, or to what extent, prior auding facilitates reading-task performance; (3) studies that measure various aspects of comprehension of passages, presented either for auding or reading; (4) studies that have evaluated the effects of training in auding on subsequent reading-test performance; (5) preschool and K-3 intervention programs; and (6) research concerned with the concept of reading to auding transfer, which should also occur if auding and reading share and develop the same internal language.

Simultaneous auding and reading.   The oral and written shared-language position suggests that in learning to read, the person becomes capable of forming internal-language representations from written-language displays that are the same as those formed from spoken-language displays. This was examined by Sticht and Beck (1976) for adults with reading skills ranging from the 2nd-grade level to the 12th-grade level, as measured by the *Gates-MacGinitie Reading Tests, Survey D* (Gates & MacGinitie, 1965). The subjects were asked to participate in the development of an experimental literacy assessment battery, a section of which involved a simultaneous auding and reading task. In this task, subjects were asked to aud a tape-recorded message of ninth-grade-reading difficulty and simultaneously to read a printed version of the passage. At varying intervals, the taped message was arranged to speak a different word than was printed on the written message, though the spoken and printed words both made sense in the context of the message. The person was asked to circle the mismatches between the spoken and printed messages. It was assumed that to perform this task, the person had to transform the externally displayed oral and written language into the same form of internally represented language and to make a same-different judgment. In developing the task, it was first assumed that the people performing the simultaneous auding and reading task all had adequate oral language vocabulary and syntax to represent internally the spoken message. Then, we reasoned that poor readers would not be able efficiently to transform the written version of the story into the same internal form as the spoken version, then to make a same-difference judgment, circle the mismatch, maintain the auding of the message, pick up their place in the written display, and track along at the rate of the voice presenting the spoken display. As reading skill improved, it was reasoned that the people would more efficiently transform the written form into internal forms, like those resulting from auding, and perform the remaining components of the task in a more efficient manner. In this task, then, it was reasoned that the internal oral language form provides a type of template to which the written-language form could be fit for making a match/mismatch judgment. In this case, then, transfer from auding to reading means making the oral-language form available as a template which can serve both as a cue for recoding the written word and as a template for making same-different decisions.

An additional factor in the simultaneous auding and reading task, is the use of grammatical knowledge. It was reasoned that poorer readers would not be able to utilize oral language grammatical knowledge to facilitate the holding of messages in working memory while also allocating the focal attention needed in making required transformations of written language into internal language forms, performing the mismatch response task, and so on. More proficient readers were expected to have more focal attention to perform the mismatch, and so on, components of the task because they can transform written words automatically into internal language, and they can automatically utilize grammar knowledge to hold and efficiently process language information in working memory.

Following the above reasoning, it was anticipated that performance of the simultaneous auding and reading task, with the detection of mismatches, should be positively correlated with reading ability.

The results confirmed the expectation, with correlations of .58, .66, .74, and .71 for Gates-MacGinitie reading and the mismatch task when the rate of presentation of the spoken message was increased from 100 wpm to 150, 200, and 250 wpm for four different segments of the 1200-word message. To detect 60% of the mismatches at each of the four rates of presentation of the spoken message, Gates-MacGinitie reading grade-level scores of 5.6, 6.6, 7.6, and 9.8 were needed. Thus, within and between rates of speech, higher performance on the mismatch task was positively correlated with reading skill. These findings are interpreted as indicating that it is possible to map reading onto the same internal language forms as those previously developed for auding or, stated otherwise, that the earlier developed oral language forms can be transferred to the reading task to facilitate it. The discrepancy between the deaf and hearing discussed above is consistent with this interpretation of the facilitative role of oral language in learning to read.

Auding and then reading messages. If knowledge acquired by auding transfers to become accessible by reading when that skill is acquired, then it can be expected that people who first aud a message and then complete a written cloze test made up of the same message should perform better on the written test than people who take the cloze test without previously having auded the message. Research by Sticht and Glasnapp (1972) applied this procedure, using young men of high- and low-verbal abilities and materials of 5th-, 8th-, and 14th-grade reading difficulty. Results showed that auding the passage before taking the reading test facilitated the performance on the reading test for men of both verbal aptitude groups and for all levels of difficulty. Additional research reported in the Sticht and Glasnapp study (1972) and by Sticht (1968, 1969a, 1969b) shows the same transfer from auding to reading-test performance, using fill-in-the-blank recall-reading tests in addition to cloze tests, indicating that the transfer is independent of the recall-task-response requirements.

Comprehension following auding or reading. If oral and written languages share the same vocabulary and syntax, then we can expect that the meaning or comprehension that results from auding will be activated by reading, once skill in that language process is achieved and, thus, comprehension following auding or reading of the same materials should produce the same meaning structure. Tests of this hypothesis have been made by Kintsch and various collaborators, utilizing techniques for analyzing the micropropositional and macropropositional structures that comprise a spoken or written message.

Kintsch, Kozminsky, Streby, McKoon, and Keenan (1975, Experiment 3) presented paragraphs for reading or auding that were equated for the number of propositions but differed in length and number of different word concepts used as arguments of the propositions. Using college students as subjects and limiting the time allowed for reading to that needed to present the paragraphs aurally, they found that level of recall was identical for both methods of presentation (49 percent recalled following reading, 50 percent following auding). More important, Kintsch and his associates report that while the variables of paragraph length and number of different arguments contained in the paragraphs affected recall, these effects did *not* differ for auding or reading.

In a second investigation, Kintsch and Kozminsky (1977) analyzed college students' story-recall summaries in terms of their propositional content, using an objective scoring technique devised by Kintsch (1974), following auding (presentation rate fixed) and reading (presentation-rate subject controlled). Although subjects were found to add more idiosyncratic detail to their summaries following an auding presentation, recall following auding or reading was similar in terms of recall of the propositions used in the stories and in the relationship among the relative weights of three identified structural categories of the stories (i.e., exposition, complication, and resolution of the single episode contained in each story) and the number of propositions recalled in each. The results were taken as support for the assumption that a "common core of comprehension processes . . . underlie both listening and skilled reading" (p. 491).

The same conclusion emerges from a study conducted by Smiley et al. (1977). These researchers analyzed recall summaries of stories presented for auding or reading (presentation time matched) to groups of good and poor reading ability seventh graders. The stories presented were divided into individual idea units by majority consensus of 21 judges as to the existence of consecutive sections of prose which "contained an idea and/or represented a pausal unit, that is, a place where a reader might pause" (p. 384). These units were then ranked for relative importance. Four rankings were used, with a rank of 4 going to the most important units and a rank of 1 to the least important units. The subjects' written recall protocols were scored for retention of the "main point of each idea unit . . . irrespective of the wording" (p. 384). Results showed that the comprehension of both groups bore some relationship to the variable of ranked importance of prose units, albeit to a lesser degree with the poor readers, and this relationship obtained whether the material was presented for auding or reading. As pointed out by the authors, this finding is "consistent with the notion that comprehension of heard or read material involves the same processes" (p. 386).

Walker (1976) had eleventh-grade students view and aud a videotape discussion about three topics and then either produce a written recall protocol or read a written version of the discussion, with all "um's," "ah's," and verbal "mazes" that are characteristic of spontaneous speech removed. Following the reading of the passages, students produced written recall protocols. These protocols were scored for number of recalled ideas, number of nondistorted recalled ideas, number of recalled ideas demonstrating appropriate relationships to the context of the messages, and percentage of response units that were imported from outside the discussions. Results showed that both listening while viewing the videotape and reading the more focused written passages permitted students to perform the recall tasks, though recall following reading was greater.

Regarding importations, or intrusions of ideas not in the messages, in two out of three passages, listening while viewing the videotape produced more importations than followed reading. In the third passage, there was no difference. Thus, again, the capabilities involved in auding, such as selective attending to speech to reconstruct an internal message, were demonstrated to transfer to reading. The fact that the written passages had already been focused may have permitted more selective attention to be brought to bear on the central ideas. This plus the fact that people at the eleventh-grade level will usually have had a great deal of practice in learning from written language may account for the observation that recall *quantity* was greater following reading than auding, but the same *types* of information were recalled following both modes of presentation.

The work by Kintsch and colleagues, Smiley and colleagues, and Walker is consistent in revealing that comprehension following both auding and reading is structurally similar—as indicated by propositions recalled, important ideas recalled, and relationships established to knowledge not given in the messages, as in Walker's importation measure. However, it does not necessarily indicate auding to reading transfer. It may represent reading to auding transfer because the ages/grades of subjects mean they had time to learn the peculiarities of written language. Either way, however, the results support the suggestion that, internally, reading and auding are the same language (see Carr & Evans, 1981; Carr, Varus, & Brown, 1983; Royer, 1983, for similar conclusions).

Effects of auding training on reading.   A large number of studies have evaluated the effects upon subsequent reading-task performance of prior training in various auding tasks. An earlier review of much of this literature (Sticht et al., 1974) indicated that whereas many of the studies were methodologically flawed, 12 were found adequate to meaningfully evaluate transfer from auding to reading. Of these, 10 reported successful transfer of comprehension skills trained by auding to reading situations, whereas only 2 studies failed to demonstrate successful transfer.

The successful demonstrations of transfer used a variety of training programs. Some included training in listening to recall events, ideas, or details; some trained listening to predict outcomes or to draw conclusions or inferences; some trained listening to follow directions. In testing for transfer, similar skills were performed by reading. The variety of transferred skills makes more impressive the findings of transfer from auding to reading.

Intervention programs.   An extensive review of early childhood programs to develop the intellectual and verbal (oral) skills of preschool children and K-3 children is given by Beller (1973). Programs have focused on direct training of children or the training of parents, mostly mothers, to interact in special nurturing ways with their children. Beller's review seems to indicate that a great many approaches to intervention can produce significant improvements in children's preschool and, later, in-school achievement. Thus, these programs, though they confound strict oral language training with other treatments, support the concept of oracy to literacy transfer.

Literacy to oracy transfer.   The concept of literacy to oracy transfer is important for its potential as a means of understanding why some children arrive at school with a high level of skill in oral language and subsequently do well in the written language, as indicated by Loban's data above. Two types of transfer may be considered in the literacy to oracy transfer concept. On the one hand, there is the transfer of new vocabulary and conceptual knowledge that is learned by reading (and writing) to the individual's language and semantic memory which, according to the reading-potential concept, are common to auding and speaking. In this case, then, we expect the more highly educated, widely read person to have a larger vocabulary and knowledge base to draw upon in speaking and auding and to speak in a more "literate" manner of speech, with more precision and less redundancy, fewer word mazes, and so on. As indicated by Wilkinson (1971), this is what is observed in higher-socioeconomic, better-educated groups.

Significantly, a second form of literacy to oracy transfer seems to occur when the more highly literate parents transfer their literacy to the oral language skill of their children. Hess and Holloway (1979) review considerable literature which suggests that more highly educated (higher-socioeconomic) mothers produce children with higher preschool oral language skills, such as measured by Loban (1964), and that this is accomplished by the mother speaking more with the child, in a more intelligible manner, and about a wider range of topics known to the child. In addition, the more highly educated parents are more likely to spend more time reading books to their children, thereby exposing them to a literate manner of speech, and the more highly educated are likely to have more reading materials around the house and to spend more time reading, thus, modeling the value of reading and how reading materials are used. Although the last two activities do not directly provide literacy to oracy experiences for the child, they provide implicit knowledge about books and how to use them that may permit the child to understand more readily what the teacher is talking about when formal schooling begins. In this sense, such knowledge may improve the comprehension of oral language.

Summary. To summarize briefly this section on the oracy to literacy transfer concept, we have presented evidence to suggest that (1) in learning to read, people become capable of transferring what they know about aurally received words to the recognition of words presented in written passages; (2) auding messages prior to reading them permit greater recall of what was read; (3) elementary school students and college students comprehend both auding and reading passages by developing comparable recall structures, suggesting that comparable comprehension structures are developed while auding and reading; (4) experimental studies of the effects of auding training on subsequent reading-test performance as well as large-scale preschool and early-school intervention studies, have indicated that such training facilitates later achievement in reading; and (5) in the concept of literacy to oracy transfer, we come full cycle and note that the language skills and knowledge acquired through literacy become accessible to the oracy skills and, through processes of child-parent communication and the modeling of literacy behaviors by parents, an intergenerational transfer of the parent's literacy skills to the child's oracy skills may take place. Then, as Loban's (1964) data indicate, these children arrive at school with the oracy skills that provide for a high reading potential and (as indicated in the next section) this gap between oracy and literacy is closed as the child acquires reading skill.

Closing the Gap between Auding and Reading

According to the reading-potential concept, if auding and reading ability are assessed developmentally, we should find a decreasing difference between auding and reading-test scores. Figure 10.4 presents the results from 31 studies that compared auding and reading ability in groups of subjects ranging from first graders through adults (see Sticht et al., 1974, for a more thorough description of the data base of Figure 10.4). The figure shows, for data grouped into five grade levels, the proportion of comparisons for which auding performance surpassed reading performance (A > R), auding and reading performance were equivalent (A = R), and auding performance was inferior to reading performance (A < R). The figure indicates that up to the seventh grade, auding surpasses reading on the average, whereas at the seventh grade, one is equally likely to find auding surpassing reading and reading equal to or surpassing auding. At the adult level, almost half the studies reviewed showed reading surpassing auding, reflecting, we surmise, the extensive practice in learning from written texts that characterizes schooling in the middle and secondary schools. With the exception of the blind, little learning of difficult materials by auding is required in school (or outside of school for that matter).

The data of Figure 10.4, which are composed of a great variety of auding and reading tasks, are confirmed by the data obtained by Durrell and Brassard (1969) in the norming of the Durrell Listening-Reading series, a test battery designed to assess the gap between auding and reading skills. The national standardization and norming data indicate that auding and reading scores converge in the middle of the sixth grade for paragraph comprehension and around the eighth grade for paragraph comprehension and vocabulary scores combined. These data are clearly consistent with those of Figure 10.4.

Rate of auding and reading.   As discussed earlier, the concept of reading potential includes not only the development of parity between eye and ear in

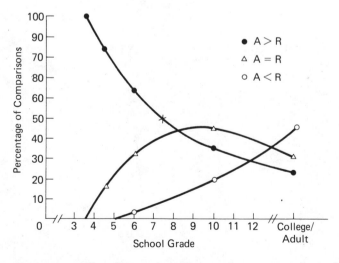

FIGURE 10.4 Comparison of auding and reading performance at five schooling levels.

what can be comprehended and how well, but also the development of parity in rate of processing. In other words, in learning to read, one should become both as accurate *and efficient* in processing language by eye as he or she is at processing language by ear.

Table 10.1 presents data obtained by Taylor (1964) in a study of silent reading rates of subjects ranging from first grade through college. Here, we see that reading rate gradually increases with grade level to 280 wpm as students reach the college level. This reading rate is quite similar to that reported by Carver (1973a, 1973b), who found that a rate of 300 wpm was optimal for both auding and reading in college students, suggesting that when reading ability is fully developed no gap between auding and reading rates exists. Although the necessary developmental studies have not been conducted, it is reasonable to assume that such a gap in auding and reading rates does exist early in the reading training period of the child, and quite obviously this is so before the child has learned to read (see Carver, 1982, 1983 for additional analyses of auding and reading rates).

Assessing the auding and reading gap. In research by Sticht and Beck (1976), a Literacy Assessment Battery (LAB) was developed to measure the effectiveness and efficiency with which middle-grade, secondary, and adult students aud and read. Among other things, this battery assesses the person's ability to store information presented orally or in writing and to recall factual information in tests immediately following auding or reading. Reading time is strictly controlled to match the time available for auding, so that auding and reading efficiency is assessed.

Figure 10.5 presents the results obtained when the LAB was administered, along with the *Gates-MacGinitie Reading Tests, Survey D* (1965), to a group of adult men. Figure 10.5 plots the results of the LAB paragraph subtests as a

TABLE 10.1   READING
RATES ACROSS GRADE
LEVELS

Grade Level	Reading Rate (wpm)
1	80
2	115
3	138
4	158
5	173
6	185
7	195
8	204
9	214
10	224
11	237
12	250
College	280

After Taylor (1964).

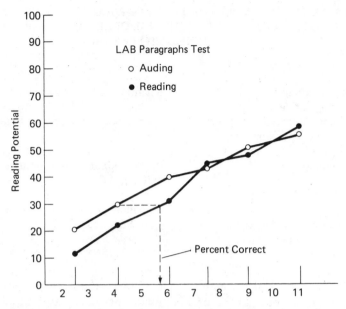

FIGURE 10.5   Mean percent correct for the LAB paragraphs test as a function of reading ability measured by the Gates-MacGinitie Reading Tests, Survey D.

function of Gates-MacGinitie reading-grade-level score. These data indicate that auding surpasses reading until a measured skill at the seventh-grade level is obtained; at that point, and beyond, there is equivalence in accuracy and efficiency of processing by ear and by eye.

The data for adults, the data of Figure 10.4, of Durrell and Brassard (1969), and the data on reading rates (Taylor, 1964) are consistent with the idea that in learning to read, one closes the gap between tasks which, at one time, can only be performed by auding or are performed much better by auding, and that later can be performed equally as well by reading as by auding. Further, the data indicate that the development of performance parity between auding and reading may require, on the average, seven years or so. This is considerably longer than the end of the third grade, which traditionally has been regarded as when students stop "learning to read" and start "reading to learn." Precisely what is happening that makes this additional time necessary is not certain, though it may be that in the first three or four years of school, children learn the rudiments of reading-decoding (including the decoding of phrase and sentence units), while an additional two to three years of practice is required for the automaticity of reading to equal that of auding.

DISCUSSION

The various lines of research reviewed above firmly establish that a strong interdependence exists between auding and reading and that, in many respects, it is useful to regard reading as a second signaling system for speech. There is bountiful evidence that a great number of tasks can be identified that follow the *oracy*

TABLE 10.2   EXAMPLES OF TASKS IN WHICH RECODING OF
WRITTEN LANGUAGE INTO INTERNAL ORAL LANGUAGE *IS* OR
IS NOT LIKELY TO OCCUR

IS	*IS NOT*
Reading aloud	Scanning alphabetical lists
Reading connected discourse	Looking up serial numbers
Holding information in working memory for application (e.g., a telephone number, a procedural step)	Searching print for target letters, words
	Responding to simple signs (e.g., exit, stop)
Studying a difficult text	Encountering a difficult to pronounce word in a text (e.g.,
Memorizing words, phrases, or longer linguistic units	sphygmomanometer)

to literacy developmental sequence, that is, tasks that are performed at one stage of development only in the oral language mode are later capable of being performed using the written language. Furthermore, the data for hearing persons compared to the deaf indicate that though reading *can* be accomplished without the mediation of an oral language comprehension system, the presence of such a system greatly facilitates the rate of acquisition and the extent of skill that is achieved in reading. Thus, hearing persons may have an option in reading: they may process the written language as visual symbols, as the deaf must, or they may mediate reading by means of the oral language system. Whether the latter is done or not is most likely a complex function of the person's instructional history and current skill, the task, and the situation at hand. In this regard, it has been suggested that tasks which involve the maintenance of information in working memory are likely to induce the recoding of written into internal oral language (Kleiman, 1975). In some cases, this may even be accompanied by speech movements of the lips, perhaps with accompanying subdued speaking aloud. Table 10.2 presents a cursory and not mutually exclusive list of tasks in which recoding to internal oral language is or is not likely to occur, assuming a moderately skilled reader.

Theoretical Concerns

Given the large body of research on reading and the continuous debate over which approach to reading is the best, we should emphasize the importance of the finding of agreement among the three major theoretical positions currently holding sway in the reading research literature: the code, meaning, and psycholinguistic positions. As indicated earlier, all three positions share these fundamental understandings:

1. Oral language skills develop to a fairly high level prior to the development of written language skills.
2. Oral and written languages share much the same lexicon (vocabulary) and syntax (grammar).

In contrast and like Smith, the Goodmans focus on reading for meaning at the outset. Also, as with Smith, the Goodmans consider that, on the one hand, "the deep structure and rules for generating the surface structure are the same for both language modes," yet, on the other hand, "oral- and written-language processes become parallel for those who become literate; language users can choose the process that better suits their purposes" (Goodman & Goodman, 1977, p. 323).

These statements, like those quoted earlier by Smith, seem somewhat contradictory. It is not clear how the oral and written languages can be based on the same rules for generating surface structure and yet be parallel rather than convergent. Nor does the extensive literature reviewed earlier regarding oracy to literacy transfer support the idea that, in the typical case, oral and written languages develop in parallel. Rather, as also noted by the Goodmans, "As children become literate, the two systems become interactive, and children use each to support the other when they need to" (Goodman & Goodman, 1979, p. 150).

The latter statement implies that, perhaps in the early stages of reading, the oral and written languages are developed more or less independently and in parallel, as suggested by the Goodmans. This would account for the ability of the congenitally deaf to acquire some skill in reading. However, in order for high levels of written language skills to develop, as the person becomes more literate, the oral and written languages converge, or become interactive, drawing on the same internal lexicon and syntax to encode and decode meaning rapidly. This would account for the oracy to literacy transfer phenomenon and the observation that the deaf have great difficulty in achieving high levels of reading.

History and Individual Development

Interestingly, the foregoing account, which seems to accommodate code, meaning, and psycholinguistic approaches to reading, appears to parallel the historical development of the written language. Historically, the eventual *similarities* and *functional* equivalences (for some purposes) of oral and written languages appear to have occurred, in large measure, because the more or less permanent nature of the graphic display permitted the study of graphic symbols as communication tools. This study, in turn, may have led to reflection on the nature of speech, which led to the discovery of the structural elements of speech, which (turning the wheel again) led to the discovery of graphic marks for representing elements of speech—the alphabet (Wrolstad, 1976).

This design process has been an evolutionary process, not necessarily a process of conscious design, though some individuals may have understood explicitly what they were doing when they introduced graphic symbols that stood for sounds rather than ideas. In his review of the history of reading, Huey (1908/1968) makes this point, and he succinctly expresses the urge that motivated the development, over centuries, of an alphabetic writing system to represent the spoken language. Following a chapter in which he discusses the historical beginnings of reading in gesture ("The first pictures, however, were drawn in the air and were read as fast as drawn" [p. 189]) and picture writing, Huey describes the functional motivators that lead to the historical convergence of oral and written language:

During the ages in which picture-writing was practically the sole means of written communication, the various *spoken* languages had been keeping pace in their development with the needs of the civilization in which they were used. The further need was of some sort of "graphs" which would represent to the eye the sounds of these spoken languages *as* sounds. This would solve for all time the problem of facile communication, in writing, of all that man had to communicate. But it was very long before it dawned upon men that all of the words which men utter are expressed by a few sounds, and that all that was needed was "to select from the big and confused mass of ideograms, phonograms, and all their kin, a certain number of signs to denote, unvaryingly, certain sounds." Such a step meant the birth of an alphabet, "one of the greatest and most momentous triumphs of the human mind." By the use of only twenty-six simple characters we may represent to the eye all that men say or have said, in languages whose vocabularies have enlarged until they number hundreds of thousands of words. (p. 203)

The evolution of the alphabet from early gestural signing, through pictographic representation, to phonographic representation seems to be recapitulated in the typical child who grows up in a literate society. Children, and adults, retain the skills of our preliterate ancestors in comprehending and representing thought in nonlinguistic visual-graphic displays. We gesture, we draw pictures, we use logographs. But because of the wit of our ancestors in perceiving the functional utility of being able to represent efficiently in a permanent record our ephemeral speech, we command today a most powerful tool for communication, problem solving, and learning: literacy. And because of the oracy to literacy transfer effect, we have the opportunity to develop strategies for education that will increase literacy through activities to improve oracy skills, while we work in an efficient manner to bring about the oracy to literacy transfer through code, meaning, and psycholinguistic approaches.

SUMMARY

In this chapter, the three most prevalent theoretical positions regarding listening and reading were identified as the code (Chall, 1967), meaning (Smith, 1971), and psycholinguistic (Goodman & Goodman, 1979) theories. It was noted that, whereas the latter theories seem to hold that listening and reading are independent and parallel processes, careful reading of these positions reveals that they, like the code position, actually regard reading as building upon and becoming interactive with earlier developed oral language skills.

In addition to the theoretical evidence to suggest that reading and listening both build upon a common language and knowledge base, empirical studies were reviewed bearing upon three concepts derived from the interactive view of listening and reading. The *reading-potential* concept suggests that if a person's reading skills build upon earlier acquired listening (auding) skills, then the latter establish a goal or early potential for reading in the novice reader.

Closely related to the reading-potential concept is the idea that in learning to read, one *closes the gap* between auding and reading, that is, people become capable of recognizing and comprehending in printed form words and sentences that they previously could comprehend only in the spoken form. Finally, and closely related to the previous concepts, there is the notion of the *oracy to literacy transfer sequence,* which forms the basis for reading intervention programs which aim at improving student's oral language skills as means for improving their reading language skills.

An extensive literature exists supporting the veracity of the three concepts derived from the interactive position regarding oral and written language. Taken together, both the empirical evidence and the three theoretical positions argue for the soundness of an approach to reading development which includes extensive activities to develop oral language knowledge and skills, while activities which focus upon bridging the gap between oral and written language (e.g., sound decoding programs) are emphasized at other times in the instructional day.

While it is recognized that the unique properties of the written language, for example, its permanence, use of contrast and color, and capability of being arrayed in space, makes possible the performance of tasks using writing and other graphic representations that do not directly build on oral language (see Sticht, 1978, for a further discussion of differences between oral and written language), these *unique* properties of the written language should not lead to approaches to teaching reading, especially early reading, which deny the fundamental *commonalities* among oral and written languages that have been achieved through the ages by "one of the greatest and most momentous triumphs of the human mind," the alphabet.

REFERENCES

Beller, E. K.   Research on organized programs of early education. In R. W. Travers (Ed.) *Second handbook of research on teaching.* Chicago: Rand McNally, 1973.

Brown, D. P.   *Auding as the primary language ability.* Unpublished doctoral dissertation, Stanford University, 1954.

Carr, T. H., Vavrus, L. G., & Brown, T. L.   *Cognitive skill maps of reading ability.* Paper presented at the annual meeting of the American Educational Research Association, April 1983.

Carr, T. H., & Evans, M. A.   Influence of learning conditions on patterns of cognitive skill in young children. *Paper presented at the biennial meeting of the Society for Research in Child Development.* Boston, April 1981.

Carroll, J. B.   *Language and thought.* Englewood Cliffs, N.J.: Prentice-Hall, 1964.

Carroll, J. B.   Developmental parameters of reading comprehension. In J. Guthrie (Ed.) *Cognition, curriculum, and comprehension.* Newark, Del.: International Reading Association, 1977.

Carver, R. P.   Effect of increasing the rate of speech presentation upon comprehension. *Journal of Educational Psychology,* 1973, 65, 118–126. (a)

Carver, R. P.   Understanding, information processing, and learning from prose materials. *Journal of Educational Psychology,* 1973, 65, 118–126. (b)

Carver, R. P.   *Reading comprehension and auding theory.* Springfield, Ill.: Charles C. Thomas, 1981.

Carver, R. P.   Optimal rate for reading prose. *Reading Research Quarterly*, 1982, *18*, 56–89.

Carver, R. P.   Is reading rate constant or flexible? *Reading Research Quarterly*, 1983, *18*, 190–215.

Chall, J. S.   *Learning to read: The great debate.* New York: McGraw-Hill, 1967.

Danks, J. H.   Comprehension in listening and reading: Same or different? *Report of the Interdisciplinary Institute in Reading and Child Development*, University of Delaware, July 1977.

Downing, J.   *Reading and reasoning.* New York: Springer-Verlag, 1979.

Durrell, D. D., & Brassard, M. B.   *Manual for listening and reading tests,* New York: Harcourt, Brace and World, 1969.

Fries, C. C.   *Linguistics and reading.* New York: Holt, Rinehart & Winston, 1963.

Fullmer, R.   *Maximal reading and auding rates.* Unpublished doctoral dissertation, Harvard University, 1980.

Gates, A. I., & MacGinitie, W. H.   *Gates-MacGinitie reading tests, survey D.* New York: Columbia University, Teachers College Press, 1965.

Gibson, E. J., & Levin, H.   *The psychology of reading.* Cambridge: MIT Press, 1975.

Goodman, K. S.   The psycholinguistic nature of the reading process. In K. S. Goodman (Ed.), *The psycholinguistic nature of the reading process.* Detroit: Wayne State University Press, 1968.

Goodman, K. S., & Goodman, Y. M.   Learning about psycholinguistic processes by analyzing oral reading. *Harvard Educational Review*, 1977, *47*, 317–333.

Goodman, K. S., & Goodman, Y. M.   Learning to read is natural. In L. Resnick & P. Weaver (Eds.) *Theory and practice of early reading* (Vol. 1). Hillsdale, N.J.: Erlbaum, 1979.

Hammill, D. D., & McNutt, G.   Language abilities and reading: A review of the literature on their relationships. *Elementary School Journal*, 1980, *80*, 269–277.

Hess, R. D., & Holloway, S.   *The intergenerational transmission of literacy.* Washington, D.C.: National Institute of Education, June 1979.

Huey, E. B.   *The psychology and pedagogy of reading.* New York: Cambridge: MIT Press, 1968. (Originally published, 1908.)

Kintsch, W.   *The representation of meaning in memory.* Hillsdale, N.J.: Erlbaum Associates, 1974.

Kintsch, W., & Kozminsky, E.   Summarizing stories after reading and listening. *Journal of Educational Psychology*, 1977, *69*, 491–499.

Kintsch, W., Kozminsky, E., Streby, W., McKoon, G., & Keeman, J.   Comprehension and recall of text as a function of content variables. *Journal of Verbal Learning and Verbal Behavior*, 1975, *14*, 196–214.

Kleiman, G. M.   Speech recoding in reading. *Journal of Verbal Learning and Verbal Behavior*, 1975, *14*, 323–339.

Lenneberg, E. H.   *Biological foundations of language.* New York: Wiley, 1967.

Levy, B. A.   Speech processes during reading. In Lesgold, A., Pellegrino, J., Fokkema, S., & Glass, R. (Eds.), *Cognitive psychology and instruction.* New York: Plenum, 1978.

Loban, W.   *Language ability: Grades seven, eight, and nine* (Project No. 1131). University of California, Berkeley, March 1964.

Resnick, L. B.   Theories and prescriptions for early reading instruction. In: L. Resnick, and P. Weaver (Eds.), *Theory and practice of early reading* (Vol. 2). Hillsdale, N.J.: Erlbaum, 1979.

Royer, J. M.   *The sentence verification technique as a measure of listening and reading comprehension.* Paper presented at the annual meeting of the American Educational Research Association, April 1983.

Smiley, S. S., Oakley, D. D., Worthen, D., Campione, J. C., & Brown, A. L.   Recall of thematically relevant material by adolescent good and poor readers as a function of written versus oral presentation. *Journal of Educational Psychology*, 1977, *69*, 381–387.

Smith, F.   *Understanding reading.* New York: Holt, Rinehart & Winston, 1971.

Smith, F.   *Comprehension and learning.* New York: Holt, Rinehart & Winston, 1975.

Smith, F.   Making sense of reading—and of reading instruction. *Harvard Educational Review*, 1977, *47*, 386–395.

Sticht, T. G.   Some relationships of mental aptitude, reading and listening using normal and time-compressed speech. *Journal of Communication*, 1968, *18*, 243–258.

Sticht, T. G.   Comprehension of repeated time—compressed recordings. *Journal of Experimental Education*, 1969, *37*, 60–62. (a)

Sticht, T. G.   Some interactions of speech rate, signal distortion, and certain linguistic factors in listening comprehension. *AV Communication Review*, 1969, *17*, 159–171. (b)

Sticht, T. G.   The acquisition of literacy by children and adults. In F. Murray and J. Pikulsky (Eds.), *The acquisition of reading.* Baltimore, Md.: University Park Press, 1978.

Sticht, T. G., Beck, L. B., Hauke, R. N., Kleiman, G. M., & James, J. H.   *Auding and reading: A developmental model.* Alexandria, Va.: Human Resources Research Organization, 1974.

Sticht, T. G., & Beck, L. J.   *Experimental literacy assessment battery (LAB)* (Final Rep.: AFHRL–TR–76–51, Air Force Human Resources Laboratory, Technical Training Division). Lowry Air Force Base, Colo., August 1976.

Sticht, T. G., & Glassnapp, D. R.   Effects of speech rate, selection difficulty, association strength and mental aptitude on learning by listening. *Journal of Communication*, 1972, *22*, 174–188.

Taylor, S. E.   *Listening.* Washington, D.C.: National Education Association, 1964.

Walker, L.   Comprehending writing and spontaneous speech. *Reading Research Quarterly*, 1976, *11*, 144–167.

Wilkinson, A.   *The foundations of language.* London: Oxford University Press, 1971.

Wrolstad, M. E.   A manifesto for visible language. *Visible Language*, 1976, *10*, 5–40.

Ziegler, E., & Valentine, J. (Eds.), *Project head start.* New York: Macmillan, 1979.

11 THE STRUCTURE OF TEXT

Bonnie J. F. Meyer and
G. Elizabeth Rice

In recent years, researchers in the area of reading have been investigating the effects of the structure among the ideas presented in a text on what the reader learns and retains from the text. Texts are obviously more organized than simple lists of sentences or ideas, and understanding their organization can shed light on important aspects of the reading process. This chapter is designed to provide an overview of some of the ways the structure of text can be described. It will include a brief historical review of contributions from a number of disciplines, a review of the more commonly used descriptive systems in present-day reading research, and a discussion of the issues of current concern to researchers in the area.

We use the term text structure to refer to how the ideas in a text are interrelated to convey a message to a reader. Some of the ideas in the text are of central importance to the author's message, while others are of less importance. Thus, text structure specifies the logical connections among ideas as well as subordination of some ideas to others.

From the point of view of reading research, specifying the structure of a text or passage to be read can provide several benefits. First, text structure is a significant dimension along which text selections may be evaluated as to their similarities and differences. Second, specifying the text structure allows the researcher to identify the amount and type of information which readers remember from text. Third, it allows identification of variations which may arise between the text and the reader's understanding of the text.

The problem of specifying variables on which passages are similar or different is crucial for research on learning or reading prose. Unless these variables can be identified, results obtained from one passage cannot be generalized to another passage. In the past, attempts at solving this problem have involved the classification of passages on the basis of measures of readability. These measures have included such variables as sentence length, vocabulary density and rarity, and idea density (Chall, 1958). These measures have had limited success; they deal with surface factors of prose and are not concerned with the meaning of prose and the manner in which the content is organized to convey this meaning to the reader. More recent readability theorists have found it essential to include text structure variables in their theories (Kintsch & Vipond, 1979; Swanson, 1979; see the chapter by Klare, this volume). The structure of a passage depicts the relationships among the ideas in the passage. It shows how authors of text have organized their ideas to convey a message, the primary purpose of their writing endeavor. Therefore, the structure of a passage captures one of the primary attributes of prose. This structure dimension in prose has potential for becoming an important and useful variable by which to characterize passages.

A second problem for reading researchers often is to identify the amount and type of information which a reader remembers from a text. An essential element of this problem is finding a method of scoring what is remembered from the passage. One option for solving this problem is to write questions about information in the passage and then to evaluate readers' responses to these questions. This is the approach that has been taken by most educators. Instead of asking questions after a passage, psychologists have tended to ask readers to write down all they can remember from a passage. This presents the problem of whether to count as correct only word for word (verbatim) recall or deciding also to count as correct substantive paraphrase of the ideas from a passage. The former is completely objective, while the latter requires judgment on the part of the scorer as to whether or not an idea is substantially correct. If recall protocols from passages of lengths greater than a few sentences are scored only for verbatim recall, important information is lost about the meaning of the passage that is remembered by readers in their own words, rather than the words of the passage. However, if the passage's structure is analyzed so that the information it contains is divided into units of content and relations, then this analysis can be used to help score just which of the content and relation units were remembered by a reader.

Furthermore, such an analysis and scoring procedure can be used to evaluate variations between the text and the reader's understanding of it. Where the content and structure of both the text and the reader's recall of the text can be specified, these two structures can be compared. In this way, it is possible to discover those aspects of a given text which are easiest and/or hardest for readers to understand. It is also possible to determine if a given reader exhibits a systematic pattern of difficulties with different aspects of text. In this way, analysis of text structure can illuminate important features of both the texts' and the readers' contributions to the reading and understanding process.

Given the potential benefits of a system for specifying the structure of a text, one might expect that researchers would by now have converged on a simple, universally accepted system. Unfortunately, this is not the case. Some of the obstacles are historical: as will be described below, the multiplicity of disciplines involved serves to diversify the text structures proposed at the same time as it enriches our understanding of them.

The more difficult obstacles are those which are inherent in the study of text understanding. Part of the problem arises from the complexity of the reading process. Because the text and the reader interact in this process, it is difficult to isolate purely textual variables. The structure of the text may appear differently to different readers. The most reasonable escape from this problem is to analyze the text from the point of view of the author. However, unless the author provides clear signaling of his/her intended structure or unless the author is available for querying as to intent, problems arise here also. It is sometimes necessary for the analyst to make inferences about the organization intended by the author. Individual differences among analysts in making such inferences can produce variability in the analyses produced.

A final, and very important, reason for the variety of text analysis systems in use at present has to do with the purposes for which they were developed. It is not surprising that different disciplines have different goals for analyzing text structure. Even within reading research, specification of text structure may serve several purposes, as described above. For example, Meyer's system (1975) was designed to provide a hierarchical description of text in a manner suitable for scoring recall protocols for information remembered, while Dawes (1966) and Frederiksen (1975) were more interested in memory storage of logical relationships.

ATTEMPTS TO OUTLINE THE STRUCTURE OF TEXT

A Historical Review of Contributions from a Number of Disciplines

Any discipline which is concerned with either text itself or with the understanding of text will have an interest in theories of text structure. In this section, we will consider briefly the approaches of a number of concerned disciplines, including rhetoric, folklore, linguistics, education, psychology, and artificial intelligence. Research in the area is both multidisciplinary and interdisciplinary, so that dividing the discussion into disciplines is a rather arbitrary procedure, undertaken here for the sake of organization and clarity.

Rhetoric

Classical rhetoric, found in such books as Aristotle's *Rhetoric* (1960) and Cicero's *De Inventione et Topica* (1954), dealt with developing a structure for exposition. Aristotle's rhetoric presented three basic ingredients for communicative discourse: invention, arrangement, and style. Invention guided the development of ideas for writing. Arrangement was the organizational structure of a discourse. Style was the syntactic and semantic devices used by a writer to present his/her message. Invention and arrangement are closely related to text structure; invention assists the writer in developing a logical structure for investigating a topic and arrangement fixes this logical structure into the structure of a text. Invention begins with Aristotle's *topoi* or ways of thinking about a topic; they include causative, possible/impossible, definition, division into parts, and genus/species. They suggest probing questions that a writer can use to explore a topic, such as what causes it? What are its effects? And to what can it be compared? These categories are similar to the relationships which are used to interrelate sentences and paragraphs in present-day systems for analyzing the structure of exposition and narration.

Some contemporary rhetoricians (D'Angelo, 1975, Chapter 2; Gorrell, 1963; Mills, 1977; Williams, 1981) stress the importance of structure and encourage composition instructors to place greater emphasis of this aspect of writing than it has been given in the last two centuries. D'Angelo (1979) stresses teaching students about paradigms, or patterns of organization, which are the structural counterparts of *topoi*. These paradigms are equivalent to the top-level structures of Meyer's prose analysis system (Meyer, 1979, 1981; Meyer & Freedle, in press). Flower and Hayes (1977) encourage writers to use similar patterns of organization or to organize their ideas into a clear hierarchy or issue tree. These trees parallel the macropropositions, or top third of Meyer's hierarchical text structure, as well as Kintsch and van Dijk's (1978) macrostructure; however, the issue trees contain only sketches of the topic content and do not specify interrelationships. Thus, rhetorical theorists of past and present have encouraged writers to write in a manner compatible with many aspects of current discourse analysis procedures.

Folklore

Much of the early work with folktales consisted of classifying similar folktales on the basis of their motifs or subunits of their plots (Bedier, 1893; Propp, 1958; Thompson, 1928, 1932–1936; Volkov, 1924). Propp's work, *Morphology of the Folktale,* marked a move away from particularistic studies of folklore content towards a more abstract approach to story structure. Propp identified a group of 31 functions which, together with rules describing the order in which they could occur, accounted for the content and organization of all the narratives in his collection of Russian stories. In addition, Lord (1960) investigated the patterns which producers of tales (singers) used to create epic Slavic tales.

Expanding on Propp's basic methodology, Colby, an anthropologist, has developed eidochronic analyses or grammars of Eskimo (1973b) and of Ixil Maya (Colby & Cole, 1973) folktales. These grammars describe the hierarchy of rules which govern the occurrence of the different categories of story content, or eidons.

A cautionary note about the application of story grammars from folklore to school and other everyday materials is in order. This has to do with the cultural specificity of some aspects of story structures (Kintsch & Greene, 1978; Rice, 1978). As Colby (1973a) points out, Propp's analysis of Russian tales is not applicable to Eskimo tales, nor is his Eskimo grammar appropriate for Mayan stories. Nevertheless, the general principle of searching for regularities in the organization of prose has stimulated important work in psychology. Much of the story structure research currently underway in psychology (Mandler & Johnson, 1977; Stein & Glenn, 1979; Thorndyke, 1977) uses story descriptions which derive from the work in folklore (see Rumelhart, 1975).

Linguistics

The development of interest in text structure within linguistics has some striking parallels to that experienced in psychology. Early linguists of the structuralist school focused on language units ranging in size from single sounds to complete sentences. Within this paradigm, Harris (1952) examined the distribution of various linguistic features within discourse but did not concern himself with its content or with the organization of that content. The revolution brought about by the transformational-generative grammar approach of Chomsky (1957) did not expand the scope of interest in mainstream linguistics beyond the sentence.

However, inadequacies in the transformational-generative paradigm have led some linguists to increase their scope to encompass larger and larger linguistic contexts (e.g., sociolinguistics—Hymes, 1964; Labov, 1972; and others; experiential linguistics—Lakoff, 1977). A recent review by van Dijk (1979a) describes the development of text grammars, which aim at providing explicit structural descriptions of the linguistic properties of texts. The development of text grammar approaches is largely European and less than a decade old.

Recent work by some linguists (Fillmore, 1968; Grimes, 1975; Halliday, 1968; Halliday & Hasan, 1976; van Dijk, 1977a, 1977b) has attempted to analyze prose in a manner which classifies ideas in a passage according to their role in conveying the total meaning of the passage. Halliday and Grimes have proposed similar theories of discourse. They have identified three distinct sets of relationships in discourse. The first is the organization of the content of discourse. The second relates to the presentation of new information to a listener. The third system is concerned with expressing the speaker's perspective on what information is being related. Most of the examples of the occurrence of these systems of relationships have been in sentences. Although Halliday and Grimes's writing both deal primarily with sentences, they intend the basic principles to be applied to longer discourses and prose. The Meyer analysis system, which is commonly used in reading research, draws heavily from Grimes's theory of prose structure.

Education

Since much of what is learned in the schools is communicated through text or lectures, educators have been interested in studying learning from reading or listening to prose. Carroll (1971) has reviewed the research on learning from discourse by educators. In general, educators have tended not to examine the influence of aspects of the prose itself on which aspects of it are remembered. Instead, the effects of aids, such as special instructions (Flanagan, 1939; Welborn & English, 1937), interspersed questions (Faw & Waller, 1976; Rothkopf & Bisbicos, 1967), training programs (Deverell, 1959), or other variables external to the text itself have been examined to ascertain their usefulness in increasing recall from a passage.

Although, until recently, educational research has not dealt with structure in text, educators (Anderson, 1978; Dechant, 1969; Gainsburg, 1967; Herber, 1970; Niles, 1965; Smith, 1963) in reading and study skills have pointed out its importance for instruction. For examples, Niles's (1965) program for teaching perception of structure in text begins with showing students how ideas are arranged in patterns; common patterns listed are enumerative order (simple listing), time order, cause-effect, and comparison-contrast. These relationships are similar to those identified by rhetoricians and used in current prose analysis systems. However, these educators did not detail a systematic way to identify text structure.

Currently, research relating prose structure to reading comprehension is an active area of research in educational psychology and reading (Drum & Lantaff, 1977; Flood, 1978; Meyer, Haring, Brandt, & Walker, 1980; Mosenthal, 1979; Swanson, 1979). However, educational research has tended to look to other disciplines for its theories of text structure (Meyer, 1981).

Psychology

In contrast to educators' frequent use of prose in studies, in the past, psychologists generally have tended to avoid research with natural prose. This avoidance resulted from a view that learning processes could better be studied with less complex and more easily controlled stimuli, such as lists of nonsense syllables or words, or pairs of these items. Thus, verbal learning research rarely involved the use of sentences or prose. However, some of the learning principles consistently found with lists or words were not found with prose (Kircher, 1971). Not only is prose more complicated, but it contains an organizational structure designed to deliver a message; this primary attribute of prose materials is not found in lists of words or nonsense syllables.

Until the last few years, most investigations in psychology which used prose investigated the generalizability of the effects of variables studied with word lists. In the first few studies in which the organization of prose was considered, the goal of the research was to examine which ideas were remembered from a passage under free-recall conditions and then to relate those ideas to aspects of the information in the passage. These studies include the work of F. C. Bartlett (1932), Gomulicki (1956), Johnson (1970), and Meyer and McConkie (1973) as well as the studies of Crothers (1972), Dawes (1966), Frederiksen (1972), Kintsch and Keenan (1973), and Meyer (1975), all of which relate recall to aspects of structure in a passage.

Prose comprehension is currently one of the most active research areas in psychology (Freedle, 1977, 1979; Trabasso, 1978). In the last 10 years, there has been a dramatic increase in the number of investigators involved in such research. Organization, which has long been a key principle in learning and memory research (Shimmerlik, 1978), is now being examined in relation to structure and comprehension of prose. Beaugrande (1980), Crothers (1972), Frederiksen (1975, 1979), Graesser (1981), Kintsch (1974), and Meyer (1975), among others in psychology and related disciplines, have presented systems for analyzing the structure of expository prose. The Kintsch, Meyer, and Frederiksen systems are the most widely used. These and others will be discussed more fully in a later section of this chapter. Psychologists have also been interested in the analysis of narrative prose, or stories, with quite similar analysis systems being suggested by Mandler and Johnson (1977), Rumelhart (1975), Stein and Glenn (1979), and Thorndyke (1977).

Artificial Intelligence

Several aspects of text structure are relevant to workers in the field of artificial intelligence. Almost all the work in this field is concerned with either the comprehension or the production of natural language which occurs in units larger than single sentences. Systems which concern themselves with the overall or top-level structure of discourse have tended to be top-down; these are production systems which operate with rules for the unfolding of plots. An early system was that of Klein, Aeschlimann, Balsiger, Converse, Court, Foster, Lao, Oakley, and Smith (1973) which generated short mystery stories. More recent and sophisticated work includes that of Simmons (1978) and an interactive story-generating system called TALE-SPIN (Meehan, 1977). This last is based on a problem-solving schema which is similar to those being investigated by psychologists.

With respect to comprehension systems, Charniak's (1972) work with comprehension of children's stories was among the first to deal with problems of discourse. A review of first- and second-generation natural language understanding systems can be found in Wilks (1976). More recent work includes that of Schank and Abelson (1977), which is concerned with explicating the kinds of knowledge structures (including scripts, plans, and goals) which a reader/understander must bring to a text in order to comprehend it, and Wilensky (1978) who has developed a story understanding system (PAM).

Summary

From this brief review, it can be seen that there has been a continuing concern across a number of disciplines with the structure of text. The manner in which an author organizes his ideas is of intrinsic interest to students of literature and of pragmatic interest to those concerned with the communicative aspects of text. Continuing research is beginning to explicate the complex interaction between text structure and reader's knowledge which informs the comprehension process.

Structure Employed to Organize Sentences, Paragraphs, and the Text

In this section, we will begin a more detailed discussion of various structural characteristics of texts. There are three primary levels at which the structure of a text can be analyzed (Meyer, 1981; van Dijk, 1979c). The first is the sentence or micropropositional level, which is concerned with the way sentences cohere and are organized within a text. The second is the paragraph or macropropositional level, which pertains to issues of logical organization and argumentation. The third is that of the top-level structure of the text as a whole.

Micropropositions

A salient property of texts is that they cohere or hang together. Thus, the concern at the lowest level of text structure is with the interrelationships among individual propositions, that is, with how each new proposition or item of information given relates to what has already been presented. A text coheres when the interpretation of one element depends upon or presupposes another (Halliday & Hasan, 1976). Halliday and Hasan have identified five general kinds of cohesive ties to be found in texts, ranging in scope from the syntactic to the pragmatic. These include reference, substitution, ellipsis, conjunction, and lexical cohesion. These are mechanisms by which authors tie their materials together.

Haviland and Clark (1974) have suggested that both the writer and reader participate in a "given-new contract." Under this contract, the writer is constrained to be relevant (i.e., not confuse the reader with extraneous information), to cooperate, and to consider what the reader knows or doesn't know. Thus, the writer constructs his/her sentences so that the "given" or antecedent information (what the reader is expected to know) and the "new" information (what the author is adding to this knowledge) are clearly differentiated. The topic-comment ideas of Clements's (1979), Grimes's (1975), and Halliday's (1968) analysis of staging also address this issue. Research has shown that readers' comprehension is impaired when this contract is violated by putting "new" information into the topic or "given" position in a sentence (Carpenter & Just, 1977; Clark & Haviland, 1974, 1977; Haviland & Clark, 1974; Yekovich & Walker, 1978).

Most of the research on the issue of coherence has been done with two sentence pairs, attempting to systematize our understanding of the way one sentence can relate to another (Clark, 1977). Halliday and Hasan provide analyses of complete texts; however, these simply list all the pairwise relations among sentences. Kintsch and van Dijk (1978) have constructed "coherence graphs" for longer texts. However, they use a very limited notion of coherence, with only a single type of cohesive tie, that of reference (through argument repetition) being represented in the graph. On the other hand, even this limited representation appears to be helpful in accounting for some aspects of a text's readability (see Kintsch & Vipond, 1979).

Macropropositions

The term macroproposition, equivalent to van Dijk's (1977a) macrostructure, is used here to refer to the level of prose analysis at which the topic or gist of portions of the text becomes important. Whereas at the micropropositional level, the relationships between individual sentences or concepts was at issue, at the macropropositional level, the concern is with the relationships among ideas represented in complexes of propositions or paragraphs (cf., Vipond, 1980). The relationships at this level tend to be of a logical or rhetorical sort, as opposed to the more mechanical or syntactic relations discussed in the previous section. Van Dijk gives the following example of a series of sentences which are "linearly coherent" at the micropropositional level, but lack essential macropropositional structuring:

> I bought this typewriter in New York. New York is a large city. Large cities often have financial problems. (van Dijk, 1977a, p. 149)

A number of classifications of the types of logical relations which operate in text have been proposed (Beaugrande, 1980; Frederiksen, 1975; Grimes, 1975; Halliday & Hasan, 1976; Meyer, 1975). Many of the relations proposed are applicable at the micropropositional level of text as well, though they may also be used to relate textual units at the macropropositional level. As an example, Meyer (1975, 1981, 1982, in press, drawing from Grimes, 1975) recognizes five basic groups of rhetorical relations which may hold among segments of text:

a. An *antecedent/consequent* or *covariance* rhetorical relationship shows a causal relationship between topics.

b. A *response* rhetorical relationship includes the remark and reply, question and answer, and problem and solution formats.

c. A *comparison* relationship points out differences and similarities between two or more topics.

d. A *collection* relationship shows how ideas or events are related together into a group on the basis of some commonality.

e. A *description* relationship gives more information about a topic by presenting attributes, specifics, explanations, or settings.

In a similar vein, Frederiksen (1975) proposes five classes of logical relations, including conditions, order and proximity, conjunction and alternation, exhaustive differentiation, and algebraic relations. Of these, the last two are meant to operate primarily at the micropropositional level; the others can be used to identify relations among larger segments of text.

While Meyer and Frederiksen each focus on logical or rhetorical relations at this level, van Dijk (1977a) adds a further element for consideration. He suggests appealing to the content of the topic of discourse, as organized in a "frame," to describe certain macrostructural attributes. For example, a text about a war will derive some of its organization from a war "frame," in which is represented component states and the necessary or probable conditions and consequences of wars in general. The advantage to applying this sort of content analysis in an educational setting is that it can help identify the background information which students will need to understand a given text. The disadvantage is that it is not possible to specify in advance a bounded set of relations to be used in the analysis, as is possible for both Meyer and Frederiksen.

Top-level Structure

The top-level structure of a text corresponds to its overall organizing principles. For example, the rhetorical relations described by Meyer (listed above) may serve to organize the text as a whole. It may be written as a comparison of two views, a description of an item or scene, or possibly as a problem-with-possible-solution. In addition to such general rhetorical patterns, it is possible to identify certain genres of writing which have specific and typical structures. There may be further specifications of these more general patterns (Meyer, 1982, in press). Such genres include texts, such as stories (see below), scientific articles (Kintsch & van Dijk, 1978), and others.

With respect to the more general, rhetorical structures, Meyer and her colleagues have found a relationship in recall between the use of the author's top-level structure and the amount that is recalled. Readers who are able to identify and use the author's structure in a passage recall more of the ideas in that passage (B. J. Bartlett, 1978; Brandt, 1978; Meyer, 1979, 1982; Meyer, Brandt, & Bluth, 1980; Swanson, 1979).

Most of the work pertaining to the more specific top-level structures has been done with narrative or story structures (Mandler & Johnson, 1977; D. E. Rumelhart, 1975; Stein, 1979; Thorndyke, 1977; van Dijk, 1979b). These systems all describe the typical top-level structure of a simple story, suggesting that any given story follows a predictable, rule-governed sequence, typically involving one or more episodes. Thus, it is possible to describe the top-level structure of stories independent of the content of any given text. These story structures and their implications for reading will be discussed more fully below.

An Examination of Prominent Text Analysis Procedures

Prominent Prose Analysis Systems

The purpose of the section is to compare briefly the most commonly used prose analysis systems. The goal of the discussion is not to make a choice of a single system, but to demonstrate that each may be more or less appropriate, depending on the characteristics of the text under analysis and the purpose of the investigator.

The three most widely used prose analysis systems in educational research are those of Frederiksen (1975, 1977, 1979), Kintsch (1974), and Meyer (1975, in press). We will, thus, focus on these three systems, making only brief comments about the other available systems. Comparisons will be made utilizing the three structural levels described above. For each system, the types of materials for which it is appropriate, a brief description and a sample analysis of a passage will be given.

Meyer's system.   The Meyer (1975) system is applicable to all types of expository prose and has also been applied to story materials (Meyer, Haring, Brandt, & Walker, 1980). The minimal unit of analysis is the idea unit, which includes both actual content units named in the text and relational terms inferred from the text. The analysis produces a single, hierarchically organized representation of a passage's structure, called the content structure. It is a propositional structure with the relationships (predicates) at the micropropositional level held primarily by verbs from the text, while at the macropropositional level they are held by the previously described rhetorical relations, such as comparison. The arguments are individual content units from the text or content units which are parts of other propositions.

The relations at the micropropositional level are defined by lexical predicates and role relationships, or case relations adapted from Fillmore (1968). Reference, substitution, ellipsis, and lexical cohesion are not explicitly treated by the system, rather they are used as cues to guide the analysis. The Meyer system provides a classification system for mechanisms of conjunction (e.g., collection, comparison, causation).

Because of the hierarchical form of the analysis, the text is easily segmented at the macropropositional level and relations at this level are labeled by rhetorical predicates (described above), including problem/solution, antecedent/consequent, and so on. These relations are identified by various key words or signals used by authors.

As a natural outgrowth of the hierarchical structure, the top-level structure corresponds to the rhetorical relation which governs the highest level of the hierarchy. Thus passages can be classified as having an overall comparison, or descriptive, and so on, structure. The top-level structure of a sample passage depicted in Figure 11.1 is response: problem/solution; the passage was adapted from an article appearing in *Read* magazine and is reproduced in the Appendix.

The Meyer system was developed to allow investigations of the effects of such text variables as text structure or organization on the recall of prose materials. Six basic research findings have emerged using this system. First, ideas which are located at the top levels of a structural analysis of prose are recalled and retained better than ideas which are located at the lower levels (B. J. Bartlett, 1978; Britton, Meyer, Simpson, Holdredge, & Curry, 1979; Duchastel, 1979; Haring & Fry, 1979; Meyer, 1971, 1975, 1977; Swanson, 1979). Second, different items of information located high in the structure are more likely to be integrated in memory than items located low in the structure (Walker & Meyer, 1980). Third, the type and structure of relationships among ideas in prose dramatically influence recall when they occur at the top levels of the structure; however, when the same relationships occur low in the structure, they have little effect on recall (Meyer, 1975). Fourth, different types of relationships at the top levels of the structure differentially affect memory (Meyer & Freedle, in press). Fifth, students who are able to identify and use these top-level structures in prose remember more from their reading than those who do not (Meyer, Brandt, & Bluth, 1980; Meyer, 1979). Sixth, training in how to recognize and use these top-level structures improves recall for text materials (B. J. Bartlett, 1978).

Kintsch's system.   The Kintsch (1974) system also produces a hierarchical representation but follows the surface structure more closely. The minimal unit of analysis is the proposition, which is defined as a relationship and its arguments (e.g., John loves Mary is [LOVES, JOHN, MARY]). Analysis of a passage with this system produces a text base, a list of propositions, and a hierarchical ordering of these propositions. The hierarchy is formed on the basis of argument repetition. The system is applicable to expository prose in which a hierarchy of conceptual relations is not particularly significant, though it has been applied to all varieties of prose. It is particularly appropriate where the concern is with content items rather than their interrelationships. Since the hierarchy is built on the basis of repetition of content, rather than identification of logical relationships as in the Meyer (1975) system, it is a simpler system to learn and to apply. However, Bieger and Dunn (1980) have found Meyer's model of text structure more sensitive to developmental differences in recall than Kintsch's model; the crucial difference being that Meyer's approach explicitly represents both inferred and explicit semantic relationships in text, while Kintsch's approach does not.

The text base and its hierarchical structure are the facts of the text which correspond to the micropropositional level. As just described, they consist of propositions arranged in a hierarchy through argument repetition (repetition of content). Other forms of cohesion are not considered in making the hierarchy.

Many of the expository texts used by Kintsch (1974) do not have summary or preview statements (signaling, Meyer, 1975), while Meyer's texts (frequently *Scientific American* articles) do. Thus, the macropropositions of Meyer's system are the gist or summary. The top third of the propositions in Kintsch's text base are the most important facts of the text, as indicated by the repetition of their concepts in the rest of the text. However, they do not provide a summary of the passage's gist.

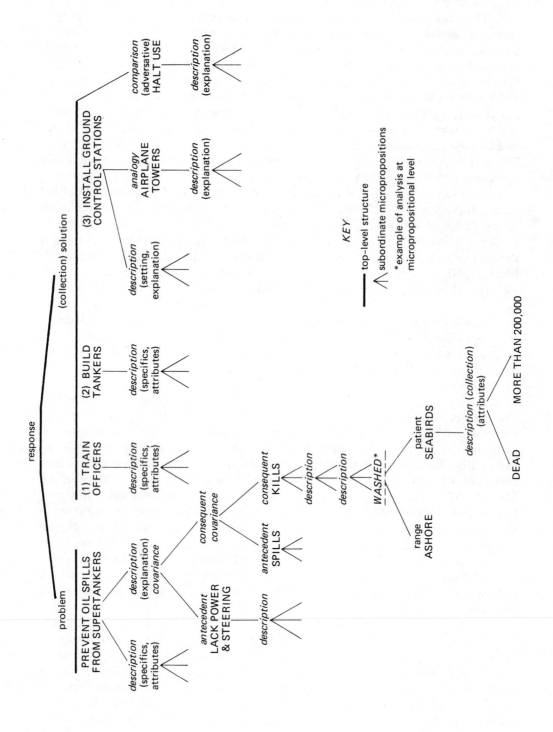

330

Text: A problem of vital concern is the prevention of oil spills from supertankers. A typical supertanker carries a half-million tons of oil and is the size of five football fields. A wrecked supertanker spills oil in the ocean; this oil kills animals, birds, and microscopic plant life. *For example,* when a tanker crashed off the coast of England, more than 200,000 dead seabirds washed ashore. Oil spills *also* kill microscopic plant life which provide food for sea life and produce 70 percent of the world's oxygen supply. Most wrecks result from the lack of power and steering equipment to handle emergency situations, such as storms. Supertankers have only one boiler to provide power and one propeller to drive the ship.

The solution to the problem is not to immediately halt the use of tankers on the ocean since about 80 percent of the world's oil supply is carried by supertankers. *Instead, the solution lies in the training of officers of supertankers, better building of tankers, and installing ground control stations to guide tankers near shore. First,* officers of supertankers must get top training in how to run and maneuver their ships. *Second,* tankers should be built with several propellers for extra control and backup boilers for emergency power. *Third,* ground control stations should be installed at places where supertankers come close to shore. These stations would act like airplane control towers, guiding tankers along busy shipping lanes and through dangerous channels.

FIGURE 11.1   Meyer system sample that shows top-level, macropropositions, and example of micropropositions for a segment of a magazine article on supertankers.

Thus, Kintsch and van Dijk's model (1978) of text comprehension has the reader operating on the text to construct the macrostructure, which is equivalent to Meyer's macropropositions. The macrostructure results from the operation of the macro-operators, which are a set of abstraction, or summarization, rules (van Dijk, 1977a).

Kintsch and van Dijk (1978) use a top-down rather than bottom-up approach to the top-level structure of text. That is, the top-level structure is an independent organization overlaying the propositional analysis, rather than an emergent structure as in the Meyer system. This is because only highly conventionalized top-level structures are utilized, for example, stories or scientific articles.

A sample passage analyzed by the system appears as Figure 11.2. The Kintsch system was developed originally to aid in determining what information in a passage was available to the learner, so that recall could be more easily scored. In more recent years, it appears as a key element in a model of text comprehension which is being developed by Kintsch, van Dijk, and colleagues (Kintsch & van Dijk, 1978; Kintsch & Vipond, 1979; Miller & Kintsch, 1980). Salient findings from studies using this system include the levels effect (high structural information recalled and retained better than low structural information [Kintsch & Keenan, 1973; Kintsch, Kozminsky, Streby, McKoon, & Keenan, 1975]), as described above for the Meyer system; a lawful relationship between the time subjects take to read text and the number of propositions they process (Kintsch & Keenan, 1973); and a relationship between readability of text and argument repetition (Kintsch, et al., 1975).

Frederiksen's system.   The Frederiksen (1975, 1977) system applies to various types of expository prose. The minimal units of analysis are the concept, which may be a single word or word group, depending on the specificity desired, and the relation. Analysis does not produce a hierarchical structure, but rather "structure graphs" which have more of the quality of networks. The Frederiksen system is particularly appropriate in situations where investigators require a method for scoring inferences made by readers.

At the micropropositional level, Frederiksen describes an elaborate set of relations which hold among concepts, including both semantic and conditional (causal). The system at this level is very similar to the micropropositional level of Meyer's system; however, Frederiksen's system makes more distinctions within types of relationships.

The analysis system does not provide natural segmentation into hierarchical levels. However, some logical relations defined at the micropropositional level could be adapted for use at a macropropositional level. There are no provisions for the top-level structure. The system was designed to exemplify a model of text knowledge in the mind apart from the organization of the original text with its emphasis of some ideas and subordination of others.

A sample analysis from an early version of the system appears in Figure 11.3. The Frederiksen system was developed to handle issues in the learning and recalling of logical relations and makes finer distinctions among relationships than the other two approaches. The system was also formulated to study inferences (Frederiksen, 1975); the approach provides an exhaustive classification of different types of inferences that can occur in children's recall of stories (Frederiksen, 1979). Also, Frederiksen (1975) has defined types of information in recall

The *Asteroid* Paragraph: Long, Few Different Arguments

1 (ISA, ASTEROID, PLANET)

2 (MINIATURE, PLANET)

3 (ORBIT, ASTEROID, SUN)

4 (IDENTIFY, ASTEROID)

5 (NUMBER OF, 4, HUNDRED)

6 (CONTRAST, 4, 7)

7 (DIFFICULT, 8)

8 (KEEP, TRACK, ASTEROID)

9 (CONSEQUENCE, 10, 7)

10 (ALIKE, ASTEROID)

11 (ALL, ASTEROID)

12 (IDENTIFY, ASTEROID, POSITION)

13 (HAS, POSITION, ORBIT)

14 (ONLY, 12)

15 (DETERMINE, ORBIT)

16 (AFTER, 15, 18)

17 (EVEN, 16)

18 (LOOSE, ORBIT)

19 (CONSEQUENCE, 18, 21)

20 (OFTEN, 18)

21 (CHANGE, ORBIT)

22 (CONSEQUENCE, 21, 23)

23 (INFLUENCE, PLANET, ASTEROID)

24 (LARGE, PLANET)

25 (DEFLECT, PLANET, ASTEROID, ORBIT)[a]

Arguments: ASTEROID, PLANET, SUN, HUNDRED, POSITION, ORBIT (6)

Text: Asteroids are miniature planets that orbit around the sun. Hundreds of asteroids have been identified, but it is difficult to keep track of them, since all asteroids are alike. An asteroid is identified only by the position of its orbit. Even after an orbit has been determined, it is often lost because the orbit changes due to the influence of the large planets which deflect the asteroid from its orbit (70 words).

[a] The case of ORBIT is *Source*, from which *from orbit* is derived.

FIGURE 11.2 Kintsch system sample that shows analysis of a paragraph on asteroids (*from Kintsch, Kozminsky, Streby, McKoon, & Keenan, 1975*).

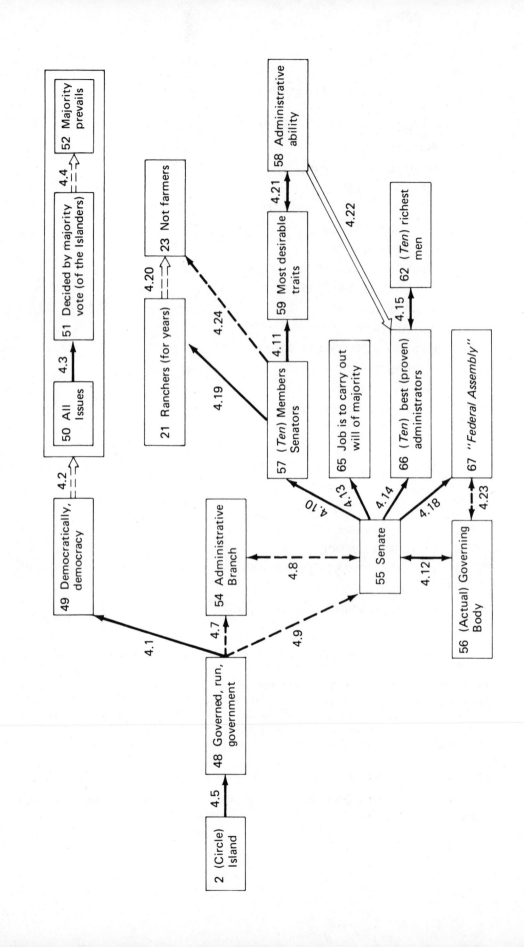

Text: The island is run democratically. All issues are decided by a majority vote of the islanders. The actual governing body is a ten-man senate called the Federal Assembly, whose job is to carry out the will of the majority. Since the most desirable trait in a senator is administrative ability, the senate consists of the island's ten best proven administrators, the ten richest men. For years all senators have been ranchers.

FIGURE 11.3   Frederiksen system sample that shows analysis of a passage about a fictional "Circle Island" (*from Frederiksen, 1975*).

protocols more descriptively: veridical recall, overgeneralizations, pseudodiscriminations, text-implied inferences, and elaborations (inferences from prior knowledge). The first four are scored as present in a protocol in Meyer's system, but distinctions among them are not made. None of the systems provide a way to conceptualize elaborations other than recognizing their presence.

Some important findings which derive from the Frederiksen approach are that overgeneralizations, pseudodiscriminations, and text-generated inferences occur at the time of comprehension, while elaborations occur during recall (Frederiksen, 1975) and that explicit statements of logical relationships facilitates the comprehension of poorer readers (Marshall & Glock, 1978–79).

In summary, these three prose analysis systems differ in their strengths and suitability for different types of passages and research questions. Meyer's and Frederiksen's systems are better suited to examining logical relationships and comprehension of these relationships explicitly or implicitly stated in the text. The logical relationships in Meyer's model closely follow those suggested by the text, while the superordinate level of Frederiksen's are drawn not from the text but from semantic knowledge (see Meyer, 1975). Thus, Meyer's system would probably be more effective for studying writing; it closely parallels work in rhetoric as previously mentioned. In Meyer's and Frederiksen's systems, protocols can be scored for recall of relationships independent from correct recall of content; this is not the case in Kintsch's system, where propositions are the units for scoring, rather than their component relation and arguments. Both Meyer's and Kintsch's systems provide clearly specified hierarchies, while this is not the case for Frederiksen's approach. Kintsch's system is probably the easiest to apply and quickest to score. However, Meyer's approach gives a more articulated structure (Cofer, Scott, & Watkins, 1978).

Meyer (in press) presented an in-depth comparison of the analysis procedures of the Kintsch and Meyer approaches; the "Saint passage" (used by Miller & Kintsch, 1980), a short paragraph comprised of three information-packed sentences, was analyzed with both approaches and the resultant hierarchies were related to recall frequency data. The data showed that the hierarchy formed with the Meyer approach was the best predictor of recall. The Meyer approach is built upon knowledge of logical relationships and discourse organization; these components are not found in the microprocesses component of the Kintsch and van Dijk model (1978), where coherence is only examined in terms of word repetition. Even with this single paragraph, the model which emphasized learner's knowledge of text organization matched recall better than one that focused on word repetition. This pattern would be expected to be stronger with longer passages where there are a greater number of logical relations among propositions. Also, Meyer (in press) compared the scoring systems of the two different approaches; recall protocols from subjects of different ages and vocabulary levels under various task conditions were scored with the two systems. The Kintsch scoring system was more efficient for scoring immediate free-recall protocols with close correspondence to text content. The Meyer approach was more time consuming but more informative when scoring less accurate recall protocols (e.g., delayed recall, recall of older adults, children and less proficient learners). The correlation on total recall scores was .96 between the two scoring systems for the wide range of protocols examined.

Other systems.   Other prose analysis systems include those of Beaugrande (1980), Crothers (1979), Drum and Lantaff (1977), Graesser (1981), Turner and Greene (1977). Two of these are adaptations of Kintsch's approach, Turner and Greene for analysis and Drum and Lantaff for further distinctions in scoring protocols. In general, these systems are less widely used because they do not lend themselves to use for accomplishing the goals which were described at the outset of this chapter, namely those of providing dimensions along which to classify texts, and providing mechanisms for measuring and scoring content learned from a passage during reading.

Crothers's (1979) system is limited to the analysis of prose no longer than a few paragraphs. It provides a very detailed structural description, which does not appear to result in dimensions which could be readily used for classifying texts.

Beaugrande's (1980) system produces elaborate networks of content with relations, both syntactic and conceptual, clearly marked. An important attribute of this model is that it applies the same type of relationships to the text as to prior knowledge of readers and attempts to mesh the two. The system is complex and subject to the same criticism as that mentioned for Crothers. Both, however, make contributions to reading research, in that they explicate the organizational principles involved in text structuring and thus can be used by educators to help determine the cognitive skills which readers will need.

Graesser (1981) recently has presented a system for identification of a representational structure constructed during prose comprehension. This representational structure, called the conceptual graph structure, results from four steps. First, inferences are generated from the explicitly stated statements in the text. Subjects read or listen to a passage and then go back through each text statement to answer *why* and *how* questions. Answers to each question must fill up four typed lines. Inferences generated by at least two subjects become part of the representational structure. The next step involves segmenting the obtained inferences and explicit information into statement nodes. In the third step, each node is assigned to one of six node categories (Physical State, Physical Event, Internal State, Internal Event, Goal, and Style). The final step involves interrelating the nodes by directed arcs, which are labeled by Reason, Initiate, Manner, Consequence, or Property.

The first step in this system, generation of inferences, draws directly from artificial intelligence but is unique to discourse analysis approaches in psychology. These approaches have included explicit statements and a minimal number of inferences necessary to maintain continuity. In contrast, in Graesser's approach there are an average of 15 inference statements in his structure for each explicit statement in a narrative. The crucial issue is how many of these inferences are actually generated during comprehension and how many are a function of the task demands of the question-probe technique. For example, it seems doubtful that a reader would actually construct the inference "Czar liked boys more than girls" (inference included in Graesser's conceptual graph) when reading the following statement in a narrative: "Once there was a Czar who had three lovely daughters."

The second step in Graesser's system involves a propositional analysis. The smallest unit of analysis, the statement node, is not a simple proposition (e.g.,

Kintsch, 1974), but a lexical proposition (e.g., Meyer, 1975) which is equivalent to a simple sentence. The third step, assignment of nodes to categories, is similar to Beaugrande's (1980) approach. The final step, labeling relational links, is similar to the approaches of Beaugrande (1980), Frederiksen (1975), and Meyer (1975), but disparate from that of Kintsch (1974) where structural connectivity is based on repetition of words, rather than logical relationships. Thus, the construction of the representational structure is similar to other psychological approaches; the major difference involves the inclusion of a large number of inferences and the empirical method for their generation.

Story Grammar Approaches

While the text analysis systems just described are bottom-up, in that they build up or produce a structure for a given passage, the story grammar approaches tend to have a "top-down" orientation. In the story grammar literature, what is presented is a conventional organization for a particular category or genre of texts—stories. This organization is independent of the specific content of any given story, though the usual procedure followed is to demonstrate that any story is a specification of the structure. As was described above, this approach has its origins in folklorists' efforts at describing tales of various sorts. Because of its highly conventionalized form, the story is the one type of textual top-level structure that has been most widely studied (Kintsch, 1977; Kintsch & van Dijk, 1975; Lakoff, 1972; Mandler & Johnson, 1977; Rice, 1980; Rumelhart, 1975; Stein & Glenn, 1979; Thorndyke, 1977; van Dijk, 1979b).

A story grammar is analogous to a sentence grammar, in that each is composed of a set of rules which describes the possible structures of the class of items which can be called well-formed stories or sentences. In principle, a story grammar is generative, that is, it can produce structural descriptions of stories which have never been told but would be considered to be acceptable stories. In practice, the rules are more often used to describe the organization of a particular story under consideration.

Given the conventionalized form of stories, it is not surprising that the many story grammars which have been proposed share significant features (see Black & Wilensky, 1979). Almost all describe stories as consisting of a setting and a series of one or more episodes. Episodes, in turn, are usually seen to have a problem/solution internal structure. The usual formalism for describing the story grammar is a series of rewrite rules. As an example, the rewrite rules for Rumelhart's (1975) original grammar are given in Figure 11.4. These rewrite rules specify the possible constituents of the various story parts. For example, Rule 1 says that a Story can be rewritten as a Setting plus an Episode. An Episode, in turn, is constituted by an Event and a Reaction. Another way of representing these rules is in a tree diagram which illustrates their hierarchical relations. An example of such a diagram for the first seven of Rumelhart's rules is given in Figure 11.5.

These rewrite rules and their associated hierarchical diagrams correspond to the syntax of a story structure. In addition to these syntactical or structural descriptions, most story grammarians also provide a description of semantic relations. For example, Rumelhart lists semantic corollaries to each of his rewrite

(1) Story − > Setting + Episode
     = > ALLOW (Setting, Episode)

(2) Setting − >(States)*
     = > AND (State, state,.......)

(3) Episode − > Event + Reaction
     = > INITIATE (Event, Reaction)

(4) Event − > {Episode | Change-of-state | Action | Event + Event}
     = > CAUSE (Event$_1$, Event$_2$) or ALLOW (Event$_1$, Event$_2$)

(5) Reaction − > Internal Response + Overt Response
     = > MOTIVATE (Interval-response, Overt Response)

(6) Internal Response − > {Emotion | Desire}

(7) Overt Response − > {Action | (Attempt)*}
     = > THEN (Attempt$_1$, Attempt$_2$,......)

(8) Attempt − > Plan + Application
     = > MOTIVATE (Plan, Application)

(9) Application − > (Preaction)* + Action + Consequence
     = > ALLOW (AND(Preaction, Preaction,...),
          {CAUSE | INITIATE | ALLOW} (Action, Consequence))

(10) Preaction − > Subgoal + (Attempt)*
     = > MOTIVATE [Subgoal, THEN (Attempt,......)]

(11) Consequence − > {Reaction | Event}

FIGURE 11.4   Syntactic rules and semantic interpretation rules (*from Rumelhart, 1975*).

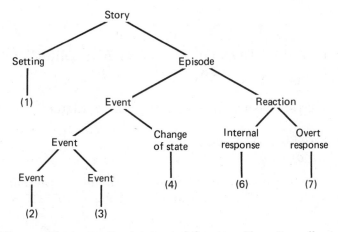

FIGURE 11.5   The syntactic structure of the story (*from Rumelhart, 1975*).

rules: the corollary to Rule 3 (Episode − Event + Reaction) is INITIATE (Event, Reaction), which indicates that the Event is in the relation of Initiator to the Reaction within a given Episode. Other story grammarians, including Mandler and Johnson (1977) and Stein and Glenn (1979) have incorporated these logical/ semantical relations into their rewrite rules. A story grammar, then, provides both a structural and a logical description of the conventional form of stories.

In addition to being a descriptive tool, the story grammar has some implications for comprehension processes as well. The assumption here is that the reader already possesses a story grammar, and that the grammar functions during reading to aid him in identifying significant items in the text to be remembered. In addition, the grammar may provide a strategy for retrieval of the information contained in the story (Mandler & Johnson, 1977).

In the area of reading research, the usual procedure is to apply the story grammar to a given story passage. Thus, the components of the passage are identified according to their position or role in the story. This makes it possible to compare stories with respect to their structure, regardless of the content of the story. As a result of this feature of story grammars, Thorndyke (1977) was able to show facilitation in recall for a second story with the same structure as an earlier story.

Other significant findings which rely on the description of the structure of stories include the ability to predict comprehensibility ratings for stories (Bower, 1976; Rice, 1978, 1980), ability to describe the sorts of summaries which subjects will make of target stories (Kintsch, 1977; Kintsch & van Dijk, 1975; Rumelhart, 1977), ability to predict which items will be remembered from a story (Mandler & Johnson, 1977; Thorndyke, 1977). Developmental studies of story grammar acquisition in children (Kintsch, 1977; Mandler, 1978; Mandler & Johnson, 1977; Stein, 1979; Stein & Glenn, 1979) suggest that even very young children have knowledge of and utilize story grammars.

Recent investigations (Black & Wilensky, 1979; Pollard-Gott, McCloskey, & Todres, 1979) have examined the adequacy of story grammars. In addition, emphasis with narratives has switched lately from a focus on top-down, conventionalized story structures to more content-sensitive analyses of stories, such as identifying causal links among story content units (e.g., Lehnert, 1982; Trabasso & van der Broek, 1983).

AN EVALUATION OF THE PAST AND DIRECTIONS FOR THE FUTURE

Current Issues in Specifying Text Structure

Should the Structure Be Represented as a Hierarchy or as a Network?

This question asks us to choose between the hierarchical representation systems (Kintsch, 1974; Meyer, 1975; Rumelhart, 1975; Schank, 1975; Thorndyke, 1977) and those which are arranged in a network (Anderson, 1976; Anderson & Bower, 1973; Beaugrande, 1980; Frederiksen, 1977; Rumelhart, Lindsay, & Norman, 1972). At first glance, this looks like a real issue: Is text hierarchically organized or not? However, the differences between the two types of textual representation are more apparent than real. Hierarchical representations can easily be reinterpreted as networks, and a certain amount of hierarchical structuring (some nodes govern others, some nodes have more links) is implicit in any network account. This question is really one of emphasis. Should the inclusion relations be considered dominant and thus be singled out for representation (as in the hierarchical forms) or should a variety of relations be represented (as in network forms)? As was discussed earlier in this chapter, previous research has shown the inclusion of hierarchical relations to be significant factors in a reader's perception of a text. Further research into the influences of other kinds of relations will be necessary to determine their relative saliency. The "best" representation of a text will depend not only on such research, but also on the purposes of the investigator.

McKoon (1977) pointed to an encoding versus retrieval distinction between hierarchical and network models. She explained that better or faster recall of superordinate propositions over subordinate propositions could be explained only by encoding processes with nonhierarchical, network theories (e.g., Anderson & Bower, 1973; Rumelhart, Lindsay, & Norman, 1972), while encoding or retrieval processes could account for such a levels effect with hierarchical models (e.g., Kintsch, 1974; Meyer, 1975; Rumelhart, 1975; Schank, 1975). She explained that for the nonhierarchical theories, text propositions are combined with prior knowledge of the world in long-term memory by repetition of concepts. The resulting structure of the text representation is determined entirely by these long-term memory connections and not by emphasis given to the concepts by the writer (or reader) of the text. Thus, the writer's emphasis in the text could only influence whether or not a concept was encoded, but could not affect speed of retrieval from the long-term memory structure or lack of retrieval over time. In contrast, the hierarchical structures of text represented in memory are organized by the importance of the propositions; these memory structures are thought to be new memory constructions and more independent of previous long-term memory structures. Thus, the emphasis in the text on certain propositions over others could result in the more frequent selection of these propositions for encoding (Cirilo & Foss, 1981; Meyer, 1975) into the memory structure of the text or from a top-down retrieval search of a memory structure built with the same importance judgments of the propositions as that found in the text (Thorndyke & Yekovich, 1980). McKoon's (1977) study showed that superordinate propositions in a text verified faster and also more accurately identified over time; thus, she believed her data to support hierarchical rather than nonhierarchical, network representations of text in memory.

However, Kintsch and van Dijk (1978), proponents of a hierarchical model, present a different explanation for the levels effect. They attribute it to multiple processing of high-level information in the short-term memory buffer. That is, due to repetition of concepts from superordinate propositions in subordinate propositions, the superordinate propositions stay or get pulled more frequently into short-term memory for relating to other propositions; more practice is allotted to superordinate propositions. This same explanation for the levels effects was proposed by Anderson (1976) in relation to his network model. He explained that the central propositions in the network of his computer simulation model (propositions with the most links to other propositions or high-level propositions in a hierarchy) are more frequently called up to help interpret the more peripheral (or subordinate) propositions. This constitutes extra rehearsal of high-level propositions and results in increasing the probability of their recall. Thus, in this network model, a writer's emphasis (or reader's perspective) will not affect the form of the memory representation, but will affect practice with rehearsing its components and thus affect retrieval processes. (For further discussions of causes of the levels effect, see Britton et al., 1979; Cirilo & Foss, 1981; Meyer, 1983.) Thus, the distinction over involvement of retrieval processes between hierarchical and network models made by McKoon (1977) becomes less clear.

Should Content Structure, Cohesion, and Emphasis Be Represented in Separate or Integrated Manners?

As should be clear from earlier discussion, a number of different elements operate in the organization of prose. It is possible to describe a passage from the point of view of the content it presents, from a purely structural standpoint (as in story grammars), in terms of the cohesive relations which tie sentences together, or from the point of view of the emphasis patterns being used by the author to underscore his/her own interpretation of the relative importance of the ideas expressed. At present, no single system attempts to combine all of these possible organizations, and it is not clear that such a combination is desirable. The story grammar approach abstracts the structural features of a passage and does not deal with the others. Systems used for expository prose tend to combine content and structural elements (argument sharing in Kintsch, rhetorical relations in Meyer). Systems which represent cohesive relations and emphasis patterns are limited to very short passages (Beaugrande, 1980; Crothers, 1979). It is possible that a representation system which integrated all these elements would be too unwieldy. On the other hand, it is important to recognize that each of these elements may contribute significantly to the organization of a prose passage.

How Many and What Types of Distinction Should Be Made in Text?

In the discussion of the various prose analysis systems, we have seen that different investigators choose to make different kinds of distinctions. For instance, Frederiksen distinguishes many varieties of causal relations, while Meyer (1975) distinguishes only a more general antecedent/consequent relationship. The number and variety of prose units and relationships which can be distinguished at any given level of the analysis is very large. What is necessary is to determine which distinctions are salient and useful, and again, this determination will depend to large extent on the purposes of the investigator.

To What Degree of Specificity Should the Analysis Be Carried?

This question is analogous to the last one about the number of distinctions which should be made. Again the issue has to do with the most salient and useful size for units of prose. The issue of specificity arises when the analyst must decide at what point to terminate his/her analysis. Must each word be identified? Should "a large red balloon" be considered a single concept or two or three? The answer is also analogous to that for the last question. If the investigator is interested in color recall, she/he will want "red" to appear as a separate concept in the analysis. For other purposes, this may not be necessary.

Each of these first four questions has dealt with issues in the representation of prose passages. None can be given a definitive answer. This is because it is unreasonable to expect that there will emerge a single "correct" and unassailable method for representing the structure of a text. Each system may be more or less useful for different research questions. This is not to say that there are no criteria for evaluating analysis systems. A consideration of some of these follow in the next questions.

Can the Procedures Be Generalized across Types of Text?

As discussed earlier, the various prose analysis procedures may be more or less appropriate for various types of texts. Clearly, the story grammar analyses are applicable only to story texts, though the general approach of identifying the structural principles of a given genre of texts could be generalized. This has, in fact, been done with scientific reports (Kintsch & van Dijk, 1978) and political communiques (Flammer & Hinder, 1979). With respect to less conventionalized expository prose, analysis systems may still differ greatly in their generality. The Kintsch and Meyer systems have been most widely applied and have been used to analyze material from classroom texts, magazine articles, and stories among other types. A high degree of generalizability is desirable because it allows comparison of results across various kinds of prose.

Can the Procedures Describe Recalled Information Which Varies from the Original Text, Such as Generalization, Deletions, Constructions, Distortions, and Elaborations?

The question of analyzing reader-generated text arises in situations where the investigator is interested in studying recall protocols. In such a case, it is desirable to be able to compare the original passage to that recalled by the reader and to be able to measure changes which may occur, such as generalizations, deletions, constructions, distortions, and elaborations. While any of the analysis procedures which we have discussed could be applied to the reader's production, most do not provide any mechanism for comparing the recall and the original. Frederiksen (1977, 1979) does address this issue and provides a method for scoring various inferences, generalizations, and distortions made by readers. The top-level structure categories of Meyer have been used to compare top-level structures employed by readers in their written recall of text to the top-level structure employed in the original text (Meyer, Brandt, & Bluth, 1980). Rice (1980) has developed a measure for assessing the degree of structure in a story passage which has been used to compare the structure of recalled stories to the original. In general, research which is oriented towards understanding the processes by which readers identify and respond to text structure will need more such comparative mechanisms.

Can Text Analysts Be Taught to Make Equivalent Inferences When Analyzing Text?

This question of equivalent inferences in analysis is essentially one of reliability. If the analysis system is either so complex or so intuitive that only its originator can apply it, then it obviously has little scientific use. At the present stage of prose analysis development, however, a certain amount of subjectivity and intuitive judgment is required for all the systems. Many of these inferences we make so automatically that we scarcely recognize them as problematic. This includes issues of reference and other cohesive inferences. When it comes to complex issues, such as determining the author's message or point of view, the problems of interpretation are even clearer. Similar problems arise during the scoring of recall protocols where it is necessary to decide if a subject has recalled an item or not. Scorers must be able to agree on what constitutes an acceptable paraphrase. The systems described in the earlier sections of this chapter are all fairly reliable in these respects, which is part of the reason why they are widely used. Still, we are a long way from complete objectivity and the possibility of computer scoring and analysis.

A FINAL NOTE

Models of the structure of text are crucial to research on reading comprehension. As we have seen, at present, a number of models are available for use in research. Both their development and effective use are dependent on the goals of particular research investigations. Without these models, we would be confined to looking at task variables, such as postquestion effects, without any way to specify their interaction with the materials variable. Knowledge about the structure of text has made it possible to predict quite adequately which ideas will be recalled and how long subjects will need to study text. Specifying the structure of text permits theorizing about how readers process text. Future research will require integrating task, material, and reader variables to understand the reading process better.

REFERENCES

Anderson, J. R. *Language, memory, and thought.* Hillsdale, N.J.: Erlbaum, 1976.

Anderson, J. R., & Bower, G. H. *Human associative memory.* Washington, D.C.: Winston, 1973.

Anderson, T. H. *Study skills and learning strategies* (Tech. Rep. No. 104). Urbana: University of Illinois at Urbana-Champaign, Center for the Study of Reading, 1978.

Aristotle. *The rhetoric of Aristotle* (L. Cooper, trans.). New York: Appleton-Century-Crofts, 1960.

Bartlett, B. J. *Top-level structure as an organizational strategy for recall of classroom text.* Unpublished doctoral dissertation, Arizona State University, 1978.

Bartlett, F. C. *Remembering.* Cambridge: Cambridge University Press, 1932.

Beaugrande, R. *Text, discourse, and process.* Norwood, N.J.: Ablex, 1980.

Bedier. *Les Fabliaux.* Paris, 1893.

Bieger, G. R., & Dunn, B. R. *Sensitivity to developmental differences in recall of prose: A comparison of two prose grammars.* Paper presented at the meeting of the American Educational Research Association, Boston, April 1980.

Black, J. B., & Wilensky, R. An evaluation of story grammars. *Cognitive Science,* 1979, *3,* 213–230.

Bower, G. H. Experiments on story understanding and recall. *Quarterly Journal of Experimental Psychology,* 1976, *28,* 511–534.

Brandt, D. M. *Prior knowledge of the author's schema and the comprehension of prose.* Unpublished doctoral dissertation, Arizona State University, 1978.

Britton, B. K., Meyer, B. J. F., Simpson, R., Holdredge, T. S., & Curry, C. Effects of the organization on memory: Tests of two implications of a selective attention hypothesis. *Journal of Experimental Psychology: Human Learning and Memory,* 1979, *5,* 496–506.

Carpenter, P. A., & Just, M. A. Integrative processes in comprehension. In D. LaBerge & S. J. Samuels (Eds.), *Basic processes in reading: Perception and comprehension.* Hillsdale, N.J.: Erlbaum, 1977.

Carroll, J. B. *Learning from verbal discourse in educational media: Review of the literature* (Final Report Project 7–1069). Princeton, N.J.: Educational Testing Service, 1971.

Chall, J. W. *Readability: An appraisal of research and application.* Columbus: Ohio State University, 1958.

Charniak, E. *Towards a model of children's story comprehension.* MIT AI Lab. Memo TR–266, 1972.

Chomsky, N. *Syntactic structures.* The Hague: Mouton, 1957.

Cicero. *De inventione et topica* (H. M. Hubbell, trans.). London: William Heinemann, Ltd., 1954.

Cirilo, R. K., & Foss, D. J. Text structure and reading time for sentences. *Journal of Verbal Learning and Verbal Behavior,* 1981, *19,* 96–109.

Clark, H. H. Inferences in comprehension. In D. LaBerge & S. J. Samuels (Eds.), *Basic processes in reading: Perception and comprehension.* Hillsdale, N.J.: Erlbaum, 1977. Pp. 243–263.

Clark, H. H., & Haviland, S. E. Psychological process as linguistic explanation. In D. Cohen (Ed.), *Explaining linguistic phenomena.* Washington, D.C.: Hemisphere, 1974.

Clark, H. H., & Haviland, S. E. Comprehension and the given-new contract. In R. O. Freedle (Ed.), *Discourse production and comprehension.* Norwood, N.J.: Ablex, 1977.

Clements, P. The effects of staging on recall from prose. In R. O. Freedle (Ed.), *New directions in discourse processing.* Norwood, N.J.: Ablex, 1979.

Cofer, C. N., Scott, C., & Watkins, K. *Scoring systems for the analyses of passage content.* Paper presented at the meetings of the American Psychological Association, Toronto, 1978.

Colby, B. N. Analytical procedures in eidochronic study. *Journal of American Folklore,* 1973, *86,* 14–24. (a)

Colby, B. N. A partial grammar of Eskimo folktales. *American Anthropologist,* 1973, *75,* 645–662. (b)

Colby, B. N., & Cole, M. Culture, memory, and narrative. In R. Horton & R. Murray (Eds.), *Modes of thought.* London: Faber & Faber, 1973. Pp. 63–91.

Crothers, E. J. Memory structure and the recall of discourse. In R. O. Freedle & J. B. Carroll (Eds.), *Language comprehension and the acquisition of knowledge.* New York: Wiley, 1972. Pp. 247–284.

Crothers, E. J. *Paragraph structure inference.* Norwood, N.J.: Ablex, 1979.

D'Angelo, F. J. *A conceptual theory of rhetoric.* Cambridge, Mass.: Winthrop, 1975. Pp. 9–17.

D'Angelo, F. J. Paradigms as structural counterparts of *topoi.* In D. McQuade (Ed.), *Linguistics, stylistics, and the teaching of composition.* Akron, Ohio: University of Akron Press, 1979. Pp. 41–51.

Dawes, R. M. Memory and distortion of meaningful written material. *British Journal of Psychology,* 1966, *57,* 77–86.

Dechant, E. V. *Improving the teaching of reading.* Englewood Cliffs, N.J.: Prentice-Hall, 1969.

Deverell, A. F. Are reading improvement courses at the university level justified? *Invitational Conferences on Education,* Canadian Education Association, 1959. Pp. 19–27.

Drum, P. A., & Lantaff, R. E. *Scoring categories for protocols.* Paper presented at the 2nd Annual Language Conference, Boston University, October 1977.

Duchastel, P. C. Learning objectives and organization of prose. *Journal of Educational Psychology,* 1979, *71,* 100–106.

Faw, H. W., & Waller, T. G. Mathemagenic behaviors and efficiency in learning from prose materials: Review, critique and recommendations. *Review of Educational Research,* 1976, *46,* 691–720.

Fillmore, C. J.   The case for case. In E. Bach & R. T. Harms (Eds.), *Universals in linguistic theory.* New York: Holt, Rinehart & Winston, 1968.

Flammer, A., & Hinder, H.   *A text grammar for political communiques.* Paper presented at the meeting of the Psychonomic Society, Phoenix, 1979.

Flanagan, J. C.   A study of the effect on comprehension of varying speeds of reading. In *American Educational Research on the Foundations of American Education,* 1939, 47–50.

Flood, J.   A system for scoring reader's recall of propositions from texts. In P. D. Pearson & J. Hansen (Eds.), *Reading: Disciplined inquiry in process and practice.* Clemson, S.C.: National Reading Conference, 1978. Pp. 99–105.

Flower, L. S., & Hayes, J. R.   Problem-solving strategies and the writing process. *College English,* 1977, *39,* 449–461.

Frederiksen, C. H.   Effects of task-induced cognitive operations on comprehension and memory processes. In R. O. Freedle & J. B. Carroll (Eds.), *Language comprehension and the acquisition of knowledge.* New York: Wiley, 1972. Pp. 211–246.

Frederiksen, C. H.   Acquisition of semantic information from discourse: Effects of repeated exposures. *Journal of Verbal Learning and Verbal Behavior,* 1975, *14,* 158–169.

Frederiksen, C. H.   Semantic processing units in understanding text. In R. O. Freedle (Ed.), *Discourse production and comprehension.* Norwood, N.J.: Ablex, 1977.

Frederiksen, C. H.   Discourse comprehension and early reading. In L. B. Resnick & P. A. Weaver (Eds.), *Theory and practice of early reading* (Vol. 1). Hillsdale, N.J.: Erlbaum, 1979.

Freedle, R. O. (Ed.)   *Discourse processes: Advances in research and theory.* Vol. 1, *Discourse production and comprehension.* Norwood, N.J.: Ablex, 1977.

Freedle, R. O. (Ed.).   *Advances in discourse processes.* Vol. 2, *New directions in discourse processing.* Norwood, N.J.: Ablex, 1979.

Gainsburg, J. C.   *Advanced skills in reading.* New York: Macmillan, 1967.

Gomulicki, B. R.   Recall as an abstractive process. *Acta Psychologica,* 1956, *12,* 77–94.

Gorrell, R. M.   Structure in thought. *College English,* 1963, *24,* 592–594.

Graesser, A. C.   *Prose comprehension beyond the word.* New York: Springer-Verlag, 1981.

Grimes, J. E.   *The thread of discourse.* The Hague: Mouton, 1975.

Halliday, M. A. K.   Notes on transitivity and theme in English, Part 3. *Journal of Linguistics,* 1968, *4,* 179–215.

Halliday, M. A. K., & Hasan, R.   *Cohesion in English.* London: Longman, 1976.

Haring, M. J., & Fry, M. A.   Effect of pictures on children's comprehension of written text. *Educational Communication and Technology,* 1979, *27,* 185–190.

Harris, Z. S.   Discourse analysis. *Language,* 1952, *28,* 1–30.

Haviland, S. E., & Clark, H. H.   What's new? Acquiring new information as a process in comprehension. *Journal of Verbal Learning and Verbal Behavior,* 1974, *13,* 512–521.

Herber, H. L.   *Teaching reading in the content areas.* Englewood Cliffs, N.J.: Prentice-Hall, 1970.

Hymes, D. (Ed.).   *Language and culture in society.* New York: Harper & Row, 1964.

Johnson, R. E.   Recall of prose as a function of the structural importance of the linguistic units. *Journal of Verbal Learning and Verbal Behavior,* 1970, *9,* 12–20.

Kintsch, W.   *The representation of meaning in memory.* New York: Erlbaum, 1974.

Kintsch, W.   On comprehending stories. In M. A. Just & P. A. Carpenter (Eds.), *Cognitive processes in comprehension.* Hillsdale, N.J.: Erlbaum, 1977. Pp. 33–62.

Kintsch, W., & Greene, E.   The role of culture-specific schemata in the comprehension and recall of stories. *Discourse Processes*, 1978, *1*, 1–13.

Kintsch, W., & Keenan, J. M.   Reading rate as a function of number of propositions in the base structure of sentences. *Cognitive Psychology*, 1973, *6*, 257–274.

Kintsch, W., Kozminsky, E., Streby, W. J., McKoon, G., & Keenan, J. M.   Comprehension and recall of text as a function of content variables. *Journal of Verbal Learning and Verbal Behavior*, 1975, *14*, 196–214.

Kintsch, W., & van Dijk, T.   Recalling and summarizing stories. *Languages*, 1975, *40*, 98–116.

Kintsch, W., & van Dijk, T. A.   Toward a model of text comprehension and production. *Psychological Review*, 1978, *85*, 363–394.

Kintsch, W., & Vipond, D.   Reading comprehension and readability in educational practice and psychological theory. In L.-G. Nilsson (Ed.), *Proceedings of the conference on memory: University of Uppsala*. Hillsdale, N.J.: Erlbaum, 1979.

Kircher, M. C.   *The effects of presentation order and repetition on the free recall of prose*. Unpublished master's thesis, Cornell University, 1971.

Klein, S., Aeschlimann, J. F., Balsiger, D. F., Converse, S. L., Court, C., Foster, M., Lao, R., Oakley, J. D., & Smith, J.   *Automatic novel writing: A status report* (Technical Report No. 186, WIS–CS–186–73). University of Wisconsin, Madison, 1973.

Labov, W.   *Sociolinguistic patterns*. Philadelphia: Pennsylvania University Press, 1972.

Lakoff, G.   Structural complexity in fairy tales. *The Study of Man*, 1972, *1*, 128–190.

Lakoff, G.   Linguistic gestalts. *Proceedings of the Chicago Linguistic Society*, 1977, 236–287.

Lehnert, W. G.   Plot units: A narrative summarization strategy. In W. G. Lehnert & M. H. Ringle (Eds.), *Strategies for natural language processing*. Hillsdale, N.J.: Erlbaum, 1982.

Lord, A. B.   *The singer of tales*. Cambridge: Harvard University Press, 1960.

Mandler, J. M.   A code in the node: The use of a story schema in retrieval. *Discourse Processes*, 1978, *1*, 14–35.

Mandler, J. M., & Johnson, M. S.   Remembrance of things parsed: Story structure and recall. *Cognitive Psychology*, 1977, *9*, 111–151.

Marshall, N., & Glock, M. D.   Comprehension of connected discourse: A study into the relationship between the structure of text and information recalled. *Reading Research Quarterly*, 1978–79, *14*, 10–56.

McKoon, G.   Organization of information in text memory. *Journal of Verbal Learning and Verbal Behavior*, 1977, *16*, 247–260.

Meehan, J. R.   TALE-SPIN, an interactive program that writes stories. In *Proceedings of the 5th international joint conference on artificial intelligence*. Cambridge, Mass.: 1977. Pp. 91–98.

Meyer, B. J. F.   *Idea units recalled from prose in relation to their position in the logical structure, importance, stability, and order in the passage*. Unpublished master's thesis, Cornell University, 1971.

Meyer, B. J. F.   *The organization of prose and its effects on memory*. Amsterdam: North-Holland Publishing Co., 1975.

Meyer, B. J. F.   The structure of prose: Effects on learning and memory and implications for educational practice. In R. C. Anderson, R. J. Spiro, & W. E. Montague (Eds.), *Schooling and the acquisition of knowledge*. Hillsdale, N.J.: Erlbaum, 1977.

Meyer, B. J. F.   Organizational patterns in prose and their use in reading. In M. L. Kamil & A. J. Moe (Eds.), *Reading research: Studies and applications*. Clemson, S.C.: National Reading Conference, 1979. Pp. 109–117.

Meyer, B. J. F.   Basic research on prose comprehension: A critical review. In D. F. Fisher & C. W. Peters (Eds.), *Comprehension and the competent reader: Inter-specialty perspectives.* New York: Praeger, 1981.

Meyer, B. J. F.   Reading research and the composition teacher: The importance of plans. *College Composition and Communications,* 1982, *33,* 37–49.

Meyer, B. J. F.   Text dimensions and cognitive processing. In H. Mandl, N. Stein, & T. Trabasso (Eds.), *Learning and comprehension of text.* Hillsdale, N.J.: Erlbaum, 1983.

Meyer, B. J. F.   Prose analysis: Purposes, procedures, and problems. In B. K. Britton & J. Black (Eds.), *Analyzing and understanding expository text.* Hillsdale, N.J.: Erlbaum, in press.

Meyer, B. J. F., & Freedle, R. O.   Effects of discourse type on recall. *American Educational Research Journal,* in press.

Meyer, B. J. F., Haring, M. J., Brandt, D. M., & Walker, C. H.   Comprehension of stories and expository text. *Poetics,* 1980, *9,* 203–211.

Meyer, B. J. F., & McConkie, G. W.   What is recalled after hearing a passage? *Journal of Educational Psychology,* 1973, *65,* 109–117.

Miller, J. R., & Kintsch, W.   *Readability and recall of short prose passages.* Paper presented at the meeting of the American Educational Research Association, Boston, April 1980.

Miller, J. R., & Kintsch, W.   Readability and recall of short prose passages: A theoretical analysis. *Journal of Experimental Psychology: Human Learning and Memory,* 1980, *6,* 335–354.

Mills, H. *Commanding paragraphs.* Glenview, Ill.: Scott, Foresman, 1977.

Mosenthal, P.   Three types of schemata in children's recall of cohesive and noncohesive text. *Journal of Experimental Child Psychology,* 1979, *27,* 129–142.

Niles, O. S.   Organization perceived. In H. H. Herber (Ed.), *Perspectives in reading: Developing study skills in secondary schools.* Newark, Del.: International Reading Association, 1965.

Pollard-Gott, L., McCloskey, M., & Todres, A. K.   Subjective story structure. *Discourse Processes,* 1979, *2,* 251–281.

Propp, V.   *Morphology of the folktale* (L. Scott, trans.). Bloomington: Indiana University Research Center in Anthropology, Folklore, and Linguistics, Pub. 10, 1958.

Rice, G. E.   *The role of cultural schemata in narrative comprehension.* Social Sciences Research Reports No. 10. Irvine: University of California, Irvine, 1978.

Rice, G. E.   On cultural schemata. *American Ethnologist,* 1980, *1,* 152–171.

Rothkopf, E. Z., & Bisbicos, E.   Selective facilitative effects of interspersed questions on learning from written material. *Journal of Educational Psychology,* 1967, *58,* 56–61.

Rumelhart, D. E.   Notes on a schema for stories. In D. G. Bobrow & A. M. Collins (Eds.), *Representation and understanding.* New York: Academic Press, 1975.

Rumelhart, D. E.   Understanding and summarizing brief stories. In D. LaBerge & S. J. Samuels (Eds.), *Basic processes in reading: Perception and comprehension.* Hillsdale, N.J.: Erlbaum, 1977.

Rumelhart, D. E., Lindsay, P., & Norman, D.   A process model for long-term memory. In E. Tulving & W. Donaldson (Eds.), *Organization of memory.* New York: Academic Press, 1972.

Schank, R. C.   The structure of episodes in memory. In D. G. Bobrow & A. M. Collins (Eds.), *Representation and understanding.* New York: Academic Press, 1975.

Schank, R. C., & Abelson, R. P.   *Scripts, plans, goals, and understanding.* Hillsdale, N.J.: Erlbaum, 1977.

Shimmerlik, S. M.   Organization theory and memory for prose: A review of the literature. *Review of Educational Research,* 1978, *48,* 103–120.

Simmons, R. F.   *Towards a computational theory of textual discourse* (TR NL–37). Austin: University of Texas, Department of Computer Sciences, 1978.

Smith, N. B.   *Reading instructions for today's children.* Englewood Cliffs, N.J.: Prentice-Hall, 1963.

Stein, N. L.   How children understand stories: A developmental analysis. In L. Katz (Ed.), *Current topics in early childhood education* (Vol. 2). Norwood, N.J.: Ablex, 1979.

Stein, N. L., & Glenn, C. G.   An analysis of story comprehension in elementary school children. In R. O. Freedle (Ed.), *New directions in discourse processing.* Norwood, N.J.: Ablex, 1979.

Swanson, C.   *The effects of readability and top-level structure on ninth graders' recall of textual materials.* Unpublished doctoral dissertation, Arizona State University, 1979.

Thompson, S.   *The types of the folktale.* F F Communications, No. 74. Helsinki, 1928.

Thompson, S.   *Motif-index of folk-literature.* Indiana University Studies Nos. 96–97, 100, 101, 105–106, 108–110, 111–112. Bloomington: Indiana University, 1932–1936.

Thorndyke, P. W.   Cognitive structures in comprehension and memory of narrative discourse. *Cognitive Psychology,* 1977, *9,* 77–110.

Thorndyke, P. W., & Yekovich, F.   A critique of schema-based theories of human story memory. *Poetics,* 1979, *2,* 113–126.

Trabasso, T.   *Cognitive prerequisites to reading.* Paper presented at the meeting of the American Educational Research Association, Toronto, March 1978.

Trabasso, T., & van den Broek, P. W.   Coherence in narrative text. In H. Mandl, N. Stein, & T. Trabasso (Eds.), *Learning and comprehension of text.* Hillsdale, N.J.: Erlbaum, 1983.

Turner, A., & Greene, E.   *The construction and use of a propositional text base.* Boulder: University of Colorado Institute for the Study of Intellectual Behavior (TR 63), 1977.

van Dijk, T. A.   Semantic macrostructures and knowledge frames in discourse comprehension. In M. Just & P. Carpenter (Eds.), *Cognitive processes in comprehension.* Hillsdale, N.J.: Erlbaum, 1977. (a)

van Dijk, T. A.   *Text and context: Explorations in the semantics and pragmatics of discourse.* London: Longman, 1977. (b)

van Dijk, T. A.   *From text grammar to interdisciplinary discourse studies.* Paper given at the La Jolla Conference on Cognitive Science, 1979. (a)

van Dijk, T. A.   Recalling and summarizing complex discourse. In W. Burghardt & K. Hölker (Eds.), *Text processing: Papers in text analysis and text description.* Berlin/New York: de Gruyter, 1979. (b)

van Dijk, T. A.   Relevance assignment in discourse comprehension. *Discourse Processes,* 1979, *2,* 113–126. (c)

Vipond, D.   Micro- and macroprocesses in text comprehension. *Journal of Verbal Learning and Verbal Behavior,* 1980, *19,* 276–296.

Volkov, R. M.   *The investigations on formation of the folktale,* I. Ukrainian State Publishing House, 1924.

Walker, C. H., & Meyer, B. J. F.   Integrating different types of information in text. *Journal of Verbal Learning and Verbal Behavior,* 1980, *19,* 263–275.

Welborn, E. L., & English, H. B.   Logical learning and retention: A general review of experiments with meaningful verbal materials. *Psychological Bulletin,* 1937, *34,* 1–20.

Wilensky, R.   Why John married Mary: Understanding stories involving recurring goals. *Cognitive Science,* 1978, *2,* 235–266.

Wilks, Y.   Natural language understanding systems within the A. I. paradigm. In *Artificial intelligence and language comprehension*. National Institute of Education, 1976.

Williams, J.   *Style: Ten lessons in clarity and grace*. Glenview, Ill.: Scott, Foresman, 1981.

Yekovich, F. R., & Walker, C. H.   Identifying and using referents in sentence comprehension. *Journal of Verbal Learning and Verbal Behavior*, 1978, *17*, 265–277.

12 METACOGNITIVE SKILLS AND READING

Linda Baker and Ann L. Brown

In this chapter, we discuss the relationship between metacognitive skills and effective reading. One of the most influential trends in developmental cognitive psychology has been a growing interest in the child's metacognitive status, that is, the knowledge and control the child has over his or her own thinking and learning activities, including reading. As the concept of metacognition is somewhat fuzzy, it seems appropriate to begin by explaining how the term has been used, the phenomena to which it refers, and its particular relevance to reading.

The term has been used to refer to two somewhat separate phenomena and we would like to make this separation explicit here. Flavell (1978) defined metacognition as "knowledge that takes as its object or regulates any aspect of any cognitive endeavor." Two (not necessarily independent) clusters of activities are included in that statement: knowledge about cognition and regulation of cognition.

The first cluster is concerned with a person's knowledge about his or her own cognitive resources and the compatibility between the person as a learner and the learning situation. Prototypical of this category are questionnaire studies and confrontation experiments, the main purpose of which is to find out how much children know about certain pertinent features of thinking, including themselves as thinkers. The focus is on measuring the relatively stable information that children have concerning the cognitive processes involved in any academic task. This information is stable, in that one would expect that a child who knows pertinent facts (e.g., that organized material is easier to learn than disorganized material, that passages containing familiar words and concepts are easier to read than those composed of unfamiliar ones) would continue to know these facts if interrogated properly. This information is also stateable, in that the child is able to reflect on the processes and discuss them with others.

The ability to reflect on one's own cognitive processes, to be aware of one's own activities while reading, solving problems, and so on, is a late-developing skill with important implications for the child's effectiveness as an active, planful learner. If the child is aware of what is needed to perform effectively, then it

353

is possible for him or her to take steps to meet the demands of a learning situation more adequately. If, however, the child is not aware of his or her own limitations as a learner or the complexity of the task at hand, then the child can hardly be expected to take preventive actions in order to anticipate or recover from problems.

The second cluster of activities studied under the heading *metacognition* consists of the self-regulatory mechanisms used by an active learner during an ongoing attempt to solve problems. These indexes of metacognition include *checking* the outcome of any attempt to solve the problem, *planning* one's next move, *monitoring* the effectiveness of any attempted action, and *testing*, *revising*, and *evaluating* one's strategies for learning. These are not necessarily stable skills in the sense that although they are more often used by older children and adults, they are not always used by them, and quite young children may monitor their own activities on a simple problem (Brown, 1978). Learners of any age are more likely to take active control of their own cognitive endeavors when they are faced with tasks of intermediate difficulty (since if the task is too easy, they need not bother; if the task is too hard, they give up). Effective learning requires an active monitoring of one's own cognitive activities. Failure to monitor can lead to serious reading problems, as we shall document.

A third concern of psychologists interested in metacognition is the development and use of compensatory strategies. Given that learners have some awareness of their own cognitive processes and are monitoring their progress sufficiently well to detect a problem, what type of remedial activity will they introduce to overcome that problem? Strategies vary, depending on the goal of the activity; for example, reading for meaning demands different skills than reading for remembering (studying). What types of strategies are available to learners and with what efficiency can they be orchestrated are important developmental questions with obvious implications for the study of reading.

Since effective readers must have some awareness and control of the cognitive activities they engage in as they read, most characterizations of reading include skills and activities that involve metacognition. Some of the metacognitive skills involved in reading are: (a) clarifying the purposes of reading, that is, understanding both the explicit and implicit task demands; (b) identifying the important aspects of a message; (c) focusing attention on the major content rather than trivia; (d) monitoring ongoing activities to determine whether comprehension is occurring; (e) engaging in self-questioning to determine whether goals are being achieved; and (f) taking corrective action when failures in comprehension are detected (Brown, 1980).

Although the current focus on such planning and monitoring activities falls within the framework of research on metacognition, reading researchers and educators will recognize that the issues are not new. Researchers since the turn of the century (e.g., Dewey, 1910; Huey, 1908/1968; Thorndike, 1917) have been aware that reading involves the planning, checking, and evaluating activities now regarded as metacognitive skills. Moreover, numerous studies have attempted to determine differences between good and poor readers in the strategies that are crucial to effective reading (Golinkoff, 1975–1976; Ryan, 1981). Thus, although the term metacognition may be new, the knowledge and skills to which it refers have long been recognized. Therefore, in this chapter, we will consider research both explicitly and implicitly concerned with problems of metacognition in reading.

In this chapter, we will deal with two broad areas of research: reading for meaning (comprehension) and reading for remembering (studying). Reading for meaning involves the metacognitive activity of comprehension monitoring, which entails keeping track of the success with which one's comprehension is proceeding, ensuring that the process continues smoothly, and taking remedial action if necessary (Baker, 1979b). The metacognitive aspects of reading for remembering include identifying important ideas, testing one's mastery of material, developing effective study strategies, and allocating study time appropriately.

In the next two sections, we will consider the research on reading for meaning and then some selected research on studying. Under both broad headings, we will concentrate on the three main types of metacognitive skills: awareness, monitoring, and the deployment of compensatory strategies. In the final section, we will consider the potential application of this research for developing instructional routines to help alleviate some of the more disabling consequences of inadequate knowledge and control of reading activities.

READING FOR MEANING

Reading for meaning is essentially an attempt to comprehend, and any attempt to comprehend must involve comprehension monitoring. In this section, we will begin by briefly considering theories of comprehension monitoring from both cognitive psychology and reading research. We will then proceed to a consideration of the existing data on children's knowledge of such activities and their ability to monitor their own comprehension both in listening and reading tasks. Finally, we will review recent research on comprehension monitoring in adults that dispels the tacit assumption that inadequate metacognition is a disease of childhood.

Experts' Theories about Comprehension Monitoring

Comprehension monitoring activities are implicitly, if not explicitly, incorporated into several recent models of comprehension (e.g., Collins, Brown, & Larkin, 1980; Goodman, 1976; Ruddell, 1976; Rumelhart, 1980; Woods, 1980). These theories view comprehension as an active process of hypothesis testing or schema building. Readers make hypotheses about the most plausible interpretation of the text as they are reading and test these hypotheses against the available information. As more information is acquired, hypotheses can be further refined or modified. If a reasonable set of hypotheses cannot be found, comprehension suffers. Markman (1981) specifically considers the relationship between comprehension and comprehension monitoring with respect to the reader's expectations or hypotheses about meaning. She argues that if one is able to confirm or disconfirm one's hypotheses, one can acquire knowledge about how well one is comprehending the text. Markman suggests that one need not continually ask whether or not one understands; often information about one's comprehension is a byproduct of the active comprehension process itself. In some cases, all that may be necessary to detect failures to comprehend is the active attempt to understand.

Recent theories of reading incorporate similar comprehension strategies. Ruddell's (1976) model involves evaluating information adequacy, data gathering, hypothesis building, organizing and synthesizing data, and hypothesis testing. According to Goodman (1976), readers must test their hypotheses against the "screens" of meaning and grammar by frequently asking themselves if what they are reading makes sense. The reader must "monitor his choices so he can recognize his errors and gather more cues when needed" (p. 483).

This characterization of comprehension as an active constructive process is certainly not new. Thorndike (1917) suggested that comprehension problems arise if the reader "is not treating the ideas produced by the reading as provisional [so that he can] inspect and welcome them or reject them as they appear." Moreover, he argued that, "The vice of the poor reader is to say the words to himself without actively making judgments concerning what they reveal." In his research, Thorndike found that many sixth graders did not spontaneously test their understanding; although they often felt they understood, they in fact did not. Such behavior reflects poor comprehension monitoring.

A number of researchers have speculated about the conditions under which comprehension failures occur (Brown, 1980; Eller, 1967; Flavell, 1981; Markman, 1981; Rumelhart, 1980; Woods, 1980). There seem to be three main types of comprehension failures: (a) the appropriate schemata are not available; that is, the reader does not have enough knowledge about the topic to impose an interpretation upon the text; (b) the appropriate schemata are available, but the author has not provided enough clues to suggest them; that is, the author is at fault in not conveying his or her ideas clearly enough; (c) the reader finds a consistent interpretation of the text, but not the one the author intended; that is, the reader "understands" the text, but misunderstands the author. Readers who understand incorrectly have much the same feelings as readers who understand correctly. Hence, they can hardly be expected to take remedial action when comprehension fails, since they don't realize that comprehension has in fact failed. Readers who have failed to understand because they were unable to construct any coherent interpretation are more likely to initiate attempts to clarify their understanding.

If we broaden the conception of comprehension to include critical reading, a fourth cause of comprehension failure can be identified: the reader interprets the material in a manner desired by the author, rather than considering an alternative interpretation and "thus is deluded to some degree" (Eller, 1967). Critical reading involves not only imposing sense on the material in the way the author intended, but also going beyond the information given and critically evaluating it. Thus, good comprehension also depends on an awareness that authors write for a variety of purposes and that they may employ propaganda techniques to sway readers to a particular point of view.

Although mature readers typically engage in comprehension monitoring, it is not often or even usually a conscious experience. For example, Brown (1980) distinguishes between an automatic and debugging state. The skilled reader is one who can be characterized as operating with a lazy processor. All her top-down and bottom-up skills (Rumelhart, 1980) are so fluent that she can proceed merrily on automatic pilot, until a *triggering event* alerts her to a comprehension failure. While the process is flowing smoothly, her construction of meaning is very rapid, but when a comprehension failure is detected, she must slow down and allot extra processing to the problem area. She must employ debugging devices and strategies, which take time and effort. T. H. Anderson (1980) has also suggested that mature readers need not devote constant attention to evaluating their understanding. He postulated the existence of an "automated monitoring mechanism" which "renders the clicks of comprehension and clunks of comprehension failure." Similarly, Flavell (1981) argues that there are probably few conscious metacognitive experiences when comprehension is proceeding smoothly; such experiences are more likely to become conscious when progress is blocked and some obstacle to comprehension arises.

One commonly experienced triggering event is the realization that an expectation we have been entertaining about the text is not to be confirmed. Another triggering situation is when we encounter unfamiliar concepts too often for us to remain tolerant of our ignorance. Whatever the exact nature of the triggering event, we react to it by slowing down our rate of processing, allocating time and effort to the task of clearing up the comprehension failure. And in the process of disambiguation and clarification, we enter a deliberate, planful, strategic state that is quite distinct from the automatic pilot state, where we are not actively at work on debugging activities. The debugging activities themselves occupy the lion's portion of our limited processing capacity, and the smooth flow of reading abruptly stops.

Realizing that one has failed to understand is, of course, only a part of comprehension monitoring; one must also know what to do when comprehension failures occur. This involves a number of important strategic decisions. The first decision is whether or not remedial action is even necessary, a decision that will depend largely on the purposes for reading (Alessi, Anderson, & Goetz, 1979). If the reader decides to take strategic action, a number of options are available. He or she may store the confusion in memory as a pending question (T. H. Anderson, 1980), in the hope that the author will soon provide clarification. Or the reader may decide to take action immediately, which may involve rereading, jumping ahead in the text, or consulting a dictionary or knowledgeable person.

Whimbey's (1975) characterization of a good reader captures much of the essence of comprehension monitoring:

> A good reader proceeds smoothly and quickly as long as his understanding of the material is complete. But as soon as he senses that he has missed an idea, that the track has been lost, he brings smooth progress to a grinding halt. Advancing more slowly, he seeks clarification in the subsequent material, examining it for the light it can throw on the earlier trouble spot. If still dissatisfied with his grasp, he returns to the point where the difficulty began and rereads the section more carefully. He probes and analyzes phrases and sentences for their exact meaning; he tries to visualize abstruse descriptions; and through a series of approximations, deductions, and corrections he translates scientific and technical terms into concrete examples. (p. 91)

The preceding description of comprehension monitoring has focused on what theorists believe are essential skills and strategies of mature, competent readers. It is assumed that poor readers are deficient in these skills and strategies. Whimbey (1975) compares the poor reader's performance to that of a novice biology student looking through a microscope for the first time, unable to make sense of what he sees. Both are characterized by a lack of attention to relevant dimensions and a lack of task-appropriate strategies. Similar differences have been observed between novice and expert chess players (Chi, 1978) and X-ray technicians (Thomas, 1968). Novice technicians fail to scan as exhaustively as necessary and fail to focus on the most informative areas, a problem of immaturity analogous to poor readers' failure to concentrate on main ideas and failure to reread critical sections. The fact that novices exhibit similar patterns of behavior, regardless of age, demonstrates the crucial role of experience and expertise in cognitive monitoring (Brown & DeLoache, 1978).

Successful comprehension monitoring may also depend on individual differences other than reading ability. Some students are less willing to admit, even to themselves, that they have failed to understand, and they frequently will not ask questions for fear of appearing stupid (Holt, 1964). Personality characteristics such as dogmatism and closed-mindedness may also impair comprehension monitoring by leading readers to jump to conclusions without careful analysis (Kemp, 1967; Sullivan, 1978). Similarly, differences in cognitive style may influence comprehension monitoring. Field-independent students are more likely than field-dependent students to adopt an active hypothesis-testing approach to many learning situations (Goodenough, 1976). Similar differences between reflective and impulsive children have far-reaching effects on their school performance in a variety of domains, including reading (Kagan, Moss, & Sigel, 1963).

Children's Theories about Comprehension Monitoring

Most theories of reading for meaning acknowledge the crucial role of comprehension monitoring activities. Experts agree that such activities are essential for adequate understanding of texts. Here we consider what children know about reading for meaning. One simple way of assessing what children know is to ask them. A primary source of evidence that young children and poor readers have metacognitive deficits in reading comes from interview investigations of children's conceptions of the purposes of reading. In general, younger and poorer readers have little awareness that they must attempt to make sense of text; they focus on reading as a decoding process, rather than as a meaning-getting process (Canney & Winograd, 1979; Clay, 1973; Denny & Weintraub, 1963, 1966; Johns & Ellis, 1976; Myers & Paris, 1978; Reid, 1966). Two recent studies have provided representative findings of this type of research and will be discussed below.

Canney and Winograd (1979) studied children's conceptions of reading by using an experimental manipulation as well as an interview technique. Children in grades 2, 4, 6, and 8 were presented with passages that were either intact or disrupted at four levels of severity: (a) correct syntax, but some semantically inappropriate words; (b) semantic and syntactic violations, but some semblance to connected discourse; (c) strings of random words; and (d) strings of random letters. The children were asked if each type of passage could be read and why; they were also given a questionnaire probing their conceptions of reading. Children in second and fourth grades, and even sixth graders identified as poor comprehenders, focused on the decoding aspect of reading. In contrast, the better readers in sixth grade and all eighth graders knew that meaning-getting was the primary goal of reading. Moreover, poorer comprehenders often reported that all but the passage containing letter strings could be read. Since these children believed that reading is being able to say the words correctly, a passage of unrelated words seemed just as readable as an intact passage.

Thus, younger and poorer readers seem to be unaware that they must expend additional cognitive effort to make sense of the words they have decoded. They seem to lack "sensitivity" (Flavell & Wellman, 1977) to the demands of reading for meaning. Myers and Paris (1978) examined another aspect of children's metacognitive knowledge about reading, their understanding of how different variables affect performance. Children in second and sixth grades were asked a series of interview questions assessing their knowledge about person, task, and strategy variables (Flavell & Wellman, 1977) involved in reading. Many differences were apparent in children's knowledge about comprehension monitoring. For example, older readers understood that the purpose of skimming was to pick out the informative words, while younger readers said they would skim by reading the easy words. These different skimming strategies reflect conceptions of reading as meaning-getting and as word decoding respectively. Kobasigawa, Ransom, and Holland (1980) also found that it was not until eighth grade that the majority of children could describe "how to skim," although from fourth grade on, approximately half the children could do so. The older children in the Myers and Paris (1978) study also had more awareness of appropriate strategies for coping with words or sentences they didn't understand. They were more likely than younger children to say they would use a dictionary, ask someone for help, or reread a paragraph to try to figure out the meaning from context.

Although the interview studies provide tantalizing glimpses of the child's understanding, or lack of understanding, of the actual demands of reading for meaning, there are serious problems associated with self-report techniques (Brown, 1978; 1980). Briefly, even adults are less able to introspect about their cognitive knowledge than one would like (Nisbett & Wilson, 1977; but cf. White, 1980), and the problems of eyewitness testimony are no less acute when asking the witness to testify about the workings of his mind than about the activities of the world around him. For this reason we advise that conclusions concerning what a child knows and can do when reading should not rely exclusively on self-report techniques of the kind favored in interview studies, where the child is asked to imagine a reading situation and to predict how best to perform in it. Convergent evidence concerning metacognitive skills must come from observations of children actually undertaking the reading tasks in question. In the next section, we will consider the research on children's comprehension monitoring during ongoing attempts to understand messages.

Comprehension Monitoring while Listening

A great deal of developmental research has focused on the young child's difficulty in comprehending a message when listening. If children have difficulty monitoring their comprehension while listening, it is not surprising that they are similarly plagued when attempting the more difficult task of reading. Because of the obvious parallel, we will review briefly the aural comprehension data before considering analogous reading situations.

Some of the earliest evidence of poor comprehension monitoring was provided by Piaget (1926). When young children listened to a story or a technical description about how an object such as a faucet functioned, they often indicated that they had understood the message when in fact they had not. This was revealed both by later questioning and the fact that the message quality itself was poor, having been conveyed by another youngster with poor understanding. Moreover, the listeners seldom sought clarification or asked additional questions of the speaker. Modern experiments on referential communication skills have corroborated Piaget's observations (see Asher, 1979, and Patterson & Kister, 1981, for reviews of this literature). Young elementary school children frequently indicate that they have understood a message even when it was ambiguous or incomplete (Ironsmith & Whitehurst, 1978; Karabenick & Miller, 1978). They often fail to question the speaker or seek additional information when their understanding is poor (Cosgrove & Patterson, 1977).

In a recent experiment, Flavell, Speer, Green, and August (1981) examined the development of comprehension monitoring and knowledge about communication. Kindergarten and second-grade children listened to taped instructions for constructing block buildings given by a young girl serving as a confederate. The children were told to make a building exactly like the instructor's using blocks that were available to them. They were shown how to use the tape recorder and were encouraged to stop and replay the instructions as often as they wished. Flavell and his associates used a ploy popular in examinations of comprehension monitoring: they manipulated the instructions, so that their comprehensibility was adversely affected. Thus, some of the instructions contained ambiguities, unfamiliar words, insufficient information, or unattainable goals. Failure to notice such deliberately introduced inadequacies or confusions was taken as evidence of ineffective comprehension monitoring.

The children were videotaped as they attempted to carry out the instructions, and the videotapes were analyzed for nonverbal signs of problem detection, for example, looking puzzled or replaying the tape. The children were later asked if they had succeeded in making a building exactly like the instructor's and whether they thought the instructor did a good job in conveying the instructions. As expected, the older children were more likely to notice the inadequacies in the messages than the younger children. Even though both kindergarteners and second graders gave nonverbal signs of puzzlement during the task, the kindergarteners were less likely to report later that some of the messages were inadequate. This finding further attests to the lack of reliability of young children's verbal reports (Brown, 1978, 1980; Winograd & Johnston, 1982).

Markman (1977, 1979) has also examined children's ability to analyze oral messages for completeness and consistency. In her first study (Markman, 1977), children in first and third grades listened to simple instructions on how to play a game or perform a magic trick; crucial information was omitted. For example, the instructions for the card game were as follows:

We each put our cards in a pile. We both turn over the top card in our pile. We look at the cards to see who has the special card. Then we turn over the next card in our pile to see who has the special card this time. In the end the person with the most cards wins the game.

The instructions were incomplete, because, among other things, there was no mention of what the "special card" might be. Third graders realized the instructions were incomplete much more readily than did the younger children. It was often not until the first graders actually tried to carry out the instructions that they realized that they did not understand. It seems clear that the first graders did not actively evaluate whether the instructions made sense as they were listening.

These results suggest that first graders often fail to monitor their comprehension, even though it is comparatively easy to test one's understanding of instructions by evaluating whether a goal can be attained. Monitoring comprehension of text is more difficult because the criteria for successful comprehension are less explicit and readers must select their own standards for evaluation. Thus, the effectiveness of comprehension monitoring may depend not only on age, but also on the nature of the materials. This suggestion receives some support in Markman's second (1979) study. Children in third, fifth, and sixth grades listened to short essays containing inconsistent information and then answered questions designed to assess awareness of the inconsistencies. Following is an example from a passage about fish:

> Fish must have light in order to see. There is absolutely no light at the bottom of the ocean. It is pitch black down there. When it is that dark the fish cannot see anything. They cannot even see colors. Some fish that live at the bottom of the ocean can see the color of their food; that is how they know what to eat.

The obvious inconsistency here is that fish cannot see colors at the bottom of the ocean, yet some can see the color of their food. Children in all grades tested were equally unlikely to report the inconsistencies. Although third graders in the card game study did report failures to understand instructions, children of the same age and older failed to report confusions in the essays. However, when specifically warned about the inconsistencies, a greater proportion of children, primarily sixth graders, reported them. This indicates that comprehension monitoring is easier when one has some idea of what to look for, that is, when the criteria for evaluation are more explicit.

The experiments reviewed in this section show that young school children are poor at analyzing oral messages for clarity, completeness, and consistency. These shortcomings may be due to children's failures to monitor their understanding effectively. Nevertheless, failures to report message inadequacies may occasionally be due to factors other than poor comprehension monitoring (Baker, 1979a, 1979b; Brown, 1980; Winograd & Johnston, 1982). Perhaps the children believed they understood the message (i.e., they evaluated their understanding and found it adequate), but their interpretation did not match the author's interpretation. It is also possible that the children made inferences to resolve the potential sources of confusion and were unable, for reasons of verbal ability or memory, to convey this when questioned. The children may also have been unwilling to point out problems in the messages or to say they didn't understand, despite efforts to make them feel comfortable doing so.

One additional point to keep in mind is that these studies evaluated comprehension monitoring in a listening task rather than a reading task. Despite many similarities, there are some important differences between listening and reading that may contribute to differences in comprehension monitoring in the two situations (Kleiman & Schallert, 1978; Rubin, 1980). In oral communication situations, listeners have the opportunity to interact with the message source (the speaker): they can ask questions, request clarification, look puzzled, and so on. Readers are unable to interact directly with their message source (the author) and so must depend on their own resources to make sense of the message. In this respect, a listener has an advantage over a reader in clarifying comprehension difficulties, but in other respects, a reader is at an advantage. Due to the permanence of text, readers can adjust the rate of input depending on the success of their understanding. They can also reread previous sections of text and look ahead in search of clarification (Kleiman & Schallert, 1978). However, in order to take advantage of these sampling options, the reader needs to know that they are available and must also know how to use them efficiently. It is precisely in these skills that differences exist between good and poor comprehenders (e.g., Golinkoff, 1975–1976; Ryan, 1981; Smith, 1977; Strang & Rogers, 1965). In the following section, we will consider children's comprehension monitoring during reading by examining performance on a variety of representative reading tasks.

Comprehension Monitoring while Reading

Ratings of felt understanding.   One way of assessing feelings of understanding is to ask people to rate their certainty that they have answered a comprehension question correctly or incorrectly. Readers are considered good comprehension monitors if they indicate that they are sure their answers are correct when in fact they are or if they indicate that their answers are wrong when the answers are indeed incorrect. On the other hand, readers are considered poor comprehension monitors if there is a mismatch between their confidence ratings and the correctness of their answers. A study by Forrest and Waller (1979) investigated children's skills at evaluating their understanding by using this confidence rating technique. The subjects were third and sixth graders, identified by test scores as good, average, or poor readers. Each child read two different stories for each of four different purposes: (a) for fun, (b) to make up a title, (c) to find one specific piece of information as quickly as possible (skim), and (d) to study. After reading each story, the children were given a comprehension test and then rated their confidence in their answers.

The result of primary interest was that older children and those who were better readers were more successful at evaluating their performance on the comprehension test than the younger and poorer readers. Not surprisingly, the older and better readers scored higher on the comprehension tests and were more likely to adjust their reading strategies in response to the task instructions. In addition, a posttest questionnaire showed that the younger and poorer readers had less knowledge about comprehension monitoring and fix-up strategies, a result which replicated the findings of Myers and Paris (1978).

Although the Forrest and Waller (1979) study showed differences as a function of age and reading ability, the confidence rating approach to the study of comprehension monitoring has certain limitations. One problem is that young children frequently respond to questions affirmatively, regardless of the truth of their assertions (see Brown & Lawton, 1977). Thus, the third graders may have felt their answers were wrong, yet responded that they were sure they were right simply because of a positive response bias. This bias would lead to lower comprehension monitoring scores relative to the sixth graders, who used more mature criteria for making their decisions. A second limitation of the technique is that it tests one's ability to judge the correctness of an answer given *after* reading, rather than assessing one's feelings of understanding or misunderstanding *during* reading.

Self-corrections during reading.   More direct evidence of monitoring one's understanding during reading comes from self-corrections of errors. Several studies of oral reading have revealed differences between good and poor readers both in the types of errors made and in the likelihood of spontaneous corrections. Clay (1973) found that beginning readers in the upper half of their class spontaneously corrected 33 percent of their errors, while beginners in the lower half corrected only 5 percent of their errors. Weber (1970) reported that good and poor readers in the first grade did not differ in the extent to which they corrected errors that were grammatically acceptable to the sentence context but that good readers were twice as likely to correct errors that were grammatically inappropriate. In a comparison of average and above-average sixth-grade readers, Kavale and Schreiner (1979) found that the average readers were more likely to make meaning-distorting errors and were less likely to correct those errors that did occur. Similar patterns have even been observed with adults (Fairbanks, 1937; Swanson, 1937). The results of these studies suggest that good readers, even those as young as first grade, monitor their comprehension as they are reading; if they make an error that does not fit in with the previous context, they will stop and correct themselves. If the error is semantically acceptable, however, good readers may not correct it since their comprehension still seems to be proceeding smoothly.

One explanation for these differences between good and poor readers is that poor readers have difficulty decoding the words and so are unable to benefit from the contextual information that signals meaning distortions. However, recent experiments by Isakson and Miller (1976, 1978) have shown that when good and poor readers were matched on the ability to decode words in isolation, good readers still made fewer errors when reading in context. In addition, good fourth-grade readers were more likely to detect semantic and syntactic anomalies introduced into the sentences than were poor readers. When the good readers encountered an anomalous word, they frequently tried to fix up the resulting comprehension difficulty by substituting a more sensible word. Poor readers, on the other hand, read the anomalous words without apparent awareness of the problem. Thus, good readers, in addition to keeping track of the success or failure with which their comprehension was proceeding, also took measures to deal with any difficulties which did arise.

Comprehension monitoring measured by the cloze technique.   A recent study by Di Vesta, Hayward, and Orlando (1979) explored the development of comprehension monitoring strategies by using a cloze technique. In a cloze test, people are presented with passages containing word deletions and they are asked to supply the missing words. Because good readers make better use of contextual information and redundancy than poor readers, they are typically more successful on such tasks (Neville & Pugh, 1976–1977). Di Vesta et al. (1979) constructed passages such that to fill in the missing words, a subject either needed to read ahead for relevant contextual information or could rely on previous context. They predicted that whereas better readers would perform equally well on both types of tests, younger and poorer readers would perform less well on the cloze task requiring use of subsequent context. This prediction was based on a hypothesized developmental shift from believing that the printed word is inviolate to realizing that writers may be at fault. Less mature readers, who attribute comprehension failures to their own shortcomings, should deal with such failures by rereading previously read text. More mature readers, on the other hand, should adopt a strategy of searching subsequent text for clarification.

High school students of high- and low-reading ability served as subjects in one study, and good and poor readers from sixth, seventh, and eighth grades participated in a second. As expected, the older and better readers performed equally well on both cloze tasks, while the younger and poorer readers performed more poorly when they were required to make use of subsequent context. The authors concluded that younger and poorer readers made less efficient use of the strategy of searching subsequent text for clarification of information. Mastery of this strategy may be an important development in the ability to monitor one's comprehension, but it is not clear that searching subsequent text if a failure to comprehend arises is necessarily a better or more mature strategy than rereading previously read sections of text. While it may be true that the rereading strategy develops earlier, there are times when it is a more appropriate and efficient strategy (Alessi et al., 1979). A good comprehension monitor will select whatever strategy is most appropriate to the situation at hand. In addition, because the demands of the cloze test are quite different from those of a typical reading situation, the failure to use a strategy of looking ahead may not extend to normal reading.

On-line measures of processing during reading. One of the best sources of information about processing behaviors are on-line measures obtained while a subject is actually reading. Such measures include eye movements, eye-voice span (EVS), and reading times. Studies have shown that good readers modify their eye movements when faced with difficult materials and adapt them appropriately when given different instructions for reading such as reading for the general idea versus reading to obtain a detailed understanding (I. H. Anderson, 1937; Levin & Cohn, 1968). Good readers also have longer EVS than poor readers, indicating they use a scan-for-meaning strategy rather than a word-by-word approach. In addition, good readers reread previous sections of text only if they are unable to understand an entire chunk of text, while poor readers, when they make regressive movements, do so within single words (Buswell, 1929). It is unfortunate that most of the studies which have obtained on-line measures of reading behavior have not assessed comprehension. Equally unfortunate is the fact that most comprehension studies have not obtained processing measures. We clearly need information of both types to attain a better understanding of the monitoring processes crucial to good comprehension (Ryan, 1981).

Self-reports during reading.   Although many of the observed differences between good and poor readers implicate metacognitive factors, few studies have examined the metacognitive experiences of their subjects during reading. The interview studies, which questioned children about the strategies they would use in hypothetical situations, revealed differences in knowledge about reading but did not address actual differences in reading skills. Are readers aware of using particular strategies as they read? Do they consciously modify their reading strategies in response to changes in task demands? How carefully do they evaluate their ongoing comprehension processes? Some researchers have attempted to answer such questions by asking readers to comment on their thoughts and behaviors while they are engaged in reading.

Introspective reports collected from adults have provided evidence that mature readers do possess some awareness and control of their comprehension processes (Collins et al., 1980; Olson, Duffy, & Mack, 1978). For example, Collins et al. presented short, difficult-to-understand passages to adults and asked them to describe how they had processed the text. Analysis of the protocols revealed the complex processes involved in attempting to construct an interpretation of a passage such as evaluating it for plausibility, completeness, and interconnectedness.

Several self-report studies have been conducted in an effort to identify differences in strategy use between good and poor readers in high school (Olshavsky, 1976–1977, 1978; Smith, 1967; Strang & Rogers, 1965). Olshavsky (1976–1977) presented students with stories to read, clause by clause, and instructed them to talk about what happened in the story and about what they were doing and thinking as they read. Good and poor readers were quite similar in their attempts to monitor comprehension; when they failed to understand words or clauses, they used contextual cues, inferential reasoning, and rereading as strategies for resolving comprehension difficulties. In a second study, Olshavsky (1978) used the same procedure but varied the difficulty of the passages. Contrary to her predictions, strategy use decreased rather than increased with passage difficulty, for both good and poor readers. Olshavsky attributed her unexpected results to the fact that students simply gave up trying to understand the difficult passages.

Though strategy differences between good and poor readers were minimal in Olshavsky's studies, other investigators have found interesting differences due to reading ability. Strang and Rogers (1965) observed that good readers often tried to describe their process or method of reading a short story, while poor readers seemed almost completely unaware of the processes of reading. In addition, poor readers were less likely to take remedial measures when they encountered ideas and words they did not understand. Similarly, Smith (1967) reported that good readers adjusted their reading behaviors depending on whether they were reading for details or general impressions, while poor readers used the same behaviors for both purposes. In addition, the poor readers were less able to report the procedures they used. Interestingly, Smith found that neither good nor poor readers remembered being taught how to read for different purposes; it seems this is a skill that good readers develop on their own.

Finally, to strike a positive note, it is not always the case that poor readers are found deficient in metacognitive awareness. Ngandu (1977) obtained retrospective reports over a four-month period from high school sophomores enrolled in remedial reading classes. Over time, these poor readers came to use many of the strategies characteristic of good readers, and they often knew which behaviors were effective and which were ineffective in helping them comprehend. Variables that promote and foster the development of such awareness in poor readers deserve special attention.

Comprehension Monitoring in Mature Readers

The research discussed thus far has been concerned with the comprehension monitoring limitations of young children and older children who are poor readers. Underlying this research is the tacit assumption that competent readers always monitor their comprehension effectively. But do they? Given that students tend not to receive formal instruction in evaluating and regulating their understanding, perhaps there is room for improvement even among college students. Two recent studies by Baker and her colleagues have shown that this is in fact the case (Baker, 1979a; Baker & Anderson, 1982). In both studies, confusions were introduced into expository passages to pinpoint segments that should cause comprehension difficulties, and students were asked to report the confusions after reading. Additional evidence of comprehension monitoring was obtained by collecting retrospective reports and recall protocols (Baker, 1979a) and by recording on-line reading behaviors (Baker & Anderson, 1982). (See T. H. Anderson, 1979, for a discussion of the pilot phases of this research.)

In the first study (Baker, 1979a), college students were instructed to read six expository passages carefully in preparation for subsequent discussion questions. Each passage contained one of three types of confusions (inappropriate logical connectives, ambiguous referents, and inconsistent information), but subjects were not informed of their existence before reading. After subjects answered discussion questions calling for recall of the deficient sections of text, they were informed that the paragraphs did, indeed, contain confusions and were asked to report them, rereading the paragraphs if necessary. The students were also asked whether or not they noticed the confusions during reading, how they had interpreted them, and how the confusions affected their overall understanding of the paragraph.

The study provided several findings of interest. A surprisingly large percentage of the confusions (62 percent) were not detected, and students claimed to have noticed less than one quarter of the confusions during reading. Nevertheless, the recall protocols and retrospective reports made it apparent that many failures to report confusions were not due to failures to monitor comprehension but rather to the use of fix-up strategies for resolving comprehension problems. (See Baker, 1979a, for a detailed discussion of these strategies.) For example, students frequently made inferences to supplement the information explicitly presented in the text; they decided that some relevant information had been omitted and used their prior knowledge to bridge the gap. They also reported strategies of rereading and looking ahead in search of clarification. Some students reported using criteria for evaluating their understanding that did not require fix-up strategies. For example, they realized there was a problem but decided it was trivial and not worth the effort of attempting resolution. Moreover, they occasionally failed to detect confusions because they had assigned alternative interpretations to the text; they felt they understood but in fact did not get the intended meaning.

These findings suggest that mature readers do engage in comprehension monitoring during reading, but we should not overinterpret data that are dependent on retrospective reports and measures of recall obtained after reading. In order to obtain more conclusive evidence of comprehension monitoring during reading, Baker and Anderson (1982) obtained on-line measures of reading behavior. Passages containing inconsistencies were presented on a computer terminal, sentence by sentence, under individual readers' control. Thus, students advanced to subsequent sentences at their own pace and were free to look back at previous sentences. The computer automatically recorded reading times on each exposure to a sentence and the pattern of movement through the text. After reading the passages, the students were asked to indicate which sentences, if any, contained inconsistencies. Half of the students were informed prior to reading that inconsistencies were present, while the remainder were told after reading.

As expected, students spent more time reading inconsistent passages than consistent passages, and they looked back at previous sentences more frequently when inconsistencies were present. Students were considerably more successful at detecting confusions in this study than in the previous one, perhaps because inconsistencies are more salient than the other types of confusions used. Surprisingly, students who were explicitly instructed to monitor for inconsistencies during reading did not differ from uninformed readers in either reading behavior or confusion detection. Our interpretation of this finding is that under favorable conditions adults are able to monitor their comprehension effectively with or without specific instructions. In sum, these experiments have shown that, in general, college students evaluate their understanding during the actual process of reading. If they encounter a confusion, they devote extra time to studying it, and they reread previous sentences in an effort to clarify their understanding. It is these processes of self-regulation that children need to acquire in order to become effective readers.

READING FOR REMEMBERING

Reading for remembering, or studying, involves all the activities of reading for meaning and more. It is obviously helpful, if not absolutely necessary, to understand the material one is studying. Failures to comprehend materials to be remembered would result in a reliance on difficult rote-remembering techniques to ensure retention of the material. While students have been known to approach a studying task via rote-learning methods, and there is a very large body of data examining the processes underlying such procedures (Brown, 1975), we will restrict our attention here to attempts to study that rely on an initial effort to understand, followed by additional efforts aimed at ensuring retention of critical or important information. In order to study, the learner must take purposive action to ensure that the material is not only comprehensible but also memorable. In this section, we will consider some selected evidence from the developmental literature that highlights the problems immature learners face when attempting to read for remembering.

We would like to emphasize, however, that the work focusing on metacognitive aspects of studying is but a small part of the large area of research on effective

techniques for studying. Anderson and Armbruster (this volume) review the literature on study techniques and the how-to-study programs that have been developed to teach effective study skills. Therefore, this section should be regarded
as complementary to their much more extensive review. Here we will concentrate on a few selected studies that have been carried out recently, within the
framework of metacognitive skills in children's studying. Interestingly, few investigators in the traditional study-skills literature have been primarily concerned
with what the student does *during* reading to facilitate learning from text. For
example, Robinson's (1941) SQ3R technique instructs the student to engage in
survey and question activities *before* reading and to engage in recitation, reflection, and review activities *after* reading. However, what a student does while
actually processing the material may be one of the most important aspects of
effective study, and it is this aspect that the metacognitive research focuses upon.

In order to be an efficient studier, one must engage in "study monitoring"
(Locke, 1975), which is similar to comprehension monitoring:

> Studying actually requires a double or split mental focus. On the one
> hand, you need to be focused on the material itself (that is, on learning
> it). At the same time, however, you need to be constantly checking to see
> that you are actually performing those mental operations that produce learn-
> ing. In short, you need to monitor your mental processes while studying.
> (Locke, 1975, p. 126)

Study monitoring involves the ability to concentrate on the main ideas, to
introduce some deliberate tactic to aid learning, and the concurrent ability to
self-test the effectiveness of the strategy one has called into service. Adequately
dispensing the available study time involves at least an appreciation of which
material is important and which material is not known sufficiently to risk a test.
When faced with the common task of attempting to commit to memory a set
of materials or when time limitations or other restrictions impede leisurely study,
how do we plan our time for most efficient results? Such a task can involve
very fine degrees of metacognitive judgment, as any student can attest. In this
section, we will consider recent work that focuses on various components of
study activity: concentrating on main ideas, making use of logical structure in
the material, self-interrogation during studying, self-testing the results of studying,
and employing macrorules to ensure comprehension and retention.

Selecting and Studying Main Ideas

Children are commonly exhorted to concentrate on the main ideas when studying, but in order to be responsive to this suggestion, they must be aware of
what the main points of a passage are. This is a gradually developing skill, and
although children as young as 6 can often indicate the main character and sequence of events in a simple narrative, they tend to experience difficulty isolating
central issues in more complex prose (Brown & Smiley, 1977; Smiley, Oakley,
Worthen, Campione, & Brown, 1977). For example, grade school children who
were perfectly able to recall the main ideas of folk stories had much more difficulty

rating sections of the stories in terms of their importance to the theme (Brown & Smiley, 1977; Brown, Smiley, & Lawton, 1978). This finding has important implications for studying. In order to go beyond retention of just a few main points, that is, to achieve a more complete fleshed-out memory of the text, one must engage in active strategies to ensure increased attention to material that will not be retained automatically. This need for active intervention is particularly pressing if the contents of lengthy texts are to be retained over some period of time, a typical school-learning situation.

As children mature, they become better able to identify the essential organizing features and crucial elements of texts (Brown & Smiley, 1977; Pichert, 1979). Thanks to this foreknowledge, they should be able to make better use of extended study time. Brown and Smiley (1978) found that when given an extra period for study, children from seventh grade up improved their recall considerably for important elements of text; recall of less important details did not improve. Children below seventh grade did not show such effective use of additional study time. As a result, older students' recall protocols following study included all the essential elements and little trivia. Younger children's recall, though still favoring important elements, had many such elements missing.

Older students benefit from increased study time as a direct result of their insights into the workings of their own memory and their ability to identify the important elements of the texts. Younger students, not so prescient, cannot be expected to allocate extra time intelligently; they do not concentrate on the important elements of text, since they do not know what they are. Evidence to support this claim came from an examination of the activities the students engaged in while studying. The young children rarely appeared to be doing anything more than rereading. The older students, however, underlined or took notes during studying. Students who spontaneously engaged in underlining or note taking tended to use these devices to highlight the main ideas and, as a result of this selective attention, increased their recall of these central ideas on subsequent tests.

Once they have ensured that the main ideas are well understood, efficient students will take steps to fill in the details. One method of achieving this is to test oneself to determine which details one has failed to recall and then to devote extra attention to the previously missed information. Even grade school children can initiate some efforts to test their current state of memory (Masur, McIntyre, & Flavell, 1973), and mildly retarded children can also be taught to do so (Brown & Campione, 1977; Brown, Campione, & Barclay, 1979). But again, this can become a much more difficult task if the material is complex.

The ability to concentrate on information one has previously failed to recall was examined in a laboratory task analogous to the process of studying (Brown & Campione, 1979; Brown et al., 1978). Students from fifth through twelfth grade, together with college students, were asked to study prose passages until they could recall all the details in their own words. They were allowed repeated trials. The passages were divided into constituent idea units rated in terms of their importance to the theme; there were four levels of rated importance. On each trial, the students were allowed to select a subset of the idea units (printed on cards) to keep with them while they attempted recall. After recall and a rest period, the entire process was repeated.

Of interest are the idea units selected as retrieval aids to enhance recall. On the first trial, the majority of students at all ages selected the most important units to help them recall, and children below high school age continued to do this, even though across trials they became perfectly able to recall the most important information without aid but persistently failed to recall additional details. College students, however, modified their selection as a function of trials: on the first trial they selected predominantly important (Level 4) units for retrieval aids. On the second trial they shifted to a preference for Level 3 units, while on the third trial they preferred Level 2 units. On all three trials, Level 1 units were treated appropriately as trivia. As they learned more and more of the material, college students shifted their choice of retrieval cues to reflect their estimated state of knowledge.

Older high school students showed the same basic pattern as the college students, but they were one trial behind; they did not begin to shift to less important units until the third trial. This lag could be due to slower learning, that is, both groups shifted when they reached the same level of learning, but the younger students took an extra trial to reach that level. It could also be due to a slower selection of the effective study strategy of switching to less important units, that is, both groups learned as much on each trial, but it took high school students longer to realize that they needed to shift cue selection. The latter appears to be the correct interpretation, for even when students were matched on the basis of degree of learning, the younger students still took longer to shift their choice of retrieval cues. Thus, the ability to select suitable retrieval cues is a late-developing skill because it requires a fine degree of sensitivity to the demands of studying. The successful user of the flexible retrieval plan illustrated in these studies (Brown & Campione, 1979; Brown et. al., 1978) must have (a) information concerning the current state of knowledge, that is, what he knows of the text and what he does not yet know; (b) knowledge of the fine gradation of importance of various elements of texts, that is, what is important to know and what can be disregarded; and (c) the strategic knowledge to select for retrieval cues information that he has missed previously.

Although the retrieval-cue-selection task is a somewhat artificial analogue to "true" studying, it does demonstrate the complexity of concentrating first on main ideas and then, via a process of self-testing, gradually filling in the details. A process similar to this is involved in studying. In order to succeed, the student must have at least rudimentary self-knowledge (i.e., myself as a memorizer), task knowledge (gist recall vs. verbatim recall), and text knowledge (importance vs. trivia, organization of text, etc.). The orchestration and coordination of these forms of knowledge demand a sophisticated learner, and it is, therefore, not surprising that efficient studying is a late-emerging skill.

Making Use of Logical Structure

Another important rule for effective studying is to capitalize on any inherent structure in the text. If the material is essentially meaningless to the student, she will have a great deal of difficulty retaining it. If the student can detect the logical structure of the material, she will be better able to learn from it.

Children have some difficulty detecting even gross violations of logical structure. For example, Danner (1976) constructed two short expository passages containing four topics related to an overall theme. In organized versions of the passages, each paragraph dealt with one topic, while in disorganized versions, each paragraph contained sentences about different topics. Children in grades two, four, and six listened to the taped passages, with each subject hearing an organized version of one passage and a disorganized version of the second.

The children were asked to recall the passages and then they were asked which passage was more difficult to learn and were asked to justify their answers. The younger children showed similar recall patterns to the older children, in that organized passages were better recalled than disorganized ones. However, the younger children had less awareness of the cause of the difference in difficulty. All children reported that the disorganized passages were more difficult, but only the older children could show the experimenter how the two passages differed or could actually state that one passage was mixed up and the other in the correct order.

A recent series of studies by Bransford, Stein, Shelton, and Owings (1981) also shows that less able students have little awareness of the text and task characteristics that should be taken into account when studying, even though their memory is affected by the structure of the text. Bransford et al. presented fifth-grade students in the top and bottom quartiles of their classes with short stories which differed in the extent to which descriptions of characters were congruent with their behaviors. Examples of sentences from a congruent, or precise, story are: "The hungry boy ate a hamburger. The sleepy boy went to bed." In the less precise stories, the pairing of characters and events was reversed: "The hungry boy went to bed. The sleepy boy ate a hamburger." The students were allowed to spend as much time reading and studying the passages as they wished and were tested for memory with such questions as, "What did the hungry boy do?" The children were then asked which passage was harder to learn and were asked to justify their responses.

Children from both quartiles had better memory for the precise passages than the imprecise, indicating a facilitative effect of congruence with past experience. However, the better students were more likely to identify the imprecise passages as more difficult and to include appropriate justifications for their answers. In addition, the better students spent more time studying the less precise passages than the precise, while the study times of the poorer students did not differ across the two passage types. These results show clear differences in the metacognitive knowledge brought to bear on the task. However, in subsequent work, Bransford et al. found that the poorer students were quite capable of evaluating whether the passages made sense when they were asked to evaluate them with respect to their own experiences. Moreover, with training, these students also showed differential study time for the two passage types. This suggests that although poor students do not spontaneously monitor their understanding and mastery of prose material, they are capable of doing so with relevant instruction.

Self-Interrogation during Studying

One way to facilitate learning from text during reading is to engage in self-interrogation. André and Anderson (1978–1979) recently developed and tested a self-questioning study technique in which high school students were taught to locate sections of text containing important points and generate questions about them. They found that generating such questions facilitated learning better than simply reading and rereading text or making up questions without regard to important points. In addition, the training was more effective for students of lower ability, suggesting that the better students had developed effective self-questioning techniques of their own. André and Anderson suggest that self-questioning may be more effective than such passive strategies as rereading because it incorporates many metacognitive components. That is, it encourages the reader to (a) set purposes for study, (b) identify and underline important segments of the material, (c) generate questions which require comprehension of the text to be correctly answered, and (d) think of possible answers to the questions. The questioning strategy leads the student to an active monitoring of the learning activity and to the engagement of strategic action.

Student-generated questions are valuable not only as an aid to studying, but also as an aid to comprehension itself. Singer's (1978) conception of "active comprehension" involves reacting to a text with questions and seeking answers with subsequent reading. His preliminary work has shown that student-generated questions are more effective in promoting comprehension than teacher-generated questions, even for children in elementary school. The ability to ask relevant questions of oneself during reading is, of course, crucial to comprehension monitoring and studying. Thus, training in effective question asking may be an important first step in the development of monitoring skills. Collins et al. (1980) suggest that many failures of comprehension are in fact due to a failure to ask the right questions; and a study by Nash and Torrance (1974) has shown that participation in a creative reading program designed to sensitize readers to gaps in their knowledge, such as inconsistencies and ambiguities, led to a significant improvement in the kinds of questions first graders asked about their reading material. Perhaps training in creative reading is a good technique for teaching children to monitor their comprehension as they read.

Instruction in critical reading may also be useful in fostering the evaluation skills required to monitor one's own understanding while reading and studying. However, although most elementary school curricula include units in critical reading, the instruction is often inadequate. Because instruction is typically postponed until children have become fluent readers, "the habit of indiscriminate acceptance of printed material may become so well established that later instruction in these skills would be extremely difficult" (Wolf, King, & Huck, 1968, p. 435). A second problem lies in the practice of limiting emphasis on critical reading to a specific class period, rather than attempting to promote critical reading in a variety of contexts (Goodman, 1976). As many educators have noted, all too few college students today are critical readers (Wolf, 1967), and this certainly poses a barrier to their development of an adequate repertoire of study skills.

Macrorules for Comprehension and Retention

An essential element of effective studying is the ability to estimate one's readiness to be tested. This can be a simple form of knowledge or it can involve very complex forms of evaluation. Consider a simple form that young children can engage in quite successfully. Presented with a set of pictures, grade school children were asked to continue studying them until they were sure they would remember all of them verbatim (Flavell, Friedrichs, & Hoyt, 1970). By third grade, the majority of normal children can accomplish this task, and with training, even mentally retarded children can greatly improve their performance (Brown et al., 1979).

Estimating that one can recall a list of items verbatim is a relatively simple task for those who engage in simple strategies like rehearsal or anticipation, thus providing immediate feedback that one can or cannot recall the list. It is not such a simple task when one must recall the gist of a prose passage. Although strategies of anticipation or rehearsal are still useful, selection of what to anticipate or rehearse is more difficult, and the criteria of successful retention are much less precise. The learner must gauge when he has grasped the main ideas, a much more subjective experience than estimating verbatim recall of a list of items. Encouragingly, training on the simple list-learning task does improve the performance of retarded children in the more complex prose-learning situation (Brown et al., 1979).

A commonly reported sophisticated method of testing one's level of comprehension and retention and, therefore, one's preparedness for a test, is to attempt to summarize the material one has been reading. Composing such a summary is a complex task and requires considerable skill. Brown and Day (1983) identified five basic rules that are essential to summarization, operations that are very similar to the macrorules described by van Dijk and Kintsch (1978) as basic operations involved in comprehending and remembering prose. Two of the five rules involve the deletion of unnecessary material. One should obviously delete material that is trivial, and even grade school children are quite adept at this (Brown & Day, 1983; Brown, Day, & Jones, 1983). One should also delete material that is redundant. A third rule of summarization is to provide a superordinate term or event for a list of items or actions. For example, if a text contains a list such as *cats, dogs, goldfish, gerbils,* and *parrots,* one can substitute the term *pets.* Similarly, one can substitute a superordinate action for a list of subcomponents of that action, that is, *John went to London* for *John left the house, John went to the train station, John bought a ticket,* and so on. The two remaining rules have to do with providing a summary of the main constituent unit of text, the paragraph: first find a topic sentence, if any, for this is the author's summary of the paragraph. If there is no topic sentence, invent your own. The five operations, then, are: (a) delete redundancy, (b) delete trivia, (c) provide superordinates, (d) select topic sentences, and (e) invent topic sentences where missing.

These operations are used freely by experts when summarizing texts (Brown & Day, 1983), but do less sophisticated readers realize that these rules can be applied? Brown and Day examined the ability of children from grades 5, 7, and 10 and college students to use the rules while summarizing. They used specially constructed texts that enabled them to predict when each rule should be applied, or at least would be applied by experts (college rhetoric teachers). Even the youngest children were able to use the two deletion rules with above 90 percent accuracy, showing that they understood the basic idea behind a summary: get rid of unnecessary material. On the more complex rules, however, developmental differences were apparent. Students became increasingly adept at using the superordination and topic-sentence rules, with college students performing extremely well. However, the most difficult rule, invention, was almost never used by fifth graders, used on only a third of those occasions when it would be appropriate by tenth graders, and used by college students on only half of the appropriate occasions. Junior college students (remedial studiers) performed like seventh graders, having great difficulty with the invention rule and using only the deletion rules effectively.

Brown and Day explained this developmental progression in terms of the degree of cognitive intervention needed to apply each rule. The easier deletion rules require only that the child omit information in the text, and the intermediate topic-sentence rule requires only that the child identify and select the main sentence contained in a paragraph. But the more difficult invention rule requires that the child supply a synopsis in his or her own words, that is, add information, rather than just delete, select, or manipulate sentences already provided for him or her. It is these processes of invention that are the essence of good summarization, that are used with facility by experts, and that are most difficult for novice learners.

It is encouraging, however, that these rules can be taught. Day (1980) trained junior college students of varying levels of reading sophistication to apply the five rules and to check that they were using the rules appropriately. They were given various colored pencils and told to delete redundant information in red, delete trivial information in blue, write in a superordinate for any lists, underline topic sentences if provided, and write in a topic sentence if needed. Then, they were to use the remaining information to write a summary. After many examples and some practice, performance improved dramatically. For the more sophisticated students, training in the rules alone was sufficient to bring about large improvements. For students with more severe learning problems, training in using the rules and procedures for self-management (checking, monitoring, etc.) were both necessary to effect improvement. But they did improve, dramatically.

The macrorules of summarization may also facilitate studying directly. Constructing an adequate summary for oneself serves as a check that one has both understood and remembered the material. Moreover, there is some evidence that it is easier to study from a summary than from the original text (Reder & Anderson, 1981). Many college students learn to use such macrorules for themselves, but others do not. If we make it explicit that such rules exist, that such rules can be applied regularly, and that the application of such rules does improve performance, the study skills of the less able can be much improved.

Implications for Instruction

Throughout this chapter, we have indicated some of the quite striking problems that children experience when reading. Awareness of these difficulties should sensitize teachers to possible lines of remediation. In this last section, we will examine the types of skills that we feel should readily respond to training and those that should prove less tractable. Finally, we will discuss the emergence of self-awareness and self-regulation, which are fundamental to effective reading.

There are two general classes of problems that can impede effective reading: inefficient application of rules and strategies and impoverished background knowledge. The child may lack the necessary strategies to make reading an active learning experience, and we have given ample evidence of children's lack of strategic knowledge in this chapter. Alternatively, or in addition, the child may lack the requisite knowledge of the world to understand texts that presuppose adequate background experience. Instruction aimed at instigating strategic reading is somewhat easier to design than instruction aimed at instilling relevant knowledge, although, unfortunately, the two forms of knowledge interact in quite complex ways (Brown, in press).

Consider, first, instruction in rules and strategies. If adequate performance depends on the application of a set of rules, and these rules can be specified exactly, then it should be possible to design instructional routines that introduce the uninitiated to this possibility. For example, merely making children aware that they should continue studying and self-testing until ready for a test improves study performance in young children (Brown et al., 1979). Instructing students in efficient self-questioning techniques is also an effective training procedure (Andre & Anderson, 1978–1979). Sensitizing young readers to the logical structure of text and the inherent meaning in certain passages again helps the less able reader (Bransford et al., 1980). The more explicit and detailed understanding one has of effective rules for reading, the more readily can those rules be trained. Brown and Day's work with summarization rules is a case in point. Instructing students to make their summaries as brief as possible and to omit unnecessary information was not an explicit enough guide for junior college students. Exact specification of the rules that could be used to achieve this aim, however, was an extremely effective instructional routine (Day, 1980). The more we are able to specify the rules used by expert readers, the more we will be able to successfully instruct the novice.

The second major impediment to effective reading is a deficient knowledge base. If the text deals with topics unfamiliar to the reader, it will be difficult for her to understand the significance of the material, to select main points, and to disregard trivia. One has to understand the meaning of the material one is reading to be able to identify just what is important and what is trivial. One solution to this problem is to select texts that do deal with familiar material, but this is not always possible. And whereas the teacher may actively attempt to provide the requisite background knowledge for a particular text, she or he cannot always do this. The only answer is to increase the reader's store of information, and this takes time. The only prescription for training is one of general enrichment, which few schools have the resources to provide.

One strategy that can be instructed, however, is the general routine of attempting to fit what one is reading into a framework of whatever background knowledge one has. Efficient readers do this routinely (R. C. Anderson, 1977), and there is some evidence that young children will use background knowledge to flesh out their understanding of texts (Brown, Smiley, Day, Townsend, & Lawton, 1977). Good teachers engage in four main activities to help children comprehend a lesson (Schallert & Kleiman, 1979). They tailor the message to the child's level of understanding; they continually focus the student's attention on the main points; they force the students to monitor comprehension by asking them questions about their degree of understanding; and, finally, they activate schemata, that is, they help the students see how the new information is related to knowledge they already have. Instructing children to engage in these activities on their own while they read should be both possible and profitable.

This brings us back to a general theme running throughout the paper, the notion of self-awareness. An essential aim is to make the reader aware of the active nature of reading and the importance of employing problem-solving, trouble-shooting routines to enhance understanding. If the reader can be made aware of (a) basic strategies for reading and remembering, (b) simple rules of text construction, (c) differing demands of a variety of tests to which his knowledge may be put, and (d) the importance of attempting to use any background knowledge he may have, he cannot help but become a more effective reader. Such self-awareness is a prerequisite for self-regulation, the ability to monitor and check one's own cognitive activities while reading.

METACOGNITIVE SKILLS AND READING: AN UPDATED PERSPECTIVE

At the time the original chapter was written, interest in the metacognitive aspects of reading was in its infancy. Indeed, much of the research we cited was carried out under rather different auspices. One of the more formidable tasks involved in writing the chapter was to seek pertinent evidence in sources that never used key words such as metacognition and comprehension monitoring. The fact that pertinent studies existed, of course, indicates that researchers have been interested in similar issues for quite some time. However, because of the variations in terminology, these similarities were not apparent to the casual peruser of the literature. One of the main contributions of the chapter, we feel, was its attempt to integrate a previously unintegrated body of literature.

In the four years that have elapsed since the chapter was written, metacognition has come of age. The number of studies specifically examining metacognitive aspects of reading has increased dramatically, as has the number of integrative reviews (e.g., Baker, in press; Baker & Brown, in press; Brown, 1982; Brown, Armbruster, & Baker, in press; Wagoner, 1983; Yussen, Mathews, & Hiebert, 1982). Given the availability of these reviews, we will not attempt to provide a comprehensive update of the literature here. Rather, we will focus selectively on some of the major developments in the field. In so doing, we will follow the basic organizational scheme of the original chapter, maintaining the distinction between reading for meaning and reading for remembering.

Reading for Meaning

This part of the chapter was devoted to examining theoretical and empirical research on comprehension monitoring. The first section, "Experts' Theories about Comprehension Monitoring" served to introduce the concept and needs no revision.

Children's Theories about Comprehension Monitoring

The second section was primarily concerned with children's knowledge about the strategies, tasks, and goals of reading, that is, their metacognitive knowledge about reading. This knowledge has typically been tapped through the use of structured interviews, as in the Myers and Paris (1978) and Canney and Winograd

(1979) studies described in this section and in more recent studies by Garner and Kraus (1981–82), Paris and Myers (1981), and Gambrell and Heathington (1981). The general consensus, then and now, is that younger and less proficient readers tend to focus on reading as a decoding process rather than as a meaning-getting process.

We concluded the section with a word of caution about overreliance on interview data, and we encouraged researchers to seek convergent behavioral evidence. Data are now available indicating that our concerns were well founded. Studies incorporating both interview and behavioral components have often revealed a lack of correspondence between what children say they would do while reading and what they in fact do (Garner & Kraus, 1981–1982; Paris & Myers, 1981). Moreover, this lack of correspondence has also been found among college students (Phifer & Glover, 1982), leading the authors to title their report, "Don't take students' word for what they do while reading."

Though it may appear that such findings render self-report data useless, such is not the case. The lack of correspondence between saying and doing is theoretically important. Why does it obtain? And in what direction? Usually the relationship is such that readers indicate they know that a strategy is effective, but they do not use it. Sometimes, however, a reader does not describe how to use a particular strategy but does in fact use it (e.g., skimming [Kobasigawa et al., 1980]). In the former case, metacognitive knowledge seems to precede strategy use, while in the latter case, it seems to follow. Perhaps we need to make a distinction here between declarative knowledge (knowing *that*) and procedural knowledge (knowing *how*). Intuitively, declarative and procedural knowledge differ in the ease with which they can be subjected to deliberate examination. Consider, for example, the relative difficulty of *reporting that* tying your shoe is a good way to avoid tripping as compared to *describing how* to tie your shoe. Moreover, one would also expect to find that knowledge that a particular strategy is useful precedes its routine use, which in turn precedes the ability to describe how it is used. In short, rather than dismissing self-reports for lack of validity, we should seek to understand why there is not always a correspondence between what readers say they would or should do in a given situation and what they in fact do.

Comprehension Monitoring while Listening

This section of the chapter focused primarily on three studies, two of which already have become classics: Markman's 1977 and 1979 studies of children's evaluation of inadequate instructions and essays and Flavell, Speer, Green, and August's (1981) monograph on children's evaluation of inadequate instructions. These studies portrayed young children as very ineffective evaluators of their own comprehension, who frequently indicated they understood material that by design was not comprehensible. Although we pointed out some alternative explanations for why the children did not report the problems (e.g., they believed they understood but their interpretation did not match the author's interpretation), we concluded that young children are poor at monitoring their understanding of oral messages.

In light of more recent empirical evidence, however, this conclusion seems overly harsh. For example, several investigations have shown that when the problems inherent in the messages are made more salient, children show considerably more competence at identifying them (e.g., Pace, 1980; Patterson, O'Brien, Kister, Carter, & Kotsonis, 1981; Pratt & Bates, 1982; Stein & Trabasso, 1982; Wimmer, 1979). In addition, when children are informed in advance that the materials will contain problems and are given specific examples, their problem identification also improves (e.g., Baker, 1983a; Markman & Gorin, 1981). Finally, when children are given feedback as to the success of their initial efforts and are given a second opportunity to identify missed problems, even five-year-olds show substantial gains (Baker, 1983a). Such findings clearly indicate that performance factors must be taken into account when appraising children's comprehension monitoring skills. The fact that children do show considerable success at evaluating their understanding under optimally structured conditions provides important insight into the kinds of procedures that could be used to foster effective comprehension monitoring in more naturalistic settings and in the absence of external supports (i.e., in settings more similar to those initially studied by Markman and Flavell et al.).

The section closed with a reminder that comprehension monitoring in listening situations may differ in important ways from comprehension monitoring in reading situations. As yet, we still lack empirical evidence addressing this possibility. However, it may well be that the *evaluation* component of comprehension monitoring is similar in the two situations, that is, both listeners and readers may use the same standards or criteria to evaluate their state of understanding. What may differ is the *regulation* component, that is, once a problem has been identified, listeners and readers may deal with it in different ways. These are the strategies that were discussed in the chapter, for example, listeners can request clarification from the speaker; readers can reread or look ahead in the text.

Comprehension Monitoring while Reading

The section of the chapter was organized according to the different types of tasks that have been used to examine comprehension monitoring during reading. Since the purpose of this organizational scheme was simply to highlight the variety of research methods, we will not maintain this separation here. In fact, most of the recent studies have combined two or more approaches in order to acquire converging evidence, a research strategy that is particularly valuable given the difficulties inherent in operationalizing comprehension monitoring. Because the extent to which readers evaluate and regulate their own comprehension is an issue of such obvious educational significance, it has attracted dozens of researchers from diverse backgrounds. So much additional empirical evidence has become available since the chapter was written that we can't begin to do it justice and so must again refer the reader to other reviews (e.g., Baker, in press; Brown, Armbruster, & Baker, in press; Wagoner, 1983).

The studies we discussed in this section were essentially unanimous in their conclusion that younger and poorer readers do not monitor their comprehension as effectively as older and better readers. Many of the more recent studies have strengthened this intuitively predictable conclusion by using more refined procedures and collecting multiple-response measures (e.g., Baker, 1983c; Garner & Taylor, 1982; Garner, Wagoner, & Smith, in press; Harris, Kruithof, Terwogt, & Visser, 1981; Paris & Myers, 1981). A few of the important issues that have arisen from these studies will be considered.

One such issue concerns the relationship between verbal and nonverbal indexes of comprehension monitoring. Harris et al. (1981) found that 11-year-olds were more likely than 8-year-olds to identify sentences that were incompatible with the themes of simple stories, in line with previous findings. But both the older and younger children spent more time reading the incompatible sentences than the compatible. Similar discrepancies have been observed in several other studies (e.g., Flavell, Speer, Green, & August, 1981; Patterson, Cosgrove, & O'Brien, 1980) and seem to be more common among younger children than older. Harris et al. interpret their data as showing that children of both ages generate an internal signal that an obstacle to comprehension has been encountered but that older children have more capacity to notice or interpret the signals. A similar conclusion was reached by Flavell et al. (1981) in their efforts to explain why kindergarten children who gave nonverbal signs that they were confused nonetheless did not identify instructions as problematic. These observations are important because they implicate an early stage in the development of comprehension monitoring during which the child generates signals of comprehension failure but does not recognize their significance.

Two additional issues involve problems which arise from the tendency of many researchers to treat comprehension monitoring as a unitary phenomenon. The first concerns the distinction between the evaluation and regulation components of comprehension monitoring. Even though most researchers do not differentiate the two components, those who operationalize comprehension monitoring as success at identifying embedded problems are in effect studying the evaluation phase. Once the evidence for problem detection has been collected, the researcher draws a conclusion about comprehension monitoring in general. The problem with this approach is that only one component of comprehension monitoring has been examined; the data do not address how readers regulate their comprehension. There is no reason to believe that a child who knows she doesn't understand will also know what to do about it. This is not to say that it is inappropriate to focus only on evaluation, but rather that researchers must be aware of how this restricts the range of permissible inferences.

The second problem arises even when researchers do restrict their conclusions to the evaluation phase. The problem is that detection of different types of text disruptions requires that the reader use different standards or criteria for evaluating his or her understanding. For example, in order to notice contradictions, the reader needs to use an internal consistency standard, checking that all of the ideas within the passage are consistent with one another. In order to notice nonsense words, the reader need only apply a lexical standard, checking that individual word meanings are known (see Baker, in press, for a detailed discussion of different types of standards). Baker (1983a, 1983b, 1983c) has shown that there are differences both in the likelihood that different standards will be adopted and in the effectiveness of their use. Therefore, it is not justifiable to conclude that children are poor at evaluating their comprehension simply because they failed to notice a particular type of problem. All that can be said is that they either did not adopt or did not effectively use a particular standard of evaluation; they may well have used others. In short, comprehension monitoring involves many different skills. The only way we can acquire a better understanding of these skills and their interactions with one another is to avoid treating comprehension monitoring as a unitary construct.

Comprehension Monitoring in Mature Readers

This section of the chapter focused on two studies by Baker (1979a, Baker & Anderson, 1982) which provided both encouraging and discouraging information about the comprehension monitoring skills of college students: adult readers evaluate their understanding more effectively than children, but they are far from perfect. A recent study (Baker, 1983b) has extended these findings by demonstrating differences as a function of verbal ability and the specificity of the instructions the students are given. Most of the other recent studies with adults, however, have focused on metacognitive knowledge about reading (e.g., Garner, 1982; Hare & Pulliam, 1980; Phifer & Glover, 1982), rather than comprehension monitoring per se. It is unfortunate that there is not more research activity in the area of adult metacognition. Anyone who has ever taught a group of college students must know that their metacognitive skills in a variety of domains could stand considerable enhancing!

Reading for Remembering

In the "Reading for Meaning" section, we adopted the procedure of updating the original chapter by following its existing headings and commenting on advances in these fields in the last four years. We abandoned this procedure in the "Reading for Remembering" section for two main reasons. First, the original section headings corresponded to a set of ongoing research projects. As there has been a great deal of new data generated by these projects, it would be possible to update these sections one by one. For example, Bransford and his colleagues have expanded their work on making use of logical structures and implicit connection in texts (Franks, Vye, Auble, Mezynski, Perfetto, Bransford, Stein, & Littlefield, 1982), and Brown and her colleagues have considerably refined our understanding of the study technique of selecting suitable retrieval aids (Brown, McPhee, Jones, Fields & Campione, work in progress). But it would make for a fragmentary commentary to proceed by updating these ongoing projects one by one.

The second and most important reason for abandoning the original outline is that there has been a major shift in the type of research conducted in this area, a change that the interest in metacognition has helped spur. This is a change in focus from examining how, when, and where students have difficulty studying to an emphasis on interventions designed to overcome these problems. The Bransford and Brown ongoing projects are cases in point. The Franks et al. (1982) paper is a training study where academically less successful fifth graders were trained to engage in elaboration strategies to make explicit logical connections only implicit in the surface structure of the text. The work of the Brown group on effort allocation and retrieval-cue selection while studying has also passed into an instructional phase. Fifth- to eighth-grade students have been helped to design a suitable study plan via various ploys, including explicit training in (a) selecting main ideas, (b) checking on one's existing state of knowledge, and (c) selecting as study aids, important information that is not known well enough to risk a test.

In the original chapter, only one training study, that by Day (1980), was mentioned and then only in passing. Today, such studies are proliferating. Rather than reviewing the emergent studies in detail, we will discuss some unique factors of the new wave of instructional studies and why we think that such studies are resulting in considerable success, whereas the outcomes of previous attempts to train reading comprehension were less satisfactory. We will illustrate these points by considering one training project that is typical of the new wave (Palincsar & Brown, in press).

We would like to argue that there are three main factors that distinguish the new wave of instructional research from its predecessors and that all three have followed from some aspect of the research on metacognition. These factors are: (1) attention to the *metacognitive environment* in which the skills are trained; (2) adequate *diagnosis* of the learner's needs; and (3) training in the *context* of reading with the *goal* of understanding and remembering.

Metacognition and training.   In a number of recent reviews of the litera-ture (Brown, Armbruster, & Baker, in press; Brown, Bransford, Ferrara, & Campione, in press; Brown & Palincsar, 1982; Brown, Palincsar & Purcell, in press), we have argued that successful cognitive skills training programs include three main factors: (1) training and practice in the use of task-specific strategies (skills training); (2) instruction in the orchestration, overseeing, and monitoring of these skills (self-regulation training); and (3) information concerning the significance and outcome of these activities and their range of utility (awareness training). Students who receive only instruction in the skills often fail to use them intelligently and on their own volition because they do not appreciate the reasons why such activities are useful, nor do they grasp where and when to use them. Adding instruction in "awareness," or knowledge, about a skill's evaluation, rationale, and utility greatly increases the positive outcomes of training studies (e.g., see Paris, Newman, and McVey, 1983). This is, in effect, training for lateral transfer (Gagné & Smith 1967), that is, explicitly instructing students about where, when, and how to use a strategy in a variety of appropriate domains.

It is also true that students who receive only skills training often fail to benefit as much as they might because they do not receive practice at overseeing and regulation of their own employment of the activity, relying on a teacher, tutor, or experimenter to check and monitor that they are using the activity effectively. When left to their own devices, they often fail to adopt the overseeing role themselves. Training in self-regulation, together with task-specific strategies, also results in considerably more improvement in the use of study strategies (e.g., see Day, 1980). This is roughly equivalent to training for vertical transfer (Gagné & Smith 1967). As it is well documented that both vertical transfer (spontaneously assembling learned subskills into an integrated whole) and lateral transfer (applying skills broadly) are problematic for all learners, and particularly for the slow learner, it is not surprising that instructional programs that specifically train for vertical and lateral transfer, by paying attention to the student's awareness of the skill's utility and ability to regulate her own activities, are more successful than programs that leave the problem of transfer entirely up to the learner (Brown et al., 1983). Metacognitive supplements to skills training are proving successful.

Diagnosis. A daunting problem for those who would engage in the explicit training of comprehension skills is that there are so many putative strategies involved and descriptions of them are so vague. A common argument against the feasibility of explicitly training cognitive skills takes two forms. First, the necessary skills are legion, and one cannot train them all. Hayes (in press), for example, claimed that there were over 100 basic study skills, and they could not all be accommodated even in an intensive, well-designed study-skills curriculum. Second, if the researcher concentrates on a particular subset, the argument is—why those strategies and not other equally viable candidates? The only answer to these arguments is *diagnosis*. True, one cannot train all skills, but not every learner needs explicit training at every stage of the game. Given a reasonable start, many learners can fill some gaps for themselves. And, just as a doctor would not treat every patient alike, beginning at remedy 1 and proceeding to remedy 100 until a cure is found, it is just as important to diagnose the presenting symptoms of problem readers and tailor instruction accordingly.

The second implication of the importance of diagnosis is the interaction between the teacher and student. Many of the successful training studies that are now being reported have been influenced by the Vygotskian notion of guided learning within a student's *zone of proximal development* (Vygotsky, 1978) or *region of sensitivity to instruction* (Wood & Middleton, 1975).

The current interest in dynamic learning situations has seen a move away from experimenter-controlled, or teacher-controlled, instruction of the traditional kind towards a concentration on interactive processes. It is through interactions with a supportive, knowledgeable adult that the student is led to the limits of her own understanding. The teacher does not tell the student what to do and then leave her to work on unaided; she enters into an interaction where the child and the teacher are mutually responsible for getting the task done. As the child adopts more of the essential skills initially undertaken by the adult, the adult relinquishes control.

Although the supportive other in the laboratory is usually an experimenter, these interactive learning experiences are intended to mimic real-life learning. Mothers (Ninio & Bruner, 1978; Wertsch, 1978; Wood & Middleton, 1975), teachers (Collins & Stevens, 1982), and mastercraftsmen (Childs & Greenfield, 1980) all function as the supportive other, the agent of change responsible for structuring the child's environment in such a way that she can first observe, then participate, and gradually increase the level of participation until she assumes the adult role. In order to perform this essential role, however, the adult must be sensitive to the child's needs at any stage of the process. She must engage in on-line diagnosis that will inform her level of participation, a level of participation that is finely tuned to the child's changing cognitive status.

Vygotsky (1978) has argued that many cognitive activities are initially experienced in such interactive settings but, in time, the activities of the teacher are adopted by the child to form part of her own repertoire of skills; that is, they become *internalized.* Initially, the supportive other acts as the model and interrogator, leading the child to use more powerful strategies. The interrogative, regulatory role becomes internalized by the child during the interactive process and the child becomes able to fulfill some of these functions for herself via self-regulation and self-interrogation (Binet, 1909; Brown, in press). Mature readers are those who practice thought experiments, question their own basic assumptions, provide counterexamples to their own rules, and so on. Through the process of internalization, mature readers become capable of providing the supportive-other role for themselves. Under these dynamic systems of tutelage, the child learns not only how to get a particular task done independently, she also learns how to set about learning new problems (Brown, Bransford, Ferrara, & Campione, in press). In the domain of reading, the student learns how to learn from reading (Brown, 1982).

Contextualized skills.   The final contrast we would like to make between the new wave of instructional research and the old is the contextualization of skills. Skill-package curricula of the kind that dominate American schools and traditional instructional research share a common feature; they both provide practice on certain basic skills such as paraphrasing, finding the main idea, clarifying inconsistencies, sequencing, and so on. But this practice takes the form of exercises in isolation from the actual process of reading or studying. The student reads in a reading group, but then practices the skills in the workbooks, and so on. In experiments, the child practices and is tested on the trained skill and transfer to "real" reading situations is hoped for—a vain hope, given what we know about transfer propensity in the young, or not so young for that matter (Brown & Campione, 1981). The new wave of training studies (Brown, Palincsar, & Armbruster, in press) and curricula (Tharp, 1982) teach essential strategies in the *context* of actually reading or studying with the *goal* of arriving at a coherent interpretation of the text. We will illustrate these three points, *metacognitive training, student diagnosis, and contextualization* in one recent study conducted by Palincsar and Brown (in press).

The Palincsar and Brown Training Studies

The main aim of the series of studies conducted by Palincsar and Brown (in press) was to design a package that would meet strict criteria of success, including reliable, durable, and generalizable improvement in comprehension processes, by paying careful attention to the three points mentioned above, metacognitive training, student diagnosis, and contextualization.

Processes.   Palincsar and Brown concentrated on four main cognitive activities that occur in almost every description of critical reading. These were *summarizing* (self-review), *questioning, clarifying,* and *predicting.* In addition to being recognizable school exercises, the four activities serve a double function; they can enhance comprehension and they afford an opportunity for the student to check whether it is occurring. That is, they can be both *comprehension fostering* and *comprehension monitoring* activities if properly used. Summarization as a process of self-review is an excellent example. Monitoring one's progress while reading, to test whether one can pinpoint and retain important material, provides a check that comprehension is progressing smoothly. If the reader cannot produce an adequate synopsis of what he is reading, this is a clear sign that comprehension is *not* proceeding smoothly and that remedial action is called for.

Palincsar and Brown (in press) combined the four activities of self-directed summarizing (review), questioning, clarifying, and predicting in a package of activities with the general aim of enhancing understanding. Each "separate" activity, however, was used in the *context* of actual reading and in response to a concrete problem of text comprehension. Clarifying occurred only if there were confusions either in the text (unclear referent, etc.) or in the student's interpretation of the text. Summarizing was introduced as an activity of self-review; it was engaged in to state to oneself, the group, or to the teacher what had just happened in the text and as a test that the content had been understood. If an adequate synopsis could not be reached, this fact was regarded not as a failure to perform a particular decontextualized skill, but as an important source of information that comprehension was not proceeding as it should and remedial action (such as rereading or clarifying) was needed. Questioning, similarly, was not practiced as a teacher-directed isolated activity, but as a concrete task— what question could a teacher or test reasonably ask about that section of the text?

Metacognitive environment.   In addition to the cognitive skills, every attempt was made to enhance the students' understanding of the activities and their sense of competence and control. The adult teacher provided praise and feedback; the students kept their own graphed record of success. The students received explicit instruction, extensive modeling, and repeated practice in concrete versions of the trained activities; they were constantly reminded to engage in these activities while reading, indeed to read for the purpose of performing these activities for themselves. They were instructed not to proceed until they could summarize, clarify, and answer questions on each segment of text. Finally, the students were constantly reminded that the target activities were to help them improve and monitor their own comprehension, shown that their performance improved dramatically when they did so, and told that they should always engage in them while reading for academic purposes, all forms of metacognitive instruction.

Diagnosis.   First, consider the initial diagnosis. Seventh-grade disadvantaged students were referred by their teachers because, although they were decoding at grade level, they were experiencing difficulties with reading comprehension (two- to three-year delays). They had particular difficulty performing well on a common test of comprehension in schools, reading expository passages and then answering questions on the content; this became the target task for training.

Second, consider the on-line continuous process of diagnosis embedded in the teacher-pupil interaction. The activities of summarizing, questioning, clarifying, and predicting were embedded within a training procedure that was very similar to prototypical interactive mother-child, teacher-student dyads. Termed *reciprocal teaching,* the procedure consisted of student and teachers taking turns leading a dialogue concerning each segment of text. The teacher thereby modeled the appropriate activities and the student was forced to participate at whatever level he or she could. Teachers could then provide guidance and feedback at the appropriate level for each student.

The general procedure was that the adult teacher assigned a segment of the passage to be read (usually a paragraph) and either indicated that it was her or his turn to be the teacher or assigned one of the students to teach that segment. The adult teacher and the students then read the assigned segment silently. After reading the text, the teacher (student or adult) for that segment summarized the content, discussed and clarified any difficulties, asked a question that a teacher or test might ask on the segment, and finally made a prediction about future content. All of these activities were embedded in as natural a dialogue as possible, with the teacher and other students giving feedback to each other.

Initially, the adult teacher modeled appropriate activities, but the students had great difficulty assuming the role of dialogue leader when their turn came. The adult teacher was sometimes forced to resort to constructing paraphrases and questions for the students to mimic. In this initial phase, the adult teacher was modeling effective comprehension monitoring strategies, but the students were relatively passive observers.

In the intermediate phase, the students became much more capable of playing their role as dialogue leader and by the end of approximately 20 sessions were providing paraphrases and questions of some sophistication. For example, in the initial sessions, 46 percent of the questions produced by the students were judged as nonquestions or as needing clarification. By the end of the sessions, only 2 percent of responses were judged as either needing clarification or nonquestions. Unclear questions dropped out and were replaced over time with questions focusing on the main idea of each text segment. A similar improvement was found for summary statements. At the beginning of the sessions, only 11 percent of summary statements captured main ideas, whereas at the end, 60 percent of the statements were so classified.

Close inspection of the dialogues revealed repeated examples of the teachers providing modeling, feedback, and practice to students at exactly the level they needed. As students became better able to perform segments of the task, the teacher increased her or his demands accordingly, until the students' behavior became increasingly like that of the adult model, who in turn decreased her or his level of participation and acted as a supportive audience.

In addition to the qualitative changes in the students' dialogues, there was a significant improvement in the level of performance on daily comprehension tests. Each day, following the interactive learning sessions, the students read novel passages and independently answered 10 comprehension questions on the passage (from memory). During pretesting prior to the introduction of the interactive sessions, students averaged 20% correct on such tests. After the experience of the reciprocal teaching sessions, students reached accuracy levels of 80-to-90 percent correct. The improvement on the daily comprehension tests was large and reliable; 90 percent of the students taking part in the first two studies (when an experimenter served as the adult teacher to individual students or dyads) improved to the level set by good comprehenders. Of the 31 students in Study 3 (where volunteer teachers introduced the procedure in the already-existing reading groups), all met this level. The effect was durable; there was no drop in the level of performance for up to an eight-week period. Although there was a decline after six months (levels dropping from 80 percent to 60 percent), only one session with the reciprocal teaching procedure was sufficient to raise performance back to the short-term maintenance level.

The effect also generalized to the classroom setting. During the course of the study, the students took comprehension tests that were given as part of their regular science and social science instruction. They were not informed that these tests were related to the study. All seventh graders in the school took the tests (approximately 150). The trained students began the study with scores of below the 20 percentile rank compared with their age peers, but after the study, 90 percent of the students showed a clear pattern of improvement, averaging a 36 percentile-rank increase, thus bringing them up to at least the average level for their age mates.

Training also resulted in reliable transfer to dissimilar laboratory tasks that demanded the same underlying processes. In writing summaries (on the Brown and Day task, see page 373), predicting questions a teacher might ask, and detecting incongruities (on the Harris et al., 1981, comprehension monitoring task) all improved significantly, bringing the trainees up to the level set by "normal" seventh-grade students. In addition, sizable improvements in standardized comprehension scores were recorded for the majority of subjects (67 percent improving over two years on standardized tests). And, of prime importance, the intervention was no less successful in natural group settings conducted by regular classroom teachers than it was in the laboratory when conducted by an experimenter.

Implications for Instruction

The success of recent studies in training comprehension and study strategies enables us to be much more concrete in suggesting implications for instruction than we could be in the original chapter. Indeed, until the middle 1970s, the prognosis of worthwhile educational gains from cognitive skills training studies was poor. Although some success had been achieved in obtaining improvement on a particular skill in isolation, this improvement was often slight and fleeting, and there was very little evidence of transfer. Maintenance over time, generalization across settings and transfer within conceptual domains was rarely found. The more difficulties the learner experienced initially, the more fleeting and bounded was the effect of training (Brown & Campione, 1981; Meichenbaum, in press). But the picture has changed in the last few years; the success of the Palincsar and Brown studies is not an isolated phenomenon (see Chipman, Segal, & Glaser, in press). The current outlook is quite optimistic. From a practical point of view, it is clear that we can train the cognitive skills for comprehending and studying texts even with students who would be regarded as recalcitrant by many teachers. This training can be carried out under the pressure of normal classroom settings. And it does result in worthwhile and reliable improvements, in the Palincsar and Brown studies bringing students from the very bottom of the distribution of their age peers to the average set by their "normal-reading" classmates. The necessary research needed now consists of extensions across skills and settings that would permit us to test the limits of these exciting findings and streamline our instructional packages. Study skills can be trained, and such training can be durable and generalizable.

We would like to argue that it is developments in theory and research on metacognition that has led to greater success in designing instruction aimed at improving study skills. Interventions that include training in both the skills themselves and the student's control and understanding of the skills are proving successful. We look forward to further studies of this kind and an extension to classroom curricula.

REFERENCES

Alessi, S. M., Anderson, T. H., & Goetz, E. T.   An investigation of lookbacks during studying. *Discourse Processes*, 1979, *2*, 197–212.

Anderson, I. H.   Eye-movements of good and poor readers. *Psychological Monographs*, 1937, *48*, 1–35.

Anderson, R. C.   The notion of schemata and the education enterprise. In R. C. Anderson, R. J. Spiro, & W. E. Montague (Eds.), *Schooling and the acquisition of knowledge.* Hillsdale, N.J.: Erlbaum, 1977.

Anderson, T. H.   Study skills and learning strategies. In H. F. O'Neil, Jr., & C. D. Spielberger (Eds.), *Cognitive and affective learning strategies.* New York: Academic Press, 1979.

Anderson, T. H.   Study strategies and adjunct aids. In R. J. Spiro, B. C. Bruce, & W. F. Brewer (Eds.), *Theoretical issues in reading comprehension.* Hillsdale, N.J.: Erlbaum, 1980.

Andre, M. D. A., & Anderson, T. H.   The development and evaluation of a self-questioning study technique. *Reading Research Quarterly*, 1978–1979, *14*, 605–623.

Asher, S. R.   Referential communication. In G. J. Whitehurst, & B. J. Zimmerman (Eds.), *The functions of language and cognition.* New York: Academic Press, 1979.

Baker, L.   Comprehension monitoring: Identifying and coping with text confusions. *Journal of Reading Behavior*, 1979, *11*, 363–374 (a).

Baker, L.   *Do I understand or do I not understand: That is the question* (Reading Education Report No. 10). Urbana: University of Illinois, Center for the Study of Reading, 1979. (ERIC Document Reproduction Service No. ED 174 948) (b).

Baker, L.   *Children's effective use of multiple standards for evaluating their comprehension.* Unpublished manuscript. University of Maryland, 1983 (a).

Baker, L.   *Differences in the standards used by college students for evaluating their comprehension of expository prose.* Unpublished manuscript, University of Maryland, 1983 (b).

Baker, L.   *Spontaneous versus instructed use of multiple standards for evaluating comprehension: Effects of age, reading ability, and type of standard.* Unpublished manuscript, University of Maryland, 1983 (c).

Baker, L.   How do we know when we don't understand? Standards for evaluating text comprehension. In D. L. Forrest, G. E. MacKinnon, & T. G. Waller (Eds.), *Metacognition, cognition, and human performance*. New York: Academic Press, in press.

Baker, L. & Anderson, R. I.   Effects of inconsistent information on text processing: Evidence for comprehension monitoring. *Reading Research Quarterly*, 1982, *17*, 281–294.

Baker, L. & Brown, A. L.   Cognitive monitoring in reading. In J. Flood (Ed.), *Understanding reading comprehension*. Newark, Del.: International Reading Association, in press.

Binet, A.   *Les idées modernes sur les enfants*. Paris: Ernest Flammarion, 1909.

Bransford, J. D., Stein, B. S., Shelton, T. S., & Owings, R. A.   Cognition and adaptation: The importance of learning to learn. In J. Harvey (Ed.), *Cognition, social behavior and the environment*. Hillsdale, N.J.: Erlbaum, 1981.

Brown, A. L.   The development of memory: Knowing, knowing about knowing, and knowing how to know. In H. W. Reese (Ed.), *Advances in child development and behavior*. (Vol. 10). New York: Academic Press, 1975.

Brown, A. L.   Knowing when, where, and how to remember: A problem of metacognition. In R. Glaser (Ed.), *Advances in instructional psychology*. Hillsdale, N.J.: Erlbaum, 1978.

Brown, A. L.   Metacognitive development and reading. In R. J. Spiro, B. C. Bruce, & W. F. Brewer (Eds.), *Theoretical issues in reading comprehension*. Hillsdale, N.J.: Erlbaum, 1980.

Brown, A. L.   Learning to learn how to read. In J. Langer & T. Smith-Burke (Eds.), *Reader meets author, bridging the gap: A psycholinguistic and social linguistic perspective*. Newark, Del.: International Reading Association, Dell Publishing, 1982.

Brown, A. L.   Mental orthopedics: A conversation with Alfred Binet. In S. Chipman, J. Segal, & R. Glaser (Eds.), *Thinking and learning skills: Current research and open questions* (Vol. 2). Hillsdale, N.J.: Erlbaum, in press.

Brown, A. L., Armbruster, B. B., & Baker, L.   The role of metacognition in reading and studying. In J. Orasanu (Ed.), *Reading comprehension: From research to practice*. Hillsdale, N.J.: Erlbaum, in press.

Brown, A. L., Bransford, J. D., Ferrara, R. A., & Campione, J. C.   Learning remembering, and understanding. In J. H. Flavell & E. M. Markman (Eds.), *Handbook of child psychology* (Vol. 3). New York: Wiley, in press.

Brown, A. L., & Campione, J. C.   Training strategic study time apportionment in educable retarded children. *Intelligence*, 1977, *1*, 94–107.

Brown, A. L., & Campione, J. C.   The effects of knowledge and experience on the formation of retrieval plans for studying from texts. In M. M. Gruneberg, P. E. Morris, & R. N. Sukes (Eds.), *Practical aspects of memory*. London: Academic Press, 1979.

Brown, A. L., & Campione, J. C.   Introducing flexible thinking: A problem of access. In M. Friedman, J. P. Das, & N. O'Connor (Eds.), *Intelligence and learning*. New York: Plenum, 1981.

Brown, A. L., Campione, J. C., & Barclay, C. R.   Training self-checking routines for estimating test readiness: Generalization from list learning to prose recall. *Child Development*, 1979, *50*, 501–512.

Brown, A. L., & Day, J. D.   Macrorules for summarizing texts: The development of expertise. *Journal of Verbal Learning and Verbal Behavior*, 1983, *22* (1), 1–14.

Brown, A. L., Day, J. D., & Jones, R.   The development of plans for summarizing texts. *Child Development*, 1983, *54*, 968–979.

Brown, A. L., & DeLoache, J. S.   Skills, plans and self-regulation. In R. S. Siegler (Ed.), *Children's thinking: What develops?* Hillsdale, N.J.: Erlbaum, 1978.

Brown, A. L., & Lawton, S. C.   The feeling of knowing experience in educable retarded children. *Developmental Psychology*, 1977, *13*, 364–370.

Brown, A. L., & Palincsar, A. S.   Inducing strategic learning from texts by means of informed, self-control training. *Topics in Learning and Learning Disabilities,* 1982, *2,* 1–17.

Brown, A. L., Palincsar, A. S., & Armbruster, B. B.   Instructing comprehension-fostering activities in interactive learning situations. In H. Mandl, N. Stein, & T. Trabasso (Eds.), *Learning from texts.* Hillsdale, N.J.: Erlbaum, in press.

Brown, A. L., Palincsar, A. S., & Purcell, L.   Poor readers: Teach, don't label. In U. Neisser (Ed.), *The academic performance of minority children.* Hillsdale, N.J.: Erlbaum, in press.

Brown, A. L., & Smiley, S. S.   Rating the importance of structural units of prose passages: A problem of metacognitive development. *Child Development,* 1977, *48,* 1–8.

Brown, A. L., & Smiley, S. S.   The development of strategies for studying texts. *Child Development,* 1978, *49,* 1076–1088.

Brown, A. L., Smiley, S. S., Day, J., Townsend, M., & Lawton, S. C.   Intrusion of a thematic idea in children's recall of prose. *Child Development,* 1977, *48,* 1454–1466.

Brown, A. L., Smiley, S. S., & Lawton, S. C.   The effects of experience on the selection of suitable retrieval cues for studying texts. *Child Development,* 1978, *49,* 829–835.

Buswell, G.   An experimental study of the eye-voice-span in reading. *Supplementary Educational Monographs,* 1929 (Whole No. 17), 1–105.

Canney, G., & Winograd, P.   *Schemata for reading and reading comprehension performance* (Tech. Rep. No. 120). Urbana: University of Illinois, Center for the Study of Reading, 1979. (ERIC Document Reproduction Service No. ED 169 520).

Chi, M. T. H.   Knowledge structures and development. In R. S. Siegler (Ed.), *Children's thinking: What develops?* Hillsdale, N.J.: Erlbaum, 1978.

Childs, C. P., & Greenfield, P. M.   Informal modes of learning and teaching: The case of Zinacanteco weaving. In N. Warren (Ed.), *Studies in cross-cultural psychology* (Vol. 2). London: Academic Press, 1980.

Chipman, S., Segal, J., & Glaser, R.   (Eds.), *Thinking and learning skills: Current research and open questions* (Vol. 2). Hillsdale, N.J.: Erlbaum, in press.

Clay, M. M.   *Reading: The patterning of complex behavior.* Auckland, N.Z.: Heinemann Educational Books, 1973.

Collins, A., Brown, J. S., & Larkin, K. M.   Inference in text understanding. In R. J. Spiro, B. C. Bruce, & W. F. Brewer (Eds.), *Theoretical issues in reading comprehension.* Hillsdale, N.J.: Erlbaum, 1980.

Collins, A., & Stevens, A.   Goals and strategies of inquiry teachers. In R. Glaser (Ed.), *Advances in instructional psychology* (Vol. 2). Hillsdale, N.J.: Erlbaum, 1982.

Cosgrove, J. M., & Patterson, C. J.   Plans and the development of listener skills, *Developmental Psychology,* 1977, *13,* 557–564.

Danner, F. W.   Children's understanding of intersentence organization in the recall of short descriptive passages. *Journal of Educational Psychology,* 1976, *68,* 174–183.

Day, J. D.   *Training summarization skills: A comparison of teaching methods.* Unpublished doctoral dissertation, University of Ilinois, 1980.

Denny, T., & Weintraub, S.   Exploring first graders' concepts of reading. *Reading Teacher,* 1963, *16,* 363–365.

Denny, T., & Weintraub, S.   First-graders' responses to three questions about reading. *Elementary School Journal,* 1966, *66,* 441–448.

Dewey, J.   *How we think.* Boston: Heath, 1910.

Di Vesta, F. J., Hayward, K. G., & Orlando, V. P.   Developmental trends in monitoring text for comprehension. *Child Development,* 1979, *50,* 97–105.

Eller, W.   Reading and semantics. In M. L. King, B. D. Ellinger, & W. Wolf (Eds.), *Critical reading.* Philadelphia: Lippincott, 1967.

Fairbanks, G.   The relation between eye-movements and voice in oral reading of good and poor readers. *Psychological Monographs,* 1937, *48,* 78–107.

Flavell, J. H.   Metacognitive development. In J. M. Scandura & C. J. Brainerd (Eds.), *Structural/process theories of complex human behavior.* Alphen a. d. Rijn, The Netherlands: Sijthoff & Noordhoff, 1978.

Flavell, J. H.   Cognitive monitoring. In W. P. Dickson (Ed.), *Children's oral communication skills.* New York: Academic Press, 1981.

Flavell, J. H., Friedrichs, A. G., & Hoyt, J. D.   Developmental changes in memorization processes. *Cognitive Psychology,* 1970, *1,* 324–340.

Flavell, J. H., Speer, J. R., Green, F. L., & August, D. L.   The development of comprehension monitoring and knowledge about communication. *Monographs of the Society for Research in Child Development,* 1981, *46,* (Whole No. 192).

Flavell, J. H., & Wellman, H. M.   Metamemory. In R. V. Kail, Jr., & J. W. Hagen (Eds.), *Perspectives on the development of memory and cognition.* Hillsdale, N.J.: Erlbaum, 1977.

Forrest, D. L., & Waller, T. G.   *Cognitive and metacognitive aspects of reading.* Paper presented at the meeting of the Society for Research in Child Development, San Francisco, March 1979.

Franks, J. J., Vye, N. J., Auble, P. N., Mezynski, K. J., Perfetto, G. A., Bransford, J. D., Stein, B. S., & Littlefield, J.   Learning from explicit vs. implicit text. *Journal of Experimental Psychology: General,* 1982, *111*(4), 414–422.

Gagné, R. M., & Smith, E. C.   *Learning and individual differences.* Columbus, Ohio: Charles E. Merrill, 1967.

Gambrell, L. B., & Heathington, B. S.   Adult disabled readers' metacognitive awareness about reading tasks and strategies. *Journal of Reading Behavior,* 1981, *13,* 215–222.

Garner, R.   Verbal report data on reading strategies. *Journal of Reading Behavior,* 1982, *14,* 159–167.

Garner, R., & Kraus, C.   Good and poor comprehender differences in knowing and regulating reading behaviors. *Educational Research Quarterly,* 1981–1982, *6,* 5–12.

Garner, R., & Taylor, N.   Monitoring of understanding: An investigation of attentional assistance needs at different grade and reading proficiency levels, *Reading Psychology,* 1982, *3,* 1–6.

Garner, R., Wagoner, S., & Smith, T.   Externalizing question-answering strategies of good and poor comprehenders. *Reading Research Quarterly,* in press.

Golinkoff, R.   A comparison of reading comprehension processes in good and poor comprehenders. *Reading Research Quarterly,* 1975–1976, *11,* 623–659.

Goodenough, D. R.   The role of individual differences in field dependence as a factor in learning and memory. *Psychological Bulletin,* 1976, *83,* 675–694.

Goodman, K. S.   Behind the eye: What happens in reading. In H. Singer & R. B. Ruddell (Eds.), *Theoretical models and processes of reading* (2nd ed.). Newark, Del.: International Reading Association, 1976.

Hare, V. C., & Pulliam, C. A.   College students' metacognitive awareness of reading behavior. In M. L. Kamil & A. J. Moe (Eds.), *Perspectives on reading research and instruction.* Washington, D.C.: National Reading Conference, 1980.

Harris, P. L., Kruithof, A., Terwogt, M. M., & Visser, P.   Children's detection and awareness of textual anomaly. *Journal of Experimental Child Psychology,* 1981, *31,* 212–230.

Hayes, R.   Training thinking skills. In S. Chipman, J. Segal, & R. Glaser (Eds.), *Thinking and learning skills: Current research and open questions* (Vol. 2). Hillsdale, N.J.: Erlbaum, in press.

Holt, J.   *How children fail.* New York: Dell, 1964.

Huey, E. B.   *The psychology and pedagogy of reading.* Cambridge: MIT Press, 1968. (Originally published, 1908).

Ironsmith, M., & Whitehurst, G. J.   The development of listener abilities in communication: How children deal with ambiguous information. *Child Development*, 1978, *49*, 348–352.

Isakson, R. L., & Miller, J. W. Sensitivity to syntactic and semantic cues in good and poor comprehenders. *Journal of Educational Psychology*, 1976, *68*(6), 787–792.

Isakson, R. L., & Miller, J. W. *Comprehension and decoding skills of good and poor readers.* Paper presented at the meeting of the American Educational Research Association, Toronto, March 1978.

Johns, J., & Ellis, D. Reading: Children tell it like it is. *Reading World*, 1976, *16*(2), 115–128.

Kagan, J., Moss, H. A., & Sigel, I. E. Psychological significance of styles of conceptualization. In J. C. Wright & J. Kagan (Eds.), Basic cognitive processes in children. *Monographs of the Society for Research in Child Development*, 1963, *28*, 73–112.

Karabenick, J. D., & Miller, S. A. The effects of age, sex, and listener feedback on grade school children's referential communication. *Child Development*, 1977, *48*, 678–683.

Kavale, K., & Schreiner, R. The reading processes of above average and average readers: A comparison of the use of reasoning strategies in responding to standardized comprehension measures. *Reading Research Quarterly*, 1979, *15*, 102–128.

Kemp, C. G. Improvement of critical thinking in relation to open-closed belief systems. In M. L. King, B. D. Ellinger, & W. Wolf (Eds.), *Critical reading*. Philadelphia: Lippincott, 1967.

Kleiman, G. M., & Schallert, D. L. Some things the reader needs to know that the listener doesn't. In P. D. Pearson & J. Hansen (Eds.), *Reading: Disciplined inquiry in process and practice*. Clemson, S.C.: National Reading Conference, 1978.

Kobasigawa, A., Ranson, C. C., & Holland, C. J. Children's knowledge about skimming. *Alberta Journal of Educational Research*, 1980, *26*, 169–182.

Levin, H., & Cohn, J. A. Studies of oral reading: XII. Effects of instructions on the eye-voice span. In H. Levin, E. J. Gibson, & J. J. Gibson (Eds.), *The analysis of reading skill* (Final report, Project No. 5–1213, Contract No. OE6–10–156). Cornell University & U.S. Office of Education, 1968.

Locke, E. Q. *A guide to effective study.* New York: Springer, 1975.

Markman, E. M. Realizing that you don't understand: A preliminary investigation. *Child Development*, 1977, *46*, 986–992.

Markman, E. M. Realizing that you don't understand: Elementary school children's awareness of inconsistencies. *Child Development*, 1979, *50*, 643–655.

Markman, E. M. Comprehension monitoring. In W. P. Dickson (Ed.), *Children's oral communication skills*. New York: Academic Press, 1981.

Markman, E. M., & Gorin, L. Children's ability to adjust their standards for evaluating comprehension. *Journal of Educational Psychology*, 1981, *73*, 320–325.

Masur, E. G., McIntyre, C. W., & Flavell, J. H. Developmental changes in apportionment of study time among items in a multitrial free recall task. *Journal of Experimental Child Psychology*, 1973, *15*, 237–246.

Meichenbaum, D. Cognitive behavior modification. In S. Chipman, J. Segal, & R. Glaser (Eds.), *Thinking and learning skills: Current research and open questions* (Vol. 2). Hillsdale, N.J.: Erlbaum, in press.

Myers, M., & Paris, S. G. Children's metacognitive knowledge about reading. *Journal of Educational Psychology*, 1978, *70*, 680–690.

Nash, W. A., & Torrance, E. P. Creative reading and the questioning abilities of young children. *Journal of Creative Behavior*, 1974, *8*, 15–19.

Neville, M. H., & Pugh, A. K. Context in reading and listening: Variations in approach to cloze tasks. *Reading Research Quarterly*, 1976–1977, *12*, 13–31.

Ngandu, K. What do remedial high school students do when they read? *Journal of Reading*, 1977, *21*, 231–234.

Ninio, A., & Bruner, J. S.   The achievement and antecedents of labelling. *Journal of Child Language*, 1978, *5*, 1–15.

Nisbett, R. E., & Wilson, T. D.   Telling more than we know: Verbal reports on mental processes. *Psychological Review*, 1977, *84*, 231–279.

Olshavsky, J.   Reading as problem solving: An investigation of strategies. *Reading Research Quarterly*, 1976–1977, *12*, 654–674.

Olshavsky, J.   Comprehension profiles of good and poor readers across materials of increasing difficulty. In P. D. Pearson, & J. Hansen (Eds.), *Reading: Disciplined inquiry in process and practice*. Clemson, S.C.: National Reading Conference, 1978.

Olson, G. M., Duffy, S., & Mack, R.   *The reader's knowledge of the conventions of story writing*. Paper presented at the meeting of the Psychonomic Society, San Antonio, Tex., November 1978.

Pace, A. J.   *Further exploration of young children's sensitivity to word-knowledge-story information discrepancies*. Paper presented at the meeting of the Southeastern Conference on Human Development, Alexandria, Va., April 1980.

Palincsar, A. S., & Brown, A. L.   Reciprocal teaching of comprehension-monitoring activities. *Cognition and Instruction*, in press.

Paris, S. G., & Myers, M.   Comprehension monitoring, memory, and study strategies of good and poor readers. *Journal of Reading Behavior*, 1981, *13*, 5–22.

Paris, S. G., Newman, R. S., & McVey, K. A.   Learning the functional significance of mnemonic actions: A microgenetic study of strategy acquisition. *Journal of Experimental Child Psychology*, 1983, 34(3), 490–509.

Patterson, C. J., Cosgrove, J. M., & O'Brien, R. G.   Nonverbal indicants of comprehension and noncomprehension in children. *Developmental Psychology*, 1980, *16*, 38–48.

Patterson, C. J., & Kister, M. C.   The development of listener skills for referential communication. In W. P. Dickson (Ed.), *Children's oral communication skills*. New York: Academic Press, 1981.

Patterson, C. J., O'Brien, C., Kister, M. C., Carter, D. B., & Kotsonis, M. E.   Development of comprehension monitoring as a function of context. *Developmental Psychology*, 1981, *17*, 379–389.

Phifer, S. J., & Glover, J. A.   Don't take students' word for what they do while reading. *Bulletin of the Psychonomic Society*, 1982, *19*, 194–196.

Piaget, J.   The language and thought of the child (M. Gabain, trans.). London: Routledge & Kegan Paul, 1926.

Pichert, J. W.   *Sensitivity to what is important in prose* (Tech. Rep. No. 149). Urbana: University of Illinois, Center for the Study of Reading, November 1979. (ERIC Document Reproduction Service No. ED 179 946).

Pratt, M. W., & Bates, K. R.   Young editors: Preschool children evaluation and production of ambiguous messages. *Developmental Psychology*, 1982, *18*, 30–42.

Reder, L. M., & Anderson, J. R.   A comparison of texts and their summaries: Memorial consequences. *Journal of Verbal Learning and Verbal Behavior*, 1981.

Reid, J. F.   Learning to think about reading. *Educational Research*, 1966, *9*, 56–62.

Robinson, R. P.   *Effective study*. New York: Harper & Row, 1941.

Rubin, A.   Comprehension processes in oral and written language. In R. J. Spiro, B. C. Bruce, & W. F. Brewer (Eds.), *Theoretical issues in reading comprehension*. Hillsdale, N.J.: Erlbaum, 1980.

Ruddell, R. B.   Psycholinguistic implications for a systems of communication model. In H. Singer & R. B. Ruddell (Eds.), *Theoretical models and processes of reading* (2nd ed.). Newark, Del.: International Reading Association, 1976.

Rumelhart, D. E.   Schemata: The building blocks of cognition. In R. J. Spiro, B. C. Bruce, & W. F. Brewer (Eds.), *Theoretical issues in reading comprehension*. Hillsdale, N.J.: Erlbaum, 1980.

Ryan, E. B.   Identifying and remediating failures in reading comprehension: Toward an instructional approach for poor comprehenders. In T. G. Waller, & G. E. MacKinnon (Eds.), *Advances in reading research* (Vol. 2). New York: Academic Press, 1981.

Schallert, D. L., & Kleiman, G. M.   *Why the teacher is easier to understand than the textbook* (Reading Education Report No. 9). Urbana: University of Illinois, Center for the Study of Reading, 1979. (ERIC Document Reproduction Service No. ED 172 189).

Singer, H.   Active comprehension from answering to asking questions. *Reading Teacher,* 1978, *31,* 901–908.

Smiley, S. S., Oakley, D. D., Worthen, D., Campione, J. C., & Brown, A. L.   Recall of thematically relevant material by adolescent good and poor readers as a function of written versus oral presentation. *Journal of Educational Psychology,* 1977, *69,* 381–387.

Smith, H. K.   The responses of good and poor readers when asked to read for different purposes. *Reading Research Quarterly,* 1967, *3,* 53–84.

Stein, N. L., & Trabasso, T.   What's in a story: Critical issues in comprehension and instruction. In R. Glaser (Ed.), *Advances in instructional psychology* (Vol. 2). Hillsdale, N.J.: Erlbaum, 1982.

Strang, R., & Rogers, C.   How do students read a short story? *English Journal,* 1965, *54,* 819–823, 829.

Sullivan, J.   Comparing strategies of good and poor comprehenders. *Journal of Reading,* 1978, *21,* 710–715.

Swanson, D. E.   Common elements in silent and oral reading. *Psychological Monographs,* 1937, *48,* 36–50.

Tharp, R. G.   The effective instruction of comprehension: Results and description of the Kamehameha early education program. *Reading Research Quarterly,* 1982, *17*(4), 503–527.

Thomas, E. L.   Movements of the eye. *Scientific American,* 1968, *219,* 88–95.

Thorndike, E. L.   Reading as reasoning: A study of mistakes in paragraph reading. *Journal of Educational Psychology,* 1917, *8,* 323–332.

van Dijk, T. A., & Kintsch, W.   Cognitive psychology and discourse: Recalling and summarizing stories. In W. U. Dressler (Ed.), *Trends in text linguistics.* New York: de Gruyter, 1978.

Vygotsky, L. S.   Mind in society: *The development of higher psychological processes* (M. Cole, V. John-Steiner, S. Scribner, & E. Souberman, Eds. and trans.). Cambridge: Harvard University Press, 1978.

Wagoner, S. A.   Comprehension monitoring: What it is and what we know about it. *Reading Research Quarterly,* 1983, *17,* 328–346.

Weber, R. M.   A linguistic analysis of first-grade reading errors. *Reading Research Quarterly,* 1970, *5,* 427–451.

Wertsch, J. V.   Adult-child interaction and the roots of metacognition. *Quarterly Newsletter of the Institute for Comparative Human Development,* 1978, *1,* 15–18.

Whimbey, A.   *Intelligence can be taught.* New York: Dutton, 1975.

White, P.   Limitations on verbal reports of internal events: A refutation of Nisbett and Wilson and of Bem. *Psychological Review,* 1980, *87,* 105–112.

Wimmer, H.   Processing of script deviations by young children. *Discourse Processes,* 1979, *2,* 301–310.

Winograd, P., & Johnston, P.   Comprehension monitoring and the error detection paradigm.

Wolf, W.   Teaching critical reading through logic. In M. L. King, B. D. Ellinger, & W. Wolf (Eds.), *Critical reading.* Philadelphia: Lippincott, 1967.

Wolf, W., King, M. C., & Huck, C. S.   Teaching critical reading to elementary school children. *Reading Research Quarterly,* 1968, *3,* 435–498.

Wood, E., & Middleton, D.   A study of assisted problem-solving. *British Journal of Psychology*, 1975, *66*, 181–191.

Woods, W. A.   Multiple theory formation in high-level perception. In R. J. Spiro, B. C. Bruce, & W. F. Brewer (Eds.), *Theoretical issues in reading comprehension.* Hillsdale, N.J.: Erlbaum, 1980.

Yussen, S. R., Mathews, S. R., & Hiebert, E.   Metacognitive aspects of reading. In W. Otto & S. White (Eds.), *Reading expository material.* New York: Academic Press, 1982.

13 DIRECTIONS IN THE SOCIOLINGUISTIC STUDY OF READING

David Bloome and Judith Green

In the last decade, a new conceptualization of reading has emerged. This conceptualization is grounded in recent theory and research in sociolinguistics and in the ethnography of communication. From this perspective, reading is viewed not only as a cognitive process, but also as a social and linguistic process. As a social process, reading is used to establish, structure, and maintain social relationships between and among people. As a linguistic process, reading is used to communicate intentions and meanings, not only between an author and a reader, but also between people involved in a reading event.

The purpose of this article is to identify the directions that researchers have taken in the study of the sociolinguistic nature of reading and to explore two of these directions in depth: (1) reading as a cognitive activity embedded in social and linguistic contexts and (2) reading as a social and linguistic process. In the first direction, reading is viewed as a cognitive activity embedded in social and linguistic contexts. The social and linguistic contexts influence the nature of the cognitive processes involved in reading. To date, researchers have examined the social and linguistic nature of *instructional contexts of reading* (e.g., Au, 1980; Au & Mason, 1981; Bloome & Green, 1982; Cochran-Smith, in press; Collins, 1981; DeStefano, Pepinsky, & Sanders, 1982; Green, 1977, in press; Griffin, 1977; Gumperz & Tannen, 1979; Heap, 1980; McDermott, 1967/1976, 1976; Mehan, 1979a, 1979b; Michaels, 1981; Morine-Dershimer, 1982; Mosenthal & Na, 1980; Wilkinson & Calculator, 1982a, 1982b), *noninstructional contexts of reading* (e.g., Bloome & Green, 1982; Fiering, 1981; Gilmore, 1981; Griffin, 1977), and *home and community contexts of reading* (e.g., Bloome & Green, 1982; Goodman & Goodman, 1979; Heath, 1982a, 1982b; Scollon & Scollon, 1981; Taylor, 1983; Taylor & Gaines, 1982).

In addition, researchers have looked across contexts comparing the social and linguistic nature of instructional with noninstructional school contexts of reading (e.g., Bloome, 1983; Gilmore, 1981; Smith, 1981), and home-community with classroom-school contexts of reading (e.g., Cook-Gumperz & Gumperz, 1981;

The authors gratefully acknowledge the help of James Heap for critical comments on an earlier draft and the help of Michael Kamil and P. David Pearson for editorial comments.

Cook-Gumperz, Gumperz, & Simons, 1981; Fiering, 1981; Florio & Shultz, 1979; Gilmore, 1981; Heath 1982a, 1982b; McDermott, Goldman, & Varenne, in press; Scollon & Scollon, 1982; Smith, 1981; Varenne, Hamid-Buglione, McDermott, & Morison, 1982).

In the second direction, researchers have viewed reading itself as a social and linguistic process. Within this second direction, researchers have been concerned with *how reading structures social interaction* (Bloome, 1981; Hymes, 1981; McDermott, 1967/1976, 1976; McDermott et al., in press; Stubbs, 1980; Szwed, 1977; Taylor, 1983) and *how reading—and literacy in general—are part of the processes of cultural transmission, enculturation, and socialization* (e.g., Bloome, in press; Cochran-Smith, in press, Cook-Gumperz & Gumperz, 1982; Heath, 1982b; Reder & Green, in press; Scollon & Scollon, 1981; Scribner & Cole, 1978, 1981; Smith, 1981; Tannen, 1978, 1980b; Varenne et al., 1982).

Research in each of the above directions will be discussed later, as will the historical antecedents of emerging directions within sociolinguistic research in reading. First, however, we offer a discussion of what constitutes the sociolinguistic perspectives described in this chapter.

THE NATURE OF A SOCIOLINGUISTIC PERSPECTIVE

Sociolinguists have tended to avoid defining sociolinguistics. Part of the avoidance is based on Labov's (1972b) view that the term sociolinguistics is itself "an oddly redundant term" (p. 183) since language and linguistics are always social. Gumperz (1972), Hymes (1974), and Labov (1972b) describe sociolinguistics as a movement away from the study of language outside of social interaction toward the study of linguistic and social processes as an integrated whole. Thus, Hymes (1974) suggests that correlations between social data and linguistic data, while worthwhile and important, do not constitute a sociolinguistic perspective. Rather, a sociolinguistic perspective requires viewing language as a social and cultural phenomena (Trudgill, 1974). The basis for doing so is the similarity between social and linguistic rules for communication. As Gumperz (1972) states:

> Social rules, therefore, are much like linguistic rules; they determine the actor's [or speaker's] choice among culturally available modes of action or strategies in accordance with the constraints provided by communicative intent, setting, and identity relationships. (p. 16)

A sociolinguistic perspective requires exploring how language is used to establish a social context while simultaneously exploring how the social context influences language use and the communication of meaning. To paraphrase, a sociolinguistic perspective of reading requires exploring how reading is used to establish a social context while simultaneously exploring how the social context influences reading praxis and the communication of meaning.

Methodologically, it is extremely difficult to explore how reading is used to establish a social context while simultaneously exploring how social contexts influence reading praxis. Thus, researchers have tended to emphasize one or the other dimension of a sociolinguistic perspective of reading. It is this difference in emphasis that leads to the directions in research on reading as a social and linguistic process described earlier.

The definition of sociolinguistics will become clearer as both the antecedents of this emerging approach to reading and the research undertaken within this perspective are considered. The discussion of reading research that follows is divided into five sections. The first section describes antecedents of emerging sociolinguistic perspectives for research on reading and reading instruction. These historical antecedents involve the fields of anthropology, linguistics, and literary analysis. The second section discusses reading research that emphasizes how social contexts influence reading praxis. Since research in this area has emphasized classroom contexts of reading, the discussion also emphasizes the classroom context. In addition, research that has looked across classroom and home-community contexts is discussed. In the third section, the focus shifts to research that views reading itself as a social and linguistic process. The section begins with a review of the few studies that show how reading is used to structure social interactions, followed by a lengthy discussion of studies concerned with how reading and literacy in general are part of the processes of cultural transmission. The fourth section briefly discusses efforts at bridging sociolinguistic and psychological perspectives of reading. The last section presents conclusions and future directions.

HISTORICAL ANTECEDENTS OF A SOCIOLINGUISTIC VIEW OF READING AND READING INSTRUCTION

The roots of emerging sociolinguistic views of reading and reading instruction involve three fields: anthropology, linguistics, and literary analysis. Contributions from these three fields include methodology, theoretical constructs, and conceptualizations. In the sections that follow, contributions to the conceptualization of reading as a sociolinguistic process will be presented. (For those interested in methodological contributions, see Chapter 4 by Hall and Guthrie.)

Anthropological Roots of Sociolinguistic Perspectives of Reading

The contributions from anthropology come primarily from work on the nature and development of literacy. Two different phases exist in anthropological research on literacy. In the early phase of this research, the development of literacy by a culture was viewed as an indication of historical, cultural, and social progress. Literate societies were viewed as more advanced than nonliterate societies. Therefore, in this phase, anthropological research was concerned primarily with whether or not a culture was literate, when literacy within a culture evolved, and what the nature of the literacy practices within a culture were like.

Within the last 25 years, anthropological research on literacy has shifted. Rather than viewing literacy as a benchmark of cultural and historical progress, anthropologists have been concerned primarily with the nature of literacy and its impact on cultural organization, social practices, and other cultural phenomena (e.g., Deshen, 1975; Goody & Watt, 1968; Gough, 1968; Lewis, 1968; Meggit, 1968; Tambiah, 1968). Characteristics of printed language—for example, being linear, capable of being stored and studied—were viewed as influencing cultural practices, such as law, the transmission of history, and (most important) schooling. In nonliterate societies, children learned information needed for their social and work roles through participation, apprenticeship, and the oral transmission of knowledge from an adult. With the availability of printed language, children could also learn information by studying written materials. The studying of written materials occurred outside of the contexts in which the information was to be used. For example, information about when, where, and how to plant a crop was learned in school rather than just the field. Since information was learned outside of either its original context or its context of use, knowledge became increasingly abstract and decontextualized (Goody & Watt, 1968).

Recent discussions and definitions of culture (e.g., Geertz, 1973; Goodenough, 1971) have provided a means of applying anthropological perspectives to literacy events at the level of face-to-face interaction. These definitions and discussions of culture have influenced recent sociolinguistic studies of reading. For example, Geertz (1973) defines culture as the 'webs' of meaning and interpretations that are created through the interactions of people. Thus, rather than viewing culture as a general set of knowledge carried around in one's head, culture is viewed as a dynamic process created and recreated through what people do in interaction with each other and through interpretive meanings that are created and shared through interactions. Although different from Geertz, Goodenough (1971) also defines culture in ways applicable to studying literacy events at the level of face-to-face interaction. Goodenough (1971) views culture as ways of perceiving, believing, behaving, and evaluating events of social life (Goodenough, 1971).

Based on these views of culture, anthropologists, such as Cook-Gumperz et al. (1981), Gumperz (1981), Heath (1982a, 1982b), and Scribner and Cole (1978, 1981), have explored reading and writing events as cultural events. Their concern has been with how people in interaction with each other create cultural contexts that influence what they do with written language and how they interpret both text and what they are doing.

From anthropology, therefore, researchers of reading processes and reading instruction obtain constructs that help broaden the definition of reading, place reading in the broader context within society, and identify what is being learned and acquired from engaging in reading events and reading instruction. In other words, by viewing reading as a cultural phenomenon, the reading researcher becomes concerned with the interpersonal nature of reading as well as the intrapersonal nature of reading.

Linguistic Roots of Sociolinguistic Perspectives of Reading

The development of sociolinguistics within the field of linguistics is often viewed as a movement away from the analysis of language in isolation to analysis of language as it is used in natural, everyday situations (e.g., Hymes, 1974; Labov, 1972b; Trudgill, 1974). Within this movement four trends are apparent.

One trend can be called the sociology-of-language trend because of its concern with "large scale social factors and their mutual interaction with language and dialects" (Labov, 1972b, p. 183). Research has focused on *language differences between social classes* (e.g., Bernstein, 1972a, 1972b, 1982; Robinson, 1979; Tough, 1982) and *language change and stability as a result of social, geographical, and political developments* (cf. Fishman, 1972a, 1972b).

A second trend involves the study of language diversity, language structures, language variations, and change within a speech community. Of primary concern are changes and variation in phonology, morphology, syntax, and semantics. Among the issues explored have been *standard and nonstandard dialects* (e.g., Fasold & Wolfram, 1970; Labov, 1972a; Smitherman, 1977), *institutional and societal responses to nonstandard dialects* (e.g., Baratz & Shuy, 1969; DeStefano, 1973; Labov, 1982, 1972b; Piestrup, 1973), *language features and variations related to social status and situation* (e.g., Ferguson, 1972; Scherer & Giles, 1979), and *underlying linguistic rules governing language variation and change* (e.g., Ervin-Tripp, 1982; Kay, 1977; Kay & McDaniel, 1979; Labov & Fanshel, 1977; Sankoff & Labov, 1979).

In these trends, social context is viewed as background against which language is studied. By contrast, the other trends emphasize social context as part of the foreground, that is, both language and social context are explored as an integrated whole.

One of the foreground trends concerns descriptions of language according to social functions (cf. Halliday, 1969; Stubbs, 1980; among others); while the other involves ethnography of communication (cf. Erickson & Shultz, 1981; Gumperz & Hymes, 1972; Hymes, 1974; Philips, 1982; among others). Since these two trends are important antecedent components of the sociolinguistic perspectives of reading discussed previously, they are discussed in more detail below. It should be emphasized, however, that the four trends described here are interrelated and that each provides important contributions to sociolinguistic perspectives of reading. (For additional examples of other perspectives on sociolinguistic approaches to reading see Hall & Guthrie, 1981, 1982; Labov & Robins, 1969.)

Social Functions of Language

Language, including language development, can be viewed in terms of its social functions (Halliday, 1969, 1973), that is, language is a tool and like any tool it is defined in terms of how it is used. Therefore, a focus on social functions requires a focus on the way language is functioning both within a specific context and at a specific point within a conversation. Halliday (1973) suggests that language is a tool for categorizing, ordering, and representing the world. In addition, he suggests that through interactions with adults, children learn appropriate ways of conceptualizing their experiences and the phenomena of their world. Therefore, by adopting a focus on language functions and how language is used, researchers can begin to explore the ways in which children view their world and to identify factors that influence what is acquired and how it is acquired.

Reading researchers have used Halliday and other discussions of social functions of language and language development (e.g., Britton, 1970) to explore relationships between the social functions of language and reading development (e.g., Goodman & Goodman, 1979; Stubbs, 1980; Teale, 1982). This research suggests that children learn to read because reading will serve social functions, like getting something they need or controlling someone's behavior. The social functions provide a framework within which children play with written language, learning how it can be used to get things done.

By viewing language and reading in terms of social functions, researchers can explore one set of influences for reading development and praxis. However, a social function, itself, does not constitute a social context. That is, social functions are only one set of social and linguistic influences involved in communicative contexts of reading events.

Ethnography of Communication

Research on context and functions of language has also been undertaken by ethnographers of communication. Researchers have explored patterns of activity organization; language use; and the rights, obligations, and demands within and across everyday contexts of social life. One basic premise of this work is that within face-to-face interactions, participants make communicative demands on each other as they work together to construct conversations. (An important influence on the work of ethnographers of communication has been the work of ethnomethodologists—e.g., Garfinkel, 1967; Sacks, 1972.)

Communicative rights, obligations, and demands (e.g., who gets to talk, when, where, and about what) do not remain constant across situations. Therefore, researchers interested in the nature and function of everyday conversations and language use have explored how and when demands—obligations and rights for participants shift and change. The premise underlying this work is that as people come together in face-to-face interactions, they must signal and negotiate communicative rights, demands, and obligations for that specific context. As contexts shift and evolve, so do the rights, obligations, and demands for participation. Consider a classroom for example. In classrooms, different sets of communicative rights and obligations for participation exist for teacher-led reading instruction, whole class instruction, and peer-to-peer lessons (e.g., how one gets a turn to talk in each setting differs). Therefore, within each situation or context, communicative rights and obligations are negotiated by participants based on how they define what they are doing and who they are.

One way to view the establishment of communicative rights and obligations is as the establishment of participation structures (cf. Erickson & Shultz, 1981; Florio & Shultz, 1979; Philips, 1982). Research on participation structures of reading events, like reading instruction, has provided insights into how students get to display competence, how students may be evaluated, and how cultural differences may be manifested in the classroom (e.g., Au, 1980; Shultz, Erickson, & Florio, 1982; Philips, 1982).

Explorations of the participation structures of face-to-face interaction constitute part of the research conducted under the rubric of the ethnography of communication (also called sociolinguistic ethnography). The ethnographer of communication seeks to explore cultural patterning of language in face-to-face interaction and the functions of language in social interaction (Gumperz, 1982; Gumperz & Hymes, 1972; Hymes, 1974). In addition to studies of participation structures, educational research within the field of ethnography of communication has been concerned with how people communicate and interpret intentions and meaning within face-to-face interaction (Gumperz, 1981); with how people gain access to face-to-face interactions, such as instructional conversations (e.g., Green & Wallat, 1981; Green & Harker, 1982; Michaels, 1981; Stoffan-Roth, 1981); and how people use language to structure a broad range of communicative situations, such as teacher-led instruction, for the transmission of knowledge (e.g.,

Mehan, 1979a) and for the transmission of social and cultural roles (McDermott, 1976, 1977).

Research and theoretical constructs from the ethnography of communication provide a language for discussing contexts of reading, evolution, and construction of reading events as well as providing directions for exploring the relationship between the contexts in which reading occurs.

Literary Analysis Roots of Sociolinguistic Perspectives of Reading

Although literary analysis has provided many contributions to reading research, of special importance to the development of sociolinguistic perspectives of reading are contributions concerned with the location of meaning. Locating meaning within reading events can be viewed heuristically as a two-level process.

The first level is concerned with the meaning of a text being read. Golden (in press, a) presents this location problem succinctly by asking, "If there is a text and there is no reader, is there meaning?" (p. 1). For Golden, the answer is no. She bases her response on the comparison of three different traditions in literary analysis: the phenomenological tradition, the rhetorical tradition, and the structuralist tradition. Each of these traditions views meaning as constructed by the reader within the literary constraints imposed by the text. Texts are viewed as capable of evoking more than one legitimate interpretation and, thus, different readers may generate different meanings for a single text. Within the three literary traditions, the reader is viewed as moving back and forth across the literary features of the text and creating a coherent representation of the text based not only on the text features, but also on his or her background knowledge and experience. Thus, meaning is located neither in the text nor the reader but in their interaction. Similar views of reader-text interaction and the location of meaning have been offered under the rubrics of hermeneutics and semiotics (e.g., Fish, 1980). The reader's task is essentially viewed as a dialectical task in which the reader must choose between competing interpretations.

In many ways, the task facing a reader described above is similar to the task facing an ethnographer or social scientist. Just as a reader must choose among competing interpretations of a text, a social scientist must choose among competing interpretations of an event. This is the second level of concern with the location of meaning. The discussion that follows suggests that the field of literary analysis, and in particular hermeneutics—originally an approach to biblical exegesis—can provide a philosophical context for helping choose among competing interpretations of an event.

Applied to the interpretation of events, hermeneutics calls for the interpretation of "parts" in terms of the "whole" and the interpretation of the "whole" in terms of its "parts" (cf. Agar, 1980). In other words, the social and communicative acts that make up an event need to be interpreted in terms of the social and cultural meaning of the event itself. For example, oral reading within a low-track reading group needs to be interpreted in terms of the social and cultural meaning of that group. However, just as social and communicative acts need to be interpreted in terms of the event itself, the event itself needs to be interpreted in terms of the social and communicative acts that constitute the event.

For example, the social and cultural meaning of a low-track reading group needs to be interpreted in terms of what the participants in that group actually do.

SOCIAL AND LINGUISTIC CONTEXTS OF READING

From a sociolinguistic perspective, contexts of reading consist of the social and communicative behaviors of participants engaged in face-to-face interaction and the meanings and interpretations that the participants give to their behavior. Because of the way that sociolinguistic studies of reading define context, these studies need to be read in ways that may be different from reading research based on psychological paradigms.

Research based on psychological paradigms is typically read in a cumulative manner. Each study adds information to studies that precede it. Sociolinguistic studies of reading need to be read in terms of what Hymes (1982) has called "comparative generalization," that is, descriptions of contexts of reading need to be compared within and across levels of context. For example, knowledge about reading within the context of reading groups is built (a) by comparing descriptions of reading groups, (b) by comparing descriptions of reading groups with analogous contexts in other settings (e.g., comparing the context of reading in a reading group with bedtime storyreading), and (c) by comparing descriptions of reading groups with descriptions of the context of reading at other, perhaps broader, levels (e.g., comparing the context of reading in a reading group with whole-class contexts for reading).

The research studies discussed in this section are organized to facilitate comparative generalization. However, before discussing the research studies, it is important to understand how sociolinguistic studies of contexts of reading define and identify reading.

In order to capture and describe contexts of reading, incidents of reading must first be identified. Within sociolinguistic studies of the contexts of reading, researchers have identified reading (a) as any type of interaction with text (e.g., looking at a book, carrying a note, orally rendering a text, etc.), (b) as comprehension of a text, and (c) as defined by the participants themselves. Although there are problems with any criteria used for identifying reading (see Heap, 1980, for a discussion of problems in identifying reading), the means for identifying what counts and what does not count as a reading event needs to be made explicit. When criteria for identifying reading events are omitted, left vague, or merely implied, the process of comparative generalization (described above) is made more difficult.

Reading as a Classroom Process

Part of being a student member of a classroom involves participating in a number of different reading events, such as reading groups, whole-class teacher-led instruction, individualized reading-skills instruction. One focus of sociolinguistic studies of reading has been to describe the nature of participation in different classroom reading events.

Sociolinguistic studies of reading groups have focused primarily on differences between high and low reading groups. McDermott (1976) found differences in the amount of time actually spent on reading instruction between high and low groups and in the turn-taking procedures used in high and low groups. High groups spent more time on reading instruction, partly because their turn-taking procedures did not divert their attention from their instructional tasks. The low reading group, which met for as much time as the high reading group, spent less time actually engaged in reading, partly because turn-taking procedures diverted attention away from the instructional task and partly because the group was frequently interrupted by other class members (including interruptions from members of the high reading group). McDermott (1967/1976) views what happens in the low reading group, not as a failure, but rather as an "achievement." Teacher and students work together to avoid, as much as possible, the frustration, embarrassment, and difficulty associated with reading while getting through the reading lesson.

Collins's (1981) study of reading groups found both similarities and differences with McDermott's study. Although Collins found differential treatment between the high and low reading groups, the differences primarily involved the kinds of instructional tasks they were given rather than turn-taking protocols. (Like McDermott, Collins found that the amount of time spent engaged in actual reading instruction in the low group was less than that for the high group.) Collins explains the differential treatment in terms of students' prosodic behavior (how they used intonation, stress, pausing, etc.) during the oral rendition of texts. The intonation patterns and prosodic behavior students used in segmenting orally rendered texts was linked to the teacher's strategies for correcting errors, which itself was linked to the time spent on comprehension-type tasks versus penmanship-type/sounding-out-type tasks. Interpreting his findings, Collins suggests [emphasis added]:

> Teachers appear to have certain implicit models of literate behavior, of discourse prose, *what it sounds like and how it is put together.* They appear to have differing expectations about students' readiness or ability to assimilate the skills necessary for literacy. (p. 21)

That is, differences in the prosodic behavior of students in high and low reading groups are interpreted by the teacher to require different instructional treatments. Because differences in students' prosodic behavior are not necessarily an indication of lack of reading ability or potential but rather may derive from students' home and community culture, Collins suggests that the basis for differential treatment in the high and low groups is questionable.

Although McDermott (1976) and Collins (1981) describe how reading events in reading groups are different, sociolinguistic studies of classroom contexts of reading suggest similarities across classroom reading events not revealed by explorations of reading groups.

DeStefano et al. (1982) closely studied the communicative behavior of reading instruction in one first-grade, inner city classroom. In addition, they studied the communicative behavior of three culturally diverse male students (a black student, a mainstream white student, and an Appalachian student) within reading lessons in the classroom. They found that the discourse of reading instruction emphasized (a) how students were to behave and (b) how students should become literate. That is, the discourse of reading instruction emphasized procedures and rules for social and communicative behavior within the classroom reading events. However, they "found no substantial evidence that [the] students were being helped to perceive and comprehend as coherent text the words, phrases or sentences to which they were being exposed one at a time" (p. 125). Examinations of the students' language during reading instruction showed that they had learned how to participate appropriately in classroom reading events, but the students' relative success in becoming literate was masked by the heavy emphasis on appropriate participation. In effect, DeStefano et al. (1982) suggest that what may count as becoming literate in a classroom may have more to do with learning to participate appropriately in classroom reading events than with the development of processes for comprehending text.

Bloome (1983) presents a similar finding based on a study of junior high school classrooms. He suggests that teachers and students engage each other in procedural display. He defines procedural display as teachers and students displaying to each other the accomplishment of procedures that count as accomplishing the lesson. Simply put, procedural display involves getting through the lesson rather than learning the substantive content of the lesson.

Similar findings are also reported by Heap (1982), who explored the function of the vocabulary segment of directed reading lessons. In directed reading lessons, a review or lesson on "new" or "difficult" vocabulary is presented prior to reading a story or other written passage. Heap found that the vocabulary segment provided a means of helping students and teacher get through the lesson but was unrelated to reading comprehension (although it may help in word attack, or vocabulary knowledge). That is, the vocabulary segment played a social role in facilitating getting through the lesson.

The studies by Bloome (1983), DeStefano et al. (1982), and Heap (1982) raise questions about what kinds of differences make a difference in the nature of classroom reading events. Differences between what occurs in high and low reading groups may be overshadowed by similarities at other levels (e.g., at the level of the classroom context).

Reading as a Developmental Process

One way to look at differences and similarities in classroom reading events is through process-product and process-process research models. Differences identified through the sociolinguistic analysis of classroom reading events can be linked to processes involved in reading comprehension or to measures of reading comprehension.

For example, Green (1977) analyzed videotapes of the teacher-student interaction of 11 teachers teaching the same lesson. After accounting for differences in student ability, Green (1977) found that differences in student recall of text used in the reading lesson were related to differences in how the teachers organized their instruction conversations. Teachers who asked questions and who initiated teacher-student discussion throughout the reading of the story, rather than at the end of the story, had high student-recall scores.

In a secondary analysis of this study, Green (in press), Golden (in press, b), and Harker (in press) undertook a contrastive case study of two of the teachers, one top-ranked teacher and one low-ranked teacher (based on student-recall performance). The three analyses represented different disciplines. Green (in press) undertook a sociolinguistic ethnographic analysis of social demands and instructional patterns of the evolving lesson. Harker (in press) built on this analysis and added a propositional analysis to explore the development of theme and academic content. Golden (in press, b) used an episodic analysis to explore the relationship between the original story text, the student reconstructed (recalled) text, and the teacher mediated text. The three analyses showed that (a) the rights and obligations for participation were different for each group, therefore, the lesson was not the same lesson socially (Green, in press); (b) the teachers emphasized different aspects of the story and stressed different content, therefore, the academic demands for student learning were different (Harker, in press); and (c) the teachers segmented the story differently and stressed different literary elements, therefore, the story, was not the same (Golden, in press, b). The two groups were comparable, however, in terms of age, sex, ability, ethnic composition, and teacher background. The findings suggest that setting, materials, and students may not be the major factors that lead to differences in learning; rather, differences may be attributed to individual teacher differences in delivery, structure, and intent. These studies suggest a need to look in depth at reading processes and the need to explore similarities and differences in teaching within and across lessons as well as teachers.

In another set of process-product studies of reading comprehension, the relationship between the way language is used in teacher-student interaction and students' responses to comprehension questions was explored (Mosenthal, in press; Mosenthal & Na, 1980; Mosenthal & Davidson-Mosenthal, 1982). For example, in one study Mosenthal and Na (1980) categorized students' responses to teacher initiatives as occurring at an imitative register level, a contingent register level, or a noncontingent register level. They found that "children adopt the same registers they use to converse with their teachers as they do to recall text for their teacher" (pp. 17–18).

One of the implications of these process-product studies is that the language of teacher-student interaction provides a context that influences the nature of reading comprehension processes. The language of classroom interaction has also been linked to students' gaining access to literacy learning opportunities. Michaels (1981) found that differential access to literacy events during sharing time (show and tell) in one first grade was based on the nature of students' narrative style. Students who had a narrative style that was topic centered (e.g., about one topic with verbally explicit links between concepts) were provided greater access to literacy learning events within sharing time. Students whose narrative style was topic associated (e.g., about the relationship of events with implied and prosodically signaled links between concepts) were provided less access to literacy learning events. Michaels (1981) suggests that differential access to literacy-learning events in sharing time was due, in part, to the teacher's implicit model of what constituted literate behavior, namely being topic centered.

Implied in Michaels's study is a process-process orientation. Processes involved in gaining access to literacy events are implicitly linked to processes involved in literacy learning events. That is, learning to read and write requires participation in literacy learning events and gaining access to such events is a necessary first step.

Wilkinson (Wilkinson & Calculator, 1982a, 1982b; Wilkinson & Dollaghan, 1979) has used a process-process model to look at the relationship between the language of classroom interaction and student access to literacy learning resources. For example, Wilkinson and Calculator (1982a) explored how students get information they need in peer-directed reading groups. They found that student requests which were on task, in direct form, sincere, made to a designated listener, and revised if unsuccessful at first attempt were more likely to obtain appropriate responses from other students. Wilkinson's findings suggest that students' communicative competence (e.g., ability to make effective requests) is related to getting access to resources needed for literacy learning.

Cochran-Smith (in press) explored the acquisition and development of formal and informal literacy processes by students in nursery school. She explored the relationship between naturally occurring literacy events and students' participation and knowledge about both uses and skills of literacy. Cochran-Smith identified both contextualized and decontextualized literacy events. Contextualized literacy is print which gets meaning from context (e.g., stop sign, an envelope). Decontextualized literacy involved a focus on print itself without the support from the contextual surround (e.g., on print in a storybook as the sole source of meaning). The nursery school that she studied was print rich, that is, print was an ongoing part of both formal and informal events. Children and teachers used print throughout the day in a variety of ways (e.g., as labels, for letters and notes) and at specific times (e.g., during rug time, storyreading). Exposure to print was a consistent part of the environment and of the day. Formal reading instruction, however, was not part of the curriculum (e.g., reading-readiness tests, auditory-discrimination activities).

Cochran-Smith found that from the formal and informal interaction, children acquired both technical skills of decoding and encoding as well as knowledge of the "appropriate ways print could be used in various situations in order to achieve specific goals in their community" (p. 141). By documenting literacy events, student-student interactions and teacher-student interactions systematically and carefully, Cochran-Smith was able to identify and document the ways in which "learning about reading and writing was the result of a gradual process of socialization that was indirect, informal and embedded into the routine social interactions of adults and children" (p. 99).

The studies by Green, Harker, Golden, Mosenthal, Wilkinson, and Cochran-Smith are primarily concerned with the classroom context of students' development of literacy skills. What they suggest is that in the classroom, both the nature of literacy learning skills (such as learning how to respond to comprehension questions) and opportunities for literacy development (such as gaining access to literacy learning events) are socially negotiated. Simply put, what is learned and who learns it is linked to the nature of the classroom context created by teacher-student and student-student interactions.

So far, we have discussed two sets of sociolinguistic studies concerned with the contexts of reading. The first set was concerned with reading as a classroom process and the second set was concerned with the development of reading. Both sets of studies suggest that appropriate and effective participation in classroom reading events, whether linked to classroom processes or to reading development, depend on at least the following: (a) teachers' and students' abilities to interpret accurately each others' behavior and what communicative expectations each holds for the other and (b) teachers' and students' abilities to act and to communicate in ways consistent with the social and linguistic expectations held by classroom participants.

Difficulties in how students and teachers interpret classroom communicative behavior, form communicative expectations, and attempt to communicate their intentions may be due, in part, to differences between home-community and school contexts of reading.

Home-Community/School Issues

Goodman and Goodman (1979) suggest three possible relationships between reading at home and reading in home-community situations: (a) complementary relationship in which what schools do builds on what children do with reading in home-community situations, (b) a null relationship in which what schools do and what happens in home-community situation is unrelated, and (c) a negative relationship in which what schools do hinders or harms reading development begun and fostered in home-community situations. Although sociolinguistic studies of the contexts of reading in home-community and school situations have shown both complementary and negative relationships, the reports of these studies have tended to emphasize negative relationships. This emphasis on negative relationships between reading in home-community situations and in school may be due, in part, to the schools and communities chosen for study. That is, the studies concerned with contexts of reading and home-community/school issues have been conducted primarily in schools and communities with a predominately black or minority-group population or, at least, an integrated population. Second, the explicitly stated intent of many of the studies was to explore reading failure in school and the studies may have chosen research sites that reflected their intent.

One potential source of a negative relationship between reading in home-community contexts and school contexts is the misevaluation of student reading ability and potential. For example, students who use a narrative discourse style that differs from that expected in school situations may be misevaluated regarding their reading ability and potential (Collins, 1981; Cook-Gumperz et al., 1981; Michaels, 1981). That is, teachers may evaluate students' reading ability and potential based on the students' culturally based communicative/interactional style rather than on other criteria more directly related to reading.

Misevaluation may also occur when students interpret text during classroom reading events in ways consistent with reading in home-community contexts. For example, Bloome (1981) reports a ninth-grade student failing a fourth-grade-level multiple-choice comprehension task because the student answered the questions in terms of his own experience rather than in terms of the answers expected by the publishers. Scollon and Scollon (1982) also report the misevaluation of students based on differences in approaches to text interpretation between home-community and school contexts. In their study of Athabascan Indian students, Scollon and Scollon (1981, 1982) found that in home-community narrative events, like storytelling, individuals were allowed to make their own sense of the narrative discourse. Audience participation in generating the narrative discourse was also allowed. However, in school situations, when students used approaches to text interpretation similar to approaches used in their home-community culture, they were negatively evaluated by the teacher. That is, not only was their approach negatively sanctioned but also judgments were made about their underlying ability to decode print.

The studies above describe factors that contribute to misevaluation of student reading behavior. But misevaluation can also occur when students do not have the opportunity to display competence.

Gilmore (1981) and Heath (1982a, 1982b) discuss misevaluation of student reading based on how difference in the ways classroom and home-community events are constituted. In effect, the nature of classroom reading events constrains students' display of competence and ability with reading and literacy tasks. For example, Gilmore (1981) describes how students in informal, peer-group, non-classroom settings engage in verbal games that require sophisticated word- and phrase-analysis skills. However, the same students in classroom situations did not display the competence and ability they displayed on the playground. Heath (1982a) describes how questioning at home and at school differ in terms of the communicative expectations made of children. While at home, children may demonstrate competence in responding to questions; at school, the same children may fail to respond to questions. The nature and organization of questions at school often fail to elicit from children the competence they show in responding to questions in home-community situations.

Not all studies of home-community and school contexts of reading reveal a discontinuity or negative relationship. Au's (Au, 1980; Au & Mason, 1981) research suggests that classroom reading lessons can be constructed in ways consistent with students' home-community culture and that allows students opportunities to display competence and engage in achievement-related behaviors. Au's study focused on reading lessons that were successful with native Hawaiian children. She found that there were many similarities between turn-taking protocols in the reading lesson and turn-taking protocols in native Hawaiian narrative discourse events. Au suggests that similarities in the turn-taking protocols provided students with a means for displaying competence and allowed them to gain access to literacy learning events in the classroom.

Summary: Contexts of Reading

Sociolinguistic studies of classroom contexts of reading have suggested (a) that differences exist between the contexts of reading in high and low reading groups, (b) that what counts as reading may have more to do with following participation and display procedures than with substantive and meaningful interpretations and interactions with text, (c) that the nature of teacher-student and student-student interactions in classrooms is related to gaining access to literacy resources and to the approach that students take in interacting with texts, and (d) that cultural differences between contexts of reading and reading-related events in school and in home-community settings may result in the misevaluation of student reading ability. These general findings need to be interpreted in terms of the underlying assumptions of these studies. A primary assumption is that reading is a cognitive process embedded in social and linguistic contexts. By describing the nature of the social and linguistic contexts of reading, processes influencing the nature of reading as a cognitive process are revealed.

However, it should be emphasized that reading is not only a cognitive process, but also a social and linguistic process. The findings above need to be reinterpreted when reading is viewed as a social and linguistic process rather than only a cognitive process. To accomplish this task, the following questions need to be asked: Within reading groups and classrooms, how is reading used to structure or establish social and communicative relationships among people? How is reading used as a social and linguistic response to cultural differences manifested in the classroom?

READING AS A SOCIAL AND LINGUISTIC PROCESS

Only recently have researchers begun to view and explore reading as a social and linguistic process. Because of the small number of studies employing a view of reading as a social and linguistic process, the discussion in this section is necessarily brief.

Reading and Social Relationships

During reading events, people not only interact with a text, but also interact with other people. For example, during bedtime reading, children not only interact with the book, but also with a parent. Indeed, from both the child's and the parent's point of view, the interaction with the book may be secondary to their interaction with each other.

Taylor's (1983) study of young children and family literacy describes how reading and writing are used to establish and negotiate relationships between parents and children, between siblings, and between children and their friends. For example, the children used writing to establish and reestablish membership in informal clubs. They wrote lists—and revised them—of "who's in and who's out" (p. 43). Taylor reports that the content of the children's writing could be irrelevant to the purpose or function of the written communication. For example, she describes a letter written by a 3½-year-old to a friend. The letter consisted of a page of circles with lines through them. However, the child who received the letter stated that he had understood the letter and was pleased to receive it (p. 42).

Taylor also describes how literacy events can be a context for sharing among parents and children:

> If Sandy Lindell did not want to read, then her parents read to her. She listened to stories. She wrote notes and letters and drew pictures. She received notes from her family and did her chores according to a list taped to the refrigerator door. For Sandy, as with other children, reading and writing were activities to be shared. They were meaningful, concrete tasks dictated in many ways by the social setting, literate events that occurred

as part of family life, a way of building and maintaining the relational contexts of everyday life. (1983, p. 82)

However, literacy events can also lead to dissent and separate parents and children. For example, Taylor reports how a mother was rejected by her children because she was not literate.

Taylor suggests that part of the ways in which literacy structures social relationships involves social status. As Taylor states, "Literacy gave the children both status and identity as it became the medium of shared experience" (p. 87). Not being literate precluded the children (or a parent) from some aspects of social status within their family.

Taylor's study focused on young children within six families in suburban communities. Bloome's (1981) study focused on adolescents in both school and community contexts in an urban community. His findings concern differences in the social configurations of students across reading events. He describes two types of configurations: (a) isolated reading and (b) social reading. Isolated reading configurations consist of one reader and one text, as if the reader and text were isolated from anything else occurring around them. He found that in instructional settings, teachers promoted isolated reading configurations. Students sat at individual desks and had their own text; students were not allowed to share; students were not allowed to talk with friends or others while engaged in reading. Social reading configurations consist of multiple readers simultaneously interacting with each other, usually with a single text. Social reading configurations were found in noninstructional situations, such as comic book reading, note reading, newspaper reading, and menu reading.

Bloome (1981) also describes how students could use both isolated and social reading configurations to negotiate social interactions. For example, he describes how a student used an isolated reading configuration to separate herself from a classroom activity. Students in class were engaged in a modified version of "Password," in which the whole class could give clues to a designated student. The activity was boisterous. After briefly participating, one student shifted how she was sitting, opened her book, and seemed to be reading. When asked why she did so, she replied that the class would get in trouble and she did not want to be included.

Reading and Cultural Transmission

Researchers have primarily been concerned with three issues related to reading and cultural transmission. The first is sociological—how reading influences who gets what social and economic roles in a society. The second issue concerns the framework to approaching text that children are taught. The third issue concerns how reading is involved in conflicts between cultural transmission as a school process and cultural transmission in home-community settings.

One way to view reading as a process of cultural transmission is in how reading events define and determine people's roles and identities. For example, McDermott (1967/1976, 1976, 1977) describes how the social organization and conduct of reading activities in one first-grade classroom was linked to the social roles that students played out in the classroom. McDermott suggests that the differentiation of social roles and status is based on the competitive context of schooling. That is, one sociological function of schools is viewed as dividing students into different kinds of futures that have greater or lesser social status. Since not all students can fit into the top categories, mechanisms are needed for differentiating students. Reading events may be an important part of that differentiation.

A second way to view reading as a process of cultural transmission is in the frameworks for approaching text taught to children. Tannen (1978, 1980a, 1980b, 1982) suggests that a distinction can be made between reading/writing/ speaking/listening and literacy/orality frameworks. Reading, writing, speaking, listening describe the expressive or receptive uses of written or oral language. Reading, writing, speaking and/or listening can occur in either a literate or an oral framework. Literate frameworks are characterized as involving decontextualized language, explicit verbal links between concepts, and little audience participation. Orality frameworks are characterized as involving contextualized language, implied and prosodically linked concepts, and audience participation.

Cook-Gumperz and Gumperz (1982) suggest that one of the tasks facing children in learning to read is becoming literate. That is, children need to make a transition between contextualized language (in which the concepts or items being discussed are nearby or can be assumed to be known) and decontextualized language. The transition is necessary because in school, reading is primarily defined in terms of a literate (decontextualized) framework.

Differences between definitions of reading in school and home-community contexts may result in conflicts. These conflicts often highlight how reading is used as a process of cultural transmission. For example, Smith (in press) discusses how schools count as reading only a small set of events that involve interaction with text:

> What counts as reading or writing in school (or, for that matter, as learning in general) is usually determined by what is taught. Texts are designed for the display of not what may have been learned naturally, but what the teacher believes has been taught. Lessons are planned to lead students systematically through stages that the teacher establishes. . . . The effects of this counting only-what-is-taught syndrome on the acquisition and display of reading and writing skills is far-reaching. A child, for example, coming to school, able as Heath's subjects were to "read to learn" [Heath, 1982a, 1982b, states that in some communities young children focus on using reading to learn activities rather than on learning to read activities] may soon find that what s/he can do doesn't count as reading. (p. 8)

The issue Smith (in press) presents goes beyond evaluation of student reading. He suggests that reading in schools is a cultural activity related primarily to student participation and membership in school rather than reading development per se.

Research on reading as a social and linguistic process, while a newly emerging area, holds promise for researchers concerned with factors that influence the acquisition of reading and related literacy abilities. The work on reading and social relationships (e.g., Bloome, 1981; Taylor, 1983) suggests that how reading influences student relationships and family relationships is an area for further study. The work on reading and cultural transmission (e.g., Cook-Gumperz & Gumperz, 1982; McDermott, 1967/1976, 1976, 1977; McDermott et al., in press; Smith, 1981, in press; Tannen, 1978, 1980a, 1980b, 1982) suggests further research is needed on (a) how literacy functions in schools, families, and communities as a social and cultural process; (b) how conflicting definitions of literacy across school and home-community settings affect students and families; and (c) the role of oral and literate frameworks in the acquisition of reading and other literacy skills.

BRIDGING SOCIOLINGUISTIC AND PSYCHOLOGICAL PERSPECTIVES OF READING

The need for bridging sociolinguistic and psychological perspectives of reading is based upon the assumption that reading is both a cognitive and a social/linguistic process. However, there are a number of difficulties in bridging sociolinguistic and psychological perspectives of reading. While these difficulties tend to manifest themselves as methodological problems, there are philosophic problems involving the underlying assumptions upon which sociolinguistic and psychological research are based.

Psychological paradigms are typically viewed as embedded in a positivist philosophic tradition. Knowledge is objective and cumulative. Sociolinguistic perspectives (at least those based partially or fully upon anthropology, ethnomethodology, and/or the ethnography of communication) are typically viewed (perhaps incorrectly) as embedded in a phenomenological philosophical tradition in which knowledge is primarily subjective and dialectical in nature. Bridging sociolinguistic and psychological perspectives would require bridging at the level of underlying philosophic assumptions.

Failure to acknowledge differences between underlying philosophic assumptions has lead to miscommunication and misunderstanding among researchers. As Cole and Scribner (1976) state:

> The general failure of anthropologists [or sociolinguists working within an anthropological framework] and psychologists to share the same definitions, facts, and theoretical constructs is a fundamental impediment to our understanding of the relation between culture and the development of cognitive processes; all the more so because this failure often goes unnoticed. Because they share a common interest and a common terminology, psychologists and anthropologists tend to make the assumption that they share a common topic of inguiry—each in his own way pursues the link between social experiences and cognition. We believe this assumption is unfounded on both sides of the equation: anthropologists and psychologists do not mean the same thing when they speak of cognitive "consequences"; they do not agree on the characteristics of culture that are potential "antecedents"; and they distrust each other's method for discovering the links between the two. (p. 159)

Cole and Scribner's (1976) concern for the language used by researchers is reiterated by McDermott and Hood (1982). They raise at least two issues that have importance for building bridges between psychological and sociolinguistic perspectives of reading. First, educational research has been dominated by educational psychology to the extent that the language used to describe educational processes is—with few exceptions—the language of psychology. This influences the kinds of problems and issues that researchers explore. McDermott and Hood (1982) argue that researchers need to explore educational problems and issues other than those defined by the language of educational psychology. What is needed is the application of a different language—for example, the language of anthropology—to the description of educational processes. This leads to a second issue raised by McDermott and Hood. They argue that researchers cannot merely take research techniques from one discipline (e.g., sociolinguistics or anthropology) and apply those techniques to problems or issues raised by another discipline (e.g., educational psychology). They argue that unless the framework is changed (i.e., unless the research problem is reconceptualized), the research effort will not provide a new perspective and may falsely suggest the convergence of multiple perspectives.

Despite difficulties in bridging sociolinguistic and psychological perspectives of reading, recently researchers have suggested directions for building bridges.

Bridging by Reformulating the Concept of Context

Psychological perspectives of reading are primarily concerned with the individual reader and how that reader establishes a meaning for a text. Of primary concern are the background knowledge and skills that a reader brings to the task of interpreting a text as well as individual differences in the reader's knowledge and skills. The individual's background knowledge, skills, and general approach to reading can be viewed as the *intra*personal context of reading. The *inter*personal context of reading would involve the organization of reading events, the interaction of participants involved in reading events, the influences that the interaction of participants had on the reading process, as well as how the reading process influenced the interaction of participants. The interpersonal context of reading is of primary concern in sociolinguistic perspectives of reading.

By reformulating the concept of context to account for both the intrapersonal context and the interpersonal context, researchers have attempted to bridge sociolinguistic and psychological perspectives. For example, Harste, Burke, and Woodward (1982) argue that reading is a sociopsycholinguistic process involving a language setting, a mental setting, and strategy utilization. Harste et al. (1982) explain (emphasis in original):

> In considering a given text, the *language setting* which includes where the language is found (home, school, store), in what culture (United States, Israel, Saudia Arabia), and for and by whom it was produced (peer, superior, subordinate) modifies the *mental setting* in terms of what schema the reader accesses. The accessed schemata direct strategy utilization and, hence, sampling of language setting. (p. 108)

The language setting is the *inter*personal context, while the mental setting is the *intra*personal context.

Calls for not separating the intrapersonal context from the interpersonal context have recently been made by Bussis, Chittenden, Amarel, and Klausner (1982), Cazden (1979, 1981), and Sulzby (1981) among others. However, difficulties arise in specifying relationships between the intrapersonal context and the interpersonal contexts. Part of this difficulty is related to the nature of the phenomena themselves. That is, in order to explore the intrapersonal context, the interpersonal context must be "frozen" or stopped. However, in "freezing" the interpersonal context, the nature of the interpersonal context is distorted since the interpersonal context is an evolving, ongoing, dynamic process.

One way in which researchers have attempted to capture both the intrapersonal and interpersonal context without distorting either has been through juxtaposing different research perspectives.

Bridging through the Juxtaposition of Different Perspectives

As stated earlier, before combining findings and/or methods from sociolinguistic and psychologically based studies of reading, a theoretical basis for their juxtaposition needs to be established. By building on Gumperz's (1981) concept of conversational inference, Frederiksen (1981) and Green and Harker (1982) provide a theoretical basis for juxtaposing propositional analysis and sociolinguistic analysis. Simply put, participants engaged in face-to-face interaction need to make inferences about how to interpret each other's communicative behavior and participants need to make inferences about what they should say, and about how, where, and when they should say it. The inferences participants make are based on their own background knowledge and the constraints involved in communicative interaction. These constraints involve social-interactive constraints, such as turn-taking rights and obligations, and semantic structure constraints, such as the propositional structure of the conversational discourse. In order to explore the conversational framework within which inferences are made, both the social-interactive nature and the propositional-structure nature of conversational discourse need to be explicated.

Though somewhat differently, both Frederiksen (1981) and Green and Harker (1982) juxtapose sociolinguistic and cognitive science approaches to discourse analysis. Frederiksen (1981) is concerned with the kinds of inferences students need to make during instructional conversations. He presents a method for the close analysis of instructional conversations that provides for analysis of conversational inferences based on the social-interactive context and the propositional structure of the discourse. Through his approach, Frederiksen (1981) is able to show the interplay of contextual constraints and propositional constraints in instructional conversations.

Green and Harker (1982) are primarily concerned with the demands of instructional conversations. These demands are both social interactive and propositional content in nature. By juxtaposing a sociolinguistic analysis with a propositional analysis, Green and Harker (1982) present a method for close analysis of the evolving social-interactive and propositional-content demands. That is, they show how the propositional-content demands are reflected in the social-interactive demands and how the social-interactive demands are reflected in the propositional demands.

SUMMARY: CONCEPTS, ISSUES, AND
DIRECTIONS REVISITED

The discussion of reading from a sociolinguistic perspective presented in this chapter centers around concepts, issues, and directions. Conceptually reading was defined as a cognitive, intrapersonal process embedded in a social and linguistic process and as an interpersonal social/linguistic process. In both views of reading, reading is defined as a contextualized activity and context is seen as a factor influencing both the nature of practice and what is learned. The studies reviewed showed that (a) the ways in which teachers structure the interpersonal context influences student performance within the lesson and on related tasks and outcome measures; (b) the ways in which students use language in their interactions with teachers within lessons influences teacher evaluation of their reading performance; (c) differences in the nature of reading, in the ways in which reading is structured, and in expectations for reading performance and participation exist for high and low group students; (d) the interpersonal context of reading mediates the reading-learning process; (e) definitions of reading held by members of the group may vary, based on past experiences with literacy-type events (e.g., storytelling, narrative performance) and with expectations for language use; (f) ways in which children use language may constrain or support their ability to gain access to reading and literacy events; and (g) literacy learning is a process of gradual socialization to print, which can be supported by formal and informal contexts for literacy in classrooms and other settings. The findings highlighted above are representative, not all-inclusive.

All of the studies suggest the need for an expanded definition of reading and a more refined understanding of the nature of literacy learning and literacy functions in home-community settings and at school. This work also suggests the need to explore further the relationships between home-community learning and school-learning demands.

In addition to the expanded conceptualizations of reading, issues in the study of reading are important. The studies raise a series of questions and issues when engaged in reading research in natural settings. Issues include the need to consider (a) the theoretical grounding of the research and its match to the question and (b) the language of the research approach selected and how it influences what is studied, what counts as reading, and how processes are viewed. The work shows that sociolinguistics and ethnography of communication can provide a systematic language for talking about everyday reading/literacy events, their structure, their function, and the interrelationship between their structure and function.

Finally, the research presented here points to several promising directions. The studies suggest that future work needs to consider: (a) both the interpersonal and intrapersonal context of reading, (b) the perceptions of the activity and process held by participants, (c) the functions of literacy in home-community settings and school settings, (d) the resources students bring to reading activities and tasks, (e) what is being learned about reading from participating in reading and literacy activities in home-community settings and at school, (f) the relationship among language use, functions of literacy, and reading/literacy participation and performance, (g) sources of misevaluation of reading ability (e.g., patterns of language use, expectations for appropriate participation), and (h) what counts as reading in and across different settings.

REFERENCES

Agar, M.   Hermeneutics in anthropology: A review essay. *Ethos,* 1980, *8,* 253–272.

Au, K.   Participation structures in a reading lesson with Hawaiian children. *Anthropology and Education Quarterly,* 1980, *11,* 91–115.

Au, K., & Mason, J.   Social organizational factors in learning to read: The balance of rights hypothesis. *Reading Research Quarterly,* 1981, *17,* 115–151.

Baratz, J., & Shuy, R.   *Teaching black children to read.* Washington, D.C.: Center for Applied Linguistics, 1969.

Bernstein, B.   Social class, language and socialization. In P. Giglioli (Ed.), *Language and social context.* Middlesex, Eng.: Penguin, 1972.(a)

Bernstein, B.   A sociolinguistic approach to socialization; with some reference to educability. In J. Gumperz & D. Hymes (Eds.), *Directions in sociolinguistics.* New York: Holt, Rinehart & Winston, 1972.(b)

Bernstein, B.   Codes, modalities, and the process of cultural reproduction: A model. *Language in Society.* 1982, *11,* 165–201.

Bloome, D.   *An ethnographic approach to the study of reading among black junior high school students.* Unpublished doctoral dissertation, Kent State University, Ohio, 1981.

Bloome, D.   *Definitions and functions of reading in two middle school classrooms.* Paper presented at the meeting of the American Educational Research Association, Montreal, Can., 1983.

Bloome, D.   Reading as a social process. In B. Hutson (Ed.), *Advances in reading/language research* (Vol. 2). Greenwich, Conn.: JAI Press, in press.

Bloome, D., & Green, J.   *Capturing social contexts of reading for urban junior high school youth in home, school and community settings* (Final report to the National Institute of Education). Washington, D.C.: U.S. Department of Education, 1982.

Britton, J.   *Language and learning.* Coral Gables, Fla.: University of Miami Press, 1970.

Bussis, A., Chittenden, E., Amarel, M., & Klausner, E.   *Inquiry into meaning* (Final report to the National Institute of Education). Washington, D.C.: U.S. Department of Education, 1982.

Cazden, C.   Learning to read in classroom instruction. In L. Resnick & P. Weaver (Eds.), *Theory and practice of early reading* (Vol. 3). Hillsdale, N.J.: Erlbaum, 1979.

Cazden, C.   Social context of learning to read. In J. Guthrie (Ed.), *Comprehension and teaching: Research reviews.* Newark, Del.: International Reading Association, 1981.

Cochran-Smith, M.   *The making of a reader.* Norwood, N.J.: Ablex, in press.

Cole, M., & Scribner, S.   Theorizing about socialization of cognition. In T. Schwartz (Ed.), *Socialization as cultural communication: Development of a theme in the work of Margaret Mead.* Berkeley: University of California Press, 1976.

Collins, J.   Differential treatment in reading instruction. In J. Cook-Gumperz, J. Gumperz, & H. Simons. *School-home ethnography project* (Final report to the National Institute of Education). Washington, D.C.: U.S. Department of Education, 1981.

Cook-Gumperz, J., & Gumperz, J.   From oral to written culture: The transition to literacy. In M. Whiteman (Ed.), *Variation in writing.* Hillsdale, N.J.: Erlbaum, 1981.

Cook-Gumperz, J., & Gumperz, J.   Communicative competence in educational perspective. In L. C. Wilkinson (Ed.), *Communicating in the classroom.* New York: Academic Press, 1982.

Cook-Gumperz, J., Gumperz, J., & Simons, H.   *School-home ethnography project* (Final report to the National Institute of Education). Washington, D.C.: U.S. Department of Education, 1981.

Deshen, S.   Ritualization of literacy: The works of Tunisian scholars in Israel. *American Ethnologist,* 1975, *2,* 251–260.

DeStafano, J.   *Language, society and education: A profile of black English.* Worthington, Ohio: C. A. Louer, 1973.

DeStefano, J., Pepinsky, H., & Sanders, T.   Discourse rules for literacy learning in a first grade classroom. In L. C. Wilkinson (Ed.), *Communicating in the classroom.* New York: Academic Press, 1982.

Erickson, F., & Shultz, J.   When is a context? Some issues and methods in the analysis of social competence. In J. Green & C. Wallat (Eds.), *Ethnography and language in educational settings.* Norwood, N.J.: Ablex, 1981.

Ervin-Trip, S.   Structures of control. In L. C. Wilkinson (Ed.), *Communicating in the classroom.* New York: Academic Press, 1982.

Fasold, R., & Wolfram, W.   Some linguistic features of negro dialect. In R. Fasold & R. Shuy (Eds.), *Teaching standard English in the inner city.* Washington, D.C.: Center for Applied Linguistics 1970.

Ferguson, C. Diglossia. In P. Giglioli (Ed.), *Language and social context.* Middlesex, Eng.: Penguin, 1972.

Fiering, J.   Commodore school: Unofficial writing. In D. Hymes (Project Director), *Ethnographic monitoring of children's acquisition of reading/language arts skills in and out of the classroom* (Final report to the National Institute of Education). Washington, D.C.: U.S. Department of Education, 1981.

Fish, S.   *Is there a text in this class?* Cambridge: Harvard University Press, 1980.

Fishman, J.   Domains and the relationship between micro and macrosociolinguistics. In J. Gumperz & D. Hymes (Eds.) *Directions in sociolinguistics.* New York: Holt, Rinehart & Winston, 1972. (a)

Fishman, J.   The sociology of language. In P. Giglioli (Ed.), *Language and social context.* Middlesex, Eng.: Penguin, 1972. (b)

Florio, S., & Shultz, J.   Social competence at home and school. *Theory into practice,* 1979, *18,* 234–243.

Frederiksen, C.   Inference in preschool children's conversations—a cognitive perspective. In J. Green & C. Wallat (Eds.), *Ethnography and language in educational settings.* Norwood, N.J.: Ablex, 1981.

Garfinkel, H.   *Studies in ethnomethodology.* Englewood Cliffs, N.J.: Prentice-Hall, 1967.

Garfinkel, H.   Remarks on ethnomethodology. In J. Gumperz & D. Hymes (Eds.) *Directions in sociolinguistics.* New York: Holt, Rinehart & Winston, 1972.

Geertz, C.   *The interpretation of cultures.* New York: Random House, 1973.

Gilmore, P.   Shortridge school and community: Attitudes and admission to literacy. In D. Hymes (Project Director), *Ethnographic monitoring of children's acquisition of reading/language arts skills in and out of the classroom* (Final report to the National Institute of Education). Washington, D.C.: U.S. Department of Education, 1981.

Golden, J.   If a text exists without a reader, is there meaning? Insights from literary theory for reader-text interaction. In B. Hutson (Ed.), *Advances in reading/language research* (Vol. 2). Greenwich, Conn.: JAI Press, in press. (a)

Golden, J.   Structuring and restructuring text. In J. Green & J. Harker (Eds.), *Multiple perspective analysis of classroom discourse.* Norwood, N.J.: Ablex, in press. (b)

Goodenough, W.   *Culture, language, and society.* Reading, Mass.: Addison-Wesley, 1971.

Goodman, K., & Goodman, Y.   Learning to read is natural. In L. Resnick & P. Weaver (Eds.). *Theory and practice of early reading* (Vol. 1). Hillsdale, N.J.: Erlbaum, 1979.

Goody, J., & Watt, I.   The consequences of literacy. In J. Goody (Ed.), *Literacy in traditional societies.* London: Cambridge University Press, 1968.

Gough, K.   Literacy in Kerala. In J. Goody (Ed.), *Literacy in traditional societies.* London: Cambridge University Press, 1968.

Green, J.   *Pedagogical style differences as related to comprehension performances: Grades one through three.* Unpublished doctoral dissertation, University of California at Berkeley, 1977.

Green, J.   Lesson construction and student performance. In J. Green & J. Harker (Eds.), *Multiple perspective analysis of classroom discourse.* Norwood, N.J.: Ablex, in press.

Green, J., & Harker, J.   Gaining access to learning: Conversational, social and cognitive demands of group participation. In L. C. Wilkinson (Ed.), *Communicating in the classroom.* New York: Academic Press, 1982.

Green, J., & Wallat, C.   Mapping instructional conversations. In J. Green & C. Wallat (Eds.), *Ethnography and language in educational settings.* Norwood, N.J.: Ablex, 1981.

Griffin, P.   How and when does reading occur in the classroom? *Theory into Practice,* 1977, *16,* 376–383.

Gumperz, J.   Introduction. In J. Gumperz & D. Hymes (Eds.), *Directions in sociolinguistics.* New York: Holt, Rinehart & Winston, 1972.

Gumperz, J.   Conversational inference and classroom learning. In J. Green & C. Wallat (Eds.), *Ethnography and language in educational settings.* Norwood, N.J.: Ablex, 1981.

Gumperz, J.   *Discourse strategies.* London: Cambridge University Press, 1982.

Gumperz, J., & Hymes, D. (Eds.) *Directions in sociolinguistics.* New York: Holt, Rinehart & Winston, 1972.

Gumperz, J., & Tannen, D.   Individual and social differences in language use. In C. Filmore et al. (Eds.), *Individual differences in language ability and language behavior.* New York: Academic Press, 1979.

Hall, W., & Guthrie, L.   Cultural and situational variation in language function and use— methods and procedures for research. In J. Green & C. Wallat (Eds.), *Ethnography and language in educational settings.* Norwood, N.J.: Ablex, 1981.

Hall, W., & Guthrie, L.   Situational differences in the use of language. In J. Langer & M. Smith-Burke (Eds.), *Reader meets author/bridging the gap: A psycholinguistic and sociolinguistic perspective.* Newark, Del.: International Reading Association, 1982.

Halliday, M.   Relevant models of language. *Educational Review,* 1969, *22,* 1–128.

Halliday, M.   Language as a social semiotic: Towards a general sociolinguistic theory. In M. Makkai & L. Heilman (Eds.), *Linguistics at the crossroads.* The Hague: Mouton, 1973.

Harker, J.   The relationship between the evolving oral discourse and the discourse of a story. In J. Green & J. Harker (Eds.), *Multiple perspective analysis of classroom discourse.* Norwood, N.J.: Ablex, in press.

Harste, J., Burke, C., & Woodward, V.   Children's language and world: Initial encounters with print. In J. Langer & M. Smith-Burke (Eds.), *Reader meets author/bridging the gap: A psycholinguistic and sociolinguistic perspective.* Newark, Del.: International Reading Association, 1982.

Heap, J.   What counts as reading? Limits to certainty in assessment. *Curriculum Inquiry,* 1980, *10* 265–292.

Heap, J.   *Word recognition, in theory and in classroom practice.* Paper presented at the Ethnography in Education Research Forum, Philadelphia, 1982.

Heath, S.   Questioning at home and at school: A comparative study. In G. Spindler (Ed.), *The ethnography of schooling.* New York: Holt, Rinehart & Winston, 1982. (a)

Heath, S.   What no bedtime story means: Narrative skills at home and school. *Language in Society,* 1982, *11,* 49–76. (b)

Hymes, D.   *Foundations in sociolinguistics: An ethnographic approach.* Philadelphia: University of Pennsylvania Press, 1974.

Hymes, D. (Project Director),   *Ethnographic monitoring of children's acquisition of read-*

ing/language arts skills in and out of the classroom (Final report to the National Institute of Education). Washington D.C.: U.S. Department of Education, 1981.

Hymes, D.   What is ethnography? In P. Gilmore & A. Glatthorn (Eds.), *Children in and out of school.* Washington, D.C.: Center for Applied Linguistics, 1982.

Kay, P.   Language evolution and speech style. In B. Blount & M. Sanchez (Eds.), *Sociocultural dimensions of language change.* New York: Academic Press, 1977.

Kay, P., & McDaniel, C.   On the logic of variable rules. *Language in Society.* 1979, *8,* 151–188.

Labov, W.   The logic of nonstandard English. In P. Giglioli (Ed.), *Language and social context.* Middlesex, Eng.: Penguin, 1972. (a)

Labov, W.   *Sociolinguistic patterns.* Philadelphia: University of Pennsylvania Press, 1972. (b)

Labov, W.   Objectivity and commitment in linguistic science: The case of the black English trial in Ann Arbor. *Language in Society,* 1982, *11,* 165–202.

Labov, W., & Fanshel, D.   *Therapeutic discourse.* New York: Academic Press, 1977.

Labov, W., & Robins, C.   A note on the relation of reading failure to peer group status in urban ghettos. *Teachers College Record,* 1969, *70,* 395–404.

Lewis, I.   Literacy in a nomadic society: The Somali case. In J. Goody (Ed.), *Literacy in traditional societies.* London: Cambridge University Press, 1968.

McDermott, R.   Achieving school failure: An anthropological approach to illiteracy and school stratification. In H. Singer & R. Ruddell (Eds.), *Theoretical models and processes of reading* (2nd ed.). Newark, Del.: International Reading Association, 1976. (Originally published, 1967.)

McDermott, R.   *Kids make sense: An ethnographic account of the interactional management of success and failure in one first-grade classroom.* Unpublished doctoral dissertation, Stanford University, 1976.

McDermott, R.   Social relations as contexts for learning in school. *Harvard Educational Review,* 1977, *47,* 198–213.

McDermott, R., & Goldman, S., & Varenne, H.   When school goes home. *Teachers College Record,* in press.

McDermott, R., & Hood, L.   Institutionalized psychology and the ethnography of schooling. In P. Gilmore & A. Glatthorn (Eds.) *Children in and out of school.* Washington, D.C.: Center for Applied Linguistics, 1982.

Meggit, M.   Uses of literacy in New Guinea and Melanesia. In J. Goody (Ed.), *Literacy in traditional societies.* London: Cambridge University Press, 1968.

Mehan, H.   *Learning lessons: Social organization in the classroom.* Cambridge: Harvard University Press, 1979. (a)

Mehan, H.   "What time is it, Denise?" Asking known information questions in classroom discourse. *Theory into Practice,* 1979, *18,* 295–294. (b)

Michaels, S.   "Sharing time": Children's narrative styles and differential access to literacy. *Language in Society,* 1981, *10,* 423–442.

Morine-Dershimer, G.   *The literate pupil.* Syracuse: Syracuse University, School of Education, 1982.

Mosenthal, P.   The influence of social situation in children's classroom comprehension of text. *Elementary School Journal,* in press.

Mosenthal, P., & Davidson-Mosenthal, R.   Individual differences in children's use of new and old information during reading lessons. *Elementary School Journal,* 1982, *83,* 24–34.

Mosenthal, P., & Na, T.   Quality of text recall as a function of children's classroom competence. *Journal of Experimental Child Psychology,* 1980, *30,* 1–21.

Philips, S.   *The invisible culture: Communication in classroom and community on the Warm Springs Indian reservations.* New York: Longman, 1982.

Piestrup, A.   *Black dialect interference and accommodation of reading instruction in first grade* (Monographs of the Language-Behavior Research Laboratory). Berkeley: University of California, 1973.

Reder, S., & Green, K.   Contrasting patterns of literacy in an Alaska fishing village. *International Journal of Sociology of Language*, in press.

Robinson, W.   Speech markers and social class. In K. Scherer & H. Giles (Eds.), *Social markers in speech*. Cambridge: Cambridge University Press, 1979.

Sacks, H.   An initial investigation of the usability of conversational data for doing sociology. In D. Sudnow (Ed.), *Studies in social interaction*. New York: Free Press, 1972.

Sankoff, D., & Labov, W.   On the uses of variable rules. *Language in Society*, 1979, *8*, 189–222.

Schegloff, E.   Sequencing and conversational openings. In J. Gumperz & D. Hymes (Eds.), *Directions in sociolinguistics*. New York: Holt, Rinehart & Winston, 1972.

Scherer, K., & Giles, H. (Eds.).   *Social markers in speech*. Cambridge: Cambridge University Press, 1979.

Scollon, R., & Scollon, S.   *Narrative, literacy, and face in interethnic communication*. Norwood, N.J.: Ablex, 1981.

Scollon, R., & Scollon, S.   Cooking it up and boiling it down. In D. Tannen (Ed.), *Spoken and written language: Exploring orality and literacy*. Norwood, N.J.: Ablex, 1982.

Scribner, S., & Cole, M.   Literacy without schooling: Testing for intellectual effects. *Harvard Educational Review*, 1978, *48*, 448–461.

Scribner, S., & Cole, M.   *The psychology of literacy*. Cambridge: Harvard University Press, 1981.

Shultz, J., Erickson, F., & Florio, S.   Where is the floor? Aspects of cultural organization of social relationships in communication at home and at school. In P. Gilmore & A. Glatthorn (Eds.), *Children in and out of school*. Washington, D.C.: Center for Applied Linguistics, 1982.

Smith, D.   General findings. In D. Hymes (Project Director), *Ethnographic monitoring of children's acquisition of reading/language arts skills in and out of the classroom* (Final report to the National Institute of Education). Washington, D.C.: U.S. Department of Education, 1981.

Smith, D.   Reading and writing in the real world: Explorations into the culture of literacy. In R. Parker & F. Davis (Eds.), *Developing literacy: Young children's use of language*. Newark, Del.: International Reading Association, in press.

Smitherman, G.   *Talkin and testifyin: The language of black America*. Boston: Houghton Mifflin, 1977.

Stoffan-Roth, M.   *Conversational access gaining strategies in instructional contexts*. Unpublished doctoral dissertation, Kent State University, Ohio, 1981.

Stubbs, H.   *Language and literacy: The sociolinguistics of reading and writing*. London: Routledge & Kegan Paul, 1980.

Sulzby, E.   *Kindergartners begin to read their own compositions: Beginning readers' developing knowledge about written language project* (Final Report to the Research Foundation of the National Council of Teachers of English). Urbana, Ill.: 1981.

Szwed, J.   *The ethnography of literacy*. Paper presented to the National Institute of Education Conference on Writing, Los Angeles, 1977.

Tambiah, S.   Literacy in a Buddhist village in north-east Thailand. In J. Goody (Ed.), *Literacy in traditional societies*. London: Cambridge University Press, 1968.

Tannen, D.   A cross-cultural study of oral/literate narrative style. *Berkeley Linguistic Studies*, 1978, *4*, 640–650.

Tannen, D.   *Implications of the oral/literate continuum for cross-cultural communication*. Paper presented at 31st Annual Georgetown Roundtable on Language and Linguistics, Washington, D.C., 1980. (a)

Tannen, D.   Spoken/written language and the oral/literate continuum. *Proceedings of the 6th annual meeting of the Berkeley Linguistic Society.* Berkeley: University of California at Berkeley, 1980. (b)

Tannen, D.   The oral/literate continuum in discourse. In D. Tannen (Ed.), *Spoken and written language: Exploring orality and literacy.* Norwood, N.J.: Ablex, 1982.

Taylor, D.   *Family literacy: Young children learning to read and write.* Exeter, N.H.: Heinemann Educational Books, 1983.

Taylor, D., & Gaines, C.   *The cultural context of family literacy.* Paper presented at the National Reading Conference, Clearwater, Fla., 1982.

Teale, W.   Toward a theory of how children learn to read and write naturally. *Language Arts,* 1982, *59,* 555–570.

Tough, J.   Language, poverty and disadvantage in school. In L. Feagans & D. Farran (Eds.), *The language of children reared in poverty.* New York: Academic Press, 1982.

Trudgill, P.   *Sociolinguistics.* Middlesex, Eng.: Penguin, 1974.

Varenne, H., Hamid-Buglione, V., McDermott, R., & Morison, A.   *"I teach him everything he learns in school": The acquisition of literacy for learning in working class families.* New York: Elbenwood Center for the Study of the Family as Educator, Teachers College, 1982.

Wilkinson, L. C., & Calculator, S.   Effective speakers: Students' use of language to request and obtain information and action in the classroom. In L. C. Wilkinson (Ed.), *Communicating in the classroom.* New York: Academic Press, 1982. (a)

Wilkinson, L. C., & Calculator, S.   Requests and responses in peer-directed reading groups. *American Educational Research Journal,* 1982, *19,* 107–120. (b)

Wilkinson, L. C., & Dollaghan, C.   *Peer communication in first grade reading groups.* Madison: Wisconsin Research and Development Center for Individualized Schooling, 1979.

14 SOCIAL AND MOTIVATIONAL INFLUENCES ON READING

Allan Wigfield and Steven R. Asher

There has been a long-standing interest in how motivational and socialization factors influence children's reading skills (Athey, 1976; Bloom, 1976; Burt, 1917; Entwisle, 1979; Ladd, 1933; Matthewson, 1976; Purkey, 1970; Resnick & Robinson, 1975; Wattenberg & Clifford, 1964). However, the research literatures addressing these topics have remained relatively fragmented. On the one hand, researchers interested in the development of achievement motivation processes generally have not explored how such processes operate in particular achievement contexts such as reading. On the other hand, reading researchers and those studying home and school socialization practices often have conceptualized motivation in rather general terms and have not attended to specific processes or components of achievement motivation. Integrating these literatures should provide a more complete account of social and motivational influences on reading.

The purpose of the present chapter is to integrate findings from these disparate research traditions and to provide suggestions for future inquiry. In addition, a particular focus of this chapter is on how race and social class differences in children's reading performance are influenced by social and motivational factors. The problems of race and socioeconomic status (SES) differences in achievement have been at center stage in educational research for nearly three decades. Research has clearly demonstrated that such differences exist; black children experience more difficulty with reading than white children, and the discrepancy increases across the school years (Coleman, Campbell, Hobson, McPartland, Mood, Weinfeld, & York, 1966; Singer, Gerard, & Redfearn, 1975). Similarly, children from lower SES homes perform less well than children from middle-class homes (Armor, 1972; Coleman et al., 1966; St. John, 1970), and here too the difference increases over age (Coleman et al., 1966; Jencks, 1972). Like others (e.g., Entwisle, 1979; Resnick & Robinson, 1975), we believe that a social-motivational perspective can make an important contribution to understanding and overcoming such differences.

In the first section of this chapter, we will examine current trends in achievement motivation theory. Subsequent sections will focus on socialization research in the home and school as it relates to reading. Throughout our discussion, we will highlight research that is needed to bridge the motivation and socialization of reading literatures.

ACHIEVEMENT MOTIVATION THEORY:
CURRENT TRENDS

Achievement motivation has interested social and educational psychologists for several decades. While a complete review of achievement motivation theory is beyond the scope of this chapter (see Eccles & Wigfield, in press; Heckhausen, 1982, for more complete reviews), we will briefly discuss motivational processes thought to be most important for high achievement, and developmental differences in those processes.

In early theoretical views (McClelland, 1961; McClelland, Atkinson, Clark, & Lowell, 1953), the achievement motive was conceptualized as a relatively enduring personality trait. Individual differences in this trait were said to be due to different child rearing practices, and researchers assessed how parental practices influenced children's developing achievement motivation (e.g., Rosen & d'Andrade, 1959; Winterbottom, 1958; see more complete discussion below). Subsequent theorists (Atkinson, 1964) specified that the achievement motive is a function of expectancy and value; motivation to pursue a goal is determined by the expectancy one has of attaining that goal and the value one places on attaining it. Atkinson emphasized affective processes, especially the motive to approach success and the motive to avoid failure. Research in this tradition has concentrated mostly on how individuals differing in the motives to approach success and avoid failure differ in the risks they are willing to take in achievement situations (see Atkinson & Raynor, 1974).

More recently, there has been interest in cognitive determinants of achievement motivation. Weiner and his colleagues (Weiner, 1972, 1974, 1979; Weiner, Frieze, Kukla, Reed, Rest, & Rosenbaum, 1971) have argued that individuals' causal reasoning or attributions about achievement outcomes influence their motivation and behavior in achievement situations. Like Atkinson, Weiner views achievement motivation as a function of expectancy for success and the value one places on the outcome. However, in contrast to Atkinson, he emphasizes that reasoning about causes of success and failure rather than affective processes determines expectancies and values. This view has gained wide acceptance as a powerful explanation for achievement motivation, and so we will consider it in more detail. We will focus on the two questions posed earlier: What are the important motivational processes? How do they develop?

Initially, Weiner and his colleagues posited four factors that are used most often to explain achievement outcomes—ability, effort, task difficulty, and luck.[1] They classified these factors into two dimensions, stability and locus of control. Stability refers to whether the cause is changeable or not, and locus of control refers to whether the cause is believed to be personal (internal) or environmental (external) (see Rotter, 1954, 1966). In this classification scheme, ability is an internal, stable cause; effort an internal, unstable cause; task difficulty an external, stable cause; and luck an external, unstable cause.

The attributions people give to explain success and failure are postulated to have consequences for achievement motivation, expectations for success, achievement value and affect, and achievement behavior. For instance, Weiner and Kukla (1970) classified subjects as high or low in achievement motivation based on their responses to an achievement motivation scale. Individuals high in achievement motivation (particularly males) were more likely to assume personal responsibility for success than were those low in achievement motivation. Individuals low in achievement motivation were more likely to believe that failure was due to lack of ability, whereas the group high in achievement motivation was more likely to believe failure was due to lack of effort. Thus, at least for males, positive achievement motivation was related to attributing success to ability and failure to lack of effort, and negative achievement motivation was related to attributing failure to lack of ability and success to luck or other variable factors (see also Covington & Omelich, 1979b, 1979c; Ickes & Layden, 1978).

Expectations for future performance are said to be related to attributional stability (Weiner, 1979; Weiner et al., 1971). If performance on a task is attributed to stable factors, then the person will be relatively sure about his or her level of future performance on similar tasks. For example, if success on a task is attributed to ability, then expectations for future performance will be high. Similarly, if failure is attributed to a stable factor, then expectations for future success will be low. If success (or failure) is attributed to a variable factor (e.g., effort), then expectations about future success will be less certain. This description has been supported by results of several studies (Fontaine, 1974; McMahon, 1973; Valle & Frieze, 1976; Weiner, Nierenberg, & Goldstein, 1976).

Weiner et al. (1971) initially linked achievement value and affect to the locus of control dimension; stronger affective reactions were said to occur when outcomes were attributed to internal factors. More recently, Weiner (1979) proposed two different sources of affect in achievement situations. First, people generally feel good about success and bad about failure with more differentiated reactions occurring, depending upon the attribution made for the outcome (see Weiner, 1979). Ability attributions have the greatest impact on self-esteem, and so individuals tend to feel best when they attribute success to ability and feel worst when failure is attributed to lack of ability (see Sohn, 1977).

Finally, attributions influence subsequent achievement behavior. Attributing success to ability and failure to lack of effort means the person generally will expect to succeed and will be willing to try more challenging tasks. When the person fails, the failure can be overcome by trying harder, so the person will persist in the face of failure. In contrast, attributing success to a variable factor and failure to lack of ability means that the person will not expect to succeed. When the person fails, he or she will give up quickly since extra effort will not overcome the person's perceived lack of ability.

What about race and SES differences in attributional processes? Weiner et al. (1971) hypothesized that race and SES differences in achievement could be due to differences in attributional processes. For instance, individuals from poverty backgrounds may make more external attributions for success since they likely feel less control over their environment (see Hess, 1970). Few studies have assessed this possibility. However, some support for this hypothesis was obtained by Murray and Mednick (1975) in a study of success and failure attributions of high- and low-achievement-motivated black men and women. Murray and Mednick found that black male subjects were more likely than females to make external attributions for success. Friend and Neale (1972) investigated social class and race differences in fifth-grade children's attributions for success and failure. White children ranked ability and effort as more important than did black children in explaining successful outcomes. All groups were equally ashamed of failure, but black children did not experience as much pride in success as white children did. Overall, however, there were few differences among the different groups in terms of their attribution patterns.

Studies to date, then, have not fully tested the hypothesis of Weiner et al. that race and SES differences in achievement could be due to attributional differences. More research is needed to assess this possibility. Additionally, given black and low-SES children's relatively poor reading achievement, the attribution model would predict that these children will have low expectations for future success in reading and negative affect toward reading. We will discuss these points more fully below.

Developmental Differences in Achievement Motivation

There is increasing evidence that children differ across age in how they interpret the information they receive in achievement situations and thus differ in their achievement motivation. Parsons and Ruble (1977) found that young children maintained higher expectancies for future success after experiencing failure than did older children. Younger children were more likely to ignore the information that they were not doing well and naively continue to expect that they would succeed. Similarly, Nicholls (1978, 1979) demonstrated that young children overestimated their attainment in school and did not perceive school success as related to ability. Older children more accurately estimated their attainment and saw school success as due to ability. Nicholls (1978, 1980) also showed that 5- and 6-year-old children often could not judge which of a set of tasks was most difficult or realize that difficult tasks require more ability. Young children generally are happy about success and unhappy about failure, regardless of the degree of task difficulty or the cause of the success or failure (see Veroff, 1969).

Research also indicates developmental change toward making more differentiated attributions. Nicholls (1978) found that during the early elementary school years, children did not conceptually distinguish effort and ability as separate causes of outcomes. Instead, being able also meant trying hard. Only at about age 12 or 13 were the two causes fully distinguished. Similar results were obtained by Kun (1977).

These studies indicate that children in the early grades interpret success and failure information differently than older children and adults and also have different conceptions of ability and effort. Interestingly, in simple situations in which success and failure were quite obvious (Frieze & Snyder, 1980; Karabenick & Heller, 1976), children's attributions did not differ as much across age as shown in the Nicholls (1978) and Kun (1977) studies. However, since the success and failure feedback children receive in school often is rather unclear (see Blumenfeld, Pintrich, Meece, & Wessels, 1982), it seems that young children may not interpret that information accurately.

Although the development of attributions has been the focus of some attention, the antecedents of the attribution process have not been studied extensively. Weiner et al. (1971) made some general inferences about how different attribution patterns may begin. For instance, they proposed that people's judgments about their ability are a function of past success or failure on different tasks as well as the consistency of that past success or failure. However, little work has been done on how parents influence their children's attributions, expectations, and affective reactions to success and failure. More work has been done on how teacher feedback influences these processes. In general, there is a need for more research on the socialization of achievement motivation. As we discuss the influence of different socialization agents, we will indicate how they may influence motivational processes and will suggest avenues for future inquiry.

Recently, several studies (e.g., Covington & Omelich, 1979a; Parsons, in press) have shown that attributions obtained in real-world achievement situations have less of an influence on subsequent achievement motivation than Weiner predicted. Other variables, notably expectancies and values, had a stronger influence on subjects' task persistence and performance. These results suggest that we need to take a somewhat broader approach to the study of achievement motivation rather than focusing nearly exclusively on attributions. Because constructs such as expectancies and values are particularly important ones to consider, we will discuss them in sections on home and school environments.

In summary, the attribution model emphasizes the role of cognition in achievement motivation. There are important developmental differences in reasoning about achievement outcomes, and other achievement-related constructs have been shown to be important predictors of achievement motivation in real-world settings. We turn next to a discussion of how the home environment influences children's acquisitions of reading skills and motivation to read.

✓HOME INFLUENCES ON READING

Several large-scale studies of educational achievement have demonstrated that factors in the home environment play a critical role in determining children's achievement motivation and performance in school. The best known of these studies in the United States was conducted by Coleman et al. (1966), who found that home factors outweighed school factors in determining children's achievement. Although the methodology of this study has been criticized (e.g., Dyer, 1968; Shea, 1976), the major finding has been relatively well accepted. Research in other countries also points to the importance of home influences (e.g., Davie, Butler, & Goldstein, 1972; Douglas, 1964). Since parent-child interaction is the most important home influence on children's later achievement behavior in school, we will focus on how parents facilitate or constrain the development of reading skills and motivation to read by structuring the home environment and interacting with their children. We will consider studies which have assessed how parents influence children's achievement motivation and also studies looking at how parent-child interactions relate to the acquisition of reading skills per se. Although race and SES differences in reading will be a main focus of the discussion, we hope to show that particular parental behaviors are the most important variables.

Parental Influence on the Development of Achievement Motivation

Although currently there is little research on the home antecedents of particular motivational processes such as attributions, earlier research in the achievement motivation area did attempt to assess home influences on the development of achievement motivation (see Parsons, 1981, for a detailed review). The studies assessed various hypotheses of McClelland's (1961) achievement motivation theory. A major tenet of McClelland's theory is that experiences involving independent mastery are essential to the development of achievement motivation. Several studies have assessed this hypothesis. In a retrospective interview study, Winterbottom (1958) found that mothers of 8- to 10-year-old boys who were high in achievement motivation (as measured by the Thematic Apperception Test [TAT]), made more independence demands earlier on, were less restrictive, and were more rewarding for their children's successes.

In an observational study, Rosen and d'Andrade (1959) compared how middle- and lower-SES parents and their sons interacted on various analogue achievement tasks, ranging from block-stacking and ring-toss tasks to an anagrams task. Results showed that parents of 9- to 11-year-old boys who were high in need for achievement had higher performance expectations for their sons and were generally more involved and interested in their sons' achievement-related behavior. This pattern was especially true of mothers and held even when performance differences between children were controlled for. Middle-class parents had higher performance expectations for their children than did lower-class parents and evaluated their sons' performance more carefully. These results suggest that parents can foster the development of achievement motivation in their children by: (a) holding high expectations and evaluating their performance carefully and (b) being involved in the achievement-related activities of their children (see also Katkovsky, Crandall, & Preston, 1964, for evidence that parents who value intellectual competence tend to become more involved in their children's achievement activities; and Parke, 1978, for a discussion of how involvement which is contingent on children's responses seems particularly important). The results also suggest that middle-class parents are more likely to hold higher performance expectations and be more involved in achievement activities than are lower-class parents. Others have conducted similar studies and obtained quite similar results (Hermans, ter Laak, & Maes, 1972; Rosen, 1959; Smith, 1969).

There is a need for research to assess the home antecedents of children's understanding of success-failure feedback and attributions. Recently, Hess, King, and Holloway (1981) showed that parents make attributions differently than do their children; mothers attributed their fifth-grade children's school success more to ability and failure to lack of effort, whereas the children attributed their success more to effort and failure to lack of ability. While these results are intriguing, more work is needed to answer several important questions concerning the home antecedents of children's attributions. For instance, what kinds of attributions do parents give when their children succeed or fail on reading and other achievement tasks and how does this influence children's own interpretations of success and failure? Do parents' attributions for their children's performance change as children get older? Work addressing these questions would increase our understanding of parental influences on achievement motivation.

Parental Aspirations, Expectations, and Values

A related literature concerns parents' educational aspirations for their children. It would seem that parents who have confidence in their children's abilities and have high expectations for their performance would have higher educational aspirations for their children. Several studies have examined race and SES differences in parental aspirations for their children. The most common finding is that lower-SES and black parents often have *educational* aspirations for their children that are as high as those of middle-SES and white parents (Brook, Whiteman, Peisach, & Deutsch, 1974; Dreger & Miller, 1968; Rosen, 1959), though there are exceptions (R. R. Bell, 1965). However, black and lower-SES parents' *occupational* aspirations for their children are usually lower than those of white and middle-SES parents, perhaps reflecting a realistic view of the opportunity structure of society.

Further, while educational aspirations for children are high, black and lower-SES parents often do not expect their children to attain those high goals (Dreger & Miller, 1968; Resnick & Robinson, 1975), and they do not make adequate plans for their children to attain the goals (Wolff, 1966). This discrepancy between aspirations and expectations likely has a number of causes. One could be parental perceptions about schools. Hess and Shipman (1968) interviewed middle- and lower-SES black mothers about their perceptions about school and their aspirations for their children in school. Lower-SES mothers thought that education was very important, but they viewed school as a place where they had little input or control. For instance, when asked to imagine working with a teacher, the lower-SES mothers described themselves as passive or subservient to the teacher, whereas middle-class mothers described themselves as actively involved and more equal to the teacher (see similar findings in Entwisle & Hayduk, 1978). Lower-SES mothers stressed the importance of obedience when they were asked what they would tell their children as they started school (see also Clausen & Williams, 1963). Middle-class mothers stressed the importance of positive interactions with teachers and other children. These views likely influence the kind of relationships children develop with their teachers. Given this pattern, middle-SES children likely feel more comfortable in the school environment.

Another reason for the discrepancy between aspirations and attainment could be the way lower-SES parents interact with their children in learning situations. Many studies have shown that compared to middle-SES parents, lower-SES parents use less effective teaching strategies (Bee, Van Egereth, Streissguth, Nyman, & Leckie, 1969; Brophy, 1970; Hess & Shipman, 1965; Nottleman, 1978). These studies indicate that lower-SES mothers provide their children with poorer problem-solving strategies, and they tend to take over for their children rather than letting them do the task (see Laosa, 1978, 1980, for work suggesting that level of parent education is an important mediating variable here). As Parsons (1981) suggests, taking over for their children could be due to lower-SES parents' lack of confidence in their children's ability to do learning tasks. That lower-SES parents view the school as a distant, rather formidable institution over which they have little control; engage in less effective teaching strategies; and lack confidence in their children's ability does not bode well for their children's school performance.

It seems, then, that lower-SES parents do not provide their children with certain experiences that would help them do well in school, even though the parents value education and want their children to do well in school. This issue of parental values deserves closer scrutiny. Recall that lower-SES parents' occupational aspirations for their children were lower than those of middle-SES parents. Since a primary function of education is preparation for an occupation, perhaps low-SES children place less value on school because they, like their parents, do not set their occupational aspirations as high as middle-class children do (see Wylie, 1979). Recently, Parsons and Goff (1980) argued that achievement values have a strong impact on achievement choices. One aspect of achievement values (called utility value by Parsons and Goff) is the degree to which successfully doing a task contributes to a long-term goal. School probably has less utility value for low-SES students because school success does not fit into their career plans (see Maehr & Nicholls, 1980, for discussion of tasks that may have greater utility value for low-SES children). Low-SES parents' lower career aspirations for their children perhaps contribute to their children's beliefs that school has less utility value for them.

In summary, parents' involvement in achievement activities and the value they place on school success appear to be particularly important contributors to the development of children's achievement motivation. They are also likely to give rise to race and SES differences in achievement orientation. Little work has been done on the home antecedents of attributional processes, and there is a clear need for research in this area.

The Home Reading Environment

The studies reviewed in the previous sections show how parents can influence their children's achievement motivation by the ways in which they become involved in their children's achievement activities. Turning to the acquisition of reading skills, more specifically, how do parents become involved to help their children? One way is by providing appropriate reading materials in the home. Research indicates a positive relationship between the number of books in the home and children's reading ability (Lamme & Olmsted, 1977; Sheldon & Carrillo, 1952). Durkin (1966) interviewed mothers whose children learned to read during the preschool years. The mothers frequently referred to the availability of reading materials in the home as an important factor in their children's early acquisition of reading skills.

The influence of material availability likely is mediated by the ways in which parents become involved with those materials. For instance, the extent to which parents model reading activity, read to their children, and otherwise encourage their children to read should influence whether children become good readers. Ransbury (1973) provided anecdotal evidence from interviews with children that their parents' attitudes toward reading were an important influence on their own reading attitudes. Several studies have shown that parental involvement in reading to their children and parental provision of reading materials predicts later reading ability (e.g., Bing, 1963; Brezinski, 1964; Dix, 1976). There is at least one exception to this general finding (Briggs & Elkind, 1977); however, even this study indicated that parents of early readers provided them with more reading materials and took them to the library more. Thus, research points to the importance of having reading-related materials in the home as well as having parents being involved with their children in reading-related activities.

This kind of involvement should have a number of positive influences. From a cognitive perspective, parents who read to their children are increasing their children's reading-relevant skills. From a social-motivational perspective, this involvement communicates that reading is a pleasurable activity, and one that provides children with an opportunity to interact positively with their parents. This sort of pleasurable interaction should motivate children to read more. There is a need for research to test how the cognitive and social benefits associated with parental involvement interact to aid children's acquisition of reading skills.

It is apparent that there are social class differences in children's home reading environments. Briggs and Elkind (1977) noted that parents of early readers were more likely to be in the middle and upper classes than the lower class, and a similar finding was reported by Sutton (1964). Miller (1969) interviewed mothers about children's prereading experiences. In comparison to lower-class mothers, middle-class mothers reported that their children had been read to more and had more contact with books and other reading-related materials in the home. These kinds of experiences likely provide middle-class children with more positive attitudes toward reading.

Although social class is an important factor, it appears that the home reading environment is actually a better predictor of children's attitudes toward reading than social class membership per se. For instance, Hansen (1969) measured four aspects of the home reading environment—availability of reading materials in the home, amount of reading done with children, amount of reading guidance and encouragement, and the extent to which parents served as models by engaging in reading. This composite process measure correlated more highly with fourth-grade children's reading attitudes than did a measure of parent SES. Similar findings were reported by Krus and Ruben (1974). These findings have important implications for intervention programs. By encouraging reading and by reading to children, it should be possible for low-SES parents to help their children acquire positive attitudes toward reading and improve their reading skills. Indeed, intervention programs which have focused on getting low-SES parents involved in their children's education have been successful in improving children's academic performance (see Chilman, 1973, and Horowitz & Paden, 1973, for reviews).[2]

There are some limitations of this work that need to be addressed. The first is the use of SES as a descriptive measure. Recall Hansen's (1969) results that particular aspects of the home reading environment were a better predictor of reading attitudes than was a more general SES measure. A growing set of findings supports the point that particular environmental measures correlate more strongly with children's academic performance than do SES measures (e.g., Bradley, Caldwell, & Elardo, 1977; Elardo, Bradley, & Caldwell, 1977; Marjoribanks, 1976; Walberg & Marjoribanks, 1973; Wolff, 1966). The implication here is that a better understanding of *why* SES differences in achievement exist can only be obtained by looking at particular parent-child interactions in the home. From the work of Bradley et al. (1977), some of the important factors include the responsivity of the parent, the kinds of discipline techniques used, the organization of the physical environment, parental involvement, and provision of appropriate play materials. Most of the studies listed above have looked at how such environmental factors relate to performance on tests of general ability. There is a need to conduct such studies with specific reading-related skills as the dependent measures in order to extend Hansen's (1969) work.

A second limitation is that studies on parent involvement with reading have conceptualized reading in global terms rather than examining component subskills. Certain practices in the home might help children acquire particular skills such as learning the alphabet, whereas other factors may influence processes such as children's reading comprehension. For instance, Hess, Holloway, Price, and Dickson (1979) classified reading into a number of component skills such as attention, decoding, and knowledge of vocabulary. They also distinguished different kinds of features of the home that influence the acquisition of reading skills such as parent-child verbal interaction, parental values associated with reading, and availability of reading materials. Hess et al. argued that these different environmental variables likely influence the various component reading skills in specifiable ways.

Hess et al. examined how some of these environmental variables influenced children's ability to decode letters. The environmental variables selected for study were availability of materials related to recognizing letters, verbal-eliciting techniques of the mother, and parental emphasis on achievement. Results indicated that parents whose children were good letter decoders had more materials available and tended to make their children respond verbally to a greater extent. Parental press for achievement was found to be quite important as well, even more so than some of the particular environmental features. For example, parents who stressed the importance of achievement but provided fewer relevant materials had children who were better decoders than parents low in press but who provided more materials. This work could be extended to assess other dependent measures in order to obtain a better understanding of how specific environmental variables influence particular reading skills.

Another limitation of the work on the home reading environment is that the primary focus has been on how mothers influence their children's interest in reading. Fathers' potential influence has either been neglected, or in some cases, fathers have been characterized as having little influence (see Durkin, 1966). However, other evidence suggests that fathers do have an important influence, especially on their sons' cognitive development. Radin's work (Radin, 1972, 1973; Radin & Epstein, 1975) indicates that paternal nurturance relates to preschool boys' test-score performance. Mutimer, Laughlin, and Powell (1966) found that boys aged 8 to 12 who read well preferred to be with their fathers. Gruenebaum, Hurwitz, Prentice, and Sperry (1962) found that elementary school boys of average intelligence, but one to two years below the achievement test-score norm for their age, tended to have poor relationships with their fathers.

Some evidence suggests that father absence contributes greatly to the academic problems of low-SES children. Biller (1974) has reviewed the many studies which show that father-absent lower-class black children score much lower on intelligence tests than father-present lower-class black children. Middle-class father-absent children are not as adversely affected, especially in the verbal-skill areas (Carlsmith, 1964; Lessing, Zagorin, & Nelson, 1970). Generally, then, this research shows how the achievement of lower-class, father-absent children is adversely affected. Research is needed on how fathers influence children's acquisition of particular reading skills since previous studies have primarily examined general achievement measures.

Additionally, there is a need to investigate how children's behavior influences their parents' behavior. Socialization is not a unidirectional process of parents shaping their children's behavior; children also have a strong impact on how their parents treat them (R. Q. Bell, 1968). This bidirectionality of the socialization process has not been investigated in the areas reviewed here. It seems plausible that children who show more interest in reading cause their parents to become more involved in reading activities with them.

Finally, researchers need to integrate the two research traditions we have been reviewing. Presumably the way parents involve themselves in their children's reading activities influences children's motivation to learn to read. Few, if any, studies have assessed how (or whether) parents make attributions for their children's reading performance, the kinds of expectations they have for their children's performance, or their perceptions of their children's reading ability. While some work has begun to look at more specific features of the environment and how those features influence reading, motivational variables have not yet been included in this work. Studies assessing such variables would increase our understanding of how parental involvement influences reading. Further, such work would provide important field tests concerning the role of motivational processes in children's acquisition of reading skills.

In summary, studies of parental involvement suggest that parents greatly influence children's achievement orientation and acquisition of reading skills. Some of the evidence indicates that particular factors in the home are better predictors of children's reading attitudes than general measures of SES. Nonetheless, higher-SES parents are more likely to be involved in the kinds of activities that promote skills and interest in and positive feelings about reading. Middle-class children are more likely to come to school with the idea that reading is an important activity, they are more likely to be familiar with reading-related materials, and they have been exposed to parental teaching styles that foster school-relevant cognitive skills and motivational styles.

SCHOOL INFLUENCES ON READING

In this section, we will examine how motivational and social factors in the school situation influence children's reading skills. Although home factors influence race and SES differences in school attitudes and performance, the school environment certainly is important as well. For instance, studies have shown that there are few differences in self-concept of ability between SES groups early in the school years, but low-SES children's self-concepts of ability decline more quickly than those of their middle-class peers (Bridgeman & Shipman, 1978; Eshel & Klein, 1981). These results suggest that factors in the school environment are contributing to low-SES children's lower self-concepts of ability. In conceptualizing social and motivational influences in school, of particular importance would seem to be children's attitudes toward reading, the teacher-student relationship, the reading materials used in classrooms, and peer influences on achievement. We will discuss how these affect race and SES differences in reading performance and also how they affect achievement motivation processes.

Children's Attitude toward Reading

Numerous studies have assessed the relationship between children's reading attitudes and reading performance (see Alexander & Filler, 1976, for a review). Not surprisingly, the results generally show that good readers have more positive attitudes toward reading than poor readers (Askov & Fischbach, 1973; Groff, 1962; Hake, 1969; Kenneday & Halinski, 1978; Shepps & Shepps, 1971; Zimmerman & Allebrand, 1965). Still, the relationships found in most studies are modest, ranging from correlations of .2 to .4. Further, the correlational design of these studies does not allow for any causal assessment of the obtained relationships.

Since black and low-SES children tend to be poorer readers, the results just summarized would suggest that they should be more negative in their attitudes to reading and school. Research assessing this suggestion has produced mixed results. Some studies have shown that lower-SES children do indeed have less positive attitudes toward school than middle- and upper-SES children (Coster, 1958; Yee, 1968), whereas others have not found a relationship (Heimberger, 1970; Neale & Proshek, 1967). These discrepant results could be due to different measuring techniques, to social desirability demands, or to the different ages of the children in the different studies.

Generally, results of these studies are rather disappointing. What is needed are more sophisticated correlational designs that allow causal inferences to be drawn with more confidence. It would also be more fruitful to investigate specific dimensions of reading attitudes and motivation to read rather than simply examining the global "attitude toward reading" construct. Some recent work on children's attitudes toward mathematics could serve as an exemplar for future work on children's reading attitudes. Parsons and her co-workers (Parsons, Adler, & Kaczala, 1982; see also Parsons, Adler, Futterman, Goff, Kaczala, Meece, & Midgley, 1983) conducted a longitudinal investigation of elementary, junior high, and high school students' attitudes, self-concepts of ability, values, expectations for, and planned participation in mathematics courses. Additionally, they obtained children's perceptions of their parents' beliefs concerning these variables as well as parents' own beliefs about their children. This study thus goes far beyond assessing a global "attitudes toward math"; instead, variables of theoretical and practical interest were assessed. Parsons et al. identified three clusters of variables which predicted students' plans to enroll in math courses, and showed how parents have different notions about boys' and girls' math ability (because the study dealt with math, a detailed results summary is not presented here). Similar studies of parents' and children's reading attitudes would greatly improve upon previous studies and perhaps help clarify the results of previous research.

The Teacher-Student Relationship

The way teachers interact with their students exerts a significant influence on students' achievement in reading and motivation to achieve. Although a comprehensive review of the teacher-student interaction literature is beyond the scope of this chapter, two aspects are particularly relevant to our focus here, teacher expectations and the influence teachers have on motivational processes.

Teacher expectations. There is a large literature on the topic of teacher expectations for their students' performance (see Brophy & Good, 1974; Cooper, 1979; and Dusek, 1975, for reviews). In general, research indicates that teachers' perceptions of and expectations about their students are affected by student race and social class (see Brophy & Good, 1974). For instance, Yee (1968) found that teachers expressed more positive attitudes toward middle-class students and Datta, Schaeffer, and Davis (1968) found that teachers described white students more favorably than black students. Cooper, Baron, and Lowe (1975) found that teacher trainees, when describing hypothetical middle- and lower-SES students, said the middle-SES students would have higher grades and that their successes would be due more to factors such as their ability and effort. Goodwin and Sanders (1969) found that for first-grade pupils, teachers believe that student social class is the most important factor for predicting school success.

What is unclear from these studies is whether teachers are accurate in their perceptions of individual students, even though they may hold general negative expectations concerning the academic potential of black and low-SES students. West and Anderson (1976) highlight this point in their review of the teacher expectancy literature. It is quite possible that teachers' expectations are often an outcome or consequences of the child's performance rather than the cause of that performance. Indeed, results of studies reviewed by West and Anderson (1976) can often be accounted for in terms of student behavior causing teacher expectancy rather than vice versa. When teachers and students interact together for a period of time, teachers use the information obtained to form expectancies for students rather than letting initial attitudes determine student behavior. When teacher expectancy appears to cause certain student behaviors, it is usually in situations in which students and teachers have little time to interact and get to know one another (Brophy & Good, 1974; West & Anderson, 1976).

Still, teachers could be guilty of a more subtle form of bias, even if their perceptions are data based. It is an educator's task to go beyond the data given, that is, to expect that a child's behavior can be transformed with appropriate instruction and structuring of the educational environment. The teacher who does not hold this view is failing to construe education as a process that can significantly influence children's development. In this sense, the teacher is failing to decenter from the observable data of the child's present behavior to the possibility of future growth. Thus, it is the teacher's expectations for children's teachability that ultimately is at issue, not just whether teachers perceive children's current behavior in a negative light. Paladry (1969) conducted a study which has some relevance to this point. He compared first-grade reading achievement scores of two different groups of teachers. One group of teachers thought that boys and girls had an equal chance to learn to read. The other group believed that girls learn to read more easily. Reading achievement scores for the students did not differ in September. However, by May, the group of students whose teachers believed girls learned to read more easily showed significant sex differences favoring girls. There were no sex differences in reading achievement in the other group. This study suggests how teachers' beliefs in children's educability influences children's achievement.

A major limitation of much of the work on teacher expectations discussed above is the failure to assess how such expectations are translated into behavior. Results of studies in which teacher behaviors have been observed indicate that teachers treat students differently for whom they have high versus low expectations; for instance, students who teachers expect to do well get more praise, are called on to answer questions more, receive more classroom privileges, and are allowed more time to answer questions, (see Brophy & Good, 1970; Good & Brophy, 1977; Good, Cooper, & Blakely 1980; Parsons, Kaczala, & Meece, 1982; Weinstein, 1976). Students, too, are aware of differences in teacher treatment of high- and low-achieving children (Weinstein & Middlestadt, 1979).

Since teachers have lower expectations for black and low-SES children, these same behavioral differences in teacher treatment may apply to them, though this contention has not received a direct test. Rubovits and Maehr (1973) found that teacher trainees criticized and ignored black students more than white students, especially when the black students were described as bright. However, this study was done in a laboratory rather than a classroom setting and with teacher trainees rather than teachers. Rist (1970), in an observational study, found that teachers grouped kindergarten students based on their SES level and proceeded to treat the higher-SES children much more favorably. A two-year follow-up observation showed that the groupings of children were still relatively intact in second grade. Results of this study have to be viewed with some caution since the classroom observations were informal in nature and done in only one school. There is a need to assess further whether teacher expectations about different racial and SES groups are translated into specific behaviors that affect how children learn to read.

Teacher influences on children's achievement motivation.   Results of the work just discussed show that teacher expectations are sometimes translated into behavior that influences children's learning. Differential praise and criticism by teachers likely influences children's motivation to achieve. Recall the claim of Weiner et al. (1971) that the kinds of attributions one makes about achievement outcomes depend on the consistency of the successes or failures one experiences. One theme running through the literature is that black and lower-SES children feel less control over their environment and experience more failures in both home and school environments. In an interesting series of experiments, Dweck has investigated the consequences of repeated failure experiences on children's achievement motivation and behavior. Dweck's concern is with learned helplessness, which is the perception that failure cannot be overcome. As Dweck and Goetz define it, "learned helplessness in achievement situations exists when an individual perceives the termination of failure to be independent of his responses" (Dweck & Goetz, 1978, p. 157).

Dweck and Repucci (1973) conducted an initial investigation of helplessness with fourth- through sixth-grade children. Children worked on soluble and insoluble problems given by two different experimenters. After several trials with each kind of problem, the experimenter giving insoluble problems began to administer soluble ones. Many children were unable to solve these problems, even though they had received quite similar problems from the other experimenter in earlier trials. These children were showing helplessness in response to initial failure.

Using Crandall, Katkovsky, and Crandall's (1965) Intellectual Achievement Responsibility Scale, Dweck and Repucci assessed children's attributions for success and failure. Those children who persisted, even though they were failing, emphasized motivational factors like effort as determining the failure outcomes. Those who did not persist emphasized more uncontrollable factors such as ability or external factors like task difficulty. Hence, these children believed failure was hard to overcome. Finally, girls were more likely than boys to attribute failure to lack of ability.

Butkowsky and Willows (1980) assessed whether poor readers could be characterized as learned helpless about failures on a reading-related task. Good, average, and poor reading fifth-grade children were given soluble and insoluble anagrams. In comparison to good and average readers, poor readers had lower initial expectancies for success, attributed success to external factors and failure to internal factors (especially to lack of ability), and persisted less under failure. Following failure, poor readers' expectations for future success had a greater negative shift than those of the other groups. Thus, this study shows that poor readers do exhibit learned helplessness in the face of failure.

There is a need to assess race and SES differences in learned helplessness. It is likely that black and low-SES children experience more criticism in school (e.g., Brophy & Good, 1974; Rubovits & Maehr, 1973), yet it has not been determined whether this criticism is directed primarily toward ability or to other aspects of performance. Since these children generally experience more failure in school than their white and middle-class peers, they may be more likely to attribute failure to lack of ability (see Katz, 1967) and thus show helplessness in response to failure. Several observational studies have assessed whether teacher feedback patterns influence children's tendency to exhibit helplessness in response to failure (Blumenfeld, Hamilton, Bossert, Wessels, & Meece, 1982; Dweck, Davidson, Nelson, & Enna, 1978; Parsons et al., 1982; see also Fennema, in press, and Parsons, in press, for discussions of whether there are indeed sex differences in learned helplessness). It would be useful to do similar observational research focusing on teacher feedback patterns to black and low-SES children.

What can be done about the problem of learned helplessness? Dweck (1975) showed that training learned helpless children to attribute failure to lack of effort helped them overcome helplessness—the children were more likely to persist when later faced with failure. In contrast, simply providing helpless children with success experiences was not enough to overcome helplessness; when they faced failure again, their performance deteriorated. These results indicate that changing children's attributions about their performance improved their subsequent performance. Similar results have been reported by Andrews and Debus (1978).

On the other hand, attribution retraining may sometimes be insufficient, particularly when children lack skills. Schunk (1981), based on Bandura's (1977a) self-efficacy theory, trained slow-learning students in an attempt to improve their math performance. Children received one of two training programs or were in a control group. One training program was a modeling program in which children observed an adult do math problems, verbalizing his or her strategy. Children then practiced some problems and received feedback. The other program involved practice on math problems; when children had difficulty, they were told where to look for help in a training manual. Half the children in each training group also received attribution retraining; when they succeeded or failed on some of the practice problems given in training, the experimenter attributed the outcome to effort. Although both training conditions improved children's persistence, accuracy (the modeling condition was especially effective here), and perceived efficacy, there were no differences between the children who received attribution retraining and those who did not in either training group. Thus, attribution retraining may not always be the most effective way to improve children's performance (see also Chapin & Dyck, 1976, and Fowler & Peterson, 1981). This may be particularly true for children who lack critical basic academic skills.

A potential problem with attribution retraining is that if children continue to fail even after the retraining, they may eventually conclude that they lack ability. Covington and Beery (1976), Covington and Omelich (1979b, 1979c), as well as Kukla (1972, 1978), discuss how the degree of effort expended in a situation is an important indicator of one's ability. Attribution retraining teaches children to try harder; if children continue to do poorly even after this training, they may be forced to conclude that they lack ability. Trying hard is therefore risky in potential failure situations. Given that black and low-SES children more often lack specific academic skills, training programs such as Schunk's may be more successful than attribution retraining programs in improving these children's performance and persistence.

Finally, the developmental issues discussed earlier should be considered here. Since young children are not very accurate at judging their abilities and do not make success-failure attributions with adult logic (Nicholls, 1978; Parsons & Ruble, 1977), failure experiences in the early elementary school years may not influence as strongly children's perceptions of their ability. In support of this, Rholes, Blackwell, Jordan, and Walters (1980) demonstrated that children younger than 10 or 11 (the age of children in most of Dweck's work) did not demonstrate learned helplessness in response to failure feedback. Also, Entwisle and Hayduk (1978) found that working-class children in the first grade who were receiving poor grades in school were very inaccurate in predicting the relationship between their work and their grades, and they continued to think that they would do well in school. Thus, even children who have had many failure experiences early on could become better achievers if they are given tasks at which they can succeed, and they learn to attribute failure to nonability factors. With Resnick and Robinson (1975), we would suggest that it is vitally important for children to experience as much success as possible during reading instruction, especially those children who are struggling with reading.

Learned helpless children have often been found to be highly anxious (see Dweck, 1975; Hill, 1980). Studies investigating the relationship between children's anxiety and their school performance have found that the correlation between test anxiety and achievement test performance increased across the elementary school years (see Dusek, 1980; Hill, 1972, 1977, 1980; Hill & Sarason, 1966). This negative relationship is particularly strong on measures of reading achievement, perhaps because of the more independent and comprehension-oriented nature of reading instruction in the later elementary years. Studies have also shown that black and low-SES children tend to be more anxious than their white and middle-class peers (Fyans, 1979; Willig, Harnisch, Hill, & Maehr, in press).

Teachers may contribute to student anxiety through their interactions with students, for instance, through excessive criticism. Since black and low-SES children appear to be more anxious about school than other children, they especially may need more praise and less criticism in order to do well. In support of this point, Brophy and Evertson (1976) reported that most successful teachers of low-SES children motivate them with praise and encouragement (see also Brophy, 1981). Brophy and Evertson contend that lower-SES children can begin to overcome their alienation from school when the school atmosphere is a warm and friendly one. It is important that lower-SES children begin participating, and encouragement helps accomplish this. Similarly, Cooper (1977) showed that when teachers stop criticizing children, those children who were criticized frequently begin to interact more positively with the teachers. The use of encouragement may allow low-SES children to participate in school without feeling threatened, and thus negative anxiety dynamics may be avoided.

How exactly does anxiety interfere with learning and task performance? Many theorists (e.g., Dusek, 1980; Geen, 1980; Sarason, 1972, 1975; Wine, 1971, 1980) believe that anxious persons (both children and adults) divide their attention between the tasks they are doing and their own self-preoccupation with how well they are doing, whereas low-anxious persons tend to stay focused more on the task. Research with children supports this view; studies show that high-anxious children have more difficulty focusing on task-relevant information (Dusek, Kermis, & Mergler, 1975; Dusek, Mergler, & Kermis, 1976; Nottleman & Hill, 1977). Perhaps teaching children to focus more on the task at hand would help them improve their performance. Wigfield (1982) showed that children achieved better prose recall in a condition where instructions emphasized concentrating on the task than in a condition which described the task as a test of ability. However, the specially designed set of task-focus instructions were not especially beneficial to high-anxious children, as would be expected from the studies just reviewed.

Recently, much has been written about how important academic engaged time and attentiveness are to learning (see Bloom, 1976; Brophy, 1979; Jenkins & Jenkins, 1981; Rosenshine, 1979; Rosenshine & Berliner, 1978, see also the chapter by Rosenshine & Stevens, this volume). For instance, Bloom (1976) reviewed studies showing that attentiveness relates positively to school achievement, with correlations ranging from .4 to .5. Other studies have shown that inattention to reading instruction is a good predictor of low reading achievement (Camp & Zimet, 1975; Lambert & Nicoll, 1977; Soli & Devine, 1976). The research on anxiety suggests that some children's problems in attending in school could be due to their anxiety, and thus it is important to reduce anxiety in the classroom in order that high-anxious children can better maintain their attentiveness in the classroom. Hill (1980) provides many suggestions for how schools can be restructured to reduce evaluative pressure and anxiety in testing situations; perhaps similar things could be done to reduce anxiety in classroom learning situations. Direct attentional training could be one way to deal with this problem. A series of studies by Cobb and Hops (Cobb & Hops, 1973; Hops & Cobb, 1974;

Walker & Hops, 1976) has shown that training attention skills in first-grade children improved their reading performance and that this program was as effective as a direct instructional reading program in improving children's reading.

Reading Materials

Students' involvement in reading is undoubtedly influenced by the kinds of reading materials schools provide. Uninteresting reading primers would cause special problems for children having little prior exposure to reading materials in the home. Research by Asher (1979) assessed whether children's interest in the material they are given relates to race differences in reading comprehension (for complete reviews of this work, including a discussion of methodological issues, see Asher, 1977, 1980). Fifth-grade children's interests were assessed by showing photographic slides representing different topics. About a week later, children received, from a different experimenter, reading passages, three of which corresponded to the child's three highest-rated topics and three of which corresponded to the child's three lowest-rated topics. Results indicted that white children comprehended the passages better than black children and that black and white children better comprehended the high-interest than the low-interest material. The performance gap between black and white children's performance was the same on both kinds of materials. Postreading preference ratings indicated that both black and white children strongly preferred the high- to the low-interest material.

In an earlier study, Asher and Markell (1974) found that boys did as well as girls on high-interest material, even though boys did worse than girls on low-interest material. A parallel finding was hoped for with respect to race differences. Still, it is encouraging that the interest level of the material did have an effect for black children. The data used in this study were obtained from the *Britannica Junior Encyclopaedia* (1970), a source with a rather dry style of prose. Perhaps stronger results would occur with different types of text. Since black children have greater reading problems than white children, providing personally interesting materials may keep them engaged in reading, even if those materials do not immediately lessen the gap in reading achievement. Indeed, Daniels (1971) has provided anecdotal evidence that a steady diet of high-interest material can greatly improve black children's reading performance.

An important question still to be answered is why children better understand high-interest material. One explanation is that interesting material better maintains the reader's attention, that is, the reader is more motivated when presented with high-interest materials. Another explanation is that readers have more knowledge about topics they are interested in, and thus can more easily understand passages about those topics. Research is needed to evaluate these alternatives. Another issue for future research is whether the effects associated with topic interest would be obtained with younger children. Nearly all research on topic interest has been conducted with older elementary school children, and it would be instructive to do similar work with younger children. Such studies would more clearly indicate how topic interest influences early reading. Furthermore, studies of the long-term effects of a steady diet of high-interest material on children's reading skills and continuing motivation to read (see Maehr, 1976) are clearly needed.

In concluding this section, it is important to stress that the phrase high-interest material describes an interaction between the reader and the material. Material that is fascinating for one child may be dull for another; hence, in both research and instruction, individualized assessment of children's interests and individualized assignments of material should be done. A related point is that children's interests in topics change, and thus there is a need to monitor interests over the school year. Accurate monitoring of children's interests and the provision of reading materials that children are interested in should increase the amount of time children spend reading.

Peer Influences on Achievement

Children's school performance is influenced by peers as well as teachers and text. Indeed, a salient feature of school is the presence of a large number of age mates. As children enter school, they begin to compare themselves with others to evaluate their own behaviors and attitudes (Campbell, 1964; Ruble, Boggiano, Feldman, & Loebl, 1980; Ruble, Feldman, & Boggiano, 1976; Veroff, 1969). They also come to conform to peer group standards (Berends, 1950), and this tendency seems to increase through the elementary school years (Constanzo & Shaw, 1966; McDonnell, 1963).

Because peer group influences can be powerful, a child wishing to be accepted may choose not to work as hard in school if the peer group does not value achievement. Coleman's (1960, 1961) research has demonstrated the contribution of the peer group to patterns of achievement. In schools where students valued achievement highly, there was a closer relationship between academic excellence and intelligence than in schools where achievement was less valued. Similarly, studies of educational aspiration have shown that children's and adolescents' aspirations are quite similar to those of their peers, especially valued peers (Haller & Butterworth, 1960; Kardel & Lesser, 1969; McDill & Coleman, 1965; Simpson, 1962).

Because peers influence the extent to which children value academic achievement, it is of concern that low-SES children do not seem to value academic-related activities to the extent middle-class children do (Coster, 1959; Pope, 1953). Other evidence indicates that low-SES children tend to be more conforming (see Hess, 1970) and that the peer group may be especially prominent in forming low-SES children's values. For instance, Psthas (1957) found that low-SES parents showed less concern and exercised less control over their children's activities outside the home. One implication of this finding is that more low-SES children may be influenced to do poorly in school in order to gain acceptance from peers.

One's social status within the peer group also plays a role. Researchers interested in the correlates of popularity have found that children who are intelligent tend to be more popular and that slow-learning children tend to be less popular (Campbell, 1964; Green, Forehand, Beck, & Vosk, 1980; Hartup, 1970; Porterfield & Schlichting, 1961). Children from low-SES backgrounds also are less likely to be popular (Hartup, 1970; Hess, 1970). Thus, low-SES children who are low achievers are likely to be among the least accepted children in the classroom. In response to this, these children may form their own groups, with one characteristic of the group being that little value is placed on achieving in school. McMichael (1980) has provided evidence of this dynamic; boys who were both poor readers and lacked social skills tended to be accepted only by other boys with similar academic and social problems. As McMichael suggests, such groups of children likely become more and more alienated from school.

It appears, then, that the peer group exerts a negative influence on low-SES children's achievement and that strategies are needed for involving low-SES children more in the school situation. One strategy may be to enlist children in the educational process by having them serve as peer tutors. Peer tutoring can be quite effective in improving other children's academic performance (e.g., Jenkins, Mayhall, Peschka, & Jenkins, 1974) and both the tutor and the learner make academic and social gains as a result of the tutoring experience (Feldman, Devin-Sheehan, & Allen, 1976). These gains occur in both reading and mathematics, and with children from different SES and racial groups (see Allen, 1976). Thus, involving low-SES children in tutoring programs could increase the value they place on reading and other academic skills. Care should be taken when designing peer tutoring programs, however. In a review of studies on peer tutoring, Hartup (in press) concluded that to be successful, tutoring programs should use tutors who are several years older than tutees, the tutors should be trained and supervised closely, and intervention should be implemented for a relatively long time.

CONCLUSIONS

Specific suggestions for future research have been made throughout this chapter. In concluding, we will make several general points concerning future research efforts. Central to this chapter is the belief that research on achievement motivation and socialization influences on reading should become more closely integrated. Researchers interested in attributional processes need to look more closely at the antecedents of these processes in the home and school to learn how and when children and parents make attributions in naturally occurring situations related to reading. Such research would provide important field tests of the validity of attribution theory. Similarly, researchers interested in how socialization agents influence reading achievement should attend more to processes postulated by achievement motivation theorists to mediate achievement behavior. The work of Parsons and her colleagues on mathematics is a good example of such an approach; similar work needs to be done in reading. This sort of research would further understanding in both areas and help bridge the gap.

Inquiry is also needed into how particular features of the home and school environments influence the development of reading skills. Research like that of Hess, Elardo, and their colleagues on the home environment is an important first step, as is that of Brophy, Weinstein, and others on the school environment. From such research it will be possible to identify particular features of each environment which may be especially beneficial to children's acquisition of reading skills. Work on particular environmental features would allow researchers to go beyond the more general demographic variables of race or SES in explaining performance differences in reading.

NOTES

1. Weiner (1979) has added some additional causal factors to his model. These are not central to the points we will make about Weiner's view, and thus we will not discuss them here.

2. One of the beneficial side effects of greater parental involvement in reading-related activities with children is that as a result of such involvement parents likely control things in the home that, if left uncontrolled, might have a negative influence on the acquisition of reading skills. An example is excessive television viewing. Several studies (e.g., Robinson, 1971; Schramm, 1976; Stein & Friedrich, 1975) have shown that high rates of television viewing have a negative influence on the development of reading skills.

REFERENCES

Allen, V. L. (Ed.)   *Children as teachers.* New York: Academic Press, 1976.

Alexander, J. E., & Filler, R. C.   *Attitudes and reading.* Newark, Del.: International Reading Association, 1976.

Andrews, G. R., & Debus, R. L.   Persistence and the causal perception of failure: Modifying cognitive attributions. *Journal of Educational Psychology,* 1978, *70,* 154–166.

Armor, D. J.   The evidence on busing. *The Public Interest,* 1972 (Serial No. 28), 90–128.

Asher, S. R.   *Sex differences in reading achievement* (Reading Education Report No. 2). Urbana: University of Illinois, Center for the Study of Reading, 1977. (ERIC Document Reproduction Service No. ED 145 567.)

Asher, S. R.   Influence of topic interest on black children's and white children's reading comprehension. *Child Development,* 1979, *50,* 686–690.

Asher, S. R.   Topic interest and children's reading comprehension. In R. J. Spiro, B. C. Bruce, & W. F. Brewer (Eds.), *Theoretical issues in reading comprehension.* Hillsdale, N.J.: Erlbaum, 1980.

Asher, S. R., & Markell, R. A.   Sex differences in comprehension of high- and low-interest reading material. *Journal of Educational Psychology,* 1974, *66,* 680–687.

Askov, E. N., & Fischbach, J. W.   An investigation of primary pupils' attitudes towards reading. *Journal of Experimental Education,* 1973, *41,* 1–7.

Athey, I. G.   Reading research in the affective domain. In H. Singer & R. B. Ruddell (Eds.), *Theoretical models and processes of reading* (2nd ed.). Newark, Del.: International Reading Association, 1976.

Atkinson, J. W.   *An introduction to motivation.* Princeton, N.J.: Van Nostrand, 1964.

Atkinson, J. W., & Raynor, J. O.   *Motivation and achievement.* Washington, D.C.: Winston, 1974.

Bandura, A.   Self-efficacy: Toward a unifying theory of behavioral change. *Psychological Review,* 1977, *84,* 191–215. (a)

Bandura, A.   *Social learning theory.* Englewood Cliffs, N.J.: Prentice-Hall, 1977. (b)

Bee, H. L., Van Egereth, K. F., Streissguth, A. P., Nyman, B. A., & Leckie, M. S.   Social class differences in maternal teaching strategies and speech patterns. *Developmental Psychology,* 1969, *1,* 726–734.

Bell, R. Q.   A reinterpretation of the direction of effects in studies of socialization. *Psychological Review,* 1968, *75,* 81–95.

Bell, R. R.   Lower class Negro mothers' aspirations for their children. *Social Forces,* 1965, *43,* 493–500.

Berends, R. W.   *The influence of the group on the judgments of children.* New York: King's Crown Press, 1950.

Biller, H. B.   Parental and sex-role factors in cognitive and academic functioning. In J. K. Cole & R. Dienstbier (Eds.), *Nebraska Symposium on Motivation* (Vol. 21). Lincoln: University of Nebraska Press, 1974.

Bing, E.   Effect of childrearing practices on development of differential cognitive abilities. *Child Development*, 1963, *34*, 631–648.

Bloom, B. S.   *Human characteristics and school learning.* New York: McGraw-Hill, 1976.

Blumenfeld, P., Hamilton, V. L., Bossert, S. T., Wessels, K., & Meece, J.   Teacher talk and student thought: Socialization into the student role. In J. M. Levine and M. C. Wang (Eds.), *Teacher and student perceptions: Implications for teaching.* Hillsdale, N.J.: Erlbaum, 1982.

Blumenfeld, P. C., Pintrich, P. R., Meece, J., & Wessels, K.   The formation and role of self-perceptions of ability in elementary classrooms. *Elementary School Journal*, 1982, *82*, 401–420.

Bradley, R., Caldwell, B. M., & Elardo, R.   Home environment, social status, and mental test performance. *Journal of Educational Psychology*, 1977, *69*, 697–701.

Brezinski, J. E.   Beginning reading in Denver. *Reading Teacher*, 1964, *18*, 16–21.

Bridgeman, B., & Shipman, V. C.   Preschool measures of self-esteem and achievement motivation as predictors of third-grade achievement. *Journal of Educational Psychology*, 1978, *70*, 17–28.

Briggs, C., & Elkind, D.   Characteristics of early readers. *Perceptual and Motor Skills*, 1977, *14*, 1231–1237.

Britannica Junior Encyclopaedia.   Chicago: Encyclopaedia Britannica, 1970.

Brook, J. S., Whiteman, M., Peisach, E., & Deutsch, M.   Aspiration levels of and for children: Age, sex, race and socioeconomic correlates. *Journal of Genetic Psychology*, 1974, *124*, 3–16.

Brophy, J.   Mothers as teachers of their own preschool children: The influence of socioeconomic status and task structure on teaching specificity. *Child Development*, 1970, *41*, 79–94.

Brophy, J.   Teacher behavior and its effects. *Journal of Educational Psychology*, 1979, *71*, 733–750.

Brophy, J.   Teacher praise: A functional analysis. *Review of Educational Research*, 1981, *51*, 5–32.

Brophy, J., & Evertson, L. M.   *Learning from teaching: A development perspective.* Boston: Allyn & Bacon, 1976.

Brophy, J., & Good, T. L.   Teachers' communications of differential expectations for children's classroom performance: Some behavioral data. *Journal of Educational Psychology*, 1970, *61*, 365–374.

Brophy, J., & Good, T. L.   *Teacher-student relationships.* New York: Holt, 1974.

Burt, C.   The unstable child. *Child Study*, 1917, *10*, 61–79.

Butkowsky, I. S., & Willows, D. M.   Cognitive-motivational characteristics of children varying in reading ability: Evidence for learned helplessness in poor readers. *Journal of Educational Psychology*, 1980, *72*, 408–422.

Camp, B. W., & Zimet, S. G.   Classroom behavior during reading instruction. *Exceptional Children*, 1975, *42*, 109–110.

Campbell, J. D.   Peer relations in childhood. In M. L. Hoffman & L. W. Hoffman (Eds.), *Review of child development research* (Vol. 1). New York: Russell Sage Foundation, 1964.

Carlsmith, L.   Effects of early father absence on scholastic aptitude. *Harvard Educational Review*, 1964, *34*, 3–21.

Chapin, M., & Dyck, D. C.   Persistence in children's reading behavior as a function of N length and attribution retraining. *Journal of Abnormal Psychology*, 1976, *85*, 511–515.

Chilman, C. S.   Programs for disadvantaged parents: Some major trends and related research. In B. M. Caldwell & H. N. Ricciuti (Eds.), *Review of child development research*
(Vol. 3). Chicago: University of Chicago Press, 1973.

Clausen, J. A., & Williams, J. R.   Sociological correlates of child behavior. In H. W. Stevenson (Ed.) *Child psychology*. Chicago: University of Chicago Press, 1963.

Cobb, J. A., & Hops, H.   Effects of academic survival skill training on low-achieving
first graders. *Journal of Educational Psychology*, 1973, *67*, 108–113.

Coleman, J. S.   The adolescent subculture and academic achievement. *American Journal
of Sociology*, 1960, *65*, 337–347.

Coleman, J. S.   *The adolescent society*. Glencoe, Ill.: The Free Press, 1961.

Coleman, J. S., Campbell, E. Q., Hobson, C. J., McPartland, J., Mood, A. M., Weinfeld,
F. D., & York, R. L.   *Equality of educational opportunity*. Washington, D.C.: Department of Health, Education, and Welfare, U.S. Government Printing Office, 1966.

Constanzo, P. R., & Shaw, M. E.   Conformity as a function of age level. *Child Development*, 1966, *37*, 967–975.

Cooper, H. M.   Controlling persoal rewards: Professional teachers' differential use of feedback and the effects of feedback on the student's motivation to perform. *Journal of
Educational Psychology*, 1977, *69*, 419–427.

Cooper, H. M.   Pygmalion grows up: A model for teacher expectation communication
and performance. *Review of Educational Research*, 1979, *49*, 389–410.

Cooper, H. M., Baron, R. M., & Lowe, C. A.   The importance of race and social class
information in the formation of expectancies about academic performance. *Journal
of Educational Psychology*, 1975, *67*, 312–319.

Coster, J. K.   Attitudes toward school of high school pupils from three income levels.
Journal of Educational Psychology, 1958, *49*, 61–66.

Coster, J. K.   Some characteristics of high school pupils from three income groups. *Journal
of Educational Psychology*, 1959, *50*, 55–62.

Covington, M. V., & Beery, R.   *Self-worth and school learning*. New York: Holt, Rinehart
& Winston, 1976.

Covington, M. V., & Omelich, C. L.   Are causal attributions really causal? A path analysis
of the cognitive model of achievement motivation. *Journal of Personality and Social
Psychology*, 1979, *37*, 1487–1502. (a)

Covington, M. V., & Omelich, C. L.   Effort: The double-edged sword in school achievement. *Journal of Educational Psychology*, 1979, *71*, 169–182. (b)

Covington, M. V., & Omelich, C. L.   It's best to be able and virtuous too: Student and
teacher evaluative responses to successful effort. *Journal of Educational Psychology*,
1979, *71*, 688–700. (c)

Crandall, V. C., Katkovsky, W. A., & Crandall, V. J.   Children's beliefs in their own control
of reinforcement in intellectual-academic situations. *Child Development*, 1965, *36*,
91–109.

Daniels, S.   *How 2 gerbils, 20 goldfish, 200 games, 2000 books and I taught them how
to read*. Philadelphia: Westminster Press, 1971.

Datta, L., Schaeffer, E., & Davis, M.   Sex and scholastic aptitude as variables in teachers'
ratings of the adjustment and classroom behavior of Negro and other seventh-grade
students. *Journal of Educational Psychology*, 1968, *59*, 94–101.

Davie, R., Butler, M., & Goldstein, H.   *From birth to seven*. London: Longman, 1972.

Dix, M.   *Are reading habits of parents related to reading performance of their children?*
Paper presented at the annual meeting of the National Council of the Teachers of
English, 1976.

Douglas, J.   *The home and the school*. London: MacGibbon and Kee, 1964.

Dreger, R. M., & Miller, K. S.   Comparative psychological studies of Negroes and whites
in the U.S.: 1959–1965. *Psychological Bulletin*, 1968, *70*(No. 3, Pt. 2), 1–58.

Durkin, D. R. *Children who read early.* New York: Teachers College Press, 1966.

Dusek, J. B. Do teachers bias children's learning. *Review of Educational Research,* 1975, *45,* 661–684.

Dusek, J. B. The development of test anxiety in children. In I. G. Sarason (Ed.), *Test anxiety: Theory, research and applications.* Hillsdale, N.J.: Erlbaum, 1980.

Dusek, J. B., Kermis, M. A., & Mergler, N. C. Information processing in low- and high-test anxious children as a function of grade level and verbal labeling. *Developmental Psychology,* 1975, *11,* 651–652.

Dusek, J. B., Mergler, N. L., & Kermis, M. D. Attention, encoding, and information processing in low- and high-test anxious children. *Child Development,* 1976, *47,* 201–207.

Dweck, C. S. The role of expectations and attributions in the alleviation of learned helplessness. *Journal of Personality and Social Psychology,* 1975, *11,* 674–685.

Dweck, C. S., Davidson, W., Nelson, S., & Enna, B. Sex differences in learned helplessness: (II) The contingencies of evaluative feedback in the classroom and (III) An experimental analysis. *Developmental Psychology,* 1978, *14,* 268–276.

Dweck, C. S., & Goetz, T. E. Attributions and learned helplessness. In J. H. Harvey, W. I. Ickes, & R. F. Kidd (Eds.), *New directions in attribution research* (Vol. 2). Hillsdale, N.J.: Erlbaum, 1978.

Dweck, C. S., & Repucci, N. D. Learned helplessness and reinforcement responsibility in children. *Journal of Personality and Social Psychology,* 1973, *25,* 109–116.

Dyer, H. S. School factors and equal educational opportunity. *Harvard Educational Review,* 1968, *38,* 38–56.

Eccles, J., & Wigfield, A. Teacher expectations and student motivation. In J. B. Dusek (Ed.), *Teacher expectancies.* Hillsdale, N.J.: Erlbaum, in press.

Elardo, R., Bradley, R., & Caldwell, B. M. A longitudinal study of the relationship of infant's home environments to language development at age 3. *Child Development,* 1977, *48,* 595–603.

Entwisle, D. R. The child's social environment and learning to read. In *Reading research: Advances in theory and practice* (Vol. 1). New York: Academic Press, 1979.

Entwisle, D. R., & Hayduk, I. A. *Too great expectations: The academic outlook of young children.* Baltimore: Johns Hopkins University Press, 1978.

Eshel, Y., & Klein, Z. Development of academic self-concept of lower-class and middle-class primary school children. *Journal of Educational Psychology,* 1981, *73,* 187–193.

Feldman, R. S., Devin-Sheehan, L., & Allen, V. L. Children tutoring children: A critical review of research. In V. L. Allen (Ed.), *Children as teachers.* New York: Academic Press, 1976.

Fennema, E. Attribution theory and achievement in mathematics. In S. R. Yussen (Ed.), *The development of reflection.* New York: Academic Press, in press.

Fontaine, G. Social comparison and some determinants of expected personal control and expected performance in a novel task situation. *Journal of Personality and Social Psychology,* 1974, *29,* 487–496.

Fowler, J. W., & Peterson, D. L. Increasing reading persistence and altering attributional style of learned helpless children. *Journal of Educational Psychology,* 1981, *73,* 251–260.

Friend, R. N., & Neale, J. M. Children's perceptions of success and failure: An attributional analysis of the effects of race and social class. *Development Psychology,* 1972, *7,* 124–128.

Frieze, I. H., & Snyder, H. N. Children's beliefs about the causes of success and failure in school settings. *Journal of Educational Psychology,* 1980, *72,* 186–196.

Fyans, L. J. *Test anxiety, test comfort, and student achievement test performances.* Paper presented at the Educational Testing Service, 1979.

Geen, R. G.   Test anxiety and cue utilization. In I. G. Sarason (Ed.), *Test anxiety: Theory, research and applications.* Hillsdale, N.J.: Erlbaum, 1980.

Good, T. L., & Brophy, J.   *Educational psychology: A realistic approach.* New York: Holt, Rinehart & Winston, 1977.

Good, T. L., Cooper, H., & Blakely, S. C.   Classroom interaction as a function of teacher expectations, student sex, and time of year. *Journal of Educational Psychology,* 1980, *72,* 378–385.

Goodwin, W., & Sanders, J.   *An exploratory study of the effect of selected variables upon teacher expectations of pupil success.* Paper presented at the annual meeting of the American Educational Research Association, 1969.

Green, K. D., Forehand, R., Beck, S. J., & Vosk, B.   An assessment of the relationship among measures of children's social competence and children's academic achievement. *Child Development,* 1980, *51,* 1149–1156.

Groff, P. J.   Children's attitudes toward reading and their critical reading abilities in four content-type materials. *Journal of Educational Research,* 1962, *55,* 313–317.

Gruenebaum, M. G., Hurwitz, I., Prentice, N. M., & Sperry, B. M.   Fathers of sons with primary neurotic learning inhibition. *American Journal of Orthopsychiatry,* 1962, *32,* 462–473.

Hake, J. M.   Covert motivations of good and poor readers. *The Reading Teacher,* 1969, *22,* 731–738.

Haller, A. O., & Butterworth, C. E.   Peer influence on levels of occupation and educational aspiration. *Social Forces,* 1960, *38,* 289–295.

Hansen, H. S.   The impact of the home literary environment on reading attitude. *Elementary English,* 1969, *46,* 17–24.

Hartup, W. W.   Peer interaction and social organization. In P. H. Mussen (Ed.), *Carmichael's manual of child psychology* (Vol. 2). New York: Wiley, 1970.

Hartup, W. W.   Peer relations. In P. H. Mussen (Ed.), *Handbook of child psychology* (Vol. 4). New York: Wiley, in press.

Heckhausen, H.   The development of achievement motivation. In W. W. Hartup (Ed.), *Review of child development research* (Vol. 6). Chicago: University of Chicago Press, 1982.

Heimberger, M. J.   *Sartain reading attitudes inventory.* Paper presented at the Pennsylvania Educational Research Association, Pittsburgh, April 1970.

Hermans, H. J. M., ter Laak, J. J. F., & Maes, P. C. J. M.   Achievement motivation and fear of failure in family and school. *Developmental Psychology,* 1972, *6,* 520–528.

Hess, R. D.   Social class and ethnic influences upon socialization. In P. H. Mussen (Ed.), *Carmichael's manual of child psychology* (Vol. 2). New York: Wiley, 1970.

Hess, R. D., King, D. R., & Holloway, S. D.   *Causal explanations for high and low performance in school: Some contrasts between parents and children.* Paper presented at the biennial meeting of the Society for Research in Child Development, Boston, 1981.

Hess, R. D., & Shipman, V. C.   Early experience and the socialization of cognitive modes in children. *Child Development,* 1965, *36,* 369–386.

Hess, R. D., & Shipman, V. C.   Maternal attitudes toward the school and the role of the pupil: Some social class comparisons. In A. H. Passow (Ed.), *Developing programs for the educationally disadvantaged.* New York: Teachers College Press, 1968.

Hess, R. D., Holloway, S., Price, G. E., & Dickson, W. P.   *Family environments and acquisition of reading skills: Toward a more precise analysis.* Paper presented at the conference on the Family as a Learning Environment, Educational Testing Service, 1979.

Hill, K. T.   Anxiety in the evaluative context. In W. W. Hartup (Ed.), *The young child* (Vol. 2). Washington, D.C.: National Association of the Education of Young Children, 1972.

Hill, K. T.   The relation of evaluative practices to test anxiety and achievement motivation. *UCLA Educator*, 1977, *19*, 15–21.

Hill, K. T.   Motivation, evaluation and educational testing policy. In L. J. Fyans, Jr., (Ed.), *Achievement motivation: Recent trends in theory and research*. New York: Plenum, 1980.

Hill, K. T., & Sarason, S. B.   The relation of test anxiety and defensiveness to test and school performance over the elementary school years. *Monographs of the Society for Research in Child Development*, 1966, *31*(Serial No. 104).

Hops, H., & Cobb, J. A.   Initial investigation into academic survival skill training, direct instruction, and first grade achievement. *Journal of Educational Psychology*, 1974, *66*, 548–553.

Horowitz, F. D., & Paden, L. Y.   The effectiveness of environmental intervention programs. In B. M. Caldwell & H. N. Ricciuti (Eds.), *Review of child development research* (Vol. 3). Chicago: University of Chicago Press, 1973.

Ickes, W., & Layden, M. A.   Attributional styles. In J. H. Harvey, W. Ickes, & R. F. Kidd (Eds.), *New directions in attribution research* (Vol. 2). Hillsdale, N.J.: Erlbaum, 1978.

Jencks, C.   *Inequality: A reassessment of the effects of family and schooling in America*. New York: Basic Books, 1972.

Jenkins, J. R., & Jenkins, L. M.   *Cross-age and peer tutoring: Help for children with learning problems*. Reston, Va.: Council for Exceptional Children, 1981.

Jenkins, J. R., Mayhall, W. F., Peschka, C. M., & Jenkins, L. M.   Comparing small group and tutorial instruction in resource rooms. *Exceptional Children*, 1974, *40*, 245–250.

Karabenick, J. D., & Heller, K. A.   A developmental study of effort and ability attributions. *Developmental Psychology*, 1976, *12*, 559–560.

Kardel, D. B., & Lesser, G. S.   Parental and peer influence in college plans of adolescents. *American Sociological Review*, 1969, *34*, 213–223.

Katkovsky, W. A., Crandall, V. C., & Preston, A.   Parent attitudes toward their personal achievements and toward the achievement behavior of their children. *Journal of Genetic Psychology*, 1964, *104*, 67–82.

Katz, I.   The socialization of academic motivation in minority group children. In D. Levine (Ed.), *Nebraska Symposium on Motivation* (Vol. 15). Lincoln: University of Nebraska Press, 1967.

Kenneday, L. D., & Halinski, R. S.   Measuring attitudes: An extra dimension. *Journal of Reading*, 1978, *18*, 518–522.

Krus, P. H., & Ruben, R. A.   *Use of family history data to predict educational functioning from ages 5–7*. Paper presented at the annual meeting of the American Educational Research Association, 1974.

Kukla, A.   Foundations of an attributional theory of performance. *Psychological Review*, 1972, *79*, 454–470.

Kukla, A.   An attributional theory of choice. In L. Berkowitz (Ed.), *Advances in experimental social psychology* (Vol. 11). New York: Academic Press, 1978.

Kun, A.   Development of the magnitude-covariation and compensation schemata in ability and effort attributions of performance. *Child Development*, 1977, *48*, 862–873.

Ladd, M. R.   *The relation of social, economic, and personal characteristics to reading ability*. New York: Columbia University Press, 1933.

Lambert, N. M., & Nicoll, R. G.   Conceptual model for nonintellectual behavior and its relationship to reading achievement. *Journal of Educational Psychology*, 1977, *69*, 481–496.

Lamme, L., & Olmsted, D.   *Family reading habits and children's progress in reading*. Paper presented at the annual meeting of the International Reading Association, 1977.

Laosa, L. M.   Maternal teaching strategies in Chicano families of varied educational and socioeconomic levels. *Child Development*, 1978, *49*, 1129–1135.

Laosa, L. M.   Maternal teaching strategies in Chicano and Anglo-American families: The influence of culture and education on maternal behavior. *Child Development*, 1980, *51*, 759–765.

Lessing, E. E., Zagorin, S. W., & Nelson, D.   WISC subtest and IQ score correlates of father absence. *Journal of Genetic Psychology*, 1970, *67*, 181–195.

Maehr, M. L.   Continuing motivation: An analysis of a seldom considered educational outcome. *Review of Educational Research*, 1976, *46*, 443–462.

Marjoribanks, K.   Environment, social class, and mental ability. *Journal of Educational Psychology*, 1976, *63*, 103–109.

Matthewson, G. C.   The function of attitude in the reading process. In H. Singer & R. B. Ruddell (Eds.), *Theoretical models and processes of reading* (2nd ed.). Newark, Del.: International Reading Association, 1976.

McDill, E. L., & Coleman, J. S.   Family and peer influence in college plans of high school students. *Sociology of Education*, 1965, *38*, 112–116.

McDonnell, T. R.   Suggestibility in children as a function of chronological age. *Journal of Abnormal and Social Psychology*, 1963, *67*, 286–289.

McClelland, D. C.   *The achieving society*. New York: The Free Press, 1961.

McClelland, D. C., Atkinson, J. W., Clark, R. W., & Lowell, E. L.   *The achievement motive*. New York: Appleton-Century-Crofts, 1953.

McMahon, I. D.   Relationships between causal attributions and expectancy of success. *Journal of Personality and Social Psychology*, 1973, *28*, 108–114.

McMichael, P.   Reading difficulties, behavior and social status. *Journal of Educational Psychology*, 1980, *72*, 76–86.

Miller, W. H.   Home prereading experiences and first grade reading achievement. *Reading Teacher*, 1969, *22*, 641–645.

Murray, S. R., & Mednick, M. T. S.   Perceiving the causes of success and failure in achievement: Sex, race and motivational comparisons. *Journal of Consulting and Clinical Psychology*, 1975, *43*, 881–885.

Mutimer, D., Laughlin, L. & Powell, M.   Some differences in the family relationships of achieving and underachieving readers. *Journal of Genetic Psychology*, 1966, *109*, 67–74.

Neale, D. C., & Proshek, J. M.   School-related attitudes of culturally disadvantaged elementary school children. *Journal of Educational Psychology*, 1967, *58*, 238–244.

Nicholls, J. G.   The development of the concepts of effort and ability, perception of academic attainment, and the understanding that difficult tasks require more ability. *Child Development*, 1978, *49*, 800–814.

Nicholls, J. G.   Development of perception of own attainment and causal attributions for success and failure in reading. *Journal of Educational Psychology*, 1979, *71*, 84–100.

Nicholls, J. G.   The development of the concept of difficulty. *Merrill-Palmer Quarterly*, 1980, *26*, 271–281.

Nottleman, E. D.   *Parent-child interaction and children's achievement-related behavior.* Unpublished doctoral dissertation, University of Illinois at Urbana-Champaign, 1978.

Nottleman, E. D., & Hill, K. T.   Test anxiety and off-task behavior in evaluative situations. *Child Development*, 1977, *48*, 225–231.

Paladry, J. M.   What teachers believe, what children achieve. *Elementary School Journal*, 1969, *69*, 370–374.

Parke, R. D.   Children's home environments: Social and cognitive effects. In I. Altman & J. F. Wohlwill (Eds.), *Children's environments* (Vol. 3). New York: Plenum, 1978.

Parsons, J. E.   *The development of achievement motivation*. Report No. 117, Developmental Psychology Program, University of Michigan, 1981.

Parsons, J. E.   Attributions, learned helplessness, and sex differences in achievement. In S. R. Yussen (Ed.), *The development of reflection*. New York: Academic Press, in press.

Parsons, J. E., Adler, T. F., Futterman, R., Goff, S. B., Kaczala, C. M., Meece, C., & Midgley, C.   Expectancies, values and academic behaviors. In J. T. Spence (Ed.), *Assessing achievement*. San Francisco: W. H. Freeman, 1983.

Parsons, J. E., Adler, T. F., & Kaczala, C. M.   Socialization of achievement attitudes and beliefs: Parental influences. *Child Development*, 1982, *53*, 310–321.

Parsons, J. E., & Goff, S. B.   Achievement motivation and values: An alternative perspective. In L. J. Fyans, Jr., (Ed.), *Achievement motivation: Recent trends in theory and research*. New York: Plenum, 1980.

Parsons, J. E., Kaczala, C. M., & Meece, J. L.   Socialization of achievement attitudes and beliefs: Classroom influences. *Child Development*, 1982, *53*, 322–339.

Parsons, J. E., & Ruble, D. N.   The development of achievement-related expectancies. *Child Development*, 1977, *48*, 1075–1079.

Pope, B.   Socio-economic contrasts in children's peer culture prestige values. *Genetic Psychology Monographs*, 1953, *48*, 157–220.

Porterfield, O. V., & Schlichting, H. F.   Peer status and reading achievement. *Journal of Educational Research*, 1961, *54*, 291–297.

Psthas, G.   Ethnicity, social class and adolescent independence from parental control. *American Sociological Review*, 1957, *22*, 415–423.

Purkey, W. W.   *Self-concept and school achievement*. Englewood Cliffs, N.J.: Prentice-Hall, 1970.

Radin, N.   Father-child interaction and the intellectual functioning of four-year-old boys. *Developmental Psychology*, 1972, *6*, 353–361.

Radin, N.   Observed paternal behaviors as antecedents of intellectual functioning in young boys. *Developmental Psychology*, 1973, *8*, 369–376.

Radin, N., & Epstein, A. S.   *Observed paternal behavior and the intellectual functioning of preschool boys*. Paper presented at the biennial meeting of the Society for Research in Child Development, Denver, 1975.

Ransbury, M. K.   An assessment of reading attitudes. *Journal of Reading*, 1973, *17*, 25–28.

Resnick, L. B., & Robinson, B. H.   Motivational aspects of the literacy problem. In J. B. Carroll (Ed.), *Towards a literate society*. New York: McGraw-Hill, 1975.

Rholes, W. S., Blackwell, J., Jordan, C., & Walters, C.   A developmental study of learned helplessness. *Developmental Psychology*, 1980, *16*, 616–624.

Rist, R. C.   Student social class and teacher expectations. *Harvard Educational Review*, 1970, *40*, 411–451.

Robinson, J. P.   Television's impact on everyday life: Some cross-national evidence. In *Television and social behavior* (Vol. 4). Washington, D.C.: U.S. Government Printing Office, 1971.

Rosen, B. C.   Race, ethnicity and the achievement syndrome. *American Sociological Review*, 1959, *24*, 47–60.

Rosen, B. C., & d'Andrade, R.   The psychosocial origins of achievement motivation. *Sociometry*, 1959, *22*, 185–218.

Rosenshine, B. V.   *Direct instruction for skill mastery*. Paper presented to the School of Education, University of Wisconsin at Milwaukee, April 1979.

Rosenshine, B. V., & Berliner, D. C.   Academic engaged time. *British Journal of Teacher Education*, 1978, *4*, 3–16.

Rotter, J. B.   *Social learning and clinical psychology*. Englewood Cliffs, N.J.: Prentice-Hall, 1954.

Rotter, J. B.   Generalized expectancies for internal versus external control of reinforcements. *Psychological Monographs*, 1966, *80*(1, Whole No. 609).

Ruble, D. N., Boggiano, A. K., Feldman, N. S., & Loebl, J. H.   A developmental analysis of the role of social comparison in self-evaluation. *Developmental Psychology,* 1980, *16,* 105–115.

Ruble, D. N., Feldman, N. S., & Boggiano, A. K.   Social comparison between young children in achievement situations. *Developmental Psychology,* 1976, *12,* 192–197.

Rubovits, P., & Maehr, M. L.   Pygmalion in black and white. *Journal of Personality and Social Psychology,* 1973, *25,* 210–218.

St. John, N. H.   Desegregation and minority group performance. *Review of Educational Research,* 1970, *40,* 111–134.

Sarason, I. G.   Experimental approaches to test anxiety: Attention and the uses of information. In C. D. Spielberger (Ed.), *Anxiety: Current trends in theory and research* (Vol. 2). New York: Academic Press, 1972.

Sarason, I. G.   Test anxiety, attention and the general problem of anxiety. In C. D. Spielberger & I. G. Sarason (Eds.), *Stress and anxiety* (Vol. I). Washington, D.C.: Hemisphere, 1975.

Schramm, W.   *Television and the test scores.* Paper prepared for the Educational Testing Service, August 1976.

Schunk, D. H.   Modeling and attribution effects on children's achievement: A self-efficacy analysis. *Journal of Educational Psychology,* 1981, *73,* 93–105.

Shea, R. M.   Schooling and its antecedents: Substantive and methodological issues in the status attainment process. *Review of Educational Research,* 1976, *46,* 463–526.

Sheldon, W. D., & Carrillo, R.   Relation of parent, home and certain developmental characteristics to children's reading ability. *Elementary School Journal,* 1952, *52,* 262–270.

Shepps, F. P., & Shepps, R. R.   Relationship of study habits and school attitudes to achievement in mathematics and reading. *Journal of Educational Research,* 1971, *65,* 71–73.

Simpson, R. L.   Parental influence, anticipatory socialization and social mobility. *American Sociological Review,* 1962, *27,* 517–552.

Singer, H., Gerard, H. B., & Redfearn, D.   Achievement. In H. B. Gerard & N. Miller (Eds.), *School desegregation.* New York: Plenum, 1975.

Smith, C. P. (Ed.)   *Achievement-related motives in children.* New York: Russell Sage Foundation, 1969.

Sohn, D.   Affect-generating powers of effort and ability self-attributions of academic success and failure. *Journal of Educational Psychology,* 1977, *69,* 500–505.

Soli, S. D., & Devine, V. T.   Behavioral correlates of achievement: A look at high and low achievers. *Journal of Educational Psychology,* 1976, *68,* 335–341.

Stein, A. H., & Friedrich, L. K.   Impact of television on children and youth. In E. M. Hetherington (Ed.), *Review of child development research* (Vol. 5). Chicago: University of Chicago Press, 1975.

Sutton, M. H.   Readiness for reading at the kindergarten level. *Reading Teacher,* 1964, *17,* 235–240.

Valle, V. A., & Frieze, I. H.   Stability of causal attributions as a mediator in changing expectations for success. *Journal of Personality and Social Psychology,* 1976, *33,* 579–587.

Veroff, J.   Social comparison and the development of achievement motivation. In C. P. Smith (Ed.) *Achievement-related motives in children.* New York: Russell Sage Foundation, 1969.

Walberg, H. J., & Marjoribanks, K.   Differential mental abilities and home environments: A canonical analysis. *Developmental Psychology,* 1973, *9,* 363–368.

Walker, H. M., & Hops, H.   Increasing academic achievement by reinforcing direct academic performance and/or facilitative non-academic response. *Journal of Educational Psychology,* 1976, *68,* 218–225.

Wattenberg, W. W., & Clifford, C.   Relation of self-concepts to beginning achievement in reading. *Child Development*, 1964, *35*, 461–467.

Weiner, B.   *Theories of motivation.* Chicago: Markham, 1972.

Weiner, B.   *Achievement motivation and attribution theory.* Morristown, N.J.: General Learning Press, 1974.

Weiner, B.   A theory of motivation for some classroom experiences. *Journal of Educational Psychology*, 1979, *71*, 3–25.

Weiner, B., Frieze, I., Kukla, A., Reed, A., Rest, S., & Rosenbaum, L. M.   *Perceiving the causes of success and failure.* Morristown, N.J.: General Learning Corporation, 1971.

Weiner, B., & Kukla, A.   An attributional analysis of achievement motivation. *Journal of Personality and Social Psychology*, 1970, *15*, 1–20.

Weiner, B., Nierenberg, R., & Goldstein, M.   Social learning (locus of control) versus attributional (causal stability) interpretations of expectancy of success. *Journal of Personality*, 1976, *44*, 52–68.

Weinstein, R.   Reading group membership in first grade: Teacher behaviors and pupil experience over time. *Journal of Educational Psychology*, 1976, *68*, 103–116.

Weinstein, R., & Middlestadt, S. E.   Student perceptions of teacher interactions with male high and low achievers. *Journal of Educational Psychology*, 1979, *71*, 421–431.

West, C. K., & Anderson, T. H.   The question of preponderant causation in teacher expectation research. *Review of Educational Research*, 1976, *46*, 613–630.

Wigfield, A.   *The influence of task- versus self-focus on children's achievement performance and attributions.* Unpublished doctoral dissertation, University of Illinois at Urbana-Champaign, 1982.

Willig, A. C., Harnisch, D. L., Hill, K. T., & Maehr, M. L.   Sociocultural and educational correlates of success-failure attributions and evaluation anxiety in the school setting for Black, Hispanic and Anglo children. *American Educational Research Journal*, in press.

Wine, J. D.   Test anxiety and the direction of attention. *Psychological Bulletin*, 1971, *76*, 97–104.

Wine, J. D.   Cognitive-attentional theory of test anxiety. In I. G. Sarason (Ed.), *Test anxiety: Theory, research and applications.* Hillsdale, N.J.: Erlbaum, 1980.

Winterbottom, M. R.   The relation of need for achievement to learning experiences in independence and mastery. In J. W. Atkinson (Ed.), *Motives in fantasy, action, and society.* Princeton, N.J.: Van Nostrand, 1958.

Wolff, R.   The measurement of environment. In A. Anastasai (Ed.), *Testing problems in perspective.* Washington, D.C.: American Council on Education, 1966.

Wylie, R. S.   *The self-concept: Theory and research on selected topics.* Lincoln: University of Nebraska Press, 1979.

Yee, A.   Interpersonal attitudes of teachers and advantaged and disadvantaged pupils. *Journal of Human Resources*, 1968, *3*, 327–345.

Zimmerman, I. L., & Allebrand, G. N.   Personality characteristics and attitudes toward achievement of good and poor readers. *Journal of Educational Research*, 1965, *59*, 28–31.

15 UNDERSTANDING FIGURATIVE LANGUAGE

Andrew Ortony

There probably is no person on earth, however erudite and however skilled a reader, who has not at some time or other chanced upon a text that seemed to be incomprehensible. Obvious examples of texts that are essentially unintelligible to all but a select few are the highly technical texts that are typically written by specialists for specialists. It is important to remember that the uninitiated would-be readers of such texts do not upon encountering them come to doubt that they really are skilled and competent readers after all. Rather, they recognize that to a great extent the problem has to do with extratextual factors—they simply lack the necessary background knowledge and special vocabulary that such texts presuppose for their proper comprehension.

The question to be addressed in this chapter is whether figurative language is an important source of comprehension failures (particularly, but not exclusively, for the beginning reader), and if so, whether such failures have to do with reading or reading-related skills, with extratextual factors, or with both. It is theoretically possible that figurative uses of language are a potential source of comprehension difficulty at every level of linguistic analysis, from the word level through to that of the entire discourse. At the word level, a reader might fail to understand a metaphor or might fail to grasp its full force or implications. This could also be true at the phrase level, where, in addition, certain clichés and idiomatic expressions might be unfamiliar to the reader. At the sentence level, a reader might have difficulty understanding, say, a proverb; at the level of the text itself, a reader might fail to recognize that what had been read was a fable or an allegory. In each case, the nature and cause of the comprehension "failure" could be rather different and, so, accordingly, would a reader's awareness of it.

So, the main question to be addressed is this: Are figurative uses of language more difficult to understand than literal uses? A more precise way to formulate this question would be to ask whether, if figurative uses of language do give rise to comprehension difficulties, do they do so just *because* they are figurative uses?

THE NATURE OF FIGURATIVE LANGUAGE

Figurative language comes in many varieties, each with its own, often obscure, name, such as litotes, zeugma, synecdoche, metonymy, syllepsis, oxymoron, and hyperbole, as well as the more familiar irony, simile, and metaphor. A reasonable starting point is to ask what it is that makes these various rhetorical devices all instances of figurative language. A first approximation is that they are all cases of "saying one thing and meaning another." One problem with this proposal is that it fails to distinguish certain rhetorical devices that are not figurative from those that are figurative. Suppose that one receives an invitation to dinner for some particular evening and one replies by saying that one already has an engagement for that evening. This would be an example of saying one thing and meaning another, but it would not normally be regarded as a figurative use of language. In this case, what has happened is that one has *indirectly* declined the invitation—one has performed an *indirect speech act* (Searle, 1969, 1975). Such indirection is a critical component of figurative uses of language, but insofar as it is also a widespread component of nonfigurative uses, it cannot be the whole story.

What else is needed then? One candidate immediately comes to mind, namely, that an important characteristic of figurative uses of language is that if they are not interpreted figuratively—that is, if they are taken at face value—they often appear to be either false, bizarre, or nonsensical. After all, it is not literally true that all the world's a stage, nor does it really rain cats and dogs, and foolish people are not really asses. This suggests that we need to modify our account by reference to the unreasonableness of (asserting) the literal meaning of a figurative use of language. As a second approximation, therefore, we might try to say that a figurative use of language is one in which one says one thing that one does not believe to be true while meaning another, that one does believe to be true. So, when one says that it is raining cats and dogs, one does not really believe *that* to be true. On the other hand, one does believe its intended, or figurative, meaning (i.e., that it is raining hard) to be true.

However, such an account is still not adequate because some figurative uses of language are literally true if taken at face value. For example, if I say that life is not a bed of roses, what I have said is literally true, yet it is clearly figurative in intention. So, too, are many proverbs, for example, *good things come in small packages* can be true both literally and figuratively. Except in very rare cases where there is a double entendre on both the literal and the figurative meaning, the literal meaning is not intended, even if it is true. The key here seems to have something to do with the bizarreness of the literal meaning in the context of the discourse—elsewhere I have referred to this as *contextual anomaly* (e.g., Ortony, 1975). Presumably various factors can give rise to the bizarreness. What is said can be patently false *or* (trivially) true if taken literally; in either case, it would be pointless to say it. Then, the mere fact that it was said would suggest that something else might have been intended. If one is explaining to a child that whales are not fish, it is reasonable to assume that one does so precisely because one knows or suspects that the child wrongly thinks that they are; consequently, there is nothing bizarre about it. If on the other hand, everybody knows that the Pope is Catholic, someone who says that he is could reasonably be expected to be (indirectly) saying something else, for otherwise there would appear to be no point in saying it at all. As Grice (1975) has emphasized through his "cooperative principle," people engage in linguistic interchanges against a background of expectations that the participants are cooperating in their effort to communicate. For a speaker or writer to communicate something without a purpose would violate this principle (see also Wilensky, in press, on "points").

Another source of bizarreness seems to have something to do with the categories from which the juxtaposed terms are drawn. Figurative uses of language often involve similarities between essentially incompatible or wildly disparate categories. Life and beds of roses are entirely different kinds of things, nor are persistent and large raindrops much like cats and dogs. The juxtaposition of incongruous categories seems to be highly correlated with figurative uses of language, although it is neither a necessary nor sufficient condition for such uses (consider, for example, proverbs).

We are now in a position to summarize our findings so far. It seems that figurative uses of language are ones in which what is said is different from what is meant. Furthermore, what is said usually appears to be anomalous with respect to the surrounding context, so that one would not expect the speaker to intend it to be taken at face value, even if it is, technically speaking, true. Rather, one would expect it to be an indirect way of conveying something else. Clearly, however, the relationship between what is said and what is meant cannot be arbitrary. It is differences in the type of relationship between what is said and what is meant or intended that give rise to the different kinds of figures of speech.

Similes and Metaphors

Variations in the nature of the relationship between what is said and what is meant are not always easy to characterize, and they are not always sufficient to account for differences between particular figures of speech. Accordingly, to reduce our task to manageable proportions, I shall concentrate on similes and metaphors since these are common figurative uses of language—ones that seem to receive attention in basal readers from about the third grade on. Let us consider the following examples, first of a simile then of a metaphor, both taken from a popular basal reader: *The people on the street below were like columns of ants moving along the sidewalk* and *The fog was a curtain [blocking our view]*.

In each case, what is said is different from what is meant, but the manner in which it is different varies subtly from the one case to the other. Consider first the simile, *The people on the street below were like columns of ants moving along the sidewalk*. At first sight, it might appear that there is no discrepancy at all between what is said and what is meant. What is said is that two things were alike, and that is what is meant. I shall argue that this is a thoroughly misleading position to take. If one were to deny any difference between what is said and what is meant in this case, one would be denying that similes were figurative. Such a conclusion would have unacceptable ramifications for other types of figurative language. In particular, I shall argue that we need to understand what it is about similes that makes them figurative because that will form the basis of our account of metaphors too. It is at this point, therefore, that we are going to have to make a theoretical commitment.

When we ordinarily say that two things are similar, what we mean is that they share some important property or properties. If two things do not share some property that is important to both of them, then we are inclined to say that they are not *really* similar. So, for example, termites *are* like ants, but people are not really like ants. It makes much better sense to say that people are only like ants *metaphorically speaking*, whereas it makes no sense at all to say that termites are only like ants metaphorically speaking. In other words, if two things are really alike, they cannot be metaphorically alike and vice versa.

The importance of these simple observations (which are discussed more fully in Ortony, Reynolds, & Arter, 1978, and in Ortony, 1979a, 1979b, 1981) is that they suggest that some statements of comparison are metaphorical, while others are literal. In particular, of course, they suggest that similes are metaphorical statements of comparison to be contrasted with literal statements of comparison. This immediately leads us to the question of what the difference is between literal and metaphorical statements of comparison. The answer to this question is not at all easy. Since I have discussed it at length elsewhere (e.g., Ortony, 1979a, and Ortony, Vondruska, Foss, & Jones, 1983), I shall only sketch my proposed answer here. Briefly, it is this: Statements of comparison vary in the extent to which they are metaphorical; in other words, every statement of comparison can, in principle, be assigned a degree of metaphoricity. The most important variable that influences metaphoricity has to do with the relative importance of the shared properties for each of the two terms. If the shared properties are important for both, then the degree of metaphoricity is low and we consider the statement to be a literal statement of comparison. Thus, the two things really are alike, as in, *Sermons are like lectures.* If, on the other hand, the shared properties are important for the second term, but normally less important for the first term, and if there are important properties of the second term that cannot be applied to the first term at all, then the statement of comparison is a metaphorical one, as in, *Sermons are like sleeping pills.* According to this account, the degree of metaphoricity depends on the extent to which the shared properties differ in their relative salience. Now, there are many caveats that need to be added to give this account credence; most of them are discussed in Ortony (1979a) and Ortony et al. (1983). But even with this skeletal account, we can make progress.

To start with, let us simplify our earlier example to, *The people were like columns of ants.* If one were to write down the important things one knew to be true about people and the important things one knew to be true of columns of ants, one would almost certainly find no overlap on the two lists. The properties that people and columns of ants share are not important for both of them. They are either important for columns of ants (e.g., bustling, weaving in and out, orderly) and rather unimportant for people or they are unimportant for both (e.g., being living creatures). Notice that "importance" here is being used in the sense of "diagnostic." In one sense, of course, it is an important property of people that they are living things, but that is not the sense of concern to us. Being a living thing is not a property that is *particularly* important for people (no more so than for any other animal). In other words, it is not a property that helps to discriminate people from, for example, other animals. Thus, the sense of "importance" that we are using is one such that the fewer the kinds of things that have the property in question, the more important or diagnostic it is. So, in our example, there are matching properties that are important for columns of ants that are not so important for people, and to that extent, it is a metaphorical statement of comparison.

The difference between the original example and our modified version is that the original, *"The people on the street below were like ants moving along the sidewalk,"* makes it easier to understand the ways in which the people and the ants are supposed to be perceived as being similar. It can be argued (see Ortony, 1979a) that such specification of the dimensions of similarity actually reduces the perceived metaphoricity (compare the original simile with *"the people on the street below looked like columns of ants moving along the sidewalk"*), but a discussion of such refinements is not really necessary here.

We can now return to the question of what makes similes figurative uses of language at all. How is a simile a case of saying one thing and meaning something different? The answer that has to be given is that a simile, in having the form *"a is like b,"* purports to claim that *a* and *b* are *really* alike, that is, it purports to claim that the two things share important properties. What is meant, however, is something different, namely, that they share properties that are differentially important, specifically properties that are important for the *b* term but much less so for the *a* term. So, similes are figurative uses of language because the two things being compared are not really alike at all. They are only *metaphorically* alike. Since we have defined metaphoricity independently of figurative language, our account is not circular, even though, on the face of it, to say that a use of language is figurative because it is metaphorical is circular.

Armed with the above account of similes, it becomes relatively easy to give an account of (at least straightforward cases of) metaphors. When we read that, *"The fog was a curtain,"* all we need say is that the metaphor is an *indirect* way of asserting a metaphorical comparison (i.e., a simile). So, the metaphor is indirectly the simile, *"The fog was like a curtain."* This element of indirection presumably adds to the complexity of the form since it is one step further removed from the underlying meaning than is the simile. The simile, taken at face value, suggests that fog and curtains share important properties. Its underlying meaning is that there are some important properties of curtains that are normally thought to be less important for fog, while there are some important properties of curtains that cannot be applied to fog. The metaphor has the same underlying meaning, but taken literally, it does not suggest a comparison at all. Again, notice that in the original example, the particular property of interest is specified ("view blocking"). The specification of this dimension tends to reduce the perceived metaphoricity (Ortony, 1979a). Notice also that the metaphor depends to some extent on the subtle difference between the kind of view blocking typically thought to be applicable to curtains (impenetrable, designed specifically for that purpose, etc.) and the kind of view blocking typically thought to be applicable to fog (penetrable—to a degree, and incidental).

THE COMPREHENSION OF FIGURATIVE LANGUAGE

Although figurative language has been studied by scholars of philosophy and rhetoric for hundreds of years, it is only quite recently that research has been undertaken investigating issues related to how it is understood and whether its comprehension is in some way different from, and more difficult than, that of literal language. Much of this research as well as discussions of the philosophical and linguistic underpinnings of figurative language can be found in a number of recent books and review articles (e.g., Billow, 1977; Honeck & Hoffman, 1980; Johnson, 1981; Lakoff & Johnson, 1980; Miall, 1982; O'Hare, 1981; Ortony, 1979b; Ortony et al., 1978; Sacks, 1978). The work represented in this literature gives a very diverse array of perspectives on figurative language.

One of these perspectives derives from recent work in linguistics and the philosophy of language. It is an approach that, on the surface at least, fits naturally with the account of figurative language that I sketched in the last section. In recent years, philosophers and linguists have become increasingly interested in the communicative functions of language. It may seem surprising that theorists interested in language were not always interested in those functions. The fact is, however, that previous research often devoted itself to the analysis of, for example, the meanings of individual words, abstract theories of grammatical structure, and other aspects of language more remote from the banality of everyday linguistic interactions. The increase in interest in the realities of language as a medium of communication is realized in an area of study called *pragmatics* (e.g., see Cole, 1978), which Stalnaker (1972) characterizes as "the study of linguistic acts and *the contexts in which they are performed*" (p. 383, emphasis added).

Two central concepts of pragmatics are that of a *speech act* (e.g., see Austin, 1962, on "performatives"; and Searle, 1969) and that of *indirection* (e.g., see Searle, 1975). Essentially, the idea behind the notion of a speech act is that when we ordinarily use language we are performing one of a number of possible actions. We can be asserting, asking, ordering, apologizing, warning, and so on. The second notion, indirection, has to do with the fact that sometimes we can indirectly achieve the goals of one kind of speech act (e.g., requesting) by actually performing another kind of speech act (e.g., asserting). So, to take a simple example, one can indirectly ask someone to shut the door behind them by asserting that one hates the draft caused by the open door.

By now the reader will probably have noticed the similarity between the notion of indirection and the account of figurative language offered in the last section. That account was partly in terms of a discrepancy between what is said and what is meant, and I claimed that a metaphor could be regarded as an indirect statement of a (metaphorical) comparison. I also claimed that a simile was a case of saying that two things were alike which were not really alike at all. Thus, in a sense, metaphors involve two levels of indirection, similes involve one, while literal comparisons involve none. I also argued that not all indirect uses of language were metaphorical. In fact, Searle (1979) has proposed that the difference between an indirect speech act (of the nonmetaphorical variety) and a metaphor is that in the first case we mean both what we say *and* something different (i.e., one means to communicate one's dislike for drafts *as well as* a desire for the door to be closed), whereas in the case of metaphors, we mean only what is intended and not what is said (i.e., one does not mean, for example, that John is *really* a buffoon, but only that he is a buffoon *metaphorically speaking*). I think there is merit in this proposal, although I prefer to stick with my account in terms of the contextual anomaly associated with the nonfigurative interpretation.

Processing Mechanisms

Any view of figurative language that is based on the contextual anomaly of the literal meaning leads rather naturally to a stage model of the comprehension process. In such a model, the first main stage involves the recognition that some particular text element is incongruous or anomalous with respect to the surrounding context. The second main stage requires an appropriate reinterpretation of the text element to remove the apparent anomaly. Searle (1979) proposes just such an account for metaphor comprehension. This view, however, has received little empirical support. Studies by Clark and Lucy (1975) provided weak support for a model of this type as an account of the comprehension of certain indirect speech acts (indirect requests), but in later work, Clark (1979) abandoned it in favor of a model in which the literal meaning and the conveyed (or intended) meaning are "computed as parts of a single package."

More recent studies have not only failed to support a stage model but actually suggest that, in many cases, the nonliteral meaning of an expression may force itself upon readers, even when the literal interpretation is contextually more appropriate. For example, using a sentence priming paradigm, Gibbs (1983) found that for conventional indirect forms (e.g., *Can/can't you do X?* meaning "Please do/don't do X") subjects were able to determine that a succeeding target sentence was a meaningful English sentence significantly more quickly if it were related to the conventional (indirect) meaning of the prime than if it were related to the literal meaning of the prime. He concluded that people do not always interpret the literal meaning of indirect requests in order to arrive at the intended meaning. Perhaps, the most dramatic empirical evidence against a stage model of the comprehension of figurative language is that provided in a series of experiments by Glucksberg, Gildea, and Bookin (1982). They found that when subjects were asked to make true/false judgments about statements, like *Some jobs are jails*, the reaction times were significantly slower when (as in the example given) a metaphorical interpretation was available than in cases (e.g., *Some birds are eagles*) where there is no metaphorical potential. Since the task required only a literal interpretation, they argued that the metaphorical meaning must have interfered with the true/false judgments. A stage model could not possibly predict such a result because it could offer no explanation for why processing should continue beyond the literal meaning when the literal meaning is all that the task required.

Nevertheless, it might be that there are some cases in which the stage model provides an appropriate description of the comprehension process, even though it might not always do so. Ortony, Schallert, Reynolds, and Antos (1978) investigated the stage model's applicability to the comprehension of metaphors and idioms. In one experiment, they had subjects indicate that they had understood a target sentence after they had read a context that either induced a literal or a metaphorical interpretation of it. The amount of context preceding the target was also manipulated. Reaction times for understanding the sentences in these four conditions (long/short context, literal/metaphorical target) were recorded. The results showed that whereas targets following short contexts always took significantly longer to understand than those following long contexts, metaphorical interpretations only took significantly longer when they followed the semantically impoverished, short contexts. Ortony et al. (1978) concluded that the stage model might conceivably be applicable to the comprehension of metaphors in cases where the context provided inadequate semantic support for their comprehension. But the model, requiring as it does more time for the additional reinterpretation stage, was not supported in cases more like those normally encountered in which there is adequate semantic support for a metaphor, since in such cases metaphorical interpretations took no longer to reach than literal ones. In their second experiment, Ortony et al. (1978), using a similar procedure, found some evidence that idioms, such as *Let the cat out of the bag* are actually interpreted more quickly in their figurative sense than in their literal sense; again, a discouraging finding for those who would postulate that figurative language is normally understood by first rejecting the literal meaning on the basis of its contextual incongruity and then reinterpreting it figuratively.

Thus, it seems that the stage model does not constitute a viable general model of the comprehension of indirect uses of language, including metaphorical uses, even though there may be certain cases in which it does apply. The lack of general empirical support for it might, therefore, appear to constitute a challenge to the account of figurative language offered in the previous section. However, I think that the challenge is only apparent. Just as mathematical models of the behavior of projectiles are not invalidated by the fact that flying objects do not actually compute the equations that may perfectly describe their trajectories, so, too, a descriptive theory of figurative language is not invalidated by the fact that people do not normally engage in operations that correspond to such a description. What the descriptive theory provides is a way of distinguishing instances from noninstances. It need not, and in this case apparently does not, also provide an explanation of how people understand figurative language.

This may be a tenable philosophical escape from a potentially embarrassing conflict between theory and data, but it says little about how figurative language is understood. Perhaps a more fruitful way to view the comprehension issue is to adopt a more general model of language comprehension. Such a model could employ the notion of "accounting" for the input (a particular word, phrase, sentence, or even larger linguistic unit) in terms of the already active set of concepts that has resulted from understanding the preceding context (see Ortony, 1978; Rumelhart & Ortony, 1977; and Anderson's chapter in this volume). In general, it can then be argued, as it is by Rumelhart (1979), that figurative uses of language can be accommodated by this same processing model. It may be that the "fit" between the currently available concepts, or schemata, may not be quite as good as for literal uses of language, but comprehension will still occur if the fit exceeds some criterion that, presumably, every reader has for understanding something. A model of this kind is proposed in Ortony (1980).

This kind of account is compatible with the findings of Ortony et al. (1978), and it also leaves open the possibility that in some cases a reader may fail to understand a figurative use of language to his or her satisfaction and may be aware of that failure. The reader could then employ more conscious problem-solving procedures, of which the stage model might be an example. Certainly, most of us have experienced the need to consciously try to understand some text, or part of a text, in this way, as when, for example, we read certain figure-laden literary texts. However, the occasional employment of such "problem-solving" strategies is not restricted to the comprehension of figurative language. It can occur in texts of all types in which comprehension may require certain nonobvious inferences. Expository texts that are at slightly too high a level, given the reader's existing knowledge, provide one kind of example, complicated detective stories provide another.

It has been suggested, for example, by Cunningham (1976), that texts containing metaphors are more difficult to understand than parallel texts without them, even though both texts might have identical readability estimates. Cunningham concludes that "if a metaphorical passage can be considered more difficult than a non-metaphorical passage in ways which readability estimates do not measure, selections from children's literature may be generally more difficult than previously thought." This conclusion is not warranted by Cunningham's research, even though it might be true independently of it. The passages employed in Cunningham's experiment, which involved collecting cloze scores, may have yielded identical readability scores, but they were vastly different along a number of dimensions not specifically related to the presence or absence of metaphors per se. For example, a description, be it metaphorical or not, can be more or less appropriate to the situation described. By way of illustration, consider the following paragraph from Cunningham's nonmetaphorical passage: *She smiled, "This is a great picture, but tell me all about it, Bill."* In the parallel (*sic*) metaphor version, the same paragraph read: *Her face was a sun. "This is heaven's painting, but tell me all about it."* The trouble is that the metaphors seem forced and unnatural. The paragraph is indeed less comprehensible, but not, I think, because it contains metaphors, but because it is less coherent; the metaphors are not good ones; they seem awkward and inappropriate. Although I have not discussed what makes a figurative use of language a good figurative use, it is likely to be the case that stylistic and descriptive quality is going to be another variable that influences text comprehensibility quite independently of whether the text contains figurative language.

However, one aspect of the difference between texts with and without figurative language is highlighted by Cunningham's study. It appears that texts containing metaphors (if not other figurative uses) have less redundancy. Compare the phrase *she smiled* with the sentence, *Her face was a sun.* Regardless of the quality and naturalness of the expression, it seems reasonable to suppose that even if smiling could have been predicted from the context, her face being a *sun,* as opposed to something else, is much less predictable. If the redundancy of a text, or its analogue, the predictability of parts of it from preceding parts, is an important ingredient in the comprehensibility of a text, as it might well be, then it is quite possible that texts containing certain kinds of nonconventionalized figurative uses would be more difficult to understand, even if the figurative uses were stylistically superior.

Developmental Issues

The next question that needs to be addressed is whether or not there are limitations over and above general language-processing facility on the ability of children to understand figurative language, and if so, what is the nature of those limitations. This topic has received much more attention.

There are really two kinds of views on this question. One, associated with

Piagetian approaches to cognitive development, maintains that the comprehension of figurative language often involves certain cognitive prerequisites relating to such things as intersectional classification (classification of items based on sets of intersecting properties, e.g., see Cometa & Eson, 1978) or the ability to deal with proportions (e.g., see Billow, 1975). According to such views, genuine comprehension of, for example, metaphors, would not be expected to emerge until middle childhood or early adolescence. In fact, researchers who take this position have not normally generalized their claims to include all forms of figurative language but have restricted them, most typically, to the comprehension of metaphors.

The alternative view frequently starts from the common observation that the oral language even of preschool children seem to include an abundance of figurative language. This observation leads quickly to the belief that young children *can* understand figurative language (again, typically metaphors) together with a suspicion that any empirical evidence showing that they cannot is probably confounding the comprehension of metaphor with other, uncontrolled characteristics of the stimuli (e.g., see Gardner, 1974; Gentner, 1977; Winner, Engel, & Gardner, 1979).

A representative study of the first approach is that of Cometa and Eson (1978). They hypothesized that "the child's operationalization of intersection, which develops during the stage of concrete operations, serves as a necessary, logical precondition to the child's interpretation of metaphor" (p. 651). Cometa and Eson administered tests to children (Grades K, 1, 3, 4, and 8) on the basis of which children were assigned to one of four groups: preoperational, concrete operational (but not intersectional), intersectional, and formal operational. Children were then asked to paraphrase the meanings of words that required metaphorical interpretations in each of seven presented sentences (e.g., *What does it mean to say that the leaves "dance" in the sentence "When the wind blew, the leaves began to dance?"*). They were also asked to explain their paraphrases. Results showed that children in the preoperational group could not adequately paraphrase the items and that acceptable explanations of their responses were only obtainable from children if they were in the intersectional or formal operational group. Cometa and Eson concluded:

> The stages which occur in the development of metaphor comprehension (i.e., syncretism, paraphrase, and explanation) appear to reflect the gradual evolution and application of intersectional classification. Children's entry into the stage of concrete operations signals the onset of intersection and, as such, enables children to begin to paraphrase metaphors; children with access to a fully developed system of intersectional classes are not only able to paraphrase metaphors but can explain the reasoning inherent in metaphoric figures of speech. (p. 658)

The alternative view, that even kindergarten children can interpret figurative language (under suitable conditions), has been proposed by Malgady (1977) who presented children (Grades K, 3, and 6) with a list of 11 simple similes, such as *"The tree is like a friend,"* and *"The pond is like a mirror."* Children were asked to provide as many meanings for each sentence as they could (the interpretation task) and then to select which of the two sentences in all possible pairings did the better job of "saying what one thing is by describing it as if it were something else" (the preference, or appreciation, task). Of particular interest in the present context was the finding that the kindergarten children provided a high level of simile interpretations that were acceptable to adults (about 67% of their responses being judged adequate compared with about 71% in Grade 3 and about 83% in Grade 6), even though they tended to give only one characterization for each simile.

Since the research described both by Cometa and Eson (1978) and by Malgady (1977) carefully avoids making any generalizations about the relationship between metaphor comprehension and age, it may be worth spelling out the essential similarities and dissimilarities between the two studies. Cometa and Eson claimed that a precondition for metaphor comprehension was the ability to construct new classes from the intersection of old ones, an ability which they claim (following Inhelder & Piaget, 1964) does not reach completion until the later phases of the stage of concrete operations (say, ages 9 to 11). If such intersectional classification skills were truly a necessary condition for the comprehension of metaphors, one would not have expected Malgady's youngest two groups (kindergarten and third grade) to have shown evidence of comprehension; but they did. Assuming (see Wadsworth, 1971) that the preoperational period is roughly from ages 2 to 7, the concrete operational period is roughly from ages 7 to 11, and the stage of formal operations is roughly from ages 11 to 15, it is strange to find Malgady assuming that "most of the preadolescent children in [his] study were in the concrete operational stage" (p. 1738). If one accepts that assumption as valid, then the results of the two studies appear to be compatible since both seemed to demonstrate that children in the preoperational stage were not able to understand figurative uses. However, that would require the concrete operational stage to span the years from about age 5 to age 11 and claims pertaining to the dependence on reaching that stage would become correspondingly less interesting.

It is important to notice that both studies suffer from their reliance on children "giving the meaning of" (or paraphrasing) words or sentences. The problem with this approach is that, in general, whereas success can certainly be taken as an indication of comprehension, failure cannot be taken as a guarantee of lack of understanding. Suppose someone describes the voice of an opera singer as being *thin*. It would be absurd to establish an ability to paraphrase the word *thin* in that context as a criterion for understanding it. Paraphrasing it may be impossible for anybody but an expert in voice, and it is certainly a lot more difficult to do than merely understanding it. Similarly, but even more so, measures of children's cognitive abilities based on their ability to explain their understandings are likely to be unreliable and misleading.

Ortony et al. (1978), in reviewing the developmental literature on the comprehension of metaphorical language, concluded that most developmental studies suffer from various common problems, of which the nature of the task was one. Others included the presentation of stimuli in the absence of context, a lack of control over the children's background knowledge, and the failure to employ a coherent definition of metaphorical language. Ortony et al. argued that the general incompatibility between claims suggesting that metaphor comprehension does not occur until late childhood (e.g., Asch & Nerlove, 1960; Billow, 1975; Cometa & Eson, 1978; Winner, Rosenstiel, & Gardner, 1976) and claims suggesting early metaphoric competence (e.g., Billow, 1981; Carlson & Anisfeld, 1969; Chukovsky, 1968; Gardner, 1974; Gardner, Winner, Bechhofer, & Wolf, 1978; Gentner, 1977; Winner, McCarthy, & Gardner, 1980) is largely explicable in terms of these shortcomings. When these shortcomings are avoided, the picture looks rather different.

Much of our own research has concentrated on investigating the young child's ability to understand metaphorical language using techniques designed to circumvent the difficulties associated with earlier studies. For example, Reynolds and Ortony (1980) had children (Grades 2 to 6) read a series of short, paragraph-length stories. These stories provided a context for the interpretation of a succeeding sentence. After each story, children were asked to select one of four presented sentences on the basis of which one best fitted the story. Sometimes the intended sentence (the target) was a literal continuation, sometimes it was a metaphor, and sometimes a (corresponding) simile. Results showed that mean performance on similes was above chance level for all grades, while the same items transformed into metaphors did not result in above-chance performance until the fifth grade. Children's ability to perform the task and understand the stories was confirmed by their success at all grade levels with the literal items. In a second experiment slight changes were made to the materials. All ambiguous-referring expressions were replaced with explicit references to the intended referent. Thus, for example, if in Experiment 1 the target had been *The worn out shoe was thrown onto the trash* (in the metaphor condition) and *It was like a worn out shoe thrown onto the trash* (in the simile condition)— both alluding in the story to a no-longer-cared-for racehorse called Jack Flash— now, those same targets would read, *Jack Flash was a worn out shoe thrown onto the trash* and *Jack Flash was like a worn out shoe thrown onto the trash* respectively. These changes, although not affecting children's overall better performance on similes over metaphors, resulted in a higher level of performance on both, with children at all grade levels now performing better than chance on both similes and metaphors. Interpreted uncritically, the first experiment might lead one to conclude that children cannot understand metaphors until about age 10, much as Cometa and Eson (1978) concluded, whereas they can understand similes by age 7, which is consistent with Malgady (1977). The second experiment, however, shows that such a conclusion is unwarranted since it revealed a high level of performance, even on metaphors, by age 7. The difference between the materials in the two experiments had to do with variables not normally controlled in empirical studies of children's ability to deal with metaphorical uses of language. Together what they show is that variables having nothing specifically to do with figurative language may be responsible for apparent differences in performance.

It seems reasonable to conclude, therefore, that several factors can contribute to making metaphorical uses of language difficult for young children to understand. These include not only the elements of indirection, but also any additional general language-processing factors that are involved in the specific occurrence. Such factors (e.g., vague referring expressions) are potential sources of comprehension difficulty, whether they occur in the context of literal or metaphorical uses of language. If this is right, then metaphors would be more difficult for children to understand than similes because they involve an additional level of indirection. In other words, the problem that the child faces has to do with pragmatic aspects of language comprehension rather than some fundamental cognitive constraints pertaining to metaphors as such (see also Winner et al., 1979). It would not be unreasonable to suppose that this is true for the comprehension of figurative uses of language in general. Indeed, Honeck, Sowry, and Voegtle (1978) report a study which suggests that 7-year-olds are, in principle, able to understand proverbs.

The Reynolds and Ortony (1980) results are reinforced by the findings of a more recent study involving younger (preschool through third grade) children (Vosniadou, Ortony, Reynolds & Wilson, in press). The experiments were similar in spirit to those reported in Reynolds and Ortony (1980), however, they involved a methodological improvement, the enactment paradigm, that made it possible to examine the performance of preschool children while imposing minimal extraneous demands. In the enactment paradigm, the child need not rely only on his or her memory for the context-setting story, nor is the child's interpretation of the target sentence restricted to one of a set of predetermined choices. Rather, the child is read the story while in the presence of a "toy world" which includes some of the buildings that are referred to in the story and which includes toy figures that represent the "characters" in the story. As the story is read to the child, he or she acts it out with the toys, finally using the toys to act out the target sentence (be it literal or metaphorical). Comprehension is assessed in terms of the number of correct enactments of targets.

The experiments manipulated three variables thought to influence the difficulty of metaphor comprehension. One of these variables was patently a metaphor-independent variable having to do with the predictability of the intended meaning of the target from the preceding (story) context. In some trials, the event described by the target (either literally or metaphorically) was relatively more predictable than in others. The other variables had to do with the linguistic form (or complexity) of the metaphorical targets themselves. One of these was, as in Reynolds and Ortony (1980), the simile versus metaphor manipulation. The other was whether or not the metaphorical target employed only nouns used metaphorically (as opposed to nouns and the verb). The results showed that all three variables had a marked effect on the ease of comprehension. Furthermore, the variables appeared to contribute to difficulty cumulatively, especially for the preschoolers. Thus, when all three variables were set at the "easy" level (i.e., relatively predictable similes with literal verbs), preschoolers attained better than 75% correct responses. When any one of the three variables was set at the "difficult" level, performance, while still high, dropped to about 60% correct. When all three were set at the "difficult" level, performance reduced to about 5% correct. The conclusion was that, given an appropriate method of measuring comprehension, even four-year-old children show evidence of understanding metaphorical uses of language.

To conclude this section, then, I want to propose that the comprehension of figurative language by adults is often a fairly automatic process that functions in much the same way as the comprehension of literal uses of language. However, there are certainly many cases in which, for various reasons, the ordinary processes fail to yield a satisfactory interpretation of the text. For example, the connection between what is said and what was or could have been intended may be obscure. In such cases, additional inferential processes will be required, and these are more likely to require sensitivity to pragmatic factors, such as knowledge about the communicative functions, that can be served by various rhetorical devices, like indirection. Young children may well lack this sensitivity, so that if they cannot understand a figurative use of language more or less immediately, their ability to "figure it out" is likely not to be well developed. Nevertheless, if one thinks of figurative uses of language as being one of the most common ways in which we stretch language to suit our communicative purposes, it is worth remembering that the real masters at that game are young children.

SOME IMPLICATIONS FOR RESEARCH

From our discussion so far, it is tempting to conclude that figurative (or at least, metaphorical) uses of language do not require any special cognitive mechanisms. This conclusion is suggested both by the fact that there is little evidence that a stage model of the comprehension of indirect uses of language is generally applicable (suggesting that some sort of "direct" comprehension model may be more appropriate) and from the fact that what seems to effect the difficulty of understanding metaphorical language for very young children is the degree to which the particular linguistic usage imposes sources of general linguistic difficulty. This does not mean, of course, that there are no theoretical questions that remain to be investigated. I suspect we have only scratched the surface in uncovering variables that influence metaphor difficulty. Furthermore, there remains much work to be done in exploring the relationship between metaphor and similarity, especially when the metaphors take on different structures (e.g., genitive metaphors). This quickly leads to the territory of the relation between metaphor, similarity, and analogy, an area which has received relatively little attention (but see Gentner, 1983; Miller, 1979; Vosniadou & Ortony, in press). And if there has been little empirical research investigating the connection between metaphor and analogy, there has been even less on other forms of figurative devices, although a first attempt at an empirical examination of irony can be found in Jorgensen, Miller, and Sperber (in press).

Thus, there remains much basic research to be done. Nevertheless, I think that we have made enough progress to be able to shift the focus of basic research from questions about comprehension mechanisms to rather more detailed issues. I also think that the most urgent need now is for more applied research, especially research having to do with instructional issues. Our conclusion that metaphor comprehension may not involve any special cognitive processes beyond those ordinarily involved in language comprehension would seem to justify a rather optimistic view of young children's abilities to handle figurative uses of language. I have suggested that, whereas figurative language can certainly be a source of comprehension problems, these problems are frequently due to factors unrelated to the fact that some particular text segment is figurative. These factors include various syntactic variables as well as, of course, constraints resulting from children's relatively limited, and perhaps idiosyncratic, knowledge of the world. If I am right that indirection is the most important ingredient of figurative language, then it would follow that a sensitivity to indirection would be a prerequisite for figurative awareness. However, it seems that some figurative language might even be understood in the absence of such an awareness.

This kind of perspective on the problem has some quite different implications from a perspective which supposes there to be the kind of high-level cognitive constraints on the comprehension of figurative language that are suggested by, for example, the Piagetian approaches. For one thing, it suggests that the judicious introduction of figurative language to 5- and 6-year-olds will not necessarily pose insurmountable comprehension problems for them. This is not to say, of course, that instruction pertaining to the nature of figurative language at such early ages is advisable. Nevertheless, it would be worth comparing traditional instructional techniques with those suggested by the kind of view I have been proposing in order to determine which is more effective.

Clearly, the "judicious" introduction of figurative language would involve paying careful attention to the other variables. So, for example, even though one might know that a first-grade child knew the meanings of *king, Brazil, jungle, coffee,* and *lion* (or knew to what the words referred), one might expect such a child to understand the metaphor, *The lion is the king of the jungle,* while one would not expect such a child to understand the statement, *Coffee is king in Brazil.* Understanding the latter requires all kinds of extratextual knowledge about trade and commerce and the economic importance of products for countries that no first-grade child could reasonably be expected to possess. If comprehension should fail in such a case, it would not be due to the metaphorical nature of the statement, for otherwise one would not expect success with the king-of-the-jungle metaphor. One would expect quite comparable results if, in both cases, the words "the king (of)" were replaced by "important (in)."

It would not be unreasonable at this juncture to wonder why one should bother to introduce figurative uses of language to young children. There are at least two answers to this. First, figurative language is a powerful way of relating old knowledge to new (e.g., see Pearson, Raphael, TePaske & Hyser, 1981; Petrie, 1979; Vosniadou & Ortony, in press). Second, figurative language increases the expressive power of the available linguistic resources by permitting the expression of what might otherwise be difficult or impossible to express. How else can the opera singer's voice be described, if not by the metaphorical use of some word like *thin?* And, if ships don't plow the seas, what do they do literally? I have proposed arguments for the utility, at least of metaphors and similes, in Ortony (1975). More research is needed to determine when and under what conditions figurative language, especially metaphorical and analogical uses, enhance the acquisition of new knowledge.

The introduction of figurative uses of language probably should not be postponed until the middle grades as is the current practice. While figurative language should not be forced into the linguistic experiences of young children regardless of their appropriateness, their introduction in contexts where they are stylistically and descriptively appropriate is likely to be valuable. In fact, it would be interesting to investigate the extent to which young children are exposed to figurative language in ordinary conversational settings. Is the 4-year-old child, in fact, routinely exposed to figurative language which he or she generally understands?

In conclusion, it seems to me that our state of knowledge about at least the comprehension of metaphorical uses of language is such that we should start to move away from investigations of comprehension mechanisms toward more instructionally oriented research. In particular, I think that serious attention should be devoted to investigating the extent to which the child's early potential to understand metaphorical uses of language can be used to facilitate the cognitive exploitation of old information in new domains.

REFERENCES

Asch, S., & Nerlove, H.   The development of double function terms in children: An exploration study. In B. Kaplan & S. Wapner (Eds.), *Perspectives in psychological theory.* New York: International University Press, 1960.

Austin, J. L.   *How to Do Things with Words.* Oxford, Eng.: Oxford University Press, 1962.

Billow, R. M.   A cognitive developmental study of metaphor comprehension. *Developmental Psychology,* 1975, *11,* 415–423.

Billow, R. M.   Metaphor: A review of the psychological literature. *Psychological Bulletin,* 1977 *84,* 81–92.

Billow, R. M.   Observing spontaneous metaphor in children. *Journal of Experimental Child Psychology,* 1981, *31,* 430–445.

Carlson, P., & Anisfeld, M.   Some observations on the linguistic competence of a two-year-old child. *Child Development,* 1969, *40,* 565–575.

Chukovsky, K.   *From two to five.* Berkeley: University of California Press, 1968.

Clark, H. H., & Lucy, P.   Understanding what is meant from what is said: A study in conversationally conveyed requests. *Journal of Verbal Learning and Verbal Behavior,* 1975, *14,* 56–72.

Clark, H. W.   Responding to indirect speech acts. *Cognitive Psychology,* 1979, *11,* 430–477.

Cole, P. (Ed.).   *Syntax and semantics,* Vol. 9, *Pragmatics.* New York: Academic Press, 1978.

Cometa, M. S., & Eson, M. E.   Logical operations and metaphor interpretation: A Piagetian model. *Child Development,* 1978, *49,* 649–659.

Cunningham, J. W.   Metaphor and reading comprehension. *Journal of Reading Behavior,* 1976, *8,* 363–368.

Gardner, H.   Metaphors and modalities: How children project polar adjectives onto diverse domains. *Child Development,* 1974, *45,* 84–91.

Gardner, H., Winner, E., Bechhofer, R., & Wolf, D.   The development of figurative language. In K. Nelson (Ed.), *Children's language.* New York: Gardner Press, 1978.

Gentner, D.   Children's performance on a spatial analogies task. *Child Development,* 1977, *48,* 1034–1039.

Gentner, D.   Structure-mapping: A theoretical framework for analogy. *Cognitive Science,* 1983, *7,* 155–170.

Gibbs, R. W.   Do people always process the literal meanings of indirect requests? *Journal of Experimental Psychology: Learning, Memory, and Cognition,* 1983, *9,* 524–533.

Glucksberg, S., Gildea, P. G., & Bookin, H. B.   On understanding nonliteral speech: Can people ignore metaphors? *Journal of Verbal Learning and Verbal Behavior,* 1982, *21,* 85–98.

Grice, H. P.   Logic and conversation. In P. Cole & J. L. Morgan (Eds.), *Syntax and seman-tics*, Vol. 3, *Speech acts.* New York: Academic Press, 1975.

Honeck, R. P., & Hoffman, R. R. (Eds.).   *Cognition and figurative language.* Hillsdale, N.J.: Erlbaum, 1980.

Honeck, R. P., Sowry, B. M., & Voegtle, K.   Proverbial understanding in a pictorial context. *Child Development*, 1978, *49*, 327–331.

Inhelder, B., & Piaget, J.   *The early growth of logic in the child.* New York: W. W. Norton, 1964.

Johnson, M. (Ed.).   *Philosophical perspectives on metaphor,* Minneapolis: Minnesota University Press, 1981.

Jorgensen, J., Miller, G. A., & Sperber, D.   A test of the mention theory of irony. *Journal of Experimental Psychology: General,* in press.

Lakoff, G., & Johnson, M.   *Metaphors we live by.* Chicago: University of Chicago Press, 1980.

Malgady, R. G.   Children's interpretation and appreciation of similes. *Child Development,* 1977, *48*, 1734–1738.

Miall, D. S. (Ed.).   *Metaphor: Problems and perspectives.* Atlantic Highlands, N.J.: Humanities Press, 1982.

Miller, G. A.   Images and models, similes and metaphors. In A. Ortony (Ed.), *Metaphor and thought.* New York: Cambridge University Press, 1979.

O'Hare, P. (Ed.).   *Psychology and the arts.* Atlantic Highlands, N.J.: Humanities Press, 1981.

Ortony, A.   Why metaphors are necessary and not just nice. *Educational Theory,* 1975, *25*, 45–53.

Ortony, A.   Beyond literal similarity. *Psychological Review,* 1979, *86*, 161–180. (a)

Ortony, A. (Ed.).   *Metaphor and thought.* New York: Cambridge University Press, 1979. (b)

Ortony, A.   Metaphor. In R. J. Spiro, B. C. Bruce, & W. F. Brewer (Eds.), *Theoretical issues in reading comprehension.* Hillsdale, N.J.: Erlbaum, 1980.

Ortony, A.   Understanding metaphors. In D. O'Hare (Ed.) *Psychology and the arts.* Atlantic Highlands, N.J.: Humanities Press, 1981.

Ortony, A., Reynolds, R. E., & Arter, J. A.   Metaphor: Theoretical and empirical research. *Psychological Bulletin,* 1978, *85*, 919–943.

Ortony, A., Schallert, D. L., Reynolds, R. E., & Antos, S. J.   Interpreting metaphors and idioms: Some effects of context on comprehension. *Journal of Verbal Learning and Verbal Behavior,* 1978, *17*, 465–477.

Ortony, A., Vondruska, R., Foss, M. A., & Jones, L. E.   *Salience, similes, and the asymmetry of similarity.* Unpublished manuscript, Center for the Study of Reading, University of Illinois, Urbana, 1983.

Pearson, P. D., Raphael, T., TePaske, N., & Hyser, C.   The function of metaphor in children's recall of expository passages. *Journal of Reading Behavior,* 1981, *13*, 249–261.

Petrie, H. G.   Metaphor and learning. In A. Ortony (Ed.), *Metaphor and thought.* New York: Cambridge University Press, 1979.

Reynolds, R. E., & Ortony, A.   Some issues in the measurement of children's comprehension of metaphorical language. *Child Development,* 1980, *51*, 1110–1119.

Rumelhart, D. E.   Some problems with the notion of literal meanings. In A. Ortony (Ed.), *Metaphor and thought.* New York: Cambridge University Press, 1979.

Rumelhart, D. E., & Ortony, A.   The representation of knowledge in memory. In R. C. Anderson, R. J. Spiro, & W. E. Montague (Eds.), *Schooling and the acquisition of knowledge.* Hillsdale, N.J.: Erlbaum, 1977.

Sacks, S. (Ed.).   *On metaphor.* Chicago: University of Chicago Press, 1978.

Searle, J. R.   *Speech acts.* Cambridge, Eng.: Cambridge University Press, 1969.

Searle, J. R.   Indirect speech acts. In P. Cole & J. L. Morgan (Eds.), *Syntax and semantics,* Vol. 3, *Speech acts.* New York: Academic Press, 1975.

Searle, J. R.   Metaphor. In A. Ortony (Ed.), *Metaphor and thought.* New York: Cambridge University Press, 1979.

Stalnaker, R. C.   Pragmatics. In D. Davidson & G. Harmon (Eds.), *Semantics of natural language.* Dordrecht, The Netherlands: Reidel, 1972.

Vosniadou, S., & Ortony, A.   The influence of analogy in children's acquisition of new information from text. In J. Niles (Ed.), *Searches for meaning in reading/language processing and instruction* (31st yearbook of the National Reading Conference), in press.

Vosniadous, S., Ortony, A., Reynolds, R. E., & Wilson, P. T.   Sources of difficulty in children's understanding of metaphorical language. *Child Development,* in press.

Wadsworth, B. J.   *Piaget's theory of cognitive development.* New York: McKay, 1971.

Wilensky, R.   Story grammars versus story points. *The Behavioral and Brain Sciences,* in press.

Winner, E., Engel, M., & Gardner, H.   *Misunderstanding metaphor: What's the problem?* Paper presented at the biennial meeting of the Society for Research in Child Development, San Francisco, March 1979.

Winner, E., McCarthy, M., & Gardner, H.   The ontogenesis of metaphor. In R. T. Honeck & R. R. Hoffman (Eds.), *Cognition and figurative language.* Hillsdale, N.J.: Erlbaum, 1980.

Winner, E., Rosenstiel, A. K., & Gardner, H.   The development of metaphoric understanding. *Developmental Psychology,* 1976, *12,* 289–297.

16 INDIVIDUAL DIFFERENCES AND UNDERLYING COGNITIVE PROCESSES IN READING

Rand J. Spiro and Ann Myers

The subject of individual differences has numerous applications in the context of reading and learning to read. Individuals differ in their reading ability, both with respect to decoding and in *understanding* what may have been accurately decoded. Differences in reading performance may be due to inequalities of general and fundamental mental abilities, of one or many of the component skills specific to reading, of environmental influences, of personality, of motivation, and of varying combinations of these and many other factors. Furthermore, individuals of comparable *ability* may differ in their *style* of reading, again for many possible reasons.

We are making a case for a complex rather than a simple phenomenon. And we have yet to mention what a broad and irregularly overlapping family of activities is subsumed by the rubric "reading." Reading can be shown to involve every conceivable activity of the mind, from visual perception to verbal memory to logical reasoning to highly heuristic and judgmental "seat of the pants" problem solving. A chapter on individual differences in a book on reading has an interesting relationship to the rest of the volume: every psychological component of reading, every aspect of a theory of reading, *any* way you can divide up the reading pie, is a possible source of differences among individuals (in short, this whole volume is, in a sense, about individual differences in reading).

So, if the terms "individual differences" and "reading" can mean so many different things, all of them of some interest, how should a paper such as this one be written? Obviously, with a good deal of selectivity. We have chosen to emphasize the *cognitive processes* involved in understanding written text. Such central noncognitive issues as effects of socioeconomic status, motivation, and teacher and classroom variables are dealt with elsewhere (see the chapters by Asher & Wigfield and by Bloome & Greene, this volume).

The authors wish gratefully to acknowledge helpful discussions on the topic of this paper with Joan Boggs, Richard Brummer, Tsivia Cohen, Judy DeLoache, Peter Freebody, William Tirre, and Terence Turner. We owe a special note of appreciation to David Pearson and Michael Kamil for numerous helpful suggestions on an earlier draft. This work was supported in part by Contract No. US–NIE–C–400–07716 from the National Institute of Education.

This chapter marks a fairly radical departure from the preceding ones in this section on basic processes in reading. Unlike its companions, it is not a comprehensive review of basic research (although considerable research is reviewed). Instead, we have adopted a more forward-looking orientation, focusing on individual difference directions to which current theories of reading point. There are several reasons for this departure, all hinging on recent advances in the science of differential psychology.

First, the entire field of individual differences has recently undergone a radical transformation. Where once there were "two disciplines of scientific psychology" (Cronbach, 1957), the experimental and correlational traditions have been increasingly merged. The study of individual differences in mental tasks is no longer divorced from experimentally validated cognitive processing theories for the task domains where individual differences are observed. Second, the development of cognitive models of the structures and processes involved in reading, upon which systematic individual difference research must partly depend, is a fairly recent phenomenon (see the chapter by Samuels and Kamil, this volume). Finally, the cognitive theories that have emerged reinforce old beliefs about the high degree of complexity of the reading process, a complexity that further complicates the search for individual differences.

Our forward-looking orientation should not be interpreted as an implied criticism of the nearly century-old tradition of individual difference research in reading. Indeed, our view in many ways hearkens back to an earlier period in reading research. We prefer to conclude that any problems in earlier individual differences research were an unavoidable result of subsuming trends in psychological research generally. Given so many recent changes in the rules of the game that guide individual difference inquiry (i.e., methodological advances, the movement toward integration with experimental approaches and cognitive modeling, and the rapid growth of processing models of reading), it is not surprising that progress has been slow. Individual difference research now has a built-in lag factor behind the advance of cognitive theories. When those theories are as complex as reading theories must be, the lag is greater still. In summary, it has only recently been possible to begin to develop an adequate framework for studying individual differences in reading. Accordingly, we devote most of our efforts to reflecting upon state-of-the-art considerations that will shape the direction of future developments.

Our plan for the chapter is as follows: First, we sketch a brief history of efforts at studying individual differences in reading. Second, we discuss some conceptual and methodological guidelines for conducting and evaluating individual differences research. Third, we present a brief theoretical account of the framework in which we wish to conceptualize individual differences. Fourth, we discuss individual difference variables consistent with that framework. Finally, we conclude with the observation that to study individual differences in reading is to study thinking in all its richness and complexity.

THE ROOTS OF INDIVIDUAL DIFFERENCES RESEARCH IN READING

Attempts to identify and explain differences between individuals have a long history (see Tyler, 1978). The earliest approaches sought to classify individuals into types according to their physical, physiological, or "temperamental" characteristics. At the turn of the century, the mental-testing movement began; instruments were developed that attempted to assess mental abilities, interests, and attitudes. Later, the advent of powerful new statistical techniques enabled the study of correlational patterns involving large numbers of traits and the identification of groups of individuals who shared patterns of trait combination. Another recent strand of individual difference research has employed longitudinal studies of individual development or detailed case studies of individuals. Most recently, advances in the experimental psychology of information processing have permitted the coordinated study of highly specific aspects of mental functioning and individual characteristics.

All of these methods have figured to some degree in the study of individual differences in reading. Although the various research strands all share the common goal of discovering characteristics of successful and problem readers, six types of approaches may be distinguished by the varying means they employ to attain that goal. The first derived from Binet's early attempt to build an intelligence test to predict school learning. Binet's early attempts were successful; intelligence tests did (and still do) predict learning in school settings quite well. The belief that intelligence tests measured learning spilled over quite directly into reading research in the 1920s and 1930s that related intelligence test performance to a specific kind of learning: learning to read. A good example is the debate on the issue of whether (sometimes *how*) one could determine the appropriate mental age to begin reading or phonics instruction (Gates, 1937; Gates & Russell, 1929; Morphett & Washburne, 1931).

This concern for predicting probable success by using intelligence tests led fairly soon to the quest for reading-specific abilities that might provide even stronger predictors of future reading success. Gates and his colleagues (Gates & Bond, 1936; Gates, Bond, & Russell, 1939) conducted a series of studies trying to determine "readiness" prerequisites to reading, as did Durrell and his colleagues (see Durrell & Murphy, 1953). A logical next step in this line of inquiry was to use the results of tests given to assess allegedly prerequisite behaviors as a blueprint for instruction prior to teaching children to read. Research along these lines was pursued with varying degrees of success (none of it too successful) by deHirsch (deHirsch, Jansky, & Langford, 1966) and Durrell and Murphy (1953).

A second line of individual difference research in reading can be thought of as an operationalization of the oft-heard homily, "There is no one best way to teach reading; you can only find the best way to teach reading for *an individual child.*" In research circles, this homily gets translated into the search for aptitude by treatment interactions, the basic premise being that students with varying degrees of some aptitude (say, intelligence or certain reading-readiness factors) will benefit differentially from different instructional approaches. Begun as far back as the 1920s (see Chall, 1967, for a summary), this work reached its apex in the 1960s in the first-grade studies of Bond and Dykstra (1967) and in the seminal work of Robinson (1972). Besides intelligence and traditional readiness factors, aptitude measures have included language proficiency, auditory versus visual modality preference, reading achievement, and even such obviously group-membership factors as race and social class. Unfortunately, treatments have usually been grossly defined as either code emphasis or meaning emphasis (and they often contained instructional activities that were highly similar); hence, the inquiry has not often proven fruitful.

The third research strand involves a search for correlates of *overall* reading skill. The work of Davis (1944) was one of the earliest examples of this approach. He gave high school students a battery of reading-comprehension subskill tests and, armed with the then novel statistical technique of factor analysis, tried to determine the number of distinctive factors involved in reading comprehension. The most ambitious research program of this kind is the work of Holmes and his successor, Singer. Dubbed the substrata-factor theory of reading (see an entire collection of articles about this theory in Singer & Ruddell, 1976), Holmes and Singer tried to isolate, from among a set of 80 candidate variables, the most significant causal factors accounting for reading success. This work remains as a landmark effort to discover underlying causal factors within the then-prevailing psychometric tradition of reading research (see the Samuels and Kamil chapter, this volume).

In a fourth line of research, good and poor readers are compared on a single hypothesized component of reading proficiency (e.g., syntactic competence, contextual facilitation of word recognition, etc.). This work has been extensively reviewed (e.g., Golinkoff, 1975–1976); an excellent methodological critique is provided by Kleiman (1982). A multitude of general intellectual and specifically reading-related factors that distinguish good from poor readers have been identified. Ideally, when such performance differences are found, a conclusion about the causes of reading difficulty and success would be drawn. However, great care must be taken in inferring causation from correlational data. This type of research may best be viewed as a prerequisite step to an experiment in which direct instruction might be provided to improve poor readers' ability on the correlate to see whether or not improvement in general reading performance occurs (see Fleisher, Jenkins, & Pany, 1978). We must be able to distinguish between factors which cause reading ability and those which are mere symptoms of it.

A fifth line of inquiry involves differential diagnosis based on the examination of patterns of reading errors or miscues within the context of psycholinguistic theories. This approach is represented by the work of Goodman and his colleagues (e.g., Goodman 1969, 1975; Goodman & Burke, 1972; K. Goodman & Gollasch, 1980; for a complete review, see Allington's chapter, this volume). An intriguing aspect of the work of Goodman and his colleagues is the discovery that it is not so much the sheer quantity of miscues as it is the quality of miscues that is symptomatic of different levels of comprehension (e.g., the greater the incidence of semantically congruent miscues, the higher the overall level of comprehension). Others have emphasized differential error patterns of students of different ability or developmental levels (e.g., Weber, 1968) or different "stages" of error patterns along the path to fluent reading (e.g., Biemiller, 1970).

The sixth and most recent approach to individual differences in reading is similar to those that preceded it, with the exception that the selection of reading components and correlates to be studied is more closely linked to finely specified and experimentally validated cognitive information processing models. An example of this approach is Calfee's adaptation of Sternberg's (1969) independent cognitive process model for analyzing individual differences in early reading development (see the chapter by Calfee & Piontkowski, this volume). The bulk of our chapter will address individual differences from the cognitive processes perspective, employing current schema-theoretic models of reading as a point of departure. First, however, we discuss some methodological criteria pertinent to the investigation of individual differences in reading.

THE METHODOLOGICAL AND CONCEPTUAL FOUNDATIONS OF INDIVIDUAL DIFFERENCES INQUIRY

The careful scientific investigation of individual differences is a methodologically demanding enterprise. Here we will do no more than highlight some procedural considerations, stressing issues related to the initial conceptualization and ultimate interpretation of individual difference studies. The reader who wants a full, technical treatment of methodological issues might begin by consulting Cronbach and Snow (1977) or Kleiman (1982). Let it suffice to say that the pitfalls for the unwary may be quite devastating. A sobering example is the critique by Calfee, Arnold, and Drum (1976) of an oft-cited study by Cromer (1970). What had appeared to be some impressive and important individual difference findings turned out to be mere artifacts of subject classification processes and statistical regression to the mean.

Causal Inferences

While researchers would like to conclude that an observed difference in performance between good and poor readers on a cognitive component of reading indicates that problems with that component are causing the difference in reading ability, such conclusions are often unwarranted. There are a number of other reasons such results could be observed (Kleiman, 1982). The component in question could be a *symptom* rather than a cause of reading difficulty. For example, even if good and poor readers differ systematically in their eye-movement patterns, the way they move their eyes might not be responsible for their difference in reading ability; if not, training poor readers to move their eyes in a fashion similar to that of better readers probably would not lead to improvements in reading. In general, the old dictum that correlation does not imply causation needs to be heeded—many things are correlated with reading ability, and it is always possible that a component of reading that distinguishes between good and poor readers is merely correlated with reading ability without either causing the reading problem or even being caused by it. If some aspect of cognitive processing is suspected of being a cause of reading difficulty, the best way to demonstrate that hypothesis is to show that *training* randomly selected students on that process leads to an alleviation of reading difficulty that is not observed for comparable students who are not selected for training. In addition, in situations where it is difficult to use ideal experimental designs, statistical techniques are available that allow for some causative conclusions (cf. Kenny, 1979).

Reliability and Generalizability

Individual difference research is notorious for failures to replicate, especially when there are changes from one study to another, however subtle they may first appear. Part of the reason is statistical (see Cronbach & Snow, 1977). Part of the reason is the instability of many individual difference tendencies: people process information differently, depending on variations in the kinds of purposes for reading, in the relative demandingness of reading tasks, in the type of text being read and its structural characteristics, and in the relative familiarity of the material, among other things.

However, when one considers the many ways in which one reading situation can differ from others, it begins to make less sense to talk about "instability" and more sense to shift attention to the nature of changes in reading situations that produce what appears to be intra-individual inconsistency in processing style. What might appear to be a failure to replicate (or generalize) may, in fact, be a case where alterations in the reading environment induced the changes in performance. In such a case, replication (or generalization) would not have been expected if the complete reading situation had been appropriately *classified*, both as to the type of reading purpose involved and the cognitive processes required in that context. Before concluding that some individual difference measure produces unreliable data on the same person or that some set of findings do not replicate or generalize as well as they should (including generalizations from laboratory to naturalistic and instructional settings), researchers should demonstrate that the apparent failure to replicate is not due to theoretically significant variability across situations in characteristics of texts, tasks, criterial tests, or the individuals being studied (cf. Brown, Jenkins, Bransford, Ferrara, & Campione, 1983; Jenkins, 1979).

Ecological Validity

This last observation underscores the importance of examining separate aspects of the reading process in contexts sufficiently like those in which the complete activity occurs so that meaningful generalizations will be possible. For too long in experimental psychology, tasks were stripped down and isolated in order to study them scientifically. However, all the precisely controlled studies of memory for nonsense syllables that can be imagined will not lead people to process more natural verbal materials in a like fashion. The point is that the goal of precision associated with the task-analytic cognitive correlates and components approaches to individual differences in reading (discussed in the section after next) must never be achieved at the expense of rendering the results of that research inapplicable to real, naturally occurring reading situations in which the conceptually separable aspects of cognitive processing must function together as part of an integrated system.

Specifying Models of Reading Failure

Kleiman (1982), following Appleby (1971), points out that appropriate interpretation of studies comparing performance of good and bad readers on a single aspect of reading hypothesized to be related to proficiency requires consideration at a more global level of the way reading disabilities are produced. For example, a single cognitive component may be so central that it is responsible for most of the variability in ability across readers. Or problems with a single cognitive component could always be the main source of reading disability, but which single component is responsible may be different across individuals. Or there may be various cognitive components contributing to reading disability, each weighted for its contributions to an individual's disability along the lines of a multiple regression model (which would permit many combinations of weighted component contributions across the regression models of different individuals). Or it may be the case that sources of reading disability are discoverable only in the way components are combined rather than by considering the components singly. Indications that more complex models are required may be found in recent methodologically sophisticated studies that have shown a high degree of interdependence among reading components (e.g., Fredericksen, 1982; Jackson & McClelland, 1979). Complexity will be a theme of this chapter.

Analysis of the Cognitive Components of Reading Tasks

One of the most important theoretical developments in the history of individual difference research has been the employment of increasingly more sophisticated analyses of the cognitive processes involved in all sorts of mental activities, including the many facets of reading. This development has seen an integration of the "two disciplines of scientific psychology" (Cronbach, 1957): (1) the experimental tradition (with its concern for theory building and precise modeling of psychological phenomena based on group data and without much concern for characteristics of the individuals that make up those groups) and (2) the correlational/psychometric tradition (emphasizing measurement of interrelationships of characteristics within individuals and with differences across individuals, usually with scant consideration of theoretical models of the processes studied). For many years, individual difference research suffered from not being related to cognitive processing theories. Put simply, one could not know for sure what individual differences were differences in. Also, there was no principled basis for knowing where to look for individual differences. In reaction to this shortcoming of past approaches (and because of the rapid advances in cognitive process modeling), a fairly strong consensus has emerged that the processes that contribute to the behavior individuals may differ on must be specified in detail and have a theoretical basis. We need to analyze reading tasks carefully and then match the cognitive demands found to be involved to dimensions of underlying difference between individuals. (For an illustration of this principle in the context of text processing, see Spiro & Tirre, 1980.)

The precise, theory-based specification of the cognitive process origin of individual differences is not only necessary for a rigorous cognitive science of individual differences, but also for the emergence of systematic differential instruction. If we want to provide different instructional treatments as a result of individual difference analyses, we need specific knowledge of what cognitive outcomes the instructional approaches should be designed to achieve. Otherwise, we will be "shooting in the dark." The more precise the basic research findings, the narrower the ballpark of possible instructional interventions that may be tried.[1] It is precisely to this endeavor of specifying the cognitive components of individual differences in reading that we now turn our attention.

A THEORETICAL FRAMEWORK: CONSTRUCTIVISM, SCHEMA THEORIES, AND THE LIMITED CAPACITY INTERACTIVE MODEL OF READING

Since one of our central contentions is that individual difference research must be guided by overarching cognitive theories of the reading process, we will begin with a discussion of our best current knowledge of the basic processes in reading. The theory we present will then serve as a basis for our explorations throughout the rest of the chapter.

Before proceeding, it should be noted once again that our goal is not scholarly exhaustiveness or definitiveness (for more detailed theoretical accounts see the chapters by Anderson & Pearson, Gough, and Samuels and Kamil, this volume). Rather, we want to illustrate some of the ways one might traverse the current theoretical terrain of reading in looking for and at individual difference issues. We hope that what will emerge is not so much a catalogue of important findings on the topic of individual differences in reading (the field changes so fast that such an aim would result in fairly rapid obsolescence) but an improved ability to think about individual difference issues as they develop in the coming years or as the reader investigates them. As such, this chapter is thought of less as a didactic presentation and more as a modest demonstration, a "showing" rather than a direct "telling."

The following is a greatly oversimplified account of the historical development of what we take to be the currently dominant view of the reading process. Our discussion is at a very general level (for more detail, see Spiro, 1980).

We pick up the story in the 1960s. At that time most models of reading had a predominantly bottom-up emphasis (e.g., Gough, 1972). According to this view, readers go through a series of processing stages that progress from smaller units of analysis in text to larger ones. Roughly, features of letters are detected, letters are recognized, strings of letters are identified as words, concatenated words are analyzed to determine sentence meaning, and, finally, sets of sentences are considered together to produce the meaning of a connected discourse. A corollary of the bottom-up view is an emphasis on *text-based* aspects of reading. In working from the bottom up, the reader was working mainly *from the text*.

The bottom-up and text-based view of reading was undermined by research beginning in the late 1960s that demonstrated strong influences on language processing resulting from factors outside the text, especially pragmatic (i.e., not logically necessary) inferential importations in comprehension and recall based on preexisting knowledge of the topics dealt with in the text and knowledge-based determination of the relative importance of information in text (cf. Anderson & Pichert, 1978; Bransford & McCarrell, 1975; Spiro, 1977). Given the ubiquitous role of contextual factors, such as prior knowledge, in even what appeared to be the most routine cases of comprehension and recall, it became clear that information that could be gleaned solely on the basis of text-based processing of any discourse was insufficient to characterize the complete comprehension process. Rather, understanding is *actively constructed,* much like buildings, from "blueprints" based in part on text information and in part on contextual factors (top-down processing). Systematic bases for this inferential, constructive activity were provided by advances in the field of knowledge-structure representation under various rubrics, such as schemata, scripts, and frames (e.g., R. C. Anderson, 1977; Minsky, 1975; Rumelhart & Ortony, 1977; Schank & Abelson, 1977; Spiro, 1977). All of these approaches in one way or another organized commonly co-occurring information into packets describing the relationships among elements (or variables) in the structure; they also allowed for a constrained variety of possible instantiations of those elements in individual texts and specified the most likely instantiations in the absence of explicit information in the text (hence the notion of pragmatic inferences as instantiations of schema variables "by default").

Along with the recognition of the importance of top-down or knowledge-based processing came the view of reading as an *interactive* process (Rumelhart, 1977), in which both bottom-up and top-down processes operate simultaneously or alternately, with information from each processing direction feeding into the other and influencing the other's course. Details on the ongoing course of interactive processing during reading comprehension may be found in Collins, Brown, and Larkin (1980) and in Rumelhart (1980) (also see the chapters by Anderson and Pearson, and Samuels and Kamil, this volume).

A key feature of the interactive models is that all the interacting processes share a total system of limited capacity. Thus bottom-up and top-down processes not only may influence (and sometimes facilitate) each other by their informational interaction, but they may also interfere with each other, depending on the amount of the system's total resources they each require (e.g., if more resources are used by bottom-up processes, the ability to execute top-down processes may be lessened).

As indicated earlier, we will repeatedly return to this theoretical orientation to illustrate our discussion as well as to reinforce the larger point that theorizing about individual differences in reading must take place in the context of an overarching reading theory. Before proceeding, it is important to note that our most detailed current theories (e.g., Frederiksen, 1982; Just & Carpenter, 1980; Kintsch & van Dijk, 1978; Schank & Abelson, 1977; see also the reading models discussed in the Samuels and Kamil chapter, this volume) all have a restricted scope: as yet, we lack any precisely specified theory that integrates all aspects of reading (Sternberg, Powell, & Kaye, 1982).

From Reading Theory to Individual Differences

The theoretical orientation presented in the last section suggests four natural categories for investigating individual differences in reading performance: bottom-up (or text-based) processing, top-down (or knowledge-based or schema-based) processing, the interaction of top-down and bottom-up processing, and the control processes that manage the entire system. These will be considered in turn. Then, in the next major section, we will address issues that are not easily dealt with in terms of current reading theory.

Bottom-Up Processing and the Centrality of Decoding

We will not undertake a review of individual differences in decoding ability, a topic that can be analyzed from a variety of perspectives (visual-perceptual and auditory-perceptual, neurological, etc.). It is probably the most studied topic in reading (cf. Downing & Leong, 1982, for a fairly exhaustive recent survey of this literature). One point, however, is clear: Fluent verbal coding is a common characteristic of proficient reading comprehension. Fluent verbal coding includes such skills as accurate, rapid, and effortless decoding and word recognition (LaBerge & Samuels, 1974; Perfetti & Lesgold, 1978); accurate representation of temporal and order information (Hunt, Lunneborg, & Lewis, 1975); and the efficient coding of *verbal* information in short-term memory—but not short-term memory capacity in general—(Perfetti & Goldman, 1976).

Necessity versus sufficiency.   While it is clear that proficiency in decoding is necessary for reading-comprehension success, it by no means follows that such proficiency is *sufficient* to insure successful comprehension. Actually, a study by Fleisher et al. (1978) provides evidence of insufficiency: When children were trained to process fluently the words that would appear in a story, their comprehension of the story did not improve compared to children in a control condition.

The confusion of necessary and sufficient conditions that is sometimes encountered regarding this issue is attributable to the once widespread belief that the attainment of reading-comprehension proficiency is merely a matter of tacking a newly acquired decoding skill onto a set of skills already available from oral comprehension—if a child was not having trouble with listening comprehension, it was thought, then teaching the child to read simply involved instruction in the written code, with the oral comprehension skills merely being transplanted to the reading situation. Careful comparative studies of the listening and reading situations have dispelled these notions (e.g., Kleiman & Schallert, 1978; Rubin, 1980). Systematic differences between the physical characteristics of the two media and among the kinds of messages that are typically found in each suggest many points at which processes of oral comprehension would not overlap with or transfer to the written language-comprehension situation. The development of proficiency in reading comprehension involves the acquisition of a rich set of new processing skills beyond those involved in acquiring the written code.

"Decoding versus comprehension" and "bottom-up versus top-down" are not equivalent distinctions.   It should be noted that the relationship of decoding to comprehension is a different issue from the interactive relationship of bottom-up and top-down processing. To take one case, although the work of Perfetti and Lesgold (1978) is indirectly related to the interaction of bottom-up and top-down processing, the relation that they intentionally address directly is that between decoding and comprehension. The reason is that they mix text-based processes with prior-knowledge-based processes. For example, the increasing utilization of text structure as one reads further in a text is likely to covary with increasing importance of prior knowledge as the reader encounters more schema-signaling information, tests some schema hypotheses, and instantiates some slots within a hypothesized schema. Or, to take another factor considered in their

research, effects related to the use of "given" information in text are partly text based, but also partly knowledge based to the extent that information already processed has led to schema activation. Another example is a study by Curtis (1980) in which decoding skills were related to listening-comprehension ability: there are many aspects of listening comprehension that are bottom-up in the sense of that term as *"text based"*—or, as it is sometimes called, data based, in contradistinction to conceptually based (Bobrow & Norman, 1975). We will consider issues related to text-based versus knowledge-based patterns of reading in the section on interactive processing.

Knowledge-Based Processes

Beginning at a global level, there is evidence that some individuals underutilize their knowledge, while others maladaptively overrely on preexisting knowledge structures to guide text processing. An example of the former is a study by Spiro and Tirre (1980). Overreliance on preexisting knowledge was demonstrated in a study by Derry and Spiro (in preparation) in which college students of low verbal ability switched from one personality-stereotype schema to its opposite when the first was disconfirmed, despite the fact that the texts were written and normed to insure that the personality information was *randomly* selected for inclusion and, thus, the best strategy (and the one employed by subjects with high verbal ability) was to shift resources to a predominantly text-based processing mode.

Not only are there these two possibilities for maladaptive knowledge-based processing, but they can each be caused by a multitude of reasons (Spiro, 1979, 1980). Consider the case of underutilization of preexisting knowledge. The most obvious source of this processing style would be a general lack of background knowledge—one cannot use knowledge one does not have. However, the same problem could be caused by a misconception of reading as a primarily text-based process. In a study by Myers and Spiro (in preparation) some children who were diagnosed as overreliant on text were found to know the answers to knowledge-based inference questions they had missed on a reading test; when asked why they had not chosen the correct answer on the earlier test, a typical response was "It didn't say that anywhere in the story." Another cause of schema underutilization might be a problem elsewhere in the system; for example, laborious decoding might leave too little capacity for effectively executing knowledge-based processes (although that same decoding problem could lead to an overreliance on knowledge-based processes if the child opts to escape from his or her decoding difficulties—cf. Stanovich, 1980).

The last cause of failure of knowledge-based processing, breakdowns in component processes, has quite general implications for the theme of *complexity* that runs through the rest of the paper. Progress in the area of cognitive components and correlates (Pellegrino & Glaser, 1979) of top-down processing is limited by an obvious obstacle: As yet, we lack finely specified models of top-down processing that could guide empirical research. By far, the largest share of attention in cognitive psychology in the last 15 years has concerned the role of schema availability; numerous studies have demonstrated that without relevant background knowledge, comprehension and recall of otherwise well-structured text may fail (e.g., Bransford & Johnson, 1972; Dooling & Lachman, 1972) and that when knowledge is available, it exerts a directing effect on text processing (e.g., Anderson & Pichert, 1978; Spiro, 1977). Here we encounter another "necessary versus sufficient conditions" problem.

The assumption that is often drawn is that top-down reading failure is a problem of schema unavailability: some people lack the knowledge structures required for reading the texts they are encountering, and the natural remedy is to build more knowledge into their heads. However, although problems of schema unavailability can indeed be disabling, particularly for children of minority cultures, it is *not* true that schema availability is a *sufficient* condition for successful top-down processing—available schemata also have to be used correctly and efficiently (Spiro, 1980).

Spiro suggests various kinds of knowledge-based processing breakdowns that could lead to reading comprehension failure. Some children might have lots of knowledge stored in memory but have difficulty accessing the needed knowledge when it is signaled by a text (due either to inefficient, cluttered representation of the information or to difficulties with strategies for retrieving information from long-term memory). Or a child might possess sufficient background knowledge and be somewhat adept at locating and retrieving relevant knowledge when a text fairly clearly signals what knowledge is required, but have difficulty with determining which schemata are relevant in the absence of explicit signaling in a text. (This problem relates to the oral versus written-language issue discussed earlier: there is less contextual support in most written situations compared to the rich extralinguistic context of oral discourse, and such contextual support is an important source of clues as to which schemata are relevant. Thus, the schema-access problem is increased in reading as compared to oral comprehension.)

It might be that some children access their schemata effectively but do not combine them adaptively to fit the needs of a given text-processing situation. Or they might have difficulty maintaining schema activation for the right amount of time, either discarding a schema prematurely or maintaining one past the point where it is any longer useful. The result would be text representations insufficiently integrated across nonadjacent text segments. Or a child who executes all of these top-down processes accurately may carry them out so inefficiently and effortfully that limitations of processing capacity are exceeded. Or some children might adequately use their prior knowledge to understand text but fail to use comprehended information from text to update and modify their existing knowledge structures.

As this partial set of possibilities suggests, it is conceivable that top-down processing could break down in *many* ways. However, we need to develop better models of the psychological processes involved in utilizing prior knowledge during reading if we are to be able to design studies to determine whether any single aspect of top-down processing is most often implicated in reading failure, or a set of processing aspects is so implicated, or perhaps whether there is a pattern of top-down processing breakdowns that tend to co-occur and mutually reinforce each other (Spiro, 1980). We need to know the parts that comprise top-down processing and how those parts are interrelated before looking for "seams" in the process.

We have just seen a partial glimpse of the richness that characterizes top-down processing. The complex manifold of cognitive processes involved in using prior knowledge to understand may pose serious problems for the individual difference researcher after simpler aspects become well studied. The cognitive correlates of this diverse set of processes could conceivably tap as many aptitude clusters as can be identified. We will return to the theme of the problem of complexity after discussing factors that provide further complications: interactive processing and executive control.

The Interaction between Bottom-Up and Top-Down Processes

By most accounts, the dominant view of reading today is that of an interactive activity (Rumelhart, 1977). Processing goes on from the bottom-up *and* from the top-down (either simultaneously or alternatingly). Furthermore, these two kinds of processes must operate under a limitation: they both involve what might be called cognitive "effort" (e.g., use of memory space, directed consciousness, etc.), and they both must operate within a system that, as a whole, is limited in the amount of cognitive effort that can be supported at any one time (i.e., bottom-up and top-down processes must *share* a *limited processing capacity*).

The interactive model and its implications for reading are far from a settled issue (cf. Stanovich, 1980). Regardless of how controversies concerning the model itself turn out, the most fundamental (and least controversial) characteristics of interactive models suggest some potent sources of individual differences. For example, it seems fairly obvious that if a component process requires much effort, that is, it is not "automatic" (e.g., LaBerge & Samuels, 1974), the execution of that process will *detract* from the ability to execute other processes—when one process uses more of the limited capacity, less is left for other processes. This notion of *"bottlenecks"* in the reading process has inspired considerable research (e.g., Perfetti & Lesgold, 1978).

A caution is required however: things are rarely as simple as they seem. For example, even the seemingly obvious point about excesses in the effortfulness of one process detracting from another need not necessarily hold. In some cases, it might be that more effort for one process (e.g., schema selection) *reduces* the effort required for others (e.g., effort to select more carefully the most appropriate schema for a text might facilitate pragmatic inferencing in connection with the text). In other words, processes could be *mutually facilitative* (Spiro, 1979). In general, bottleneck effects might be more likely for processes relatively unrelated to effortful process, especially to the extent that the effort is expended *ineffectively*. We need to know more about when process interactions take the form of complementary facilitations, when there are unidirectional bottlenecks with little interaction, and when bottlenecks are due to ineffective compensatory interactions (also see Fredericksen, 1982, on processing interdependencies). To achieve this aim, studies must be designed that include contexts that are sufficiently well specified and inclusive so that radically different kinds of interactive processing patterns would be appropriate and observable.

As was the case with bottom-up and top-down processes individually considered, there are various ways "seams" in the interactive aspect of reading could be envisioned. For example, the exact role of top-down processes in facilitating rapid word recognition is a matter of dispute. Smith (1971) hypothesized that a primary characteristic of better readers is that they use top-down processing to facilitate the ongoing recognition of words. Thus, a problem of less able readers is a failure to use interactive processes when they ought to do so. This point of view is widely held among reading theorists.

A conflicting viewpoint is that of Stanovich (1980), who claims that poor readers maladaptively bolster ongoing word-recognition processes by interactive top-down support, that is, they attempt to *compensate* for their bottom-up deficiency by *overrelying* on top-down processes. Support for the compensatory claim comes from a few studies that have shown greater contextual facilitation effects on word-recognition speed for less able than for more able readers (see Stanovich, 1980). However, as was mentioned earlier, scaling factors are the likely explanation of a large share of these findings. A related orientation to this issue is the limited-capacity bottleneck approach (e.g., Perfetti & Lesgold, 1978): effort that goes into verbal coding detracts from the cognitive capacity to execute other reading processes. Or the effort to use top-down processes to support bottom-up activities may divert top-down attention from more proper knowledge-based processes, such as constructing thematic cohesion and drawing pragmatic inferences.

There is another possibility that has been mentioned occasionally but that has not received the sustained theoretical and empirical attention it deserves. The crucial contributor to reading success may be *flexibility*—the ability to adapt *all* the interacting components skills to situational needs (see Wagner & Sternberg, 1983, for a recent study that demonstrates a central role for flexibility in executive control). Thus, it may sometimes be more efficient to escape to a second level of processing to compensate for difficulty at one level. In other contexts, perseverance as a reaction to processing difficulty may be preferable. Perhaps better readers are distinguished by their ability to adapt interactive tradeoffs to meet varying situational needs. A related possibility is that skilled readers have all their processes simultaneously primed, even when they are not in use. That is, nonfocal processes may be kept sufficiently active at any one time in the reading process so that they are at least *ready* to make a contribution if called on during the rapidly changing flux of ongoing reading comprehension. So, at the more general level of top-down and bottom-up processing, even when there is no immediate use for top-down expectation formation during reading a passage that is better suited to a bottom-up approach, some low-level top-down processing would still be going on in order that top-down processes will be ready to execute as needed. Or, to take another example, even if it turns out to be the case that less able readers make just as much use of top-down constraints in facilitating the ongoing recognition of words as better readers do, the crucial difference may be whether poor readers are simultaneously ready to make other, less bottom-up uses of their top-down processing (see Stanovich, 1980).

Recently, we have found some preliminary support in our laboratory for the notion that *breadth and flexibility* of reading skills is responsible for important differences in reading proficiency. When passages are presented that either interfere with top-down processing (information necessary for ready schema selection is built into passage titles that are then left off in experimental conditions) or impede syntactic parsing aspects of comprehension (by leaving out all capitalization and punctuation of sentences), the best predictor of fifth-graders' level of reading ability is the tendency not to be seriously affected by *either* of these two types of experimental text degradation (using performance on intact passages as a statistical control). That is, the better readers seem to be those that do not have any single dominant processing style. Note that the demonstration of this effect is independent of reading ability since performance on the degraded passages is measured by regression residuals from predicting performance on those passages from the individual's performance on intact passages; that is, the extent to which a child does better than would be expected (given that child's performance on the same task when passages are left intact) when processing is disrupted in *both* the top-down and bottom-up ways is positively correlated with scores on standardized reading-comprehension tests. Also, if we are right that interactive packaging can go on in many ways, then our processing interference manipulations would be only two of many ways to discover overreliant, inflexible reading styles, in which case, our small but significant correlation may *underestimate* the magnitude of processing-style overreliance for poor readers.

There is probably a measure of truth to all plausible interactive processing orientations. We believe that a detailed investigation of individual reading patterns (Kleiman, 1982) and of reading contexts (Jenkins, 1979; Spiro, 1977) would indicate that readers combine the various interactive components of the reading process in many ways. For example, just to consider problems in acquiring decoding skill, some children might try to *persevere* in the effortful decoding task at the expense of knowledge-based processes; other readers may try to *escape* from the unpleasant decoding process by ignoring bottom-up processes and by trying to rely too exclusively on knowledge-based processes; still others may stay with bottom-up processing with an inefficient compensatory "boost" from top-down processes; and some may switch repeatedly among styles, with the less able readers showing less adaptive flexibility (Spiro, 1979).

This plurality would likely be obscured by any of the nomothetic approaches used by researchers who are investigating reading difficulty from a single theoretical perspective. It is interesting to observe that compensation theorists tend to pay little attention to the perseverance notion, while bottleneck theorists, on the other hand, often ignore the possibilities of compensation. Systematic neglect is made possible by the fact that researchers in different camps do different kinds of studies and, thus, do not address the possibilities espoused by each other. It is, however, also symptomatic of the individual difference tension mentioned earlier, namely, that there is a great deal of *indeterminacy* in the manner in which a specific reading problem may affect other aspects of reading. We have once again encountered the problem of complexity.

It is worth noting again that we have illustrated only one of the tradeoffs that is involved in comprehension and that requires its own species of cost-benefit analysis. There are many others. For example, there are tradeoffs concerning the quality of initial representation and characteristics of later use of that information. It might be the case that as more information is explicitly represented at the time of initial understanding, less processing effort is required for subsequent use. However, that would be true only to the extent that retrieval of information uses less system capacity than generation of information. If representations get cluttered, then generation might be easier than retrieval. It is possible that some children store too much information explicitly, mistakenly believing that they cannot infer what information had been previously encountered if it is not explicitly stored or "memorized." Other readers may store too little information, assuming that they can generate it later as needed; these readers may find they have overestimated their reconstructive powers. Anecdotal accounts indicate that the latter problem is common in studying—students often feel that they know everything while they are examining their texts, only to be disappointed by their misjudgment when they later have to answer test questions without their texts in front of them.

So, if the interactive processing mix can take many forms and is best kept flexibly adaptable, perhaps a natural next place to look for simpler and more general answers to the problem of complexity in individual differences is in the processes that direct and manage the various interactive coordinations required in a given reading situation. This brings us to the subject of executive control processes and metacognition.

Metacognitive Control

Our hope as we left the last section was that the problem of indeterminately proliferating possibilities for the individual packaging of interactive processing might be resolved by clarification at the level of metacognitive management or executive control. Any such hopes for simpler answers in this domain are unwarranted. The problem is that there is even greater complexity in coordinating these diverse processes than in the processes themselves. As an illustration, we will look in some detail at the complex individual difference possibilities related to a single aspect of metacomprehension, knowing when you know and when you do not know. (See Brown, 1980, and in this volume as well as Sternberg et al., 1982, for discussions of other aspects of metacognition and for reviews of comprehension monitoring.)

Knowing when you know. It is difficult to repair one's failures to comprehend without being aware that failure has occurred. Yet, despite advances in the last few years (Brown, 1980; Brown et al., 1983), we still know little about the clues one should look for as indicators of when one knows and does not know. Such knowledge would be invaluable for attempts to remedy the problems many children have in monitoring their comprehension and would set the stage for instruction in fix-up strategies (the latter being a topic we know a bit more about; see Collins et al., 1980).

Among the problems children might have with knowing when they know are failures to monitor, failures to distinguish adequate from inadequate understanding, overly conservative criteria for concluding that understanding has occurred (resulting in attentional bottlenecks), and overly optimistic criteria of understanding (resulting in false alarms). If one considers the "click of comprehension" to be a signal of sorts, then the kinds of problems one can encounter in accurately "detecting" that click are in many ways like those that can occur in the detection of auditory signals: (1) problems of discriminating signals from noise (and the potential sources of "noise" in reading-comprehension situations, the misleading signs of *partial* understanding, are considerable) and (2) problems of maladaptive criteria (thresholds) for deciding that one has understood.

Here again, we encounter the problems of complexity and indeterminacy, which so confuse the individual difference picture. Unlike auditory signal-detection situations, in reading comprehension there is usually not a single signal. Rather, the "click" of comprehension results from the integration of the many factors that contribute to comprehension. Furthermore, the integration of these factors must be flexibly adapted as they relate to a multitude of possible reading tasks and purposes, many of which provide highly vague criteria at best, and all of which have their own unique requirements. To illustrate, consider just one common context in which knowing when you know is vital: studying for end-of-semester exams.

As in any language-processing context, there are many metacognitive activities that are relevant to studying (e.g., selective deployment of attention, fixing up inadequate understandings, etc.). Once again, however, we will only be focusing on that aspect of metacomprehension that concerns assessing the adequacy of one's understanding (i.e., self-assessment of the readiness to perform adequately in a given task context; in this case, to take a test). Among the special characteristics of the studying situation is the relatively large quantity of material that must be processed, the fact that that material will have received some prior processing, that the earlier processing will vary in quality and degree of integration across topics, and the considerable amount of time and newly encountered information since initial reading. For example, one might need to make decisions about the quality of understanding and recall of information contained in an entire subject-area textbook that has been read over the course of several months, not to mention information from class discussions and lectures that must be integrated with the text material. These unique features of studying place special demands on metacognitive processes, any of which can be the source of individual differences.

Additional aspects of the studying process that make special metacognitive demands include the following:

1. *Knowing what to study.* Readers must be able to decide which aspects of the material are most important and/or most likely to be tested. Hence, readers must possess and apply finely differentiated schemata for the topic, for the kind of test to be taken, and for the biases of the instructor.
2. *Knowing when one has studied enough.* Often in studying situations, finite explicit criteria are not available for determining whether one is prepared for a test. That is, it is usually not possible to generate a list of all the questions that could be asked so that a complete self-examination may be administered. The demands for assessment of test-readiness in such contexts are very different from those involved in metacomprehension assessments concerning, say, individual sentences. Combinations of such factors as the representativeness of a student's sampling of self-examination items and the ability of the student to make appropriate judgments about likely test performance based on outcomes of the self-examination sample are likely to be involved. Each of these elements involve many potential sources of individual differences.

3. *Knowing how to study.* Many systems for effective studying have been proposed (T. H. Anderson, 1980). Not only do we know little about their relative effectiveness across individuals, but also the possibility of interaction between the kinds of facilitation in self-assessment of knowledge and task readiness provided by different study techniques and the characteristics of students (e.g., amount of prior knowledge, cognitive style, verbal ability, degree of motivation, etc.) is largely unexplored. Taking one of many possible examples, one study technique might be better for individuals who tend to represent information in a highly compartmentalized form, while another is better for individuals whose knowledge structures are characterized by high interconnectivity.

As we can see, there are many individual difference issues that may be involved in the "knowing when you know" aspect of just one kind of comprehension activity, studying. And we have not even considered a further complicating factor: the relationships between initial reading and later studying. The term "studying" implies that the material is not being read for the first time. The many possible variations on the nature and quality of initial comprehension will interact in complex ways with the kinds of studying that wi' be required. Once again, a long and involved story of individual difference "ins and outs" could be told here. However, our goal has never been exhaustiveness. (For example, we have not even considered the metacognitive complexities of studying in a context that concerns aspects other than knowledge self-assessment.) Rather, we have been trying to make a point: our earlier hope that the problem of complexity might be resolved by discovering simplicity at the higher level of metacognition has not been borne out. We have found more rather than less complexity.

Flexibility of Adaptation to Reading Tasks and Contexts

There are a multitude of reading purposes and contexts in which reading occurs. We will use "task" to refer to the goals and purposes of reading, while a "context" is the source of information about reading tasks. Thus, contexts may convey information about reading tasks explicitly or implicitly. Obviously, as in understanding any situation, comprehension of task demands involves a constructive interpretation, in this case an interpretation of contexts—part of the task information will be explicitly presented and part will be implicit and, thus, will have to be inferred, based on an individual's schemata for tasks and contexts. Two possible sources of reading deficiency, then, are impoverished task-context schemata and processing difficulties in applying such schemata.

One reason some students may have inadequate task-context schemata is that they have never been instructed on the intended nature of comprehension activities in school settings when vague instructions are given. The oft-mentioned difficulty many children experience in moving from stories to subject-area expository text may be due in part to their never finding out what the vague reading task "learn about X" means.

It is an item of belief for many that an important characteristic of skilled readers is their ability to adapt to the demands of varying reading tasks. Before we can test the validity of this belief and its individual difference implications, we must be able to define and identify context-dependent characteristics of desirable reading behavior. There are a rich variety of contextual factors that can significantly alter the reading process in natural situations. Partial taxonomies of learning contexts have been developed, many of which are variants of Jenkins's (1979) well-known tetrahedral classification: characteristics of learners, the material to be learned, the mental processes involved in acts of learning, and the criterial tasks that are used to determine the quality of learning that has been achieved. Development of instruments to assess contextual sensitivity in adapting reading purposes requires application of such a taxonomy, as does the development of instructional approaches to foster flexibility of contextual adaptation. And it should not be concluded that only learner characteristics are the domain of individual difference studies. Contextual space is highly "intertwined," and an understanding of individual differences in contextual sensitivity and adaptiveness requires a full understanding of reading and learning contexts. It is also possible that some aspects of reading deficiency might be context-dependent; if it could be determined that a reading problem may be lessened by altering contextual conditions, that might form a basis for improving reading by the direct manipulation of contexts (see the chapter by Bloome & Greene in this volume).

Understanding criterial tasks is equally as important as understanding task contexts. As we have already indicated, many reading contexts, especially in school, have the vague requirement that the student "learn" about some subject. What is successful comprehension in such a case? The answer to that question has at least two parts. One goal is local adequacy of understanding: a reader must build a complete and consistent model or representation of the meaning of the text, and the important aspects of that model must endure in long-term memory. However, more is usually desired. We want readers to integrate the information from a particular text with other related knowledge they already possess so that knowledge-acquisition episodes will become interrelated, building upon each other rather than coexisting in mutual isolation. New information should affect interpretations of previously stored knowledge, when appropriate, and should induce accommodative restructuring of that knowledge. Further, we want readers to be able to use newly comprehended information in new situations, unanticipated at the time of original acquisition. In other words, successful understanding includes the ability to apply information in novel contexts and in interaction with other knowledge. A troublesome question for reading researchers is how readers can possibly know the future uses for which knowledge may be relevant. And if uses cannot be anticipated, how can readers assess their state of preparedness? Clearly, however, some readers predict better than others (Campione, Brown, & Bryant, in press).

One consequence of rich contextual variability is that, in the measurement of comprehension, we may need to turn more to multiple-dependent variables and/or optional correct answers. This will probably require the development of new assessment procedures to measure kinds of performance not presently targeted by conventional tests (e.g., the demonstration of understanding when there is no single best answer and justification of a selected response is required). The real world in which school knowledge will need to be applied is often not so considerate as to provide a single answer to the questions it poses nor to make its demands in neat packages. Perhaps the transfer of knowledge from schooling to uses in the world outside of school might be smoother if some of the real world's "messiness" were incorporated in the school curriculum. In other words, an apt application of the old rallying cry of the 1960s, "relevance in education," might have less to do with offering nontraditional courses in specialized areas of contemporary student interest and more to do with making the structure of materials and tasks in traditional courses conform better to the structures that will be encountered in the intellectual pursuits of everyday life. That is, important individual difference variables may be flexibility and adaptability in applying comprehended information to the novel (and often indeterminate) circumstances the world provides for us.

Reading Is Thinking

Our message should be clear: The question of what it is to read with understanding is highly complex. To take one further example, after studying the phenomena of memory for what has been previously read, we were led to the inescapable conclusion that remembering is no mere matter of passive retrieval or even straightforward and routinizable reconstruction; rather, remembering seemed to be a mental activity as complex as all of thought (Spiro, 1977). What then of reading comprehension, which includes the act of remembering as only one part of a richly interconnected set of mental activities? Here it is surely the case that all the ancient riddles of the mind will come into play. These are not fresh insights, as indicated by the remarks of the following two luminaries of the past, Thorndike and Huey:

> Understanding a paragraph is like solving a problem. . . . The mind is assailed as it were by every word in the paragraph. It must select, repress, soften, emphasize, correlate and organize, all under the influence of the right mental set or purpose or demand. (Thorndike, 1917)

> To completely analyze what we do when we read would almost be the acme of a psychologist's achievements, for it would be to describe very many of the most intricate workings of the human mind. (Huey, 1980/1968)

The moral of our recurring references to complexities and indeterminacies in reading (and the concomitantly diverse possibilities for individual difference analysis) is that we need considerably more theoretical knowledge about reading comprehension processes, products, and purposes before all the important potential sources of individual differences may be imagined, much less fully investigated. If reading comprehension is itself so complex a process, the possibilities for individual differences in that process can only be more complex, helping to explain why we do not as yet have very many answers. Put another way, if solid individual difference research depends on cognitive task analyses (another of our recurring themes), then such research will be hampered in reading, where numerous cognitive processes contribute in complexly (and often indeterminately) intermingled patterns.

And if our knowledge about individual differences in reading is still in a fairly primitive state when considering only those areas where considerable basic research gains have been made, our message should be considerably reinforced if we now turn briefly to even less well-explored territory: gaps in current reading comprehension theory.

Problems with Prepackaged Knowledge Schemata

Advances in schema-theoretic approaches to comprehension have rested upon the employment of knowledge structures corresponding to highly *routinized* situations, such as scripted everyday events—like trips to restaurants and the structure of children's stories. Routinizability allows the construction and use of prepackaged knowledge structures that work in pretty much the same way across the occasions in which they are used.

A major problem has resulted from our dependence on routinized schemata, and it may be easily stated: *One cannot have a prepackaged knowledge structure for everything!* Yet, we are very good at figuring out what to do when we encounter situations for which we lack "prescriptions" for thought and action in prior knowledge. Thus, it must be that we can either accommodatively refine preexisting schemata or build radically new schemata to fit these situations. That is, we are not limited to processes that are *imitative* of past uses of knowledge. Rather, we are able to operate *productively*, adapting to novelty in extemporaneous fashion (see Anderson & Pearson's chapter, this volume).

We should say that *ideally* we operate in this fashion, for it has often been proposed that one characteristic of many students, perhaps due to characteristics of schooling which stress imitative forms of testing, is a tendency to overrely on retrieval of prepackaged information from highly compartmentalized memory structures (cf. Spiro, 1977); the consequence is an inability of these students to "think for themselves," to treat unique aspects of contexts as unique rather than trying to fit these aspects to familiar but tired molds. Evidence of pervasive inability to deal with novelty is also found in the frequent observation from laboratory studies of failures to transfer available information to new uses (recent reviews of the literature on transfer may be found in Brown et al., 1983, and Campione et al., in press).

The development of productive thought capabilities has to be considered one of the most important goals of schooling—surely we want students who are adaptive and independent in their ability to deal with the complexities presented by the ever-changing world around them. Unfortunately, we know very little about how ongoing schema acquisition occurs. It is ironic that one likely reason for this gap in our theories is the very success of those theories: the empirically demonstrated power of prepackaged knowledge schemata has caused us to stress what one already knows to the neglect of what one does not yet know. It is no coincidence that, until quite recently, there was very little research in the last 20 years that purports to deal with *learning*.

How may this serious gap in our theories of comprehension be remedied? How is it that some individuals are able to carry out the difficult task of performing successfully in conditions of novelty? First, we must consider the typical attributes of such situations. Most obviously, when processing directions are indeterminate, it is not clear what information sources will be most relevant, what principles of organization should be imposed upon those sources, or, given general principles, how they should receive specific and detailed instantiation.

What sort of processing strategy is likely to be effective in cases where one has few clues about how he or she will eventually represent the information that is being gathered? We propose that the best approach to such situations is to tentatively *encode as much information as possible in as many ways as possible*. Then, when sufficient data have emerged from the environment to guide the construction of more uniform representations and processing modes, the learner will have enough of the previously unforseeable necessary information available (and available in enough different, easily scannable forms) to be prepared to notice and act upon the patterns that permit appropriate understandings to be developed. If you do not know what you will have to be ready for, then you have to be ready for anything!

The obvious problem with this proposal is that the strategy is ambitious and will be cognitively taxing. The solution to this problem is simple: in indeterminate situations and situations where one cannot be certain that preexisting schemata will be adequate, one should make *simultaneous* or parallel use of as many available cognitive resources as possible. In other words, the most proficient readers and learners may be those who prepare themselves for the largest number and greatest variety of plausible but unanticipatable conceptual outcomes. Hence, they need to use *all* the parallel processing modes available to support human thought as efficiently as possible in ways tailored to the special features of those various modes.

Thus, we are proposing a threefold set of operating principles for maximizing productive thought in highly indeterminate situations: (1) encode a lot of information because you do not know what information will eventually be needed, (2) encode the same information simultaneously in many different ways because you do not know how you will eventually organize the information, and (3) use many modes or styles of thought because different modes are suited in different ways to fulfilling the first two principles (e.g., the verbal processing system has strengths and weaknesses different from the visual-perceptual system; the ability to effect rapid figural closure is useful for different things than is memory span for discrete items; fluid processing abilities are best employed toward different cognitive ends than are crystallized processing abilities; etc.). We illustrate with the example of uses of the visual-perceptual system in verbal processing situations characterized by novelty.

A New Research Agenda

In this section we distinguish two kinds of conceptual domains (well structured versus entangled), two kinds of reduction of information processing demands (through conceptual abstraction versus through imaging), and two kinds of information processing style (simple-mindedness versus muddle-headedness). We then suggest a theoretical alignment of these distinctions.

Entangled conceptual domains. Some knowledge domains are better structured than others. The same is true of texts. The well-structured domains and texts often exhibit neat hierarchical organization, examples are well tied to classes, and the features that permit classification are clear and unambiguous.

Further, instances of these domains exhibit these clear relationships, thus permitting easy recognition (*"Aha! He's talking about birds."*) and comparison across instances (*"Birds, again!"*). Within the realm of text, examples would include most of the domains studied by analysts of discourse structure (e.g., Kintsch, 1974; Meyer, 1975). That those interested in modeling text structure, a difficult activity in the best of situations, would select domains and texts that have clear-cut structures is not surprising.

On the other hand, it is often the case (some, e.g., Wittgenstein, 1953, would say that it is *usually* the case) that domains (and texts and tasks) are *ill structured* or ill defined. Across occasions of a domain's use (or across parts of a given text that reflect the structure of such domains), there is at best a *partial and irregular overlap* of thematic features of the domain and of the ways relevant features relate to each other on each occasion (or across parts of text). Examples of domains that have this structure are easy to find. First, any domain that is nonentangled in principle will be represented in entangled fashion prior to learning the principles that permit disentanglement or conceptual unification (or prior to having sufficient data for such learning). Second, examples of conceptual domains that are inherently entangled include many everyday concepts, such as "criterion" (for making a judgment; notice that this relates to the task-context adaptiveness and metacognition issues discussed earlier—what should determine processing adequacy in different contexts), "reading," and "guiding" (Wittgenstien, 1953). Also, most subject-area domains are entangled (e.g., "causes of wars," most areas of medical diagnostics, etc.), although it might be argued from inspection of subject-area textbooks that these domains are well structured. We believe, however, that such structure is often *artificially imposed* for the convenience of authors and the purported convenience of students. Further, we suspect a connection between the problems students frequently have with *using* school information in settings that they have not been explicitly prepared for and the *inappropriate compartmentalization* of information that results from treating information as well structured when, in reality (i.e., in the context in which it should be usable), it is ill structured. In other words, we believe that many of the problems of *transfer failure* so prevalent in our schools and in our laboratory experiments (see the earlier discussion of transfer problems) are due to an inculcation of strategies fit to well-structured situations that then have to be applied in less well-structured contexts.

It is in entangled contexts—such as those we have just described, where information reduction by conceptual chunking is either premature or impossible in principle because of inherent irregularities—that we believe the three guidelines for productive adaptiveness mentioned earlier must be applied. We contend that the first two principles, encoding a lot of detailed information and encoding the same information in many ways, are achieved best by invoking the third principle, namely, using alternative processing modes. In particular, we argue that the *visual-perceptual* processing mode has special features not found in the discursive or verbal mode that suit it to economical representation of large amounts of irregularly interrelated information according to the dictates of the first two principles.

Entangled domains and the visual-perceptual system. In irregular domains and situations of the sort we have described, it is not possible *by definition* to reduce the information that needs to be incorporated in memory by logical or analytical processes of schema abstraction without considerable inaccuracy resulting—if such abstractive reduction were possible, the domain (text, task) would not be entangled. If information cannot be analytically reduced or "*chunked,*" then it must be retained in more detail, reflecting the actual complex and irregular patterns of occurrence of the information and the need to keep available whatever information may later be needed but cannot be anticipated. The obvious drawback that results is an increase in pressures on long-term memory capabilities: without a basis in domain regularity for chunking information and with an ever-expanding set of occurrences of information in an entangled domain, possibly over many years of exposure, how is the goal of retaining more and more of the irregular intricacies of use patterns to be reconciled with the memory problems such extensive storage would produce? It is here, we suggest, that the third principle comes into play: the answer may lie in a shift in the *kind* of memorial processing required.

The verbal/analytic/discursive/propositional processing system (although these terms are not synonymous, we will use them interchangeably since it is only their common features that we are addressing) is characterized by a reliance on discrete serial processes. This characteristic is well suited to situations that either have a small number of elements or have principles for generating elements, and that have regular linear patterns of relationship among elements. Those are not the characteristics of entangled domains and tasks. The verbal system would quickly become overloaded in trying to attain the multiple irregular encoding goals of the first two principles.

The visual-perceptual system, on the other hand, has its strengths just where the verbal system is weak (and vice versa). An excellent description of these strengths has been provided by Jonas (1954):

> Sight is *par excellence* the sense of the simultaneous or the coordinated, and thereby the extensive. A view comprehends many things juxtaposed, as coexistent parts of one field of vision. It does so in an instant: as in a flash one glance, an opening of the eyes, discloses a world of co-present qualities. . . . Sight is unique already in beholding a co-temporaneous manifold as such. . . . All other senses construct their perceptual "unities of manifold" out of a temporal sequence of sensations which are in themselves time-bound and non-spatial. Their synthesis therefore, [is] ever unfinished and depend[ent] on memory. (p. 507)

It can readily be seen that the above comparison retains its accuracy if instead of talking about "other senses," "perceptual" unities, and "sequence of sensations," we substitute "discursive processing," "abstract conceptual unities," and "sequence of conceptual elements." In other words, the visual-perceptual processing system encodes the multiple irregular overlap of elements spontaneously and effortlessly as a gestalt, whereas the discursive verbal system must continually expand its resource commitments as multiplicity and irregularity increase. Where the visual-perceptual system can overlay relationships one upon the next in the same image (think about the complexities simultaneously represented in memory for faces), the verbal system must add on each variant of a relationship separately (if the relationships do not have a basis for conceptual chunking, that is, if there is a lack of specifiable analytic relationships among the relationships). Thus, increments in domain complexity and the explosion of information as entangled concepts are encountered on succeeding new occasions are far less taxing to the visual-perceptual than to the verbal system.

So, the visual-perceptual system has special capabilities that suit it to processing demands in entangled abstract conceptual domains and is also a system that almost everybody has and uses efficiently (differences in relative tendencies to rely on visual processing styles aside; see below). Furthermore, suggestive support for the notion that we use the visual-perceptual system in productive thought comes from a study by Snow, Lohman, Marshalek, Yalow, and Webb (1977), who found that while spatial visualization and fluid thinking were distinguishable abilities from crystallized thinking ability, they were not distinguishable from each other. In addition, there is widespread support for these notions from anecdotal accounts of the cognitive processes of inventive thinkers in many fields (cf. Hadamard, 1945).

There is a large problem however: abstract conceptual material is by definition nonimageable. That is, there is no obvious or direct way for the visual-perceptual processing system to be applied to abstract material. The question then becomes how this powerful and specially qualified system's resources can be harnessed to serve nonconcrete conceptual ends. People *have* it—it would be wasteful not to *use* it in nonvisual situations, especially since its special qualities should be helpful just where analytic schema-type representations fail. The question is how. In particular, how do the apparently incommensurable systems "communicate" with each other? We believe that the answer involves a *metaphorical* transformation of conceptual properties into perceptual properties, suitable as inputs to the visual-perceptual system (Spiro, in preparation).[2] However, it is just this question that the various currently popular cognitive-style dichotomies in the analytic-holistic family—and these are the ones that bear affinities to our discussion of the role of the visual system—either fail to answer or do not even address (see Dunn, in press; Ornstein, 1977; Paivio, 1971, for reviews of this literature).

In other words, we need *process models*, not just vague labels. For example, theories that employ an analytic-holistic dichotomy or that suggest a role for nonverbal or nondiscursive modes in abstract conceptual thought must specify in detail what abstract intellectual tasks holistic or nondiscursive processes are best suited to perform, how those tasks are carried out in these alternative modes, and in what contexts the nondiscursive processes tend to operate. Our suggestion is that such processes are specialized for memory storage and productive conceptual pattern detection (hypothesis generation) within irregular, entangled domains where expansive representations that do not tax memory load will be required. Underlying these functions are processes of perceptual (and affective) analogue conversion of conceptual content (and discursive relations between content elements) in order to enable that information to be input to our perceptual processing system.

And what individual differences would such a theory suggest? We believe that the most important distinction would be that between *simple-minded* and *muddle-headed* processors (Alfred North Whitehead's labels for Bertrand Russell and himself respectively, which originated during the writing of the *Principia Mathematica*—cited in Barrett, 1967. Naturally, given the context of their origin, the terms merely reflect stylistic preferences and are not intended to have negative connotations). The simple-minded individual tends to employ representational principles based on abstractive reduction, using a minimum of conceptual unifying criteria, and performs better in well-structured and/or highly scripted domains. The muddle-headed individual constructs irregular expansive representations that are united by multiple overlapping conceptual threads (such that no single thread runs through the whole structure) and encounters difficulty in neat domains for which this more complex and approximate form of representation is overly cluttered and unnecessarily confusing and inexact. Where the thoughts of the muddle-headed individual often go off in too many directions, the simple-minded individual may juxtapose too few trains of thought. The ideal, naturally, is a *balance* between both styles, a "level-headedness" that enables the opposed modes to complement each other, with the strengths of one compensating for the weaknesses of the other in a contextually appropriate blend.

This is not the place to go into detail on the specifics of our theory and the empirical approaches to testing it (see Spiro, in preparation)—we have by now surely taxed the patience of even our most forgiving readers without extending this already lengthy chapter still further. In keeping with the importance of theory as a basis for individual difference inquiry, our intention was merely to point to one area where schema theories were deficient and to suggest the possibility of alternative conceptualizations of knowledge structures that might remedy those deficiencies. Whether new developments in comprehension theories take this or some other form is really not the issue—the point is that new directions of some kind are inevitable, given the state of the art. And we can be certain that future generations of individual difference research will follow those same directions because we have now learned the lesson that the building of theories of cognitive processing and the study of individual differences are inseparable parts of the same enterprise.

NOTES

1. It is important to note that two further steps are required before information about individual differences gleaned from empirical investigations can be applied to the classroom. First, the same problem that causes reading difficulty may itself have different possible causes; hence, any possible "cause" must itself be traced to its etiological origin. To take one example that will be discussed in greater detail later, suppose one finds that comprehension difficulties arise because people fail to use requisite prior knowledge to support comprehension. This failure could itself stem from many sources: (a) the knowledge may not be available, (b) the cognitive processes that relate prior knowledge to texts may be deficient, (c) the reader may mistakenly conceive the purposes of reading to be primarily text based, or (d) a decoding problem that uses up limited capacity could be responsible (Spiro, 1979). Although the problem is the same in each case (i.e., insufficient use of prior knowledge), it seems likely that instructional interventions would be differentially effective as a function of which of the possible causes of the problem is implicated in an individual case.

   Second, basic cognitive process research does not tell you very much about the everyday issues of instruction, which themselves require research directed toward the development of a *theory of instruction* that would mediate between basic cognitive research findings and the actual practice of instruction. Should you teach to an individual's strengths (and, thus, perhaps keep motivation up), or toward weaknesses (possibly risking debilitating discouragement), or to both simultaneously? What is the best sequence to remediate a problem uncovered by basic research? Should students with problems of a certain kind be taught individually or in groups, directly or indirectly? Questions such as these require their own basic research in the area of instructional psychology. Although we will not be treating these issues in this chapter, it is clear that we need far more research in this area in order to complement the kinds of cognitive-process-related notions that we will be addressing (see also the chapter by Barr, this volume).

2. Note that the recently developed and successful expository text-mapping techniques (e.g., Armbruster & Anderson, 1982), in which text structural characteristics are visually displayed, do not use the visual system in the way that we suggest. First, the maps have been applied only to neatly organized structures. It would appear difficult to generalize the mapping technique to entangled domains without the map becoming overly cluttered. Second, and probably the reason for the latter unsuitedness of these maps to entangled situations, the visual characteristics of the map do not correspond to the structural properties of the text; for example, it does not matter if one conceptual entity that is related to another is placed in a box that is to the left or the right of the other, or above it or below it, or is larger or smaller. For the visual system to serve the encoding principles we have proposed, the specifics of the visual representation should have direct symbolic conceptual significance and should be capable of being repeatedly overlayed upon other visual details so that multiple information about patterns of conceptual relatedness can be conveyed without loss of information. This is not to say the mapping techniques lack value; they are most useful, but for different purposes than we are currently discussing. Similarly, Paivio's (1971) dual-processing model uses imagery in different ways and toward different ends than in our approach.

Note as well that much of what we have said about indirect or metaphorical uses of the visual system for productive processing in entangled situations can be applied to other modes too, including especially the affective, aesthetic, and motor systems. (See Spiro, 1980, and Spiro, Crismore, & Turner, 1982, for suggestions on the role and nature of affective representation of conceptual information in memory. Also see Osgood, Suci, & Tannenbaum, 1957, on connotative aspects of meaning.) Interestingly, in many ways the purposes that motivated our proposal resemble those of the original formulations of the schema notion, including Head's (1920) idea of the schema as a fluid bodily image used to recognize the endless variety of postural configurations and Bartlett's (1932) largely affective "attitude" (which was strongly influenced by Head's theory). To take another example, Piaget (1959) stressed the role of sensorimotor schemata in early stages of the development of thought (also see Bruner, 1964). We believe that those schemata continue to play a vital role long beyond the stage in which they are dominant, except their manner of use becomes more indirect (once again, if you already have it, why not continue to use it; see also McNeill, 1979).

REFERENCES

Anderson, R. C.   The notion of schemata and the educational enterprise. In R. C. Anderson, R. J. Spiro, & W. E. Montague (Eds.), *Schooling and the acquisition of knowledge.* Hillsdale, N.J.: Erlbaum, 1977.

Anderson, R. C., & Pichert, J. W.   Recall of previously unrecallable information following a shift in perspective. *Journal of Verbal Learning and Verbal Behavior*, 1978, *17*, 1–12.

Anderson, T. H.   Study strategies and adjunct aids. In R. J. Spiro, B. C. Bruce, & W. F. Brewer (Eds.), *Theoretical issues in reading comprehension*. Hillsdale, N.J.: Erlbaum, 1980.

Appleby, A. N.   Research in reading retardation: Two critical problems. *Journal of Child Psychology and Psychiatry*, 1971, *12*, 91–113.

Armbruster, B. B., & Anderson, T. H.   *Idea-mapping: The technique and its use in the classroom* (Reading Education Rep. No. 36). Urbana-Champaign: University of Illinois, Center for the Study of Reading, October 1982.

Barrett, W.   *The illusion of technique*. Garden City, N.Y.: Anchor Books, 1967.

Bartlett, F. C.   *Remembering*. Cambridge: Cambridge University Press, 1932.

Biemiller, A.   The development of the use of graphic and contextual information as children learn to read. *Reading Research Quarterly*, 1970, *6*, 75–96.

Bobrow, D. G., & Norman, D. A.   Some principles of memory schemata. In D. G. Bobrow & A. M. Collins (Eds.), *Representation and understanding: Studies in cognitive science*. New York: Academic Press, 1975.

Bond, G. L., & Dykstra, R.   The cooperative research program in first grade reading instruction. *Reading Research Quarterly*, 1967, *2*, 5–141.

Bransford, J. D., & Johnson, M. K.   Contextual prerequisites for understanding: Some investigations of comprehension and recall. *Journal of Verbal Learning and Verbal Behavior*, 1972, *11*, 717–726.

Bransford, J. D., & McCarrell, N. S.   A sketch of a cognitive approach to comprehension. In W. B. Weimer & D. S. Palermo (Eds.), *Cognition and the symbolic processes*. Hillsdale, N.J.: Erlbaum, 1975.

Brown, A. L.   Metacognitive development and reading. In R. J. Spiro, B. C. Bruce, & W. F. Brewer (Eds.), *Theoretical issues in reading comprehension*. Hillsdale, N.J.: Erlbaum, 1980.

Brown, A. L., Bransford, J. D., Ferrara, R. A., & Campione, J. C.   Learning, remembering, and understanding. In J. H. Flavell & E. M. Markman (Eds.), *Handbook of child psychology* (Vol. 3) (4th ed.). New York: Wiley, 1983.

Bruner, J. S.   The course of cognitive growth. *American Psychologist*, 1964, *19*, 1–15.

Calfee, R. C.   Sources of dependency in cognitive processes. In D. Klahr (Ed.), *Cognition and instruction*. Hillsdale, N.J.: Erlbaum, 1976.

Calfee, R. C., Arnold, R., & Drum, P.   Review of Gibson and Levin's "The Psychology of Reading." *Proceedings of the National Academy of Education*, 1976, *3*, 1–80.

Calfee, R. C., Chapman, R., & Venezky, R. L.   How a child needs to think to learn to read. In L. W. Gregg (Ed.), *Cognition in learning and memory*. New York: Wiley, 1972.

Campione, J. C., Brown, A. L., & Bryant, N. R.   Individual differences in learning and memory. In R. J. Sternberg (Ed.), *Human abilities: An information processing approach*. Hillsdale, N.J.: Erlbaum, in press.

Chall, J.   *Learning to read: The great debate*. New York: McGraw-Hill, 1967.

Collins, A., Brown, J. S., & Larkin, K. M.   Inference in text understanding. In R. J. Spiro, B. C. Bruce, & W. F. Brewer (Eds.), *Theoretical issues in reading comprehension*. Hillsdale, N.J.: Erlbaum, 1980.

Cooper, L. A.   Spatial information processing: Strategies for research. In R. E. Snow, P. Federico, & W. E. Montague (Eds.), *Aptitude, learning, and instruction*. Hillsdale, N.J.: Erlbaum, 1980.

Cromer, W.   The difference model: A new explanation for some reading difficulties. *Journal of Educational Psychology*, 1970, *61*, 471–483.

Cronbach, L. J.   The two disciplines of scientific psychology. *American Psychologist*, 1957, *12*, 671–684.

Cronbach, L. J., & Snow, R. E.   *Aptitudes and instructional methods.* New York: Irving-ton, 1977.

Curtis, M. E.   Development of components of reading skill. *Journal of Educational Psy-chology,* 1980, *72,* 656–669.

Davis, F. B.   Fundamental factors of comprehension in reading. *Psychometrika,* 1944, *9,* 185–197.

deHirsch, K., Jansky, J. J., & Langford, W. S.   *Predicting reading failure: A preliminary study.* New York: Harper & Row, 1966.

Derry, S., & Spiro, R. J.   *Overreliance on knowledge structures in text processing.* In preparation.

Dooling, D. J., & Lachman, R.   Effects of comprehension on retention of prose. *Journal of Experimental Psychology,* 1972, *88,* 216–222.

Downing, J., & Leong, C. K.   *Psychology of reading.* New York: Macmillan, 1982.

Dunn, B. R.   Bimodal processing and memory from text. In V. M. Rentel & S. Corson (Eds.), *Psychophysiological aspects of reading.* London: Pergamon, in press.

Durrell, D. D., & Murphy, H. A.   The auditory discrimination factor in readiness and reading ability. *Education,* 1953, *73,* 556–560.

Fleisher, L. S., Jenkins, J. R., & Pany, D.   *Effects on poor readers' comprehension of training in rapid decoding* (Tech. Rep. No. 103). Urbana-Champaign: University of Illinois, Center for the Study of Reading, September 1978.

Frederiksen, J.   *A componential theory of reading skills and their interactions* (Tech. Rep. No. 227). Urbana-Champaign: University of Illinois, Center for the Study of Reading, January 1982.

Gates, A. I.   The necessary mental age for beginning reading. *Elementary School Journal,* 1937, *37,* 497–508.

Gates, A. I., & Bond, G.   Reading readiness: A study of factors determining success and failure in beginning reading. *Teachers College Record,* 1936, *37,* 679–685.

Gates, A. I., Bond, G. L., & Russell, D. H.   *Methods of determining reading readiness.* New York: Bureau of Publications, Teachers College, Columbia University, 1939.

Gates, A. I., & Russell, D. H.   The effects of delaying beginning reading a half year in the case of underprivileged pupils with IQs of 75–95. *Journal of Educational Research,* 1929, *32,* 321–328.

Golinkoff, R. M.   A comparison of reading comprehension processes in good and poor comprehenders. *Reading Research Quarterly,* 1975–1976, *11,* 623–659.

Goodman, K. S.   Analyses of oral reading miscues: Applied psycholinguistics. *Reading Research Quarterly,* 1969, *5,* 9–30.

Goodman, K. S.   Influences of the visual peripheral field in reading. *Research in the Teaching of English,* 1975, *9,* 210–222.

Goodman, K. S., & Gollasch, F. V.   Word omissions: Deliberate and non-deliberate. *Reading Research Quarterly,* 1980, *16,* 6–31.

Goodman, Y. M., & Burke, C. L.   *Reading miscue inventory: Procedure for diagnosis and evaluation.* New York: Macmillan, 1972.

Gough, P. B.   One second of reading. In J. F. Kavanagh & I. G. Mattingly (Eds.), *Language by ear and by eye.* Cambridge: MIT Press, 1972.

Hadamard, J.   *The psychology of invention in the mathematical field.* New York: Dover, 1945.

Head, H.   *Studies in neurology.* London: Oxford University Press, 1920.

Huey, E. D.   *The psychology and pedagogy of reading.* Cambridge: MIT Press, 1968. (Originally published, 1908.)

Hunt, E., Lunneborg, C., & Lewis, J.   What does it mean to be high verbal? *Cognitive Psychology,* 1975, *7,* 194–227.

Jackson, M. D., & McClelland, J. L.   Processing determinants of reading speed. *Journal of Experimental Psychology: General,* 1979, *108,* 151–181.

Jenkins, J. J.   Four points to remember: A tetrahedral model and memory experiments. In L. S. Cermak & F. I. M. Craik (Eds.), *Levels of processing in human memory*. Hillsdale, N.J.: Erlbaum, 1979.

Jonas, H.   The nobility of sight: A study in the phenomenology of the senses. *Philosophy and Phenomenological Research*, 1954, *14*, 507–519.

Just, M. A., & Carpenter, P. A.   A theory of reading: From eye fixations to comprehension. *Psychological Review*, 1980, *87*, 329–354.

Kenny, D. A.   *Correlation and causality*. New York: Wiley, 1979.

Kintsch, W.   *The representation of meaning in memory*. New York: Wiley, 1974.

Kintsch, W., & van Dijk, T. A.   Toward a model of text comprehension and production. *Psychological Review*, 1978, *85*, 363–394.

Kleiman, G. M.   *Comparing good and poor readers: A critique of the research* (Tech. Rep. No. 246). Urbana-Champaign: University of Illinois, Center for the Study of Reading, June 1982.

Kleiman, G. M., & Schallert, D. L.   Some things the reader needs to know that the listener doesn't. In P. D. Pearson & J. Hansen (Eds.), *Twenty-seventh Yearbook of the National Reading Conference*. Clemson, S.C.: National Reading Conference, 1978.

LaBerge, D., & Samuels, S. J.   Toward a theory of automatic information processing in reading. *Cognitive Psychology*, 1974, *6*, 293–323.

Lakoff, G., & Johnson, M.   *Metaphors we live by*. Chicago: University of Chicago Press, 1980.

McNeill, D.   *The conceptual basis of language*. Hillsdale, N.J.: Erlbaum, 1979.

Meyer, B. J. F.   *The organization of prose and its effects on memory*. Amsterdam, The Netherlands: North-Holland Publishing Co., 1975.

Minsky, M.   A framework for representing knowledge. In P. H. Winston (Ed.), *The psychology of computer vision*. New York: McGraw-Hill, 1975.

Morphett, M. V., & Washburne, C.   When should children begin to read? *Elementary School Journal*, 1931, *31*, 496–503.

Myers, A., & Spiro, R. J.   *Sources of schema underutilization*. In preparation, 1983.

Ornstein, R. E.   *The psychology of consciousness*. San Francisco: W. H. Freeman, 1977.

Osgood, C. E., Suci, G. J., & Tannenbaum, P.   *The measurement of meaning*. Urbana: University of Illinois Press, 1957.

Paivio, A.   *Imagery and verbal processes*. New York: Holt, Rinehart & Winston, 1971.

Pellegrino, J. W., & Glaser, R.   Cognitive correlates and components in the analysis of individual differences. *Intelligence*, 1979, *3*, 187–214.

Perfetti, C. A., & Goldman, S. R.   Discourse memory and reading comprehension skill. *Journal of Verbal Learning and Verbal Behavior*, 1976, *15*, 33–42.

Perfetti, C. A., & Lesgold, A. M.   Discourse comprehension and sources of individual differences. In P. Carpenter & M. Just (Eds.), *Cognitive processes in comprehension*. Hillsdale, N.J.: Erlbaum, 1978.

Piaget, J.   *The language and thought of the child*. London: Routledge & Kegan Paul, 1959.

Robinson, H. M.   Visual and auditory modalities related to methods for beginning reading. *Reading Research Quarterly*, 1972, *8*, 7–39.

Rubin, A. D.   Comprehension processes in oral and written language. In R. J. Spiro, B. C. Bruce, & W. F. Brewer (Eds.), *Theoretical issues in reading comprehension*. Hillsdale, N.J.: Erlbaum, 1980.

Rumelhart, D. E.   Toward an interactive theory of reading. In S. Dornic (Ed.), *Attention and performance VI*. Hillsdale, N.J.: Erlbaum, 1977.

Rumelhart, D. E.   Schemata: The building blocks of cognition. In R. J. Spiro, B. C. Bruce, & W. F. Brewer (Eds.), *Theoretical issues in reading comprehension*. Hillsdale, N.J.: Erlbaum, 1980.

Rumelhart, D. E., & Ortony, A.   The representation of knowledge in memory. In R. C. Anderson, R. J. Spiro, & W. E. Montague (Eds.), *Schooling and the acquisition of knowledge.* Hillsdale, N.J.: Erlbaum, 1977.

Schank, R. C., & Abelson, R. P.   *Scripts, plans, goals, and understanding.* Hillsdale, N.J.: Erlbaum, 1977.

Singer, H., & Ruddell, R.   *Theoretical models and processes of reading* (2nd ed.). Newark, Del.: International Reading Association, 1976.

Smith, F.   *Understanding reading.* New York: Holt, 1971.

Snow, R. C., Lohman, D. F., Marshalek, B., Yalow, E., & Webb, N.   *Correlational analyses of reference aptitude constructs* (Tech. Rep. No. 5, Aptitude Research Project). Palo Alto, Calif.: Stanford University, School of Education, September 1977.

Spiro, R. J.   Remembering information from text: The "State of Schema" approach. In R. C. Anderson, R. J. Spiro, & W. E. Montague (Eds.), *Schooling and the acquisition of knowledge.* Hillsdale, N.J.: Erlbaum, 1977.

Spiro, R. J.   Etiology of reading comprehension style. In M. Kamil & A. Moe (Eds.), *Twenty-eighth Yearbook of the National Reading Conference.* Clemson, S.C.: National Reading Conference, 1979.

Spiro, R. J.   Constructive processes in prose comprehension and recall. In R. J. Spiro, B. C. Bruce, & W. F. Brewer (Eds.), *Theoretical issues in reading comprehension.* Hillsdale, N.J.: Erlbaum, 1980.

Spiro, R. J.   *Configural conceptual representations and productive processing in entangled domains.* In preparation, 1983.

Spiro, R. J., Crismore, A., & Turner, T. J.   On the role of pervasive experiential coloration in memory. *Text,* 1982, *2,* 253–262.

Spiro, R. J., & Esposito, J.   Superficial processing of explicit inferences in text. *Discourse Processes,* in press.

Spiro, R. J., & Taylor, B. M.   *On investigating children's transition from narrative to expository discourse: The multidimensional nature of psychological text classification* (Tech. Rep. No. 195). Urbana-Champaign: University of Illinois, Center for the Study of Reading, December, 1980. [To appear in R. J. Tierney, P. Anders, & J. Mitchell (Eds.), *Understanding readers' understanding.* Hillsdale, N.J.: Erlbaum, in press.]

Spiro, R. J., & Tirre, W. C.   Individual differences in schema utilization during discourse processing. *Journal of Educational Psychology,* 1980, *72,* 204–208.

Stanovich, K. E.   Toward an interactive-compensatory model of individual differences in the development of reading fluency. *Reading Research Quarterly,* 1980, *16,* 32–71.

Sternberg, R. J., Powell, J. S., & Kaye, D. B.   The nature of verbal comprehension. *Poetics,* 1982, *11,* 155–187.

Sternberg, S.   The discovery of processing stages: Extensions of Donder's method. In W. G. Koster (Ed.), *Attention and performance* (Vol. 2). Amsterdam: North-Holland Publishing Co., 1969.

Thorndike, E. L.   Reading as reasoning: A study of mistakes in paragraph reading. *Journal of Educational Psychology,* 1917, *8,* 323–332.

Tyler, L. E.   *Individuality.* San Francisco: Jossey-Bass, 1978.

Wagner, R. K., & Sternberg, R. J.   Executive control of reading. Submitted for publication, 1983.

Weber, R. M.   The study of oral reading errors: A review of the literature. *Reading Research Quarterly,* 1968, *4,* 96–119.

Wittgenstein, L.   *Philosophical investigations.* New York: Macmillan, 1953.

PART THREE

Instructional Practices: The State of the Art

Rebecca Barr, Editor

17 EARLY READING FROM A DEVELOPMENTAL PERSPECTIVE

Jana M. Mason

Interest in early reading, while it has important links to the past, is a relatively recent concern, because until this century high levels of literacy were not required (Resnick & Resnick, 1977). Nonetheless, there are links to early education which need to be traced, for they help show how and why reading instruction of young (preschool) children has been controversial.

A Brief Historical Perspective

A central issue, which some would argue can be traced back many centuries, is what sort of instruction young children ought to receive. Plato argued:

> Now you know that in every enterprise the beginning is the main thing, especially in dealing with a young and tender nature. For at that time it is most plastic, and the stamp sinks in deepest which it is desired to impress upon anyone.
>
> Just so.
>
> Shall we then quite lightly give licence for our children to hear any chance fables imagined by any chance people, and to receive in their souls impressions opposed to those which, when they have come to maturity, we shall think that they ought to possess?
>
> We must not permit it in the smallest degree.
>
> To begin with, as it seems, we must control the composers of fables, and select any good ones which they compose, and reject what are not good. And we will persuade the nurses and mothers to tell the children those fables which we have selected, seeing that they mould their souls with the tales they tell, far more really than their bodies with their hands. (Plato, 1917, p. 51)

The research reported herein was supported in part by the National Institute of Education under Contract No. HEW–NIE–C–400–76–0116 and was prepared principally during a sabbatical leave from the University of Illinois in 1979 at Stanford University. Revised from Tech. Rep. No. 198, Center for the Study of Reading, University of Illinois, Champaign.

Aristotle spoke less confidently:

> There is no agreement as to what the young should learn, either with a view to the production of goodness or the best life, nor is it settled whether we ought to keep the intellect or the character chiefly in view. If we start from the education we see around us, the inquiry is perplexing, and there is no certainty as to whether education should be a training in what is useful for life or in what tends to promote goodness or in more out-of-the-way subjects. (Aristotle, 1967, p. 107)

Plato focused on the development of goodness in order that it lead to virtuosity and obedience to law. Aristotle, while of a similar mind, expressed in a more tentative manner the nature of a fitting program of instruction. While education in Plato and Aristotle's time was very different from our own, we still are concerned about whether to emphasize intellect or character in our early instruction.

Erasmus, speaking on the education of young children in 1529, appears to argue for the development of the intellect:

> First, the beginnings of learning are the work of memory, which in young children is tenacious. Next, as nature has implanted in us the instrument to seek for knowledge, can we be too early in obeying her behest? Third, children can learn more readily at an early age. Fourth, since children can learn manners at that age, why not begin to learn elements of letters, grammar, fables, and stories? By disciplining, the mind gains far more in alertness and vigour than the body is ever likely to lose. (Cited in Cohen, 1974, p. 114)

Comenius, who, in the seventeenth century, proposed to teach "all things to all men," wrote a guide to mothers for instructing their young children, recommending that training of the soul begin at age 2 when "reason, as a little flower, begins to unfold itself." He asserted that:

> children do not train themselves spontaneously, but are shaped only by tireless labor . . . [for] whatever seed one sows in youth, such fruit he reaps in age, according to the axiom, the pursuits of youth are the delights of maturity. (Comenius, 1956, p. 67)

An alternative principle was presented in the eighteenth century by Rousseau that the child's early education follow the order of nature:

> Nature wants children to be children before they are men. If we deliberately pervert this order, we shall get premature fruits which are neither ripe nor well flavoured, and which soon decay. We shall have youthful sages and grown-up children. Childhood has ways of seeing, thinking and feeling, peculiar to itself: nothing can be more foolish than to seek to substitute our ways for them. (Rousseau, 1979, p. 22)

Pestalozzi, who was influenced by Rousseau's argument, formulated later that century a practical scheme for a natural approach to education. It relied initially on informal instruction at home by mothers, using the principle of *An-*

schauung (roughly translated to mean awareness of objects or situations through direct, concrete experiences or spontaneous appreciation). He determined that instruction ought to be based on observing three aspects of objects: their number and type, their appearance, and their names.

The instruction was always to be placed in the context of the whole object. Here, for example, are Pestalozzi's comments about instruction (cited in Rusk & Scotland, 1979): "Nature gives the child no lines, she only gives him things, and lines must be given him only in order that he may perceive things rightly"; or similarly, "Like nature with the savage, I always put the picture before the eye, and then sought for a word for the picture." Hence, while formal methods devised for analyzing objects and words (e.g., a syllabic representation of words) ally him with the direct instruction espoused by Commenius, his insistence on concrete experiences and familiar topics draw upon some of Rousseau's ideas. His compromise is evident in his advice about gifted children: "Unusual capacity should be given every possible chance, and above all, it should be rightly guided."

Froebel, a nineteenth century philosopher, argued that the child's mind should be allowed to unfold from within according to its predetermined pattern:

> Education in instruction and training, originally and in its first principles, should necessarily be passive, following (only guarding and protecting), not prescriptive, categorical, interfering. (Froebel, 1887/1905, p. 7)

Also:

> . . . the grapevine must, indeed, be trimmed; but this trimming as such does not insure the wine. On the other hand, the trimming, although done with the best intention, may wholly destroy the vine, or at least impair its fertility and productiveness, if the gardener fails in his work passively and attentively to follow the nature of the plant. (Froebel, 1887/1905, p. 7)

He maintained that play is the self-active representation of the inner impulse, and from his influence came the notion of kindergartens centered on child-directed play.

Froebel's views about early education were like those stated by Dewey:

> As a general principle no activity should be originated by imitation. The start must come from the child. . . . [A teacher's] suggestion must fit in with the dominant mode of growth in the child; it must serve simply as stimulus to bring forth more adequately what the child is already blindly striving to do. (Dewey, 1900/1943, pp. 124–125)

A contrasting view, more like Comenius and Pestalozzi, was espoused by Montessori as she centered on a need for early training of the senses and orderly management of everyday life. This was to be carried out with simple but useful sensory training activities that would lead children through progressive practice in small steps to mastery of a task or concept. She argued that materials should be:

ordered to a definite end, not disorderly noise which distracts the attention. To employ the sensory training apparatus for any other purpose than that for which it is devised would appear as meaningless to the child as to use the pieces of a jigsaw puzzle for some other game. (Montessori, 1912/1964, p. 180)

The materials also provided instruction which allowed children to discover and correct their own errors. She wrote:

It is precisely in these errors that the educational importance of the didactic materials lies. . . . [It is not] the active work of the teacher, who busies herself furnishing knowledge, and making haste to correct any error. It is the work of the child, the auto-correction, the auto-education which acts, for the teacher must not interfere in the slightest way. . . . It is necessary that the pupil perfect himself through his own efforts. (Montessori, 1912/ 1964, p. 172)

So, into this century, with a lessening of the Calvinist view that the purpose of education is the "inculcation of humility, industry, and obedience" (Gammage, 1982) and with an initiation of the child-study movement to form a scientific basis for education (Hall, 1883), the issue of the extent of intrusion by adults into young children's learning is not resolved. Many developmental psychologists in the period from 1930 to 1960, believing that maturation played an overriding role in learning to read, were reluctant to advocate instruction. Thus, reports and textbooks for teachers generally recommended reading readiness instruction but not reading instruction. Here are three examples of this view.

A 1960 Educational Policies Commission of the National Education Association argued against reading instruction for all kindergarten children. They said that research shows that while some children gain from an early start, others do not or are not ready to learn, even in first grade. They believed that the relative function of maturation and experience had not been resolved because some skills seem to develop regardless of practice opportunities, others require both training and practice, and still others develop only with maturation, even though practice is given. Reading skill was thought to be characterized as a function primarily of maturation.

K. Read (1971), a long-standing authority on preschool education, mentioned reading only in the context of providing and arranging books and reading to children. She espoused instruction through games that encourage use of senses, imagination, and problem solving and through conversations with children. "A great part of the teacher's role is in helping children learn how to learn . . . respect[ing] the individual interests, styles and rates of learning of the children" (K. Read, 1971, p. 28).

Leeper, Dale, Skipper, and Witherspoon (1974) took a position against formal teaching of reading, arguing that research indicates a lack of permanence of reading skills taught in kindergarten and that gains are dependent upon subsequent reading instruction. They concluded that instruction for all five-year-olds is questionable and may be harmful for some. Instead, they advocated the use of learning situations which they believed would provide a readiness for reading:

visual perception—distinguishing colors and geometric shapes; visual recall—playing games of remembering what was seen; eye-hand coordination—working with puzzles, balls, clay, painting, and hammering; hearing—awareness of loud and soft and high and low sounds, naming sounds by people and animals and things, hearing words that begin or end with the same sound; and other factors—for example, being read to, having trips and visits in the community.

The fallacy of these views lies in the extreme position that early instruction will have a harmful effect. However, it is apparent in a reanalysis of developmental studies (Razel cited by Hunt, 1983) and long-term training studies (Herber, 1978; Hunt, 1983; Lazar & Darlington, 1978; Levenstein, 1976; Meyer & Gersten, 1983) that early training is not only unharmful but also may be beneficial. Since none of these studies involved only early reading instruction, it remains to be determined whether preschool reading instruction will have positive long-term effects.

Against this backdrop and given the wide ranging descriptive studies on early reading that have been published since 1930 (surveyed by Hammill & McNutt, 1981), I reviewed early reading development literature through the constraint of a model of early reading. The ensuing review, while reflecting an assumption that learning to read has deep roots in early childhood experiences, also proposes explanations of research findings and implications for instruction. Its force, then, is similar to that espoused by G. Stanley Hall (1883): to help form a scientific basis for reading education so that instruction is based on the developing needs and interests of the child.

Issues and Assumptions

> I struggled through the alphabet as if it had been a bramble-bush; getting considerably worried and scratched by every letter. After that, I fell among those thieves, the nine figures, who seemed every evening to do something new to disguise themselves and baffle recognition. But, at last I began, in a purblind groping way, to read, write, and cipher, on the very smallest scale. (Pip in Dickens, *Great Expectations*)

What does a child know about reading before beginning to read in school? The answer depends not only upon the opportunities a child has to learn about how to read but also upon the research approach chosen to study the question and the assumptions made about the role of spoken language in reading. While language research has relied on diary studies, reading has more often been studied cross-sectionally in terms of its correlations with social, educational, cognitive, or linguistic factors. While language competency is assumed to derive from the child's understanding of its principles, reading acquisition is usually assumed to be a function of explicit instruction. While parents are seen to play a crucial role in children's language development, there is no more than a token acceptance that reading could be learned through interaction with parents. Thus, even though it is generally agreed that reading and language are related, research methodology and expected outcomes have obscured the tie to language.

I will assume that there is a tie between language and beginning reading. For purposes of this chapter, I will focus on the tie between children's speech and their interpretation of written language. For example, when children begin learning to read, they will notice that their language is comprised of words and phrases that correspond to similar units of print, they will recognize and distinguish sounds in words in terms of letters and sounds, and they will find out how speech differs from written language in form and function. From this perspective, then, learning to read involves understanding how to relate meaningful utterances to discrete written units, acquiring strategies to analyze words into phonemes and distinguish phonemes as single letters and letter clusters, and using print in ways that serve different purposes from speech. With this perspective, how children should be instructed is deferred to the question of how children learn and understand printed language. But see Hiebert (1981), Morris (1981), or Resnick and Weaver (1979) for other views.

When children begin to notice printed words, they are likely to assume that printed words stand for names of things. In so doing, they will realize that many familiar words are represented in print as discrete units, bound by spaces, replicable by a more-or-less uniform sequence of letters, studied from a left-to-right direction, and so on. Through tasks of attempting to recognize, print, and spell words or through instruction, they figure out or learn that words can be broken into smaller units, which in many cases correspond to names or sounds of letters. These phonological considerations suggest an entirely new insight about printed and spoken words and the possibility of constructing hypotheses about print in order to solve the deeper problem of how meaningful utterances, speech sounds, and printed symbols are related. Furthermore, as children carry out tasks that involve reading, they learn about its untaught aspects, such as the terms describing reading and the rules governing the act of reading. Thus, there appear to be three characteristics of language that are woven into children's understanding about reading: (a) determining how words and concepts are shared by speech and print, (b) realizing how to break speech sounds into the abstract phonemic units that correspond to letters and letter groups, and (c) acquiring conventional information—labels, rules, and procedures—needed to describe and carry out reading tasks.

If one assumes that attention to this information is initiated, even though not fully understood, before a child reads independently, then reading concepts can be grouped into three distinct knowledge strands. The first mentioned strand, closely related to language meaning, is called the *function* of print. It carries a sense of the term segmentation (Menyuk, 1976) and that of amalgamation (Ehri, 1979). When the child begins to try to read, words in print are related to their meanings (Goodman & Goodman, 1979; Mason, 1980; Smith, 1971). The child probably starts by recognizing signs, labels, names, and familiar words, especially those on television, billboards, traffic signs, and labeled food products. The second, distinguished from meaning in terms of its visual and phonological features, is termed *form and structure* of print. Not a new concept, it has been identified as an important aspect of beginning reading by Barron (1979), Calfee (1977), Downing (1973, 1979), Gleitman (1979), Liberman (1970), Mattingly (1972, 1979), Rozin and Gleitman (1977), Samuels (1979), and Valtin (1979), among others. For children who have not yet been instructed in reading, it is an explicit awareness that letters have distinct forms and can be related to word sounds. Extending letter names to sounds, children realize they can match letter-name sounds with initial phonemes in words. The third strand, describing the social and task constraints of reading, is the *conventions* of reading (Clay, 1972; Downing, 1972; Hardy, Stennett, & Smythe, 1974; Hillerich, 1978; Johns, 1972; Reid, 1966). It is an understanding of terms that are used to talk about reading (e.g., "find a word . . . ," "look at the top of the page," or "read the first sentence") as well as the arbitrary rules that govern the act of reading (e.g., knowing that one reads from left to right, that punctuation is important, and what spaces between letters mean) and, later, the procedures and social rules for engaging in reading lessons.

While these strands have been suggested separately, it is the joint construct I want to emphasize. I propose that early reading can be defined as the acquisition of concepts related to functional, formal and conventional strands of print. Initially, I propose that concepts surrounding each strand are acquired in their separate nature, with concepts related to the function of print playing a prominent early role and concepts associated with the other strands joined to those already learned. To consider this model visually, imagine three ribbons (strands) that are hung vertically. The top one is labeled early reader, or prereader, the middle one elementary school reader, while the bottom one is mature reader. Before children are formally instructed, the ribbon labeled function of print predominates because it forms the central focus at first for understanding reading. Later, but depending upon children's experiences and instruction in reading, one and then the other ribbon is woven into the pattern. At the bottom all three strands are woven together to form an integrated whole.

STUDIES OF EARLY READING

One must devise ways of investigating the constituent skills involved in language. And typically one begins well before language begins, following the communicative behavior of particular children until a particular level of linguistic mastery is achieved, testing as well for other, concomitant indices of growth. (Bruner, 1979, p. 65)

Because of the close connection between language learning and early reading learning, the methodology favored to investigate early language development is ideally suited for the study of children's development of concepts about reading.

This review will follow Bruner's recommendation by considering studies which begin well before skilled reading is achieved through longitudinal studies of progress in early reading, surveys of children's attempts to read, and effects of early instruction. The model constructed from that work and organized sectional research in terms of the three hypothesized strands is filled in with cross-sectional research on early and beginning reading.

The child's knowledge about print and plausible supportive environments for learning to read are featured rather than formal instruction. I hope, thereby, to avoid the instructional controversies regarding the centrality of decoding, how beginning readers recognize and analyze words, and whether reading is a top-down or bottom-up process. The aim instead is to demonstrate that children acquire knowledge about reading before they are formally taught to read. The proposed three-strand construct is used to catalog early reading characteristics. Throughout this chapter, the term reading will refer to an ability to recognize and verbalize novel printed words as well as to comprehend some texts. Early reading, or prereading, will refer to conceptual knowledge and skill that precedes independent reading.

Longitudinal Studies

Unlike research into the inception of speech, there are few reported studies of children's acquisition of reading. Many offer no more than anecdotal evidence of children's progress. Even so, and in spite of the fact that parents could help their children learn about reading in dissimilar ways, the reports are remarkably alike. The first examples are taken from authors' summaries of parent interviews.

A 5-year-old black child from a low-middle social class home who could read and write before beginning kindergarten was studied by Torrey (1969). The mother reported no one had taught him or even encouraged him to learn. However, they noticed that before he began reading, he had learned to recite all the TV commercials. Subsequently, he began reading labels from food packages, boxes, and cans. Torrey determined that his language development was typical for the age and his verbal IQ was 96 with a performance IQ of 111.

Durkin (1966) found 49 children out of 5103 in Oakland, California, (in 1958) and 180 children out of 4465 in New York (in 1961) who, at the beginning of first grade, could read a list of primary-level words. Deemed early readers, Durkin asked the parents of these readers, "How did your child first show an interest in reading?" and "Can you remember what might have encouraged the interest?"

> . . . it was a combination of people who had helped Paul to read early, chiefly by answering his many persistent questions about words that interested him. In time, the mother said, she herself grew tired of "running to Paul to see what word he was asking about," so she encouraged him to spell out the word, and she would tell him what it was. According to his mother, Paul knew the names of most of the letters by the time he was four. (p. 62)

> In the beginning, she would copy words from the papers John (older brother) brought home from school, and then she would ask, "What do these say?" (p. 64)

> It was the [television] weather reports and, later, the television commercials that seemed to create his excitement about letters, spelling, writing, and then reading. She said she herself was unaware of Jack's ability to identify written words until he began reading aloud some of the advertisements on television. She said his recognition of the same words on food products in the grocery store was a source of great delight to him. (p. 120)

Söderbergh (1977) reports in detail the responses by her daughter to reading materials, beginning at age two years four months and continuing for a year. During the first six weeks, the child was presented word cards denoting familiar things and actions. After six weeks, the words of a short book were put on cards so that after learning words on cards, the child read them in a book. During this period, the author observed that the child treated word cards as if they had been persons or things and that functors were difficult to learn out of context.[1] Then, at the child's instigation similarly spelled words were commented on and compared; it seems that visual images of words were formed as they were learned. The child learned about 150 words during the first three months. During the next nine months, and after learning the words, she read books that contained only the learned words, rereading them many times and relating characters and events to herself. She was able to learn five to ten new words a day and began to decode new words by herself by analysis into letters or letter clusters, noting to her mother the similarity with previously learned words. By the eighth month, she was learning 130 to 140 words a month. After one year of reading and practicing new words on cards, she was able to read almost any new word that was put on a card. Then she was given new books directly without the preliminary card reading and learning. Söderbergh noted that it was in rereading the stories aloud to herself that the child learned phrasing and intonation, practicing different intonations and stress patterns. In spite of learning words on cards, the child always connected reading with reality. New words on cards were put into context through the child's comments (e.g., "Mother, I get so frightened when it says 'frightful' on a reading card."). Contents of a story were frequently criticized if they conflicted with her knowledge of the world (e.g., "That is not what gives people grey hair. It is only when they get old." was her retort when she read that waiting turned hair grey) or served as inspiration for her games and play and enhanced some later experiences (e.g., she was delighted to be able to label new experiences using words she had only read, such as her first view of a pasture). Writing, which had not been fostered, was initiated by the child after her first year of reading. She began with the capital letters, then lower-case letters, to write to invented people. She seldom made spelling errors.

The case study demonstrates how and under what circumstances the written word might be acquired. Söderbergh had predicted that if a child learns to talk without formal instruction, solely by being exposed to language, then, if exposed to written language, a child ought to be able to learn to read at about the same time by forming hypotheses, building models, and thus discovering written language's morphemic, syntactic, and semantic systems. Here, exposure to written language was not haphazard but was structured by giving the child words on cards to learn, with the first words being those that were extremely familiar to the child. Later word cards were derived from books that the child would next read. The author noted that the child herself constructed notions about visual features of words, how they could be pronounced, how they were related to objects and events and how they were used in stories. She read and reread words and stories many times, just as children recite words and phrases when learning to talk.

While the report demonstrates that a very young child can learn to read, the hypothesis that the processes of learning to read and speak are the same remains unproven since the printed words and the order of learning were not chosen by the child. Nonetheless, the study does support the important notion that children can learn to read without being taught rules—that they can discover the regularities of morphemic, syntactic, and semantic systems as they learn words and read stories and that it can take place as the child is learning to talk.

A study conducted by MacKinnon (1959) documents first-grade children's progress in learning to read, measuring test results as well as changes in errors from oral reading. The study contrasts three types of instruction:

(a) Groups of children met with an experimenter to read aloud simple, repetitive sentences.[2] The sentences were partly cued with pictures and gradually included new words and a larger variety of consonants. Lessons were arranged so that children took turns reading aloud each succeeding sentence. If a child could not read something, then the group as a whole tried to figure out the print. The experimenter-teacher helped only when asked by the children.

(b) Individual children met with an experimenter to read aloud the sentences described above. Since instruction was one to one, each child had to read all the sentences and had no opportunity to work together with others to figure out words.

(c) Groups of children read aloud with an experimenter, utilizing standard reading materials[3] and a standard instructional format.

The results were quite conclusive, showing that the use of letter-restricted materials with *groups* of children was the most successful; instruction with the same materials but in a child/experimenter dyad was next best. Summarizing from MacKinnon's data of the second, fifth, seventh, and last sessions of the average number of errors made and not corrected (Table 17.1), it is evident that the advantage of the group instruction was greater at the end of the ten sessions than earlier and appeared only for function words. Further, a comparison of the two group instruction treatments revealed that only children using the letter-restricted materials maintained their practice of helping one another (see Table 17.2). Finally, the groups using letter-restricted materials obtained higher scores than the other groups on the *Gates Reading Readiness Test* and *Diagnostic Tests in Reading*. MacKinnon noted that while these children took longer to complete the tests and even though they had been exposed to half as many letters and fewer words, they attempted to do more of the test items. They appeared to focus on the letters they knew, using them as cues to identify whole words. They also seemed to look more carefully at letter order, using word parts that needed to be discriminated, to compare and identify words. They had learned to approach reading as a problem that they could solve.

Mason (1980) followed groups of nursery school children for 9 months during which time they received informal early reading instruction. The children's parents filled out a questionnaire at the beginning and end of the school year which described their child's interest in learning about letters and words and any roles they played in fostering their child's reading. Word and letter identification and word-learning tasks were devised to measure when and under what circumstances the children began to read and were able to remember printed words. The results indicated that all the children made progress in reading and four were reading on their own by the end of the school year.

The changes made in knowledge of reading and skill in recognizing letters

TABLE 17.1   MEAN NUMBER OF WORD-READING ERRORS MADE DURING INSTRUCTION

INSTRUCTION TYPE	MEETING NO. 2		MEETING NO. 5		MEETING NO. 7		MEETING NO. 10	
	NOUNS	FUNCTORS	NOUNS	FUNCTORS	NOUNS	FUNCTORS	NOUNS	FUNCTORS
Letter-restricted materials, group setting $N = 8$ groups	9	18	7	13	5	8	3	5
Letter-restricted materials, individual setting $N = 42$	9	15	9	20	8	15	5	9
Traditional Materials group setting $N = 8$ groups	3	28	3	35	6	36	3	28

Source: MacKinnon, 1959.

TABLE 17.2   PERCENTAGES OF CHILDREN IN GROUPED INSTRUCTION WHO
OFFERED SUGGESTIONS DURING READING

INSTRUCTION TYPE	MEETING NO. 2	MEETING NO. 5	MEETING NO. 7	MEETING NO. 10
Letter-restricted materials	55	41	64	85
Traditional materials	65	30	25	12

Source: MacKinnon, 1959.

and words, spelling, and writing were best described in terms of three levels of development.[4] The first level is denoted by children's ability to read at least one printed word, usually their name or a few signs and labels. They can also recite the alphabet, recognize a few letters, and may print letters. At the second level, they read a few short and very common words from books, print, and spell short words and begin to try reading new words by looking at the first consonant. At the third level, they notice and begin to use the more complex letter-sound to word-sound congruences and letter-pattern configurations. Thus, first-level children recognize words by context, second-level children begin to use letter- and word-sound cues, and third-level children rely on a sounding-out strategy to identify words. Mason defines third-level children as readers; first- and second-level children, as prereaders.

Case study descriptions of children's progress during their year in a preschool (from the Mason, 1977, study) show that each child made progress in learning to read but at a different level of development. That is, every child's prereading knowledge advanced gradually throughout the school year and showed a predictable change in understanding about print.

A subsequent study was carried out to determine whether the three levels of development would be apparent through testing children's reading knowledge and, if so, whether that test would predict reading after a year of instruction (Mason & McCormick, 1979; McCormick & Mason, 1981). Three classrooms of kindergarten children were tested in late spring, retested during the first week of first grade, and given a Gates-MacGinitie Primary Reading Test at the end of first grade. The children were separated into three levels based on their end-of-first-grade achievement test scores. The 6 children who at the end of kindergarten had obtained deviantly low scores were still Level I prereaders in first grade. The remaining 44 children were at Level II (38 children) or Level III (6 children).

Children's test scores at the end of kindergarten and progress over the summer suggest that they were categorized accurately by the three-leveled model (see Table 17.3). Children in Level I who did very poorly in spelling, letter sounding, and word reading were the only children who had not learned their letters by the end of kindergarten. Predictably, they made great progress over the summer in letter naming and some progress in spelling. Level II children, knowing the alphabet at the end of the school year and able to read a few words, made the greatest progress on consonant identification and the reading of two- and three-letter words. Level III children, having mastered the alphabet and consonant-sound correspondences, showed progress on vowel sounds and recognition of words. Thus, all the children gained knowledge over the summer

TABLE 17.3 AVERAGE PERCENTAGE PREREADING TEST CHANGE BETWEEN THE END OF KINDERGARTEN AND BEGINNING OF FIRST GRADE

	LEVEL I PERFORMERS (N = 6)		LEVEL II PERFORMERS (N = 38)		LEVEL III PERFORMERS (N = 6)	
	PERCENT CHANGE	TIME 2 PERCENT	PERCENT CHANGE	TIME 2 PERCENT	PERCENT CHANGE	TIME 2 PERCENT
LEVEL I TESTS						
Upper-case letter naming	25	77	1	100	0	100
Lower-case letter naming	12	67	4	94	2	100
LEVEL II TESTS						
Spelling 2- or 3-letter words	28	55	4	91	6	100
Consonant-sound identification	8	12	16	78	10	98
LEVEL III TESTS						
Word reading (isolated words)	1	4	15	39	33	93
Vowel-sound identification	1	2	4	22	22	68

Source: McCormick and Mason, 1981.

about how to read, but, in keeping with the construct, learned about different aspects of reading.

A follow-up study (Mason & McCormick, 1981) determined whether training prereaders to recognize letters and words and to read stories can accelerate interest in or knowledge about reading. To this end, 10 lessons were arranged that were thought to foster Level I or Level II development. One group was taught to recognize and print six consonants; to read (or recite) short, very simple stories (Level I constructs); and to relate letters to their initial sound in words (Level II constructs). Another group was given lessons that fostered only Level I constructs. They learned to recite the books but talked about the stories instead of receiving instruction in letter-sound identification. They also took turns extending stories and categorizing pictured objects.

Children's responses to the tasks indicated a clear hierarchy of difficulty. Most children did not seem to understand what it meant to point, for example, to the t's in words from a story. While willing to comply, they did not understand why they were drawing pictures of objects that, for example, began with t. They continually forgot to draw a t to go with their picture. Also, only two children could name words beginning with a particular consonant; the others mimicked the teacher's choices. On the other hand, the six-to-seven-page stories,[5] which contained a handful of words on each illustrated page, did not require children to understand or remember sounds of letters. After listening to the teacher read a story, they were able, in one or two readings, to recite most of the text. They were eager for their turn to read aloud. Even easier were the tasks of selecting letters and naming pictures. Thus, a hierarchy of instructional difficulty was: letter naming = picture categorization < story recitation = letter copying < letter-sound tasks. According to parental report, the children subsequently displayed much greater interest in reading, printing, spelling, and having words identified. Five months later, nearly all the parents reported their children to have greater interest in and more knowledge about reading.[6] These results, which are being confirmed in follow-up work, suggest that helping children attend to words in context can substantially advance their knowledge about print.

One other longitudinal study, a diary study in beginning reading, was reported by Calfee and Piontkowski (1981). Fifty first-grade students who had not yet learned to read but were considered on the verge by their teacher were observed and tested throughout their first year of reading instruction. While details about individual students were not available, the growth of decoding skills was described in terms of mastery of particular skills during first grade.

> During September and October students demonstrated functional prereading skills—they learned the letter-names, could identify rhyming words, and could match letters to the initial consonant in words. In November, however, when students were asked to read lists of rhyming words, significant differences were observed. Those differences increased during winter and spring. By the end of the school year, five levels of skill mastery could be discerned among the 50 students. Eleven students had succeeded on every decoding task in the entire system. Six students could handle vowel contrasts but had difficulty with polysyllabic words. Eight students had some success in identifying consonant blends and digraphs, but could not pronounce these words by themselves. Eleven students were still having trouble decoding CVC words. (p. 359)

The 11 most troubled students, most of whom continued to obtain low reading scores in second grade, were described further. In January, when asked to read three-letter words, 7 of the students gave no response, a response unrelated to the word, or a word that contained one letter, usually the first, of the word to be read. In May, however, they all were able to use the correct initial consonant and often, also, the final consonant. Vowels were still generally incorrectly rendered.

This description of the 11 children matches very closely the growth observed in the earlier reported study of preschool children (Mason, 1980). December responses were like Level I word-reading behavior, being either a no-response or an unrelated word. Many responses were like Level II behavior, that of matching the initial or initial plus final consonant. At both levels, vowels were usually wrong. Thus, the children in the Calfee and Piontkowski study who knew the least about the phonology seemed to be most like prereaders. It is also important that these children, although failing to make significant progress in decoding, did acquire some skill in reading stories orally. Possibly, these children were late in understanding the function of print so that they were also behind other children in achieving the form and structure of print.

Results from these longitudinal studies, which by themselves are insufficient (they need to be both replicated and extended in scope and population type), help to explain some individual differences in reading achievement that appear at the beginning of first grade or before a year of reading instruction has been completed. The reason for these differences, Mason's model suggests, is not due principally to the teacher or the method of reading instruction but to the differences in children's already-acquired knowledge of print. It took Söderbergh's child a full year—given concerted parental help—to pass through the prereading levels; only half the four-year-olds Mason (1980) tested moved through one level of prereading during the 9 months they were observed. Hence, it seems likely that children who are given next to no help at home are unlikely to recognize printed words or letters, let alone letter sounds, and may need a year of instruction before reaching the level of their more fortunate, parent-assisted peers.

While a one- or two-level developmental lag sounds disastrous, it needs to be tempered by the reminder that more longitudinal studies are needed to determine (a) whether recognition of words, printing, and spelling are sufficient indicators of reading; (b) whether formal early reading instruction can affect children's later reading success; and (c) whether parents can be taught to provide relevant informal early reading instruction. In so doing, we can begin to understand how to improve the prereading milieu for preschool and kindergarten children.

Cross-sectional Research

The division of early reading into concepts related to the function, form and structure, and conventions of print, as noted earlier, reflects the speculation that there are three interrelated strands of prereading competency, one being initiated by learning that context cues help to identify object names as printed words, a second begun by recognizing that letters have particular graphic forms and sounds and that sounds in words are related to letters, and a third that is based on the assumption that, as concepts about reading are acquired, so are rules, procedures, and uses for reading. These distinctions are maintained in this section. While research on early reading processing will be based on the original question, "What does a child know about reading before becoming a skillful reader?", it will be discussed under the proposed strands: function, form, and convention.

The Function of Print

A child was overheard asking a teacher, "How do you spell 'Mom'?" As it was spelled, the child wrote it out, studied the word, and said, "M–O–M, mommy." (Observed by Mason at a nursery school)

Understanding the function of print probably occurs in a fumbling manner, for at first the child does not realize, for example, that the printed word *rabbit* cannot be called "bunny" (Mason, 1980), or, as noted by Harste (1980), the word *CREST* is not read "toothpaste" or "brush your teeth." In likeness to speech, realizing the meaningfulness of print involves knowledge of how to separate speech into words that correspond to printed words and to relate both to an appropriate meaning. It requires a child to learn about the relationships among speech, concepts, objects, or events and the printed word or phrase.

A number of researchers have studied some aspects of children's acquisition of knowledge about print and speech, using the terms word consciousness or segmentation. Studying children's abilities to segment speech into words, Karpova in 1955 (abstracted by Slobin, 1966) described three stages of development. Three- and four-year-old children regarded the sentence as composed of semantic units; words were not distinguished. For example, the sentence, "Galyla and Vova went walking" was said to contain two words, "Galyla went walking" and "Vova went walking." At the next stage, children were able to identify object nouns or to separate sentences into subject and predicate. In the third stage, children understood the notion of wordness, except that compound or multisyllable words were sometimes mismarked and functors were often not distinguished. Huttenlocher (1964) gave children two-word sequences and asked children to reverse the order of the units. She found that 35% of the four- and five-year-old children could not do the task. Those who could had the most trouble reversing common phrases (e.g., when asked to say, "runs man" after presentation of "man runs"). Holden and MacGinitie (1972) simplified Karpova's task of sequencing sentences by asking children to point to a poker chip as they repeated each separate word in sentences that they had just heard. Testing four- to six-year-olds, they found that most of the children were in Karpova's second or third stage.

Ehri (1975) extended the Holden and MacGinitie study by testing whether sentence-segmentation performance would be improved if sentences were read in a monotone with a demonstration of the correct division into words. Preschool children improved little, changing from 17% when performing under normal conditions to 22% with a monotonic demonstration. Kindergarten children who could not read benefited considerably, obtaining first an average score of 20%, then a score of 43%; however, kindergarteners and first graders who could read made little improvement, changing from 58% to 59%. One possible explanation for the low scores is that children may have been confused by an accompanying syllable-sequentation task. Another possibility is that the task quite accurately reflects children's understanding of the relationship between print and speech (after all, readers performed better than did prereaders) but that mimicry is not sufficient to affect conceptual knowledge. Further, while children who could read obtained the higher scores, their overall scores of less than 60% suggest that even beginning readers do not have a complete understanding of print/speech referencing. This interpretation is in agreement with work completed by Holden and MacGinitie (1972), Meltzer and Herse (1969), and Mickish (1974).

The lack of understanding of the relationship between print and speech could be used to explain results obtained by Francis (1977). Five-year-old children who had begun to read, all of whom could read some or all the words in a book, were asked to read (a) the exact sentences from the book, (b) unfamiliar but meaningful sentences comprised of words from the original sentences, and (c) a listing of the words from the sentences. Combining children's scores from two social classes and three ability levels reveals that the number of word errors was higher for unfamiliar sentences (30%) and words in lists (32%) than for familiar sentences (20%). Differences were particularly marked for low-ability children. The results suggest that many first graders identify words by their context; they do not necessarily transfer word/print information to other contexts.

Perhaps they are still treating sentences as an unbroken stream rather than in terms of individual words. That is, it is possible that at this early level of development, words are not the child's unit of analysis but are treated in terms of the meaning or message.[7] Children's errors support this interpretation as they often rendered unfamiliar sentences as the sentences originally learned. A similar result was obtained by MacKinnon (1959).

It is plausible that when children begin to acquire an understanding of the function of print, they remember print in terms of its meaning and do not consider word-sized units; if so, they may not even realize that their textbooks contain a large number of the same words.[8] Hence, instruction to use context clues to figure out a new or a forgotten word could, in some circumstances, not be helpful to early readers. In that case, reading words in a list would be no harder than reading an unfamiliar sentence—a result which is nicely documented in the Francis (1977) study.

The research that was just presented highlighted the fact of individual differences in knowledge about the function of print. To understand how to help children learn, we need to ask what could be guiding children's different viewpoints, that is, what could lead them to learn about the function of print? The question is speculative, there being no concerted research on the topic. However, results from the earlier presented longitudinal research suggest what and how children acquire this knowledge.

Parents frequently report that their child began reading by watching television advertisements closely, noticing words on food-product containers, or attending to traffic signs. Consider that each of these provides occasions of nearly direct matching between speech and print. For example, a television announcer describes a product, emphasizing its name, and the name or a picture of the labeled product is prominantly displayed. Young children grocery shopping with a parent hear products named and see what is selected, often even helping to choose a particular product. In these informal ways, children can observe that print is used to express or label named objects. Television commercials, food and household products, store and traffic signs, and billboards are intended to attract attention to print as a reference to objects or (in the case of traffic signs) actions. These obviously provide some of the necessary knowledge about separate words in speech (and might explain the suggested effect of television viewing on first-grade reading scores found by Barth and Swiss, 1976, and by Scott, 1975).

Even while children may not be coached by their parents to begin reading words in books, they are often helped to recognize labels on food products or signs and in this way are likely to acquire some notions about how speech can be coded. Note, however, that in these instances print is highly contextualized; words often appear embedded in a picture, or design, or logo. Note, also, that the meaning referencing the printed word may not be voiced in the same way each time. While STOP occurs next to a crossroad on an octagonally shaped board and is called, stop or stop sign by adults, food labels are often difficult to discern because they can be referenced in various ways by parents (by their brand name [Crest], a generic name [toothpaste], function [brush your teeth]). Also, some two- or three-word phrases are always together (e.g., corn flakes, Nature Valley Granola, Cap'n Crunch, Coca-Cola), so children may not realize the importance of spaces to identify separate words. As a result, while the child can begin to learn how objects and speech are related, incorrect deductions about reading can be made easily.

The segmentation research suggests that an understanding of print/speech relationships is clarified through experiences of reading and reading lessons in first grade. Thus, even after repeated experiences of listening to someone read and receiving coaching on word recognition by parents, children usually enter school with an inadequate understanding of how words in print are related to meaning. Not only are word junctures poorly understood, but object noun words may be related to speech inaccurately (or freely translated, as noted earlier) and function words may be enirely unnoticed. Differences found between pre-school children's ability to learn to read words that vary in meaningfulness favor nouns over function words (e.g., Mason, 1977; MacKinnon, 1959; Ollila & Chamberlain, 1979; Steinberg & Yamada, 1978) and thus support this interpretation.

An instructional implication is that beginning reading instructors ought to be well aware of the conceptual problem young children face when confronted by whole sentences, many of which are written in a style that poorly matches children's speech utterances.[9] It may be very difficult for many children to figure out how printed phrases and sentences are related to meaningful speech. This is perhaps the point of "reading for meaning," stressed by Goodman (1972a, 1972b) and Smith (1971).

Form and Structure of Print

It was my very own child who first embroiled me in the nettlesome issue of "metalinguistic knowledge." At about 3½ she asked me: "Mom, is it *an a*-dult or *a nuh*-dult?" (Gleitman, 1979, p. 1)

According to Halliday (1975), there are two functions of speech: *pragmatic* (interactive and manipulative aspects) and *mathetic* (declarative and observational utterances that lead the speaker to become aware of language itself).[10] It is the mathetic function which relates to the form and structure of print, describing the graphic, phonological, and morphophonemic structures of printed information. While this function extends beyond the prereading period into later development of reading knowledge, we shall necessarily center on its inception. As such, the ability to verbalize the rules for letter-to-sound relationships is not the issue here; what is important instead is the information children appear to use when confronted with printed words and how their understanding changes through experiences of reading, printing, or spelling. Two aspects will be considered here: (a) differentiation of the graphic forms of letters and (b) phonemic analysis of words.

Letter identification.   When children are able not only to recite the alphabet but also to name and print letters, they have acquired considerable knowledge about the critical attributes for distinguishing letters. They then know that particular strokes and orientations of straight and curved lines, not thickness or color of lines, are to be noticed; that letters can appear in various type fonts; and that letters have more than one form (e.g., Aa, Ee, Rr). What may be more remarkable is that this information is seldom taught in school, yet it must be known—letters must be recognized accurately—in order to learn to read. How then do children acquire this information?

Letter knowledge has been tested principally with three types of tasks, letter or symbol discrimination, letter recognition, and letter naming. A discrimination task measures the child's ability to match pairs of symbols. Gibson, Gibson, Pick, and Osser (1962) tested children aged four to eight on discrimination of novel letterlike forms (e.g., $\perp$, $\triangleright$) by comparing discrimination on each form in 12 different transformations. The child was asked to select exact copies of the standard form. Four types of transformations were compared across age:

(a) break-and-close (e.g., $\perp$ or $\pm$),

(b) line-to-curve (e.g., $\downarrow$, $\not\perp$, or $\triangleright$),

(c) rotation or reversal (e.g., $\mp$, $\curlyvee$, or $\triangleleft$), and

(d) perspective ($\perp$, $\triangleright$).

Break-and-close transformations were least frequently confused with standard forms; errors decreased over the age span from 15% to 5%. Line-to-curves were reduced from 38% to 7%, rotations and reversals went from 46% to 4%, and perspectives changed from 79% to 60%. The differences in the four types of transformations demonstrate what young children observe about print before learning to read and how they alter their perceptions, presumably in response to learning to read. Break-and-close transformations are infrequently chosen as copies, even by 4-year-olds, while rotations, reversals, and line-to-curve transformations are not initially recognized.[11] But by age eight, these initially contrary transformations are rejected as often as are break-and-close transformations. However, perspective changes continue to be accepted, even by eight-year-olds, as exact copies more than half the time. Foreshortening or tilting of letters, unless excessive, are usually tolerated, as either would be by skilled readers. The study indicates, then, that over the time period that young children are learning to read, they gradually learn which features of symbols are critical for letter recognition. They learn to discriminate features that distinguish different letters and ignore features that do not.

Hillerich (1966) cites an unpublished study by Nicholson in which 2188 first graders were tested after three weeks of school. Results of a letter-discrimination test, with mean scores of 25.34 in matching capital letters and 24.48 in matching lower-case letters, suggested to her that gross discrimination reading readiness activities are a waste of children's time. This conclusion is not generally disputed. The value of letter naming, by contrast, has not been settled. Olson (1958), who followed 1172 of the children Nicholson had tested through the middle of second grade, determined that the mean for lower-case letter naming was much lower at the beginning of first grade (9.0) and that letter naming correlated .55 with second-grade reading. Similarly, de Hirsch, Jansky, and Langford (1966) found that of 19 tests given in kindergarten, letter naming was the best predictor of second-grade reading (.55). This high correlation has also been confirmed by many others (see reviews by Barrett, 1965, or Chall, 1967).

However, a causal link is disputed. According to Venezky (1978), "a significant advantage in letter name training over other forms of initial training for benefiting first grade achievement [has not been realized]" (p. 12). Gibson and Levin (1975) suggested that "untaught knowledge (or reasonably spontaneous learning) of the names of letters is simply a symptom of a child's awareness of linguistic concepts or of his interest in language and reading, and not in itself something to build on" (p. 251). Venezky (1970) thought that "letter-name knowledge at the beginning of first grade reflects the presence of a variety of factors which themselves are important for learning to read; e.g., level of cognitive development, emotional stability, attention span, and proper interaction with adults outside of school" (p. 10). A third alternative is that letter names orient the child to analysis of words and serve as partial labels for identifying phonemes in words and for relating letter symbols to their sounds (Durrell & Murphy, 1953).

The longitudinal studies described earlier provide evidence that letter naming typically precedes an early awareness of letter sounds in words. Four-year-old children (Mason, 1980) learned to recite the alphabet, recognize and name letters, and print letters before they learned to identify letters in spoken words and figure out how parts of words were pronounced. Other studies show that letter naming is highly correlated with other aspects of reading. For example, kindergarten children's lowercase letter-naming scores (Mason & McCormick, 1979) were correlated .46 with word reading, .57 with spelling, .57 with the knowledge of consonant sounds in three-letter words, and .59 with end-of-first-grade vocabulary achievement test scores.

If letter naming is important to reading, why have training experiments not been able to demonstrate its value? Two possible overlapping explanations are indicated. First, to return to the point made at the beginning of this section, letter naming is a task which measures much more than discrimination of letter forms; it approximates underlying conceptual knowledge of how to distinguish and name symbols. So, children could have been taught in an experimental situation to label differently *C, O, G,* and *Q* or *b, d, p, q,* and *a,* but the instruction might have been carried out without communicating the distinctive visual features of letters. While Samuels (1973) showed that letter-name learning was facilitated by visual-discrimination training on distinctive features of letters, in other studies a single type font or letter case might have been used in training and testing. Hence, children may not have learned to be sufficiently flexible in identifying letters. When eventually tested in another setting or with slightly different materials, the children might have failed to see the connection between the training and testing forms of letters. Thus, letter-name experiments could have failed because training has been defined too narrowly.

The second explanation is that letter naming may provide an important function as a verbal label, both to help children differentiate letter forms visually and to aid them in identifying or remembering sounds of letters. Verbal labeling was found in paired associate work to aid preschool children's learning (Spiker, 1963). With respect to its value in affixing sounds, the principal opposing argument comes from Venezky (1978). He states that letter-name training cannot be justified on grounds of mediation for sounds: "40% of the letter names are not usable as sound mediators (letters such as *h* or *w* do not name the sound, also vowels and the consonants *c* and *g* name the less frequently appearing sound) and the remaining 60% must be differentiated according to where the mediated sounds occurs" (p. 12) (i.e., at the beginning or end of the name). However, an alternative analysis of letter names allows the opposite conclusion. Children's attempts to read and spell words (Chomsky, 1971, 1979; Mason, 1980; Mason & McCormick, 1979; Paul, 1976; Read, 1971) show that children learn letter names somewhat before they begin to relate the sound of consonants to words. This suggests that when uninstructed children begin to recognize and analyze words into letters, most consonant names can serve a sound mediation role. While 2 consonants, *h* and *w*, do not describe a sound that the letter makes and 3 others, *y*, *c*, and *g*, are misleading[12] in describing less frequently used sounds, the remaining 16 consonants contain in their names the principal germ of the sound. The fact that the sound is either displayed at the beginning (e.g., *b*, *d*) or the end (e.g., *f*, *l*) of the letter name is not necessarily a serious impediment. Our unpublished research on this question has not found differences of applying to words initial-name and final-name consonants.

Letter naming, then, ought to be considered as a mask for more enveloping concepts about print. If so, cursory letter-name training is not likely by itself to make a difference in reading. Children who learn letters at home spend months learning to differentiate letters, recognizing their various upper- and lower-case forms, and labeling those forms. Since they generally learn letter names from parents' presentation of letter names, rather than sounds, letter names become children's first means of differentiating and labeling letter forms; later these labels appear to mediate between the grapheme and the phoneme. The latter point, while attested to by Durrell and Murphy (1978), and suggested by children's spelling and word-reading errors (C. Read, 1971), is discussed more fully in the next section.

Another aspect of letter identification is seen in letter writing. According to Gibson and Levin (1975), previous studies of writing indicate that children's early productions can be classified into levels of development (Hildreth, 1936). Testing children between the ages of three and six, children were asked to write their names or any letters or numbers they could make. Five levels were observed: *one*, unorganized, aimless scribbling; *two*, up and down zigzags; *three*, contrasts of straight lines and curves; *four*, close approximations to real letters and words; and *five*, construction of real letters or words. Since none of the children had been encouraged by parents to write, it was concluded that writing skill can occur without direct instruction. Wheeler (1971) analyzed kindergarten children's drawings and writings, dividing the school year into 15 periods of 10 days each in order to study more closely the development of writing. A change from designs and pictures to letters and words in isolation to words in phrases and sentences occurred. Construction of letters improved, apparently by self-correction, since the teachers did not intervene to correct errors or to teach children how to write.

Some research has found a positive relationship between parents' perceptions of preschool children's prereading knowledge and tests of the children's letter- and word-printing ability. Mason (1980) found that preschoolers began to write at about the same time that they began to recognize printed words. Thus, writing (actually printing letters and words, usually in upper case) seems frequently to accompany preschoolers' increasing interest in naming letters and reading words. It appears to be a self-motivated activity, requiring little or no correction by adults. While it is not an easy task for some four-year-olds, it is often highly valued by children themselves. What we do not know yet is what the parents' role is in encouraging their children to write. Durkin (1966) reported important differences based on home interviews between parents of early readers and nonearly readers. For example, between 47% and 83% of parents of early readers said that paper, pencil, blackboards and reading materials were available, while only between 14% and 23% of parents of nonearly readers provided these supports. Thus, since many preschool children begin to write as they acquire prereading knowledge about letters and words, writing as an avenue to learning about the form and structures of print might be more important than we yet realize (see work by Calkins, 1980; Graves, 1982).

Phonemic analysis of words. In order to utilize an alphabetic language properly (by which I mean that a child can take advantage of the structure implicit in an alphabetic code and thereby learn to read words never before seen in print) what must a prereader understand? In some way unknown to us as yet, the child must work analytically to distinguish sounds in words and relate those to letters. However, phones, which are the minimal units of speech, are not necessarily represented in the orthography. Instead, collections of phones which are regarded as the same by speakers of the language are distinguished. These are called *phonemes.* Phonemes, then, are more or less well represented by the graphemes, our alphabet. In the case of English, the representation is complex since we distinguish more phonemes (about 44) than letters (26). To further confuse the child, some phonemes (e.g., $/k/$ as in *kill* and *call*) are represented by two graphemes, some letters (e.g., $/c/$ as in *candy* and *cindy*) have very different sounds, and some letters represent two distinct phoneme clusters (e.g., $/x/$ as in *exact*—$/gz/$—and *exercise*—$/ks/$).[13] Finally, in seeming disregard of the child's need for labels that might help match letters to sounds, alphabet names, as noted earlier, do not always describe a letter's principal phoneme.

Given the importance of understanding the phonological structure of the language, how *do* children learn to attach sounds to letters and match those to sounds in words? Gibson and Levin (1975) offer three possibilities: (a) by induction, (b) by being told a verbalization of a rule, or (c) by practice with contrasting patterns. The question, however, is complicated by the fact that the phonological and orthographic rule systems have not been completely defined by linguists. It is even difficult to estimate how many rules there are in English for describing correspondences (see Venezky, 1970, for one classification). There is controversy over whether English orthography is related primarily to phonemes or to larger lexical units (morphemes and words). Finally there is very little evidence, assuming that children learn primarily by induction, about which structures they understand first or how. Also, assuming that children learn primarily by being given rules or contrasting patterns, how much deliberate instruction is required and how should it be ordered?

Although there is no doubt that knowledge of letters and their sounds in words is aided by rule learning in reading lessons, the orientation of this chapter is toward learning that occurs during the preschool period. Since few children are given deliberate instruction at that time, we will consider evidence regarding inductive learning.

Earlier, three levels of reading development were proposed and related to three knowledge strands: function, form and structure, and convention. Possibly, as children begin to distinguish words in speech that can be recognized in print (Level I), they notice that words starting with the same sound usually have the same letter. This paves the way for further analyses—segmenting words into phonemes and remembering words by their letter composition (Level II). If children have learned letter names but not sounds (which, among preschoolers, is typical), they are likely to make use of names to segment words into letter-corresponding phonemes. This may be the way that uninstructed children begin to acquire knowledge of the phonology. Evidence evaluating this issue comes from phonetic segmentation research, invented spellings, and word pronunciation errors.

The segmentation research seems to indicate that children understand phonetic segmentation (separation of words into sounds that can be represented by letters) as a result of reading instruction. Bruce (1964) gave children age 5 to 7½ common words to segment. They were asked to report what word remained when an initial, medial, or final sound was deleted (e.g., /h/ from hill, /s/ from nest, or /d/ from card). Children below age 7 had great difficulty with the task, particularly segmentation of the medial sound. Similarly, Rosner and Simon (1971) asked children age 5 to 11 to delete one sound (syllable or consonant in initial, medial, or final position) from a pronounced word. The greatest grade-to-grade difference occurred between kindergarten and first grade. Since the test was given at the end of the school year, the results suggest that first-grade reading instruction facilitated performance. However, a simpler version of phonetic awareness was devised by Calfee (1977). Training children first to recognize an ending sound as a picture (e.g., pictures of "eyes," "eat," and "ache"), kindergarten children were able to select the picture that contained the respective ending sound, such as choosing "eyes" if given the word *spies*. Even when new pictosounds were introduced, the children were able to carry out the task (though the average correct response was then reduced from 90% to 70%).

Phonetic segmentation was also investigated by Liberman, Shankweiler, Fischer, and Carter (1974) who asked preschool children to tap on a table the number of segments they heard in a word. They were asked, after practicing the task, to segment 42 words into syllables or into phonemes. No word was longer than three syllables for the one condition or three phonemes for the other. The results showed that syllable segmentation was easier than phonetic segmentation. None of the nursery school children could correctly segment as few as six consecutive words by phoneme, whereas nearly half could segment that number by syllable. Only 17% of the kindergarten children but 70% of the first graders succeeded in phoneme segmentation, while, in syllable segmentation, the percentages were 48% and 90%, respectively.

The last two mentioned studies indicate that, while preschool children as a whole do not perform well on phonetic segmentation tasks, some can segment by phonemes and many more can separate words into syllables or can distinguish ending sounds, implying that preschool children acquire some knowledge of the phonology by induction. The leap in performance after receiving reading instruction probably indicates that a fairly substantial amount of learning also occurs by reading practice and direct phonics instruction. Nevertheless, since the relative success of a preschool or kindergarten child in a phonetic segmentation task strongly predicts later achievement in reading (e.g., Calfee, Chapman, & Venezky, 1972; Calfee, Lindamood, & Lindamood, 1973; Fox & Routh, 1976;

Liberman et al., 1977), it is possible that preschoolers' understanding of the phonology aids them in their later reading.

An explanation of the role played by phonological awareness can be extrapolated from a comparison of good and poor readers' use of phonetic recoding. In a study reported by Liberman et al. (1977), 46 second-grade children with similar IQ scores but dissimilar reading grade equivalent scores were presented five-letter unpronounceable strings; in one condition they were asked to recall them immediately and in another condition to recall them after a 15-second delay. The letter strings were either confusable (i.e., rhyming, drawn from the set *B C D G P T V Z*) or nonconfusable (i.e., nonrhyming, drawn from the set *H K L Q R S W Y*). While the superior readers (second graders with an average grade equivalent score of 4.9) made fewer errors altogether, the more interesting result is that confusable letter strings more severely hampered the superior readers than it did the marginal readers (with a grade equivalent score of 2.5) or the poor readers (grade equivalent score of 2.0), particularly in the delayed recall condition. The result suggests that superior readers make more efficient use of phonetic recoding than do marginal or poor readers. This works to their advantage ordinarily but not in a task where they must recall letters that are phonologically confusing (rhyming). By contrast, marginal and poor readers may be using nonphonetic memory strategies and so are not appreciably hampered by the rhyming set of letters.

More direct evidence that linguistic awareness is often initiated by preschool children comes from studies of invented spelling. When C. Read (1971) showed that some preschool children were able to spell words (i.e., they invented spellings that could be interpreted on the basis of linguistic analysis), the response initially was that this behavior is atypical (e.g., "It seems to the writers that this is a rather unusual accomplishment and that these were not run-of-the-mill children," Gibson & Levin, 1975; p. 253). It has since been found to be not so unusual (see Chomsky, 1979; Lamb, 1979; Mason & McCormick, 1979; Paul, 1976; Söderbergh, 1977) and provides further evidence that young children acquire by induction some phonological principles.

Read (1971) analyzed 20 children's attempts to spell common and uncommon, short and long words. He found that the children seemed to rely on letter names for they often encoded the initial consonant and front (long) vowels correctly (e.g., *day* was DA, *lady* was LADE, *feel* was FEL and *my* was MI). They invented spellings for sounds that were not easily identified by letter names (e.g., *chicken* and *track* were begun with *h*—HCICN and HCRAK respectively— perhaps because the sound of the letter-name *h* can be heard in the initial part of those words). These attempts to spell, when parents had given no instruction in letter sounds or how to spell, suggest that the children applied their knowledge of letter names. They figured out how sounds in words might be segmented based on information contained in letter names.

Paul (1976), who taught kindergarten children and gave them many opportunities to write, noted four stages of spelling development which fit with Read's interpretation: (a) recognition of words by their initial sound and letter (e.g., TB for *toy box*), (b) recognition of initial and final sounds—consonants and some front vowels—(e.g., WZ for *was* or BOT for *boat*), (c) using vowels to mark a place for vowels (e.g., DORRDY WOTAR for *dirty water*), (d) acknowledgment of the correct spelling of sight words. By this classification, most of Read's subjects were at the second stage of development.

In the Mason and McCormick (1979) study, 75 middle-class[14] kindergarten children were given 10 magnetic uppercase letters and asked to spell *cat, top, at,* and *pot.* There were 41 children who spelled the four words correctly, while only 2 children gave letter-unrelated responses. The remaining children used the correct initial phoneme (although 5 used *k* for *c* in *cat* and 4 sometimes misordered the consonants), half also chose the correct final phoneme of the word but usually ignored or used the wrong vowel. Correlations with other reading-task variables were all very high: .60 with uppercase letter naming, .63 with word recognition, .76 with consonant-sound matching, and .65 with short-vowel-sound matching. The correlation with reading achievement given the following year was .67 for vocabulary and .50 for comprehension. These results indicate that spelling of two- and three-letter words is very closely tied to letter-sound recognition skills and reading of common words; hence to beginning reading achievement.

Conventions of Print

Ian failed to sort out his confusions about print through the whole of his first year at school. He claimed that his teacher who wrote his name as "Ian" could not spell it; it should be written "IAN." But in a bookshop he pointed to the title of a scrapbook, "GIANT," and said, "There's my name," unconcerned by the presence of extra letters. (Clay, 1972, p. 59)

It is patently obvious that children begin learning about reading with very fuzzy definitions about reading terms, how words are read, and what to say about print. Since it is altogether too easy for teachers to use language that might be misinterpreted by beginning readers and to use tasks and procedures that are unclear to children, researchers have studied children's knowledge of reading terms and their ability to carry out directives.

An extensive study on knowledge of reading terms and concepts was conducted by Hardy et al. (1974). Sixty children from three socioeconomic levels were tested in October, February, and June of their kindergarten year. The data are reported in terms of the percent of children who achieved a mastery score of 90% or better on a subtest or term. They found that children's alphabet recitation advanced from 44% to 75% mastery between October and June, letter naming changed from 38% to 56%, and an ability to rhyme went from 13% to 62%. All of the children were instructed on these concepts during the school year. With regard to reading terms, children were asked to show the examiner parts of a book or items in a book (e.g., *front, cover, back, letter, word*). The children were very competent at the beginning of the year on most of these items, above 80% on book parts and 77% on identification of a letter but 46% on identification of a word. By June, and after all had received instruction on the terms, they were at 76% mastery on words and 93% on the others. Directional terms were also asked. Only about 30% of the children in October knew the *right* and *left* side of a page, but about 65% could identify *top, bottom,* and *across.* By the end of the year, another 15% knew these five terms. Action terms were, for the most part, understood by the children in October. They were asked to put something *on top of, over, beside, above, below, between, under,* or to *make a circle around* or *through, make a box around,* or to *underline.* Except for *under* (56%) and *underline* (51%), mastery in October was at 70% to 95%. In June, percentages were generally in the 90s, except for *through* (72%), *box around* (71%), and *underline* (83%). These terms, however, were not taught to all children. They were also asked to find the *middle, last, first, end,* and *beginning* of words. Mastery in October ranged from 61% to 87% for all but *beginning* (54%). In June, the range was 8% to 36% higher (88% to 95%). Lastly, children's scores in October were in the middle range when asked to point out a *big* word (74%), a *long* word (69%), a *little* word (57%), and a *short* word (57%). In June, mastery was at or above 90% for all the length terms, except *short* (62%). All of these terms were taught to the children.

Clay (1972) reports somewhat lower changes over the first year of instruction: locating one letter advanced from 34% to 53%, locating one word went from 22% to 47%, and locating the first letter changed from 28% to 41%.

Downing and Oliver (1973–74) asked children aged five, six, and seven, to say yes when they heard a single word. They were presented with abstract sounds, real-life sounds, isolated phonemes and syllables, phrases, sentences, and long and short words. None of the children correctly said that syllables were not words; only one seven-year-old identified phonemes as not being words. However, about half of the five-year-olds correctly realized that short and long words were words or phrases, while real-life sounds were not. They made more errors on sentences and abstract sounds. Most of the older children knew that short words were words, but inexplicably, they did no better than the five-year-olds on long words and phrases. They made fewer errors, however, on abstract and real-life sounds and syllables.

Meltzer and Herse (1969) had first-grade students count, cut, and circle words in sentences. Of the 39 children, 26 made errors. The number of errors was related to the reading level of the child. The children in the lowest reading level (28%) made 73% of the errors.

This research, then, shows that we should not necessarily expect young children to know the terminology or the procedures we use to teach reading. While much of it is learned easily through instruction, some important terms (e.g., *word, syllable, right, left, beginning*) are not understood by many children even after a year of instruction.

A related aspect of the research on reading terminology concerns children's judgments about when a word is a word. In an earlier study, Rosinski and Wheeler (1972) found that not until the end of first grade are children able to say that letter strings, such as *tup, dink,* or *blasps,* are more like words than are *nda, xogl,* or *ikiskr.* More recently, Pick, Unze, Brownell, Drozdal, and Hopmann (1978) showed young children from three to eight years of age letter strings and asked them whether each was a word. Since the younger children more often answered yes than no to words or nonwords, only error responses of yes to nonwords are interpretable (see Table 17.4). These indicate that false recognition of nonwords as words extends even into first grade. Preschool children do not yet realize very basic orthographic rules (such as that a word must contain at least one vowel). They are, however, very suspicious of one-letter units, while

TABLE 17.4 MEAN PERCENT ERROR RESPONSES THAT
LETTER STRINGS WERE WORDS

GROUP	SINGLE-LETTER NONWORDS	5-LETTER NONWORDS	4-LETTER CONSONANT CLUSTERS	4-LETTER VOWEL CLUSTERS	11-LETTER NONWORDS
Three to four years	54	83	80	80	87
Five years of age	6	80	83	71	75
Kindergartners	29	62	59	51	53
Grade 1	16	30	23	17	34
Grade 2 and 3	23	18	5	4	8

Source: Adapted from Pick, Unze, Brownell, Drozdal, and Hopmann, 1978.

much more accepting of longer pronounceable or unpronounceable strings of letters.

Another aspect of this research describes what preschoolers attend to when asked to look at or learn words. In a study conducted in 1923 by Gates and Bocker, kindergarten children were given 48 nouns to learn, 6 each from lengths of 3 through 10 letters. Contrary to their expectations, they found greater variation in word learning within each list length than across it. Short words were not easier to learn than long words, probably because the children were Level I prereaders. When the authors asked the children later how they had learned the words, only idiosyncratic cues were noted. Of the 60 children 6, for example, remembered *pig* by the dot over the *i*, 4 remembered *box* by the "funny cross," 3 remembered *window* because the beginning was like the end, and 2 noticed that *monkey* had a tail at the end.[15]

Marchbanks and Levin (1965) inquired how cues about words are noticed by nonreaders and beginning readers. Children were shown a word on a card, then, after the card was withdrawn, they picked out a word that was most like the one seen. Alternatives included a word that began or ended with the same letters or had the same pattern of ascenders and descenders (thus, being similar in shape). The children were most likely to choose first or last letters; the least used cue was word shape. In a follow-up study, Williams, Blumberg, and Williams (1970) questioned whether the Marchbanks and Levin task would produce similar results with socioeconomically disadvantaged urban children. They found that while kindergarten children used no single cue, first-grade children matched most often on the first letter and next most often on the last letter. With a different type of task (Pick et al., 1978)—testing first, third, and fifth graders—children were asked to judge from two pairs of three-letter words, the pair that was "most alike." In every case, one pair had the same initial consonant and medial vowel (e.g., *bum, bug*), while the other had the same medial vowel and final consonant (e.g., *hop, pop*). The procedure was carried out first by having children choose one pair after reading the word pairs from cards and later by having them listen to the words. First graders based more of their judgments on the beginnings of words that they read than did older children. Also, first graders gave more judgments of word-ending similarity when they heard them than when they read them.

In a second experiment, Pick and associates taught kindergarten children (who were not yet reading but knew some letters and sounds) 12 CVC words (e.g., *bum, bug*). Then, they were asked to try reading 18 new CVC words, 6 of which had the same initial CV, 6 having the same ending VC, and 6 having no letter clusters that matched. All contained letters that had appeared in the trained words. Children read more CV matched words (27 on the first try) than VC words (14 on the first try), or cluster unmatched words (9 on the first try). Also, errors were more likely to appear at the end than at the beginning of the word. The results suggest that when words taught together contain discernible letter cluster to sound patterns and the children are Level II prereaders, children seem to observe and use the initial clusters in trying to read new words.

These studies suggest that young children are more likely to recognize words by noticing idiosyncratic cues than letter-to-sound cues. Children who used letter-sound cues were apparently Level II prereaders. This interpretation expands on Söderbergh's (1977) findings (1) that a child's first attempt at word learning is to relate a word to the object or event it describes, rather than to other learned words and (2) that words that are the most difficult to learn at first are those which contain no meaningful mnemonic. Later attempts at word learning involve more careful analysis of letter information.

Early Reading Instruction

TEACHER: Let's all make an *M*, just like at the top of your paper.
J.E.:   I'm goin' to make both *M*'s.
TEACHER: Both *M*'s. Very nice. Very good.
T.O.:   I can't make *M*'s.
J.E.:   I made a *M*, a small *m*.
TEACHER: Very nice.
K.R.:   I can't make one.
J.E.:   I'm goin' to make a picture of mud [to go with the *M*].
(Portion of a reading lesson to 4-year-old children, Mason & Au, 1981, p. 17)

The lack of a strong theoretical model of early reading has placed us in double jeopardy: we have ignored differences in young children's knowledge about print in setting up beginning reading lessons, and we have failed to resolve the questions of *what* early reading instruction to provide and *when* to provide it. First, we must address the question of whether any instruction is justified and, if so, to consider whether our proposed three-strand model of prereading (function, form, and convention) is a sufficient construct for instructional planning and decision making.

Questioning prereading instruction.   There are two principal arguments against preschool instruction. One is that young children need to learn through self-initiated activity, rather than through guided instruction; the other is that a child must be mentally ready for instruction. The first will be finessed here by asserting that teachers can set up early reading activities that balance child-initiated learning with teacher guidance. The second argument, however, is more problematic.

Claims that a certain level of mental readiness, or maturation, is necessary for successful reading were first espoused by Patrick in 1899.

> It is a well-known fact that a child's powers, whether physical or mental, ripen in a certain rather definite order. There is, for instance, a certain time in the life of the infant when the motor mechanism of the legs ripens, before which the child cannot be taught to walk, while after that time he cannot be kept from walking. Again, at the age of seven, there is a mental readiness for some things and an unreadiness for others. (Cited in Coltheart, 1979, p. 3)

While lacking empirical support, this view has experienced acceptance. For example, "We have a mountain of evidence to prove that a perfectly 'normal' child—IQ 100—cannot learn to read until he is about six years six months old." (Hefferman, 1960, cited in Coltheart, 1979, p. 9). Arguments for the notion of maturational readiness, according to Coltheart, result from two studies: Morphett and Washburne (1931) and Dolch and Bloomster (1937). Morphett and Washburne found that children with a mental age of 6.5 or above obtained reading scores at or above a certain value. Disregarding the arbitrariness of the value they chose, they concluded that children with lower mental ages could have obtained higher reading scores if their instruction had been delayed until the critical mental age had been reached. Dolch and Bloomster, obtaining correlations of .41 to .52 between mental age and performance on a phonics test and noting that children with mental ages below 7.0 made only chance scores, concluded too hastily that "A mental age of seven years seems to be the lowest at which a child can be expected to use phonics" (cited in Coltheart, 1979, p. 11). While research that explained the errors of these conclusions has since been published (e.g., Bliesmer, 1954; Chall, Roswell, & Blumenthal, 1963; Davidson, 1931) and the notion of physical readiness upon which the original notion depended discarded, reading readiness is still widely accepted. What is the attraction to the idea of maturation? One is that it provides an easy explanation for instructional failure. A child who fails to learn can be judged unready, rather than poorly instructed. However, Hall, Salvi, Seggev, and Caldwell (1970) suggest, "When a task proves too difficult for a group of subjects [a more plausible solution] is to continue searching for other possible training conditions rather than using labels (such as maturation) as explanations" (p. 427).

It would seem from comparing the predictors of second-grade reading from tests given by de Hirsch et al. (1966) that emotional maturity plays an important role in beginning reading because correlations of .43 to .46 were obtained between reading and hyperactivity, distractibility, ego strength (a clinical evaluation of grit and energy), and a goal-directed attitude. These emotional maturity measures have dubious value, though, when we learn that the scores were based on judgments made by the experimenters while conducting the other 16 tests. Since all the tests correlated positively with reading, children's interest in the task, willingness to keep trying, and remain attentive would naturally be related to success on the task.

Clay (1972), who studied one group of children for a year and another for six months, argued that "to relax and wait for 'maturation' when there are many concepts and skills to be developed would appear to be deliberately retarding the child in relation to what is usual in his culture" (p. 6). This conclusion was based in part on a follow-up study of 100 children two and three years after school entry. "Where a child stood in relation to his age-mates at the end of his first year at school was roughly where one could expect to find him at 7.0 or 8.0" (p. 7).

Thus, the notion that children will eventually read if they are allowed a longer time to mature, may be actually harmful. Children who obtain experience at home in learning letters, writing, reading labels and memorizing stories may be better ready to learn about reading in school because they know more about how to read; this can be unrelated to their emotional or social maturity. The very children who have not obtained early reading experiences are likely to be those who need such experiences when they start school. Since children who are behind at the beginning of first grade often continue to be poor readers, catching up may be a myth. Hence, a more effective course of action may be to plan an early reading program for children in preschool programs and in kindergartens, especially for children who demonstrate little or no knowledge about letters, printed words, and books.

Reading instruction components.   As recently as the 1960s, visual discrimination was assumed to play a major role in reading instruction and achievement, as evidenced by the fact, according to Barrett (1965), that all available reading readiness tests devoted attention to it. Barrett's review of over 30 years of research helped to show that word- or letter-identification tasks generally resulted in higher predictions of first- or second-grade reading achievement than did visual tasks, such as copying shapes or identifying figures. This conclusion was also affirmed by de Hirsch et al. (1966) who found letter and word tasks to be better predictors than visual or auditory discrimination, expressive language, or fine motor-coordination tasks. Barrett also showed that knowledge of letter names (correlations usually around .55 to .65) was a better predictor than an ability to match letters directly or from memory (with correlations around .25). However, as argued earlier in this chapter, measures of letter and word knowledge may include knowledge of concepts about letters and sounds in words, not simply an ability to discriminate one form from another. We are still correcting misinterpretations of those earlier obtained correlations.

Auditory-discrimination tasks have also been found to correlate with reading ability or to differentiate good from poor readers (e.g., Calfee et al., 1973; Chall et al., 1963; Durrell & Murphy, 1953; Dykstra, 1966; Gates, Bond, & Russell, 1939; Harrington & Durrell, 1955; Monroe, 1932; Schonell, 1948; Thompson, 1963; Wheeler & Wheeler, 1954). Correlations obtained are generally .40 or better. With respect to differentiation of good and poor readers, Thompson (1963), for example, found out of the best 24 second-grade readers tested that 16 could perform adequately on an auditory-discrimination task at the beginning of first grade. By contrast, out of the poorest readers, only 1 demonstrated adequate skill. In general, weakness in auditory discrimination of speech or word sounds has continued to emerge as a major correlate of reading disability.

Visual-discrimination studies, if reinterpreted in terms of knowledge about letter and word forms, suggest that instruction which helps young children differentiate and recognize letters and common words affects later reading success. Auditory-discrimination studies suggest that instruction which features analysis of words into letter sounds is important. Neither of these suggestions, however, is novel. Beginning reading programs and first-grade teachers have long advocated teaching letter recognition, word recognition, and phonics. The problem is that these suggestions are easily misinterpreted without a well-articulated model illustrating why they can be effective.

I will use the three-strand model here both to explain the value of visual- and auditory-discrimination training and to show why it is an inadequate conceptualization of early reading instruction.

An alternate formulation for early reading instruction. Visual- and auditory-discrimination abilities are represented by one strand of the three-strand model, *form and structure* of print. Cross-sectional studies show that children learn not only to discriminate letters one from another in upper- and lowercase, but also to name and print letters. Many then learn to distinguish phonemes in words and to match phonemes with letters and letter sounds. Longitudinal studies indicate that graphic discrimination of letters is accompanied by recognition and naming of letters and followed by discrimination of letter sounds and used to spell and identify words. However, visual and auditory discrimination, recognition, and labeling of letters represent only one strand of the hypothesized three-strand model. Children need to understand the *functional* relationship between printed words and language and meaning and to learn *conventions*, rules, and labels for carrying out and practicing reading (see Mason, 1982, for a more complete presentation of this argument). We should not assume that all children will acquire information about these strands through incidental or informal experiences with print. Some will, but those who do not should receive clearly organized instruction or opportunities for self-learning before they reach first grade.

While the question, "What should be the nature of early reading instruction?" is a complex question that extends beyond the purview of this chapter, it is apparent from the vast differences among kindergarten children in knowledge about reading that more efficient means to help children should be devised. The approach suggested here is to utilize the three-strand construct, devising opportunities for children in preschool programs to acquire knowledge about reading and writing, learning letters, reading simple words, signs, and stories. Evidence from both longitudinal and cross-sectional research suggests that informal reading helps children to understand print meaning and figure out how to break speech into word units. It can also help children to realize that letters provide cues for spelling and recognizing words. Informal reading thus allows children to acquire procedures, terms, and rules that characterize reading experiences. And, perhaps most important, if reading is presented as a problem for children to solve, the act of making and evaluating hypotheses can help children think about the structure of print and its meaning and usefulness. Children who are not so prepared at home may be likely to flounder in first grade unless helped in kindergarten or preschool programs. Although more instructional research is needed to test the necessity and sufficiency of the three strands, the model provides a footing from which to study children's developing knowledge and to consider intervention procedures for preschool children.

CONCLUSION

Early constructs of reading readiness were once thought to be inseparable from more general cognitive characteristics and motor skills. An outcome of that view was an assumption that one prepared children for reading by insuring that they could distinguish colors and shapes, sequence pictures, separate bell from drum sounds, hold and draw with a crayon, or even crawl, hop and skip. Since then, because of a theoretical shift from analyses of products of learning to the process of learning, which has helped differentiate overall maturation from particular skill and knowledge acquisition, cognitive psychologists have found that what children learn is overwhelmingly task- and situation-specific. Turning to reading, it is now apparent that preparation for reading is better addressed with specific experiences that are closely related to reading than to general cognitive and motor tasks. Recognition of the change has even affected our labels. For example, reading readiness, which implied general task instruction, has been discarded in favor of early reading, or prereading. Hence, while some educators still argue for a maturational approach for reading preparation, their position has been severely eroded by mounting evidence that early reading instruction benefits young children. Barr (personal communication) argues further that because first-grade reading books are more difficult than those used a decade ago, kindergarten reading instruction is necessary for many children and has become the rule, rather than the exception.

If it is increasingly the case that kindergarten teachers are considering or providing formal reading instruction, on what model or construct are they establishing a program? Are they ignoring the issue by assuming that kindergarten children need only be given the preprimers and primers from first-grade materials or have they formulated an instructional model? If so, which one? They might construct a reading-readiness program based on a maturational view (give instruction only to the most mature), a general cognitive view (provide picture, shape, and problem-solving tasks to everyone), a language-facilitation view (provide practice in oral communication and listening), an early reading view (provide letter discrimination, letter and word writing, word recognition, and story reading and writing), or an eclectic view (provide some combination of the above). How can this chapter advise kindergarten teachers about a program based on the best evidence available?

The work reviewed here does not yield absolute conclusions about how to prepare young children for reading but can offer the following interpretations and tentative conclusions: (a) many children begin to learn about how to read at a very early age through being read to, learning to identify and name letters and words, and learning to print, spell, and use printed labels in their drawings. This early knowledge is positively related to later reading and should be encouraged in kindergarten and preschool programs. Hence, preschool teachers should not transform first grade materials but should rely on program ideas arising from a less formal approach to learning. (b) While language experience is assumed to be closely related to reading, the research-into-practice evidence has not delineated the boundaries for instruction. Hence language facilitation experiences ought to be encouraged, such as tasks that use full sentences and specific vocabulary terms to name objects and events and express ideas, stories that are organized and communicated through listening, activities that require following oral directions, and practice in putting oral expressions into a written form. However, the limited research means that teachers should take an eclectic attitude about materials, tasks, and procedures, for example, using children's interest as evidence of appropriateness.

At this point, we need more extensive studies of young children's incipient reading development and the effect of language and instruction on later reading interest and achievement. This review, for example, suggesting three levels of early reading development that mesh with three knowledge strands, could provide a framework, though it also needs further validation. Moreover, it is clearly important to understand how parents and kindergarten teachers begin preparing children for reading in middle- and lower-class families, in majority and minority cultures, and within rural and urban areas. Eventually we may be confident that we understand how young children develop and change their views of reading; only then will it be possible to achieve major progress in reducing illiteracy.

NOTES

1. Also disliked. Söderbergh noted her daughter's explanation of this fact for the word *what:* "When we read 'tongue' we do like this"—she puts out her tongue—"but 'what'?"
2. Materials contained 36 nouns and 20 pictures with a token count of nouns being 278. There were 29 different function words, qualities, and operations with a token count of 876. To make the words, 12 different letters were used, 5 in upper and lower case. Stories were from Richard-Gibson Reading Materials.
3. Materials contained 19 nouns and 5 pictures with a token count of nouns being 103. Fifty-nine different function words, qualities, and operations appeared with a token count of 713. Twenty-three different letters were used to make the words, 17 in upper and lower case. Stories were from Nisbet Reading Materials.
4. No knowledge of print (5 children in September but no one in May); Level I, context dependency (18 in September and 12 in May); Level II, visual recognition of letters and words (14 in September and 22 in May); and Level III, letter-sound analysis (reading) (1 in September and 4 in May).
5. One story, *Stop Sign,* was: Stop, car (picture of stop sign and car). Stop, bus (picture of stop sign and bus). Stop, truck (picture of stop sign and truck). Stop (picture of a train crossing and track). For the train (picture of train). Tooot (no picture).
6. According to parents, 13 of the 14 children were still interested in the books that we had given them at the end of the training and were reading them to parents, stuffed animals, imaginary friends, and baby-sitters, all but 2 reading them "occasionally" or "frequently." Seven of the 14 parents reported heightened interest in naming letters, 8 in printing letters, 6 in spelling words, 11 in reading or recognizing words, and 8 in reading stories.
7. Eventually, of course, the reader must consider the longer, sentence segment since phrases or sentences transcend the meaning of individual words. Liberman, Shank-

weiler, Liberman, Fowler, & Fischer (1977) suggest that skilled readers hold the shorter segments in short-term store until the meaning of the longer segments has been constructed. It is not known when, how, or even whether beginning readers learn this.

8. When we were teaching three- and four-year-olds to read stories and asked them to point to each word as they read, they either ignored the pointing instruction or made a sweeping gesture under the whole line of print. They seemed to view each page, apparently, as a separate unit of print.

9. An example from Menyuk (1976), where a child read the printed sentence "He didn't go to school" as "He no do go school," indicates how verbs and functors in print and speech are often not well matched.

10. See Mattingly (1972, 1979), also Downing (1979) for further discussion of linguistic awareness.

11. Calfee (1977) showed that if children are told explicitly that a reversal is not an exact copy, they seldom select it. Thus, they *can* make the discrimination but before schooling are probably unaccustomed to consider rotations as different things.

12. We have found that preschool children often believe that *c* has an /s/ sound. One child asked, "*Stop* has a *c* in it, right?" Another laughed at us for asserting that *c* said /k/. Several others named words beginning with *s* when we discussed the letter *c*. Thus, it appears that letter names are used as clues for their sounds since there is no other explanation for the substitutions. This interpretation is supported also by work on preschool children's invented spellings of words (C. Read, 1971).

13. This point is more fully discussed in Gleitman & Rozin (1977). Two of their examples suggest the complexity: the /t/ sounds in *grate* and *grater* are not the same but are represented by the single grapheme *t*. Also, there are differences in dialect (e.g., *these* spoken by a New Yorker is different from the same word spoken by a midwesterner).

14. Social class is noted because Read's subjects as well as a group we tested (Mason, 1980) were upper-middle class. It is important to show that these linguistic insights have occurred among more typical children.

15. Preschool children we tested best remembered the "biggest" word (e.g., *elephant*). Also, in testing remedial readers, the two poorest readers knew only one word on our list, *look*, perhaps because its shape could be rendered in terms of meaning—it appears to have two eyes.

REFERENCES

Aristotle. *Aristotle on Education: Extracts from Ethics and Politics* (J. Burnet, Ed. and trans.). Cambridge: Harvard University Press, 1967.

Barrett, T. The relationship between measures of prereading, visual discrimination and first grade reading achievement: A review of the literature. *Reading Research Quarterly*, 1965, *1*, 51–76.

Barron, R. *Rule generated and lexical information in reading and spelling.* Paper presented at the meeting of the American Educational Research Association, San Francisco, April 1979.

Barth, R., & Swiss, T. The impact of television on reading. *Reading Teacher*, 1976, *30*, 236–239.

Bliesmer, E. Reading abilities of bright and dull children of comparable mental ages. *Journal of Educational Psychology*, 1954, *45*, 321–331.

Bruce, D.   Analysis of word sounds by young children. *British Journal of Educational Psychology,* 1964, *34,* 148–169.

Bruner, J.   From communication to language—a psychological perspective. In V. Lee (Ed.), *Language development.* New York: Wiley, 1979.

Calfee, R.   Assessment of independent reading skills: Basic research and practical applications. In A. Reber & D. Scarborough (Eds.), *Toward a psychology of reading.* Hillsdale, N.J.: Erlbaum, 1977.

Calfee, R., Chapman, R., & Venezky, R.   How a child needs to think to learn to read. In L. Gregg (Ed.), *Cognition and learning in memory.* New York: Wiley, 1972.

Calfee, R., Lindamood, P., & Lindamood, C.   Acoustic-phonetic skills and reading—kindergarten through twelfth grade. *Journal of Educational Psychology,* 1973, *64,* 293–298.

Calfee, R., & Piontkowski, D.   The reading diary: Acquisition of decoding. *Reading Research Quarterly,* 1981, *16,* 346–373.

Calkins, L.   Children learn the writer's craft. *Language Arts,* 1980, *57,* 2.

Chall, J.   *Learning to read: The great debate.* New York: McGraw-Hill, 1967.

Chall, J., Roswell, F., & Blumenthal, S.   Auditory blending ability: A factor in success in beginning to read. *Reading Teacher,* 1963, *17,* 113–118.

Chomsky, C.   Write first, read later. *Childhood Education,* 1971, *47,* 296–299.

Chomsky, C.   Approaching reading through invented spelling. In L. Resnick & P. Weaver (Eds.), *Theory and practice of early reading* (Vol. 2). Hillsdale, N.J.: Erlbaum, 1979.

Clay, M.   *Reading, the patterning of complex behavior.* Auckland, N.Z.: Heinemann, 1972.

Cohen, S. (Ed.)   *Education in the United States: A documentary history.* New York: Random House, 1974.

Coltheart, M.   When can children learn to read? In T. Waller & G. MacKinnon (Eds.), *Reading research: Advances in theory and practice.* New York: Academic Press, 1979.

Comenius, J.   *The school of infancy* (E. Eller, Ed.). Chapel Hill: University of North Carolina Press, 1956.

Davidson, H.   An experimental study of bright, average, and dull children at the four-year mental level. *Genetic Psychology Monographs,* 1931, *9,* 119–289.

de Hirsch, K., Jansky, J., & Langford, W.   *Predicting reading failure.* New York: Harper & Row, 1966.

Dewey, J.   *The child and the curriculum: The school and society.* Chicago: University of Chicago Press 1943. (Originally published 1900)

Dolch, E., & Bloomster, M.   Phonic readiness. *Elementary School Journal,* 1937, *38,* 201–205.

Downing, J.   Children's developing concepts of spoken and written language. *Journal of Reading Behavior,* 1972, *4,* 1–19.

Downing, J. (Ed.)   *Comparative reading: Cross-national studies of behavior and processes in reading and writing.* New York: Macmillan, 1973.

Downing, J.   *Cognitive clarity and linguistic awareness.* Paper presented at the International Seminar on Linguistic Awareness and Learning to Read, University of Victoria, Can., June 1979.

Downing, J., & Oliver, P.   The child's conception of "a word." *Reading Research Quarterly,* 1973–74, *9,* 568–582.

Durkin, D.   *Children who read early.* New York: Teachers College Press, 1966.

Durrell, D., & Murphy, H.   The auditory discrimination factor in reading readiness and reading disability. *Education,* 1953, *73,* 556–560.

Durrell, D., & Murphy, H.   A prereading phonics inventory. *Reading Teacher,* 1978, *31,* 385–390.

Dykstra, R.   Auditory discrimination abilities and beginning reading achievement. *Reading Research Quarterly*, 1966, *1*, 5–34.

Educational Policies Commission.   *Contemporary issues in elementary education.* Washington, D.C.: NEA, 1960.

Ehri, L.   Word consciousness in readers and prereaders. *Journal of Educational Psychology*, 1975, *67*, 204–212.

Ehri, L.   Linguistic insight: Threshold of reading acquisition. In T. Waller & G. MacKinnon (Eds.), *Reading research: Advances in theory and practice.* New York: Academic Press, 1979.

Fox, B., & Routh, D.   Phonemic analysis and synthesis as word attack skills. *Journal of Educational Psychology*, 1976, *68*, 70–74.

Francis, H.   Symposium: Reading abilities and disabilities: Children's strategies in learning to read. *British Journal of Educational Psychology*, 1977, *47*, 117–125.

Froebel, F.   *The education of man* (Translated and annotated by W. Hailmann). New York: Appleton, 1905. (Originally published, 1887)

Frederiksen, J.   *A chronometric study of component skills in reading* (BBN Report No. 3757). Cambridge, Mass.: Bolt Beranek and Newman, 1978.

Gammage, P.   *Children and schooling.* Boston: George Allen & Unwin, 1982.

Gates, A.   An experimental evaluation of reading readiness tests. *Elementary School Journal*, 1939, *39*, 497–508.

Gates, A.   A further evaluation of reading readiness tests. *Elementary School Journal*, 1940, *40*, 577–591.

Gates, A., & Bocker, E.   A study of initial stages in reading by preschool children. *Teachers College Record*, 1923, *24*, 469–488.

Gates, A., Bond, G., & Russell, D.   *Methods of determining reading readiness.* New York: Columbia Teachers College, 1939.

Gibson, E., Gibson, J., Pick, A., & Osser, H.   A developmental study of the discrimination of letter-like forms. *Journal of Comparative and Physiological Psychology*, 1962, *55*, 897–906.

Gibson, E., & Levin, H.   *The psychology of reading.* Cambridge: MIT Press, 1975.

Gleitman, L.   *Metalinguistics is not kid-stuff.* Paper presented at the International Seminar on Linguistic Awareness and Learning to Read, University of Victoria, Can., June 1979.

Gleitman, L., & Rozin, P.   The structure and acquisition of reading I: Relations between orthographies and the structure of language. In A. Reber & D. Scarborough (Eds.), *Toward a psychology of reading.* Hillsdale, N.J.: Erlbaum, 1977.

Goodman, K.   Orthography in a theory of reading instruction. *Elementary English*, 1972, December, 1254–1261. (a)

Goodman, K.   Reading: The key is in the children's language. *Reading Teacher*, 1972, March, 505–508. (b)

Graves, D.   *Let's take another look at the development of young writers.* Keynote address at the National Reading Conference, Clearwater Beach, Fl., December 1982.

Hall, G. S.,   *Content of Children's Minds,* New York: Harper, 1883.

Hall, V., Salvi, R., Seggev, L., & Caldwell, E.   Cognitive synthesis, conservation, and task analysis. *Developmental Psychology*, 1970, *2*, 423–428.

Halliday, M.   *Learning how to mean.* London: Edward Arnold, 1975.

Hammill, D., & McNutt, G.   *The correlates of reading: The consensus of thirty years of correlational research.* Austin, Tex.: Pro-Ed, 1981.

Hardy, M., Stennett, R., & Smythe, P.   Development of auditory and visual language concepts and relationship to instructional strategies in kindergarten. *Elementary English*, 1974, *51*, 525–532.

Harrington, M., & Durrell, D.   Mental maturity versus perceptual abilities in primary reading. *Journal of Educational Psychology*, 1955, *46*, 375–380.

Harste, J.   *Written language learning as social event*. Paper presented at the annual meeting of the American Educational Research Association, Boston, April 1980.

Herber, F.   Sociocultural mental retardation: A longitudinal study. In D. Forgays (Ed.), *Primary prevention of psychopathology, VII: Environmental influences*. Hanover, N.H.: University Press of New England, 1978.

Hildreth, G.   Developmental sequences in name writing. Child Development, 1936, *7*, 291–303.

Hillerich, R.   An interpretation of research in reading readiness. *Elementary English*, 1966, April, 359–364.

Hillerich, R.   A diagnostic approach to early identification of language skills. *Reading Teacher*, 1978, *31*, 357–364.

Holden, M., & MacGinitie, W.   Children's conceptions of word boundaries in speech and print. *Journal of Educational Psychology*, 1972, *63*, 551–557.

Hunt, J. McVicker.   *The role of early experience in the development of intelligence and personality*. University of Illinois, 1983.

Huttenlocher, J.   Children's language: Word-phrase relationship. *Science*, 1964, *143*, 264–265.

Johns, J.   Children's concepts of reading and their reading achievement. *Journal of Reading Behavior*, 1972, *4*, 56–57.

Lamb, P.   *Preschool children's knowledge of phoneme-grapheme correspondences*. Paper presented at the meeting of the American Educational Research Association, San Francisco, April 1979.

Lazar, I., & Darlington, R. (Eds.),   *Lasting effects after preschool*. Final Report, HEW Grant 900–1311, 1978.

Leeper, S., Dale, P., Skipper, J., & Witherspoon.   *Good schools for young children*. New York: Macmillan, 1974.

Levenstein, P.   The mother-child home program. In M. Day & R. Parker (Eds.), *The preschool in action* (2nd ed.). Boston: Allyn & Bacon, 1976.

Liberman, I.   Segmentation of the spoken word and reading acquisition. *Bulletin of the Orton Society*, 1970, *23*, 65–77.

Liberman, I., Shankweiler, D., Fischer, F., & Carter, B.   Explicit syllable and phoneme segmentation in the young child. *Journal of Experimental Child Psychology*, 1974, *18*, 201–212.

Liberman, I., Shankweiler, D., Liberman, A., Fowler, C., & Fischer, F.   Phonetic segmentation and recoding in the beginning reader. In A. Reber & D. Scarborough (Eds.), *Toward a psychology of reading*. Hillsdale, N.J.: Erlbaum, 1977.

MacKinnon, A.   *How do children learn to read?* Vancouver, Can.: Copp Clark, 1959.

Marchbanks, G., & Levin, H.   Cues by which children recognize words. *Journal of Educational Psychology*, 1965, *56*, 75–61.

Mason, J.   *Reading readiness: A definition and skills hierarchy from preschoolers' developing conceptions of print* (Tech. Rep. No. 59). Urbana: University of Illinois, Center for the Study of Reading, 1977.

Mason, J.   When *do* children begin to read: An exploration of four-year-old children's letter and word reading competencies. *Reading Research Quarterly*, 1980, *15*, 203–227.

Mason, J.   *Acquisition of knowledge about reading*. Paper presented at the meeting of the American Educational Research Association, New York, 1982.

Mason, J., & Au, K.   *Learning social context characteristics in prereading lessons* (Tech. Rep. No. 205). Urbana: University of Illinois, Center for the Study of Reading, 1981.

Mason, J., & McCormick, C. *Testing the development of reading and linguistic awareness* (Tech. Rep. No. 126). Urbana: University of Illinois, Center for the Study of Reading, 1979.

Mason, J., & McCormick, C. *An investigation of prereading instruction: A developmental perspective* (Tech. Rep. No. 224). Urbana: University of Illinois, Center for the Study of Reading, 1981.

Mattingly, I. Reading, the linguistic process and linguistic awareness. In J. F. Kavanagh & I. Mattingly (Eds.), *Language by ear and by eye: The relationships between speech and reading.* Cambridge: MIT Press, 1972.

Mattingly, I. *The psycholinguistic basis of linguistic awareness.* Unpublished paper, 1978.

Mattingly, I. *Linguistic awareness and learning to read.* Paper presented at the International Seminar on Linguistic Awareness and Learning to Read, University of Victoria, Can., June 1979.

McCormick, C., & Mason, J. What happens to kindergarten children's knowledge about reading after a summer vacation? *Reading Teacher,* 1981, *35,* 164–172.

Meltzer, N., & Herse, R. The boundaries of written words as seen by first graders. *Journal of Reading Behavior,* 1969, *1,* 3–14.

Menyuk, P. Relations between acquisition of phonology and reading. In J. Guthrie (Ed.), *Aspects of reading acquisition.* Baltimore: Johns Hopkins University Press, 1976.

Meyer, L., & Gersten, R. *Long-term academic effects of direct instruction follow through: Graduates from cohorts 1 & 2, P.S. 137.* University of Illinois, 1983.

Mickish, V. Children's perceptions of written word boundaries. *Journal of Reading Behavior,* 1974, *6,* 19–22.

Monroe, M. *Children who cannot read.* Chicago: University of Chicago Press, 1932.

Montessori, M. *The Montessori Method.* New York: Schocken Books, 1964. (Originally published, 1912)

Morphett, V., & Washburne, C. When should children begin to read? *Elementary School Journal,* 1931, *31,* 495–503.

Morris, D. Concept of a word: A developmental phenomenon in the beginning reading and writing process. *Language Arts,* 1981, *58,* 659–668.

Ollila, L., & Chamberlain, L. The learning and retention of two classes of graphic words: High-frequency nouns and non-noun words among kindergarten children. *Journal of Educational Research,* 1979, May–June.

Olson, A. Growth in word perception abilities as it relates to success in beginning reading. *Journal of Education,* 1958, *140,* 25–36.

Paul, R. Invented spelling in kindergarten. *Young Children,* 1976, *31,* 195–200.

Pick, A., Unze, M., Brownell, C., Drozdal, U., & Hopmann, M. Young children's knowledge of word structure. *Child Development,* 1978, *49,* 669–680.

Plato. *The education of the young in the Republic of Plato* (Translated with notes and introduction by B. Bosanquet). Cambridge: Harvard University Press, 1917.

Read, C. Preschool children's knowledge of English phonology. *Harvard Educational Review,* 1971, *41,* 1–34.

Read, K. *The nursery school: A human relationships laboratory.* Philadelphia: Saunders, 1971.

Reid, J. Learning to think about reading. *Educational Research,* 1966, *9,* 56–62.

Resnick, D., & Resnick, L. The nature of literacy: An historical exploration. *Harvard Educational Review,* 1977, *47,* 370–385.

Resnick, L., & Weaver, P. (Eds.) *Theory and practice of early reading* (3 vols.). Hillsdale, N.J.: Erlbaum, 1979.

Rosinski, R., & Wheeler, K. Children's use of orthographic structure in word discrimination. *Psychonomic Science,* 1972, *26,* 97–98.

Rosner, J., & Simon, D.   The auditory analysis test: An initial report. *Journal of Learning Disabilities*, 1971, *4*, 384–392.

Rousseau, J.   *Emile* (A. Bloom, Trans.). New York: Basic Books, 1979.

Rozin, P., & Gleitman, L.   The structure and acquisition of reading II: The reading process and the acquisition of the alphabetic principle. In A. Reber & D. Scarborough (Eds.), *Toward a psychology of reading.* Hillsdale, N.J.: Erlbaum, 1977.

Rusk, R., & Scotland, J.   *Doctrines of the great educators.* New York: St. Martin's Press, 1979.

Samuels, S. J.   Effect of distinctive feature training on paired-associate learning. *Journal of Educational Psychology*, 1973, *64*, 164–170.

Samuels, S. J.   *Linguistic awareness as a prerequisite for learning to read.* Paper presented at the International Seminar on Linguistic Awareness and Learning to Read, University of Victoria, Can., June 1979.

Schonell, F.   *Backwardness in the basic subjects.* Edinburgh: Oliver & Boyd, 1948.

Scott, R.   Shifts in reading readiness profiles during the past decade. *Journal of Genetic Psychology*, 1975, *126*, 269–273.

Slobin, D.   English abstract of Soviet studies of child language. In F. Smith & G. Miller (Eds.), *The genesis of language.* Cambridge: MIT Press, 1966.

Smith, F.   *Psycholinguistics and reading.* New York: Holt, Rinehart & Winston, 1971.

Söderbergh, R.   Reading in early childhood: A linguistic study of a preschool child's gradual acquisition of reading ability. Washington, D.C.: Georgetown University Press, 1977.

Spiker, C.   Verbal factors in the discrimination learning of children. In J. Wright & J. Kagan (Eds.), Basic cognitive processes in children. *Monographs of the Society for Research in Child Development*, 1963, *28*.

Steinberg, D., & Yamada, J.   Are whole word kanji easier to learn than syllable kana? *Reading Research Quarterly*, 1978, *14*, 88–99.

Thompson, B.   A longitudinal study of auditory discrimination. *Journal of Educational Research*, 1963, *56*, 376–378.

Torrey, J.   Learning to read without a teacher: A case study. *Elementary English*, 1969, *46*, 550–556.

Valtin, R.   *Increasing awareness of linguistic awareness in research on beginning reading and dyslexia.* Paper presented at the International Seminar on Linguistic Awareness and Learning to Read, University of Victoria, Can., June 1979.

Venezky, R.   Reading acquisition: The occult and the obscure. In F. Murray, H. Sharp, & J. Pikulski (Eds.), *The acquisition of reading: Cognitive, linguistic and perceptual prerequisites.* Baltimore: University Park Press, 1978.

Venezky, R.   *The Structure of English Orthography.* The Hague: Mouton, 1970.

Wallach, L., Wallach, M., Dozier, M., & Kaplan, N.   Poor children learning to read do not have trouble with auditory blending but do have trouble with phoneme recognition. *Journal of Educational Psychology*, 1977, *69*, 36–39.

Wheeler, L., & Wheeler, V.   A study of the relationship of auditory discrimination to silent reading abilities. *Journal of Educational Research*, 1954, *48*, 103–113.

Wheeler, M.   *Untutored acquisition of writing skill.* Unpublished doctoral dissertation, Cornell University, 1971.

Williams, J., Blumberg, E., & Williams, D.   Cues used in visual word recognition. *Journal of Educational Psychology*, 1970, *61*, 310–315.

18 BEGINNING READING INSTRUCTION

FROM DEBATE TO REFORMATION

Rebecca Barr

How should children be taught to read? No other issue has piqued the interest and emotions of educators and lay persons as has this one. From the onset of literacy instruction, teachers have voiced strong and often opposing views about the proper way to teach reading (Mathews, 1966). In the United States, the alphabetical methods of colonial and revolutionary days gave way to two major alternatives in the mid-1900s. The first expanded on the previous approach by teaching the sounds of letters. The second, representing a distinct departure, initiated children into reading by having them learn whole words. This dichotomy in approach continued into the current century but with some changes. The phonics approach became modernized by abandoning an earlier emphasis on alphabet learning and spelling while incorporating blending practice. The word method became elaborated into sentence and story methods with analysis of larger units into their components (i.e., sentences into words, words into phonemes). At the same time, the hornbook of the early period gave way to graded readers and finally to basal series (N. B. Smith, 1934/1970).

A major dimension was added to the advocacy of reading approach with the advent of systematic study of educational practice. Although a few early reading studies were characterized by imaginative research questions and a richness of evidence (e.g., see Gates, 1927; Gates & Russell, 1938; W. E. Wiley, 1928), most investigations of the effectiveness of alternative reading approaches have involved the comparison of an innovative method with a traditional approach. But alternative methods were not examined to determine their features as used in classes; rather, they were characterized in a global fashion, simply

Marilyn Sadow, Chicago State University, served as editorial consultant during the preparation of this chapter. I would like to thank her for her helpful comments.

as a "word" or a "phonics" or a "sentence" method. Accordingly, variations in types of approaches were not identified. Not surprisingly, innovative methods were typically found to be more effective in terms of student achievement than the traditional alternatives with which they were compared (Chall, 1967; Pflaum, Walberg, Karegianes, & Racher, 1980).

The 1960s was a period of "taking stock" among educational researchers. Chall (1967) undertook the monumental task of summarizing the research on beginning reading approaches conducted prior to the 1960s. She asked whether methods stressing meaning or those emphasizing decoding were better in general and for children of different abilities. Based on her review, Chall contended that "a code emphasis tends to produce better overall reading achievement by the beginning of fourth grade than a meaning emphasis" (p. 137) and that the advantage of the code emphasis is observed earlier for high-ability children and later for below-average and average-ability children. Her conclusions, however, should be compared with the more conservative opinions expressed by Gray (1960), Russell and Fea (1963), and Bond and Dykstra (1967) who argue that no firm conclusions can be drawn on the basis of inconsistent evidence.

It is the purpose of this review to examine trends in the study of beginning reading approaches during the past two decades—to take up the question where Chall left off. Not only are the findings from recent investigations considered, but also more important, the manner of studying the effectiveness of alternative reading approaches is evaluated. The chapter is organized into three main sections, followed by a concluding section with implications for further research. In the first, I describe trends in reading method investigations undertaken during the past two decades and argue that we have learned relatively little from research that compares the effectiveness of one approach with another when both are characterized in a global fashion. Second, based on studies that consider the relative effectiveness of reading approaches for students of different aptitude, I suggest that future study should continue to focus on the learning of low-aptitude children. Finally, based on an in-depth consideration of innovative investigations of the effectiveness of reading approaches, both from within the field of reading and from related disciplines, I argue that alternative research techniques and formulations are not only feasible, but also promise to increase our understanding of the role of instructional approaches in the classroom.

The scope of the review is limited in several respects. In general, it is based on published reports. Relatively few studies other than those of primary-reading methods exist, and those that do are not of the same type (Pflaum et al., 1980). Because of this characteristic of the methods literature, the review focuses on classroom studies of primary-grade reading instruction and does not consider studies of reading methods conducted in later grades and remedial instruction. Similarly, the review does not consider studies of methods in other curricular areas, such as social studies, mathematics, and spelling, nor those that pertain only to other aspects of instruction, such as grouping arrangements, tutorial supplementation, and time scheduling. The review examines only those investigations that consider the consequence of reading approaches for learning. Further, it considers only those that studied classroom instruction over a minimal period of a semester; in other words, it does not consider short-term experimental investigations.

EFFECTIVENESS OF READING APPROACHES

Research of the 1960s

General Trends

Concern with reading methods during the 1960s appears to be the result of a coincidence of forces. At the national level, the 1960s was a period of social concern and economic prosperity. It is not surprising that those wishing to build the "Great Society" should view education as the main road to social equality. Reading skill, particularly among the disadvantaged, appeared to many as an important means to achieve this goal. Educators debated about effective reading instruction and particularly about the merits of phonics. Reading scholars agreed that the inconsistency and inconclusiveness of earlier methods studies encouraged conflicting recommendations for practice. They suggested, therefore, "that large-scale cooperative experimentation undertaken with proper, clearly defined controls could provide better evidence on whether some approaches were indeed more effective than others for specific outcomes in reading, for particular kinds of children, with particular kinds of teachers, and in particular kinds of school situations" (Chall, 1967, p. 5).

During the 1960s, the number of methods studies included in the annual summaries of reading research (Robinson, annual studies 1961 through 1965; Robinson, Weintraub, & Smith, annual studies 1965 through 1970; Weintraub et al., annual studies 1971 through 1982) increased dramatically, as shown in Figure 18.1.[1] A major impetus in the United States was the massive funding of the Cooperative Reading Projects by the U.S. Office of Education (USOE). Nevertheless, as can be seen from Figure 18.1, an increase in methods comparisons began prior to the cooperative-research funding and continued after it. Whereas the Cooperative Research Projects usually compared several different methods within each project, other investigations usually contrasted an innovative with a traditional approach.

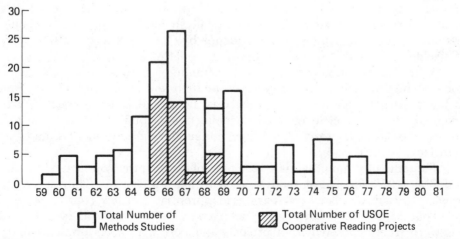

FIGURE 18.1 Number of reports on reading methods investigations conducted in the primary grades, based on the annual *Summary of Investigations Relating to Reading*, 1961–1982.

USOE Sponsored Reading Studies

The USOE First Grade Reading Studies are of special interest because of their design and the total number of classrooms studied. Of 27 funded projects, 15 explored the efficacy of different methods with typical samples of children, and four more examined the same question for special groups of children. Not all projects examined the same approaches, but all included a traditional basal approach to serve as a control against which to compare the effectiveness of alternative approaches. As described by Chall (1967), the traditional basal approaches of the time emphasized meaning with phonics introduced relatively later and unsystematically.

The projects exploring methods were cooperative in the sense that they used a common research design and common measures to assess the prereading capabilities of pupils, socioeconomic characteristics of the community, teacher characteristics, school characteristics, and outcomes, such as reading vocabulary, comprehension and speed, attitude toward reading, and facility in writing. Nevertheless, as noted by Stauffer, methods "given the same label were often not the same" (1966b, p. 563).

A coordinating center assumed responsibility for assembling, analyzing, and reporting data common to those projects that compared methods (Bond & Dykstra, 1967; Dykstra, 1968). Five innovative approaches, basal plus phonics, i.t.a., linguistics, language experience, and phonics/linguistics, were compared with traditional basal approaches. Generally, the newer approaches, particularly those involving more systematic instruction in phonics, tended to be similar to or more effective at the end of first grade than traditional basal approaches, particularly in word reading. Table 18.1 summarizes the trends for word reading, vocabulary, and paragraph meaning. The results from the second year of the study are generally consistent with those from the first (Dykstra, 1968). Based on these findings, Bond and Dykstra concluded that no approach is so much better in all situations that it should be considered the best method. However, since programs that emphasized the systematic study of sound-symbol correspondences tended to produce higher word-reading scores (one or two months grade equivalence advantage), they recommended that word-study skills should be emphasized and taught systematically. (A reanalysis of the evidence by Guthrie & Tyler, 1978, pp. 65–66, yielded results that strongly supported the latter conclusion.)

With the exception of one project beginning with noncomparable subjects, none of the interaction effects between method and pupil aptitude was found to be statistically significant. On this basis, Bond and Dykstra concluded that "no method was especially effective or ineffective for pupils of high or low readiness as measured by tests of intelligence, auditory discrimination, and letter knowledge" (1967, p. 5).

Subsequently, a multivariate reanalysis of the data was conducted by Lohnes and Gray (1972) for five methods studied within ten projects. They argued that previously used covariance analysis was inappropriate because controls were partialed out from outcome criteria but not from treatments. Instead, because methods were freely chosen within projects and not all projects implemented all five methods, a multivariate analysis taking treatment-control correlations into account was appropriate. When methods were evaluated from this viewpoint,

TABLE 18.1 COMPARISON OF BASAL AND NONBASAL SUBJECTS ON THE STANFORD WORD READING, VOCABULARY, AND PARAGRAPH MEANING SUBTESTS

METHODS COMPARED	NUMBER OF STUDIES	WORD READING			VOCABULARY			PARAGRAPH MEANING		
		NON-BASAL METHOD SUPERIOR*	NO SIGNIFICANT DIFFERENCE	BASAL READER SUPERIOR*	NON-BASAL METHOD SUPERIOR*	NO SIGNIFICANT DIFFERENCE	BASAL READER SUPERIOR*	NON-BASAL METHOD SUPERIOR*	NO SIGNIFICANT DIFFERENCE	BASAL READER SUPERIOR*
i.t.a. vs. Basal	5	3	2	0	0	5	0	1	4	0
Linguistic vs. Basal	3	1	2	0	0	3	0	0	3	0
Basal + Phonics vs. Basal	4	0	4	0	1	3	0	1	3	0
Language Experience vs. Basal	4	2	2	0	1	3	0	1	2	1
Phonic/ Linguistic vs. Basal	3	3	0	0	0	3	0	2	1	0

* $p < .05$.
Source: From Tables 76 and 77, Bond & Dykstra, 1967, p. 98.

the differences among methods were not significant. Only one trend showed a methods effect; negative partial correlations for the language experience method suggest that this method may have been slightly less effective. The general findings concerning the relative equivalence of methods were neatly summarized by Lohnes and Gray: A model including methods as well as pretest measures accounted for 48 percent of outcome variance in contrast to 45 percent accounted for by readiness pretests alone.

As Lohnes and Gray note, "pessimism and gloom . . . prevailed regarding the outcomes of the studies" (1972, p. 54). Not only did methods as operationalized in the Cooperative Research Projects fail to predict learning outcomes to a significant degree, there was also considerable variance in learning outcomes that was unaccounted for. Bond and Dykstra properly note the substantial variation among classrooms within methods and the superior results of certain projects over others, regardless of method. On this basis, they recommended that "future research might well center on teacher and learning situation characteristics rather than methods and materials" (Bond & Dykstra, 1967, p. 123; see also Dykstra, 1968, pp. 66–67).

Although variation within methods and between projects may reflect characteristics of teaching and of instructional context, other alternative explanations exist. Most obviously, method conceptualized in a global fashion may not reflect the aspects of reading instruction that influence learning. Further, standardized outcome measures may contribute error to the criterion variance and may be insensitive to instructed content.

Research of the 1970s

General Trends

The most striking feature of methods research in the 1970s compared with that of the 1960s is the decline in the number of primary-reading investigations undertaken. As shown in Figure 18.1, even if one disregards the USOE Cooperative Research Projects, the average number of studies is lower. Thus, decrease in funding is not the sole explanation for the decline in methods studies. Rather, it is likely that the findings from the earlier studies persuaded many researchers that the question of method effectiveness had been answered and that other foci, such as teacher characteristics, would be more productive.

The second most striking feature of the investigations of the 1970s is that they resemble those of the 1960s in most respects: research design, reading methods, outcome measures, and results. Thus, although interest in methods investigations declined, most of those undertaken followed earlier patterns. In particular, most studies of the 1970s continued to assess reading outcomes and many researchers measured affective and language behavior in addition to reading and spelling. This range of outcome measures reflected those used in the USOE First-Grade Reading Studies.

Two trends in outcome measures are of particular interest: the use of measures directly related to instructional objectives or content and the analysis of oral reading errors. Whereas differences among alternative reading approaches may not be revealed on general standardized measures of reading achievement which bear an undefined relation to instructed content, they become apparent on instructionally relevant measures (e.g., see Atkinson, 1967; Briggs, 1972–1973; Calfee & Piontkowski, 1981; Hartley, 1971; Lesgold & Curtis, 1981). Similarly, students instructed with eclectic basal programs produce oral reading responses that differ in predictable ways from those instructed with phonics emphases (Barr, 1974, 1974–1975; Biemiller, 1970; Cohen, 1974–1975; Dank, 1976; DeLawter, 1975; Elder, 1971; also, for a review of this literature, see Allington, this volume).

The specific reading approaches studied during the past decade reflect those being tried in schools. For example, beginning in the late 1960s, we see evaluations of computer-assisted instruction (Atkinson, 1967; Hartley, 1971) and programmed linguistic materials (Briggs, 1972–1973; Feldhusen, Lamb, & Feldhusen, 1970; Shore & Marascuilo, 1974). During the 1970s, researchers became interested in programs that combined listening with reading (Schneeberg & Mattleman, 1973; Schneeberg, 1977) and writing or composition with reading (Callaway, McDaniel, & Mason, 1972; L. B. Smith, 1976; Smith & Morgan, 1975). Nevertheless, most method comparisons examined more traditional approaches: phonics programs in new packages, such as Distar (Kaufman, 1976; Ryckman, McCartin, & Sebasta, 1976), linguistic programs (Sabaroff, 1971; Wooden & Pettibone, 1973), language experience approaches (Pienaar, 1977; Stauffer & Pikulski, 1974) and transformed orthographies (e.g., Abiri, 1976; Downing, 1968, 1969; Johnson, Jones, Cole, & Walters, 1972; Mazurkiewicz, 1975; Robertson & Trepper, 1974; Trepper & Robertson, 1975). The tendency for innovative methods to be found superior to traditional methods continued in the research of the 1970s.

Many researchers examined the effectiveness of these methods with disadvantaged groups of children, possibly as part of the Right to Read initiative. Only one reading study (Holland, 1977) involved a Piagetian-based program and this was conducted in Ireland. The limited interest in child-centered approaches was unexpected because of the intense interest shown by child development experts in the development of new language-reading programs as part of the Follow Through investigations of the early 1970s.

Follow-Through Studies

Reading researchers tend to be unfamiliar with Follow Through programs developed mainly by child development specialists for primary-aged children during the early 1970s. Because research evidence indicated that pupil gains realized during the Head Start Program years were not maintained in the primary years of schooling, the USOE sponsored the development of model programs for disadvantaged children. In all, 22 different models were developed and implemented in over 180 sites. The goals of the different models varied, some emphasizing mainly affective social development, others conceptual development, and still others the development of academic skills. All, however, concerned reading acquisition in some form. For example, among the 7 programs studied by Stallings (1975), 2 emphasized reading-skill development through structured programs (programmed materials for individuals and Distar for groups). The remaining 5 models, influenced by the theories of Piaget, Dewey, and the British Infant School Movement, created responsive environments that encouraged an integration between learning and social development. Reading and writing skills were developed as part of ongoing communication through language experience approaches and even through the programmed typewriter in one case.

It is instructive to consider the Follow Through models in comparison with the Cooperative Reading research methods. Whereas reading researchers specified only the reading program to be followed by classroom teachers, Follow Through sponsors stipulated in great detail what the classroom environment should look like: what materials should be included, the role of the teachers, the treatment of pupils individually or in groups, time scheduling, and the like (Stallings, 1975).

The most extensive evaluation of Follow Through model effectiveness in terms of outcome measures involved three cohorts (samples) followed during the primary years (Stebbins, St. Pierre, Proper, Anderson, & Cerva, 1977). Similar to the USOE reading studies, the first major finding concerned the great variation from site to site in the results for each model. Methods which on the average yielded high achievement also included sites with relatively low achievement. Second, small differences were found between Follow Through and non-Follow Through programs, although investigators noted that "where differences were apparent, Follow Through groups scored lower more frequently than they scored higher" (Anderson, St. Pierre, Proper, & Stebbins, 1978, p. 162; Stebbins et al., 1977, p. 158). And third, with few exceptions, Follow Through groups still scored substantially below grade-level norms after three or four years of intervention.

Only as a secondary finding did the evaluators report differences between models. In particular, they found that methods classified together as emphasizing the mechanics of reading, writing, and arithmetic realized higher average achievement on subtests emphasizing skills (word knowledge, spelling, language, and math computation) than did other programs. By contrast, no model proved more effective than the others on conceptual measures (reading comprehension, math concepts, and math problem solving). Although these findings, in particular, were the basis of considerable controversy (see House, Glass, McLean, & Walker, 1978), they are nearly identical to those from the USOE Cooperative Reading findings described earlier.

Other Reviews

Although several reviews of the recent reading methods literature have been conducted (e.g., see Chall, 1979; Maxwell, 1972; Popp, 1975), the most comprehensive (Pflaum et al., 1980) employs the approach of meta-analysis (Glass, 1978). Pflaum and her associates developed systematic procedures and criteria for identifying a "population" of reading methods studies from which to select a subset for further analysis. Each study was then examined in order to determine the emphasis of instruction and to specify other characteristics of the instruction, the sample, and the learning outcomes. This set of evidence from the studies was analyzed statistically in order to determine the existence and magnitude of the difference between experimental and control methods in outcomes and to explore the interaction between program characteristics, such as the length of treatment and learning effects. The superiority of the experimental over control methods was demonstrated, as was the greater effectiveness of synthetic phonics methods over those involving analytic phonics.

The advantage of meta-analysis over traditional reviews lies in the rigor with which the results from different studies can be evaluated and the possibility of comparing across studies the influence of conditions which are constant for individual studies. The approach is limited, however, by the quality of the studies that serve as cases within the meta-analysis.

Summary

What have we learned from this vast amount of research conducted on reading methods? First, substantively, we have learned that the emphasis of instructional method is reflected in learning; children tend to learn what they are taught. In particular, methods that promote the development of decoding skills tend to yield higher learning of decoding-related skills. Second, we have learned that no single method or approach is consistently more effective in developing general reading skill than any other. Third, the wide variation among classes instructed with the same approach attests to the fact that conditions other than the reading program, at least when characterized globally, have consequences for learning to read.

Methodologically, we should have learned that the procedure of comparing globally defined programs is unproductive. It fails to account for the conditions other than method that influence learning—that is, it does not place method in a proper context—and it does not formulate the aspects or dimensions of an approach that may be relevant to learning. For example, it fails to consider the amount of time children actually spend working with the materials and how much of the program they actually cover. However, the continued use of this methodological approach in the majority of reading method investigations conducted during the 1970s suggests that we have yet to appreciate its limitations.

The survival of an inadequate research methodology in spite of repeated criticism is enigmatic. Its resistence to extinction or elaboration may reflect conceptual commitments of researchers or the failure of alternative methodologies to present themselves. Regarding the first explanation, it appears that the distinction between meaning-emphasis and code-emphasis methods does not arise simply because of the nature of English orthography. Downing (1977) concluded, following a study of reading methods in 14 countries, that a "similar dichotomy of methods existed in every language." (p. 25). Nevertheless, it does not follow that because a conceptual dichotomy in methods exists, the feature on which this dichotomy is based is the only significant one, overriding all other aspects of a particular method or of instruction generally. In other words, while the question "Which is best?" has an understandable hold on our attention, we may not be able to answer that question without first specifying more fully the distinctive features of each method and identifying the secondary aspects of instruction that influence achievement.

INFLUENCE OF PUPIL CHARACTERISTICS ON METHOD EFFECTIVENESS

The question of the best program was not the only one being posed during the 1960s and 1970s. Investigators were also concerned with whether a particular method might be better for some children than for others. In research circles, this is known as the aptitude-treatment interaction (ATI) hypothesis. It suggests, quite simply, that students who possess one level of aptitude (e.g., low intelligence or readiness) may respond better to one treatment (e.g., code emphasis), while students who possess another level of the same aptitude (e.g., high intelligence or readiness) will respond better to another treatment (e.g., meaning emphasis).

This sort of hypothesis is reflected in the old belief, shared by teachers and researchers, that certain children respond better to one method than to another. If such interactions were established, differential instruction of pupils in classes might be warranted. The first set of pertinent findings is based mainly on data derived from the USOE sponsored reading methods investigations. In this research, aptitude is either treated in a general fashion or in terms of specific components, while method is characterized globally. The second set of reports identifies abilities which pertain specifically to reading acquisition and explores their interaction with reading methods, characterized along a decoding-meaning continuum.

General Abilities and Reading Methods

Chall (1967) and Bond and Dykstra (Bond & Dykstra, 1967; Dykstra, 1968) in their extensive analyses of methods investigations examined whether children's abilities influenced their response to different reading methods. As described earlier, they drew different conclusions about the effectiveness of different methods for pupils of different ability. Whereas Chall found that low-aptitude children instructed by meaning-emphasis materials achieved higher than similar children instructed with a systematic phonics approach at the end of first grade, those instructed with decoding emphases achieved higher by the end of second grade. By contrast, Bond and Dykstra reported no difference in method effectiveness for groups of different ability. One reason for the discrepancy may be their methods of analysis: Chall used differential achievement of pupils instructed by different methods within groups of low, average, and high ability as evidence for an interaction effect, while Bond and Dykstra used the more stringent criterion of a statistically significant interaction effect.

Cronbach and Snow (1977), in their comprehensive review of ATI investigations, criticized the methodology used by Bond and Dykstra: "Blocking on aptitude led to extraordinarily weak statistical tests. Furthermore, applying uniform cutting scores across all projects created markedly uneven cell sizes within projects, undermining the anova. . . . Cell sizes also varied between treatments within projects. Regression methods would have minimized these difficulties, and would have made it possible to compare relations across projects" (1967, p. 220). Although Cronbach and Snow undertook a regression analysis of the data, inconsistencies between their results and those of individual project reports led them to abandon the effort.

An extensive reanalysis of the USOE Cooperative Reading second-grade data was also undertaken by Lo (1973). Five aptitude factors (intelligence, perceptual speed, spatial relations, listening, and learning rate), extracted from pretest and posttest measures, were reduced to a single composite score. Using multiple regression, Lo found a number of suggestive ATI effects; indeed, nearly all comparisons of the traditional basal approach with other methods were statistically significant.

The Cronbach and Snow (1977, pp. 222–231) interpretation of the results from the Lo (1973) and the Bond and Dykstra (1967) analyses is particularly useful. Their study of the original project reports as well as the two analyses led them to conclude that evidence suggesting ATIs existed. In particular, they proposed that general ability predicted a steeper regression slope for the language experience method, i.t.a., and combined phonic/linguistic methods respectively in comparison with the slope for whole-word emphases. In other words, there was less difference between the reading achievement of low- and high-ability children instructed by whole-word methods than by the other approaches. The pattern for linguistic methods appeared to be different, with a steeper regression slope for the whole-word methods than for the linguistic approaches. In addition, they suggested that some special abilities may interact to influence the relationships.

While Cronbach and Snow attempted to learn as much as possible concerning ATI effects from existing data, they urge caution in interpreting the evidence because of inconsistencies among projects employing the same method: "Treatments are multivariate in nature—to characterize a treatment as "phonic" is to leave a great deal unspecified" (1977, p.221).

Newman and Lohnes (1972) reanalyzed data gathered by Reid and Beltramo (1965, 1966) which compared seven beginning reading methods used in instructing 310 children from the lowest third of the aptitude distribution in readiness. Three orthogonal criterion factors, intellectual development, vocabulary, and paragraph reading, were derived from the outcome measures. Multiple regression coefficients, with paragraph reading as the criterion, revealed markedly different patterns for aptitude predictors, indicating ATI effects. To illustrate, two methods showed the strongest effects: the language method involving reading, writing, listening, and speaking (Ginn Elementary English) depended primarily on general intelligence, while the same language method used in conjunction with instruction involving recognition of letters and their sounds and the use of context clues (Houghton Mifflin) capitalized mainly on letter knowledge. This means that among children low in readiness, when paragraph reading was the criterion, more intelligent children did best with the language method alone, while those low in general intelligence but high on letter names profited from the addition of a program that emphasized letter sounds.

Cooley and Lohnes (1976), with reference to the Lo (1973) and the Newman and Lohnes (1972) investigations, describe the potential usefulness of ATI inquiry: "The potential value of ATI phenomena is that replicable findings of this type, if strong enough, may permit the prescription of optimal curriculum systems, units, or processes to individual students on the bases of their differential aptitude profiles" (p. 73).

This research provides evidence supporting the existence of ATI effects, particularly when aptitude is treated in general terms. Furthermore, the analysis of Newman and Lohnes suggests the usefulness of focusing on low-aptitude pupils and of examining their special abilities. Still, inconsistent findings among classes and projects indicate that there is significant variance in achievement unaccounted for. The treatment of method in a global fashion may, at least in part, account for the difficulty in identifying ATI effects. As suggested by Cronbach and Snow (1977), neither the multidimensional aspects of treatment are accounted for nor are other schooling conditions which may confound the relationship considered. Until method is properly formulated, it may be extremely difficult to determine what makes a method effective for pupils of different general and specific abilities.

Specific Aptitudes and Reading Methods

Studies in this section differ from those in the previous section in that an analysis of reading processes logically presumed by different methods provides the basis for suggesting that certain special abilities are important. Similar to the previous section, method is treated globally.

One theoretical tradition in reading derives from the medical literature which examines the processing characteristics of persons who have sustained brain injury. The similarity between adults with processing disruptions and children who encounter difficulty in acquiring oral- and printed-language competencies was noted in the nineteenth century (Hinshelwood, 1917). It was a small step to the hypothesis that differences in perceptual processing capabilities influence how easily a child responds to different instructional methods, and, accordingly, this view became common in the clinical literature of reading (Mills, 1956). In the past two decades, partly due to increased interest in the learning disabilities of children, the hypothesis has been applied to classrooms of normal learners as well as clinical samples of disabled readers (Wepman, 1968).

During the 1960s and 1970s, a number of reading investigators (Bateman, 1968; Cullinan, 1969; Miller, 1974, 1979; Robinson, 1972) undertook systematic studies to determine whether children with good visual processing skills (e.g., discrimination, sequencing, memory) learn to read most easily by methods which emphasize sight word learning while children with good auditory processing abilities learn most easily by approaches which emphasize letter-sound associations. The research evidence, however, offers little support for the expected interaction between pupil modality and reading method. Both Bateman and Robinson found that children with an auditory modality superiority performed higher with both approaches; Cullinan and Miller found no main effect differences in method or aptitude. No investigators found significant interaction effects with the exception of Miller, who found, in opposition to the hypothesis, that those with auditory preferences achieved higher in a class taught with a visual emphasis than similar children instructed with a phonics approach.

Part of the difficulty with this type of research lies in the definition of modality deficiency. A difference on two measures (one visual and one auditory) taken from a battery of tests may not constitute enough of a deficiency to interfere with reading development. Further, there are problems with the global classification of phonics as an auditory method and of a sight-word emphasis as a visual method since both approaches pose visual and auditory processing demands. But finally, as suggested by Miller, "It may turn out that cognitive skills are more important to initial reading success than perceptual ones" (1979, p. 104).

There has been some investigation of the specific conceptual abilities related to reading. For example, the research of Lesgold and Curtis (1981) is based on an analysis of the conceptual demands of reading. They argue that the cognitive processing ability which they call "phonological proficiency" relates directly to the ease a child has in learning to read.

An alternative treatment of conceptual ability focuses on the relationship between reading method and conceptual stage of development. The basic argument is that eclectic methods, which entail mainly whole-word learning, depend on preoperational strategies and memory capabilities available to most beginning readers. In contrast, the processes demanded by synthetic-phonics methods, involving part-whole relationships and reversibility, may be possible only for children who conserve (Ferreiro, 1978) or perceptually decenter (Elkind, 1967; Elkind, Koegler, & Go, 1964).

In sum, although it is tempting to conclude that perceptual modality strength represents an unproductive formulation of abilities related to reading method effectiveness, the failure of existing research to define reading method in other than a global fashion makes this conclusion premature. Similarly, even though phonological proficiency and conceptual stage appear to interact in plausible ways with beginning reading methods, replication of current findings with more detailed specification of instructional methods is needed.

Conclusions

Research findings suggest that different groups of children do respond differently to alternative reading approaches. Accordingly, viewing the effectiveness of reading methods as conditionally influenced by pupil aptitude seems to be productive. Questions remain, however, concerning the most useful way to characterize and identify those aptitudes of children that bear on learning to read. Further and repeatedly in the ATI research, investigators identify the inadequate formulation of reading approaches as a major limitation in the attempt to determine the most appropriate methods for instructing different groups of children.

Determining which reading approach is best for certain children represents a highly practical quest. One important step in this inquiry is to think about the problem of how reading methods might be conceptualized usefully. If an obvious or easy solution existed, the problem would have been solved by now; but none does. The final section of this chapter concerns the attempt to provide an answer to this problem. It examines selected studies that have defined reading approaches in alternative ways.

REFORMULATION OF THE PROBLEM
OF READING METHODS

Cooperative Research Studies

Two of the investigations examined in this section were conducted in the mid-1960s as part of the Cooperative Reading Studies. They merit examination because they describe reading methods in some detail and reflect the influence of observational methods developed for the study of classroom teaching and climate (Flanders, 1965, 1970; Medley & Mitzel, 1963).

Chall and Feldmann (1966a, 1966b) examined how 12 classes using the same eclectic reading program differed in classroom instruction and learning. Because they studied only teachers who used the same program, they did not characterize the program as a variable resource; they treated it as a constant. To characterize reading instruction, an observer recorded a factual description of reading activities at least once a month in each class and then rated such dimensions of instruction as the proportion of teacher talk, reading error rate, approach to learning, teacher distance, and the quality and amount of time devoted to these activities: whole-word recognition, word analysis and phonics, and connected reading.

Having gathered a large number of teacher and instructional ratings (83 in all), Chall and Feldmann then attempted to organize the evidence into a more limited and coherent representation. Two of their solutions are interesting. The first, following Chall's theoretical distinction between decoding versus meaning emphases in reading instruction, involved derivation of an average rating composed of dimensions that varied along the decoding to meaning continuum. They found that a decoding emphasis in the context of eclectic instruction predicted higher reading achievement at the end of the first grade.

The second solution, involving factor analysis, yielded seven factors. Four of these, designated as teaching competence, learning approach, reading emphasis, and instructional appropriateness, were associated with higher reading achievement, while a fifth factor referred to as teacher approval-disapproval was unrelated (Chall & Feldmann, 1966b, pp. 74–78). However, it is difficult to interpret the significance of these findings for instruction because factors are derived from a variety of components. For example, the "primary emphasis in reading" factor loaded highly not only on ratings reflecting the use of sound-symbol versus meaning activities and time allocated to these activities, but also the ratio of teacher talk to pupil practice.

We learn from this research the value of observing instruction rather than simply characterizing a program globally in terms of its emphasis. Further, in addition to primary reading emphasis within curricular program emphasis, other conditions, such as teaching competence, learning approach, and instructional appropriateness, are seen to bear on learning.

In this investigation, we confront the problem that has plagued subsequent researchers: Once the phenomenon of reading instruction has been divided into a myriad of variables, how can a subset be selected and recombined in a useful fashion? Although the solution of recombining ratings along the continuum of decoding to learning emphasis represents an advance over a global rating of a curricular program, it too masks or overlooks other conditions that influence learning. While the solution of factor analysis suggests what some of these other significant instructional influences might be, the factors themselves are statistical abstractions which combine a variety of underlying elements that do not necessarily form a coherent package in reality.

A second Cooperative Reading Study reflects the belief that reading programs may be used in different ways. Harris and Serwer (1966a, 1966b, 1966c) characterized four programs in terms of method emphasis (basal reader, basal reader with phonovisual, language experience, and language experience with audiovisual) and then observed the instruction associated with each program. Eight measures of reading method and five of teaching style were derived; however, none (including one representing emphasis on skills) correlated significantly with subsequent reading achievement.

As a second method for documenting aspects of classroom instruction, Harris and Serwer asked teachers to keep a daily log of the time they spent engaged in various reading activities and supportive activities. Based on reports from five consecutive days per month from January to May, teachers using the four reading programs were found to differ considerably in total instructional time devoted to reading and in their emphasis on reading versus activities supportive of reading (e.g., language arts, art).

Two major conclusions were drawn about the relationship between activity emphasis and reading achievement. First, substantial investment of time in activities involving little or no reading practice (e.g., art with reading, audiovisual activities) was not productive in fostering reading achievement, while more time devoted to reading activity was. Second, emphasis on the activities characteristic of a particular program was productive. For example, instruction using the basal reader method profited from more time reading the basal and teaching sight words; instruction using the language experience method was facilitated by time spent in writing, dramatization, social studies and science; audiovisual activities were most productive for teachers using the language experience plus audiovisual method. Inconsistent with this trend were the results for pupils who were instructed with the basal plus phonovisual methods; emphasis on phonics was not particularly productive, but storytelling was.

We learn two main things from this analysis. First, combined ratings based on direct observation of instruction may be as ineffective in predicting learning outcomes as programs characterized in a global fashion. Yet, why was the Chall and Feldmann characterization of teaching productive, while the Harris and Serwer was not? The latter ratings pertained to the "range and varieties of materials and activities observed in the classroom," using a checklist-tally procedure and served to distinguish among the instructional methods of the four programs. It may be that the Chall and Feldmann factors were useful because they were examined in the context of a single curricular program. Accordingly, their measure of skill emphasis may have referred to skill emphasis and elaboration by teachers above and beyond that inherent in the program, whereas the Harris and Serwer measure of skill emphasis may have confounded program emphasis with teacher emphasis.

Second, characterization of reading instruction in terms of the time a teacher reports allocating to alternative reading and supporting activities appears to be promising. Indeed, as we shall see later in this section, this method of characterizing instruction achieved prominence in the 1970s. Equally significant is the treatment of method (program) as a conditional influence, as when teaching sight words enhanced learning when a basal program was used. Such interactions suggest that examining activities without reference to curricular program context may be unproductive.

Recent Instructional Studies

Five investigations of beginning reading instruction were selected for detailed examination in order to think about how reading approaches might be usefully conceptualized. Each of the five represents research enterprises that have spanned several years. Not all were undertaken by reading researchers. Four of the five approach the problem of instruction from psychological perspectives, whereas the fifth is sociological in orientation. They were selected because their varied treatment of instruction and their findings concerning the linkages between instructional conditions and learning permit a comparative consideration of how the problem of reading methods might be usefully formulated.

Prescriptive Approach (Texas)

In their study of primary instruction, Brophy and Evertson (1974) identify teaching processes which predict the acquisition of fundamental "tool skills." They draw on the work of earlier investigations (Brophy & Good, 1970; Flanders, 1965, 1970; Kounin, 1970; Smith & Meux, 1962; see also Dunkin & Biddle, 1974, for a review of teaching process-product studies) for a collection of about 350 different variables. Most indexes pertain to interaction during instruction, in particular to the rate of different types of verbal response by teachers and pupils (questions, comments, responses, reactions). Some, however, reflect more global ratings of classroom climate and activity, and others refer to teacher solutions to such common classroom problems as handling catch-up work, allocating time to different activities, setting rules for conduct, and giving rewards and punishment.

Although the descriptive scheme is comprehensive, including most variables examined in other process-product studies, no theory about what aspects of teaching influence learning explicitly guides the selection and organization of teaching variables. As a consequence, teaching-process variables are considered seriatim as isolated conditions in relation to measures of achievement. Aside from the methodological problems of considering a large number of variables in small samples, a major conceptual problem arises. The results are difficult to make sense of because the complex phenomenon of teaching has been atomized into many parts, and there are no guidelines for recombining elements back into an integral conception of teaching.

A second Texas investigation (Anderson, Evertson, & Brophy, 1979) was limited to a single setting: first-grade reading groups. The researchers organized teaching variables around 22 principles believed to promote effective teaching in small group settings. These principles pertain to such aspects of group management as getting and maintaining student attention, introducing lessons and new materials, calling on individuals, dealing with individual learning rates, and the like. The authors refer to this list as an instructional model; however, interconnections among teaching activities are not specified.

Slightly more than half of the teaching activities were significantly associated with reading achievement, and it is tempting to try to make some sense of this array of independent findings. For example, does minimizing pupil choral responses and call-outs and teacher feedback after correct answers lead to higher achievement directly or because their absence permits the occurrence of other more productive activities, such as overviews and pupil practice? We cannot know the answer to this question since we do not know how the selected teaching procedures were combined during instruction.

In addition to the dimensions related to the 22 principles that make up the model, other conditions, such as time use, curriculum content, and reading method emphasis were examined. These conditions are of particular interest to us since two conditions, curriculum used and content covered, pertain directly to reading program characteristics and two others, use of phonic clues and use of word-attack questions, reflect reading method emphasis. Consistent with previous reading research, materials and methods that emphasize word-study skills predicted higher achievement.

Two other conditions derive from models of classroom learning which propose time as a major determinant of learning (Carroll, 1963). Again, consistent with previous research, time spent on instructionally relevant tasks predicted learning.

This work makes a noticeable conceptual advance over earlier process-product research, which selected and classified teaching-process variables arbitrarily, in that teaching activities are related conceptually to salient instructional issues, such as control of groups, consideration of individual learning rates, and the provision of incentives. Nevertheless, in each of these categories, the investigators consider seriatim the relationship between some aspect of teacher behavior and achievement. Treating teaching activities one at a time cannot yield an understanding of the nature of the complex set of interrelationships that hold in classroom instruction—particularly, the question of whether certain conditions are independent or contextually determined and whether their influence on achievement is direct, indirect, or negligible.

As noted, the variables of particular interest to reading researchers are not included as part of the model nor is a rationale provided for their inclusion in the study. Yet, the empirical evidence indicates their relationship to reading achievement. One might, therefore, view this listing as a beginning attempt to include in a teaching model other important aspects of instruction. Note, however, that no formulation is provided concerning how these other aspects of instruction go together and interact with teaching methods.

Beginning Teacher Evaluation Study (BTES)

A second series of investigations were based in part on the process-product approach to teaching. Initiated by the California Commission for Teacher Preparation and Licensing, BTES was limited in focus to reading and mathematics and to the second and fifth grades. An interdisciplinary group that included teacher educators, administrators, subject matter specialists, and educational researchers cooperated in the conception and conduct of the BTES; nevertheless, the psychological perspective shared by the majority of researchers is reflected in the evolving formulation. After a planning year, Phase II involved field work to develop measuring instruments, formulate hypotheses, and test relationships between teaching, environmental, and pupil characteristics and learning outcomes (McDonald & Elias, 1976a, 1976b).

Several methods were used in Phase II to document classroom instruction. One, the Reading and Mathematics Observation System (RAMOS) (Calfee & Calfee, 1976) involved observation during a period of reading (or math) instruction. Four main categories were evaluated: the role of the instructor, the aim of instruction, the instructional activities, and the main materials used. Each time instruction changed along one of these major dimensions, the time and the nature of the change were recorded. Calfee and Calfee (1976) found that the dominant role of the 41 second-grade teachers studied during reading lessons was that of direct instruction and the dominant aim involved practicing skills. Books were the main instructional material and workbooks were common, but children worked with no materials for about 20 percent of the time. Most time was spent in seatwork activities; discussion accounted for about 20 percent of the time and oral reading recitation for about 10 percent. Little time was spent on new concepts or application.

Elias and Wheeler (1976) examined the results from a Reading Work Diary completed by BTES teachers on two occasions, each of a week's duration. Teachers were asked to check a list containing subcategories of decoding, vocabulary, comprehension, and application according to the skills they introduced during the week and those they reviewed. In addition, for each skill marked, they described the teaching strategy, the activity of pupils, the time spent, and the materials used. Elias and Wheeler explored an important methodological question: What is the relationship between teacher reports and observational evidence? They found that teacher reports about the organization of pupils for reading instruction were consistent with observed organizational patterns, whereas teacher reports on time spent teaching specific reading skills were not consistent with observed time allocations.

Generally, the conditions examined in BTES-Phase II were not unlike those examined in the Texas studies, although reading activities and content were described more comprehensively. Both investigations were atheoretical, in that no logical basis was developed for specifying the importance of certain dimensions over others. Analysis of the relationships between instructional conditions and achievement proceeded variable by variable, although in BTES-Phase II some variables were combined and multiple-regression procedures were employed to determine the unique and joint contribution of conditions to achievement gain.

By contrast, Phase III of BTES develops a formulation of instructional effectiveness (Fisher, Filby, Marliave, Cahen, Dishaw, Moore, & Berliner, 1978). The theory contains three components: the first, which includes instruction and other conditions of the classroom, is viewed as having direct consequences for the second, the time a student is involved in curricular tasks. The second, in turn, predicts the third, pupil achievement. The theory draws from two distinct traditions of school research. The notion of academic learning time (ALT) was derived from the formulation of school learning by Carroll (1963), which was subsequently refined and elaborated by Bloom (1968) and D. E. Wiley (1976), among others, so as to include not only the time allocated by the teacher to a particular curricular area, but also the proportion of the time the student is actually engaged in a relevant task. The BTES group carried the conceptual refinement one step further by adding the qualification that the task must not be too difficult if the time was to be effective for learning. ALT, then, refers to "the amount of time a student spends engaged on a task that produces few student errors and which is directly related to a defined content area" (Fisher et al., 1978, p. 1-7).

The formulation of teaching follows directly from earlier process-product studies in general and the BTES-Phase II investigation in particular. It goes beyond this earlier work by conceptualizing teaching as a cyclical process consisting of planning and instructional interaction. Planning involves diagnosis and pre-scription, whereas teaching interaction entails presentation, feedback, and moni-toring. Teacher planning is expected to influence error rate within ALT, that is, less adequate diagnosis and prescription should result in less appropriate tasks as reflected in high error rates. Teacher interaction is expected to affect pupil engagement through the direct involvement of the teacher and error rate through more complete information about how pupils are doing.

In addition to teaching-process characteristics, the BTES researchers pro-pose that the classroom environment moderates the influence of teaching on ALT or influences ALT directly. Classroom environment is also conceptualized consistently with earlier process-product work in its emphasis on climate, includ-ing observational assessment of warmth, cooperation, and instructional appropri-ateness.

The following summary gives the flavor of the results for second- and fifth-grade reading instruction. (1) Contrary to expectations, neither the instructional planning measures, with one exception, nor the interactive measures were corre-lated with error rates. However, the interactive teaching measure of monitoring, feedback, and presentation were significantly correlated with pupil engagement rates. Teaching then seems to keep pupils on task in second grade, but does not necessarily make the task appropriate in difficulty. The pattern was somewhat different for fifth-grade reading. Most significant, and surprisingly, interactive measures were associated with high error rates. (2) The global measures of class-room environment did not predict engagement rates in second grade, but were effective predictors in fifth grade. (3) Multiple-regression analyses, after account-ing for the influence of pretest variance, revealed that ALT and teaching-process variables accounted for a similar proportion of variance, about 18 percent each, in total reading in second grade and about 10 percent each in fifth grade. This means that although teaching process variables may influence achievement gain through ALT, they also contribute independently to learning.

Although not a part of their formulation, the BTES researchers considered the consequence of two setting conditions: self-paced (seatwork) and other paced (group instruction typically guided by a teacher). Setting was shown to have clear impact on the frequency of interactive teaching and engagement rate, and engagement rate within setting varied according to interactive teaching. That is, in seatwork, an average engagement rate of about 70 percent increased to about 98 percent when substantive instructional interaction occurred. Never-theless, setting was not part of the formulation as a contextual condition.

The differences observed between Phase II and Phase III of the research are instructive. The instructional formulation, by identifying and relating a set of conditions, solved the problem of previous investigators of how a large number of instructional variables should be treated. In particular, the concept of ALT appears to have important implications for learning. Nevertheless, the formula-tion is content free in form. While Phase II contained a detailed description of reading methods, materials, goals, and activities, in Phase III, reading and math instruction became the setting in which the proposed interrelations of the ALT formulation were tested. How the contexts of instructional activity (reading vs. math) conditionally influenced instruction and learning process was not formu-lated.

Both the Texas investigation and the BTES-Phase III increase our understanding of how instructional management may contribute directly or indirectly to learning; they are less useful in thinking about what aspects of reading methods and material allocations influence learning and how these conditions relate to the instructional management of teachers. Indeed, the final formulations of both groups of researchers are content free. By contrast, the approach of the reading conceptions group of the Institute for Research on Teaching (IRT) to be considered next is directly concerned with reading methods in the context of classroom instruction.

Reading Conceptions (IRT)

The research of the IRT at Michigan State University rests on the belief that the mental life and decision making of teachers have significant consequence for their instructional effectiveness (Shulman, 1975). Accordingly, the research on classroom reading instruction undertaken by the reading conceptions research group focuses not only on classroom practices, but also on the mental framework or conceptions of teachers. Not unlike the earlier research of Chall and Feldmann, this group characterizes teacher belief systems in relation to their instructional practice.

The conceptions of teachers about reading were measured in two major ways. The first involved an inventory in which a teacher agreed or disagreed (on a 5-point scale) with propositions about reading instruction. Propositions were selected to represent five main views of reading instruction, but the statistical analysis of the results yielded a single continuum, ranging from "content centered" (basal text and linear skills) to "pupil centered" (natural language, interest, and integrated curriculum models) (Duffy & Methany, 1978).

A second, more complex manner of characterizing teacher belief systems was based on teacher statements made during formal and informal interviews and in classroom instruction. Statements were classified into a two-by-two matrix that included the categories of pupil-centered versus content-centered and child-environment versus reading-learning (Buike & Duffy, 1979).

Case studies of the reading instruction in 23 elementary school classrooms were undertaken. Detailed observations, using unstructured written accounts and selective tape recording, were made for at least one full and four half-days, four times during the school year. Eight areas of instructional practice were identified: judging pupil progress, evaluating instructional materials, forming instructional groups, allocating time to reading activities, allocating time to pupils of various ability, using word-recognition prompts, emphasizing comprehension, and identifying the instructional role favored by the teacher.

Based on the observational notes, the practices of each of the teachers were rated in the eight areas. One end of each continuum was identified as being child centered and the other content centered, although it is not clear that this characterization applies to all dimensions (e.g., allocating time to groups of different ability and emphasizing comprehension). In addition, the percentages of time devoted to affective considerations, oral language development, basal reading and skill development during reading instruction were determined. It is difficult to judge the adequacy of the methodology because the criteria and procedures for classifying teacher behavior along the eight dimensions and for determining time allocations are not described.

Visual inspection and comparison appear to have been the method for determining whether the representations of teacher conceptions conformed to the characterizations of observed reading practice. While Duffy and Anderson (1981) observe that teachers' reading beliefs were reflected in practice, they conclude that "instruction appears to be based not on various reading theories which trigger qualitatively different instructional decisions but, rather, on situational conditions in the classroom context, primarily the use of the basal textbook" (p. 33). They note as well the influence of student age and ability on teacher statements about instruction. For example, teachers of younger and less able students preferred more structured, content-centered reading approaches, while those with older and more able students emphasized student-centered approaches.

Reading achievement gain scores and attitude measures from a sample of eight children from each of eight primary rooms revealed no systematic differences between those taught by the content-oriented versus the pupil-oriented teachers. It should be noted that all students were instructed with eclectic basal readers.

The reading conceptions research shows that other dimensions than those typically included under the rubric of reading methods must be considered in accounting for instruction. That is, the traditional reading categories of eclectic basal, linear skill, natural language, interest, and integrated curriculum (or content centered vs. child centered) neither represent the conceptions of teachers about reading instruction nor describe their practice. Nevertheless, the IRT researchers did not resolve the problem of how to characterize instruction successfully. Although the delineation of eight instructional categories represents a conceptual advance over characterizing instructional practice simply as child or content centered, the use of the child-content dichotomy in characterizing each of the other dimensions suggests its hold over reading researchers in thinking about instruction. No rationale supporting the choice of the eight dimensions was provided, nor were the interconnections among these categories formulated. Thus, the main contribution of this research lies in its demonstration that other than traditional reading conceptions are important in thinking about instruction and its identification of instructional materials and student characteristics as being significant influences on the instructional planning of teachers.

Social Organization (Chicago)

The work of Barr and Dreeben (1983) considers three related problems. The first is how the prevailing conditions of the classroom—its students, instructional materials, time schedules, and teaching goals and expertise—become established through allocation decisions at the school and district levels of educational organizations. The second is how classroom instruction becomes organized and is managed given these prevailing conditions. The third is how instruction and student characteristics interact to influence the learning outcomes of individuals.

Barr and Dreeben argue that work in schools is characterized by a division of labor among levels of school organization, each with its own productive activities and outcomes. Work at the district level, for example, involves the securing of personnel and materials, the acquisition and maintenance of buildings, the establishment of yearly and daily time schedules, and the like. Some activities at the school level include the assignment of teachers and students to classes, the development of the school time schedule, the distribution of instructional materials, and the assessment and coordination of learning. Instruction is the province of the classroom and teachers. Although levels of school organization are distinguished by different sorts of activity, they are also interconnected, in that the problems solved at one level bear directly on the work of adjacent levels. Most obviously, the work of teachers is influenced by decisions made by district and school personnel concerning the scheduling of time, the selection of materials, and the composition of classes.

In order to test this formulation, Barr and Dreeben elaborated its form with respect to classroom instruction. They argue that the first activity of teachers in preparing for instructional activity is to consider the class, particularly its distributive properties, and to determine the appropriate social arrangement for instruction. This decision influences the design of instruction, for if teachers group children for instruction, they solve to some extent the problem of matching the difficulty of materials with the aptitudes of children. But this solution makes teachers less available to direct the work of pupils who are not in the immediate subgroup they are teaching. Correspondingly, the solution of total class instruction may solve the problem of teacher availability, but because it typically involves use of a single set of materials, the work is usually inappropriate for a number of students. Barr and Dreeben argue that instruction is responsive to the characteristics of the group for which it is designed; accordingly, the mean aptitude of groups should exert major influence on instructional productivity, which they define in terms of the content actually covered by groups. They further propose that the relationship between group mean aptitude and content coverage is influenced by other conditions of the class, such as the difficulty of curricular materials, the time schedule developed by the teacher, and the teacher's management and supervision of instruction.

Reanalyzing data available on the reading instruction in 15 first-grade classes, they found that the mean aptitude of groups ($n = 43$) accounted for a substantial proportion (47%) of the variance in the number of new words covered in the basal materials. The difficulty of the reading materials (the number of words introduced in the first-grade materials) and the time teachers reported spending on basal instruction also accounted for a significant proportion of the variance (19% and 17%) in word coverage. Because of collinearity between these conditions (37% shared variance), only the condition of material difficulty contributed significantly to the prediction of coverage along with group mean aptitude (accounting for 65% of the variance, an increase of 18%). The collinearity between allocated time and the difficulty of materials is particularly interesting; it means that teachers with more difficult reading programs allocate more time to reading instruction. Further, it is the combination of these conditions that bear on coverage, over and above what might be predicted on the basis of the mean aptitude of the group for which instruction is planned.

A similar analysis was undertaken for phonics instruction. The number of phonics concepts covered during the first grade was less responsive to the group mean aptitude than to the number of phonics concepts contained in the first-grade materials and the time allocated to phonics activities. Further, the amount of time during which the teacher directly supervised phonics activities had a bearing on the pace of phonics instruction; a similar relationship was not found for basal instruction.

With regard to the influence of content coverage on learning, they found different patterns for word learning versus phonics learning. Basal coverage accounted for 86% of the variance in basal word learning and no other instructional or class condition contributed to the relationship. In contrast, phonics coverage accounted for only 38% of the variance in phonics learning and other conditions, such as teacher supervision, teacher experience teaching first grade, and instructional group size, contributed significantly to the variance accounted for in phonics learning. Whereas in basal learning, the influence of time, materials, and other conditions was mediated through basal coverage to influence learning, in phonics learning, other conditions influenced it directly as well as indirectly through phonics coverage. In other words, phonics learning appears to be more sensitive to the way in which instruction is actually conducted.

Barr and Dreeben (Barr, 1983; Dreeben, 1983) have replicated and refined the study with 13 additional first-grade classes. Instead of teacher reports on instructional time allocations, coverage, grouping, and other instructional conditions, the classes were observed 12 times during the school year. The basic findings, reported for 10 of the classes, replicated those from the first study. The difficulty of materials and observed time use were found to covary with each other, and both predicted coverage at a level higher than in the previous investigation and at a level comparable with that of the mean aptitude of instructional groups. Again coverage was found to be the condition most closely associated with learning, accounting for 83% and 71% of the variance in basal and phonics learning respectively and for 50% in general achievement.

Several things are interesting about this approach. First, as with the BTES investigation, we see the value of theory in identifying and ordering the interconnections among conditions. Unlike the BTES, which examines the linkages among instructional conditions and pupil outcome measures (involved time, error rate, learning), the Chicago formulation selects a condition of instruction, content coverage, and examines how other instructional conditions influence it. The theory treats classroom instruction in the context of school organization and draws attention to how instruction is influenced by the resources available in classrooms. Unlike the content-free formulations of the Texas and BTES research, the approach is directly concerned with the nature of materials and documents their difficulty (number of words and phonics concepts in first-grade-level materials) and the extent to which students experience them (coverage) in a precise fashion. Similar to the BTES research, the investigation includes instructionally sensitive measures of learning as well as general measures of reading achievement.

Word-Processing Efficiency

The longitudinal study of reading acquisition by the Learning Research and Development Center (LRDC) at the University of Pittsburgh shows the influence of two major strands of work in psychology. From instructional psychology, we find interest in the nature of the instructional task: component stages of learning necessary for a desired outcome are identified and sequenced through logical analysis, and then task materials and activities are designed in order to promote each learning component. From cognitive psychology comes interest in the processing characteristics of children as they acquire skill in word recognition.

In a series of instructional investigations, Lesgold and associates (Lesgold

& Curtis, 1981; Lesgold & Resnick, 1982) explore the association between slow word processing and poor reading comprehension. For example, Lesgold and Resnick argue that when certain processes are inefficient, requiring too much direct attention or too much working memory capacity, the cognitive resources available for other processes may be insufficient. In particular, they propose that word processing may preoccupy poor readers and, thus, impoverish processes associated with comprehension. Their emphasis is on speed, not accuracy, of word recognition. In discussing the nature of word processing, Lesgold and Curtis (1981) argue that it involves "phonological code access" rather than direct ideographic recognition.

In order to examine the relationship between word-processing efficiency and comprehension, Lesgold and colleagues studied four samples (or cohorts) of beginning readers, three taught with an individualized reading program emphasizing phonics and comprehension skills (NRS) and one with an eclectic word- and language-oriented approach (Houghton Mifflin), each over a three-year period. Children were tested after they had completed each level within the curricular program with tests bearing a specified relationship to instructed content. Tests were of two main types: (1) those assessing speed of verbal processing, composed of words previously introduced in the curriculum, including a word-recognition test (word vocalization), and (2) those assessing contextual oral reading proficiency on familiar passages and transfer passages which related systematically to the curricular materials. In addition, standardized tests of reading comprehension were administered at the beginning of each school year, including first grade. Ability groups within each cohort were determined on the basis of second- and third-grade standardized reading comprehension scores.

We will consider the findings reported by Lesgold and Resnick (1982) in some detail. Significant differences were found in the processing characteristics of code-instructed and word-emphasis cohorts, as shown in Figure 18.2. Whereas the code-instructed cohort showed a pattern of decrease in word-recognition response time and a two-second spread among groups, the word-emphasis cohort maintained a consistent response time across the four levels with considerably less difference among groups. For both cohorts, ability groups become more similar in response time over the four levels.

As shown in Figure 18.3, the rate at which children read familiar passages reflects a pattern of change similar to that of word reading for groups in the two cohorts. However, the word-emphasis group showed greater spread in oral reading rate than might be predicted from word-recognition speed. Lesgold and Resnick (1982) interpret the trends as reflecting the nature of alternative instructional methods: "As the materials get harder in successive tests, constant speed of the basal-cohort pattern can be interpreted as reaching a constant level of mastery for progressively harder text. In contrast, the speed increases of the code-emphasis cohort suggest positive transfer effects that make each level's performance better than that of earlier levels—even for new and harder material" (p. 179).

In order to determine whether lack of word-processing efficiency accounts for the inadequate reading comprehension of learning-disabled readers, they examined the relationship between a speed variable, composed of word-vocalization rate and oral reading speed, and reading comprehension for the cohort of

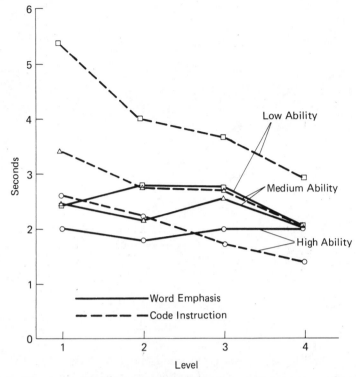

FIGURE 18.2   Word-vocalization task: Mean times for correct responses for ability groups within the word (eclectic) and code-instructed cohorts. (From Lesgold & Resnick, 1982, figs. 5, 9, pp. 167, 180.)

children instructed with the word-emphasis (eclectic) materials. They argue that in order to demonstrate a causal connection, speed measures should predict subsequent comprehension measures but that comprehension measures should not predict subsequent speed measures.

While they report results in accord with their expectations, several problems complicate the interpretation of their findings. First, with respect to design, word-processing and oral reading efficiency were measured at the completion of curricular levels, whereas reading comprehension was measured at the beginning of each school year. Thus, one set of measures controls for content and the other for time. In order to compare the two, the curricular measures were assigned a common time value that reflected "the underlying distribution of level completion dates" (p. 175). But according to the assigned time line, the only reading comprehension test preceding the four speed measures was administered at the beginning of first grade; so it cannot be taken seriously as a valid measure of reading comprehension.

Second, a speed measure representing isolated word processing alone, rather than one including contextual reading rate as well, might have provided a cleaner test of the predicted relationship between word-processing efficiency and comprehension. Inspection of the results in Figures 18.2 and 18.3 for the word-emphasis ability subgroups suggests that differences among the ability groups are considerably greater for contextual speed than for isolated word-vocalization speed.

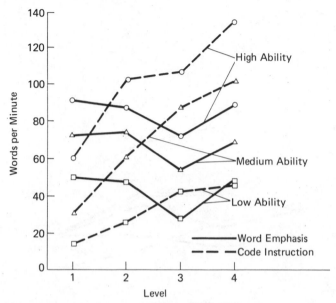

FIGURE 18.3   Familiar passage reading speeds for ability groups within the word (eclectic) and code-instructed cohorts. (From Lesgold & Resnick, 1982, figs. 6, 11, pp. 169, 182.)

Indeed, when the three groups completed the fourth level of the curricular materials, there was virtually no difference among them in word-vocalization speed. Thus, the magnitude of the relationship between speed and comprehension in the analysis actually reflects mainly the contribution of contextual reading speed. Simple word processing may not be as important an issue for children instructed with word-emphasis materials, as the speed of processing connected words. By contrast, speed of word processing appears to be associated with the comprehension of code-instructed children (Lesgold & Curtis, 1981).

This series of instructional investigations is interesting as a prototype of much research in the instructional psychology of reading. In contrast to the prior four investigations, it focuses on individual instruction and learning, even though all children in the samples learn in classes managed by teachers. Instruction is defined very narrowly: it includes a description of materials, but does not treat other conditions, such as teaching methods and style. Even instructional time is allowed by design to vary without being considered in relation to learning outcomes. Materials have been carefully considered in the design of outcome measures. Moreover, by examining outcomes at specific points in the materials, instruction is held constant for all groups experiencing the same method. The inquiry is designed, then, both to study the influence of instructional method on learning and to examine differences in learning and processing over and above those related to rate of progress through instructional materials.

The LRDC researchers share with the Chicago group a belief that content coverage is a major instructional influence on learning; they choose, however, to control its influence rather than to examine its influence as a variable. That is, they have disregarded learning time so that they can consider the learning of children in response to comparable units of curricular materials. This control of materials, however, does not preclude documentation of the materials that children encounter from unit to unit. Without such characterization, Lesgold and associates cannot account for observed patterns of response rate. Although they speculate that the code materials allow transfer of skill, while the basal materials do not, and that changes in the characteristics of materials account for the different response patterns, they cannot demonstrate that case given their failure to characterize changes in the reading materials and their corresponding tests. Similar to earlier methods investigations, they characterize the two instructional methods globally, although their speculations about what may account for the different response patterns represent the beginnings of a formulation about what aspects of instructional method may influence learning.

Summary

Whereas the methods studies reviewed in the first two sections of the chapter characterized reading programs in a global fashion, without reference to classroom use, the seven investigations considered in this section reveal some of the problems as well as solutions that arise in reformulating the study of classroom reading instruction. We must now consider what lessons these investigations hold. Two questions guide our pursuit. First, what does the research teach us about the study of classroom instruction? Second, how should reading methods and associated instructional conditions be characterized?

Study of Classroom Instruction

In several studies, the process of reading instruction was fractionated into a myriad of variables. While some investigators then proceeded to analyze the linkages between instruction and learning, considering one variable at a time in a bivariate fashion, others attempted to combine variables through statistical procedures. Neither approach was productive. The first procedure yielded a vast array of correlations, some of which achieved statistical significance on the basis of chance, some of which were inconsistent, and many of which were difficult to interpret out of context. The second approach, combining conditions statistically into factors, yielded factors composed of underlying conditions that did not necessarily go together. That is, no counterpart existed in reality because the factors were abstractions. A third solution, that of combining conditions along a selected continuum, such as a meaning versus decoding emphasis represents a conceptually based approach to data organization. Though this solution does not take us much further conceptually than the global characterizations of reading approach, it has the advantage of being based on observational evidence.

In addition, when instructional conditions are related one at a time or in combination to outcome measures using correlational or regression analysis, we learn little about the status of the conditions considered. Are they independent of other conditions or dependent on or derivative of other conditions? Are the conditions effective only in certain situations and not others? Consideration of conditions singly or in combination in relation to learning ignores the question of the interconnections among instructional conditions. The attempts to explore these interconnections in some of the studies reviewed were limited and ill conceived. For example, the treatments of socioeconomic status and climate do not seem to bring us any closer to understanding how instruction may be influenced or limited by prevailing conditions in classes or schools. By contrast, exploration of reading programs, instructional materials, and pupil characteristics (aptitude and age) as conditional influences on instruction appears to be more productive.

A solution to these problems—the proliferation of instructional conditions and the failure to explore interconnections among conditions—was derived from theoretical formulations of instructional phenomena. In both the BTES and the Chicago research, formulations of how instruction works served to identify certain conditions as centrally important and others as trivial and to specify the manner in which conditions interconnect. Observational evidence was then used to test how well samples of instructional reality conformed to the theoretical representation. Much instructional research has been undertaken without theoretical guidance. As a result, there is no basis for determining which conditions should be included in an analysis, and there is considerable difficulty making sense of a mass of sometimes conflicting evidence.

Further, a formulation should be comprehensive. We see in the Texas research a formulation which focused on the activity of teachers. Other conditions were included on an ad hoc basis, and because they were not represented in the prescriptive model, there was no theoretical basis for examining their interaction with teaching activity. Indeed, the attempts of formulations to be "content free" so as to apply to all content areas is misguided. To formulate how characteristics of curricular programs interact with other conditions of instruction is not to specify content, but rather to identify instructional methods and materials as conditions that cannot be overlooked when one thinks about classroom instruction. That is, the notion of curricular materials may be included in formulations in generic form; characteristics that have import for instruction can cross-cut specific curricular areas. For example, in the Chicago research, curricular programs are characterized in terms of their difficulty. The same sort of characterization would apply as well to mathematics and other curricular areas.

Characterization of Reading Methods

The examined studies provide some basis for thinking about how reading methods should be conceptualized and for identifying other conditions that interact with method to influence learning. First, it is important to distinguish between the characteristics of a curricular program that is available for use in a classroom and how it is actually used. The Chicago research suggests that reading programs can be characterized usefully in terms of difficulty, that is, the number of new words and phonics concepts introduced. While this characterization may work well for first-grade materials, other approaches (see Chall, 1980) may be useful in characterizing the difficulty of subsequent reading materials. In addition to the difficulty of the reading inherent in a curricular program, it is important to determine the amount of reading involved. The emphasis of a curricular program along the meaning-decoding continuum may also represent an important characterization, but emphasis should be evaluated in specific terms. The research of Beck and colleagues (Beck & Block, 1979; Beck & McCaslin, 1978) provides a useful model for evaluating the development of phonics concepts in beginning reading materials.

While a curricular program may be available in a classroom, it is well known that not all children complete all materials designated to a particular grade level and that some students progress beyond what is identified as grade-appropriate work. Accordingly, reading method needs to be measured in group- or pupil-specific terms. The LRDC research monitored completion of units in an individualized reading program. The Texas research recorded the number of books completed, and the Chicago investigations recorded the number of word and phonics concepts covered. How much content children covered in their reading materials was a major determinant of their learning to read. Accordingly, it is important not only to characterize a reading program, but also to know how much of it children have actually experienced.

It is important to assess the effectiveness of instruction using measures of learning that relate directly to instructed content. If general measures of reading achievement are used as the only outcome measures of learning, they may overlap inconsistently with instructed content from program to program and therefore be biased in favor of some programs. More important, they may simply be insensitive to the effects of instructional conditions. However, not only is it important to assess the influence of instruction on learning, but also to trace the transfer of specific learning to more general measures of achievement using procedures such as those developed by Lesgold and colleagues (Lesgold & Curtis, 1981; Lesgold & Resnick, 1982).

The research also indicates that it is important to represent reading instruction in terms other than the content covered. Many investigators focused on instructional time and the Chicago research found that the time spent on certain reading activities is closely associated with the amount of content that is covered. Nevertheless, it appears that time does not distinguish among groups within classes, but rather among the instructional programs developed by different teachers (Allington, 1983). Research is needed to examine further the influence of instructional time in relation to content coverage and learning. Perhaps, one of the most suggestive findings concerning time was reported by Harris and Serwer (1966c): time allocations may be differentially effective depending on the general reading approach. The specific program used by a teacher determined whether time invested in certain reading activities was productive or not.

Finally, it may be important to characterize the behavior of teachers. Whether the teacher emphasized decoding or not was found to predict learning in some studies, but not in others. Perhaps the effectiveness of emphasizing certain strategies over others depends on the reading program being used. The results from the studies reviewed suggest that more structured teaching activities that orient pupils toward instructional tasks result in higher achievement. It should be noted, however, that in the research reviewed, teaching behavior was described for classes. A general description of teaching may not adequately represent that received by different groups in a class; indeed, an average value may characterize the teaching of no group in a class. When groups or individuals in classes receive differential instruction, the teaching activities studied must be specified in terms of the proper unit of instructional focus for their effectiveness to be properly assessed.

CONCLUSIONS AND DIRECTIONS
OF FUTURE RESEARCH

This review of reading methods research leads to several conclusions. First, the quest to establish the best method continued into the 1970s through the comparison of programs, globally characterized, in spite of criticism. This form of research neither answers the practical question of which program is more effective because outcomes are not simply a reflection of method conditions nor does it increase our understanding of the complexities of classroom instruction of which reading method is a part.

Second, strong forces operate that should modify the character of classroom instructional research. New approaches developed during the 1970s incorporate formulations and research strategies from such disciplines as psychology, sociology, and anthropology. But because these new approaches have been underway for a relatively short period of time, they do not yet provide completed formulations and methodologies. Further, it is clear that the alternative approaches are complementary in the study of classroom instruction and that they have clear implications for the study of beginning reading methods in general and as they pertain to the learning of low-readiness and learning-disabled students. In the current decade, the study of multidimensional aspects of instruction, including reading methods and materials, should become more common and global comparisons less frequent.

Third, the problem of how to facilitate the learning of low-aptitude children, which has occupied educators, researchers, and politicians during the past two decades, will continue to be a major preoccupation. ATI research has been of limited use for two major reasons. First, aptitude has not been formulated in a useful and comprehensive fashion. We need to do a better job of conceptualizing the aptitudes of children that are of major importance in reading acquisition. Although we are learning more about how prereading abilities may be examined (see Mason, this volume), we are only beginning to come to terms with the nature of perceptual, linguistic, conceptual, and social aptitudes that bear directly on a child's ability to respond to the set of conditions that constitute reading instruction. The identification of relevant aptitudes must be based not only on an assessment of children's functioning, but also on an examination of the demands of alternative forms of beginning reading instruction.

Just as important, the "treatment" in the ATI paradigm must be specified. As noted in the preceding discussion, we are beginning to learn how to think about reading instruction. Such aspects of instruction as the difficulty and emphasis of the reading program, content coverage, time allocated to different reading activities, and teacher supervision and activities form a comprehensive description of the instructional treatment experienced by groups of readers. Better characterization of children's aptitudes and their instructional treatment should form the basis of studies of conditions that enhance the progress of children who encounter difficulty learning to read.

NOTES

1. All studies included in the section entitled, "Teaching Reading—Primary Grades" in the annual Summary of Investigations Relating to Reading (Robinson et al., 1961–1970; Weintraub et al., 1971–1982) were examined and classified in terms of *duration* (semester or longer vs. short-term or summer), *setting* (classroom vs. other), and *focus* (reading methods vs. other instructional conditions and research reviews). Figure 18.1 pertains to long-term classroom studies of reading methods.
2. The fifteen studies were conducted by Bordeaux (1966), Cleland (Vilscek, Morgan, and Cleland, 1966), Fry (1966), Hahn (1966), Hayes (1966), Kendrick (1966), Manning (1966), Mazurkiewicz (1965, 1966), Murphy (1966), Ruddell (1966), Schneyer (1966), Sheldon (1966), Stauffer (1966a), Tanyzer and Alpert (1966), and Wyatt (1966). See Bond and Dykstra (1967) for a description of the projects.
3. The four studies were conducted by Harris and Serwer (1966a, 1966b, 1966c), McCanne (1966), Niles (1967), and Reid and Beltramo (1965, 1966).

REFERENCES

Abiri, J. O. Using i.t.a. and standard orthography in teaching English reading in Nigeria. *Reading Teacher,* 1976, *30,* 137–140.

Allington, R. L. The reading instruction provided readers of differing ability. *Elementary School Journal,* 1983, *83,* 255–265.

Anderson, L. M., Evertson, C. M., & Brophy, J. An experimental study of effective reading in first-grade reading groups. *Elementary School Journal,* 1979, *79,* 193–233.

Anderson, R. B., St. Pierre, R. G., Proper, E. C., & Stebbins, L. B. Pardon us, but what was the question again?: A response to the critique of the follow through evaluation. *Harvard Educational Review,* 1978, *48,* 161–170.

Atkinson, R. C. Instruction in initial reading under computer control: The Stanford project. *Journal of Educational Data Processing,* 1967, *4,* 165–192.

Barr, R. Influence of instruction on early reading. *Interchange,* 1974, *5,* 13–22.

Barr, R. The effect of instruction on pupil reading strategies. *Reading Research Quarterly,* 1974–1975, *10,* 555–582.

Barr, R. *A sociological approach to classroom instruction.* Paper presented to the American Educational Research Association, Montreal, April 1983.

Barr, R., & Dreeben, R. *How schools work.* Chicago: University of Chicago Press, 1983.

Bateman, B. The efficacy of an auditory and visual method of first-grade reading instruction with auditory and visual learners. In H. Smith (Ed.), *Perception and reading.* Newark, Del.: International Reading Association, 1968.

Beck, I. L., & Block, K. K. An analysis of two beginning reading programs: Some facts and some opinions. In L. B. Resnick & P. A. Weaver (Eds.), *Theory and practice of early reading* (Vol. 1). Hillsdale, N.J.: Erlbaum, 1979.

Beck, I. L., & McCaslin, E. S. *An analysis of the dimensions that affect the development of code-breaking ability in eight beginning reading programs.* Learning, Research, and Development Center, University of Pittsburgh, 1978.

Biemiller, A. The development of the use of graphic and contextual information as children learn to read. *Reading Research Quarterly,* 1970, *6,* 75–96.

Bloom, B. S. Learning for mastery. *Evaluation Comment.* UCLA-CSEIP, 1968, *1.*

Bond, G. L., & Dykstra, R. The cooperative research program in first-grade reading instruction. *Reading Research Quarterly,* 1967, *2,* 5–142.

Bordeaux, E. A., & Shope, N. H. An evaluation of three approaches to teaching reading in first grade. *Reading Teacher,* 1966, *20,* 6–11.

Briggs, B. C.   An investigation of the effectiveness of a programmed graphemic option approach to teaching reading to disadvantaged children. *Journal of Reading Behavior*, 1972–1973, *5*, 35–46.

Brophy, J. E., & Evertson, C. M.   *The Texas Teacher Project: Presentation of non-linear relationships and summary observations* (Rep. 74–6). University of Texas at Austin, 1974.

Brophy, J. E., & Good, T.   The Brophy-Good didactic interaction system. In A. Simon & E. Boyer (Eds.), *Mirrors for behavior: An anthology of observation instruments continued, 1970 supplement* (Vol. A). Philadelphia: Research for Better Schools, Inc., 1970.

Buike, S., & Duffy, G. G.   *Do teacher conceptions of reading influence instructional practice?* Paper presented to American Educational Research Association, San Francisco, April 1979.

Calfee, R., & Calfee, K. H.   Reading and mathematics observation system: Description and measurement of time usage in the classroom. *Journal of Teacher Education*, 1976, *27*, 323–325.

Calfee, R., & Piontkowski, D.   The reading diary: Acquisition of decoding. *Reading Research Quarterly*, 1981, *13*, 346–373.

Callaway, B., McDaniel, H., & Mason, G. E.   Five methods of teaching language arts: A comparison. *Elementary English*, 1972, *49*, 1240–1245.

Carroll, J. B.   A model of school learning. *Teachers College Record*, 1963, *64*, 723–733.

Chall, J. S.   *Learning to read: The great debate*. New York: McGraw-Hill, 1967.

Chall, J. S.   *Textbook difficulty, reading achievement, and knowledge acquisition*. Research proposal, Harvard University, Graduate School of Education, 1980.

Chall, J. S.   The great debate: Ten years later, with a modest proposal for reading stages. In L. B. Resnick & P. A. Weaver (Eds.), *Theory and practice of early reading*, Vol. 1, Hillsdale, N.J.: Erlbaum, 1979.

Chall, J. S., & Feldmann, S. C.   First grade reading: An analysis of the interactions of professed methods, teacher implementation and child background. *Reading Teacher*, 1966, *19*, 569–575. (a)

Chall, J. S., & Feldmann, S. C.   *A study in depth of first-grade reading: An analysis of the interactions of professed methods, teacher implementation and child background*. Unpublished report, City College of the City University of New York, 1966. (ERIC Document Reproduction Service No. ED 010 036) (b)

Cohen, A. S.   Oral reading errors of first grade children taught by a code emphasis approach. *Reading Research Quarterly*, 1974–1975, *10*, 616–650.

Cooley, W. W., & Lohnes, P. R.   *Evaluative inquiry in education*. New York: Irvington Press, 1976.

Cronbach, L. J. & Snow, R. E.   *Aptitudes and instructional methods*. New York: Irvington Press, 1977.

Cullinan, B.   *Preferred learning modalities and differentiated presentation of learning task*. Unpublished report, 1969. (ERIC Document Reproduction Service No. ED 042 589)

Dank, M. E.   *A study of the relationship of miscues to the mode of formal reading instruction received by selected second graders*. Unpublished doctoral dissertation, University of Massachusetts, 1976. (ERIC Document Reproduction Service No. ED 126 431)

DeLawter, J. A.   Three miscue patterns: The relationship of beginning reading instruction and miscue patterns. In W. D. Page (Ed.), *Help for the reading teacher: New directions in research*. Urbana, Ill.: National Conference on Research in English, ERIC Clearinghouse on Reading and Communication Skills, 1975.

Downing, J.   Some difficulties in transfer of learning from i.t.a. to T.O. In J. A. Figurel (Ed.), *Forging ahead in reading. Proceedings of the International Reading Association,* 1968, *12,* 541–546.

Downing, J.   Comparison of failure in i.t.a. and T.O. *Reading Teacher,* 1969, *23,* 42–47.

Downing, J.   *The child's understanding of the function and processes of communication.* Unpublished paper, University of Victoria, Can., 1977.

Dreeben, R.   *Aptitude, instructional organization, and reading achievement.* Paper presented to the American Educational Research Association, Montreal, April 1983.

Duffy, G., & Anderson, L.   *Final report: Conceptions of reading project.* Unpublished report, Institute for Research on Teaching, Michigan State University, 1981.

Duffy, G., & Methany, W.   *The development of an instrument to measure teacher beliefs about reading.* Paper presented to the National Reading Conference, St. Petersburg, Fla., 1978.

Dunkin, M. J., & Biddle, B. J.   *The study of teaching.* New York: Holt, Rinehart & Winston, 1974.

Dykstra, R.   Summary of the second grade phase of the Cooperative Research Program in primary reading instruction. *Reading Research Quarterly,* 1968, *4,* 49–70.

Elder, R. D.   Oral reading achievement of Scottish and American children. *Elementary School Journal,* 1971, *71,* 216–230.

Elias, P., & Wheeler, P.   Instructional activities as reported by teachers. *Journal of Teacher Education,* 1976, *27,* 326–328.

Elkind, D.   Piaget's theory of perceptual development: Its application to reading and special education. *Journal of Special Education,* 1967, *1,* 357–361.

Elkind, D., Koegler, R., & Go, E.   Studies in perceptual development: II. Part-whole perception. *Child Development,* 1964, *35,* 81–90.

Feldhusen, H. J., Lamb, P., & Feldhusen, J.   Prediction of reading achievement under programmed and traditional instruction. *Reading Teacher,* 1970, *23,* 446–454.

Ferreiro, E.   What is written in a written sentence? A developmental answer. *Journal of Education,* 1978, *160,* 25–39.

Fisher, C. W., Filby, N. N., Marliave, R., Cahen, L. S., Dishaw, M. M., Moore, J. E., & Berliner, D. C.   *Beginning teacher evaluation study* (Technical Report, V–1). Far West Laboratory, San Francisco, 1978.

Flanders, N. A.   *Teacher influence, pupil attitudes, and achievement.* Washington, D.C.: U.S. Department of Health, Education, and Welfare, 1965.

Flanders, N. A.   *Analyzing teacher behavior.* Reading, Mass.: Addison-Wesley, 1970.

Fry, E. B.   First grade reading instruction using diacritical marking system, initial teaching alphabet and basal reading system. *Reading Teacher,* 1966, *19,* 666–669.

Gates, A. I.   Studies of phonetic training in beginning reading. *Journal of Educational Psychology,* 1927, *18,* 217–226.

Gates, A. I., & Russell, D. H.   Types of materials, vocabulary burden, word analysis and other factors in beginning reading. *Elementary School Journal,* 1938, *39,* 27–35, 119–128.

Glass, G. V.   Integrating findings: The meta-analysis of research. In L. S. Shulman (Ed.), *Review of research in education* (Vol. 5). Itasca, Ill.: F. E. Peacock, 1978.

Gray, W. S.   The teaching of reading. In *Encyclopedia of educational research.* New York: Macmillan, 1960.

Guthrie, J. T., & Tyler, S. J.   Cognition and instruction of poor readers. *Journal of Reading Behavior,* 1978, *10,* 57–78.

Hahn, H. T.   Three approaches to beginning reading instruction—ITA, language arts and basic readers. *Reading Teacher,* 1966, *19,* 590–594.

Harris, A. J., & Serwer, B. L.   Comparing reading approaches in first grade teaching with disadvantaged children. *Reading Teacher*, 1966, *19*, 631–635, 642. (a)

Harris, A. J., & Serwer, B. L.   *Comparison of reading approaches in first-grade teaching with disadvantaged children.* Unpublished report, City University of New York, New York, 1966. (b)

Harris, A. J., & Serwer, B. L.   The CRAFT project: Instructional time in reading research. *Reading Research Quarterly*, 1966, *2*, 27–57. (c)

Hartley, R. N.   A method of increasing the ability of first-grade pupils to use phonetic generalizations. *California Journal of Educational Research*, 1971, *22*, 9–16.

Hayes, R. B.   ITA and three other approaches to reading in first grade. *Reading Teacher*, 1966, *19*, 627–630.

Hinshelwood, J.   *Congenital word-blindness.* London: Lewis, 1917.

Holland, S.   The evaluation of a programme in reading instruction for five- and six-year old children. In V. Greaney (Ed.), *Studies in reading*. Dublin: The Educational Co., 1977.

House, E. R., Glass, G. V., McLean, L. D., & Walker, D. F.   No simple answer: Critique of the follow through evaluation. *Harvard Educational Review*, 1978, *48*, 128–160.

Johnson, H., Jones, D. R., Cole, A. C., & Walters, M. B.   The use of diacritical marks in teaching beginners to read. *British Journal of Educational Psychology*, 1972, *42*, 120–126.

Kaufman, M.   Comparison of achievement for Distar and conventional instruction with primary pupils. *Reading Improvement*, 1976, *13*, 169–173.

Kendrick, W. M.   A comparative study of two first grade language arts programs. *Reading Teacher*, 1966, *20*, 25–30.

Kounin, J.   *Discipline and group management in classrooms.* New York: Holt, Rinehart & Winston, 1970.

Lesgold, A. M., & Curtis, M. E.   Learning to read words efficiently. In A. M. Lesgold & C. A. Perfetti (Eds.), *Interactive processes in reading*. Hillsdale, N.J.: Erlbaum, 1981.

Lesgold, A. M., & Resnick, L. B.   How reading difficulties develop: Perspectives from a longitudinal study. In J. P. Das, R. F. Mulcahy, & A. E. Wall (Eds.), *Theory and research in learning disabilities*. New York: Plenum, 1982.

Lo, M. Y.   *Statistical analysis of interaction and its application to data from the cooperative research program in primary reading instruction.* Unpublished doctoral dissertation, State University of New York at Buffalo, 1973.

Lohnes, P. R., & Gray, M. M.   Intellectual development and the cooperative reading studies. *Reading Research Quarterly*, 1972, *8*, 52–61.

Manning, J. C.   Evaluation of levels designed visual-auditory and related writing methods of reading instruction in grade one. *Reading Teacher*, 1966, *19*, 611–616.

Mathews, M. M.   *Teaching to read: Historically considered.* Chicago: University of Chicago Press, 1966.

Maxwell, M. J.   Results of the survey of the literature on methods and materials in reading. In F. P. Greene (Ed.), *21st yearbook of the National Reading Conference: Investigations relating to mature reading*, 1972, *1*, 203–211.

Mazurkiewicz, A. J.   Second year evaluation—interim report: Lehigh University—Bethlehem schools i/t/a study. *Journal of Reading Specialist*, 1965, *4*, 35–38.

Mazurkiewicz, A. J.   ITA and TO reading achievement when methodology is controlled. *Reading Teacher*, 1966, *19*, 606–610.

Mazurkiewicz, A. J.   Comparative attitudes and achievements of the 1963 i.t.a. and T.O. taught students in the tenth and eleventh grades. *Reading World*, 1975, *14*, 242–251.

McCanne, R.   Approaches to first grade English reading instruction for children from Spanish-speaking homes. *Reading Teacher*, 1966, *19*, 670–675.

McDonald, F. J., & Elias, P. M.   *Executive summary report: Beginning teacher evaluation study, Phase II.* Princeton, N.J.: Educational Testing Service, 1976. (a)

McDonald, F. J., & Elias, P. M.   A report of the results of phase II of the beginning teacher evaluation study: An overview. *Journal of Teacher Education,* 1976, *27,* 315–316. (b)

Medley, D. M., & Mitzel, H. E.   Measuring classroom behavior by systematic observation. In N. L. Gage (Ed.), *Handbook of research on teaching.* Chicago: Rand McNally, 1963.

Miller, E.   *Relationships among modality preference, method of instruction and reading achievement.* Unpublished doctoral dissertation, State University of New York at Albany, 1974.

Miller, E.   First-grade reading instruction and modality preference. *Elementary School Journal,* 1979, *80,* 99–104.

Mills, R. E.   An evaluation of techniques for teaching word recognition. *Elementary School Journal,* 1956, *56,* 221–225.

Murphy, H. A.   Growth in perception of word elements in three types of beginning reading instruction. *Reading Teacher,* 1966, *19,* 585–589, 600.

Newman, A. P., & Lohnes, P. R.   *Relations of readiness factors and beginning reading methods to first grade achievement, with an interaction effect.* Unpublished manuscript, Indiana University, 1972.

Niles, O. S.   Methods of teaching reading to first grade children likely to have difficulty with reading. *Reading Teacher,* 1967, *20,* 541–545.

Pflaum, S. W., Walberg, H. J., Karegianes, M. L., & Racher, S. P.   Reading instruction: A quantitative method. *Educational Researcher,* 1980, *9* (7), 12–18.

Pienaar, P. T.   Breakthrough in beginning reading: Language experience approach. *Reading Teacher,* 1977, *30,* 489–496.

Popp, H. M.   Current practices in the teaching of beginning reading. In J. B. Carroll & J. S. Chall (Eds.), *Toward a literate society: The report of the committee in reading of the National Academy of Education.* New York: McGraw-Hill, 1975.

Reid, H. C., & Beltramo, L.   *The effect of different approaches of initial instruction on the reading achievement of a selected group of first grade children.* Unpublished report, Cedar Rapids, Iowa, Community School District, 1965. (ERIC Reproduction Service Document No. ED 003 488)

Reid, H. C., & Beltramo, L.   Teaching reading to the low group in the first grade. *Reading Teacher,* 1966, *19,* 601–605.

Robertson, D. J., & Trepper, T. S.   The effects of i.t.a. on the reading achievement of Mexican-American children. *Reading World,* 1974, 13, 132–138.

Robinson, H. M.   Summary of investigations relating to reading. *Journal of Educational Research,* 1961, *54,* 203–220.

Robinson, H. M.   Summary of investigations relating to reading. *Reading Teacher,* 1962, *15,* 293–321; 1963, *16,* 285–322; 1964, *17,* 326–392; 1965, *18,* 331–428.

Robinson, H. M.   Visual and auditory modalities related to methods for beginning reading. *Reading Research Quarterly,* 1972, *8,* 7–39.

Robinson, H. M., Weintraub, S., & Smith, H. K.   Summary of investigations relating to reading. *Reading Research Quarterly,* 1965, *1;* 1966–1967, *2;* 1968, *3;* 1969, *4;* 1970, *5.*

Ruddell, R. B.   Reading instruction in first grade with varying emphasis on the regularity of grapheme-phoneme correspondences and the relation of language structure to meaning. *Reading Teacher,* 1966, *19,* 653–660.

Russell, D. H., & Fea, H.   Research on teaching reading. In N. L. Gage (Ed.), *Handbook of research on teaching.* Chicago: Rand McNally, 1963.

Ryckman, D. B., McCartin, R., & Sebasta, S.   Do structured reading programs hamper intellectual development? *Elementary School Journal*, 1976, *77*, 71–73.

Sabaroff, R. E.   A comparative investigation of six reading programs: Two basal, four linguistic. *Education*, 1971, *91*, 303–314.

Schneeberg, H. E., & Mattleman, M. S.   The listen-read project: Motivating students through dual modalities. *Elementary English*, 1973, *50*, 900–904.

Schneeberg, H. E.   Listening while reading: A four year study. *Reading Teacher*, 1977, *30*, 629–635.

Schneyer, J. W.   Reading achievement of first grade children taught by a linguistic approach and a basal approach. *Reading Teacher*, 1966, *19*, 647–652.

Sheldon, W. D., & Lashinger, D. R.   Effect of first grade instruction using basal readers, modified linguistic materials and linguistic readers. *Reading Teacher*, 1966, *19*, 576–579.

Shore, R. E., & Marascuilo, L.   Programmed approach vs. conventional approach using a highly consistent sound-symbol system of reading in 3 primary grades. *California Journal of Educational Research*, 1974, *25*, 11–31.

Shulman, L. S.   Teaching as clinical information processing. In N. L. Gage (Ed.), *National conference on studies in teaching*. Washington, D.C.: National Institute of Education, 1975.

Smith, B. O., & Meux, M. O.   *A study of the logic of teaching*. Urbana: University of Illinois Press, 1962.

Smith, L. B.   They found a golden ladder . . . stories by children. *Reading Teacher*, 1976, *29*, 541–545.

Smith, L. B., & Morgan, G. D.   Cassette tape recording as a primary method in the development of early reading material. *Elementary English*, 1975, *52*, 534–538.

Smith, N. B.   *American reading instruction* (Rev. ed.). Newark, Del.: International Reading Association, 1970. (Originally published 1934.)

Stallings, J.   Implementation and child effects of teaching practices in Follow Through classrooms. *Monographs of the Society for Research in Child Development*, 1975, *40*.

Stauffer, R. G.   The effectiveness of language arts and basic reader approaches to first grade reading instruction. *Reading Teacher*, 1966, *20*, 18–24. (a)

Stauffer, R. G.   The verdict: Speculative controversy. *Reading Teacher*, 1966, *19*, 563–564, 575. (b)

Stauffer, R. G., & Pikulski, J. J.   A comparison and measure of oral language growth. *Elementary English*, 1974, *51*, 1151–1155.

Stebbins, L. B., St. Pierre, R. G., Proper, E. C., Anderson, R. B., & Cerva, T. R.   *Education as experimentation: A planned variation model, (Vol. IV–A), An evaluation of follow through*. Cambridge, Mass.: Abt Associates, 1977.

Tanyzer, H. J., & Alpert, H.   Three different basal reading systems and first grade reading achievement. *Reading Teacher*, 1966, *19*, 636–642.

Trepper, T. S., & Robertson, D. J.   The effects of i.t.a. on the reading achievement of Mexican-American children: A follow-up. *Reading Improvement*, 1975, *12*, 177–183.

Vilscek, E., Morgan, L., & Cleland, D.   Coordinating and integrating language arts instruction in first grade. *Reading Teacher*, 1966, *20*, 31–37.

Weintraub, S., et al. (including Robinson, H., Smith, H., Plessas, G. P., Roser, N. L., & Rowls, M.).   Summary of investigations relating to reading. *Reading Research Quarterly*, 1971, *6;* 1972, *7;* 1973, *8;* 1973–1974, *9;* 1974–1975, *10;* 1975–1976, *11;* 1976–1977, *12;* 1977–1978, *13;* 1978–1979, *14*.

Weintraub, S., et al.   *Summary of investigations relating to reading July 1, 1978 to June 30, 1979*. Newark, Del.: International Reading Association, 1980.

Weintraub, S., et al. *Summary of investigations relating to reading July 1, 1979 to June 30, 1980.* Newark, Del.: International Reading Association, 1981.

Weintraub, S., et al. *Summary of investigations relating to reading July 1, 1980 to June 30, 1981.* Newark, Del.: International Reading Association, 1982.

Wepman, J. *The modality concept—including a statement of perceptual and conceptual levels of learning.* University of Chicago, 1968. (ERIC Document Reproduction Service No. ED 012 678)

Wiley, D. E. Another hour, another day: Quality of schooling, a potent path for policy. In W. J. Sewel, R. M. Hauser, & D. L. Featherman (Eds.), *Schooling and achievement in American society.* New York: Academic Press, 1976.

Wiley, W. E. Difficult words and the beginner. *Journal of Educational Research,* 1928, *17,* 278–289.

Wyatt, N. M. The reading achievement of first grade boys versus first grade girls. *Reading Teacher,* 1966, *19,* 661–665.

Wooden, S. L., & Pettibone, T. J. A comparative study of three beginning reading programs for the Spanish-speaking child. *Journal of Reading Behavior,* 1973, *5,* 192–199.

19 WORD IDENTIFICATION

Dale D. Johnson and James F. Baumann

The purpose of this chapter is to present research on instructional practices in word identification, that is, studies investigating how children are taught to read words. Our focus—contrasted to Gough's review (this volume) of basic processes in word identification—will be to *highlight research conducted with children in their classrooms* (research Bronfenbrenner, 1976, would consider to be "ecologically valid"). Consequently, highly controlled, laboratory studies on word identification will receive much less attention than research that has been conducted with children in schools. We realize, however, that at times this distinction is arbitrary, subjective, or both. It should be noted that given the charge to review research relevant to instructional practices in word identification, the logical emphasis of the present chapter will be on children's decoding ability. While this may tacitly involve some consideration of vocabulary development (e.g., basic and/or accumulating sight vocabularies), research on the development of children's meaning vocabulary is not directly explored. Our major concern is with research related to the efficacy of instructional strategies in specific word identification skills.

After a brief look at historical research in word-identification instruction, our review turns to more recent investigations. Studies are organized under three main categories: research on the teaching of (a) phonics analysis, (b) structural analysis, and (c) contextual analysis. Space has not permitted review of such other word-identification skills as use of configuration or picture cues. We conclude with a summary, a discussion of implications, and a consideration of what course future research in word-identification instruction should take.

AN HISTORICAL PERSPECTIVE

What constitutes "historical" research in word-identification instruction and what should be considered "current" becomes a subjective judgment. Although research in reading was produced at a reasonably slow and steady pace for about the first 50 years of this century, since the mid-1950s, reading theorists and educators have conducted research at an accelerated, almost geometric, rate. Given the constraint of a single chapter, only a fraction of the total number of relevant studies can be possibly reviewed. Consequently, one must be selective. This selectivity can take the form of choosing only those studies deemed to be "significant," or one can arbitrarily designate a cut-off date that eliminates the critique of research conducted prior to that time.

Our approach to this problem involves a compromise: We somewhat arbitrarily select a date that discriminates between "historical" and "current" research in word-identification instruction, concentrating our review on studies conducted after this date. But, in light of the proliferation of reading research, we attempt to be selective by reviewing in detail only those studies considered to be most significant. Our review, therefore, is comprehensive, in that all relevant research will have been considered, but it will be selective in the sense that only those studies we have judged to be of greater importance are critiqued in detail. Because of this selectivity, when appropriate, we direct the reader to previous reviews of research in word-identification instruction for additional references.

The date we have chosen as an historical/current cut-off point is 1965; a date that not coincidentally marks the initiation of the USOE First Grade Reading Studies (Bond & Dykstra, 1967; Stauffer, 1967). While limiting a research review to the most recent 20 years may appear to be unduly restrictive, we feel that 1965 is a logical demarcation point for several reasons. First, a bountiful, if not excessive, number of relevant studies on word-identification instruction have been conducted since 1965, which provides a plentiful source of current, pertinent research. Second, we believe that the vast majority of research on word-identification pedagogy prior to 1965 dealt with one issue: the efficacy of phonic instruction. These studies typically addressed one of two questions: (a) Is a phonics or look-say approach more effective? or (b) Which of several forms of phonic instruction (e.g., systematic/intrinsic, analytic/synthetic) results in better reading ability?

While these issues are important (and will be considered in following sections), we are charged in this review to go beyond such questions and explore other specific instructional problems in word identification. Since the First Grade Studies marked the close of this era of general research in word-identification instruction and signaled the beginning of a period of specific-issue-related research, we feel that concentrating this review on the more diverse and recent studies is appropriate. But before this most recent research is presented, let us first consider the historical investigations in word identification.

Early Studies: Pre-1940

Research on the teaching of word-identification skills prior to about 1940 typically addressed one issue: the relative merits of a phonics versus a look-say approach to reading. This research perspective is not surprising when one considers that a debate over the efficacy of one or the other methodology predates 1800. Prior to 1800, reading instruction in America typically consisted of an alphabetical system (e.g., Noah Webster's *The Elementary Spelling Book, The New England*

Primer, The Hornbook), which essentially was a synthetic-phonics approach. In the early 1800s, Horace Mann introduced a new whole-word method of teaching reading. This method prospered until the later half of the nineteenth century when phonics again became popular. Very rigorous phonic programs were the rule, therefore, from about 1880 to 1915. Dissatisfaction with this heavy emphasis on word analysis to the exclusion of concern for comprehension caused the pendulum to swing toward a new look-and-say method, which, in fact, was the predecessor of the first basal reading programs that emerged in the 1930s. It is not very surprising, given this vacillation between a whole-word and phonics emphasis, that the research interest in the early twentieth century involved a preoccupation with determining which approach to word identification was more effective.

During this early period, the majority of researchers comparing phonics and look-say methodologies noted superior results for phonics instruction. Valentine (1913) reported that word recognition and oral reading ability of 6½- to 8-year-olds taught by a phonics method was superior to that of children receiving only look-say instruction. Currier and Duguid (1916) and Currier (1923) also compared these two methodologies. While their research was only descriptive and qualitative, they also agreed that phonics instruction aided word identification; they did mention, however, that phonics drills are not essential for every child and that they should be employed with discretion. A study conducted in Britain by Winch (1925) and research in the United States by Garrison and Heard (1931) and Tate (1937) also reinforced the position that intensive phonics instruction promoted word-recognition ability. Results of a classic study by Agnew (1939) that also investigated the effectiveness of a phonics versus a "conventional" (i.e., look-say) method were in agreement with these findings: Agnew found that primary-grade children receiving reading instruction that contained a heavy, consistent emphasis on phonics scored higher on tests of phonic ability, word pronunciation, oral reading, and vocabulary. Agnew tempered these findings, however, by noting that:

> If the basic purpose in the teaching of primary reading is the establishment of skills measured in this study (namely: independence in word recognition, ability to work out the sounds of new words, efficiency in word pronunciation, accuracy in oral reading, certain abilities in silent reading, and the ability to recognize a large vocabulary of written words), the investigations would support a policy of large amounts of phonetic training. If, on the other hand, the purposes of teaching primary reading are concerned with "joy in reading," "social experience," "the pursuit of interests," etc., the investigations reported offer no data as to the usefulness of phonetic training. (p. 47)

Agnew, thus, noted the effectiveness of phonics instruction in teaching children word identification and oral reading skills, but tempered these findings by acknowledging that such instruction has unknown effects on children's affective behavior.

It should be noted that results of several studies run contrary to the above findings. Gill (1912) found that preschool and primary-grade children instructed

in a "thought or sentence method of word identification" (i.e., look-say) outperformed their peers who were taught by a phonics method. Similarly, for upper
elementary and high school students, Dumville (1912) found that phonics instruction resulted in poorer performance on an oral reading task than did whole
word instruction. A study of 1000 first graders (Sexton & Herron, 1928) in Newark,
N.J., revealed that teacher effectiveness—not the presence or absence of phonics
instruction—was the better predictor of successful word-identification ability.
In summary, however, it is fair to state that the preponderance of studies from
this early period of research in word-identification instruction suggests that a
phonics approach to teaching word-recognition skills produces superior scores
on measures of phonics knowledge, word-identification ability, and oral reading
than does a look-say instructional methodology.

Research: 1940–1965

Just as the debate concerning the effectiveness of a phonics over a look-say approach to teaching word-identification skills was the central theme of research
in the first four decades of the twentieth century, so, too, the next 25 years
possess a singular focus: namely, the issue of whether a systematic or intrinsic
form of phonics instruction was more effective. (The terms systematic and intrinsic
are Chall's, 1967; we will use them synonymously and interchangeably with synthetic and analytic. Our definition of a systematic/synthetic phonics approach
is an instructional method in which early, intensive phonic rules are taught in
a deductive, part-to-whole manner by teaching letter sounds in isolation, which
are then blended into words. In contrast, an intrinsic/analytic method involves
an inductive, whole-to-parts strategy in which learned sight words are analyzed
and phonics rules are inferred and discovered.) Apparently researchers were
generally convinced, indeed, that phonics instruction had some merit, and based
on this assumption, they sought to determine what form of instruction was the
most effective. Consequently, the preponderance of research in word identification during this period investigated this issue; and it was the most comprehensive
study of all—the First Grade Studies—that marked the close of the era.

A number of studies reported that children instructed in a systematic/syn-
thetic phonics approach outperformed children taught by an intrinsic/analytic
methodology in word-identification tasks. Studies by Russell (1943), Wohleber
(1953), Henderson (1955), Sparks (1956), Bear (1959, 1964), and Duncan (1964),
in addition to the previously cited study by Agnew (1939), all supported the
contention that intensive, systematic phonics instruction resulted in better word
recognition, oral reading, and vocabulary achievement than that produced by
"conventional," less intensive, intrinsic phonics instruction. For example, in Bear's
1959 study, first graders who had been instructed using Hay-Wingo materials
(i.e., Lippincott's synthetic phonics materials) exhibited significantly higher
achievement on a number of measures (e.g., Gates Primary Reading Test, Metropolitan Achievement Test: Primary I, etc.) when compared to first graders using
"conventional" materials. In a follow-up study in 1964, Bear found that these
same children, now in sixth grade, maintained their advantage over their classmates receiving conventional instruction only.

There have been studies, however, that reported either no significant differences between the two phonics approaches or results that favored the intrinsic/ analytic approach. A study by Gates (1927) found no difference in first graders' word recognition, oral reading ability, and application of phonics knowledge between a systematic and intrinsic phonics program; furthermore, he reported superior performance by the intrinsic group on measures of vocabulary and comprehension. Additional studies by McDowell (1953), Gates (1961), and Morgan and Light (1963) also reported either mixed results or results favorable to the intrinsic/analytic methodology.

In summary, however, the majority of studies that investigated the relative effectiveness of a synthetic versus an analytic approach to phonics instruction have reported findings in support of the position that intensive, systematic instruction in phonics will result in superior word-identification ability. While this conclusion may be justified on the basis of sheer numbers of studies favoring this position, one should be aware that there are some problems associated with reviewing historical research. Gurren and Hughes (1965), for example, omitted several studies from their phonics review because of (a) inappropriate types of comparisons, (b) inaccurate group-matching procedures, (c) failure to control for intelligence across groups, or (d) the use of inappropriate statistical procedures. In addition to the research methodological kinds of problems associated with historical studies, one should also be cognizant of the fact that various reviewers have interpreted the same research differently. A good example of this occurs regarding a study by McDowell (1953). McDowell compared one group of children taught to read using a synthetic phonics approach and a second group using a basal reading approach where phonics was taught as a part of the word-attack skills. Interestingly, in reviews of research on phonics, Betts (1956) and N. B. Smith (1957) interpreted McDowell's results as indicating that the basal reader plus phonics group outperformed the synthetic phonics group, whereas Gurren and Hughes (1965) and Bond and Dykstra (1967) analyzed this study as suggestive of no difference between the two groups.

We are not implying that the above mentioned reviewers are inaccurate in their accounts of the research they considered; the example was only meant to be illustrative of the problem associated with historical research, that is, the difficulty in evaluating research methodology and statistical procedures and interpreting results in light of current definitions and practices. And it was because of this dissatisfaction with the extant research in instructional practices that the First Grade Studies were commissioned, for these comprehensive investigations in the methodologies and accompanying materials of beginning reading were to be the "definitive" studies in this area. Unfortunately, they were not. While results tended to support the efficacy of phonics as a means of teaching word-identification skills, no dominant set of instructional practices emerged. Rather, they tended to support the notion that some children learn to read well and some do not, almost irrespective of the instructional emphasis. Bond and Dykstra (1967, p. 123) express this sentiment:

> Children learn to read by a variety of materials and methods. Pupils become successful readers in such vastly different programs as the Language Experience approach with its relative lack of structure and vocabulary control and the various Linguistic programs with their relatively high degree of

structure and vocabulary control. Furthermore, pupils experienced difficulty in each of the programs utilized. No one approach is so distinctly better in all situations and respects than the others that it should be considered the one best method and the one to be used exclusively.

In conclusion, what did we learn about the effectiveness of instructional practices in word identification from research prior to 1965? Regarding children's ability to identify unknown words, read orally, and accumulate sight-vocabulary words, there is little doubt that intensive, systematic instruction in phonics results in better performance in all these areas when compared to instruction based on a whole-word methodology or a program based on an instrinsic/analytic phonics approach. While there most certainly is not universal agreement on this analysis, when one considers the previous research of this period, this conclusion is unavoidable. It should be noted, however, that this evaluation of research makes no statements about program effectiveness in teaching comprehension skills nor does it address the issue of affect and reading. While these issues are not the concern of this chapter, one should be aware that the evaluation of systematic, intensive phonics programs regarding comprehension and affective variables are not so clear-cut and frequently run contrary to results in the area of word-identification instruction.

CURRENT RESEARCH

This section discusses more recent investigations in the effectiveness of instructional practices in the teaching of word-identification skills. Studies are organized under the categories of phonics analysis, structural analysis, and contextual analysis. In keeping with the purpose of this chapter, and in contrast with Chapter 8 by Gough, studies involving classroom practice are of major concern.

Phonics Analysis

Although more recent research in phonics has tended to look at the effects of instruction in specific phonics skills, there still remains some interest in general methodological questions, like those addressed in the First Grade Studies, that is, comparative research exploring the effectiveness of phonics versus no-phonics programs or studies looking at different kinds of phonics instruction. We will briefly update this continuing line of inquiry before moving on to a review of more specialized studies.

Recent Comparative Research

Dykstra (1968), in reporting the second-grade findings of the First Grade Studies, noted a pattern of achievement in word-identification abilities in second graders similar to that found in first grade: the code-emphasis programs (linguistic readers and phonics-first basals) resulted in better oral word pronunciation and silent word-recognition skills than did the conventional meaning-emphasis basal reader programs. Dykstra did, however, temper these findings by suggesting that there was no clear-cut evidence that the early code emphasis was the major reason for the relative effectiveness of those programs. Rather, he suggested that the project itself appeared to have a greater influence on reading achievement than did the particular instructional method or material. In essence, Dykstra suggested that there may have been a grandiose Hawthorne effect operating in the First Grade Studies.

Regardless of Dykstra's cautionary statements, there still remains little contradictory evidence to the position that early, intensive instruction in phonics generally results in *highly proficient word-calling ability*—word calling being defined as a measure of ability to pronounce words correctly without assurance that the caller understands the meaning of the word. Additional studies by Potts and Savino (1968) and Hartlage, Lucas, and Main (1972) comparing either synthetic phonics or linguistic programs to basal or whole-word approaches reinforces this position; in both instances, first graders' oral word-pronunciation and silent word-recognition abilities were superior when reading was taught by a code-emphasis methodology. Kaufman (1976) reported similar results when a very intensive, systematic, and formalized phonics program (Distar) was compared to a conventional basal program: first and second graders' word-identification abilities were superior when instructed by Distar methods and materials.

Perhaps because the continuing line of research comparing phonics to other word-identification methodologies produced similar results, researchers began to address more qualitative questions; that is, acknowledging the fact that intensive phonics instruction produces superior word-calling ability, are there any qualitatively interesting differences in the kinds of word-analysis skills these methodologies produce?

Barr (1972) pursued this question when she investigated the type of responses first graders made on a word-identification task. She found that children taught words by a phonics method produced many more nonsense words or untaught words than did children receiving sight-word instruction. Children taught with a sight method produced fewer nonresponses than the phonic-method children, although the latter group's error responses were more graphically similar to the tested word. In a study conducted with second graders who had been taught reading with either a decoding or meaning emphasis, DeLawter (1975) found a similar pattern when miscues were analyzed. Decoding group children produced about twice as many nonword miscues as real word errors when administered either an isolated word or in-context word identification test. Conversely, real word errors by the meaning group outnumbered nonword miscues, although the decoding group demonstrated better performance in the use of graphophonic elements and syllabication in decoding (as evidenced by the tendency for their miscues to look and sound more like the target word than errors for the meaning-emphasis group).

In a dissertation by Dank (1976), a similar comparison of second graders' miscues was made. Children taught reading by a program that emphasized letter-sound correspondences generated miscues that were frequently nonwords but had a high graphic and sound similarity to the attempted word. Second graders who received reading instruction by using a popular meaning-emphasis basal reader produced miscues that were typically real words and semantically appropriate, though less graphically and aurally appropriate. Norton and Hubert (1977) found a similar pattern when first-grade students taught by a phonics-emphasis approach and an eclectic basal-reader approach were compared. Miscues generated by the basal-reader group were usually syntactically and semantically acceptable, while the phonics group produced more miscues that had high graphic or phonic proximity but were more frequently nonwords.

In summary, there are two main findings that emerge from a great volume of comparative research: (a) programs emphasizing a phonics or code approach to word identification produce superior word-calling ability when compared to programs applying an analytic phonics or meaning emphasis—superior being typically defined as fewer words mispronounced on either isolated word or in-context word-reading tasks and (b) there seem to be distinct differences in the quality of error responses made by children instructed in the two general methodologies—readers' errors tend to be real words, meaningful, and syntactically appropriate when instruction emphasizes meaning, whereas code-emphasis word-identification instruction results in more nonword errors that are graphically and aurally like the mispronounced words.

While there is little doubt that early, reasonably intensive phonics instruction results in word-identification skills in advance of those produced by programs deemphasizing phonics, these studies do not clearly display improved comprehension ability. Resnick (1977, p. 7) expresses this same opinion after considering several decades of applied research:

> When skill in word recognition is the primary dependent variable, code-oriented programs tend to show up better than language-oriented programs. This is especially true for low socioeconomic groups and for low achievers in general. However, when comprehension beyond the very simplest levels is the criterion, there is no clear advantage for either code- or language-oriented programs.

Bond and Dykstra (1967) also noted that the code-emphasis programs—though definitely superior in teaching word-recognition skills—were not consistently superior when comprehension was the dependent variable. And in some instances (e.g., Norton & Hubert, 1977), a reverse pattern was observed: the phonics groups were superior in word-identification ability, while the meaning groups excelled in comprehension.

While the purpose of this chapter is to review relevant research on the topic of instructional practices in teaching word-identification skills, not comprehension skills, the reader should be aware that favorable results in word-identification ability as a result of a particular set of instructional methods and materials does not necessarily imply that such an advantage carries over to other aspects of reading ability. This is mentioned so that generalizations beyond only those justified are not made.

Specialized Phonics Research

Studies investigating specific issues in phonic instruction fall into three general categories: research in (1) the effectiveness of segmenting and blending, (2) the usefulness of training in pattern recognition, and (3) training children to cue on specific word parts. This section considers research within these three categories.

Training in segmenting and blending.   The purpose of phonic instruction, of course, is to teach children how to pronounce "unknown" words. In order for phonics analysis to be effective, one must assume that the "unknown" word is in a child's speaking and/or listening vocabulary. If it is, one assumes that the ability to pronounce the unknown word will automatically cue its meaning in semantic memory.

One approach to teaching phonics is based on the premise that if children are able to analyze words and segment them into parts, they should be able to recombine them into new units, thus enabling them to transfer and apply this skill in decoding unfamiliar words. Research has shown, however (see Jeffrey & Samuels, 1967; Jenkins, Bausell, & Jenkins, 1972; Muller, 1973), that both processes—segmentation and blending—must be mastered before this skill is transferable to the reading of unfamiliar words. While many children independently learn these skills either intuitively or through exposure to traditional beginning reading instruction (basal readers), one should not assume that these skills are automatically acquired. Ramsey (1972) found that disabled second-grade readers were generally lacking in the ability to recombine sets of known sounds. Similarily, Haddock and Tiano (1976) found a high correlation between blending and reading achievement for second, fourth, and sixth graders. It is apparent, therefore, that there is indeed a relationship between word-identification facility and segmenting/blending skills; and it is, furthermore, reasonably well substantiated that both skills must be present if transfer to decoding unknown words is to occur.

Perhaps not surprisingly, the skill of segmentation appears to be a prerequisite for the ability to blend successfully. Fox and Routh (1976) found that children already proficient at segmenting syllables into phonemes benefited from training in auditory blending. Furthermore, facility with both these skills appeared to transfer to word learning: children who could segment syllables were successful in blending training, which, in turn, facilitated the learning of words. Support for the existence of this apparent hierarchy can also be inferred from the previously cited studies by Jeffrey and Samuels (1967), Jenkins et al. (1972), and Muller (1973).

Regarding what are the most appropriate teaching techniques for these subskills, research and opinion is mixed. Most studies investigating training in segmentation (e.g., Skjelfjørd, 1976) have revealed a fairly consistent pattern: grapheme/phoneme correspondences are taught followed by direct instruction in phonemic analysis. There is no similar consensus, however, as to the most appropriate method for teaching blending. Brown (1971), for example, after studying acquisition of blending skills in preschoolers, concluded that emphasis should initially be placed on blending syllables rather than individual phonemes. In a similar study, Sullivan, Okada, and Niedermeyer (1971) compared a single-letter versus a letter-combination approach to blending. Results suggested that neither method was generally more effective in assisting first graders in pronouncing unfamiliar words, although an ATI was found: High-ability first graders applied the letter-combination approach more effectively, whereas the single-letter method assisted low-ability children more in decoding unknown words.

Haddock (1976, 1978) conducted several studies investigating the effectiveness of three techniques in teaching blending. Preschool children (1976) and kindergartners (1978) received one of three training methods: (a) an auditory method in which teachers pronounced word parts (e.g., *sh—eet*) and asked the children to recombine them into words; (b) an auditory-visual method in which a word was visually presented and pronounced (e.g., *feet*) and then consonants were substituted (e.g., *sheet*) followed by pronunciation of the new word; or (c) a basic letter-sound training method devoid of specific blending instruction (i.e., a form of control group). Results of the 1976 study revealed that both the auditory and auditory-visual methods were significantly more effective than the letter-sound-only group; and the auditory-visual method was significantly more effective than the visual-only method. Results of the 1978 study indicated that only the auditory-visual method was superior to the letter-sound group. Based on these two investigations, Haddock (1978, p. 657) reaches the following conclusion:

> These two studies along with previous evidence from laboratory studies strongly suggest that beginning readers would profit from specific instruction in blending sounds and letters, along with other basic decoding skills. Only two of the children in the control group of the original [1976] study were able to induce the principle on their own by practicing sound-letter associations. Presumably, those children who would eventually induce the blending principle independently would not be harmed by such instruction—they would merely acquire the principle sooner—while the children who are unable to learn to blend without explicit instruction would get the help they need.

Haddock further concludes that the auditory-visual method is to be preferred over the auditory-only approach. This method, which in effect involves a consonant-substitution task, has been recommended by others (e.g., Cunningham, 1975, 1977), although it has been pointed out (see Griffin, 1972; Railsback, 1970) that the crucial operation in applying this strategy is the ability to recall a known word visually similar to the unknown word.

One additional finding of Haddock's research of interest is evidence suggesting that there is no substance to the long-held belief that pronouncing sounds in isolation is detrimental to children's blending ability and, hence, decoding skill. This belief was based on the assumption that the necessary inclusion of a schwa sound (or intruded vowel) when pronouncing consonants that are stops interferes with blending ability and will never produce a fused unit. Haddock found that children performed equally well in blending stops and continuants, which can be pronounced without the schwa or added vowel. She concluded, therefore, that criticizing code-emphasis programs on this basis was unjustified.

Williams (1980, p. 1) described a program which provided explicit training in phoneme analysis and phoneme blending, letter-sound correspondences, and decoding:

> The results of two years of program evaluation in New York City classrooms for learning-disabled children indicated that the program successfully teaches general decoding. That is, instructed children were able to decode novel combinations of letters that were not presented in training.

In conclusion, what can be said for the efficacy of blending instruction as a tactic in teaching word-identification ability? First, there certainly appears to be a sequence of skills (analysis, segmentation, blending, transfer) involved in applying blending as a word-identification strategy. Second, one must not always assume automatic transfer to unpracticed blending patterns. And finally, although there is no conclusive research base, it does appear that an auditory-visual (i.e., consonant substitution) method is reasonably effective in teaching children to apply this strategy in phonics analysis.

Training in pattern recognition. Studies in pattern-recognition training and its transfer effects to word reading fall into two categories: aural/oral training programs and visual training programs. The former category, typified by a study by Rentel and Kennedy (1972), has generally investigated effects of oral-language training for speakers of nonstandard dialects. Rentel and Kennedy, for example, found that intensive aural/oral training (i.e., modeling of sentences) for low socio-economic status (SES) first graders from Appalachia resulted in oral-language patterns with significantly fewer structural deviations from the standard South Midland dialect of this area when compared to a control group. Reading ability (as measured by the Word Reading subtest of the Stanford Achievement Test), however, was shown to be unaffected by oral pattern drill: children in the experimental group performed no better on a word-identification measure than those children who received no such training. Rentel and Kennedy concluded that, at least for short-term intervention programs, oral pattern drill does not positively affect word-identification ability.

Regarding visual pattern training, there is some evidence that beginning readers do benefit from specific training in identifying the essential components of letters. Although for years it has been known (see Witty & Kopel, 1936) that prereading training that involved discrimination practice only for nonletter and nonword shapes and symbols did not transfer directly to reading, a more recent study by Montgomery (1977) has shown that training in identifying letter components does benefit beginning readers in identifying words. Montgomery instructed 5-year-old children in British primary schools for four weeks in pattern-training exercises: booklets and manipulative materials (jigsaws, sticks, and dots) that required children to construct letter shapes by assembling essential letter components (sticks and dots). Results showed that children receiving the visual pattern training not only did significantly better on a criterion measure of visual pattern recognition when compared to control-group children, but the experimental group also performed significantly better on a measure of word recognition. Montgomery concluded that visual pattern training for prereaders and beginning readers does constitute an effective component for a beginning reading program.

So, while there is little evidence that oral-language training by a pattern-matching method directly affects word-reading ability, there is some support for the use of visual pattern training as an aid to word recognition at the beginning reading levels. Obviously, much additional research is needed to further evaluate this latter phenomenon and assess its effectiveness in teaching word-identification skills.

Word-part saliency and word recognition.   Several studies (e.g., Bertrand, 1976; Guthrie & Seifert, 1977; Hafner, Weaver, & Powell, 1970; Jeffrey & Samuels, 1967; Mason, 1977) have investigated a different important issue within phonics instruction: the saliency of different parts of words. Jeffrey and Samuels (1967), for example, found that specific training in letter-sound correspondences (followed by blending instruction) was found to be more effective in transfer to reading new words than was a whole-word approach. Similarly, Mason (1977) reported that at the word level, decoding is dependent upon letter properties, although she also indicated that whole-word familiarity positively affects word recognition as well.

Studies by Hafner et al. (1970) and Bertrand (1976) explored which word parts are most helpful in decoding unfamiliar words. Hafner et al. reported that for fourth graders, the first two letters of a word plus configuration provided the most powerful combination of cues in word identification. Cues provided by the first letter plus configuration were the next most helpful, followed by the last two letters of a word. Bertrand also noted that for both first and fifth graders, the beginnings of words were much more helpful in making a correct word identification than were cues supplied by the middle and end portions of words.

Guthrie and Seifert (1977) also examined how complexity of letter-sound correspondence rules and instruction affect word identification. They conducted a longitudinal study of first-, second-, and third-grade children and reported that a hierarchy of difficulty emerged: consonant vowel combinations were least difficult, followed by short vowel words, long vowel words, special rule words, and nonsense words. In addition, it was noted that there were two phases of acquisition: short vowel words and simpler tasks were learned before long vowel words and more difficult tasks.

In summary, there is little doubt that the beginnings of words provide readers the most powerful phonic cues in identifying unknown words. In addition, the research of Guthrie and Seifert (1977) suggests that there may also be a hierarchy of phonics instruction. A justifiable implication may be that phonics instruction should, at least initially, emphasize beginning word cues; and, if the hierarchy of instruction is verified by subsequent research, publishers of instructional materials may finally possess some rationale for decisions regarding which phonics skills to teach and in what order to teach them.

Phonics Instruction: Summary and Conclusions

What general conclusions can be reached concerning the current research in phonics instruction? First, the results of recent comparative studies still suggest that programs emphasizing early, reasonably intensive phonics instruction produce readers who are more proficient at word pronunciation than programs emphasizing meaning. And although this conclusion is unavoidable, when one analyzes research assessing more qualitative aspects of word identification (e.g., oral reading miscues), it becomes apparent that the strategies children use in word analysis differ markedly as a function of program emphasis. The argument is thus frequently made that heavy phonics emphasis—though effective in producing accurate word readers—may negatively affect meaning acquisition in reading.

Although research has not conclusively verified this charge, there still remains a possibility that heavy emphasis on phonics may negatively affect comprehension ability and perhaps affective aspects of reading as well.

A second general set of conclusions centers on the issues related to specific phonics instruction; that is, what programs have been successful in teaching letter-sound correspondences and generalizations and how effectively have these analysis skills transferred to the reading of unfamiliar words? There is accumulating evidence that a sequence of analysis-segmentation-blending successfully accomplishes these goals. Children are initially taught letter-sound correspondences by analyzing words in their speaking/listening vocabulary; they are then taught to segment words into phonemic units; and finally, they are instructed in the skill of blending these isolated sounds into known and previously unknown words. It is this last step—blending—that has been shown to be most crucial in the transfer of phonic analysis skills to the reading of unfamiliar words. Additional research has shown that perhaps an auditory-visual method (essentially consonant substitution) is most effective in teaching the skill of blending sounds, although one should not assume that children automatically generalize blending skills to untaught patterns; thus, there is no substitute for direct instruction.

A third, somewhat tentative, conclusion can be reached concerning pattern-recognition training. While there is no research evidence that aural/oral pattern training is effective, there is some indication that visual pattern-recognition training in letter components does facilitate word identification for beginning readers. And finally, research investigating which word part provides the strongest phonic cues rather conclusively suggests that readers should and do direct their efforts toward the beginnings of words.

What then do these research findings imply for the reading teacher and for the reading researcher? Regarding the teaching of reading, the message is clear: if you want to improve word-identification ability, teach phonics. But teach phonics in special ways. Instruction in both the visual and aural modes that emphasize the segmenting and then blending of sounds may be the most effective way to teach phonics subskills. And if word pronunciation is the singular goal, a synthetic or systematic approach to phonics will most likely be more effective than analytic methods. Adherence to a specific sequence for the introduction and teaching of phonics skills may also be beneficial as will emphasis on the beginning parts of words. Teachers should not assume, however, that children will generalize skills not specifically taught, nor should one assume that transfer to unknown words will automatically occur. Again, direct instruction provides the most expeditious method to achieve a specific goal.

And while the above-stated procedures will probably be effective in teaching children to become proficient word readers, the wise and experienced teacher will not lose sight of the ultimate goal of reading: meaning acquisition. For it may be that excessive reliance upon code-emphasis instruction obscures the more important goal of obtaining meaning from print. Our position is that phonics instruction is necessary and essential for many children; consequently, it should be an integral part of all beginning reading programs.

Regarding future research in phonics instruction, several fertile areas remain unexplored. Additional research into the potential skills-hierarchy issue is warranted; that is, research that will (1) identify what specific phonics subskills are necessary in learning to read words and (2) determine the most effective order for presenting and teaching these skills. Research investigating what relationships exist between phonics instruction and comprehension is also needed. There currently is much conjecture and opinion concerning a possible negative impact that early, intensive phonics instruction may have on children's comprehension ability and on their attitude about reading. This debate, however, needs to be empirically resolved. Finally, additional methodological research exploring the long-term effects of intensive phonics instruction is needed. Most phonics research has investigated only reading behavior (usually only word identification) for primary-grade children. This research needs to be continued into the intermediate grades in order to determine whether initial gains made by heavy phonics instruction is maintained in later grades. And above all, future research in phonics should emphasize ecological validity; that is, studies need to be conducted with children in elementary classrooms using materials taken directly from the curriculum. In only this way will future research result in any valid generalizations for instructional methods and materials.

Structural Analysis

Structural analysis is a word-identification strategy through which a reader determines the meaning and pronunciation of an unfamiliar word by examining its meaningful parts. This involves analyzing words and dismantling them into units of meaning (i.e., free and bound morphemes—base words, affixes, and inflected endings), identifying the individual meanings, and then recombining these parts into a meaningful whole. Instruction in structural analysis typically involves the teaching of base words and common prefixes, suffixes, and inflected endings (plurals, possessives, comparatives, and tense morphemes), the assumption being that if a reader is familiar with these meaningful units, they will be recognized when encountered in unknown words and will thus aid in their identification. The ability to syllabicate—though not directly a structural analysis skill—is also intimately related to success in structural analysis, for in many instances, the structural subunits (i.e., the roots, affixes, and inflections) consist of syllables (e.g., *foot/ball, jump/ing, un/clear, small/er*). Consequently, syllabication instruction will also be considered in this section (although one could argue that it is more a phonic decoding skill than a structural analysis skill). The research in the area of structural analysis instruction, therefore, will be organized into two sections: (a) instruction in syllabication and (b) the teaching of base words, affixes, and inflections.

Syllabication Instruction

The rationale for teaching syllabication is based on the belief that if children can segment unknown words into more manageable parts, decoding will be facilitated; that is, phonics, phonogram identification, or structural skills can then be effectively applied. This position has been bolstered by the popular opinion that the syllable, not the phoneme, is the basic unit of language (although linguists continue to disagree on both the definition of a syllable and the rules for boundary determination). In addition, there is evidence that children are reasonably facile at identifying the number of syllables in words and that better readers intuitively divide unfamiliar words into syllables (cf. Schell, 1967; Sherwin, 1970). There remains, however a considerable controversy over the efficacy of teaching children to syllabicate words as an aid to word identification. Proponents of syllabication instruction (e.g., Gates, 1947; Gray, 1960; Karlin, 1971; N. B. Smith, 1963) have maintained that this ability is indispensable as a first-step process in decoding polysyllabic words. Opponents (e.g., Durrell, 1956; Groff, 1971; Johnson & Pearson, 1984; Spache & Baggett, 1966; Zuck, 1974) have essentially argued that in order for readers to segment a word into syllables accurately, they must first pronounce the word itself: the supposed goal of syllabication.

Several studies have been conducted to evaluate empirically the effectiveness of instruction in syllabication. Gleitman and Rozin (1973) instructed kindergartners in a simple syllabary and reported that these children were subsequently able to blend, read, and comprehend previously untaught combinations of syllables. Canney and Schreiner (1977) instructed second-grade pupils in the skill of syllabication or phonogram identification. When compared to controls, Canney and Schreiner reported that neither instructional strategy was effective in improving word-identification skills or comprehension. Biggins and Uhler (1978) also investigated syllabication instruction in children from grades 2 through 8 and reported a slight advantage for experimentals in vocabulary measures but no significant differences in comprehension.

Cunningham (1979; Cunningham, Cunningham, & Rystrom, 1981) acknowledged the conceptual flaw in expecting syllabication instruction to be effective as a word-pronunciation strategy when traditional syllabication rules presuppose word pronunciation. Instead, she proposed a synthesized theory of mediated word identification (Cunningham, 1975) in which readers use a compare/contrast strategy in word identification. Cunningham taught second-grade children to compare and contrast unknown low-frequency one-syllable words and nonwords to known high-frequency one-syllable words. A posttest revealed that children who received this instruction outperformed controls in ability to pronounce not only other low-frequency monosyllabic words, but also new two-syllable words.

In a follow-up study, Cunningham (1979) formally evaluated the effectiveness of the compare/contrast technique in promoting children's pronunciation of two-syllable words. Fourth- and fifth-grade students were taught to compare and contrast unknown two-syllable words to known one-syllable words that rhymed with individual syllables of the two-syllable words (e.g., *problem—Bob, them*). Posttesting revealed significant gains in students' ability to pronounce previously unpronounceable two-syllable words when compared to the performance of a control group. Interestingly, students in the experimental group were no more skillful in their ability to divide words into syllables as a result of the compare/contrast instruction. Cunningham interpreted this finding as "more support to the theory that syllabication rules have more to do with dictionaries than with decoding unfamiliar words" (1979, p. 778).

In another study, Cunningham et al. (1981) developed a new syllabication strategy which did not require prior pronunciation of the word to be divided, and they sought to determine the relationship between the new syllabication system and reading achievement. Third- and fourth-grade teachers instructed in the new strategy taught it to their students for a period of 15 weeks. Results revealed that these students were no more proficient than control peers on various vocabulary and comprehension measures. Cunningham et al. concluded "there is currently no empirical support for teaching pupils to divide words into syllables as an aid to successful reading. Until some evidence can be presented, we invite the readers to join us in calling for a moratorium on syllabication instruction" (p. 213).

In summary, both opinion and research remain mixed concerning the effectiveness of syllabication instruction, although the weight of evidence calls for caution in expecting syllabication instruction to result in improved decoding ability. And considering the relatively few studies that have been conducted, further research in this area is warranted. As Canney and Schreiner (1977) stated: "Certainly, additional research following carefully designed procedures is required to adequately resolve the many issues surrounding syllabication" (p. 123).

The Teaching of Base Words, Affixes, and Inflections

As previously stated, the rationale for teaching structural analysis is based on the belief that recognition of meaningful parts of words will facilitate the identification of unknown words containing these elements. While this argument is logical and intuitively appealing, there is little research evidence supportive of this opinion. In fact, our review uncovered only one study each in the areas of instruction in affixes and the teaching of inflected endings.

Otterman (1955) implemented a study in which seventh graders received 30 ten-minute lessons in structural elements. Results revealed that the experimental group outperformed controls in spelling, and not surprisingly, displayed a greater knowledge of the meanings of the elements studied. No significant differences were found, however, for the identification of new words nor for general reading vocabulary and comprehension. And while Otterman fails to make any general conclusions based on her study, Groff (1972) interprets the findings as follows:

> Otterman's study seems to suggest a conclusion, namely, that even when extra instructional time is given to the study of the meanings of affixes, such study will not be worthwhile for reading instruction. (p. 29)

Concerning the effectiveness of teaching inflected endings, Hanson (1966) evaluated first graders who received 18 periods—each of 20 minutes—in direct instruction of variant word endings (*s, ed, ing, er, est*). Results of the study revealed when compared to controls that children receiving special instruction in these inflected endings performed significantly better on a specially constructed Variant Endings Test, although no significant differences were reported in general reading ability. (No measure of word identification was administered to the subjects.) Hanson concluded that inflected endings can be taught to beginning readers and that there is no reason to delay instruction in this area.

Structural Analysis Instruction: Summary and Conclusions

Based on the absence of relevant research in the area of structural analysis, there is little empirical evidence that supports the effectiveness of teaching syllabication or structure skills involving affixes or inflections. This does not mean that structural analysis is not a potentially powerful word-identification strategy, but rather, it simply demonstrates once again that all too frequently educational practice is not founded on educational research. Certainly, further research is warranted—research involving children of different grade levels being instructed in a variety of structural and syllabic skills. Only then will it be possible to evaluate objectively the effectiveness of these instructional strategies and the efficacy of this method of identifying words and its overall contribution to reading ability.

Contextual Analysis

Contextual analysis is a word-identification strategy whereby a reader attempts to determine the meaning and pronunciation of an unknown word by the way it is used in a sentence or passage. Contextual clues include pictorial and graphic aids, such as pictures, charts, graphs, and diagrams, and typographical clues, such as quotation marks, parentheses, and definitional footnotes. But the most powerful contextual clues are linguistic clues provided by the positional nature of English (i.e., syntactic clues) and by the knowledge a language user has of the meanings of other words (i.e., semantic clues). It has been theorized (cf. Goodman, 1967, 1973; F. Smith, 1978) that a reader applies this tacit knowledge of language by reducing the number of possible alternative candidates for an unfamiliar word and thereby enhances his/her chances of making an accurate identification.

Because of the potential power of contextual clues as a word-identification strategy, reading educators, researchers, and theorists (e.g., Ames, 1966; Artley, 1943; Aulls, 1970; Jongsma, 1971; McCullough, 1945; Spache & Spache, 1977; Timian & Santeusanio, 1974) have promoted the teaching of contextual clues as a word-identification strategy. And unlike structural analysis (and to a certain extent phonic analysis), there is a reasonably firm psychological base for a reader's use of contextual aids and the subsequent teaching of these skills in word-identification instruction.

Sternberg, Powell, and Kaye (in press) believe that "a vocabulary-training program that uses learning from context is incomplete if it fails to provide instruction in how to use context" (p. 13). They identify specific cues which should be taught and differentiate external cues (from surrounding context) from internal cues (from morphemes within the word). Eight external cues—temporal, spatial, value, attribute, functional, enablement, class, and equivalence—and four internal cues—prefix, stem, suffix and interactive—are described. The authors report research which supports their notions of contextual analysis, a notion which is, to us, a sensible combination of contextual and structural analysis.

Psychological Research in Contextual Analysis

Goodman (1965) reported that young readers were much more accurate in identifying words when they were situated in a surrounding context than when included in simple lists. Weber (1970) investigated first graders' use of grammatical context in reading by analyzing their oral reading errors and noted that:

> Beginning readers use their knowledge of grammar to narrow down the words that compete for a given sentence slot, just as they surely do in

understanding speech. . . . It is as though the children resisted uttering a sequence that did not conform to an acceptable sentence. (p. 162)

Other more recent investigations have further explored a reader's use of contextual clues in word identification. Pearson and Studt (1975) found that both word frequency and context affected word-identification abilities for first- and third-grade children—contextual richness was more pronounced for high-frequency words than for less common lexical items. Klein, Klein, and Bertino (1974) found that both fourth and sixth graders effectively used context, but not in equivalent amounts: the older children relied more on contextual clues than did the younger children. This developmental effect was substantiated by further research with children (Klein, Klein, & Doris, 1973) and with mature readers (Klein & Klein, 1973), although an interesting discrepancy was apparent: Klein et al. (1974) showed that context use was lower at both the fourth- and sixth-grade levels than did Klein et al. (1973). This apparent anomaly was resolved in a further study (Klein, 1976) when the use of context was shown to be linked to the difficulty of the reading material. Although Klein (1976) found the same developmental trend for students in the third, fifth, seventh, and ninth grades and for college students, it was also noted that there were much greater increments in the use of contextual clues when the reading material was less complex.

Schvaneveldt, Ackerman, and Semlear (1977) attempted to differentiate the effects of syntactic and semantic context in word recognition. They found that contrary to previous findings (Klein, 1976; Klein & Klein, 1973; Klein et al., 1973; Klein et al., 1974), young readers do take advantage of certain kinds of contextual clues as much as older readers. Schvaneveldt et al. (1977) found that readers of all ages took equal advantage of the *semantic clues* in identifying unknown words. Thus, it appears that syntactic context may be developmentally related, whereas semantic context is not. West and Stanovich (1978) sought to further clarify this issue by investigating contextual facilitation in light of automaticity in decoding (see LaBerge & Samuels, 1974). West and Stanovich found that while congruous contexts facilitated reading times for groups of fourth graders, sixth graders, and adults, incongruous context negatively affected the children's reading times (as expected) but did not influence those of the adults. West and Stanovich concluded that while context certainly enhances word identification, it is mediated, at least in part, by automatic processes, that is, by immediate word identification—reading automaticity.

Research in the Teaching of Contextual Analysis

So, while there seems to be a sound psychological base that supports the notion that children effectively use contextual clues in word identification, there unfortunately is little research evaluating the effectiveness of specific instructional techniques used to teach contextual analysis. Although opinion abounds concerning what constitutes the best way to teach context clues (cf. Ames, 1966; Artley, 1943; Emans, 1969; Emans & Fisher, 1967; Johnson & Pearson, 1984; McCullough, 1943, 1945), there is little research evidence supportive of any specific methodology. And of the few extant relevant studies to be reviewed, there is little conclusive evidence regarding the effectiveness of any specific program.

Askov and Kamm (1976) instructed third, fourth, and fifth graders in the specific context clues of cause and effect and description. After a total of four hours of training distributed over ten sessions, the children's ability to use these clues effectively was evaluated using a criterion-referenced test specifically designed to measure mastery of these skills. Results indicated that the children receiving the special instruction significantly outperformed children who did not receive special context clue training. Askov and Kamm concluded that:

> Teaching a classification of context clues, such as cause/effect and direct description, will promote greater use of such clues and enhance the student's ability to determine the meaning of an unknown word in a sentence. (1976, p. 343)

Fleisher and Jenkins (1977) investigated the effects of contextualized practice (i.e., the exclusive reading of connected discourse) and decontextualized practice (i.e., supplemental drill on isolated words) on learning-disabled children's word-identification ability. Results indicated that decontextualized practice produced significantly greater isolated word recognition than did contextualized practice (as would be expected), but neither treatment differentially affected oral reading in context as measured by rate or accuracy.

Bender (1975) similarly investigated nine- and ten-year-old corrective readers' ability to apply context clues after completing a special audiotutorial training program in contextual analysis. Results on a posttreatment cloze exercise showed no significant difference in performance between experimentals and controls.

Contextual Analysis: Summary and Conclusions

The psychological research in children's use of context clues as aids in word identification leaves us with several general findings: (a) it is apparent that children do indeed use contextual information in identifying words (Goodman, 1965; Weber, 1970); (b) there appears to be a developmental trend in children's use of *syntactic* contextual clues (Klein & Klein, 1973; Klein et al., 1973; Klein et al., 1974), although *semantic* contextual information seems to be equally applied by both developing and mature readers (Schvaneveldt et al., 1977); (c) children's use of context seems to be linked to the type of reading material—both word frequency (Pearson & Studt, 1975) and difficulty level (Klein, 1976) affect the power of contextual clues; and (d) contextual clues are, at least in part, mediated by automaticity in reading (West & Stanovich, 1978).

The scanty educational research in the teaching of contextual analysis also leaves us with several tentative findings: (a) it appears as though nonreading-disabled children can be taught to make use of specific contextual clues as aids in identifying words (Askov & Kamm, 1976) and (b) disabled readers have difficulty in learning to apply contextual aids in identifying unknown words (Bender, 1975; Fleisher & Jenkins, 1977), which of course, reinforces the finding (see Steiner, Wiener, & Cromer, 1971; Weinstein & Rabinovitch, 1971) that poor readers do not take advantage of the contextual clues present in text.

What conclusions, therefore, can be drawn? First, the psychological studies may suggest that instruction in contextual analysis is indeed practical and feasible and that teaching how to make use of both the syntactic and semantic contextual clues may be productive. In addition, both the level of difficulty and the frequency of the targeted words should be considered when constructing instructional materials, that is, less difficult and more frequent words may negate children's need to use contextual information. Second, while the educational studies tell us that it may be profitable to teach contextual analysis, we are left with little concrete information concerning the best methodology and most efficient instructional materials. So, while there is little doubt that contextual clues are potentially powerful aids in identifying unknown words, much additional educational research is warranted in order to determine what specific pedagogical procedures will be most effective in teaching children to learn and apply this skill.

WORD IDENTIFICATION: SOME CONCLUSIONS AND IMPLICATIONS

Our overwhelming impression of word-identification research findings is that, pedagogically, few of the answers are in. This is especially true as it relates to the overarching question: How does word-identification ability affect one's ability to comprehend what is read? The question seems not to have received much research attention in the past decade and a half, nor in the previous half century for that matter. We do not yet know to what degree and in what ways mastery of the word-identification skills of phonics analysis, structural analysis, and contextual analysis contributes to reading comprehension. Do, in fact, "skill masters" read better (or more or with greater enthusiasm) than "nonmasters"? Which word-identification skills seem to contribute most to the comprehension of written discourse? But before discussing needs, let's reiterate what we've learned.

We have learned that "what you train is what you get." Children taught a good deal of intensive phonics will do well at pronouncing words and at measures of phonics ability for example. Children taught with a meaning-emphasis approach will tend to produce more errors which are semantically or syntactically appropriate than children taught with a code-emphasis approach, whose errors are more phonetically appropriate.

We have learned that blending is important to phonics and that a sequence of analysis-segmentation-blending is effective. We have learned that the beginnings of words are more significant identifiers than middles or ends of words.

Research has shown that children do use context to identify words: they make use of semantic cues at all levels, but application of syntactic cues proceeds developmentally. It has been further demonstrated that children can be taught to use specific context clues.

Virtually no evidence was uncovered supporting the effectiveness of instruction in structural analysis or syllabication. This does not mean such instruction is not warranted, it simply means it has received little research attention, and the few relevant studies were inconclusive.

Our experience as teachers, our intuition, and our belief in conventional wisdom cause us to value instruction in the word-identification skills of phonics and structural and contextual analysis. We believe they can significantly help children independently expand their vocabularies and, thus, comprehend better what they read. *But* empirically, we have been unable to document strong support for such belief.

We think a good deal of instructional research in word identification is needed. Questions such as the following need, in our opinion, to be addressed by present and future reading researchers:

1. What relationships exist between the various and sundry word-identification skills and reading comprehension?
2. Is comprehension ability dependent upon or enhanced by training in word identification?
3. Are there word-identification skills hierarchies? Which skills of phonics, structure, or context are essential and what sequences are required?
4. What methodologies are most successful for teaching the various elements of phonics and structural and contextual analysis?
5. What can ATI research in word identification tell us? Tirre, Freebody, and Kaufman (1980) present a strong argument for the need for ATI research in real-school settings.
6. What instructional techniques best assist a reader to *apply* the various word-identification strategies *in conjunction* with one another to discern meanings of unfamiliar words?
7. What is the nature and impact of the way individual teachers structure word-identification lessons, independent of the method they are teaching? Teacher interruption behaviors, such as those identified by Allington (1980), and a host of other variables *besides* methods need investigation.

In summary, what is needed is research which attempts to identify what *ought to be* taught, what *can* be taught, how best to help children *learn* it, and how best to help children *apply* it. We feel such questions can best be answered through studies done in classrooms with children and teachers in realistically natural educational settings. There is always a compromise between the experimental rigor that can accompany laboratory studies and the generalizability permitted by the ecological validity inherent in field studies. Because of the purpose of the present chapter—the review of and recommendations about research on instructional practices in word identification—we urge that the greatest experimental care be taken, but that research on instruction in word identification be done in real-life situations.

REFERENCES

Agnew, D. C. *The effect of varied amounts of phonetic training on primary reading* (Duke University Research Studies in Education, No. 5). Durham, N.C.: Duke University Press, 1939.

Allington, R. L. Teacher interruption behaviors during primary-grade oral reading. *Journal of Educational Psychology*, 1980, *72*, 371–377.

Ames, W. S. The development of a classification scheme of contextual aids. *Reading Research Quarterly*, 1966, *2*, 57–82.

Artley, A. S. Teaching word meaning through context. *Elementary English Review*, 1943, *20*, 68–74.

Askov, E. N., & Kamm, K.   Context clues: Should we teach children to use a classification system in reading? *Journal of Educational Research*, 1976, *69*, 341–344.

Aulls, M. W.   Context in reading: How it may be depicted. *Journal of Reading Behavior*, 1970, *3*, 61–73.

Barr, R. C.   The influence of instructional conditions on word recognition errors. *Reading Research Quarterly*, Spring 1972, *7*, 509–529.

Bear, D. E.   Phonics for first grade: A comparison of two methods. *Elementary School Journal*, 1959, *59*, 394–402.

Bear, D. E.   Two methods of teaching phonics: A longitudinal study. *Elementary School Journal*, 1964, *64*, 273–279.

Bender, S. S.   *The effectiveness of audio-tutorial training in context skills for improving reading comprehension*. Unpublished doctoral dissertation, Auburn University, 1975. (ERIC Document Reproduction Service No. ED 119 159)

Bertrand, C. V.   *The effect of letter deletion on word recognition*. Unpublished master's thesis, Rutgers University, 1976. (ERIC Document Reproduction Service No. ED 124 876)

Betts, E. A.   Phonics: Practical considerations based on research. *Elementary English*, 1956, *33*, 375–371.

Biggins, C. M., & Uhler, S.   Is there a "workable" word decoding system? *Reading Improvement*, 1978, *15*, 47–55.

Bond, G. L., & Dykstra, R.   The cooperative research program in first-grade reading instruction. *Reading Research Quarterly*, Summer 1967, *2*, 1–142.

Bronfenbrenner, U.   The experimental ecology of education. *Educational Researcher*, October 1976, *5*, 5–15.

Brown, D. L.   Some linguistic dimensions in auditory blending. In F. P. Greene (Ed.), *Reading: The right to participate: Twentieth yearbook to the national reading conference*. Clemson, S.C.: National Reading Conference, 1971.

Canney, G., & Schreiner, R.   A study of the effectiveness of selected syllabication rules and phonogram patterns for word attack. *Reading Research Quarterly*, 1977, *12*, 102–124.

Chall, J. S.   *Learning to read: The great debate*. New York: McGraw-Hill, 1967.

Cunningham, P. M.   A compare/contrast theory of mediated word identification. *Reading Teacher*, 1979, *32*, 774–778.

Cunningham, P. M.   Investigating a synthesized theory of mediated word identification. *Reading Research Quarterly*, 1975, *11*, 127–143.

Cunningham, P. M.   Supplying the missing links from consonant substitution to "real reading." *Reading Horizons*, 1977, *17*, 279–282.

Cunningham, P. M., Cunningham, J. W., & Rystrom, R. C.   A new syllabication strategy and reading achievement. *Reading World*, 1981, *20*, 208–214.

Currier, L. B.   Phonics and no phonics. *Elementary School Journal*, 1923, *23*, 448–452.

Currier, L. B., & Duguid, O. C.   Phonics or no phonics? *Elementary School Journal*, 1916, *17*, 286–287.

Dank, M. E.   *A study of the relationship of miscues to the mode of formal reading instruction received by selected second graders*. Unpublished doctoral dissertation, University of Massachusetts, 1976. (ERIC Document Reproduction Service No. ED 126 431)

Delawter, J. A.   Three miscue patterns: The relationship of beginning reading instruction and miscue patterns. In W. D. Page (Ed.), *Help for the reading teacher: New directions in research*. Urbana, Ill.: National Conference on Research in English, ERIC Clearinghouse on Reading and Communication Skills, National Institute of Education, 1975.

Dumville, B.   The methods of teaching reading in the early stages. *School World*, 1912, *14*, 408–413.

Duncan, R. L.   A comparative study: Two methods of teaching reading. *Tulsa School Review*, 1964, *21*, 4–5.

Durrell, D.   *Improving reading instruction*. Chicago: Harcourt, Brace and World, 1956.

Dykstra, R.   The effectiveness of code- and meaning-emphasis beginning reading programs. *Reading Teacher*, 1968, *22*, 17–23.

Emans, R.   Use of context clues. In J. A. Figural (Ed.), *Reading and realism, proceedings of the thirteenth annual convention*. Newark, Del.: International Reading Association, 1969.

Emans, R., & Fisher, G. M.   Teaching the use of context clues. *Elementary English*, 1967, *44*, 243–246.

Fleisher, L. S., & Jenkins, J. R.   *Effects of contextualized and decontextualized practice conditions on word recognition* (Technical Report No. 54). Urbana, Ill.: Center for the Study of Reading, 1977.

Fox, B., & Routh, D. K.   Phonemic analysis and synthesis as word-attack skills. *Journal of Educational Psychology*, 1976, *68*, 70–74.

Garrison, S. C., & Heard, M. T.   An experimental study of the value of phonetics. *Peabody Journal of Education*, 1931, *9*, 9–14.

Gates, A. I.   Studies of phonetic training in beginning reading. *Journal of Educational Psychology*, 1927, *18*, 217–226.

Gates, A. I.   *The improvement of reading* (3rd ed.). New York: Macmillan, 1947.

Gates, A. I.   Results of teaching a system of phonics. *Reading Teacher*, 1961, *14*, 248–252.

Gill, E. J.   Methods of teaching reading: A comparison of results. *Journal of Experimental Pedagogy*, 1912, *1*, 243–248.

Gleitman, L. R., & Rozin, P.   Teaching reading as a syllabary. *Reading Research Quarterly*, 1973, *8*, 447–483.

Goodman, K. S.   A linguistic study of cues and miscues in reading. *Elementary English*, 1965, *42*, 639–643.

Goodman, K. S.   Reading: A psycholinguistic guessing game. *Journal of Reading Specialist*, 1967, *6*, 126–135.

Goodman, K. S.   Psycholinguistic universals in the reading process. In F. Smith (Ed.), *Psycholinguistics and reading*. New York: Holt, Rinehart & Winston, 1973.

Gray, W. S.   *On their own in reading*. Chicago: Scott, Foresman, 1960.

Griffin, M.   Consonant substitution—a diagnostic technique in word identification. In L. A. Harris & C. B. Smith (Eds.), *Individualizing reading instruction, a reader*. New York: Holt, Rinehart & Winston, 1972.

Groff, P.   *The syllable: Its nature and pedagogical usefulness*. Portland, Ore.: Northwest Regional Educational Laboratory, 1971.

Groff, P.   Teaching affixes for reading improvement. *Reading Improvement*, Spring 1972, *9*, 28–30.

Gurren, L., & Hughes, A.   Intensive phonics vs. gradual phonics in beginning reading: A review. *Journal of Educational Research*, 1965, *58*, 339–347.

Guthrie, J. T., & Seifert, M.   Letter-sound complexity in learning to identify words. *Journal of Educational Psychology*, 1977, *69*, 686–696.

Haddock, M.   Effects of an auditory and an auditory-visual method of blending instruction on the ability of prereaders to decode synthetic words. *Journal of Educational Psychology*, 1976, *68*, 825–831.

Haddock, M.   Teaching blending in beginning reading instruction *is* important. *Reading Teacher*, 1978, *31*, 654, 658.

Haddock, M., & Tiano, K.   *The relationship between blending ability and reading comprehension*. Unpublished paper, Arizona State University, 1976.

Hafner, L. E., Weaver, W. W., & Powell, K.   Psychological and perceptual correlates of reading achievement among fourth graders. *Journal of Reading Behavior*, 1970, *2*, 281–290.

Hanson, I. W.   First grade children work with variant word endings. *Reading Teacher*, 1966, *19*, 505–507, 511.

Hartlage, L. C., Lucas, D. G., & Main, W. H.   Comparison of three approaches to teaching reading skills. *Perceptual and Motor Skills*, February 1972, *34*, 231–232.

Henderson, M. G.   *Progress report on reading study 1952–55*. Champaign, Ill.: Board of Education, 1955.

Jeffrey, W. E., & Samuels, S. J.   The effect of method of reading training on initial learning and transfer. *Journal of Verbal Learning and Verbal Behavior*, 1967, *6*, 354–358.

Jenkins, J. R., Bausell, R. B., & Jenkins, L. M.   Comparison of letter name and letter sound training as transfer variables. *American Educational Research Journal*, 1972, *9*, 75–86.

Johnson, D. D., & Pearson, P. D.   *Teaching reading vocabulary* (2nd ed.). New York: Holt, Rinehart & Winston, 1984.

Jongsma, E.   *The cloze procedure as a teaching technique*. Newark, Del.: International Reading Association, 1971.

Karlin, R.   *Teaching elementary reading*. Chicago: Harcourt Brace Jovanovich, 1971.

Kaufman, M.   Comparison of achievement for Distar and conventional instruction with primary pupils. *Reading Improvement*, Fall 1976, *13*, 169–173.

Klein, H. A.   The role of material level on the development of word identification. *Journal of Psychology*, 1976, *94*, 225–232.

Klein, G. A., & Klein, H. A.   Word identification as a function of contextual information. *American Journal of Psychology*, 1973, *86*, 399–406.

Klein, H. A., Klein, G. A., & Bertino, M.   Utilization of context for word identification: Decisions in children. *Journal of Experimental Child Psychology*, 1974, *17*, 79–86.

Klein, H. A., Klein, G. A., & Doris, A.   Some developmental trends in context utilization. In *Proceedings 81st annual convention, American Psychological Association*. Washington, D.C.: American Psychological Association, 1973.

LaBerge, D., & Samuels, S. J.   Toward a theory of automatic information processing in reading. *Cognitive Psychology*, 1974, *6*, 293–323.

Mason, J. M.   Questioning the notion of independent stages in reading. *Journal of Educational Psychology*, 1977, *69*, 288–297.

McCullough, C. M.   Learning to use context clues. *Elementary English Review*, 1943, *20*, 140–143.

McCullough, C. M.   The recognition of context clues in reading. *Elementary English Review*, 1945, *22*, 1–5.

McDowell, J. B.   A report on the phonetic method of teaching children to read. *Catholic Education Review*, 1953, *51*, 506–519.

Montgomery, D.   Teaching prereading skills through training in pattern recognition. *Reading Teacher*, 1977, *30*, 616–623.

Morgan, E., & Light, M.   A statistical evaluation of two programs of reading instruction. *Journal of Educational Research*, 1963, *57*, 99–101.

Muller, D.   Phonic blending and transfer of letter training to word reading in children. *Journal of Reading Behavior*, 1973, *5*, 13–15.

Norton, D. E., & Hubert, P.   *A comparison of the oral reading strategies and comprehension patterns developed by high, average, and low ability first grade students taught by two approaches—phonic emphasis and eclectic basal*. College Station: Texas A & M University, 1977. (ERIC Document Reproduction Service No. ED 145 393)

Otterman, L. M.   The value of teaching prefixes and word-roots. *Journal of Educational Research*, 1955, *48*, 611–616.

Pearson, P. D., & Studt, A.   Effects of word frequency and contextual richness on children's word identification abilities. *Journal of Educational Psychology*, 1975, *67*, 89–95.

Potts, M., & Savino, C.   The relative achievement of first graders under three different reading programs. *Journal of Educational Research*, 1968, *61*, 447–450.

Railsback, C. E.   Consonant substitution in word attack. *Reading Teacher*, 1970, *23*, 432–435.

Ramsey, W.   *Evaluation of assumptions related to the testing of phonics skills*. St. Louis: National Center for Educational Research and Development, 1972. (ERIC Document Reproduction Service No. ED 068 893)

Rentel, V. M., & Kennedy, J. J.   Effects of pattern drill on the phonology, syntax, and reading achievement of rural Appalachian children. *American Educational Research Journal*, 1972, *9*, 87–100.

Resnick, L. B.   *Theory and practice in beginning reading instruction*. Pittsburgh: Pittsburgh University, 1977. (ERIC Document Reproduction Service No. ED 149 292)

Russell, D. H.   A diagnostic study of spelling readiness. *Journal of Educational Research*, 1943, *37*, 276–283.

Schell, L.   Teaching structural analysis. *Reading Teacher*, 1967, *21*, 133–137.

Schvaneveldt, R., Ackerman, B. P., & Semlear, T.   The effect of semantic context on children's word recognition. *Child Development*, 1977, *48*, 612–616.

Sexton, E. K., & Herron, J. S.   The Newark phonics experiment. *Elementary School Journal*, 1928, *28*, 690–701.

Sherwin, J. S.   Research and teaching of English. *English Record*, 1970, *21*, 2.

Skjelfjørd, V. J.   Teaching children to segment spoken words as an aid in learning to read. *Journal of Learning Disabilities*, 1976, *9*, 297–306.

Smith, F.   *Understanding reading: A psycholinguistic analysis of reading and learning to read* (2nd ed.). New York: Holt, Rinehart & Winston, 1978.

Smith, N. B.   What research says about phonics instruction. *Journal of Educational Research*, 1957, *51*, 1–9.

Smith, N. B.   *Reading instruction for today's child*. Englewood Cliffs, N.J.: Prentice-Hall, 1963.

Spache, G. D., & Baggett, M.   What do teachers know about phonics and syllabication? *Reading Teacher*, 1966, *19*, 96–99.

Spache, G. D., & Spache, E. B.   *Reading in the elementary school* (4th ed.). Boston: Allyn & Bacon, 1977.

Sparks, P. E.   *An evaluation of two methods of teaching reading*. Unpublished doctoral dissertation, Indiana University, 1956.

Stauffer, R. G. (Ed.),   *The first grade reading studies: Findings of individual investigations*. Newark, Del.: International Reading Association, 1967.

Steiner, R., Wiener, M., & Cromer, W.   Comprehension training and identification for poor and good readers. *Journal of Educational Psychology*, 1971, *62*, 506–513.

Sternberg, R. J., Powell, J. S., & Kaye, D. B.   Teaching vocabulary-building skills: A contextual approach. In A. C. Wilkinson (Ed.), *Classroom computers and cognitive science*. New York: Academic Press, in press.

Sullivan, H. J., Okada, M., & Niedermeyer, F. C.   Learning and transfer under two methods of word-attack instruction. *American Educational Research Journal*, 1971, *8*, 227–239.

Tate, H. L.   The influence of phonics on silent reading in grade 1. *Elementary School Journal*, 1937, *37*, 752–763.

Timian, J. E., & Santeusanio, R. P.   Context clues: An informal inventory. *Reading Teacher*, 1974, *27*, 706–709.

Tirre, W. C., Freebody, P., & Kaufman, K.   *Achievement outcomes of two reading programs: An instance of aptitude treatment interaction* (Tech. Rep. No. 174, University of Illinois at Urbana-Champaign). Cambridge, Mass.: Bolt Beranek and Newman, 1980.

Valentine, C. W.   Experiments on the methods of teaching reading. *Journal of Experimental Pedagogy*, 1913, *2*, 99–112.

Weber, R. M.   First-graders' use of grammatical context in reading. In H. Levin & J. P. Williams (Eds.), *Basic studies on reading*. New York: Basic Books, 1970.

Weinstein, R., & Rabinovitch, M. S.   Sentence structure and retention in good and poor readers. *Journal of Educational Psychology*, 1971, *62*, 25–30.

West, R. F., & Stanovich, K. E.   Automatic contextual facilitation in readers of three ages. *Child Development*, 1978, *49*, 717–727.

Williams, J. P.   Teaching decoding with an emphasis on phoneme analysis and phoneme blending. *Journal of Educational Psychology*, 1980, *72*, 1–15.

Winch, W. H.   Teaching beginners to read in England: Its methods, results, and psychological bases. *Journal of Educational Research Monographs*, 1925, No. 8. Bloomington, Ill.: Public School Publishing Company.

Witty, P., & Kopel, D.   Factors associated with the actiology of reading disability. *Journal of Educational Research*, 1936, *29*, 449–459.

Wohleber, Sister M.   *A study of the effects of a systematic program of phonetic training on primary reading*. Unpublished doctoral dissertation, University of Pittsburgh, 1953.

Zuck, L. V.   Some questions about the teaching of syllabication rules. *Reading Teacher*, 1974, *27*, 583–588.

20 RESEARCH ON TEACHING READING COMPREHENSION .

Robert J. Tierney and
James W. Cunningham

INTRODUCTION

The present chapter represents an update of an earlier attempt (Tierney & Cunningham, 1980) to address the "state of the art" relative to research on teaching reading comprehension. The reading researcher and practitioner will find the chapter a review of what we know about reading-comprehension instruction, and a framework for addressing the adequacy and promise of existing and forthcoming lines of inquiry. Two basic questions drive our discussion: With whom, in what situations, and in what ways does teaching improve reading comprehension? How should research in teaching reading comprehension proceed?

Our purpose is threefold: (1) describe the nature and distribution of research in teaching reading comprehension in the context of stated and/or implied instructional goals, (2) consider issues of methodological significance as they emerge, and (3) suggest some reasonable guidelines for future research in accord with rising research interests and alternative approaches to investigation. To these ends, we adopt two discussion headings which represent the nature and scope of this research in terms of two fundamental goals for instruction: increasing comprehension from text and increasing ability to comprehend from text. The former reviews the large array of studies which examine the efficacy of teacher intervention intended to improve students' ability to understand, recall, or integrate information from a specific text passage or passages. The latter addresses those studies whose goal is to improve general and specific reading-comprehension abilities which will transfer to students' reading of passages they later encounter on their own. The two discussions will then merge in the final section of the paper, which addresses considerations for future reading-comprehension instructional research.

During its inception we recognized that a review which exhausted the literature was neither realistic nor within the bounds of our goals. Instead we decided
that studies cited in the context of our remarks should be selected largely for
their representativeness, significance, or promise. And, with respect to research
paradigms, an attempt was made to include descriptive studies dealing with
theoretical issues of relevance to teaching reading comprehension, empirical
studies involving such prototypical methodology as treatment-group comparison,
and discussions relating aspects of pedagogical intuition. To these ends, we believe
the present review is comprehensive.

INCREASING COMPREHENSION AND LEARNING FROM TEXT/PROSE

It is the purpose of this section to highlight research which studies instructional
intervention as a means to improve students' understanding, recall, and integration of information stated in or inferable from specific text passages. Our review
of such interventions includes prereading activities, guided reading activities,
and postreading activities. Note that we have drawn a distinction between activities or strategies based upon when intervention takes place. This distinction might
be characterized in the following trichotomy: building background knowledge;
activating readers' existing background knowledge and attention focusing *before*
reading; guiding reader/text interactions *during* reading; and providing review,
feedback, or cognitive stimulation *after* reading.

Prereading Activities

Most reading lessons include a prereading activity which provides a bridge of
sorts between a reader's knowledge base and the text. Most lesson frameworks
used in conjunction with basals and content-area textbooks consider this step a
preparatory one in which purpose setting and concept development are primary
goals. In principle, most of these activities are directed at the reader's background
knowledge; implicitly, they reflect at least tacit acceptance of the role of background knowledge and the importance of building and activating readers' knowledge before reading (see Anderson & Armbruster, this volume).

Building Background Knowledge Prior to Reading

When readers apparently lack the prior knowledge necessary to read, what can
be done to compensate? Three suggestions appear most often in instructional
literature: teach vocabulary as a prereading step; provide experiences, vicarious
or otherwise, which fill in and expand upon students' existing knowledge; or
introduce a conceptual framework analogous to that of the text which will enable
students to build appropriate background for themselves.

Preteaching vocabulary.   An enduring piece of conventional wisdom in
reading education is the recommendation that students be taught crucial word
meanings prior to encountering them in text. In most directed reading lessons

which accompany basals and content-area textbooks, introduction to new vocabulary is an integral first step. As Bridge (in press) suggests, introduction to new vocabulary is perceived as serving "the function of arousing previous conceptual associations and providing new associations . . . to help students to relate the unfamiliar concepts to familiar ones." In a similar vein, Pearson and Johnson (1978) describe such activities as providing anchors for new information. Or as Beck, McKeown, McCaslin, and Burkes (1979) have suggested, teaching vocabulary is a specialized aspect of developing background knowledge essential for comprehension and is widespread in most reading programs. In fact, one person (Becker, 1977) has recommended that disadvantaged students be taught 25 word meanings per week, starting in third grade and continuing through twelfth grade, in order to compensate for the students' lack of conceptual knowledge.

The fact that vocabulary development is such a widespread instructional focus may be partially a function of that research which alludes to the relationship between vocabulary and reading comprehension. Correlations between knowledge of word meanings and ability to comprehend passages containing those words, between knowledge of word meanings and verbal intelligence, as well as between word difficulty and passage difficulty are all high and well established. (For a review of this work, see Anderson & Freebody, 1981; Davis, 1971.) These relationships have been further demonstrated by studies which show that not only do good and poor readers appear to differ with respect to knowledge of word meanings (Belmont & Birch, 1966), but also replacing high-frequency words with low-frequency synonyms in texts decreases subjects' passage comprehension (Freebody & Anderson, 1981a, 1981b; Marks, Doctorow, & Wittrock, 1974; Wittrock, Marks, & Doctorow, 1975). A strong relationship between meaning vocabulary and comprehension still obtains, even when intelligence is held statistically constant (Johnston, 1981; Vineyard & Massey, 1957). Such evidence, of course, fails to establish knowledge of word meanings as a *cause* of comprehension. Direct support for a causal relationship must be sought in the several instructional studies which have investigated the effect of preteaching vocabulary on passage comprehension.

Comprehension studies employing prereading instruction in word meanings have been both successful and unsuccessful in accomplishing a significant effect. While any conclusions drawn from an analysis of only a few studies should be seen as tentative, several characteristics seem to distinguish effective from ineffective programs. Preteaching vocabulary in order to increase learning from text probably requires that the words to be taught must be key words in the target passages (Beck, Perfetti, & McKeown, 1982; Kameenui, Carnine, & Freschi, 1982), that words be taught in semantically and topically related sets so that word meanings and background knowledge improve concurrently (Beck, Perfetti, & McKeown, 1982; Stevens, 1982), that words be taught and learned thoroughly (Beck, Perfetti, & McKeown, 1982), and that only a few words be taught per lesson and per week (Beck, Perfetti, & McKeown, 1982; Kameenui et al., 1982; Stevens, 1982). Attempts to teach word meanings without determining that they are key to the target passages (Ahlfors, 1980; Pany & Jenkins, 1978), without teaching word meanings and background knowledge concurrently (Ahlfors, 1980; Evans, 1981; Jenkins, Pany, & Schreck, 1978; Pany & Jenkins, 1978), without teaching words thoroughly (Evans, 1981; Jenkins et al., 1978; Pany & Jenkins,

1978; Tuinman & Brady, 1974), or without teaching only a few words per lesson or per week (Evans, 1981; Jenkins et al., 1978; Pany & Jenkins, 1978; Tuinman & Brady, 1974) are probably doomed to failure.

These conclusions lead us to question the practice of cursorily introducing new word meanings before having students read. This practice is probably only justified when just one or two crucial words are taught at some depth. Rather, to be effective, an extensive and long-term vocabulary strand accompanying a parallel schemata or background-knowledge-development strand is probably called for. Instead of preteaching vocabulary for single passages, teachers should probably be preteaching vocabulary and background knowledge concurrently for sets of passages to be read at some later time. In effect, this recommendation would result in a type of "spiral curriculum" (Bruner, 1960) wherein knowledge and vocabulary taught about a topic would assume knowledge and vocabulary learned previously about that topic and provide knowledge and vocabulary on which later knowledge and vocabulary about that topic could be built.

Our conclusions must remain tentative, however, for what is lacking in the research on teaching vocabulary is a substantial data base which addresses the subtleties and various effects which arise from vocabulary instruction across a variety of classroom situations.

Enriching background knowledge. Intervention research has supported the existence of a causal relationship between background knowledge and comprehension. McWhorter (1935), cited in Smith (1963), provided enriching experiences to children lacking in background of information and noted significant improvement in reading. McDowell (1939), cited in Smith (1963), improved reading readiness for kindergarten students by providing them with an "enriched curriculum." Graves and his associates (Graves & Cooke, 1980; Graves & Palmer, 1981; Graves, Cooke, & La Berge, 1983) developed previews for short stories that had, as one component, the building of prior knowledge important to understanding the selection. These several experiments produced data documenting that reading the previews before reading the stories increased students' learning from stories by a significant and impressive amount. Stevens (1982) increased learning from text compared with a control group for tenth-grade students reading a history passage by teaching them relevant background information for that passage. Hayes and Tierney (1982) found that presenting background information related to the topic to be learned helped readers learn from text regardless of how that background information was presented or how specific or general it was.

Unfortunately, while these studies support the notion that background knowledge development *can* improve comprehension and learning from text, they do not together or separately give us very clear or very specific guidelines on how to build background knowledge prior to having students learn from text. It is not certain what steps should be taken in determining what background knowledge a written selection requires, what quantity or quality of that knowledge a set of learners has or lacks, or what particular approach to use in developing that background knowledge for those learners. Furthermore, a number of issues need to be resolved before effective practices for developing background knowledge to increase reading to learn can be established: direct versus symbolic experience, direct versus incidental instruction, explicit versus inductive instruction, and so on. Obviously, more instructional research employing background-knowledge development before reading to learn is called for.

Analogy. A specialized instance of enriching background is the use of analogy. Analogy might be defined as an expositional method for comparing sets of information which are similar enough in essential respects to permit transposition of attributes across sets, usually from familiar to unfamiliar information. The classroom being what it is, explanation must often suffice for experience. Teachers, therefore, have long operated under the assumption that while explanation via analogy is not a substitute for experience, it affords a practical means for introducing students to unfamiliar information in the context of a familiar framework. Many philosophers (Black, 1962; Campbell, 1920) and psychologists (Rumelhart & Ortony, 1977), especially those advocating a schema-theoretic point of view, concur on this point.

Despite the potential utility of analogy claimed by educators, philosophers and psychologists, research on its pedagogical efficacy has been examined by only a few studies and many of these studies have only indirectly explored analogy's use in reading comprehension. In a listening situation, Vosniadou and Ortony (in press) showed that analogies are effective mechanisms for acquiring new information but their worth varied in accordance with their "goodness of fit." In problem-solving situations, several researchers have examined the effect of reading analogous story problems (e.g., Gick & Holyoak, 1980, in press; Perfetti, Bransford, & Franks, 1983). They have shown that many individuals fail to access analogies unless prompted to do so or presented with more than a single analogical possibility. Several studies have dealt with analogy only indirectly and results from these studies are mixed and rather unrevealing. For example, Dowell (1968) and Drugge (1977) found no significant effects stemming from instructional use of analogy, whereas Mayer (1975) and Royer and Cable (1975, 1976) obtained results which favored the advance presentation of analogous material on readers' comprehension of other passages. Of most direct relevance to reading comprehension, the most positive evidence of the value of analogy comes from a study by Ausubel and Fitzgerald (1961) who found a superiority for readers given an advance expository passage on an analogous familiar topic and from a study by Hayes and Tierney (1982) who found that students given different modes of presenting or embedding analogous information had an advantage on certain transfer measures over students not given analogies. Hayes and Mateja (1981) replicated this latter finding for immediate and delayed posttest measures using different materials. Taken together, the results suggest that if analogy is to be used effectively to increase comprehension or background knowledge as a requisite for comprehension, care must be taken on several points: (a) one must alert students to the analogy or passages with analogies which could possibly prompt readers to notice the relationship or "fit" between two sets of information, (b) the presentation of the analogous information matters—it is likely that different modes will have different impacts, and (c) the methods used to assess effects may influence the conclusions one draws. In terms of our third point, we hold that any research attempting to improve background knowledge needs to consider that a complex interaction will exist among teaching methodology, texts, topics, and readers. Also, the influence of changes in background knowledge of the familiar or unfamiliar information may be subtle and difficult to measure without on-line as well as posttest measures sensitive to such variations. Apart from providing students with analogies in the text they read, researchers might consider training students to create their own analogies. We are unaware of any research which has studied when and how readers might enlist their own analogies to improve their own reading comprehension.

Activating Background Knowledge and Attention Focusing

If readers have the necessary background knowledge prior to reading to learn, what can or should be done to activate that knowledge or focus attention in order to expedite their learning from text? Many theorists and practitioners advocate strategies which encourage students actively to relate the new information they gain from reading to their prior knowledge. Such strategies are based on the assumption that learning is a constructive rather than a merely reproductive process. A number of suggestions for activating background knowledge have arisen. Many are directed to teachers, a very few are directed to students, and still fewer are directed to texts (or rather to text authors). For the purposes of discussion, we have selected the following as illustrative of teacher initiated/ directed strategies for activating background knowledge: advance organizers, objectives, and pretests and prequestions. From among those strategies indicative of student generated/monitored activity, we will consider student-centered discussion and student generated questions and purposes. With respect to text adjuncts we will discuss prefatory statements, pictures, and titles.

Advance organizers.   One of the most widely researched and controversial strategies designed to activate a reader's background knowledge is that of the advance organizer, proposed by Ausubel (1963, 1968). In Ausubel's (1968) words, the intent of the advance organizer is "to bridge the gap between what the reader already knows and what the reader needs to know before he/she can meaningfully learn the task at hand" (p. 148). Based upon Ausubel's theory of verbal learning, which posits the existence of hierarchically organized cognitive structures, the function of the organizer is to provide ideational scaffolding for the stable incorporation and retention of the more detailed and differentiated material that follows in the passage. In a practical sense, its purpose is to prepare readers to gain information from reading they could not have otherwise gained (Bransford, 1979).

Ausubel (1978) has suggested that for advance organizers to function effectively, they must be written at a higher level of abstraction or generality than the material to be learned, address the conditions of their specific use, account for both the reader's existing subsumers and the unfamiliar concepts presented within the text, and take into account those factors involved in posttesting. In the case of unfamiliar material, Ausubel prescribes the use of an expository organizer to provide "relevant proximate subsumers." With familiar material, he suggests a comparative organizer to facilitate the integration of new ideas and to increase discrimination between ideas.

There is some evidence that advance organizers affect the subsequent learning of some students some of the time with some texts when readers have some prerequisite knowledge (Ausubel, 1978; Bransford, 1979). However, despite the fact that several hundred research studies and any number of synthesis attempts have explored the differential worth of advance organizers, we still lack any "real" closure regarding their instructional value. Over the years researchers intent on synthesizing the bulk of advance organizer research have resorted to extensive literature reviews (Barnes & Clawson, 1975; Hartley & Davies, 1976; Lawton & Wanska, 1977; Mayer, 1979) and, most recently, meta-analysis, a statistical technique suggested by Glass (1978) to standardize and compare treatment effects (Luiten, Ames, & Ackerson, 1980; Moore & Readence, 1980). One such review of the research by Sledge (1978), which focused on the use of advance organizers with secondary students, reported that the majority of studies did not favor advance organizers and, in studies for which differences did favor advance organizers, less capable students benefited most. A more recent synthesis, a meta-analysis which examined trends across 135 advance organizer studies (Luiten et al., 1980), suggested the following: most advance organizer treatment groups tended to perform better than control groups; the effect of advance organizers had a variable impact across special education, elementary, secondary, and college students; the impact of aural and visual organizers varied with the age level of students; and the effect of advance organizers tended to increase rather than decay over time.

Two major problems have had the effect of diminishing the worth of most individual advance organizer research studies and synthesis attempts. The first problem, the lack of a clearly specified operational definition of advance organizers, has left advance organizer research largely nonreplicable. Theoretical position papers, research reviews, and research reports have virtually failed to provide either teachers or researchers with specific guidelines for developing advance organizers. Unfortunately, Ausubel (1978) suggests that "apart from describing organizers in general terms with an appropriate example, one cannot be more specific about the construction of an organizer. For this always depends on the nature of the learning material, the age of the learner, and his degree of prior familiarity with the learning passage" (p. 251). These "general terms" to which Ausubel refers are scattered throughout his writings and in what appears to us to be poorly articulated examples. The result is such that for any single text, a variety of advance organizers might be generated and the differential effect of any one might become a legitimate research question. Clark and Bean (1982), after arguing the seriousness of this problem, called for theorists and researchers to employ text analysis and free-recall measures of comprehension and learning to define operationally advance organizers.

The second problem relates to the global nature of those questions researchers tend to ask about advance organizers. Given Ausubel's warning with respect to the differential nature of learning material and varying needs of learners, it seems misguided for researchers and practitioners to continue to explore the efficacy of the advance organizer without regard for the different potential effects these variables may have. Questions should be pursued that go beyond the general issue of whether or not advance organizers work. Clearly, only in the context of examining a variety of data across a variety of specific texts and types of learners can researchers hope to develop descriptions which address the instructional and theoretical significance of the advance organizer in a useful manner. Literature reviews and meta-analyses already suggest that, while advance organizers tend to increase conceptual learning and problem solving, they decrease recall of technical information and specific details (Mayer, 1979, 1983) and that advance organizers are of more benefit to older and more able learners than they are to younger and less able ones (Luiten et al., 1980). More recently, research studies have found that advance organizers aid sixth graders who can selectively attend, but not those with selective attention deficits (Borer, 1981), and that EMR adolescents benefit more when reading to learn from an advance organizer than they do from a traditional introduction (Peleg & Moore, 1982). Clearly, more research in how advance organizers interact with text characteristics, learner characteristics, and type of learning desired is called for.

In content classes, such as social studies and science, there exists a hybrid of the advance organizer—the structured overview—whose widely advocated use deserves some comment. In theoretical papers, both Barron (1969) and Earle (1969b) proposed the development and use of a visual overview to introduce students to the concepts and relationships represented within a text or a unit within a course. They proposed that the overview incorporate the terms arranged in outline form effectively to highlight to students the content of a text or unit, including its logical structure. In so doing, it was believed that the overview assumed the properties of Ausubel's advance organizer, that is, it related "new content to relevant subsuming concepts that have previously been learned" (Barron, 1969, p. 33). Fortunately, structured overviews are operationally defined more clearly than traditional advance organizers. Unfortunately, to date the research dealing with the effectiveness of these graphic overviews suffers from one of the same major problems ailing advance organizer research—namely, the probes which have driven the research have failed to examine systematically the impact of the strategy beyond whether or not it works. Studies conducted so far have provided support that under certain conditions with certain students structured overviews have a positive effect on learning (Dean-Guilford, 1981; Kelleher, 1982; Moore & Readence, 1980); however, these investigations have provided little in the way of specific guidelines for developing, using, or evaluating structured overviews. In general, students with high verbal ability seem to benefit more from structured overviews and they seem to work better with expository passages (Moore & Readence, 1980), but there are exceptions. The issue of the *quality* of the structured overview in determining its effect on learning from text has yet to be adequately addressed.

Another hybrid of the advance organizer—the story preview—has been developed by Graves to be used with students before they read to learn stories in either literature or reading classes. In research conducted by Graves and his associates, story previews have been shown to increase learning from stories for high- and low-ability fifth- and sixth-grade students (Graves & Palmer, 1981); for low-ability seventh- and eighth-grade, inner-city students (Graves, Cooke, & LaBerge, 1983); for tenth-grade, rural students (Hood, 1981); and for eleventh-grade, suburban students (Graves & Cooke, 1980). In reviewing this work, Graves and Slater (1981) concluded that story previews generally have a moderate and positive effect on story comprehension and retention, especially when the stories being read are difficult for the students. They also concluded that story previews can assist students in making inferences from their reading and that, in general, students like them. Story previews seem a promising intervention for activating background knowledge and attention focusing before having students read to learn from stories. The story preview is operationally defined, and initial investigations have attempted to determine how well story previews work for students of different ages and abilities.

Objectives.   Providing students with objectives before they read is a practice that has long been advocated by reading educators under the heading "setting purposes for reading." Common sense would suggest that providing students with objectives before they read to learn will enhance that learning (Levin & Pressley, 1981) on the assumption that if students know what they are expected to learn, they will tend to pursue their learning more systematically. The few studies which have used objectives as a prereading intervention to increase learning from text have generally supported their use. Duell (1974) found that students receiving detailed purposes for reading in advance learned targeted, unimportant information better than students who were just told they would have to take a multiple-choice test after reading. There was no difference between groups in their learning of targeted, important information. Borer (1981) found that behavioral objectives help sixth-grade students who can attend selectively, but not those with selective attention deficits. Maier (1980) found that giving learning-disabled students purposes for reading increased their learning of two folk tales.

Objectives do appear to focus readers' attention on the information targeted by the objectives, as evidenced by the fact that they have a positive learning effect on targeted information (intentional learning) and a negative learning effect on untargeted information (incidental learning) (Petersen, Glover, & Ronning, 1980). If teachers know what they want students to learn from reading a specific text, using prereading objectives/purposes to focus students' attention seems a good idea; if teachers do not know what they want students to learn or if they want them to learn everything, using prereading objectives/purposes seems a bad idea. Beyond this rather general advice based on common sense and a few studies, little can be said. What kinds of objectives there are, how to formulate or match them to specific passages, and their effect on different types and ages of learners are questions without even tentative answers.

Pretests and prequestions.   Two teacher-directed preinstructional strategies somewhat related to objectives are pretests and prequestions. In the context of the classroom, both pretests and prequestions tend to be used most frequently for purposes of assessment. But as Pressey (1926) points out, questions asked prior to reading a text can serve a learning producing function as well. Specifically, Pressey (1926) has claimed that pretests increase a student's sensitivity to learning by alerting him or her to the nature of the task and its relevance as well as providing a means to evaluate, categorize, or generalize.

The claim that pretests and prequestions have a beneficial effect upon learning continues to be supported empirically, although with qualification. There is a general pretest effect (Willson & Putnam, 1982). Moreover, as Anderson and Biddle (1975), Hartley and Davies (1976), Levin and Pressley (1981), and Rickards (1976) suggest, pretests (often in the form of adjunct prequestions) can have a facilitative effect if the material to be read is difficult to comprehend (Hartley & Davies, 1976; Levin & Pressley, 1981) *and* if the goal of the pretest is intentional learning (to have students learn only the information from reading which is necessary to answer the pretest questions) (Anderson & Biddle, 1975) *and* if the information tested on the pretest is among the most important in the text (Rickards, 1976). If, on the other hand, the goal is to improve general understanding and retention of a passage, pretests and prequestions tend to have a restricting effect on incidental learning (Anderson & Biddle, 1975). One may suppose, therefore, that if students know something about the topic to be learned, if the material to be used is difficult for them to read, and if the teacher wants students to gain specific learnings from reading, then either a pretest or prequestions in advance of reading will likely facilitate subsequent learning from that text. When prequestions are given to students *again* after they read, as postquestions, their effect on intentional learning can increase (White, 1981).

Such a claim, however, falls short of addressing the issue of variability across texts, readers, and teachers in the following respects. First, whatever effects pretests may have, it is doubtful they can overcome the lack of prerequisite information necessary to process a text. Logically, a pretest can only be expected to facilitate activation of existing knowledge if a reader has such knowledge (Bransford, 1979). Second, pretests and prequestions interact with passages to produce differential effects (Richmond, 1976). The relationships which exist between questions and texts are obviously complex and cannot be considered realistically outside the purposes for which the questions are posed, as well as the purposes for which the answers to them are interpreted. Like research on advance organizers and objectives, research on prequestions and pretests awaits further elaboration.

Student-centered reading activities.   The three previous subsections have discussed prereading instructional strategies which tend to be teacher directed in nature; for while they may address student-related issues, they are nonetheless generated and/or directed on behalf of students rather than by students. We wish to contrast this approach to activating students' background knowledge and attention focus with that of student-centered prequestions, predictions, and discussion of purposes for reading. As is the case with most prereading activities, student-centered prequestions, predictions, and discussion are principally directive in their effect. They differ, however, from teacher-directed preactivity, in that their intended function is to encourage and make use of spontaneous student response in terms of directing both the focus of activity and its outcome. And, characteristically, these procedures result in some degree of student-teacher and/or peer interaction, as opposed to simple exchanges limited to one-way question-response sequences. In the main, student-centered prereading activities are based on the notion that such activity has the potential to activate problem-solving behavior (i.e., inquisitiveness) as well as the ability and desire to examine ideas and generate alternatives.

Most basal reading lessons and a number of reading educators advise teachers to begin with either selected questions or a discussion of the story topic designed to facilitate student-teacher and peer interaction in the context of the reading lesson. Stauffer's (1959, 1969) Directed Reading-Thinking Activity

(DR-TA) is one such procedure where purpose setting together with interaction are integral. As Stauffer has described the approach:

> . . . either the reader declares his own purposes or if he adopts the purposes of others, he makes certain how and why he is doing so. He also speculates about the nature and complexity of the answers he is seeking by using his fullest experience and knowledge relevant to circumstances. Then he reads to test his purposes and assumptions. (Stauffer, 1969, p. 40)

Another recommended strategy, Manzo's (1969) ReQuest Procedure, uses a simple questioning format whereby students are given the opportunity to generate as well as respond to questions based upon a text selection or a portion of it. The procedure is typically done in pairs, student-teacher or individual students, and as sections from a text are read silently, each participant, in turn, poses a number of questions based upon his or her reading.

Research examining the efficacy of procedures similar to those described above provides some support for student-generated questions and discussion, but little mention is made with regard to either the type of text and student for which specific procedures are most appropriate or the extent to which the rationale for each such procedure is justified. For example, Manzo (1970) and Manzo and Legenza (1975) found general support for the use of the ReQuest Procedure with kindergarten children and poor readers. Palincsar (1982) supported the use of a variation of this procedure with seventh graders. Similarly, Bisken, Hoskisson, and Modlin (1976) reached the general conclusion from their study that first- and third-grade Title I children learned considerably more from passages taught by the DR-TA than from listening to the stories without discussion. Davidson (1970) and Petre (1970) found a similar advantage for the DR-TA over other types of directed reading lessons for fourth-grade students of different ability groups.

Outside the context of research based on selected strategies, there has been little support for the student-centered approach until more recently. Using both immediate and delayed passage-dependent recall questions, Chodos, Gould, and Rusch (1977) found that having fourth-grade students generate four questions from a brief summary of a passage before they read the passage significantly improved the students' learning of that passage as well as their ability to maintain what they had learned. Using a paradigm suggested by Swaby (1977), Schachter (1978) used discussion to link "to be read text" with prior experience. Swaby (1977) had presented sixth-grade students, prior to their reading a passage, with a written statement designed to create a link to prior experience. The procedure did not facilitate comprehension, but Swaby speculated that a discussion of prior experiences may have had an effect—especially an effect on inferential comprehension. Schachter (1978) took Swaby's suggestion and examined the impact of linking with prior experience through discussion. As predicted, Schachter's procedure yielded results which reflected an enhancement of inferential comprehension.

In general, research on student-centered prereading activities leaves us with an overriding concern. Despite the fact that informal prequestioning and discussion are widespread classroom practices, we could find little research which examined the effect of these activities as actually carried out in classrooms on students' learning from reading. Durkin (1978–1979) and Guszak (1967) describe teacher-questioning, but the effect of teacher-questioning behavior upon students is not clear.

Pictures, prefatory statements, and titles.   To what extent do pictures, prefatory statements, and titles (text adjuncts described by Hartley and Davies [1976] as content clarifying) improve a reader's ability to learn information in a specific text? While it is clear that such adjuncts can provide relevant contextual information and thereby improve comprehension for ambiguous or unclear passages (Arnold & Brooks, 1976; Bransford & Johnson, 1972, 1973; Bransford & McCarrell, 1974), it is less clear whether they are effective aids when the adjunct reiterates information provided directly in the prose (Aulls, 1975). Certainly, no one argues that having students read titles, prefatory statements, or illustrations makes them better comprehenders in any general sense (Jenkins & Pany, 1981), but there does exist evidence both to support and disclaim their facilitative effect when students are reading to learn from text.

With respect to pictures, Samuels concluded in 1970 that there was "almost unanimous agreement that pictures, when used as adjunct to the printed text, do not facilitate comprehension" (p. 405). Since that time, Thomas (1978) investigated the effectiveness of pictorial illustrations as adjunct aids in science texts using fourth-grade students of three ability levels as subjects; he found the illustrations to have no facilitative effect. Marr's research (1979) led her to a similar conclusion, namely, that it is often the case that pictures fail to have a facilitative effect on learning.

In contrast, a growing number of studies have found evidence to the contrary. Specifically, pictures have been shown to increase the prose learning of: (a) young children when their effect is measured in terms of responses to short-answer questions (Guttmann, Levin, & Pressley, 1977; Lesgold, Levin, Shimron, & Guttmann, 1975; Levin, Bender, & Lesgold, 1976); (b) fourth-grade students, (Peeck, 1974); (c) sixth-grade students, as measured by main idea responses (Koenke & Otto, 1969); (d) undergraduates (Dwyer, 1968; Snowman & Cunningham, 1975); and (e) the retarded (Bender & Levin, 1978; Riding & Shore, 1974). These and other studies have led Ruch and Levin (1977) and Levin and Lesgold (1978) to argue strongly in support of the notion that pictures have a facilitative effect on children's learning from prose. This effect is said to be a special effect for pictures over and above an effect due to more repetition of ideas (Levin et al., 1976).

The picture becomes murky when one considers that Rasco, Tennyson, and Boutwell (1975) found a facilitative effect for pictures but suggested that true effects were confounded with subjects' use of strategies. Dwyer (1967, 1968, 1969, 1971, 1972) found that not only were some pictures more effective than others, but also suggested that even when pictures were effective, they caused learners to slow down. We might argue that since strategy utilization arose from picture use, the relationship between picture and strategy use may be worthwhile to pursue as a positive effect rather than as a confounded outcome. Several of these studies have used listening rather than reading modes and assumed results were generalizable. When Readence and Moore (1980) meta-analyzed those studies where pictures were used when subjects read to learn (as opposed to listening to learn), they found the effect size for those studies to be generally positive but nonetheless quite small. Clearly, pictures do not have an equally facilitative effect for all subjects (Levin, Divine-Hawkins, Kerst, & Guttmann, 1974).

It is the differential effect of pictures in interaction with a host of variables that leads us to conclude again that certain students, when reading certain texts for certain purposes with certain adjunct aids, are helped dramatically by those aids; however, such facilitative effects are significantly reduced when no regard is given to the likelihood of interaction. Indeed, this conclusion seems quite compatible with one Schallert (1980) reached following a review of the role of illustrations in prose comprehension. She stated:

> . . . where research has found pictures to be helpful, the illustrations have seemed to be related to the text in certain ways. A reasonable hypothesis is that pictures are likely to help readers learn from written material if they represent spatial information or information that is important to the total message. In addition, there may be differences in the effectiveness of illustrations between situations in which the information to be derived from a picture is explicitly repeated by the text and situations in which the text provides merely the framework for certain information left to be derived from appropriate illustrations (p. 519).

Accordingly, she suggests that three issues need to be addressed: How might the information represented in pictures be measured? What kind of information should be represented in pictures? How do students read or learn to read pictures? These and other questions about the effect of pictures on learning from text have yet to be answered (Brody, 1980; Duchastel, 1980).

Research findings are in a similar state with respect to titles and prefatory statements. With children and adults as subjects, neither titles nor prefatory statements (Christensen & Stordahl, 1955; Cole, 1977; Landry, 1966) were found to have a facilitative effect on comprehension. Conventionally written introductions did not increase learning from text for EMR adolescents (Peleg & Moore, 1982). In contrast, studies by Doctorow, Wittrock, and Marks (1978) as well as Memory (1979) suggest that the inclusion of titles and prefatory statements provide certain adolescent readers advantages in terms of their ability to recall and answer selected questions. Kosoff (1981) found that different types of prefatory statements failed to increase learning from text but that *scripturally implicit* introductions increased the integration of prior knowledge with textual information in subjects' recalls. Unfortunately, in all but a few studies, we are given only sparse descriptions of the adjunct aid and the teacher, text, and reader variables. Rarely were multiple measures employed to address systematically the impact of the adjunct aid upon strategy use during and comprehension after reading.

Guiding Reader/Text Interactions during Reading

A variety of interventions have been used by teachers and researchers in an attempt to influence how readers process text in order to increase comprehension.

Among these interventions are those adjuncts and activities which accompany the presentation and processing of the to-be-read text. Essentially such adjuncts and exercises appear to have a twofold purpose: increasing the extent to which to-be-learned material is accessible to readers and improving students' ability to comprehend the text. We shall address briefly each of the following: inducing imagery, inserted questions, self-questioning, and oral reading, lesson frameworks, and study guides.

Inducing Imagery

In a recent paper, Tierney and Pearson (1983) argued that as an aid to comprehension readers and writers might try to visualize a scenario from the vantage point of an eyewitness or character in a story. Unfortunately, direct evidence of the worth of their suggestion is restricted to examining the effects of such encouragement in rather constrained text situations. The attempts at so doing in experimental situations suggest that imaging may not facilitate learning from text for very young children (Dunham & Levin, 1979; Gambrell, 1982) or even for adolescent EMR students (Bender & Levin, 1978). It may be that these students cannot image on command or that they do not learn well from pictures (Levin et al., 1974). This seems quite likely since a number of studies demonstrate that careful instructions and/or training to image can improve prose learning of third-grade students (Gambrell, 1982; Lesgold, McCormick, & Golinkoff, 1975; Pressley, 1976, 1977); fourth-grade students (Lesgold, McCormick, & Golinkoff, 1975; Levin, 1973; Lin, 1982); and fifth- and sixth-grade students (Gambrell, Koskinen, & Cole, 1981; Kulhavy & Swenson, 1975; Lin, 1982; Linden & Wittrock, 1981; Mazur-Stewart, 1983; Pressley, 1977). Other studies have found a facilitative effect for readers imaging about prose with twelfth-grade students (Anderson & Kulhavy, 1972; Mazur-Stewart, 1983) and college students (Steingart & Glock, 1979). While it must be noted that there are imagery-inducing strategies which do not help learning from text (Tirre, Manelis, & Leicht, 1979), that with longer passages it is difficult to get readers to maintain an imaging strategy (Anderson & Kulhavy, 1972), and that students who do not learn well from pictures do not seem to benefit from imaging (Levin et al., 1974), it seems fair to conclude that inducing imagery is likely to increase learning from text for selected students in and above grade 3.

In 1971, Paivio expressed concern for the fact that imagery researchers could only speculate about the instructional effects of imagery. Now there is sufficient data for educators to be optimistic that imaging activity is effective. However, given that most increases in learning from prose due to inducing imagery are slight and given that some students apparently have difficulty imaging, more research needs to be conducted in which the two concerns are addressed: (a) a variety of effects are examined; (b) care is taken to determine and describe how well imagery is induced. At the same time researchers might begin to explore the nature and role of spontaneous imaging by students as well as other vicarious reading experiences (e.g., identification with characters, the sensation of being "on the page," and so on).

Inserted Questions

Providing students with questions during reading is a common instructional practice. In an attempt to guide students' reading of a text selection, teachers frequently stop students who are in the process of reading to pose a number of text-related questions. These questions are often either retroactive in nature, requiring the reader to refer to something just read, or proactive, requiring the reader to read ahead in order to search out an answer or confirm a prediction.

Research seems to bear out teachers' intuitions concerning the facilitative effect of inserted questions. Hershberger's (1964) original study and Rothkopf's follow-up work (1966) have not only provided a great deal of research impetus in the area of questioning, but also have clarified the role of inserted questions in reading to learn. Hershberger's (1964) original investigation reported that students given self-evaluative review questions outperformed a control (i.e., no-question) group on a posttest based on those same questions. This issue has since been examined by Rothkopf (1966, 1971, 1972a), who initiated a number of studies addressing the direct influence of questions inserted in text. Rothkopf's line of research and methodology prompted a rash of investigations (Boyd, 1973; Frase, 1967, 1968; Frase, Patrick, & Schumer, 1970; McGaw & Grotelueschen, 1972; Rothkopf & Bisbicos, 1967; Rothkopf & Bloom, 1970; Snowman & Cunningham, 1975; Graves & Clark, 1981; White, 1981) which, with few exceptions, confirm that students responding to inserted factual questions perform better on those same questions given as a posttest than students who only read the text passage. Further, when the questions which are given involve applying information gleaned from text, students who respond to the questions both in the inserted and the posttest situations perform better not only on the application questions, but also on the others as well (Watts & Anderson, 1971).

Of interest to educators, however, is not just the fact that inserted questions have an effect. Since the strategy is used by a great many teachers on a day-to-day basis, it seems imperative that their use be examined more closely. The available research provides only partial information on the value of inserted questions across different texts and purposes for reading, especially if time on task is held constant (Carver, 1972). Only a limited number of studies have addressed the type of attention-focusing functions inserted questions prompt as well as the extent to which learning is tied to attention or vice versa (Britton, Westbrook, & Holdredge, 1978; Reynolds & Anderson, 1980; Reynolds, Standiford, & Anderson, 1979). Too few studies have examined the effectiveness of using questions within classroom settings—for example, their value with repeated use and the worth of questions tied to a rational model of the text or reader.

Self-Questioning

In an earlier section, we addressed self-questioning and purpose-setting strategies as they occur in prereading situations. We shall now extend that discussion to include literature which deals with self-questioning *during* reading.

Research-based information on self-generated questions is not only conflicting, but also far from complete. Studies by Duell (1974) and Morse (1976) demonstrated that college students induced to self-question had no advantage over other students not induced to question, while André and Anderson (1978–1979), Frase and Schwartz (1975), Schermerhorn, Goldschmid, and Shore (1975), and Weiner (1978) found reason to support their use. Darwazeh (1983) found self-generated questions inferior to teacher-generated ones. There are a number of reasons why a more comprehensive and rigorous research program is needed to investigate further the effects of self-questioning as a prose-learning strategy. First, very few studies to date have trained students to ask questions or given them the opportunity to practice that strategy. In those studies where training did take place, peer training procedures were most often used. Second, in some instances, the instructions which were given to students severely limited the types of questions students would tend to ask. This criticism would hold with respect to both the Frase and Schwartz (1975) study—where students were required to identify those lines from the text that contained answers to their questions—and the Weiner (1978) study—where students were asked to generate a singular set of question types across different texts—with little regard for the idiosyncratic purposes for which the students might be reading. Third, and typical of reading comprehension instructional studies, very few self-questioning studies have used more than a single achievement measure to assess the effectiveness of a self-questioning strategy. And no study used text-analysis methodology to indicate the different types of inferences students generated. Fourth, a majority of the studies failed to use a sufficient number of comparison groups to separate out the effects of different components of the question-generation process. In summary, as Weiner (1978) has suggested in the conclusion of her paper, analyzing training programs, comparing various types of strategies, and using multiple-comparison groups and different measures of effect across a variety of texts are essential if we are to make explicit what has only been implied about the strategy of self-questioning. A recent study on self-questioning and other strategies by Palincsar and Brown (1983), which is discussed later in this chapter, addresses some of these issues.

Oral Reading, Lesson Frameworks, and Study Guides

While questioning strategies are undoubtedly the most widespread approach to guiding student-text interactions during reading to learn, with imagery-inducing strategies achieving a less frequent second place, there are countless other adjunct devices and practices suggested in the literature. We will comment briefly upon three which are frequently recommended for classroom use: oral reading, lesson frameworks, and study guides.

Oral reading. When students find a textbook difficult to read, teachers often ask that those students read the textbook aloud. This is not only an observed classroom practice, but also one to which teachers readily admit. Research on oral reading as a strategy is sparse and equivocal, although there exists a slight edge in favor of oral reading over silent reading for purposes of comprehension. Poulton and Brown (1967) and Rogers (1937) found no differences between learning from text after oral reading as compared with silent reading, while Collins (1961), Elgart (1978), Graham (1979), and Rowell (1976), all found comprehension and retention to be superior after oral reading for students at several different age levels. We found no studies which examined the differential effects oral reading might have had upon recall of explicit and likely to-be-inferred information across texts read for different purposes by students of varying abilities. Nor did we find any students that addressed the long-term effects of oral reading versus silent reading in classrooms where boredom, inattention, and other factors might mediate the apparent superiority of oral reading.

Lesson frameworks.   Cunningham (in press) and Cunningham, Moore, Cunningham, and Moore (1983) have suggested, based upon their analyses of lesson frameworks, that there are four steps essential for comprehension lessons to be effective:

Step 1: Establish purpose(s) for comprehending.
Step 2: Have students read or listen for the established purpose(s).
Step 3: Have students perform some task which directly reflects and measures accomplishment of each established purpose for comprehending.
Step 4: Provide direct informative feedback concerning students' comprehension based on their performance on that (those) task(s).

They also concluded that many, but not all, effective comprehension lesson frameworks have a readiness step preceding Step 1:

Readiness Step: Cue access to or develop background knowledge assumed by the text.

Similar steps are apparent in several widely used and highly recommended learning frameworks. For example, the Directed Reading Activity (Betts, 1946), the DR-TA (Stauffer, 1959, 1969), and the Guided Reading Procedure (Manzo, 1975), recommend lesson formats with similar phases to content teachers and publishers as strategies for aiding students in their efforts to learn from text as well as for guiding the development of teacher's editions for basals. While they may be designed to provide readers with a way to approach a text, they are as much an aid to teachers as to students.

Despite their widespread use and advocacy, there is a dearth of research based on these practices. In two experiments with seventh-grade poor readers in a geography class, Bean and Pardi (1979) found better learning from text when the Guided Reading Procedure was used in combination with prereading assessment and structured discussion. Biskin et al. (1976) found that first- and third-grade Title I students remembered story elements better after being engaged in a DR-TA than after listening to the stories without discussion. Also, Davidson (1970) and Petre (1970) examined student responses and found results which favored the DR-TA over the Directed Reading Activity (DRA) with fourth-grade students—especially higher-ability students. Lovelace and McKnight (1980) also found DR-TA to be effective.

Because the directed reading activity is essentially a set of prequestions given to students before they read and then given to the students again as postquestions after they read, the literature on prequestioning and postquestioning can be said to evaluate indirectly the DRA. Anderson and Biddle (1975) concluded from their review that prequestions facilitate learning for the information sought by the questions and that postquestions facilitate learning for all textual information. Additional indirect support of the DRA comes from White (1981) who compared getting the same questions prereading *and* postreading with getting them just prereading or just postreading and found the before-and-after questioning superior to the other two approaches and a control condition. Sachs (1981) actually compared a version of the DRA with a worksheet activity and found the DRA superior.

Recently, several new lesson frameworks have appeared for teachers to use in aiding students to learn from reading. Stetson (1981) used Survey-Read-Recite-Record-Review (S4R) as a lesson framework in three pilot studies with different types of subjects and found that it increased learning from text dramatically. Hansen (1981) and Hansen and Pearson (in press) used a strategy method, a question method, and a combined method to increase inferential comprehension during reading to learn. Beck, Omanson, and McKeown (1982) reported that their redesigned DRA was superior to the DRA they found in a basal reading series.

While these lesson frameworks are supported both by tradition and the existing research, a multitude of questions remain. Not only is it not clear why or what part of each framework is causing learning from text to occur, but also little research exists to guide the users of these frameworks in matching frameworks with different learners or with different texts. Nor is it clear how teachers actually implement these frameworks in classrooms.

Study guides.   Study guides are widely advocated adjuncts to textbook material. As described by Earle (1969a) and Herber (1970, 1978), study guides use various adjunct activities and questions to structure as well as guide students' reading of difficult subject matter prose. It is the purpose of a study guide to facilitate readers' understanding of text content while improving their ability to deal with patterns of ideas (cause and effect; comparison and contrast; sequence or time order; and simple listing) as well as levels of text presentation. While there is not an extensive body of research on the effectiveness of study guides at this time, several studies involving some permutations of this methodology have produced encouraging but differential results. Namely, for some subjects on some variables with selected texts, study guides have proven effective (Anthony, 1981; Berget, 1977; Carney, 1977; Estes, 1970, 1973; Maxon, 1979; Phelps, 1979; Riley, 1979; Vacca, 1977). With the growth of interest in cataloging text characteristics as well as describing readers' inferences with and without adjuncts, research should be forthcoming which will provide the differential information needed to examine those intuitions which prompted Herber's and Earle's original rationales for study guides. At the present, however, research does not show how different types of guides might and should be developed to facilitate prescribed reading outcomes.

Teacher Interventions Following Reading

There undoubtedly exists as much variability within teacher interventions following reading (postreading activities) as between postreading activities and either prereading or during-reading activities. This state of affairs seems reasonable since postreading activities have come to imply anything from recall exercises tied exclusively to explicit information represented by the text to long-term projects of an applied nature, which may be only tangentially related to what has been read. Under the assumption that such activities will provide for the retention, reinforcement, extension and/or application of previous learnings from text, teachers are frequently encouraged to consider postreading activity an integral part of reading to learn. A perusal of most basal reading material, content area texts, and lesson frameworks will confirm this observation. The notion of postreading activity raises the issue of whether interventions occurring after the fact have any influence upon student performance. Furthermore, do they do what they purport to do? We will attempt to pursue these issues as we address the effects of a select group of postreading strategies.

Postquestions

Anyone who has visited public school classrooms very much will recognize this scenario: students are assigned to read a selection from a textbook, either in class or for homework; the teacher then asks a series of oral questions based on that selection which the students answer orally or assigns students a series of written questions to answer (generally with their books closed); at some later time, the students take a test which includes questions based on that selection.

Experimental results addressing the effect of postquestions upon student learning are quite conditional, as one would suspect. As in the case of inserted questions, students responding to postquestions perform better on those same questions given as a test than students who only read the passage. The facilitative effect of postquestions on "intentional learning" is reported by Anderson and Biddle (1975) to have occurred in 37 out of 40 such studies they examined. Nungestor and Duchastel (1982) found postquestions far superior to simple text review in producing intentional learning. Likewise, Ellis, Konoske, Wulfeck, and Montague (1982) found postquestions superior to prereading instruction on intentional learning. Results in the context of "incidental" learning, however, are much more equivocal. While Anderson and Biddle (1975) reported that 26 out of 39 studies found a facilitative effect of postquestions on new questions appearing on a later test, they did demonstrate that the size of this effect was less than dramatic. In addition, others suggest that postquestions might under some circumstances have a restrictive effect on incidental learning (Frase, 1975; Hiller, 1974; Rothkopf, 1972b; Sagaria & DiVesta, 1978; Wixson, 1981).

Another factor related to the issue of postquestioning is question focus/ question type. Rickards (1976) found that postquestions derived from information with high structural importance in a selection facilitated intentional learning from text; however, questions based on information of low structural importance did not. Watts and Anderson (1971) and Rickards and Hatcher (1977–1978) suggest that application-type or meaningful learning questions facilitate intentional learning while rote-learning questions do not. Friedman (1977); Yost, Avila, and Vexler (1977); and Denner (1982) report that "higher-level" questions produce a greater learning effect than "lower-level" questions. Biskin et al. (1976) consider reflective questions, such as those used by the Great Books Foundation (1967), to enhance comprehension and retention of stories.

It is less clear what other factors might interact with the effect of postquestioning upon learning. Richmond (1976) found the effect differed across passages. Watts (1973) found the effect diminished as the time increased between postquestioning and testing. Shavelson, Berliner, Ravitch, and Loeding (1974) found better readers gained much less than poorer readers from postquestioning.

Based on what evidence we do have, however, it seems reasonable to conclude that if teachers use text materials which students find challenging, if teachers know specifically what they want students to learn from that material, and if what teachers want students to learn is information which the author also deems important, it is likely that teachers can facilitate learning by asking application-type or inference questions based on such text-derived information, assuming such facilitation is measured by a test which asks the same questions and assuming little time elapses between postquestioning and testing. Related to classroom practice, however, very few studies have examined the value of sets of related questions tied to either the pedagogical assumptions inherent within published reading programs or the discourse flow within texts, for example, networks of inferences and their prerequisite textual information.

Feedback

When students answer questions or take posttests based on what they have read, teachers typically provide feedback, that is, let students know how well they have performed. In general, research supports this practice. Gagné (1978), Kulhavy (1977), and LaPorte and Voss (1975) all conclude that feedback which occurs subsequent to postquestions or posttests results in greater gains in learning than when feedback does not follow such activity. The timing of such feedback, however, does not appear to be a significant factor (Gagné, 1978; Kulhavy, 1977). Rather, it is the quality of feedback which most often results in its differential effects. While this may seem counterintuitive, Kulhavy (1977) and Barringer and Gholson (1979) note that it is feedback following wrong answers which has the most dramatic effect on learning. In fact, LaPorte and Voss (1975) found that feedback did not increase students' learning for questions correctly answered, but did for those questions which were incorrectly answered. Further, Barringer and Gholson (1979) have shown verbal feedback to be consistently superior to tangible feedback with respect to conceptual learning, but as Kulhavy (1977) has pointed out, if students can cheat (obtain feedback *before* answering the questions) or if material is too difficult, feedback will matter little if at all. These findings, as they stand, are quite interesting. It would be useful, however, to extend this research to address the questions of *how* learners use feedback following reading to learn and to what degree students need to understand and/or be convinced by feedback for it to have a facilitative effect on learning.

Group and Whole-Class Discussions

Beyond postquestioning and feedback, there are numerous other postreading strategies teachers use as a means of facilitating comprehension. Discussion bears specific mention as it surfaces in some form or another during a great many of them. From the initiation of group projects to the culmination of such individual pursuits as book reviews, teachers frequently either schedule group discussion of some preread text or assign projects which will necessitate interaction to some degree. Support for the use of discussion as a strategy to increase learning from text emerges, but quite indirectly, through research related to group discussion.

A study which examined the use of guide material and small-group discussion with social studies text led Estes (1970, 1973) to suggest there were no direct benefits from small-group discussions. In contrast, a study by Vacca (1977) which incorporated the use of group discussion, claimed that group discussion together with the specific text material and study guide upon which it was based was both productive and beneficial in terms of the student's acquisition of content. Galda (1982) found discussion superior to drawing for primary-grade students. And Barron and Melnick (1973), in a longitudinal vocabulary study in the area of biology, alluded to the differential effectiveness of teacher-led full-class discussion and student-led small-group discussion. They suggested that both the full-class discussion and the small-group discussion were better than no discussion but that whole-class discussion tended to be easier to operationalize given specific guidelines and a purpose for the discussion.

Intuitively it would seem that the effects of discussion, when it occurs as part of some larger postreading activity, are confounded somewhat due to the likelihood that discussion facilitates some aspects of the activity and the activity, in turn, feeds into discussion. Further, the effects of discussion as a postreading activity in and of itself have yet to be fully addressed. Researchers should be encouraged to examine discussion's influence upon reading to learn, strategy acquisition, the nature of a reader's interpretation, and the reader's self-initiated pursuits. In so doing, they should remain cognizant of both the significance of discussion in the light of other classroom strategies and the nature of reader-text-teacher interactions. This implies measuring systematically the impact of the text before, during, and after discussion as well as the characteristics of the group—for example, cohesiveness, composition, goals, purposefulness, inquiry orientation, and nature of peer-teacher interactions.

INCREASING ABILITY TO COMPREHEND AND LEARN FROM TEXT/PROSE

A principal question in research on comprehension and learning from text/prose is: What teacher interventions before, during, and/or after reading can increase what students learn from their reading beyond what they might learn when reading without such interventions? A principal question in research on improving students' ability to comprehend what they read is: What teacher interventions can increase students' ability to comprehend or learn from new passages (passages students must handle on their own) beyond the increase which might occur when students simply read independently? Clearly, the concern here is with transfer: Can students be taught knowledge, skills, or strategies that will transfer to their reading of passages with which teachers have not helped them?

In one sense, any study on reading can be viewed as a potential source for instructional implications, in which case the term instructional research on reading is synonomous with the term research in reading. If, however, it is worthwhile to distinguish between the two, then instructional research must be characterized as that which tends toward more direct and obvious implications for reading instruction than those studies whose only link to instruction is that subjects read text. Certainly, it is important to know what the characteristics of good and poor readers are and what the characteristics of comprehensible texts are. Further, it is important to know how classrooms function during reading instruction and the nature of practices presently in use. It seems, however, that such knowledge is only useful when it is examined in the context of what *causes* readers to comprehend better than they would under other circumstances.

Just four years ago, we suggested that there was a dearth of research which addressed the issue of improving students' independent comprehension abilities. Since that time the number of studies which have pursued this issue have multiplied. In our past review, we suggested that the studies with which we were familiar fell into two categories: (1) metacomprehension and inference training and (2) meeting the text-based needs of readers. At that time we felt that our categories were adequate to encompass what we believed was the domain of this research. Our present categorization represents a more specific breakdown of the nature of the pursuits which have emerged.

Enhancing Comprehension Strategies of Readers

Comprehension strategies can be defined as those cognitive activities which good readers engage in to foster comprehension. Specifically, comprehension strategies might include: engaging background knowledge, goal setting, identifying task demands, allocating attention, evaluating content, self-appraisal, self-correction, predicting, self-questioning, and so on. While the pursuit of these strategies seems a rather obvious goal of any comprehension instructional program, our review of instructional research and programs has found only a few attempts to develop deliberate use of such strategies by readers.

Engaging Prior Knowledge

As we have discussed in previous sections of the present review, the notion of prior-knowledge engagement has been a recurring theme or activity for helping students prepare for a selection. In recent years, the research on metacomprehension has prompted researchers to consider ways they might encourage students to monitor their engagement of prior knowledge. With this as a goal, there have emerged a number of curriculum projects (e.g., Langer, 1982; Smith-Burke & Ringler, in press) in which teachers are directed to help students monitor what they know and to consider how this knowledge might be integrated with the text. Unfortunately, substantial research evidence to recommend these pursuits is lacking. For still unanswered from the research is whether students will spontaneously engage in such activities without teacher prompting, except in situations similar to those within which training has occurred. Consider the research evidence to this point.

A study by Hansen (1981) examined the effectiveness of instruction intended to make second-grade students more aware of how their prior knowledge might be enlisted in story comprehension. Based upon the work of schema theorists

(Anderson, Reynolds, Schallert, & Goetz, 1977) and others (Brown, 1977; Omanson, Warren, & Trabasso, 1978; Paris & Lindauer, 1976; Riley & Trabasso, 1974), Hansen set up three treatment groups. A control group received a mixture of literal and inferential questions. A question group received a "steady diet" of inferential questions. A strategy group focused on integrating text and background knowledge prior to reading. In this third condition, students received the traditional question diet but, prior to each story were asked to do the following: (1) relate what they would do in circumstances similar to those which would be upcoming in the story, (2) predict what the main character in the story would do, (3) write down on strips of paper (1) + (2) which would be then woven together. By weaving together the strips of paper, Hansen hoped to make students more conscious of the fact that reading involves weaving together what one knows with what is in the text. After ten stories across a 40-day period, Hansen's treatments were tested on a variety of measures, including passages intended to assess the transfer value of the training. In general, the results she obtained reflected a rather localized effect due to the treatment conditions and little, if any, effect as measured on transfer tasks. As rationalization of these results, Hansen questioned whether it was reasonable to expect students to apply spontaneously the training strategies.

In a follow-up study, Hansen and Pearson (in press) pursued a similar study with fourth-grade students whose teachers they trained to administer the treatments. Also the treatment in which teachers were trained represented a combination of the strategy-training and inference-question approach. Their results suggested an advantage of the treatment condition over the control condition, especially for the poor readers. On inference measures embedded within the instructional materials as well as on measures from three new passages, the poor readers exceeded their control counterparts. Together with the data from the earlier study, Hansen and Pearson suggested that the data supported the worth of strategy training for younger readers or poor older readers; other older readers, they suggested, may not need such instruction.

A study by Gordon (1979) looked into the effects of an even more explicit attempt to improve the readers' ability to engage prior knowledge. She compared the effects of two intervention strategies upon 42 fifth-grade students. One treatment focused on activating and fine tuning prior knowledge for instructional selections along with an awareness of text structure (helping students develop a sense of the framework for a story). The second treatment focused on providing students with strategies for inferring. A control group received the normal language-related curriculum. In general, Gordon's results were consistent with the findings of Hansen (1981) and Hansen and Pearson (in press). On inference items, including transfer items, the inference-treatment group fared best: on recall measures, the background-knowledge group fared best.

Carr (1983) tested a comprehension improvement program consisting of three procedures: a structured overview, cloze, and a self-monitoring checklist. These procedures were selected and combined to train subjects to activate background knowledge, find information in the text and relate it to background knowledge, and to organize new information in a hierarchical structure. This total strategy improved students' ability to infer on passages not taught in the treatment in both immediate and delayed testing.

Identifying Task Demands

Metacomprehension research findings suggest that successful readers are more aware of the strategies they use during reading than less successful readers. On the basis of this finding an argument can be made for heightening the reader's awareness of task demands. With this as their rationale, a study by Raphael and Pearson (1982) examined instruction in the use of a strategy intended to make readers more aware of the task demands of questions accompanying story selections. During four 45-minute sessions, students from three grade levels (fourth, sixth, and eighth) were taught to differentiate questions which required them to locate the answer in the text (labeled "right there"), derive an answer from one's own background knowledge (labeled "on my own"), and derive answers that involved inferring relationships between text segments (labeled "think and search"). Over the duration of the treatment, trained students surpassed an "orientation only" group in the quality of their responses to questions (except textually implicit or "think and search" questions), performance on other measures, and their use of the question-answering strategy they were taught.

Allocating Attention: Summarizing

A number of studies have pursued transfer training in conjunction with improving summarization skills. Because a summary of a text or text section is selective and abstractive, it is logical to assume that learning to summarize texts might actually cause readers to be able to allocate their attention better to important information when reading. Several attempts at improving summarization ability have been made.

One such study by Day (1980) was reported by Brown, Campione, and Day (1981). Working with low-ability community college students, Day studied the effectiveness of summarization training with and without explicit cueing intended to facilitate self-monitoring. Specifically, college students were given either: (a) encouragement to summarize and capture main ideas, (b) instructions for modeling certain rules, (c) instructions for modeling certain rules and encouragement, or (d) instruction for modeling certain rules and rules for using these rules. Across pretest and posttest measures, Day found that providing students rules for summarizing influenced the students' abilities to summarize, detect main ideas, and delete trivial information, but the influence of this training varied with the sophistication of the students. In other words, although all students profited from the training conditions, less sophisticated students (students with writing problems) needed more explicit training (i.e., training in the rules and their application). As Brown, Campione, and Day reported:

> Training results in greater use of the rules, and improvement is effected with less explicit instruction with more advanced students. For those students with more severe learning problems, training results in less improvement and more explicit training is needed before we can get any effect of training. (1981, p. 16)

In a similar vein, Taylor (Taylor, 1982; Taylor & Beach, in press) conducted a series of studies in which intermediate grade-level students were instructed to build summaries of expository text by relating the superordinate and the subordinate information. Across the various studies, a modest transfer effect was found within content area but not across content areas.

Cunningham (1982) compared the (GIST) procedure to a placebo with regard to its effectiveness in improving fourth-grade students' ability to write one-sentence summaries of paragraphs. GIST differs from other instructional methods for teaching summarization, in that students are taught no explicit rules. Rather, they are led through a systematic procedure for developing summaries designed to enable them to induce whatever the rules for summarization are. In Cunningham's study, experimental subjects were better at composing one-sentence summaries than control subjects after nine days of treatment.

General Metacomprehension Training

In recent years a number of developmental psychologists have examined the role of heightening the awareness of students in conjunction with comprehensive studies of reading-comprehension instruction. The two studies which we describe in this section are representative of the creativity with which such pursuits are being undertaken and their variations. Palincsar (1982) pursued the deliberate control of four comprehension strategies (summarizing, self-questioning, predicting, clarifying unclear text) with seventh-grade poor readers. Across three related studies, Palincsar enlisted a reciprocal teaching method where the teacher and students took turns assuming the role of teacher in a dialogue centered on pertinent features of texts. In Study 1 and Study 2, the investigator worked with students in pairs. In Study 3, four reading teachers worked with students in small groups in their classrooms. Across baseline, intervention, maintenance, and follow-up condition, students who received strategy training acquired a great deal of facility with the strategies. They typically achieved 70% accuracy by the fifteenth day of training and the effects of the training carried over to other measures including transfer measures and delayed posttests. For example, modest but reliable transfer gains were apparent on tasks similar to but distinct from, the training tasks and on regular classroom assignments.

On a different scale, Lipson (1982) and Paris (1982) developed a 20-week "course" designed to improve third- and fifth-grade students' understanding and control of comprehension strategies. At the heart of the course was the use of a variety of metaphors intended to make the various strategies more concrete for students. For example, they would develop bulletin board displays tied to metaphors, such as "Being a Reading Detective," "Reading Is Like a Puzzle," "Following Reading Maps." These metaphors would then be applied by the students in conjunction with sets of focal questions and other guidelines. The results of the study are quite encouraging. Those students who were involved in strategy training proved more capable at using the various strategies than control-group subjects and outperformed the control group on various measures, including various transfer measures and measures administered several months after instruction ceased.

Future Research on Enhancing Comprehension Strategies

Although the results of the studies done so far are encouraging, much work in the area of instructional research on enhancing comprehension strategies of readers remains. The strategies researched to date do not represent the universe of behaviors readers might employ across different texts. Also, it is not clear yet what is required for students to acquire self-initiated and flexible control over any or all strategies in transfer situations.

We have serious reservations about the degree to which many of the studies assume the worth of explicit teaching of strategies (Pearson & Gallagher, 1983). Teaching children our theories about how they think in order to get them to think better seems to us to be fraught with danger. It is true that we should be concerned with process, but to the extent that comprehension is like gardening, we must be more interested in the vegetables produced than the tools in the shed. Student understanding is more important than tacit or meta-understanding.

Likewise, we are concerned with the narrowness with which learning how to learn is currently defined. *Identifying task demands, allocating attention,* and *metacomprehension* have broad social dimensions that have to do with real-world requirements like completing homework and seatwork adequately and on time as well as taking turns, and not interrupting others when they are working; in short, behaving in a student-like manner.

Finally, we are uneasy with the linear and mechanical approach to presenting reading to students. However the brain functions, the experience of reading has all the components of art and experience. To date our comprehension instruction has tended to emphasize the systematic, sequential, and piecemeal at the expense of the aesthetic, experiential, vicarious, and the wonder of reading.

Meeting Text-Based Needs of Readers

Given that certain readers have difficulty dealing with certain text features, there has been a tendency for researchers to subscribe to one of two approaches: either pursue instruction which will prepare students to process better texts with these features or develop text in such a way as to avoid such difficulties. Those studies adopting the former approach are a potential source of instructional implications for improving the ability of readers to comprehend or learn from passages not taught.

Improving Sentence-Level Processing

Several studies have attempted to increase comprehension and text-learning ability by treatments that seem primarily aimed at improving students' sentence-level processing. Such studies ranged from a study by Weaver (1979) that had subjects rearrange jumbled sets of words into sentences to having students pursue sentence combinations. Studies of the latter type have tended to predominate.

Sentence combining/sentence reduction.   Disenchanted with the methodology associated with teaching writing via formal grammar, but nonetheless encouraged by the interrelationships shown to exist between syntax and reading, many have come to acclaim sentence combining as a potential means for improving both writing and reading comprehension (Combs, 1975; Mellon, 1969; O'Hare, 1973). In terms of improving reading comprehension, sentence combining and its more recent counterpart, sentence reduction (Ney, 1976), is based upon the assumption that sensitizing students to the methods by which ideas are expressed and related in text will likely develop their ability to comprehend text structures. Unfortunately, attempts to validate these notions have produced limited results due to what we perceive to be a failure on the part of researchers to reflect upon those situations and measures which training in sentence combining would most likely influence. A study by Howie (1979) is an appropriate example. Howie attempted to examine the influence of sentence combining and sentence reduction upon the reading comprehension of ninth-grade students. Howie obtained no impact upon cloze reading performance nor any significant gains on the Gray Oral Reading Test. Howie attempted to rationalize these results by questioning whether the influence of sentence combining upon reading could be measured.

Three studies using fourth-grade students as subjects illustrate the same shortcoming and the equivocal nature of the findings so far on the effectiveness of sentence combining in increasing reading-comprehension ability. Crews (1971) compared an extended sentence-manipulation treatment with a traditional grammar program and found no difference in silent reading ability between the two treatment groups. Machie (1982), however, found that sentence-combining groups did better on the Gates-MacGinitie Primary Reading Test than did a traditional composition group. Straw and Schreiner (1982) reported that sentence combining affected growth on a transfer cloze test and on both writing and listening measures but not on the Nelson-Denny Reading Test when compared to instruction in a basal language arts series.

Apart from the failure of past research to enlist measures likely to be sensitive to sentence-combining training, we believe that these conflicting outcomes resulted from the fact that sentence combining/sentence reduction can only be expected to improve reading-comprehension ability for those students who have special problems with syntactic processing. If a study happens to include such students as subjects, the treatment will probably be effective; if a study happens not to include them, the treatment will probably not be effective.

Improving Text-Level Processing

A number of instructional studies have evolved from recent developments in the area of text analysis. Two main lines of research have emerged, one primarily concerned with informational or expository text and one primarily concerned with stories.

Structure of ideas.   Most text analysis procedures for use with exposition attempt to provide a diagrammatic representation for the patterns of ideas structured in text. Four such thrusts, networking (Dansereau, 1979), mapping (Anderson, 1978), flowcharting (Geva, 1980), and rhetorical structures (Meyer, 1975), have been adapted for use as instructional tools. Students use text cues to define the fundamental relationships as they manifest themselves in expository text. Networking, mapping and flowcharting require students to diagram how the ideas and their relationships are represented within text; rhetorical structuring requires students to label these patterns as well as identify the hierarchy of ideas. Apart from these four approaches, a more common classroom strategy for schematically representing collected key ideas, their interrelationships, and subordinates is the structured overview (Barron, 1969; Earle, 1969b). Used as a prereading or postreading activity, the structured overview frequently serves as a device for presenting or organizing the key ideas from a textbook unit in a diagrammatic form.

Studies examining mapping (Armbruster & Anderson, 1980) and the creation of structured overviews (Baker, 1977; Barron, 1971; Berget, 1977; Earle, 1969c, 1973; Estes, Mills, & Barron, 1969; Vacca, 1977; Walker, 1979) have yet to address whether these strategies have any transfer value to passages which are not mapped or overviewed. Studies which have addressed the transfer value of other such strategies are few in number. Studies by Dansereau, Holley, and Collins (1980); Geva (1980); and Margolis (1982) have provided some data supporting the transfer value of training in the use and application of diagrammatic representations of text. Among the most encouraging sets of findings, however, are those offered by Bartlett (1978) and Mosenthal (1983) who coupled their instruction on texts with a consideration of author's purpose.

Bartlett, for example, examined the effects of teaching ninth-grade students to recognize commonly found rhetorical structures and their purpose on subjects' ability to identify and use these structures in their own recall protocols and on the amount of information they could remember. The instruction focused on how to identify and use four commonly found top-level structures in classroom text. Special aids for identifying the top-level structure were faded out over the week of instruction, while the passages studied became increasingly more complex. Students in the training group and control group read and recalled passages prior to training, one day after the training program and three weeks after the completion of the program. The instruction resulted in significantly increased use and identification of the top-level structure as well as almost a doubling in the amount of information recalled by the training group on the posttest measures.

Mosenthal (1983) examined the influence of teaching students procedures for analyzing an author's goals against the text itself. Experimental and control training methods were contrasted in two comparable sections of an eighth-grade course in physical science and in two comparable sections of a sixth-grade social studies course. Training occurred over a six-week period. Experimental and control conditions were identical, except for the inclusion of discussion and questioning related to discerning the writer's goals. Across the various baselines, training, posttest, and delayed posttests, experimental students maintained a consistent advantage, which was greatest for those texts identified as most difficult.

Structure of stories.   Although Gates (1947) recognized the importance of a "story sense" in student comprehension of narratives, it was not until 30 years later that explicit teaching procedures were forthcoming to aid readers' development and use of a sense of story. In 1978, Cunningham and Foster reported a series of encounters between a classroom teacher and a reading education professor in which the teacher sought help from the professor in guiding her poorest readers' comprehension of the high-interest/low-vocabulary short stories they read each day in their reading group. The college professor suggested that the teacher use a simplified version of a story schema/grammar as a generic reading guide with this group of students. The teacher reported that these bottom students liked reading stories in order to complete the slots in the generic reading guide and that she believed they were improving in their ability to understand the stories they were reading. Dreher and Singer (1980) criticized Cunningham and Foster on the ground that they did not formally evaluate the effectiveness of their classroom application before reporting it. Moreover, they suggested that, if such an evaluation had been conducted, the generic reading guide for stories would not have been an effective treatment. Their evidence for this assertion was the report of a study they conducted with a range of intermediate students using a different approach to story grammar instruction. In their study, students' comprehension did not improve as a result of their treatment. They concluded, based on their study, that there is little if any need for story grammar instruction with intermediate elementary students because they already have a well-developed sense of story.

More recently, Bowman (1981) found that a story structure questioning strategy improved the reading-comprehension ability of sixth-grade students when reading folktales as compared to a control group who received traditional questions at three levels. Fitzgerald and Spiegel (1983) identified 20 average and below-average fourth-grade students lacking a keen sense of narrative structure and randomly assigned them to experimental and placebo treatments. The experimental group developed enhanced story structure knowledge and were superior to the control group on transfer measures of reading comprehension.

Based on the few studies done so far, it seems safe to conclude that story grammar instruction (loosely defined) can, but does not necessarily, improve reading-comprehension ability. We see the current controversy in this area as centered on two questions:

(1) Are there students beyond first grade who still lack a keen sense of story?
(2) Is the availability of story schemata sufficient for comprehension of stories?

Regarding the first question, Dreher and Singer (1980) conclude that there are few if any, while Fitzgerald and Spiegel (1983) report having found that at least 20 percent of their fourth-grade students lacked such a sense. Regarding the second question, Dreher and Singer (1980) conclude that since intermediate students have an internal sense of story structure, story grammar instruction is unjustified, while Hoover (1982) has concluded that:

> . . . improvement in the ability to deal with story information does not appear to be attributable to the developmental acquisition of schemata but rather to its increased accessibility, engagement, and efficiency as a processing and production mechanism. [abstract]

It would appear that some readers have a keen sense of the structure of stories and can use this sense; other readers appear to lack such a sense of story or fail to use it effectively. We hope future instructional research will delineate more carefully the characteristics of subjects with regard to their knowledge and use of the structure of stories.

Future Research on Meeting Text-Based Needs

Research which addresses the domain of meeting text-based needs of readers is in its infancy. While research has provided some clarification of those text characteristics which influence comprehension and results from training studies seem encouraging, we contend that scholars interested in the area of "text" have just begun to move into research which addresses the question:

> Can students be taught knowledge, skills, or strategies which will meet their text-based needs and transfer to their reading of unfamiliar passages?

Researchers need to undertake concurrent analyses of: (a) the discourse features evident in the texts which students encounter, (b) an examination of the type of situation within which these features either enhance or detract from learning, (c) the strategies successful readers might enlist to maximize their comprehension of texts with certain discourse features in certain types of situations. It would seem that systematic research programs could begin on several fronts: engineering texts for purposes of improving their quality; providing students with problem-solving strategies to monitor and "debug" comprehension problems; increasing students' awarenesses of text features; including adjuncts intended to meet readers' text-based needs; and improving reader-based strategies to enhance the readers' use of the text or to override text-based problems.

METAMETHODOLOGICAL FACTORS

Whether it is directed primarily at enhancing readers' comprehension strategies or meeting their text-based needs, reading-comprehension instruction functions within the context of general instructional principles. In recent years, researchers have formulated what some of these principles might be. In each case, a formulated principle represents a conclusion based on a literature review too extensive to reproduce here. Some of these principles are:

> Students achieve less in classrooms in which there is a strong emphasis on students working alone. (Stevens & Rosenshine, 1981; Rosenshine, this volume)

> Teachers should have students read easy materials and perform comprehension tasks they can complete with high success. (Cunningham, in press)

> The more time students are engaged with academic materials or activities [that yield a high success rate], the greater their achievement. (Berliner, 1981)

> For each particular group of students reading a particular set of materials in a particular allocated time, there is a pace of content coverage that will maximize student achievement in reading. (Barr, 1982)

The support for these general instructional principles is strong but problems remain. General instructional principles regarding the *quality* of instruction are lacking. How these principles and others interact is not completely clear. Why principles like Berliner's and Barr's are often corrupted during implementation to mean "increase time on task" and "increase pacing" is frustratingly unclear!

It seems reasonable to expect that those who would attempt to apply the limited findings of reading instructional research on increasing ability to comprehend and learn from text would conduct these applications with these general instructional principles in mind. Moreover, future instructional research in reading comprehension should describe carefully the nature of the metamethodological factors of student isolation, material and task difficulty, academic engaged time, and pacing of content coverage. In addition, we hope that the questions that we and others have raised about these factors will be addressed by future reading comprehension instructional research.

In 1980, when our first review of research on teaching reading comprehension appeared, we expressed a great deal of concern for an apparent lack of commitment among reading educators to pursue instructional research. Since that time, numerous researchers have ventured willingly into this area. The emergence of such studies is testimony to a commitment to classrooms; we predict that the eventual outcomes will see the advancement of our understanding not only of the basic processes of reading, but also reading pedagogy. Still many challenges remain.

FUTURE CHALLENGES AND THE NEED
TO REEXAMINE OUR GOALS

In 1980, the following guidelines for conducting research on teaching reading comprehension were discussed:

1. Apply a greatest likelihood principle to experimental research.
2. Design studies where the complexities of texts, teaching, and context are addressed and can reveal their impact.
3. Design studies where the complexities of classroom learning can be addressed.
4. Design and implement research which can be coherently interpreted in the light of literature from all the relevant disciplines.

Nowadays, researchers seem more sensitive to research paradigms and data which consider the influence of a variety of variables whether they may be manipulated or allowed to emerge. While we are encouraged by these advances we simultaneously fear them. Our fear is that researchers have adopted an overly analytic approach to comprehension and research on teaching reading comprehension at the expense of vision. Most breakdowns of comprehension, including what was used in the present paper, tend to establish a catalogue of differentiated strategies and denies that the process is unitary, multifaceted and dynamic. Similarly, most research guidelines inflate the researcher's technical qualifications rather than the need for intuition and for vision. It is the need for vision that concerns us most.

The Need for a Vision

When we say that someone has "vision," we generally mean two things. We mean that the person has the ability to see what is possible to achieve or accomplish, given the strongest concerted effort. We also mean that the person has the ability to see how all the parts of a complex operation can fit together and work together dynamically. We generally speak of leaders having vision, but specialists need vision too. A maker of custom cabinets with vision will design them so that they are more useful and attractive than ordinary cabinets would be because he will anticipate how the customer can use them and how they can fit into their location. A person who does reading comprehension instructional research is a specialist who needs vision. A piece of reading-comprehension instructional research will be of more value to our field if the researcher has a vision of what is being researched as well as how the instruction being researched can fit and work together with the other parts of a possible "best" program to improve reading-comprehension ability or comprehension and learning from text. We believe that those who conduct the most important reading-comprehension instructional research will invariably have such a vision.

A vision will probably have at least four components or "levels of vision." They are a vision of readers, learning groups, and teachers as well as teacher support and change.

A vision of readers. There are various ways we might develop a vision of readers and their characteristics. For example, we might take a schema-theoretic view and adopt goals for readers which emphasize the role of a reader's background knowledge as well as the strategies used to refine or negotiate meaning. We might take the view offered by some developmental psychologists that successful readers have or need metacognitive control and awarenesses. Accordingly, we might adopt goals which emphasize the readers' ability to determine what they are trying to do and how they might go about doing it. In contrast to either a schema-theoretic or developmental position, we might take the view that reading is an interpersonal experience either between readers and authors, involving different types of collaboration between the two, or between readers and "the world of the text." Consequently, we might emphasize a sense of readership, authorship, different modes of criticism and the vicarious nature of a reader's experience. Alternatively, we might adopt a more functional view of readers and develop goals based upon literacy demands across school, home, and the workplace. There are countless views which might be held, one must recognize the potential that each alternative offers. They can force us to rethink just what our goals for readers have been and should be. They might prompt us to invest our energies in research on other strategies and concerns and, thus, extend our reading-comprehension research and practices beyond the categories into which most studies to date can be so easily arranged.

A vision of learning groups. As we consider the individual reader, we should not forget that learning is a social event usually occurring among individuals within a learning community, whether that group be a classroom, reading group, or a network of independent workers. The nature of this community cannot be disregarded. Indeed, the characteristics of one's community interface with and affect the goals being pursued for individual students or research subjects. For example, our vision of possible optional learning groups might consider the group's metacognitive abilities (recognizing the group's goals and different strategies for achieving such goals), the group's independence (self-initiating goals or procedures for the accomplishment of such pursuits), the nature of the group's participation (teacher dependence or teacher independence; haphazard or rule governed) and the quality of the group's learning experiences (interpersonal, critical, ideational, aesthetic). Obviously, intertwined with such visions or goals for groups is a sense of the teacher's role.

A vision of teachers. Throughout the present chapter, we have made incidental references to the teacher's role. We shortchange our endeavors when we fail to appreciate their role, take advantage of them as collaborator, or disregard their multifaceted character. Our sense is that to develop a vision or visions of teachers, demands a willingness to begin pursuing instruction and instructional ideas within classrooms with teachers as collaborators in a research endeavor wherein we appreciate their role, take advantage of their insights, and consider the demands of their positions. In classrooms, with teachers, we can begin to understand the different concerns (management, curriculum, social, mental hygiene), behaviors (questioning, information giving, directing, responding), and realities (interruptions, time restraints, and materials) that should condition and shape our research and the implications we can draw from it.

A vision of teacher support and change. Our last component, or level of vision, relates to implementation and dissemination. Often our research may appear carefully planned and implemented, but its worth is diminished by its lack of potential value to teachers. Often our research is directed at studying the effects of a new strategy, but our findings fall short because we become bogged down with hostile subjects as teachers. As researchers, we must recognize that we are in the business of change involving a marketplace in which ideas may be bought, sold, discredited or nurtured. Whatever the nature of our research, we must recognize that we need to consider how to effect change, whether we are at the point of research dissemination, follow-up, or implementation. Having a vision of a support system forces us to consider how to put our research to use and compels us to recognize that to leave this critical step to the whims and follies of chance is to guarantee that the gap between research and practice will remain wide.

REFERENCES

Ahlfors, G.   Learning word meanings: A comparison of three instructional procedures (Doctoral dissertation, University of Minnesota, 1979). *Dissertation Abstracts International*, 1980, *40*, 5803–A. (University Microfilms No 80-11,754)

Anderson, R. C., & Biddle, W. B.   On asking people questions about what they are reading. In G. H. Bower (Ed.), *The psychology of learning and motivation* (Vol. 9). New York: Academic Press, 1975.

Anderson, R. C., & Freebody, P.   Vocabulary knowledge. In J. T. Guthrie (Ed.), *Comprehension and teaching: Research reviews.* Newark, Del.: International Reading Association, 1981.

Anderson, R. C., & Kulhavy, R. N.   Learning concepts from definitions. *American Educational Research Journal*, 1972, *9*, 385–390.

Anderson, R. C., Reynolds, R. E., Schallert, D. L., & Goetz, E. T.   Frameworks for comprehending discourse. *American Educational Research Journal*, 1977, *14*, 367–381.

Anderson, T. H.   *Study skills and learning strategies* (Tech. Rep. No. 104). Urbana: University of Illinois, Center for the Study of Reading, 1978. (ERIC Document Reproduction Service No. ED 161 000)

André, M. E. D. A., & Anderson, T. H.   The development and evaluation of a self-questioning study technique. *Reading Research Quarterly*, 1978–1979, *14*, 605–623.

Anthony, P. E.   An evaluation of an inductive method for teaching three skills necessary for reading narrative fiction (Doctoral dissertation, Boston University, 1981). *Dissertation Abstracts International*, 1981, *42*, 2587A–2588A. (University Microfilms No. 81-26,668)

Armbruster, B. B., & Anderson, T. H.   *The effect of mapping on the free recall of expository text* (Tech. Rep. No. 160). Urbana: University of Illinois, Center for the Study of Reading, 1980. (ERIC Document Reproduction Service No. ED 182 735)

Arnold, D. J., & Brooks, P. H.   Influence of contextual organizing material on children's listening comprehension. *Journal of Educational Psychology*, 1976, *68*, 711–716.

Aulls, M. W.   Expository paragraph properties that influence literal recall. *Journal of Reading Behavior*, 1975, *7*, 391–400.

Ausubel, D. P.   *The psychology of meaningful verbal learning*. New York: Grune & Stratton, 1963.

Ausubel, D. P.   *Educational psychology: A cognitive view*. New York: Holt, Rinehart & Winston, 1968.

Ausubel, D. P.   In defense of advance organizers: A reply to the critics. *Review of Educational Research*, 1978, *48*, 251–257.

Ausubel, D. P., & Fitzgerald, D.   The role of discriminability in meaningful verbal learning and retention. *Journal of Educational Psychology*, 1961, *52*, 266–274.

Baker, R. L.   The effects of informational organizers on learning and term relationships in ninth grade social studies. In H. L. Herber & R. T. Vacca (Eds.), *Research in reading in the content areas: The third report*. Syracuse, N.Y.: Syracuse University, Reading and Language Arts Center, 1977.

Barnes, B. R., & Clawson, E. U.   Do advance organizers facilitate learning? Recommendations for further research based on an analysis of 32 studies. *Review of Educational Research*, 1975, *45*, 637–659.

Barr, R.   Classroom reading instruction from a sociological perspective. *Journal of Reading Behavior*, 1982, *14*, 375–389.

Barringer, C., & Gholson, B.   Effects of type and combination of feedback upon conceptual learning by children: Implications for research in academic learning. *Review of Educational Research*, 1979, *49*, 459–478.

Barron, R. F.   The use of vocabulary as an advance organizer. In H. L. Herber & P. L. Sanders (Eds.), *Research in reading in the content areas: First year report*. Syracuse, N.Y.: Syracuse University, Reading and Language Arts Center, 1969.

Barron, R. F.   *The use of an iterative research process to improve a method of vocabulary instruction in tenth grade biology*. Unpublished doctoral dissertation, Syracuse University, 1971.

Barron, R. F., & Melnick, R.   The effects of discussion upon learning vocabulary meanings and relationships in tenth grade biology. In H. L. Herber & R. F. Barron (Eds.), *Research in reading in the content areas: Second year report*. Syracuse, N.Y.: Syracuse University, Reading and Language Arts Center, 1973.

Bartlett, B. J.   *Top-level structure as an organizational strategy for recall of classroom text*. Unpublished doctoral dissertation, Arizona State University, 1978.

Bean, T. W., & Pardi, R.   A field test of a guided reading strategy. *Journal of Reading*, 1979, *23*, 144–147.

Beck, I. L., McKeown, M. G., McCaslin, E. S., & Burkes, A. M.   *Instructional dimensions that may affect reading comprehension: Examples from two commercial reading programs.* Pittsburgh: University of Pittsburgh, Learning Research and Development Center, 1979.

Beck, I. L., Omanson, R. C., & McKeown, M. G.   An instructional redesign of reading lessons: Effects on comprehension. *Reading Research Quarterly,* 1982, *17,* 462–481.

Beck, I. L., Perfetti, C. A., & McKeown, M. G.   Effects of long-term vocabulary instruction on lexical access and reading comprehension. *Journal of Educational Psychology,* 1982, *74,* 506–521.

Becker, W. C.   Teaching reading and language to the disadvantaged—What we have learned from field research. *Harvard Educational Review,* 1977, *47,* 518–543.

Belmont, L., & Birch, H. G.   The intellectual profile of retarded readers. *Perceptual and Motor Skills,* 1966, *22,* 787–816.

Bender, B. G., & Levin, J. R.   Pictures, imagery, and retarded children's prose learning. *Journal of Educational Psychology,* 1978, *70,* 583–588.

Berget, E.   The use of organizational pattern guides, structured overviews and visual summaries in guiding social studies reading. In H. L. Herber & R. T. Vacca (Eds.), *Research in reading in the content areas: The third report.* Syracuse, N.Y.: Syracuse University, Reading and Language Arts Center, 1977.

Berliner, D. C.   Academic learning time and reading achievement. In J. T. Guthrie (Ed.), *Comprehension and teaching: Research reviews.* Newark, Del.: International Reading Association, 1981.

Betts, E. A.   *Foundations of reading instruction.* New York: American Book Company, 1946.

Biskin, D. S., Hoskisson, K., & Modlin, M.   Prediction, reflection, and comprehension. *Elementary School Journal,* 1976, *77,* 131–139.

Black, M.   *Models and metaphors: Studies in language and philosophy.* Ithaca, N.Y.: Cornell University Press, 1962.

Borer, G. S.   Effect of advance organizers and behavioral objectives on reading of sixth graders with selective attention deficits (Doctoral dissertation, Fordham University, 1981). *Dissertation Abstracts International,* 1981, *42,* 1052A. (University Microfilms No. 81-19,760)

Bowman, M. A.   The effect of story structure questioning upon the comprehension and metacognitive awareness of sixth grade students (Doctoral dissertation, University of Maryland, 1980). *Dissertation Abstracts International,* 1981, *42,* 626A. (University Microfilms No. 81-16,456)

Boyd, W. M.   Repeating questions in prose learning. *Journal of Educational Psychology,* 1973, *64,* 31–38.

Bransford, J. D.   *Human cognition: Learning, understanding and remembering.* Belmont, Calif.: Wadsworth, 1979.

Bransford, J. D., & Johnson, M. K.   Contextual prerequisites for understanding: Some investigations of comprehension and recall. *Journal of Verbal Learning and Verbal Behavior,* 1972, *11,* 717–726.

Bransford, J. D., & Johnson, M. K.   Considerations of some problems of comprehension. In W. G. Chase (Ed.), *Visual information processing.* New York: Academic Press, 1973.

Bransford, J. D., & McCarrell, N. S.   A sketch of a cognitive approach to comprehension: Some thoughts about understanding what it means to comprehend. In W. B. Weimer & D. S. Palermo (Eds.), *Cognition and the symbolic processes.* Hillsdale, N.J.: Erlbaum, 1974.

Bridge, C. A.   Strategies for promoting reader-text interactions. In R. J. Tierney, P. L. Anders, & J. N. Mitchell (Eds.), *Understanding readers' understanding: Bridging theory and practice.* Hillsdale, N.J.: Erlbaum, in press.

Britton, B. K., Westbrook, R. D., & Holdredge, T.   Reading and cognitive capacity usage:

Effects of text difficulty. *Journal of Experimental Psychology: Human Learning and Memory,* 1978, *4,* 582–591.

Brody, P. J.   Research on pictures and instructional texts: Difficulties and directions. Paper presented at the meeting of the Association for Educational Communications and Technology, Denver, Colo., 1980. (ERIC Document Reproduction Service No. ED 196 422).

Bronfenbrenner, U.   The experimental ecology of education. *Educational Researcher,* 1976, *5,* 5–15.

Brown, A. L.   *Knowing when, where and how to remember: A problem of metacognition* (Tech. Rep. No. 47). Urbana: University of Illinois, Center for the Study of Reading, 1977. (ERIC Document Reproduction Service No. ED 146 562)

Brown, A. L., Campione, J. C., & Day, J. D.   Learning to learn: On training students to learn from texts. *Educational Researcher,* 1981, *10,* 14–21.

Bruner, J. S.   *The process of education.* New York: Vintage Books, 1960.

Campbell, N. R.   *Physics, the elements.* Cambridge: Cambridge University Press, 1920.

Carney, J.   The effects of separate vs. content-integrated reading training on content mastery and reading ability in social studies. In H. L. Herber & R. T. Vacca (Eds.), *Research in reading in the content areas: The third report.* Syracuse, N.Y.: Syracuse University, Reading and Language Arts Center, 1977.

Carr, E. M.   The effect of inferential and metacognitive instruction on children's comprehension of expository text (Doctoral dissertation, University of Toledo, 1982). *Dissertation Abstracts International,* 1983, *43,* 2294–A. (University Microfilms No. 82-28,549)

Carver, R. P.   A critical review of mathemagenic behaviors and the effect of questions upon the retention of prose materials. *Journal of Reading Behavior,* 1972, *4,* 93–119.

Chodos, L., Gould, S. M., & Rusch, R. R.   Effect of student-generated prequestions and post-statements on immediate and delayed recall of fourth grade social studies content: A pilot study. In P. D. Pearson & J. Hansen (Eds.), *Reading: Theory, research, and practice.* Clemson, S.C.: National Reading Conference, 1977.

Christensen, C. M., & Stordahl, K. E.   The effect of organizational aids on comprehension and retention. *Journal of Educational Psychology,* 1955, *46,* 65–74.

Clark, C. H., & Bean, T. W.   Improving advance organizer research: Persistent problems and future directions. *Reading World,* 1982, *22,* 2–10.

Cole, J. N.   The effects of non-prose textual characteristics on retention of major concepts and supporting details with and without specific instructions in their use. In P. D. Pearson & J. Hansen (Eds.), *Reading: Theory, research, and practice.* Clemson, S.C.: National Reading Conference, 1977.

Collins, R.   The comprehension of prose materials by college freshmen when read silently and when read aloud. *Journal of Educational Research,* 1961, *55,* 79–83.

Combs, W. E.   *Some further effects and implications of sentence-combining exercises for the secondary language arts curriculum.* Unpublished doctoral dissertation, University of Minnesota, 1975.

Crews, R.   A linguistic versus a traditional grammar program—The effects on written sentence structure and comprehension. *Educational Leadership,* 1971, *29,* 145–149.

Cunningham, J. W.   Generating interactions between schemata and text. In J. A. Niles & L. A. Harris (Eds.), *New inquiries in reading research and instruction* (31st Yearbook of the National Reading Conference). Rochester, N.Y.: National Reading Conference, 1982.

Cunningham, J. W.   A research base for improving reading comprehension. In R. Anderson, J. Osborn, & P. Wilson (Eds.), *Research Foundations for a Literate America,* Lexington, Mass.: Heath, in press.

Cunningham, J. W., & Foster, E. O.   The ivory tower connection: A case study. *Reading Teacher,* 1978, *31,* 365–369.

Cunningham, P. M., Moore, S. A., Cunningham, J. W., & Moore, D. W. *Reading in elementary classrooms: Strategies and observations.* New York: Longman, 1983.

Dansereau, D. F. Development and evaluation of a learning strategy training program. *Journal of Educational Psychology,* 1979, *71,* 64–73.

Dansereau, D. F., Holley, C. D., & Collins, K. W. *Effects of learning strategy training on text processing.* Paper presented at the annual meeting of the American Educational Research Association, Boston, April 1980.

Darwazeh, A. N. Student-generated versus teacher-generated adjunct questions: Their effects on remember- and application-level learning (Doctoral dissertation, Syracuse University, 1982). *Dissertation Abstracts International,* 1983, *43,* 2281A. (University Microfilms No. 82-29,037.

Davidson, J. L. *The relationship between teachers' questions and pupils' responses during a directed reading activity and a directed reading-thinking activity.* Unpublished doctoral dissertation, University of Michigan, 1970.

Davis, F. Psychometric research in reading comprehension. In F. Davis (Ed.), *Literature of research in reading with emphasis upon models.* Brunswick, N.J.: Rutgers University Press, 1971.

Day, J. D. *Teaching summarization skills: A comparison of training methods.* Unpublished doctoral dissertation, University of Illinois, 1980.

Dean-Guilford, M. E. An investigation of the use of three prereading strategies on the comprehension of junior high school students (Doctoral dissertation, University of Houston, 1981). *Dissertation Abstracts International,* 1981, *42,* 1576A–1577A. (University Microfilms No. 81-21,305)

Denner, P. R. The influence of spontaneous strategy use on the development of provided and generated self-test questioning (Doctoral dissertation, Purdue University, 1981). *Dissertation Abstracts International,* 1982, *42,* 4778–A. (University Microfilms No. 82-10,184)

Doctorow, M., Wittrock, M. C., & Marks, C. Generative processes in reading comprehension. *Journal of Educational Psychology,* 1978, *70,* 109–118.

Dowell, R. E. *The relation between the use of analogies and their effects on student achievement on teaching a selected concept in high school biology.* Unpublished doctoral dissertation, Indiana University, 1968.

Dreher, M. J., & Singer, H. Story grammar instruction unnecessary for intermediate grade students. *Reading Teacher,* 1980, *34,* 261–268.

Drugge, N. L. *The facilitating effect of selected analogies on understanding of scientific explanations.* Unpublished doctoral dissertation, University of Alberta, 1977.

Duchastel, P. C. *Research on illustrating in instruction text* (Occasional Paper No. 3). Bryn Mawr, Penn.: American College, 1980. (ERIC Document Reproduction Service No. ED 215 324).

Duchastel, P. C., & Merrill, P. F. The effects of behavioral objectives on learning: A review of empirical studies. *Review of Educational Research,* 1973, *43,* 53–69.

Duell, O. K. Effect of types of objective, level of test questions, and judged importance of tested materials upon posttest performance. *Journal of Educational Psychology,* 1974, *66,* 225–232.

Dunham, T. C., & Levin, J. R. Imagery instructions and young children's prose learning: No evidence of "support." *Contemporary Educational Psychology,* 1979, *4,* 107–113.

Durkin, D. What classroom observations reveal about reading comprehension instruction. *Reading Research Quarterly,* 1978–1979, *14,* 481–533.

Dwyer, F. M., Jr. The relative effectiveness of varied visual illustrations in complementing programmed instructions. *Journal of Experimental Education,* 1967, *36,* 34–42.

Dwyer, F. M., Jr. The effectiveness of visual illustrations used to complement programmed instruction. *Journal of Psychology,* 1968, *70,* 157–162.

Dwyer, F. M., Jr. The effect of varying the amount of realistic detail in visual illustrations designed to complement programmed instruction. *Programmed Learning and Educational Technology,* 1969, *6,* 147–153.

Dwyer, F. M., Jr. Assessing students' perceptions of the instructional value of visual illustrations used to complement programmed instruction. *Programmed Learning and Educational Technology,* 1971, *8,* 73–80.

Dwyer, F. M., Jr. The effect of overt responses in improving visually programmed science instruction. *Journal of Research in Science Teaching,* 1972, *9,* 47–55.

Earle, R. A. Developing and using study guides. In H. L. Herber & P. L. Sanders (Eds.), *Research in reading in the content areas: First year report.* Syracuse, N.Y.: Syracuse University, Reading and Language Arts Center, 1969. (a)

Earle, R. A. Reading and mathematics: Research in the classrooms. In H. A. Robinson & E. L. Thomas (Eds.), *Fusing reading skills and content.* Newark, Del.: International Reading Association, 1969. (b)

Earle, R. A. Use of the structured overview in mathematics classes. In H. L. Herber & P. L. Sanders (Eds.), *Research in reading in the content areas: First year report.* Syracuse, N.Y.: Syracuse University, Reading and Language Arts Center, 1969. (c)

Earle, R. A. The use of vocabulary as a structured overview in seventh grade mathematics classes. In H. L. Herber & R. F. Barron (Eds.), *Research in reading in the content areas: Second year report.* Syracuse, N.Y.: Syracuse University, Reading and Language Arts Center, 1973.

Elgart, D. B. Oral reading, silent reading, and listening comprehension: A comparative study. *Journal of Reading Behavior,* 1978, *10,* 203–207.

Ellis, J. A., Konoske, P. J., Wulfeck, W. H., II, & Montague, W. E. Comparative effects of adjunct postquestions and instructions on learning from text. *Journal of Educational Psychology,* 1982, *74,* 860–867.

Estes, T. H. *Use of guide material and small group discussion in reading ninth grade social studies assignments.* Unpublished doctoral dissertation, Syracuse University, 1970.

Estes, T. H. Guiding reading in social studies. In H. L. Herber & R. F. Barron (Eds.), *Research in reading in the content areas: Second year report.* Syracuse, N.Y.: Syracuse University, Reading and Language Arts Center, 1973.

Estes, T. H., Mills, D. C., & Barron, R. F. Three methods of introducing students to a reading-learning task in two content subjects. In H. L. Herber & P. L. Sanders (Eds.), *Research in reading in the content areas: First year report.* Syracuse, N.Y.: Syracuse University, Reading and Language Arts Center, 1969.

Evans, B. *Pre-teaching vocabulary from superordinate propositions.* Paper presented at the meeting of the National Reading Conference, Dallas, December 1981.

Fitzgerald, J., & Spiegel, D. L. Enhancing children's reading comprehension through instruction in narrative structure. *Journal of Reading Behavior,* 1983, *15*(2), 1–17.

Frase, L. T. Learning from prose material: Length of passage, knowledge of results and position of questions. *Journal of Educational Psychology,* 1967, *58,* 266–272.

Frase, L. T. Effect of question location, pacing, and mode upon retention of prose material. *Journal of Educational Psychology,* 1968, *59,* 244–249.

Frase, L. T. Prose processing. In G. H. Bower (Ed.), *The psychology of learning and motivation* (Vol. 9). New York: Academic Press, 1975.

Frase, L. T., Patrick, E., & Schumer, H. Effect of question position and frequency upon learning from text under different levels of incentive. *Journal of Educational Psychology,* 1970, *61,* 52–56.

Frase, L. T., & Schwartz, B. J. The effect of question production and answering on prose recall. *Journal of Educational Psychology,* 1975, *67,* 628–635.

Freebody, P., & Anderson, R. C. *Effects of differing proportions and locations of difficult vocabulary on text comprehension* (Tech. Rep. No. 202). Urbana: University of Illinois,

Center for the Study of Reading, 1981. (ERIC Document Reproduction Service No. ED 201 992) (a)

Freebody, P., & Anderson, R. C. *Effects of vocabulary difficulty, text cohesion, and schema availability on reading comprehension* (Tech. Rep. No. 225). Urbana: University of Illinois, Center for the Study of Reading, November 1981. (b)

Friedman, F. H. *The effects of inferential processing induced by inserted questions on prose recall.* Unpublished doctoral dissertation, Purdue University, 1977.

Gagné, E. D. Long-term retention of information following learning from prose. *Review of Educational Research,* 1978, *48,* 629–665.

Galda, L. Playing about a story: Its impact on comprehension. *Reading Teacher,* 1982, *36,* 52–55.

Gambrell, L. B. Induced mental imagery and the text prediction performance of first and third graders. In J. A. Niles & L. A. Harris (Eds.), *New inquiries in reading research and instruction* (31st Yearbook of the National Reading Conference). Rochester, N.Y.: National Reading Conference, 1982.

Gambrell, L. B., Koskinen, P. S., & Cole, J. N. The effects of induced mental imagery upon comprehension: A comparison of written versus oral presentation. In M. L. Kamil (Ed.), *Directions in reading: Research and instruction* (30th Yearbook of the National Reading Conference). Washington, D.C.: National Reading Conference, 1981.

Gates, A. L. *The improvement of reading* (3rd ed.). New York: Macmillan, 1947.

Geva, E. *Meta-textual notions of reading comprehension.* Unpublished doctoral dissertation, University of Toronto, 1980.

Gick, M. L., & Holyoak, K. J. Analogical problem-solving. *Cognitive Psychology,* 1980, *12,* 306–355.

Gick, M. L., & Holyoak, K. J. Schema induction and analogical transfer. *Cognitive Psychology,* in press.

Glass, G. V. Integrating findings: The meta-analysis of research. In L. S. Schulman (Ed.), *Review of research in education* (Vol. 5). Itasca, Ill.: Peacock, 1978.

Gordon, C. J. *The effects of instruction in metacomprehension and inferencing on children's comprehension abilities.* Unpublished doctoral dissertation, University of Minnesota, 1979.

Graham, S. R. *A study of the effects of oral reading on comprehension of content material in the elementary grades.* Unpublished doctoral dissertation, University of North Carolina, 1979.

Graves, M. F., & Clark, D. L. The effect of adjunct questions on high school low achievers' reading comprehension. *Reading Improvement,* 1981, *18,* 8–13.

Graves, M. F., & Cooke, C. L. Effects of previewing difficulty short stories for high school students. *Research on Reading in Secondary Schools,* 1980, *6,* 38–54.

Graves, M. F., Cooke, C. L., & La Berge, M. J. Effects of previewing difficult short stories on low ability junior high school students' comprehension, recall, and attitudes. *Reading Research Quarterly,* 1983, *18,* 262–276.

Graves, M. F., & Palmer, R. J. Validating previewing as a method of improving fifth and sixth grade students' comprehension of short stories. *Michigan Reading Journal,* 1981, *15,* 1–3.

Graves, M. F., & Slater, W. H. *Some further thoughts on validating teaching procedures to be used by content area teachers.* Unpublished manuscript, 1981.

Great Books Foundation, *A manual for co-leaders.* Chicago: Great Books Foundation, 1967.

Guszak, F. J. Teacher questioning and reading. *Reading Teacher,* 1967, *21,* 227–234.

Guttmann, J., Levin, J. R., & Pressley, M. Pictures, partial pictures, and young children's oral prose learning. *Journal of Educational Psychology,* 1977, *69,* 473–480.

Hansen, J. The effects of inference training and practice on young children's reading comprehension. *Reading Research Quarterly,* 1981, *16,* 391–417.

Hansen, J., & Pearson, P. D.   An instructional study: Improving the inferential comprehension of fourth grade good and poor readers. *Journal of Educational Psychology*, in press.

Hartley, J., & Davies, I. K.   Preinstructional strategies: The role of pretests, behavioral objectives, overviews and advance organizers. *Review of Educational Research*, 1976, *46*, 239–265.

Hayes, D. A., & Mateja, J. A.   *Long-term transfer effect of metaphoric allusion.* Paper presented at the annual meeting of American Educational Research Association, April 1981.

Hayes, D. A., & Tierney, R. J.   Developing readers knowledge through analogy. *Reading Research Quarterly*, 1982, *17*, 256–280.

Herber, H. L.   Teaching reading in the content areas. Englewood Cliffs, N.J.: Prentice-Hall, 1970.

Herber, H. L.   *Teaching reading in content areas* (2nd ed.). Englewood Cliffs, N.J.: Prentice-Hall, 1978.

Hershberger, W.   Self-evaluational responding and typographical cueing: Techniques for programming self-instructional reading materials. *Journal of Educational Psychology*, 1964, *55*, 288–296.

Hiller, J. H.   Learning from prose text: Effects of readability level, inserted question difficulty, and individual differences. *Journal of Educational Psychology*, 1974, *66*, 202–211.

Hood, M.   *The effect of previewing on the recall of high school students.* Unpublished master's thesis, University of Minnesota, 1981.

Hoover, N. L.   A study of story schema acquisition and its influence on beginning reading (Doctoral dissertation, Virginia Polytechnic Institute and State University, 1981). *Dissertation Abstracts International*, 1982, *42*, 4378A. (University Microfilms No. 82-06,751)

Howie, S. M.   *A study of the effects of sentence combining on the writing ability and reading level of ninth grade students.* Unpublished doctoral dissertation, University of Colorado, 1979.

Jenkins, J. R., & Pany, D.   Research on teaching reading comprehension: Instructional variables. In J. Guthrie (Ed.), *Reading comprehension and education.* Newark, Del.: International Reading Association, 1981.

Jenkins, J. R., Pany, D., & Schreck, J.   *Vocabulary and reading comprehension: Instructional effects* (Tech. Rep. No. 100). Urbana: University of Illinois, Center for the Study of Reading, August 1978. (ERIC Document Reproduction Service No. ED 160 999)

Johnston, P.   *Prior knowledge and reading comprehension test bias.* Unpublished doctoral dissertation, University of Illinois, 1981.

Kameenui, E. J., Carnine, D. W., & Freschi, R.   Effects of text construction and instructional procedures for teaching word meanings on comprehension and recall. *Reading Research Quarterly*, 1982, *17*, 367–388.

Kelleher, A.   The effect of pre-reading strategies on comprehension (Doctoral dissertation, University of Pittsburgh, 1982). *Dissertation Abstracts International*, 1982, *43*, 707A. (University Microfilms No. 82-18,172)

Koenke, K., & Otto, W.   Contribution of pictures to children's comprehension of the main idea in reading. *Psychology in the Schools*, 1969, *6*, 298–302.

Kosoff, T. O.   The effects of three types of written introductions on children's processing of text. In M. L. Kamil (Ed.), *Directions in reading: Research and instruction* (30th Yearbook of the National Reading Conference). Washington, D.C.: National Reading Conference, 1981.

Kulhavy, R. W.   Feedback in written instruction. *Review of Educational Research*, 1977, *47*, 211–232.

Kulhavy, R. W., & Swenson, I.   Imagery instructions and the comprehension of text. *British Journal of Educational Psychology*, 1975, *45*, 47–51.

Landry, D. L.   *The effect of organizational aids on reading comprehension*. Unpublished doctoral dissertation, University of Connecticut, 1966.

Langer, J. A.   Facilitating text processing: The elaboration of prior knowledge. In J. A. Langer & M. Smith-Burke (Eds.), *Reader meets author/bridging the gap: A psycholinguistic and sociolinguistic perspective*. Newark, Del.: International Reading Association, 1982.

LaPorte, R. E., & Voss, J. F.   Retention of prose materials as a function of postacquisition testing. *Journal of Educational Psychology*, 1975, *67*, 259–266.

Lawton, J. T., & Wanska, S. K.   Advance organizers as a teaching strategy: A reply to Barnes and Clawson. *Review of Educational Research*, 1977, *47*, 233–244.

Lesgold, A. M., Levin, R., Jr., Shimron, J., & Guttmann, J.   Pictures and young children's learning from oral prose. *Journal of Educational Psychology*, 1975, *67*, 636–642.

Lesgold, A. M., McCormick, C., & Golinkoff, R. M.   Imagery training and children's prose learning. *Journal of Educational Psychology*, 1975, *67*, 663–667.

Levin, J. R.   Inducing comprehension in poor readers: A test of a recent model. *Journal of Educational Psychology*, 1973, *65*, 19–24.

Levin, J. R., Bender, B. G., & Lesgold, A. M.   Pictures, repetition, and young children's oral prose learning. *AV Communication Review*, 1976, *24*, 367–380.

Levin, J. R., Divine-Hawkins, R., Kerst, S. M., & Guttmann, J.   Individual differences in learning from pictures and words: The development and application of an instrument. *Journal of Educational Psychology*, 1974, *66*, 296–303.

Levin, J. R., & Lesgold, A. M.   On pictures in prose. *Educational Communication and Technology*, 1978, *26*, 233–243.

Levin, J. R., & Pressley, M.   Improving children's prose comprehension: Selected strategies that seem to succeed. In C. M. Santa & B. L. Hayes (Eds.), *Children's prose comprehension: Research and practice*. Newark, Del.: International Reading Association, 1981.

Lin, Y.   The effect of imagery instruction on the comprehension of social studies by fourth and fifth grade bilingual students (Doctoral dissertation, Boston University, 1982). *Dissertation Abstracts International*, 1982, *43*, 1068A. (University Microfilms No. 82-20,948)

Linden, M., & Wittrock, M. C.   The teaching of reading comprehension according to the model of generative learning. *Reading Research Quarterly*, 1981, *17*, 44–57.

Lipson, M. Y.   Promoting children's metacognition about reading through direct instruction. Paper presented at the annual meeting of the International Reading Association, Chicago, April 1982.

Lovelace, T. L., & McKnight, C. K.   The effects of reading instruction on calculus students' problem-solving. *Journal of Reading*, 1980, *23*, 305–308.

Luiten, J., Ames, W., & Ackerson, G.   A meta-analysis of the effects of advance organizers on learning and retention. *American Educational Research Journal*, 1980, *17*, 211–218.

Machie, B. C.   The effects of a sentence-combining program on the reading comprehension and written composition of fourth grade students (Doctoral dissertation, Hofstra University, 1982). *Dissertation Abstracts International*, 1982, *42*, 4779A–4780A. (University Microfilms No. 82-07,744)

Maier, A. S.   The effect of focusing on the cognitive processes of learning disabled children. *Journal of Learning Disabilities*, 1980, *13*, 143–147.

Manzo, A. V.   The request procedure. *Journal of Reading*, 1969, *13*, 123–126.

Manzo, A. V.   Reading and questioning: The request procedure. *Reading Improvement,* 1970, *7,* 80–83.

Manzo, A. V.   Guided reading procedure. *Journal of Reading,* 1975, *18,* 287–291.

Manzo, A. V., & Legenza, A.   Inquiry training for kindergarten children. *Educational Leadership,* 1975, *32,* 479–483.

Margolis, K.   *An instructional strategy for helping readers identify the gist in expository texts.* Unpublished doctoral dissertation, University of Illinois, 1982.

Marks, C. B., Doctorow, M. J., & Wittrock, M. C.   Word frequency and reading comprehension. *Journal of Educational Research,* 1974, *67,* 259–262.

Marr, M. B.   Children's comprehension of pictorial and textual event sequences. In M. L. Kamil & A. J. Moe (Eds.), *Reading research: Studies and applications.* Clemson, S.C.: National Reading Conference, 1979.

Maxon, G. A.   An investigation of the relative effect between questions and declarative statements as guides to reading comprehension for seventh grade students. In H. L. Herber & J. D. Riley (Eds.), *Research in reading in the content areas: The fourth report.* Syracuse, N.Y.: Syracuse University, Reading and Language Arts Center, 1979.

Mayer, R. E.   Different problem-solving competencies established in learning computer programming with and without meaningful models. *Journal of Educational Psychology,* 1975, *67,* 725–734.

Mayer, R. E.   Can advance organizers influence meaningful learning? *Review of Educational Research,* 1979, *49,* 371–383.

Mayer, R. E.   Can you repeat that? Qualitative effects of repetition and advance organizers on learning from science prose. *Journal of Educational Psychology,* 1983, *75,* 40–49.

Mazur-Stewart, M. E.   Differences between sixth and twelfth graders comprehension when using imagery and paraphrasing strategies (Doctoral dissertation, University of Toledo, 1982). *Dissertation Abstracts International,* 1983, *43,* 2296A. (University Microfilms No. 82-28,561).

McDowell, H. R.   A comparative study of reading readiness. Unpublished master's thesis, University of Iowa, 1939.

McGaw, B., & Grotelueschen, A.   Direction of the effect of questions in prose material. *Journal of Educational Psychology,* 1972, *63,* 580–588.

McWhorter, O. A.   Building reading interests and skills by utilizing children's first-hand experiences. Unpublished master's thesis, Ohio University, 1935.

Mellon, J.   *Transformational sentence combining: A method for enhancing the development of syntactic fluency in English composition* (NCTE Research Rep. No. 10). Urbana, Ill.: National Council of Teachers of English, 1969.

Memory, D.   *Prequestions, prestatements, causal expressions and cause-effect passages: A comparative study of adjunct aids and instructional approaches with low average and good readers in sixth grade.* Unpublished doctoral dissertation, University of Georgia, 1979.

Meyer, B. J. F.   *The organization of prose and its effects on memory.* Amsterdam: North-Holland Publishing Co., 1975.

Moore, D. W., & Readence, J. E.   A meta-analysis of the effect of graphic organizers on learning from text. In M. L. Kamil & A. J. Moe (Eds.), *Perspectives on reading research and instruction.* Washington, D.C.: National Reading Conference, 1980.

Morse, J. M.   Effect of reader-generated questions on learning from prose. In W. D. Miller & G. H. McNich (Eds.), *Reflections and investigations on reading.* Clemson, S.C.: National Reading Conference, 1976.

Mosenthal, J.   *Instruction in the interpretation of a writers argument: a training study.* Unpublished doctoral dissertation, University of Illinois, 1983.

Neilsen, A., Rennie, B., & Connell, A.   Allocation of instructional time to reading comprehension and study skills in intermediate grade social studies classrooms. In J. A. Niles
   & L. A. Harris (Eds.), *New inquiries in reading research and instruction*. (31st Yearbook
   of the National Reading Conference). Rochester, N.Y.: National Reading Conference,
   1982.
Ney, J. W.   The hazards of the course: Sentence-combining in freshman English. *English
   Record*, 1976, *27*, 70–77.
Nungester, R. J., & Duchastel, P. C.   Testing versus review: Effects on retention. *Journal
   of Educational Psychology*, 1982, *74*, 18–22.
O'Hare, F.   *Sentence combining: Improving student writing without formal grammar
   instruction*. Urbana, Ill.: National Council of Teachers of English, 1973.
Omanson, R. C., Warren, W. H., & Trabasso, T.   Goals, themes, inferences and memory:
   A developmental study. *Discourse Processes*, 1978, *1*, 337–354. (a)
Paivio, A.   *Imagery and verbal processes*. New York: Holt, Rinehart & Winston, 1971.
Palinscar, A.   *Improving the reading comprehension of junior high students through
   the reciprocal teaching of comprehension-monitoring strategies*. Unpublished doctoral
   dissertation, University of Illinois, 1982.
Palinscar, A., & Brown, A.   *Reciprocal teaching of comprehension-monitoring activities*
   (Tech. Rep. No. 269). Urbana: University of Illinois, Center for the Study of Reading,
   January 1983.
Pany, D., & Jenkins, J. R.   Learning word meanings: A comparison of instructional proce-
   dures and effects on measures of reading comprehension with learning disabled stu-
   dents. *Learning Disabled Quarterly*, 1978, *1*, 21–32.
Paris, S. G.   *Combining research and instruction on reading comprehension in the class-
   room*. Paper presented at the annual meeting of the International Reading Association,
   Chicago, April 1982.
Paris, S. G., & Lindauer, B. K.   The role of inference in children's comprehension and
   memory for sentences. *Cognitive Psychology*, 1976, *8*, 217–227.
Paris, S. G., Lipson, M. Y., Cross, D. R., Jacobs, J. E., De Britto, A. M., & Oka, E. R.   *Metacog-
   nition and reading comprehension*. Research colloquium presented at the annual
   meeting of the International Reading Association, Chicago, April 1982.
Pearson, P. D., & Gallagher, M. C.   The instruction of reading comprehension. *Contemporary Educational Psychology*, 1983, *8*, 317–344.
Pearson, P. D., & Johnson, D.   *Teaching reading comprehension*. New York: Holt, Rinehart & Winston, 1978.
Peeck, J.   Retention of pictorial and verbal content of a text with illustrations. *Journal
   of Educational Psychology*, 1974, *66*, 880–888.
Peleg, Z. R., & Moore, R. F.   Effects of the advance organizer with oral and written
   presentation on recall and inference of EMR adolescents. *American Journal of Mental
   Deficiency*, 1982, *86*, 621–626.
Perfetti, G. A., Bransford, J. D., & Franks, J. J.   Constraints on access in a problem-solving
   contest. *Memory and Cognition*, 1983, *11*, 24–31.
Peterson, C., Glover, J. A., & Ronning, R. R.   An examination of three prose learning
   strategies on reading comprehension. *Journal of General Psychology*, 1980, *102*, 39–
   52.
Petre, R. M.   *Quantity, quality and variety of pupil responses during an open-communi-
   cation structured group directed reading-thinking activity and a closed-communica-
   tion structured group directed reading activity*. Unpublished doctoral dissertation,
   University of Delaware, 1970.
Phelps, S.   The effects of integrating sentence-combining activities and guided reading
   procedures on the reading and writing performance of eighth grade students. In
   H. L. Herber & J. D. Riley (Eds.), *Research in reading in the content areas: The*

fourth report. Syracuse, N.Y.: Syracuse University, Reading and Language Arts Center, 1979.

Poulton, C. E., & Brown, C. H.   Memory after reading aloud and reading silently. *British Journal of Psychology,* 1967, *58,* 219–222.

Pressey, S. L. A.   A simple apparatus which gives tests and scores—and teaches. *School and Society,* 1926, *23,* 373–376.

Pressley, G. M.   Mental imagery helps eight-year-olds remember what they read. *Journal of Educational Psychology,* 1976, *68,* 355–359.

Pressley, G. M.   Imagery and children's learning: Putting the picture in developmental perspective. *Review of Educational Research,* 1977, *47,* 585–622.

Raphael, T. E., & Pearson, P. D.   *The effects of meta-cognitive strategy awareness training on students' question answering behavior* (Tech. Rep. No. 238). Urbana: University of Illinois, Center for the Study of Reading, 1982.

Rasco, R. W., Tennyson, R. D., & Boutwell, R. C.   Imagery instructions and drawings in learning prose. *Journal of Educational Psychology,* 1975, *67,* 188–192.

Readence, J. E., & Moore, D. W.   *A meta-analysis of the effect of adjunct aids on learning from text.* Paper presented at the annual meeting of the American Educational Research Association, Boston, April 1980.

Reynolds, R. E., & Anderson, R. C.   *The influence of questions during reading on the allocation of attention* (Tech. Rep. No. 183). Urbana: University of Illinois, Center for the Study of Reading, 1980.

Reynolds, R. E., Standiford, S. N., & Anderson, R. C.   Distribution of reading time when questions are asked about a restricted category of text information. *Journal of Educational Psychology,* 1979, *71,* 183–190.

Richmond, M. G.   The relationship of the uniqueness of prose passages to the effect of question placement and question relevance on the acquisition and retention of information. In W. D. Miller & G. H. McNinch (Eds.), *Reflections and investigations on reading.* Clemson, S.C.: National Reading Conference, 1976.

Rickards, J. P.   Type of verbatim question interspersed in text: A new look at the position effect. *Journal of Reading Behavior,* 1976, *8,* 37–45.

Rickards, J. P., & Hatcher, C. W.   Interspersed meaningful learning questions as semantic cues for poor comprehenders. *Reading Research Quarterly,* 1977–1978, *13,* 538–553.

Riding, R. J., & Shore, J. M.   A comparison of two methods of improving prose comprehension in educationally subnormal children. *British Journal of Educational Psychology,* 1974, *44,* 300–303.

Riley, C. A., & Trabasso, T.   Comparatives, logical structures and encoding in a transitive inference task. *Journal of Experimental Child Psychology,* 1974, *17,* 187–203.

Riley, J. D.   The effect of reading guides upon students' literal, interpretative, and applied level comprehension of word problems. In H. L. Herber & J. D. Riley (Eds.), *Research in reading in the content areas: The fourth report.* Syracuse, N.Y.: Syracuse University, Reading and Language Arts Center, 1979.

Rogers, M. V.   Comprehension in oral and silent reading. *Journal of General Psychology,* 1937, *17,* 394–397.

Rothkopf, E. Z.   Learning from written instructive materials: An exploration of the control of inspection behavior by test-like events. *American Educational Research Journal,* 1966, *3,* 241–249.

Rothkopf, E. Z.   Experiments on mathemagenic behavior and the technology of written instruction. In E. Z. Rothkopf & P. E. Johnson (Eds.), *Verbal learning research and the technology of written instruction.* New York: Teachers College Press, 1971.

Rothkopf, E. Z.   Structural text features and the control of processes in learning from written materials. In R. O. Freedle & J. B. Carroll (Eds.), *Language comprehension and the acquisition of knowledge.* Washington, D.C.: Winston, 1972. (a)

Rothkopf, E. Z.   Variable adjunct question schedules, interpersonal interaction, and incidental learning from written material. *Journal of Educational Psychology*, 1972, *63*, 87–92. (b)

Rothkopf, E. Z., & Bisbicos, E. E.   Selective facilitation effects of interspersed questions on learning from written materials. *Journal of Educational Psychology*, 1967, *58*, 56–61.

Rothkopf, E. Z., & Bloom, R. D.   Effects of interpersonal interaction on the instructional value of adjunct questions in learning from written material. *Journal of Educational Psychology*, 1970, *61*, 417–422.

Rowell, E. H.   Do elementary students read better orally or silently? *Reading Teacher*, 1976, *30*, 367–370.

Royer, J. M., & Cable, G. W.   Facilitated learning in connected discourse. *Journal of Educational Psychology*, 1975, *67*, 116–123.

Royer, J. M., & Cable, G. W.   Illustrations, analogies, and facilitative transfer in prose learning. *Journal of Educational Psychology*, 1976, *68*, 205–209.

Ruch, M. D., & Levin, J. R.   Pictorial organization versus verbal repetition of children's prose: Evidence for processing differences. *AV Communication Review*, 1977, *25*, 269–280.

Rumelhart, D. E., & Ortony, A.   The representation of knowledge in memory. In R. C. Anderson, R. J. Spiro, & W. E. Montague (Eds.), *Schooling and the acquisition of knowledge.* Hillsdale, N.J.: Erlbaum, 1977.

Sachs, A. W.   The effects of three prereading activities on learning disabled children's short-term reading comprehension (Doctoral dissertation, George Peabody College for Teachers, Vanderbilt University, 1981). *Dissertation Abstracts International*, 1981, *42*, 1593A. (University Microfilms No. 81-21,592)

Sagaria, S. D., & DiVesta, F. J.   Learner expectations induced by adjunct questions and the retrieval of intentional and incidental information. *Journal of Educational Psychology*, 1978, *70*, 280–288.

Samuels, S. J.   Effects of pictures on learning to read, comprehension and attitudes. *Review of Educational Research*, 1970, *40*, 397–407.

Schachter, S. W.   *An investigation of the effects of vocabulary instruction and schemata orientation upon reading comprehension.* Unpublished doctoral dissertation, University of Minnesota, 1978.

Schallert, D. L.   The role of illustrations in reading comprehension. In R. J. Spiro, B. C. Bruce, & W. F. Brewer (Eds.), *Theoretical issues in reading comprehension.* Hillsdale, N.J.: Erlbaum, 1980.

Schermerhorn, S. M., Goldschmid, M. L., & Shore, B. M.   Learning basic principles of probability in student dyads: A cross-age comparison. *Journal of Educational Psychology*, 1975, *67*, 551–557.

Shavelson, R. J., Berliner, D. C., Ravitch, M. M., & Loeding, D.   Effects of position and type of question on learning from prose material: Interaction of treatments with individual differences. *Journal of Educational Psychology*, 1974, *66*, 40–48.

Sledge, A. C.   The advance organizer: A review of research at the secondary level. In J. L. Vaughan, Jr., & P. J. Gaus (Eds.), *Research on Reading in Secondary Schools*, 1978, *2*, 41–60.

Smith, N. B.   *Reading instruction for today's children.* Englewood Cliffs, N.J.: Prentice-Hall, 1963.

Smith-Burke, T., & Ringler, L.   In J. Grasanu (Ed.) *Reading comprehension: From research to practice.* Hillsdale, N.J.: Erlbaum, in press.

Snowman, J., & Cunningham, D. J.   A comparison of pictorial and written adjunct aids in learning from text. *Journal of Educational Psychology*, 1975, *67*, 307–311.

Stauffer, R. G.   A directed reading-thinking plan. *Education*, 1959, *79*, 527–532.

Stauffer, R. G. *Directing reading maturity as a cognitive process.* New York: Harper & Row, 1969.

Steingart, S. K., & Glock, M. D.   Imagery and the recall of connected discourse. *Reading Research Quarterly,* 1979, *15,* 66–83.

Stetson, E. G.   Improving textbook learning with S4R: A strategy for teachers, not students. *Reading Horizons,* 1981, *22,* 129–135.

Stevens, K. C.   Can we improve reading by teaching background information? *Journal of Reading,* 1982, *25,* 326–329.

Stevens, R., & Rosenshine, B.   Advances in research on teaching. *Exceptional Education Quarterly,* 1981, *2,* 1–9.

Straw, S. B., & Schreiner, R.   The effect of sentence manipulation on subsequent measures of reading and listening comprehension. *Reading Research Quarterly,* 1982, *17,* 339–352.

Swaby, B. *The effects of advance organizers and vocabulary introduction on the reading comprehension of sixth grade students.* Unpublished doctoral dissertation, University of Minnesota, 1977.

Taylor, B.   Text structure and children's comprehension and memory for expository material. *Journal of Educational Psychology,* 1982, *74,* 323–340.

Taylor, B., & Beach, R.   The effects of text structure instruction on middle grade students' comprehension and production of expository text. *Reading Research Quarterly,* in press.

Thomas, J. L.   The influence of pictorial illustrations with written text and previous achievement on the reading comprehension of fourth grade science students. *Journal of Research in Science Teaching,* 1978, *15,* 401–405.

Tierney, R. J., & Cunningham, J. W.   *Research on teaching reading comprehension* (Tech. Rep. No. 187). Urbana: University of Illinois, Center for the Study of Reading, 1980. (ERIC Document Reproduction Service No. ED 195 946)

Tierney, R. J., & Pearson, P. D.   Toward a composing model of reading. *Language Arts,* 1983, *60,* 568–580.

Tirre, W. C., Manelis, L., & Leicht, K. L.   The effects of imaginal and verbal strategies on prose comprehension by adults. *Journal of Reading Behavior,* 1979, *11,* 99–106.

Tuinman, J. J., & Brady, M. E.   How does vocabulary account for variance on reading comprehension tests? A preliminary instructional analysis. In P. L. Nacke (Ed.), *Interaction: Research and practice for college-adult reading (23rd Yearbook of the National Reading Conference).* Clemson, S.C.: National Reading Conference, 1974.

Vacca, R. T.   An investigation of a functional reading strategy in seventh grade social studies. In H. L. Herber & R. T. Vacca (Eds.), *Research in reading in the content areas: The third report.* Syracuse, N.Y.: Syracuse University, Reading and Language Arts Center, 1977.

Vineyard, E. E., & Massey, H. W.   The interrelationship of certain linguistic skills and their relationship with scholastic achievement when intelligence is ruled constant. *Journal of Educational Psychology,* 1957, *48,* 279–286.

Vosniadou, S., & Ortony, A.   The influence of analogy in children's acquisition of new information from text: An exploratory story. In J. A. Niles & L. A. Harris (Eds.), *Directions in reading: Research and instruction* (31st Yearbook of the National Reading Conference). In press.

Walker, N. M.   The effect of graphic organizers on the learning of social studies content and attitude toward reading. In H. L. Herber & J. D. Riley (Eds.), *Research in reading in the content areas: The fourth report.* Syracuse, N.Y.: Syracuse University, Reading and Language Arts Center, 1979.

Watts, G. H.   The "arousal" effect of adjunct questions on recall from prose materials. *Australian Journal of Psychology,* 1973, *25,* 81–87.

Watts, G. H., & Anderson, R. C.   Effects of three types of inserted questions on learning from prose. *Journal of Educational Psychology*, 1971, *62*, 387–394.

Weaver, P. A.   Improving reading comprehension: Effects of sentence organization instruction. *Reading Research Quarterly*, 1979, *15*, 129–146.

Weiner, C. J.   *The effect of training in questioning and student question generation on reading achievement.* Paper presented at the annual meeting of the American Educational Research Association, Toronto, March 1978.

White, R. E.   The effects of organizational themes and adjunct placements on childrens' prose learning: A developmental perspective (Doctoral dissertation, Northwestern University, 1981). *Dissertation Abstracts International, 42*, 1981, 2042A–2043A. (University Microfilms No. 81-25,038)

Willson, V. L., & Putnam, R. R.   A meta-analysis of pretest sensitization effects in experimental design. *American Educational Research Journal*, 1982, *19*, 249–258.

Wittrock, M. C., Marks, C., & Doctorow, M.   Reading as a generating process. *Journal of Educational Psychology*, 1975, *67*, 484–489.

Wixson, K. K.   The effects of postreading questions on children's comprehension and learning. In M. L. Kamil (Ed.), *Directions in reading: Research and instruction* (30th Yearbook of the National Reading Conference). Washington, D.C.: National Reading Conference, 1981.

Yost, M., Avila, L., & Vexler, E. B.   Effect on learning of postinstructional responses to questions of differing degrees of complexity. *Journal of Educational Psychology*, 1977, *69*, 399–408.

21 STUDYING

Thomas H. Anderson
and Bonnie B. Armbruster

Studying is a special form of reading. The way that studying differs from "ordinary reading" is that studying is associated with the requirement to perform identifiable cognitive and/or procedural tasks. This performance-related aspect of studying was acknowledged several decades ago by Butterweck (1926) who suggested that the one definition of studying applicable to every possible school situation is "a pupil activity of the type required to satisfy the philosophy of education held by the teacher" (p. 2). "Satisfying the philosophy of education held by the teacher" translates as meeting the criteria on tasks, such as taking a test, writing a paper, giving a speech, and conducting an experiment.

Although studying has been the object of investigation since early in this century, the traditional studying research has little to offer theorists or practitioners. However, when the traditional research on studying is supplemented with theory and research from other areas of education and psychology, a clearer picture of studying begins to emerge. The purpose of this chapter is to portray that picture.

We use an organizational scheme that has two major components: *state variables* and *processing variables*. The *state variables* are those related to the status of the student and the to-be-studied material at the time of studying. Important student variables include knowledge of the criterion task, knowledge of the content in the to-be-studied material, and motivation. Important text variables include content covered, organization or structure, and other features which affect the "readability" of the prose. The *processing variables* are those involved in getting the information from the written page into the student's head. Processing variables include the initial focusing of attention, the subsequent encoding of the information attended to, and the retrieval of the information as required by the criterion task. As we see it, the outcomes of studying are a function of the interaction of state and processing variables. In this chapter, we discuss some of these components and review related research.

STATE VARIABLES

Although state variables include several student- and text-associated variables, we will discuss only student knowledge of the criterion task. We focus on this variable because it is uniquely associated with studying as opposed to other types of reading.

Knowledge of the Criterion Task

According to our definition, studying involves reading in preparation for performing a criterion task. The nature of the task and associated criteria are known to students in varying degrees. Students' cognizance of the task may range from having complete knowledge (e.g., a copy of the test to be administered) to almost no knowledge (e.g., information that the test will be paper and pencil and that it will cover World War I). The degree of knowledge that a student has about the criterion event is one important state variable that influences studying outcomes.

The underlying assumption about the relationship between knowledge of the criterion task and studying outcomes is simple: when the criterion task is made explicit to the students before they read the text, students will learn more from studying than when the criterion task remains vague. This notion is supported by several lines of related research in which degree of knowledge of the criterion task is manipulated.

The first line of research addresses the situation in which students have complete knowledge of the criterion test. This research involves the use of questions inserted in text which students are required to answer as they read. In a comprehensive review of the adjunct-question literature to date, Anderson and Biddle (1975) concluded that, in general, the availability of these questions facilitates learning from text. Of particular relevance is the situation in which the criterion test items exactly match the inserted questions. Data from 14 studies show that performance on such repeated items is 10.8 percent higher than performance on items that had not been available during studying. Clearly, this result from adjunct-question studies shows that when the criterion task associated with studying is made explicit to students early in the studying session, it can have a reliable, beneficial effect on criterion-task performance.

Other research investigates the middle ranges of knowledge about the criterion task—students have some information but not the actual test items. This area of investigation includes research on the use of behavioral objectives and research on typographical cueing of text. The behavioral-objectives research investigates the effect on learning of giving students a set of behavioral objectives, which typically include information about the topic to be learned and how the student can demonstrate that the information has been mastered. The research on typographical cueing investigates the effect on learning of underlining and other techniques of physically highlighting sections of prose. Presumably these techniques cue information that is likely to be tested. The effects of objectives and typographical cueing on criterion-test performance are similar. Combining the conclusions of T. H. Anderson (1980) with respect to objectives, and T. H. Anderson (1980) and Glynn (1978) with respect to typographical cueing, both techniques appear to facilitate learning, at least of those text ideas specifically cued by the objectives or typographical devices. Furthermore, with regard to objectives, the more specific the objective (i.e., the closer in form to the test item), the greater the effectiveness. In sum, providing less than complete information in the form of objectives or typographical cueing is effective but less potent than providing complete information in the form of adjunct questions. This finding is consistent with the hypothesis that performance on the criterion task is a function of knowledge of the task.

A final line of research to be discussed pertains to the situation in which students have little knowledge of the criterion task. In this research, students are told and/or shown the *type* of items that will be used on the criterion test. They then study the content material with the expectation of being tested in the prescribed test mode. In most designs, they are tested in the prescribed as well as one or more other modes.

This line of research blossomed in the 1930s in response to the then "new" mode of testing—multiple choice. Seemingly, researchers at the time were attempting to show that the new objective tests were detrimental because (a) students would not study as thoroughly for the multiple-choice exams as they would for the tried-and-true essay or completion exams and (b) students would study for the multiple-choice exams by learning details of the text at the expense of the main ideas. It is important to note that at this time multiple-choice tests *were* used primarily to assess knowledge of details. Therefore, when students in the early experiments were told that they would have an objective test, it was easy for them to interpret this to mean a test over details in the passage.

Two studies by G. Meyer (1934, 1935, 1936) confirmed the hypothesis that when students anticipated essay and completion exams they performed generally better on all types of tests than when anticipating true-false and multiple-choice types. Because he conducted the experiments in a laboratory where he could observe studying behavior, G. Meyer was able to determine that students who were studying for an essay exam tended to write more summary statements, while students studying for an objective exam did more "random" note taking and underlining.

Other early studies by Class (1934) with college students and by Vallance (1947) with high school students failed to find performance differences in students expecting different kinds of tests. It should be noted, however, that Class used only a true-false criterion test. Judging from G. Meyer's data, true-false tests seem to be the least sensitive measure of the effects of test expectation. Therefore, Class's choice of criterion test may have biased the results.

In more recent years, Hakstian (1971); Kulhavy, Dyer, and Silver (1975); Lucas (1977); and Rickards and Friedman (1978) also report no effect of anticipated test type on overall criterion-test scores. However, the latter two researchers approached the question in a somewhat different way by separating the criterion-test items into those measuring idea units of high structural importance and those measuring idea units of low structural importance. A reanalysis of the data organized in this way revealed that students instructed to study for an essay exam learned more ideas of high importance than did the group instructed to study for multiple-choice tests. Conversely, students studying for a multiple-choice test learned more ideas of low importance than high importance.

In conclusion, the results from several lines of research generally support the hypothesis that the more specific the knowledge about the criterion event, the greater the effectiveness of studying. In those conditions where the criterion task is known exactly (e.g., inserted questions identical to criterion test questions), performance is much higher than that found in a control condition. The effectiveness of studying decreases as knowledge of the criterion task decreases. Finally, when the nature of the criterion task is only vaguely known (e.g., only the type of test is known), facilitative effects are seldom demonstrated.

However, knowledge of the criterion task will not affect performance unless students change their studying strategy accordingly. For several *good* reasons, students might opt *not* to change their normal studying strategy. First, the text to be learned may be so short that the students feel they can learn it all anyway. Second, the information to be learned may be so extensive (e.g., long lists of objectives or dense underlining) that students believe they cannot possibly master it no matter what strategy they use. Third, the information about the criterion task may be at odds with the content and/or expectations about what a reasonable task should be; because the information has low credibility, students may reject it. In sum, for information about the criterion task to have an effect on students, it must lead the students to believe that if they modify their studying behavior in accordance with the expected outcomes of the studying session, they will do better on the criterion task. The actual studying behavior—what students *do* in response to their knowledge or beliefs about the task demands—is the topic of the next section.

PROCESSING VARIABLES

Knowledge of the criterion task may be a necessary condition for optimal studying, but it is obviously not a sufficient condition. Knowledge of the criterion task must be accompanied by processing of the relevant information. That is, students must get the information from the text into their heads. In realistic studying situations, this processing demand is very heavy. For example, it is not unusual for a single page of expository text to have at least 50 idea units which could be interrelated in a vast number of ways. In a chapter of text, the number of ideas and relationships is mind-boggling indeed. Consequently, it is folly to think that a student could (or should) learn and remember all, or even most, of the content in a textbook chapter. Therefore, the prime tasks of the student are to (a) *focus attention* and (b) *engage in encoding activities* in a way that will increase the probability of understanding and retrieving the high pay-off ideas and relationships. In other words, the students must select the segments of text that contain the important ideas and ensure that they are well understood and likely to be remembered.

Focusing Attention

Historically, there has been little research on attention focusing. Although earlier researchers included attention focusing as part of their operational theories (i.e., by collecting retrospective questionnaire data from students about how they processed the material), it was not until recently that more novel techniques have been used to monitor and, at times, control attention focusing. Four of these techniques are described in this section: induced pacing, inspection times on short text segments, eye movement observations, and cognitive effort.

McConkie, Rayner, and Wilson (1973) investigated the effects of attention focusing by inducing college students to read six 500-word passages at a fast pace or at a moderate pace by manipulating the pay-off conditions for learning the content. In addition, students received different types of inserted questions (related to numbers, facts, recognition, higher order, etc.) after each passage. On the criterion test, students received all types of questions. Results indicated that the slower paced students scored higher than the faster paced and that increasing speed had little effect on the retention of information for which a person is specifically reading, but it reduces the learning of task-irrelevant information. Thus, if time constraints force them, students may continue to direct attention to the more task-relevant information, even at the expense of not learning well the other information.

Of course, the technique of inducing reading speed does not reveal where attention is being directed. Reynolds, Standiford, and Anderson (1979) investigated the question about where attention is being focused by presenting the text and inserted questions on a computer terminal. This procedure allowed the measurement of reading times on short segments of materials, about 33 words in length. Targeted segments of text had information about (a) a technical term, (b) a number, or (c) a proper name. Each of the 43 college students received periodic inserted questions about one of these three categories or no questions at all.

Results showed that question groups performed better, relative to controls, on posttest items that repeated inserted questions and also on new posttest items from the same categories as the inserted questions. Although there was no overall reading time difference between the question and no-question groups, subjects who received inserted questions spent more time on the parts of the text that contained information of the type needed to answer the questions.

In another study using text presentation under computer control, Alessi, Anderson, and Goetz (1979) manipulated rate and investigated attention focusing in yet another way. An underlying assumption of the study, and one that was empirically determined in pilot studies, was that some expository texts have a strict prerequisite dependency among ideas; that is, mastery of concept A is necessary before concept B can be learned well. The text was administered to subjects in a way similar to that used in the Reynolds et al. (1979) experiment. The experimental manipulation occurred after students answered an inserted question requiring knowledge about concept A, and just prior to reading about concept B. Half of the students who did not answer the question correctly were allowed to proceed directly to concept B, as were the students who answered the question correctly. The other half of the students who did not answer the question correctly were branched back in the text to that segment that dealt specifically with concept A before they were allowed to read concept B. Results showed that students who received lookbacks showed better comprehension of the later information (about concept B) than when lookbacks were not provided. Thus, these results support the important relationship between attention focusing and performance on related criterion test items. Furthermore, the study shows that if students fail to process important text adequately when first encountering it, additional opportunities to read it can have beneficial effects. Of course, in this study, the computer was deciding for the student where and when the look-back focusing should occur. Presumably, successful students eventually learn this skill themselves.

Rothkopf and Billington (1979) investigated attention focusing by collecting inspection times and eye movement records as high school and college subjects read a 1500-word text. The text was divided into 12 segments and presented on slides at whatever pace the student desired. Experimental students memorized five or ten learning goals before reading, whereas students in the control group were given no goals. Results showed that compared to the incidental text, the goal-relevant text was processed slower and prompted twice as many eye fixations, with each fixation 15-msec longer on the average. Achievement scores from a short-answer test showed a pattern of results similar to those found in earlier studies where preinserted questions were used (Anderson & Biddle, 1975). That is, the goal-learning group scored higher on relevant items than did the control group, but the control group scored higher on items testing knowledge of the incidental text.

In sum, three types of experimental measures, that is, induced pacing, gross inspection time on short text segments, and eye movement measures, have been used to demonstrate that students "naturally" spend more time on the text segments that are relevant to learning goals. In addition, time spent on these text segments is correlated positively with achievement scores.

Another technique to investigate attention focusing during reading allegedly assesses the amount of cognitive capacity or effort being used by a reader. This is accomplished by requiring a student to participate in a less important task while reading—such as pressing a button when a buzzer sounds. The slower a reader is at pressing the button, the more cognitive capacity the reader is presumably directing to the primary task of reading. Britton, Piha, Davis, and Wehausen (1978) report two experiments using an inserted-question paradigm. College students read a lengthy text passage and were periodically asked text-relevant questions, text-irrelevant questions, or no questions. Results showed that cognitive-capacity usage increased when text-relevant questions were introduced but not when irrelevant questions began or when no questions were given. Indeed, results from this measure seem consistent with those from inspection-time measures.

A study by Reynolds (1979) followed up on these results. College students read a 27-page text from Rachel Carson's *The Sea Around Us*, a light technical and descriptive exposition. Students read information about technical terms, proper names, and filler information from a computer screen. As with the adjunct-question research, some students received a question inserted at equal intervals in the text that they were required to answer before continuing. Some students answered questions about proper names and others about technical terms. Still other students received no questions. On a later criterion test, all students received items about technical terms and proper names.

While the students read the text, the computer kept track of the inspection time for each text cluster. In addition, reaction time to a secondary task was also recorded by the computer. The secondary task required the student to press the space bar on the terminal keyset when a tone sounded. The reaction time to this secondary task was used as an index of cognitive effort being expended at the time of the tone.

Achievement results from this study reveal the same pattern as those reported in earlier work (e.g., Reynolds et al., 1979) on the effects of adjunct questions. That is, students scored better on criterion-test items of the same type as the inserted questions. The important new finding was that the inspection and reaction times were greater when students were studying "relevant" text segments than when studying the filler or irrelevant segments. In addition, positive correlations were found between inspection time and test performance and between cognitive effort and test performance.

These results for all the techniques discussed suggest the following scenario. In these experimental conditions, students process the entire text in a general "reading to comprehend" mode. When they determine that a segment of text is relevant to the criterion task, two processing changes occur: (a) the amount of inspection time on that text segment increases compared to that on task-irrelevant text segments and (b) the amount of cognitive effort or concentration increases. These increases in inspection time and cognitive effort are reflected in improved performance on the corresponding test items. Note that cognitive effort does not appear to be an "all or none" phenomenon. The fact that students do remember *some* task-irrelevant information indicates that they are at least processing it at a minimal level. The focusing seems to involve a burst of processing energy or a quantum leap in cognitive effort beyond the baseline condition.

Even though increased recall of information seems to be caused by greater effort and/or inspection time when reading specific segments of the text, the reverse is not necessarily true. That is, specific segments of text which are recalled at different levels of completeness under experimental conditions are not always accompanied by corresponding differences in inspection times and measures of effort.

Britton, Meyer, Simpson, Holdredge, and Curry (1979) report results from students who read two different expository passages about the same general topic. The passages contained an identical target paragraph at different levels of structural importance. When the target paragraph was high in the content structure (main ideas), compared to being low in that structure (supporting details), recall of information from the paragraph was much higher. However, the inspection times and the cognitive-effort measures related to the target showed no difference due to its importance in the content structure.

The authors suggest several hypotheses to account for this finding, but the most compelling one to us is the so-called retrieval hypothesis proposed earlier by B. J. F. Meyer (1975). This hypothesis accounts for the difference in what the students did at the time they recalled the information rather than what they did at the time of encoding. The task demands of free recall and the tendency of information from high in a cognitive structure to be recalled first probably accounts for the differential performance of the two groups.

An inspection of the experimental procedures shows that the students were told "that reading to remember the information in the text was the primary task." The inference probably made by most students was that virtually any information in the passage was equally likely to appear on a test later, so they applied attention and cognitive effort rather uniformly over the entire passage, including the target paragraph, at the time of encoding. Had the students known that they were going to be tested over the main ideas only, results from Reynolds et al. (1979) would lead us to suspect that greater inspection time and cognitive effort would have been spent on the segments that contained those ideas. A corresponding increase in recall of those ideas is also hypothesized.

So, we see that the results of Britton et al. (1979), which at first glance seem inconsistent with the scenario portrayed earlier, actually may be compatible with it. At any rate, after making the point that students do direct and focus their attention and cognitive effort while reading text, we next stress the point that the type of processing or encoding in which a student engages is also an important variable in studying.

What cognitive processes actually occur when students focus attention and concentrate harder is only conjecture at this point. However, two theoretical frameworks suggest in a very general way some processing variables relevant to studying.

The first theoretical framework is the principle of "levels of processing" (R. C. Anderson, 1970, 1972; Craik & Lockhart, 1972). According to this principle, discourse is analyzed in a hierarchy of processing stages, from an analysis of physical or sensory features to extraction of meaning. The durability of memory traces is a function of "depth of processing," where greater depth implies a greater degree of semantic analysis. In other words, what is stored in memory is determined by the kinds of operations performed on the input.

The second theoretical framework is a modification of the principle of levels of processing proposed by Morris, Bransford, and Franks (1977). Morris et al. report research suggesting the need to replace the concept of "levels of processing" with one emphasizing "transfer-appropriate processing."[1] According to the concept of transfer-appropriate processing, the value of particular processing activity must be defined relative to particular goals and purposes of the learner. That is, particular types of processing are not inherently deep/meaningful or shallow/superficial: it depends on the learner's goals. For example, if the learner's purpose is to attend to so-called superficial aspects of text, such as number of multisyllabic words, deeper, more meaningful processing is not appropriate and may actually impede encoding of the target material.

The concept of transfer-appropriate processing helps explain the earlier conclusions about the effect of knowledge of the criterion task on performance and on attention focusing. The more specific students' knowledge of the criterion task, the more able and likely they are to focus attention on relevant material and engage in processing activities appropriate to performing that task.

In sum, the theoretical framework of transfer-appropriate processing (or the principle of encoding specificity) suggests that studying will be effective if

[1] The concept of transfer-appropriate processing is very similar to "the principle of encoding specificity" presented by Tulving and Thomson (1973). According to the principle of encoding specificity, the way in which information is encoded determines how it is stored, which, in turn, determines which retrieval cues will access it effectively. This principle calls attention to the important interaction between initial encoding and subsequent retrieval operations: the optimal form of processing is ultimately dependent on the nature of the retrieval task.

students process the right information in the right way, where "rightness" is defined in relationship to the criterion task. In other words, studying will be facilitated to the extent that students know the performance requirements of the criterion task and encode the information in an optimal form to meet those requirements. In most school-learning situations, the usual criterion tasks require comprehension and recall. The implication for studying from the levels of processing framework, therefore, is that performance on school-related learning tasks will be facilitated to the extent that students attend to, interact with, and elaborate on the underlying "meaning" of the text.

Students can and do engage in a variety of covert and overt activities to help them process the right information in the right way. Most of the common studying techniques, such as underlining, note taking, summarizing, and outlining are commonly used because teachers of studying and students alike intuitively believe that these methods will help the student learn and remember the required information. Unfortunately, empirical research fails to confirm the purported benefits of the popular strategies. So far, the effort to find the one superior method has not been successful; the few studies that have been done present a confusing array of inconsistent results. In the next section, we propose that the confusion stems from a failure to consider the interaction of the state and processing variables discussed in this chapter. We will develop the case that, for the most part, research on common studying techniques has so far ignored the influence of the student's knowledge or beliefs about the criterion task and the match (or mismatch) between the encoding processes during the studying session and the retrieval processes required for performance of the criterion task. Usually the reader of the research report knows neither what subset of presented information the subject selected for processing nor the depth of the processing effort. Information about the studying condition to which a subject was assigned does not reveal the precise nature of the processing activities used by the subjects. For example, a subject who is "taking notes" could be merely copying the author's words, which entails a very superficial level of processing, or he or she could be engaging in deep processing, as reflected in notes that reorganize or elaborate the input.

In addition, readers are often uninformed about the criterion task. Even if the researcher reported the general type of test (e.g., constructed response or multiple choice), this information is insufficient to convey the depth of processing required to perform the task. For example, multiple-choice questions could test knowledge ranging from detail or recognition to application of principles (R. C. Anderson, 1972).

RESEARCH ON COMMON STUDYING TECHNIQUES

Underlining

Perhaps because it is quick and easy, underlining is probably the most popular aid used in studying text. However, by far the majority of research done on student-generated underlining shows it to be no more effective than other studying techniques (Arnold, 1942; Hoon, 1974; Idstein & Jenkins, 1972; Kulhavy et al., 1975; Stordahl & Christensen, 1956; Todd & Kessler, 1971; Willmore, 1966).

It is difficult to comment on these results because insufficient information is provided about the encoding and retrieval-processing variables—what the subjects underlined and the requirements of the criterion test.

Three studies showed positive results for underlining (or its equivalent, highlighting). Rickards and August (1975), Schnell and Rocchio (1975), and Fowler and Barker (1974) all used designs comparing groups who produced their own text cues, groups who read cued materials, and groups who used uncued text. The results of the three studies are similar. In the Rickards and August study, college students who had actively underlined the passage recalled significantly more idea units and spent considerably more time on the task than subjects in the other treatment groups. The increased studying time and greater recall may indicate that students who underline may be processing the text more thoroughly than they otherwise would.

In the Schnell and Rocchio study, high school students who received an underlined text or who underlined their own text recalled a greater number of idea units on immediate and delayed free-recall tests than students who read an uncued text. In addition, students who did their own underlining scored significantly higher than the other two groups on the immediate recall test.

Fowler and Barker found no overall difference between treatments in performance by college students on a delayed multiple-choice test. However, subjects who highlighted the text outperformed subjects who received a highlighted text on items corresponding to highlighted materials, but not on items corresponding to unhighlighted material. Also, for active highlighters, the probability of getting an item correct, given that the corresponding information had been highlighted, was significantly greater than the probability of getting an item correct if the corresponding information had not been highlighted.

The results of these studies indicate that the major benefit of underlining does not come from the mere cueing of information, for text with supplied underlining cues information but does not necessarily enhance recall. Rather, the primary facilitative effect of underlining occurs when the student generates the underlining, presumably because of the amount of processing required to make the decision about what to underline.

Note Taking

Note taking vies with underlining for popularity as a studying aid. Theoretically, note taking has great potential as a studying aid, for it allows the student to record a reworked (perhaps more deeply processed) version of the text in a form appropriate for the criterion task. However, the few studies that have been done on note taking from prose have mixed results, with most studies showing that note taking is no more effective than other studying techniques. In this section, the results of empirical studies of note taking will be discussed with respect to state and processing variables. Studies showing positive effects for note taking will be discussed first.

In two experiments, Shimmerlik and Nolan (1976) had high school students read a 1200-word passage organized in one of two ways. Students were instructed to take notes that either maintained the presented organization or imposed an alternate organization. On immediate and delayed free-recall measures, students who reorganized the passage in their notes recalled significantly more idea units than students who maintained the original organization. A possible explanation for this finding is that reorganizing the passage forces deep processing of the text; the subject has to understand the original organization as well as think through how the content and relationships must be restructured to form the new organization. Repeated semantic operations on the content and relationships led to more durable memory traces. This type of encoding was well suited to a free-recall criterion test, in which the subject's score reflects ability to reproduce content and relationships in the absence of retrieval cues. On the other hand, subjects who took notes that maintained the original organization did not necessarily have to process the material at a deep level; they, therefore, had less information available and/or accessible.

In an experiment by Kulhavy et al. (1975), high school students either read, underlined a limited amount, or took limited notes on a narrative. In addition, they were either given no instructions about the criterion test or told to expect either a multiple-choice or constructed-response test. On the criterion measure consisting of both multiple-choice and constructed-response items, note takers significantly outperformed underliners and read-only subjects, who did not differ from each other. These results are difficult to interpret because no information is provided about the type of notes taken, which might indicate the nature of encoding. However, as the authors point out, since the note takers significantly outperformed the underliners, they seemed to be doing "something more" than merely identifying information. The limitation on the amount of notes taken per page may have induced subjects to record summary statements, which would presumably require a deeper level of processing.

Bretzing and Kulhavy (1979) had high school subjects read a 2000-word passage in one of four conditions designed to promote different levels of processing: (a) write summaries of each page, (b) take paraphrase notes of the main idea, (c) take verbatim notes, and (d) record words beginning with a capital letter. A control group simply read the passage. On a test of constructed response items requiring integration of information, summary writers and paraphrase note takers performed equally well and significantly higher than verbatim note takers, who performed the same as the reading-only control group. Subjects who were assigned the letter-search task fared worst of all. The authors explained the results in terms of levels of processing—writing summaries and taking paraphrase notes require greater cognitive effort than do the other treatments. A supplementary explanation might be that the subjects who summarized and took paraphrase notes were encoding the information in a transfer-appropriate manner, which subjects in the other conditions were not. Indeed, the studying activity least similar to the criterion task (searching for capitals) produced the worst performance.

In another study by Bretzing and Kulhavy (1981), college students read passages in one of three conditions: (1) read only, (2) take notes in preparation for delivering a lecture to high school students, or (3) take notes in preparation for delivering a presentation to professionals. For the purposes of this paper, the important results were (1) on a free-recall test, both groups of notetakers recalled significantly more idea units than the read-only group; (2) an idea unit had significantly greater chance of being recalled if it was originally written in notes; and (3) for the most part, subjects took verbatim notes. As in their earlier study, the authors offer a "levels of processing" explanation for the results. Taking notes, even verbatim notes, involves "deeper" processing of the material than reading only. An additional explanation might be that taking notes was a transfer-appropriate way of encoding the text in preparation for free recall. In effect, subjects were "practicing" for free recall as they took their notes.

One of the results of an early study by Mathews (1938) provides additional support for the effectiveness of note taking: 735 high school students studied a 2000-word passage by either reading and rereading, reading and taking marginal notes, or reading and taking notes in outline form. Overall, the groups did not differ significantly in performance on a test consisting of multiple-choice items and items requiring outlining or organizing of information. However, subjects who read and took notes in outline form tended to score highest on the outlining half of the test. In terms of transfer-appropriate processing, this situation reflects an optimal match of encoding and retrieval processes.

In contrast to the few studies showing positive results for note taking, most studies do not show an advantage for note taking compared to other studying strategies (see T. H. Anderson, 1980). These results are difficult to interpret because of a lack of information about state variables (what students knew or expected the task demands to be) and processing variables (encoding as reflected in the focus and nature of the notes taken and the retrieval demanded by the nature of the criterion task). In most of these studies, however, subjects are probably either not processing the right information with respect to the criterion task or are not encoding the information as deeply as they might be in another condition. This conclusion is based on the following line of reasoning.

The first possibility is that subjects may not be processing the right information. In most experiments, subjects have a limited studying time, which is usually the same for all treatments. Obviously, taking notes requires more time than simply reading the text. The time that note takers use to record some information is time subtracted from processing other information. In the absence of knowledge of the criterion task, subjects take notes over what they think will be tested. Probably, subjects select the "main idea" or "most important" information as the focus of their note-taking efforts; they may not have time to process less important information. Research has shown, however, that people tend to remember the "most important" information anyway (e.g. Johnson, 1970; Meyer & McConkie, 1973; B. J. F. Meyer, 1975). Therefore, note takers may be learning "main ideas" very well, but at the expense of learning other information. On the other hand, subjects who use less time-consuming studying techniques (e.g., read-reread and underline) are able to distribute their attention and effort more evenly over the passage. Therefore, a read-reread group, for example, might have an advantage over a note-taking group when the criterion task taps information of lesser importance or when the criterion task is free recall (in which case the score reflects total number of idea units recalled without respect to importance). The second possibility for the apparent ineffectiveness of note taking is that subjects may not be taking notes in a way that entails deep processing. For example, subjects may choose to record information verbatim from the text rather than recording a reworked, paraphrased representation of text meaning. Either or both of those analyses may help explain the results of the following studies.

Arnold (1942) had college students study history in one of four conditions: reading with underscoring and marginal notation, reading and outlining important ideas, reading and summarizing, or repetitive reading. The criterion test consisted of both factual questions and higher-level comprehension questions. A reanalysis of the data by T. H. Anderson (1980) revealed that on both immediate and delayed tests, repetitive reading was the most effective strategy. In a study by Todd and Kessler (1971), college students studied a short story using strategies of underlining, note taking, or reading only. Total number of idea units recalled on a free-recall test did not differ for the three groups. Howe and Singer (1975) had college students study a 286-word passage in the following conditions: take verbatim notes (copy), summarize each paragraph, or read-reread. Results on both immediate and delayed free-recall measures showed that the read-reread group outperformed the summarizing group, who, in turn, outperformed the verbatim notetakers.

In two experiments by Poppleton and Austwick (1964), postgraduate students and 12-to-13-year-olds either worked through a programmed text and filled in the blanks or read and took notes on the same material presented in the form of a textbook. On an immediate-criterion test consisting of constructed-response, multiple-choice, and application items, the adults performed equally well in either condition, but the children scored significantly higher in the programmed-text than in the note-taking condition. Compared to taking notes, working through the programmed text may have elicited deeper processing as subjects actively searched their semantic store or engaged in lookback behavior in the text itself. It may also be that subjects in the programmed-text condition were forced to make the kinds of responses required by the criterion test, while those in the note-taking condition were spending the available study time recording information unrelated to the criterion test.

In some studies, the ineffectiveness of note taking compared to other studying strategies may occur because the potentially deeper processing associated with note taking is not the right way to process the particular passage with respect to the criterion task. One example of this situation is a study by Schultz and DiVesta (1972). The stimulus passage used in this study consisted of statements about six attributes of six imaginary nations. The passages were organized in one of three ways: (a) name organization—the six attributes of a single nation were presented together, (b) attribute organization—for a given attribute, the different values associated with each nation were presented together, or (c) random organization. Thus, the stimulus passages were lists of facts. List learning can proceed smoothly without requiring deep processing. Therefore, it is not surprising that the high school subjects who took notes had no advantage over subjects who (presumably) spent the studying time in reading and mental rehearsal. In fact, under such circumstances, note taking could be detrimental— if notetakers do engage in deeper processing, they may actually store a less accurate representation of the text meaning—a representation colored by their prior knowledge, perspective, and interests. This outcome was realized in the Schultz and DiVesta study, for note takers introduced a significantly greater number of errors and had a greater tendency to recall information in a different organization from that of the stimulus passage.

Another example in which the type of processing associated with note taking may have biased the results is the previously cited Todd and Kessler (1971) experiment. The stimulus passage used in this study was "The War of the Ghosts" (the story used in Bartlett's, 1932, well-known prose-learning research). "The War of the Ghosts" is a very unusual passage—it is a story from another culture with a structure and content unfamiliar to most American college students. Distortions and intrusions in the recall of this passage are the rule rather than the exception. With the potential of deeper processing, a note-taking condition might accentuate the tendency to alter the structure and content of this passage, thus depressing the accuracy of free recall. In sum, the Schultz and DiVesta (1972) and Todd and Kessler (1971) experiments suggest that note taking may not be an asset to processing if the material to be learned is a list of facts or has some very unusual characteristics.

In conclusion, our analysis of the research on note taking from prose suggests that note taking can be an effective strategy if it entails attention focusing and processing in a way compatible with the demands of the criterion task. In studies where note taking has not been found too effective, it may be because students were either focusing attention on and processing information unrelated to the demands of the criterion task or failing to take notes in a manner that elicited sufficiently deep or thorough processing.

Summarizing

Research in support of summarizing as a studying activity is sparse indeed. One study with results in support of summarizing was the Bretzing and Kulhavy (1979) study (discussed in the previous section) in which summarizers significantly outperformed a reading-only control group. A second study in support of summarizing was reported by Taylor (1982). In this study, fifth-grade students received seven hours of instruction in how to prepare and study "hierarchical summaries." The hierarchical-summarization task consisted of preparing an outline corresponding to the hierarchical organization of the text. A control group received directed reading lessons over the same material studied by the experimental group. The lessons involved prereading discussion, reading, and answering, as well as reviewing and discussing answers to questions.

On immediate- and delayed-criterion tests, subjects read and studied test passages; the next day they wrote free recalls and answered short-answer questions about the passages. Compared to the control group, the group trained in the hierarchical-summarization task recalled more idea units and had better organized recalls but did not have higher short-answer test scores. Taylor explained the results using the notion of transfer-appropriate processing: in generating their hierarchical summaries, the subjects in the experimental treatment had practiced for organized recall. The advantage of the experimental treatment on a free-recall task was not replicated in a second study. However, the results of both experiments revealed that children who generated better summaries tended to recall more than children who generated poorer summaries. Taylor's results suggest that students need fairly extensive training in how to summarize text before they can use summarizing as an effective studying strategy.

To our knowledge, no other research besides the Bretzing and Kulhavy (1979) and Taylor (1982) studies have found summarizing to be more effective than repetitive reading. In fact, studies by Germane (1921a, 1921b), Arnold (1942), and Howe and Singer (1975) found summarizing to be inferior to a read-reread strategy. In a study by Stordahl and Christensen (1956), the effect of summarizing was no different than the effect of using other techniques, including repetitive reading.

The explanation for the apparent lack of effectiveness of summarizing in these studies parallels that used with regard to note taking: in the summarizing conditions, subjects were probably focusing attention on or engaging in transfer-appropriate processing. In producing their summaries, subjects were presumably using the available studying time locating, organizing, and recording the main ideas, which they would have recalled relatively well anyway. Summarizers probably did not have time to process information of low structural importance. In contrast, the reading-only subjects had time to process information at all importance levels. The criterion tests for all studies, except the Howe and Singer (1975) experiment, were objective tests that probably included items tapping knowledge of less important passage information. Therefore, in accordance with the transfer-appropriate processing notion, it is not surprising that the repetitive readers scored higher on the criterion measures. On the free-recall tests of the Howe and Singer study, on the other hand, summary writers recalled significantly more items than subjects who merely copied the text, which probably reflects the transfer-appropriate processing that subjects were using as they wrote their summaries.

According to our analysis, summary writing is likely to be most effective as a studying strategy if (1) students receive instruction in how to produce summaries and (2) the criterion-task demands reflect the kind of processing used in writing a summary.

Student Questioning

The questioning technique requires that students *generate* questions about the prose they are studying. This technique is similar to note taking, in that the student makes a written record of selected information from the text. The questioning technique differs from note taking, in that the format of the recorded idea is that of a question. Theoretically, the processing effort required to generate questions should result in studying gains.

Several studies have compared the effects of questioning behaviors when the student generates the question versus when questions are given to the student. Significant differences favoring student construction of questions were found in three investigations. In a study by Duell (1978), college students who constructed multiple-choice questions from instructional objectives outperformed students who simply studied the passage with the list of objectives on a criterion test consisting of lower-level recognition items and higher-level application items. In a study by Frase and Schwartz (1975), both high school and college students who wrote questions scored significantly higher than reading-only controls. Furthermore, students scored significantly higher on "targeted" test items (test items for which they had written similar studying items) than on nontargeted items (test items with no corresponding student-generated item). Finally, Schmelzer (1975) demonstrated positive effects on a multiple-choice-criterion test for a strategy of generating questions *after* reading.

Positive results for student generation of questions were also obtained in a study by André and Anderson (1979). In this study, one group of high school students was trained to write questions about main ideas. On tests over two passages, a questioning with training group and a group who wrote questions without training obtained higher scores than a read-reread control group. The two question-writing groups did not differ from each other, but low- and middle-verbal-ability students benefited from training in question writing more than did high-verbal-ability subjects.

In other studies, the student-generated-questions treatment had no effect. Specifically, Pederson (1976) used Schmelzer's (1975) materials and failed to replicate the earlier results. In addition, Bernstein (1973), Morse (1975), and Owens (1977) were unable to find an effect for student questioning.

It seems plausible that when student questioning *is* effective, it is so because students are forced to encode the information more than they might if they simply read it. Writing questions probably requires students to at least paraphrase or perform some other transformation of the presented text; these activities entail "deeper processing" (see R. C. Anderson, 1972).

Outlining

Since outlining presumably requires deeper processing in order to produce an alternative representation of text meaning, it should theoretically be a relatively effective studying technique. Two early studies did find outlining after training to be superior to a reading-only strategy. In an extensive training program, Barton (1930) taught outlining to 96 high school students in three schools. The general processing strategy was (a) skim the article to find the main divisions, (b) skim the article a second time to find the main subdivisions, and (c) read the article again carefully to find the facts corresponding to each subdivision. Students then applied the outlining strategy to two units of geography, ancient history, or American history materials. Performance on objective tests was significantly higher for students who had been trained in outlining than for matched groups who had similar instruction, except for the outlining training.

Salisbury (1935) administered a 30-lesson training program in outlining and summarizing to seventh-, ninth-, and twelfth-grade English students. Compared with matched control subjects who received no training, the trained subjects showed significant gains on a standardized reading test (equivalent to one or two grades of improvement) and on a standardized test of reasoning ability.

In contrast to the positive results of the Barton and Salisbury studies, four studies found outlining to be no more effective than other strategies, including repetitive reading (Arnold, 1942; Stordahl & Christensen, 1956; Todd & Kessler, 1971; Willmore, 1966). In none of these studies were students taught how to outline.

Two studies, therefore, suggest that with fairly extensive training in how to process information logically, students can learn to use outlining as an effective attention-focusing and processing device. It is not surprising that students need to be taught this complex skill in order to use it effectively. When students are told to outline but are given no training in how to do so, they may use the format of an outline but only process the text superficially. A potential problem with outlining as a studying aid is that it is very time consuming to think through the logical relationships in text and represent the meaning in outline form.

Elaboration

Elaboration refers to the formation of a relationship between previously learned information and new, unfamiliar material by means of mental images or verbal elaborations, such as inferences and analogies. We were able to locate very few studies investigating the effects of elaboration on learning from text.

In a study reported by Diekhoff, Brown, and Dansereau (1982), undergraduates were given three hours of instruction in a four-step studying procedure that involved elaboration. The four steps were (1) identification of key concepts; (2) definition of key concepts by finding related information; (3) elaboration of key concepts by activities, such as thinking of examples or potential applications of information; and (4) relationship-guided comparison of key concepts, involving the search for similarities, differences, and other relationships among the concepts being compared. The trained group and an untrained control group read and studied two passages and completed essay tests asking for definitions and comparisons one week later. Trained subjects received significantly higher scores than untrained subjects. The results can be interpreted in terms of the concept of transfer-appropriate processing. As the authors admit, the tests required recall of the same information in much the same format as generated by the trained students during the studying session.

Bransford, Stein, Shelton, and Owings (1980) discuss several studies designed to explore how children learn new information. Those students that knew and could access relevant information from memory about what they were reading could remember better the information that they read. For example, fifth-grade students read about camels and encountered facts, such as: "camels can close their nasal passages and have special eyelids to protect their eyes." Students who understood the adaptation notion of animal features made use of their prior knowledge of sand storms by linking the "closing of nasal passages" and "special eyelids" as a means of coping with the damaging effects of sand. It is clear in these studies that students who were able to elaborate their prior knowledge with information that they were reading, remembered the facts better.

Weinstein, Underwood, Wicker, and Cubberly (1979) report some studies in which training in a variety of elaborative learning strategies resulted in higher performance on comprehension and recall measures. However, on the whole, their results in favor of elaboration as a technique for learning and remembering connected discourse are not particularly robust.

Techniques for Representing Text Diagrammatically

Recently, three groups working independently have developed methods for visually representing the important relationships among ideas in text. These techniques make possible the transformation of linear prose into nonlinear symbolic representations that are presumably more closely matched to the way knowledge is stored in memory.

Two of the techniques, networking and mapping, are conceptually very similar. Networking was developed at Texas Christian University and expanded at the National Technical Institute for the Deaf in Rochester, N.Y. Mapping is the product of a development team at the Center for the Study of Reading, University of Illinois. Both networking and mapping are based on the assumption that there are a few fundamental relationships in text (including example, characteristic, definition, temporal, causal, compare and contrast) which are cued by standard lexical and syntactic devices. The third technique, schematizing, a product of the University of Amsterdam, allows for the representation of coordinate and subordinate relationships among ideas but does not distinguish the precise nature of the relationships.

Because these text-representation techniques are so new, little research has been completed to test their effectiveness. However, studies by Dansereau (1979) with hearing college students and by Long, Hein, and Coggiola (1978) with deaf college students showed promising results for networking. A study by Armbruster (1979) showed facilitative effects for mapping as a reading-comprehension/studying technique for middle school students.

The promise of methods like networking, mapping, and schematizing as studying aids probably lies in the fact that they force the student to attend to and process the relationships among *all* idea units in order to translate the prose into a coherent diagram. The benefit of this intense processing must be weighed against the costs. As with outlining, these techniques need to be taught to students before they can be used effectively. Also, with any of these strategies, students must spend considerable time constructing a visual representation of text.

Conclusion about the Research on Studying Techniques

Using the notions of state and processing variables, particularly the theoretical perspectives of levels of processing and transfer-appropriate processing, we have attempted to impose some order on the otherwise confusing array of results of research on studying techniques. We believe that the following conclusions are warranted. Almost any technique *can* be effective if its use is accompanied by focused attention and encoding in a form and manner appropriate to the criterion task. However, some techniques have more potential than others for promoting the deeper processing suited to criterion tasks requiring greater comprehension and/or recall. These techniques include outlining, networking, mapping, and schematizing, which all force students to identify or impose relationships that convey the meaning of text. Not surprisingly, these techniques that are likely to yield the highest learning benefits also have the greatest costs in student time and energy.

CONCLUSIONS

This review leads us to some simple notions about the complex phenomenon of studying. First, regarding state variables, we see that when the criterion tasks associated with studying are made explicit, as compared to remaining vague, students spend more time and effort on the relevant segments of texts and learning outcomes generally improve. Second, regarding processing variables, when students know the nature of the criterion task as well as the type of relevant encoding activities in which to engage, their performance on the criterion task improves.

There is some evidence that those studying techniques which encourage students to process virtually all of the ideas found in text at a deep level improve learning of main and less important points. Examples of these techniques are outlining, mapping, and networking. These techniques demand a tradeoff, however, in that a lot of time and substantial amounts of effort are required to learn and employ them properly. Both of these commodities are at a premium for most students.

Consequently, we seem to be portraying a potential dilemma. On the one hand, we know that students will never have a list of clear criteria available at every studying session to make their efforts more efficient. On the other hand, the incentive is not high enough for students to devote the time and effort required for outlining and networking/mapping/schematizing. However, the picture is not a true dilemma. For example, good students know when to employ deep processing strategies and when it would be a waste of time to do so. They also know whether they understand an idea or not and what to do if comprehension has failed. In other words, there is a higher-order processor, metacognition, which students can and do use in the studying process. In fact, Brown and Baker present a convincing case in their chapter in this volume and elsewhere (e.g., Brown & Palincsar, 1982) that instruction in studying strategies is most effective if it includes training in metacognitive skills.

FUTURE RESEARCH

Much of the research in studying has been guided by the quest to find the perfect strategy. Once located, the perfect strategy could be taught to all students and learning by reading would generally improve. Our review of research shows that the quest has not been very successful. To continue the quest for a perfect strategy is probably not a very good strategy either. Rather, we suggest that research be focused on ways to make the studying techniques compatible with the demands of different instruction programs, disciplines, and student backgrounds. How is studying earth science different from studying American literature? How should a seventh-grade student study photosynthesis, compared to how a college freshman should study photosynthesis? How is studying to take a test different from studying to write a term paper? How should a student who has only two hours, compared to one who has two weeks, study for a test?

We remain concerned about the time and effort required to use some of the more heavy-handed techniques, such as outlining and mapping. Perhaps a profitable line of research could investigate how technologies, like computer-based word processors and video/audio recorder systems, might ease the student effort and shorten the time required to use some of the in-depth studying techniques. Other, more appropriate techniques might evolve out of this line of research.

Finally, we suspect that advances in studying techniques will ride on the heels of advances in several other reading research areas. The more we under-

stand about the nature of text, the role of prior knowledge in learning, the structure of content-area disciplines, and the psychological processes in reading, the
more likely it is that studying techniques can be fine tuned to meet students'
immediate studying needs.

REFERENCES

Alessi, S. M., Anderson, T. H., & Goetz, E. T.   An investigation of lookbacks during study-
    ing. *Discourse Processes,* 1979, *2,* 197–212.
Anderson, R. C.   Control of student mediating processes during verbal learning and in-
    struction. *Review of Educational Research,* 1970, *40,* 349–369.
Anderson, R. C.   How to construct achievement tests to assess comprehension. *Review
    of Educational Research,* 1972, *42,* 145–170.
Anderson, R. C., & Biddle, W. B.   On asking people questions about what they are reading.
    In G. H. Bower (Ed.), *The psychology of learning and motivation* (Vol. 9). New
    York: Academic Press, 1975.
Anderson, T. H.   Study strategies and adjunct aids. In R. J. Spiro, B. C. Bruce, & W. F.
    Brewer (Eds.), *Theoretical issues in reading comprehension: Perspectives from cogni-
    tive psychology, artificial intelligence, linguistics, and education.* Hillsdale, N.J.: Erl-
    baum, 1980.
André, M. E. D. A., & Anderson, T. H.   The development and evaluation of a self-question-
    ing study technique. *Reading Research Quarterly,* 1978–1979, *14,* 605–623.
Arkes, H. R., Schumacher, G. M., & Gardner, E. T.   Effects of orienting tasks on the
    retention of prose material. *Journal of Educational Psychology,* 1976, *68,* 536–545.
Armbruster, B. B.   *An investigation of the effectiveness of "mapping" text as a studying
    strategy for middle school students.* Unpublished doctoral dissertation, University
    of Illinois, 1979.
Arnold, H. F.   The comparative effectiveness of certain study techniques in the field of
    history. *Journal of Educational Psychology,* 1942, *33,* 449–457.
Bartlett, F. C.   *Remembering.* Cambridge: Cambridge University Press, 1932.
Barton, W. A.   *Outlining as a study procedure.* New York: Teachers College, Columbia
    University, 1930.
Bernstein, S.   *The effects of children's question-asking behaviors on problem solution
    and comprehension of written material.* Unpublished doctoral dissertation, Columbia
    University, 1973.
Bransford, J. D., Stein, B. S., Shelton, T. S., & Owings, R. A.   Cognition and adaptation:
    The importance of learning to learn. In J. Harvey (Ed.), *Cognition, social behavior,
    and the environment.* Hillsdale, N.J.: Erlbaum, 1980.
Bretzing, B. B., & Kulhavy, R. W.   Note taking and depth of processing. *Contemporary
    Educational Psychology,* 1979, *4,* 145–153.
Bretzing, B. H., & Kulhavy, R. W.   Note-taking and passage style. *Journal of Educational
    Psychology,* 1981, *73,* 242–250.
Britton, B. K., Meyer, B. J. F., Simpson, R., Holdredge, T. S., & Curry, C.   Effects of
    the organization of text on memory: Tests of two implications of a selective attention
    hypothesis. *Journal of Experimental Psychology: Human Learning and Memory,* 1979,
    5, 496–506.
Britton, B. K., Piha, A., Davis, J., & Wehausen, E.   Reading and cognitive capacity usage:
    Adjunct question effects. *Memory and Cognition,* 1978, *6,* 266–273.
Brown, A. L., & Palincsar, A. S.   Inducing strategic learning from texts by means of
    informed, self-control training. *Topics in Learning and Learning Disabilities.* 1982,
    2, 1–17.

Butterweck, D. S.   *The problem of teaching high school pupils how to study.* New York: Teachers College, Columbia University, 1926.

Class, E. C.   The effect of the kind of test announcement on students' preparation. *Journal of Educational Research,* 1934, *28,* 358–361.

Craik, F. I. M., & Lockhart, R. S.   Levels of processing: A framework for memory research. *Journal of Verbal Learning and Verbal Behavior,* 1972, *11,* 671–684.

Dansereau, D. F.   Development and evaluation of a learning strategy training program. *Journal of Educational Psychology,* 1979, *71,* 64–73.

Diekhoff, G. M., Brown, P. J., Dansereau, D. F.   A prose learning strategy training program based on network and depth-of-processing models. *Journal of Experimental Education,* 1982, *50,* 180–184.

Duell, O. K.   Overt and covert use of objectives of different cognitive levels. *Contemporary Journal of Educational Psychology,* 1978, *3,* 239–245.

Fowler, R. L., & Barker, A. S.   Effectiveness of highlighting for retention of text material. *Journal of Applied Psychology,* 1974, *59,* 358–364.

Frase, L. T., & Schwartz, B. J.   Effect of question production and answering on prose recall. *Journal of Educational Psychology,* 1975, *67,* 628–635.

Geiselman, R. E.   Memory for prose as a function of learning strategy and inspection time. *Journal of Educational Psychology,* 1977, *69,* 547–555.

Germane, C. E.   Outlining and summarizing compared with reading as methods of studying. In G. M. Whipple (Ed.), *20th Yearbook of the National Society for the Study of Education, Part II.* Bloomington, Ill.: Public School Publishing Co., 1921. (a)

Germane, C. E.   The value of the written paragraph summary. *Journal of Educational Research,* 1921, *3,* 116–123. (b)

Glynn, S. M.   Capturing reader's attention by means of typographical cueing strategies. *Educational Technology,* 1978, *18,* 7–12.

Hakstian, A. R.   The effects of type of examination anticipation on test preparation and performance. *Journal of Educational Research,* 1971, *64,* 319–324.

Hoon, P. W.   Efficacy of three common study methods. *Psychology Reports,* 1974, *35,* 1057–1058.

Howe, M. J. A., & Singer, L.   Presentation variables and students' activities in meaningful learning. *British Journal of Educational Psychology,* 1975, *45,* 52–61.

Idstein, P., & Jenkins, J. R.   Underlining versus repetitive reading. *Journal of Educational Research,* 1972, *65,* 321–323.

Johnson, R. E.   Recall of prose as a function of the structural importance of the linguistic units. *Journal of Verbal Learning and Verbal Behavior,* 1970, *9,* 12–20.

Kulhavy, R. W., Dyer, J. W., & Silver, L.   The effects of note-taking and test expectancy on the learning of text material. *Journal of Educational Research,* 1975, *68,* 363–365.

Long, G., Hein, R., & Coggiola, D.   *Networking: A semantic-based learning strategy for improving prose comprehension* (Tech. Rep.). Rochester, N.Y.: Rochester Institute of Technology and the National Technical Institute for the Deaf, 1978.

Lucas, P. A.   *Anticipation of test format: Some effects on retention.* Paper presented at the annual meeting of the American Educational Research Association, April 1977.

Mathews, C. O.   Comparison of methods of study for immediate and delayed recall. *Journal of Educational Psychology,* 1938, *29,* 101–106.

McConkie, G. W., Rayner, K., & Wilson, S.   Experimental manipulation of reading strategies. *Journal of Educational Psychology,* 1973, *65,* 1–8.

Meyer, B. J. F.   *The organization of prose and its effects on memory.* Amsterdam: North-Holland Publishing Co., 1975.

Meyer, B. J. F., & McConkie, G. W.   What is recalled after hearing a passage? *Journal of Educational Psychology,* 1973, *64,* 72–75.

Meyer, G.   An experimental study of the old and new types of examination: I. The effect of the examination set on memory. *Journal of Educational Psychology*, 1934, *25*, 641–660.

Meyer, G.   An experimental study of the old and new types of examination: II. Methods of study. *Journal of Educational Psychology*, 1935, *26*, 30–40.

Meyer, G.   The effects on recall and recognition of the examination set in classroom situations. *Journal of Educational Psychology*, 1936, *27*, 81–99.

Morris, C. D., Bransford, J. D., & Franks, J. J.   Levels of processing versus transfer appropriate processing. *Journal of Verbal Learning and Verbal Behavior*, 1977, *16*, 519–533.

Morse, J. M.   *Effect of reader-generated questions on learning from prose.* Unpublished doctoral dissertation, Rutgers University, 1975.

Owens, A. M.   The effects of question generation, question answering, and reading on prose learning (Doctoral dissertation, University of Oregon, 1976). *Dissertation Abstracts International*, 1977, *37*, 5709A–5710A. (University Microfilms No. 77–4750)

Pederson, J. E. P.   *An investigation into the differences between student-constructed versus experimenter-constructed post-questions on the comprehension of expository prose.* Unpublished doctoral dissertation, University of Minnesota, 1976.

Poppleton, P. K., & Austwick, K.   A comparison of programmed learning and note-taking at two age levels. *British Journal of Educational Psychology*, 1964, *34*, 43–50.

Reynolds, R. E.   *The effect of attention on the learning and recall of important text elements.* Unpublished doctoral dissertation, University of Illinois, 1979.

Reynolds, R. E., Standiford, S. N., & Anderson, R. C.   Distribution of reading time when questions are asked about a restricted category of text information. *Journal of Educational Psychology*, 1979, *71*, 183–190.

Rickards, J. P., & August, G. J.   Generative underlining strategies in prose recall. *Journal of Educational Psychology*, 1975, *67*, 860–865.

Rickards, J. P., & Friedman, F.   The encoding versus the external storage hypothesis in note-taking. *Contemporary Educational Psychology*, 1978, *3*, 136–143.

Rothkopf, E. Z., & Billington, M. J.   Goal-guided learning from text: Inferring a descriptive processing model from inspection times and eye movements. *Journal of Educational Psychology*, 1979, *71*, 310–327.

Salisbury, R.   Some effects of training in outlining. *English Journal*, 1935, *24*, 111–116.

Schmelzer, R. V.   The effect of college student constructed questions on the comprehension of a passage of expository prose. (Doctoral dissertation, University of Minnesota, 1975). *Dissertation Abstracts International*, 1975, *36*, 2162A. (University Microfilms No. 75–21,088)

Schnell, T. R., & Rocchio, D.   A comparison of underlining strategies for improving reading comprehension and retention. In G. H. McNinch & W. D. Miller (Eds.), *Reading: Convention and inquiry* (24th yearbook of the National Reading Conference). Clemson, S.C.: National Reading Conference, 1975.

Schultz, C. B., & DiVesta, F. J.   Effects of passage organization and note-taking on the selection of clustering strategies and on recall of textual materials. *Journal of Educational Psychology*, 1972, *63*, 244–252.

Shimmerlik, S. M., & Nolan, J. D.   Reorganization and the recall of prose. *Journal of Educational Psychology*, 1976, *68*, 779–786.

Stordahl, K. E., & Christensen, C. M.   The effect of study techniques on comprehension and retention. *Journal of Educational Research*, 1956, *49*, 561–570.

Taylor, B. M.   Text structure and children's comprehension and memory for expository material. *Journal of Educational Psychology*, 1982, *74*, 323–340.

Todd, W., & Kessler, C. C.   Influence of response mode, sex, reading ability and level of difficulty on four measures of recall of meaningful written material. *Journal of Educational Psychology*, 1971, *62*, 229–234.

Tulving, E., & Thomson, D. M.   Encoding specificity and retrieval processes in episodic memory. *Psychological Review*, 1973, *80*, 352–373.

Vallance, T. R.   A comparison of essay and objective examinations on learning experiences. *Journal of Educational Research*, 1947, *41*, 279–288.

Weinstein, C. E., Underwood, V. L., Wicker, F. W., & Cubberly, W. E.   Cognitive learning strategies: Verbal and imaginal elaboration. In H. F. O'Neil, Jr., and C. D. Spielberger (Eds.), *Cognitive and affective learning strategies*. New York: Academic Press, 1979.

Willmore, D. J.   *A comparison of four methods of studying a textbook*. Unpublished doctoral dissertation, University of Minnesota, 1966.

22 READABILITY

George R. Klare

INTRODUCTION

The term *readable* may refer to any one of three characteristics of reading matter:

1. Legibility, of either the handwriting or the typography.
2. Ease of reading, owing to the interest-value of the writing.
3. Ease of understanding, owing to the style of writing.

Though the first and second meanings still occur, usage now clearly favors the third meaning, especially in the field of reading. This chapter on readability, thus, concerns itself with qualities of writing which are related to reader comprehension.

The importance of being able to understand seems so obvious as to need no emphasis. Writers in general and teachers in particular have long acknowledged this. The importance of readability as an area of research and the rationale for discussing it rests instead upon three other related considerations.

First, the amount of reading our technological society requires for success—or even survival—has been growing rapidly. Comparing job-related reading requirements for the last half century or so provides some dramatic examples. The field of aviation offers several. The "flight manual" provided for the Curtiss "pusher" airplane of 1911 was barely one-page long; by contrast, the U.S. Navy's Cougar aircraft of 1952 required 1800 pages of documentation and the modern F–14 requires 260,000 pages. Overall, the Navy listed 25 million pages of technical manuals in use in 1979 and adds or revises 300,000 to 500,000 pages annually (Naval Ocean Systems Center, 1979). The U.S. Government itself now prints about 1 million words of regulations and notices in the Federal Register on an average day (*New York Times*, 1977). Many of these become part of the myriad forms and documents which must be read and/or filled out by citizens for such social programs as health, unemployment, and retirement payments. A survey

(R. Murphy, 1973) showed that, as one might expect, readers consider this to be among the most important reading they have to do in a typical day.

Second, reading skills, as measured for U.S. high school graduates over the past two decades or so, have been declining. Though the drop in test scores seems to be leveling off, the reasons for it are still unclear (*ACTivity,* 1979). This gives added meaning to the results of several surveys. Louis Harris and Associates (see DeCrow, 1972), using the kind of social forms and documents mentioned above as testing materials, projected approximately 13 million functionally illiterate adults in the U.S. at the time of its analysis. More recently, Duffy (1976) surveyed a large sample of Navy recruits and found that 18 percent read below an eighth-grade level. A General Accounting Office study (1977), similarly, strongly implies that the average reading ability within selected groups of servicemen may be well below ninth-grade level.

Third, making writing easier to understand offers a partial solution to this pincerlike attack of increased reading combined with decreased reading skills. But can the field of readability research, as currently studied, contribute significantly? Pyrczak, in his article, "Reducing Reading Illiteracy by Improving Reading Materials" (1976), reflects the positive answer given by many current advocates of "plain talk." Bormuth (unpublished) also answers positively, but more specifically, by providing equations to predict the tradeoffs between making material easier and providing more schooling. In fact, the question itself may seem odd when:

- well over 1000 readability references can be found in the library;
- readability ratings of textbooks are widely used in American school systems (Vaughan, 1976);
- over half of the states in the United States have considered or established desirable readability levels for insurance policies (survey of April 1977, conducted by Mr. Rob LaRue, Texas State Board of Insurance);
- the U.S. Department of Defense requires certain readability levels in the manuals prepared by contractors (see Kniffin, 1979);
- President Jimmy Carter, in an executive order on March 23, 1978, requested that U.S. regulations be "as simple and clear as possible" (Carter, 1978);
- seven of the states in the United States had enacted "plain language" laws for consumer contracts as of February 1982 (*Simply Stated,* 1982b) and two more were added as of November 1982 (*Simply Stated,* 1982a);
- the problems predicted by opponents in the five years since New York's pioneer law was passed have not occurred (*Simply Stated,* 1982–1983);
- Great Britain has established a Plain English Campaign complete with Golden Bull Plaques for unreadable writing (*New York Times,* 1982).

Yet a procession of critics, from general commentators to respected scholars, have questioned both the validity and the value of readability measures. A sample from the 1930s to the present includes:

- Moore's prediction of readers "recoiling from reading" rewritten classics (1935);
- S. E. Fitzgerald's criticism of "literature by slide rule" (1953);
- McLaughlin's warnings about "temptations of the Flesch" readability measure (1970);

- Manzo's indictment of readability research as a "construct without a point of reference" (1970);
- Maxwell's conclusion that maybe we have "gone too far" with readability and that an obsession with readability may even be an important factor in the decline of inferential reading skills of teenagers from 1970 to 1974 (1978).
- Chall's study which found the current decline in SAT scores to be associated with a decline in the difficulty of textbooks over a 30-year period (Chall, 1979; Chall, Conrad, & Harris, 1977);
- Walmsley's finding that the readability of a document is a poor indicator of its comprehensibility (Trapini & Walmsley, 1981; Walmsley, Scott, & Lehrer, 1981);
- Wagner's tale of Beowulf battling the Dale and Chall monster (1981);
- McConnell's questions about the usefulness of formulas (1982);
- Davison and Kantor's case study of adaptations which shows that readability formulas fail to define readable texts (1982);
- Lange's "second looks, second thoughts" concerning readability formulas (1982).

In view of this contradictory state of affairs, Coupland's query "Is readability real?" (1978) should come as no surprise. His comments present a major aspect of the issue very concisely, and bear repeating here.

> Traditional objective techniques for assessing the readability level of texts are often said to lack face validity. This may be because the simplicity of these techniques, particularly of readability formulas, does not seem compatible with the extreme complexity of what is being assessed. . . . the problem of validity remains; if readability is not measurable in its own right, how do we know that the simple variables that we are measuring are really indexing something larger, something that we might want to call "readability"? (Coupland, 1978, p. 15)

To spare any reader suspense, Coupland answers affirmatively. On the basis of intercomparisons of values from 5 readability formulas, 2 cloze-testing methods, and 15 teachers' judgments on 5 randomly chosen passages, he concludes that

> . . . readability *is* a variable that can be quantified on a single scale, and can be indexed in quite different ways." (Coupland, 1978, p. 17)

Chall (1979) answers the question about the problematic role of readability in another way: teachers, not formulas, are responsible for the trend to easy books since that is the kind they ask of publishers. Parkhurst (1979) agrees that this is where the problem lies, and Jorgenson (1977) has even provided the rationale: in general, classroom behavior improves as reading material becomes easier. Yet, as Chall (1979) again points out, recent adoption of more difficult texts in some primary schools has led to increased reading scores, and readability formulas can help in the selection of harder as well as easier ones. Hartley, Trueman, and Burnhill (1980) agree that formulas, despite their faults, can predict whether one piece of text will be easier than another.

Such views have not convinced all doubters, leading several journals to devote all or part of recent issues to readability, with contributors presenting different opinions. These journals include *IEEE Transactions on Professional Communication* (1981), *Journal of Business Communication* (1981), and *Information Design Journal* (1981). Since use of readability formulas has now spread so widely as one answer to society's reading dilemma, a closer look at the issues seems timely. As usual, a simple question, such as Tibbetts's "How Much Should We Expect Readability Formulas to Do?" (1973) does not yield the desired simple answer; instead, a new set of questions emerges. A brief look at the history of readability measurement can provide a useful introduction to these questions.

SOME HISTORY

Fortunately, several authors (Chall, 1958; Gilliland, 1972; Klare, 1963, 1974–1975) have presented historical accounts of readability measurement. These readily available sources review the details up to about 1974 and need be supplemented here only with new material appearing since. This makes it possible to emphasize instead certain high points in the history of readability research and then to pose some significant questions raised by that research.

High Points up to 1974

Reviewing the extensive literature on readability tempts a writer to include more material than a chapter permits. Assembling the list of references for discussion must itself be a subjective task, and cutting this information down to manageable size, to highlights, must be even more so. Consequently, readers may wish more detail in some cases, may disagree with the interpretations presented, or may wish to consult the sources mentioned above for a more complete picture.

Concern for how easily messages can be understood can be traced back to Biblical times. For the purpose of understanding current readability approaches, however, Thorndike's *The Teacher's Word Book* (1921) stands as the first milestone. His tabulations of the frequency with which words occur in print were expanded later (Thorndike, 1932; Thorndike & Lorge, 1944), but publication of the first book set the stage for readability research by providing an objective way of estimating word difficulty. This led Lively and Pressey (1923) to develop the first of the so-called readability formulas. Since such formulas have become the most visible, the most often used, and the most controversial product of readability research, a few words should be said here about their treatment.

1. Readability formula refers to a *predictive* device (Klare, 1963, p. 33) intended to provide quantitative, objective estimates of reading difficulty. Though this qualifier may seem obvious, much of the controversy surrounding readability has arisen from a failure to recognize, or perhaps to remember, the implications of this term. One concerns the distinction between predictors of readability and measures of readability (Klare, 1974–1975); another concerns the distinction between prediction of readable writing and production (preparation) of readable writing. These distinctions will be considered more fully later in drawing some conclusions about the value of readability research.

2. Space limitations prohibit inclusion of readability formulas, except for new ones not included in previous reviews. But even for those formulas presented, original references must be consulted before attempting to apply them because detailed and lengthy steps would otherwise have had to be included.

Readability formulas have appeared in a rather steady progression since Lively and Pressey's pioneer effort. Vogel and Washburne's formula (1928) took the form of a regression equation involving more than one language variable and, thus, became the prototype for most formulas since their time. Gray and Leary's *What Makes a Book Readable* (1935) has become a classic because of its comprehensive look at the many possible contributors to readability. A sample of librarians, publishers, and teachers and directors of adult education classes contributed 288 suggested "factors," classified under four headings:

1. Content (judged most important).
2. Style of expression and presentation (a close second).
3. Format (a more distant third).
4. General factors of organization (judged least important).

Gray and Leary considered only style factors for the readability formulas they developed, and for this they found only 44 of these precise, objective, and frequent enough to become candidates for inclusion. Formula developers since have almost universally followed the same pattern of omitting content, format, and organization variables out of an inability rather than an unwillingness—as such critics as Harris and Jacobson (1979) have occasionally implied—to do so successfully (e.g., see Björnsson, 1968). This restriction does, of course, place a logical limit on both the face validity and predictive validity of formulas and will, therefore, be discussed again later.

Prior to World War II, few except educators and librarians used formulas, but their application in deciding whether particular books were appropriate to the reading skill of particular readers grew rapidly. Washburne and Morphett (actually the Vogel and Washburne referred to above) took the helpful step of providing a formula (1938) which yielded scores on a grade-placement scale. Such a scale now appears as controversial as it was helpful, with the Delegates Assembly of the International Reading Association passing a resolution in April 1981, advocating that grade-equivalent scores be abandoned for reading tests (*Reading Research Quarterly*, 1981). Once again, the concept and value of a grade-level scale must be considered (as it will be later) in evaluating the contribution of readability research.

Lorge (1939) refined the formulas up to his time by introducing two innovations which became trends.

1. Use of the McCall and Crabbs *Standard Test Lessons in Reading* (1925) as a criterion. This extensive set of passages provides for grade-placement scores, and came to be used in its revisions (1950, 1961) almost exclusively for formula development until about the middle 1960s. Harris and Jacobson (1974, 1975, 1976; Jacobson, Kirkland & Selden, 1978) later argued that many of the grade scores were inaccurate and restandardized them before using the McCall and

Crabbs passages in developing their formulas. Stevens, after corresponding with William McCall, went even farther, stating that, "The lessons were never meant to be used for rigorous testing, and were never intended for use as a criterion for readability formulae" (Stevens, 1980, p. 414). The *Standard Test Lessons in Reading* was not, as it happens, abandoned for these reasons, but rather (as will be seen later) because of the advent of a more convenient criterion. Nevertheless, with so many still-used formulas based on *Standard Test Lessons in Reading*, their appropriateness (as part of the larger question of developmental criteria) will be reconsidered later.

2. Use of a simple, efficient formula. Lorge felt that the predictive power of the complex formulas did not justify the labor they entailed and provided a three-variable formula almost as powerful.

Since Lorge's time, developers have often limited themselves to two-variable formulas, one covering the semantic factor and one the syntactic factor, as a reasonable tradeoff between the labor involved and the predictive power achieved. Flesch's Reading Ease formula (1948) provides a good example; the two readily counted variables of word length in syllables and average sentence length in words helped the formula (combined with Flesch's skillful popularization) become the most widely used of all readability formulas. Dale and Chall (1948) published another two-variable formula, which became widely used, especially in educational circles. They also used average-sentence length in words as their index of syntactic difficulty, but they used a list of familiar words (rather than word length) to determine semantic difficulty. This variation, because of number of application rules, adds labor but also adds a small but consistent amount of predictive power. Word list and word length remain the most common competitors as indexes of semantic difficulty. Spache (1953) chose the word-list approach for his popular formulas designed for Grades 1–3 (the formulas of Flesch and of Dale and Chall did not reach down that far). Wheeler and Smith (1954) chose the word-length approach for their (less popular) formula for these lower grades.

The effort to make formulas easier to apply has been a consistent trend. Fry (1963) provided one of the most popular manual aids in his "readability graph"; Danielson and Bryan (1963) took advantage of the growing popularity of computers by providing the first two known programs for applying readability formulas. Klare (1974–1975) provided a review of manual and machine aids available up to about 1974; since that time a number of other computer programs have appeared (Carlson, 1980; Gerbens, 1978; Goodman & Schwab, 1980; Irving & Arnold, 1979; Keller, 1982; Schuyler, 1982). Certain of these authors have included their programs in their articles; Schuyler's article is particularly recommended since his published program will provide scores for nine different formulas.

Wide usage of both the Fry graph and the various computer programs (especially those coupled with such other computer programs as ones for typesetting or editing) emphasizes the important role of efficiency in formula application. Fry's suggestion of selecting only three samples further increases ease of application but, at the same time, raises questions about sampling adequacy and range of variation of scores. Fitzgerald (1980, 1981) has been particularly critical of Fry's sampling procedure, even though he qualifies his number of three by suggesting additional samples if difficulty seems to range widely. The critical questions concern what formula users *actually do,* how this influences their decisions, and when (most important of all) this affects reader behavior (Bradley & Ames, 1976). This matter receives further attention later in this chapter.

Growing use of readability formulas for the English language led to application of formulas to other languages. Some research workers adapted English-language formulas for their use, among the first being Kandel and Moles's modification of the Flesch Reading Ease formula for use with French text (1958). Other workers developed formulas specifically for another language, among the first being Spaulding's two formulas for Spanish (1951). A summary of the research up to 1954 in languages other than English can be found in Klare (1974–1975, pp. 91–96). Since this is a rapidly growing area, it will be taken up again later in the section of this chapter dealing with research since 1974.

In 1953, Taylor proposed cloze procedure as a new tool for measuring readability, but Coleman (1965) became the first to use this fill-in-the-blank method as a criterion for the development of a readability formula. Cloze criteria have since supplanted the multiple-choice-based *Standard Test Lessons in Reading* (McCall & Crabbs, 1925, 1950, 1961) as the most popular criterion to serve as a measure of comprehension. The 36 passages calibrated by Miller and Coleman (1967) in terms of cloze percentages correct have been among the most often used. Since the criterion plays a critical role in the predictive power of statistical methods, the widespread use of cloze procedure must be considered later in discussing the value of readability research.

Bormuth began experimenting with cloze criteria at much the same time as E. B. Coleman and in 1969 published the most extensive readability analyses yet made. He used large numbers of subjects, covered a wide range of subject matters, examined most of the newer linguistic variables, employed several criterion levels, and developed formulas for different purposes. His results, as well as the 330 cloze passages he calibrated in terms of percentages correct, continue to provide the basis for much readability research. He found, among his many comparisons, a surprising result: his "unrestricted" formulas with up to 20 variables gained slightly in predictive power over his simpler formulas in the validation process but dropped considerably in cross-validation. This yielded an unexpected answer to those who felt that the availability of computers would lead to more complex and, therefore, necessarily more powerful predictors.

Most formula developers, for reasons of both probable area of application and availability of good criteria, used children and/or children's material in the development process. This has raised validity questions, particularly in the now large-scale applications of formulas outside the field of education. Caylor, Sticht, Fox, and Ford (1973), however, in developing their FORCAST formula for military applications, used only U.S. Army materials and subjects in the process. The effort involved in this thorough approach must, of course, be evaluated against predictive validity as well as face validity.

This brief summary of readability research up to about 1973 (the extent of published reviews) points up the following major trends.

• Early emphasis on word frequency as an indicator of word difficulty supplied the basis for the first objective measures of readability, the first readability formulas.
• Readability formulas evolved quickly into statistical regression equations involv-

ing a number of different language variables which could be subsumed under word (semantic) or sentence (syntactic) factors.

• Attempts to involve variables other than semantic or syntactic (e.g., format, organization, content) in formulas failed almost entirely, but attempts to improve upon these two major sources of variance have continued.

• Developers began to provide formulas which yielded grade-level scales so that mismatches between readers' tested ability and school-text readability could be assessed more easily. Various writers have, however, questioned the validity of grade-level scales.

• Early criticisms of the criteria for formula development led first to the use of the multiple-choice-based McCall and Crabbs *Standard Test Lessons in Reading*, which has recently received its own share of criticism. Later work evolved in two directions: use of the cloze procedure as an alternative criterion and specialized criterion development for specialized formulas.

• Users found early formulas tedious to apply (and sometimes, therefore, also unreliable); efficiency grew in importance as formulas became more widely used (and led, in turn, to still wider usage). Two major directions have emerged: manual application aids and computer programs.

With this analysis of trends in mind, high points from 1974 to the time of writing can be reviewed.

Developments Since 1974

By 1973, formula developers had tried well over 200 different language variables and had, in fact, developed almost as many different formulas. Computers have helped to make this possible since they permit complex analyses, combinations, and comparisons of variables which would have been impossibly time-consuming—if possible at all—in the past. One could have predicted this trend to complexity in the new formulas developed more recently. But in addition, many of the trends apparent up to 1973 have been carried on to new levels in the formulas which have appeared. A review, in fact, suggests that, since many formulas appeared at about the same time in this recent period, they be grouped according to these trends rather than in purely chronological order. Four trends, involving ease of application, development of new criteria, use of new approaches, and work in languages other than English received new emphases, and each will be considered in turn.

Ease of application.   In 1975, Bormuth proposed a new formula designed for manual use by teachers. He selected word-length and sentence-length variables that would be "easy to analyze without getting involved in word lists or complex grammar analyses" (Bormuth, 1975, p. 83).

$$d = 1.069 - \left(.106\,\frac{1}{w}\right) - \left(.0036\,\frac{1}{s}\right) + \left[.000002\left(\frac{1}{s}\right)^{2}\right]$$

where d = difficulty of passage in terms of cloze means

$\dfrac{1}{w}$ = average number of letters per word in a randomly chosen 250-word passage

$\dfrac{1}{s}$ = average number of letters per sentence in a randomly chosen 250-word passage

Though the formula may look difficult in this form, Bormuth has published a table which provides grade placement norms directly upon entry with $1/w$ and $1/s$ values (for cloze criterion scores of 35%, 45%, and 55%). Bormuth also suggests (1975, p. 86) that labor may be reduced by estimating number of letters. He indicates a validity correlation of about .81 for the formula, but says this increases to about .89 when taking 2 passages from the same material and to about .94 when taking 5 (1975, p. 84). He also says that using more than 12 passages becomes inefficient and indicates the standard error of estimate is about .8 of a year (or about 6 cloze percentage points) for a single passage.

Also in 1975, M. Coleman and Liau presented a formula quite similar to Bormuth's formula in terms of variables used.

$$\text{Estimated cloze \%} = 141.8401 - .214590L + 1.079812S$$

where   Estimated cloze % = percentage of cloze deletions that can be
filled in by a college undergraduate
L = number of letters per 100 words
S = number of sentences per 100 words

Coleman and Liau also provide a table (1975, p. 284) and a formula for translating cloze percentages into grade levels (using values based upon the McCall and Crabbs *Standard Test Lessons in Reading*). They suggest their method be made even more efficient by using an optical scanner (with a computerized version of the formula). As to validity, they report a multiple R of .92 with the cloze percentages on the Miller and Coleman passages (Miller & Coleman, 1967).

In 1976, Liau, Bassin, Martin, and Coleman modified the earlier Coleman formulas (1965, 1971). They used the same 36 criterion passages and the same 32 predictor variables as Coleman had used earlier, but modified the criterion and tested several hundred possible computer-derived formulas. From these they selected four which they felt represented a good compromise between ease of scaling and percentage of variance explained.

$$
\begin{aligned}
\text{Estimated cloze \%} &= 159.76 - .24\ Let \\
&= 141.84 - .21\ Let + 1.08\ Sent \\
&= 39.84 - .10\ Let + 1.36\ Sent + .66\ 1\text{-}Syl \\
&= 43.49 - .10\ Let + 1.22\ Sent + .67\ 1\text{-}Syl - .44\ Cord\ Conj
\end{aligned}
$$

where   Estimated cloze % = the percentage of deletions likely to be
inserted correctly in a typical cloze test
Let = number of letters per 100 words
$Sent$ = number of sentences per 100 words
$1\text{-}Syl$ = number of one-syllable words per 100 words
$Cord\ Conj$ = number of coordinate conjunctions per 100 words

They report multiple R^2 values of .816, .851, .880, and .884, respectively. M. Coleman and Liau had, as they say, already discussed (1975) the second of these formulas, and they repeat for all formulas the Coleman and Liau suggestion of using an optical scanning device and a computer program for further ease of use. Note that the R value for this second formula, .94, corresponds to that Bormuth reports for his similar two-variable formula when taking five samples.

It comes as no surprise, therefore, that Liau et al. found a correlation of .867 in cross-validating their second formula against the cloze scores of thirty-two 250-word passages Bormuth had used with school-aged children.

In 1977, Fry extended his readability graph (1963) "through the college years by simple extrapolation" (1977, p. 251). His graph had proved highly popular with users, and many had asked for such an extension which he supplied with "considerable trepidation." He has shown similar concern about Maginnis's extension of the graph downward into preprimer levels (1969) and Kretschmer's suggestion (1976) of adding a set of words to his count of word length in syllables and sentence length in words. Validation studies at the graph's several levels by Crook (1977), Paolo (1977), and Longo (1982) should at least have helped to put his mind at ease. And the availability of a simple hand calculator (Fry, 1977) has added to the popularity of his method; in fact, it seems safe to say that it is one of the most, if not *the* most, widely used of all current methods.

Flesch's Reading Ease (1948) has also remained among the most popular formulas over the years, and various proposals have been made for easier application. First, more computer programs have been developed to apply the Reading Ease than any other formula. Second, several different kinds of manual aids have been developed. Notable among these have been the tables by Farr and Jenkins (1949), Flesch's own direct reading chart (appearing in several of his books), the hand calculator developed at General Motors Corporation, Kincaid and McDaniel's metronome method (1974), and Biersner and Bunde's stylus counter (1979). Foulger (1978) has provided a way of simplifying the manual count by reducing the steps needed to get a score.

New manual aids have also been proposed for other popular formulas. Burmeister (1976) developed a chart for the new Spache formula, and Layton (1980) has provided a companion chart for the Dale and Chall formula. Layton points out that using the two together provides "an easy way to estimate readability level from beginning reading through college-level reading" (Layton, 1980, p. 244). Maginnis (1982, p. 598) says the SMOG readability formula "is probably the fastest and simplest way to arrive at an objective difficulty rating for reading material." He believes his Smogometer makes the process of getting SMOG scores still faster and more likely to be free of errors.

Raygor (1977) has also emphasized ease of use in his new "Raygor readability estimate." He, like Fry, has provided a graph for getting readability grade levels, but has substituted a count of words of six or more letters for Fry's syllable count; sentence length remains the same for both. Raygor indicates that "informal experimentation" has shown that his word count takes only about half as long as Fry's syllable count. Baldwin and Kaufman found the Raygor graph easier and 25 percent faster to use than the Fry graph, yet "for all practical purposes, the two graphs yield the same results" (Baldwin & Kaufman, 1979, p. 153). Raygor himself reports that the two variables in his formula, when combined in the work of Harris and Jacobson (1974), gave a multiple R of .888 with their criterion, a standard error of estimate of .402 grades, and a Spearman-Brown reliability value of .916. Putting Baldwin and Kaufman's and Raygor's comments together, one might expect that the Fry graph and the Harris and Jacobson formula for the primary grades would yield the same results when applied to primary reading materials. Fry (1980) indeed says they do, but Harris and Jacobson (1980) say they do not.

Whatever the merits of that argument, Bormuth, in a recent paper carefully examining a number of readability formulas (Bormuth, unpublished), has opted for the same variables as Raygor's in presenting a new manual formula.

Criterion developments. Bormuth has for some time pointed to the problem that most formulas, by providing only a single estimate of readability, assume a particular level of comprehension to be desirable. In his formulas of 1969 and 1975, therefore, he provided for cloze criterion scores of 35 percent, 45 percent, and 55 percent. In his most recent formulas (Bormuth, unpublished), he has again provided for different criterion-score levels (and curvilinearity of regressions), but he has also provided for different grade levels of intended student readers in order to reduce the biasing effect otherwise found. And, in the process, he has developed not only a basic formula, β, but also variants for computer use, κ, and for manual use μ.

$$S_\beta = .9162G + .2046M + .9247CM + 5.456CD + .006496GY - .02174GM$$
$$- 6.335FD - .06565MA - 1.268NA$$
$$S_\kappa = .9759G - 1.388C + .8722F - .02690GW + 1.301CW - .3112WF$$
$$+ .1032WP$$
$$S_\mu = .8564G - .6063C + .9137CW + .2959CP + .07939WP$$

where S = the formula's estimate of the level of reading achievement, expressed as a grade equivalent score, that a reader enrolled in grade G must have in order to answer the proportion C of the items on a cloze test made from a passage having the linguistic characteristics indicated by the numbers substituted for those variables

G = the grade level of schooling reached by the readers for whose use the material is being evaluated

C = the proportion of cloze items that the evaluator would want these readers to be able to answer were they to be tested on the material being evaluated

M = transformed M [letters per minimal sentence] = $\ln(m)$

D = density of derived forms

Y = letters per syllable

F = transformed f (Dale familiar words) = $\sqrt{2f} - \sqrt{2(1-f)}$

N = transformed n [numerical nouns] = $\frac{1}{2}\zeta n[n/(1-n)]$

A = transformed a [total density of anaphora = $\frac{1}{2}\zeta n[a/(1-a)]$

W = letters per word

P = transformed p [words per sentence] = $\zeta n(p)$

Bormuth reports identical multiple R values of .882 and standard error of estimate values of 1.441 for each of the three formulas. He cross-validated each formula against the cloze scores on a set of twenty 250-word passages and found values of $-.93$, $-.90$, and $-.90$ respectively. He also points out that the computer formula can provide analysis entirely by machine and that the manual formula can be used by persons who have minimal resources for learning to use and apply a formula. The more complex basic formula, he indicates, can provide for increased precision, can make it difficult for a clever writer to fool it, and can yield considerable construct validity (Bormuth, unpublished, pp. 140–141).

Harris and Jacobson (1976; Jacobson, Kirkland, & Selden, 1978) have provided a different approach to improving the criterion for readability measurement. They had found that the norms for the McCall and Crabbs *Standard Test Lessons in Reading* (1961) were no longer accurate, and that the rank order of difficulty of the selections had changed somewhat over the years. They, therefore, took a sample of 190 of the lessons and gave them in various combinations to over 22,000 pupils in Grades 4, 6, 9, and 12. They then selected mean comprehension scores of 18,000 of the pupils as representative of the national norms on aptitude and reading-comprehension tests taken recently. Finally, they developed separate readability formulas for each of the four grades. All four of the formulas (not presented as such in the publications because of complexity) contain the Harris and Jacobson first- and second-grade word list (see Harris & Jacobson, 1972) and mean sentence length in words. All four also contain a set of spelling patterns, 10 at Grades 4, 9, and 12, and 11 at Grade 6, but all sets are different (see Jacobson, 1974). Finally, the formulas for Grades 4 and 9 include percentage of words with more than five letters and that for Grade 6 includes mean letters per word. These formulas yielded multiple R's with the renormed McCall and Crabbs passages of .93, .89, .88, and .96 respectively. Note also that use of 37 spelling patterns as a readability variable correlates .92 with primary grade difficulty (Jacobson, 1974).

Finally, Harris and Jacobson (1982) have recently presented a wide-range readability formula covering first- through eighth-grade levels, and by extrapolation through eleventh-grade level.

Predicted raw score = .245 (% of hard words) + .160 (average sentence length)
+ .642

where % of hard words = percentage in the sample of noncapitalized words not on the Harris and Jacobson Basic Reading Vocabularies list
average sentence length = average length of sentences, in words, in the sample analyzed

Predicted raw scores are converted to readability scores by means of a table. The new formula is said to have a multiple R with the 118 books in eight basal reader series of .93, with an R^2 of .86 and a standard error estimate of .501, or half a grade. The new formula was cross-validated against the McCall and Crabbs *Standard Test Lessons in Reading*. The word list and directions for using the formula are presented in Harris and Jacobson (1982).

Kincaid, Fishburne, Rogers, and Chissom (1975) followed the lead of Caylor et al. (1973) in deriving new versions of existing readability formulas for Navy use. They tested over 500 enlisted personnel on a reading-comprehension test and also on passages from Navy rate-training manuals in cloze form. This enabled them to derive versions of the Automated Readability Index (ARI) (Smith & Kincaid, 1970; Smith & Senter, 1967), Fog Count (Air Force Manual, 1953), and the Flesch Reading Ease formula (1948), which yield reading grade-level scores specific to Navy personnel. (Only the new versions of these older formulas appear below.)

ARI

$$GL = 0.37 \text{ (words/sentence)} + 5.84 \text{ (strokes/word)} - 26.01$$
$$GL = .4 \text{ (words/sentence)} + 6 \text{ (strokes/word)} - 27.4 \begin{cases} \text{simplified} \\ \text{version} \end{cases}$$

Fog Count

$$GL = \frac{\left[\dfrac{\text{easy words} + 3 \text{ (hard words)}}{\text{sentences}} - 3 \right]}{2}$$

Flesch Reading Ease formula (recalculated Flesch or Flesch and Kincaid)

$$GL = .39 \text{ (words/sentence)} + 11.8 \text{ (syllables/word)} - 15.59$$
$$GL = .4 \text{ (words/sentence)} + 12 \text{ (syllables/word)} - 16 \begin{cases} \text{simplified} \\ \text{version} \end{cases}$$

where GL = grade level
      easy words = words of one or two syllables
      hard words = more than two syllables

The U.S. military services recently adopted the recalculated Flesh formula as the basis for deciding whether military technical manuals from suppliers meet newly established readability requirements.

Kane, Byrne, and Hater (1974) developed a new criterion for their formulas but, even more important, took a new approach to readability measurement. Consequently, their work fits more appropriately into the following section.

New approaches.   In 1974, Kane et al. presented two readability formulas for the language of mathematics. These investigators used the cloze scores on sets of 12, 22, and 70 mathematical passages as their criteria, with scores obtained from students in the 6th through 12th grades (most of them in the 7th through 9th range). Both formulas below require samples of 400 tokens (both word and math tokens) for analysis.

Formula I

$$\text{Predicted readability} = -0.23X - 0.53Y + 61.88$$

Formula II

$$\text{Predicted readability} = -0.15A + 0.10B - 0.42C - 0.17D + 35.52$$

where   Predicted readability = mean score on a 75-item cloze test
      A = words not on Dale list of 3,000 words that are also not on 80% Mathematics list
      B = number of changes from a word token to a math token and vice versa
      C = number of different mathematics symbols not on 80% Mathematics

list plus number of different math symbols not on 90% Symbols
list

D = number of question marks

X = number of mathematics words not on the 80% Mathematics list

Y = number of different words with three or more syllables

Formula I yielded an R^2 of .60, while II yielded an R of 0.55 (R^2 = .30). The authors recommend Formula II despite the difference because they based it on more extensive data; they do indicate, however, that the simpler Formula I may fit some users' purposes (Kane et al., 1974, pp. 30–35).

Carver (1974, 1975–1976) and Singer (1975) have provided yet another new approach in using human judges of readability. Carver's method involves the average judgments of three qualified raters who have matched a passage against an anchor set of six passages. This set, called the Rauding Scale, consists of "six passages ostensibly representing grades 2, 5, 8, 11, 14, and 17" (Carver, 1975–1976, p. 663) Raters become qualified by rating accurately five sample passages using this scale. A table then provides a final grade-level difficulty value for a passage when entered with the average judgment of the three qualified raters. Carver (1975–1976, p. 680) finds that his method is highly reliable; is slightly more valid than the Dale and Chall and Flesch Reading Ease techniques; provides valid grade-level scores through the entire school range (Grades 1 to 18); and (elsewhere), yields rapid evaluations.

Singer calls his method the SEER (Singer Eyeball Estimate of Readability) technique. It involves the judgment of one or preferably two accurate SEER judges (Singer, 1975, p. 260) matching a sample of text against one of two readability scales. Standard Scale I consists of eight paragraphs at grade levels 1.5 to 6.8 taken from children's literature and rated according to the Spache formula (1953) for Grades 1–3 and according to the Dale and Chall formula (1948) for Grades 4–6. Eight comparably rated passages (range = 1.8–6.4) with difficulties not given to raters serve as "unknown" passages for matching. Standard Scale II consists of eight paragraphs at grade levels 1.8 to 6.5 taken from *Diagnostic Reading Scales* (Spache, 1963). Candidates for selection as accurate SEER judges try to match the unknown passages to Standard Scale I or II. If the difference between computed and SEER estimated readability levels averages less than 0.5 grade for the eight passages, a candidate qualifies as a SEER judge. Singer indicates that SEER scores, in an experiment using 32 judges, differed less than 1.0 grade level from computed readability scores, yielded more accurate values than McLaughlin's SMOG (1969) and as accurate values as Fry's graph, and proved more efficient than either the SMOG or Fry graph techniques.

Comparison of Carver's and Singer's methods was inevitable, and disagreement between different evaluators perhaps also inevitable. Froese (1980) found the SEER approach superior to the Rauding approach, but only when using several raters rather than the single rater suggested by Singer. Duffelmeyer (1982), however, found that the Rauding Scale gave results closer to Spache and Dale and Chall formula values than the SEER technique.

One might suppose that, by now, research workers had examined all possible language variables as potential indexes of readability. The long history of attempts at measurement, combined with the detailed examinations of Bormuth, E. B.

Coleman, and Harris and Jacobson, would seem to have exhausted all the possibilities. And, in fact, the recent attempts at making formulas easier to use seem to bear this out since the variables used for this purpose have almost all been seen before. But one must never underestimate the richness of the English language: new variables, or at least new variants, still seem to be appearing.

Both Cohen (1975) and Colby (1981) propose using a count of abstract words. This variable is not itself new; Flesch suggested it in 1943 and a formula using level of abstraction in 1950. But Cohen and Colby define abstractness differently, the former in terms of certain words and word endings plus weak verbs, the latter as a ratio of extensional words to intentional words. Extensional words are considered concrete because they can be pointed to or demonstrated; intentional words are considered abstract because they are not extensional or are unknown to the reader. Neither of these authors presents a new formula as such (though they do suggest evaluative standards), and neither has as yet presented rigorous developmental or support data.

Williams, Siegel, Burkett, and Groff (1977) have, on the other hand, examined some new variables, provided a formula, and presented detailed supporting data. These authors examined two categories of variables: (1) psycholinguistically oriented variables, many of them previously examined by some readability investigator; and (2) structure-of-intellect oriented variables (see Guilford & Hoepfner, 1971), none of them previously examined by a readability investigator. They used cloze procedure scores on 14 passages of approximately 600 words, each drawn from Air Force career-development-course texts as a criterion. They employed an unusual deletion ratio of 1:10 (with one of the ten possible versions) on 30 subjects with high-reading ability and 21 with low-reading ability, using standard cloze scoring procedure.

$$\text{Estimated cloze} = .169CMU - .173MMU + .156ESI + .19DMU + .335YD \\ - .26TC - .14CE + .242RB - .344$$

where   Estimated cloze = cloze percentage correct
CMU = cognition of semantic units
MMU = memory for semantic units
ESI = evaluation of symbolic implications
DMU = divergent production of semantic units
YD = Yngve depth
TC = transformational complexity
CE = center embedding
RB = right-branching

The authors found little shrinkage in their multiple R's when they split their subject pool in half and compared values; they, therefore, combined the halves and found a multiple R of .601 ($R^2 = .36$) with cloze percentage correct. They interpret the low R value as resulting from attenuation in range of difficulty of their criterion materials since they were technical and intended for adults. They also indicate that their variables, as contrasted with traditional ones, can have diagnostic and prescriptive value as "rules for writing."

The work of Cohen, Colby, and Williams et al. described above is in line with the recent emphasis on specialized analysis of the readability of technical text and on the special need for rewriting to improve readability. Two recent reports, Hull (1979) and Jarman (1979), add further evidence that readability of technical text represents a trend. Hull began with the hypothesis that an increase in the number of adjectives and adverbs before a noun decreases a reader's understanding of material. He used five of the criterion passages of Kincaid et al. (1975) as a basis for examining this and other variables. He prepared three experimental versions of the original passages, with increases in density of modifiers in one, ambiguity of modifiers in another, and prepositional density in the third. Adding in sentence length in words and word length in syllables, he was able to account for 68 percent of the variation in passage difficulty (cloze scores) with this five-variable formula. Using only the two variables of sentence length and density of modifiers (called prenominal modifiers), he could account for 48 percent with the formula below:

Grade level = 0.49 (average sentence length)
+ 0.29 (prenominal modifiers/100 words) − 2.71

Hull indicates that his prototype formula, in using modifier load, provides a word variable almost as predictive as a traditional syllable count. He considers it preferable, however, because it stands in a causal relationship to difficulty and can, thus, provide some assurance that rewriting to formula will produce more readable writing.

Jarman (1979) has not produced a readability formula for technical text, but he has provided correlations of 48 factors of writing style with readability ratings of five samples of technical text. He reports that 17 common factors characterize the writing style of the easiest-to-read samples and notes the following particulars:

1. The frequent use of active verbs is not necessarily an indication of readable writing.
2. The more frequent use of verbs over adjectives as an element of readable writing does not hold true.
3. The Fog Index does not correlate with readability.
4. Sentences can be crammed with ideas as long as the ideas are punctuated effectively.

Jarman's criticism runs almost counter to that of Hull by questioning sentence length and more frequent use of verbs over adjectives. The developers of the next three formulas also have questioned some of the accepted practices in readability measurement. Kintsch, the first of the three, has argued that traditional formulas are deficient because they consider only the text; they should, he says (Kintsch & Vipond, 1979), take both reader and text into account. He practices what he advocates in his own formula (Kintsch, 1979).

Reading difficulty = 2.83 + .48RS − .69WF + .51PD + .23INF + .21C

where RS = number of reinstatement searches
WF = average word frequency

PD = proposition density
INF = number of inferences
C = number of processing cycles
ARG = number of different arguments in the proposition list

Although he says he does "not want to suggest a new readability formula," he does report a "proud .97" correlation between his six predictor variables and reading difficulty, which he defines as number of seconds of reading time per proposition recalled on an immediate free-recall task. This criterion measure is, he says, preferable to multiple-choice or cloze measures.

The next formula also takes a direction somewhat different from more traditional approaches. The formula itself was developed by Bormuth (1969), but was adapted by the College Entrance Examination Board (1980) for use in the recent degrees of reading power (DRP) system.

$$Readability\ (R) = .886593 - .083640\ (LET/W) + .161911\ (DLL/W)^3$$
$$- 0.021401\ (W/SEN) + .000577\ (W/SEN)^2 - .000005\ (W/SEN)^3$$

where LET = letters in passage X
W = words in passage X
DLL = Dale long-list words in passage X
SEN = sentences in passage X

Readability (R) is a traditional cloze score; however, it is transformed into new units called *DRP* units by means of the conversion formula below. Such units range from about 30 (very easy) to 100 (very hard).

$$DRP = (1 - R) \times 100$$

The reason for the transformation is to make readability scores and scores on the College Board's reading test, DRP, "run in a consistent direction (and to convert to percents)" (College Entrance Examination Board, 1980, p. 13). The purpose, in other words, is to get around the criticism that readability scales and reading-test scales, though both are in grade levels, do not compare perfectly with each other. The readability formula itself is said to have a higher validity in original development (r = .83 for 110-word passages) than the best of other formulas, a higher cross-validation coefficient (r = .92 for 250- to 300-word passages), and relatively low standard errors of measurement (*S.E.* = .06 in original development; *S.E.* = .04 in cross-validation). The DRP system is being used to provide a series of readability reports on instructional materials for use by school systems (College Entrance Examination Board, 1982).

The British Index of Reading Difficulty (BIRD), like the DRP system, uses a scale other than the typical U.S. grade-level scale. Being British, it uses reading age and provides scores for selected newspapers as a frame of reference. It is also said to differ from other measures "in that it comprises a family of related formulae" (Caffyn & Mills, 1980, p. 340). The formulas, not presented because they are presumably "Company secret," are described as follows. *F*1 is designed to assess the readability of books, newspaper items, and other relatively long texts; $F2$ is intended for leaflets and other short texts; $F3$ is an extension of $F2$ that takes account of ungrammatical constructions. $B1/B2/BE$ are said to be modifications of $F1$, $F2$, and $F3$, which incorporate a "difficult words" index. A "C" series of formulas which take conceptual difficulty into account is said to be under development.

The next four approaches were designed to supplement traditional readability formulas. Harris and Jacobson (1979) argue that such formulas, with their reliance on style difficulty variables, have not moved beyond the suggestions of Herbert Spencer, the nineteenth-century British essayist. They argue that new formulas must consider the following kinds of new variables: cognitive-affective, orthographic-phonic, graphic design, and developmental reading. Exactly how this is to be done is not made clear.

The second of these approaches, ThUS, is called a "non-formula readability measure" (Lowe, 1979) and was designed to help users recognize thought units and gauge their difficulty. It has been used together with the Flesch and Fog formulas, and the Fry graph.

The third approach, the PHAN system, is a phrase-analysis system modestly called a "simplistic stepchild" of the approach of Kintsch and his colleagues (C. H. Clark, 1981). Passages are compared to determine relative ease or difficulty of comprehension; this information can then be used in conjunction with that from conventional readability formulas.

The fourth approach is called "subjective text difficulty" (Tamor, 1981). It uses text-based (objective) and performance-based (behavioral) information in a combination (subjective) approach. Objective approaches, such as readability formulas, are said to be text based because they take "difficulty" to be a characteristic residing in the text itself. Behavioral approaches, such as recall scores, are said to be performance based because they focus only on the individual. The subjective approach "matches *a priori* estimates of reading ability to objective measures of text difficulty to establish a criterion for each individual reader" (Tamor, 1981, p. 165). This so-called alternative approach, thus, relates to Kintsch's emphasis on the reader and the DRP's emphasis on matching text and reader.

If Tamor's "subjective" alternative is one step away from traditional readability formulas, the next four approaches are several additional steps away. Irwin developed her checklist approach as an alternative that "incorporates important factors not considered by formulas" (Irwin & Davis, 1980, p. 124). The major sections of her checklist, which teachers are to use in evaluating classroom texts, are: understandability, organization, reinforcement, motivation, and, learnability. All items within these sections, she says, have been carefully selected on the basis of accepted or current psychological research. They will, she says, provide a teacher with a reasonably complete description of the specific readability factors interacting in the specific set of materials being examined.

Holland (1981), in her "psycholinguistic alternatives to readability formulas," discusses critical variables beyond readability as traditionally measured and provides examples of revisions in public documents that take such variables into account.

Rubin (1981) provides new ways to look at text under the rubric of "conceptual readability." Her edited report includes papers on: categories and strategies of adaptation in children's reading materials; conflict—analysis of a higher-level story feature and its application to children's literature; mapping—representing text structure diagrammatically; and, an educational technique to encourage practice with high-level aspects of texts.

The final approach, called "a new definition of readability" (Amiran & Jones, 1982), is based on structure-of-text research, specifically the three textual variables of the structure, texture, and informational (content) density of text. Structure includes three kinds of superstructures—narrative, expository, and persuasive— and three categories of sectional structures—subordinating, coordinating, and sequential. For texture, or explicitness, there is at present only a "very general or tentative" continuum. Informational or content density is also a hard-to-describe continuum, according to the authors, which interacts with structure and texture. Emphasis, as in the work of Kintsch and others, is placed on comprehension as an interaction between text and reader.

Work in Languages Other Than English

As noted earlier, readability work in languages other than English has been growing steadily. Klare's earlier review (Klare, 1974–1975) covered the work up to about 1974, but inadvertently omitted a major contribution, the work of Björnsson (1968) in Sweden, which uses his lix formula. The formula name is an abbreviation for läsbarhetsindex (readability index).

$$\text{lix} = \text{sentence length} + \text{word length}$$

where   Sentence length is measured in words
Word length is measured as the percentage of words with more than six letters

Scores range from about 20, which is very easy text, to 60, which is very difficult text. Björnsson reports the use of a large number of judges in developing his criterion of difficulty and the checking of his results with reading time and cloze procedure. He reports applying his method to many thousands of books and reading passages during the 1960s and 1970s; these applications have included work with the Danish, English, Finnish, French, and German languages as well as Swedish; in Sweden, the formula is routinely applied to school and library books. Björnsson's is, thus, among the most influential of techniques, and he has published widely on his work.

Another non-English formula appeared about the time that the Klare review was published. It was developed by Park (1974) for Korean textbooks, and it accounted for 89.4 percent of the variance in the 32 textbooks used in the study. The variables in the formula are: easy words, different words, different hard words, simple sentences, and pronouns.

Evidence for the influence of Björnsson's work can be seen in the recent Rix formula of Anderson (1983). He had been applying the lix formula to English materials, checking validity and developing a method of converting lix scores to grade levels, when he observed that "even quicker readability estimates could be obtained by just counting the number of long words per sentence" (1983, p. 495). He, therefore, presented this new version of lix.

$$\text{Rix} = \frac{\text{number of long words}}{\text{number of sentences}}$$

where   Rix = rate index
          long words = words of more than six letters

Anderson emphasizes that Rix is actually a two-factor not a one-factor index, since the concept of ratio of long words per sentence takes into account number of words per sentence and number of long words. Scores from the new formula are said to correlate .99 with those from lix, and an interpretation table provides equivalent grade levels for Rix scores.

Dickes and Steiwer (1977) developed several formulas for the German language shortly after this. Their formula with eight variables had a multiple correlation with cloze scores on 60 German texts of .91; with six variables the value was .89; and with three it became .87. The three-variable formula is similar to that of Flesch.

Three recent methods for Spanish are similar to, and in fact based upon, the Fry graph. Garcia (1977) adapted the Fry graph by changing both the vertical and the horizontal numbers to reflect language differences in sentence length and syllable length respectively. His developmental criterion was a basal reader series in Spanish. Gilliam, Peña, and Mountain (1980) adapted the Fry graph by changing only syllable length, stating that a change in sentence length was not necessary. They proposed a correction factor of −67 syllables when using the graph for 100-word samples of Spanish. Their basis was a comparison of the Spanish version and the English translation of 13 Spanish textbooks and 9 juvenile books. (The authors recognize that material may not remain at the same grade level after translation but consider this a workable assumption for a first study.) Vari-Cartier (1981) actually developed a new graph, on the order of Fry's, for use with Spanish, and called it the FRASE graph (Fry Readability Adaptation for Spanish Evaluation). FRASE is similar to Fry in its use of both sentence and syllable length, but dissimilar in giving four difficulty levels (beginning, intermediate, advanced intermediate, and advanced) rather than grade levels. Eight textbooks served as the criterion for development, with additional validity data based on correlations with subjective teacher ratings, Spaulding (1956) formula ratings, cloze test scores, and informal multiple-choice test scores.

Nguyen and Henkin (1982) have recently presented a formula for Vietnamese. They had former Vietnamese teachers rate the grade levels of twenty 300-word passages according to the Vietnamese educational system. Using these criterion data, they developed the following formula.

$$RL = 2.88\,WL + .21\,SL - 8.79\,WD - 7.69$$

where RL = judged readability level
          WL = word length in letters
          SL = sentence length in words
          WD = percentage of difficult words

This formula accounts for about 76 percent of the variance in the criterion and has a standard error of 1.59. The authors provide both a readability table and readability scale for ease of usage.

A number of books on readability have appeared in languages other than

English, most of them fairly recently. These include books in: Finnish (Wiio, 1968); French (Henry, 1975; Richaudeau, 1969, 1976); Danish (Togeby, 1971); Swedish (Platzack, 1974); Dutch (van Hauwermeiren, 1975); and, German (Groe-ben, 1978). Numerous applications of formulas and cloze procedure have also been made to languages other than English.

It is perhaps fitting to close out this review of research in the prediction of readability since 1974 with mention of a new book in English, the language for which most of the research has been done. The book, *Readability in the Classroom*, is by Harrison (1980b). It is also fitting that the "classroom" is mentioned since that is where most of the concern about readability has centered. The following section presents a series of questions designed both to provide some notion of where research has led and some suggestions for needed research in the future.

WHERE DO THINGS STAND NOW?

References to readability can be found in many areas of the professional litera-ture—education, journalism, linguistics, psychology, speech, to name the most common—and in many languages. Consequently, not knowing exactly how many exist, aside from what they say, indicates part of the problem in trying to answer the above question. Making sense of those available can be difficult enough, even without the itchy feeling there may be something critical among the unavail-able. The answer, as a result, has been largely the time-honored one of asking some new questions.

The writer intends these questions as a basis for examining more closely, and relating, the research which has been done and the controversies which have arisen. At the same time, they should call attention, through obvious gaps or tangles in the research, to some things which still need to be done or, at least, to be done better than they have been done so far. Finally, these questions should enable readers to see discrepancies in, or disagreements with, the writer's framework itself.

Highlights in the history of readability have typically involved formulas, as the brief history shows. Their apparent objectivity and precision have consider-able appeal for many, but not all, potential users, as the earlier criticisms of formulas clearly indicated. Before getting farther into this issue, one might para-phrase Coupland's question, and ask: Are readability formulas necessary?

Other ways of estimating readability can be used. Taylor (1953) originally developed cloze procedure as a possible substitute for formulas, calling it "a new tool for measuring readability" in the title of his paper. This description provides a first important distinction in discussing readability research. As noted earlier, formulas predict readability; cloze procedure and other similar compre-hension methods measure readability. Formulas do not require the testing of human subjects to provide readability scores for passages; cloze procedure does. On the other hand, while cloze procedure and other test-based techniques require more time and effort of the user, they can and have served as useful criteria of readability. They have the advantage when accuracy of comprehension scores is at a premium since formulas can be no more accurate than the criteria on which they are based. Getting adequate criteria for formula development thus becomes a major problem and deserves attention later. At this point, however, the question of the need for formulas still awaits an answer.

Since using formulas (even computer-based ones) involves users, why not have the users make judgments of readability themselves? Can humans make accurate judgments and thus dispose of formulas? A body of studies (see Klare, 1963, pp. 137–143) shows that human judgments and formula scores can be closely related. More recently, it has been argued that humans can be excellent judges of (1) simple versus complex sentences (Schwartz, Sparkman, & Deese, 1970; Wang, 1970) and (2) of the difficulty of books (Porter & Popp, 1973). Carver (1974, 1975–1976) and Singer (1975) have argued, further, that humans can be as accurate as formulas in providing reading-grade levels for passages.

Yet Jongsma (1972) found that school and public librarians rated one Newbery Award-winning book from 3rd-grade to 12th-grade in difficulty; Klare's professional writers (1976a) rated five passages at each of the five possible levels of difficulty (except one). Jorgenson (1975) and Miller and Marshall (1978) found that teachers made judgments of reading level that varied widely from teacher placement; Harrison (1977, 1979, 1980a) found teacher ratings to vary by six to nine grade levels in his studies.

Why the contradictions? The answer, though complex, appears to be due primarily to the following. Unselected and untrained *individuals cannot* be relied upon as judges. Untrained *groups can* provide quite good consensus *rankings* of sets of passages (Klare, 1976a), and specially trained and/or selected groups can even provide good *ratings* using Carver's Rauding (1974, 1975–1976) or Singer's SEER (1975) techniques. Singer has even argued that one trained and selected individual may be enough, but this was not the case in Froese's (1980) comparison of the two techniques. Furthermore, the contradiction in the comparisons of Froese (1980) and Duffelmeyer (1982) cited earlier suggests caution in using either technique without further research support.

Even assuming relatively good accuracy of these techniques, there is a question of how much time and effort they require. Singer has argued that his SEER technique is quicker than formula estimation. Though the time actually needed for a judge to read and rank (or rate) a passage can be measurably less than that needed to apply even a simple formula, the total time including training and selection of judges must clearly be greater. In summary, judgments seem unlikely to supplant formulas where formal estimates of readability are needed. This should not seem to disparage individual human judgments, especially those sharpened by feedback. Most estimates of readability are, in fact, made by writers in the process of writing—in most cases subjectively and perhaps even unconsciously. Human judgments and formulas can better be considered complements than competitors: formulas can help to screen writing and, thus, provide feedback; human judgments can under certain circumstances act as criteria and can, at least, help to prevent misuse of formulas and formula scores (in ways described more fully below).

Both tests and judges require more time and effort than readability formulas in getting estimates of readability. At this point, therefore, the answer to the question of the need for formulas is: yes, if users want convenience. That, however, is not the only concern. Two major questions can frame the other issues more clearly.

Prediction Research versus Production Research

Users of readability research typically have one or the other, or both, of the following general questions in mind:

1. How can I tell how readable a piece of writing is likely to be for intended readers?
2. How can I write readably (or more readably) for intended readers?

These can, for convenience, be called the prediction question and the production question (Klare, 1976b). Though closely related in certain ways, they lead to quite different implications in other ways which have not always been made clear in the literature. A comparison of the general steps involved in prediction versus production research can set the stage for reviewing these problems. Table 22.1 provides a set of typical steps; keep in mind that they are necessarily stated in general terms and that the order of applying them can vary somewhat.

Prediction research has a largely psychometric orientation, and formulas can be compared on such typical standards as validity, reliability, sampling, and scale. Production research, on the other hand, has a largely psycholinguistic orientation, and certain of the above standards do not apply. Nevertheless, many users wish to answer both the prediction and production questions, so, comparisons and contrasts are needed where possible.

A first comparison concerns the success investigators have had with each process. As the brief history of readability showed, modern readability formulas achieve surprisingly high correlations with their criteria, with values in the low .90s becoming possible. This holds true for simple as well as complex formulas, with relatively little shrinkage in cross-validation. Could higher values reasonably be expected? Prediction research in readability clearly seems to compare very favorably with such other kinds of psycho-educational prediction as school grades or sales (Chall, 1979). Yet there are persistent concerns about the accuracy of readability scores, particularly those in grade levels.

Production research, by contrast, has not even produced a comparable statistical success story. Klare's comparison of 36 studies (1976b) showed that more readable versions of material produced significant increases in comprehension in only about 60 percent of the cases. Why the disagreement? Perhaps one could not expect to find a higher degree of success in production research; human language and human users of language are much too complex, to say nothing of the complex measurement problems which are also involved. Much more goes into writing than word and sentence considerations. With that in mind, the degree of success in prediction research becomes all the more surprising. But the results of production research cast a disturbing shadow over prediction research as well since users of readability research so often have both purposes in mind. Certainly no simple answer can be given to the question of disagreement, but an examination of critical issues in prediction and production research can

TABLE 22.1   STEPS FOLLOWED IN CARRYING OUT PREDICTION AND PRODUCTION RESEARCH IN READABILITY

PREDICTION RESEARCH	PRODUCTION RESEARCH
1. Choose (or develop) a large set of criterion-text passages of varied content and measured difficulty (typically, comprehension) values.	1. Select one or more language variables for experimental variation.
2. Identify a number of objectively stated language variables.	2. Choose (or develop) an appropriate text passage or passages for experimental use.
3. Count the occurrences of the language variables in the criterion passages and correlate them with the difficulty values of the criterion passages.	3. Modify the text, using the selected language variables, to produce easier and/or harder versions.
4. Select the variables with the highest correlations as potential indexes of readability.	4. Hold constant other critical variables, such as content, technical terms, and length.
5. Combine the indexes, usually using multiple-regression techniques, into a formula.	5. (Optional) Apply a readability formula to indicate differences between the versions.
6. (Optional) Cross-validate on a set of new criterion passages.	6. Compare the versions on subjects, using some dependent variable (typically, comprehension scores).

help to throw some light on the answer as well as raise problems for future research.

Selection of Text Passages

Prediction research.   In the case of prediction research, the text passages serve as the criterion passages. Investigators generally hope to find, or develop, a criterion with the following characteristics:

- a large number of passages; with
- a wide range of difficulty; and with
- highly varied content.

The first and second of these characteristics, number and range of difficulty, provide statistical conditions for maximizing correlations. The third characteristic, varied content, further raises the likelihood of a high correlation by providing a range of interests for readers. Or, as McMahon, Cherry, and Morris (1978) put it, the passages are intended for different audiences (which itself raises problems when compared to production research, where the same audience is involved).

The McCall and Crabbs *Standard Test Lessons in Reading* (1925), with their large number of passages, varied content, objective questions, and detailed reading-grade levels, proved more convenient than earlier developmental criteria, and a number of formulas were based on them. These included several still widely used today, notably the Dale and Chall (1948) and the Flesch Reading Ease (1948). Cloze-based criterion passages, such as those of Coleman (1965) and Bormuth (1969) have now largely supplanted the McCall and Crabbs and other multiple-choice-based passages. Cloze criteria have certain advantages in analysis (see Klare, Sinaiko, & Stolurow, 1972, pp. 81–83 for a review of these). In addition, Miller (1972, 1975) has shown this criterion easier to predict than the McCall and Crabbs criterion using the same formulas. One might be tempted to assume this difference in predictability to be solely a matter of cloze versus multiple-choice item types. Harris and Jacobson (1974, 1979), however, started with the assumption that after 50 years the McCall and Crabbs norms were out of date and that restandardizing might provide better criterion values. Comparing an early correlation of .74 they reported for four of their variables, and their later correlations in the high .80s and low to middle .90s, this seems to be the case. The comparison is not a direct one, however, so the better assumption remains that cloze scores are somewhat easier to predict.

More significant than this limitation of the McCall and Crabbs *Standard Test Lessons in Reading* as a criterion, however, is the one by Stevens (1980) mentioned earlier. She points out, on the basis of correspondence with McCall, that the *Lessons* were intended only to be practice exercises in reading and that the grade-level scores were only rough equivalents provided for students to track their progress. They were never, she says, intended for use as a criterion for readability formula development. This is a serious charge, not only since the popular Dale and Chall and Flesch Reading Ease formulas were based directly on them, but also since certain other formulas were validated by comparison with these two formulas and, thus, based indirectly on them. Concern about accuracy in the grade-level designations from these formulas might, it seems, be traceable to weaknesses in the McCall and Crabbs criterion.

Two findings are of interest in this connection. The first deals with correlations. Powers, Sumner, and Kearl (1958) found that the Dale and Chall formula actually correlated slightly higher, .71, in a cross-validation on the 1950 edition of the *Lessons* than on the 1925 edition originally used in development, .70. A higher value of this sort in cross-validation is quite unusual statistically. The Flesch Reading Ease formula dropped somewhat, from .70 to .64, in cross-validation, which is the more common occurrence. The second deals with grade-level designations. Klare (1979) found the grade-level values from the Flesch Reading Ease formula to vary only slightly from those based on the recalculated Flesch and Kincaid formula in the middle range of grades (i.e., 7 to 12); the difference was greater in the lower grades of 5 and 6 and at college level. This is of interest because the Flesch and Kincaid formula was based on cloze versions of Forms E and F (Grades 6 to 16) of the *Gates-MacGinitie Reading Tests* (1972) and, thus, on an entirely different set of grade-level designations. A more recent informal comparison (Klare, 1983) shows that the Fry graph grade levels differ only slightly from those of the Flesch Reading Ease and the Flesch and Kincaid formulas. Since the Fry graph was based on publishers' grade-level assignments (Fry, 1968, p. 515), this is still a third different set of grade-level designations. Yet in this comparison the Fry and Flesch and Kincaid differ no more than one grade level in the range of 6 to 16 grades, and neither differs more than two grade levels from the Flesch Reading Ease in this range; there is, in fact, agreement among the three for most grades. Perhaps, then, the statistical and grade-level foundations provided by the McCall and Crabbs *Standard Test Lessons in Reading* are more substantial than the recent criticisms imply, at least for the formulas in question. However, there are other statistical and conceptual concerns.

First, a statistical question. A major reason for the high correlations of modern formulas lies in the nature of the criterion—it is almost ideal for statistical prediction. As noted, correlation coefficients are increased when there are a large number of passages of varying content and with a wide range of difficulty. If a wide range of talent among the readers is added, they can be maximized. What happens when these conditions are not present can be seen in a study by Rodriguez and Hansen (1975) in which they renormed four of Bormuth's general-purpose formulas (1969). They used the same variables as in the original formulas, but limited their subjects to seventh graders and their materials to textbook, newspaper, and leisure reading passages generally appropriate for that level. The correlation coefficients dropped from around .90 in the original norming to around .45 in the renorming. It is understandable why the correlation coefficient is sometimes called a rubber yardstick and why the standard error of estimate is a preferable statistic in many cases.

Second, a conceptual question. The conditions for maximizing the correlation between modern formulas and their criteria are most often found in the recent studies using cloze-based criterion passages but is the cloze procedure an ideal measure of reader comprehension? Some writers have maintained that it is at least superior to a multiple-choice measure for several reasons. For one, cloze uses the text itself as the test; this avoids the problem of easy questions on hard text and hard questions on easy text. For another, use of the possible n (e.g., five) forms of an every-nth (e.g., every fifth) deletion ratio means that the entire text has been tested; this avoids the sampling problem. Bormuth (unpublished, p. 148) summarizes the case for cloze by saying that tests made by the cloze procedure have "survived all the challenges so far raised against their validity as measures of comprehensibility."

Well, perhaps. Cloze procedure can be, and often is, misused as a criterion. Perhaps the most common way is to use only one of the n forms to collect criterion data when studies have shown that all n forms are seldom equal in difficulty. Entin (1980; Entin & Klare, in press), for example, compared two of the five possible forms on standard and difficult versions of 12 passages. Of the 24 comparisons, 16 yielded significant differences in scores at the .05 level or beyond.

Putting aside the question of misuse, basic conceptual issues remain. Kintsch and colleagues (Kintsch & Vipond, 1979; Kintsch & Yarbrough, 1982) consider the various criteria used in developing formulas to be "quite unsatisfactory." They consider cloze procedure to be "probably actually misleading" since it is a measure of statistical redundancy rather than comprehensibility. They finally say with apparent resignation that "reading time, recall, and question answering are probably the most useful measures available" (Kintsch & Vipond, p. 13), though only if theory dependent. They feel that recall or summarizing of a text should be used more often, at the same time admitting the problems of scoring. In developing his own readability formula, Kintsch (1979) used recall per unit of time as his measure of comprehension. Carver (1977–1978b, p. 31) has also criticized cloze procedure, calling it a rubber yardstick. He points out that a cloze-based estimate of difficulty depends both upon the ability level of the group being tested and the difficulty level of the material.

The Kintsch and Carver discussions call attention once again to the need for more and better criteria of readability. Certain of the problems below require long-term study before satisfactory solutions can be found, of course.

Writers do not agree on what comprehension is. A study of definitions in the literature, from 1697 (John Locke's) to the present (see Klare, in press), shows that authors tend to fall back on their own conceptions of human behavior and make their definitions fit. Readers in several demonstrations could tell which famous writer wrote which definition by their knowledge of the writers, because of the highly individualistic (and even contradictory) definitions.

The term comprehension covers many kinds of behavioral and cognitive activities, some of them quite different. The reader may, for example, be asked to answer comprehension questions with the text either present or absent; as Carroll (1972) has pointed out, the latter arrangement overemphasizes the memory component. Or the reader may be asked to study text and/or learn it, implying repeated readings, perhaps at different times. Guthrie (1972) has compared "learnability" with readability; perhaps "studyability" and other criteria should also be examined separately.

Criteria seem to have been used primarily because of their statistical convenience. This is understandable but has put the emphasis upon gains in predicting the criterion; more effort needs to be put upon examining the adequacy of the criterion. In recent work, Bormuth (1969, 1975, unpublished) has taken a step in this direction by examining the relationship of cloze criterion scores to such student behaviors as information gain, willingness to study, difficulty-preference ratings, and rate of reading and has also provided several different percentage-correct criteria for his formulas. And as noted earlier, the College Entrance Examination Board (1980) provides readability ratings for books on the same scale as the reading abilities scores for its DRP test.

A related problem concerns the reading-grade-level ratings assigned to the criterion passages. Different readability formulas can yield different grade-level ratings (e.g., see Pauk, 1969; Vaughan, 1976), which users find to be a major problem. These discrepancies arise at least partly from the different grade-level values on the different criterion passages used in development. But other factors, such as sampling, also contribute to the problem. Some work has been done on formula comparison; for example, both Pauk (1969) and Vaughan (1976) have found that Dale and Chall and Fry scores agree rather consistently but that SMOG (McLaughlin, 1969) scores run about two grades higher. Comparisons of the ratings from the more common formulas on standard sets of materials would be helpful, and a further comparison with some accepted criterion would be still more helpful. Harrison (1980b) has made a good start by comparing nine formulas on validity, ease of application, and grade-level accuracy. He gave particular attention to the latter, using the pooled judgments of teachers on 24 first-year secondary texts and 16 fourth-year secondary texts used in British schools as his criterion. The teachers' judgments yielded average reading-age scores of 11.30 and 13.14 respectively. The two most predictive formulas, the Dale and Chall (1948) and Mugford (1970), differed by half a year or less, up or down, from these values. The Flesch Reading Ease formula (1948) differed by one year; the FORCAST (Caylor et al., 1973) and SMOG (McLaughlin, 1969) by about two years; and the Fog Index (Gunning, 1952) differed by almost three years. The latter three less predictive formulas, incidentally, yielded higher (more difficult) ratings than the teachers. More work of this kind might help users like Morris, Thilman, and Myers (1980) avoid becoming misusers. They applied 13 readability formulas to an information sheet on valium and were surprised to find a range of over 12 grade levels in the scores they provided. However, they uncritically lumped together formulas:

• intended for children with formulas for adult materials;
• designed to provide different levels of reading comprehension;
• equipped to give grade levels in some cases but not in others; and
• developed at an early stage and little used, or new and untried, with formulas of better established validity.

Existing criterion passages have been quite short, typically around 100 words and seldom as long as 250 words in length. This may well contribute to the observation that word and sentence factors, both short range, predominate in factor analyses of readability matrices (Entin & Klare, 1978a). The problem of dealing with such long-range factors as prior knowledge, organization, and certain cohesiveness characteristics (Halliday & Hasan, 1976; Irwin, 1980) can be quite complex under any conditions of course. But the immediate concern is that they cannot easily be observed in criterion passages that are short.

A standard set of passages for comparison and contrast of different formulas could be valuable. This need not imply only one set of criterion passages; in fact, several would be better (especially considering the number of comparisons involved). But it does imply a criterion designed carefully enough to permit comparing the major contending formulas. This comparison could take several forms, with regressions of each formula's grade assignments upon those of the others being an ideal solution as far as most users are concerned. Coleman (1965; Miller & Coleman, 1967) and Bormuth (1969) have provided extensive sets of passages with difficulty scores for each, but no regressions of formulas on each other have been published. Comparing very many formulas on an extensive set of materials would task even a large computer, but this might be considered for a selected group of the more popular formulas.

The criterion question can be summarized as one which has been given more attention statistically than conceptually. Significant attempts have been made recently to attack the question conceptually, many under the stimulus of the Center for the Study of Reading at the University of Illinois. Some of the valuable recent books in this area are those by: Bobrow and Collins (1975); Anderson, Spiro, and Montague (1977); LaBerge and Samuels (1977); Spiro, Bruce, and Brewer (1980); and Lesgold and Perfetti (1981). Applications to the teaching of reading comprehension can be found in such books as those by Pearson and Johnson (1978) and Guthrie (1981).

Production research.   In the case of production research, the text passages serve as the materials to be varied experimentally. Thus, the requirements differ from those for the criterion passages in prediction research. Typical characteristics include:

• readily manageable number and/or size; with
• easily manipulable variables (of the desired type); and with
• a relatively small number of contents (often as few as one).

These characteristics lend themselves to convenient experimentation but also limit generalization of results. Considering the many difficulties in carrying out production research, this is understandable. The problem, of course, lies in the extent to which the usefulness of the research has been limited. This question cannot be answered in a simple fashion, but critics of production research have pointed to a number of issues deserving attention; including those below.

Experimental designs used often do not permit generalizing to a language population. Coleman (1964) first pointed out that typical designs used in language-research studies provide for proper generalization to a subject population but not to a language population. He has followed this paper with several other comments and suggestions on the problem (Coleman, 1973; Coleman & Miller, 1974; Miller & Coleman, 1972). H. H. Clark (1973) has raised similar questions about designs in language research, precipitating arguments in the literature (Carver, 1978; Clark, Cohen, Smith, & Keppel, 1976; Wike & Church, 1976), which each reader will have to resolve for himself or herself.

A related problem involves the fact that the experimental passages have often been specially selected to meet the experimenter's needs. This is not unreasonable but, as noted, it can contribute to generalization problems. Kintsch and Keenan (1973) have shown in texts equated for length that reading time varies with the number of propositions. Yet Kling and Pratt (1977) have found in other passages that number of syllables yields a higher correlation with passage complexity ratings (.70) than does number of propositions (.60). The issue may well revolve around questions of how many propositions a reader actually derives from a text rather than the number an experimenter has counted or the number of arguments (Kintsch & Keenan, 1973). Or it may be a matter of different dependent variables (time vs. ratings), or other unspecified conditions. But it may simply be the passages used; experimenters seldom really sample randomly from the content of language material they wish to generalize to.

Still another related issue concerns the use of at least two contents rather than just one. It may seem sufficient to select passages on a random basis, but in practice, the number of variables which may contribute to a given result is too large to be reassured by this. For example, Denbow (1973) found increased readability related to a significant increase in information gain for two different contents. But he also found the amount of gain to be significantly greater for the nonpreferred content. Though objectively describing content may not be easy, use of even two crudely different contents can be informative.

The length of the experimental material is generally small. Much of the relevant production research has been done by or has developed from the work of psycholinguists, and it has been done on sentence-length samples. But even where longer samples have been used, as in the typical readability studies, Rothkopf (1972) points out that they have been quite small in relation to typical amounts of instructional text.

The problem of selecting desirable experimental passages may be summarized by saying that the passages often seem desirable for the experimenter without being equally desirable for the user. Or, to put matters more directly, the user cannot feel confident of generalizing from the published results to his or her own practical situation.

Selection of Language Variables

Prediction versus production research.   Prediction and production research logically require somewhat different characteristics in the language variables used, as the comparison in Table 22.2 shows. To summarize the contrast, the variables in prediction research need only show an index relationship to the criterion of readable writing; they may, but need not, show a causal relationship. Correlation, as we all know, does not prove causation. The variables in production research, on the other hand, must show a causal relationship, in that they must produce significant differences in reader comprehension.

This contrast can be seen in several examples. Jacobson (1974) found that words beginning with the letter *e* contribute to reading difficulty, while those ending in *ll* contribute to reading ease. Yet, as he says, a better understanding of why the difference occurs can be obtained by looking at the words actually placed in each category. Inspection clearly shows that the underlying (causal) factor is the degree of correspondence between the letters and the sounds. Words

TABLE 22.2   CHARACTERISTICS OF LANGUAGE VARIABLES NEEDED IN CARRYING OUT PREDICTION AND PRODUCTION RESEARCH

PREDICTION RESEARCH	PRODUCTION RESEARCH
1. Yield high correlations with the criterion values, but low correlations with each other.	1. Produce significant differences in subjects' scores on the experimental passages.
2. Show high reliability of application.	2. Can be manipulated reliably.

3. Are appropriate for:
  (a) manual application and/or
  (b) machine application.
	3. Are appropriate in writing, i.e., do not produce awkward written material.

ending in *ll* represent only one sound and are easily read. By contrast, the letter *e* in the beginning position represents at least seven sounds and, thus, contributes to difficulty.

Similarly, sentence complexity appears to be a cause of difficulty in comprehension. Writers have used various methods of measuring it, including the recent complex count called "sum of Yngve word depths per sentence." Yet Bormuth (1966) found that the simple count of number of words per sentence correlated .99 with Yngve word depth. Which raises a question: How highly does an index variable have to correlate with a causal variable or, better yet, with a criterion of difficulty, to qualify as a causal variable itself? Or, to phrase the question differently: Is an index variable always an index variable? Sentence length within the range of, say, 5 to 25 words per sentence may well be primarily an index of reading difficulty; at the level of 100 words per sentence, is it still an index or has it shifted over to causal status?

The problem qualifies as more than academic since it touches several issues of considerable importance in readability. First, can a writer fool a formula, that is, write so that a formula score grossly misrepresents the true degree of readability? Yes. To take an extreme case, all a writer need do is randomly rearrange the sentences or—worse yet—the words within the sentences also, after writing a long passage. The simple and efficient two-variable formulas of modern times would clearly not predict difficulty in such cases. Or, as Taylor (1953) has pointed out, in somewhat less drastic cases, such as the writings of James Joyce or Gertrude Stein. Or even, as Clive and Russo (1981) have pointed out, in the parody in which a hooker's appeal was found to have a less readable score than an advanced calculus theorem and proof. Would a more complex formula have made better predictions? The answer is unclear since, apparently, no one has ever felt called upon to try it (or at least publish the results).

Such extreme misapplications of formulas appear unlikely; human judges could too easily spot them. The more serious question concerns the unscrupulous writer who wishes to fool a formula in a way which cannot be detected. This might, for example, occur when a book (or, more likely, a series of books) appears too difficult for an intended grade and the author doctors the text. Can the writer fool the formula? Bormuth (1975) believes this possible with simple formulas but suggests that complex formulas can be foolproof. Once again, studies of the extent to which complex—or even simple—formulas can be fooled deliberately would be informative.

A related, and perhaps more serious, question to many critics concerns writing to formula. Occasionally, someone actually suggests this procedure, as happened in the case of a contractor for the U.S. Navy Technical Information Presentation Program (Naval Ocean Systems Center, 1979). Most writers on readability, however, have condemned this practice as ineffective if not dangerous. They point out further that the increasing use of readability standards for such publications as reading series, technical manuals, and insurance policies inclines writers to write to formula whether they wish to do so or not. Even scrupulous writers may fall into the habit of making changes they know will improve formula scores when under pressure. Davison and Kantor (1982) detail this problem in their comparison of two versions of four reading texts, the original version intended mainly for adult readers and the adapted version intended for less skilled readers.

The problem of index-causal variables can be given a different focus by using Bormuth's "manipulable" versus "nonmanipulable distinction" (1969). The question remains, of course, one of testing each candidate variable to see whether manipulating it experimentally will produce significant changes in reader comprehension. Some recent formula developers, such as Williams et al. (1977) and Hull (1979), have begun to argue that their formulas contain variables which *can* serve as guidelines and, thus, make writing to formula safe. They have not, however, provided convincing evidence of this, which emphasizes once more the need for research in this very complex area. A brief review of the research done on prediction variables and that done for production purposes can, at least, help to define the problem somewhat more clearly.

Prediction variables. Formula developers have examined well over 250 variables as potential predictors of readability. In the process, a number of issues have been raised which deserve further study, as noted below.

Variables have sometimes been chosen for increased convenience in counting and at other times for improved predictive value, but the research evidence can be difficult to assess. For example, Flesch originally proposed the syllable count in his Reading Ease formula (1948) as an easier alternative to the count of affixes in his original formula (1943). Farr, Jenkins, and Peterson (1951) proposed a count of one-syllable words as easier than a count of syllables; Gunning (1952) proposed counting only words of three or more syllables instead. McDaniel and Kincaid (1978) found counting syllables in time with a metronome (see Kincaid & McDaniel, 1974) to be faster than manual counts; Biersner and Bunde (1979) found a stylus wired to an electromechanical counter to be still faster.

On the other hand, Thomas, Hartley, and Kincaid (1975) found the typewriter-based ARI, which uses a count of character spaces, to be faster than a syllable count. Bormuth (1975) and Coleman and Liau (1975) also proposed letter counts (by hand or machine). And more recently Raygor (1977) proposed counting only words of six or more letters as a further improvement.

Comparisons of the relevant variables prove hard to find and, when found, even harder to interpret (but see Klare, 1979, for a number of these). The answers they provide have not been simple. For example, Dunnette and Maloney (1953) found that a count of all syllables was performed more accurately than a count of one-syllable words for easy material, with the reverse being the case for hard material. At this stage the most helpful comparisons would seem to be those which indicate how important any differences really are in practical use.

Baldwin and Kaufman (1979) made a useful start of this sort. They compared the recent Raygor graph (1977) with the well-established Fry graph (1963, 1977). They found, in extensive comparisons, that the values from the two methods correlated .875 and that the levels they yielded differed more than one grade in only 6 percent of the passages. At the same time, they found the Raygor method to be applied 25 percent faster without a significant difference in errors. A further useful step would have been to see whether applications changed in rate or number of errors with experience—and then to compare other contending formulas. But these are both large-scale tasks, which explains why practical comparisons of the relative convenience variables are so rare.

One might, at least, expect the distinction between more convenient versus more predictive variables to be clearer; but there the results can also be cloudy.

Bormuth (unpublished) found that his complex and simpler formulas yielded almost identical correlations with criterion values in both validation and cross-validation. Furthermore, Liau et al. (1976) found that their simple formula using only word length in letters and sentence length in words yielded very close to the same cross-validation values as Bormuth's on some of Bormuth's passages.

The above discussion has not raised the issue of machine application, although it is now becoming common. Where computer programs are available, the problem of convenience versus predictive power becomes of less concern. At the same time, such programs can create their own application problems, especially in terms of user flexibility. Recently, however, programs have been published for the kinds of microcomputers a user is likely to have available; as noted earlier, the article of Schuyler (1982) is particularly valuable.

A related problem concerns predictive validity versus face validity. Where users plan to apply a formula in a specific area (e.g., technical manuals) or a specific industry, the question of how to count commonly known technical jargon often comes up. Word lists (in formulas which use them) do not include such terms since they typically contain only highly frequent words. Syllable counts (in formulas which use them) seem to yield suspiciously high counts, especially since these special words tend to get repeated. Such words can be dropped from syllable counts, with the intent of concentrating on the rest of the text. Or, they can be added to word lists, with the notion that they are really familiar. This kind of modification must be made cautiously; even when based upon research, adding such words seems to have relatively little effect on predictive validity, at least at the lower reading levels (see Klare, 1974–1975, p. 72). Predictive validity might increase at adult reading levels, of course (see Klare, 1979, pp. 53–55), and it is at such levels where the face validity issue comes up most often.

Bormuth has raised a question several times (1966, 1969, 1975) about the linearity of readability variables. He has indicated that certain ones are curvilinear and that this can lead to inaccuracy if not taken into account. Many recent formulas are linear regression equations and do not consider this. Bormuth has built corrections into his formulas and has indicated that Fry's graph (1963, 1977) almost alone among other measures provides for curvilinearity. As it happens, Raygor's recently published method (1977) also employs a curvilinear graph.

This leads to the question of whether the corrected grade-equivalent tables used by Dale and Chall (1948), Flesch (1949, 1962), and Harris and Jacobson (1974) might be having the same effect. They do modify raw scores but apparently chiefly to account for the reduced variability of scores predicted from a regression equation.

This would not appear to modify curvilinearity directly. But, the use of less precise grade values in the place of seemingly more precise raw scores might well render a correction for curvilinearity unnecessary. Furthermore, such a correction can itself yield puzzling results. Lower grades are typically assigned to shorter word-sentence combinations, which at most seem to level off at the longer word-sentence values. A shift where the longer combinations actually again yield lower grades seems puzzling at best; yet the correction appears responsible for this (see Bormuth, 1975, Table 2, p. 85).

Formula developers discovered rather quickly that many variables intercorrelate and, therefore, that continuing to add variables quickly runs into diminishing returns in predictive power. The evidence from a review of existing formulas (Klare, 1974–1975, pp. 97–98), from factor analyses (Entin & Klare, 1978a), and from a recent analysis using a sophisticated computer system and new variables (McMahon et al., 1978) supports this point of view. In general, two factors stand out, semantic difficulty and syntactic difficulty, with the former typically accounting for much the greater amount of variance. Other factors appear in factor analyses, of course, but usually account for small amounts of variance. Contradictions also arise, as would be expected; for example, Bormuth (unpublished) did not find it worthwhile to add spelling variables to his formulas, whereas Harris and Jacobson (1974) found them useful.

The "good news" and the "bad news" pretty well summarizes the matter of selecting language variables in prediction. The good news is that two language variables, and simple ones at that, account for so much of the variance in the prediction of readable writing. Kintsch and Vipond (1977, p. 9), call this "amazing." The bad news is that adding new and different variables, however promising they may sound, usually turns out to be a frustrating task. They seem to account for little, if any, new or added variance. Kintsch's attempt (1979) to take reader characteristics into account in his formula may well be a useful exception. Studies comparing his approach to a traditional approach on a wider range of materials and readers than he has used would be helpful. Such work, unfortunately, is difficult and time consuming, but could be especially interesting in helping users decide whether the extra work his approach requires pays off. With the ability of modern formulas to correlate in the .90s with existing criteria, this is a significant question for prediction variables. And it leads directly into related questions regarding production variables.

Production variables. Writers about writing have suggested that a large number of variables can contribute to clarity. Klare (unpublished), for example, found 156 variables listed in 15 books on clear writing even after grouping them together as well as possible when they seemed to say the same thing. The problem, as with prediction, is not a shortage of variables. But there are other problems for writers who wish to use them in producing readable writing, as noted below.

Most of the above variables have not been studied experimentally, since production research is difficult to do well. More and more receive attention as time goes on, of course. Wright, in a series of recent papers (1977, 1978b, 1978c, 1979a) provides an excellent summary of research in this area.

A related problem, with the number of variables available, is that of knowing when each might be appropriate. Klare's study of books on clear writing (Klare, unpublished) found some pairs of suggestions actually contradictory. The problem appeared to be that one of the pair might apply in a particular set of circumstances and the other in another set. But the problem of which to use and when to use it remains unclear. Once again, Wright has written some very useful papers on this issue recently (1978a, 1979b). She suggests three stages in the production of written materials: establishing the reader's purpose, applying the relevant research, and evaluating the final product. As this indicates, she feels that even where relevant research is available, it needs to be tested under realistic conditions before being judged effective.

Another related problem concerns the extent to which writers *can* keep the available suggestions for producing readable writing in mind while writing. Certainly, the number a writer can remember and apply, even when consciously attempting to do so, must be limited. This is the rationale for computer programs designed to help writers recognize and repair potential trouble spots in their writing. The Writer's Workbench developed by Frase and his associates at Bell Laboratories (Frase, 1980; Macdonald, Frase, Gingrich, & Keenan, 1982) is perhaps the best known and most extensive of these systems. It contains programs which provide information on the following aspects of writing:

- Proofreading, including spelling, punctuation, consecutive occurrences of the same word, faulty phrasing, and split infinitives.
- Stylistic analysis, including several readability indexes (grade levels), information on the average lengths of words and sentences, distribution of sentence lengths, grammatical types of sentences used (simple and complex), percentage of verbs in the passive voice, percentage of nouns that are nominalizations, number of sentences beginning with expletives, sets of style standards, and stylistic problem locators.
- Reference information on English usage and on its own programs, including descriptive information about the use of words and about correct spelling.
- Other information, including organization, sexist language, and text abstractness.

Of particular interest in connection with the style analyses are the programs which provide different sets of standards for the various style statistics and which help writers find stylistic problems associated with all forms of "to be." There were over 1000 users of The Writer's Workbench in the Bell System in 1982; a survey of a sample found them to be highly satisfied with it.

Kincaid, Aagard, and O'Hara (1980; see also Kincaid, Aagard, O'Hara, & Cottrell, 1981) have developed CRES, a computer readability editing system for writers in the U.S. Navy. Applied to text, it:

- provides a readability formula score (grade level and related statistics),
- flags and lists uncommon words,
- flags long sentences,
- offers the writer simpler and more common options in the text itself alongside the uncommon words and phrases.

A program similar to CRES in many ways is being developed at Westinghouse Electric by Kniffin and Pierce (1981). Other programs of this general type include JOURNALISM (Bishop, 1975) and EPISTLE (Miller, Heidorn, & Jensen, 1981). JOURNALISM provides some proofreading assistance as well as comments on the organization and content of the articles being analyzed. EPISTLE is a business-office system which corrects grammatical errors in letters being sent out as well as abstracts the contents of letters being received.

Users of The Writer's Workbench commented especially on the fact that this system called attention to problems of unclear writing they had not thought about previously, or to problems they were aware of but would have missed in their own writing. Of course, some writers can and do write readably even without computer assistance. How do they keep the various necessary considerations in mind? Part of the explanation would seem to lie, as in the case of prediction, in intercorrelation among the variables. For example, Paivio, Yuille, and Madigan (1968) report intercorrelations from .56 and .83 between the ratings of the word characteristics of meaningfulness, concreteness, and imagery; the correlations involving Thorndike and Lorge frequency and the above variables were .12 to .33. The latter values are surprisingly low, perhaps because of restriction of range; other comparisons involving frequency typically yield higher values (e.g., see Klare, 1968 or Noble, 1963, for a review). Toglia and Battig (1978) extended the ratings of word characteristics to include categorizability, number of attributes, and pleasantness. They found very high intercorrelations between concreteness, imagery, and categorizability—ranging from .88 to .91—and, in fact, consider the three to represent a single higher-order semantic dimension. Low intercorrelations—between .22 and .31—were found whenever the dimension of pleasantness was involved, and the other intercorrelations ranged between .3 and .6. It is interesting to note that familiarity (along with frequency), meaningfulness, concreteness, and imagery were among the more common characteristics found in Klare's survey of books on clear writing (Klare, unpublished). Similarly, the correlation of frequency and length (especially of content words) has long been recognized (Thorndike, 1937; Zipf, 1935). In addition to the matter of intercorrelation, another part of the explanation would seem to lie in writers gaining experience—with feedback of some sort—in using readable words and constructions while writing. Still another related part of the explanation would seem to lie in the editing, or self-editing, process. Whatever the explanation (and there may well be more), writers do seem to vary a great deal in their ability to write readably. And with the recent emphasis on making informative writing of so many kinds more readable, a better understanding of the explanation would be helpful.

In summary, the selection and use of language variables in producing readable writing has not progressed nearly so far as in predicting readable writing. At least several reasons must be involved. For one thing, word and sentence variables (or style variables) are not the only contributors to readability. Among the more obvious missing candidates are organization, format, and illustrations (verbal and pictorial). For another thing, variables in the subjects serving as readers must play a part in the outcome of experimentation (this matter is discussed more fully below). Still another thing concerns the conditions of experimentation and their inevitable effects upon the psychometric adequacy of the results (again, explained more fully below). These considerations play a lesser role in prediction studies, especially with a good criterion, since the variability tends to be cancelled out across the different kinds of readers.

For these reasons, many writers have warned against making changes in the index variables used in formulas and then expecting comparable changes in reader behavior (comprehension). For example, Pearson and Camperell (1981) remind writers that chopping sentences in half will affect formula score without necessarily affecting comprehension (see also Pearson, 1974–1975). Selzer (1981) summarizes this problem using Klare's analogy—merely shortening words and sentences to improve readability is like holding a lighted match under a thermometer when you want to make your house warmer. Yet, recent writers, such as Williams et al. (1977) and Jarman (1979), argue that the variables in their methods are conceptually different and directly affect comprehension. Williams et al. have even provided normative values for their variables in the kind of Air Force writing for which they developed their formulas. Whether or not writers could produce more readable writing by using such guidelines has not been demonstrated. And, yet again, as a review of production studies has shown (Klare, 1976b), writers *can* produce readable writing—writing which raises comprehension scores significantly. Exactly how they have accomplished or do accomplish this deserves further close scrutiny.

Other Prediction Problems

Scaling.   The adequacy of the scale used and the scale indexes the formulas provide constitute the biggest problem in the prediction of readable writing. Most users, both within and outside the field of education, want readability indexes in terms of reading-grade levels. Such scores provide users with a way to compare, and presumably match, readers' ability levels to the difficulty levels of written material. Even for readers not in school, the grade-level scale has an appeal lacking in other scales (descriptive terms varying from "easy" to "hard," typical magazines, percentage correct in cloze tests, etc.). A number of attempts have been made to look at mismatch as well as match of reader and reading-grade levels (e.g., Coke, 1976a; Johnson, Relova, & Stafford, 1972; Sticht, 1975; Kniffin, Stevenson, Klare, Entin, Slaughter, & Hooke, 1980).

The widespread desire for a grade scale has led most formula developers to provide one. Flesch, for example, avoided such a scale in the first report on his widely used Reading Ease formula (1948) but soon adopted one—in fact, two (1949). British writers typically have a version more appropriate to their terminology, a reading-age scale based on automatic addition of five years to the reading-age values (e.g., see Harrison, 1980b, p. 74). The situation resembles that of using the IQ scale with tests of mental ability, with both its good and bad ramifications.

Many users first become aware of the problem when they notice that different formulas can yield different grade-level scores. Confusing as this may be, the problem goes much deeper, beginning with the question, noted earlier, of just what comprehension is. Such long-term issues are best avoided here, with concentration instead upon the practical issues formula users must face. A definition, in the time-honored manner, provides a good place to begin a brief discussion (a more complete discussion can be found in Klare, 1979, pp. 45–67).

A grade-level score for an individual based upon a typical reading test means that he or she reads as well as some normative group. Such a score does not mean that the individual cannot read with understanding below, of course, or even quite far above that level under proper conditions. It is that score, however, which readability formulas attempt to predict—recently, as noted earlier, with great success when the criterion values are good ones and the statistic is a correlation coefficient. But there the problems begin.

High intercorrelations among the scores yielded by different formulas do not assure equivalent grade-level ratings. For example, Vaughan (1976) found intercorrelations of .87 between the SMOG (McLaughlin, 1969) and the Dale and Chall (1948) and the SMOG and Fry (1963, 1977) values respectively; yet, the SMOG consistently gave values two grades higher than the other two. The Dale and Chall and Fry, on the other hand, correlated .87 and consistently gave very similar grade values. Such intercorrelations and grade-level comparisons have been made for some time (see Klare, 1963, pp. 115–121, for a review of early studies) and have continued down to the present (e.g., see Guidry & Knight, 1976; Harrison, 1980b; Vaughan, 1976). High intercorrelations and roughly equivalent grade ratings do sometimes occur, but not necessarily, apparently for several reasons (a few of which appear below). Some recent formulas come equipped with a standard error of estimate in terms of grade level, which can be helpful. Where this value has been given for recent formulas, it typically falls below one grade level and sometimes even below half a grade level (e.g., Harris & Jacobson, 1973). However good this may be, one must remember that standard errors of estimate are, strictly speaking, specific to the criterion being used. Comparisons between formulas, therefore, cannot often be made, as the next point indicates.

Different formula developers have used different criteria, as noted earlier. Adequacy of the criterion values as well as applicability to different groups of readers becomes a first possible cause of differences. Several attempts have been made to reduce the possible error. Caylor et al. (1973) tied the grade-level scores from their formula directly to the actual reading grade levels of Army readers, for example. Kincaid et al. (1975) used a similar approach in revising the Flesch Reading Ease formula for Navy readers. Bormuth (unpublished) went a step farther by actually introducing, as a variable in the formula, the grade level of schooling reached by readers for whom the material is intended. And as noted, the College Entrance Examination Board (1980) accomplished this by using a common scale for both the values from their version of Bormuth's formula and their reading test. These approaches have the desirable property of making comparisons of readability scores and reading-ability scores more meaningful, which permits improved matching of readers to reading material. However, they would seem, at the same time, to tie formula scores even more closely to a particular criterion test, making formula comparisons even more difficult. Fortunately, this problem is not necessarily as serious as it sounds. As indicated, the comparisons by Klare cited earlier show that grade-level scores from the Flesch Reading Ease and Flesch and Kincaid formulas and from the Fry graph relate quite closely, despite their very different developmental criteria. Furthermore, a close relationship is typically found between Reading Ease and Dale and Chall scores.

Most readability formulas are based upon counts in criterion passages of a particular range of difficulty. Because most formulas are linear regression equations, however, scores can be extrapolated beyond the range of difficulty of the criterion passages. This can lead to grade levels as high as 34 if one uses the circular developed by the U.S. Army for use with the Flesch and Kincaid formula. School grades do not go this high, for one thing. For another, content becomes so much more critical to comprehension beyond high school and the early college years that such a value can be seriously misleading. Carver (1974), for example, encountered special problems in prediction at the level of the more difficult passages. Tables of corrected or interpreted grade levels, such as those of Dale and Chall (1948) or Flesch (1948), which extend only up to college graduate level, are more convincing, although even they represent a small amount of extrapolation beyond the McCall and Crabbs passages on which they were based. Fry recently extrapolated his graph through the same college-year period, as noted earlier, but fortunately received support for this from the validity check of Longo (1982). The solution of Kincaid et al. (1975), in basing the Flesch and Kincaid formula on the *Gates-MacGinitie Reading Tests* (1972), which goes up to grade-level 16, is still more satisfactory. The Army, as noted, did not terminate its table for the Flesch and Kincaid at that level but continued beyond with a linear interpolation. To show how unfortunate such a linear arrangement is, Klare submitted a long passage from the California probate code for analysis, using a computer program for this formula. The results indicated that a reader would need 122 years of schooling to comprehend the passage!

M. Coleman and Liau's procedure (1975) of translating cloze percentages directly into grade levels presents a still different problem. The percentages correct on cloze passages change with the language skill of the readers as well as the difficulty of the passages, as Carver (1977–1978) and others have pointed out. Consequently, a high percentage correct on the cloze version of a passage could result from either a simple style in the passage or a high level of skill in the reader. Bormuth (1967, 1968) and Rankin and Culhane (1969) have found that cloze percentages correspond roughly to particular levels of multiple-choice percentages, which can aid interpretation. However, Peterson, Peters, and Paradis (1972) and Peterson, Paradis, and Peters (1973) found such correspondence in one study but puzzling differences in another.

In summary, several conclusions can be drawn. If one uses formulas only to provide reminders or rough guides to readability levels, the scale problem is not a serious one. Because a reading-grade scale seems convenient and easily understood, it need not be misleading, especially if it does not go beyond college level. If a more precise grading of material is needed, as in selection of school texts, readability levels must be interpreted more cautiously and the best formula sought. As noted, the International Reading Association has gone further and recommended that the use of grade levels be abandoned altogether (*Reading Research Quarterly*, 1981). In such a case, derived units like those of the College Entrance Examination Board (1980) may get around some of the objections to grade levels. Further guidance in use of formula scores could be provided by additional studies, like that of Harrison (1980b), in relating the scores of a set of formulas to a consensus of teacher ratings. Another approach that could be helpful would be regression equations which permit a user to relate grade levels from one formula to those from another. This sounds easier to do than it is, as the preliminary work of Stokes (1978) shows. All formulas must be compared in terms of ratings on the same satisfactory criterion passages, of course. If the number of passages gets large, the application process becomes very costly in time and effort. If the number of formulas gets large, the analysis of the much larger number of comparisons can soon tax even large computers. Perhaps a compromise representing logical groups of the most used formulas would be possible. At any rate, the question of scale, particularly grade-level scale, deserves more attention, as the coming sections emphasize further. The grade-level scale appears, on the one hand, to be too useful to discard but, on the other hand, too questionable to accept—at least uncritically.

Sampling. Another problem, and one related to scaling in certain ways, concerns the selection of samples for analysis. Use of samples to reduce the labor of application was suggested early in the history of readability measurement, with a recent trend to reducing the number of samples which parallels that of simplifying of formulas. This trend has, however, come under increasing criticism.

All sorts of sampling schemes have been suggested by formula developers; a few of the common ones will be noted here. Dale and Chall (1948), for example, recommended a 100-word sample every tenth page; Flesch (1948) recommended 25 to 30 samples of 100 words per book. Fry (1977) and Raygor (1977) suggested 3 samples of 100 words should be enough, unless a great deal of variability is noted. Yarnell (1971) actually suggested using only 1 "typical" or "random" sample of 100 words for use with his small "readability calculator." How many samples are enough?

Early evaluations of sampling adequacy tended to emphasize mean-score comparisons, and results typically indicated that the recommended numbers of samples could be cut. As recently as 1977, Burkhead and Ulferts (1977) found that mean Dale and Chall scores based on 100-word samples taken at intervals of 20, 30, 40, and 50 pages were as reliable as the 10-page intervals recommended by Dale and Chall.

A number of research workers have found, however, that samples of books are likely to vary considerably in difficulty. Coke and Rothkopf (1970), using 200 continuous 100-word samples of material on modern physics, found Flesch Reading Ease scores from 40 to over 110, that is, from about college level to fourth-grade level. Bradley and Ames (1977) found that even samples from a single level of a basal reader showed variations of at least seven grade levels in Fry graph scores. Bradley, Ames, and Mitchell (1980) found an even greater range of Fry scores, from Grade 4 to college, in American history texts intended for junior high school.

Such findings have raised anew the question of how many samples are needed to get a reliable estimate of readability. Moll (1975) suggested a simple square root sampling method, which involves taking the square root of the number of paging units (pages of 100-plus words) as the required number of samples. McCuaig and Hutchings (1975) commented that the three samples suggested for the Fry graph were certainly not enough since they could so easily mask the variation in a book. They suggested taking six samples and using the standard deviation of the sentences and syllables to create an interval on the graph which would contain 68 percent of all 100-word samples in the book. Luiten, Ames, and Bradley (1979), however, found this method to underestimate consistently the observed readability variation in whole-book samplings, covering 46 percent rather than 68 percent in their research. They suggested further research to determine sample size.

G. G. Fitzgerald (1980, 1981) made the most complete sampling studies to date, computing both confidence intervals and power functions. She also found three samples on the Fry graph to be inadequate since they resulted in:

• high standard errors among samples;
• confidence intervals so broad as to be almost useless; and,
• probabilities of Type II errors that were unacceptably high.

In determining the critical (necessary) number of samples for the 36 workbooks in her study, she found that to achieve the desired degree of power (.80), the entire of 11 of the books had to be analyzed. The critical number in all cases, she reports, "was discouragingly large" (1981, p. 408). This appears to take users back to the situation in the 1930s. At that time, Dolch (1930), who was apparently the first to call attention to sampling problems, noted that a formula should be applied to the entire contents of a book to get the most accurate evidence of its true readability. This might seem to be an almost impossible order and, at the least, suggests looking at two things:

1. the needed research recommended by G. G. Fitzgerald to find out more about "how samples reflect a whole text" and
2. the use of much larger samplings than is common nowadays, which available computer programs render feasible.

The question of how a wide level of variation affects reader behavior is even less well understood. Stokes, as part of a doctoral dissertation underway in England, found a rather close parallel between readability scores and cloze scores on successive samples in a textbook. The tracking of the two appears fairly good, with certain exceptions, such as figurative language, where the readability score underestimates difficulty. Exactly how readers react when faced with a wide range of difficulty has not been examined sufficiently. On the one hand, the challenge of difficult passages may be desirable. On the other hand, readers may fail to comprehend difficult passages and become frustrated. If, when, and where such behavior becomes likely, though difficult to study, it deserves greater attention. The information available, as expected, suggests that the question is not an easy one. Bradley and Ames (1976) found that intrabook variability did indeed adversely affect oral reading performance. Jorgenson (1977), in a study of the match between material difficulty and reader ability, found further that classroom behavior improved as material became easier. Yet, as noted earlier (Chall, 1979; Chall et al., 1977), there is also reason to use more difficult material to raise reading scores. The question is more than merely one of readability measurement.

Other Production Problems

Content variables. One of the steps in production research, as described earlier, requires that variables other than those being studied be held constant in the several experimental versions. Otherwise, of course, one cannot properly attribute any resulting differences among the versions. Unfortunately, this step is easier to prescribe than to achieve—or even describe. There are several significant problems encountered in this kind of research.

One immediate concern relates to keeping meaning, or content, the same while changing readability variables. This seems obvious enough, but the problem lies in knowing how to measure or count meaning or content units; no convenient metric exists. A review of production studies (Klare, 1976b) shows that where research workers took this into account (and not all did, at least in an obvious way), the most common method was to use judges. This is helpful, and requiring judges to use something like thought units or idea units might be still more helpful. Carver (1977–1978b) has used this in building his approach around a count of thought units in reading material. Significant attempts have been made recently to use propositions in the analysis of content by Kintsch (Kintsch, 1974; Kintsch & Keenan, 1973), by Meyer (1977), and by Frederiksen (1975, 1979). Kintsch (1979) has used this approach in conjunction with traditional readability measures in development of his readability formula.

A characteristic which would seem easy to equate in studies is length of experimental passages. But even this is complicated in readability studies, chiefly because more readable words tend to be shorter. As noted earlier, Zipf (1935) and Thorndike (1937) pointed out that length and frequency of usage (and thus familiarity) relate quite consistently, especially for content words. In addition to this effect, the more readable active-voice form is shorter than the passive-voice form of sentences. Thus, readability changes can show up in terms of brevity, even in carefully controlled studies. Klare, Mabry, and Gustafson (1955), for example, equated the number of words in their easy, standard, and hard experimental versions and noted that the hard version had a greater overall length than the standard, and the standard had a greater overall length than the easy. This kind of observation has raised questions about the proper unit for measuring the effect of readability upon reading speed. Significant differences may be found using words as a measure, but other measures, such as lines (Klare et al., 1955) or syllables (Carver, 1971–1972; Coke, 1974; Rothkopf, 1972), tend not to show these differences. The problem centers around which measure of length should serve as a control. If a measure like number of lines or syllables is used as a control instead of number of words, the results are biased against the effects of readability. When more and less readable versions are required to have the same number of syllables, the more readable version must have a larger number of words if the powerful variable of frequency is used (Klare, 1968). Yet, length of word, indexing as it does such other variables as word familiarity, concreteness, and meaningfulness, is a major contributor to readability and cannot be adjusted as an alternative. Perhaps research workers should report rate in both words and syllables.

The problem is only a bit less acute with other variables. For example, writers have pointed out for some time that mechanical changes, such as making arbitrary substitutions of words or chopping sentences in half (Pearson & Camperell, 1981) are ineffectual. They will change the score on readability formulas without making a corresponding change in comprehensibility; they may, indeed, reduce comprehensibility if deliberately or even carelessly done. Furthermore, such a construction may be "awkward" and, thus, have no effect or even a negative effect on readers. But this cannot easily be shown, on the one hand, or perhaps easily avoided, on the other hand, when mechanical changes are made. Studies of this sort (Duffy & Kabance, 1982) are, therefore, difficult to evaluate. As one writer put it, the aim should be to produce "considerate" prose rather than mechanical changes. That is why such developers of computer aids for writers as Frase (1980), Kincaid et al. (1980), and Kniffin and Pierce (1981) have been careful in describing what their programs can do. They can provide the writer with evaluations and information for possible alternative changes. However, the suggestions are just that, suggestions, and the writer must decide whether or not to use them. A related problem in research concerns restricting the kinds of variables changed according to which other variables can be most satisfactorily—or justifiably—controlled. This can, again, produce ineffectual writing. But lack of controls, or inadequate controls, can be just as serious, if not more serious, for research.

Subject variables. Experimental attempts to modify comprehension through changes in the level of readability are necessarily very complex. The comparison of 36 such production studies cited previously (Klare, 1976b) began with a review of 40 characteristics in the attempt to discover those which raised or lowered the probability of finding significant differences between more and less readable versions. Of these, 28 grouped in the following areas received special attention.

1. The experimental passages and how they were modified.
2. The tests and other dependent measures used.
3. Descriptions of the subjects and their characteristics.
4. The instructions given to the subjects.
5. Details of the experimental situation.
6. The statistical analyses employed.
7. The results, and detailed discussions based on them.

Of these, the characteristics associated with the subjects appeared to play the largest part in raising or lowering the probability of significant differences between easy and hard versions. As noted in the paper, the review could not be specific enough to indicate that a given variable *would* make a difference; the interactions, particularly, were too complex for that. However, certain possibilities stood out clearly enough for testing.

Motivation of subjects, as might be expected, assumed a major role. McLaughlin (1966), for example, showed the kind of effect motivation can have in comparing comprehension scores on the easier and harder versions of a pamphlet. He found that for subjects who were *not* highly motivated, the mean comprehension scores significantly favored the easier version; for subjects who *were* highly motivated by threat, the mean comprehension scores no longer significantly favored the easier version. Denbow (1973) showed the same general kind of effect comparing easier and harder versions of two contents, one of higher and one of lower reader interest, with information gain as the dependent measure. He found that the easier versions of both contents produced significantly greater gain than the harder, as expected; however, the amount of gain was significantly greater on the content which was lower in interest value. Fass and Schumacher (1978) tested the effect of motivation directly using two groups, one of which had a special monetary incentive. Once again, the easier version produced significantly greater comprehension only under lower motivation (points given toward course grade). Entin (1980; Entin & Klare, in press) provided further evidence of the effect of motivation by altering reader interest. She used 12 experimental passages, 6 shown previously to be of high interest to college freshmen and 6 of low interest. These passages were modified so that one version (standard) was at approximately Grade 12 according to the Flesch Reading Ease formula and one was at approximately Grade 16, yet with the same content according to judges. Both readability and interest resulted in a significant difference in cloze scores on the passages. She concluded that she did not find the interaction effect found by Denbow and by Fass and Schumacher because the material was *at* (standard version) and *above* (difficult version) the readers' normed ability levels, so that the effects of readability and interest were cumulative.

The degree of subjects' prior knowledge can also have an effect upon whether readability changes will affect comprehension scores significantly. This was suggested by two earlier studies (Klare et al., 1955; Funkhouser & Maccoby, 1971) but could only be presumed because of experimental conditions. Both studies seemed to indicate that as degree of prior knowledge increased, the effect of readability decreased. In recent analyses, Entin and Klare (1978, 1980) showed that a measured degree of prior knowledge had a clear effect. Correlations between passage readability levels and multiple-choice comprehension scores on a published reading test were essentially zero, but became moderately positive when corrections were made for prior knowledge of readers. Entin (1980; Entin and Klare, in press) varied prior knowledge experimentally in her study of the effects of interest and readability and again found a significant effect for this variable. The effect was not as clear-cut as with interest and readability, however, because of problems of getting a completely satisfactory measure of prior knowledge. Had this been possible, an interesting chicken-egg conundrum—which comes first, interest or knowledge—could have been examined, at least in a preliminary way. Rothkopf (1978) has presented a detailed theoretical analysis of the reciprocal relationship between previous experience and processing in determining learning outcomes, which should help such studies along.The conditions under which an investigator works can, of course, have marked effects on the results of most studies. In studies of the effect of readability upon comprehension this shows up especially clearly. In the laboratory, subjects may feel compelled for any number of reasons to comply with the investigator's wishes. Furthermore, the level of motivation tends to be high and, in most cases, the investigator helps this tendency along to the extent possible. In the field, however, certain effects which might be obscured in the laboratory can be seen more clearly. Readership goes up along with improved readability in split-run studies of newspapers (D. R. Murphy, 1947a, 1947b; Swanson, 1948), now a widely accepted conclusion. Readability can also have a significant effect upon use of military manuals (Kern, Sticht, & Fox, 1970), discrepancies in following military procedures (Johnson et al., 1972), and reader perseverance in correspondence instruction (Klare & Smart, 1973). This effect could also be seen in the analysis of the 36 studies relating comprehension to changes in readability. In 10 of the 16 studies which yielded nonsignificant or mixed results on comprehension scores, subjects had been asked to pick out or indicate their preference for the more or less readable version. They chose the more readable, even though the comprehension differences were not found to be significant (Klare, 1976b, pp. 139–140). As these results suggest, more research should be done in a field setting when motivation and other relevant variables are typical of the real world situation. And, to keep the effects clear, the measures of effects should themselves ideally be unobtrusive.

A GLANCE AHEAD

Attempts to peek into the future can, at best, be risky ventures. The future soon enough becomes the present and too often reclassifies judgments as misjudgments. Nevertheless some guesses, or perhaps hopes, always seem clear enough to hazard.

One might be tempted to say that investigators appear unlikely to produce many new readability formulas. Most useful language variables seem to have been used—and, in fact, reused many times. Furthermore, correlations in the .90s between formula values and criterion measures would seem to be discouraging to further research. Two observations make this unlikely however. The first is the growing criticism of existing readability formulas. The second is the recent emphasis on plain talk in public documents, insurance policies, financial agreements, and job-related civilian and military materials. Though increased efforts appear to be stemming the slide in reading skills among high school and college graduates, the growth in essential documents in our technological society seems certain to continue. Consequently new formulas and new "nonformulas" are likely to continue to appear. The current structure-of-text orientation in reading research offers a significant new direction for such work. Kintsch's additional emphasis on readability as an interaction between a text and the reader's prose-processing capabilities appears particularly promising, with his formula prediction (Kintsch, 1979) and subsequent multiple-regression predictions of readability measures (Miller & Kintsch, 1980) producing correlation coefficients in the .80s and .90s.

Applications of readability measures, both older and newer, seem likely to be increasingly oriented to particular practical needs. Use continues to be heaviest in the area of education, but can be found in many other applied fields, and concern has grown about the adequacy and accuracy of the grade-level scale commonly used with formulas. The approach of the College Entrance Examination Board (1980) to this problem is of special interest. A common scale, called DRP units, is used with both their readability formula measurements and their reading test, providing an improved method of matching text difficulty to readers' ability scores.

Investigators have for some time, of course, been interested in validating readability measures against such practical kinds of reader behaviors. The accumulated evidence now clearly supports the notion that improved readability can produce increases in the following kinds of reader behaviors (reviews are covered in Klare, 1963, 1976b, and in this chapter):

- comprehension, learning, and retention;
- reading speed and efficiency; and
- acceptability (a general term intended to cover readership, preference, perseverance, etc.).

Improved readability *can* produce these effects but does not *always* do so. The application of readability formulas to texts in psychology is a good case in point. At an early date, Stevens and Stone (1947) pointed out that the "personal references" variable in Flesch's original formula (1943) inappropriately raised the readability score in certain very difficult texts. This led Flesch (1948) to remove this variable from his then new Reading Ease formula and to suggest a separate Human Interest formula to parallel it. The Human Interest formula has been little used, especially in comparison with the popular Reading Ease formula. But the many writers about the readability of psychology texts (e.g., see Gillen, 1973; Hofmann & Vyhonsky, 1975; Ogdon, 1954) have continued to use both—and, in fact, to find both to be valid, invalid, and of mixed validity (e.g., see Croll & Moskaluk, 1977; Gillen, Kendall, & Finch, 1977; *Teaching of Psychology*, 1977).

The discovery of *when* and *how* the above effects on reader behavior are likely to occur constitute two major questions that are only poorly understood at present and that are likely to get increased research attention. Klare (1976b), for example, has presented a "when" model suggesting that the probability of an increase in comprehension depends upon interactions among the factors below (as well as others).

1. The test situation, particularly as it affects the reader's level of motivation and the opportunity for it to have an effect.
2. Reader motivation, particularly as a function of interest and typical level of motivation.
3. Readability level of material, particularly in terms of degree of difference between more and less readable versions.
4. Content of material, particularly where amount of old/new information and maturity level are concerned.
5. Reader competence, particularly where size of mismatch between reader skill and reading difficulty are concerned.

Studies by Denbow (1973), Fass and Schumacher (1978), and Entin and Klare (Entin, 1980; Entin & Klare, 1978, 1980, in press) have supported the predictions from this model.

Coke, as another example, has studied the question of when readability level will affect reading rate. In a first study (Coke, 1974), she showed that, when measured in terms of syllables, more difficult text was read at essentially the same rate as less difficult. In later studies (Coke, 1976b, 1977), she found that the effect of readability upon rate was affected by the kind of processing the reader was doing. Readability had no effect on rate of search for literal information, but it did affect rate of search for semantic information, with more difficult material slowing the rate in the latter case. Sticht (1975) has provided another example, showing when readability will affect reader acceptability of material. Military readers, he has shown, will turn from manuals to colleagues for help when manuals become difficult for them to read, that is, when there is a so-called literacy gap. Yet, Kniffin et al. (1980) have shown that, as predicted, the effect of a literacy gap upon comprehension can be greatly weakened where motivation is raised and the experimental situation allows it to affect reader behavior. This is an example of the kind of interaction among variables which makes the study of readability's effects so complex and interpretation of a study like that of Duffy and Kabance (1982) appear deceptively simple.

The question of *when* readability will and will not be likely to produce changes in reader behavior clearly needs, and will likely get, further study. But equally needed—and likely—will be new research on *how* readability produces its effects. Changes in readability level might profitably be related, for example, to other concepts in psychology and linguistics. There have recently been more studies of this sort, notable among them the following.

- Hardyck and Petrinovich (1970) have shown that subvocalization increases as the reading difficulty of material increases.
- Klare and Smart (1973) have found a close relationship between readability level and the probability correspondence students would persevere and complete their courses.
- Holgerson (1977) has shown that the eye-voice span is related to readability (and thus, presumably, to efficient use of short-term or working memory).
- Britton and associates (Britton, Westbrook, & Holdredge, 1978; Britton, Ziegler, & Westbrook, 1980) have used a secondary-task technique to observe cognitive-capacity usage in easy and difficult text; they have found that easy text fills cognitive-capacity usage more fully than difficult text.
- Rothkopf (1978, 1980) has shown the level of readability to be related to several measures of typists' "copying span," that is, the amount they can copy (in letters) without looking at the text and, thus, their efficient use of short-term memory.
- Kintsch (1979) found that level of readability was related to the reading times of his passages and to ratings of subjective readability but not to reading time per proposition recalled in an immediate test.
- Schwantes (1982) found that readability level was related to vocalization latency for target words in context; developmental differences favoring older children were reduced for material beyond appropriate grade level, showing the relationship of readability level to the helpful effect of context.

The work above has been moving in a direction likely to continue to grow: the attempt to fit readability research and findings more completely into the larger picture of reading behavior and human behavior more generally. There have been several recent and notable attempts of this sort.

Carver (1977–1978b, 1981), for example, has presented a theory of reading comprehension and rauding (the phenomenon of general language comprehension in which readability plays a central part). The theory proposes that the rate at which most individuals typically raud (i.e., comprehend each thought) is constant and that the accuracy of comprehension can be predicted from measures of material difficulty (readability) and the individual's ability. The number of thoughts in a passage that have been comprehended may be predicted from:

- two characteristics of the reader, rauding rate, R_r, and level of reading ability, L_a;
- two characteristics of the material, number of thoughts presented, T_p, and level of difficulty of the material, L_d, and
- amount of time spent in reading, t.

Carver (1983) has been continuing to provide research data for a number of the notions in his theory.

Bormuth (unpublished) has centered his approach upon how to achieve the most effective literacy program. He points out that literacy can be increased either by adjusting reading material to suit the needs of intended readers or by adapting the skills of the readers to meet the demands of the materials. In his approach, readability formulas play a pivotal role in articulating these two methods. He has developed formulas which include components for:

- different degrees of reader comprehension desired by users;
- the bias and the changing variance of reading tests at different levels; and
- the curvilinearity in the relationship between formula variables and measures of comprehensibility.

He has also provided formulas for three major types of users: those who need a simple formula for day-to-day use; those whose extensive use requires a computerized formula; and those for whom accuracy demands a sophisticated formula. He argues that they provide a needed step in the direction of a scientific as opposed to the practical approach of earlier work. A formula of his, noted earlier, became the basis for the College Entrance Examination Board's readability analyses.

Kintsch argues strongly for a clearer theoretical approach to readability. The problem of predicting reader comprehension, he says, "is not with the formulas but with our theories" (Kintsch & Vipond, 1979, p. 335); he believes that readability must be defined for specific texts and specific readers. His "formula" (Kintsch, 1979) used the following predictor variables and yielded a multiple correlation of .97 with readability (reading time per proposition recalled) on ten passages:

- number of reinstatement searches;
- word frequency;
- proposition density;
- number of inferences;
- number of processing cycles; and
- number of different arguments in the proposition list.

In his later study (Miller & Kintsch, 1980), he found a multiple correlation of .86 between the same measure of readability on 20 passages by adding the following predictor variables to those above:

- input size (related to the earlier processing cycles);
- sentence length (related to the earlier processing cycles);
- short-term memory stretches (overloads); and
- buffer size.

Each of the above writers takes care to point out the tentative nature of his model and especially its current limitations. Questions can certainly be raised, as shown by the comments of Hill (1977–1978) and Pearson and Kamil (1977–1978) on Carver's model, but they can also be a spur to further thought, as Carver's reply (1977–1978a) testifies. Whatever their fate, these models do represent interesting new attempts to integrate readability research into reading theory. One can hope, if not expect, that such work will continue. As Rothkopf points out (1980, pp. 571–572), this kind of work represents "an important step away from surface indicators such as the Flesch Reading Ease index toward more fundamental psychological analysis. [But] in the meantime, practical considerations require the continued use of surface readability indicators."

In that case, what can we expect of readability formulas today? Here are some suggestions for users (Klare, 1982):

- Remember that different formulas may give different grade-level scores on the same piece of writing. Though they resemble thermometers in giving index values, they differ in that (like most educational and psychological tests) they do not have a common zero point.
- Look over existing formulas and pick a good one for the purpose at hand; but consider all formulas to be screening devices and all scores to be probability statements, as Monteith (1976) puts it.
- Choose a formula with two index variables for rough screening purposes; having only one variable decreases predictiveness, but having more than two usually increases effort more than predictiveness. For critical applications or for research, apply more than one formula or try one of the newer, more complex formulas.
- Increase the value of an analysis by taking a large random (or numerically spread) sampling. For critical applications or for research, analyze the entire piece of writing (a computer program can be of help); three samples can, at best, give an indication of the average level of difficulty but cannot say anything useful about variations in difficulty.
- Bear in mind that formula scores derive from counts of style difficulty. Therefore they become poorer predictors of difficulty at higher grade levels (especially college), where content weighs more heavily.
- Consider again the purpose of the intended reading material. Training readers calls for more challenging material than merely informing or, especially, entertaining them.
- Take into account other recognized contributors to comprehension, especially higher levels of motivation or of prior knowledge; otherwise formula scores may overestimate or underestimate difficulty. For example, using special interests or incentives to get above-average motivation can help to keep challenging material from being frustrating.
- Do not rely on formulas alone in selecting reading materials when this can be avoided; include judges for characteristics that formulas cannot predict and to be sure formulas have not been misused in preparing materials. But not just any judges—select experts or get more reliable consensus opinions.
- Prepare to shift material after tentative placement; where to draw the line between reading material that frustrates readers or that challenges them cannot be specified easily with or without formulas.
- Keep formulas out of the writing process itself; if you use them for feedback, try the writing-rewriting cycle described by Macdonald-Ross (1979):

Write→Apply formula→Revise→Apply formula . . .

To summarize, the two encompassing questions raised earlier by Coupland (1978) and Maxwell (1978) might again be considered.

1. Is readability real? The thousand-plus references and the growing interest in theory as well as applications suggest it is at least alive and thriving. And every now and then we can expect a "new approach" (Bormuth, 1966; Flesch, 1942), a "new framework" (Harris & Jacobson, 1979), or a "new definition" (Amiran & Jones, 1982) to enliven the research contests.
2. But, have we gone too far with readability? In terms of research, the answer must clearly be no. In terms of application, the answer must be a more cautious sometimes no, but sometimes yes.

We clearly *can* go too far with readability findings, both in attempts at predicting and producing readable writing, but we need not. Arguable issues remain in the areas of criteria and grade-level assignments and in application to the preparation of reading materials. Formulas selected and used properly can be helpful as screening devices, but this does not mean they can at the same time serve as guides for readable writing. Humans and language are too complex to expect such simple cause-effect relationships. Research has now clearly begun, however, to move in the direction of understanding *when* and *how* changes in readability can work for the individual reader. That seems certain to be the future test for readability research.

REFERENCES

ACTivity.   No final answer yet on questions about test score decline. May 1979, *17*, 4–5.

Air Force Manual.   *Guide for air force writing* (Air Force Manual 11–3). Maxwell, Ala.: Air University, Maxwell AFB, June 1953.

Amiran, M. R., & Jones, B. F.   Toward a new definition of readability. *Educational Psychologist*, 1982, *17*, 13–30.

Anderson, J. Lix and Rix: Variations on a little-known readability index. *Journal of Reading*, 1983, *26*, 490–496.

Anderson, R. C., Spiro, R. J., & Montague, W. E.   *Schooling and the acquisition of knowledge*. Hillsdale, N.J.: Erlbaum, 1977.

Baldwin, R. S. & Kaufman, R. K.   A concurrent validity study of the Raygor readability graph. *Journal of Reading*, 1979, *23*, 149–153.

Biersner, R. J., & Bunde, G. R.   An alternative method of performing automated readability counts. *Human Factors Society Bulletin*, 1979, *22*, 1–3.

Bishop, R. L.   The JOURNALISM programs: Help for the weary writer. *Creative Computing*, 1975, *1*, 28–30.

Björnsson, C. H.   *Läsbarhet* [Readability]. Stockholm, Swed.: Liber, 1968, 248–249.

Bobrow, D. G., & Collins, A. M.   (Eds.), *Representation and understanding*. New York: Academic Press, 1975.

Bormuth, J. R.   Readability: A new approach. *Reading Research Quarterly*, 1966, *1*, 79–132.

Bormuth, J. R.   Comparable cloze and multiple-choice comprehension test scores. *Journal of Reading*, 1967, *10*, 291–299.

Bormuth, J. R.   Cloze test readability: Criterion scores. *Journal of Educational Measurement*, 1968, *5*, 189–196.

Bormuth, J. R.   *Development of readability analyses* (Final Report, Project No. 7–0052, Contract No. 1, OEC–3–7–070052–0326). Washington, D.C.: USOE, Bureau of Research, HEW, March 1969.

Bormuth, J. R.   The cloze procedure: Literacy in the classroom. In W. D. Page (Ed.), *Help for the reading teacher: New directions in research.* Urbana, Ill.: National Conference on Research in English, ERIC Clearinghouse on Reading and Communication Skills. National Institute of Education, 1975.

Bormuth, J. R.   *Readability formulas and the literacy production function.* Unpublished paper, University of Chicago, n.d.

Bradley, J. M., & Ames, W. S.   The influence of intrabook variability on oral reading performance. *Journal of Educational Research,* 1976, *70,* 101–105.

Bradley, J. M., & Ames, W. S.   Readability parameters of basal readers. *Journal of Reading Behavior,* 1977, *9,* 175–183.

Bradley, J. M., Ames, W. S., & Mitchell, J. N.   Intrabook readability: Variations within history textbooks. *Social Education,* 1980, *44,* 524–528.

Britton, B. K., Westbrook, R. D., & Holdredge, T. S.   Reading and cognitive capacity usage: Effects of text difficulty. *Journal of Experimental Psychology: Human Learning and Memory,* 1978, *4,* 582–591.

Britton, B. K., Ziegler, R., & Westbrook, R.   Use of cognitive capacity in reading easy and difficult text: Two tests of an allocation of attention hypothesis. *Journal of Reading Behavior,* 1980, *12,* 23–30.

Burkhead, M., & Ulferts, G.   Sample frequency in application of Dale-Chall readability formula. *Journal of Reading Behavior,* 1977, *9,* 287–290.

Burmeister, L. E.   A chart for the new Spache formula. *Reading Teacher,* 1976, *29,* 384–385.

Caffyn, J. M., & Mills, P.   From information to understanding and action in social research. *Proceedings of the MRS Conference.* United Kingdom, 1980, 335–346.

Carlson, R.   Reading level difficulty. *Creative Computing,* 1980 (April), 60–61.

Carroll, J. B.   Defining language comprehension: Some speculations. In J. B. Carroll & R. O. Freedle (Eds.), *Language comprehension and the acquisition of knowledge.* Washington, D.C.: Winston, 1972.

Carter, J.   *Executive order: Improving government regulations.* Washington, D.C.: Office of the White House, March 23, 1978.

Carver, R. P.   Evidence for the invalidity of the Miller-Coleman readability scale. *Journal of Reading Behavior,* 1971–1972, *4,* 42–47.

Carver, R. P.   *Improving reading comprehension: Measuring readability* (Final Report, Contract No. N00014–72–C0240, Office of Naval Research). Silver Spring, Md.: American Institutes for Research, 1974.

Carver, R. P.   Measuring prose difficulty using the Rauding scale. *Reading Research Quarterly,* 1975–1976, *11,* 660–685.

Carver, R. P.   Another look at rauding theory. *Reading Research Quarterly,* 1977–1978, *13,* 116–132. (a)

Carver, R. P.   Toward a theory of reading comprehension and rauding. *Reading Research Quarterly,* 1977–1978, *13,* 8–63. (b)

Carver, R. P.   Sense and nonsense about generalizing to a language population. *Journal of Reading Behavior,* 1978, *10,* 25–33.

Carver, R. P.   *Reading comprehension and rauding theory.* Springfield, Ill.: Charles C. Thomas, 1981.

Carver, R. P.   Is reading rate constant or flexible? *Reading Research Quarterly,* 1983, *18,* 190–215.

Caylor, J. S., Sticht, T. G., Fox, L. C., & Ford, J. P.   *Methodologies for determining reading requirements of military occupational specialties* (Tech. Rep. No. 73–75). HumRRO

Western Division. Presidio of Monterey, California: Human Resources Research Organization, March 1973.

Chall, J. S. *Readability: An appraisal of research and application.* Columbus: Bureau of Educational Research, Ohio State University, 1958.

Chall, J. S. Readability: In search of improvement. *Publishers Weekly,* October 29, 1979, 40–41.

Chall, J. S., Conrad, S., & Harris, S. *An analysis of textbooks in relation to declining S.A.T. scores.* Princeton, N.J.: College Entrance Examination Board, 1977.

Clark, C. H. Assessing comprehensibility: The PHAN system. *Reading Teacher,* 1981, *34,* 670–675.

Clark, H. H. The language-as-fixed-effect fallacy: A critique of language statistics in psychological research. *Journal of Verbal Learning and Verbal Behavior,* 1973, *12,* 335–359.

Clark, H. H., Cohen, J., Smith, J. E. K., & Keppel, G. Discussion of Wike and Church's comments. *Journal of Verbal Learning and Verbal Behavior,* 1976, *15,* 257–266.

Clive, M., & Russo, F. The plain English movement in America: A view from the front. *Information Design Journal,* 1981, *2/3 & 4,* 208–214.

Cohen, G. I. *A new key to better writing.* Paper presented at the 22nd International Technical Communication Conference, Anaheim, Calif., May 1975.

Coke, E. U. The effects of readability on oral and silent reading rates. *Journal of Educational Psychology,* 1974, *66,* 406–409.

Coke, E. U. *Are Bell System practices difficult to read? Measurement of the readability of a sample of BSP's.* Unpublished paper, Bell Laboratories, July 15, 1976. (a)

Coke, E. U. Reading rate, readability, and variations in task-induced processing. *Journal of Educational Psychology,* 1976, *68,* 167–173. (b)

Coke, E. U. The effect of altering the context cues in prose on reading rate in a search task. *Journal of Reading Behavior,* 1977, *9,* 365–380.

Coke, E. U., & Rothkopf, E. Z. Note on a simple algorithm for a computer-produced reading ease score. *Journal of Applied Psychology,* 1970, *54,* 208–210.

Colby, J. The i/e ratio—a measure of comprehensibility. *Technical Communication,* 1981, *28,* no. 1, 4–9.

Coleman, E. B. Generalizing to a language population. *Psychological Reports,* 1964, *14,* 219–226.

Coleman, E. B. *On understanding prose: Some determiners of its complexity* (NSF Final Report GB–2604). Washington, D.C.: National Science Foundation, 1965.

Coleman, E. B. Developing a technology of written instruction: Some determiners of the complexity of prose. In E. Z. Rothkopf & P. E. Johnson (Eds.), *Verbal learning research and the technology of written instruction.* New York: Teachers College Press, 1971.

Coleman, E. B. Generalization variables and restricted hypotheses. *Journal of Reading Behavior,* 1973, *5,* 226–236.

Coleman, E. B., & Miller, G. R. The simplest experimental design that permits multiple generalization. *Journal of Reading Behavior,* 1974, *6,* 31–40.

Coleman, M., & Liau, T. L. A computer readability formula designed for machine scoring. *Journal of Applied Psychology,* 1975, *60,* 283–284.

College Entrance Examination Board. *Degrees of reading power* (Readability report, 1980–81 academic year). New York: The College Board, 1980.

College Entrance Examination Board. *Degrees of reading power* (Readability report, 1982–83 academic year). New York: The College Board, 1982.

Coupland, N. Is readability real? *Communication of Scientific and Technical Information,* April 1978, 15–17.

Croll, W., & Moskaluk, S.   Should Flesch counts count? *Teaching of Psychology*, 1977, *4*, 48–49.

Crook, N. M.   A study of the validity of the Fry readability graph. *Journal of Social Studies Research*, 1977, *1*, 53–59.

Dale, E., & Chall, J. S.   A formula for predicting readability. *Educational Research Bulletin*, 1948, *27*, 11–20, 37–54.

Danielson, W. A., & Bryan, S. D.   Computer automation of two readability formulas. *Journalism Quarterly*, 1963, *39*, 201–206.

Davison, A., & Kantor, R. N.   On the failure of readability formulas to define readable texts: A case study from adaptations. *Reading Research Quarterly*, 1982, *17*, 187–209.

DeCrow, R.   (Ed.) *Adult reading development: An information awareness service*. Washington, D.C.: National Reading Center Foundation, 1972. (ERIC Document Reproduction Service No. ED 068–808).

Denbow, C. J.   *An experimental study of the effects of a repetition factor on the relationship between readability and listenability*. Unpublished doctoral dissertation, Ohio University, 1973.

Dickes, P., & Steiwer, L.   [Formulation of a readability formula for the German language.] *Zeitschrift für Entwicklungspsychologie und Pädagogische Psychologie*, 1977, *9*, 20–28.

Dolch, E. W.   Sampling of reading matter. *Journal of Educational Research*, 1930, *22*, 213–215.

Duffelmeyer, F. A.   A comparison of two non-computational readability techniques. *Reading Teacher*, 1982, *36*, 4–7.

Duffy, T. M.   Literacy research in the Navy. In T. G. Sticht & D. W. Zapf (Eds.), *Reading and readability research in the armed services* (HumRRO RF–WO–CA–76–4). Alexandria, Va.: Human Resources Research Organization, September 1976.

Duffy, T. M., & Kabance, P.   Testing a readable writing approach to text revision. *Journal of Educational Psychology*, 1982, *74*, 733–748.

Dunnette, M. D., & Maloney, P. W.   Factorial analysis of the original and the simplified Flesch reading ease formula. *Journal of Applied Psychology*, 1953, *37*, 107–110.

Entin, E. B.   *Relationships of measures of interest, prior knowledge, and readability to comprehension of expository passages*. Unpublished doctoral dissertation, Ohio University, 1980.

Entin, E. B., & Klare, G. R.   Factor analyses of three correlation matrices of readability variables. *Journal of Reading Behavior*, 1978, *10*, 279–290. (a)

Entin, E. B., & Klare, G. R.   Some interrelationships of readability, cloze, and multiple-choice scores on a reading comprehension test. *Journal of Reading Behavior*, 1978, *10*, 417–436. (b)

Entin, E. B. & Klare, G. R.   Components of answers to multiple-choice questions on a published reading comprehension test: An application of the Hanna-Oaster approach. *Reading Research Quarterly*, 1980, *15*, 228–236.

Entin, E. B., and Klare, G. R.   Relationships of measures of interest, prior knowledge, and readability to comprehension of expository passages. In B. Hutson (Ed.), *Advances in reading/language research*, Vol. III. Greenwich, Conn.: JAI Press, in press.

Farr, J. N., & Jenkins, J. J.   Tables for use with the Flesch readability formulas. *Journal of Applied Psychology*, 1949, *33*, 275–278.

Farr, J. N., Jenkins, J. J., & Peterson, D. G.   Simplification of Flesch Reading Ease formula. *Journal of Applied Psychology*, 1951, *35*, 333–337.

Fass, W., & Schumacher, G. M.   Effects of motivation, subject activity, and readability on the retention of prose materials. *Journal of Educational Psychology*, 1978, *70*, 803–808.

Fitzgerald, G. G.   Reliability of the Fry sampling procedure. *Reading Research Quarterly,* 1980, *15,* 489–503.

Fitzgerald, G. G.   How many samples give a good readability estimate?—The Fry graph. *Journal of Reading,* 1981, *24,* 404–410.

Fitzgerald, S. E.   Literature by slide rule. *Saturday Review,* February 14, 1953, *36,* 15–16, 53–54.

Flesch, R. F.   Readability—a new approach. *Library Journal,* 1942, *67,* 213–215.

Flesch, R. F.   *Marks of readable style: A study in adult education.* New York: Bureau of Publications, Teachers College, Columbia University, 1943.

Flesch, R. F.   A new readability yardstick. *Journal of Applied Psychology,* 1948, *32,* 221–233.

Flesch, R. F.   *The art of readable writing.* New York: Harper & Bros., 1949. (Collier Books edition, 1962.)

Flesch, R. F.   Measuring the level of abstraction. *Journal of Applied Psychology,* 1950, *34,* 384–390.

[Flight Manual]   *Rules governing the use of aeronautical apparatus. First known airplane flight manual: Instructions issued with the 1911 Glen Curtiss "pusher."* Washington, D.C.: Engineering and Manufacturing Branch, FAA Academy.

Foulger, D.   A simplified Flesch formula. *Journalism Quarterly,* 1978, *55,* 167, 202.

Frase, L. T.   *Computer aids for writing and text design.* Symposium presented at the annual meeting of the American Educational Research Association, Boston, April 1980.

Frederiksen, C. H.   Representing logical and semantic structure of knowledge acquired from discourse. *Cognitive Psychology,* 1975, *7,* 371–458.

Frederiksen, C. H.   Discourse comprehension and early reading. In L. B. Resnick & P. A. Weaver (Eds.), *Theory and practice of early reading* (Vol. 1). Hillsdale, N.J.: Erlbaum, 1979.

Froese, V.   Rauding and SEERing: Judging global readability. *Perspectives on reading research and instruction.* (29th yearbook of the National Reading Conference.) Washington, D.C.: National Reading Conference, 1980.

Fry, E. B.   *Teaching faster reading.* London: Cambridge University Press, 1963.

Fry, E. B.   A readability formula that saves time. *Journal of Reading,* 1968, *11,* 513–16 and 575–78.

Fry, E. B.   Fry's readability graph: Clarifications, validity, and extension to level 17. *Journal of Reading,* 1977, *21,* 242–252. (Hand calculator for the Fry readability scale (extended) available from Jamestown Publishers, P.O. Box 6743, Providence, R.I. 02940.)

Fry, E. B.   Comments on the preceding Harris and Jacobson comparison of the Fry, Spache, & Harris-Jacobson readability formulas. *Reading Teacher,* 1980, *33,* 924–926.

Funkhouser, G. R., & Maccoby, N.   *Study on communicating science information to a lay audience, Phase II.* (Report based upon a study funded by the National Science Foundation [NSF GZ–996]. Institute for Communication Research, Stanford University, September 1971.

Garcia, W. F.   *Assessing readability for Spanish as a second language: The Fry graph and cloze procedure.* Unpublished doctoral dissertation, Columbia University Teachers College, 1977.

Gates, A. I., & MacGinitie, W. H.   Gates-MacGinitie reading tests. Boston: Houghton Mifflin, 1972.

General Accounting Office.   *A need to address illiteracy problems in the military services* (Report No. FPCD–77–13). Washington, D.C.: U.S. General Accounting Office, March 31, 1977.

Gerbens, A.   Read any good books lately? *Kilobaud,* 1978, *14,* 104–106.

Gillen, B.   Readability and human interest scores of thirty-four current introductory psychology texts. *American Psychologist,* 1973, *28,* 1010–1011.

Gillen, B., Kendall, P. C., & Finch, A. J.   Reading ease and human interest scores: A comparison of Flesch scores with subjective ratings. *Teaching of Psychology,* 1977, *4,* 39–41.

Gilliam, B., Peña, S. C., & Mountain, L.   The Fry graph applied to Spanish readability. *Reading Teacher,* 1980, *33,* 426–430.

Gilliland, J.   *Readability.* London: University of London Press for the United Kingdom Reading Association, 1972.

Goodman, D., & Schwab, S.   Computerized testing for readability. *Creative Computing,* 1980 (April), 46–51.

Gray, W. S., & Leary, B. E.   *What makes a book readable.* Chicago: University of Chicago Press, 1935.

Groeben, N.   *Die Verständlichkeit von Unterrichtstexten* [The comprehensibility of educational texts]. Münster, W. Ger.: Aschendorff, 1978.

Guidry, L. J., & Knight, D. F.   Comparative readability: Four formulas and Newbery books. *Journal of Reading,* 1976, *19,* 552–556.

Guilford, J. P., & Hoepfner, R.   *The analysis of intelligence.* New York: McGraw-Hill, 1971.

Gunning, R.   *The technique of clear writing.* New York: McGraw-Hill, 1952.

Guthrie, J. T.   Learnability versus readability of texts. *Journal of Educational Research,* 1972, *65,* 273–280.

Guthrie, J. T. (Ed.)   *Comprehension and teaching: Research reviews.* Newark, Del.: International Reading Association, 1981.

Halliday, H. A. K., & Hasan, R.   *Cohesion in English.* London: Longman, 1976. (English Language Series).

Hardyck, C. D., & Petrinovich, L. F.   Subvocal speech and comprehension level as a function of the difficulty level of reading material. *Journal of Verbal Learning and Verbal Behavior,* 1970, *9,* 647–652.

Harris, A. J., & Jacobson, M. D.   *Basic elementary reading vocabularies.* New York: Macmillan, 1972.

Harris, A. J., & Jacobson, M. D.   *The Harris-Jacobson primary readability formulas.* Paper presented at the annual convention of the International Reading Association, Denver, Colo., May 1973.

Harris, A. J., & Jacobson, M. D.   *Revised Harris-Jacobson readability formulas.* Paper presented at the annual meeting of the College Reading Association, Bethesda, Md., October 1974.

Harris, A. J., & Jacobson, M. D.   *Comparative predictions of tested reading comprehension of high school seniors.* Paper presented at the annual convention of the American Psychological Association, September 1975.

Harris, A. J., & Jacobson, M. D.   Predicting twelfth graders' comprehension scores. *Journal of Reading,* 1976, *19,* 43–47.

Harris, A. J., & Jacobson, M. D.   A framework for readability research: Moving beyond Herbert Spencer. *Journal of Reading,* 1979, *22,* 390–398.

Harris, A. J., & Jacobson, M. D.   Comparison of the Fry, Spache, and Harris-Jacobson readability formulas for primary grades. *Reading Teacher,* 1980, *33,* 920–924.

Harris, A. J., & Jacobson, M. D.   *Basic reading vocabularies.* New York: Macmillan, 1982.

Harrison, C.   Assessing the readability of school texts. In J. Gilliland (Ed.), *Reading: Research and classroom practice.* London: Ward Lock Educational, 1977.

Harrison, C.   Assessing the readability of school texts. In E. A. Lunzer & W. K. Gardner (Eds.), *The effective use of reading.* London: Heinemann, 1979.

Harrison, C.   *Readability and pupil response in relation to samples of 11- and 14-year-olds'* reading material in four subject areas. Unpublished doctoral dissertation, University of Nottingham, Eng., 1980. (a)

Harrison, C.   *Readability in the classroom.* Cambridge: Cambridge University Press, 1980. (b)

Hartley, J., Trueman, M., & Burnhill, P.   Some observations on producing and measuring readable writing. *Programmed Learning and Educational Technology,* 1980, *17,* 164–174.

Henry, G.   *Comment mesurer la lisibilité* [How to measure readability]. Brussels, Belg.: Editions Labor; Paris: Fernand Nathan, 1975.

Hill, W.   Concerning reading theory: A reaction to Carver's "Toward a theory of reading comprehension and rauding." *Reading Research Quarterly,* 1977–1978, *13,* 66–91.

Hofmann, R. J., & Vyhonsky, R. J.   Readability and human interest scores of thirty-six recently published introductory educational psychology texts. *American Psychologist,* 1975, *30,* 790–792.

Holgerson, A. S.   *The relationship of eye-voice span to reading ability and readability.* Unpublished master's thesis, Rutgers University, June 1977. (Available through ERIC.)

Holland, V. M.   *Psycholinguistic alternatives to readability formulas* (Tech. Rep. No. 12, Document Design Project). Washington, D.C.: American Institutes for Research, 1981.

Hull, L. C.   *Measuring the readability of technical writing.* Paper presented at the 26th International Technical Communication Conference, Los Angeles, Calif., May 1979. (See *ITCC Proceedings,* E–73 to E–78.)

IEEE Transactions on Professional Communication, 1981 (March), *PC–24,* (1). (Special issue on making information usable.)

Information Design Journal.   The design of forms and official information. 1981, *2/3, 4.*

Irving, S. L., & Arnold, W. B.   Measuring readability of text. *Personal Computing,* 1979 (September), 34–36.

Irwin, J. W.   The effect of linguistic cohesion on prose comprehension. *Journal of Reading Behavior,* 1980, *12,* 325–332.

Irwin, J. W., & Davis, C. A.   Assessing readability: The checklist approach. *Journal of Reading,* 1980, *24,* 124–130.

Jacobson, M. D.   Predicting reading difficulty from spelling. *Spelling Progress Bulletin,* 1974, *14,* 8–10.

Jacobson, M. D., Kirkland, C. E., & Selden, R. W.   An examination of the McCall-Crabbs Standard Test Lessons in Reading. *Journal of Reading,* 1978, *22,* 224–230.

Jarman, B. D.   *Measurement of writing-style factors in readability-rated samples of technical text.* Paper presented at the 26th International Technical Communication Conference, Los Angeles, Calif., May 1979. (See *ITCC Proceedings,* E–79 to E–84.)

Johnson, K. H., Relova, R. P., Jr., & Stafford, J. P.   *An analysis of the relationship between readability of Air Force procedural manuals and discrepancies involving non-compliance with the procedures.* Unpublished master's thesis, Air Force Institute of Technology, Air University, August 1972. (Document No. AD 750 917, National Technical Information Service.)

Jongsma, E. A.   The difficulty of children's books: Librarian's judgments versus formula estimates. *Elementary English,* 1972, *49,* 20–26.

Jorgenson, G. W.   An analysis of teacher judgments of reading level. *American Educational Research Journal,* 1975, *12,* 67–75.

Jorgenson, G. W.   Relationship of classroom behavior to the accuracy of the match between material difficulty and student ability. *Journal of Educational Psychology,* 1977, *69,* 24–32.

Journal of Business Communication, 1981 (Fall), *18*, (4). (Special issue on readability.)

Kandel, L., & Moles, A.   Application de l'indice de Flesch à la langue français. *Cahiers d'Etudes de Radio-Télévision*, 1958, *19*, 253–274.

Kane, R. B., Byrne, M. A., & Hater, M. A.   *Helping children read mathematics.* New York: American Book Co., 1974.

Keller, P. F. G.   Maryland micro: A prototype readability formula for small computers. *Reading Teacher*, 1982, *35*, 778–782.

Kern, R. P., Sticht, T. G., & Fox, L. C.   *Readability, reading ability, and readership* (Professional Paper 17–70). Alexandria, Va.: Human Resources Research Organization, June 1970.

Kincaid, J. P., Aagard, J. A., & O'Hara, J. W.   *Development and test of a computer readability editing system (CRES)* (TAEG Report No. 83). U.S. Navy Training Analysis and Evaluation Group, Orlando, Fla., 1980.

Kincaid, J. P., Aagard, J. A., O'Hara, J. W., & Cottrell, L. K.   Computer readability editing system. *IEEE Transactions on Professional Communications*, March 1981.

Kincaid, J. P., Fishburne, R., Rogers, R. L., & Chissom, B. S.   *Derivation of new readability formulas (Automated Readability Index, Fog Count, and Flesch Reading Ease formula) for navy enlisted personnel* (Branch Report 8–75). Chief of Naval Training, Millington, Tenn., 1975.

Kincaid, J. P., & McDaniel, W. C.   *An inexpensive automated way of calculating Flesch Reading Ease scores.* Washington, D.C.: Patent Disclosure Document No. 031350, U.S. Patent Office, 1974.

Kintsch, W.   *The representation of meaning in memory.* Hillsdale, N.J.: Erlbaum, 1974.

Kintsch, W.   On modeling comprehension. *Educational Psychologist*, 1979, *14*, 3–14.

Kintsch, W., & Keenan, J. M.   Reading rate and retention as a function of the number of propositions in the base structure of sentences. *Cognitive Psychology*, 1973, *5*, 257–274.

Kintsch, W., & Vipond, D.   Reading comprehension and readability in educational practice and psychological theory. In L-G. Nilsson (Ed.), *Perspectives on memory research.* Hillsdale, N.J.: Erlbaum, 1979.

Kintsch, W., & Yarbrough, J. C.   Role of rhetorical structure in text comprehension. *Journal of Educational Psychology*, 1982, *74*, 828–834.

Klare, G. R.   *The measurement of readability.* Ames: Iowa State University Press, 1963.

Klare, G. R.   The role of word frequency in readability. *Elementary English*, 1968, *45*, 12–22. (Also reprinted in J. R. Bormouth (Ed.), *Readability in 1968.* Champaign, Ill.: National Conference on Research in English, 1968.)

Klare, G. R.   Assessing readability. *Reading Research Quarterly*, 1974–1975, *10*, 62–102.

Klare, G. R.   Judging readability. *Instructional Science*, 1976, *5*, 55–61. (a)

Klare, G. R.   A second look at the validity of readability formulas. *Journal of Reading Behavior*, 1976, *8*, 129–152. (b)

Klare, G. R.   Readability standards for Army-wide publications (Evaluation Report 79–1). Fort Benjamin Harrison, Ind.: Directorate of Evaluation, U.S. Army Administration Center, 1979.

Klare, G. R.   Readability. In H. E. Mitzel (Ed.), *Encyclopedia of educational research,* 5th Ed. New York: Free Press, 1982, 1520–1531.

Klare, G. R.   *Comparisons of grade-level estimates from readability measures based on three different developmental criteria.* Unpublished paper, Ohio University, 1983.

Klare, G. R.   Readability and comprehension. In R. S. Easterby & H. Zwaga (Eds.), *Visual presentation of information.* London: Wiley, in press.

Klare, G. R.   Some suggestions for clear writing found in fifteen source books. Unpublished, n.d.

Klare, G. R., Mabry, J. E., & Gustafson, L. M.   The relationship of style difficulty to immediate retention and to acceptability of technical material. *Journal of Educational Psychology*, 1955, *46*, 287–295.

Klare, G. R., Sinaiko, H. W., & Stolurow, L. M.   The cloze procedure: A convenient readability test for training materials and translations. *International Review of Applied Psychology*, 1972, *21*, 77–106.

Klare, G. R., & Smart, K.   Analysis of the readability level of selected USAFI instructional materials. *Journal of Educational Research*, 1973, *67*, 176.

Kling, M., & Pratt, D. F.   *Readability: A re-examination and new directions for further research*. Paper presented at the annual meeting of the National Reading Conference, New Orleans, La., December 1977.

Kniffin, J. D.   The new readability requirements for military technical manuals. *Technical Communication*, 1979, *26*, 16–19.

Kniffin, J. D., & Pierce, E.   *The story of Westinghouse technical data research on readability, comprehensibility, text processing, and computer-aided translation*. Unpublished paper, Technical Data and Training Systems Department, Columbia, Md., September 1981.

Kniffin, J. D., Stevenson, C. R., Klare, G. R., Entin, E. B., Slaughter, S. L., & Hooke, L.   *Operational consequences of literacy gap* (AFHRL–TR–79–22). Brooks AFB, Tex.: Air Force Systems Command, May 1980.

Kretschmer, J. C.   Updating the Fry readability formula. *Reading Teacher*, 1976, *29*, 555–558.

LaBerge, D., & Samuels, S. J.   (Eds.)   *Basic processes in reading: Perception and comprehension*. Hillsdale, N.J.: Erlbaum, 1977.

Lange, R.   Readability formulas: Second looks, second thoughts. *Reading Teacher*, 1982, *35*, 858–861.

Layton, J. R.   A chart for computing the Dale-Chall readability formula above fourth grade level. *Journal of Reading*, 1980, *24*, 239–244.

Lesgold, A. M., & Perfetti, C. A.   (Eds.)   *Interactive processes in reading*. Hillsdale, N.J.: Erlbaum, 1981.

Liau, T. L., Bassin, E. B., Martin, C. J., & Coleman, E. B.   Modification of the Coleman readability formulas. *Journal of Reading Behavior*, 1976, *8*, 381–386.

Lively, B. A., & Pressey, S. L.   A method for measuring the "vocabulary burden" of textbooks. *Educational Administration and Supervision*, 1923, *9*, 389–398.

Longo, J. A.   The Fry graph: Validation of the college levels. *Journal of Reading*, 1982, *26*, 229–234.

Lorge, I.   Predicting reading difficulty of selections for children. *Elementary English Review*, 1939, *16*, 229–233.

Lowe, A. J.   ThUS: A non-formula readability measure. *Reading Improvement*, 1979, *16*, 155–157.

Luiten, J., Ames, W. S., & Bradley, J. M.   Using Fry's graph to describe the variation of readability: A corrected procedure. *Reading World*, 1979, *18*, 361–367.

Macdonald, N. H., Frase, L. T., Gingrich, P. S., & Keenan, S. A.   The writer's workbench: Computer aids for text analysis. *Educational Psychologist*, 1982, *17*, 172–179.

Macdonald-Ross, M.   Language in texts. In L. S. Shulman (Ed.), *Review of research in education* (No. 6, 1978). Itasca, Ill.: Peacock, 1979.

Maginnis, G. H.   The Readability Graph and informal reading inventories. *The Reading Teacher*, 1969, *22*, 516–518, 559.

Maginnis, G. H.   Easier, faster, more reliable readability ratings. *Journal of Reading*, 1982, *26*, 598–599.

Manzo, A.   Readability: A postscript. *Elementary English*, 1970, *47*, 962–965.

Maxwell, M.   Readability: Have we gone too far? *Journal of Reading*, 1978, *21*, 525–530.

McCall, W. A., & Crabbs, L. M. *Standard test lessons in reading: Teacher's manual for all books.* New York: Bureau of Publications, Teachers College, Columbia University, 1925 (Revised 1950; Revised 1961).

McConnell, C. R. Readability formulas as applied to college economics textbooks. *Journal of Reading,* 1982, *26,* 14–17.

McCuaig, S. M., & Hutchings, B. Using Fry's graph to describe the variation of readability. *Journal of Reading,* 1975, *18,* 298–300.

McDaniel, W. C., & Kincaid, J. P. Inter-analyst reliability and time measures for the automated and manual Flesch counts. *Human Factors Society Bulletin,* 1978, *21,* 1–2.

McLaughlin, G. H. Comparing styles of presenting technical information. *Ergonomics,* 1966, *9,* 257–259.

McLaughlin, G. H. SMOG grading—A new readability formula. *Journal of Reading,* 1969, *12,* 639–646.

McLaughlin, G. H. *Temptations of the Flesch.* Unpublished paper, Communications Research Center, Syracuse University, 1970.

McMahon, L. E., Cherry, L. L., & Morris, R. Statistical text processing. *Bell System Technical Journal,* 1978, *57* (6, Pt. 2), 2137–2154.

Meyer, B. J. F. The structure of prose: Effects on learning and memory and indications for educational practice. In R. C. Anderson, R. J. Spiro, & W. E. Montague (Eds.), *Schooling and the acquisition of knowledge.* Hillsdale, N.J., Erlbaum, 1977.

Miller, G. R., & Coleman, E. B. A set of thirty-six passages calibrated for complexity. *Journal of Verbal Learning and Verbal Behavior,* 1967, *6,* 851–854.

Miller, G. R., & Coleman, E. B. The measurement of reading speed and the obligation to generalize to a population of reading materials. *Journal of Reading Behavior,* 1972, *4,* 48–56.

Miller, J. R., & Kintsch, W. Readability and recall of short prose passages: A theoretical analysis. *Journal of Experimental Psychology: Human Learning and Memory,* 1980, *6,* 335–354.

Miller, J. W., & Marshall, F. W. *Teachers' abilities to judge the difficulty of reading materials.* Paper presented at the annual meeting of the International Reading Association, Houston, Tex., May 1978.

Miller, L. A., Heidorn, G. E., & Jensen, K. *Text-critiquing with the EPISTLE system: An author's aid to better syntax.* Paper presented at the National Computer Conference, Chicago, May 1981.

Miller, L. R. *A comparative analysis of the predictive powers of four readability formulas.* Unpublished doctoral dissertation, Ohio University, 1972.

Miller, L. R. Predictive powers of multiple-choice and cloze-derived readability formulas. *Reading Improvement,* 1975, *12,* 52–58.

Moll, J. K. *Children's access to information in print: An analysis of the vocabulary (reading) levels of subject headings and their application to children's books.* Graduate School of Library Service, Rutgers University, January 1975.

Monteith, M. K. Readability formulas. *Journal of Reading,* 1976, *19,* 604–607.

Moore, A. C. Recoiling from reading: A consideration of the Thorndike Library. *Library Journal,* 1935, *60,* 419–422.

Morris, L. A., Thilman, D., & Myers, A. M. Application of the readability concept to patient-oriented drug information. *American Journal of Hospital Pharmacy,* 1980, *37,* 1504–1509.

Mugford, L. A new way of predicting readability. *Reading,* 1970, *4,* 31–35.

Murphy, D. R. How plain talk increases readership 45 per cent to 66 per cent. *Printer's Ink,* 1947, *220,* 35–37. (a)

Murphy, D. R.   Test proves short words and sentences get best readership. *Printer's Ink,* 1947, *218,* 61–64. (b)

Murphy, R.   *Adult functional reading study* (Final Report, Project No. 0–9004, PR 73–48). Princeton, N.J.: Educational Testing Service, December 1973.

Naval Ocean Systems Center.   U.S. Navy Technical Information Presentation Program (Solicitation No. N66001–79–R–0403). San Diego, Calif.: Supply Officer, Naval Ocean Systems Center, July 30, 1979.

New York Times. As per paragraph (i)(2)(ii)(B) or (D). February 6, 1977, p. 14E (Editorial).

New York Times. Britons take aim at gibberish. December 26, 1982.

Nguyen, L. T., & Henkin, A. B.   A readability formula for Vietnamese. *Journal of Reading,* 1982, *26,* 243–251.

Noble, C. E.   Meaningfulness and familiarity. In C. N. Cofer & B. S. Musgrave (Eds.), *Verbal behavior and learning.* New York: McGraw-Hill, 1963.

Ogdon, D. P.   Flesch counts of eight current texts for introductory psychology. *American Psychologist,* 1954, *9,* 143–144.

Paivio, A., Yuille, J. D., & Madigan, S. A.   Concreteness, imagery, and meaningfulness values for 925 nouns. *Journal of Experimental Psychology: Monograph Supplement,* 1968, *76* (Whole Pt. 2).

Paolo, M. F.   *A comparison of Readability Graph scores and oral reading errors on trade books for beginning reading.* Master's thesis, Rutgers University, 1977.

Park, Y.   *An analysis of some structural variables of the Korean language and the development of a readability formula for Korean textbooks.* Unpublished doctoral dissertation, Florida State University, 1974.

Parkhurst, W.   Textbooks: Dull is null, spice is nice. *Change,* 1979, *11,* 18–22.

Pauk, W.   A practical note on readability formulas. *Journal of Reading,* 1969, *13,* 207–210.

Pearson, P. D.   The effects of grammatical complexity on children's comprehension, recall, and conception of certain semantic relations. *Reading Research Quarterly,* 1974–1975, *10,* 155–192.

Pearson, P. D., & Camperell, K.   Comprehension of text structures. In J. T. Guthrie (Ed.), *Comprehension and teaching: Research reviews.* Newark, Del.: International Reading Association, 1981.

Pearson, P. D., & Johnson, D. P.   *Teaching reading comprehension.* New York: Holt, Rinehart & Winston, 1978.

Pearson, P. D., & Kamil, M.   What hath Carver raud? A reaction to Carver's "Toward a theory of reading comprehension and rauding." *Reading Research Quarterly,* 1977–1978, *13,* 94–115.

Peterson, J., Paradis, E., & Peters, N.   Revalidation of the cloze procedure as a measure of the instructional level for high school students. In P. L. Nacke (Ed.), *Diversity in mature reading: Theory and research* (22nd Yearbook of the National Reading Conference). Boone, N.C.: National Reading Conference, 1973.

Peterson, J., Peters, N., & Paradis, E.   Validation of the cloze procedure as a measure of readability with high school, trade school, and college populations. In F. B. Greene (Ed.), *Investigations relating to mature reading* (21st Yearbook of the National Reading Conference). Milwaukee, Wis.: National Reading Conference, 1972.

Platzack, C.   *Språket och läsbarheten* [Language and readability]. Lund, Swed.: Gleerup, 1974.

Porter, D., & Popp, H. M.   *An alternative to readability measures: Judging the difficulty of children's trade books.* Paper presented at the annual meeting of the American Educational Research Association, February 1973.

Powers, R. D., Sumner, W. A., & Kearl, B. E.   A recalculation of four readability formulas.

Journal of Educational Psychology, 1958, *49,* 99–105.

Pyrczak, F.   Reducing reading illiteracy by improving reading materials. *Reading Improvement,* 1976, *13,* 159–162.

Rankin, E. F., & Culhane, J. W.   Comparable cloze and multiple-choice comprehension test scores. *Journal of Reading.* 1969, *13,* 193–198.

Raygor, A. L.   The Raygor readability estimate: A quick and easy way to determine difficulty. In P. D. Pearson (Ed.) *Reading: Theory, research, and practice* (26th Yearbook of the National Reading Conference). Clemson, S.C.: National Reading Conference, 1977. (Raygor Readability Estimator hand calculator available from Twin Oaks Publishing, Inc., 134 Mason Street, Rehoboth, Mass. 02769.)

Reading Research Quarterly.   Resolutions passed by Delegates Assembly—April, 1981. 1981, *16* (following p. 613).

Richaudeau, F.   *La lisibilité* [Readability]. Paris: Denoel, 1969. (New edition, 1976).

Rodriguez, N., & Hansen, L. H.   Performance of readability formulas under conditions of restricted ability level and restricted difficulty of materials. *Journal of Experimental Education,* 1975, *44,* 8–14.

Rothkopf, E. Z.   Structural text features and the control of processes in learning from written materials. In J. B. Carroll & R. O. Freedle (Eds.), *Language comprehension and the acquisition of knowledge.* New York: Winston, 1972.

Rothkopf, E. Z.   On the reciprocal relationship between previous experience and processing in determining learning outcomes. In A. M. Lesgold, J. W. Pellegrino, S. D. Fokkema, & R. Glaser (Eds.), *Cognitive psychology and instruction.* New York: Plenum, 1978.

Rothkopf, E. Z.   Copying span as a measure of the information burden in written language. *Journal of Verbal Learning and Verbal Behavior,* 1980, *19,* 562–572.

Rubin, A. (Ed.)   *Conceptual readability: New ways to look at text* (Reading Education Report No. 31, Center for the Study of Reading). Cambridge, Mass.: Bolt, Beranek and Newman, 1981.

Schuyler, M. R.   A readability program for use on microcomputers. *Journal of Reading,* 1982, *25,* 560–591.

Schwantes, F. M.   Text readability level and developmental differences in context effect. *Journal of Reading Behavior,* 1982, *14,* 5–12.

Schwartz, D., Sparkman, J. P., & Deese, J.   The process of understanding and judgments of comprehensibility. *Journal of Verbal Learning and Verbal Behavior,* 1970, *9,* 87–93.

Selzer, J.   Readability is a four-letter word. *Journal of Business Communication,* 1981, *18,* 23–34.

Simply Stated.   New plain language laws, 1982 (November), 1, 4. (a)

Simply Stated.   Plain language laws: Update. 1982 (February–March), 3. (b)

Simply Stated.   Plain language laws—myth and reality. 1982–1983 (December–January), 3–4.

Singer, H.   The SEER technique: A non-computational procedure for quickly estimating readability level. *Journal of Reading Behavior,* 1975, *7,* 255–267.

Smith, E. A., & Kincaid, J. P.   Derivation and validation of the automated readability index for use with technical materials. *Human Factors,* 1970, *12,* 457–464.

Smith, E. A., & Senter, R. J.   *Automated readability index* (AMRL–TR–66–22). Wright-Patterson AFB, Ohio: Aerospace Medical Division, 1967.

Spache, G.   A new readability formula for primary-grade reading materials. *Elementary School Journal,* 1953, *53,* 410–413.

Spache, G.   *Diagnostic reading scales.* Monterey, Calif.: McGraw-Hill, 1963.

Spaulding, S.   Two formulas for estimating the reading difficulty of Spanish. *Educational Research Bulletin,* May, 1951, *30,* 117–124.

Spaulding, S. A.   A Spanish readability formula. *Modern Language Journal*, 1956, *40*, 433–441.

Spiro, R. J., Bruce, B. C., & Brewer, W. C.   (Eds.), *Theoretical issues in reading comprehension*. Hillsdale, N.J.: Erlbaum, 1980.

Stevens, K. C.   Readability formulae and McCall-Crabbs *Standard test lessons in reading*. *Reading Teacher*, 1980, *33*, 413–415.

Stevens, S. S., & Stone, G.   Psychological writing, easy and hard. *American Psychologist*, 1947, *2*, 230–235.

Sticht, T. G. (Ed.)   *Reading for working: A functional literacy anthology*. Alexandria, Va.: Human Resources Research Organization, 1975.

Stokes, A.   The reliability of readability formulas. *Journal of Research in Reading*, 1978, *1*, 21–34.

Swanson, C. E.   Readability and readership: A controlled experiment. *Journalism Quarterly*, 1948, *25*, 339–343.

Tamor, L.   Subjective text difficulty: An alternative approach to defining the difficulty level of written text. *Journal of Reading Behavior*, 1981, *13*, 165–172.

Taylor, W. L.   Cloze procedure: A new tool for measuring readability. *Journalism Quarterly*, 1953, *30*, 415–433.

Teaching of Psychology. Reading readability formulae. 1977, *4*, 50–51.

Thomas, G., Hartley, R. D., & Kincaid, J. P.   Test-retest and inter-analyst reliability of the Automated Readability Index, Flesch Reading Ease score, and Fog Count. *Journal of Reading Behavior*, 1975, *7*, 149–154.

Thorndike, E. L.   *The teacher's word book*. New York: Teacher's College, Columbia University, 1921.

Thorndike, E. L.   *A teacher's word book of 20,000 words*. New York: Bureau of Publications, Teachers College, Columbia University, 1932.

Thorndike, E. L.   On the number of words of any given frequency of use. *Psychological Record*, 1937, *1*, 399–406.

Thorndike, E. L. & Lorge, I.   *The teacher's word book of 30,000 words*. New York: Bureau of Publications, Teachers College, Columbia University, 1944.

Tibbetts, S–L.   How much should we expect readability formulas to do? *Elementary English*, 1973, *50*, 75–76.

Togeby, O.   *Sprog og laeseproces*. Copenhagen, Den.: Gjellerup, 1971.

Toglia, M. P., & Battig, W. F.   *Handbook of semantic word norms*. Hillsdale, N.J.: Erlbaum, 1978.

Trapini, F., & Walmsley, S.   Five readability estimates: Differential effects of simplifying a document. *Journal of Reading*, 1981, *24*, 398–403.

van Hauwermeiren, P.   *Het leesbaarheidsonderzoek* [Readability research]. Groningen, The Netherlands: H. D. Tjeenk Willink, 1975.

Vari-Cartier, P.   Development and validation of a new instrument to assess the readability of Spanish prose. *Modern Language Journal*, 1981, *65*, 141–148.

Vaughan, J. L.   Interpreting readability assessments. *Journal of Reading*, 1976, *19*, 635–639.

Vogel, M., & Washburne, C.   An objective method of determining grade placement of children's reading material. *Elementary School Journal*, 1928, *28*, 373–381.

Wagner, B. J.   Blood and gore, fens and fears: Beowulf battles the Dale-Chall monster. *Reading Teacher*, 1981, *34*, 502–510.

Walmsley, S. A., Scott, K. M., & Lehrer, R.   Effects of document simplification on the reading comprehension of the elderly. *Journal of Reading Behavior*, 1981, *13*, 237–248.

Wang, M. D.   The role of syntactic complexity as a determiner of comprehensibility. *Journal of Verbal Learning and Verbal Behavior*, 1970, *9*, 398–404.

Washburne, C., & Morphett, M. V.   Grade placement of children's books. *Elementary School Journal*, 1938, *38*, 355–364.

Wheeler, L. R., & Smith, E. H.   A practical readability formula for the classroom teacher in the primary grades. *Elementary English*, 1954, *31*, 397–399.

Wiio, O. A.   *Readability, comprehension, and readership*. Tampere, Fin.: Tampereen Yliopisto, 1968.

Wike, E. L., & Church, I. D.   Comments on Clark's "Language-as-fixed-effect fallacy." *Journal of Verbal Learning and Verbal Behavior*, 1976, *15*, 249–255.

Williams, A. R., Siegel, A. I., Burkett, J. R., & Groff, S. D.   *Development and evaluation of an equation for predicting the comprehensibility of textual material*. AFHRL–TR–77–8. Brooks AFB, Tex.: Air Force Human Resources Laboratory, Air Force Systems Command, February 1977.

Wright, P.   Presenting technical information: A survey of research findings. *Instructional Science*, 1977, *6*, 93–134.

Wright, P.   Feeding the information eaters: Suggestions for integrating pure and applied research in language comprehension. *Instructional Science*, 1978, *7*, 249–312. (a)

Wright, P.   *Is legal jargon a restrictive practice?* Paper presented at the SSRC Law and Psychology Seminar Group Meeting, Trinity College, Oxford, Eng., September 1978. (b)

Wright, P.   *Strategy and tactics in the design of forms*. Paper presented at the NATO Conference on Visual Presentation of Information, Het Vennenbos, The Netherlands, September 1978. (c)

Wright, P.   Helping lawyers communicate. *Legal Action Group Bulletin*, July 1979. (a)

Wright, P.   The quality control of document design. *Information Design Journal*, 1979, *1*, 33–42. (b)

Yarnell, E. A.   *Everyone has the right to read at his own level*. Charleston, S.C.: Nova Company, 1971.

Zipf, G. K.   *The psycho-biology of language*. Boston: Houghton-Mifflin, 1935.

23 CLASSROOM INSTRUCTION IN READING

Barak Rosenshine and Robert Stevens

This chapter contains research reviews on a number of topics: general and specific classroom instructional procedures, the content covered, academic engaged time and allocated time, and the error rate. For each topic, we present the research results, offer suggestions for improving instruction, and make suggestions for future research.

Because of the length and because the topics do not easily fit into a single whole, we have divided the chapter into three sections. The first section is on general instructional procedures, the second is on specific instructional procedures, and the third presents the research on three major indicators of effective instruction: content covered, academic-engaged minutes, and student error rate. All of these areas are fairly new, and most of this research does not, as yet, appear in reading methods textbooks.

The first two sections, general and specific instructional procedures, represent a line of research which began in the 1950s with the work of Flanders and Medley and Mitzel. This research took place in regular classrooms with regular teachers and students. This line of research has witnessed important advances since 1974. Most results have been replicated across a number of correlational and experimental studies, leading to some convergence on the issue of what classroom practices are associated with student achievement gain. Fortunately, for this volume of research in reading, a great many of these studies have investigated reading instruction in elementary grades, and the results will be one focus of this review.

The third section begins with a review of the research on content covered. This is a fairly recent concern. The first cited study in this area is Husen (1967) and the research has continued since that time. The review on academic-engaged time represents a line of research which Jackson (1968) notes began with the work of Morrison in 1927. The research waned in the 1940s, but the modern resurgence began with the work of Carroll (1963). The research on error rate was drawn from a number of sources, and error rate was a particular focus of the Beginning Teacher Evaluation Study (BTES) (Fisher, Filby, Marliave, Cahen, Dishan, Moore, & Berliner, 1978).

GENERAL INSTRUCTIONAL PROCEDURES

The three topics reviewed in this section—teacher-directed instruction, instruction in groups, and academic emphasis—have been controversial topics in reading instruction for years. In this review, we bring together the data on each of these topics. We have prepared extensive tables of results in order to provide evidence that is as concrete and comprehensive as possible. Across a large number of studies, investigators have found that (1) students who receive much of their instruction from the teacher do better than those expected to learn on their own or from each other and (2) students learn to read most efficiently when teachers use systematic instruction, monitor student responses, and give students feedback about their performance (Brophy, 1980).

Teacher-Directed Instruction

There has been a long-standing debate over whether instructional activities should be chosen and directed by the teacher or whether the students should choose the activities. However, the research in the 1970s has yielded extremely consistent results. As measured by achievement gains in reading and math, students make more progress when teachers select and direct classroom activities.

Studies by Soar (1973); Stallings, Cory, Fairweather, and Needles (1977); Stallings and Kaskowitz (1974); and Solomon and Kendall (1979) indicate that teachers who most successfully promote achievement gain take the role of a strong leader. That is, they select and direct the academic activities; approach the subject matter in a direct, businesslike way; organize learning around questions they have posed; and occupy the center of attention. In contrast, the less successful teachers make the students the center of attention, organize learning around the students' own problems, and join or participate in students activities (see Table 23.1).

A consistent finding—but one which is surprising to many—is that student choice of activities yields negative results. Classrooms organized so that students have a great deal of choice about the activities are usually ones with less academic-engaged time and lower achievement. For example, in the study by Soar (1973), student free choice, student limited choice, and student selection of work groups were associated with lower achievement gain. For Stallings and Kaskowitz (1974) and Stallings et al. (1977), child selection of seating and work groups yielded similarly consistent negative correlations with achievement gain. These three studies were limited to children of low SES backgrounds. However, Solomon and Kendall (1979) obtained the same results in their study of children in 30 fourth-grade suburban classrooms. They found that classrooms in which students chose their own activities, followed their own interests, were responsible for class planning, and were not teacher dependent were also the classrooms which were characterized by rowdiness, shouting, noise, and disorderliness. In addition, these factors of permissiveness, spontaneity, and lack of control were *negatively* related, not only to achievement gain, but also to growth in creativity, inquiry,

TABLE 23.1   CORRELATION BETWEEN TEACHER OR STUDENT SELECTION OF ACTIVITY AND ACHIEVEMENT GAIN

STUDY	TEACHER-DIRECTED ACTIVITIES	CORRELATIONS
Stallings et al. (1977) 3rd grade	Teacher assigns students to groups	.46**
Solomon & Kendall (1979) 4th grade	Teacher control/students follow prescribed plan	.54**
	STUDENT CHOICE	
Stallings & Kaskowitz (1974) 1st grade	Student selection of seating and work groups	−.26**
Stallings & Kaskowitz (1974) 3rd grade	Student selection of seating and work groups	−.23
Stallings et al. (1977) 3rd grade	Students select work groups	−.24
Soar (1973) kindergarten	Student choice of activities	−.27**
Soar (1973) entering 1st grade	Student choice of activities	.16
Soar (1973) nonentering 1st grade	Student choice of activities	−.51**
Soar (1973) 2nd grade	Student choice of activities	−.34
Stallings et al. (1979) secondary	Adult offers students a choice of activities	−.32*

* $p < .05$.
** $p < .01$.

writing ability, and self-esteem for the students in those classrooms. Similarly, in a study by Good and Beckerman (1978) on student engagement in six sixth-grade middle and lower socioeconomic classrooms, students were more engaged when the teacher assigned the work than when the students chose the work. The same is true for remedial reading students in secondary schools (Stallings, Needles, & Stayrook, 1979) where offering students a choice of activity had consistently negative correlations with student achievement gain.

Some data from the BTES (Fisher et al., 1978) may provide an explanation for these consistent results (Table 23.2). In each grade and subject area, students were more engaged when they were in teacher-led settings. In fact, the engagement rate was about 14% higher in teacher-led settings. As shown in Table 23.2, students were less engaged when working alone, even when they selected the activities (Good & Beckerman, 1978). Thus, classrooms which are more teacher directed have more engagement and higher achievement.

Instructing Students in Groups

The issue of how to group students for instruction in classrooms has been debated since the 1920s. Proponents of "individualized" instruction have argued that a teacher cannot "meet the needs" of children by placing them in "lock-step"

TABLE 23.2 TIME SPENT AND ENGAGEMENT RATE IN TEACHER-LED SETTINGS AND IN SEATWORK

GRADE AND SUBJECT	SETTING	PERCENTAGE OF TIME IN SETTING (%)	ENGAGEMENT RATE (%)
2 Reading	Teacher-Led	36	84
	Seatwork	63	68
2 Math	Teacher-Led	27	82
	Seatwork	73	67
5 Reading	Teacher-Led	30	84
	Seatwork	70	70
5 Math	Teacher-Led	24	85
	Seatwork	76	72

Source: From Fisher et al. 1978.

groups. Yet, in the 1960s, when Englemann was developing new reading programs for low socioeconomic children, he decided that instruction should take place in small groups because "it is more efficient than one-to-one instruction and provides better teacher direction, supervision, and individualization than large group instruction. In addition, small group instruction provides a setting in which the repetitious practice necessary for some important skills is made more fun by transforming drill into a challenging game" (Becker, 1977, p. 523).

One reason for the differences in opinion is that we tend to equate "individualizing" with one-to-one instruction. However, each child actually receives very little one-to-one instruction in a classroom of 20 to 25 students. If a teacher had only 20 students and gave each of them one-to-one instruction, then each child would receive only 3 minutes of instruction per hour and would be expected to work alone for 57 minutes each hour. In "individualized" approaches, then, a student is expected to learn a great deal on his or her own, to teach himself or herself through the worksheets. The research presented below found that, for the early grades, it is more effective if the children receive their instruction from the teacher and this occurs most effectively when the instruction occurs in groups.

Since 1973, a number of studies provide data to evaluate the grouping issue. Without exception, the studies support group instruction. Stallings and Kaskowitz (1974) found that teacher time spent working with only one or two students, was negatively related to class achievement gain, whereas time spent working with small groups (three to seven students) or with large groups was consistently and positively related to achievement. Three studies by Stallings, one on early childhood education and two on remedial reading in junior and senior high, also found the same pattern of teacher time with groups being positively related to achievement gain and teacher time spent with individual students being negatively related to achievement gain (see Table 23.3 for a summary of these results.) Likewise, Soar (1973) discovered that when students worked in groups under adult supervision, correlations with achievement were positive and often significant, but when small groups met *without* an adult, correlations between this pattern and achievement were negative and often significant.

In a study of California elementary schools, 21 schools which were high in student achievement on basic skills for two consecutive years were paired with 21 schools which were low achieving. Each pair of schools was similar in selection variables, such as school size, type of location, ethnic makeup, and parental income. One of the differences between the two groups of schools was that "Teachers in higher-achieving schools divided their classes into several groups working at different paces; teachers at lower-achieving schools more frequently reported individualization of instruction" (California State Department of Education, 1977, p. 36). In addition, observers reported that in the higher achieving schools, "Students were perceived to be happier, more engaged in their work, and less disruptive, restless, or bored" (California State Department of Education, 1977, p. 36).

Similar results were obtained in Philadelphia in a study of teachers in first to fourth grades who obtained high achievement gain and low achievement gain in reading. Based on teacher interviews, the investigators found that, "Pupils in classes taught in a small group/whole group class combination achieved better than pupils who were taught individually only, in small groups only, or in whole class only" (Kean, Summers, & Raivetz, 1979, p. 9). The investigators concluded that "the active presence of the teacher plays a major role. A hypothesis is that . . . individual and small groupings are less effective [because] the teacher can then only be involved with a few students at a time, while, in large groupings, the teacher is actively involved with more students more of the time" (Kean et al., 1979, p. 47).

The results are equally dramatic in the BTES study (Fisher et al., 1978) as noted in Table 22.2. When students were working with a teacher or another adult, they were usually engaged about 84% of the time, whereas when students were working alone they were engaged only 70% of the time.

An observational study of six British junior high school teachers who used informal methods (Boydell, 1974) provides additional evidence on the minimal amount of teacher-student contact which occurs when students are working alone. In this study, students were working alone an average of 76% of the time (a percentage somewhat higher than reported in the second- and fifth-grade classrooms in the BTES). The investigator found that when working alone the students had *no contact* with the teacher 89% of the time, and academic contacts (e.g., explanation, feedback, praise, and supervision) occurred only 7% of the time. The author concludes that these data are at variance with the popular view of the informal teacher who stimulates students to formulate their own ideas and probes and extends their level of understanding. There simply is not time to do this with each individual child.

Surprisingly, the findings that students are more engaged when working in groups than when they are working alone is not new. It was known as early as 1926, and again in 1968, but we did not attend to it. In a delightful review on student attention in his book, *Life in Classrooms,* Jackson (1968) describes a study by Washburne, Vogel, and Gray 60 years ago which compared student attention in a traditional school and in a progressive (Winnetka) school. They wrote that "the results show a small but remarkably consistent tendency of children working under the class method to be more uniformly at attention than those working under the individual method" (Washburn, Vogel, & Gray cited in Jackson, 1968, p. 93).

TABLE 23.3   CORRELATION BETWEEN SIZE OF INSTRUCTIONAL GROUP AND ACHIEVEMENT GAIN

STUDY	VARIABLE	CORRELATIONS WITH GAIN IN READING ACHIEVEMENT
Stallings & Kaskowitz (1974) 1st grade	Teacher with one child	−.34**
	Teacher with two children	−.29**
Stallings & Kaskowitz (1974) 3rd grade	Teacher with one child	−.12
Stallings et al. (1977) 3rd grade	Teacher with two children	−.37**
	Teacher with one child	−.38**
Kean et al. (1979) grades 1–4	Individual instruction only	lower achievement
Stallings et al. (1979) secondary	Adult interaction with individuals	−.25
Stallings & Kaskowitz (1974) 1st grade	Teacher with small group (3–7 students)	.23*
3rd grade	Teacher with small group (3–7 students)	−.39**
Stallings et al. (1977) 3rd grade	Teacher with small group (3–7 students)	.32
Kean et al. (1979) grades 1–4	Small group instruction only	lower achievement
	Small group and individual instruction	achievement equal large group

Stallings & Kaskowitz (1974)		
1st grade	Teacher with large group (8–12 students)	.14
3rd grade	Teacher with large group (8–12 students)	.49**
Stallings et al. (1977)		
3rd grade	Teacher with large group (8–12 students)	.15
Kean et al. (1979) grades 1–4	Large group instruction combined with small group or individual instruction	higher achievement
Soar (1973) kindergarten	Teacher directed group instruction	−.22
Soar (1973) entering 1st grade	Teacher-directed group instruction	.45*
Soar (1973) nonentering 1st grade	Teacher-directed group instruction	−.53**
Soar (1973) 2nd grade	Teacher-directed group instruction	.52**
Stallings et al. (1979) secondary	Adult interaction with the entire group	.23

* $p \leq .05$
** $p \leq .01$

The results, then, are quite consistent across these studies. Students show both more engagement and higher achievement gain when they are placed in groups for instruction. Students are less engaged when they are working alone and achieve less in classrooms where there is a strong emphasis on independent work. One advantage of grouping may be that, when students are in groups, they receive more teacher demonstrations and more corrective feedback than when they are working alone.

Yet, we need to be cautious in generalizing these results. In these studies, when students are working alone, they are usually not receiving demonstration or feedback. These results might be different if the students who are working alone are working with a computer terminal or hand-held calculator. With this technology, students can receive immediate feedback, correctives, and knowledge of their "percentage correct." The feedback and correctives may reduce the error rate, and the flashing of the "percent correct" may motivate the students to continue. Thus, the use of low-cost computers and microprocessors (and good software) might lead to increased engagement when students are working alone.

Academic Emphasis

Across a number of studies, the successful teachers were those who maintained a strong academic focus. That is, their classrooms were rated as being high in "task orientation" and "businesslike," a good deal of time was spent on academic activities, and much less time was spent on nonacademic activities.

Stallings and her associates studied classroom activities and student achievement gain in reading in three studies: Stallings and Kaskowitz (1974—first grade and third grade), Stallings et al. (1977—third grade); and Stallings et al. (1979—secondary remedial reading). Table 23.4 contains a summary of results on academic emphasis showing that student time spent on reading and math activities and student time spent using texts, workbooks, and instructional materials all yielded positive, consistent, and usually significant correlations with achievement gain.

In a study comparing the effects of formal and informal styles of teaching (Bennett, Jordan, Long, & Wade, 1976), the students in formal classrooms had the highest achievement gain in reading and math, and these formal teachers reported more emphasis on assigning regular homework, giving weekly tests, marking and grading student work, and expecting students to be quiet. One of the teachers who used an informal style also obtained high student achievement gain in her classroom, but a case study of this teacher showed that she also had a particularly strong academic emphasis in her classroom.

Another study (California State Department of Education, 1977) investigated 20 pairs of schools. In each pair, both schools were of comparable social and demographic characteristics, but one school was much higher performing and one was much lower performing on achievement tests. Observers found that teachers in the higher-achieving schools were more task oriented. This relationship was also found in an observational study of fourth-grade classrooms (Solomon & Kendall, 1979), where teachers who were rated as task oriented also had the greatest achievement gain. Similarly, Brophy and Evertson (1976) characterized the successful teachers in their study as "determined that their students learn." Academic focus appears similar to Rosenshine's (1971) term "task oriented," and this variable now has increased support in recent studies.

Nonacademic activities.   Throughout these studies, nonacademic activities tended to yield negative correlations with achievement gain. Stallings and Kaskowitz (1974) found that activities involving group time, teacher reading of stories to the class, arts and crafts, active play, use of toys and puzzles, and even use of academic games consistently had negative correlations with achievement gain. Similarly, in Brophy and Evertson (1976) and Stallings et al. (1977), there were negative correlations with reading achievement gain for teacher questions about family background or personal experience, social interactions, and for student initiated contacts involving personal concerns. Similar results also hold true for secondary school students (Stallings et al. 1979), where the frequency of social interactions had consistently negative correlations with student reading achievement gain.

Throughout these studies, there was no nonacademic activity which yielded positive correlations with reading and mathematics achievement. This result is somewhat surprising because it has frequently been argued that some nonacademic activities contribute to academic gain by motivating students or by providing additional stimulation. Such indirect enhancement was not evident in any of these studies.

The task orientation of the school principal is also important. Two studies comparing high-achieving and low-achieving schools of similar socioeconomic composition (Maryland State Department of Education, 1978; Venezky & Winfield, 1979) found that schools which had more efficient and effective instruction also had principals who were achievement and task oriented. Principals who tended to emphasize human relations (often at the exclusion of academic emphasis) had schools which were less effective.

Affect in academically focused classrooms.   One worries whether academic emphasis means an academic sweatshop where kids are drilling in a harsh, humorless, cold, rote classroom. Despite these fears, none of the data, to date, suggests that this is so. The data do not support the stereotype of the cold task-oriented teacher. Further, the personal accounts of the authors of these studies—people who have observed hundreds of elementary classrooms—do not support even one instance of a task-oriented teacher who was also cold and humorless.

Surprisingly, teacher criticism is relatively rare in traditional classrooms (Anderson, Evertson, & Brophy, 1979; McDonald, 1975; Stallings et al., 1977). For example, Anderson et al. found that only 1% of all academic interactions included teacher criticism and the standard deviation was only 1 across 20 first-grade classrooms.

In the study by Solomon and Kendall (1979), the group of classrooms which were highest on the variable "calm, orderly, task orientation" were at about the same level as other classrooms on variables, such as "relaxed, friendly," "warmth, praise" and "emphasis on student comprehension and exploration." In a study comparing the ten highest achieving teachers with the ten lowest achieving teachers who taught special units in reading to their second- and fifth-grade classrooms (Tikunoff, Berliner, & Rist, 1975), the highest achieving teachers

TABLE 23.4   CORRELATION BETWEEN ACADEMIC ACTIVITIES AND ACHIEVEMENT GAIN

STUDY	VARIABLE	CORRELATIONS WITH READING ACHIEVEMENT GAIN
	POSITIVE CORRELATIONS	
Stallings & Kaskowitz (1974) 1st grade	Adult instruction, academic	.11
	Approximate number of students involved in reading	.40**
	Reading, alphabet, language development	.40**
	Time spent using texts, workbooks	.24**
	Numbers, math, arithmetic	.29**
	Approximate number of students involved in math	.35**
	Total academic verbal interactions	.41**
Stallings & Kaskowitz (1974) 3rd grade	Adult instruction, academic	.29*
	Approximate number of students involved in reading	.18
	Numbers, math, arithmetic	.52**
	Approximate number of students involved in math	.53**
	Total academic verbal interactions	.34**
Stallings et al. (1977) 3rd grade	Adult instruction, academic	.30*
	Time spent by teacher (and other adults) on academic instruction	.25

Study	Variable	Correlation
	Average occurrence of reading per child	.31*
	Percent of activities on academics	.41**
	Total academic interactions	.43**
Solomon and Kendall (1979) 4th grade	Businesslike and task-oriented, e.g., orderly sequence of activities, calm and quiet classrooms	.54**

NEGATIVE CORRELATIONS

Study	Variable	Correlation
Stallings & Kaskowitz (1974) 1st grade	Activities involving arts and crafts	-26*
	Activities involving games and puzzles	-10
	Activities involving group time	-22*
	Active play	-23*
	Use of games, toys, or play equipment	-20*
	Story, music, dancing	-15
Stallings & Kaskowitz (1974) 3rd grade	Activities involving arts and crafts	-18
	Activities involving games and puzzles	-17
	Activities involving group time	-20
	Use of games, toys, or play equipment	-32*
	Story, music, dancing	-22
Stallings et al. (1977) 3rd grade	Group sharing time	-42**
	Use of games, play equipment	-43**
	Number of social interactions	-43**
Stallings et al. (1979) secondary	Social interactions	-30*

*$p < .05$
**$p < .01$

were described by ethnographers as being significantly higher in monitoring learning, structuring, and pacing—variables which appear to reflect academic focus. But these same teachers were also rated as significantly higher in "accepting students," "promoting self-sufficiency," and rated higher in "conviviality" and "cooperation." Their classrooms were also rated lower in "belittling."

In Phase III of the BTES (Filby & Cahen, 1977), teachers who were high in academic focus, clarity, and task orientation, also tended to be moderate to high on conviviality, warmth, and knowledge of each individual student. The worst situation, both for student engagement and for achievement gain, were teachers who were high in affect but low in cognitive emphasis.

Thus, although many readers fear that classrooms with an academic emphasis would be harsh and cold, this has not occurred. In three studies on this topic, classrooms which were high in academic emphasis were also moderate to high on conviviality, warmth, and praise.

Student reports of affect.   How do students feel in academically focused classrooms? The most relevant study we found on this topic was the Abt Associates (1977) report on the evaluation of eight different follow-through programs for low-income children in grades K to 3. The study was experimental, in that it compared the effects of different instructional models implemented in different school districts around the United States. The Abt Associates found that programs which were high in achievement gain were also highest in academic focus and had students with the highest scores on the Coopersmith Self-Esteem Inventory. Programs which had less academic emphasis had students with lower scores in reading and math and on the Coopersmith Self-Esteem Inventory.

There is, however, another set of studies for which the results on attitude toward school are not as clear. In a review of research, Peterson (1979) concluded that open approaches surpass traditional ones in improving students' attitudes toward school, but the size of the effect was small. However, she also concluded that there was little or no difference between open and traditional approaches on outcomes, such as self-concept, locus of control, and anxiety.

Thus, across a number of studies and personal reports, there is no evidence, at this time, that academically focused classrooms are taught in an overbearing manner or that students' attitudes toward school or self are affected adversely. Rather, such classrooms have reasonable teacher warmth and lead to reasonably positive student attitudes. These studies indicate that decent, humane, genuine interactions occur in many classrooms which are highly structured and teacher directed. The image of the formal classroom as humorless, cold, and regimented, was not found to be true. Today, teachers in formal classrooms are warm, concerned, flexible, and allow much more freedom of movement. But they are also task oriented and determined that children shall learn.

Training teachers in academic emphasis.   One experiment was reported in which intern elementary teachers were trained in businesslike behavior (Gabrys, 1979). Teachers were trained in specific skills in general areas, such as goal orientation, deliberateness, and organization. Some of the skills included:

—Clear, precise goal statements

—Well-developed, systematic lessons

—Few digressions from task

—Efficient and systematic movement toward goal

—Well-developed follow-through activities

—Precise use of student input

—Buoyancy but not lighthearted

—Natural humor without sarcasm

The ten experimental-group and ten control-group teachers were each observed in their classrooms on four occasions: prior to training, immediately after training, five weeks after training, and ten weeks after training. The experimental-group teachers were significantly higher than the control-group teachers on the rating scale items immediately after training and ten weeks after training. Although not part of the training, all teachers were also rated on "warmth" (e.g., ratings on openness, friendliness, sensitivity to personal needs, encouragement, supportiveness) because of a concern that businesslike might mean cold, calculating, and uncaring. Both groups of teachers were high on these items, scores were stable across observations, and the differences between the groups were small and not statistically significant.

Specific behaviors of academic focus.   It will probably be difficult to isolate all the behaviors which comprise "academic emphasis" because these behaviors probably overlap with other areas, such as effective classroom management, well-developed lessons, and monitoring of student progress. The specific variables used by Gabrys (1979) seem useful as do some developed by Bennett et al. (1976) and by Good and Grouws (1979). Some of the variables one might add to the Gabrys (1979) list are:

—Systematic, goal-related activities

—Lessons and content related to attaining specific goals

—Rapid pacing of lessons

—Few vacillating, aimless comments/questions/discussions

—Ready availability of materials

—All students participate in answering and responding

—Efficient use of time

—Emphasis on assigning regular homework

—Giving weekly and monthly tests

—Students accountable for classroom work

—Students accountable for homework

—Emphasis on marking and grading student work

—Positive encouragement of good work habits

Intercorrelations of these three variables.   One would expect that the three variables discussed in this section—academic focus, teacher-directed activities, and students working in groups—would be closely related. Only one study was found which had all three of the above variables (Solomon & Kendall, 1979), and in that study, the three variables were intercorrelated and were also related to student gain in achievement, creativity, inquiry skill, writing quality, and self-esteem.

These findings on the importance of academic focus, teacher-led activities, and group instruction make a case for traditional teaching.There is no reason to stigmatize this method, as has frequently happened, because traditional education as it is practiced today is neither mindless, nor meaningless, nor demeaning, nor punitive to children. The research shows that variations of traditional teaching can be an effective and humane method to enhance student achievement. The fact that this pattern emerges consistently in a large number of correlational and experimental studies adds to its credibility. We hope that these results will not be forgotten when the pendulum of educational fancy swings again to some form of "open" education.

In summary, three general instructional procedures have frequently been correlated with reading achievement: teacher-directed instruction, instruction in groups, and academic emphasis. Students who receive instruction from a teacher consistently do better in reading achievement than those who are expected to learn on their own. Teacher-led instruction is done most efficiently with groups of children. Teachers who group their children for instruction usually obtain higher reading achievement. Equally consistent results have been found for teachers who maintain a strong academic emphasis in their classrooms. Across a number of studies, teachers who are task oriented and determined that students learn are more successful in obtaining reading achievement.

SPECIFIC INSTRUCTIONAL PROCEDURES

We now turn from the three general variables discussed above to the question of specific methods for instruction in groups. An effective instructional procedure, which might be labeled demonstration-practice-feedback has emerged from at least four independent research and development efforts.

An Instructional Model

A general model of this demonstration-practice-feedback approach probably includes:

1. A short demonstration in which the new material or skill is presented to the group.
2. Guided practice, in which the practice is guided by the teacher through factual or process questions and/or teacher demonstration. During this practice, the teacher provides feedback, evaluates understanding, and provides additional demonstration if necessary.

3. Independent practice, where the students practice without teacher guidance and continue until their responses are rapid and firm. If necessary, the specific stages are recycled, although if the instruction consists of small steps and explicit directions, there should be little need to do so.

That the model is valid is evidenced by the fact that the major studies investigating it (or variations of it) have used experimental designs and have shown significant results (Anderson et al., 1979; Becker, 1977; Bloom, 1976; Good & Grouws, 1979).

The research summarized in this section focuses on effective procedures for carrying out the demonstration, practice, feedback, and independent practice components. Although all classrooms have these components, they are not always carried out effectively. All classrooms have demonstrations, but frequently they are too short, there are too few examples, and examples are imprecise or unclear. All classrooms have guided practice, but often it is infrequent or too brief, there are too few questions and examples, and there is too little checking for student understanding. All teachers also correct student errors, but frequently the corrections are uninformative, consisting of only a single word or sentence; reteaching in small steps occurs seldom. All classrooms have independent practice, too, but frequently too great a proportion of classroom time is allocated to independent practice, especially without immediate feedback, and students are expected to learn too much from worksheets.

The problem, then, is that even when teachers employ demonstration, practice, and feedback in their teaching, it is often ineffective. However, there is recent research regarding specific instructional variables, and we hope that this new data will stimulate further research as well as diminish some of the controversy surrounding these variables.

The topics which are reviewed are presented below in four major categories: demonstration, guided practice, feedback and correctives, and independent practice. We will also discuss two additional topics of high interest: higher cognitive level questions and classroom management.

Demonstration

Although demonstration (or development) is regarded as important in the experimental studies of Bloom (1976), Englemann and Carnine (1982), Becker (1977), Good and Grouws (1978), and Anderson et al. (1979), very little research exists evaluating the effectiveness of different forms of demonstration or the value of different demonstration variables. However, the findings of Anderson et al. (1979) on first-grade instruction reported positive correlations between reading achievement gain and beginning lessons with an overview and with demonstrating the pronunciation of new words.

Aside from the above, little research was found on the demonstration phase of a lesson. In teaching phonics and word analysis, the instructions to the teacher are written in the teacher's guide, but no study was found on the adequacy of these instructions, on the size of the step of the material to be taught, on the number of repetitions a teacher should use, or when repetitions are necessary.

Until recently, little was known about how to demonstrate reading-comprehension skills explicitly. This was particularly evident in the study by Durkin (1978–1979), where she observed 24 fourth-grade teachers during the reading period. Durkin found that most comprehension instruction involved "assessment," that is, teachers asking questions and telling students whether their answers were right. Specific instruction directed toward helping a student learn a rule or process for answering reading comprehension questions occurred less than 1% of the time. However, this lack of demonstration and explicit instruction was not due to teacher apathy. Rather, it occurred because explicit rules which students could use to comprehend reading passages did not exist (see Durkin, 1981, for a study illustrating the lack of direct instruction guidelines in basal reading manuals).

More recently, studies by Day (1980); Raphael (1980); Hansen (1981); Patchings, Kameenui, Colvin, and Carnine (1979); and Singer and Donlon (1982) have explicated rules for specific comprehension skills and taught them to students. Although each of the studies focuses on different comprehension skills, taken together, they exemplify an area of research which may remedy the lack of explicit demonstration in reading comprehension which Durkin found.

An example of a comprehension skill which has been investigated in one study is summarization. Day (1980) developed five rules for writing summaries of passages. They were:

a. Delete unnecessary trivial information
b. Delete redundant information
c. Substitute superordinate concepts or propositions for a list of concepts or propositions
d. Use topic sentences from the passage
e. Invent a summary sentence when none is provided in the passage (Day, 1980, p. 40)

The students were taught how to use each of these rules and then given practice writing summaries using the rules. As a result of this training the students (1) wrote better summaries than they had prior to instruction, (2) utilized these rules when writing summaries, and (3) wrote better summaries than those students who did not receive this training. Thus, this study provides an excellent example of how explicitly to demonstrate and teach a comprehension skill.

Guided Practice

During group instruction, the practice phase frequently consists of students responding to teacher questions about the material that was demonstrated or about the story that was read. This type of practice through questions might be labeled teacher-guided practice. It takes place under the guidance of teachers so that they can correct errors and add additional explanation or demonstration when necessary. Five topics under guided practice are reviewed below: frequent practice, types of questions, patterns of guided practice, individual versus group responding, and calling on students.

The importance of frequent, teacher-led practice.   A number of studies provide evidence to support a large amount of teacher-led practice (Table 23.5). Like adults, elementary students need a great deal of practice. In the five studies considered here (Table 23.5), the frequency of academic verbal interactions and the frequency of child responses yielded consistently positive correlations with achievement gain in reading.

In two experimental studies (Anderson et al., 1979; Good & Grouws, 1979), the experimental instructions asked teachers to increase the amount of time they spent on guided practice—asking questions and guiding the students through problems. The control teachers continued their regular teaching. In both cases, the experimental classrooms had significantly higher achievement than did the control classrooms. Furthermore, the experimental teachers in the Anderson et al. study (a) spent more time asking questions to their reading group, (b) had more academic interactions per minute, and (c) asked a higher percentage of questions involving word-attack skills. This study thus provides support for the effectiveness of asking factual questions in guided practice situations.

The large number of positive correlations in Table 23.5 indicates that frequency of practice, particularly practice when students are correct, is positively and consistently correlated with achievement gain. There are two ways to obtain a high frequency of teacher-led questions and both are reflected in the studies. One way is to increase the number of questions per minute and the other is to increase the amount of time spent in the teacher-led setting.

Types of teacher questions.   In addition to studying the frequency of teacher questions, these investigators have also studied different types of teacher questions. Stallings and Kaskowitz (1974) found that the frequency of academically focused direct questions at the two lower levels of the Bloom taxonomy resulted in increased acquisition of basic arithmetic and reading skills. They identified a "factual question-student response-teacher feedback" pattern as the most functional. Using a sample of low-income students, similar to those in the Stallings and Kaskowitz study, Soar (1973) also found that factors with high loadings from variables, such as convergent questions, drill, or questions that have single answers, usually correlated positively with achievement. In two subsequent studies by Stallings (Stallings, et al. 1977, 1979), frequent use of factual questions again emerged as a significant correlate of reading achievement. Similarly, a study of first-grade classrooms of mixed SES (Coker, Lorentz, & Coker, 1980) found that narrow questions followed by immediate feedback were positively correlated with reading and math achievement gain. These results, as summarized in Table 23.6, suggest that teacher-guided practice using factual questions is correlated with achievement gain.

Patterns of guided practice.   In a review of the literature on this topic, Medley (1978) described two types of guided practice which were correlated with student achievement gains. For children of low SES, the successful pattern was one with a high frequency of fairly simple questions, a high percentage of correct answers (about 80% or higher), teachers responding to student errors by giving the student help or a hint, and infrequent criticism of the student. For students of high SES, the successful pattern included harder questions, fewer (about 70%) correct answers, and calling on another student when the student

TABLE 23.5 CORRELATION BETWEEN FREQUENCY OF PRACTICE AND ACHIEVEMENT GAIN

STUDY	VARIABLE	MEAN FREQUENCY	CORRELATION
Anderson et al. (1979) 3rd grade	Number of academic interactions per minute with individual students both in reading turns and for questions not in reading turns	2.03	.30[+]
	Number of academic interactions per minute with individual student for questions not in reading turns	1.42	.46[**]
	Number of oral reading turns per minute given to individual student	.38	−.20
	Number of academic interactions per minute with individual student in oral reading turns	.61	−.32[+]
	Number of choral responses per minute	.14	−.34[*]
Stallings & Kaskowitz (1974) 1st grade	Total academic verbal interactions (adult focus)		.33[**]
	Total academic verbal interactions (child focus)		.50[**]
	Child responses, academic (adult focus)		.33[**]
	Child responses, academic (child focus)		.35[**]

Study	Measure	Mean	Correlation
Stallings & Kaskowitz (1974) 3rd grade	Total academic verbal interactions (adult focus)	37.41	.29*
	Total academic verbal interactions (child focus)		.34**
	Child responses, academic (adult focus)	7.32	.15
	Child responses, academic (child focus)		.20
Stallings et al. (1977) 3rd grade	Total academic verbal interactions	31.29	.43**
	Child responses, academic	6.38	NS
	Individual child response to academic questions	2.43	.30*
Stallings et al. secondary	Discussion/review (Phase I)		.40**
	Discussion/review (Phase II)		.63**
	Drill and practice (Phase I)		NS
	Drill and practice (Phase II)		.38**
	Student response to an adult, task or reading (Phase I)	30.2	NS
	Student response to an adult, task or reading (Phase II)	27.0	.54**

+ $p < .10$
* $p < .05$
** $p < .01$
NS = not significant.

TABLE 23.6   CORRELATION BETWEEN FACTUAL QUESTIONS AND ACHIEVEMENT GAIN

STUDY	VARIABLE	CORRELATIONS WITH READING ACHIEVEMENT
Stallings & Kaskowitz (1974) 1st grade	Adult commands, requests, and directs questions to groups of children, academic	20*
	Child group responses to academic command, request, or direct question	22*
3rd grade	Adult commands, requests, and directs questions to groups of children, academic	.32*
	Child group responses to academic command, request, or direct question	34**
Stallings et al. (1977) 3rd grade	Adult asks academic question of an individual child	30*
	Child responds to academic question	30*
	All adult direct academic questions	29*

Study / Grade	Variable		(PHASE I)	(PHASE II)
Soar (1973)				
kindergarten	Convergent questions	.26*		
	Drill	.37**		
entering 1st grade	Convergent questions	−11		
	Drill	−18		
nonentering 1st grade	Convergent questions	42**		
	Drill	53**		
2nd grade	Convergent questions	52*		
	Drill	26		
Coker et al. (1980)				
2nd grade	Narrow questions with immediate feedback	positive correlation		
Stallings et al. (1979)				
secondary	Adult commands, requests, and directs questions to students, task or reading		NS	35*
	Student responses to an adult, task, or reading		NS	.33*

* $p \leq .05$
** $p \leq .01$
NS = not significant.

did not know the answer. A pattern similar to the second pattern had a positive but nonsignificant relationship with achievement in the study by Solomon and Kendall (1979).

There is probably an upper limit to the amount of desirable guided practice. Soar and Soar (1973) found that a factor which they labeled as recitation was most successful in moderate amounts with fifth-grade children of middle SES. After a point, they found that recitation yielded diminishing returns. However, Soar and Soar did not discuss the point at which these diminishing returns appear, and more research on this topic is needed.

Individual versus group responding.   During guided practice, should the teacher ask for choral (group) responses, individual responses, or some combination of the two? Only a few studies have investigated this question. Anderson et al. (1979) and Brophy and Evertson (1976) each found that a teacher's use of group choral responses was negatively related to achievement gain. However, McKenzie (1979) and McKenzie and Henry (1979) found that questions to the whole group with the entire group responding produced greater attention and higher achievement than questions eliciting individual responses. But the studies by McKenzie were limited to questions involving yes-no answers in which students responded by raising their hands and voting for one of the two alternatives.

In contrast, the Oregon Direct Instruction Follow-Through Program (Becker, 1977), which has been the most successful of all follow-through programs in obtaining student achievement relies heavily upon choral responses during the controlled practice phase. Choral responses are initiated by a specific signal from the teacher so that the entire group responds at the same time (much like a conductor and an orchestra). Indeed, students are trained in this type of specific response. Becker (1977) argues that choral response (to a signal) (1) allows a teacher to monitor the learning of all students effectively and quickly (by watching the responses of all students), (2) allows the teacher to correct the entire group when an error is made, thereby diminishing the potential embarrassment of the individual students who make errors, and (3) makes the drill more like a game because of the whole group participation. Further, the *Direct Instruction Model Guidebook for Teachers* (Witcher, Skillman, & Becker, 1977) recommends that the children most likely to make errors be seated closest to the teacher so that she or he can monitor their responses closely. The Oregon Direct Instruction Model suggests a mixture of both choral responses and individual turns in the controlled practice phase, with choral responding occurring about 70% of the time. The individual turns allows for testing of specific children.

Becker, Englemann, and their associates have suggested (personal communication) that the negative correlations obtained for group responding by Brophy and Evertson (1976) and Anderson et al. (1979) occurred because the students were not responding *in unison.* They argue that when students do not respond in unison, the slower students wait a fraction of a second and echo the response of the faster students, thus merely creating the impression of giving the correct answer.

Calling on students.   How should a teacher select students during controlled practice? Volunteers or nonvolunteers? Random calling on students or ordered turns? The question has not received much attention.

In their study of first-grade reading groups, Anderson et al. (1979) found that the percentage of academic interactions where the student was selected by an ordered turn were positively related to student achievement. When the teacher selected either volunteers or nonvolunteers not in ordered turns, the results were consistently negative. Apparently, the ordered turns served to insure that all students had an opportunity to respond and receive feedback.

When teaching lower achieving students, the frequency of academic interactions involving students calling out the answers was positively related to achievement (Anderson et al., 1979). This supports the conclusion made by Brophy and Evertson (1976) that it is best *to get low-achieving students to respond in any fashion.* But due to the lack of other studies in this area, these conclusions are regarded as tentative.

Feedback and Correction of Student Responses

During guided practice or during any recitation or drill part of a lesson, how should teachers respond to a student's answers? Student responses to questions can be classified into at least five types: correct, incorrect, partly correct, don't know, and no response. Although one is curious as to the effective teacher feedback to each type of response, the research in this area is far from complete. Only the studies by Brophy and Evertson (1976) and Anderson et al. (1979) contained results on all five types of student responses. Combining results across a number of studies (not all of which match up as neatly as one would wish), we can offer some tentative suggestions.

Correct response.   Stallings and Kaskowitz (1974) and Stallings et al. (1977) have found positive correlations for adult acknowledgment of correct academic responses for first-grade students ($r = .23$ to $.49$). However, positive feedback was found to be nonsignificant in third grade (Stallings & Kaskowitz, 1974) as well as in the first-grade study done by Anderson et al. (1979). Instead the Anderson et al. study offers strong evidence for no feedback, and it suggests that the teacher follow a correct response with another question. The latter conclusion is supported by experimental research on feedback conditions. That research indicates that "children exhibit a tendency to interpret the absense of overt feedback as positive feedback" (Barringer & Gholson, 1979, p. 469). From their review of experimental studies, they concluded that the "no feedback to correct answers" was just as effective for student learning as telling students they were correct when they gave a correct answer.

In short, these studies indicate that when a student makes a correct response to an academic question, the most effective feedback is for the teacher to ask a new question, maintaining the momentum of the practice session. However, a teacher might also wish to provide short statements of acknowledgment (such as, "OK" or "right"), particularly in cases where the student is correct but hesitant.

Incorrect response.   In two correlational studies (Anderson et al. 1979; Stallings & Kaskowitz, 1974), investigators found that when a student gave an incorrect response, the best teacher behavior was to ask a simpler question, provide a hint which guided the student to the correct answer, or remind the student of the process used to arrive at the answer. But, in both of these studies (as well as in Stallings et al., 1977) this "sustaining feedback" occurred infrequently. More frequently teachers followed an incorrect answer with "terminal feedback," that is, they gave the student the correct answer and moved on. Anderson et al. found that 53% of incorrect answers received terminal feedback and that the frequency of terminal feedback was negatively correlated with achievement gain ($r = -.45$). However, three other studies (Stallings et al., 1977; Stallings et al., 1979; and Stallings & Kaskowitz, 1974) indicated nonsignificant results for terminal feedback. Unfortunately, there is confounding here. Classrooms with lower success rates are those where students give more incorrect answers (which receive more terminal feedback). Alternatively, terminal feedback to incorrect answers allows students to persist in their incorrect answers, hence reducing the success rate. At any rate, it appears that incorrect answers are best handled by helping the student arrive at the correct answer (but not lingering too long) or by recycling the initial explanation; moving on to another student does not appear to help matters.

In studies of mathematics teaching (Good & Grouws, 1979), "process feedback" has been positively correlated with achievement gain. In process feedback, a teacher gives an explanation of the process used to arrive at the correct answer, in effect, reteaching the earlier material.

No response.   In some cases, students will not respond or say they "don't know." Two studies with low SES students (Brophy & Evertson, 1976; and Stallings et al. 1979) have found positive correlations for encouraging students to respond. And Anderson et al. (1979) found that giving a clue was also a positive correlate of achievement.

Overall, the evidence provides the clearest support for using sustaining feedback or process feedback when student answers are incorrect. Sustaining feedback means helping a student by giving hints or asking simpler questions; process feedback refers to reminding the student of the process used to arrive at the answer.

The use of sustaining feedback for incorrect answers needs to be studied further. Such feedback might slow down the pace of the lesson and lead to inattentiveness in other students. However, if the success rate is 70% or higher, then sustaining feedback is less likely to slow down the lesson.

Independent Practice

Providing time for students to practice new skills independently to the point of mastery is an important aspect of the demonstration-practice-feedback paradigm. Studies have shown that the most successful teachers of reading give students time to practice these skills independently, by having them do seatwork exercises (Brophy & Evertson, 1976; Fisher et al., 1978). Most students spend two thirds of their time working independently (Fisher et al., 1978; Stallings et al., 1977; and Stallings & Kaskowitz, 1974), but their average engagement rate during seatwork is frequently lower than when they are given instruction by the teacher (Fisher et al., 1978). Therefore, the question of how to manage students during seatwork in order to maintain their engagement becomes of primary interest.

Brophy and Evertson (1976) suggest that the teacher should monitor the students during seatwork, giving individualized feedback in the process. This point is reiterated by Fisher et al. (1978). They found that the amount of substantive instruction during seatwork was positively related to achievement and that when students have contacts with the teacher during seatwork their engagement rate increased by about 10%. Thus, it seems important that teachers not only monitor seatwork, but also that they provide academic feedback and explanation to students during their independent practice. The same investigators also found positive correlations between the amount of teacher-student interaction during groupwork and student engagement during seatwork. Perhaps the additional practice which the teacher-student interaction provides during guided practice helps the students during seatwork.

An experimental study by Mueller, Light, and Reynolds (1971), investigated the effects of long-duration and short-duration contacts in the management of seatwork of fifth- and sixth-grade remedial reading students. Long-duration contacts lasted a minute or more; short-duration contacts lasted less than a minute; both guided the students to the correct response. In general, the use of long contacts produced decreased academic performance and more off-task behavior by the students, whereas short contacts yielded greater academic performance and higher engagement. Also, because of the brevity of the contacts, the teacher had three times as many short contacts during the 40-minute period than were possible with long contacts and, presumably, was able to give more students the individualized feedback they needed. Thus, efficient management of seatwork seems to involve monitoring the students' work and providing short, academically related comments or feedback.

In a study using six students in third-grade mathematics instruction, Scott and Bushell (1974) found a similar relationship between the length of the contact and the amount of off-task behavior. As the length of the contact between the teacher and an individual student increased, the amount of off-task behavior among the other students in the small group also increased. When the contact lasted 50 seconds or more ($M = 82.6$ sec) the mean observations of off-task behavior was 68.4%. When the 20-second contact duration phase was introduced ($M = 42.4$ sec), the mean off-task behavior dropped to 39.4%. Although this study involves a small number of students, it does add validity to the conclusion made in the Mueller et al. study. Efficient management of seatwork seems to involve monitoring the students' work and providing short, academically related comments or feedback.

Other Aspects of Instruction

Use of Criticism

The results of classroom research seem to agree on the relationship between criticism and student achievement. Studies by Soar (1973), Solomon and Kendall (1979), and Stallings et al. (1977) found that teacher criticism of student behavior, harsh control, shouting, scolding and ridicule were consistently negatively related to achievement gain. However, Anderson et al. (1979) found that criticism which specified desirable alternatives was positively ($r = .33$) correlated with achievement gain, but that happened very rarely.

In most classrooms, teacher criticism occurred infrequently. Anderson et al. (1979) found that academic interactions which included teacher criticism occurred only 1% of the time ($SD = 1$) in the reading groups in the 20 classrooms they studied. Stallings et al. (1977) found similar low frequencies. In general, teachers in academically focused classrooms did not resort to threats, criticism, or ridicule; such behaviors were more characteristic of teachers in low-achieving classrooms.

Higher Cognitive Level Questions

In the section on demonstration-practice-feedback, "higher cognitive level" questions were not mentioned. Currently, this is an area of confusion. Research on higher cognitive level questions has shown that asking higher level questions is not particularly effective for mastery of either factual or higher level learning. For example, Stallings and Kaskowitz (1974) found that the frequency of open-ended questions was negatively related to student achievement gain. In Soar's study, factors with loadings from variables, like divergent questions and open-ended questions, usually correlated negatively with achievement.

In two extremely well-designed experimental studies (Gall, Ward, Berliner, Cahen, Crown, Elashoff, Stanton, & Winne, 1975; Stanford Program on Teacher Effectiveness, 1976), teachers were semiscripted, in that they were provided with scripts containing the questions to be asked and responses to be given. Overall, both studies found that classes where students were asked more recall questions did slightly better on the recall tests, whereas all classes did equally well on tests which included higher level questions no matter how many higher level questions had been asked in class. In other words, asking different numbers of higher level questions had no measurable effect on essay performance or on tests containing higher level questions.

One of the problems with this area of research may be that we have not developed a generalizable method for demonstrating how to answer interpretative or critical thinking questions. Instead, we ask students many higher level questions in the belief that if we ask enough of these questions the students will learn, somehow, how to answer them. Consider the following higher level questions which were based on the book *Huckleberry Finn*.

Why did Huck play such a trick on Jim?

Do any of you disagree with that? Do you think Huck had other motivations for playing such a trick?

Can you think of an example prior to this chapter when Huck had pangs of conscience?

As a result of this raft scene, how does the relationship between Huck and Jim change?

These appear to be excellent questions, but what rules does one use to answer them? Thus, higher cognitive level questions remain a puzzle. We want a child to learn how to answer (and ask) such questions, but the only way we have of teaching this is to ask a lot of higher cognitive level questions. But asking such questions may not teach rules for answering new questions. And the research supports the conclusion that simply asking many higher cognitive level questions does not teach the skill of answering new questions.

In addition, many questions which are coded as "higher level" may really be personal and opinion questions which do not require processing of text. Such higher cognitive level questions may not be correlated with achievement because they are, in fact, unrelated to the skills and content being tested.

Some students may be less attentive when higher level questions are being asked. In a study of preschool children Kounin and Gump (1974) found that student attention was highest when the signals they received were continuous, as when a teacher read a story to them or when the teacher interspersed the story with short questions. However, when the story telling included discussion so that there was student talk for 10 sec or more, student attention was significantly lower; Kounin and Gump believe this decrease occurred because the signal became discontinuous during the discussion.

These results have not, as yet, been replicated with elementary school children. But they suggest the possibility that asking higher cognitive level questions, which often entail longer student responses, leads to lower student attention.

Classroom Management

Although not directly related to the question of instructional procedures, classroom management has emerged as a crucial variable which is related to student achievement gain. Therefore, a brief discussion of management is included in this chapter.

The time a teacher spends managing students' behavior and correcting misbehavior is negatively correlated with achievement (Anderson et al., 1979; Coker, Lorentz, & Coker, 1980). This is probably because the time a teacher spends focused on student behavior is time that is taken away from academic instruction. Furthermore, these behavior-related interactions frequently interrupt the students who are attending; thus, they lose attention and reduce their time engaged in academic tasks (Fisher et al., 1978).

In an attempt to determine what behaviors are involved in effective classroom management, Kounin (1970) videotaped 30 first- and second-grade classrooms. Upon analyzing how the teachers managed recitation, seatwork, and transitional activities, Kounin found six teacher behaviors which were positively correlated with student work involvement and freedom from deviancy. These behaviors are:

1. Withitness—the teachers communicate to the students that they are aware of what's going on in all parts of the classroom, all of the time; the proverbial "eyes in the back of his/her head."
2. Overlapping—the teachers are able to deal with two or more activities or issues simultaneously; they are able to give their attention to more than one activity at a given time.
3. Smoothness—teachers are able to end one activity and move directly to another without making abrupt changes or jumping back and forth between

the two. Also teachers are able to deal with minor management problems without interrupting the instruction or attention of students.

4. Momentum—teachers are able to maintain the pace during an activity and make quick efficient transitions.
5. Accountability—the teachers are aware of the response performance of all the students in the group, making sure that they all respond and that they get corrective feedback if necessary.
6. Alerting—the teacher attempts to keep all the students attentive during the recitation activity and sees that the nonreciters attend to responses made by other students.

Other items relevant to management have been discussed in the section on independent practice. These include catching problems early and conducting smooth, well-paced lessons (Brophy & Evertson, 1976), circulating and providing help during seatwork (Brophy & Evertson, 1976; Fisher et al., 1978), and arranging the instruction so that seatwork contacts are less than a minute long (Mueller et al., 1971).

Smooth transitions from one activity and another are also important. The percentage of class time that is spent in transitions and the amount of time spent getting the lesson started are negatively correlated with student achievement (Anderson et al., 1979). Teachers who have well-organized transitions that quickly shift from one activity to the next have more student engagement (Arlin, 1979; Kounin, 1970) and better achievement (Brophy & Evertson, 1976). Teachers who use structured transitions have significantly less off-task behavior than those with nonstructured transitions (Arlin, 1979). These structured transitions are characterized by advanced preparation for the upcoming activity, "wrap ups" which bring the momentum of the previous activity to a halt, a short pause to gain the attention of all the students and follow through to be sure the procedures are followed consistently by the students (Arlin, 1979). In this way, the teacher ends the momentum of one activity before beginning a new activity. Through these procedures, the transitions can be quick and efficient while maintaining the attention of the students.

In summary, research on specific instructional procedures has shown that effective teaching is characterized by a predictable sequence of demonstration, guided practice, feedback and corrections, and independent practice. Although most teachers follow this general procedure, there are more and less effective ways of accomplishing these activities. From the research discussed in this section, a description of more effective behaviors has emerged.

Demonstration is more effective when the teacher proceeds in small steps, provides many examples, and intersperses the demonstration with questions designed to check for student understanding.

Guided practice is more effective when there are frequent questions (thus providing more practice), when questions focus directly upon the material, and when practice is extended so that the student success rate achieves 80% or higher. Also, using ordered turns in reading groups insures that all students have a chance to respond and receive feedback.

Feedback and correctives are more effective when correct responses are followed by brief feedback affirming the correctness of the response or simply by another question. Incorrect responses are best followed by sustaining questions (giving hints or asking simpler questions) or by providing an explanation which reteaches the material.

Independent practice is more effective when there is substantive interaction during the groupwork (thus preparing the students for the seatwork) and when the teacher or another adult actively monitors the students. Independent practice should also be sufficient to insure that students have enough practice to achieve overlearning and quickness in responding.

INDICATORS OF EFFECTIVE INSTRUCTION

The first two sections of this chapter focused upon the organization and delivery of instruction. This section focuses on three major indices of effective instruction. These are content covered, academic-engaged minutes, and student error rate. Unlike the previous section, the variables presented here represent the consequences of instruction rather than instructional variables per se. Yet, three variables have consistent positive relationships with students achievement gain, and measures of these variables provide a reasonable indication of the effectiveness of classroom instruction.

Content Covered

Relationship to Achievement

Content covered or "opportunity to learn" (Carroll, 1963) in reading has been studied by correlating one of several measures of content covered with student achievement. These measures of content covered include the content of textbooks (Chall, 1977), teacher's indications of the percentage of students who had an opportunity to learn each item on a test (Chang & Raths, 1971), the number of books students have read (Harris, Morrison, Serwer, & Gold, 1968), the number of words the teacher attempted to teach (Barr, 1973–1974; Beez, 1968; Brown, 1969; and Carter, 1969), the number of basals completed by reading groups (Anderson et al., 1979), and grade level achieved in a computer-assisted mastery-learning program in reading (Paulsen & Macken, 1978). For first-grade reading, the percentage of questions which focused on word-attack skills has been correlated with student achievement (Anderson et al., 1979). In all studies except one (Brown, 1969), significant positive relationships have been between the amount of content covered and student achievement or achievement gain.

In an experimental study designed to provide teachers with more efficient teaching procedures (Anderson et al., 1979) the first-grade reading groups with the experimental teachers completed significantly more basal books during the first grade and also obtained higher achievement scores than the control-group teachers. Moreover, for both groups combined, there was a significant positive correlation ($r = .42$ or higher) between the number of basals completed and student achievement gain. Thus, this study provided both experimental and correlational evidence on the importance of content covered.

Similar significant relationships between content covered and achievement have been obtained in other subject areas. Teacher reports of student opportunity to learn specific content has been significantly related to scores on achievement tests in math (Husen, 1967) and in science (Comber & Keeves, 1973). The pages covered by different classes using a common math textbook was significantly correlated with achievement gain (Good, Grouws, & Beckerman, 1978); the amount of content covered in short presentations on a variety of topics was significantly related to scores on a test following the presentation (Armento, 1977; Rosenshine, 1971; Shutes, 1969); and different curriculum programs have yielded different test scores commensurate with the emphasis in the program (Walker & Schaffarzick, 1974). Moreover, the correlations between content covered and achievement gain in these studies were usually larger than those obtained between teacher behaviors and achievement gain.

In one of the best examples of these studies, Good et al. (1978) studied 18 fourth-grade classrooms which were all using the same math textbook. They correlated the number of pages covered in each classroom with mean achievement score (adjusted for initial ability). The resulting correlation was .49, suggesting that teachers who moved at a faster pace and covered more content obtained higher achievement.

Based on the correlational and experimental studies cited above, we conclude that there is a close correspondence between content covered and student achievement. The correlations range from .2 to .7. It may be difficult to obtain higher correlations because there is not a perfect correspondence between the content given in a class and the content measured on the test and also because content covered is not identical with content mastered.

One can argue that the concept of content covered fits the teaching of decoding and word attack better than the teaching of comprehension. In decoding, there is a fairly strong correspondence between learning sounds and reading words. Explicit items and rules are taught. In comprehension, we do not, at present, have such neatly explicit rules to teach skills like main idea, sequence, drawing conclusions, or paraphrasing. Reading comprehension is taught by successive practice (Durkin, 1978–1979). Hence, increasing the time spent in this successive practice seems likely to improve reading comprehension, particularly for slower learners, but we need experimental studies on this topic.

Increasing Content Covered

Three methods for increasing content covered are discussed below: grouping practices, increasing the efficiency of instruction, and increasing the pacing of presentation.

Grouping practices and content covered. In a naturalistic study, Barr (1973–1974) observed nine first-grade classrooms and studied the number of new words introduced in a specified time (pace) and the number of words learned by individual students. She found that teachers who used whole-class instruction proceeded at a slower pace than did teachers who grouped students by ability for reading instruction. Middle- and high-ability students who were taught in whole-class settings learned fewer words than comparable students in classrooms which used ability grouping. Low-ability students did equally well in either setting. Unfortunately, the Barr study did not collect data on what was happening in the whole-class instruction classrooms to cause the slower pace. One explanation is that the slower pace occurred because the new words were repeated and reviewed more often in order to provide sufficient practice for the slower students.

Improving the efficiency of instruction.   In a study of fourth-grade mathematics, Good et al. (1978) compared the pacing of the 9 highest and 9 lowest teachers, as measured by class residual gain scores ($N = 41$ teachers). The high teachers as a group averaged 1.13 pages per day, whereas the low teachers averaged .71 pages per day. As stated above, the correlation between page coverage and adjusted achievement gain in mathematics was .49. Through inspection of the data and use of residual gain scores, the authors concluded that these differences in pace were the result of teacher behaviors and were independent of the characteristics of the students. Surprisingly, some teachers in each group used whole-class instruction and some used small-group instruction, and, based on the initial test scores, the classrooms of the high teachers were slightly more heterogeneous. Note in contrast to Barr's work, content covered in this study was not dependent upon grouping practices.

In discussing the study by Good et al. (1978), Brophy and Good (in press) believe that the teachers with higher achievement had lessons that moved at a brisker pace for several reasons. First, the teachers with higher achievement spent more time introducing new concepts in the development part of the lesson and giving instructions for the seatwork assignments. Thus, the emphasis was on instructing students in key concepts *before* they would be required to apply those concepts in follow-up assignments. In contrast, the teacher with lower achievement spent less time giving clear presentations. This resulted in more guessing and a higher error rate from the students. For teachers with lower achievement, the instruction came more frequently *after the students made an error,* either in responding to questions or when they were doing their seatwork. Thus, a first difference between the two groups was that the teachers with higher achievement laid a better foundation for the seatwork by making a clearer initial presentation.

A second difference between the two groups was that the higher achieving, faster paced teachers used questions *during* their explanation rather than relying more on student recitation at the end of the presentation. Third, more of the questions they did ask were direct factual questions likely to produce immediate correct answers. Fourth, when students were lost or confused, these teachers would reteach the material (i.e., give process feedback or reexplain the steps involved in getting the correct answer) rather than merely provide the correct answer or attempt to elicit correct responses through continued questioning. Fifth, because these teachers were more active during seatwork, they had more teacher-student contacts during the seatwork. Furthermore, the feedback they gave to students during seatwork was more likely to involve reteaching or extensive explanation rather than just giving the answer or brief directives.

Speed of presentation.   Another way of increasing content covered is to increase the speed of presentation. Speed has been investigated in three studies.

In an ABABAB study involving two low-achieving first-grade children, Carnine (1976) alternated slow rate and fast rate of presentation of DISTAR phonics instruction. In fast rate, there was a pause of 1 second or less between tasks; in slow rate, the delay was 5 second or more. Student attention was higher in the fast-paced condition (95% vs. 35%) and attention increased across trials in the fast-paced condition. The percentage of tasks completed correctly was also higher in the fast-paced condition (90% vs. 60%).

A subsequent study on training teachers to increase the pace of their instruction, Carnine and Fink (1978) had similar results. The researchers found that teachers with a slower instructional pace could be taught to speak more rapidly and have shorter pauses in their lesson. Not only did this treatment result in faster paced lessons, but also, as in the earlier study, the students had higher engagement rates and greater accuracy when teachers increased the pace of their instruction.

Potentially, after hearing about the research on content covered, some teachers might begin to cover pages without regard for the students' level of mastery. Although there is no evidence, as yet, such an approach would probably not be successful in increasing student mastery.

Student Attention and Engaged Minutes

A second index of effective instruction, student attention or engagement, has been investigated in both correlational and experimental studies. The most precise measure of that index is academic-engaged minutes as described in BTES (Fisher et al., 1978).

Correlational Studies on Student Engagement

Student engagement or attention is obviously necessary for student learning. Despite the difficulties of measuring attention (e.g., are reading, writing, and listening to the teacher or following another reader equal indicators of attention?) and the crude and varied procedures used to gather this data, attention consistently has been found to be positively and significantly related to reading achievement, regardless of grade level. Studies by Chall and Feldmann (1966), Lahaderne (1968), Cobb (1972), Samuels and Turnure (1976) and by Stallings et al. (1977), Luce and Hoge (1978), and Anderson et al. (1979) have all found positive correlations between student attention and unadjusted achievement scores in reading (see Table 23.7). In these studies, the average correlation between attention and unadjusted achievement was about .40.

Table 23.7 also gives the results for nine studies in reading in which student attention was correlated with reading achievement adjusted for initial achievement or ability. There is a range of results in many studies because they used a number of criterion measures, such as vocabulary and reading comprehension. Taking the highest correlation in each study, we see that the average result was between .30 and .44.

The correlations between attention and adjusted achievement scores in reading are somewhat below those typically obtained in other subject areas, such as math, science, or social studies; in these other studies, the correlations

Experimental Studies on Student Engagement and Student Achievement

In addition to the correlational studies, experimental studies have shown that attempts to increase student engagement have also resulted in increased student achievement. In two studies (Cobb & Hops, 1973; Hops & Cobb, 1974), the investigators worked with teachers to train their students to attend to classroom work more often. Cobb and Hops asked teachers to describe and model the attending behaviors for their students and to use group reinforcement to obtain criterion levels. The teachers operated a timer with a light as a cue to indicate when whole-class attention was maintained. In both studies, both attention and reading achievement were significantly higher for the experimental students than for the control students.

Of course, increasing student attention is not the only way to increase student achievement. Hops and Cobb (1974) used a classroom of students who received direct instruction in reading (this involved systematic, structured instruction in reading with immediate corrective feedback during student practice). This group had greater achievement gain than those receiving training in attending behaviors. Similarly, in an experimental study by Anderson (1975), manipulation of the type of instruction altered the attention levels of students in junior high mathematics classes. In that study, students who received instruction using a mastery learning approach had significantly higher on-task behaviors and achievement than the nonmastery learning group. Thus, students' attention can be altered both by instructional techniques and through training in skills related to attention.

The Follow-Through research by Stallings and Kaskowitz (1974) can also be regarded as an experimental study. Each of the seven programs listed in Table 23.9 represented a different approach toward the education of children

TABLE 23.9   PERCENTAGE ENGAGED TIME AND ACHIEVEMENT GAIN BY FOLLOW-THROUGH PROGRAM

	1st GRADE				3rd GRADE			
PROGRAM	READING		MATH		READING		MATH	
Oregon	54[a]	1[a]	27	5	58	2	27	1
Kansas	59	2	22	1	59	3	22	3
Non-Follow Through	50	3	18	3	48	1	22	2
Bank Street	40	6	16	4	38	7	20	4
High/Scope	40	5	20	8	46	—	16	—
Arizona	40	4	14	6	42	6	16	7
Far West	39	8	14	7	41	4	18	6
EDC	29	7	14	2	37	5	24	5

[a] In each group, the first column is average class percentage of engaged time and the second column is achievement gain rank.
Rank Order Correlations: 1st grade reading: .93; 1st grade math: .17; 3rd grade reading: .80; 3rd grade math: .78.
SOURCE: *From* Stallings & Kaskowitz, 1974. Appendix pages R–3 and R–4.

from poor families. As part of their observational study, Stallings and Kaskowitz obtained data on the percentage of time that each of 103 first-grade classrooms and 54 third-grade classrooms were engaged productively in reading or math. These results were aggregated to give an average percentage of engaged time for each of the Follow-Through models. Table 23.9 presents these percentages along with the rank order for achievement gain for each of the models and for the control classrooms (labeled non-Follow Through). Note, particularly in reading, a strong correspondence between the relative time spent engaged in reading or math activities and achievement gain. (The results on the non-Follow-Through or control classrooms are also revealing, showing that children were engaged in reading or math relatively frequently in those "traditional" settings.) Note also in Table 23.9 that, in reading, children in the top three models in achievement gain were engaged in academic activities proportionately more (50%) than were children in the lower three models.

In summary, the correlational studies reviewed in this section yielded an average correlation between student engagement rate and achievement in reading that was between .30 and .44. In the BTES, adding data on student error rate substantially increased the correlations between engagement and achievement gain in the second grade, but only slightly in the fifth grade. In four experimental studies, the investigators were successful in increasing both student engagement and student achievement. Taken as a group, these correlational and experimental studies provide strong evidence for the mediational role that engagement plays in producing academic achievement.

Normative Data from the BTES

Because students need to be engaged in academic activities in order to cover content, the question of how time is spent in elementary classrooms becomes important. We are particularly interested in how much time is allocated to reading, how much of that time students are engaged, which types of activities represent nonengaged time, and how much time is spent in these activities. The BTES (Fisher et al., 1978) provides the first set of comprehensive answers to many of these questions. The data for this study were gathered in 1976 in 24 second-grade and 21 fifth-grade classrooms in northern California. Six average students in each of these classrooms were observed *all day* for 12 days between January and May.[1]

Allocated time.   The number of engaged minutes is limited by the amount of allocated time. That is, if a teacher only allocates 60 minutes per day to reading, the maximum amount of engaged time possible is only 60 minute.

Fisher et al. (1978) showed that in the second grade (Table 23.10) an average of 1 hour and 30 minutes per day was allocated to reading and language arts. This increased to 1 hour 50 minutes in the fifth grade. Note that these figures include *all* reading and language arts activities, including those which occurred during science and social studies. Overall, about 30% of the school day was allocated to reading and language arts. If we add the time allocated to math, science, and social studies, about 2 hour 30 minutes were allocated to academic subjects. In other words, only about 58% of the school day was allocated to academic

TABLE 23.10 AVERAGE ALLOCATED TIME PER DAY IN DIFFERENT ACTIVITIES

TIME CATEGORY	GRADE 2			GRADE 5		
	MINUTES PER DAY	COMBINED MINUTES	COMBINED PERCENTAGE	MINUTES PER DAY	COMBINED MINUTES	COMBINED PERCENTAGE
Academic activities		2 hr 12 min	57%		2 hr 51 min	60%
Reading and language arts	1 hr 28 min			1 hr 50 min		
Mathematics	36 min			44 min		
Other academic	8 min			17 min		
Nonacademic activities	55 min	55 min	24%	1 hr 05 min	1 hr 05 min	23
Noninstructional activities		44 min	19%		47 min	17
Transition	34 min			34 min		
Wait	4 min			4 min		
Housekeeping	6 min			9 min		
Major in-class time	3 hr 51 min	3 hr 51 min		4 hr 44 min	4 hr 44 min	
Lunch, recess, breaks	1 hr 15 min	1 hr 15 min		1 hr 17 min	1 hr 17 min	
Length of school day	5 hr 06 min	5 hr 06 min		6 hr 00 min	6 hr 00 min	

subjects. Another hour per day (or 24%) was allocated to music, art, and physical education.

Where does the rema ing time go? About 45 minutes per day (18%) is allocated to noninstructional activities, such as waiting between activities, housekeeping (e.g., collecting papers), and transitions (students lining up and taking their seats or moving from one activity or group to another). This relatively high amount of time on noninstructional activities occurred even in those classrooms whose teachers obtained the highest number of engaged minutes from their students.

Although the average teacher in second grade allocated 1 hour 28 minutes per day to all reading activities, there was substantial variation across teachers. The three highest teachers allocated 1 hour 54 minutes per day, whereas the three lowest teachers averaged 1 hour. Thus, some classrooms had almost 2 hour per day allocated to reading and language arts, whereas other classrooms had only 1 hour per day. This same variation occurred in the fifth grade. While the average teacher allocated 1 hour 50 minutes, the three highest teachers allocated 2 hours 14 minutes, and the three lowest teachers allocated nearly 1 hour less per day—or a total of only 1 hour 18 minute.

Academic-engaged minutes.   Although the amount of time allocated to academic activities is of significant interest, we are more concerned with the number of minutes per day that students actually spend gainfully engaged in academic activities. The BTES was one of the first to report three important variables: (a) the average engagement rate of the students (i.e., the percentage of allocated time that students were engaged in academic activities), (b) the minutes per day that students were academically engaged, and (c) student engagement rates in different settings.

Overall, the students were engaged in academic activities about 72% of the allocated time, or 43 minutes for each allocated hour. The BTES obtained the academic engaged minutes by multiplying the allocated time by the engagement rate. Thus, if a teacher allocated 88 minutes to reading and language arts each day, and the engagement rate was 73%, then the engaged minutes were 64 minutes per day. Table 23.11 presents the BTES data on the average academic minutes in reading and math in Grade 2 and Grade 5. For a more detailed examination, Table 23.11 has data on the three teachers in each grade who had the highest academic-engaged minutes and on the three who had the lowest academic-engaged minutes. In each section in Table 23.11, the first column presents the allocated time, the second column presents the engagement rate, and the third column presents the number of minutes that the students were actually engaged.

In the average classroom, students were engaged in reading for approximately 1 hour per day in second grade and about 1 hour 20 minutes in fifth grade. (Note that this time also includes reading in content areas.) In the classrooms of the three highest teachers (in both second and fifth grades), the students were engaged in reading 20 minutes more per day than those in average classrooms. This adds up to over 50 hours per year. Further, the students in the classrooms of the three highest teachers were engaged in reading *twice as long* as those in the three lowest teachers' classrooms, a difference of more than 110

TABLE 23.11   HIGHEST, AVERAGE, AND LOWEST TEACHERS IN ACADEMIC-ENGAGED MINUTES

| | READING | | | MATHEMATICS | | | TOTAL |
	ALLOCATED	ENGAGEMENT RATE	ENGAGED MINUTES	ALLOCATED	ENGAGEMENT RATE	ENGAGED MINUTES	ENGAGED MINUTES
				Second Grade			
High 3	1 hr 45 min	81	1 hr 25 min	35 min	82	30 min	1 hr 55 min
Average	1 hr 30 min	73	1 hr 04 min	36 min	71	26 min	1 hr 30 min
Low 3	1 hr 00 min	72	43 min	30 min	75	22 min	1 hr 05 min
				Fifth Grade			
High 3	2 hr 10 min	80	1 hr 45 min	53 min	86	45 min	2 hr 30 min
Average	1 hr 50 min	74	1 hr 20 min	44 min	74	35 min	1 hr 55 min
Low 3	1 hr 25 min	63	1 hr 05 min	38 min	63	22 min	1 hr 25 min

hours per year. Similar and equally dramatic differences appear in the fifth grade. Thus, within this sample, there are enormous differences both in the amount of time available for reading in different classrooms and in the amount of time students spent engaged in reading activities.

Nonengaged time.   As noted above, the students were engaged in academic activities about 73% of the time, or about 43 minutes for each allocated hour. Of the 17 minutes per allocated hour that they were not engaged, about 8 minutes was spent clearly off-task, that is, daydreaming, socializing, doodling, not paying attention, sharpening pencils, and the like. The students also spent about 9 minutes each allocated hour in interim and wait activities, such as passing out and handing in papers and books, putting on headings, waiting for help from the teacher, and waiting for a paper to be graded. (Students standing in line by the teacher waiting for a paper to be graded would be coded as in nonengaged wait time.) Thus, we see that a lot of nonengaged time is not simply caused by the uninterest of the students but that an equal or larger amount is due to the difficult problems of managing, organizing, and supervising 25 individual students.

Influence of classroom grouping patterns on engagement.   As noted in the earlier section on instruction in groups (Table 23.4), the BTES data also showed that when students were in groups directed by the teacher (e.g., reading groups) their engagement rate averaged about 84%. But when students were working individually (doing seatwork), their engagement rate was 14% lower (or an average of 70%). These results were consistent in both reading and math for both the second and fifth grades. Nevertheless, students were in teacher-led settings only 25 to 35% of the time, whereas they were working alone, on seatwork, 65 to 75% of the time.

The difference in engagement rate between teacher-led and seatwork settings is probably due to the usual procedure of dividing the classroom into small groups for reading. When a teacher is working with one of the groups, the engagement in that group is high, but when the same group is doing seatwork, then the engagement drops because the teacher is not supervising that group.

Are there upper limits to engagement?   In this emphasis upon engaged minutes, one worries whether there is a point of diminishing returns, whether more allocated time leads to a lower engagement rate? More data needs to be gathered on this issue, but the data in the BTES is optimistic. Note that in each grade, the three highest teachers for total engaged time were high in allocated time and also had a high student engagement rate. Allocations of 2 hours per day for reading and math in the second grade and 3 hours per day in the fifth grade did not lead to less engagement; indeed, those three teachers in each grade who had the highest allocated time also had the highest engagement rate.

Allocated time and engagement rate.   Are allocated time and engagement rate correlated? In fact, the correlations between them in reading were .05 in the second grade and .26 in the fifth grade, suggesting that the two variables are not highly correlated. Rather, it suggests that more allocated time to academic material does not have diminishing returns on student engagement.

In summary, the BTES research was the first to present comprehensive data on allocated time and engagement rates in elementary classrooms. It found that time allocated to reading and language arts accounted for an average of 1 hour 30 minute in the second grade and 1 hour 50 minute in the fifth grade. Furthermore, the average student was engaged in academic activities for about 73% of each hour. Students were more engaged when they were in teacher-led groups, less engaged when working by themselves.

However, within each sample there were teachers who were above average in allocated time and engagement rate. The students of these teachers, in each grade, were academically engaged in reading and language arts about 23 additional minutes every day. There was no evidence of diminishing returns within this sample. That is, teachers who allocated more time did not have lower engagement rates.

Error Rate, Success Rate, and Achievement Gain

Earlier, we presented data to show that the correlation between student engagement and student achievement gain was increased when one added data on student error rate (or success rate). Because this research is fairly new, we now expand on that finding.

In an experimental study of reading group instruction in 20 middle-class first-grade classrooms (Anderson et al., 1979), a correlational analysis was performed on variables dealing with error rate across these 20 classrooms. The researchers found that "percent of academic interactions with *correct* student response" was positively related to achievement gain ($r = .49$) and that the average number of errors made during oral reading turns was negatively correlated ($r = -.36$). They also found that the treatment classrooms, which had significantly higher achievement gain than the control classrooms, also exhibited a significantly higher percentage of correct responses (73% vs. 66%), even though reducing incorrect answers was not part of the instructional treatment. In an earlier correlational study involving second- and third-grade classrooms, Brophy and Evertson (1976) found that for verbal interactions in reading, the optimal error rate was 70% for high-SES students and 80% correct for low-SES students.

The BTES (Fisher et al., 1978) has the most comprehensive data on error rate and student achievement gain (Table 23.12). For the observed students, researchers correlated the percent of time spent in low error rate and in high

TABLE 23.12   CORRELATIONS BETWEEN
ENGAGEMENT AND ERROR RATE

GRADE	SUBJECT	LOW ERROR TIME	HIGH ERROR TIME
2	Reading	.13	−.36*
2	Math	.28*	−.33*
5	Reading	.11	−.20*
5	Math	.15	−.08

* $p < .05$
SOURCE: *From* Fisher et al., 1978, Table 4–5.

error rate conditions with student achievement gain in a variety of areas in reading. The trends of the results show that low error rate was almost always positively correlated with achievement gain and high error rate was negatively correlated. All significant results followed this trend. Inspection of the original document (and Table 23.12) suggests that in the second grade, low error rate was quite important, a result which corresponds to the Anderson et al. (1979) finding. In contrast, in the fifth grade, low error rate made a much smaller contribution, suggesting that, as students become more proficient (and the nature of the work shifts from decoding to comprehension), low error rate is not as important a factor in achievement gain.

The BTES also found that there were significant negative correlations between high error rate and student engagement. That is, when the error rate was high, student engagement was lower. As before, the correlations were higher in the second grade than in the fifth grade, showing, again, that as students become more proficient, errors do not cause as many disruptions.

Difficulty level of materials.   One way of reducing error rate would be to assign students to materials below their assessed reading level. Two studies were found on this topic. Aarons, Stokes, and Bates (1977) found that greater achievement gains were obtained by first-grade teachers who assigned students to individualized reading material which was below the students' instructional levels; lesser gains were obtained by teachers who assigned students to materials at or above their instructional levels. However, Jorgenson, Klein and Kumar (1977) found no significant correlation between difficulty of reading materials and achievement gain for students in third through sixth grade. Thus, conclusions regarding the optimal level of difficulty cannot be made until further research has been done.

Jorgenson et al. (1977) also found that students were more engaged when they had reading lessons which were below their measured ability ($r = .38$). Similarly, in a study of computer-assisted mathematics, Miller and Hess (1972) found that student engagement was highest when the correct response rate was from 80 to 100%. Below 80%, student engagement dropped significantly. However, they also suggested that if material became extremely easy (e.g., second-grade material for a sixth-grade student) then engagement would drop. Note that, in each of these studies, the students were observed during seatwork, and these studies support the point made above regarding the value of relatively easy materials during seatwork when students cannot readily get help if they encounter problems.

In summary, the research on observed error rates is fairly clear and consistent. Anderson et al. (1979) and Brophy and Evertson (1976) suggest an optimal rate of 70% correct during groupwork for primary-grade middle-class students and a rate of 80% correct for slower students. The BTES (Fisher et al., 1978) data appears to support this for average second-grade students. In the fifth grade (for which only BTES data is available), a low error rate seems less important, possibly because the students are more proficient. During seatwork activities, one suspects that the error rate should be fairly low for younger or slower children so that they do not have to interrupt the teacher for help when the teacher is working with a reading group. This may be less crucial in the middle grades where the students might be able to work around the difficult sections of the seatwork.

The research on the difficulty level of materials is not as clear but seems to suggest the same conclusion. For younger children, less difficult materials led to higher achievement gain, whereas for older children the difficulty level of the materials was not related to achievement gain. However, due to the small number of studies these conclusions are tentative. Future research on the difficulty level of materials appears warranted. One suspects there is a point where extremely easy material would lead to boredom and less student attention, but this point was not reached in the context of the normal instruction observed in these studies.

SUMMARY

Knowledge of effective and efficient classroom instruction in reading has advanced a great deal in recent years. Researchers have identified both general and specific instructional procedures which are correlated with students' achievement gain. Similarly, three variables have emerged as indicators of instructional effectiveness: content covered, academic-engaged time, and success rate. While further research is required, these results provide teachers and researchers with useful information for increasing student achievement in reading.

General Instructional Procedures

Three general instructional variables have frequently been correlated with reading achievement gain. These procedures are: teacher-directed initial instruction, instruction in groups, and academic emphasis.

Students who receive their instruction from a teacher consistently do better than those who are expected to learn on their own or from other students. This result is consistent across a number of large-scale studies. It seems that students learn reading most efficiently when they are systematically taught, monitored, and given feedback by a teacher.

In addition, teachers who group their students for instruction tend to have more academic-engaged time and higher reading achievement. Although one-to-one instruction is very effective, given the reality of having 20 or more students in a classroom, this creates a problem. Given such typical classroom situations, each child can receive very little one-to-one instruction per hour. Thus, it is more efficient and effective to group students for instruction. Grouping students for instruction allows for more teacher-led demonstrations and practice. It also gives the students more opportunity to practice new skills under the teacher's guidance and to receive feedback concerning their performance. Grouping also makes it much easier for teachers to monitor the students' behavior, to keep them on task, and to avoid major classroom-management problems.

Equally consistent and positive results have been found for those teachers who maintain a strong academic emphasis in their classrooms. Across a number of studies, teachers who are more successful in getting high reading achievement are those who are "task oriented" and determined that students learn. However, such classrooms are also rated as being warm environments and the teachers are friendly toward and accepting of students.

Specific Instructional Procedures

Research on specific instructional procedures has shown that effective teaching is characterized by a predictable sequence of demonstration, guided practice, feedback and corrections, and independent practice. Although most teachers follow this general procedure, there are more and less effective ways of accomplishing these activities. From the research discussed in this section, a description of more effective behaviors has emerged.

Demonstration is more effective when the teacher proceeds in small steps, provides many examples, and intersperses the demonstration with questions designed to check for student understanding.

Guided practice is more effective when there are frequent questions (thus providing more practice), when questions focus directly upon the material, and when practice is extended so that the student success rate achieves 80% or higher. Also, using ordered turns in reading groups insures that all students have a chance to respond and receive feedback.

Feedback and correctives are more effective when correct responses are followed by brief feedback affirming the correctness of the response or simply by another question. Incorrect responses are best followed by sustaining questions (giving hints or asking simpler questions) or by providing an explanation which reteaches the material.

Independent practice is more effective when there is substantive interaction during the groupwork (thus preparing the students for the seatwork) and when the teacher or another adult actively monitors the students. Independent practice should also be sufficient to insure that students have enough practice to achieve overlearning and quickness in responding.

Finally, the time students spend in guided practice and independent practice gives the teacher an opportunity to get feedback on the adequacy of their instruction of new material. Good indicators of adequate instruction are a low error rate and lack of hesitancy. If instruction has been effective, students will be prepared to go on to the next lesson once they have sufficient independent practice. However, frequent errors, confusion, or hesitancy during guided practice and independent practice indicates that there are problems. Upon observing these types of problems during the practice sessions, it is most effective for the teacher to recycle or reteach the lesson. Also in such cases, it may be useful for the teacher to break the new content or skills into smaller components or steps. Progressing in smaller steps will then make it easier for the students to acquire the new skills with less confusion or problems.

Indexes of Effective Instruction

Content covered. Content covered is a major indicator of instructional effectiveness. A number of correlational and experimental studies have shown a close correspondence between content covered and student achievement. The correlations range from .20 to .70. Four methods for increasing content covered were discussed: dividing classes into groups when teaching sounds and words in the first grade; increasing allocated time; improving the efficiency of instruction through clearer initial presentations, asking factual questions during the explanation, and actively monitoring student seatwork; and maintaining a fairly rapid pace.

Academic-engaged time.   Student engagement is significantly correlated with reading achievement gain. The correlational studies reviewed in this section yielded an average correlation between student engagement rate and achievement in reading that was between .30 and .44. In the BTES, adding data on student error rate substantially increased these correlations in the second grade, but only slightly in the fifth grade. In three experimental studies, the experimentors were successful in increasing both student engagement and student achievement. Taken as a group, these correlational and experimental studies provide strong evidence for the mediational role that engagement plays in producing academic achievement.

The BTES (Fisher et al., 1978) was the first to present comprehensive data on allocated time and engagement rates in elementary classrooms. They found that time allocated to reading and language arts accounted for an average of 1 hour 30 minutes in the second grade and 1 hour 50 minutes in the fifth grade. Furthermore, the average student was engaged in academic activities for about 73% of each allocated hour. Students were more engaged when they were in teacher-led groups, less engaged when working by themselves.

However, within each sample, there were teachers who were above average in allocated time and engagement rate. The students of these teachers, in each grade, were academically engaged in reading and language arts about 23 additional minutes every day. There was no evidence of diminishing returns within this sample. That is, teachers who allocated more time did not have lower engagement rates.

Success rate.   Two studies (Anderson et al., 1979; Fisher et al., 1978) showed that a low error rate is significantly correlated with student achievement gain, particularly in the lower grades. The low error rates were probably achieved by proceeding in small steps, structuring each step, providing precorrections, and reviewing frequently until the new material was practiced at a high level of accuracy. In two studies (Fisher et al., 1978; Jorgenson et al., 1977), student engagement decreased as materials became more difficult.

Another way of obtaining a low error rate is to have students work on materials below their grade level. This strategy led to higher achievement gain in a first-grade study (Aarons et al., 1977) but was not replicated in Grades 3 through 6 (Jorgenson et al., 1977).

IMPLICATIONS FOR RESEARCH

The last decade of research has provided us with a valuable body of knowledge about effective classroom instruction. This recent research has helped us rethink the research of the late 1960s and early 1970s, which suggested that the home and the community—and not the teacher or the school—made all of the difference in students' achievement. As a result of this research, we have again become encouraged by the impact that effective instruction can have on students' learning and achievement. The quality and quantity of this research as well as the replication of many of the major results has helped us clarify our thinking about effective instruction. Yet, like any rich body of data, this research does not answer all the questions and raises many new ones. The unanswered questions and unresolved issues should stimulate exciting and useful research in the future.

Research on Instructional Procedures

The number of positive findings in the research on instructional procedures has grown considerably. However, most of the results are from correlational studies. There are a few experimental studies and these tend to be relatively short-term studies, such as the study on student choral responding by McKenzie (1979). Only one experimental study in reading was found in which teachers were trained in a large number of instructional procedures and that was by Anderson et al. (1979).

Therefore, our major recommendation for researchers would be to take the significant results on instructional procedures and translate them into experimental studies in which (a) teachers are trained in the specific procedures discussed above, (b) the classrooms of the experimental and control teachers are observed to record the level of implementation of these procedures, and (c) the two groups are compared in terms of students' achievement gain. Analysis of such data can also yield additional information on which behaviors are particularly difficult to change; which behaviors are most important, and the intercorrelations among these variables; and the more general variables of content covered and academic-engaged time. We believe that the best questions for future research will emerge from studies such as these.

When conducting the training part of these studies particular emphasis might be given to (1) training teachers to spend more time on guided practice, continuing the guided practice until all of the students in the reading group are at a high level of success, (2) correcting errors and repeating instruction until each student has a firm grasp of the skill or content, and (3) continuing the independent practice to overlearning, to the point where students are automatic in their responses.

Researchers interested in such classroom-based studies could refer to previously developed and validated manuals for training teachers to improve their instruction and classroom management (e.g. Emmer, Evertson, Sanford, Clements, & Worsham, 1982; Evertson, Emmer, Clements, Sanford, Worsham, & Williams, 1981; Fitzpatrick, 1981). These manuals might provide researchers with valuable information for extending these instructional procedures to classroom instruction in reading.

There is also a need for experimental studies on some specific aspects of these instructional procedures. These research issues have emerged as unanswered questions from previous classroom-based studies.

Students who need additional time and teaching.   Although it is in some sense "obvious" that lower achieving students need more instructional and/or practice time, very little research exists concerning how this time might be provided, given an already overcrowded school curriculum, or concerning the effects of providing such time. How does a teacher find that extra time for demonstration, guided practice, feedback/correction, and independent practice while keeping the rest of the class engaged in productive activities?

Even such rudimentary suggestions as carving out extra time before school, during lunch, after school, during an extra afternoon reading session, or during summer school have received little attention on the part of researchers and supervisory personnel. We need fundamental research on how the practical difficulties with any or all of these suggestions might be overcome. We also need to investigate the possibility of diminishing returns beyond some optimal threshold of extra time; many have voiced this concern but we do not know the conditions under which diminishing returns might or might not occur.

Types of teacher questions. A consistently vexing issue, and one which needs much more research, is the relative effectiveness of different types of teacher questions. The correlational research tends to support a high incidence of factual questions, while some experimental work favors higher level questions. Also, armchair recommendations (e.g., methods texts and articles for reading teachers) focus on higher level questions. The topic needs more rigorous thought and more vigorous research.

Forms of student response. Some research has shown that choral, signaled student responses provide an effective way of obtaining sufficient guided practice when new concepts are presented. Yet, many teachers remain vehemently opposed to this practice, and even oppose the combination of choral and individual responses. More studies are needed to probe the effectiveness of group versus individual response patterns. How to overcome the philosophical opposition to group responses is quite another matter.

Indexes of Effective Instruction

There are few experimental studies demonstrating that systematic changes in content covered, academic-engaged time and success rate result in changes in performance in student achievement; most of the evidence for these indexes is correlational. The need for more experimental research on these indexes is clear.

Content covered. We recommend two types of research on content covered—one on the independent variables that may contribute to differences in content coverage and the other on the issue of mastery versus coverage. In one set of studies, teachers would be trained on some or all of the techniques associated with greater content coverage: proceeding in small steps, providing precorrections, extensive guided practice, reviewing frequently to achieve overlearning, increasing speed of presentation. Dependent measures would have to include both content covered and achievement gain. The second set of studies would investigate whether continuing practice to some predetermined level of mastery (which may involve more time and less content coverage) is more or less effective than pushing on to cover new content at the expense of mastery. Although this is a hotly debated issue, we have found surprisingly little relevant research.

Academic-engaged time.   Although there are many important areas for future research on academic-engaged time, we have selected three of particular interest: what is the average number of academic-engaged minutes in schools at the present time, how many engaged minutes are needed for a child to make reasonable progress, and how can teachers increase students' engagement rate.

The major knowledge on academic-engaged minutes comes from the BTES. But those figures may be out of date because of the back-to-basics movement and the influence of the BTES itself. Because of the BTES, schools may be devoting more time to reading. More recent data is needed on the number of minutes which are allocated to reading and language arts throughout the entire day.

Underlying the emerging data on engaged time are many unanswered questions on how much engaged time is needed. For example, how much time does an average student need to make average progress in reading? How much more time will a slower student need to make as much progress as the average student? How much time can be saved by more "efficient" teaching—that is, teaching which reduces student errors, emphasizes quickness of responses, and provides strategies to use in reading comprehension? These questions are, as yet, unanswered.

The experimental studies presented two methods for increasing student engagement and student achievement: Trying to increase student engagement directly and trying to increase engagement improving the quality of instruction resulted in higher engagement and higher achievement. To date, there have been only a few studies of each type. We need to extend these studies to regular classrooms with regular teachers in order to learn (a) the particular difficulties which inhibit implementation of programs and (b) which of the program variables are most important for increasing students' engagement rate. In the process of developing, conducting, and analyzing these studies, it is likely that unforeseen but highly relevant issues will emerge and, thus, stimulate further research on academic-engaged time.

When developing programs or manuals for the experimental teachers, one might begin with the programs developed by Cobb and Hops (1973) or with the other manuals cited above, such as those by Anderson et al. (1979) or Evertson et al. (1981).

Success rate.   There have only been a few studies on success rate, and these support a success rate of 80% or higher, particularly for younger children. Yet, there are three plausible arguments concerning levels of success.

One argument would be that the most efficient learning takes place with a high success rate. Errors are wasted time because students have to spend time correcting their mistakes and then learning the correct response. According to this logic, new material should be presented in small steps, with models and prompts by the teacher and precorrections of difficult points (i.e., anticipation of errors) so that students have a high level of correct responses. Further, new material should be overlearned so that responses can be given quickly, without hesitancy or tentativeness; in other words, practice continues until a high level of mastery has been attained. Equally high standards would apply when reviewing old material. From this point of view, one would conclude that even a success rate of 80% is too low and a sign of inefficient instruction.

A counterargument is that not all errors are detrimental. Some challenge may be beneficial; some hesitancy in answering questions and some errors may be useful because they require (or at least indicate) that the student is processing the material. According to this logic, initial difficulty pays off in the form of better mastery in the end.

A third argument is that initial errors, within reason, are no great concern so long as the students are brought to mastery by the end of each unit.

Each of the above three arguments have their advocates, and, thus, they suggest future avenues of research. When doing research on error rates, it might be useful to code the context in which the error occurs. One type of error might occur when students are well prepared and the teacher seeks to challenge them by asking difficult questions on material they already know; another type might occur when students are expected to know the answer but lack the knowledge; and a third type might occur when the teacher has intentionally given a limited presentation and encourages guessing. In addition, when doing this research one might also use latency of response as a criterion measure.

A possible model. Many of our research suggestions recommend more classroom-based experimental studies. We believe that a particularly good model for conducting these studies was the one used by Anderson et al. (1979) in their study of instruction in first-grade reading groups. After a correlational study which provided suggestions for the experimental research (Brophy & Evertson, 1976), the investigators developed a manual of instructional principles in reading for teachers. One group of teachers received the manual and studied it; the control teachers were told to continue with their regular teaching. During the period of the experiment all teachers were observed at least eight times, and their frequencies on a large number of instructional variables were recorded. At the end of the experiment, the student achievement gain scores in the two groups were compared. Then, the investigators continued their analyses by computing correlations between the frequency of the observed behaviors and student gain measures. By this final procedure, they were able to determine which of the instructional variables had the strongest correlation with achievement gain. These were the variables that were retained when they rewrote their instructional principles for first-grade reading groups.

We believe that future classroom-based experimental studies should include the steps listed above, particularly the additional correlational analysis which took place after the experiment, and the revision of the manuals to take account of the new findings. When such procedures are followed, we will then have validated manuals to use in training teachers.

CONCLUDING REMARKS

Classroom research has provided us with a valuable body of knowledge about effective classroom instruction in reading. We have again become encouraged by the impact that teachers can have on students' achievement. Yet, there remains a need for more classroom-based experimental studies so that we may better understand the relative importance of the instructional variables, the interrelationship of the variables, and the potential difficulties in training teachers to implement these instructional procedures. We also hope that the classroom studies will develop training methods or manuals which can be revised as a result of the research and then later be used to help teachers implement the results of the research. In this way, future classroom research may not only provide us with more knowledge about these instructional procedures, but also provide teachers with practical applications of it.

NOTES

1. The figures for the second grade may be underestimates of "typical" classrooms because a number of classrooms in this sample were on a "split day" in which half the class arrived at 9:00 A.M. and left at 2:00 P.M.; the other half arrived at 10:00 A.M. and left at 3:00 P.M.

REFERENCES

Aarons, R., Stokes, A., & Bates, E.   *The influence of a classroom management system on the relationship between teacher assessment of pupil mastery and their standardized reading achievement scores.* Unpublished paper, College of Education, University of Georgia, 1977.

Abt Associates.   *Education as experimentation: A planned variation model* (Vol 3, 4). Cambridge, Mass.: Abt Associates, 1977.

Anderson, L. M., Evertson, C. M., & Brophy, J. E.   An experimental study of effective teaching in first-grade reading groups. *Elementary School Journal*, 1979, *79*, 193–222.

Anderson, L., & Scott, C.   The relationship among teaching methods, student characteristics, and student involvement in learning. *Journal of Teacher Education*, 1978, *29*, 52–57.

Arlin, M.   Teacher transitions can disrupt time flow in classrooms. *American Educational Research Journal*, 1979, *16*, 42–57.

Armento, B. A.   *Teacher verbal cognitive behaviors related to student achievement on a social science concept test.* Unpublished doctoral dissertation, Indiana University, 1977.

Barr, R. C.   Instructional pace differences and their effect on reading acquisition. *Reading Research Quarterly*, 1973–1974, *9*, 526–554.

Barringer, C., & Gholson, B.   Effects of type and combination of feedback upon conceptual learning of children: Implications for research in academic learning. *Review of Educational Research*, 1979, *49*, 459–478.

Becker, W. C.   Teaching reading and language to the disadvantaged—what we have learned from field research. *Harvard Educational Review*, 1977, *47*, 518–543.

Beez, W. V.   Influence of biased psychological reports on teacher behavior and pupil performance. In *Proceedings of the 76th Annual Convention of the American Psychological Association*, 1968.

Bennett, N., with Jordan, J., Long, G., & Wade, B.   *Teaching styles and pupil progress.* London: Open Books, 1976.

Bloom, B. S.   *Human characteristics and school learning.* New York: McGraw-Hill, 1976.

Boydell, D.   Teacher-pupil contact in junior classrooms. *British Journal of Educational Psychology*, 1974, *44*, 313–18.

Brophy, J. *Recent research on teaching.* East Lansing: Institute for Research on Teaching, Michigan State University, 1980.

Brophy, J. E., & Evertson, C. M. *Learning from teaching: A developmental perspective.* Boston: Allyn & Bacon, 1976.

Brophy, J., & Good, T. Teacher behavior and student learning. In M. C. Wittrock (Ed.), *Third handbook of research on teaching.* Chicago: Rand McNally, in press.

Brown, W. E. *The influence of student information on the formation of teacher expectancy.* Unpublished doctoral dissertation, Indiana University, 1969.

California State Department of Education, *California school effectiveness study: The first year, 1974–75.* Sacramento: California State Department of Education, 1977.

Carnine, D. The effects of two teacher presentation rates on off-task behavior. *Journal of Applied Behavior Analysis,* 1976, *9,* 199–206.

Carnine, D., & Fink, W. T. A comparative study of the effects of individual versus unison responding on the word reading performance of preschool children. In *Technical report 1978–2, formative research on direct instruction* (Follow-through project). Eugene: University of Oregon, 1978.

Carroll, J. B. A model of school learning. *Teachers College Record,* 1963, *64,* 723–732.

Carter, R. M. *Locus of control and teacher expectancy as related to achievement of young school children.* Unpublished doctoral dissertation, Indiana University, 1969.

Chall, J. S. *An analysis of textbooks in relation to declining SAT scores* (A Report to the Advisory Panel on Score Decline sponsored by the College Entrance Examination Board). March 1977.

Chall, J. S., & Feldman, S. First-grade reading: An analysis of the interactions of professed methods, teacher implementation, and child background. *Reading Teacher,* 1966, *19,* 569–575.

Chang, S. S., & Raths, J. The schools contribution to the cumulating deficit. *Journal of Educational Research,* 1971, *64,* 272–276.

Cobb, J. A. Relationship of discrete classroom behavior to fourth grade academic achievement. *Journal of Educational Psychology.* 1972, *63,* 74–80.

Cobb, J. A., & Hops, H. Effects of academic survival skill training on low achieving first graders. *Journal of Educational Research,* 1973, *67,* 108–113.

Coker, H., Lorentz, C. W., & Coker, J. *Teacher behavior and student outcomes in the Georgia study.* Paper presented to the American Educational Research Association annual meeting, Boston, 1980.

Comber, L., & Keeves, J. P. *Science education in nineteen countries.* New York: Wiley, 1973.

Day, J. D. Teaching summarization skills. Unpublished doctoral dissertation, University of Illinois, 1980.

Denham, C., & Lieberman, A. (Eds.) *Time to learn.* Washington, D.C.: National Institute of Education, U.S. Government Printing Office, 1980.

Durkin, D. What classroom observation reveals about reading comprehension instruction. *Reading Research Quarterly,* 1978–1979, *14,* 481–533.

Durkin, D. Reading comprehension instruction in five basal reading series. *Reading Research Quarterly,* 1981, *16,* 515–544.

Emmer, E., Evertson, C., Sanford, J., Clements, B., & Worsham, M. *Organizing and managing the junior high classroom.* Austin: Research and Development Center for Teacher Education, University of Texas, 1982.

Engelmann, S., & Carnine, D. *Theory of instruction: Principles and applications.* New York: Irvington Publishers Inc., 1982.

Evertson, C., Emmer, E., Clements, B., Sanford, J., Worsham, M., & Williams, E. *Organizing and managing the elementary school classroom.* Austin: Research and Development Center for Teacher Education, University of Texas, 1981.

Filby, N. N., & Cahen, L. S. *Teaching behavior and academic learning time in the A-B period* (Tech. Note V–lb). San Francisco: Far West Laboratory for Educational Research and Development, 1977.

Fisher, C. W., Filby, N. N., Marliave, R., Cahen, L. S., Dishaw, M. M., Moore, J. E., & Berliner, D. C. *Teaching behaviors, academic learning time, and student achievement: Final report of phase III–B, beginning teacher evaluation study.* San Francisco: Far West Educational Laboratory for Educational Research and Development, 1978.

Fitzpatrick, K. *Successful management strategies for the secondary classroom.* Downers Grove, Ill.: 1981.

Gabrys, R. E. *Training teachers to be businesslike and warm.* Paper presented to the annual meeting of the American Educational Research Association, San Francisco, April 1979. Oneonta, N.Y.: Department of Education, State University College.

Gall, M. D., Ward, B. A., Berliner, D. C., Cahen, L. S., Crown, K. A., Elashoff, J. D., Stanton, G. C., & Winne, P. H. *The effects of teacher use of questioning techniques on student achievement and attitude.* San Francisco: Far West Laboratory for Educational Research and Development, 1975.

Good, T. L., & Beckerman, T. M. Time on task: A naturalistic study in sixth grade classrooms. *Elementary School Journal,* 1978, *78,* 192–201.

Good, T. L., & Grouws, D. A. The Missouri mathematics effectiveness project. *Journal of Educational Psychology,* 1979, *71,* 143–155.

Good, T. L., Grouws, D. A., & Beckerman, T. M. Curriculum pacing: Some empirical data in mathematics. *Journal of Curriculum Studies,* 1978, *10,* 75–82.

Grobe, R. P., & Pettibone, T. J. Effect of instructional pace on student attentiveness. *Journal of Educational Research,* 1976, *70,* 131–134.

Guthrie, J. T., Martuza, V., & Seifert, M. *Impacts on instructional time in reading.* Newark, Del.: International Reading Association, 1976.

Hansen, J. The effects of inference training and practice on young children's reading comprehension, *Reading Research Quarterly,* 1981, *16,* 391–417.

Harris, A. J., Morrison, C., Serwer, B. L., & Gold, L. *A continuation of the CRAFT project.* New York: City University of the City of New York, 1968.

Hops, H., & Cobb, J. A. Initial investigation into academic survival skill training, direct instruction, and first grade achievement. *Journal of Educational Psychology,* 1974, *66,* 533–548.

Husen, T. *International study of achievement in mathematics: Comparison of twelve countries* (Vols. 1, 2). New York: Wiley, 1967.

Jackson, P. W. *Life in classrooms.* New York: Holt, Rinehart & Winston, 1968.

Jones, B. F. *Embedding structural information and strategy instructions within mastery learning units.* Paper presented at the annual meeting of the International Reading Association, St. Louis, May 1980.

Jorgenson, G. W., Klein, N., & Kumar, V. K. Achievement and behavior correlates of matched levels of student ability and material difficulty. *Journal of Educational Research,* 1977, *71,* 100–103.

Kean, M., Summers, A., Ravietz, M., & Farber, I. *What works in reading.* Philadelphia: School District of Philadelphia, 1979.

Kounin, J. S. *Discipline and group management in classrooms.* New York: Holt, Rinehart & Winston, 1970.

Kounin, J. S., & Gump, P. F. Signal systems of lesson settings and the task-related behavior of preschool children. *Journal of Educational Psychology,* 1974, *66,* 554–562.

Lahaderne, H. Attitudinal and intellectual correlates of achievement: A study of four classrooms. *Journal of Educational Psychology,* 1968, *59,* 320–324.

Luce, S., & Hoge, R. Relations among teacher rankings, pupil-teacher interactions, and academic achievement. *American Educational Research Journal,* 1978, *15,* 498–500.

Maryland State Department of Education. *Process evaluation: A comprehensive study of outliers.* College Park: Center for Educational Research and Development, University of Maryland, 1978.

McDonald, F. J. *Research on teaching and its implications for policy-making: Report on phase II of the beginning teacher evaluations study.* Paper presented at the conference on Research on Teacher Effects: An examination by policy-makers and researchers, sponsored by the National Institute of Education, School of Education, University of Texas, Austin, November 1975. Princeton, N.J.: Educational Testing Service.

McKenzie, G. Effects of questions and testlike events on achievement and on-task behavior in a classroom concept learning presentation. *Journal of Educational Research,* 1979, *72,* 348–350.

McKenzie, G., & Henry, N. Effects of testlike events on on-task behavior, test anxiety, and achievement in classroom rule-learning tasks. *Journal of Educational Psychology,* 1979, *71,* 370–374.

Medley, D. M. *The research base for teacher education.* Washington, D.C.: American Association of Colleges for Teacher Education, 1978.

Miller, R., & Hess, R. The effects upon students' motivation of fit between student ability and the level of difficulty of CAI programs. Stanford, Calif.: Center for Research and Development in Teaching, Stanford University, 1972.

Mueller, F., Light, J., & Reynolds, L. *The effects of two styles of tutoring on academic performance.* Paper presented to the annual meeting of the American Educational Research Association, April 1971.

Patchings, W., Kameenui, E., Colvin, G., & Carnine, D. An investigation of the effects of using direct instruction procedures to teach three critical reading skills to skill deficient grade 5 children. Unpublished manuscript, University of Oregon, 1979.

Paulsen, J., & Macken, M. Report on the level of achievement in CAI reading programs. Palo Alto, Calif.: Computer Curriculum Corporation, 1978.

Peterson, P. L. Direct instruction reconsidered. In P. Peterson & H. J. Walbert (Eds.), *Research on teaching.* Berkeley, Calif.: McCutchan, 1979.

Raphael, T. E. *The effect of metacognitive strategy awareness training on students' question answering behavior.* Unpublished doctoral dissertation, University of Illinois, Urbana, 1980.

Rosenshine, B. *Teaching behaviours and student achievement.* Windsor, Eng.: National Foundation for Educational Research in England and Wales, 1971.

Samuels, S. J., & Turnure, J. E. Attention and reading achievement in first-grade boys and girls. *Journal of Educational Psychology,* 1976, *68,* 29–32.

Scott, J., & Bushell, D., Jr. The length of teacher contacts and students' off task behavior. *Journal of Applied Behavior Analysis,* 1974, *7,* 39–44.

Shutes, R. E. *Verbal behaviors and instructional effectiveness.* Unpublished doctoral dissertation, Stanford University, 1969.

Singer, H., & Donlon, D. Active comprehension: Problem-solving schema with question generation for comprehension of complex short stories. *Reading Research Quarterly,* 1982, *17,* 166–186.

Smith, M. L., & Glass, G. V. Meta-analysis of research on class size and its relationship to attitudes and instruction. *American Educational Research Journal,* 1980, *17,* 419–435.

Smith, N. M. *Time allotments and achievement in social studies.* Unpublished manuscript, John F. Kennedy Institute for Habilitation, Johns Hopkins University, 1976.

Soar, R. S. *Follow-through classroom process measurement and pupil growth (1970–71): Final report.* Gainesville: College of Education, University of Florida, 1973.

Soar, R. S., & Soar, R. M. *Classroom behavior, pupil characteristics, and pupil growth for the school year and the summer.* Gainesville: Institute for Development of Human Resources, College of Education, University of Florida, 1973.

Solomon, D., & Kendall, A. J. *Children in classrooms.* New York: Praeger, 1979.

Stallings, J., Cory, R., Fairweather, J., & Needles, M.   *Early childhood education classroom evaluation.* Menlo Park, Calif.: SRI International, 1977.

Stallings, J. A., & Kaskowitz, D.   *Follow-through classroom observation evaluation, 1972–73.* Menlo Park, Calif.: Stanford Research Institute, 1974.

Stallings, J., Needles, M., & Stayrook, N.   *How to change the process of teaching basic reading skills in secondary schools.* Menlo Park, Calif.: SRI International, 1979.

Stanford Program on Teacher Effectiveness.   *A factorially designed experiment on teacher structuring, soliciting, and reacting.* Stanford, Calif.: Stanford Center for Research and Development in Teaching, 1976.

Tikunoff, W., Berliner, D. C., & Rist, R. C.   *An ethnographic study of the forty classrooms of the beginning teacher evaluation study known sample* (Tech. Rep. No. 75–10–5). San Francisco: Far West Laboratory for Educational Research and Development, 1975.

Venezky, R. L., & Winfield, L.   Schools that succeed beyond expectations in teaching reading. (University of Delaware Studies on Education, Tech. Rep. No. 1). Newark, Del.: University of Delaware, August 1979.

Walker, D. F., & Schaffarzick, J.   Comparing curricula. *Review of Educational Research,* 1974, *44,* 83–112.

Welch, W. W., & Bridgham, R. G.   Physics achievement gains as a function of teaching duration. *School Science and Mathematics,* 1968, *68,* 449–454.

Winne, P. H.   Experiments relating teachers' use of higher cognitive questions to student achievement. *Review of Educational Research,* 1979, *49,* 13–50.

Witcher, C., Skillman, L., & Becker, W. C.   *Direct instruction model guidebook for teachers* (Follow-through project). Eugene: Division of Teacher Education, University of Oregon, 1977.

24 MANAGING INSTRUCTION

Wayne Otto, Anne Wolf, and
Roger G. Eldridge

R eading instruction involves not only selecting and presenting a curriculum
to students, but also structuring a context in which teaching and learning
can occur. Setting up and maintaining a total environment—which includes curricular, organizational, and instructional aspects—either for one student or for
many is *managing instruction*. Approaches to the topic of managing instruction
are likely to stress either pragmatic or philosophical concerns. Pragmatic concerns
are often directed toward finding an optimal size for instructional groups. While
such a focus for an individual study may seem mundane or even simplistic, the
goal—to discover cost-effective environments for teaching and learning—has both
practical and theoretical significance. Philosophical concerns address such questions as whether the perceived needs of individuals or the structure of subject
matter ought to be the basis for planning and for managing instruction. Questions
like these are raised frequently when the issues related to the return-to-basics
movement or the debate about setting minimum competencies are considered.
But whatever the emphasis, the underlying quest in the literature on managing
instruction is to give proper consideration to value systems, type and structure
of content, the psychology of individual differences, and the structures and processes of effective schooling in order to enhance the learning of individual students. Americans continue to "value the individual person more than all else"
(Sartain, 1968, p. 197), and this overriding fact sets the tone for virtually all of
the work that relates to managing instruction.

Our purpose in this chapter is threefold. First, we provide a context and
a perspective for viewing the topic of managing instruction. The historical overview that is briefly developed in the section that follows provides a context for
considering the topic. Second, we offer a selective examination of the literature
related to the management of instruction in reading. The review is necessarily
selective because the literature is vast, including not only reports of empirical-
experimental studies and descriptions of promising and exemplary programs,

but also many exhortatory essays. We emphasize the empirical-experimental, acknowledge the descriptive, and try to restrain the exhortatory in order to provide a view of the literature in bold strokes. Furthermore, we attempt to limit the review to matters of administration and teaching and to keep away from the literature on learning. At the same time, we acknowledge our inability to limit the discussion strictly to reading instruction. Reading ought to be taught and must be applied in almost all areas of study, so the management of instruction must be considered in relation to the entire school operation. Third, we draw some conclusions and suggest some directions for further study and consideration.

CONTEXT AND PERSPECTIVE

From the very beginning, Americans have been inclined to value the individual student and to seek ways to accommodate the needs and aspirations of individuals in the practice of schooling. In colonial times, the teaching of reading, which was both a means and an end of religious training, was handled in dame schools, in village reading and writing schools, or through tutoring in homes and churches (French, 1964). By the middle of the nineteenth century, due largely to increased immigration, the numbers of students in schools had increased and the quality of teaching had decreased to a point where people like Horace Mann had begun to seek ways to make improvements (Tanner & Tanner, 1980). The basic question at that time remains as the basic question to this day: Given that there are more students who need to learn to read than there are teachers to teach them, what is the best way to organize students, teacher, and the curriculum—to manage instruction—for the effective teaching of reading? We will examine that question more closely in a moment, but first consider the historical context that has shaped both the question and tentative answers.

Historical Highlights

The generalizations that follow are historical highlights in the sense that they sum up major trends related to the management of reading instruction. Comprehensive historical reviews by Nila Banton Smith (1965), Mitford Mathews (1966), and H. A. Robinson (1977) are available. Also available are shorter, more specialized reviews by Sartain (1968), who focuses on organizational patterns, and by Sowards (1969) and Austin, (1969), who deal with elementary and with secondary schooling respectively.

- Managing instruction became an issue of concern in the mid-1800s when educators began to seek more efficient ways to deal with larger and more diverse student populations.
- The graded plan of school organization, developed in Prussia and advocated by Horace Mann, was soon adopted in urban schools throughout America and it continues as the most pervasive organizational plan in the nation's schools.
- Closely following the adoption of the graded-school organization, graded series of readers were developed to assist teachers with the systematic teaching of reading. Over the years these series of basal readers have been almost univer-

sally adopted and they have been made more and more comprehensive. Taken together, the basal reader series offered by the full array of publishers undoubtedly are the most potent and pervasive force in reading instruction in the nation's schools today.

- Even as graded schools and graded readers have gained in prominence, educators have, almost from the very beginning, struggled to break the lockstep that often accompanies a heavy-handed application of the graded approach. By the end of the nineteenth century, concerned educators were attempting to differentiate curriculums for different learners, to adapt instruction to individuals' progress rates, and to train specialized personnel to facilitate or augment the work of classroom teachers. These early efforts have culminated in the innovative plans for managing instruction that are used in many schools.

- Before World War I, reading instruction was virtually the exclusive business of the elementary schools. After the war, probably because the waste and inefficiency of limited literacy began to be fully recognized, the need for reading instruction at the upper levels of formal schooling and for other groups—for example, out-of-school adult illiterates and literate adults with special needs— was acknowledged and resources began to be assigned. This trend has continued to where, today, reading instruction may be directed to any population from preschool through adult.

- Between 1920 and 1935 the practice of forming three groups for reading instruction—generally students who are achieving below, at, and above grade level—was introduced and almost universally adopted in the nation's classrooms. The three-group plan remained dominant into the 1950s, when alternative plans for targeting instruction—for example, individualized instruction, open classrooms with learning centers for reading, and a variety of schemes for team teaching or for cross-class grouping—began to be more widely used. While the alternative plans continue to be refined, adopted, and adapted, the three-group plan continues as a mainstay for managing reading instruction in many schools.

- Prior to the mid-twentieth century, the major events related to managing instruction in reading were the introduction of grade-level organization in the schools and the development of basal readers. The period since mid-century can be characterized as a time when alternative proposals for managing instruction abound and, paradoxically, innovation is commonplace. Yet even as the limitations of traditional practices are recognized, as new practices are proposed, and as innovation is valued almost for its own sake, the traditional practices linger on. Schools continue to be organized by grade levels, students continue to be assigned to one of three groups for all or most of their instruction in reading, and teachers continue to rely on basal readers to teach reading.

The Problem in Perspective

Now, with some of the major historical trends identified, consider again the question of how best to organize students and teachers for the effective teaching of reading. The question has an easy answer: put one student and one teacher together and let teaching proceed through one-to-one tutoring. Such an arrangement gives the teacher maximum freedom (a) to emphasize either techniques for dealing with individual differences or techniques for presenting the curriculum in a most effective manner or (b) to strive for some reasonable balance of curriculum- and student-centered concerns. The teaching of social behaviors and values aside, the implicit goal of most schemes for managing reading instruction is to come as close as possible to one-on-one tutoring. We do not question the wisdom or the virtue of the goal; we simply acknowledge it. Unfortunately, the goal itself presents a problem insofar as managing instruction is concerned because the society has not and is not likely to commit sufficient resources to make one-on-one teaching an attainable goal.

A more workable answer to the question of how best to organize students and teachers for reading instruction is: organize the school and the classroom so as to permit maximum flexibility for dealing with student- and curriculum-centered variables. This answer is adequate insofar as it implies an attainable goal. But, it is inadequate in that it says little about bringing student and teacher characteristics, curricular aspects and issues, and situational factors into a reasonable juxtaposition. Fortunately, these are considerations that have already received some attention in the literature and they deserve to receive continued attention as techniques for managing instruction are refined. We have organized these considerations into three categories: studies of organizational plans, studies of classroom behaviors, and studies of teachers' planning and decision making. Our categories correspond roughly to those suggested by Mitzel (1960)—categories of context, process, and presage variables—as a scheme for classifying teacher effectiveness criteria.

STUDIES OF ORGANIZATIONAL PLANS

Common sense suggests that some ways of grouping students and teachers, organizing the curriculum, and organizing the classroom should be more effective than others. Consequently, there is a substantial literature that describes a variety of organizational schemes and attempts to examine their effectiveness. While the literature ranges as far afield as the effects of reorganizing school districts through federally ordered desegregation, this review is limited to studies of organizational plans at the school and classroom level. Wherever possible, we cite previous reviews and, in general, studies published before 1969 are not cited. This section is organized, first, to consider the concept of grouping and to review studies of the effects of homogeneous and heterogeneous grouping plans. Next, we assess the effectiveness of schemes for assigning students to teachers for reading instruction. Then we survey alternatives for organizing the reading curriculum for instructional purposes. Finally, we discuss specific organizational approaches, such as learning centers and tutoring, that are intended to help teachers manage reading instruction.

The literature on organizational plans for managing reading instruction includes both experimental and descriptive studies. The typical experimental study is conducted in an elementary school and it is designed to evaluate the effectiveness of one or more organizational plans in terms of students' reading achievement and, perhaps, their attitudes or other affective outcomes. Both treatment-only and control-group designs are common. An example of a typical descriptive study is a survey of teachers', administrators', or perhaps students' perceptions of one or more organizational plans.

Grouping Students: Homogeneity and Heterogeneity

The graded school brings together students who are approximately the same age and in roughly similar developmental stages. Yet, there are vast individual differences in reading achievement at any grade level, and many educators believe that students ought to be taught to read in relatively stable homogeneous groups. Reading achievement and cognitive ability are the most common criteria for homogeneous grouping; but plans range from complex arrangements for grouping students across grade levels to simpler, and much more common, arrangements for identifying multiple groups within single classrooms. Whatever the plan, the intent of homogeneous grouping is to bring together students who are more nearly alike than students in the entire population. The purpose is to facilitate planning and instruction in order to accommodate students' individual needs and to allow them to experience learning with others with similar characteristics (Esposito, 1973; Heathers, 1972).

Critics claim that homogeneous grouping provides little more than a security blanket for teachers. Grouping students on the basis of one characteristic, say, achievement or ability, gives no assurance of similarity on other characteristics, such as skill development or learning rate; but teachers may be tempted to ignore the remaining differences. Thus, the critics argue that deliberate heterogeneous grouping encourages teachers to be more sensitive to individual needs and provides a more democratic and realistic learning environment for students (Esposito, 1973). Plans for heterogeneous grouping vary as widely as those for homogeneous grouping, ranging from simple random assignment of students to self-contained classrooms to elaborate arrangements for cross-grade grouping. A popular but overly simplistic view associates homogeneous grouping with the basal reading program and heterogeneous grouping with individualized reading. In practice, there is no reliable association between the way students are grouped and the way their curriculum is ultimately organized.

Studies of homogeneous grouping.   Much of the research on homogeneous grouping for reading instruction has focused on an approach called the Joplin Plan. Interest in this specific arrangement, exemplified in the schools of Joplin, Missouri, was nurtured during the late 1950s by feature articles in popular magazines. In the Joplin Plan, intermediate-grade students are homogeneously grouped for reading instruction without regard for their grade placement; each group includes students from different grades who are similar in achievement level. Research on the Joplin Plan has been reviewed by Cushenberry (1967–1968) and Newport (1967). Both reviewers observed that studies with treatment-only designs favored the Joplin Plan, while studies with control groups generally shared no consistent differences in achievement when ability grouping was carried out through the Joplin Plan or within self-contained classrooms.

Eberwein (1972) compared two within-class grouping patterns: the traditional three-group ability plan and one that allowed for more flexibility in grouping students on criteria other than achievement. Even though the investigator provided considerable help in implementing the flexible arrangement, there were no significant achievement differences; but there was evidence that fewer students in the groups formed more flexibly were ignored by their peers. Wilkinson and Calculator (1982) reported differences in responses to requests for information in peer-directed homogeneous reading groups. Students in the low-ability group were less likely than students in the high-ability group to have their requests responded to appropriately by other students. Consequently, the low-ability-group students had more difficulty completing their assignments. More specifically, the students in the low-ability group were less likely to receive information regarding the content of the academic assignment and were less likely to obtain appropriate responses regarding the procedures and materials. Wilkinson and Calculator concluded that differences in the communicative processes within homogenous groups may serve to maintain initial differences in both reading achievement and effective use of language. Doucette and St. Pierre (1977) examined school-related variables and reading achievement scores, and found no relationship between ability grouping and gains in reading achievement.

Some reviewers of the general literature on homogeneous grouping arrangements have concluded that on the average there are no significant gains or losses in achievement when students are homogeneously grouped but that benefits for students in high-achievement groups are offset by losses for students in low-achievement groups (Esposito, 1973; Heathers, 1972; Justman, 1968; Spache and Spache, 1977). These reviews reflect findings from the early 1970s. Studies of homogeneous grouping arrangements have not been published regularly since that time. More recently, though, Glass (1976) has developed the methodology of meta-analysis to examine the magnitude of experimental effects. Kulik and Kulik (1982) used the technique to reanalyze 52 studies of homogeneous grouping arrangements, where the students were separated on the basis of ability level as measured by an IQ test, performance on a reading test, or past achievement. The results of the meta-analysis indicate that (a) grouping generally has small effects on student achievement, (b) high-ability-grouped students benefit more in terms of achievement gains, and (c) ability grouping has only trivial effects on the achievement of average and below-average students.

Hiebert (1983) says the problem with the existing research is that most of the studies that compare ability reading groups to other organizational schemes fail to consider the influence of different schemes on children of different levels. She examined studies in instructional and social psychology to determine how reading experiences differ for members of different ability groups and what effects any differences have on reading performance. While she found evidence that some experiences do differ according to ability level, she suggests that it would be premature to make unequivocal statements about the nature, effects or appropriateness of these differences. Hiebert says that one conclusive statement can be made: ability groups provide the primary context for most of the classroom reading experiences of many children.

Hart (1982) takes a somewhat different position. On the basis of an ethnographic study of the social organization of reading instruction over several grade levels in one elementary school, Hart claims that the academic characteristics of individuals are not the basis for reading-class formation. Instead, the dimensions of social organization—grades and ability levels—are used to form classes that cut across academic distinctions among individuals. The result is that reading classes formed by grade are neither the purposeful mixing of students with similar academic interests nor the purposeful separation of students with contrasting academic interests. Hart claims, therefore, that the grade dimension of the social organization for reading obscures academic differences.

In order to examine the processes by which the internal organization of schools affects students, Eder (1981) analyzed the verbal and nonverbal behaviors of students during reading-group lessons in a single classroom. Eder concluded that homogeneous grouping compounds initial learning problems by placing children who have learning problems in the same group. That is, students who are likely to have difficulty learning are assigned to groups where the social context is likely to be less conducive to learning.

If the number of special programs for the learning disabled, handicapped, and gifted continues to increase, investigators may give more of their attention to the variables and the effects of homogeneous grouping arrangements.

Studies of heterogeneous grouping.   Most studies of heterogeneous grouping practices have focused on nongraded arrangements and open classroom plans, which are intended to facilitate individualization by eliminating the grade level, curricular, and physical constraints of the traditional self-contained, graded classroom. Heathers (1972) defined nongrading as any approach to individualizing education that allows students to progress at their own rate by eliminating conventional grade leveling. In his review of the early literature on nongrading, he found conflicting and inconsistent results. Reviews of studies related to the use of the nongraded approach since the mid-1970s express views similar to those reported in two recent studies by Milburn (1981) and Way (1981). Both investigators suggest that there are no significant differences in basic skill achievement when children in multiage classrooms are compared to children in single-age classrooms, except in the area of vocabulary building. In vocabulary building, students in multiage classrooms show greater achievement than children in single-age classrooms.

Since Heathers's review, the *multiunit elementary school* has been adopted as an approach to nongraded education (Popkewitz, Tabachnick, & Wehlage, 1982). In a multiunit elementary school, students in kindergarten through Grade 3 are assigned to one or more primary units, each with a team of teachers who are jointly responsible for instruction and who may be supported by student teachers and aides. Students in Grades 4, 5, and 6 are similarly grouped (Lipham, Klausmeier, & Walter, 1977). Studies of multiunit schools have been focused primarily on organizational-administrative arrangements or on the effectiveness of these arrangements in conjunction with adoption of individualized instructional programming (Klausmeier, 1977). A study by Ironside and Conaway (1979) suggests that the multiunit label is applied to a wide range of actual practices. While some multiunit schools are committed to the underlying concept of nongraded individualization, others continue to function as a collection of graded classrooms (Popkewitz, Tabachnick and Wehlage, 1982). Insofar as reading achievement is concerned, the impact of the multiunit school is not yet clear.

The term *open education*—or *open school* or *classroom*—is also often associated with schemes for heterogeneous, individualized teaching. The term defies tidy definition, but the following statements seem generally to be accepted. Open education is characterized by sensitivity to the uniqueness of each child. The child is accepted as a significant decision maker who, in contrast to traditional expectations, participates in choosing goals, selecting materials, and planning his or her own activities (Walberg & Thomas, 1972; C. S. Weinstein, 1979). Student participation and independence are encouraged by an informal classroom organization that allows students freedom of movement and easy access to learning materials.

Horwitz (1979) reviewed approximately 200 studies of affective and cognitive outcomes associated with open education. About half the studies showed no significant differences in academic achievement, and the rest showed mixed results. Horwitz concluded that, in general, open education neither enhanced nor depressed achievement scores. His conclusion was similar for most of the affective outcomes, but students' attitudes toward school and cooperation were generally better in open classrooms.

Horwitz tabulated the number of studies with significant results favoring either open or traditional education and the number of studies with nonsignificant or inconclusive results. Such an approach is sometimes called the box score or voting method, in contrast to methods which attempt to evaluate the quality of the research or determine the magnitude of the experimental effects. Peterson (1979) used Glass's (1978) methodology to reanalyze 45 studies of open education. She concluded, in line with Horwitz, that traditional instruction appears on the average to result in slightly higher student achievement, but that open education may foster slightly more creativity, independence, and positive attitudes toward schools and teachers. Student characteristics, such as ability and personality, appear to affect how well individuals perform in either traditional or open classrooms.

One likely cause for the many inconsistent and nonsignificant findings on open education is that the term is applied to such a wide range of practices. Horwitz (1979) notes that the term is as often applied to nothing more than an architectural concept of open space as to the quality of student-teacher interactions. Bealing (1972) concluded from a survey of British junior-level teachers that many of the teachers who claimed to be working in open and informally organized classrooms actually controlled seating and student choice of activities in quite traditional ways.

While the research on student grouping plans is characterized by many nonsignificant and inconclusive findings, there is some evidence that achievement and attitude may be related to student grouping arrangements.

Assigning Students to Teachers

Whether students are grouped homogeneously or heterogeneously, they need to be assigned to teachers for instruction. At the elementary level, the most common organizational plan is the self-contained classroom, where a subject-area generalist has responsibility for teaching all, or almost all, subjects including reading to all the students in the classroom group. Research has rarely been focused on the effectiveness of the self-contained classroom per se, although it is the most commonly employed control treatment in studies of other organizational arrangements. At the secondary level, the most common organizational plan is departmentalization, where reading is taught as a separate subject, usually by a trained reading teacher or specialist who works with several groups of students each day. While educators have experimented with alternatives to these typical arrangements in both elementary and secondary schools, virtually all the research pertaining to reading instruction has been done at the elementary level.

Departmentalizing instruction in the upper elementary grades became popular during the 1960s. Proponents claimed that, with departmentalization, teachers with responsibility for reading instruction would have the time and energy to deal effectively with the requisite special methods and materials. Critics felt, on the other hand, that departmentalized teaching would be less student centered and coherent than instruction in self-contained classrooms. Studies of departmentalized teaching in upper elementary schools have produced inconsistent results regarding achievement outcomes and no evidence of adverse effects on students' personal development (Heathers, 1972).

In the 1970s, there was virtually no research on departmentalizing elementary reading instruction. Lamme's (1976) study is an exception. She examined students' reading habits as they moved from self-contained classrooms in Grade 4 to departmentalized instruction in Grades 5 and 6. Students read more books and showed fewer differences in attitude in the departmentalized situation. One cannot conclude, however, that departmentalization *caused* the change because organizational plans and grade level were confounding variables.

Like departmentalization, team teaching was in vogue with many educators during the 1960s. The term *team teaching* may refer to a variety of arrangements in which teachers share responsibility for planning instruction, but in most instances they do not teach jointly. When Heathers (1972) reviewed the literature on team teaching, he reported that few adequately controlled studies had been published. We did not locate any subsequent studies of team teaching in reading, but we did observe that interest seems to have shifted to more complex cooperative teaching arrangements, such as the multiunit school, which typically incorporate some scheme for nongrading the school and for introducing curriculum innovations as well as shared responsibility for planning instruction.

Taken together, the studies of organizational plans for assigning students to teachers suggest that it does not make much difference whether students are taught reading in self-contained, departmentalized, or team-taught classes.

Organizing the Reading Curriculum

Reading teachers are responsible for a very complex curriculum, and over the years they have devised a variety of ways to organize that curriculum and to present it to students. In this review, we identify three major patterns for organizing the reading curriculum, which we refer to as (a) the basal reader system, (b) classic individualized reading, and (c) systematic individualized reading. We use these categories more for convenience than for descriptive adequacy. While each one is popularly associated with specific teaching methodologies, they are distinguished more by the way the curriculum is structured than by the specific content that is taught.

The basal reader system.   Most American reading instruction is organized around a basal reader series (Spache & Spache, 1977). Given their present prominence, it is difficult to remember that basal readers are a relatively recent innovation, having become popular only in the 1840s (Smith, 1965). A basal reader series is characterized by its comprehensiveness. The typical series not only structures a total curriculum for teaching reading in kindergarten through Grade 6 or 8, but also provides all of the materials—readers, tests, workbooks, and reinforcement activities—needed for planning and carrying out instruction. Proponents of basal reader series claim that students benefit from the systematic and comprehensive organization of the reading curriculum. Critics claim that the series promote and encourage lockstep group instruction. Yet, despite the widespread use of basal readers, few studies have been done to test the claims of either advocates or critics. The studies that compare basal reader centered and individualized instruction are included in our discussion of classic individualized reading.

Classic individualized reading.   During the 1960s, when American educators were proposing organizational alternatives to homogeneous grouping and self-contained classrooms, reading specialists were introducing an alternative to the basal readers. The plan was called *individualized reading.* We call it *classic individualized reading* because many of its concepts and principles are now in general use. In contrast to the highly structured, teacher-directed instruction implicit in the basal reader approach, classic individualized reading is based on students' self-selection of materials and self-pacing of the reading experience. The teacher, instead of meeting with prescribed groups each day, meets as necessary with students in individual conferences to assess progress and teach any needed skills. The emphasis of classic individualized reading on student self-direction and spontaneous instruction is like that of open education.

There have been few studies of the effects of individualized reading on achievement and attitudes and the results of these studies have been mixed. Studies with treatment-only designs have favored classic individualized reading programs (Corley & Lewis, 1975; Warner, 1976) and so have comparisons of classic individualized reading and basal reader centered instruction (Greaney & Clark, 1975; R. H. Johnson, 1964; Milford, 1976; Warren & Coston, 1975). A comparison of classic individualized reading instruction with a diagnostic-prescriptive approach to instruction, however, favored the diagnostic-prescriptive plan (Peniston, 1975); yet there is some evidence that the effects of classic individualized reading may vary with grade level (Mendenhall, 1976). Results of a survey conducted during the 1960s (Blakely & McKay, 1966) indicated that classic individualized reading was most often used by classroom teachers to supplement rather than to substitute for basal readers; but we found no evidence to update this observation. Research on classic individualized reading is too limited to draw any conclusions about its effects.

Systematic individualized reading.   A frequent criticism of both basal reading systems and classic individualized reading plans is that they do not effectively provide for the systematic development of skills. Students who are grouped together because they are "ready" for the same basal reader may not have mutual needs for specific-skill development, so the skill-development activities assigned to the group may or may not be in line with the needs of individual students.

The informal diagnosis and teaching conducted in the classic individualized reading conference may be too brief and haphazard to ensure systematic skill development. Thus, a third alternative for organizing the reading curriculum has evolved during the 1970s; we call it *systematic individualized reading*.

Systematic individualized reading is a relatively structured approach characterized by explicitly stated instructional objectives, systematic diagnosis and monitoring of individuals' skill development, and explicit teaching of specific skills to individuals and groups as unique and common needs are identified. Instructional planning is usually teacher directed, but in some programs, especially in the upper grades, students may self-select the objectives or materials they will work with. The reading laboratory, popular in high school, college, and adult reading programs, often provides the setting for organizing the wide array of materials needed to implement systematic individualized reading instruction.

Materials for implementing systematic individualized reading instruction vary considerably in comprehensiveness, ranging from teacher-made activities for developing a few selected skills to commercially published programs designed to cover all of the essential skills. The latter—which typically provide sequentially ordered objectives, criterion-references tests, teaching suggestions, and a record-keeping scheme—are commonly called *skills-management systems*. Among the best known skills management systems are *Individually Prescribed Instruction* (IPI), *Project PLAN* (Program for Learning in Accordance with Needs), *Fountain Valley Teacher Support System, High Intensity Reading*, the *Prescriptive Reading Inventory*, the *Croft Inservice Reading Program*, and the *Wisconsin Design for Reading Skill Development* (see Educational Products Information Exchange Institute, 1974; Hambleton, 1974; Otto & Chester, 1976; Rude, 1974; Stallard, 1977 for descriptions of these and other skills-management systems). Most of the currently published systems are designed for elementary school use; and many of the basal reader series now offer coordinated skills-management systems.

Advocates of management systems believe that sequentially organized objectives and continuous monitoring of students' skill development enable teachers to focus their instructional efforts on the specific needs of individuals (Otto & Chester, 1976). Critics are concerned that the approach may be too mechanistic and that by fractionating the reading process it may promote negative attitudes toward reading (Johnson & Johnson, 1974). The debate has been based more on beliefs than on data, and we found few studies that might help resolve the issue. The few studies that have been published seem to suggest that skills-management systems are effective in terms of students' achievement and self-concept (Cohen, 1977; Forte, 1975; Orr, 1973; Otto, 1977; Rakes, Linz, & Payton, 1974) and that the successful programs for individualizing instruction are characterized by specific behavioral objectives, ongoing diagnosis and prescriptions, and thorough recordkeeping (Criscuolo, 1977; Jackson, 1978; Wright & Kim, 1977). But these results are still too tenuous to support firm conclusions. Surveys of skills-management users (Iverson et al., 1977; White & Demos, 1977) suggest that while teachers have generally positive attitudes toward the approach, they feel pressured to cover too many objectives in too little time and are concerned about too much testing, overemphasis on skills, insufficient teaching materials, and the time required for recordkeeping. Kamm, White, and Morrison (1977) and Kamm and White (1979) studied the strategies employed in implementing a skills-management system and found that practices varied widely among schools and among teachers.

Organizing the Classroom

The difficulty of planning worthwhile reading instruction for a class of 20 to 30 students is well recognized. It is not surprising, then, that there has been considerable interest both in examining the effects of class size and teacher-student ratios on students' achievement and in searching out ways to enhance the efforts of individual teachers. We first review studies of class size and teacher-student ratios. Then, we examine the literature on learning centers, computer-assisted and computer-managed instruction, programmed reading, instructional kits, and tutoring programs.

Small classes and a low student-teacher ratio are generally believed to be desirable, if not necessary, requisites of effective teaching. Yet, the studies of class size and reading achievement have been inconclusive, with results that favor smaller classes in three studies (Furno & Collins, 1967; Meredith et al., 1977; Schieber et al., 1979) and that show no class-size effects in three others (Doucette & St. Pierre, 1977; Johnson & Garcia-Quintana, 1978; Madison Metropolitan School District, 1976). In a general review of the literature on class size, Johnson & Johnson (1974) concluded that only younger students benefit from smaller class size and that there is no evidence that a lower student-teacher ratio is associated with higher achievement. In three recent reanalyses of class-size studies employing the methodology of meta-analysis, Glass and Smith (1978, 1979) and Smith and Glass (1980) noted that favorable teacher effects as well as favorable student effects are associated with smaller classes.

The learning center, which can be operationally described as a setting which provides and encourages self-directed activities, is often recommended as a vehicle for attaining individualized instruction and an open classroom atmosphere. Two existing studies (Powell, 1978; White, 1976) show no difference in students' achievement when learning-center and teacher-directed approaches are compared. But a study by Kosinoski and Vockell (1978), which compared the academic gains of students who used classroom learning centers with students who did not use classroom learning centers, yielded contrasting results. Kosinoski and Vockell found that students who used learning centers scored higher in achievement than students who did not use the centers.

Computers may be used in the teaching of reading in either of two ways. Students may actually interact with the computer during instruction, which is called computer-assisted instruction, or CAI; or the computer may be used for diagnosis and recordkeeping, which is computer-managed instruction, or CMI. Studies of CAI have generally yielded favorable results, but cost and the expertise needed to develop instructional programs appear to have precluded wide use of CAI in elementary and secondary reading programs (Dillingofski, 1979). While CMI procedures may pose questions regarding the validity of tests of reading performance (Venezky, Bernard, Chicone & Leslie, 1975), computer-managed recordkeeping appears to be feasible (Spuck, Bozeman, & Lawrence, 1977).

We located only one published report on programmed reading and one on instructional kits. Hammill and Mattelman (1969) compared students' achievement after instruction with a basal reader alone, programmed reading alone, and programmed reading in conjunction with a basal reader series and found no significant differences. A Philippino study of self-learning kits, summarized in the *Reading Teacher* (1978), suggested that students need considerable skill in independent learning before they can benefit from using the kits.

Studies of a wide variety of tutoring programs, including peer tutoring, tutoring by older students, and tutoring by adult aides and volunteers have, with one exception (Patterson, 1976), demonstrated favorable results for the tutoring programs (Duff & Swick, 1974; Graves & Patberg, 1976; D. W. Johnson, 1980; Klann et al., 1972; Niedermeyer & Ellis, 1971; Richardson & Havlicek, 1975; Slavin, 1980). Allen (1976) provides a comprehensive review of peer tutoring and its effects on both tutors and tutees. Applying the methodology of meta-analysis Cohen, Kulik, and Kulik (1982) reanalyzed 65 studies of tutoring programs and found that, indeed, tutoring programs do have definite and positive effects on the academic performance and attitudes of those students who received tutoring as well as those students who served as tutors.

While class size and student-teacher ratio have not been shown to have significant effects on reading achievement, it appears that teachers can effectively utilize technology and additional personnel to enhance instruction.

Summary Observations

We introduced this review with the commonsense expectation that the way in which reading instruction is organized should affect students' achievement and attitudes. But our review of studies on grouping, on assigning students to teachers, and on organizing the curriculum and classroom for instruction shows many inconsistent and inconclusive results regarding organizational plans. We could infer from this that the way in which instruction is organized does not matter much in determining cognitive and affective outcomes. But we hesitate to draw such a conclusion because we found some serious methodological limitations in the studies we reviewed and because we found some evidence, for example in the studies on open education, that achievement and attitude are indeed related to specific organizational arrangements.

Attempting to generalize about the effects of organizational arrangements is hazardous because treatments are often inadequately described. Terms, such as *homogeneous grouping* and *individualized reading*, may be used with no further clarification of actual practices and procedures. The problem is compounded by evidence that in the real world of schools and classrooms even clearly defined treatments, such as the multiunit school, are implemented in a wide variety of ways.

Aspects of research design also limit the generalizability of many of the studies we reviewed. In many studies, the duration of the treatment was very short. It is unclear, then, whether nonsignificant results should be attributed to the ineffectiveness of the treatment itself or to its limited duration. And, of course, the common practice of collecting only general attitude and achievement data may fail to reveal important but more subtle treatment effects. Other problems are inherent in flawed research designs. Many studies were limited to the effects of single treatments and most ignored probable subject-treatment interactions.

Questionable statistical procedures pose still other problems. Simple gain scores were frequently used to assess treatments; and students were the most common unit of analysis when classes or schools would probably have been more defensible. Finally, and perhaps most serious of all, there are the problems posed by compounded treatment effects. For example, if open education is more effective than the traditional classroom in producing positive attitudes, should the effect be attributed to the open space in the room, to teachers' willingness to share decision making with students, to the increased individualization after the classroom environment was opened up, to the new principal who encouraged the change, or to some combination of one or more of these? In theory there are appropriate experimental designs for answering such questions; but such studies are very difficult and virtually impossible to do on a large scale (see Chapter 3 by Calfee & Piantowski for an example of how to conceptualize such a study within an empirical framework).

Studies of organizational plans hold great promise for improving the teaching of reading. So far that promise has not been realized in any significant sense. But if a better understanding of limitations and some tentative direction can be seen as positive signs, then there is reason to continue.

STUDIES OF CLASSROOM BEHAVIORS

In the section on organizational plans, we dealt mainly with studies of different plans and the direct effects of these plans on measures of student outcomes. In the present section, the focus of attention shifts from the *context and outcomes* of instruction to the *process and outcomes* of instruction. The common purpose of the studies reviewed here was to gather data on teachers' and students' classroom behaviors. Such data provide descriptions of teachers' instructional management strategies and bases for comparing the strategies of more and less effective teachers. Despite the fact that intensive investigation of teachers' and students' classroom behaviors is a relatively recent phenomenon, the literature is already quite extensive. Our citations are limited to comprehensive literature reviews and selected major studies. The review begins with the more extensive literature related to management effectiveness and concludes with descriptions of classroom management strategies.

Studies of Management Effectiveness

Although some scholars have concluded that teachers exert little influence on student performance (e.g., see Coleman, Campbell, & Hobson, 1966), the literature on teacher effectiveness reflects the belief that the behaviors of individual teachers do affect their students' achievement and attitudes (Barr & Dreeben, 1977; Berliner, 1976, 1980; Doyle, 1977; Dunkin & Biddle, 1974; Medley, 1979; Medley & Cook, 1980). The overall purpose of teacher-effectiveness studies is to identify the teaching strategies that distinguish between more and less effective teachers. That quest has involved a wide range of variables, from teacher warmth to questioning behavior; but this review is limited to management-related strategies, like grouping arrangements and monitoring of seatwork. We refer to the latter as *management-effectiveness* variables. See Rosenshine (1979, and this volume) for a comprehensive review of the process-product literature on classroom instruction.

The typical management-effectiveness study is initiated by identifying management behaviors that may be associated with instructional effectiveness. A group of more and less effective teachers is identified, usually on the basis of student achievement scores, and several observations are made in each teacher's classroom. Since a wide variety of activities go on during any lesson, an observation schedule is used to identify and code the frequency or duration of relevant behaviors. The resulting quantitative data are then correlated with student outcome measures, typically achievement scores, in order to identify behaviors that are associated with teacher effectiveness.

Dunkin and Biddle (1974) and Medley (1977) reviewed the major teacher-effectiveness studies of the 1960s and the early 1970s. The discussion here is based on their reviews and supplemented by the results of the more recent Phase III Beginning Teacher Effectiveness Study (BTES, Phase III) which we discuss in some detail because many of its results relate to management effectiveness (Fischer, Filby, Marliave, Cahen, Dishaw, Moore, & Berliner, 1978).

Berliner and his associates at the Far West Laboratory for Research and Development organized the BTES Phase III study around a central concept called *academic learning time* (ALT), which they defined as the amount of time students spend engaged in content-related tasks on which they make few errors. They predicted that teachers who structured their classrooms to encourage more ALT would be the more effective instructors. One purpose of the BTES Phase III study was to seek support for this prediction; another was to identify the classroom management strategies that are associated with students' greater task engagement. Observations were made in second- and fifth-grade classrooms during reading and mathematics instruction. Specifically designed skills tests, rather than general achievement batteries, were administered to assess students' academic performance, and multiple-regression analysis was used to determine which variables would best predict gain scores. The results confirmed the prediction; ALT was strongly and positively associated with student outcomes (Marliave, 1978). The data also showed that task-engagement rates varied with the way that instruction was organized. Generally engagement rates were higher for group settings and for teacher-supervised activities (Filby, 1978). In a related study, Tikunoff, Berliner and Rist (1975) trained ethnographers to make subjective qualitative observations in classrooms of more and less effective second- and fifth-grade teachers. Their results indicated that at both grade levels the more effective reading teachers were more in tune with students' individual needs, more successful in adjusting instruction to these needs, and more knowledgeable about the content they were teaching.

Synthesis of major findings.   Taken together, results from the BTES Phase III study and from other studies suggest that specific classroom management strategies tend to be associated with instructional effectiveness (Fischer, Berliner, Filby, Marliave, Cahen, & Dishaw, 1980). While we fully acknowledge the danger of overstating generalizations based on investigations of similar but not identical constructs and variables, we offer the following synthesis of major findings and supporting references:

- When students spend more time working on tasks that are relatively easy for them, achievement scores tend to be higher and attitudes may be more positive (Marliave, 1978).
- When teachers do more ongoing diagnosis and utilize the information in planning appropriate instruction, achievement scores tend to be higher (Rupley, 1977; Tikunoff et al., 1975).
- When teachers spend more time on academic instruction, achievement scores tend to be higher (Medley, 1977; Rosenshine, 1979).
- When teachers or other adults spend more time supervising students as they are working on independent assignments, achievement scores tend to be higher (Medley, 1977; Tikunoff et al., 1975).
- When teachers, peers, or other adults spend more time pacing the rate at which students work, engagement rates tend to be higher (Filby, 1978). Similarly, student engagement is higher when instruction is teacher centered (Dunkin & Biddle, 1974).
- When there is less deviant or disruptive behavior, achievement scores tend to be higher (Medley, 1977).
- When students are allowed more freedom to choose the activities they will work on, achievement scores tend to be lower (Medley, 1977; Rosenshine, 1979; Soar & Soar, 1979).
- When students work independently without direct supervision, achievement scores tend to be lower (Medley, 1977; Rosenshine, 1979; Stallings, 1975).

Viewed as a whole, these findings suggest that effective elementary teachers maintain a task-oriented, but positively supportive, classroom. Berliner and Rosenshine (1977) have labeled such teaching *directed instruction.*

Limitations of the management-effectiveness studies. Again, there is reasonable support for the above generalizations, but they must be interpreted with caution. A particularly important caveat is implicit in the fact that the findings are based on observation, which limits generalizability in two ways. First, only those behaviors included on a given schedule are observed in a given study. Other, possibly more important, behaviors may be overlooked. Second, findings can be only as reliable as the observation schedule used in the research. Few of the studies cited report reliability of measures for their schedules, but other studies suggest that observation-schedule reliabilities tend to be low (Calkins, Borich, Pascone, & Kugle, 1977; Erlich & Shavelson, 1976). These low reliabilities are attributable not only to rater inconsistencies and poorly defined categories, but also to a variety and infrequency of certain behaviors. Teachers' behaviors vary from grade to grade, teacher to teacher, and even occasion to occasion (Barr, 1975, 1980; Calfee & Calfee, 1976; Crawford et al., 1976; Felsenthal & Kirsch, 1978; Fischer et al., 1978). Many schedules probably have low reliabilities simply because they are not in tune with the realities of the classroom.

Limitations of research design may also restrict the generalizability of the findings. Many of the studies cited were conducted in the lower elementary grades, often with students rated low in socioeconomic status (SES) and enrolled in compensatory programs, and frequently with outcome measures limited to achievement testing. It seems unlikely, then, that the findings we cited are equally applicable across program goals, grade levels, and student populations. Peterson (1979) suggested that different behaviors might be identified if different student outcomes were used to measure effectiveness; Medley (1977) concluded that teaching behaviors that are effective with students rated low in SES may not be effective with other student populations; Tikunoff et al. (1975) noted that different grouping strategies were effective in second and fifth grade; Stallings, Needles and Stayrook (1979) found that in remedial classrooms, students who spent time in small-group activity made greater academic gains than students who spent more time in one-to-one instruction; and Stallings (1980) concluded that the amount of time allocated to specific reading activities significantly affected students' reading gains. Because most of the findings in the management-effectiveness literature are based on measures of linear association (i.e., correlations), no cause-effect relationships may be inferred and other nonlinear associations may have been missed. Soar and Soar (1979) and Crawford et al. (1976) note that at least some teacher-effectiveness variables have significant curvilinear relationships with student outcomes. Even "good" management strategies may be effective only in moderation.

Descriptions of Classroom Interactions

The management-effectiveness literature suggests that elementary reading instruction is more effective when students are directly supervised by an adult. But how much of each student's time is actually spent in supervised activity? Descriptions of time use during reading instruction provide some tentative answers.

Filby (1978) summarized the time use data from BTES Phase III. She reports that second- and fifth-grade students spent about two thirds of their time in self-paced activities; Rosenshine (1979) and Calfee and Calfee (1976) have reported similar findings. Quirk, Tresmen, Weinberg, and Malin (1973), in a study of compensatory reading instruction, reported that students in Grades 2, 4, and 6 spent an average of 31 percent of their time working alone. In a study of Grade 2 and Grade 5 teachers implementing a skills-management system, investigators (Webb et al., personal communication, 1983) at the Wisconsin Research and Development Center for Individualized Schooling found that children paced themselves from 22 percent to 88 percent of the time. Durkin (1978–1979), on the basis of classroom observations, concluded that worksheets and written assignments comprise much of the middle grade reading program. As Rosenshine (1979) has noted, students may spend more of the time assigned for formal reading instruction (the reading period) with instructional materials than with the teacher.

Although students appear to spend a large percentage of the reading period on their own, there has been more research on teacher and student behavior during the reading period than during periods of informal, seatwork activities. Studies have been done to investigate group formation, teacher behavior with different reading groups, and social relationships within the reading group. R.

S. Weinstein (1976) observed first-grade teachers at the beginning of the school year. She concluded that teachers made the most changes in their reading groups during the first few weeks of school; after that, group membership became relatively stable. Not surprisingly, children assigned to the middle group were the most often reevaluated. Analysis of the interaction between teachers and their students suggest that the teachers interacted differently with the different groups but that they did not give the high group preferential treatment. Weinstein also noted that teachers seemed to use a wide variety of verbal cues to alert students to the relative status of the different reading groups. Barr (1975) observed grouping practices in 12 first-grade classrooms and found considerable variety in the ways the teachers grouped students for reading instruction, with all but one teacher eventually dividing students into two to four groups for basal reader instruction. Teachers appeared to establish reading groups as they identified individuals who needed differentiated instruction or attention. Once established, teachers tended to keep the number of groups stable. Tikunoff et al. (1975) reported differences in reading-group functions in second- and fifth-grade classrooms. In Grade 2 there was more group instruction, groups were usually formed on the basis of reading ability, and they served as the setting for formal instruction in reading. In Grade 5, students worked more on their own, groups were more likely to be formed on the basis of social needs or interests, and groups served less as settings for formal instruction and more as forums for the exchange of ideas.

Investigators have also been interested in reading groups as social as well as instructional settings. Alexander and Filler (1974) reviewed the research on group cohesiveness and reading instruction and concluded that cohesiveness is a postive characteristic that can be influenced by management decisions made by the teacher. Doyle (1981), in a review of research on classroom contexts, suggests that teachers must acquire constructs that reflect the realities of classroom life in order to know what to see and when to act.

Eldridge (1981) and Morrison (1982) reported studies, at the elementary and secondary level respectively, that were frank attempts to understand more fully what goes on related to reading instruction and reading performance in classrooms. Both were "qualitative" studies, in that the investigators were more interested in gaining impressions than in gathering data related to specific questions or hypotheses. The studies are noteworthy because they exemplify what appears to be a growing inclination on the part of investigators to pay attention to the experiences, motives, beliefs, and expectations of classroom inhabitants.

Summary Observations

The literature on classroom management behaviors is more enticing than definitive. Our review suggests that although teachers differ considerably in the ways that they organize their classes for reading instruction, students generally spend more time on their own with workbooks and worksheets than in group instruction. Nevertheless, the results of the management-effectiveness studies suggest that teachers' management decisions do affect student outcomes. Perhaps the most striking observation we can make is that this line of research has not yet reached adolescence. There are comparatively few studies of management-effectiveness variables and all are recent. Educators have long been advocating methods for managing reading instruction, but they are just now beginning to develop a research base in support of the methodology.

STUDIES OF TEACHERS' PLANNING AND DECISION MAKING

Classroom observation is an appropriate strategy for determining what teachers actually do in the classroom, but not for determining why they do it. To get at the reasons why, investigators have begun to examine teachers' preinstructional planning and decision making. Although attention to this area is relatively recent, the literature on teachers' planning and decision making is already quite extensive. Our citations are limited to a few comprehensive reviews and a few selected studies.

Shavelson and Stern (1981) provide a comprehensive review of numerous studies pertaining to the information teachers use to make decisions about instructional planning. They also cite studies of the cognitive processes underlying teachers' decisions. In the review, Shavelson and Stern conclude that teachers' decision making is heavily influenced by certain personal characteristics (e.g., beliefs, conceptions of subject matter) as well as by antecedent conditions (those conditions which impinge on classroom decisions, such as information about students' ability, achievement, independence, self-concept), the nature of the instructional task (e.g., materials, activities), and the physical and social context of the classroom and school environment.

After reviewing studies of teachers' thinking and planning, Clark and Yinger (1979) conclude that teachers do not follow the traditional model of instructional design that moves from specifying objectives to creating step-by-step procedures for moving students toward those objectives, to evaluating the effectiveness of the instruction once the instruction has been implemented. Instead, they suggest that teachers' planning tends to focus on creating tasks comprised of content, materials, and activities with which the teacher and students are to be involved. The need for decision making usually arose when the teaching routine was not going as planned. Doyle (1979) noted similar findings in a review of teachers' managerial decisions in a classroom setting. He described the teacher's task as one of continually monitoring and gathering information about student cooperation in order to maintain activity flow in the classroom.

Bealing (1972) surveyed teachers in British infant schools regarding their use of available diagnostic information and concluded that her subjects relied on subjective personal evaluations rather than standardized test scores or colleagues' recommendations. A study by Helton, Morrow, and Yates (1977) also suggests that teachers have idiosyncratic personal styles. The investigators involved a small group of teachers in a grouping simulation and found that participants grouped students in different ways and made a variety of instructional recommendations. Barr (1975) found that teachers' decisions on whether to group and when to group for basal reading and phonics instruction differ considerably. Barr suggests that teachers' decisions may be based on their personal conceptions of what constitutes good reading instruction. Bawden, Buike, and Duffy (1979), in a survey and follow-up case studies, found that teachers' instructional activities and time allocation to certain reading activities reflected their conceptions of reading (e.g, skill oriented, child centered). Borko, Shavelson, and Stern (1981) reviewed four studies of teachers' decisions in the planning of reading instruction. They suggest that teachers use information about students' characteristics to estimate the students' reading abilities. Then they can form reading groups on the basis of the ability estimates, consideration of selected factors in the school environment, and their own conceptions of reading. The teachers base their long-term decisions about teaching on their concern for group, not individual, considerations. Clark, Yinger, and Weldfong (1978) studied the cues teachers use to select reading activities. The teachers most frequently reported being influenced by potential student motivation and involvement, although difficulty of the material and students' potential for learning were also cited. The subjective nature of the planning process is the prominent theme through all of the reports.

Borko (1978) reported an experimental study of managerial decision making in which teachers relied on characteristics, such as academic competence and motivation, to make management decisions related to hypothetical students. Borko concludes that the teachers' decisions were influenced by their personal beliefs as well as by the cue characteristics themselves, although specific influencing variables depended on the decision being made. Duffy (1983) comes to a similar conclusion, but he goes on to argue that teachers' belief in turn taking may be the main impediment to improved reading instruction. He says that (a) turn taking—assigning turns to pupils as they move through materials—is the hub of activity in reading and (b) the problem is that, in striving for smooth, risk-free turn taking, teachers do more monitoring than explaining. Duffy concludes that poor readers are likely to remain confused until teachers are able and willing to help them view reading as a sense-making, not merely a turn-taking activity. Eder (1982) studied teacher-student interactional processes in homogeneous ability groups. Eder found that students in low-ability groups were more inattentive and required more management by the teacher during reading instruction than did students in high-ability groups. Because the teachers' management of students was found to be disruptive of the students' turns at reading, the low-ability students often were deprived of the opportunities to decode words used in the assignments. Eder concludes that low-ability students are likely to have difficulty learning when they are assigned to groups in which social interactional contexts are not conducive to learning.

The research base regarding teachers' preinstructional planning and decision making continues to grow. Meanwhile, it appears that teachers may be influenced at least as much by personal perceptions and beliefs as by ostensibly more objective information when they make plans and decisions about managing instruction. If this is so, a better understanding of the presage variables affecting teachers' plans and decisions will be needed before teachers' management practices are fully understood or, probably more important for teacher educators, influenced in any significant way.

CONCLUSIONS, LIMITATIONS, AND DIRECTIONS

In popular usage, the term managing instruction probably evokes either both or some combination of two dominant associations: *grouping students for instruc-*

tion and *controlling behavior* (i.e., *behavior problems*) in the classroom. But, as we said at the outset, the literature related to managing instruction ranges much more widely. The quest in the literature on managing instruction is to give proper consideration to value systems, type and structure of content, the psychology of individual differences, and the structures and processes of individual schooling in order to enhance the learning of individual students. Thus, broadly conceived, *managing instruction* is a many-faceted concept that eludes precise definition. We have not offered such a definition nor will we attempt to do so now. Rather, we simply acknowledge that managing instruction is a complex enterprise, the study of which may involve a wide array of variables. But the purpose of managing instruction is quite explicit: to enhance the learning of individuals by manipulating aspects of the schooling process.

Definitive conclusions based on the literature are as elusive as a precise definition for managing instruction. In fact, on the basis of our review of the literature, we are better able to identify limitations and promising ways to overcome them than to draw conclusions. In this final section, then, we offer some *conclusions* that might more properly be called *generalizations;* we discuss what we see as three major limitations of the existing research; and we identify some research directions that seem promising.

Conclusions

The general conclusion, or salient generalization, that emerges most prominently from the literature has two parts. First, with regard for present practice, the optimum or universally effective scheme or strategy for managing instruction has not been devised. This is so because such important student variables as grade level/chronological age, socioeconomic background, prior achievement, and innate ability interact with the context variables that shape various management strategies. Consequently, the effects of given practices vary from group to group and from individual to individual. A highly structured program of instruction might, for example, produce good results with students who have limited reading ability but, on the other hand, limit the performance of high achievers. Second, with regard for future research, there probably never will be an optimum or universally effective scheme or strategy for managing instruction. Student variables and context variables will always interact, so that what works with Group A may not work, or might even be harmful, with Group B. While this is hardly a highly insightful observation, the fact is that the apparent purpose of much of the research and virtually all of the practice in schools has been either to discover or to implement the ultimate scheme for managing instruction. If the quest for an all-purpose approach to managing instruction were abandoned, the way would be cleared for more promising and more realistic quests.

Three more specific but highly interrelated conclusions seem justified.

First, taken together the studies involving context variables and product variables have demonstrated either no effects at all or inconsistent effects. That is, variations in the *context of instruction*—which includes the entire array of factors related to the organization of instruction—have not been found to be associated in any regular or predictable way with the measured *products*, or outcomes, *of instruction*. We have already alluded to one of the most likely reasons for such inconclusive results: the studies generally have not been designed or interpreted with sufficient sensitivity to the fact that context variables and student variables interact. Therefore, effects may be washed out when subjects' characteristics are diverse or effects may not hold up when subjects' characteristics are systematically varied. For example, a treatment's positive effect with good readers might be washed out in a study where subjects are not stratified by reading ability. Likewise, a treatment with positive effects for poor readers might not produce similar results in a study of good readers. An equally likely reason for nonsignificant effects is that the actual outcome may not have been measured in the study. Standardized *achievement* tests have almost always been the product measures, but instruction could have a vast array of other—positive or negative—effects. And of course it is possible that many context variables selected for study are so insipid that they have no measurable or barely marginal effects.

Second, despite the generally inconclusive results of the context-product studies, evidence is accumulating from the more recent classroom-based studies that effective instruction is associated with certain management decisions. The decisions teachers make in assigning tasks, forming instructional groups, and maintaining discipline affect students' involvement in their own learning and, ultimately, their achievement. These results are still tentative, but they are encouraging. They suggest that with proper focus context-product research can be more productive than it has been in the past.

Third—and again, despite the generally inconclusive results of context-product studies—the *behavior* of both teachers and students does differ in different contexts. That is, although treatment effects have not generally been demonstrated by the existing studies, there is evidence, particularly from the more recent observational studies, that context variables do, in fact, affect the behavior of students and teachers. These results are also encouraging because they suggest that with more study, the significant and most potent context variables can be identified. Once identified, the variables can be examined more closely in systematic experiments.

Limitations

We have already alluded to two important limitations inherent in work related to managing reading instruction: (1) most studies have been designed to seek a universal system for managing instruction rather than routines that work with identifiable subgroups of students and (2) the product of instruction is almost always evaluated in terms of standardized achievement tests. Taken together, these two limitations loom large in explaining why the work to date has been largely ineffectual. They suggest not only that the focus may not have been fine enough to give a clear view of the impact of management decisions, but also that the focus may have been misdirected.

Another important limitation is the inclination to ignore the fact that teachers and students are not passively shaped by their environment—that they actively help to shape it. Consequently, a context or environment may be very different from its label. An administrator may, for example, declare a school "open," but teachers and pupils may continue to behave in quite traditional ways. In such a situation, one could hardly draw valid conclusions about the "open" context. Nevertheless, conclusions have often been drawn strictly on the basis of labels. As a result, the literature is cluttered with declarations that have little or no basis in fact.

More limitations could be identified, but a longer list would only labor the point that may already be overmade. The literature on managing instruction is limited by shortcomings that must be overcome *before* valid guidelines for managing instruction can be devised.

Directions

Although limitations are quite pervasive in the existing literature, there are some promising directions for the future. The suggestions that follow are the ones that we feel are particularly worthwhile.

Future study ought to pay much more attention to the actual activities of teachers and students in the classroom—to the process variables. The recent literature shows that a shift from context variables to process variables has already begun. This is good because research on managing instruction is seldom fruitful if it ignores the *actual, observable* activities of teachers and pupils in the classroom. Concurrent attention to context variables, process variables, and product variables in order to clarify what *really* goes on and with what results in carefully described contexts is ultimately needed.

Another trend in the recent literature is to question the "open environment" concept of the 1960s. Furthermore, evidence is accumulating to suggest that more structured environments produce better student achievement. Future study ought to pay close attention to what *actually* goes on in classrooms, whether they are labeled "open" or "structured." Once the labels are defined in terms of students' and teachers' behavior, there can be serious efforts to determine what works best with which students and for which teachers.

Still another trend is the increased use of qualitative methodologies—such as observations, participant observations, and ethnographies—to examine and clarify the bases for teachers' judgments and planning. The trend is commendable because the work should enhance our understanding of why teachers make the management decisions that they attempt to implement. Effective and ineffective teachers appear to manage instruction differently; this line of research will help to clarify both the nature and the sources of the differences.

Finally, there is reason to pay particular attention to management decisions that serve to increase students' time on tasks. There is considerable evidence that the time students spend productively on task is the best predictor of achievement.

REFERENCES

Alexander, J. E., & Filler, R. C. Group cohesiveness and reading instruction. *Reading Teacher*, 1974, *27*, 446–450.

Allen, V. L. *Children as teachers: Theory and research on tutoring.* New York: Academic Press, 1976.

Austin, D. B.   Secondary education. In R. L. Ebel (Ed.), *Encyclopedia of educational research* (4th ed.). New York: Macmillan, 1969.

Barr, R.   How children are taught to read: Grouping and pacing. *School Review*, 1975, *83*, 479–498.

Barr, R.   *School, class, group and pace effects on learning*. Paper presented at the meeting of the American Educational Research Association, Boston, April 1980.

Barr, R., & Dreeben, R.   Instruction in classrooms. In L. S. Shulman (Ed.), *Review of research in education* (Vol. 5). Itasca, Ill.: Peacock, 1978.

Bawden, R., Buike, S., & Duffy, G.   *Teacher conceptions of reading and their influence on instruction* (Research Series No. 47). East Lansing: Institute for Research on Teaching, Michigan State University, 1979.

Bealing, D.   The organization of junior school classrooms. *Educational Research*, 1972, *14*, 231–235.

Berliner, D. C.   A status report on the study of teacher effectiveness. *Journal of Research in Science Teaching*, 1976, *13*, 369–382.

Berliner, D. C.   Using research on teaching for the improvement of classroom practice. *Theory into Practice*, 1980, *19*, 302–308.

Berliner, D. C., & Rosenshine B. V.   The acquisition of knowledge in the classroom. In R. C. Anderson, R. J. Spiro, & W. E. Montague (Eds.), *Schooling and the acquisition of knowledge*. Hillsdale, N.J.: Erlbaum, 1977.

Blakely, W. P., & McKay, B.   Individualized reading as a part of an eclectic reading program. *Elementary English*, 1966, *43*, 214–219.

Borko, H.   *An examination of some factors contributing to teachers' pre-instructional classroom organization and management decisions*. Paper presented at the annual meeting of the American Educational Research Association, Toronto, March 1978.

Borko, H., Shavelson, R. J., & Stern, P.   Teachers' decisions in the planning of reading instruction. *Reading Research Quarterly*, 1981, *16*, 449–466.

Calfee, R., & Calfee, C. H.   Reading and mathematics observation system: Description and measurement of time usage in the classroom. *Journal of Teacher Education*, 1976, *27*, 323–325.

Calkins, D. S., Borich, G. D., Pascone, M., & Kugle, C. L.   *Generalizability of teacher behaviors across classroom observation systems*. Austin: Research and Development Center for Teacher Education, University of Texas at Austin, 1977.

Clark, C. M., Yinger, R. J., & Weldfong, S. C.   *Identifying cues for use in studies of teacher judgment*. East Lansing: Institute for Research on Teaching, Michigan State University, 1978.

Clark, C. M., & Yinger, R. J.   Teachers' thinking. In P. L. Peterson & H. J. Walberg (Eds.), *Research on teaching: Concepts, findings, and implications*. Berkeley, Calif.: McCutchan Publishing Corp., 1979.

Cohen, P. A., & Kulik, J. A.   Synthesis of research on the effects of tutoring. *Educational Leadership*, 1981, *39*, 227–229.

Cohen, P. A., Kulik, J. A., & Kulik, C. C.   Educational outcomes of tutoring: A meta-analysis of findings. *American Educational Research Journal*, 1982, *19*, 237–248.

Cohen, S. A.   Instructional systems in reading: A report of the effects of a curriculum design based on a systems model. *Reading World*, 1977, *16*, 158–171.

Coleman, J. S., Campbell, E. Q., Hobson, C. J., McPartland, J., Mood, A. M., Weinfeld, F. D., & York, R. L.   *Equality of educational opportunity*. Washington, D.C.: U.S. Government Printing Office, 1966.

Corley, G. B., & Lewis, C. W.   The impact of individualized instruction on low-achieving youth. *Urban Education*, 1975, *10*, 321–326.

Crawford, J., et al.   *Process-product relationships in second and third grade classrooms* (Report No. 76–11). Austin: Research and Development Center for Teacher Education,

University of Texas at Austin, 1976. (ERIC Document Reproduction Service No. ED 148 888)

Criscuolo, N. P.   Launching an effective reading program in the school. *Peabody Journal of Education*, 1977, *54*, 282–285.

Cushenberry, D. C.   The Joplin plan and cross grade grouping. *Perspectives in reading number 9: Organizing for individual differences*. Newark, Del.: International Reading Association, 1967–1968, 33–45.

Dillingofski, M. S.   *Nonprint media and reading: An annotated bibliography*. Newark, Del.: International Reading Association, 1979.

Doucette, J., & St. Pierre, R.   *Anchor test study: Correlates of fifth grade reading achievement*. Cambridge, Mass.: Abt Associates, 1977. (ERIC Document Reproduction Service No. ED 141 418)

Doyle, W.   Paradigms for research on teacher effectiveness. In L. S. Shulman (Ed.), *Review of research in education* (Vol. 5). Itasca, Ill.: Peacock, 1977.

Doyle, W.   Making managerial decisions in classrooms. In D. L. Duke (Ed.), *Classroom Management* (78th Yearbook of the National Society for the Study of Education, Part 2.) Chicago: University of Chicago Press, 1979.

Doyle, W.   Research on classroom contexts. *Journal of Teacher Education*, 1981, *32*, 3–6.

Duff, R. E., & Swick, K.   Primary level tutors as an instructional resource. *Reading Improvement*, 1974, *11*, 39–44.

Duffy, G. G.   From turn-taking to sense-making: Broadening the concept of teacher effectiveness. *Journal of Educational Research*, 1983, *76*, 134–139.

Dunkin, M. J., & Biddle, B. J.   *The study of teaching*. New York: Holt, Rinehart & Winston, 1974.

Durkin, D.   What classroom observations reveal about reading comprehension. *Reading Research Quarterly*, 1978–1979, *14*, 481–533.

Eberwein, L.   A comparison of a flexible grouping plan with a three-group achievement plan in fourth grade reading instruction. *Journal of Educational Research*, 1972, *66*, 169–174.

Eder, D.   Ability grouping as a self-fulling prophecy: A micro-analysis of teacher-student interaction. *Sociology of Education*, 1981, *54*, 151–162.

Eder, D.   The impact of management and turn-allocation activities on student performance. *Discourse Processes*, 1982, *5*, 147–159.

Eldridge, Jr., R. G.   *An ethnographic study of the acquisition and application of reading skills in one elementary school classroom* (Tech. Rep. No. 579). Madison: Wisconsin Research and Development Center for Individualized Schooling, 1981.

Educational Products Information Exchange Institute.   *An in Depth Report No. 58, Evaluating Instructional Systems*. (EPIE Educational Product Report). New York: EPIE Institute, 1974, 6–63.

Erlich, O., & Shavelson, R. J.   *Application of generalizability theory to the study of teaching* (Tech. Rep. 76–9–1). San Francisco: Far West Laboratory for Educational Research and Development, 1976.

Esposito, D.   Homogeneous and heterogeneous ability grouping: Principal findings and implications for evaluating and designing more effective educational environments. *Review of Educational Research*, 1973, *43*, 163–179.

Felsenthal, H., & Kirsch, I.   *Variations in teachers' management of and time spent on reading instruction: Effects on student learning*. Paper presented at the annual meeting of the American Educational Research Association, Toronto, March 1978. (ERIC Document Reproduction Service No. ED 159 614)

Filby, N. N.   How teachers produce "academic learning time": Instructional variables related to student engagement. In C. W. Fischer, L. S. Cahen, N. N. Filby, R. S.

Marliave, & D. C. Berliner. *Selected findings from phase III-B.* San Francisco: Far West Laboratory for Educational Research and Development, 1978.

Fischer, C. W., Berliner, D. C., Filby, N. N., Marliave, R. S., Cahen, L. S., & Dishaw, M. M.   Teaching behaviors, academic learning time, and student achievement: An overview. In C. Denham & A. Lieberman (Eds.), *Time to learn.* Washington, D.C.: USOE/NIE Printing, 1980.

Fischer, C. W., Filby, N. N., Marliave, R. S., Cahen, L. S., Dishaw, M. M., Moore, J. E., & Berliner, D. C.   *Teaching behaviors, academic learning time and student achievement: Final report of phase III-B, Beginning teacher evaluation study.* San Francisco: Far West Laboratory for Educational Research and Development, 1978.

Forte, E. J.   *The effect of individualized instruction on the improvement of self-concept of low achieving primary grade urban children.* Unpublished doctoral dissertation, Walden University, 1975. (ERIC Document Reproduction Service No. ED 119 876)

French, W. M.   *America's educational tradition: An interpretive history.* Boston: Heath, 1964.

Furno, O. F., & Collins, G. J.   *Class size and pupil learning.* Baltimore: Baltimore City Public Schools, 1967. (ERIC Document Reproduction Service No. ED 025 003)

Glass, G. V.   Primary, secondary and meta-analysis of research. *Educational Researcher,* 1976, *5,* 3–8.

Glass, G. V.   Integrating findings: The meta-analysis of research. In L. S. Shulman (Ed.), *Review of research in education.* (Vol. 5) Itasca, Illinois: Peacock, 1978.

Glass, G. V., & Smith, M. L.   *Meta-analysis of research on the relationship of class size and achievement.* San Francisco: Far West Laboratory for Educational Research and Development, 1978.

Glass, G. V., & Smith, M. L.   Meta-analysis of the research on class size and achievement. *Educational Evaluation and Policy Analysis,* 1979, *1,* 2–16.

Graves, M. F., & Patberg, J. P.   A tutoring program for adolescents seriously deficient in reading. *Journal of Reading Behavior,* 1976, *8,* 27–35.

Greaney, V., & Clarke, M.   A longitudinal study of the effects of two reading methods on leisure-time reading habits. In D. Moyle (Ed.), *Reading: What of the future?* 11th annual conference of the United Kingdom Reading Association, Edge Hill College, 1974.

Hambleton, R. K.   Testing and decision-making for selected individualized instructional programs. *Review of Educational Research,* 1974, *44,* 371–400.

Hammill, D., & Mattleman, M. S.   An evaluation of a programmed reading approach in the primary grades. *Elementary English,* 1969, *8,* 310–312.

Hart, S.   Analyzing the social organization for reading in one elementary school. In G. D. Spindler (Ed.), *Doing the ethnography of schooling: Educational anthropology in action.* New York: Holt, Rinehart & Winston, 1982.

Heathers, G.   Overview of innovations in organizing for learning. *Interchange,* 1972, *3,* 47–68.

Helton, G. B., Morrow, H. W., & Yates, J. R.   Grouping for instruction 1965, 1975, 1985. *The Reading Teacher,* 1977, *31,* 28–33.

Hiebert, E. H.   An Examination of ability grouping for reading instruction. *Reading Research Quarterly, 18,* 1983, 231–255.

Horwitz, R. A.   Psychological effects of the "open classroom." *Review of Educational Research,* 1979, *49,* 71–86.

Ironside, R. A., & Conaway, L.   *IGE evaluation, phase-II: On-site evaluation and descriptive study: Final report* (Tech. Rep. 499). Madison: Wisconsin Research and Development Center for Individualized Schooling, 1979.

Iverson, G., et al.   *Individualization, desegregation and educational decision-making in an urban decentralized school system.* Paper presented at the annual meeting of the American Educational Research Association, New York, 1977. (ERIC Document Reproduction Service No. Ed 137 495)

Jackson, S. A.   The quest for reading programs that work. *Educational Leadership,* 1978, *36,* 168–170.

Johnson, D. D., & Pearson, P. D.   Skills management systems: A critique. *Reading Teacher,* 1975, *28,* 757–764.

Johnson, D. W.   Group processes: Influences on student-student interaction and school outcomes. In J. McMillan (Ed.), *Social psychology of school learning.* New York: Academic Press, 1980.

Johnson, D. W., & Johnson, R. T.   Instructional goal structure: Cooperative, competitive or individualistic. *Review of Educational Research,* 1974, *44,* 213–240.

Johnson, L. M., & Garcia-Quintana, R. A.   *South Carolina first grade pilot project 1976–1977: The effects of class size on reading and mathematics achievement* (Office of Research Report Series: Volume 1/Number 35). Columbia: South Carolina State Department of Education, 1978. (ERIC Document Reproduction Service No. Ed 151 088)

Johnson, R. H.   Individualized and basal primary reading programs. *Elementary English,* 1964, *42,* 902–904.

Justman, J.   Reading and class homogeneity. *Reading Teacher,* 1968, *21,* 314–316.

Kamm, K., & White, S. R.   *A description of the procedures used in implementing an objective-based reading program in four schools* (Tech. Rep. No. 503). Madison: Wisconsin Research and Development Center for Individualized Schooling, 1979.

Kamm, K., White, S. R., & Morrison, B. S.   *A study of procedures used in implementing an objective-based reading program in 16 schools* (Working Paper No. 226). Madison: Wisconsin Research and Development Center for Individualized Schooling, 1977.

Klann, H., et al.   *The effects of utilizing teen tutors in a fourth and fifth grade individualizing reading program.* 1972. (ERIC Document Reproduction Service No. Ed 102 792)

Klausmeier, H. J.   IGE in elementary and middle schools. *Educational Leadership,* 1977, *34,* 330–336.

Kosinoski, G. J., & Vockell, E. L.   The learning center: Stimulus to Cognitive and affective growth. *Elementary School Journal,* 1978, *79,* 47–54.

Kulik, C. C., & Kulik, J. A.   Effects of ability grouping on secondary school students: A meta-analysis of evaluation findings. *American Educational Research Journal,* 1982, *19,* 415–428.

Lamme, L. L.   Self-contained to departmentalized: How reading habits changed. *Elementary School Journal,* 1976, *76,* 208–218.

Lipham, J. M., Klausmeier, H. J., & Walter, J. E.   The multiunit organization. In H. J. Klausmeier, R. A. Rossmiller, & M. Saily (Eds.), *Individually guided elementary education: Concepts and Practices.* New York: Academic Press, 1977.

Madison Metropolitan School District.   *Effects of class size on reading achievement in grades 1–3 in the Madison Metropolitan School District* (1974–1976). Madison, Wisc.: Madison Public Schools, 1976.

Marliave, R. S.   Academic learning time and engagement: The validation of a measure of ongoing student engagement and task difficulty. In C. W. Fischer, R. S. Cahen, N. N. Filby, R. S. Marliave, & D. C. Berliner. *Selected findings from phase III-B.* San Francisco: Far West Laboratory for Educational Research and Development, 1978.

Mathews, M.   *Teaching to read: Historically considered.* Chicago: University of Chicago Press, 1966.

Medley, D. M. *Teacher competence and teacher effectiveness: A review of process-product research.* Washington, D.C.: American Association of Colleges for Teacher Education, 1977.

Medley, D. M. The effectiveness of teachers. In P. L. Peterson & H. J. Walberg (Eds.), *Research on teaching: Concepts, findings and implications.* Berkeley, Calif.: McCutchan Publishing Corp., 1979.

Medley, D. M., & Cook, P. R. Research in teacher competency and teaching tasks. *Theory into Practice,* 1980, *19,* 294–301.

Mendenhall, S. B. *A personalized reading program in an elementary class room: Report on a tested model* (Research Monograph No. 14). Gainesville: University of Florida, 1976. (ERIC Document Reproduction Service No. ED 124 924)

Meredith, V. H., et al. *South Carolina first grade pilot project 1975–1976: The effects of class size on reading and mathematics achievement* (Office of Research Report Series Volume 1/Number 26). Columbia: South Carolina State Department of Education, 1977. (ERIC Document Reproduction Service No. ED 135 072)

Milburn, D. A study of multi-aged or family-grouped classrooms. *Phi Delta Kappan,* 1981, *62,* 513–514.

Milford, J. L. *A comparative study of two methods of reading instruction: An individualized approach using peer teachers versus a basal reader method.* Carbondale: Southern Illinois University, 1976. (ERIC Document Reproduction Service No. ED 147 762)

Mitzel, H. E. Teacher effectiveness. In C. W. Harris (Ed.), *Encyclopedia of educational research* (3rd ed.). New York: Macmillan, 1960.

Morrison, B. S. *An investigation of reading as a learning activity in grade nine social studies, science and English classes.* Madison: Wisconsin Center for Education Research, 1982.

Newport, J. F. The Joplin plan: The score. *Reading Teacher,* 1967, *21,* 158–162.

Niedermeyer, F. C., & Ellis, P. Remedial reading instruction by trained pupil tutors. *Elementary School Journal,* 1971, *71,* 400–405.

Orr, Jr., R. S. *The effect of a diagnostic-prescriptive individualized reading program on attitudes toward reading and school of remedial junior high school students.* Pullman: Washington State University, 1973. (ERIC Document Reproduction Service No. Ed 090 491)

Otto, W. R. The Wisconsin design: A reading program for individually guided education. In H. J. Klausmeier, R. A. Rossmiller, & M. Saily (Eds.), *Individually guided elementary education: Concepts and practices.* New York: Academic Press, 1977.

Otto, W. R., & Chester, R. D. *Objective-based reading.* Reading, Mass.: Addison-Wesley, 1976.

Patterson, Jr., R. T. *Planning and implementing a peer tutoring approach to individualized instruction to improve reading achievement.* Ft. Lauderdale, Fla.: Nova University, 1976. (ERIC Document Reproduction Service No. ED 131 434)

Peniston, E. Developing reading skills for low socio-economic status first grade pupils. *Reading Improvement,* 1975, *12,* 98–102.

Peterson, P. L. Directed instruction reconsidered. In P. L. Peterson & H. J. Walberg (Eds.), *Research on teaching: Concepts, findings and implications.* Berkeley, Calif.: McCutchan Publishing Corp., 1979.

Popkewitz, T. S., Tabachnick, B. R., & Wehlage, G. *The myth of educational reform.* Madison: University of Wisconsin Press, 1982.

Powell, J. V. Learning centers versus traditional instruction in alphabetizing skills. *Reading Improvement,* 1978, *15,* 43–46.

Quirk, T. J., Tresmen, D. A., Weinberg, S. F., & Malin, K. B. *The classroom behavior of teachers and students during compensatory reading instruction.* Princeton, N.J.: Educational Testing Service, 1973.

Rakes, T. A., Lintz, E., & Payton, L.   An evaluation of the reading achievement of disadvantaged freshmen enrolled in compensatory-based and traditional college reading improvement classes. In P. L. Nacke (Ed.), *Interaction: Research and practice for college-adult reading* (23rd Yearbook of the National Reading Conference). Clemson, S.C.: National Reading Conference, 1974.

Reading Teacher Staff.   Who profits from self-learning kits? *Reading Teacher*, 1978, *31*, 391–392.

Richardson, D. C., & Havlicek, L. L.   High school students as reading instructors. *Elementary School Journal*, 1975, *75*, 389–393.

Robinson, H. A.   Reading instruction and research. In H. A. Robinson (Ed.), *Reading and writing instruction in the United States: Historical trends.* Newark, Del.: International Reading Association, 1977.

Rosenshine, B. V.   Content, time, and direct instruction. In P. L. Peterson & H. J. Walberg (Eds.), *Research on teaching: Concepts, findings and implications.* Berkeley, Calif.: McCutchan Publishing Corp., 1979.

Rude, R. T.   Objective-based reading systems: An evaluation. *Reading Teacher*, 1974, *28*, 169–175.

Rupley, W. H.   Stability of teacher effects on pupils' reading achievement over a two year period and its relation to instructional emphasis. In P. D. Pearson (Ed.), *Reading: Theory, research and practice* (26th Yearbook of the National Reading Conference). 1977.

Sartain, H. W.   Organizational patterns of schools and classrooms for reading instruction. In H. M. Robinson (Ed.), *Innovation and change in reading instruction* (Part II). Chicago: University of Chicago Press, 1968.

Schieber, J. A., et al.   The effect of class size on student achievement. *Illinois School Research and Development*, 1979, *15*, 121–126.

Shavelson, R. J., & Stern, P.   Research on teachers' pedagogical thoughts, judgments, decisions, and behavior. *Review of Educational Research*, 1981, *51*, 455–498.

Slavin, R. E.   Effects of student teams and peer tutoring on academic achievement and time on task. *Journal of Experimental Education*, 1980, *48*, 253–257.

Smith, N. B.   *American reading instruction.* Newark, Del.: International Reading Association, 1965.

Smith, M. L., & Glass, G. V.   Meta-analysis of research on class size and its relationship to attitudes and instruction. *American Educational Research Journal*, 1980, *17*, 419–433.

Soar, R. S., & Soar, R. M.   Emotional climate and management. In P. L. Peterson & H. J. Walberg (Eds.), *Research on teaching: Concepts, findings and implications.* Berkeley, Calif.: McCutchan Publishing Corp., 1979.

Sowards, G. W.   Elementary education. In R. L. Ebel (Ed.), *Encyclopedia of educational research* (4th ed.). New York: Macmillan, 1969.

Spache, G. D., & Spache, E. B.   *Reading in the elementary school* (4th ed.). Boston: Allyn & Bacon, 1977.

Spuck, D. W., Bozeman, W. C., & Lawrence, B. F.   *Evaluation of the Wisconsin system for instructional management (WIS-SIM Pilot Test)* (Tech. Rep. No. 438). Madison: Wisconsin Research and Development Center for Individualized Schooling, 1977.

Stallard, C.   Comparing objective based reading programs. *Journal of Reading*, 1977, *21*, 36–44.

Stallings, J.   Implementation and child effects of teaching practices in follow through classrooms. *Monographs of the Society for Research in Child Development*, 1975, *40* (Serial No. 163).

Stallings, J.   Allocated academic learning time revisited, or beyond time on task. *Educational Researcher*, 1980, *9*, 11–16.

Stallings, J., Needles, M., & Stayrook, N.   *The teaching of basic reading skills in secondary schools phase II and phase III.* Menlo Park, Calif.: SRI International, 1979.

Tanner, D., & Tanner L. N.   *Curriculum development: Theory into practice.* New York: Macmillan, 1980.

Tikunoff, W. J., Berliner, D. C., & Rist, R. C.   *Special study A: An ethnographic study of the forty classrooms of the beginning teacher evaluation study known sample* (Tech. Rep. 75-10-5). San Francisco: Far West Laboratory for Educational Research and Development, 1975.

Venezky, R., Bernard, L., Chicone, S., & Leslie, R.   *On-line diagnosis of reading difficulties* (Tech. Rep. No. 327). Madison: Wisconsin Research and Development Center for Cognitive Learning, 1975.

Walberg, H. J., & Thomas, S. C.   Open education: An operational definition and validation in Great Britain and United States. *American Educational Research Journal,* 1972, *9,* 197–208.

Warner, D.   Pupilization of the instructional program. *Reading Horizons,* 1976, *16,* 97–103.

Warren, A., & Coston, F. E.   A comparative study of attitudes of first grade children in two reading programs—individualized and basal. *Reading Horizons,* 1975, *15,* 189–197.

Way, J. W.   Achievement and self-concept in multiaged classrooms. *Educational Research Quarterly,* 1981, *6,* 69–75.

Weinstein, C. S.   The physical environment of the school: A review of the research. *Review of Educational Research,* 1979, *49,* 577–610.

Weinstein, R. S.   Reading group membership in first grade: Teacher behaviors and pupil experience over time. *Journal of Educational Psychology,* 1976, *68,* 103–116.

White, S. R.   *Validation of the effectiveness of the learning center approach to skill instruction* (Tech. Rep. No. 384). Madison: Wisconsin Research and Development Center for Cognitive Learning, 1976.

White, S. R., & Demos, E.   *An objective-based approach to reading instruction: Implementation and evaluation* (Working Paper No. 198). Madison: Wisconsin Research and Development Center for Individualized Schooling, 1977.

Wilkinson, L. C., & Calculator, S.   Requests and responses in peer-directed reading groups. *American Educational Research Journal,* 1982, *19,* 107–120.

Wright, C. E., & Kim, Y.   *A study of the characteristics of effective individualized instruction programs.* Menlo Park, Calif.: Educational Evaluation and Research, Inc., 1977. (ERIC Document Reproduction Service No. ED 152 828)

25 ORAL READING

Richard L. Allington

Until quite recently, reading was practiced exclusively as oral reading in Western cultures (Mathews, 1966; Pugh, 1978; Resnick & Resnick, 1977). Mathews (1966) notes that St. Augustine commented on the perplexing behavior of St. Ambrose who often sat and read to himself, a rather peculiar habit in that time (fourth century). Reading as oral reading remained, by and large, until the nineteenth century when debates about educational practices in reading instruction began. The rise of silent reading practice in and out of schools seemed due to changes in the nature and availability of materials to be read, the decline in the number of listeners as literacy was expanded, and the changing purposes for which reading was used (Pugh, 1978).

The oral versus silent reading debate began around 1880 (Hyatt, 1943) when a number of basal reader manuals, textbooks, and educational leaders argued for consideration of instruction in silent reading processes. The issue was thrust to the fore when leading educators, particularly Colonel Francis Parker (1894) initiated criticism of the nearly exclusive emphasis on oral reading in school curricula and insisted that prevailing pedagogy undoubtedly contributed to the many errors prevalent then. This strong criticism of the prevailing emphasis on oral reading in instruction spawned numerous research studies over the following two decades. These studies are well sumarized in Huey (1908/1968) who was convinced of the superiority of silent reading and recommended that more attention be given it in the classroom.

Philosophical and pedagogical debate continued, as did educational research into the issue. Perhaps the work of Pitner (1913), Thorndike (1917) and Judd and Buswell (1922) best exemplify attempts of that era. Pitner studied fourth-grade children and compared comprehension after oral and silent reading, concluding that "children comprehend more when reading silently. . . ." He also argued that the observed difference would undoubtedly have been larger had the children been taught to read silently in their instructional programs. Thorn-dike examined mistakes in comprehension processes of sixth graders and by impli-cation cast oral reading in a less than positive light. Judd and Buswell investigated eye-movement behaviors and concluded that these were altered by the purpose for which one silently read.

Rapidly, three schools of thought developed about oral reading instruction and practice. The first, and perhaps yet most prevalent, depicted oral reading as a means to an ultimate end—proficient silent reading. The second held that oral reading was a detriment to the ultimate end—proficient silent reading. Fi-nally, a third school held that oral reading was not a tool, as such, but rather an art form whose techniques were worth mastering.

Regardless of which philosophical view one was aligned, the decade from 1915 to 1925 produced a relatively vigorous expansion of silent reading instruction and a concurrent decline in oral reading practice in the schools (Hyatt, 1943). N. B. Smith (1934/1965) notes that widespread publicity about the number of World War I recruits who could not read well enough to follow simple printed directions and the development of the initial assessments of silent reading com-prehension, events which occurred in the middle of this period, both contributed to public awareness of the debate and ultimately led to many of the educational modifications.

One problem which was identified by a number of educational authors of the period was that oral reading recitation was ingrained in American educational practices and teachers had not been trained in silent reading practices. Thus, the 1920s saw a number of textbooks published that emphasized silent reading, most notably Stone's (1922) *Silent and Oral Reading*, Watkins's (1922) *How to Teach Silent Reading to Beginners*, and N. B. Smith's (1925) *One Hundred Ways to Teach Silent Reading*. The impact of the Part II of the 20th Yearbook of the National Society for the Study of Education (1920) was also important. This report, entitled *Report of the Society's Committee on Silent Reading* sold over 30,000 copies in its first decade and, not surprisingly, argued for increased empha-sis on silent reading.

In the end, of course, a moderate position regarding oral reading was adopted and the debate diminished (Gray, 1955). In the next section, instructional aspects of oral reading in classroom practice are discussed and, as shall be seen, oral reading is still commonly practiced in elementary school without resolution of the debate that began over a half-century ago. Oral reading is, also, still widely employed in the evaluation of reading ability and the third section of this paper reports concerns and developments in this domain. The fourth section presents a summary of studies of the development and refinement of oral reading abilities. In the final section, a research agenda is proposed that notes what seem to be the major questions that need to be addressed.

INSTRUCTIONAL ASPECTS OF ORAL READING

Incidence of Oral Reading in Instruction

As noted in the previous section, silent reading was virtually nonexistent in ele-mentary schools prior to the beginning of the twentieth century. However, the shift in educational philosophy which began in the late 1800s had an almost immediate impact upon reading instructional practices. Initially, silent reading behaviors were cultivated in the upper grades and it was not until Zirbes's (1918) article appeared that silent reading instruction was actively encouraged prior to Grade 4. The popular opinion at that time had been that silent reading for studying informational texts was appropriate and should be developed once the child has mastered the process of reading orally. Zirbes, like Pitner (1913), demonstrated that different strategies were necessary for reading aloud than for reading silently. Her argument concluded that, "it is important to cultivate proper habits of silent reading before a child is expected to use a textbook for silent study." (p. 521).

The impact of this shift on educational practices was noted by Hyatt (1943), who reported results of two surveys completed in 1924. The first was conducted by 50 members of the National Education Association who observed reading instruction in Grades 4, 5, and 6. Lessons in which oral reading was the only observed technique accounted for nearly two thirds of the sessions studied. In the second survey of reading instruction in 375 American cities, the results indicated that oral reading instruction was still more prevalent than silent reading instruction. In 85 percent of the large cities, some attention was paid to silent reading instruction in Grade 1, though in only half of the smaller cities was silent reading instruction given any emphasis at all at this level. In a survey a decade later by the National Educational Association (1935) "successful" first-grade teachers were found to be emphasizing oral reading but integrating silent reading into the instructional program.

There developed, however, a small cadre of educators who built upon the work of Watkins's (1922) nonoral hypothesis. The major proponent was McDade (1937), an official in the Chicago public schools, who implemented a nonoral approach to beginning reading in the Chicago public schools. The nonoral approach not only required no oral reading, but also mandated that the oral and printed symbols were not to be paired at any time. Children were urged to simply "think" the meaning of the symbols based on pictures, objects, or actions. Buswell (1945) reported on the results of a study comparing children in 32 Chicago public schools, half of which received the nonoral program in Grades 1 and 2 and half a program with an emphasis on oral reading. The outcomes of these programs in Grades 3 and 4 provided some support for the nonoral approach in improving silent reading abilities and reducing subvocalization. However, both programs produced a wide range of achievement and both produced children who subvocalized, though there were slightly fewer subvocalizers from the nonoral schools. While the nonoral approach did not find wide implementation in educational practice, proponents continued to question the role of a hallmark of American reading instruction: oral reading recitation.

The shift away from nearly exclusive use of oral reading was noted by Gray (1937) who argued that there existed an "almost exclusive emphasis on silent reading in many schools and a corresponding neglect of oral reading." Thus, the debate was renewed with Dolch (1931), Gates (1935), and Durrell (1940) arguing in favor of a silent reading emphasis but noting there was a place for oral reading in the curriculum. By the late 1940s and early 1950s, the balanced view, one which argued for the judicious use of both oral and silent reading, emerged and much of the emotion was again left by the wayside (Anderson & Dearborn, 1952; Betts, 1946; Horn & Curtis, 1949).

By the late 1950s and early 1960s, oral reading was firmly established as a nearly universal practice in the elementary school, particularly in the primary grades. Austin and Morrison (1963) reported that in over two thirds of the primary-grade classrooms there was "considerable" emphasis on oral reading, while only about a third had a similar emphasis on silent reading instruction. By the middle and upper grades, silent reading received the primary emphasis, but in many schools, the emphasis on oral reading at these levels was still rated "considerable." In addition, Austin and Morrison noted widespread indiscriminate use of oral reading, without either purpose or planning, similar in many respects to the traditional oral reading recitation, with much emphasis on accuracy and little emphasis on audience communication.

More recent data on incidence of oral reading is provided by Howlett and Weintraub (1979) and Allington (1982). Howlett and Weintraub provide a summary of reading practices and note that nearly 85% of primary-grade teachers indicated children read orally every day, though fewer (44%) teachers rated the activity as an important goal. Teachers in the middle and upper grades still employed oral reading regularly with one third reporting spending "a great deal" of time on this activity.

Allington (1982) tracked the incidence of oral reading collected from teacher logs of 600 reading-group sessions in Grades 1, 3, and 5. In this study, the number of words read orally or silently were reported. The data indicate that the amount of oral reading decreases across grade levels with a dramatic decline for good reader groups. However, poor readers experience proportionally more oral than silent reading compared to good readers. In terms of daily incidence of oral reading, for instance, in Grade 1, poor readers read orally about 90% of the time, while good readers were reported to spend only about 40% of their lessons reading aloud (these data were collected during the second semester). By Grade 5, good reader groups spent less than 20% of their lessons reading aloud, while the poor reader groups read aloud in over half of their lessons.

It seems that oral reading is a relatively more common practice in the early grades and for poor reader groups in general. Hale and Edwards (1981) note that oral reading "was a daily routine" in the primary-grade classes they observed, and others have noted the predominance of oral reading as an instructional activity for poor reader groups (Gumperz & Hernandez-Chavez, 1972; McDermott, 1978; Rist, 1978).

Oral Reading as Instruction

Granted that oral reading is a traditional and commonplace activity during elementary school instruction one might ask: (1) How is the setting of oral reading instruction described? and (2) What does oral reading accomplish in terms of instruction? These questions are the focus of the following section.

Oral reading in classroom reading instruction has evolved from the "barbershop" model in which all students had the same text and simply awaited the signal "Next!" to perform an oral rendition of a paragraph. Reading instruction is now presented not so often to whole-class groups but to smaller groups formed primarily around estimates of reading ability (Pikulski & Kirsch, 1979). Each of these smaller groups typically reads in a different text, with different instructional pacing (see chapters by Barr and Rosenshine in this volume). Oral reading, as noted earlier, is a more common practice during instructional sessions with lower-achieving readers than it is with higher-achieving readers (cf. Allington, 1983; Hiebert, 1983). Still, however, once oral reading commences in a reading group, the allocation of reading turns seems to follow the traditional "one-paragraph-at-a-time" structure (Carew & Lightfoot, 1979; Eder, 1982; Hale & Edwards, 1981). There does seem to be a difference in the way reading turns are allocated in better reader groups and poorer reader groups (Eder, 1982; McDermott, 1977, 1978; Rist, 1973, 1978). Teachers seem to follow a relatively fixed pattern with better readers, moving systematically around the group. For poorer readers, teachers are more likely to open each turn for bid, often designating a student who seems to have been off task as the next oral reader. Anderson, Evertson, and Brophy (1979) presented evidence that the systematic procedure correlates well with reading achievement gains, while the open-bid process does not. Both Eder (1982) and McDermott (1977, 1978) describe how the latter strategy can lead quickly to management problems with inordinate amounts of time spent on the bidding and nominating process. Rather than flowing smoothly from reader to reader, the open-bid strategy often creates breakdowns in the activity flow, breakdowns that have to be attended to and resolved.

After being assigned or volunteering for a turn, a child begins to read aloud from the text the teacher has selected for the group. The audience now can come into play. The teacher and the other group members may offer "assistance" if the reader has difficulty. When the teacher offers help it is most often called a "prompt" (Englert & Semmel, 1981), while another student's help is termed a "call-out" (Brophy & Evertson, 1981). In either case, this assistance is most likely to be offered when the reader hesitates or mispronounces a word. Most often, the error is corrected by a member of the audience, though teachers have an extensive repertoire of verbal assistance strategies (Allington, 1980; Spiegel & Rogers, 1980). Again, however, differences in these prompts and call-outs are evident between the better-reader and poorer-reader groups (Allington, 1980; Eder, 1982). The differences in teacher prompts after oral reading errors lie in timing, frequency, and content. Poorer readers, compared to good readers, are corrected or prompted more quickly, more often, and with directions to attend to surface-level features of the text being most common.

Call-outs by other members of the group also vary by group-ability level. Eder (1982) presents convincing data that differential teacher reactions to call-outs creates an environment that supports such behavior among the poor readers and discourages it with the better-reader groups. She argues that the differences are created by differing teacher response. In any event, the incidence of call-outs seems negatively related to achievement in reading (Brophy & Evertson, 1981), though the case for teacher interruptions is not so clear (cf. McNaughton, 1981; Niles, 1980; Pany, McCoy, & Peters, 1981; Pflaum, Pascarella, Boswick, & Auer, 1980). Hoffman and Baker (1981) have recently developed a coding system for teacher interruptions that should produce clearer answers in this area.

What we see then when we observe an oral reading lesson is a rather intricate social setting with quite clearly prescribed rules (Doyle, 1978) for getting oral reading accomplished. The allocation of turns and the interruptions or assistance provided the reader are but two of the features of oral reading lessons that have been examined. While oral reading is a common instructional practice, we understand very little about the effective conduct of oral reading lessons.

We can give even less definitive responses to questions about what such oral reading lessons accomplish. While children do read aloud frequently, one can find little evidence in the literature that instruction in effective oral reading behaviors is actually offered. The most frequent teacher assistance offered is the interruption or prompt, a form of "corrective feedback" teaching (Duffy & Roehler, 1982), instruction that can hardly be described as well planned. Students do not seem to receive explicit strategy instructions, such as those suggested by Clay (1979). Rather, oral reading is a form of assessment or practice but often without a clearly developed, or delivered, instructional focus.

In terms of assessment, the classroom oral reading activity is, at best, impressionistic since teachers seldom produce written records of oral reading strategies and behaviors. Thus, while one may decide a student is not succeeding in a particular text after hearing an oral reading during an instructional session, the decision is based more on impression than quantitative evidence, and the impression is relative to the group and classroom context (Heap, 1980).

Oral reading practice in small-group sessions seems less positively related to reading achievement than does silent reading. R. M. Clark (1975) and Leinhardt, Zigmond, and Cooley (1981) found that teacher-directed silent reading activities were positively related to achievement, while oral reading activities were not. Stallings (1980), on the other hand, found the opposite in her study of secondary remedial reading programs. What we may have here, at least in part, is a difference in the task-engagement rates that oral reading will elicit in different settings. Eder (1982) presents the case most clearly for elementary classroom instruction when she notes that during oral reading one must maintain interest in an activity in which direct participation is not always possible. Silent reading, on the other hand, offers the opportunity for all members of a group to be actively engaged in the task. Given the strong relationship between task engagement and learning (Berliner, 1981), Eder's hypothesis would provide considerable explanatory power for the results available. We simply know very little about the effects of various allocations of time for oral reading during reading-group instruction. It seems most likely that a curvilinear relationship exists between oral reading practice and reading achievement. Either too much or too little will negatively affect outcomes. Unfortunately, we currently have few guidelines for determining either boundary. Beyond questions concerning the most appropriate amount of time that might be allocated, we know even less. While it seems eminently reasonable to assume that different instructional focuses (e.g., fluency training, self-correction training, absolute accuracy, etc.) during oral reading would produce different results, we have little evidence that such instructional differentiation occurs, much less the resultant effects on reader development.

In sum, then, it seems that at virtually any time in this nation's history, one could have walked into an American elementary school and expected to encounter children reading orally. Oral reading has been used exclusively, thoroughly discouraged, banned, debated, resurrected, and is still firmly entrenched in classroom practice. A primary rationale which one encounters as an explanation for such widespread acceptance relates to the perceived necessity for using oral reading to evaluate progress in the acquisition of reading ability. In the following section, the various traditions which have developed in the use of oral reading as an evaluative procedure manner are explored.

ORAL READING AS AN ASSESSMENT TECHNIQUE

Oral Reading Tests

The first formal attempt at using an oral reading performance as an assessment was Gray's *Standardized Oral Reading Paragraphs* (1915). The test passages, arranged in order of difficulty, were to be read aloud and the examiner was to record oral reading errors, including mispronunciation, omission, additions, repetitions, and so on. In addition, rate-of-reading norms were provided. Gray's error-analysis guidelines and norms seemed to receive relatively little attention in the professional literature during the decade following publication. Given the previously noted emphasis on the importance of silent reading during that period, such disregard is understandable.

As the pendulum began to swing back and oral reading again became accepted in practice, there was a resurgence of interest in profiling oral reading error types. These research efforts seemed less concerned with constructing a model of the reading process per se than with describing the types of errors made by readers in an attempt to depict, for teachers, the most common characteristics of oral reading performances. Representative of this research is Payne (1930), who presented a classification scheme for oral reading errors. Monroe (1932) also developed a classification system for errors, complete with a discussion of relative frequency, probable causes, and suggested remedial patterns. Duffy and Durrell (1935) and Daw (1938) presented descriptions of the oral reading errors of children in Grades 3 through 5. Madden and Pratt (1941) reported on the oral reading behaviors of over 1100 children in Grades 3 through 5 and presented an examination of the correlation between error types and various grammatical elements (e.g., articles, verbs, nouns, pronouns, etc.). Bennett (1942) examined errors in detail in an attempt to depict serial processing errors related to characteristics of the visual stimulus. These studies and the advent of additional diagnostic tests employing oral reading analysis influenced the way errors were viewed and examined.

Much interest developed concerning which oral reading behaviors were to be rightfully considered errors and which were important to record. Gray's (1915) oral test had been without serious challenge until Gates and McKillop (1927/1962) and Monroe (1932) presented more detailed techniques for the diagnostic analysis of errors. This lead was followed by Durrell (1953), Gilmore and Gilmore (1951), and Spache (1963/1972). In time, each of these test batteries became quite popular; they were widely used, compared, and debated (cf. Hill, 1936; Spache, 1950). While each retains some unique qualities, they exhibit a fair amount of commonality in terms of the oral reading behaviors described as important. Though scoring criteria varied, the pattern illustrated in Table 24.1 indicates that each concentrated on the analysis of errors at the word level, basically ignoring linguistic context (Weber, 1970).

To this point, no one had really viewed errors as a natural aspect of the process of reading acquisition. Rather errors were depicted as behaviors to be eradicated. However, Ilg and Ames (1950) studied developmental trends in oral reading errors across the elementary grades. They noted consistent differences in the error patterns of children at different age levels, particularly the shift from "visual form" and "non-attempts" at beginning stages to errors which reflected attention to "meaning" at higher grade levels. Their view that reading errors should not be considered simply "mistakes" or "inadequacies" was unique to the era.

The characterization of errors as behaviors to be eliminated resulted in a tendency to evaluate oral reading primarily on the number of "bad" behaviors ("bad" behaviors ranged, as indicated in Table 25.1, from additions, hesitations, and repetitions, to self-corrections). While earlier writers seemed to support the notion that only word-perfect reading was truly acceptable, Betts (1946) developed a set of criteria for evaluating oral reading performances which has had a profound impact upon educational practice. Betts developed word-recognition-accuracy and comprehension standards for three levels of reading, which he described as Independent (99% word recognition accuracy and 90% comprehension), Instructional (95% and 75%) and Frustration (below 95% and 50%). These criteria were evidently established from a doctoral dissertation completed under Betts's direction (Kilgallon, 1942, cited in Betts, 1946). However, several important factors need be noted: (1) the original data were from Grade 4 students only; (2) the students preread the passages silently; and (3) the mean accuracy ratios of the 41 subjects were lower than Betts's final criteria. Nonetheless, Betts's criteria were widely accepted at that time and remain so today, even though a variety of challenges have been raised concerning their validity.

TABLE 25.1   ORAL READING BEHAVIORS COUNTED AS "ERRORS" BY VARIOUS AUTHORS OF DIAGNOSTIC TESTS

	GRAY (1915)	GATES (1927)	DURRELL (1937)	GILMORE (1951)	SPACHE (1963)	CLAY (1975)
Omission of sound and/or word	X	X	X	X	X	X
Addition of sound and/or word	X	X	X	X	X	X
Substitution or mispronunciation	X	X	X	X	X	X
Repetition*	X	X	X	X	X	X
Self-Correction	X		X	X	X	
Word Aided	X	X	X	X	X	X
Hesitation		X	X	X		
Punctuation ignored	X		X	X		

* One-word repetitions not counted.

Beldin (1970) reviewed the development of the informal reading inventory (IRI) around which the Betts's criteria were established and pointed out deficiencies in research supporting many of the assumptions which underlie such assessment practices. Powell (1970) mounted the most direct attack on Betts's criteria, challenging them as arbitrary and without strong empirical support. In his study children with at least "tolerable" comprehension (70%–75%) averaged from 83% to 94% word recognition accuracy across Grades 1 through 6, with older readers producing more accurate renditions. Based on these results, he argued for different oral accuracy criteria at different grade levels. Pikulski (1974) reported two studies with second-grade children which attempted to replicate Powell's findings. The results of these attempts were equivocal with one supporting Betts' position (average 95.8% accuracy) and the other supporting Powell's (average 83.8% accuracy).

When children silently preread material, as was the case in the study which Betts used to establish his levels, Brecht (1977) noted that approximately 70% of the subjects reduced errors to the extent that they attained oral reading scores at least one level above performance on material not preread. Fuchs, Fuchs, and Deno (1982) found that performance at a 95% word-recognition-accuracy level on graded passages correlated well with standardized test scores and teacher placement in readers. However, they did not assess comprehension after reading but, instead, relied upon speed and accuracy of oral reading as their criterion measures. Pikulski's (1974) conclusion that much additional research is needed to establish empirical support for any word-recognition-accuracy criteria in oral reading is still valid, particularly for those evaluation procedures employed by classroom teachers.

Another challenge to Betts's criteria has come from Roberts (1976). She attempted to discover whether Betts's criteria were being employed, consciously or not, by primary-grade teachers in several schools. Her findings indicated that many children were, indeed, placed in text based upon word-accuracy criteria similar to the original Betts's standards. However, many children were also placed "incorrectly," in material that Betts would rank as frustration level. In an attempt to discover whether the negative outcomes predicted by Betts and others would accompany such placement, Roberts examined the progress and reading attitudes of children placed in frustration-level material. Results nearly contrary to the predicted negative outcomes were obtained. Children placed in frustration-level material evidenced generally positive attitudes about reading and actually seemed to be making greater progress than those placed in materials that would be considered appropriate: material which was read with 95% or greater accuracy. In her summary, Roberts notes that far too little empirical evidence exists to support the continued use of the Betts's criteria for placement decisions.

This seems a particularly pressing issue, given the evidence available from studies of classroom processes. Gambrell, Wilson, and Gantt (1981) and Berliner (1981) present evidence that student achievement in reading is positively affected by placement in materials that produce low error rates (2%–5%). Gambrell et al. (1981) and Jorgenson (1977) also noted that readers placed in reading material which produce error rates greater than 5% tend to be more frequently off-task during instruction, a point which would suggest a negative impact of such placement on achievement growth.

A basic problem with the tradition of using oral reading errors for evaluative purposes is that all reading behaviors which deviate from fluent and precisely accurate reproduction of text are typically considered errors. In the recent past, several authors have criticized this aspect of standard evaluation practices. Both Weber (1970) and Y. M. Goodman (1970) are critical of this aspect of analyses of oral reading errors, pointing out that traditional analyses emphasize quantitative rather than qualitative criteria in evaluating errors (e.g., qualitative criteria might emphasize the approximate syntactic and semantic congruence of an error to the text). Even with the weighting of various types of oral reading behaviors as equivalent, there exists little agreement among traditionalists on what degree of accuracy is required. As illustrated in Table 25.2, the most popular evaluation instruments which assess oral reading performance vary quite widely in the level of word-recognition accuracy considered satisfactory. Of particular interest, in relation to Betts's criteria, is the substantially lower accuracy level required in the primary grades, levels more in agreement with Powell's (1970) than Betts's (1946) standards.

Extended discussion has been given this topic because the tradition of different placement levels as more or less appropriate for children, and particularly the use of Betts's criteria (or something very similar for such placement), seems quite pervasive in both educational practice and the pedagogical literature. Unfortunately, too little solid empirical support is available to guide such practices. Regardless of how one defines satisfactory oral reading, there currently exists no fully adequate criteria for determining whether placement in any given text is more likely to facilitate the acquisition of reading abilities than placement in some others.

While we have advanced in our understanding of mismatches between oral reading responses and textual information, there are still few empirically supported guidelines for identifying what level of difficulty of textual materials will be most facilitative for learning to read. Perhaps this is because when we have attempted to generate such support our search has typically looked for the single best placement level. Beck (1981), on the other hand, presents a convincing argument that developing readers need to spend a substantial portion of their instructional time in relatively easy material with regular exposure to more difficult materials. Her suggestion allows the reader to develop fluent and automatic responses in less difficult text while encountering a challenge to develop new knowledge and strategies in more difficult text.

TABLE 25.2   PROPORTION WORD RECOGNITION ACCURACY* NECESSARY FOR INSTRUCTIONAL LEVEL DESIGNATION FOR VARIOUS AUTHORS

GRADE	GRAY (1915)	DURRELL (1937)	BETTS (1946)	GILMORE (1951)	SPACHE (1963)	POWELL (1971)
1	86%	67%	95%	67%	67–75%	85%
3	91%	92%	95%	88%	90%	91%
5	91%	94%	95%	92%	94%	91%

* These data are not necessarily comparable in a straightforward manner, since not all authors consider the same behaviors as "errors." However, given the degree of congruence among authors on what constitutes error behaviors these data may, in fact, be quite comparable.

Oral Reading as a Diagnostic Tool, Traditionally

In earlier eras, oral reading tests, such as Gray's (1915) *Standardized Oral Reading Paragraphs,* were used primarily as achievement tests to establish whether adequate progress was being attained. The emphasis in recording oral reading errors then was to establish an achievement level, not necessarily to use the errors as diagnostic indicators. In the following decades several authors (Durrell, 1937; Gates & McKillop, 1927/1962; Gilmore & Gilmore, 1951; Monroe, 1932; Spache, 1963/1972) developed diagnostic tests which presented strategies for analyzing errors and other behaviors in an attempt to discover the etiology of the reading disability or to identify appropriate remedial intervention techniques. Unfortunately, most, if not all, of these tests are inadequate on a number of psychometric and theoretical criteria, with none having established an adequate psychometric or theoretical base for error categories or for scoring criteria. Perhaps it is fortunate, in that sense, that only a few students, suspected underachievers, are typically administered these instruments. While several of these tests have been revised modestly since their original development, by and large they provide assessments of reading ability based upon the rather primitive view of oral reading errors prevalent a half-century ago.

Given the widespread use of these instruments, one might expect a large pool of available research on various aspects of their psychometric properties. However, relatively few such studies have been conducted with these instruments. One which challenges the ability of these instruments to provide accurate indications of achievement level is that of Eller and Attea (1966) who found significant differences in the grade-level scores obtained by subjects on each of several oral reading tests. A related problem is reported by Schell (1982) who found that the college professors who regularly taught courses involving the administration of oral reading tests had little agreement among themselves when counting errors made on such tests. He argues that examiner subjectivity in error identification results in relatively low interrater reliability. These results, in combination with criticisms leveled by various reviewers in Buros (1975), suggest that the most popular diagnostic oral reading tests seem to fall far short of meeting minimally satisfactory psychometric and theoretical standards.

Another common practice is to analyze oral reading errors in an attempt to identify instructional needs at the word-identification level. That is, to observe oral reading errors and from them to design a program to remediate word-level deficiencies. K. S. Goodman (1965) has provided a strong demonstration of the noncomparability of oral reading errors and errors in word recognition in isolation. On the other hand, Spache (1963/1972) and Shankweiler and Lieberman (1973) have argued that a relatively strong positive correlation exists between conditions, a claim generally adhered to by the authors of diagnostic reading tests. However Allington (1979) and Kreiger (1981a; 1981b) reported results which supported K. S. Goodman (1965), in that relatively few words were misidentified in both isolation and context conditions. These results suggest that an analysis of oral reading errors has limited value in identifying which words a reader might misread in other contexts. While word recognition in isolation and context are correlated generally, there exists little evidence that specific errors in either condition will reliably predict specific errors in the other. Thus, many traditional diagnostic practices centering on oral reading performance must be considered simply that—traditional and not well grounded in any empirical or theoretical base.

Oral Reading as a Diagnostic Tool, Since Goodman

In an article that was to be only the tip of the iceberg, K. S. Goodman (1965) demonstrated that readers were able to recognize words embedded in the context of a story that had gone unrecognized in isolation. He used these data to buttress his argument against the predominant view that reading a text was simply a series of one-word encounters. Shortly thereafter (1967), he presented a direct attack on the traditional notion of equivalence of various oral reading errors (which he indicated he chose to call "miscues" to avoid the negative connotation associated with the term "error"). In this article, he presented an analysis of oral reading errors, emphasizing the role of the word as part of the sentence rather than a string of graphemes and phonemes. His analysis sought to demonstrate the existence and effect of syntactic and semantic constraints on the reader's ultimate oral reading behavior. His criticism of the traditional view of oral reading behaviors was echoed in more detail by Weber (1968) who noted that "inaccurate responses are usually considered indications of perceptual inaccuracies . . . rather than responses based on reader's expectations based on his [sic] knowledge of the constraints imposed by grammatical structure" (p. 113). Thus was engaged the debate on qualitative versus quantitative criteria in analyzing oral reading errors.

While others had noted error patterns that suggested readers were attending to syntactic information (cf. Bennett, 1942; MacKinnon, 1959), this aspect of oral reading errors had generally been neglected. Rapidly though reports appeared in the literature attempting to describe the interplay of graphemic, phonemic, syntactic, and semantic information in oral reading behaviors. The nature of these reports is somewhat similar to those of a half-century earlier, in that descriptions of "normal" oral reading behaviors were developed. The differences, of course, related to the attention given the language base of oral errors and a comparison of the patterns elicited from good and poor readers. These studies had an undoubtedly profound effect on oral reading diagnostic procedures.

K. S. Goodman (1969) presented a detailed scheme for analyzing oral reading behaviors but, perhaps because of the time-consuming nature of the analysis, he did not suggest that this scheme be applied in a diagnostic manner per se. Rather, he suggested his "taxonomy" would be useful for providing detailed descriptions of oral reading behaviors with the primary purposes of evaluating and extending theoretical aspects of the reading process. This original scheme, however, seems to have served as a basis for a diagnostic procedure radically different from any developed earlier. The *Reading Miscue Inventory* (RMI) (Goodman & Burke, 1970) presented a qualitative analysis of oral reading performance with the profile sheet providing no indication of overall oral reading accuracy but with numerous analyses reflecting qualitative aspects of the performance.

In the *RMI* manual that details the "miscue analysis" procedure, no mention is made of deciding whether the material read is too difficult for the reader.

The general suggestion is to use reading material one grade level above placement level in order to elicit sufficient "miscues" to complete the analysis. Also, not all "miscues" evidently needed to be recorded, instead one typically records and analyzes only the first 25 miscues elicited. The manual also notes that for beginning readers, it may be necessary to have them read more than a single story to ensure an adequate number of "miscues." The types of behaviors to be recorded are virtually identical to those suggested in the traditional diagnostic tests, only errors are not "counted" as such but rated on general criteria, including graphic and sound similarity, grammatical acceptability, semantic acceptability, meaning change, correction, and meaning loss. Thus, rather than focusing on quantity and an analysis of graphemic and phonemic aspects of oral reading errors, "miscue analysis" is an attempt to depict which cue systems the reader uses, with the focus on whether errors will result in a meaning loss to the reader.

While one can only speculate about the proportion of individual diagnostic assessments which now incorporate the full analysis offered by the *Reading Miscue Inventory*, the influence of the miscue analysis strategy seems to have been far-reaching. Numerous authors of texts on diagnostic procedures have implemented at least partial aspects of the procedure (cf. Harris & Sipay, 1975; Rupley & Blair, 1979; Spache, 1977) and various adaptations of the procedure have appeared in professional journals (cf. Siegal, 1979; Tortelli, 1976; Williamson & Young, 1974). However, to date none of the traditional diagnostic tests have modified their scoring procedures.

While miscue analysis procedures and their resulting "reading strategy lessons" (Y. M. Goodman, 1970; 1972; Goodman & Burke, 1970) reflect advances in our understanding of the reading process, neither the procedures in general nor those outlined in the *Reading Miscue Inventory* have demonstrated adequacy on basic psychometric standards. As Wixson (1979) has noted, they are yet empirically "unvalidated as a means of identifying the relative effectiveness of the strategies used by different readers as they process printed materials" (p. 171). In her critique, Wixson notes that since "miscues" have been shown to vary as a function of the ability of the reader, the difficulty of the textual material (Christie & Alonso, 1980; Tamor, 1981), and the purpose for reading (Schwartz & Stanovich, 1981), the ultimate analysis of patterns may not reflect the reader's optimum performance abilities. She also notes that miscue analysis assumes a fully developed set of language skills which can be brought into play during the reading process, though some evidence exists that poor readers experience a delay in developing certain language abilities. These deficiencies are important because it has been suggested that miscue analysis profiles can be contrasted for different readers in order to compare relative proficiency levels and also that profiles can be contrasted across time to evaluate the effectiveness of remedial instruction. Neither of these strategies can be supported until the deficiencies noted by Wixson are ameliorated.

Another difficulty with the procedures outlined in the *Reading Miscue Inventory* is the inattention given to silent reading processes in the diagnostic session. Mosenthal (1976–1977, 1978) has questioned the assumption that oral and silent reading processes represent a unitary phenomenon, a position held by K. S. Goodman (1976–1977) and implied in the *Reading Miscue Inventory*. Mosenthal's research supports his position, that oral reading and silent reading place different demands on cognitive processes and undermine, at least, the alternative.

A final difficulty with miscue analysis procedures has been raised by Hood (1975–1976) who questioned the reliability of coding procedures among diagnosticians. While the same issue could be raised about the scoring procedures of the traditional diagnostic tests, the more complex coding scheme in miscue analysis may make it more susceptible to such variations.

Leu (1982) provides a comprehensive and updated review of oral reading error analysis which extends Weber's (1968) and Wixson's (1979) criticisms. He argues that "miscue analysis" and the other traditional error analysis systems suffer from a number of deficiencies, including: (1) the failure to arrive at any consensus on categories or oral reading behaviors, (2) the failure to define sufficiently the categories designated (e.g., wide-ranging definitions of graphic similarity and the tendency to ignore qualitative differences within categories), (3) the failure to justify theoretically the categories designated, (4) the failure to consider adequately the effects of passage difficulty on oral reading behaviors (cf. Christie & Alonso, 1980; Tamor, 1981), and (5) the ambiguity surrounding classification of multiple-source errors. He further argues that attempts to infer instructional needs from oral reading error analysis are fraught with problems. Such inferences, while common, can be considered dubious, at best, since only a portion of the oral reading behavior (i.e., errors) is used to infer the nature of the process, and this examination of errors is then used to infer the nature of silent reading behavior. From these inferences about silent reading behaviors an attempt is made to identify appropriate instructional procedures. Such attempts at instructional matching typically ignore the fact that oral reading is not a fixed process, it is affected by differences in the topical content of material and the social context of the instructional setting and passage difficulty, at the very least. Nor do such procedures consider that there is little good evidence of a strong relationship between oral and silent reading processes. Finally, these procedures assume, by and large, that teaching to a reader's weakness is more appropriate than teaching to his or her strengths.

It appears, then, that while we have advanced in our understanding of oral reading behaviors in relation to the diagnosis of reading difficulties, the state of the art is still quite primitive. Perhaps ultimately the quantity/quality issue will be resolved and more precise diagnostic instruments will be developed. Currently, though, no attempt has resulted in a diagnostic procedure which incorporates both quantity and quality dimensions and none of the available diagnostic assessments can be considered to have both strong empirical and theoretical support.

THE USE OF ORAL READING TO STUDY THE ACQUISITION OF READING SKILLS

The Development of Oral Reading Abilities

The adoption of the philosophical view (by some at least) that oral reading errors were not necessarily "bad" behaviors but rather were potentially valuable sources of information about learning processes (Ilg & Ames, 1950), leads to an expansion of interest in attempting to describe stages, strategies, or behaviors that could be characterized as "normal" aspects of oral reading behavior. Few, other than Ilg and Ames, adopted this point of view prior to 1965. However, with the reconceptualization of reading as something more than a simple (or complex, depending on your point of view) serial letter-to-sound-to-word-to-meaning process, the potential existed for the richer descriptions.

The most complete, if not the only, study prior to 1965 which examined oral reading errors in a developmental framework, is that of Ilg and Ames (1950). Too often overlooked by modern researchers, Ilg and Ames recorded the oral reading behaviors of hundreds of children across several age levels and produced a rather rich description—one, in fact, which has rarely, if ever, been equaled. They identified a pattern which portrayed children, age 5.5 to 9 years, moving from predominantly visual-similarity error responses, to a balance of visually similar and contextually appropriate error types, and finally to a stage in which contextually acceptable errors predominate. They also noted that at the more proficient levels, readers' errors tended to share both visual similarity and contextual acceptability. While certain aspects of these patterns have been challenged by more recent research, it is unlikely that their report was in error. Rather, instructional differences between programs of that era and today seem more likely sources for differences in the patterns observed. However, Ilg and Ames, like most others who have reported analyses of oral reading errors, failed to include descriptions of the instructional programs of their subjects.

Fifteen years later other reports began to appear that were philosophically compatible. K. S. Goodman (1965) presented an argument for looking beyond surface level features of written language in analyzing oral reading errors. He presented data from primary-grade readers which demonstrated an increasing ability to employ contextual information in word recognition. Clay (1967) described beginning readers' responses to written language and noted that contextual constraints seemed to exert a more powerful influence on her subjects than did graphemic or phonemic information when reading text. K. S. Goodman (1967) presented an analysis of one child's oral reading errors, demonstrating some effects contextual constraints exert upon the oral reading process. Clay (1968) presented detailed analyses of beginning readers' developmental patterns. Weber (1968) reviewed the existing literature on oral reading errors and pointed out several major shortcomings, both theoretical and psychometric. The next two years evidenced a torrent of studies of oral reading (Biemiller, 1970; Clay, 1969; Kolers, 1970; Levin & Kaplan, 1970; Nurss, 1969; Resnick, 1970; and Weber, 1970a, 1970b). The relative resplendence of studies of oral reading behaviors from that point on provides us with (1) a potent base from which to describe developmental patterns and (2) a complex task in synthesizing and interpreting the wealth of data from investigators using various populations, definitions, and tasks.

In an attempt to present the various findings as clearly and painlessly as possible, the following sections are divided first into five rough age- or school-level groups: *beginning*—readers in the first year of formal reading instruction; *primary*—readers in their second and third year of formal reading instruction; *intermediate*—years 4 through 6 of formal instruction; *secondary*—years 7 through 12 of formal instruction; *advanced*—adults who are skilled readers (most often college students). Within each of these age/school level groupings, the data are discussed relative to four broad categories: *accuracy and rate, use of textual cues, self-correction behaviors,* and *effect of method of instruction.* While other organizational schemes are possible perhaps, the present one will allow effective integration of the diverse findings.

Beginning Reading

A number of studies have analyzed oral reading behaviors during the initial year of instruction. The unequivocal trend is for children to read more accurately and more quickly (Biemiller, 1970; Clay, 1967, 1968, 1969). There is also a trend for beginning readers to become more adept at utilizing each of the textual cues available. This area is the most difficult for describing "normal" development since the influence of instructional approach is so powerful (Barr, 1972, 1974–1975; 1975; Cohen, 1974–1975; Dank, 1977). However, as Clay (1967) has pointed out, there are several stages one must go through before lifting a book to read. These involve orientation to books, print, and a notion about written languages. Unfortunately, little research is available on this aspect of beginning reading. As a further aside, M. M. Clarke (1975) argues that early readers, those who seem to acquire the ability naturally prior to the onset of the schooling process, read quite differently from those who have been taught in school. She notes that the early readers tend to make more errors and read less fluently aloud but seem to prefer silent reading and excell in it compared to their school-taught peers. The oral reading of such early readers has not, however, been studied with the rigor of other beginning reader populations. This is unfortunate since this population might be considered less bound by instructional effects than those children who are beginning reading in a formal school setting. Hence, descriptions of the oral reading behaviors of those who have learned in untutored situations might provide us with the purest view of "natural" developmental trends. Barr (1972, 1974–1975, 1975) first noted the discrepancies between published research reports and her own observation of beginning reader oral reading behaviors. While she effectively demonstrated the impact of instructional programs on word identification in isolation, other aspects of instructional influence were not examined. Her initial argument that descriptions of oral reading behaviors had to take instructional program into account have been supported by several other researchers (Cohen, 1974–1975; Dank, 1977; DeLawter, 1975; Elder, 1971).

Beginning readers seem to differ in their responses to textual cues, depending on the type of instructional program they receive. However, instructional programs often differ more as a matter of degree than by stiking contrasts (Barr, 1975). To be sure, materials reflecting a code emphasis, such as the linguistic readers with their patterns and resultant *"Rat sat on a fat hat"* sentences, preclude heavy reliance upon semantic and even syntactic cues. Similarly, materials emphasizing meaningful stories with uncontrolled vocabularies resist application of a symbol-to-sound strategy, even when children are trained to an extremely proficient level. Within the code- and meaning-emphasis categories, there also exist several subcategories. Synthetic and analytic phonics, phonogram approaches, and altered orthographies are each represented in some of the most popular code-emphasis materials. Meaning-emphasis approaches have employed whole-sentence techniques, whole-word strategies, and combinations, including either one or both of the above with a nod, at least, in the direction of teaching symbol-sound components of the written language. However, few pedagogical programs seem to be "pure." Rather, several types of material are used, often with the eclectic intent of attempting to capitalize upon the purported strengths of both emphases. Finally, there is reason to suspect that even as early as Grade 1, the low-progress readers are taught differently, with different emphases, materials, and attending directions quite irrespective of the program in which they are placed (Allington, 1980, 1983; Alpert, 1975; Hiebert, 1983; Howlett & Weintraub, 1979; Weinstein, 1976).

Given these influences and the often less than rich descriptions of the instructional milieu from which the beginning readers have been drawn, the available research is less definitive concerning the "natural" progression of behaviors in the oral reading of naive learners. The several studies which report oral reading behaviors of children in meaning-emphasis programs do present some relatively similar descriptions. MacKinnon (1959) reported that contextually constrained errors were most prominent among children at the initial stages of acquisition. This pattern shifted to nonresponse errors and finally to errors which were similar in graphic representation. However, MacKinnon simply describes these patterns, offering no data for inspection. The study is not unlike the earlier Ilg and Ames (1950) study, except in the important respect that the developmental trends are quite different. Comparing the trends, unfortunately, is virtually impossible since descriptions of subjects, observations, and error behaviors are quite barren. However, the discrepancies seem most obvious at the entry level, where Ilg and Ames found visually similar errors most common and MacKinnon found contextually appropriate errors predominant. Given the whole-word-in-isolation approach popular in the Ilg and Ames era, however, it may be that instructional program differences would account for observed differences since MacKinnon's subjects experienced a whole-sentence instructional program. It may be that Ilg and Ames simply tested children who had completed an indeterminant amount of formal instruction; thus, their first category, in reality, is MacKinnon's third stage.

Biemiller (1970) examined in substantial detail the oral reading development of beginning readers and expanded greatly on earlier descriptions. Biemiller's data also produce a three-phase developmental model. This first phase was, like MacKinnon's, typified by contextually constrained responses. The second phase was characterized by an error pattern in which more than half of the errors were nonresponses and which showed a decline in contextually constrained errors and greater proportions of errors evidencing attention to graphemic information. The third and final phase presented a decrease in nonresponse ratio to less than half and more errors constrained by both contextual and graphemic information. Biemiller also noted that high-progress readers spent only a short period in the first phase but that the duration of stay at the second phase had little relationship to final attainment.

Clay (1967, 1968, 1969) and Weber (1970a, 1970b) both expand on this description by emphasizing the role of sentence structure in shaping errant responses to text. In these studies, beginning readers' errors were shown to be constrained particularly by syntactic elements. Specifically, in each of the investigations errors of both the average and high-progress readers reflected syntactic congruity in at least 70% of the occurrences. When grammaticality was assessed only in relation to the immediately preceding context, the acceptability level rose to 90% or better.

Weber (1970b) also reported an increase in the graphic similarity of errors across time. Clay (1968) noted that a little better than 40% of the errors suggested attention to graphemic information. Thus, for meaning-emphasis programs (loosely speaking), the developmental pattern seems to be this: movement away from contextually constrained responses which indicate grammatical congruence with little attention to graphemic information, to simple omission of words as the reader comes to develop a notion of the correspondence between printed words and aural responses, to a stage that indicates increasing integration of all available textual cues (the errors which make sense *and* reflect some use of graphemic information).

Self-correction behavior also changes across time. Clay (1968, 1969) and Weber (1970a, 1970b) both note that average and high-progress readers tended to self-correct only the errors that violated contextual constraints and that were obviously incorrect, given the ending structure. Clay (1969) notes, however, that only about one-third of all errors were corrected by the better readers.

The development sketched above does not describe accurately performances of children who ultimately made less than satisfactory progress. Biemiller (1970) noted that when classified by phase, there were no differences in contextual constrained responses for high- and low-progress readers but that the low achievers had fewer errors rated as graphemically similar. Clay (1968, 1969) did not group subjects by phases. She reported that poor readers differed little in proportion of contextually constrained responses but that the poorer readers had a smaller proportion of errors reflecting graphemic or phonemic similarity, a higher proportion of errors in general, and fewer self-corrections (11% vs. 35% [1968]; 5% vs. 33% [1969]). These findings have been supported by Biemiller (1979), Whaley and Kibby (1981) and Weber (1970a, 1970b).

Biemiller had first graders read passages containing varying proportions of previously taught words. He found that as passage difficulty (measured by proportion of new words) increased both high- and low-progress readers made proportionally more no response and graphemic similarity errors, but the high-progress readers made fewer such errors than the low-progress readers. He argued that as text difficulty increased, all readers made greater use of graphemic information, not just low-progress readers. Whaley and Kibby (1981) reported that first graders' intraword (graphemic/phonemic) analysis predicted a significant portion of the variance in reading achievement, even after interword (grammatical) analysis had been partialed out. Weber found better readers corrected 85% of errors which were contextually inappropriate, while poorer readers corrected only 42% of these error types. In addition, better readers corrected contextually appropriate responses less often (27%) than contextually inappropriate responses (85%) while poorer readers had a much smaller difference in the correction rate for these errors (32%) compared to contextually unacceptable responses (42%).

Poor beginning readers in meaning-emphasis programs then, seem to employ contextual constraints like better readers, but they seem not to attend to graphemic information as frequently. More important, perhaps, these readers seem to rely on one available source of information rather than integrating all available cues. The reading rates reported for the low-progress readers suggests that they are, at best, word-by-word readers (Biemiller notes the poorest group averaged a little over two seconds per response to words in connected text). This, in itself, deserves further exploration since reported rates suggest that these low-progress readers spend an inordinate amount of time responding, indicating that they may process words serially and slowly.

The developmental pattern for the error behaviors of beginning readers in programs emphasizing decoding has been investigated less often. Cohen (1974–1975) provides a full description of oral reading error patterns of first graders across the final eight months of the school year. The children in her sample were exposed to a synthetic-phonics instructional program which was integrated into a basal reader guided-language arts program. She examined error behaviors elicited when reading the assigned instructional material and a separate material which seemed more congruent with a whole-word approach. She found few differences due to the nature of the material read for the normal readers.

While she presented neither quantitative analyses of errors nor rate, there is no reason to believe that the code-emphasis approach should elicit any trend other than more accurate and faster reading across time. Responses to textual cues do seem to differ as a function of instructional program. Code-emphasis readers produce qualitatively different oral reading behaviors from meaning-emphasis readers. The primary behaviors differentiating these code-emphasis readers were the production of nonsense words, sounding out behaviors, and the paucity of omission and insertion behaviors. On the noninstructional material, these readers tended to produce a greater proportion of nonsense words than they did on the instructional material, though this behavior is easily explainable by the difference in vocabulary-control procedures of the two materials.

Cohen found that low-progress readers exhibited different error patterns than the better readers. Poor readers always had a greater proportion of no-response errors than either nonsense or word-substitution errors, regardless of the material or time of year. They nearly doubled their nonsense word production from the beginning to the end of the year, produced slightly fewer "sounding out" behaviors than better readers, and had substantially reduced self-correction behaviors with very little, if any, improvement across the year.

As noted earlier, however, the arguments between code- and meaning-emphasis proponents may have little pedagogical relevance in an era of eclecticism and uncertainty about the "one best method." Schlieper (1977) presents a description of Grade 1 students who were exposed to an "eclectic" instructional program. These subjects read from one of three different reading series, received instruction on sight recognition of whole words and completed lesson and workbooks emphasizing development of phonic skills. The data from Schlieper's one-time sample show beginning readers in an eclectic program making both nonsense-word errors and omissions, error behaviors relatively exclusive to either a code- or meaning-emphasis in other studies. However, since she presents no data for no-response behaviors, one must assume that she, unlike other investigators, collapsed omission and no-response behaviors. In other respects, her data seem more similar to those from code-emphasis subjects. Particularly, grammaticality approximates Cohen's (1974–1975) 40%–45% acceptability level; but since different decision rules were used by each investigator, no clear resolution is available. The level of grammatical acceptability of errors for both the code-emphasis and eclectic programs is substantially lower than those reported for meaning-emphasis curricula.

In sum then, the oral reading behavior of beginning readers seems sensitive to instructional emphasis. If oral reading behaviors serve as indicators of cognitive processing (Goldman-Eislar, 1968), then different instructional programs do indeed produce different cognitive strategies. In addition, these differences appear regardless of the type of material read or ability.

Primary Reading

As children develop additional proficiency in reading, several trends are observed in oral reading error behavior. Some are similar to those noted with beginning readers, such as increases in rate (Biemiller, 1977–1978; Clay & Imlach, 1971) and overall accuracy (Clay & Imlach, 1971; Ilg & Ames, 1950; Powell, 1970; Spache, 1963/1972). In addition, children in the second and third years of formal instruction seem to continue to improve in their ability to integrate graphemic and syntactic components, as illustrated by improved proportions of errors which reflect attention to both cue systems (Burke, 1976; Y. M. Goodman, 1970; Ilg & Ames, 1950; Leslie, 1980; Lopez, 1977; Murray & Maliphant, 1982). Self-correction behavior becomes more frequent, particularly for those responses which initially violate grammaticality (Au, 1977; Burke, 1976; Y. M. Goodman, 1970; Recht, 1976). These developing readers exhibit improved fluency as well, increasingly segmenting their oral production at appropriate grammatical boundaries (Eagan, 1975; Kowal, O'Connell, O'Brien, & Bryant, 1975; Clay & Imlach, 1971). Fluency seems tied explicitly to increased eye-voice span, which is itself related to increased sensitivity to grammatical boundaries (Levin & Kaplan, 1970; Rode, 1974–1975; Wildman & Kling, 1978–1979).

Instructional programs continue to exhibit predictable effects. The errors of children in meaning-emphasis programs continue to reflect greater sensitivity to contextual constraints, while those of readers in code-emphasis programs reflect greater sensitivity to graphemic cues and less awareness of context (Dank, 1977; DeLawter, 1975; Elder, 1971). Code-emphasis programs develop readers who produce fewer omissions and more nonsense words compared to programs with a meaning emphasis.

Low-progress readers continue to produce errors which reflect less integration of graphemic and contextual cue systems (K. S. Goodman, 1976; Y. M. Goodman, 1970; Leslie, 1980; Recht, 1976; Schlieper, 1977). They also make more errors and self-correct less often (Au, 1977; Y. M. Goodman, 1970; Recht, 1977). There seems to be no empirical basis for the argument that slightly older low-progress readers perform in a manner substantially different from younger high-progress readers. That is, the error patterns of older readers making unsatisfactory progress generally are quite similar to younger readers making satisfactory progress. The low-progress readers, however, seem to become blocked at a stage prior to integration of the various cue systems. In this sense, it is important to extend the work of Clay and Imlach (1971), Resnick (1970), Siler (1973–1974), Kowal et al. (1975), Martin, Kolodziez, & Genay (1971), and Schreiber (1980) by observing under what conditions poor readers developmentally progress in fluency. Poor readers are frequently described in the literature, especially at this age level, as word-by-word readers, but most error analyses at the word level indicate relatively similar patterns, even for grammaticality, to those produced by younger high-progress readers. Since the studies noted above have demonstrated that even proficient Grade 2 readers tend to resist disruption within a syntactic constituent, it seems plausible that this aspect of oral reading behavior may provide relatively greater dissimilarities between readers of similar achievement levels but differing progress rates. The point is that poor readers seem to receive instruction that emphasizes improved accuracy rather than improved rate, fluency, or syntactic sensitivity.

Schreiber (1980) makes the clearest case for the importance of appropriate development of fluency. He argues that readers must learn to compensate for the absence of precise graphic signals corresponding to prosodic information in the speech stream by making better use of the morphological and syntactic cues that are present. Unless readers develop abilities to parse sentences appropriately, the acquisition of reading abilities will be delayed. Along this line, he presents an explanation of why instructional activities, such as repeated readings, paired reading, and reading to children, seem to have a positive impact on acquisition of oral reading fluency. Though relatively few tests of his hypotheses have been conducted, the research reported by Martin and Meltzer (1976), Morgan and Lyon (1979), Pflaum and Pascarella (1980), and Samuels (1979) seem to support both importance and trainability of oral reading fluency.

Intermediate and Secondary

As children progress into the middle school and secondary school, oral reading, as pointed out earlier, receives less instructional emphasis. This may explain the paucity of reports describing the oral reading behaviors of older elementary students. Watson and Clay (1975) did find continuing improvement in accuracy and rate generally, though one should expect wide individual variation. They also note that low-achieving readers did not utilize syntactic structure as efficiently as better readers. K. S. Goodman (1976) noted that there continues to be an increase in proportion of errors which reflect syntactic and semantic acceptability as proficiency increased, even into secondary school. He also noted (Goodman & Gollasch, 1980) an increase in word omissions as readers mature. However, the increased omissions seem to be nondeliberate and are more prevalent when reading easy material than when reading difficult material. He argues that not all omissions are equivalent and do not stem from the same processing strategies.

Several investigators have employed oral reading tasks in attempts to identify particular text features that contribute to processing difficulties in older children. Siler (1973–1974), for instance, varied syntactic and semantic constraints and found that syntactic violations were more disruptive, in terms of processing time, than were semantic violations. Nurss (1969) demonstrated that syntactically more complex sentences elicited more oral reading errors than less complex sentences, and that errors in less complex sentences were more often grammatically acceptable. Kowal et al. (1975) found that inverting the subject-object order to create an incongruous sentence produced relatively longer pauses than other transformations. They also found that there is a difference between the length and number of pauses in oral reading, arguing that length seemed primarily related to cognitive operations, while number of pauses seemed to be a function of text difficulty.

In attempts to depict differences in the reading strategies of good and poor older readers, Isakson and Miller (1976) and Allington and Strange (1977) embedded anomalous words in passages. They found that under such conditions better readers tended to read what was printed and poorer readers more often ignored graphemic information to produce a contextually appropriate response. These results, which seem to suggest that poor readers at these levels underutilize graphemic information, have recently been reinterpreted by Stanovich and West (1979) in relation to a dual-process mechanism of effective contextual utilization. This alternative theory suggests the differences are accounted for by the factors of automatic and conscious context utilization and assumes a different process for employing contextual information in good and poor readers.

Poor readers at these levels seem to read not only more slowly and less accurately (Allington, 1978; Thompson, 1978; Watson & Clay, 1957) but also exhibit error patterns much like those of younger readers (Thompson, 1978), with these exceptions: they produce more meaning-change errors (Pflaum & Bryan, 1980; Willows & Ryan, 1981), fewer self-corrections (Pflaum & Bryan, 1980; Recht, 1976), and are more affected by contextual variation. For instance, Allington (1978) found that when reading the same words in context versus a random-order condition, the good readers' accuracy suffered little, while their rate nearly doubled. Poor readers, on the other hand, showed little difference in rate but were substantially less accurate in the random-order condition.

Several investigators have examined the effect of errors on comprehension. Beebe (1980) found that generally as the number of substitution errors increased, comprehension decreased. At the same time, however, as semantically and syntactically appropriate errors and self-corrections increased, so too did comprehension. Obviously, only semantically and syntactically inappropriate errors had negative impacts on comprehension. How one assesses comprehension is important to this point however. Nicholson, Pearson, and Dykstra (1979) used embedded anomalies to simulate errors and found a greater negative impact for errors when exact recall or restoration was required. When more liberal assessments, such as summaries or allowing semantically appropriate restoration were used to check comprehension, the errors exerted less impact. Finally, Kendall and Hood (1979) identified two types of poor readers based on error patterns and comprehension. Some poor readers exhibited relatively high comprehension, even with relatively poor word accuracy. Others exhibited poor comprehension with reasonably accurate word recognition. Differences in use of contextual information, similar to that reported by Beebe (1980), seem to account for those differences within these groups of poor readers.

Beyond Grade 3, there exists an apparent lack of agreement about differences between good and poor readers' oral reading behaviors. Several investigators report no difference in context sensitivity between these groups (Allington & Strange, 1977; Kolers, 1975; Schwartz & Stanovich, 1981), while other investigators found good readers made better use of contextual information (Leslie, 1980; Pflaum & Bryan, 1980; Willows & Ryan, 1981). This inconsistency is not easily resolved since a variety of oral reading tasks and scoring criteria have been used, with different populations reading materials of different relative difficulty. These factors, combined with the distinct possibility that there are different subgroups of poor readers, point to the need for additional research in order to better understand the oral reading process in older readers.

In sum, far fewer studies describing normal oral reading behaviors exist for learners beyond Grade 3. The available research suggests continued development in rate, accuracy, self-correction, sensitivity to grammatical features, and fluency. With a few notable exceptions, poor readers at these levels produce error patterns qualitatively similar to younger high-progress readers. Instructional program effects on readers at these levels are basically unknown.

Advanced Reading

No descriptive reports of oral reading behaviors beyond a case study, have been reported for skilled adult readers. At this level, oral reading has generally been employed in an experimental design in an attempt to understand aspects of the reading process. For instance, Gilbert and Burk (1969), Lass and Lutz (1973), Silverman (1970a, 1970b), and Cecconi, Hood, and Tucker (1977) all studied effects of repeated readings of individual passages, separate passages of equivalent difficulty, or passages differing in difficulty on the oral reading rate and fluency of subjects. They found that rate and fluency increase as a function of practice, decrease as a function of passage difficulty, and vary as a function of passage topic. Brown and Miron (1971), Resnick (1970), Vazquez, Glucksberg, and Danks (1977–1978), Kolers (1970), and others have employed oral reading performance in an attempt to depict the contribution of syntactic structure in the reading process.

Oral reading performance per se then, in adult skilled readers has had little investigation, but the consensus seems to be that these subjects make relatively few errors, self-correct the vast majority of those errors which violate grammatical constraints, and read in appropriate syntactic units with generally adequate intonational features. Whether this would be the case with difficult material remains to be demonstrated.

The Task of Oral Reading

Perhaps a discussion of the processes that underlie oral reading performance should be a beginning point to any review paper such as this. However, the large community of researchers investigating oral reading has delayed serious discussion of such issues; it seems similarly justifiable to discuss this issue at the end of this review. While we have a wealth of data available on diverse aspects of oral reading, we have witnessed few attempts to describe the specific components of the oral reading process.

Danks and Fears (1979) note that traditionally it has been assumed that in oral reading, the graphemic information (letter and words) is first decoded into a phonological representation (sounds and words) and that the subsequent oral production is then comprehended in much the same way a listener processes another speaker's conversation. They call this the "decoding hypothesis"; text is turned into sounds and these sounds are recognized as language (words, phrases, sentences) and comprehended. They propose an alternative, called the "comprehension hypothesis," which suggests that oral production is begun only after comprehension has occurred (or at least after a semantic representation of the text has been constructed). Oral production then emerges from the semantic representation rather than the phonological representation. Oral production, under this hypothesis, occurs after access to meaning rather than before.

When one who is not a fluent speaker of a foreign language gives an oral rendition of a text in that language, the decoding hypothesis would, by necessity, become operative, as it would be if one read out loud a string of pseudowords; although, in both cases, there is not comprehension after production. Dialect speakers, they suggest, provide clear examples of the comprehension hypothesis since they may produce an oral rendition that includes semantically equivalent dialect-induced errors that reflect little attention to the graphemic information available in the printed text (e.g. "be" for "is" or "cah" for "car"). The fact that meaning equivalence is obtained, even in the face of an "inaccurate" phonological representation, suggests the oral production occurred after meaning had been accessed.

Danks and Fears (1979) note that the studies of oral reading errors reporting evidence of influence of semantic and syntactic constraints in oral readings (see preceding sections) offer little support for the "decoding hypothesis" since the only source of error that should be reflected is inaccurate phonological processing. That is, if words are first pronounced then comprehended, no influence of meaning, such as semantic or syntactic similarity to the target word, should be found, except in random instances. The distinct and reliable trend for the developmentally increasing influence of semantic and syntactic constraints is not consistent with the "decoding hypothesis."

On the other hand, the fact that one can read pseudoword strings or, perhaps, a foreign newspaper, suggests that oral reading *can* occur as described in the "decoding hypothesis." That it is possible does not suggest though that such processing routinely occurs. Nor does the beginning reader start with a "decoding hypothesis" system and gradually shift. The consistency of influence of semantic and syntactic information on beginning readers is powerful and denies the validity of such arguments.

Additional clarification of the processes involved in the task of oral reading is provided by Danks and Hill (1981) and Danks, Bohn, and Fears (1982). In these papers, they report the results of several studies which assess the influence of various types of information available in connected text (e.g., lexical, syntactic, semantic, factual) by measuring the hesitation induced by manipulating these textual features. In addition, they develop an interactive model of oral reading processing, extending the work of Stanovich (1980) and Marslen-Wilson (1975). In this model, the task of orally producing each word in succession is characterized as follows. Oral production is initiated after lexical access, following not immediately after any phonological mediation that might occur but only after the meaning has been identified. This lexical access is derived from the perceptual analysis and any available syntactic and semantic constraints. Potential candidates for the word are considered, evaluated, and eliminated by the various sources of information available to the reader. Once word meaning has been selected, pronunciation follows. They propose that each word is processed for meaning as it appears and that when a phrase boundary is reached, additional processing takes place in order to construct a full representation of the meaning of the text to that point. When the word-by-word meaning process fails to produce a coherent representation, junctures provided by phrase boundaries may be critical points at which the reader attempts to clarify the meaning by pausing, by orally rereading, or by silently reiterating some portion of the text.

This model of oral reading delimits three tasks required for oral readers. The first is lexical access since that is the source for pronunciation. The second is phrase understanding and integration so that meaning is obtained. The third task is ensuring that the representation is coherent and consistent with preceding text interpretations. This is essential since one can access a meaning that seems incongruous with the rest of the context (e.g., Bill lived in a big white horse). The oral production aspect of oral reading could interfere with any of these tasks as could a number of other situational variables (e.g., readers purpose, orienting instructions, text topic and difficulty, etc.).

Oral reading then, because of the oral production feature, presents different task demands from silent reading (e.g., Cambourne, 1976–1977; Mosenthal, 1976–1977). In addition, the instructional setting for oral reading imposes different demands from that of silent reading (e.g., public vs. private performance, personal vs. external monitor of performance, emphasis on accuracy of production vs. accuracy of meaning construction). Until quite recently the unique features and task demands of the oral reading activity have largely been ignored by both those who construct models of the reading process and those who deliver reading instruction. Only with a better understanding of the oral reading processes, as distinct from the silent reading processes, will we be able to address the limitations of the research reviewed earlier and the research agenda that follows. For too long, we have attempted to construct general models of reading that ignore the inherent differences between oral and silent reading.

A RESEARCH AGENDA

In my brief review of the history of oral reading as an instructional activity, I noted that there has been a distinct shift in practice in the past century. While we have available some excellent historical analyses of literacy (cf. Resnick & Resnick, 1977), no one has produced a historical essay focused solely on oral reading as an instructional activity. There seems an adequate literature available for such an inquiry. In addition, a content analysis of teachers' editions of basal readers might also improve our understanding of how commercial materials reflect social trends and influence practice.

We do know that oral reading is a frequent activity in most elementary schools, particularly in the primary grades and for poorer readers across the elementary grades. However, most studies to date have relied upon questionnaires and seldom reported direct measures of incidence. Further, we have little information on why oral reading is so commonly employed in instruction and what influences teachers to select oral reading as a pedagogical strategy.

We have less than adequate data on the incidence of oral reading in classrooms, likewise, we have little understanding of the worth of oral reading as an instructional activity. Some reports suggest little positive consequence from oral reading in terms of achievement outcomes. Others report that oral reading seems to be a valuable activity. As noted, it is most likely that a curvilinear relationship exists between incidence of oral reading and achievement gain. Unfortunately, such speculation is about as precise as one can get, given available evidence.

We have a few careful descriptions of how reading groups operate on a day-to-day basis but, most typically, these studies report intensive study of single classrooms. Upon careful inspection, several similarities are found, but striking contrasts in group procedures are also found. Given the differences in teachers, children, classrooms, schools, and communities from which these descriptions are derived, we should not be particularly surprised at the variations. However, we still are relatively ignorant of the important features of oral reading in group settings and of the factors that induce variation.

When children read aloud, teachers and other children most generally interrupt with assisting behavior. We have some understanding of the distribution of such assistance and a glimmer of information on the effects on the development of reading abilities. Still, we remain far less informed than we need to be in order to offer reliable advice on the wisdom of providing any sort of verbal feedback when readers err while reading aloud.

Clay (1979) provides evidence that oral reading strategies can be changed with instruction, as do Pflaum and Pascarella (1980). However, in the available research, such instruction was offered individually or in small groups by specially trained personnel. While these studies are important, we also need to know how to organize and deliver more effective oral reading instruction in larger groups with classroom teachers as the instructor. Oral reading behaviors seem to be seldom directly taught in regular education environments. We need to identify ways to make such instruction regularly available and to document the impact.

We need to address the inadequacies in available diagnostic assessments of oral reading. The continued use of psychometrically inadequate and theoretically outdated (or impoverished) instruments cannot add to either our professional stature or the precision of our diagnoses.

The question of determining the appropriate level of difficulty for placement in materials for instructional purposes is a most pressing issue. We continue to exercise our best guesses due to a lack of adequate evidence for any suggested criteria. Some evidence suggests that traditional standards (90%–95%) for error rates are too stringent, and other evidence suggests that those standards are too liberal. Beck's (1981) suggestion that students routinely read materials of different levels of difficulty has much logical appeal but little empirical support.

A related issue is what one counts as errors when making difficulty decisions about placement in materials. As Weber (1970) and Leu (1982) have noted, no adequate rationale or definition of error categories has been developed. The continued use of ambiguous criteria and overlapping categories will not advance our understanding. Until we adopt some common procedures, comparison, integration, interpretation, and, ultimately, understanding of oral reading research will suffer.

While we have reached some consensus on how beginning readers seem to develop oral reading abilities, relatively little is known about the influences of curricular materials or instructional contexts, particularly effects beyond the initial year of instruction. We know little about the relationship between oral language variations and the acquisition of oral reading abilities (cf. Collins, 1982). Finally, we have focused too much on errors and error counts and too little on oral reading strategies and their acquisition (e.g., What happens when an unknown word is encountered? What strategies are attempted? How do these develop?).

In our focus on errors and accuracy levels we have ignored the obviously critical feature of fluency in oral reading. While fluency has yet escaped easy operationalization, it is too central to definitions of good oral reading to continue to be ignored. We need to observe and describe the acquisition of fluency.

Another facet has been largely ignored, the social, communicative, and interactive context of oral reading practices. When reading aloud, one is performing for an audience. The work of Mishler (1972), Mehan (1979), Sinclair and Coulthard (1978), Heap (1980), and Eder (1982) all touch upon some aspect of this, but all leave many stones unturned.

The distinct tasks of oral reading, as compared to silent reading, have for too long been ignored. We need further research that details what is involved in oral reading acquisition. While the potential influence of the different variables encountered in oral reading situations have been noted, few have been detailed in depth. What role, for instance, does prior content knowledge exert on oral reading behaviors? Or different social contexts? Or different text organizational structures? Do such variations differentially affect production accuracy and comprehension?

How do different oral reading behaviors (e.g., error patterns, hesitations, fluency, rate) relate to encoding processes, or retrieval of information from short-term or long-term memory?

Finally, we might do well to examine why we have waited so long to address the mythologies and attack the traditions that pervade virtually all aspects of oral reading.

REFERENCES

Allington, R. L.   Effects of contextual constraints upon rate and accuracy. *Perceptual and Motor Skills*, 1978, *46*, 1318.

Allington, R. L.   Word identification abilities of severely disabled readers: A comparison in isolation and context. *Journal of Reading Behavior*, 1979, *10*, 409–416.

Allington, R. L.   Teacher interruption behaviors during primary grade oral reading. *Journal of Educational Psychology*, 1980, *72*, 371–372.

Allington, R. L.   *Amount and mode of contextual reading as a function of reading group membership.* Paper presented at the National Council of Teachers of English, Washington, D.C., 1982.

Allington, R. L.   The reading instruction provided readers of differing ability. *Elementary School Journal*, 1983, *83*, 255–265.

Allington, R. L., & Strange, M.   Effects of grapheme substitutions in connected text upon reading behaviors. *Visible Language*, 1977, *11*, 285–297.

Alpert, J. L.   Teacher behavior across ability groups: A consideration of the mediation of Pygmalion effects. *Journal of Educational Psychology,* 1974, *66,* 348–353.

Alpert, J. L.   Do teachers adapt methods and materials to ability groups in reading? *California Journal of Educational Research,* 1975, *26,* 120–123.

Anderson, I. H., & Dearborn, W. F.   *The psychology of teaching reading.* New York: Ronald Press, 1952.

Anderson, L. M., Evertson, C. M., & Brophy, J.   An experimental study of effective reading in first-grade reading groups. *Elementary School Journal,* 1979, *79,* 193–223.

Au, K. H.-P.   Analyzing oral reading errors to improve instruction. *Reading Teacher,* 1977, *31,* 46–49.

Austin, M. C., & Morrison, C.   *The first R: The Harvard report on reading in elementary schools.* New York: Macmillan, 1963.

Barr, R.   The influence of instructional conditions on word recognition errors. *Reading Research Quarterly,* 1972, *7,* 509–529.

Barr, R.   The effect of instruction on pupil reading strategies. *Reading Research Quarterly,* 1974–1975, *10,* 556–582.

Barr, R.   Influence of reading materials on responses to printed words. *Journal of Reading Behavior,* 1975, *7,* 123–135. (a)

Barr, R.   Processes underlying the learning of printed words. *Elementary School Journal,* 1975, *75,* 258–268. (b)

Beck, I. L.   Reading problems and instructional practices. In G. E. Mackinnon & T. G. Waller (Eds.) *Reading Research: Advances in theory and practice* (Vol. 2). New York: Academic Press, 1981.

Beebe, M. J.   The effect of different types of substitution miscues on reading. *Reading Research Quarterly,* 1980, *15,* 324–336.

Beldin, H. L.   Informal reading testing: Historical review and review of the research. In W. D. Durr, (Ed.), *Reading Difficulties: Diagnosis, correction and remediation.* Newark, Del.: International Reading Association, 1970.

Bennett, A.   An analysis of errors in word recognition made by retarded readers. *Journal of Educational Psychology,* 1942, *33,* 25–34.

Berliner, D. C.   Academic learning time and reading achievement. In J. T. Guthrie (Ed.), *Comprehension and teaching: Research reviews.* Newark, Del.: International Reading Association, 1981.

Betts, E. A.   *Foundations of reading instruction,* New York: American Book Co., 1946.

Biemiller, A.   The development of the use of graphic and contextual information as children learn to read. *Reading Research Quarterly,* 1970, *6,* 75–96.

Biemiller, A.   Relationships between oral reading rates for letters, words, and simple text in the development of reading achievement. *Reading Research Quarterly,* 1977–1978, *13,* 223–253.

Biemiller, A.   Changes in the use of graphic and contextual information as functions of passage difficulty and reading achievement level. *Journal of Reading Behavior,* 1979, *11,* 307–318.

Brecht, R. D.   Testing format and instructional level with the informal reading inventory. *Reading Teacher,* 1977, *31,* 57–59.

Brophy, J. E., & Evertson, C. M.   *Student characteristics and teaching.* New York: Longman, 1981.

Brown, E., & Miron, M. S.   Lexical and syntactic predictors of the distribution of pause time in reading. *Journal of Verbal Learning and Verbal Behavior,* 1971, *10,* 658–667.

Burke, C. L.   The three cue systems: #2—syntactic. In P. D. Allen & D. J. Watson (Eds.), *Findings of research in miscue analysis: Classroom implications.* Urbana, Ill.: National

Council of Teachers of English, ERIC Clearinghouse on Reading and Communication Skills, 1976.

Burke, E.   A developmental study of childrens' reading strategies. *Educational Review,* 1976, *29,* 30–46.

Buros, O. K.   *Reading tests and reviews.* Highland Park, N.J.: Gryphon Press, 1975.

Buswell, G. T.   *Non-oral Reading: A study of its use in the Chicago public schools* (Supplementary Educational Monographs, No. 60). Chicago: University of Chicago Press, 1945.

Cambourne, B.   Getting to Goodman: An analysis of the Goodman model of reading with some suggestions for evaluation. *Reading Research Quarterly,* 1976–1977, *12,* 605–636.

Carew, J. V., & Lightfoot, S. L.   *Beyond bias: Perspectives on classrooms.* Cambridge: Harvard University Press, 1979.

Cecconi, C. P., Hood, S. B., & Tucker, R. K.   Influence of reading level difficulty on the dysfluencies of normal children. *Journal of Speech and Hearing Research,* 1977, *20,* 475–484.

Christie, J. F., & Alonso, P. A.   Effects of passage difficulty on primary-grade children's oral reading error patterns. *Educational Research Quarterly,* 1980, *5,* 41–49.

Clark, M. M.   *Young fluent readers.* London: Heinemann, 1975.

Clark, R. M.   *A study of teacher behavior and attitudes in elementary schools with high and low pupil achievement.* Paper presented at the American Educational Research Association, Washington, D.C., 1975.

Clay, M. M.   The reading behavior of five year old children: A research project. *New Zealand Journal of Educational Studies,* 1967, *2,* 11–31.

Clay, M. M.   A syntactic analysis of reading errors. *Journal of Verbal Learning and Verbal Behavior,* 1968, *7,* 434–438.

Clay, M. M.   Reading errors and self-correction behaviour, *British Journal of Educational Psychology,* 1969, *39,* 47–56.

Clay, M. M.   *The early detection of reading difficulties: A diagnostic survey with recovery procedures* (2nd ed.). Exeter, N. H.: Heinemann, 1979.

Clay, M. M., & Imlach, R. H.   Juncture, pitch and stress as reading behavior variables. *Journal of Verbal Learning and Verbal Behavior,* 1971, *10,* 133–139.

Cohen, A. S.   Oral reading errors of first grade children taught by a code-emphasis approach. *Reading Research Quarterly,* 1974–1975, *10,* 616–650.

Collins, J.   Discourse style, classroom interaction and differential treatment. *Journal of Reading Behavior.* 1982, *14,* 361–376.

Cunningham, P. M.   Teachers' correction responses to black-dialect miscues which are non-meaning changing. *Reading Research Quarterly,* 1976–1977, *12,* 637–653.

Dank, M.   What effect do reading programs have on the oral reading behavior of children? *Reading Improvement,* 1977, *14,* 66–69.

Danks, J., Bohn, L., & Fears, R.   Comprehension processes in oral reading. In G. B. Flores d'Arcais & R. J. Jarvella (Eds.), *The process of language understanding.* Chichester, Eng.: Wiley, 1982.

Danks, J. H., & Fears, R.   Oral reading: Does it reflect decoding or comprehension? In L. B. Resnick & P. A. Weaver (Eds.), *Theory and practice of early reading* (Vol. 3). Hillsdale, N.J.: Erlbaum, 1979.

Danks, J. H., & Hill, G. O.   An interactive analysis of oral reading. In A. M. Lesgold & C. A. Perfetti (Eds.), *Interactive processes in reading.* Hillsdale, N.J.: Erlbaum, 1981.

Daw, S. E.   The persistence of errors in oral reading in grades four and five. *Journal of Educational Research,* 1938, *32,* 81–90.

DeLawter, J. A.   The relationship of beginning reading instruction and miscue patterns.

In W. D. Page (Ed.), *Help for the reading teacher: New directions in research.* Urbana, Ill.: National Conference on Research in English, ERIC Clearinghouse on Reading and Communication Skills, 1975.

Dolch, E. W.   *The psychology and teaching of reading.* Boston: Ginn, 1931.

Doyle, W.   Making managerial decisions in classrooms. In D. L. Duke (Ed.), *Classroom management.* Chicago: University of Chicago Press, 1978.

Duffy, G. B., & Durrell, D. D.   Third grade difficulties in oral reading. *Education,* 1935, *56,* 37–40.

Duffy, G. G., & Roehler, L. R.   The illusion of instruction. *Reading Research Quarterly,* 1982, *17,* 438–445.

Durkin, D.   What classroom observations reveal about reading comprehension instruction. *Reading Research Quarterly,* 1978–1979, *14,* 481–533.

Durrell, D. D.   *Durrell analysis of reading difficulties.* New York: Harcourt Brace Jovanovich, 1937, 1953.

Durrell, D. D.   *Improvement of basic reading abilities.* Yonkers, N.Y.: World, 1940.

Eagan, Sr. R.   An investigation into the relationship of the pausing phenomena in oral reading and reading comprehension. *Alberta Journal of Educational Research,* 1975, *21,* 278–288.

Eder, D.   Differences in communicative styles across ability groups. In L. C. Wilkinson (Ed.), *Communicating in the classroom.* New York: Academic Press, 1982.

Elder, R. D.   Oral reading achievement of Scottish and American children. *Elementary School Journal,* 1971, *71,* 216–229.

Eller, W., & Attea, M.   Three diagnostic tests: Some comparisons. In J. A. Figurel (Ed.) *Vistas in reading.* Newark, Del.: International Reading Association, 1966.

Englert, C. S., & Semmel, M. I.   The relationship of oral reading substitution miscues to comprehension. *Reading Teacher,* 1981, *35,* 273–280.

Fuchs, L. S., Fuchs, D., & Deno, S.   Reliability and validity of curriculum-based informational reading inventories. *Reading Research Quarterly,* 1982, *18,* 6–25.

Gambrell, L. B., Wilson, R. M., & Gantt, W. N.   Classroom observations of task-attending behaviors of good and poor readers. *Journal of Educational Research,* 1981, *24,* 400–404.

Gates, A. I.   *The improvement of reading.* New York: Macmillan, 1935.

Gates, A. I., & McKillop, A. S.   *Gates-McKillop reading diagnostic tests.* New York: Teachers College, 1927, 1962.

Gilbert, J. H., & Burk, K. W.   Rate alterations in oral reading. *Language and Speech,* 1969, *12,* 192.

Gilmore, J. V., & Gilmore, E. C.   *Gilmore oral reading test.* New York: Harcourt Brace Jovanovich, 1951, 1968.

Goldman-Eislar, F.   *Psycholinguistics: Experiments in spontaneous speech.* London: Academic Press, 1968.

Goodman, K. S.   A linguistic study of cues and miscues in reading. *Elementary English,* 1965, 639–643.

Goodman, K. S.   Reading: A psycholinguistic guessing game. *Journal of the Reading Specialist,* 1967, *6,* 126–135.

Goodman, K. S.   Analysis of reading miscues: Applied psycholinguistics. *Reading Research Quarterly,* 1969, *5,* 9–30.

Goodman, K. S.   What we know about reading. In P. D. Allen & D. J. Watson (Eds.), *Findings of research in miscue analysis: Classroom implications.* Urbana, Ill.: National Council of Teachers of English, ERIC Clearinghouse on Reading and Communication Skills, 1976.

Goodman, K. S.   From the strawman to the tin woodman: A response to Mosenthal. *Reading Research Quarterly,* 1976–1977, *12,* 575–585.

Goodman, K. S., & Gollasch, F. V.   Word omissions: Deliberate and non-deliberate. *Reading Research Quarterly*, 1980, *16*, 6–13.

Goodman, Y. M.   Using children's reading miscues for new teaching strategies. *Reading Teacher*, 1970, *23*, 455–459.

Goodman, Y. M. Reading diagnosis—qualitative or quantitative? *Reading Teacher*, 1972, *26*, 32–27.

Goodman, Y. M., & Burke, C. L. *Reading miscue inventory*. New York: Macmillan, 1970.

Gray, W. S.   *Standardized oral reading paragraphs*. Bloomington, Ill.: Public School Publishing Co., 1915.

Gray, W. S. (Ed.)   *Report of the National Committee on Reading* (24th yearbook of the National Society for the Study of Education, Part I.) Bloomington, Ill.: Public School Publishing Co., 1925.

Gray, W. S.   A decade of progress. In G. M. Whipple (Ed.), *The teaching of reading; a second report* (37th yearbook of the National Society for the Study of Education). Bloomington, Ill.: Public School Publishing Co., 1937.

Gray, W. S.   Characteristics of effective oral reading. In H. Robinson (Ed.), *Oral aspects of reading* (Supplementary Educational Monographs, No. 82, December 1955). Chicago: University of Chicago Press, 1955.

Gumperz, J. J., & Hernandez-Chavez, E.   Bilingualism, bidialectalism, and classroom interaction. In C. B. Cazden, V. P. John, & D. Hymes (Eds.), *Functions of language in the classroom*. New York: Teachers College Press, 1972.

Hale, A., & Edwards, T.   Hearing children read. In J. Edwards (Ed.), *The social psychology of reading*. Silver Spring, Md.: Institute of Modern Language, 1981.

Harris, A. J., & Sipay, E. R.   *How to increase reading ability* (6th ed.) New York: McKay, 1975.

Harste, J. C., & Burke, C. L.   A new hypothesis for reading teacher education research: Both the teaching and learning are theoretically based. In P. D. Pearson (Ed.) *Reading: Theory, research and practice*. Clemson, S.C.: National Reading Conference, 1977.

Heap, J. L.   What counts as reading: Limits to certainty in assessment. *Curriculum Inquiry*, 1980, *10*, 265–292.

Hiebert, E. H.   An examination of ability groupings for reading instruction. *Reading Research Quarterly*, 1983, *18*, 231–255.

Hill, M. B.   Experimental procedures in the study of the process of word discrimination in reading. *Journal of Educational Research*, 1936, *29*, 473–481.

Hocevar, S. P., & Hocevar, D.   The effect of meaningful versus nonmeaningful reading material on oral reading errors in first through third grade children. *Journal of Reading Behavior*, 1978, *10*, 297–298.

Hoffman, J. V., & Baker, C.   Characterizing teacher feedback to student miscues during oral reading instruction. *Reading Teacher*, 1981, *34*, 907–913.

Hood, J.   Qualitative analysis of oral reading errors: The inter-judge reliability of scores. *Reading Research Quarterly*, 1975–1976, *11*, 577–598.

Horn, E., & Curtis, J. F.   Improvement of oral reading. In N. B. Henry (Ed.) *Reading in the elementary school* (48th yearbook of the National Society of the Study of Education, Part II.) Chicago, Ill.: University of Chicago Press, 1949.

Howlett, N., & Weintraub, S.   Instructional procedures. In R. C. Calfee & P. Drum (Eds.) *Teaching reading in compensatory classes*, Newark, Del.: International Reading Association, 1979.

Huey, E. B.   *The psychology and pedagogy of reading*. New York: Macmillan, 1908. (Reprinted 1968)

Hunt, B. C.   Black dialect and third and fourth graders' performance on the *Gray oral reading test*. *Reading Research Quarterly*, 1974–1975, *10*, 103–123.

Hyatt, A. V. *The place of oral reading in the school program.* New York: Teachers College, 1943.

Ilg, F. L., & Ames, L. B. Developmental trends in reading behavior. *Journal of Genetic Psychology,* 1950, *76,* 291–312.

Isakson, R. L., & Miller, J. W. Sensitivity to syntactic and semantic cues in good and poor comprehenders. *Journal of Educational Psychology,* 1976, *68,* 787–792.

Jorgenson, G. W. Relationship of classroom behavior to the accuracy of the match between material difficulty and student ability. *Journal of Educational Psychology,* 1977, *69,* 24–32.

Judd, C. H., & Buswell, G. T. *Silent reading: A study of the various types* (Supplementary Educational Monographs, No. 23). Chicago: University of Chicago Press, 1922.

Kendall, J. R., & Hood, J. Investigating the relationship between comprehension and word recognition: Oral reading analysis of children with comprehension or word recognition disabilities. *Journal of Reading Behavior,* 1979, *11,* 41–48.

Kilgallon, P. A. Study of relationships among pupil adjustments in language situations. Unpublished doctoral dissertation, Pennsylvania State University, 1942 (cited in Betts, 1946).

Kolers, P. A. Three stages of reading. In H. Levin & J. P. Williams (Eds.) *Basic studies on reading.* New York: Basic Books, 1970.

Kolers, P. A. Pattern-analyzing disability in poor readers. *Developmental Psychology,* 1975, *11,* 282–290.

Kowal, S., O'Connell, D. C., O'Brien, E. A., & Bryant, E. T. Temporal aspects of reading aloud and speaking: Three experiments. *American Journal of Psychology,* 1975, *88,* 549–569.

Kreiger, V. K. Differences in poor readers' abilities to identify high-frequency words in isolation and context. *Reading World,* 1981, *20,* 263–272. (a)

Kreiger, V. K. A hierarchy of confusable high-frequency words in isolation and context. *Learning Disability Quarterly,* 1981, *4,* 131–138. (b)

Lass, N. J., & Lutz, D. R. Temporal patterns in a repetitive oral reading task. *Acta Symbolica,* 1973, *4,* 39.

Leinhardt, G., Zigmond, N., & Cooley, W. Reading instruction and its effects. *American Educational Research Journal,* 1981, *18,* 343–361.

Leslie, L. The use of graphic and contextual information by average and below-average readers. *Journal of Reading Behavior,* 1980, *12,* 139–149.

Leu, D. J. Oral reading error analysis: A critical review of research and application. *Reading Research Quarterly,* 1982, *17,* 420–437.

Levin, H., & Kaplan, E. L. Grammatical structure and reading. In H. Levin & J. P. Williams (Eds.) *Basic studies on reading.* New York: Basic Books, 1970.

Lopez, S. H. Children's use of contextual clues in reading Spanish. *Reading Teacher,* 1977, *30,* 735–740.

MacKinnon, A. R. *How do children learn to read?* Toronto: Copp Clark, 1959.

Madden, M., & Pratt, M. An oral reading survey as a teaching aid. *Elementary English Review,* 1941, *18,* 122–126.

Marslen-Wilson, W. D. Sentence perception as an interactive parallel process. *Science,* 1975, *189,* 226–228.

Martin, J. G., Kolodziez, B., & Genay, J. Segmentation of sentences into phonological phrases as a function to constituent length. *Journal of Verbal Learning and Verbal Behavior,* 1971, *10,* 226–233.

Martin, J. G., & Meltzer, R. H. Visual rhythms: Report on a method for facilitating the teaching of reading. *Journal of Reading Behavior,* 1976, *8,* 153–160.

Mathews, M. M. *Teaching to read: Historically considered.* Chicago: University of Chicago Press, 1966.

McCracken, R. A.   Standardized reading tests and informal reading inventories. *Education*, 1962, *82*, 362–369.

McDade, J. E.   A hypothesis for non-oral reading: Argument, experiment, and results. *Journal of Educational Research*, 1937, *30*, 489–503.

McDermott, R. P.   Social relations as contexts for learning in school. *Harvard Educational Review*, 1977, *47*, 198–213.

McDermott, R. P.   Pirandello in the classroom: On the possibility of equal educational opportunity in American culture. In M. C. Reynolds (Ed.), *Futures of exceptional children: Emerging structures*. Reston, Va.: Council for Exceptional Children, 1978.

McNaughton, S.   The influence of immediate teacher correction on self-corrections and proficient oral reading. *Journal of Reading Behavior*, 1981, *13*, 368–371.

Mehan, H.   *Learning lessons*. Cambridge: Harvard University Press, 1979.

Mishler, E. G.   Implications of teacher strategies for language and cognition: Observations in first grade classrooms. In C. B. Cazden, V. P. John, & D. Hymes (Eds.) *Functions of language in the classroom*. New York: Teachers College Press, 1972.

Monroe, M.   *Children who cannot read*. Chicago: University of Chicago Press, 1932.

Morgan, R., & Lyon, E.   "Paired-reading": a preliminary report on a technique for parental tuition of reading-retarded children. *Journal of Child Psychology and Psychiatry*, 1979, *20*, 151–160.

Mosenthal, P.   Psycholinguistics properties of aural and visual comprehension as determined by children's abilities to comprehend syllogisms. *Reading Research Quarterly*, 1976–1977, *12*, 55–92.

Mosenthal, P.   The new and given in children's comprehension of presuppositive negatives in two modes of processing. *Journal of Reading Behavior*, 1978, *10*, 267–278.

Murray, L., & Maliphant, R.   Developmental aspects of the use of linguistic and graphemic information during reading. *British Journal of Educational Psychology*, 1982, *52*, 155–169.

National Education Association.   *Better reading instruction: A survey of research and successful practice* (Research Bulletin, 8, No. 5). Washington, D.C.: Research Division of the National Educational Association, 1935.

National Society for the Study of Education.   *20th yearbook, Part II: Report of the society's committee on silent reading*, Chicago: National Society for the Study of Education, 1920.

Nicholson, T., Pearson, P. D., & Dykstra, R.   Effects of embedded anomalies and oral reading errors on childrens' understanding of stories. *Journal of Reading Behavior*, 1979, *11*, 339–354.

Niles, J. A.   The effects of selected teacher prompting strategies on oral reading performance. In M. Kamil & M. Aulls (Eds.), *Perspectives in reading research and instruction*. Washington, D.C.: National Reading Conference, 1980.

Niles, J. A., Graham, R. T., & Winstead, J. C.   Effects of teachers' response strategies on children's oral reading performance. *Reading in Virginia*, 1977, *5*, 25–28.

Nurss, J. R.   Oral reading errors and comprehension. *Reading Teacher*, 1969, *22*, 523–527.

Parker, F. W.   *Talks on pedagogics*. New York: Barnes, 1894.

Pany, D., McCoy, K., & Peters, E.   Effects of corrective feedback on comprehension of remedial students. *Journal of Reading Behavior*, 1981, *13*, 131–144.

Payne, C.   The classification of errors in oral reading. *Elementary School Journal*, 1930, *31*, 142–146.

Pflaum, S. W., & Bryan, T. H.   Oral reading behaviors in the learning disabled. *Journal of Educational Research*, 1980, *73*, 252–257.

Pflaum, S. W., & Pascarella, E. T.   Interactive effects of prior reading achievement and training in context of learning-disabled children. *Reading Research Quarterly*, 1980, *16*, 138–158.

Pflaum, S. W., Pascarella, E. T., Boswick, M., & Auer, C.   The influence of pupil behaviors and pupil status factors on teacher behaviors during oral reading lessons. *Journal of Educational Research*, 1980, *14*, 99–105.

Pikulski, J. A.   A critical review: Informal reading inventories. *Reading Teacher*, 1974, *28*, 141–153.

Pikulski, J. A., & Kirsch, I.   Organization for instruction. In R. C. Calfee & P. Drum (Eds.), *Teaching reading in compensatory classes.* Newark, Del.: International Reading Association, 1979.

Pitner, R.   Oral and silent reading of fourth grade pupils. *Journal of Educational Psychology*, 1913, *4*, 330–337.

Popp, H. M.   Current practices in the teaching of beginning reading. In J. B. Carroll & J. S. Chall (Eds.) *Toward a literate society: The report of the committee in reading of the National Academy of Education.* New York: McGraw-Hill, 1975.

Powell, W. R.   Reappraising the criteria for interpreting informal reading inventories. In D. L. DeBoer (Ed.) *Reading diagnosis and evaluation.* Newark, Del.: International Reading Association, 1970.

Pugh, A. K.   *Silent Reading: An introduction to its study and teaching.* London: Heinemann, 1978.

Quirk, T. J., Trisman, D. A., Nalin, K., Weinberg, S.   Classroom behavior of teachers during compensatory reading instruction. *Journal of Educational Research*, 1975, *68*, 185–192.

Recht, D. R.   The self-correction process in reading. *Reading Teacher*, 1976, *29*, 632–636.

Resnick, D. P., & Resnick, L. B.   The nature of literacy: An historical exploration. *Harvard Educational Review*, 1977, *47*, 370–385.

Resnick, L. B.   Relations between perceptual and syntactic control in oral reading. *Journal of Educational Psychology*, 1970, *61*, 382–385.

Rist, R. C.   *The urban school: A factory for failure.* Cambridge: MIT Press, 1973.

Rist, R. C.   *The invisible children.* Cambridge: Harvard University Press, 1978.

Roberts, T.   'Frustration level' reading in the infant school. *Educational Research*, 1976, *19*, 41–44.

Rode, S. S.   Development of phrase and clause boundary reading in children. *Reading Research Quarterly*, 1974–1975, *10*, 124–142.

Rupley, W. H., & Blair, T. R.   *Reading diagnosis and remediation.* Chicago: Rand McNally, 1979.

Samuels, S. J.   The method of repeated readings. *Reading Teacher*, 1979, *32*, 403–408.

Schell, L. M.   How accurate are oral reading tests? *Reading World*, 1982, *22*, 91–97.

Schlieper, A.   Oral reading errors in relation to grade and level of skill. *Reading Teacher*, 1977, *31*, 283–287.

Schrieber, P. A.   On the acquisition of reading fluency. *Journal of Reading Behavior*, 1980, *12*, 177–186.

Schwartz, R. M., & Stanovich, K. E.   Flexibility in the use of graphic and contextual information by good and poor readers. *Journal of Reading Behavior*, 1981, *13*, 263–269.

Shankweiler, D., & Lieberman, I. Y.   Misreading: A search for causes. In J. F. Kavanagh & I. Mattingly (Eds.) *Language by ear and eye: The relationships between speech and reading.* Cambridge: MIT Press, 1973.

Siegal, F.   Adapted miscue analysis. *Reading World.* 1979, *19*, 36–43.

Siler, E. R.   The effect of syntactic and semantic constraints on the oral reading performance of second and fourth graders. *Reading Research Quarterly*, 1973–1974, *9*, 583–602.

Silverman, F. H.   Course of nonstutterers' disfluency adaptation during fifteen consecutive oral reading of the same material. *Journal of Speech and Hearing Research*, 1970, *13*, 382–386. (a)

Silverman, F. H.   Distribution of instances of disfluency in consecutive readings of different passages by nonstutterers. *Journal of Speech and Hearing Research*, 1970, *13*, 874–882. (b)

Sinclair, J. M., & Coulthard, R. M.   *Towards an analysis of discourse.* New York: Oxford University Press, 1978.

Smith, D. D.   The improvement of childrens' oral reading through the use of teacher modeling. *Journal of Learning Disabilities*, 1979, *12*, 39–42.

Smith, N. B.   *One hundred ways to teach silent reading.* Yonkers, N.Y.: World, 1925.

Smith, N. B.   *American reading instruction.* New York: Silver Burdette, 1934. (Revised and reissued by the International Reading Association, 1965.)

Spache, G. D.   A comparison of certain oral reading tests. *Journal of Educational Research*, 1950, *43*, 441–452.

Spache, G. S.   *Diagnostic reading scales.* Monterey, Calif.: CTB/McGraw-Hill, 1963/1972.

Spache, G. D.   *Diagnosing and correcting reading disabilities.* Boston: Allyn & Bacon, 1977.

Spiegel, D., & Rogers, C.   Teacher responses to miscues during oral reading by second-grade students. *Journal of Educational Research*, 1980, *74*, 8–12.

Stanovich, K. E.   Toward an interactive-compensatory model of individual differences in the development of reading fluency. *Reading Research Quarterly*, 1980, *16*, 32–71.

Stanovich, K. E., & West, R. F.   Mechanisms of sentence context effects in reading: Automatic activation and conscious attention. *Memory and Cognition*, 1979, *7*, 77–85.

Stallings, J.   Allocated academic learning time revisited, or beyond time on task. *Educational Researcher*, 1980, *9*, 11–16.

Stevens, A. L., & Rumelhart, D. E.   Errors in reading: An analysis using an augmented transition model of grammar. In D. A. Norman & D. E. Rumelhart (Eds.) *Explorations in cognition.* San Francisco: W. H. Freeman, 1975.

Stone, C. R.   *Silent and oral reading.* Boston: Houghton-Mifflin, 1922.

Tamor, L.   Subjective text difficulty: An alternative approach to defining the difficulty level of written text. *Journal of Reading Behavior*, 1981, *13*, 165–172.

Thompson, M.   A psycholinguistic analysis of reading errors made by dyslexics and normal readers. *Journal of Research in Reading*, 1978, *1*, 7–20.

Thorndike, E. L.   Reading as reasoning: A study of mistakes in paragraph reading. *Journal of Educational Psychology*, 1917, *6*, 323–332.

Tortelli, J. P.   Simplified psycholinguistic diagnosis. *Reading Teacher*, 1976, *29*, 637–642.

Vazquez, C. A., Glucksberg, S., & Danks, J. H.   Integration of clauses in oral reading: The effects of syntactic and semantic constraints on the eye-voice span. *Reading Research Quarterly*, 1977–1978, *13*, 174–187.

Watkins, E.   *How to teach silent reading to beginners.* Chicago: Lippincott, 1922.

Watson, S., & Clay, M. M.   Oral reading strategies of third form students. *New Zealand Journal of Educational Research*, 1957, *10*, 43–51.

Whaley, J. F., & Kibby, M. W.   The relative importance of reliance on intraword characteristics and interword constraints for beginning reading achievement. *Journal of Educational Research*, 1981, *74*, 315–320.

Weber, R-M.   The study of oral reading errors: A review of the literature. *Reading Research Quarterly*, 1968, *4*, 96–119.

Weber, R-M.   First graders' use of grammatical context in reading. In H. Levin & J. P. Williams (Eds.), *Basic studies on reading*. New York: Basic Books, 1970. (a)

Weber, R-M.   A linguistic analysis of first grade reading errors. *Reading Research Quarterly*, 1970, 5, 427–451. (b)

Weber, R-M.   Dialect differences in oral reading: An analysis of errors. In J. Laffey & R. Shuy (Eds.), *Language differences: How do they interfere?* Newark, Del.: International Reading Association, 1973.

Weinstein, R. S.   Reading group membership in first grade: Teacher behaviors and pupil experience over time. *Journal of Educational Psychology*, 1976, 68, 103–116.

Wildman, D., & Kling, M.   Semantic, syntactic and spatial anticipation in reading. *Reading Research Quarterly*, 1978–1979, 14, 128–164.

Williamson, L. E., & Young, F.   The IRI and RMI diagnostic concepts should be synthesized. *Journal of Reading Behavior*, 1974, 6, 184–194.

Willows, D., & Ryan, E. B.   Differential utilization of syntactic and semantic information by skilled and less skilled readers in the intermediate grades. *Journal of Educational Psychology*, 1981, 73, 607–615.

Wixon, K. L.   Miscue analysis: A critical review. *Journal of Reading Behavior*, 1979, 11, 163–175.

Zirbes, L.   Diagnostic measurement as a basis for procedure. *Elementary School Journal*, 1918, 28, 507–523.

AUTHOR INDEX

Numbers in italics indicate the pages on which the complete references appear.

SUBJECT INDEX